FROM ANIMALS TO ANIMATS 3

Complex Adaptive Systems

John H. Holland, Christopher Langton, and Stewart W. Wilson, advisors

FROM ANIMALS TO ANIMATS 3

Proceedings of the Third International Conference on Simulation of Adaptive Behavior

edited by Dave Cliff, Philip Husbands, Jean-Arcady Meyer, and Stewart W. Wilson

A Bradford Book

The MIT Press
Cambridge, Massachusetts
London, England

This book was printed and bound in the United States of America.

Library of Congress Cataloging-in-Publication Data

International Conference on Simulation of Adaptive Behavior (3rd : 1994 : Brighton, England)
   From animals to animats 3 : proceedings of the Third International Conference on Simulation of Adaptive Behavior / edited by Dave Cliff . . . [et al.].
       p.   cm. — (Complex adaptive systems)
   "A Bradford book."
   Includes bibliographical references and index.
   ISBN 0-262-53122-4
   1. Animal behavior—Simulation methods—Congresses. 2. Animals—Adaptation—Simulation methods—Congresses. 3. Robotics—Congresses. 4. Artificial intelligence—Congresses. I. Cliff, Dave. II. Title. III. Title: From animals to animats three. IV. Series.
QL751.65.S55I58 1994
591.51—dc20   94-13152
                                                                CIP

CONTENTS

MOTIVATION AND EMOTION

INTERNAL WORLD MODELS AND COGNITIVE PROCESSES

CHARACTERIZATION OF ENVIRONMENTS

LEARNING

EVOLUTION

COLLECTIVE BEHAVIOR

APPLIED ADAPTIVE BEHAVIOR

PREFACE

When a new scientific field forms and grows, international conference proceedings serve a vital role in bringing together current research which would otherwise be distributed across publications in diverse fields. These proceedings are no exception. They contain 58 papers presented at the Third International Conference on Simulation of Adaptive Behavior (SAB94), providing comprehensive and up-to-date sources on an exciting new approach to understanding intelligence: the simulation and construction of artificial animals ('animats') which must survive and adapt in progressively more challenging environments.

The conference took place in Brighton, England, during August 8th-12th 1994. While it is true that participants at the conference represented fields as diverse as theoretical biology, ethology, robotics, machine learning, neuroscience, psychology, artificial life, and evolutionary computation, it is also probably fair to say that some of the delegates of the conference would best be described as working in the distinct scientific field known as Adaptive Behavior research. This field received initial recognition on the occasion of the first SAB conference (held in Paris in September 1990) and subsequent consolidation with both the second SAB conference (held in Hawaii in December 1992) and the publication of the MIT Press quarterly journal *Adaptive Behavior* since summer 1992. Adaptive Behavior research is distinguished by its concentration on the creation and analysis of whole, coping, animal-like systems, which—however simple at the moment—may be one of the best routes to understanding intelligence in natural and artificial systems.

To provide reviews of important issues in the field, we were fortunate to be able to host keynote lectures given by pioneering researchers. The SAB94 Keynote Lecturers were:

Professor Michael A. Arbib, University of Southern California, USA
Professor Rodney A. Brooks, Massachusetts Institute of Technology, USA
Professor John Maynard Smith, University of Sussex, UK
Professor Herbert L. Roitblat, University of Hawaii, USA and
Professor Jean-Jacques E. Slotine, Massachusetts Institute of Technology, USA

This book is divided into sections corresponding to the conference sessions. In each section, the more general papers presented as talks are followed by more specialized papers that were presented as posters.

The first section, the Animat Approach, contains papers on artificial animal research as a tool for understanding adaptive behavior and, indeed, as a new approach to artificial intelligence. The first paper reviews research since the first SAB conference in 1990, and helps to identify the most significant developments made since then.

The following sections—Perception and Motor Control, Action Selection and Behavioral Sequences, Motivation and Emotion, Internal World Models and Cognitive Processes, Characterization of Environments, Learning, Evolution, and Collective Behavior—contain papers on these themes from both the animal and animat perspectives, with several strong—and differing—theses on how to understand or achieve natural or artificial systems which exhibit adaptive behavior.

The book concludes with a two-paper section, Applied Adaptive Behavior, that describes novel techniques, inspired by results from adaptive behavior research, which could be of use in applications outside the domain of the field.

SAB94 could not have taken place without the assistance of many people and organizations. We are especially grateful to members of the Program Committee, whose punctual and conscientious reviewing selected the papers here from the 120 submitted. The Committee members were:

Michael Arbib, USA	Ronald Arkin, USA
Randall Beer, USA	Alain Berthoz, France
Lashon Booker, USA	Rodney Brooks, USA
Patrick Colgan, Canada	Thomas Collett, UK
Holk Cruse, Germany	Juan Delius, Germany
Jacques Ferber, France	Nicolas Franceschini, France
Simon Goss, Belgium	Janet Halperin, Canada
Inman Harvey, UK	Ian Horswill, USA
Alasdair Houston, UK	Leslie Kaelbling, USA
Harry Klopf, USA	Long-Ji Lin, USA
Pattie Maes, USA	Maja Mataric, USA
David McFarland, UK	Geoffrey Miller, UK
Rolf Pfeifer, Switzerland	Herbert Roitblat, USA
Jean-Jacques Slotine, USA	Olaf Sporns, USA
John Staddon, USA	Frederick Toates, UK
Peter Todd, USA	Saburo Tsuji, Japan
David Waltz, USA	Ronald Williams, USA

We thank the Financial Chair, Herbert Roitblat, for his help in attracting funding, and each of the following sponsors of the conference for their financial support:

Applied AI Systems, Inc.	Brighton Council
British Telecom	The MIT Press
Mitsubishi Corporation	Uchidate Co., Ltd.
The University of Sussex	

We are also once again indebted to John Tangney of AFOSR for his advice and intellectual support.

The members of the Organizing and Local Arrangements committee worked long and hard to make the conference a success. We thank the local organizers Inman Harvey and Alison White, and also thank Linda Thompson for secretarial support. We are very grateful to James Goodlet, who ensured that the Sussex electronic mail system remained functional at critical points in the review process. Particular thanks go to Takashi Gomi of Applied AI Systems, and Katsunori Shimohara of ATR, for their help in conference administration.

We wish to express our gratitude to Brighton Council, for having generously placed at our disposal the rooms of the Brighton Centre in which the conference was held. We also express our thanks to Ben du Boulay (Dean of the University of Sussex School of Cognitive and Computing Sciences) for his kind help in solving various administrative problems.

Finally, we are particularly indebted to Jean Solé for the artistic conception of the SAB94 poster and proceedings cover.

We invite readers to enjoy and profit from the papers in this book, and look forward to the next conference, SAB96.

Dave Cliff   Program Chair

Philip Husbands   Jean-Arcady Meyer   Stewart W. Wilson

Conference Co-Chairs

THE ANIMAT APPROACH
TO ADAPTIVE BEHAVIOR

From SAB90 to SAB94 : Four Years of Animat Research

Jean-Arcady Meyer and Agnès Guillot
Groupe de BioInformatique
Ecole Normale Supérieure, CNRS-URA 686
46, rue d'Ulm. 75230 Paris Cedex 05, France
(meyer@wotan.ens.fr - guillot@wotan.ens.fr)

Abstract

This paper builds on a previous review of significant research on adaptive behavior in animats. It summarizes the current state of the art and suggests some directions likely to provide interesting results in the near future.

1 Introduction

An animat is a simulated animal or a real robot whose rules of behavior are inspired by those of animals. It is usually equipped with sensors, with actuators, and with a behavioral control architecture that allow it to react or to respond to variations in its environment (internal or external), notably to those that might impair its chances of survival. The behavior of an animat is what the animat does. This is characterized by a sequence of actions which reflects the dynamic interplay between the animat and its environment, mediated through the animat's sensors and actuators.

The behavior of an animat is adaptive so long as it allows the animat to survive or to fulfill its mission. This requires that the animat's essential variables be monitored and maintained within their viability zone, an ability which can be enhanced, should the animat be capable of learning which actions elicit a positive or negative reward from the environment (Figure 1).

Since a previous review of significant research on adaptive behavior in animats (MEYE90), three conferences have been held on the subject. The present paper aims at updating the previous one and summarizes the current state of the art. For lack of space, it will only refer to the conference proceedings (SAB90, SAB92, SAB94), a strategical choice that, hopefully, should not leave any fundamental work aside. It is organized around the various components of Figure 1 and concludes with some possible directions for future work.

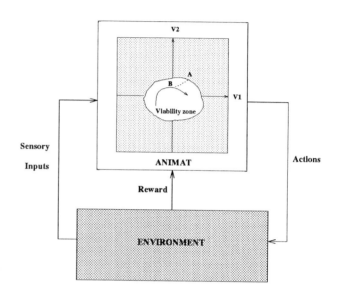

Figure 1: The interactions between an animat and its environment. The behavior of this animat is said to be adaptive because corrective action has been taken at point B so as to avoid crossing at point A the viability zone associated with the two essential variables V1 and V2. A corrective action can be preprogrammed or learned in the environment.

2 Actions

Not surprisingly - given the importance of robotic realizations in the animat community - the behavior most often exhibited by animats is motion. Thus, some animats move themselves in their environment like worms (HART92), others like bipeds (GREE94, VOGE92), quadrupeds (CHER92, CRUS90, DIGN94), hexapods (BEER90, CRUS90, CRUS92), or octopods (CRUS90). Other animats fly (MURA94), or swim (UTTA92), or even move themselves by means of brachiation (SAIT94). Still other animats are capable of moving an arm to explore their environment or to reach goals in it (FONE94, LIND92, MORA94).

If some robots are capable of pushing (KUBE92, NEHM94, SAHO94), or of grasping (MATA92) objects, their repertoire of actions is nevertheless quite limited. Animals exhibit far more diverse behaviors and many models aim at describing with as great an accuracy as possible the actual sensory-motor coordinating mechanisms which generate these behaviors. Such biomimetic models describe, for example, hierarchical dishabituation in toads (WANG90), prey-catching (ARBI90) or detour behavior (ARBI92) in anurans, visual saccades and head movements in the prey approach of salamanders (MANT90), spinal reflexes in the frog (GISZ92, GISZ94), human bodily adjustments in ball throwing tasks (ARBI94), phonotaxis in crickets (WEBB94), or fighting behavior in the Siamese fighting fish (HALP90).

Other behaviors are generated by models less dedicated to the description of precise biological mechanisms and are considered from a broader point of view. This is the case, for example, of various individual or collective behaviors involved in food seeking or foraging (ARKI92, ARKI94, BALL94, BURA94, CECC92, DENE90, DROG92, FLOR92, KUBO94, KURT90, MATA94, PARE90, SAUN94, SHAF94, STEE90, THER90, TODD92, TODD94), in herding and flocking (ARKI94, MATA92, WERN92), in predator-prey relationships (COLO92, DELU90, IBA92, MILLE94, REYN92), in mate finding (ROBB94), in exploring (GABO92) or in some sort of cleaning (ARKI94, MUNO94, PARK92) or sorting (DENEU90) tasks. Furthermore, various authors have devised special artificial environments (BERS94, BLUM94, LIN90, MAES90, TYRR90, WERN94) where animats must exhibit several of the above-mentioned behaviors in order to survive.

Within the context of social behavior, a few works are dedicated to the study of communication. For instance, de Bourcier and Wheeler (DEBO94) are interested in the signalling of aggressive intentions in animats and study how the cost of producing the corresponding signals influences the population dynamics of truth-tellers and bluffers. Likewise, McFarland (MCFA94) and Steels (STEE94) have devised a robotic ecosystem allowing the study of cooperative communications between truth-telling and bluffing robots. Yanco and Stein (YANC92) study how two robots can learn a private language in order to achieve coordinated movement and can adapt their language to cope with changing circumstances (see also PARK92 and ROBB94).

3   Perceptions

Several research efforts demonstrate the adaptive value of the long-evolved sensors of animals. For instance, Roitblat (ROIT90a, ROIT92) describes how the ear of the dolphin is used in solving intricate echolocation tasks, while Cliff (CLIF90), Lopez and Smith (LOPE92), and Mura and Franceschini (MURA94) show how the compound-eye of the fly can help tracking moving ob-

jects. Likewise, Osorio et al. (OSOR94) compare the architecture and function of the neural circuits controlling vision and olfaction in insects and suggest that these circuits implement fundamentally different computational strategies tailored to the complexities and unpredictabilities of the specific sensory signals they process. These authors conclude that the design of animats should take account of the environment in which an animat will act, and not be taken arbitrarily from a specific biological model.

Other aspects of the interaction between ad hoc sensors and perceptual strategies are also dealt with in the animat literature. For instance, Pierce and Kuipers (PIER90) studied how a robot with uninterpreted sensors and effectors could learn sequences of actions which can be taken to achieve a goal. In this case, a solution involves learning a function defined in terms of the sensory data. This function, which is maximized at the point corresponding to the goal, can be optimized by means of hill climbing. Parker (PARK92) studied how sensory filters could act as passive attention-focussing mechanisms in animats involved in a collective janitorial task. Such filters allow an animat to be more reactive to the actions of other agents. They convert communication about action of other animats into altered sensory readings, so that the animat ignores certain sensory readings or "hallucinates" others, and acts on the altered sensory feedbacks as if they were genuine. Another passive attention-focussing mechanism is studied by Foner and Maes (FONE94) whose animat learns an action model - i.e., what the perceptual consequences of a given action in a given sensory context will be. Instead of attempting to learn all that there is to know about experiencing the world, the system focusses its attention on the important aspects of its current experience and memory. The corresponding architecture implements both perceptual selectivity - which restricts the set of sensor data to which the agent attends - and cognitive selectivity - which restricts the set of internal structures that is adapted. An active attention-focussing mechanism is studied by Cliff (CLIF90) whose "computational Hoverfly" is capable of looking around and employs a foveal sampling strategy with gaze-control mechanisms repositioning the limited high-resolution area of the visual field (see also ARBI90, ARBI94, MANT90). Cohen and Atkin (COHE94) study an attention-focussing mechanism in time, instead of space. They show that paying attention to the environment according to an interval reduction monitoring strategy - i.e., monitor more frequently near a goal than far from it - is more efficient that periodic monitoring in many circumstances. They suggest that it might be worth implementing such a strategy in animats.

Finally other authors study how an evolutionary process could shape the sensory apparatus of an animat (CLIF92, HARV94, KURT90, REYN94). Kurtz (KURT90) describes the evolution, within a population of foraging animats, of the allele frequencies of three genes coding for internal, external, and relational information gathering abilities. Cliff et al. (CLIF92) describe how the angle of acceptance and the eccentricity of the photoreceptors of a visually guided robot could evolve - together with the architecture of its nervous system - and improve the robot's success at avoiding collisions with the walls surrounding its environment.

4   Architectures

In order to behave adaptively, an animat has to do the right thing at the right moment and, ideally, such a choice must depend upon the animat's perceptions of the external environment, on its physiological or internal state, on the consequences of its current behavior and on the expected consequences of its future behavior. In other words, the animat must want something and it must be endowed with a motivational system. Such a system, which selects at every moment a goal to be pursued and organizes the animat's commerce with it (TOAT90), necessitates a memory of the past consequences of the animat's activities and, eventually, a planner which relates the current behavioral choice to its future consequences (DONN94).

In several realizations, the overall architecture and the inner workings of the motivational system of an animat are fixed by its human designer or by an evolutionary process. In traditional robotics and AI, the motivational system of an intelligent agent is usually designed as a centrally controlled organization of functional modules - such as perception, modeling, planning and execution - which sequentially process information from sensors to actuators. Quite differently, animat designers conceive the motivational system of an intelligent and robust animat as a distributed agency of processing units which collectively exhibit the required functionalities. Each such module can be connected directly to sensors and actuators, and works in parallel with the others, thus endowing the animat with minimal sensory-motor faculties in the case of an internal breakdown affecting some other modules.

Often, the corresponding architectures are decisional hierarchies, more or less loosely inspired by the way many ethologists have described the action selection mechanisms of animals (BOOK90, CHER92, DIGN94, SCHN90). They involve several systems, each devoted to a specific function affecting the survival ability of the animat, which are organized as loosely overlapping hierarchies of decision centers. Each center, at each level, can take input from many different internal and external sensory stimuli and can send facilitating sensory signals to the centers of the level below. The activation of a center at a given level depends upon the combined effect of the sensory stimuli, of the facilitating control signals provided by the centers of the level above, and of inhibitory signals sent by the other centers of this level. These inhibitory signals implement some sort of winner-take-all mechanism, according to which only one center can be active at any given level. At the higher levels of these hierarchies, the activation of a center triggers a very general decision (i.e. reproduce), while such a decision becomes increasingly more specific as one goes down (i.e. court), until a final motor decision (i.e. mate) is made at the bottom level. The linear architectures in SAUN94 and HALP90 are special cases of such decisional hierarchies. Other special cases are those which implement an arbiter whose task is to merge in a single action the suggestions to perform one behavior or another afforded by several dedicated modules (BOOK90, COLL92, TENE92, YAMA94).

In free-flow hierarchies (TYRR92), the nodes at each level express multiple preferences for each of a set of lower-level candidates, rather than making a decision as to which one is most suitable. The flow of preferences travels through several nodes at each level, and it is only at the bottom level than an arbitration is done and an action selected. Another hierarchical architecture, which borrows characteristics from the two above logics, is described in BLUM94. Architectures based on feedforward neural networks (CECC92, COLL90, FLOR92, GAUS94, NEHM90, NEHM94, PARE90, VONK90, WERN92, WERN94) are special cases of free-flow hierarchies, where the top layer receives the sensory inputs and the bottom layer delivers the motor outputs.

The motivational systems of other animats are non-hierarchical and differ from each other by the degree of arbitration to which their behavioral modules are submitted. Thus, no arbitration occurs in force-field controlled architectures (ARBI90, ARBI92, ARKI92, ARKI94) whose behavioral modules each contribute a vector that is related to the animat's current goal. These vectors are normalized and summed before being transmitted to the final execution module. In subsumption architectures (KUBE92, MATA90, MATA92), each behavioral module is also active at any time, but can have its output suppressed by that of another module. In PARK92, the architecture comprises several "behavior sets" - each organized in a subsumption manner - which compete to control what the animat does. Once a behavior set is activated, other behavior sets are suppressed, so that only one behavior set is active at a time. In MAES90 or in GISZ92, the motivational system of an animat is organized as a spreading-activation network whose nodes trigger the various behaviors the animat can engage in.

These nodes are more or less active, depending upon the amount of "energy" that flows through each of them, but a winner-take-all procedure arbitrates among them and selects the behavior actually exhibited. In BEER90, no general arbitration mechanism is provided. Rather, the overall coherency of the animat's behavior depends upon specific inhibitory links which allow some active nodes to prevent others from being activated at the same time.

Although the animat community is still missing general knowledge about what kind of adaptive abilities are afforded by what kind of architecture, one can find useful contributions to such a knowledge in several papers (BROO90, BROO94, MAES92, PFEI92, ROIT90b, SCHN90, WALT90).

5   Learning

5.1   Reinforcement Learning

If the inner workings of an action selection mechanism are not fixed by the designer or by an evolutionary process, they must be learned. The corresponding animats must memorize that a given action is more rewarding than another in given circumstances, so that they will preferentially exhibit the former action instead of the latter, should the same circumstances be encountered again in the future. Furthermore, they must be capable of adjusting their behavioral policy if the relative merits of the various actions they can chose from change for whatever reason. In other words, a greater autonomy and considerable adaptive abilities are afforded to animats that are capable of learning by reinforcement.

Several systems, with increasingly adaptive functionalities, have been devised for such a purpose (see SUTT90 and LIN90 for comparisons). For instance, policy-only systems, stochastic automata (KUBO94), as well as some systems based on neural networks (GAUS94, NEHM92, NEHM94), learn a mapping from the animat's sensations to its actions and specify what the animat will do in each situation at its current stage of learning. Classifier Systems with internal messages, as well as some systems based on recurrent neural networks (LIN92, YAMA94), specify what to do according to current sensations and to a memory of past sensations and actions. Reinforcement-comparison systems and some simple Classifier Systems (VENT94) learn which immediate reward will be gained from doing a specific action in a specific sensory context. Temporal Difference algorithms (BAIR92, MILLA94, KLOP92, ROSE92), Adaptive Heuristic Critic systems (PIPE94), Q-learning systems (BERS94, DORI94, LIN92, MUNO94, SAIT94), Associative Control Process networks (BAIR92, KLOP92) and Classifier Systems (DONN94, DORI94) learn which long-term cumulative reward can be expected from a given action in a given sensory context. Finally, Dyna

systems (PENG92, SUTT90), some dedicated neural networks (CHES94, SCHMI90) and some varieties of Classifier Systems (RIOL90) not only learn such a reward, but also learn a world model - that is, how the world changes as an animat acts in it. They accordingly predict which cumulative reward and which new sensory inputs are to be expected from a given action in a given sensory context.

Various reinforcement learning algorithms have been implemented within the above mentioned motivational systems. For instance, Digney and Gupta (DIGN94) use a Temporal Difference learning algorithm to let a hierarchical action selection mechanism coordinate the locomotion of a quadruped animat. Likewise, Gistzter (GISZ94) combines a spreading-activation network, a force-field mechanism for command fusion, and a reinforcement signal to simulate the wiping behaviors of the frog.

5.2   Associative Learning

Associative learning often occurs in animats within the context of a navigational task. Such a task is usually accomplished with the aid of landmarks, which must be first categorized and recognized, then used as stepping stones, or included into a cognitive map, in order to allow the animat to reach a goal. Smart and Hallam (SMAR94) discuss the role of proprioceptive and featural cues in location recognition tasks by rats. Such cues are used by the robot of Nehmzow and Smithers (NEHM90) to train an associative Kohonen network, by the robot of Yamauchi and Beer (YAMA94) to train a dynamical neural network, and by the robot of Mataric (MATA90) to train a spreading-activation network (see also KORT92). These networks allow landmark discrimination and the building of an internal representation of the environment as the robots move around (see also MORA94). Having learned such internal representations, the robots are able to recognize where they are situated and - at least in the case of Mataric's robot - to navigate from a starting position to a goal. Such a navigation, however, implies passing through places already visited and characterized (see also DONN94 and MAZE92). The ability to estimate the distances or the visual angles of some landmarks, together with the use of cognitive maps, allow other animats to orient themselves according to these landmarks and to navigate through places never visited before (YEAP90, PRES94). For instance, the navigation system of Benhamou et al. (BENH94) relies on the use of both place cells and direction cells, that of Prescott and Mayhew (PRES92) relies on landmarks characterized by their coordinates, and that of Schmajuk and Blair (SCHMA92) relies on landmarks characterized by their visual angle. The latter model also predicts the dynamics of several spatial learning tasks.

Associative learning in animats also occurs in a variety of situations incurring habituation (SCUT94, STAD92, WANG90), sensitization (SCUT94) or conditioning (HALP90, SCHMA94, SCUT94). Its adaptive value is studied in TODD90. In the work of Aitken (AITK94), an animat detects correlations between current motor actions and future sensory inputs, and it learns to act and perceive by exposure to the sensory consequences of desired motor sequences - rather than exposure to the desired motor sequences themselves. In the presence of a teacher that provides desirable sensory sequences - as a result of its own motor sequences - the animat is capable of learning complex behavioral sequences by imitation.

6   Planning

An animat that is capable of planning will exhibit a behavioral sequence in which a specific action succeeds another, not as a mere reaction to the new environmental conditions brought about by the previous action, but because the whole sequence seems likely to fulfill the animat's current goal. In other words, a planning animat is capable of assessing the future consequences of its actions, an ability that greatly enhances its chances of surviving beyond those afforded by mere trial-and-error learning.

One way to plan a behavioral sequence is to make use of a world model that behaves like the world. With such a model, an animat can indeed perform hypothetical experiments (that is, "experiments in its head") and search for a behavioral sequence likely to reach the goal. The Dyna architecture, and the related systems which have been cited above, all allow this sort of planning.

Other planning abilities are afforded to animats that are capable of deciding what to do according to their current sensory state and their current goal or subgoal. If such animats are also capable of transforming knowledge about previously learned action sequences into appropriate subgoals for new problems, then they will solve new tasks through composition of solutions for older tasks. Thus, actions performed at a given time depend upon both a subgoal that seems likely to contribute to the achievement of the overall goal and upon the current sensory input. Accordingly, the corresponding animats exhibit reactive planning (DONN94, SCHMI92; see also SAHO94).

Another approach is described in RIBE92, where a plan is collectively achieved by a group of interacting agents, each having only local information about the state of the world and having some means of transmitting limited information to the others (see also WEIS92).

7   Evolution

As mentioned above, the overall architecture and the inner workings of an animat are sometimes determined by an evolutionary process.

Some realizations (DELU90, KURT90) involve a traditional genetic simulation model, which allows the monitoring of the dynamics of allele frequencies and the study of speciation phenomena. Other realizations implement a genotype to phenotype mapping with the help of genetic programming techniques. Such approaches seek computer programs which, given some sensors and actuators, allow an animat to exhibit behavioral sequences that improve over time, according to a given fitness function. Thus Koza (KOZA90) evolved the behavioral programs of an artificial ant capable of following a particular pheromone trail, of a pursuer chasing an optimal evader, of an evader racing away from an optimal pursuer, and of two minimaxing players. Other applications of genetic programming are to be found in REYN92 and REYN94. In particular, Reynolds (REYN94) evolves a program which determines the optimal number and orientation of the sensors that allow an animat to follow a corridor while avoiding collisions with the walls. Elsewhere, the genotype-phenotype mapping is implemented in a classical neural network (COLL90, FLOR92, PARE90, TODD90, WERN92, WERN94) or in a dynamic neural network (CLIF92, HARV92, HARV94, YAMA94). For instance, in the work of Floreano (FLOR92), a feedforward neural network allows an evolved animat to exhibit a nest-based foraging behavior. This work shows that an evolutionary process may eventually not lead to an optimal behavior, because new architectures arc necessarily built upon older ones which, although perfectly adapted to previous environmental conditions, may not be the best stepping-stones for reaching solutions to new environmental conditions.

The adaptive solutions sought by an evolutionary process usually involve predetermined sensors and actuators. As previously mentioned, however, several realizations permit the animat's sensors to evolve. Todd and Wilson (TODD92) describe a framework for exploring the evolution of adaptive behaviors in response to different environment structures, in which not only the sensors, but also the actuators and the behavioral rules of a given animat would all be allowed to evolve.

Although the improvement of the solutions to a specific problem of adaptation is usually dependent upon an explicit fitness function that helps select good solutions - that will be allowed to reproduce - and bad solutions - that will be eliminated - during the course of evolution, some realizations do not rely on such a function. They accordingly rely upon an implicit fitness and let reproduction and selection depend upon the internal dynamics of an ecosystem (DELU90, PARE90, WERN92, WERN94). Likewise, although the majority of realizations involve a simulated animat, those described in HARV94 and FLOR94 involve real robots. Thus, Harvey et al. (HARV94) encode in a pair of chromosomes both the architecture of the neural network which controls the behavior of a gantry robot and the physical organization of the robot's visual system, in order to evolve various visually-guided behaviors. Likewise, Floreano and Mondada (FLOR94) evolve the neural architecture controlling the behavior of a real robot in a navigation and obstacle-avoidance task. Although the robot has a circular shape and is equipped with two wheels that rotate at equal speeds in each direction, the evolutionary process generates a frontal direction of motion that corresponds to the side where the robot has more sensors. Accordingly, the robot faces obstacles with the side that provides a finer resolution and a larger visual angle.

Several researchers have been interested in co-evolutionary processes (DELU90, FLOR92, KOZA90, MILLE94, ROBB94, WERN92). For instance, Robbins (ROBB94) describes the evolution of a common mate-finding communication protocol within an ecosystem where immobile females guide blind moving males. Each animat is endowed with a message chromosome and an interpretation chromosome. Within such an ecosystem, it turns out that various parasites can accelerate the evolution of the protocol by increasing the evolutionary pressure put on the evolving animats.

Finally, two fundamental approaches to the mechanisms of evolution are described in TODD90 and MILLE92. The work of Todd and Miller (TODD90) helps to explore under what conditions the associative learning abilities of an animat could prove adaptive and evolve. Miller and Todd (MILLE92) compare the evolutionary forces of natural selection to those of sexual selection and explore how the dynamics of evolution may interact with the mechanisms of cognition - like those involved in directional mate preferences.

8   External environment

A given behavior might prove adaptive in one environment but not in another. Therefore, if one wants to give the animat community a chance to generate something other than fragmentary knowledge about ad hoc solutions to specific adaptive problems in specific environments (MEYE90), and if one seeks useful generalizations, one should subscribe to the general research program described by Todd and Wilson (TODD92). This program aims at characterizing the important features of environment structure in terms of the adaptive behavior they elicit and suggests studying how these features

correlate with the sensors, the actuators, and the control structures that evolve in different environments. A specific application of this program (TODD94) demonstrates that very simple animats can survive, with neither sensors nor memory, in a variety of changing and unpredictable environments and that the challenges of different types of environments are best met by different probability distributions of blind actions.

Another approach to a characterization of environments is proposed by Wilson (WILS90) on the basis of the indeterminacy of an environment with respect to the sensory capabilities of its agents. Still another suggestion is made by Littman (LITT92) who characterizes an environment by the simplest agent that can possibly achieve optimal reinforcement in it. The corresponding results show that the degree to which the adaptive problem raised by a given environment can be partially solved by a suboptimal agent may also be a significant measure of environmental difficulty (see also LITT94).

Finally, the work of Horswill (HORS92) is not unrelated to the above concerns, insofar as it aims at characterizing the environmental features that simplify the computational problem facing an animat.

9   Prospects

The short term goal of animat research is to discover architectures and working principles that allow a real animal, a simulated animal, or a robot to exhibit a behavior that solves a specific problem of adaptation in a specific environment. Undoubtedly, the present state of the art already contributes usefully to this goal.

An intermediate goal of animat research is to generalize this knowledge and make progress towards understanding what architectures and working principles can allow an animat to solve what kind of problems in what kind of environments (MEYE90). Although current attempts at categorizing architectures and environments undoubtedly constitute valuable steps in this direction, other useful contributions can probably be expected from additional research into conceptual frameworks likely to help in abstracting over incidental differences between specific architectures, behaviors, and environments. Contributions in GALL92, KISS90, SLOT94 are probably useful in this respect.

The ultimate goal of animat research - at least in our opinion - is to contribute to our understanding of the adaptive value and working principles of human cognition (MAES92, WILS90). There is certainly a lot to be gained from asking how the highest cognitive abilities of man depend upon the evolution of the simplest cognitive abilities and adaptive behaviors of animals. From such a perspective, contributions in BROO94, BURA94, DEUG92, ROIT94, SHAF94, TOAT94, VERS92 should provide insights into cognition, representations, and the inner workings of the human mind. There is also a lot to be gained from asking how processes of development and learning - those occuring at the level of the individual - interact with the process of evolution - occuring at the level of the population. Partial answers are to be found in MEYE90 and TODD90, but the field is lacking any simulation involving development, at least from this perspective (but see FONE94 and RUTK94). Finally, there is also a lot to be gained from asking how physical and social environments each contribute to the evolution of cognitive abilities. Several research efforts are aimed in such a direction (DEBO94, MCFA94, MILLE94) and might, in particular, help in studying the rise of a Machiavellian intelligence within a community where cheating animats can evolve.

10   Conclusion

Animat research is an active field of investigation which has already contributed several useful practical results and might provide valuable contributions to the understanding of human cognition in the future. However, the domain is in definite need of theoretical advances that could provide useful generalizations of still highly disparate pieces of knowledge.

References

[AITK94]   A. M. Aitken. An architecture for learning to behave. In [SAB94].

[ARBI90]   M.A. Arbib and A. Cobas. Schemas for prey-catching in frog and toad. In [SAB90].

[ARBI92]   M. A. Arbib and H.-B. Lee. Anuran visuomotor coordination for detour behavior: From retina to motor schemas. In [SAB92].

[ARBI94]   M. A. Arbib, N. Schweighofer, and W. T. Thach. Modeling the role of cerebellum in prism adaptation. In [SAB94].

[ARKI92]   R. C. Arkin and J. D. Hobbs. Dimensions of communication and social organization in multi-agent robotic systems. In [SAB92].

[ARKI94]   R. C. Arkin and K. Ali. Integration of reactive and telerobotic control in multi-agent robotic systems. In [SAB94].

[BAIR92]   L. C. Baird III, and A. H. Klopf. Extensions of the associative control process (ACP) network: Hierarchies and provable optimality. In [SAB92].

[BALL94]   N. Ball Organizing an animat's behavioral repertoire using kohonen feature maps. In [SAB94].

[BEER90]   R. D. Beer and H. J. Chiel. The neural basis of behavioral choice in an artificial insect. In [SAB90].

[BENH94]   S. Benhamou, P. Bovet, and B. Poucet. A place navigation algorithm based on elementary computing procedures and associative memories. In [SAB94].

[BERS94]   H. Bersini. Reinforcement learning for homeostatic endogenous variables. In [SAB94].

[BLUM94]   B. Blumberg. Action-selection in Hamsterdam: Lessons from ethology. In [SAB94].

[BOOK90]   L. B. Booker. Instinct as an inductive bias for learning behavioral sequences. In [SAB90].

[BROO90]   R. A. Brooks. Challenges for complete creature architectures. In [SAB90].

[BROO94]   R. A. Brooks. Coherent behavior from many adaptive processes. In [SAB94].

[BURA94]   S. Bura. Minimeme: of life and death in the noosphere. In [SAB94].

[CECC92]   F. Cecconi and D. Parisi. Neural networks with motivational units. In [SAB92].

[CHER92]   S. Cherian and W. O. Troxell. A neural network based behavior hierarchy for locomotion control . In [SAB92].

[CHES94]   W. Chesters and G. M. Hayes. Connectionist environment modelling in a real robot. In [SAB94].

[CLIF90]   D. Cliff. The computational hoverfly: A study in computational neuroethology. In [SAB90].

[CLIF92]   D. Cliff, P. Husbands, and I. Harvey. Evolving visually guided robots. In [SAB92].

[COHE94]   P. R. Cohen and M. Atkin. Preliminary evidence that the interval reduction monitoring strategy is general. In [SAB94].

[COLL90]   R. J. Collins and D. R. Jefferson. Representations for artificial organisms. In [SAB90].

[COLO92]   M. Colombetti and M. Dorigo. Learning to control an autonomous robot by distributed genetic algorithms. In [SAB92].

[CRUS90]   H. Cruse. Coordination of leg movement in walking animals. In [SAB90].

[CRUS92]   H. Cruse, U. Mueller-Wilm, and J. Dean. Artificial neural nets for controlling a 6-legged walking system. In [SAB92].

[DEBO94]   P. de Bourcier and M. Wheeler. Signalling and territorial agression: An investigation by means of synthetic behavioral ecology. In [SAB94].

[DELU90]   F. De Luigi and V. Maniezzo. The rise of interaction: Intrinsic simulation modeling of the onset of interacting behaviour. In [SAB90].

[DENE90]   J. L. Deneubourg, S. Goss, N. Franks, A. Sendova-Franks, C. Detrain, and L. Chretien. The dynamics of collective sorting: Robot-like ants and ant-like robots. In [SAB90].

[DEUG92]   D. Deugo and F. Oppacher. An evolutionary approach to cognition. In [SAB92].

[DIGN94] B. L. Digney and M. M. Gupta. A distributed adaptive control system for a quadruped mobile robot. In [SAB94].

[DONN94] J.-Y. Donnart and J.-A. Meyer. A hierarchical classifier system implementing a motivationally autonomous animat. In [SAB94].

[DORI94] M. Dorigo and H. Bersini. A comparative analysis of Q-Learning and classifier systems. In [SAB94].

[DROG92] A. Drogoul and J. Ferber. From Tom Thumb to the dockers: Some experiments with foraging robots. In [SAB92].

[FLOR92] D. Floreano. Emergence of nest-based foraging strategies in ecosystems of neural networks. In [SAB92].

[FLOR94] D. Floreano and F. Mondada. Automatic creation of an autonomous agent: Genetic evolution of a neural network Driven Robot. In [SAB94].

[FONE94] L. N. Foner and P. Maes. Paying attention to what's important: Using focus of attention to improve unsupervised learning. In [SAB94].

[GABO92] L. Gabora. Should I stay or should I go: Coordinating biological needs with continuously-updated assessments of the environment. In [SAB92].

[GALL92] J. C. Gallagher and R. D. Beer. A qualitative dynamical analysis of evolved locomotion controllers. In [SAB92].

[GAUS94] P. Gaussier and S. Zrehen. A topological neural map for on-line learning: Emergence of obstacle avoidance in a mobile robot. In [SAB94].

[GISZ92] S. Giszter. Behavior networks and force fields for simulating spinal reflex behaviors of the frog. In [SAB92].

[GISZ94] S. Giszter. Reinforcement tuning of action synthesis and selection in a 'virtual frog'. In [SAB94].

[GREE94] P. R. Green. How to watch your step: Biological evidence and a model. In [SAB94].

[HALP90] J. R. P. Halperin. Machine motivation. In [SAB90].

[HART92] R. Hartley. Propulsion and guidance in a simulation of the worm C. elegans. In [SAB92].

[HARV92] I. Harvey, P. Husbands, and D. Cliff. Issues in evolutionary robotics. In [SAB92].

[HARV94] I. Harvey, P. Husbands, and D. Cliff. Seeing the light: Artificial evolution, real vision. In [SAB94].

[HORS92] I. Horswill. A simple, cheap, and robust visual navigation system . In [SAB92].

[KISS90] G. Kiss. Autonomous agents, AI and chaos theory. In [SAB90].

[KLOP92] A. H. Klopf, J. S. Morgan, and S. E. Weaver. Modeling nervous system function with a hierarchical network of control systems that learn. In [SAB92].

[KORT92] D. Kortenkamp and E. Chown. A directional spreading activation network for mobile robot navigation. In [SAB92].

[KOZA90] J. R. Koza. Evolution and co-evolution of computer programs to control independently-acting agents. In [SAB90].

[KUBE92] C. R. Kube and H. Zhang. Collective robotic intelligence. In [SAB92].

[KUBO94] M. Kubo and Y. Kakazu. Learning coordinated motions in a competition for food between ant colonies. In [SAB94].

[KURT90] C. Kurtz. The evolution of information gathering: Operational constraints. In [SAB90].

[LIN90] L.-J. Lin. Self-improving reactive agents: Case studies of reinforcement learning frameworks. In [SAB90].

[LIN92] L.-J. Lin and T. Mitchell. Reinforcement learning with hidden states. In [SAB92].

[LIND92] A. Linden and F. Weber. Implementing inner drive through competence reflection. In [SAB92].

[LITT92] M. L. Littman. An optimization-based categorization of reinforcement learning environments. In [SAB92].

[LITT94] M. L. Littman. Memoryless policies: Theoretical limitations and practical results. In [SAB94].

[LOPE92] L. R. Lopez and R. E. Smith. Evolving artificial insect brains for artificial compound eye robotics. In [SAB92].

[MAES90] P. Maes. A bottom-up mechanism for behavior selection in an artificial creature. In [SAB90].

[MAES92] P. Maes. Behavior-based artificial intelligence. In [SAB92].

[MANT90] G. Manteuffel. A biological visuo-motor system: How dissimilar maps interact to produce behavior. In [SAB90].

[MATA90] M. J. Mataric. Navigating with a rat brain: A neurobiologically-inspired model for robot spatial representation. In [SAB90].

[MATA92] M. J. Mataric. Designing emergent behaviors: From local interactions to collective intelligence. In [SAB92].

[MATA94] M. Mataric. Learning to behave socially. In [SAB94].

[MAZE92] E. Mazer, J.-M. Ahuactzin, E.-G. Talbi, and P. Bessiere. The Ariadne's clew algorithm. In [SAB92].

[MCFA94] D. McFarland. Towards robot cooperation. In [SAB94].

[MEYE90] J.A. Meyer and A. Guillot. Simulation of adaptive behavior in animats: Review and prospect. In [SAB90].

[MILLA94] J. Millan. Learning efficient reactive behavioral sequences from basic reflexes in a goal-directed autonomous robot. In [SAB94].

[MILLE92] G. F. Miller and P. M. Todd. Evolutionary interactions among mate choice, speciation, and runaway sexual selection. In [SAB92].

[MILLE94] G. Miller and D. Cliff. Protean behavior in dynamic games I: Arguments for the co-evolution of pursuit-evasion tactics. In [SAB94].

[MORA94] P. Morasso and V. Sanguineti. Self-organizing topographic maps and motor planning. In [SAB94].

[MUNO94] R. Munos and J. Patinel. Reinforcement learning with dynamic covering of state-space: Partitioning Q-learning. In [SAB94].

[MURA94] F. Mura and N. Franceschini. Visual control of altitude and speed in a flying agent. In [SAB94].

[NEHM90] U. Nehmzow and T. Smithers. Mapbuilding using self-organising networks in really useful robots

[NEHM92] U. Nehmzow, T. Smithers, and B. McGonigle. Increasing behavioural repertoire in a mobile robot. In [SAB92]. In [SAB90].

[NEHM94] U. Nehmzow and B. McGonigle. Achieving rapid adaptations in robots by means of external tuition. In [SAB94].

[OSOR94] D. Osorio, W. Getz, and J. Rybak. Insect vision and olfaction: Different neural architectures for different kinds of sensory signal? In [SAB94].

[PARE90] J. Paredis. The evolution of behavior: Some experiments. In [SAB90].

[PARK92] L. E. Parker. Adaptive action selection for cooperative agent teams. In [SAB92].

[PENG92] J. Peng and R. J. Williams. Efficient learning and planning within the Dyna framework . In [SAB92].

[PFEI92] R. Pfeifer and P. Verschure. Designing efficiently navigating non-goal-directed robots. In [SAB92].

[PIER90] D. Pierce and B. Kuipers. Learning hill-climbing functions as a strategy for generating behaviors in a mobile robot. In [SAB90].

[PIPE94] A. G. Pipe, T. C. Fogarty, and A. Winfield. A hybrid architecture for learning continuous environmental models in maze problems. In [SAB94].

[PRES92] T. J. Prescott and J. E. W. Mayhew. Building long-range cognitive maps using local landmarks. In [SAB92].

[PRES94] T. J. Prescott. Spatial learning and representation in animats. In [SAB94].

[REYN92] C. W. Reynolds. An evolved, vision-based behavioral model of coordinated group motion. In [SAB92].

[REYN94] C. W. Reynolds. Evolution of corridor following behavior in a noisy world. In [SAB94].

[RIBE92] F. Ribeiro, J.-P. Barthes, and E. Oliveira. Dynamic selection of action sequences. In [SAB92].

[RIOL90] R. L. Riolo. Lookahead planning and latent learning in a classifier system. In [SAB90].

[ROBB94] P. Robbins. Parasitism in an artificial world. In [SAB94].

[ROIT90a] H. L. Roitblat, P. W. B. Moore, P. E. Nachtigall, and R. H. Penner. Biomimetic sonar processing: From dolphin echolocation to artificial neural networks. In [SAB90].

[ROIT90b] H. L. Roitblat. Cognitive action theory as a control architecture. In [SAB90].

[ROIT92] H. L. Roitblat, P. W. B. Moore, D. H. Helweg and P. E. Nachtigall. Representation and processing of acoustic information in a biomimetic neural network. In [SAB92].

[ROIT94] H. L. Roitblat. Mechanisms and process in animal behavior: Models of animals, animals as models. In [SAB94].

[ROSE92] B. E. Rosen and J. M. Goodwin. Dynamic flight control with adaptive course coding. In [SAB92].

[RUTK94] J. Rutkowska. Emergent functionality in infant action and development. In [SAB94].

[SAB90] J.A. Meyer and S.W. Wilson (Eds). 1991. From Animals to Animats: Proceedings of the First International Conference on Simulation of Adaptive Behavior. The MIT Press/Bradford Books.

[SAB92] J.A. Meyer, H.L. Roitblat, and S.W. Wilson (Eds). 1993. From Animals to Animats 2: Proceedings of the Second International Conference on Simulation of Adaptive Behavior. The MIT Press/Bradford Books.

[SAB94] D. Cliff, P. Husbands, J.A. Meyer, and S.W. Wilson (Eds). 1994. From Animals to Animats 3: Proceedings of the Third International Conference on Simulation of Adaptive Behavior. The MIT Press/Bradford Books.

[SAHO94] M. Sahota. Action selection for robots in dynamic environments through inter-behaviour bidding. In [SAB94].

[SAIT94] F. Saito and T. Fukada. Two-link robot brachiation with connectionist Q-learning. In [SAB94].

[SAUN94] G. Saunders, J. Kolen, and J. Pollack. The importance of leaky levels for behavior-based AI. In [SAB94].

[SCHMA92] N. A. Schmajuk and H. T. Blair. Dynamics of spatial navigation: An adaptive neural network. In [SAB92].

[SCHMA94] N. A. Schmajuk. Behavioral dynamics of escape and avoidance: A neural network approach. In [SAB94].

[SCHMI90] J. Schmidhuber. A possibility for implementing curiosity and boredom in model-building neural controllers. In [SAB90].

[SCHMI92] J. Schmidhuber and R. Wahnsiedler. Planning simple trajectories using neural subgoal generators. In [SAB92].

[SCHN90] U. Schnepf. Robot ethology: A proposal for the research into intelligent autonomous systems. In [SAB90].

[SCUT94] T. Scutt. The five neuron trick: Using classic conditioning to learn how to seek light. In [SAB94].

[SHAF94] S. Shafir and J. Roughgarden. The effect of memory length on the foraging behavior of a lizard. In [SAB94].

[SLOT94] J. J. Slotine. Stability in adaptation and learning. In [SAB94].

[SMAR94] W. D. Smart and J. Hallam. Location recognition in rats and robots. In [SAB94].

[STAD92] J. E. R. Staddon. A note on rate-sensitive habituation. In [SAB92].

[STEE90] L. Steels. Towards a theory of emergent functionality. In [SAB90].

[STEE94] L. Steels. A case study in the behavior-oriented design of autonomous agents. In [SAB94].

[SUTT90] R. S. Sutton. Reinforcement learning architectures for animats. In [SAB90].

[TENE92] J. Tenenberg, J. Karlsson, and S. Whitehead. Learning via task decomposition . In [SAB92].

[THER90] G. Theraulaz, S. Goss, J. Gervet, and J.-L. Deneubourg. Task differentation in Polistes wasp colonies: A model for self-organizing groups of robots. In [SAB90].

[TOAT90] F.Toates and P. Jensen. Ethological and psychological models of motivation – Towards a synthesis. In [SAB90].

[TOAT94] F. Toates. What is cognitive and what is not cognitive . In [SAB94].

[TODD90] P. M. Todd and G. F. Miller. Exploring adaptive agency II: Simulating the evolution of associative learning. In [SAB90].

[TODD92] P. M. Todd and S. W. Wilson. Environment structure and adaptive behavior from the ground up. In [SAB92].

[TODD94] P. M. Todd, S. W. Wilson, A. B. Somayaji, and H. Yanco. The blind breeding the blind: Adaptive behavior without looking. In [SAB94].

[TYRR90] T. Tyrrell and J. E. W. Mayhew. Computer simulation of an animal environment. In [SAB90].

[TYRR92] T. Tyrrell. The use of hierarchies for action selection. In [SAB92].

[UTTA92] W. R. Uttal, T. Shepherd, S. Dayanand, and R. Lovell. An integrated computational model of a perceptual-motor system. In [SAB92].

[VENT94] G. Venturini. Adaptation in dynamic environments through a minimal probability of exploration. In [SAB94].

[VERS92] P. F. M. J. Verschure and R. Pfeifer. Categorization, representations, and the dynamics of system-environment interaction: A case study in autonomous systems. In [SAB92].

[VOGE92] T. U. Vogel. Learning biped robot obstacle crossing. In [SAB92].

[VONK90] M. Vonk, F. Putters, and B.-J. Velthuis. The causal analysis of an adaptive system: Sex-ratio decisions as observed in a parasitic wasp and simulated by a network model. In [SAB90].

[WALT90] D. L. Waltz. Eight principles for building an intelligent robot. In [SAB90].

[WANG90] DeLiang Wang and M. A. Arbib. Hierarchical dishabituation of visual discrimination in toads. In [SAB90].

[WEBB94] B. Webb. Robotic experiments in cricket phonotaxis. In [SAB94].

[WEIS92] G. Weiss. Action selection and learning in multi-agent environments. In [SAB92].

[WERN92] G. M. Werner and M. G. Dyer. Evolution of herding behavior in artificial animals. In [SAB92].

[WERN94] G. M. Werner. Using second order neural connections for motivation of behavioral choices. In [SAB94].

[WILS90] S. W. Wilson. The animat path to AI. In [SAB90].

[YAMA94] B. Yamauchi and R. Beer. Integrating reactive, sequential, and learning behavior using dynamical neural networks. In [SAB94].

[YANC92] H. Yanco and L. A. Stein. An adaptive communication protocol for cooperating mobile robots. In [SAB92].

[YEAP90] W. K. Yeap and C. C. Handley. Four important issues in cognitive mapping. In [SAB90].

Mechanism and process in animal behavior:
Models of animals, animals as models

Herbert L. Roitblat

Department of Psychology
University of Hawaii at Manoa
2430 Campus Road
Honolulu, HI 96822 USA
roitblat@hawaii.edu

Abstract

The concept of representation is essential to understanding and predicting behavior. Arguments against the use of the concept of representation in animats are typically arguments against a certain style of representational theorizing. Animals are useful models for the development of synthetic or robotic systems, but their usefulness depends on an understanding of the mechanisms that animals actually employ to control their behavior. This paper reviews some issues in animal behavior that have important implications for the construction of control structures. Reflex-like control structures are shown to be overly simplistic to account for animal behavior, rather, animal control systems appear to employ hierarchical control structures.

1. Representations

In an interdisciplinary field such as that represented at this conference, success of the field depends on the participants' ability to share the essential findings of their component fields. By the very nature of interdisciplinary fields it is extremely difficult to be an expert in all of the components at the same time. It is very difficult, for example, to be both an expert on how to design and build robots and an expert on animal behavior, yet our success depends on our ability to apply the knowledge of one field to the development of the other. We are likely to develop better, more successful robots if we base their structure and function on that of existing animals. We are also more likely to actually understand animal functioning if we can simulate it in artificial situations and if we can use the analytic tools of systems analysis and design in animal research.

Specialists in each field tend to view the other from an idealized distance. Those who work directly with animals might think it easy to build models of animal behavior into working robotic systems. The roboticist might not be able to separate outdated views of animal behavior from current views and might, therefore, seek to use as models for

robotic developments discredited accounts of animal functionality. This is not simply a matter of theoretical style, because the value of using animals as models for robotic systems is the value of applying accurate accounts of animal control functions. Basing an artificial system on an inadequate account of animal behavior cannot lead to the development of adequate synthetic systems. It is not the behavior, per se, that serves as model and inspiration for robotic development, rather it is the behaviorist's model of the animal behavior that provides support for synthetic development. A poor account of animal behavior is likely to lead to a poorly performing synthetic system.

In the rest of this chapter, I review some of the issues in animal behavior that may appear to investigators from a distance to be straightforward and settled in a certain way. The goal of this review is to provide the reader with the current state-of-the-art in animal behavioral control structures.

Several of the participants at the preceding SAB meetings (Meyer & Wilson, 1991; Meyer, Roitblat, & Wilson, 1993) have argued strenuously that we should avoid the use of representations (e.g., Brooks, 1991). By "representation" they appear to mean symbolic rule-like systems based on arbitrary and discrete symbols manipulated according to syntactic-like rules. Clark (1990) called this kind of system a strong symbol system. Newell and Simon (1976) asserted that a physical example of such a symbol processing device is both a necessary and a sufficient mechanism for producing intelligent performance. The counter hypothesis is that discrete symbol processing is not necessary for cognition and behavior, and is rather, entirely inappropriate as an account of truly intelligent performance. This is apparently the position of the anti-representationalists.

By conflating the concept of representation with the concept of a strong symbol system, there is danger of discarding the good along with the bad. Learning organisms change as a result of their experience, and those changes are representations (Roitblat, 1982). There is no compelling reason to believe, however, that these representations must resemble the kind of word-like tokens that play a central role in strong symbol systems. Rather, organisms can use any number of alternative forms of representation. If experience at one time is to affect behavior at another, then the organism must have some means of representing that experience. Some change in the organism must depend on the experience, which can influence later behavior. Such changes are representations, even though they may not be discrete tokenized symbols (Roitblat, 1982; in press).

In psychology, behaviorists also tried to discard the concept of representation. They argued that behavior was a direct product of the animal's reinforcement history manifested as a set of reflex-like stimulus-response associations (see Roitblat, 1987 for a review). Implicit in their analysis is an assumption of a direct correspondence (Bolles, 1975; Roitblat, 1982) between observable surface variables and internal representational variables. In the behaviorist tradition, animals were assumed capable of only a single level control structure[1]. For example, Hull (1943) argued that the acquisition of knowledge was identical to the acquisition of habits and instantiated as the formation of new reflex arcs. Changes in the conditional probability of a behavior given some stimulus were assumed to correspond to and be the result of a strengthened connection between the stimulus and the response.

The reflex is a convenient unit for the representation of knowledge because it specifies both knowledge, and the behavior that results from that knowledge, as a connection between a stimulus and a particular response. Learning is equated with behavior change. Furthermore, a reflex approach has the appearance of providing objective mechanisms for the description and analysis of behavior (see Roitblat, 1987). Despite their structural simplicity, reflexes or similar control structures are not adequate to represent the range of behaviors of which animals are capable. Rather, it appears necessary to include mechanisms that are more active in seeking information from their environment, encoding it, and using it in flexible and intelligent ways (Gallistel, 1989; Roitblat, 1982, 1987; Roitblat & von Fersen, 1992).

In a strictly reflex-based control system, all control structures receive direct sensory input and directly control actions. Each reflex has a triggering stimulus condition that is sufficient to cause its activation. The reflex activates or fires whenever its sufficient stimulus conditions are present.

On activation it produces a specific response, usually a motor action.

One reflex can interact with another through chaining, potentiation, and inhibition. Chaining occurs when the action resulting from the firing of one reflex is the stimulus that triggers another reflex. Potentiation occurs, when the firing of one reflex makes another reflex more sensitive to its own triggering stimulus, and inhibition occurs when the firing of one reflex makes another reflex less sensitive to its triggering stimulus. In the stimulus-response (S-R) perspective, such mechanisms are thought to be sufficient to produce all behaviors. Complex behaviors are argued to involve more reflexes than simple behaviors, but they are still organized according to the principles of potentiation, inhibition, and chaining. Every behavior is thought to be the direct and automatic product of environmental stimuli. No internal factors are supposed to operate, except for such internal stimuli as limb position, stomach contractions, and so forth, which, although inside the organism, are just as directly sensory as visual or olfactory stimuli. Figure 1 shows an example of part of a S-R behavioral control structure.

There is a substantial body of evidence that suggests that such a simple S-R control structure is inadequate to account for animal behavior. Because of space limitations, I will discuss three of them. (1) Animals learn about features of the environment that cannot be explained by simply responding to specific stimuli (place learning, learning about dimensions), and (2) animals learn response rules that cannot be computed by single layer control structures (e.g., negative pattern learning). (3) Learning seems to involve hierarchical connections (e.g., occasion setting).

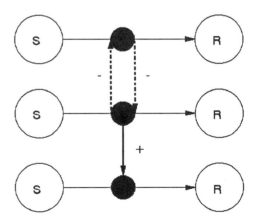

Figure 1. Three connected reflexes. The first and second reflexes are mutually inhibitory (dashed arrows), the second reflex potentiates the third reflex (solid arrow).

---

[1]They did not, of course, use terms like control architecture, but their ideas can be readily translated into such terms.

2. Place learning

According to the strong S-R view, learning is the formation of connections between specific stimulus events and specific motor events. The paradigm for this relation is the innate patellar tendon (knee jerk) reflex in which a stimulation of receptors on the patellar tendon causes leg extensors to contract, which results in a knee jerk. Place learning experiments demonstrate that learning must be more abstract than this direct connection would allow.

MacFarlane (1930) tested rats in a multi-choice-point maze consisting of several interconnected alleys. One path through the maze led to a food reward. He found that rats would successfully and correctly run in a maze after being trained to swim the maze or after being pulled through the maze on a small raft. The muscular movements involved in swimming and running are very different, yet the animals showed nearly complete transfer from one situation to the other. Hence, animals must be learning more about the maze than just the correct patterns of movement. According to the single-layer control mechanism view, the rat learned to navigate through the maze by producing specific motor patterns in response to specific cues present in the maze. Each choice point in the maze can be recognized by specific stimuli (e.g., the distance to landmark cues, the pattern of scraped paint on the floor), and has associated with it a specific response (e.g., move the legs to turn left, move the legs to walk forward). All of the serial organization of the rat's maze performance is due to the serial organization of the maze. Wherever the rat is in the maze, if it encounters the cues characteristic of that choice point it will, after learning, produce the response appropriate to that point.

By this analysis, a rat trained to swim through the maze might learn some specific motor patterns to carry it from one choice point to another, but it could not have learned useful movements when pulled through on a boat. In neither case could the rat have learned specific motor patterns adequate to move it through the drained maze. The pattern of muscular activity appropriate for swimming and for running are very different. Similarly, the stimulus patterns characteristic of the choice points in the flooded maze are also substantially different from those in the dry maze. The rat's performance after swimming and riding, both indicate that the rat also learned "higher-level" information about traversing the maze that was more abstract than the specific muscular movements necessary to move from one end to the other.

In contrast to the behaviorist single-layer control mechanism, Tolman (e.g., 1948) proposed a more elaborate control structure. Tolman called the S-R account, in which the rat learns specific muscular movements in response to specific stimuli, a molecular account. He argued that such

an account was inadequate, and that a more molar explanation of behavior was required. He argued, for example, that:

> The stimuli . . . are not connected by just simple one-to-one switches to outgoing responses. Rather the incoming impulses are usually worked over and elaborated . . . into a tentative cognitivelike map of the environment. And it is this tentative map indicating routes and paths and environmental relationships, which finally determines what responses, if any, the animal will finally release. (Tolman, 1948, p. 192)

Tolman argued that animals learn expectancies, families of which are organized into "cognitive maps," representing organism-environment interactions rather than unorganized collections of stimulus-response units.

> [An expectancy] as I conceive it, is a condition in the organism which is equivalent to what in ordinary parlance we call a "belief" (a readiness or disposition) to the effect that an instance of this *sort* of stimulus situation, if reacted to by an instance of this *sort* of response, will lead to an instance of that *sort* of further stimulus situation, or else, simply by itself be accompanied, or followed, by an instance of that *sort* of stimulus situation. (Tolman, 1959, p. 113)

In Tolman's analysis of MacFarlane's (1930) results, he argued that the rat learned a set of expectancies about the sorts of responses to be made at various points in the maze rather than about specific responses. The animal's learning was characterized by the kind of change a response would produce on the rat's local environment, rather than by the specific kind of movement that would produce that change. The rat was capable of using different patterns of movement to instantiate the same sort of action, as in switching from swimming to running when the environmental conditions changed.

Further support for Tolman's position comes from some experiments that specifically pitted response learning against place learning. In one of these experiments (Tolman, Ritchie, & Kalish, 1946), rats were trained to run in a + maze--a maze shaped like a large + sign with arms extending from a central platform in each of the cardinal directions (i.e., north, east, south, and west). One of the arms (e.g., the north one) was blocked off. The rat was always started in the south arm and rewarded with some food for going, for example, to the east arm, that is, for making a right turn. Under these circumstances, the single-layer view predicts that the rats learn a pattern of right-turning movements. They learn to turn to the right to get food. On the other hand, the expectancy view predicts that the rats learn to expect food in a particular place. They learn to go into the east arm to get food.

Both analyses predict the same results during the initial training phase of the experiment, that the rats will learn to find the food. They make different predictions, however, when the south arm is blocked off and the rat is started from the north arm of the maze during the second phase of the experiment. The single-layer analysis predicts that the rat will continue to turn right (or if the stimulus situation is sufficiently different, choose randomly), but now, because it is starting from the opposite end of the maze, it will enter the west arm if it makes a right turn. The expectancy view predicts that the rat will continue to expect food in the same *place*, and so will continue to go to the east arm. The rats in this experiment went to the east arm, whether they were started from the south arm in phase 1, or from the north arm in phase 2. They thus made opposite molecular responses in the two phases of the experiment (i.e., right turns during phase 1 and left turns during phase 2) and, therefore, showed evidence of having learned about place, rather than about the specific response they performed to get to that place. Other experiments involving adaptation to blocks and detours showed compatible evidence for place learning (e.g., Tolman & Honzik, 1930b).

The success of place-learning experiments demonstrates that animals do not learn simply by pairing specific stimuli with specific responses as a single-layer reflex-like mechanism would predict, because their behavior is controlled by more abstract properties of the situation than such a simple single-layer model would allow.

3. Timing and chaining

The traditional S-R view asserts that complex behaviors are made up of chains of simple reflex-like responses. The activation of one reflex produces a change in the stimulus situation, which then triggers the activation of the next behavior in the sequence. As Lashley (1951) pointed out, however, many behaviors such as piano playing, prey catching, or touch typing, involve responses that follow one another so quickly that there is no time for feedback from the completion of one response to be the stimulus eliciting the next response. As a result, he argued, complex acts like piano playing must be organized at higher levels than chains

of reflex-like stimulus-response units. Many behaviors, furthermore, have been found to be controlled by endogenous oscillators. Components of the behavior are controlled by their phase relation to the oscillator and not by feedback from the effects of the response (see Gallistel, 1980).

4. Negative pattern learning

Results from classical conditioning experiments also argue for a more complicated control structure than that allowed by traditional S-R theories. For example *negative pattern learning* demonstrates that rats are capable of learning about combinations of stimuli that cannot be represented by a single-layer control structure. In negative-pattern learning, an animal is trained with two conditional stimuli (CSs), each of which, when presented separately, is followed by an unconditional stimulus (US). When the two CSs are presented together, however, they are not followed by the US (A+B+/AB-). Negative pattern learning presents problems very similar to those presented by the XOR problem.

Table 1. Truth Table for the Negative Patterning Problem

Stimulus A	Stimulus B	Reinforcer R
1	0	1
0	1	1
1	1	0
0	0	0

Note: 1 = stimulus present. 0 = stimulus absent. Stimulus A is presented alone on some trials, Stimulus B is presented alone on some trials, both or which are reinforced, and both stimuli are presented together on some trials, but not reinforced. The condition in which neither stimulus is presented (and not reinforced) corresponds to the intertrial interval.

Animals learn to discriminate compound presentations from individual stimulus presentations. They continue responding to the individual stimuli, but withhold responding to the compound. This problem is revealing, because correct performance conflicts with a class of associative models that says that response level is a linear function of input activation levels. For example, according to a simple model, the animal learns to associate the CS with the US by correlating the occurrence of the two events (e.g., Rescorla, 1966; Rescorla & Wagner, 1972). The strength of the connection between the CS and the US depends on the magnitude of the correlation, and the activation of the response depends on the input value as modulated by the connection between the CS and the US. Finally, either the strength of the response or its probability is presumed to be a simple linear function of the activation level of the output. By this model, the stronger the input, the stronger or more likely is the response. If the animal responds to the individual stimuli, then it clearly has learned an association between those CSs and the US that allows activation of the response. Therefore, when the two CSs are combined, the animal should respond with even more vigor (or at least not less) to the compound than to the individual stimuli because the total input strength must be higher than that obtained with either stimulus alone.

Despite the predictions of such a linear-response model, animals do learn the negative pattern relation and withhold responding to the compound while responding to each of its elements.

In fact, no linear function of the two CSs can acquire the negative patterning relation (Minsky & Papert, 1969). Therefore, this performance rules out the class of models that says that responding is simply a learned linear function of input intensities. Solution of the negative patterning problem, and related problems (like exclusive or, XOR), requires some additional element that represents the combination of the two inputs. Some models employ a sensory unit that responds only to the joint occurrence of the two CSs, but the large number of stimuli that can effectively be trained as CSs implies a combinatorially explosive number of these joint-occurrence units, one for each pair of potential CSs (Kehoe & Gormezano, 1980).

The addition of joint-occurrence input units transforms the negative patterning problem into a linearly separable one (i.e., a problem in which some value of activity can be used to determine the class of the inputs, such as whether or not a response is appropriate), but in a somewhat ad hoc manner. Another way to solve such nonlinearly separable problems is to use an additional layer of processing units, that intervene between the stimuli and the responses, such as the hidden layer found in many connectionist networks. The hidden layer constitutes an internal representation of the relevant aspects of the input *patterns* (e.g., Elman & Zipser, 1987). Hence, application of this kind of model both solves knotty problems in animal learning, and suggests a structure for the kinds of representations animals form during learning. The units in the hidden layer form internal representations of the relations among events.

5. Contextual conditioning and occasion setting

A phenomenon known as "occasion setting" suggests that even basic conditioning is not as simple a process as traditional analyses would indicate (e.g., Colwill & Rescorla, 1990a). Three events occur during instrumental conditioning (Rescorla, 1991; Roitblat, 1987): (1) The animal is in a context, which presents specific stimulus characteristics (S). (2) The animal makes a response (R), and (3) the response is followed by an outcome(O). Generally, if the outcome is hedonically positive, the animal becomes more likely to repeat the response in that context.

The presence of three events in the instrumental conditioning situation means that there are at least three interevent relationships an animal could learn (S-R, S-O, anf R-O). Traditional S-R theories of learning (e.g., Hull, 1943; see Roitblat, 1987) describe instrumental conditioning as the result of a learned stimulus-response (S-R) association between the discriminative or contextual stimulus and the instrumental response. The reinforcer serves as a kind of catalyst to strengthen this connection, but does not otherwise participate in learning, and is not explicitly represented.

The animal could also learn about response-outcome (R-O) relations. It could learn, for example, that production of a certain behavior leads to a certain outcome. In this kind of theory, the animal's performance is controlled by an expectation that the reinforcer will follow the learned behavior. In order for such a theory to account for discrimination learning, however, it must also assume that the animal learns simultaneously about stimulus outcome relations, so that the animal can behave differentially in different contexts (e.g., press a lever when a light is on, but pull a chain when a tone is on). On this account, the contextual stimulus tells the animal when the outcome can be expected. Theories of this sort are often called two-process theories (e.g., Rescorla & Solomon, 1967; Trapold & Overmier, 1972) because they assume that learned performance is the result of two associative processes, one forming a connection between stimulus and outcome (S-O) and the other between response and outcome (R-O).

Finally a third class of theory proposes that the animal learns about more than specific associations between specific events. These theories propose that the animal learns a response outcome (R-O) association, and that this association as a unit is then associated with the contextual stimulus (S-[R-O]) These theories are called occasion-setting theories (Colwill & Rescorla, 1986, 1989; Mackintosh & Dickinson, 1979). They assume that the stimulus becomes associated with and modulates the response-outcome relation by specifying the occasion on which the response produces the outcome. On this view, the occasion-setting stimulus acts as a modulator or shunt (Grossberg & Schmajuk, 1987) that controls the activity of the response-outcome association and its ability to produce behavior.

5.1. Representation of outcome

The standard, traditional, account of instrumental conditioning is inadequate because it fails to include information about the outcome of an instrumental behavior (see Roitblat, 1987 for a discussion of this issue). A number of phenomena, including the effects of differential outcomes, and reinforcer devaluation (described below) all indicate that animals do know about the outcome of their behavior. Behavioral contrast also demonstrates that animals know about the outcome of their behavior.

In behavioral contrast (see Mackintosh, 1974), changing the outcome of a learned behavior changes the animal's performance, even if both outcomes are otherwise adequate to support conditioning. For example, rats trained to run through a maze for a preferred food reward and then switched to a less preferred reward will run more slowly after the switch than rats trained throughout with the poorer reward (e.g., Elliot, 1928). This result indicates that the rats had information about the quality of reward they would receive at the end of the maze and that their performance was affected by the relative quality of this reward.

Further evidence that animals learn directly about the outcome of their behavior is seen in experiments on reinforcer devaluation. For example, in one experiment (Colwill & Rescorla, 1985), rats were trained to perform one response (chain pull) for sucrose solution and to perform another response (lever press) for food pellets (in fact, the experiment was fully counterbalanced, another group was trained with the opposite response-outcome pair). Both of these responses were trained in the same environment under identical stimulus conditions. Following training on these two response-outcome pairs, one of outcomes was devalued by pairing it with the administration of LiCl, which produces specific aversions to flavors with which it is paired (e.g., Dickinson, Nicholas, & Adams, 1982; Holland & Straub, 1979). . The bar and chain were not present during this illness induction, so the animal presumably had no opportunity to learn about response-outcome or response-illness relations. The animal was then tested in the presence of the two response devices, without presentation of the reinforcer so again, the animal presumably had no opportunity to learn about the relationship between the response and the outcome (this is called an extinction test) Whatever effects devaluation might have, these effects would presumably have to be based on associations between the response and the outcome learned during the original training prior to

devaluation. It would not be surprising, for example, for an animal to learn to withhold a response associated with an unpleasant outcome. Nevertheless, the rats in this experiment suppressed responding to the device that formerly had produced the reinforcer that was devalued, but continued to respond to the device that delivered the other outcome. The animal seems to have learned a response-outcome association during the normal course of training and then subsequently learned that the outcome was undesirable. It was further able to combine these two pieces of information appropriately to suppress responding for the now devalued outcome.

Animals also learn about stimulus-outcome relations. For example, Trapold (1970) found that rats learned a discrimination more quickly if each choice led to a unique outcome than if both responses led the same outcome (see also Honig, 1984; Peterson, 1984). The rats were reinforced with a food pellet for pressing one lever in the presence of a tone and with sugar water for pressing another lever in the presence of a clicker. Although this difference is suggestive of the use of stimulus-outcome associations, it could also be the result of a response-outcome relation, because both the stimulus and the response were both differentially related to specific outcomes.

Stronger evidence for the representation of stimulus-outcome relations would be obtained if it can be shown that the control exerted on responding by the stimulus can be transferred to novel responses never trained in the presence of that stimulus (Colwill & Rescorla, 1988). Rats were trained to perform a nose-poke response in the presence of two stimuli. In the presence of a light, the nose poke led to one outcome (e.g., food pellets) and in the presence of a noise, the nose poke led to a different outcome (e.g., sugar water). The animals were then taught to make novel responses, chain pull and lever presses, in the absence of the light and the noise. Chain pulling led to one outcome (e.g., food pellets) and lever pressing led reliably to the other (e.g., sugar water; again everything was counterbalanced). Finally, the light and the noise were reinstated. If the animal had learned to expect one outcome in the presence of the light and a different outcome in the presence of the noise, then it should produce the response appropriate to that expectation in the presence of each stimulus. Using an extinction test, Colwill and Rescorla (1988) found that rats preferred the response appropriate to the outcome expectation in the presence of each stimulus (e.g., chain pulling in the presence of the light and lever pressing in the presence of the noise).

Evidence that animals learn about the third binary relation, between the stimulus and the response, is remarkably weaker. Rats continue to respond at nonzero rates, although at substantially lower levels than control animals following reinforcer devaluation. Even when they will no longer consume a food when presented, they will continue to produce some of the responses that formerly produced that food. It is interesting to note that S-R associations were the primary mechanism of learning proposed by the behaviorists and other early students of animal learning, but there is actually little direct empirical support for such associations (Rescorla, 1991; Colwill & Rescorla, 1990b). Reflexes clearly play an important role in animal behavior, for example in the control of locomotion, but the evidence that changes in the patterns of reflex-like mechanisms are the basis of instrumental learning is weak at best.

6. Hierarchical representation

In addition to the binary associations just described, there is substantial evidence that animals also form a hierarchical structure in which the contextual stimulus dominates and modifies the relation between the response and its outcome. On this view, the animal initially learns about the R-O relationship and then this relationship as a unit becomes associated with the contextual S. The stimulus comes to signal the relation between the response and its outcome.

The presence of three nominal stimuli in the ordinary conditioning situation does not guarantee that the animal forms a hierarchical relation among the terms. Two process accounts, as discussed earlier, argue that behavior is controlled by the interaction between two separate associations between the stimulus and the outcome and between the response and the outcome. The association between the contextual stimulus and the outcome parallels the relationship underlying classical conditioning. In classical conditioning, the crucial variable that determines the degree of conditioning is the correlation between the conditional stimulus (CS) and the unconditional stimulus (US) or reinforcer (Rescorla, 1966). Presenting the reinforcer equally often in the presence of a CS and in its absence (all other things being equal) prevents the development of a conditional response (Durlach, 1983; Gamzu & Williams, 1973; Rescorla, 1968). Under these conditions, the CS does not predict the US because the conditional probability of the US given the CS is equal to the conditional probability of the US in the absence of the CS.

In a series of experiments, Rescorla (1991) found that rats did learn about a contextual stimulus present in a situation that would not support the formation of an association between the stimulus and the outcome. In one experiment (Rescorla, 1990b), rats were trained during the first phase of the experiment in the presence of light to produce one response for one outcome and another response

for another outcome (L: R1-O1; R2-O2). During the second stage of training, the light was combined with either a tone or with noise. The same response-outcome relations were maintained in the presence of the tone-light combination (TL: R1-O1; R2-O2), but these relations were reversed in the presence of the noise-light combination(NL: R1-O2; R2-O1). Under these conditions, the tone was expected to be redundant with the light because no new information was provided by the tone plus light combination than by the light alone. In simple conditioning situations, animals appear not to learn about the addition of a redundant stimulus. The same response-outcome relations were used both before and after the tone was added. The noise, however, was not redundant, because presentation of the noise signalled a reversal in the response outcome relations (R1 was reinforced with O2, R2 was reinforced with O1). Notice that the light is equally paired with both outcomes, and that the noise and tone are also equally paired with both outcomes. As a result we would not expect these stimuli to differ in their predictability of the outcome. Notice also that the light, tone, and noise are equally paired with each of the responses, so we would not expect these stimuli to differ in their association with the responses. Because of the redundancy of the tone and light, however, we would predict that the animal might not learn about the signalling properties of the tone, but might learn about the signalling properties of the noise, because it signals a reversed response-outcome relation.

Rescorla tested this prediction by presenting the animal with opportunities to make the two responses in the presence of the tone and in the presence of the noise (the light and reinforcers were omitted during this test). The animals responded very little to the two response devices in the presence of the redundant tone, but responded substantially in the presence of the noise. Opportunities for learning about specific S-R, S-O, and R-O outcomes were controlled, but still the animals performed differentially in the presence of the noise relative to their peformance in the presence of the tone. These results show that animals learn about the ability of informative stimuli to signal the appropriate response-outcome relation. They don't just learn about pairs of events.

Additional evidence that the contextual stimulus can serve as a modulator for R-O relations was obtained in a subsequent experiment (Colwill & Rescorla, 1990a, Experiment 2) by devaluing one of the reinforcers. Rats were trained in the presence of one stimulus (e.g., noise) that one response (e.g., bar pressing) produced food pellets, and another response (e.g., chain pulling) produced another outcome (e.g., sucrose). The response outcome was reversed in the presence of the other stimulus (e.g., bar pressing produced sucrose and chain pulling produced food pellets). During the second stage of the experiment, the value of one of these reinforcers was reduced by pairing it with illness (as above). In this experiment, however, both responses were equally paired with this devalued reinforcer. Similarly, both stimuli were equally paired with both outcomes. The relationship between response and outcome, however, was signalled by the occasion-setting stimulus. Therefore, if the contextual stimuli had become modulators of the response-outcome relation, then one response should be depressed in the presence of one stimulus, and the other response should be depressed in the presence of the other stimulus. This is what they found. In the presence of each stimulus, the rats selectively suppressed the response that had produced the now devalued outcome, relative to the other response. Consistent with the hierarchical, occasion-setting view, this experiment clearly demonstrates that the stimuli came to modulate selectively the animals' expectations about the outcome of their behavior. Subsequent experiments have extended this modulation effect to higher-order relations (Arnold, Grahame, & Miller, 1991).

7. Conclusion: Representations in animals

In contrast to the traditional view of animals as passive responders to environmental change, the experiments reviewed above clearly show that animals are active processors of information about their environment. The biomimetic approach suggests that there are great benefits to using animals as models for the design of artificial control systems. The success of this approach, however, depends strongly on an appropriate analysis of the system from which we are trying to derive our lessons. As these data show, animal behavior cannot be characterized as merely reflexive, or even, as simply associative. Rather, animals appear to employ a variety of representations and mechanisms to control their behavior. Not all of these mechanisms may be strictly necessary for the construction of artificial systems, but their existence in animals suggests the possibility that they provide a level of capability not seen in systems lacking such representational structures and processes.

In contrast to the standard approach to intelligence embodied in the strong physical symbol system hypothesis, in this paper (and several others) I have advocated a complementary biomimetic approach. In this view, real progress in understanding intelligence will not come exclusively from a consideration of those behaviors that are characteristic of human technological and creative intelligence, but rather from understanding of the basic mechanisms of mundane performance. Playing chess is now relatively easy for a synthetic system, probably because chess playing can be described step by step using language or language-like representations. In contrast, such processes

as recognizing faces, or walking through a crowded room are not so easy to describe algorithmically, and have resisted solution using the traditional symbolic system approach.

Another possible explanation for the success of symbolic systems in the domains in which they have been effective is that they are often provided with symbolic information that is carefully formulated by an intelligent investigator who also interprets the system's symbolic output. Although the intelligence of many of the systems is undeniable, some of their success comes from the intelligent way in which investigators interact with the systems. A difficult problem can often be made simpler through the use of a clever representation, but it is the investigator's cleverness that produces the representation given to the system, the system does not usually do its own interpretation. In contrast, the biomimetic approach advocates modeling whole animals operating in their environments with specific sensory capacities. The biomimetic system responds to the environment rather than to some mediated interpretation of that environment.

Finally, it is probably misleading to assume that the development of an effective artificial chess player or something along the same conceptual lines would yield a generally intelligent artificial human. Solving all the problems of game playing may be of absolutely no worth for solving the problems of navigating through a complex maze of underground tunnels as rats do. Much everyday behavior, although technologically rather mundane, nevertheless appears on closer examination to require rather sophisticated processes. The animal behavior research reviewed above suggests something of that complexity.

Although animal behavior is not simple, it is also not incomprehensible. Deep understanding of behavioral control, sensory, and memory mechanisms in animals can add substantially to our understanding of intelligence in general, and the development of synthetic autonomous agents in particular.

References

Arnold, H. M., Grahame, N. J., & Miller, R. R. (1991). Higher order occasion setting. *Animal Learning and Behavior*, 19, 58-64.

Bolles, R. C. (1975) Learning motivation and cognition. In W. K. Estes (Ed.), *Handbook of learning and cognitive processes* (pp. 249-280). Hillsdale, NJ: Lawrence Erlbaum Associates.

Brooks, R. A. (1991). Intelligence without representation. *Artificial Intelligence*, 47, 139-159.

Clark, A. (1990) *Microcognition: Philosophy, cognitive science, and parallel distributed processing.* Cambridge, MA: MIT Press.

Colwill, R. M. & Rescorla, R. A. (1985). Instrumental responding remains sensitive to reinforcer devaluation after extensive training. *Journal of Experimental Psychology: Animal Behavior Processes*, 11, 520-536.

Colwill, R. M. & Rescorla, R. A. (1986). Associative structures and instrumental In G. H. Bower (Ed.), *The psychology of learning and motivation*, vol. 20 (pp. 55-104). New York: Academic Press.

Colwill, R. M. & Rescorla, R. A. (1988). Associations between the discriminative stimulus and the reinforcer in instrumental learning. *Journal of Experimental Psychology: Animal Behavior Processes*, 14, 155-164.

Colwill, R. M. & Rescorla, R. A. (1989). Associations with anticipated and obtained outcomes in instrumental learning. *Animal Learning and Behavior*, 17, 291-303.

Colwill, R. M. & Rescorla, R. A. (1990a). Evidence for the hierarchical structure of instrumental learning. *Animal Learning and Behavior*, 18, 71-82.

Colwill, R. M. & Rescorla, R. A. (1990b). Effect of reinforcer devaluation on discriminative control of instrumental behavior. *Journal of Experimental Psychology: Animal Behavior Processes*, 16, 40-47.

Dickinson, A., Nicholas, D. J. & Adams, C. D. (1983). The effect of instrumental training contingency on susceptibility to reinforcer devaluation. *Quarterly Journal of Experimental Psychology*, 35B, 35-51.

Durlach, P. J. (1983). The effect of signaling intertrial USs in autoshaping. *Journal of Experimental Psychology: Animal Behavior Processes*, 9, 374-389.

Elliott, M. H. (1928) The effect of change of reward on the maze performance of rats. *University of California Publications in Psychology, 4,* 19-30.

Elman, J. L. & Zipser, D. (1987). Representation and structure in connectionist models. CRL Technical Report 8903. Center for Research in Language, University of California, San Diego.

Gallistel, C. R. (1980). *The organization of action: A new synthesis.* Hillsdale, NJ: Lawrence Erlbaum Associates

Gallistel, C. R. (1989). Animal cognition: The representation of space time and number. *Annual Review of Psychology,* 40, 155-190.

Gamzu, E. R. & Williams, D. R. (1973). Associative factors underlying the pigeon's keypecking in autoshaping procedures. *Journal of the Experimental Analysis of Behavior*, 19, 225-232.

Grossberg, S. & Levine, D. S. (1987). Neural dynamics of attentionally modulated Pavlovian conditioning: Blocking, inter-stimulus interval, and secondary reinforcement. *Applied Optics*, 26, 5015-5030.

Grossberg, S. & Schmajuk, N. A. (1987). Neural dynamics of attentionally modulated Pavlovian conditioning:

Conditioned reinforcement, inhibition, and opponent processing. *Psychobiology*, 15, 195-240.

Holland, P. C. (1983). Occasion setting in Pavlovian feature positive discriminations. In M. L. Commons, R. J. Herrnstein, & A. R. Wagner (Eds.), *Quantitative analyses of behavior: Discrimination processes* (vol. 4, pp. 223-345). New York: Ballinger.

Holland, P. C. (1989a). Acquisition and transfer of conditional discrimination performance. *Journal of Experimental Psychology: Animal Behavior Processes*, 15, 154-165.

Holland, P. C. (1989b). Feature extinction enhances transfer of occasion setting. *Animal Learning and Behavior*, 17, 269-279.

Holland, P. C. & Straub, J. J. (1979). Differential effects of two ways of devaluing the unconditioned stimulus after Pavlovian appetitive conditioning. *Journal of Experimental Psychology: Animal Behavior Processes*, 5, 65-68.

Honig, W. K. (1984) Contributions of animal memory to the interpretation of animal learning. In H. L. Roitblat, T. G. Bever, & H. S. Terrace (Eds.), *Animal cognition.* Hillsdale, N.J.: Erlbaum, 29-44.

Hull, C. L. (1943). *Principles of Behavior.* New York: Appleton-Century-Crofts.

Kehoe, E. J. & Gormezano, I. (1980). Configuration and combination laws in conditioning with compound stimuli. *Psychological Bulletin*, 87, 351-378.

Klopf, A. H. (1988). A neuronal model of classical conditioning. *Psychobiology*, 16, 85-125.

Lashley, K. S. (1951). The problem of serial order in behavior. In L. A. Jeffress (Ed.), *Cerebral Mechanisms in Behavior.* New York: Wiley, pp. 112-136.

MacFarlane, D. A. (1930). The role of kinesthesis in maze learning, *University of California Publications in Psychology*, 4, 277-305.

Mackintosh, N. J. (1974). *The psychology of Animal Learning.* New York: Academic Press.

Mackintosh, N. J. & Dickinson, A. (1979). Instrumental (Type II) conditioning. In A. Dickinson & R. A. Boakes (Eds.), *Mechanisms of learning and motivation.* Hillsdale, NJ: Lawrence Erlbaum Associates.

Meyer, J. A., Roitblat, H. L. & Wilson, S. W. (1993). *From animals to animats 2.* Cambridge, MA: MIT Press.

Meyer, J. A. & Wilson, S. W. (1991). *From animals to animats.* Cambridge, MA: MIT Press.

Minsky, M. & Papert, S. (1969). *Perceptrons.* Cambridge, MA: MIT Press.

Newell, A. & Simon, H. A. (1976) Computer science as empirical enquiry. In J. Haugeland (Ed.), *Mind design.* Cambridge, MA: MIT Press.

Peterson, G. B. (1984). How expectancies guide behavior. In H. L. Roitblat, T. G. Bever, & H. S. Terrace (Eds.),

Animal cognition. (pp. 135-147). Hillsdale, NJ: Erlbaum.

Rescorla, R. A. (1966). Predictability and number of pairings in Pavlovian fear conditioning. *Psychonomic Science,* 4, 383-384.

Rescorla, R. A. (1968). Probability of shock in the presence and absence of CS in fear conditioning. *Journal of Comparative and Physiological Psychology,* 66, 1-5.

Rescorla, R. A. (1990a). Evidence for an association between the discriminative stimulus and the response-outcome association in instrumental learning. *Journal of Experimental Psychology: Animal Behavior Processes,* 16, 326-334.

Rescorla, R. A. (1990b). The role of information about the response-outcome relation in instrumental discrimination learning. *Journal of Experimental Psychology: Animal Behavior Processes,* 16, 262-270.

Rescorla, R. A. (1991). Associative relations in instrumental learning: The Eighteenth Bartlett memorial Lecture. *Quarterly Journal of Experimental Psychology,* 43B, 1-23.

Rescorla, R. A. (1992). Hierarchical associative relations in Pavlovian conditioning and instrumental training. *Current Directions in Psychological Science,* 1, 66-70.

Rescorla, R. A. (1992). Response-independent outcome presentation can leave instrumental R-O associations intact. *Animal Learning and Behavior,* 20, 104-111.

Rescorla, R. A. & Solomon, R. L. (1967). Two process learning theory: Relationship between Pavlovian and instrumental learning. *Psychological Review,* 88, 151-182..

Rescorla, R. A. & Wagner, A. R. (1972). A theory of Pavlovian conditioning: Variations in the effectiveness of reinforcement and nonreinforcement. In A. H. Black & W. F. Prokasy (Eds.), *Classical conditioning II: Current research and theory.* New York: Appleton-Century-Crofts.

Roitblat, H. L. (1982). The meaning of representation in animal memory. *Behavioral and Brain Sciences,* 5, 353-406.

Roitblat, H. L. (1987). *Introduction to comparative cognition.* New York: W. H. Freeman.

Roitblat, H. L. (1994) Comparative Approaches to Cognitive Science in H. L. Roitblat, & J.-A. Meyer (Eds.), *Comparative Approaches to Cognitive Science.* Cambridge, MA: MIT Press. In Press.

Roitblat, H. L. & von Fersen, L. (1992) Comparative cognition: Representations and processes in learning and memory. *Annual Review of Psychology,* 43, 671-710.

Ross, R. T. & Holland, P. C. (1981). Conditioning of simultaneous and serial feature-positive discriminations. *Animal Learning and Behavior,* 9, 293-303.

Tolman, E. C. (1948). Cognitive maps in rats and men. *Psychological Review,* 55, 189-208.

Tolman, E. C. (1959) Principles of purposive behavior. In S. Koch (Ed.), *Psychology: A study of science.* New York: McGraw-Hill, 92-157.

Tolman, E. C., & Honzik, C. H. (1930b) Introduction and removal of reward and maze performance in rats. *University of California Publications in Psychology,* 4, 257-275.

Tolman, E. C., Ritchie, B. F. & Kalish, D. (1946). Studies in spatial learning I. Orientation and the short-cut. *Journal of Experimental Psychology,* 36, 13-24.

Trapold, M. A. (1970) Are expectancies based upon different positive reinforcing events discriminably different? *Learning and Motivation,* 1, 129-140.

Trapold, M. A. & Overmier, J. B. 1972. The second learning process in instrumental learning. In A. H. Black & W. F. Prokasy (Eds.) *Classical conditioning, II: Current research and theory.* New York: Appleton-Century-Crofts. pp. 427-452.

Coherent Behavior from Many Adaptive Processes

Rodney A. Brooks
MIT Artificial Intelligence Laboratory
545 Technology Square
Cambridge, MA 02139, USA
brooks@ai.mit.edu

Abstract

Behavior-based approaches to mobile robots have yielded a number of interesting demonstrations of robots that navigate, map, plan and operate in the real world. Almost none of these robots directly manipulate the world, however. In this paper, we explore what further advances are needed in order to build artificial agents that act in the world the same way that humans do. In particular, we explore the relationships between having many adaptive processes and producing coherent global behavior.

1 Introduction

In classical AI systems, coherence of action comes from a centralized planner which orchestrates all subactions in the service of well defined goals. The cost is that such systems can not afford to be reactive to fast developing situations in the world, because in order to retain coherence they must defer decisions to the central planner.

In contrast, behavior-based systems (Maes 1990b), (Brooks 1991b), are able to react to rapidly changing circumstances, but there is a worry about how to organize larger systems so that they maintain coherence.

This problem has not been addressed directly; rather, people have been more concerned about the problem of *action selection*. This is certainly a related problem; and the action selected at any point in time can be viewed as an external indication of the, perhaps emergent, internal focus of attention of the system under observation. But it only begs the coherence question as behavior-based systems become more complex. As we increase the number of sensors and actuators, a complex behavior-based system will have many opportunites for actions which are occuring in parallel, or competing for robot resources—and when there are more resources than just a locomotion system, there will be partial allocation of these resources and apparent incoherence could easily result. In truth, no one has yet built really complex behavior-based systems. Most physically based systems have been restricted to navigation tasks, perhaps with picking up simple objects with a parallel jaw gripper (Parker 1994), (Matarić 1994). Coherence has not yet become a major problem for these systems.

Now there is movement towards building much more complex systems, such as the humanoid project of Brooks & Stein (1993). Minsky (1986) is perhaps the only attempt at a complete synthesis of a human level mind, although there are certainly many new analyses (Dennett 1991), (Crick 1994). It is clear from these modern accounts that any such synthesis of human level mind will consist of many somewhat independent adaptive processes. In such systems we will no longer be able to duck the issue of behavior coherence, and it must be addressed squarely. This does not mean to say that there must be a coherence module, but at least we must understand the sources that lead to incoherence, and the ways in which coherence can be shepherded and guaranteed.

2 Models of Thought

We are aiming eventually at human level cognitive abilities. Before concentrating on action selection and coherence, it is therefore instructive to reflect a little on our models of the human brain and mind, to see what influences those models, and what influence those models will have on our attempts at synthesis.

Throughout history our models of thought have been influenced by the most advanced technologies currently understood. In the time of Descartes, nerves were compared to the tubes of a waterworks and the pineal gland was a reservoir of animal spirits and was connected to all these tubes. As this waterlike substance, or brain fluid, flowed through the hollow nerves it puffed up the muscles.

By the late 18th century, Galvini had found a connection between electricity and nerve cells, and soon the brain became an electrical device. As electricity became better understood, the brain became a power distribution station, and then by the 1950's children's science books were depicting the brain as a telephone switching network. But cyberneticians and electrical engineers of the time had come to think of the brain as something like an analog electronic computer (Wiener 1948). As digital computers were initially built they were analyzed in terms of what was known about how the brain worked (Berkeley 1949). But by the 1960's, influenced no doubt by the mathematics of Turing (1937) and his writings on the nature of intelligence (Turing 1950), things had flipped around and the brain had become an electrical computer. Early accounts compared the human brain to a bank of vacuum tubes, but this evolved through transistor circuits, and then integrated circuits[1]. These days most AI researchers seem to share the belief that the brain is a particular sort of parallel digital computer, in essence, at least.

In Brooks (1991a) I discussed in more detail the micro-influences over the last thirty years, where detailed models of computation have influenced the models of thought used in AI research. Right now (Brooks 1991b) the situated robotics, or adaptive behavior community seems to be content with the model that intelligence can be built from a network of simple computational elements wired together in a fixed, or at most slowly changing, topology with simple semantic-free messages being sent along those connections.

Given the history of our models of brain matching our most advanced technology, who is to say that we have yet gotten things right.

(Bergland 1985) argues that such models are missing critical aspects of the brain[2]. Besides having electrical properties it is also awash in chemicals which act as transmitters, local modulators, and even long distance messengers between different parts of the nervous system. Such dissipative media have very different properties to those that are easily simulated with fixed topology local message passing networks. Just as the model of nerves as pipes for the transport of liquids eventually proved inadequate, perhaps our electrical models are insufficient.

In making such arguments, one runs the risk of falling into the errors of misunderstanding computation that have commonly been made, e.g., by (Searle 1992) and (Edelman 1992). We are not saying that computers are not sufficiently powerful to simulate cognitive processes, just that we must be careful that we choose the right abstractions to simulate. Traditional AI chose the symbol level as a higher abstraction—many now feel this was the wrong level of attack. The situated robotics com-

munity must also be prepared to carefully think, and rethink, about its levels of abstraction.

3   Action Selection

Space precludes an exhaustive analysis of the action selection literature, but here we go over the key ideas in the development of the models we have used at the MIT Artificial Intelligence Laboratory. We will then, in the next section, look at things from the point of view of maintaining coherence, rather than selecting actions.

In the original subsumption architecture (Brooks 1986) we simply used a fixed priority scheme to decide which particular behavior (or augmented finite state machine) had its output routed to the actuators. Connell (1990) used a very rigid subset of original subsumption to control a robot which could explore a laboratory world, find objects, pick them up from cluttered desks and return them to a home location. Many other early robots, e.g., the Genghis six legged robot, were able to carry out interesting navigation tasks with just this simple action arbitration scheme (Brooks 1989). Although it had many actuators within individual legs it used its state in the world (leg up or down, backward or forward, in forceful contact or not) as preconditions to provide a coherent natural sequencing of behaviors. Higher level behaviors were arranged to simply modulate the ranges of motion of lower level behaviors, so again selection was easy.

It turns out that simple fixed priority methods are sufficient to implement many other schemes, provided one chunks the control system with the right abstractions. (This is similar to that fact that although machine code looks very cumbersome for writing recursive procedures, all computer languages which allow recursion ultimately either get compiled to a machine code program, or they are interpreted by a machine code program.) The *Behavior Language* (Brooks 1990a) codifies certain of these useful abstractions, and a number of action selection mechanisms have been coded in this language, although it is a compiler which simply outputs standard but equivalent subsumption architecture programs.

While this work was proceeding there were other threads of action selection work for behavior-based robots. Arkin (1990) used selection of motor schemas, represented as navigation vector fields, and their addition to control mobile robots in a number of naviagtion-based tasks. Maes (1990a) introduced a particular type of action selection dynamics based on propagation of excitation levels between primitive behaviors. This influences the choice of abstractions in the Behavior Language.

Matarić (1992) integrated representations of the world acquired by the robot as it followed walls and categorized its surrounding as landmarks. This totally dis-

---

[1] In recent times, flummoxed by their inability so see how things might be computed, various writers have postulated hologram-like memory structures, and have even resorted to quantum mechanics as the source of intelligence (the theory roughly seems to be that quantum mechanics is deep and mysterious, and so is the brain, so they must really be the same thing).

[2] Although he does get carried away to the point of denying the importance of the electrical properties of the brain, and seems to feel some empathy with Copernicus, Galileo and Kepler, whom 'they' also laughed at...

tributed map then controlled the robot directly during goal finding tasks, as only the part of the map corresponding to where the robot was currently would send out commands to a lower level navigation system. Parker (1994) had a set of high level behaviors with a mutual inhibition network between them. Only one behavior could be activated at a time (e.g., *clean-floor*, *emtpy-trashcan*) but an underlying subsumption substrate of simpler behaviors provided a common foundation for all these high level behaviors. Matarić (1994) used two explicit behavior combination mechanisms. One was to sum the navigation vectors from a group of behaviors and the other was to explicitly switch between outputs of behaviors. All the behaviors were actually active at all time in the latter case, but only the chosen one had its output switched through to the actuators.

In (Brooks 1990*b*) we introduced the idea of implementing a model of hormones[3], in particular the lobster hormone system (Kravitz 1988). This system was fully implemented (Brooks 1990*a*) as part of a the more general Behavior Language. We have used it at MIT for a number of our robots, and others, e.g., (Gomi & Ulvr 1993), have also used it to implement behavior selection in navigating robots.

4   Sources of Coherence

In building complex adaptive systems we can gain coherence of behavior in at least two ways. There are a number of sources of natural coherence that are there to be used to our advantage through careful design. Other aspects of coherence must be achieved through specific mechanisms.

4.1   Natural Coherence

There can be a number of sources of natural coherence that are somewhat accidental, although of course natural systems have evolved to take advantage of these sources.

In particular, a complex system of many independent agents can appear coherent because:

- the world often integrates things, by forcing many systems to act in the same way—all of Simon's ants must avoid the same grain of sand when they are following a pheromone trail for instance, contributing to the coherence of the trail and the amplification of the pheremone

- the structure of the task at hand may impose a natural sequencing on actions, which when coupled

with their precondition predicates enforces a coherent sequential unfolding of events

- multiple behaviors may actually be additive in nature even if some of them contribute negatively—as long as the sum is positive it appears to an observer that the system is making coherent progress

Some of these aspects of coherence only contribute to the appearance of coherence that an observer might see, while others also contribute to the actual efficiency of a system.

From the observer's point of view, it appears that the system is paying attention to particular subtasks, or to particular aspects of the environment. Attention and coherence are thus related.

4.2   Designed Coherence

One unifying theme for designing in coherence is to try to amplify the natural sources of coherence; i.e., to artificially force the system into a state where forces that naturally drive towards coherence cannot but help take over.

We have identified three techniques which fit within this framework. They are predicated on the idea that there is a tendency for any particular behavior to be active, and that tendency can be excited or inhibited, more or less over a continuous scale. If too many behaviors are active at once, then incoherence may result.

1. **Internal drives.** Behaviors are more likely to be activated because some internal parameter says they should be activated. E.g., a hunger drive might excite a food foraging behavior. But a fear drive might inhibit such a behavior, while exciting others. This is a primary mechanism for the equivalent of action selection.

2. **Internal rewards.** Some behavior might trigger, either directly or through a coupling through the world, some internal reward, which makes the excitation of that behavior higher, while inhibiting other behaviors. This adds hystersis to the system which in turns adds to the overall coherence of the system.

3. **Mutual exclusion.** There may be subsets of behaviors, any of which when activated, inhibits the activation of another subset. This is a generalized form of lateral inhibition.

Each of these three techniques can be viewed as an attention focusing mechanism.

The question now is how to implement these coherence drivers on a complex behavior-based robot. We will consider the problem for a new robot we are building.

---

[3]Earlier Arkin (1988) had reported on implementing an endocrine system on his robots but he clearly intended it for low-level homeostatic control, rather than high level action selection.

Figure 1: The robot COG, a humanoid form from the waist up. The arms and hands are not yet attached.

5   The Humanoid, Cog

We are currently developing a humanoid robot, named 'COG' Brooks & Stein (1993).

A brief outline of the technolgy of COG follows.

5.1   The Body

COG, shown in figure 1 is approximately the size and shape of an adult human, from the waist up. It is bolted to a fixed base. Kinematically it has three degrees of freedom at its hips, three degrees of freedom at its neck, two camera mounts, or eyes, each with an independent pan and tilt motor, two six degree of freedom arms, and for now two one degree of freedom hands. This gives a total of 24 motors to control.

Each motor has its own dedicated processor, a Motorola 6811 with 2Kbytes of EEPROM, and 256 bytes of RAM, and high precision shaft encoders. Additionally the motors in the arm are linked to their loads via leaf springs with separate potentiometers measuring the

compliance. All but the eye motors have heat sensors mounted on both them and their drive transistors. All the sensed information is available on $\pi\beta$, the main processor for COG. This gives COG a kinesthetic sense of how hard its motors are working, and the potential for us to build in regulatory behaviors which ensure that the motors stay within reasonable temperature bounds by resting if necessary.

Each eye of COG, figure 2, consists of two cameras with parallel optical axes, separated by about 2cm vertically. One has a 23° field of view and corresponds in intent to a mammalian fovea. The other provides peripheral vision with approximately a 120° field of view. Each eye can carry out about three saccades per second. We digitize the images to 128 × 128 pixels, which is a rather low number by conventional standards. This can be changed later if we have more funds available to build a better real-time vision system. Altogether then we have 65,536 pixels from the four cameras at 30Hz. The ears consist of four microphones (two for lateral localization and two for vertical localization), attached to Texas Instruments C40 digital signal processing chips.

5.2   The Brain

The brain[4] of COG is called $\pi\beta$ (Kapogiannis 1994) and is a specially built MIMD machine. Each node is a 16MHz 68010-ish class machine (a Motorola 68332 to be exact) with a megabyte each of ROM and RAM. Each node runs a real-time operating system and an L image. L is a downwardly compatible subset of Common Lisp; any program that runs in L should run in Common Lisp, but the converse is not necessarily true. L is augmented with a multi-processing system, so that many concurrent processes can run in the same Lisp heap, and by a library of COG specific utilities. The idea is that each node of $\pi\beta$ should provide a certain functionality as would a small contiguous section of neuro-anatomy in an animal or human brain. Our initial version of $\pi\beta$ has room for 64 nodes, although we do not have that many actual processors at this point. With sufficient funding the number can easily be extended to 240 nodes, and with minor software revisions to 61440, should we choose to!

There are two networks associated with $\pi\beta$. One is a communication network by which the nodes communicate with each other during the normal operation of COG, and the other is a meta-level network for providing file service to the nodes and debugging tools to us the designers of COG and its programs.

The first network is implemented by movable cables that connect one of six data ports on one node to a data port on another node. In the middle of these cables is a dual ported RAM (DPRAM), 16Kbytes in size. This

---

[4] Somehow it seems scientifically unrespectable to use this word.

is mapped into the address space of each processor and may be accessed asynchronously by the two of them, although there is also some sempahore hardware coupled into the system so that safe atomic communication of large data structures can occur. Pointers can not be transferred between Lisps on separate machines through this mechanism. Only integers and arrays of integers (as small as 8 bit integers) can be written into these memories. These DPRAMs correspond to nerve bundles transmitting image and spatial data maps much as occur often in the brain, along with other more specialized signals. Because the communication is bi-directional, we can easily implement backward connections wherever there is a forward connection. The cables are plugged into the array to set up a particular network topology and can only be moved when the machine is powered down. These same DPRAMs are used as the interface to higher speed input/output devices. Frame grabbers provide images via the DPRAMs (and cause an interrupt to the host 68332 whenever an image is written). DPRAMs provide the output to frame displays, which are connected to a bank of 20 monitors which display internal processing states of the vision systems. DPRAMs are the method that the sound processing system C40 processors use to inject the results of signal processing into the rest of the system. Later, we expect to use the DPRAMs for sound output interfacing.

The second network, a high speed RS232 serial network, connects all the processors via another 68332 and a SCSI interface to a Macintosh running Common Lisp. The Mac serves as a file server, and there is a growing GUI implemented on the Mac that lets a user type to listeners on individual $\pi\beta$ nodes, and provides facilities such as multiple trace digital oscilliscopes that can be used to monitor values all the way down on the 6811 motor slave boards, along with various graphical widgets to set and monitor values in other ways.

The motor 6811 slaves can be daisy chained to any particular $\pi\beta$ node via a serial packet system that communicates with each slave processor at 32Hz. Each slave 6811 has a number of free I/O channels and we plan to add more sensors, such as tactile sensors using these channels.

The nodes of the $\pi\beta$ computer run completely asynchronously and the system is very loosely coupled. Even their individual time of day clocks bear no relationship to each other. At the operating system and language levels there is no protection against messages getting overwritten in the DPRAM, just as in the original subsumption architecture (Brooks 1986). The machine is clearly not intended to run conventional parallel processing applications.

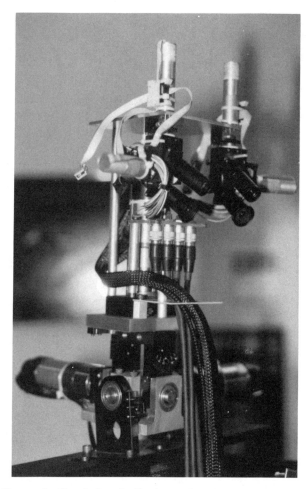

Figure 2: COG's head. Each eye has two cameras, one wide angle for peripheral vision, and one narrow angle for foveal vision.

5.3   Why this Organization?

From some points of view, the design and construction of $\pi\beta$ seems sub-optimal. If we count MIPS alone it would probably be more optimal and cost effective to use a top of the line scientific workstation.

However, we believe that the form of the computation mechanism constrains the way solutions are implemented on it, and we are particularly interested in understanding how to achieve our goals for the humanoid while satisfying certain computational constraints.

These constraints serve two purposes. First, they match what we understand about biological systems, so their existence in our hardware helps stop our solutions from losing all biological relevance. Second, the single processor solution will not be scalable to the levels that will eventually be required for human level cognition. By working with a scalable system now, any solutions we produce will be integrable with other scalable solutions.

The particular constraints that we feel are important are as follows:

- The system is totally asynchronous.

- There is no global control.

- There is no global shared memory (and hence no problems with cache coherence, etc.).

- There is no way to transmit pointers between processors.

- The system is abitrarily scalable in terms of being able to easily add more processors.

- When a subgroup of processors has been debugged and is handling real-time constraints on a particular sub-behavior (e.g., saccades or smooth pursuit in the vision system), there is no way that development in another part of the system can influence those satisfied timing constraints—this would be a significant problem in a single processor solution.

- The hardware reflects and facilitates the layered approach (Brooks 1986) to building intelligence that we have been successfully using for a number of years.

A broader goal, which $\pi\beta$ facilitates, but does not guarantee, is that as we add new layers or different sub-sytems we should not have to go back and re-link or recompile any of the existing subsystems

6 Global Dissipative Quantities For Complex Systems

The COG robot is a large complex system and there are many opportunities for incoherent behavior to arise. In Brooks & Stein (1993) we outline a long time-scale development plan for the robot, which includes the integration of many diverse behavior-based subsystems.

A simple example of problems which might arise is as follows. The foveated vision system is able to react to motion cues, to turn its foveal attention towards areas of potential interest. But the vision system is also intended to be used for visual servoing fine manipulation with the hands. Saccades to peripheral motion during such servoing will potentially disrupt the task at hand and to an observer, certainly, the robot's behavior will appear incoherent. So the system should suppress saccades during the fine motion, unless there is significantly violent motion, or potentially looming motion that should be dealt with immediately. As the saccade is made, appropriate backing off from motions in progress in the manipulation epsiode should be carried out. What is needed then is a way of adjusting thresholds on the activation of certain other visual behaviors during the recruitment of vision for a fine motion task. This is but one of tens or hundreds of examples which can be constructed from the set of capabilities we desire to implement in COG.

All of the mecanisms outlined in section 4.2 can be implemented on top of disappative *substances*. All we need is a mechanism which releases substances throughout the brain in some quantity and these substances should dissipate over time. In some cases, e.g., an internal reward, we may want the dissipation rate to be high, so that the reward will have to be almost continually received to have the desired effect, implemented through continous release of the substance.

The idea is that various processes throught the system can be simultaneously releasing different or the same substances, which then are available globally. Furthermore these substances dissipate over time.

At first sight, a distributed digital architecture such as we have described for $\pi\beta$ does not seem conducive to the implementation of such substances. The following properties of the system and the desired properties conspire to make things difficult:

- As we build each subsystem, and program each node, we do not know in advance the eventual network topology in which that node will be embedded.

- There is no global clock.

- All nodes are asynchronous.

- There is no way to access global information at reasonable speeds.

Below we present an algorithm which overcomes these problems. The key ideas that enable us to build a global dissipative substance distribution system are as follows:

- Release can be from any single source, and the global spreading is done via existing communication links and (unknown) network topology by piggy backing on a few extra bytes of "substance spread" information. The only constraint is that node connectivity does not partition the processors into more than one disjoint set.

- Dissipation should be repeated locally, rather than done singly and uniformly. Each processor node has a server process which accumulates all the locally recieved susbtances and dissipates them over time.

- Every release of a substance includes three authentification stamps: a unique processor id, a substance id, a local timestamp, a substance amount and a substance dissipation rate.

The algorithm is implemented by having a substance message server process on each processor node. Whenever a substance message arrives it checks whether it has received a similar message from the same processor with an equal or later time stamp. If so it ignores the message. Otherwise it accumulates the new substance amount locally and transmits the same message out over all its communications links (recall that there are a fixed maxmimum number of such links—6 in the case of $\pi\beta$).

It is easy to see that all substance messages eventually reach all nodes of the network, and are never double counted. Also, the latency in a node receiving a substance update is bounded by the diameter of the communication network. The skew in the level of a substance over the network is determined by this latency.

On $\pi\beta$ we handle message processing typically at 32Hz, and expect the diameter of forseeable network topologies we might build to be no more than 8. Thus we can expect at most a quarter second skew in the exact values of substances throughout the network.

Note that there needs to be no global knowledge of the network topology, nor any a priori knowledge of which substances might be transmitted around the network. This algorithm is therefore completely compatible with the incremental way in which we wish to build up the capabilities of CoG.

7   Conclusions

In this paper we have argued that the maintenance of *coherence* is a better organizing principle for the design of behavior-based systems than is *action selection*. In particular, as we try to apply behavior-based ideas to more complex systems the latter eventually will be buckle under the weight of complexity and a lack of the former will dominate the inability of the system to perform well.

To solve this problem we suggested that we need to look beyond the purely computational[5] model of cognition; we must look beyond our current electrocentric view of the world of neural activity and also consider the biochemical mechanisms at work. This view is also an organizing principle, as we then showed how to implement models of dissipative structures within a totally distributed asynchronous computation system that forms the brain of our humanoid robot CoG. We are suggesting that while real nervous systems may use checmical means to transmit global coherence signals, it is possible to do the same in a totally distributed silicon based system.

Acknowledgements

The research reported here was done at the MIT Artificial Intelligence Laboratory. Support for this research was provided in part by the Advanced Research Projects Agency under Office of Naval Research contract N00014–91–J–4038, and in part by a grant from the Matsushita Corporation.

References

Arkin, R. C. (1988), 'Homeostatic Control for a Mobile Robot: Dynamic Replanning in Hazardous Environments', *SPIE* **1007**(Mobile Robots III), 407–413.

Arkin, R. C. (1990), Integrating Behavioral, Perceptual and World Knowledge in Reactive Navigation, *in* P. Maes, ed., 'Designing Autonomous Agents: Theory and Practice from Biology to Engineering and Back', MIT Press, Cambridge, Massachusetts, pp. 105–122.

Bergland, R. (1985), *The Fabric of Mind*, Viking, New York, New York.

Berkeley, E. C. (1949), *Giant Brains or Machines That Think*, John Wiley & Sons, Inc., New York, New York.

Brooks, R. A. (1986), 'A Robust Layered Control System for a Mobile Robot', *IEEE Journal of Robotics and Automation* **RA-2**, 14–23.

Brooks, R. A. (1989), 'A Robot That Walks: Emergent Behavior from a Carefully Evolved Network', *Neural Computation* **1**(2), 253–262.

Brooks, R. A. (1990*a*), The Behavior Language User's Guide, Memo 1227, Massachusetts Institute of Technology, Artificial Intelligence Lab, Cambridge, Massachusetts.

Brooks, R. A. (1990*b*), Challenges for Complete Creature Architectures, *in* 'Proceedings of the First International Conference on Simulation of Adaptive Behavior', MIT Press, Cambridge, Massachusetts, pp. 434–443.

Brooks, R. A. (1991*a*), Intelligence Without Reason, *in* 'Proceedings of the 1991 International Joint Conference on Artificial Intelligence', pp. 569–595.

Brooks, R. A. (1991*b*), 'New Approaches to Robotics', *Science* **253**, 1227–1232.

Brooks, R. A. & Stein, L. A. (1993), Building Brains for Bodies, Memo 1439, Massachusetts Institute of Technology, Artificial Intelligence Lab, Cambridge, Massachusetts.

Connell, J. (1990), *Minimalist Mobile Robotics: A Colony-style Architecture for a Mobile Robot*, Academic Press, Cambridge, Massachusetts. also MIT TR-1151.

---

[5]Inman Harvey has a wonderful slogan: "Evolution is not optimisation, cognition is not computation".

Crick, F. (1994), *The Astonishing Hypothesis: The Scientific Search for the Soul*, Charles Scribner's Sons, New York, New York.

Dennett, D. G. (1991), *Consciousness Explained*, Little, Brown and Company, Boston, Massachusetts.

Edelman, G. M. (1992), *Bright Air, Brilliant Fire: On the Matter of Mind*, Basic Books, New York, New York.

Gomi, T. & Ulvr, J. (1993), Artificial Emotions as Emergent Phenomena, *in* 'Robot and Human Communication (RO-MAN'93)', Tokyo, Japan.

Kapogiannis, E. (1994), Design of a Large Scale MIMD Computer, Master's thesis, MIT, Department of EECS, Cambridge, Massachusetts.

Kravitz, E. A. (1988), 'Hormonal Control of Behavior: Amines and the Biasing Behavioral Output in Lobsters', *Science* **241**, 1775–1781.

Maes, P. (1990*a*), Situated Agents Can Have Goals, *in* P. Maes, ed., 'Designing Autonomous Agents: Theory and Practice from Biology to Engineering and Back', MIT Press, Cambridge, Massachusetts, pp. 49–70.

Maes, P., ed. (1990*b*), *Designing Autonomous Agents: Theory and Practice from Biology to Engineering and Back*, MIT Press, Cambridge, Massachusetts.

Matarić, M. J. (1992), 'A Robust Layered Control System for a Mobile Robot', *IEEE Journal of Robotics and Automation* **RA-8**, 304–312.

Matarić, M. J. (1994), Interaction and Intelligent Behavior, PhD thesis, MIT, Department of EECS, Cambridge, Massachusetts.

Minsky, M. (1986), *The Society of Mind*, Simon and Schuster, New York, New York.

Parker, L. E. (1994), Heterogeneous Multi-Robot Cooperation, PhD thesis, MIT, Department of EECS, Cambridge, Massachusetts.

Searle, J. R. (1992), *The Rediscovery of the Mind*, MIT Press, Cambridge, Massachusetts.

Turing, A. M. (1937), On Computable Numbers with an Application to the Entscheidungsproblem, *in* 'Proceedings of the London Math. Soc. 42', pp. 230–265.

Turing, A. M. (1950), 'Computing Machinery and Intelligence', *Mind* **59**, 433–460. also published in Feigenbaum and Feldman, Computers and Thought.

Wiener, N. (1948), *Cybernetics*, John Wiley and Sons, New York, New York.

STABILITY IN ADAPTATION AND LEARNING

Jean-Jacques E. Slotine
Nonlinear Systems Laboratory
Massachusetts Institute of Technology
Cambridge, MA 02139, USA
jjs@mit.edu

April 25, 1994

Abstract

In understanding complex, nonlinear, adaptive systems, whether natural or artificial, stability is a fundamental issue. Furthermore, in a machine, explicit, built-in stability guarantees yield high-performance designs. This paper discusses some techniques and results on stable adaptation and learning in the context of robot motion control and motion-vision coordination. While the paper is meant as a brief conceptual survey, the mathematical formalization of many of the topics is rather complete and can be found in the references. It also suggests how machines have potential for performance and learning mechanisms vastly different from those of animals.

1 Introduction

Some of the very first robots were developed by cyberneticians. In famous papers [Walter, 1950, 1951], the British neurophysiologist W. Grey Walter reported constructing simple tortoise-shaped robots which, given their simplicity and the rudimentary electronics of the time, exhibited striking "free will", goal-seeking behavior, and robustness properties. Faced with designing coordination mechanisms for the interacting subunits at the heart of his machines, Grey Walter immediately recognized that "one weakness of more elaborate systems can be predicted with confidence: extreme plasticity cannot be gained without some loss of stability[1]." Walter also identified learning mechanisms as key techniques for organizing complexity, and made simple explorations thereof.

This paper discusses some specific techniques and results on stability, adaptation, and learning in a robotics context. While it is meant as a brief conceptual survey, it is important to realize that the mathematical formalization of many of the topics is rather complete and can be found in the specific references.

---

[1] "It is therefore no wonder that the incidence of neuropsychiatric complaints marches with intellectual attainment and social complexity," he added.

2 Stability

In understanding complex, nonlinear, adaptive systems, whether natural or artificial, system stability is not a trivial issue. In most nonlinear systems (including linear adaptive systems as special cases, since their dynamics are actually nonlinear), no set of simulations can fully or even adequately account for potential system behavior given various inputs, environmental changes or disturbances, or initial conditions. Furthermore, in a machine, *explicit, built-in stability guarantees yield high-performance designs*. This can be seen time and again, e.g., in the development of adaptive manipulator controllers, where stability-based algorithms yield indeed very fast and effective approaches to simultaneous identification and control.

Casual treatments should thus be avoided. For instance, a standard result states that, in essence, closing a feedback loop about a naturally stable system (say, a passive mechanical system) will preserve stability as long as the feedback remains weak. In practice, this reassuring result has all-too-often resulted in a "small-gain" syndrome, i.e., in overlooking stability issues altogether when discussing e.g. some aspects of animal or robotic motion control. In the robotic case, such an approach, besides presenting obvious inherent risks, also totally foregoes performance.

One of the major tools for understanding stability of nonlinear systems consists of Lyapunov functions or Lyapunov-like functions. A pendulum left to itself will eventually come to rest due to friction, regardless of initial position or speed. This corresponds to the fact that its initial, finite mechanical energy is progressively dissipated. Lyapunov-like functions formalize and extend this notion of a scalar time-function "summarizing" the system behavior and yielding precise results about boundedness and convergence (for recent treatments, see, e.g., [Slotine an Li, 1991; Vidyasagar, 1992]).

As the concepts in Lyapunov theory evolved from physical considerations, similarly in *designing* feedback controllers for complex nonlinear systems, the physical properties of the system plants should be taken advantage of. For instance, the conservation of total mechanical energy allows one to show simply the stability of simple proportional-derivative position controllers for robot manipulators [Takegaki and Arimoto, 1981], and can also be systematically exploited to design trajectory controllers for these systems [Slotine and Li, 1987]. Similarly, recognizing naturally dissipative dynamics allows one to exploit the intrinsically stabilizing nature of certain "disturbance" terms such as viscous friction [Slotine, 1988]. Related approaches can also be of use in addressing problems of robustness to high-frequency unmodelled dynamics. The natural additivity of Lyapunov-like functions (in the same way that the total energy of a system is the sum of its local energy components), formalized in passivity theory [Popov, 1973], considerably simplifies dealing with complex interconnected systems (see e.g., [Colgate and Hogan, 1988]), including accounting for environment changes.

Of course, in flavor these "virtual physics" ideas are not specific to stability and control, and can be found e.g. in circuits for early vision [Horn, 1988] and analog VLSI designs [Mead, 1989] [2]. As Herbert Simon might put it [Simon, 1981], " the aesthetics of natural science and mathematics is at one with the aesthetics of music and painting - both inhere in the discovery of a partially concealed pattern."

Stability tools can be systematically used in the analysis and design of progressively more sophisticated control systems, from basic feedback loops to adaptive and learning systems.

3   Feedback

Feedback of performance measures (e.g., position error), by constantly comparing actual and desired system performances and adjusting control action accordingly, is one of the most basic tools towards robust execution. Closing a sensor-computer-actuator loop around a physical system can be "unnatural", however, and thus stability and convergence analysis should be explicit.

As explained to a 5 year-old (or similarly to a layperson by Norbert Wiener in "Cybernetics" [Wiener, 1961]), feedback can be well understood: "if you are too much to the right, push towards the left, if you are too much to the left, push towards the right, this way you'll end up in the middle". Of course, this child is being misled, and this appealing qualitative interpretation is actually wrong: apply it to an arbitrary system and you'll get oscillations, perhaps divergence. Remarkably though, the

approach does work for systems described by *first-order* differential equations. Hence the emergence of a body of techniques aiming at replacing original n-th order problems by "equivalent" first-order ones, an operation particularly attractive for complex, uncertain, nonlinear systems (see e.g., [Slotine, 1984]).

4   Adaptation and Learning

4.1   Adaptive Control

The next level of performance can be achieved by letting the controller be adaptive or learn, i.e., by letting the system model (including the environment model) on which it is based actually vary with time, according to a real-time analysis of past performance. In our context, we shall distinguish adaptation and learning as follows. Adaptation will refer to a known dynamic structure (e.g., Lagrange's equations in a robot) and unknown parameters (e.g., mass properties of the load that the robot is manipulating). Learning will refer to the case were the structure itself is unknown (or partially unknown, in which case it will be combined with adaptation), whether it be the dynamic structure (e.g., hydrodynamic terms in an underwater robot, which are difficult to model accurately) or the task structure (e.g., combined planning and control).

The recent resurgence of interest in approximation methods loosely based upon models of biological signal processing, the so-called "neural network" techniques, has led to a variety of new learning control algorithms, potentially capable of synthesizing control laws for partially known, nonlinear dynamic systems. However, if a controller design is to be viable in practice, its stability must be guaranteed and its performance quantified.

The field of adaptive control arose in the late 1950's to address these issues for the learning control models of the time, which consisted mainly of single-input *linear* systems, and since then has developed a variety of adaptive algorithms providing the required guarantees (see e.g., [Astrom and Wittenmark, 1989; Narendra and Annaswamy, 1989; Slotine and Li, 1991]).

Our own research has largely concentrated on extending classical adaptive control techniques to large classes of *nonlinear* systems, including important classes of multi-input physical systems such as robot manipulators. Most results in the field of adaptive nonlinear control, however, have required *a priori linear parametrization*, i.e., the possibility of writing the unknown terms in the physical system dynamics as products of known state-dependent nonlinear terms (e.g., reflecting system geometry) by unknown constants or slowly varying terms (e.g., reflecting mass properties).

---

[2]Conversely, they motivate research in information physics; Richard Feynman remarked "It always bothers me that, according to the laws as we understand them today, it takes a computing machine an infinite number of operations to figure out what goes on in no matter how tiny a region of space, and no matter how tiny a region of time." [Feynman, 1967]

4.2 Adaptive Robot Control

Such models apply very well to robot manipulators, where the a priori linear parametrization is provided by the structure of Lagrange's equations. Stable and effective adaptive trajectory controllers can be systematically designed, can combine high-speed and high-precision in robot manipulation, and can considerably simplify high-level programming by providing consistent performance in the face of large variations in loads, tasks [e.g., Slotine and Li, 1987], or environments. Such globally tracking-convergent adaptive controllers were illustrated experimentally [Niemeyer and Slotine, 1991] on the WAM, a high-performance 4-degree-of-freedom articulated robot arm developed at MIT [Salisbury, et al., 1988; Townsend, 1988]. Continuing research suggests a wide range of application well beyond adaptation to grasped loads.

The goal of these Lyapunov-based adaptive controllers is to adaptively converge to a specified *task performance* (e.g., accurate trajectory control) while maintaining all signals in the system within reasonable bounds. *A key ingredient in their high performance is that they do not attempt to estimate all system parameters exactly in the process, but only generate estimates which get the job done.* Whether the parameter estimates converge to exact values depends on how hard the task is, a notion formalized in the adaptive control literature as "sufficient richness" or "persistency of excitation." Consider for example a robot manipulator, initially at rest under gravity forces, and whose desired task is to just stay there; no control needs being applied and no adaptation needs occuring, and this is indeed what the adaptive controller will do. Conversely, if the robot is required to follow a desired trajectory so complicated (so "rich") that exact trajectory tracking necessarily requires all parameter estimates to be exact, then the guaranteed tracking convergence of the same adaptive algorithm will automatically guarantee accurate parameter convergence.

4.3 Gaussian and Wavelet Networks for Stable Adaptive Control and Estimation

As the problems and applications considered become *less structured* a priori, one is naturally led to wonder whether the formal methodology of adaptive control theory can be extended to the new "neural" learning models, thus providing a more general class of provably effective stable adaptive control architectures.

A successful treatment of problems in adaptive nonlinear control and identification using neural network models requires a cross-disciplinary integration, drawing techniques from fields such as learning theory, constructive approximation, nonlinear stability, and robust systems theory. Recently, such results have started to emerge, resulting both in systematic network synthesis techniques and in algorithms for adaptive prediction and control with guaranteed stability and convergence properties.

For instance, a constructive analysis can be developed [Sanner and Slotine, 1992], which, given an estimate of the smoothness of the functions driving the plant dynamics, exactly specifies the size and configuration of a network of gaussian radial basis functions (see, e.g., [Poggio and Girosi, 1990]) capable of *uniformly* approximating these functions over a prespecified subset of the state space. An adaptive controller architecture capable of exploiting this network representation can then be designed based on stability theory for a large class of uncertain nonlinear dynamic systems. The controller explicitly acknowledges the fact that the network approximation is accurate only on the prespecified subset of the state space, and smoothly transitions between adaptive and nonadaptive operation.

The need for prior assumptions about the smoothness of the vector field can actually be avoided by extending the analysis to produce stable adjustment mechanisms for the centers and variances of each gaussian node. The design can be further optimized by allowing irregular spatial sampling [Sanner and Slotine, 1992], using tools for space/frequency localization from wavelet theory [Daubechies, 1992]. A multiple-time-scale analysis can refine the stable simultaneous adjustment of the architecture and the parameters [Cannon and Slotine, 1994].

The methodology and tools thus developed can also be easily applied to create stable, convergent identifiers for nonlinear dynamic systems. They are equally applicable if the system to be identified is memoryless, and hence provide direct insight into the general problem of learning nonlinear mappings from examples. Associated analysis tools such as the notion of incremental persistency of excitation also allow one to start addressing basic issues in active learning, e.g., wondering how systems can be made to "ask the most informative questions" at critical junctures in their learning process.

The explicit use of Lyapunov-based tools for robust design (e.g., [Slotine and Coetsee, 1986]) can systematically yield precise specifications for adaptation deadzones, conceptually consistent with the notion of maintaining readiness for adapting to or learning from the unexpected while not affecting robust routine performance. In particular, it allows one to explicitly account for the finite approximation capabilities of the networks described above [Sanner and Slotine, 1992]. This, in turn, allows overtraining phenomena to be easily interpreted as the result of overlooking such limitations, and thus insisting on keeping adaptation or learning active while the network's performance has already reached its best predictable level [Slotine and Sanner, 1993]. Overtraining, and the dual phenomenon of "bursting" behavior (essentially, the slow adaptive drift of parameters ensuring the local stability of the system, towards instability regions, leading to sudden explosions of activity) are easily understandable from the mathematics of adaptation mechanisms. They may also have some relevance to the explanation of "punctuated equilibria" familiar to evolution researchers [Eldredge and Gould, 1972; Gould and Eldredge, 1994].

4.4 Real-Time Motion-Vision Coordination

We have studied experimentally real-time catching and precision throwing of tennis balls, by applying nonlinear adaptation and estimation techniques to both the robot manipulator and the visual data. The system consisted of the WAM arm equipped with a 1-d.o.f. on-off gripper, and a real-time stereo vision system, incorporating, in the case of catching, a nonlinear "Kalman-like" filter for averaging the image noise over the very few time-samples available to generate the robot trajectory.

The system is currently being upgraded to include active foveal vision (stereo, plus a third "fish-eye" lens), which, in our context of interaction with fast moving objects, allows for increased precision while maintaining an open field of view, with further precision increases as objects get closer and the catching operation proceeds. Active vision also implies that the tracking and isolation of moving targets of interest can be made to correspond to a low-pass rather than a high-pass time filtering operation, thus considerably reducing noise sensitivity.

5 Concluding Remarks

Obviously, a sound understanding of stability issues is relevant in a much broader context. As Richard Dawkins notices [Dawkins, 1976], "Darwin's survival of the fittest is a special case of a more general law of survival of the stable." The concept of an evolutionary stable strategy [Maynard Smith, 1974], for example, has had a fundamental impact on ethology and evolutionary thinking. Similarly, it may be plausibly argued [Kauffman, 1991] that fast stable adaptiveness is one of the main characteristics selected in evolution.

Cybernetic thinking permeates Braitenberg's playful and illuminating thought experiments [Braitenberg, 1984] as well as more recent embodiments (see e.g., [Brooks, 1990; Meyer and Guillot, 1990]). There is also a vast potential in exploiting "controlled instabilities", an approach sometimes found in nature (e.g., [Braitenberg, 1984], see also [Nicolis and Prigogine, 1977]) and which has been systematically used in some engineering contexts, e.g. in the design of high-performance aircraft.

Conversely, mathematical formalizations can specifically suggest how machines have potential for performance and learning mechanisms vastly different from those of animals. This is obvious in adaptive manipulator control, for instance, with robots adapting to un-

known mass properties (say, of a large unknown load) much faster and much more precisely than any animal would. Similarly, robot learning of precision throwing does not necessarily consist of trial-and-error, but rather of building and committing to memory a monotonic interpolated map between robot motion (say a fixed throwing path with a tunable constant acceleration) and object trajectory (say landing location), a much more reliable approach. Along the same lines, it is now well understood in 3D vision analysis (see e.g., [Faugeras, 1994]) that using 3 cameras rather than the obvious 2 mitigates the correspondence problem. In a robot, if necessary, many more processes can be made amenable to intensive conceptual or mathematical real-time shaping than the seven or so conscious "chunks" commonly thought (see e.g., [Simon, 1981]) to limit the attention capabilities of the brain.

Marvin Minsky once quipped that he had studied mathematics because he did not like baseball. Leaving professional sport to robots, this may be the only reasonable option.

6 References

Arbib, M.A., 1964. Brain, Machines and Mathematics, McGraw-Hill.

Ashby, W.R., 1956. An Introduction to Cybernetics, Chapman and Hall, London.

Astrom, K.J., and Wittenmark, B., 1989. Adaptive Control

Braitenberg, V., 1984. Vehicles: Experiments in Synthetic Psychology, MIT Press

Brooks, R.A., 1990. Challenges for Complete Creature Architectures, *First Int. Conf. Simulation of Adaptive Behavior*, MIT Press

Cannon, M.R., and Slotine, J.J.E., 1994, MIT Nonlinear Systems Lab. Report NSL-050594

Colgate, J.E., and Hogan, N., 1988. Robust Control of Dynamically Interacting Systems, *Int. J. Control, 48(1)*

Daubechies, I., 1992. Ten Lectures on Wavelets, SIAM, Philadelphia, PA.

Dawkins, R., 1976. The Selfish Gene, Oxford University Press

Eldredge, N., and Gould, S.J., 1972. Punctuated equilibria: an alternative to phyletic gradualism, *Paleobiology, ed. Schopf, T. J. M., 82-115,* Freeman and Cooper , San Francisco

Faugeras, O., 1994. Three-Dimensional Computer Vision, MIT Press

Feynman, R.M., 1967. The Character of Physical Law, MIT Press

Gould, S.J., and Eldredge, N., 1994. Punctuated equilibrium comes of age, *Nature, 366*

Horn, B.K.P., 1988. Parralel Networks fdr Machine Vision, *MIT AI Lab. Memo 1071*

Kauffman, S.A., 1991. Antichaos and Adaptation, *Scientific American, 78(8)*

Maynard Smith, J., 1974 The Theory of Games and the Evolution of Animal Conflict, *J. Theoret. Biol., 47*

Mead, C., 1989. Analog VLSI and Neural Systems, Addison-Wesley

Meyer, J.A., and Guillot, A., 1990. Simulation of Adaptive Behavior in Animats: Review and Prospect, *First Int. Conf. Simulation of Adaptive Behavior*, MIT Press

Narendra, K, and Annaswamy, A., 1989. Stable Adaptive Systems, Prentice-Hall.

Nicolis, G., and Prigogine, I., 1977. Self-Organization in Non-Equilibrium Systems, Wiley-Interscience

Niemeyer, G., and Slotine, J.J.E., 1991. Performance in Adaptive Manipulator Control, *Int. J. Robotics Res., 10(2)*

Poggio, T., and Girosi, F., 1990. Networks for Approximation and Learning, *Proc. IEEE, 78(9)*

Popov, V.M., 1973. Hyperstability of Control Systems, Springer-Verlag

Salisbury, J.K., Townsend, W.T, Eberman, B., and Di Pietro, D., 1988. *Preliminary Design of a Whole-Arm Manipulator System*, IEEE Int. Conf. Robotics and Automation, Philadelphia, PA

Sanner, R.M., and Slotine, J.J.E., 1992. Gaussian Networks for Direct Adaptive Control, *I.E.E.E. Trans. Neural Networks, 3(6)*

Simon, H.A., 1981. The Sciences of the Artificial, 2nd edition, MIT Press

Slotine, J.J.E., 1984. Sliding Surfaces for Nonlinear Systems, *Int. J. Control, 40(2)*

Slotine, J.J.E., and Coetsee, J., 1986. Adaptive Sliding Controller Design for for Nonlinear Systems, *Int. J. Control, 43(6)*

Slotine, J.J.E., 1988. Putting Physics in Control, *I.E.E.E. Control Systems Magazine, 8(6)*

Slotine, J.J.E., and Li, W., 1987. On the Adaptive Control of Robot Manipulators, *Int. J. Robotics Res., 6(3)*

Slotine, J.J.E., and Li, W., 1991. Applied Nonlinear Control, Prentice-Hall

Slotine, J.J.E., and Sanner, R.M., 1993. *Neural Networks for Adaptive Control and Recursive Identification: A Theoretical Framework*, Essays on Control, Trentelman and Willems, Eds., Birkhauser

Takegaki, M., and Arimoto,S., 1981. A New Feedback Method for Dynamic Control of Manipulators, *ASME J. Dyn. Sys. Meas. Control, 102*

Townsend, W., 1988. The Effect of Transmission Design on Force-Controlled Manipulator Performance, *MIT AI Lab. Report 1054*

Vidyasagar, M., 1992. Nonlinear Systems Analysis, Prentice-Hall

Walter, G.W., 1950. An Imitation of Life, *Scientific American, 182(5)*

Walter, G.W., 1951. A Machine that Learns, *Scientific American, 185(2)*

Wiener, N., 1961. Cybernetics, 2nd edition, MIT Press

PERCEPTION AND MOTOR CONTROL

Modeling the Role of Cerebellum in Prism Adaptation

Michael A. Arbib
Nicolas Schweighofer
Center for Neural Engineering
University of Southern California
Los Angeles, CA 90089-2520
arbib@pollux.usc.edu
nicolas@rana.usc.edu

W.T. Thach
Washington University School of Medicine
Department of Anatomy and Neurobiology
St. Louis MO 63110-1031
thach_wt@wums.wustl.edu

Abstract

Adaptation of sensori-motor transformations is a basic component of adaptive behavior, and an important paradigm for such adaptation has involved studying the response to wearing prisms. The present paper provides a biologically based neural net model for prism adaptation and advances the study of "eligibility" as a general and crucial feature of synaptic plasticity.

We review data showing that the cerebellum is required for adaptation of throwing when the subject wears a wedge prism. We then model this adaptation in terms of plasticity of synapses from parallel fibers to Purkinje cells in cerebellar cortex, stressing the integration of cerebellar cortex and nuclei in microzones as the units for correction of motor pattern generators (MPGs). The model uses a "window of eligibility" to ensure that error signals that elicit a corrective movement help adjust the appropriate MPGs.

1. Sensori-Motor Transforms and Prism Adaptation

In analyzing the adaptive behavior of an animal or a robot, we will often focus on the choice of the appropriate behavior (to feed or to flee) or the appropriate modification of that behavior (whether or not to detour around an obstacle to reach a goal). In many cases, then, behavior may be viewed in terms of the invocation, with appropriate timing, singly or in combination, of various motor schemas or motor pattern generators (MPGs). However, the present paper focuses not on adaptation of patterns of MPG activation, but rather on the tuning of the sensori-motor transformations involved in single MPGs. In particular, we look at a widely used probe of sensori-motor adaptation, the use of prisms to change the apparent visual input, followed by observation of the restoration of (more or less) normal responses to environmental stimuli despite this change in input representation.

Our own recent observations (work by Martin et al. 1994 in Thach's laboratory) provide new insights into the adjustment of eye, head (gaze), arm, and hand in humans throwing a dart or ball at a target while wearing wedge prism spectacles. In throwing, the eyes fixate (and the head turns toward) the target, and serve as reference aim for the arm. If wedge prism spectacles are placed over the eyes with the base to the right, the optic path is bent to the subject's right, and the eyes (and head) move to the left in order to see the target so that the arm, calibrated to the line of sight, will throw to the left of the target. But with repeated throws, the calibration will change, and the arm will throw closer to and finally on-target. When, after adaptation, the prisms are first removed, the eyes are now on-target, but the eye-head-arm calibration for the previously left-bent gaze persists: the arm throws to the right of target by an amount almost equal to the original leftward error. With repeated throws, eye-head position and arm synergy are recalibrated: each throw moves closer to and finally is on target.

A key question for our general study of behavior is whether adaptation applies to a visual representation accessed by all motor behaviors, or whether it is a specific sensori-motor transformation that is being adapted. In the present context, we asked whether the adaptation of the trained body parts carry over to their use in other tasks, or whether it is specific for the use of those body parts during the one task only. To address this question, we asked subjects to use the same arm to make underhand and overhand throws, with and without prism adaptation. On wearing prisms, all subjects adapted the overhand throw. For two subjects, the subsequent underhand throw showed absolutely no effect of prior overhand adaptation. In these subjects, prior overhand adaptation persisted in subsequent overhand throws despite intervening underhand throws, and readapted with repeated overhand throws. In 4 subjects, the results were similar, except for an apparent carry-over of the overhand prism adaptation to the first subsequent underhand throw. Nevertheless, this disappeared with the second throw, and it is therefore unclear to what extent this represented an adaptive change. In these as in the first 2 subjects, the prior overhand adaptation survived the intervening underhand throws, persisting undiminished in subsequent overhand throws, and readapting only after repeated overhand throws.

2. The Role of Cerebellum in Prism Adaptation

To model the above data biologically, we must seek information on where adaptation occurs. The following data will support the claim that adaptation does not occur in the MPG itself, but rather requires the presence of the cerebellum (Thach et al. 1992). Later sections will develop a model for this role in which the cerebellum provides a modulatory signal to the MPG to adjust its metrics. However, at least in some simple adaptations, it appears that while the cerebellum may be necessary for adaptation to occur, and to provide a corrective signal in the short run, it may not be necessary to maintain the *results* of adaptation in the long run. But this topic of how one neural network may serve to install the results of learning in another, a topic of great general interest for the simulation of adaptive behavior, must await future research.

The cerebellum has been implicated in a number of situations in which the metrics of movement must adapt to changing circumstances. In particular, prism adaptation in macaques is abolished by cerebellar lesion (Baizer and Glickstein, 1974). Martin et al.

(1994) also applied their paradigm to patients with cerebellar disease. In a patient who had multiple sclerosis, with tremor and ataxia (no other deficits), no adaptation was seen after donning and doffing the prisms. With a patient with right cerebellar hemisphere infarct, tremor and ataxia, little adaptation is seen after donning and doffing the prisms. Martin et al. also found that two patients with MRI-documented inferior olive hypertrophy (a degenerative disease of the inferior olive, which is the exclusive source of the cerebellar climbing fibers) could not adapt, despite otherwise normal performance.

3. Microcomplexes and the Modulatory Role of the Cerebellum

Our theory of cerebellar function posits that the cerebellar output affects motor repertoires resident in the MPGs located elsewhere, and that this effect is not only modulatory, controlling gain of these MPGs, but also combinatorial - mixing motor elements within and across generators such as to adapt old and develop new synergies of multiple body parts (Schweighofer et al., 1994).

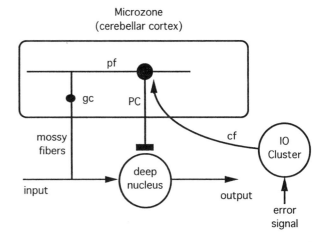

Figure 1: A corticonuclear microcomplex, the structural-functional unit of the cerebellum. IO, inferior olive; cf, climbing fiber; PC, Purkinje cell; gc, granule cell; pf, parallel fibers. See text. (Adapted from Ito 1984).

For readers unfamiliar with cerebellar circuitry, we summarize the key elements in Figure 1, showing a patch of cerebellar cortex linked with the patch of cerebellar nuclei whereby it communicates with the rest of the nervous system. Such a unit, a cerebellar corticonuclear **microcomplex** (Ito, 1984), is composed of a cerebellar microzone and a small number of nuclear cells. We view each microcomplex as providing input to some MPG, with cerebellar signals adjusted to adapt the MPG to changing circumstances.

A microzone receives (to simplify) two kinds of input, mossy fibers and climbing fibers, the output being carried by the deep nuclear cells. Moreover, both mossy fibers and climbing fibers supply collaterals to the nuclear cell group when passing to the corresponding microzone. The crucial point is that a set of mossy fibers provides inputs to many microcomplexes, since the granule cells send out long parallel fibers characterized by considerable divergence across many microzones. This "mossy set" constitutes a general context for the present sensorimotor actions, providing information about the state of activity of various structures, from the cerebral level to sensory ones.

The only output cells of a microzone are Purkinje cells (PCs). As PCs have inhibitory action upon nuclear cells (while collaterals of mossy fibers excite the nuclear cells), the signal flow from the nuclear cells is modulated by the microzone action.

The climbing fibers are commonly considered as conveying signals encoding errors in the performance of the system in which a given microcomplex is installed (see Ito 1990 for a review of the evidence). An important learning mechanism for the microcomplex follows from the fact that climbing fiber signals induce LTD (long-term depression of synaptic strength) in those parallel fiber-PCs synapses which were co-activated with the climbing fibers (within a certain time window).

Coordination of different MPGs, tuned by different microcomplexes, is effected by the parallel fibers which via Purkinje cell projections to the cerebellar nuclei spans the width of up to two different body representations within these nuclei. We concur with the evidence that adjustment of parallel fiber-Purkinje cell synapses, under the influence of the climbing fiber, is the probable mechanism for changing synergic combinations.

4. The Structure of the Model

In Figure 2, we diagram the putative mechanisms of gaze-throw adjustment. The essential adjustment is proposed to be between eye position and the synergy of the muscles in the trunk and arm involved in throwing. The target is seen, and the eye foveates and fixates the center of the target. With repeated throws, adjustments are made in the strength of the parallel fiber input to Purkinje cells such that the changing output produced from the Purkinje cells in response to the eye position and visual input modulates nuclear cells of the relevant micro-

complexes in such a way that their effect upon the MPGs is to yield a throw that will hit the target.

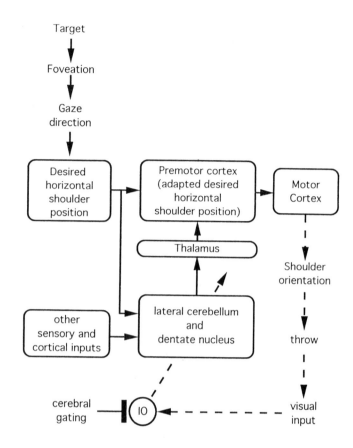

Figure 2: Putative mechanisms of adjustment between eye position and synergy of the muscles in the trunk and arm involved in throwing. Afferent information on eye position arrives in cortical motor areas that control eye, neck, arm and hand muscle synergies. With repeated throws, adjustments are made in the synaptic connections in lateral cerebellum such that its changing output (to premotor cortex via the dentate nucleus and thalamus) in response to the eye position and visual input modulates the throw sufficiently for it to hit the target.

We consider the movement to be decomposed into two parts: 1) aiming and then 2) throwing. Only horizontal shift of gaze by the prisms will be considered, and we proceed as if aiming were solely realized by orientation of the shoulder joint in the horizontal plane. Trunk, elbow and wrist rotation are not taken into account in our model. Only the desired position of the shoulder after aiming (but before throwing) is coded, i.e., we do not model the movement itself, but only the horizontal adaptation of the endpoint of aiming. This is supported by the study of Flanders et al. (1992) who showed that the pointing movement to a target is controlled independently in the elevation and horizontal directions. This parcellation may facilitate comparing a target location signal with signals of the limb position so as to yield a motor error signal. If arm position and target location are represented in a common coordinate system (centered at the shoulder, the three coordinates being: vertical and horizontal shoulder angles, and distance), a simple combination between these internal representations may suffice to compute the initial part of the movement.

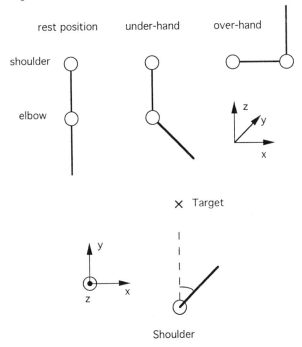

Figure 3: Simplified model of the arm with two degrees of freedom for the shoulder and one for the elbow. Top: side-view. Bottom: top-view. Adaptation in the present model is limited to horizontal shoulder rotation.

Population studies in the premotor and motor cortices show that cells code for all the possible direction of arm movements in 3D space; no separate coding for elevation or azimuth coding by two sub-populations has been found, which might suggest that the two different processing mechanisms would be coded by the same population of neurons. The segregation would therefore be based on functional assemblies and not spatial ones (Burnod and Caminiti 1992). We model one such assembly, coding for horizontal desired position.

We model the arm (Figure 3) with a reference frame centered at the shoulder, with **x** pointing towards the target, **y** to the left, and **z** upwards. In order to reproduce the data, the minimum model of the arm will have three degrees of freedom: vertical and horizontal shoulder rotations (around **y** and **z** respectively) and elbow rotation. We do not model

the third degree of freedom at the shoulder joint of the real arm. The rest position is with the arm along -**z** with the elbow joint maximally extended, while the endpoint of aiming depends on the strategy, i.e. overarm or underarm, as well as the target location. In both underarm and overarm strategies, the elbow adopts a characteristic angle prior to the throw phase, and we assume it is the shoulder rotation around **z** that provides the horizontal component of aiming — whose adaptation we study.

A subject throws where she looks. Before the throw, head and trunk are "towards the target". This ability, under normal circumstances, does not involve the cerebellum (in a first approximation: In effect, other plastic and compensatory mechanisms operate in the chronic cerebellar patient), as is shown by the accurate throwing by a cerebellar patient when not wearing prisms. Yet, from the inability of cerebellar patients to adapt their throw to prisms (Martin et al. 1994), we infer that the shoulder area of the dentate — the cerebellar nucleus for the lateral cerebellar system — is necessary for the aiming adaptation, in accord with the putative role of the dentate in planning and preparation of the movement. Moreover, the cerebellum is involved in a side path projecting to the premotor cortex, area 6, (Schell and Strick 1984) via the ventral thalamus (Figure 2).

Figure 4 shows the structure of the neural network involved in our model of aiming the throw and its adaptation: The premotor cortex "prepares" information on desired horizontal shoulder position for the motor cortex. Since the lateral cerebellum projects to premotor cortex, we postulate that it is this cerebellar signal that adjusts the premotor cortex appropriately to changing circumstances (e.g., prisms), and we here model how the cerebellar circuitry can adapt on the basis of a delayed error signal provided by vision of the where the dart lands relative to the target.

The system (human + dart) is an open loop system since the error in dart throwing is available only after the movement and so the error cannot be used to correct the given movement; however, over trials, the correct match between gaze and throw is learned. Before throwing, the subject foveates the target and therefore the internal representation of gaze and hence of the desired shoulder position (before it undergoes adaptation) is changed. This information is coded in a distributed manner, providing robustness to lesion and noise: A signal distributed over many noisy nonlinear channels may be summed to yield an accurate signal. This system has been modeled using leaky integrator neurons in our NSL simulation environment (Weitzenfeld, 1991).

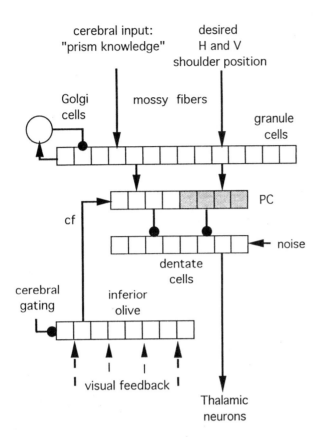

Figure 4: Detailed view of the cerebellar neural network. Mossy fibers encode desired arm configuration at the end of aiming (before adaptation), and cortical projections for some form of "mental set". The Golgi cell population acts as a gain regulator of the total granule cell activity. The granule cells project with a large convergence to the Purkinje cells, which in turn inhibit the dentate (nuclear) cells. The latter are excited by some background activity (noise). The inferior olive receives a weighted retinotopic input and sends a one-to-one projection to the PC layer. This precise projection is kept in the nuclear cell and thalamic layers (the number of neurons shown is not that which is simulated).

Our cerebellar neural network model (Figure 4) models the microcomplexes embedded in the overall model of Figure 2. The model represents granule cells, Golgi cells, Purkinje cells and the shoulder area of the deep cerebellar nucleus. The granule cells generate a statistical distribution of combinations of mossy fibers carrying retinotopic signals, two position signals and a temporal signal. (Actually, Schweighofer et al. 1994 use a simple deterministic scheme, but the connections from the mossy fibers to the granule cells are randomly generated in the model of adaptation described below. Simulations show that this does not degrade model performance, but does allow a richer combination of mossy fiber signals.)

The present model has only one PC per microcomplex. The Purkinje cells membrane potential equation is:

$$\tau_{pc}\frac{dpc}{dt} = -pc + w_{ltd}{*}GC$$

where w_{ltd} is a vector of adjustable weights (see below), and GC is the vector of firing rate of the granule cells. [By not taking into account the climbing fiber afferent in the PC equation, we implicitly make the following assumption: As the climbing fibers, on their way to the cerebellar cortex, send collaterals to the deep nuclei, the excitation of the fastigial neurons by these collaterals would nullify the strong inhibition caused by the complex spikes, which are the response of the PCs to the climbing fiber firing.] The PC axons then converge to the dentate, whose cells they inhibit. Collaterals of the mossy fibers also converge to nuclear cells, and give an excitatory projection. It is the output of the nuclear cells that provides the correction signal to the MPGs. We must demonstrate that it can be adapted in the right direction (i.e., that correcting for the prism) so long as the throw requires correction.

To reproduce all the experiments, the mossy fiber inputs that we consider are:

1) Desired arm configuration at the end of aiming. This position is calculated from eye position muscles and/or from a corollary discharge for the control of gaze. As proprioceptive inputs of the end-point are not available before aiming, a desired position of the vertical shoulder position should be available to the cerebellum via mossy fibers (this is consistent with fact that there are no direct inputs from the periphery to the lateral cerebellum). We assume that this desired position is well learned as cerebellar patients can throw if no adaptation is required (however, as mentioned above, some neural rearrangements probably occur).

2) Desired vertical shoulder position (to distinguish underarm from overarm throws).

3) Cortical projections for some form of "mental set". This does not have to explicitly code knowledge for the present purpose, but must differ depending on whether the prisms are known or unknown. This input is necessary to explain the ability of highly practiced subjects to immediately switch "gain" when donning or removing known prisms. [However, the simulations which show that our model shares this capability are not included in the present paper.] The cortical input to the cerebellar cortex is known to be large. Indeed, the cortico-pontine fibers form a very large group of fibers which arise from the whole cerebral cortex.

Adapting the observations of Georgopoulos et al. (1988) on cells associated with movement of the hand, we assume that each cell in premotor cortex associated with rotation of the shoulder has a preferred direction, i.e., a shoulder rotation for which the cell fires maximally. Georgopoulos associates with each cell's firing a vector C_i which points in the cell's preferred direction and whose length varies with the cell's firing rate. The activity of the neural population is then posited to be in the direction given by the "population vector" $P = \sum C_i$, where the sum is taken over the whole population.

To account for adaptation, we now postulate that premotor cortex combines the gaze vector G with a compensatory signal coming from the dentate deep cerebellar nucleus via the ventral thalamus. During adaptation, the cerebellum shifts the population coding of the desired shoulder position after aiming by an amount opposite to the initial deviation. Since we follow the "Georgopoulos view" that premotor cortex neurons code shoulder direction by a population vector S, it is tempting to posit that the nuclear output is a signal corresponding to a vector C in world coordinates which is added to the gaze vector G to yield the "adapted" shoulder planar vector S = G + C. Since the shoulder vector should point toward the center of the target, adaptation ends when cos(C, S) = - cos(G, S). However, when the glasses are taken off, G points towards the target, and C does not change until re-adaptation takes place. Immediately upon removal of an adapted 40° prism, the shoulder will point at -40°, yet if S = G + C, **the new S would be at - 20•**. Therefore, the actual transformation needed is a rotation and not a vectorial sum. If the cerebellum learns how to rotate the desired shoulder position coding by 40°, removal of the lenses will give a reverse error of 40°, as in the experiment.

The algorithm we used to perform this rotation was developed by Bruce Hoff (personal communication; details to be provided elsewhere) and uses sigma-pi neurons (Rumelhart and McClelland 1986). The transformation need not be too accurate since learning and can compensate for non-perfectly realized mathematical requirements.

We next turn to the **error detection system**. With Flanders et al. (1992), we assume that the target location and arm position share the same coordinate system, with error "in register" with the shoulder position. A leftward error activates a "leftward" group of IO cells. These cells receive weighted retinotopic projections from the retina so that a large error will give rise to several spikes. Therefore, the climbing fibers fire to give the direction and amplitude of the error given by a visual projection to the IO which retains some retinotopy. A large error will activate (with a certain probability) different

inferior olive neurons than a smaller error. However, there is a gradient of cf firing activities within each microzone.

5. Adaptation: Problems and Solutions

The purely feedforward nature of the movement (the error cannot be corrected during the movement since the error is not known before the dart hits the wall containing the target) and the delay between motion generation and error detection implies the need for a short term memory system capable of retaining the locus of cerebellar activity involved in the throw — especially since the throw has been made in between the aiming and the receipt of the error signal.

To address these temporal problems, we will assume synapse **eligibility** (Klopf 1982; Barto et al. 1983). The form postulated by Houk and Barto (1992) is that activation of a dendritic spine by a parallel fiber leads to the release of a chemical called a second messenger in the spine, and its concentration acts as a short term memory. The synapse is **eligible** if the concentration is above some threshold. If an error signal is provided to the whole cell by the climbing fiber, the resulting increase in Ca^{++} in the cell will only affect the eligible synapses, and therefore only their efficacies will be changed. If a parallel fiber-PC synapse participates in synaptic transmission, it becomes eligible to be weakened by LTD if a climbing fiber signal is sent somewhat later. However, we further require that when the error signal arrives, the concentration of the messenger be largest for synapses involved in the aiming and not the subsequent throw. We therefore introduced the concept of "time window of eligibility" (Schweighofer et al. 1994). Our model uses a concentration having the response of a second order system for the concentration [2nd] of the messenger (although, alternatively, we can imagine a second messenger following a first order equation but with a delay).

$$\frac{d^2[2nd]}{dt^2} + a\frac{d[2nd]}{dt} + b\,[2nd] = K.GC$$

with a and b properly chosen so that the response is damped, the concentration matches in time the occurrence of the error signal and the concentration decays relatively fast as there should be minimum interference with the throw *per se*. With w_{ltd} the vector of adjustable weights for parallel fiber-PC synapses, the synaptic adjustment rule we consider is:

$$\frac{dw_{ltd}}{dt} = \{- c.IO + d.(1 - IO)\}.[2nd]$$

Figure 5: A row showing activity of 180 mossy fiber inputs. Three different modalities are encoded, each carried by a distinct sub-population. The horizontal shoulder position (derived from the horizontal gaze direction) in the case of the 25° prism on (a) and for a case without prisms (b); the vertical shoulder position which is in overhand position; and the cognitive inputs encoding, here, an unknown prism.

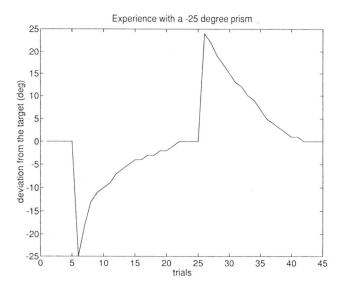

Figure 6: Simulated 25° prism adaptation experiments. This figure and the following show the adaptation of angle between the shoulder angle (derived from the premotor activity) and the "forward" direction after aiming over trials. The adaptation requires 20 trials, somewhat more than re-adaptation to the non-prism condition. Note that the irregularities in the curve are due to the probabilistic firing of the climbing fibers.

w_{ltd} at $t = 0$ is set randomly between 0 and w_{max}, with $w_{max} > w_{ltd} \geq 0$, $c \gg d > 0$, IO the binary climbing fiber error signal, c the learning coefficient (LTD) and d the "forgetting" coefficient. The d term provides some kind of LTP (long-term potentiation of synaptic strength) in this learning rule and is necessary: If only LTD were occurring, all the weights would eventually tend to zero. As the climbing fiber fires only if an error occurs, the weights decrease most of the time, but slowly since $c \gg d$. As a consequence, if the system is tuned at a certain moment, the decrease of the weights will sooner or later induce an error. One (or a few) corrective movements will then be

generated, and because $c \gg d$, the weights soon regain the correct values.

6. Results

Mossy fiber coding is shown in Figure 5, and simulated prism adaptation experiments are shown in Figures 6-8. Note that with a model performing a pure rotation, the off-prism initial error is exactly opposite to the initial error with the prism (Figure 6). Both forgetting and relearning are present in the system: forgetting is included in the learning rule, as the positive term. If there is no climbing fiber activity at a particular site, the weights are increased. As the error signal carried by the climbing fibers decreases the weights, there is forgetting of the previously learned patterns. By contrast, re-adaptation to the non-prism situation after adaptation to prisms is due to learning as can be seen on Figure 7. In the PC layer, there is a large depression after complete re-adaptation. This is how the two gains are stored.

Figure 8 show the Over/Underhand experiments. Note how in this case the vertical shoulder position is different for the two throwing strategies. The model reproduces the experimental data reported by Thach: There is some transfer from overhand to underhand in the prism adaptation ... though in some subjects there is no transfer, while in others the transfer is total. We adopted a middle ground with some overlap in the mossy fiber inputs between the two positions and a not too large mossy fiber input for the vertical shoulder position.

7. Discussion

We have studied a key problem for adaptive behavior — adjusting a sensorimotor transformation — and seen that the machinery for adapting an MPG may be external to the circuitry which enables the MPG to operate under conditions in which adaptation is not required.

The role of cerebellum in humans and monkeys thus offers suggestions for the parcellation of function and adaptation in distinct neural networks in the design of adaptive robots. Moreover, as shown by the underarm vs. overarm experiments, the adaptation is **not** a recalibration of the visual coding of space (which would be task neutral), but instead acts on a transformation specific to the task. Each motor schema is a controller with its own private transformation.

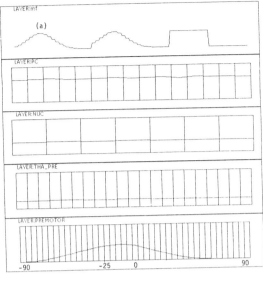

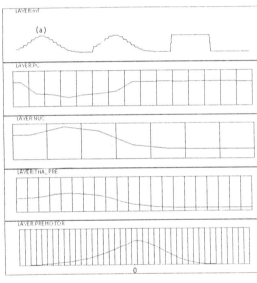

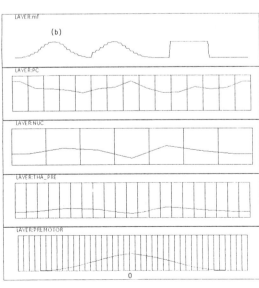

← **Figure 7:** These three simulations show the spatial behavior of the cerebellar neurons during adaptation to 25° prisms and underhand throwing with a known prism: Each row graphs the activity of a layer of cells after visual input and just prior to the throw. The first row of cell shows the mossy fiber input. The second represent the firing rates of 15 PCs (vertical scale 0-110 spikes/s, as in the following groups of neurons), the third the nuclear cell firing rates. The nuclear cells are inhibited by the PCs, and are driven by a high background rate. The fourth row shows the response of the 20 thalamic neurons and the last the 40 premotor neurons. Shoulder position is derived from the premotor layer activity by the population vector transformation (not by the peak of activity). a) situation before the first throw with prism on (as in (a) in Fig. 5). The apparent uniform background rate of the PCs is due to random connections from the parallel fibers with initial random weights. The background firing rate in the nucleus provides facilitation to the premotor activity which is deviated from the middle due to the gaze input. The premotor activity corresponds to a 25° angle between the shoulder and the forward direction b) End of adaptation to a prism. The depressed PC activities (on the left) release activity in the nuclear cells and in the thalamic neurons. The premotor distributed activity is pushed back in the middle (The corresponding shoulder position is 0°). c) After re-adaptation to the non-prism situation ((b) in Fig. 5). The PC layer shows another depression on the right side: It is not forgetting but re-learning that occurs. Also note the quasi-constant thalamic total activity (during adaptation) due to the negative feedback achieved by the reticular thalamic complex, which results in contrast enhancement and consequently in a better shift of the premotor "hump". The shoulder angle is 0° again.

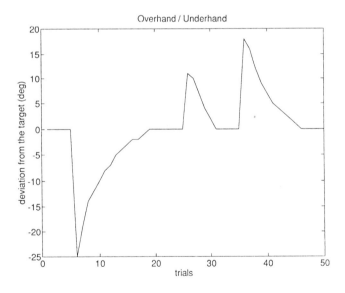

Figure 8: Over/Under arm experiment. In this case, the vertical shoulder position is different for the two throwing strategies. The first part of the learning curve shows adaptation with a overhand strategy. After the prisms are removed, an underhand throw strategy is used. Then (last peak) throwing is made overhand again. The model reproduces the experimental data reported by Martin et al.: There is some transfer from overhand to underhand in the prism adaptation.

Even though the direct mapping from sensory to motor output is somewhat plastic, adaptation to novel context does not occur reliably without cerebellum. We have used the same cerebellar model for both saccade adaptation and prism adaptation for throwing, with a similar coding of the error — but in the throwing model the cerebellum projects "upstream" to the premotor cortex instead of "downstream" to the brainstem as in the saccade model (in the sense of a stream from cortex to brainstem to spinal cord). The microzone concept holds in both cases. The unification of diverse information - from sensory signals to cerebral codes for "mental set" - is made possible by the long length of the parallel fibers, overlapping different microzones.

Finally, we note that the concept of eligibility addresses a key problem in adaptive behavior: how can reinforcement or error signals to a network affect those cells which were active some time earlier? Following Klopf, Sutton, Barto, and Houk, we use a short-term memory internal to individual synapses to do the job when the delay between activity and feedback is on the order of a few hundred milliseconds. However, although it takes us beyond the reach of the present study, a more explicit form of short-term memory seems required to link events more widely separated in time. Important clues for future modeling, and for the design of adaptive systems, may come from the phenomenon of *trace conditioning*. Here, an animal without cerebellum cannot be conditioned in a simple conditioned response; and an animal with cerebellum and without hippocampus can be conditioned only if the delay between unconditioned and conditioned stimulus is at most a few hundred milliseconds. The animal must have both cerebellum *and hippocampus* intact if it is to be conditioned when this delay is much longer (Moyer, DeYoe, and Disterhoft, 1990). The hypothesis is that the hippocampus holds a *trace* during the intervening period, bringing yet another neural network into play.

Acknowledgments

The research at USC was supported in part by Grant NOOO14-92-J-4026 from the Office of Naval Research for research on "Cerebellum and the Adaptive Coordination of Movement".

References

Baizer JS, Glickstein M (1974) Role of the cerebellum in prism adaptation. *J Physiol (London)* 236: 34-35.

Barto, A., Sutton, R., & Anderson, W. (1983) Neuronlike adaptive elements that can solve difficult learning control problems, *IEEE Transactions on Systems, Man and Cybernetics*, SMC-13:834-846.

Burnod Y, Caminiti R (1992) Cortical mechanisms of visuomotor transformations underlying arm movements to visual targets. *Behav Brain Sci* 15: 332-333.

Flanders, M., Helms, Tillery, S.I., and Soechting, J.F., (1992) Early stages in sensorimotor transformation. *Behavioral and brain sciences* 309-362.

Georgopulos, A.P., Kettner, R.E., and Schwartz, A.B. (1988) Primate motor cortex cell and free arm movements to visual targets in three dimensional space. II Coding of the direction of movement by a neural population. *J Neurosci.* 8:2928-2937.

Ito, M. (1984) *The Cerebellum and Neuronal Control*, New York: Raven Press.

Ito, M. (1990) A New Physiological Concept on Cerebellum, *Rev. Neurol. (Paris)*, 146:564-569.

Klopf, A. H. (1982) *The Hedonistic Neuron: A Theory of Memory, Learning, and Intelligence*, Washington, D.C.: Hemisphere.

Martin, T., Keating, J. G., Goodkin, H. P., Bastian, A. J., & Thach, W. T. (1994) Prism Adaptation of Human Eye-Hand Coordination: Task Specificity and Dependency on the Olivo-Cerebellar System, to appear.

Moyer, J.R., Jr., DeYoe, R.A. and Disterhoft, J.F. (1990) Hippocampectomy disrupts trace eyeblink conditioning in rabbits. *Behav. Neurosci.*, 104:243-252.

Rumelhart D.E., and McClelland J.L. (1986) *Parallel Distributed Processing - Explorations in the Microstructure of Cognition*. Cambridge, MA, The MIT Press.

Schweighofer, N., Arbib, M. A., & Dominey, P. F. (1994) A Model of the Role of Cerebellum in Adaptive Control of Saccades, to appear.

Schell, G.R. and Strick, P.L. (1984) The origin of the thalamic inputs to the arcuate premotor and supplementary motor areas. *J. Neurosci.* 4: 539-560.

Thach W.T., Goodkin, H.P., and Keating J.G. (1992) The cerebellum and the adaptive coordination of movement. *Ann. Rev. Neurosci.* 15:403-442.

Robotic Experiments in Cricket Phonotaxis

Barbara Webb

Department of Artificial Intelligence
University of Edinburgh
5 Forrest Hill, Edinburgh EH1 2QL, Scotland
bhw@uk.ac.edinburgh.aifh

Abstract

As yet there are few studies that link biological and robotic systems at the level of potential neural mechanisms. In this paper I describe the development and evaluation of a model of the neural mechanism of phonotaxis in the cricket through the building and testing of the behaviour of a robot. Robotic considerations lead to a hypothesised mechanism somewhat different to those currently put forward in neuroethological research; robotic testing demonstrates that this mechanism can coherently explain many of the neuroethological observations. These specific results demonstrate the potential power of this methodology for understanding perceptual systems, and in the process reveal some important aspects of how real (biological and artificial) sensory-motor systems function.

1 Introduction

An essential component of an intelligent agent is the capacity to interact competently with the surrounding environment, utilising sensing to successfully adapt actions to its situation. Perceptual mechanisms should be regarded as specialised structures that provide appropriate linkages between an agent and its environment (Varela et al, 1991), rather than performing processes of representation. Consequently understanding the behavioural function of sensory processing is essential to understanding perceptual systems (Gibson, 1979), and the structure of those systems will be determined by the physical details of the interaction of agent and environment.

This view of perception suggests that an appropriate approach is to study systems where the complete connection from sensors to behaviour, and the physics of the interaction with the environment, can plausibly be examined; which currently can only be done if the system is a relatively 'simple' one, such as a lower animal (insect or below) or a mobile robot (Brooks, 1986). Investigating mechanisms of sensorimotor control in simple systems has become a topic of increasing importance in AI research leading to interaction with biological rather than cognitive sciences. However the connection is often somewhat tenuous, consisting mostly of adopted vocabulary rather than substantive links in subject matter.

Robots are obviously a suitable medium for investigating sensorimotor systems as they satisfy the critical issues of completeness and physical interaction given above. But the potential connection of robotics to biology is not simply one of extracting mechanisms from biological examples to install in robotic devices as seems to be advocated by Beer (1990)—there aren't many biological perceptual systems that are well enough understood to be directly implemented. The principal idea behind the methodology presented here is that the *process* of attempting to implement physical models of biological systems can potentially contribute to our *understanding* of how perceptual systems work, both in terms of specific hypotheses and in more general terms of the features of real, functional perceptual systems.

The particular biological example of a perceptual mechanism modelled in this work was phonotaxis in the cricket (*Ensifera: Gryllidae*): the ability of the female cricket to find a conspecific male by walking or flying towards the 'calling song' the male produces. The behaviour and its neural underpinnings are one of the insect systems most thoroughly studied in neuroethology (overviews are given in Huber and Thorson (1985) and Schildberger (1988)), and thus there is a good deal of experimental data to draw upon; yet the fundamental mechanism by which the cricket uses sound sensing to control its behaviour is still not well understood.

The cricket calling song consists of short bursts of almost pure tone produced by the male drawing one wing across the other. The frequency and temporal pattern of the sound is species specific (Figure 1). The cricket has an auditory receptor on each front leg, and the female's tracking behaviour is generally explained by the principle of 'turn to the more strongly stimulated side'. An additional process of filtering the frequency and temporal pattern to identify the signal is assumed to 'turn on' this taxis behaviour when the right sort of song is detected. But as Schildberger and Horner (1988) write, "It is still entirely unclear whether or how these two aspects

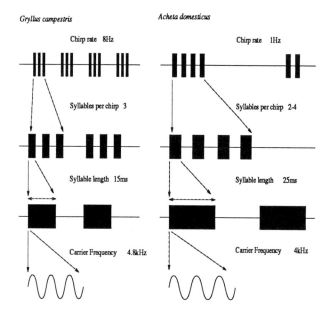

Gryllus campestris   *Acheta domesticus*

Figure 1: *Hierarchy of song features for two cricket species: from bottom to top, a tone of specific frequency occurs in short syllables at a specific rate; groups of syllables make up chirps separated by pauses.*

[the direction and the characteristic sound] of the calling song are processed independently of one another in the brain, or how the brain triggers and controls phonotactic walking". The work described here aimed to devise the simplest possible robotic mechanism that could support the observed behaviour of the cricket, and thus provide a potential answer to 'whether and how' recognition of the signal and location of the source could be combined in phonotaxis.

2   A robot-inspired hypothesis

The behaviour of phonotaxis (moving towards a specific sound source) suggests, at least to a robot-designer, that an appropriate mechanism would be one which can only successfully perform taxis to the right kind of signal, i.e. non-conspecific signals can be inherently rejected by the failure of the taxis mechanism to operate with them.

This idea arose initially from consideration of the peripheral auditory mechanism in the cricket: the tracheal connection between the ears and spiracles that results in phase cancellation producing a direction-dependent difference in intensity at each tympanum (Boyd and Lewis, 1983). This mechanism can only work if the signal is at a particular frequency, because the phase shift depends on the (fixed) length of the trachea. Thorson *et al* (1982) found that changing the frequency can result in anomalous phonotaxis, that is, moving in the wrong direction: this does require a higher signal intensity (to overcome neural tuning effects) and seems to indicate that rather than rejecting a signal with the wrong frequency, the

animal is simply less able to find it.

How might the phonotaxis system operate so that it works only for the right kind of temporal pattern, as well as frequency? Simplicity suggests that some sort of temporal comparison is involved. The operation of the auditory receptors introduces an intensity dependent latency of firing onset (inversely proportional to firing rate) that could serve as the cue (Esch *et al*, 1980). This possibility has been noted by several experimenters (for example, Mörchen, 1980) but has received little direct investigation. Of course the fact that latency and firing rate are not independent makes it difficult to separate them experimentally. However, they can be implemented separately in a model to test their effectiveness. There are aspects of the signal that make latency comparison easier to implement: the signal's low duty cycle (with sound present only about one sixth of the time) does not seem well suited to an independent comparison of firing rate, whereas the interrupted bursts and consequent frequent onsets, are well suited to latency comparison.

Thorson *et al* (1982) suggested that for the cricket, the syllable repetition rate was a necessary and sufficient temporal cue for recognition. Most of their sample of *G.campestris* would track a continuous series of syllables (a 'trill' i.e. without the chirp structure of the natural song) provided the syllables repeated at a rate within 15-50Hz, roughly the range of the syllable rate in the natural song under varied temperature conditions. They also found that varying the syllable length between 10% and 90% of the duty cycle has little effect on phonotactic behaviour.

The failure of phonotaxis at fast syllable rates is generally attributed to the time constants of decay in the auditory interneurons (particularly AN1): a rapidly changing song cannot be clearly coded after such low-pass filtering. In fact, the neural and behavioural evidence is a little less clear cut. Schildberger (1985) claims that recognition of the song requires a 7-8ms gap between syllables, and notes smaller gaps don't seem to be coded by AN1. Wohlers and Huber (1982) estimate 'critical pause length' for AN1 to be 15ms, and show a degradation of signal copying at 50Hz (i.e. with 10ms gaps), but they find the syllable structure equally masked with a 30Hz song that has long syllables with short pauses (5ms): yet such songs *are* successfully tracked by the cricket (Thorson *et al*, 1982).

Hypotheses for slow rate rejection are discussed by Huber and Thorson (1985): they consider a template matching process to be unlikely, and a correlation process is argued against by the lack of aliasing effects. However, they don't give a clear mechanism for the high-pass filtering that they suggest. The simplest possibility is summation, with more than one syllable required within a certain time period to get a response. To prevent a continuous signal being summed would require prior pro-

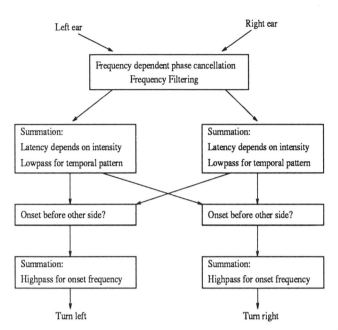

Figure 2: *Hypothesised mechanism for phonotaxis (see text).*

cessing such that only onsets contribute to the sum (i.e. an adaptive neuron that reflects changes in the firing rate). Alternatively, if the summation is done on the output of a latency comparison (i.e. neurons that fire when one side is active but not both) then only syllable onsets will be available, because only at onset will one side (the one with shorter latency) be active without the other.

This latter possibility is not generally considered as it is assumed that recognition takes place independently of location and involves combining rather than comparing the signals (Huber, 1983: note however that a straightforward combination of signals with latencies differing by up to 15ms would in fact obscure the 15ms gap in the calling song). Schildberger (1984) identified brain neurons that apparently fire only to syllable rates within a certain range. This is consistent with a summation mechanism (for example, firing doesn't start till after the second syllable occurs), but the results are not sufficiently detailed to determine exactly what neural connections and processes may be involved; nor was the effect of differences between the ears examined.

Combining these considerations of what is known about the cricket, and what would be simplest to build into a robot, gives rise to a specific hypothesis about the mechanism of phonotaxis (see Figure 2). The basic stages are:

- Phase cancellation causes a direction-dependent difference in the effective intensity at the ears: the side closer to the sound will have a stronger response, pro-

vided the signal has the right frequency.

- Intensity differences lead to a difference in firing latency in auditory neurons through summation of the input, *i.e.* threshold is reached more quickly for higher intensities.
- Above threshold (firing) level is maintained as long as input is received, and then decays over time. The decay rate is such that small gaps in the signal are missed, thus lowpass filtering occurs.
- The response on one side is compared with the other: if an onset of firing occurs on one side first, a signal for turning is generated. Requiring an onset means that there must be a detectable temporal pattern after the low-pass filtering.
- Turning also involves summation of the input: signals for turning are summed; decay occurs between signals; thus signals must occur sufficiently frequently to initiate a turn; thus high pass filtering of the signal pattern occurs. This summation could be considered a property of the motor system, i.e. turning requires a certain rate of stimulation.

Hence a sound that is closer to one side and has an appropriate frequency and temporal pattern should cause a turn to that side; these repeated corrections will result in the animal successfully moving to the sound source.

3 A robot-based implementation

The most effective way to test a model of a sensory-motor mechanism is to build it into a real sensory-motor device, i.e. a robot. There is insufficient space here to give details of the implementation: it is described in (Webb, 1993a) and full details are in (Webb, 1993b). The robot is pictured in Figure 3. The robot base is a Lego vehicle with simple bump and infrared sensors, two motor-driven wheels and one castor, controlled by a 68000 clone processor programmed in C. Miniature microphones connect to a circuit that processes the auditory signal and performs phase cancellation. The neural processes of

Figure 3: *The robot used to test the hypothesis.*

summation, firing latency, thresholding and comparison are carried out continuously in pseudo-parallel software. Movement is continuous and turning is controlled simply by stopping the wheel on the appropriate side for time intervals signalled by the neural process.

The responses from the the ears circuit occur every 35ms and indicate the intensity at each ear (after phase cancellation), ranging from 0-16. They are summated over time using the simple equation

$$value_t = value_{t-1} * 7/8 + response$$

with a 'threshold' value of 16 representing the onset of firing of the auditory interneuron, and firing being maintained until the value falls back below 8. A difference between the ear responses of 2 or more will thus result in a latency difference in the onset of firing; but if the temporal modulation of the signal (the syllables) is too rapid, the value will not decrease sufficiently between sounds for onsets (or latency differences) to be detectable.

If one side fires first, the motor will be stopped briefly on that side; but the resulting turn is very small unless several 'first onsets' occur in quick succession. Thus the signal modulation cannot be too rapid (as above) *or too slow*, if the robot is to successfully turn to approach the sound source. Parameters of robot size, processing time in the circuit and software, and of movement speed and turning inertia determined an ideal 'conspecific' signal for the robot of a 1.6Hz rate of syllables of 2kHz tone.

The robot was tested under experimental conditions comparable to those used with crickets, performing repeated runs with various sound sources, within a confined area (4x3.5 metres). The paths taken were recorded using an overhead camera system that could provide floor position co-ordinates to within a centimetre for a light mounted centrally on the robot, at video frame rate (25Hz). The following are some of the results that have most bearing on the biological hypothesis; further results are described in Webb (1993b).

3.1 Phonotaxis

The robot was able to successfully find the 'ideal' signal on every run within the arena, usually approaching quite directly. The behaviour was clearly different when no sound was present (it would wander around the enclosure). Different configurations of the sound source and the robot's start position did not affect the success, nor did adding obstacles between the start and the source (provided the gaps were not too small). Without the arena the robot would sometimes go outside the range of the signal and get lost under the furniture in the lab.

A deviation of no more than ±60° from the speaker direction is one of the criteria specified by Thorson *et al* (1982) for 'clear tracking' in the cricket. Another is corrective meandering centred on the speaker direction, i.e the zig-zag path typical of phonotaxis with the angle to the sound varying about the midline but turns tending to take the cricket back towards it. Both characteristics can be examined in the robot path by plotting the angle relative to the speaker that the robot is heading against time. In Figure 4 it can be seen that the robot stays mostly within ±60°, and shows the zig-zag characteristic: the trace is quite comparable to those produced by crickets (see, for example, Schmitz *et al*, 1982).

3.2 Recognition

It is fairly well established that the most critical feature for phonotaxis in the cricket is the rate at which the syllables repeat. The phonotactic response decreases for syllable rates faster or slower than the ideal. To test this in the robot, a series of trials was performed using syllable rates of 5Hz, 2.5Hz, 1.6Hz, 1.25Hz, 1Hz and 0.8Hz (that is, with a 50/50 duty cycle, and syllables of length 100, 200, 300, 400, 500 and 600 milliseconds). For each rate, ten trials were run, in pairs from two different starting positions. Figure 5 shows the best, worst and median track for 3 of the rates, and, by reducing each track to the set of vectors between turns and plotting all the vectors from the same origin, shows the complete range of movement relative to the sound source (vector direction 0) for all the tracks at that rate.

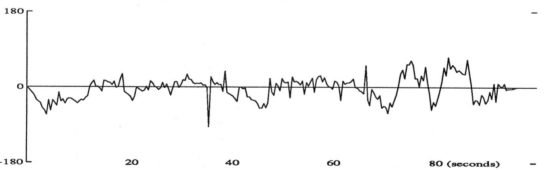

Figure 4: *Corrective meandering: the relative angle of the robot's path to the sound source during 100 seconds of tracking (several separate trials have been combined). The robot's position (tracked via camera) was averaged each 400ms, and the 'relative angle' is that between the direction of the sound source and the vector joining successive positions.*

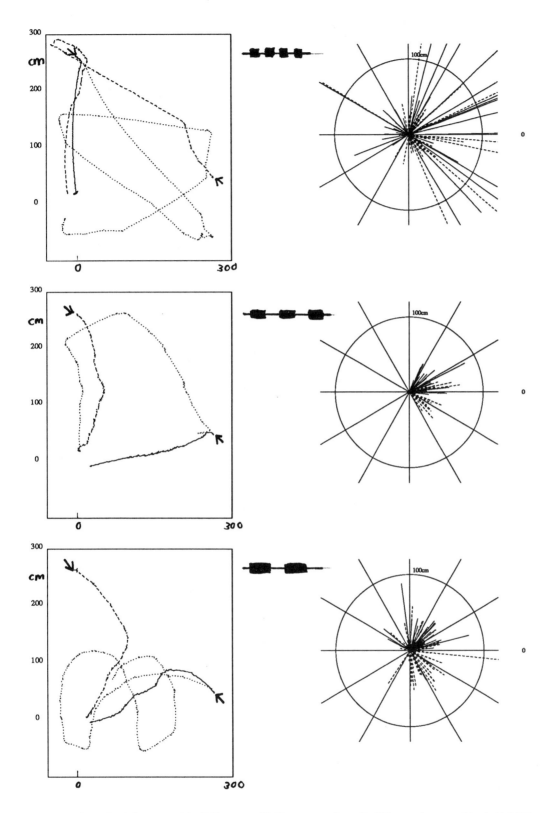

Figure 5: *Results of trials run with different syllable rates: fast (2.5Hz, top), near ideal (1.25Hz, middle) and slow (1.0Hz, bottom). The left hand side shows the shortest (solid line), median (dashed) and longest (dotted) paths towards the speaker (at 0,0) from two possible start positions (→) out of ten trials for each rate. The right hand side summarises the paths (from all ten trials) as a set of vectors between turns, showing the distance and angle relative to the sound source (direction 0) that the robot moved on each path segment: solid vectors are paths starting from the left of the speaker and dashed vectors are paths starting from the right.*

Statistical testing (details in Webb, 1993b) confirmed that the paths were significantly more direct at the ideal syllable rate, i.e. the track vectors were clustered more closely around the speaker direction. Taxis was almost non-existent at 5Hz, and is inefficient at 2.5Hz. At slower rates the robot more reliably approaches the speaker but finds it through repeated small turns that make up a curving track: for 1.25Hz the curvature is sufficiently high to result in reasonable taxis, at 1Hz and 0.8Hz the decreasing size of the curvature starts to adversely affect the directness of the path to the speaker. This difference in the paths is evident in the shorter vectors, and also in the fact that the start position (left or right) has more influence on the direction of vectors.

It is worth noting that Thorson *et al* (1982) explicitly exclude tracks of this latter kind, "segments of circling (without corrective meandering) which bring the animal near the direction of the active loud speaker" under their tracking criteria, which may partly account for the "greatly reduced tracking" they report outside the preferred syllable range. They do not present any details about what tracks looked like outside that range, but Stout *et al* (1983) note that slower rates cause a less dramatic reduction of taxis than faster ones in several cricket species, as they do in the robot.

The different rates compared above also had different syllable lengths (as duty cycle was held constant) so to check that this was not the cause of the observed difference two further sets of trials were run: using short syllables (200ms) at the 'ideal' rate of 1.6Hz, and using 'ideal' syllables (300ms) at the slower rate of 1Hz. Again ten trials of each were recorded, and statistical comparisons showed no difference between 200ms and 300ms syllables at 1.6Hz, but a significant difference between 300ms syllables at 1.6Hz and 1Hz. So the more direct tracks do appear to be associated with the rate, rather than the length, of the syllables.

Some of the tracks to 'non-ideal' rates actually resulted in faster approach (*i.e.* quicker, though less direct) to the speaker than at the ideal rate. Once the robot was headed in roughly the right direction, moving forward between small corrective turns could be quite efficient, whereas at the ideal rate there was a certain amount of unnecessary vacillation. This behaviour is interesting because it suggests a possible role for the chirp structure in the natural cricket song: within syllable groups the cricket can adjust direction and between them it can move forward, in roughly the right direction, thus increasing the speed of approach. Some evidence of this was found in experiments with the robot.

One interesting implication of this explanation for the chirp is that it predicts different results for different paradigms for measuring taxis. When the cricket's position is fixed and its *attempted* turning is measured, continuous syllables would be expected to produce a stronger (because continuous) result. On the other hand, the speed of the track in an arena would be faster with chirps than without. There does seem to be some evidence for this in crickets: with *Teleogryllus* showing a 'preference' for trills over natural song for tethered flight experiments, but not in arena experiments (Pollack and Hoy, 1981).

3.3   Choice

One aspect of cricket behaviour that is often thought to imply complex central processing is the fact that the female seems able to 'choose' to approach directly just one singing male despite a number of other males also singing well within auditory range. In an interesting series of tests, Weber and Thorson (1988) used a choice paradigm in which elements of songs were presented alternately from different locations. If a normal song was split in this way so that alternate chirps or alternate syllables came from each side, the animal would track a 'target' *between* the two speakers, apparently combining the input from each side. If each side produced a normal song, with the chirps or syllables interleaved, the cricket would track one source or the other. With a single sound source, altering the intensity of alternate syllables would not disturb tracking: if the alternate syllable came from different sources, the tracking would be biased towards the speaker with *lower* intensity. Weber and Thorson admit the difficulty of interpreting these results because of the lack of knowledge of how a complex sound field will affect the receptor mechanisms. They conclude that the "directions adopted by the females are apparently influenced not only by the 'tracking mechanism' but also by the altered activation of the 'recognizer' as the animal turns in the split-song stimulus field"—perhaps it rather suggests that the operations of localization and recognition are less separable than is generally thought.

To test whether the simple mechanism in the robot might account for some of the cricket behaviour under such complex conditions, a set of experiments examined the behaviour with two sound sources. In Figure 6 (i), the tracks of the robot in ten trials with simultaneous songs from two speakers are shown: it goes quite directly to one or other speaker. In Figure 6 (ii), with the syllables alternating between the speakers, the robot tends to move down the middle before turning to one or the other. Statistical tests show that the tendency to go towards a central 'target' is significantly stronger in the second condition, and that in the first 'choice' condition the paths are no less direct than they are when only one sound source is present.

As there is no possibility that the robot is separately processing the sounds, it is clearly not necessary to postulate such capability to explain the cricket's behaviour.

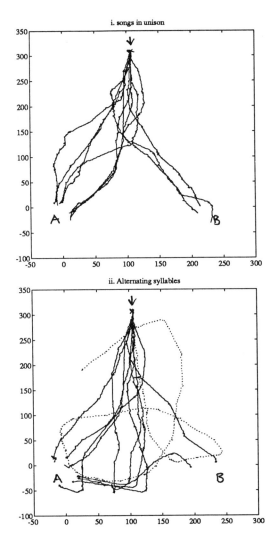

i. songs in unison

ii. Alternating syllables

Figure 6: *Ten tracks, starting at the top of the arena towards speakers at A and B, with song i. simultaneously from both speakers ii. alternating syllables between speakers.*

4   Discussion

It is evident from the above experiments that a difference in behaviour to alterations in the temporal pattern of the signal can occur as the result of a latency-based comparison mechanism for taxis. Also, those differences resemble the effects attributed to 'recognition' in the cricket. This implies that the syllable-rate dependency of the cricket's response can plausibly be explained by a combination of slow auditory neural response (effective low pass filtering) and temporal summation in motor neuron response (effective high pass filtering), where both are inherent features of the onset-dependent latency-comparison mechanism. An independent 'recognition' function is not necessary to explain the results.

A working robot is quite a convincing demonstration

that a hypothesised mechanism does account adequately for the behaviour. Theoretical descriptions of mechanisms are often difficult to evaluate. While the hypothesis regarding taxis presented here can be supported by examining evidence from crickets, it is certainly strengthened by the fact that it was possible to build it into a robot, which then produced comparable behaviour. Furthermore, it becomes possible to show what a certain mechanism will do under various conditions despite being unable to formally analyze the effect of those conditions. An example here was the use of two sound sources: by putting the robot in the situation it could be demonstrated that it *does* work, without having to first find the physical equations that describe the situation.

While the results do show the mechanism producing many of the appropriate behaviours, extending these conclusions to the cricket requires demonstrating that the robot is an adequate representation of the cricket, for the purpose of evaluating this hypothesis. Various aspects of the adequacy of representation are discussed in detail in Webb (1993b) Two general observations in favour are:

- The precision of sensing and motor control is generally much worse in the robot than would be expected for the cricket, so the success of the mechanism is unlikely to be due to abilities that the cricket could not really have. The robot constitutes a *subset* of the capabilities of the cricket rather than an *abstraction* of them.
- A number of the aspects of behaviour demonstrated *emerged* in the robot's behaviour rather than being specifically programmed. The robot wasn't tuned to get matching behaviour by readjusting parameters; nearly all the values were predetermined by the robot's sensory and motor capacities.

On the other hand there are some significant differences that may have influenced the results. These include the fact that phase cancellation is mechanical in the cricket, but based on an 'ideal' equation in the robot, which means that the sources of error and noise in the two systems may differ, and that the simplistic implementation of neural firing in the robot uses a sharp cutoff for the length of gap that could be detected which may have contributed to the significant difference found in the response to different rates. Also, having the mechanisms of high and lowpass filtering inherently bound up in the sensory and motor properties may limit the ability of the model to explain phonotactic specificity in all cricket species. The 'recognisability' of the song serves to have females attracted only to conspecific males; and although most songs can be characterised as repetitive temporal patterning, not all preferences can be subsumed under 'bandpass filtering' (for example, *Gryllodinus kerkennenis* prefer continuous to temporally-patterned sound (Ewing, 1989)).

Some of these limitations will be addressed in future work, which will also permit testing of some of the more complex elements of cricket behaviour such as the effects of duty cycle, preferences when choosing between two different songs, and the apparent ability to sometimes perform taxis with only one ear. However, such further work also requires knowing more about the cricket than is currently the case. Some specific suggestions for neuroethological investigation that arise from the work reported here are as follows:

- One noticeable aspect of the robot behaviour was that the modes of failure of taxis reflected the functioning of the mechanism: taxis was inefficient rather than non-existent at slow rates, for example. Cricket studies in general have not specified in what manner the cricket goes wrong when it does go wrong; it may be possible to determine whether the failure modes are consistent with failure of the taxis mechanism rather than a lack of recognition. Robot behaviour also suggested a possible adaptive advantage to the chirp structure of song that explains why it may improve taxis (act as a 'motivational parameter' according to Popov and Shuvalov (1977)) while not being necessary (not an 'essential recognition parameter') for taxis to occur. Examination of the response of crickets to trills and chirps under different paradigms may bear out this suggestion. In general, a more careful consideration of *what exactly* has improved when the cricket does 'better' taxis seems warranted—reporting 'percentage of time tracking' (as do Thorson *et al*, 1982) is less useful than giving values for each of the criteria applied to determine tracking.
- The ability to interpret results for complex sound fields is currently limited by the inability to estimate the tympanal response to such situations (Weber and Thorson, 1988). Measuring the tympanal, or auditory nerve, responses in these situations would certainly make reasoning about the taxis mechanism on the basis of these experiments more viable. It may also be possible to supply the cricket with tympanal or auditory nerve stimulation that separates the latency and intensity, and thus directly examine how each contributes to the turning response— experiments of this kind have been carried out on the grasshopper (Romer and Rheinlaender, 1983; von Helversen and von Helversen, 1983)
- Further examination of the response properties of brain neurons seems warranted. There does not appear to have been any replication of the widely quoted results of Schildberger (1984). In particular, the hypothesis presented here suggests that their high-pass selectivity may be based on the compared signal, so the response properties with sound from different locations should reflect the direction. Further, this

response property has been associated with requirements of the motor mechanism, so determining details of the further connections of these neurons would be interesting, although perhaps rather difficult to do.

5   Conclusion

The previous section has made clear the effectiveness of using robotic modeling to help understand a specific biological perceptual mechanism. But the process also permits some interesting observations about the way real perceptual mechanisms seem to work; and about potential advantages of using robots rather than simulation for this kind of investigation.

5.1   Behaviour and physics vs. Representations

Taxis for the cricket is not a general problem of localizing sound sources but rather a highly specific behavioural task of moving towards a particular sound. This specificity was essential to the hypothesised mechanism. The use of phase cancellation to detect interaural differences works because the wavelength of the sound is fixed. The simplicity of latency comparison (responding to first onset) depends upon the temporal variation in the signal. It is interesting to note that in this system, specificity is a feature rather than a bug. That is, the fact that the mechanism only works for particular inputs, which allows the use of a simpler device, is part of the characterisation of the task in the first place: it is not supposed to work for the wrong signals. This points to the counterproductivity of the common tendency to analyze a specific task as the intersection of several more general abilities (in this case, the ability to recognize a pattern, and the ability to approach a sound), when general abilities are actually *more* difficult to implement than specific ones (Wehner, 1987).

The importance of real physical interactions in determining the mechanism was revealed strongly in the extent to which the parameters in the program were determined by the properties of the sensors and motors. The rate and accuracy of the auditory response set a limit on processing speed, and the rate of turning and moving set a limit on response time. Even factors such as the amplitude of motor-related noise detected by the auditory circuit affected the choice of parameters for summation rates. But the effect is more fundamental than this. Perhaps the abstract principle of the mechanism 'Use the difference between the ears to control turning' can be stated without reference to how the sensory difference arises, or how the turning is controlled. But to be any more specific about the mechanism, these details need to be known: in what form, and at what rate is the difference available, and how, and with what accuracy does it reflect the direction of the robot; what form and rate of signalling do the motors require and how is the position affected? It is hard to identify any part of the control code in the robot that is not influenced by considerations of this kind.

This robot operates without any attempt to build an internal model of its environment: there is no centralised representation of the sensory situation, not even in a distributed sense (a non-iconic map at some layer of a network). This does not prove that such representation is never needed, but rather shows that it is not, as has been claimed, an essential component for successful sensory-motor behaviour (for example, Kreigman *et al* (1987) begin their paper "A mobile robot architecture must include sensing, planning and locomotion which are tied together by a model or map of the world ..."). It could be argued that the robot does contain 'representations', in the sense of variables that correspond to the strength of sensory inputs or signals for motor outputs. But does conceiving of these variables as 'representations of the external world' and thus the mechanism as 'manipulation of symbols' actually provide an explanatory function? It is not necessary to use this symbolic interpretation to explain how the system functions: the variables serve a mechanical function in connecting sensors to motors, a role epistemologically comparable to the function of the gears connecting the motors to the wheels.

5.2   Robots vs. Computer Simulation

A computational, rather than a physical, simulation of the system of cricket phonotaxis would still have supplied the impetus for a simpler mechanism, and the need to specify it in sufficient detail to express it in computer code, that contributed to devising the hypothesis. On the other hand, the validation of the hypothesis would be less direct, and would depend upon the detail of the modeling of the environmental situation. A fairly simple attempt at simulation was made early on during this project but proved to be almost useless in evaluating possible mechanisms (almost anything worked). There are some specific reasons for this:

- Taxis (approach along a sensory gradient) does not require a complex behavioural solution: the principle of turning to the side more strongly stimulated is fairly obvious, and it is not necessary to model it to accept that it will work. A simulation of taxis is only interesting to the extent that it tackles a real problem of detecting the differences in response to a sensory source, and integrating the response with the constraints on mobility. If the sensory detection and motor response are represented as reasonably reliable and regular then achieving taxis becomes fairly trivial. In passing it should be noted that 'learning' taxis in such a situation (for example in Pierce and Kuipers (1991)) is probably not particularly difficult either.

- Computer modeling of *realistic* physics of phonotaxis in a moving animal or robot is quite difficult. 'Ideal' sound propagation can be described by fairly simple equations, but in any real situation, with a directed speaker, a floor surface, reflecting walls and so on, it becomes extremely difficult to calculate with any accuracy. Likewise, the real physics of a motor response involve more interactions of forces than can be viably captured without complex equations (for wheeled robots see, for example, Alexander and Maddocks (1989)). In short, it would require a great deal of effort to build a computer model that reflected the real situation well enough to make strong claims that the mechanism actually works. And it was certainly the case here that a simple simulation was quite misleading about how the mechanism would perform. Furthermore, extending the experiment to add more obstacles or sounds would have required even further elaboration of an already complex model.

- Using a computer model rather than a robot would, in this case, substantially weaken the justification for extending the results of testing the hypothesis to the cricket. For example, it would be hard to claim that, insofar as sensors and motors differ, those in the model are substantially *worse* in accuracy than in the cricket: it would be more likely that the mechanism only works because of the idealised conditions. There would also be a lot more tuning of variables involved, which could well lead to values being specifically chosen to generate 'cricket-like' behaviour, rather than that behaviour resulting from getting the mechanism to work at all, as happened with the robot.

It seems to be the case that an *adequate* simulation would in fact be more difficult to implement than building a robot, which does suggest that for perceptual problems such as this, where sensing and motor response are tightly linked and the mechanism depends upon their specific properties, computer simulation is not necessarily the best first step in model-building—a physical robot may more easily capture the critical aspects of the problem.

It is often argued that simulation is being done because it is not yet 'viable' to build physical models of perceptual systems to test specific hypotheses. The work reported here shows that it is viable, and there seems no reason why other examples of perceptual systems could not also be approached in this way.

Acknowledgements *The author was supported during this work by a British Commonwealth Award. The Department of Artificial Intelligence at Edinburgh University has supplied the facilities for research which has been supported by the department's technical staff. Thanks to Tim Smithers and John Hallam for their assistance in this work.*

References

Alexander, J.C. and Maddocks, J.H. (1989). On the kinematics of wheeled mobile robots. *The International Journal of Robotics Research*, 8:15-27.

Beer, R.D. (1990). *Intelligence as Adaptive Behaviour* Academic Press, San Diego.

Boyd, P. and Lewis, B. (1983). Peripheral auditory directionality in the cricket. *Journal of Comparative Physiology A*, 153:523-532.

Brooks, R.A. (1986). Achieving artificial intelligence through building robots. A.I.Memo 899, M.I.T.

Esch, H., Huber, F. and Wohlers, D. (1980). Primary auditory interneurons in crickets: Physiology and central projections. *Journal of Comparative Physiology A*, 137:27-38.

Ewing, A.W. (1989). *Arthropod Bioacoustics: Neurobiology and Behaviour.* Edinburgh Universtity Press, Edinburgh.

Gibson, J.J. (1979). *The ecological approach to visual perception.* Houghton Mifflin, Boston.

Huber, F. (1983). Neural correlates of orthopteran and cicada phonotaxis. In Huber, F. and Markl, H., (eds.), *Neuroethology and Behavioural Physiology.* Springer-Verlag, Berlin.

Huber, F. and Thorson, J. (1985). Cricket auditory communication. *Scientific American*, 253:6:47-54.

Kreigman, D.J., Triedl, E. and Binford, T.O. (1987). A mobile robot: sensing, planning and locomotion. In *Proceedings of IEEE International Conference on Robotics and Automation.*

Mörchen, A. (1980). Spike count and response latency. Two basic parameters encoding sound direction in the CNS of insects. *Naturwissenschaft*, 65:656-657.

Pierce, D. and Kuipers, B. (1991). Learning hill-climbing functions as a strategy for generating behaviours in a mobile robot. In *Proceedings of the First International Conference on the Simulation of Adaptive Behaviour.*

Pollack, G.S. and Hoy, R. (1981). Phonotaxis to individual rhythmic components of a complex cricket calling song. *Journal of Comparative Physiology*, 144:367-373.

Popov, A.V. and Shuvalov, V.F. (1977). Phonotactic behaviour of crickets. *Journal of Comparative Physiology*, 119:111-126.

Romer, H. and Rheinlaender, J. (1983). Electrical stimulation of the tympanal nerve as a tool for analysing the responses of auditory interneurons in the cricket. *Journal of Comparative Physiology A*, 152:289-296.

Schmitz, B., Scharstein, H. and Wendler, G. (1982). Phonotaxis in *Gryllus campestris L.* I Mechanism of acoustic orientation in intact female crickets. *Journal of Comparative Physiology A*, 148:431-444.

Schildberger, K. (1984). Temporal selectivity of identified auditory neurons in the cricket brain. *Journal of Comparative Physiology A*, 155:171-185.

Schildberger, K. (1985). Recognition of temporal patterns by identified auditory neurons in the cricket brain. In Kalmring, K. and Elsner, N., (eds.), *Acoustic and Vibrational Communication in Insects.* Verlag Paul Parey, Berlin.

Schildberger, K. (1988). Behavioural and neuronal methods of cricket phonotaxis. *Experientia*, 44:408-415.

Schildberger, K. and Horner, M. (1988). The function of auditory neurons in cricket phonotaxis I Influence of hyperpolarization of identified neurons on sound localization. *Journal of Comparative Physiology A*, 163:621-631.

Stout, J.F., DeHann, C.H. and McGhee, R. (1983). Attractiveness of the male *Acheta domestica* calling song to females. *Journal of Comparative Physiology A*, 153:509-521.

Thorson, J., Weber, T. and Huber, F. (1982). Auditory behaviour in the cricket II Simplicity of calling song recognition in *Gryllus* and anomolous phonotaxis at abnormal carrier frequencies. *Journal of Comparative Physiology A*, 146:361-378.

Varela, F.J., Thompson, E. and Palacios, A. (1991). *The embodied mind* MIT Press, Boston, Mass.

von Helversen, D. and von Helversen, O. (1983). Species recognition and acoustic localization in acridid grasshoppers: a behavioural approach. In Huber, F. and Markl, H., (eds.), *Neuroethology and Behavioural Physiology.* Springer-Verlag, Berlin.

Webb, B. (1993a). Modeling Biological Behaviour or 'Dumb Animals and Stupid Robots'. In *Proceedings of the Second European Conference on Artificial Life.*

Webb, B. (1993b). *Perception in Real and Artificial Insects: A Robotic Investigation of Cricket Phonotaxis.* PhD. Thesis, University of Edinburgh.

Weber, T. and Thorson, J. (1988). Auditory behaviour in the cricket II Interaction of direction of tracking with perceived temporal pattern in split-song paradigms. *Journal of Comparative Physiology A*, 163:13-22.

Wehner, R. (1987). Matched filters—neural models of the external world. *Journal of Comparative Physiology A*, 161:511-531.

Wohlers, D.W. and Huber, F. (1982). Processing of sound signals by six types of neurons in the prothoracic ganglion of the cricket, *Grullus campestris L. Journal of Comparative Physiology*, 146:161-173.

How to watch your step: biological evidence and an initial model

Patrick R Green

Department of Psychology
University of Nottingham
Nottingham NG7 2RD
U.K.
prg@psyc.nott.ac.uk

Abstract

As well as avoiding obstacles, robots able to move about independently in natural, cluttered surroundings must also be able to recognize a variety of important features of the ground surface. Steep drops, deep holes and sharp projections are dangerous and must be avoided, while upwards and downwards slopes may require adjustment of motor speed or gearing. The mechanisms of visual control of the step cycle in animals, and especially in birds, provide a rich source of techniques for solving these problems, and a simulation drawing on some of this biological evidence is described. It is shown that lateral inhibitory interactions between motion sensitive units provide a means of detecting steep drops and other dangerous regions of high surface curvature, and that an array of motion sensitive units which learns patterns of retinal velocities can be used to modulate locomotion in response to changes in surface slant. Prospects for the extension of this simulation to a robot application, and implications for further biological research, are discussed.

1. Introduction

Recent successes in building robots able to navigate through natural, cluttered surroundings have come about in part through exchanges of theory and evidence with neural and behavioural biology (e.g. Brooks, 1991; Beer, Chiel & Sterling, 1991; Franceschini, Pichon & Blanes, 1992). For example, Franceschini et al. (1992) describe how a wheeled vehicle can steer around the edges of objects in its path using motion parallax information computed by an array of motion detectors modelled after those in the visual systems of insects. In applications such as this, the design problem is to avoid collision with the vertical surfaces of objects such as desk legs, filing cabinets or walls standing on a floor surface. Machines capable of doing this in biologically realistic time are a major achievement, but what new problems would arise if we relaxed the constraint that the surface over which they move is flat and smooth? What if the robot must move about in a world containing cliff edges which are dangerous to fall over, slopes which require gear changes to ascend or descend, holes in which a wheel could become stuck, or bumps which could tip it over?

In some applications, these problems can be solved mechanically, by using large squashy tyres to overcome rough surfaces, or low gearing of wheels to deal with slopes. But if the vertical scale of cliff edges, slopes and other surface features is too great, or speed requirements rule out low gearing, then the machine must be able to detect them and to control its movement accordingly. This could be achieved through mechanical sensors of various kinds - 'antennae' measuring the height of the ground just ahead, or automatic gearboxes sensitive to slope changes - but these solutions do not allow the system to *anticipate* features of the ground surface. For fast-moving, intelligent machines, the ability to anticipate is critical, just as it is for animals which walk, run and jump over natural surfaces. In this paper, I will describe a model of the visual control of walking, based on behavioural and physiological evidence from animals, and will outline how it could be developed as a robot application.

2. Biological evidence and modelling principles

In this section, the main features of a model of the visual control of the bipedal stepping cycle will be outlined and related to biological evidence. This evidence will be drawn from pigeons and other birds, which, it will be argued, provide a particularly good source of relevant findings. Then, in the following section, the details of the model will be described.

The primary requirement of the model is that it should be able to obtain information about surface features ahead of the animal quickly; at moderate walking speeds, the interval between a pigeon's footfalls is only 200-250 ms (Davies & Green, 1988). The only source of optical information computed by the model is therefore motion parallax, as it provides a faster and more robust means of obtaining spatial information than binocular disparity, texture gradients and so on (Horridge, 1987). This feature of the model also provides continuity with models based on insect visual systems (e.g. Reichardt, Poggio & Hausen, 1983) and with robotics applications based on them (Franceschini et al., 1992).

Although it is unlikely that motion parallax is the *only* source of visual information about surface features for pigeons or other birds, the prominence of responses to complex local and global patterns of image motion in the pigeon visual system (Frost, Wylie & Wang, 1990, 1994) suggests that it must be an important one. Also, there is evidence that head motion and posture during pigeon locomotion maximize the speed of image motion. The head-bobbing behaviour of walking pigeons consists of alternating 'hold' phases, in which the head is stationary relative to the surroundings, and 'thrust' phases, in which it moves forward (Friedman, 1975; Frost, 1978). Although stabilization of the retinal image during the hold phase may be important for the detection of object motion, the occurrence of head-bobbing without a hold phase in fast running and in landing flight (Davies & Green, 1988; Green, Davies & Thorpe, 1994) indicates that this cannot be the only function of the behaviour, and that effects of head-bobbing on optic flow must also be significant for vision. Further evidence for this argument is that pigeons show a close match between trajectory and head posture in landing flight, which keeps the axis of head-bobbing parallel to the direction of locomotion and so ensures maximum amplification of optic flow in the thrust phase (Green, Davies & Thorpe, 1992, 1994).

There are various ways in which the effects of head-bobbing on optic flow could be important for vision. Amplification of motion parallax during the thrust phase may aid in the detection of fine spatial structure, and particularly of small, camouflaged food items on the ground (Davies & Green, 1988). A second possibility is that optical acceleration in the thrust phase is important for controlling manoeuvres such as landing, by providing information about the time to contact of the feet with the perch, and about their trajectory relative to it (Lee, Davies, Green & van der Weel, 1993).

As well as indicating a role for image motion in visual processing, the conspicuous head-bobbing of pigeons and other birds also provides a valuable model for visual control of the step cycle. The head-bob cycle is tightly synchronized with stepping, the thrust phase occurring as the trailing leg pushes backwards against the ground (Daanje, 1951; Dagg,

1977). In humans, visual information is used to control stride length during specific phases of the step cycle (Laurent & Thomson, 1988), and head-bobbing birds provide a good model with which to investigate this relationship further. The model developed here, for example, predicts specifically that information used to modulate stepping force is obtained during the thrust phase.

In the model, two systems operate in parallel on the array of angular velocity measurements which provide its input. One system is designed to detect a steep drop ahead of the bird and to give an output which can inhibit stepping before it is reached. The other is designed to detect the relative height of the next footfall, as determined by surface slope, and to control the extension of the leading leg accordingly. The separation of these two functions is supported by evidence from the behaviour of young chicks on a visual cliff. Stepping is more strongly inhibited when a chick stands on a transparent floor at a cliff edge than when it stands above a smooth surface at the same depth below the transparent floor (Green, Davies & Davies, 1994). This finding suggests that the detection of cliff edges and the control of the height of stepping are achieved by separate systems.

The operations performed by the model are neurally realistic, and have some basis in properties of the pigeon visual system. Units are tuned to particular angular velocities, interact through lateral inhibition, and habituate to image motion through modification of synaptic strength. At no point is a single representation of the layout of the ground surface constructed. The model is tested by its ability to generate outputs which could plausibly control walking locomotion. Can the system designed to detect cliff edges reliably generate a signal to stop stepping when a dangerous edge is ahead? Can the system designed to detect slopes yield a signal varying with the height of the next footfall, which could modulate the timing and force of contraction of hind

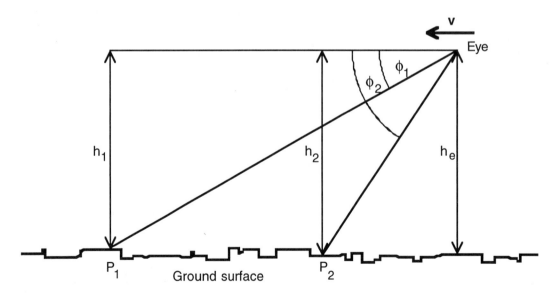

Figure 1. Calculation of angular velocities of points on a simulated flat ground surface. The eye moves parallel to the surface with velocity v and at height h_e above it. Points P_1 and P_2 on the surface are at heights h_1 and h_2 relative to the eye and at retinal elevations ϕ_1 and ϕ_2. The model calculates velocities for 10 points, at elevations from 45° to 90°, in 5° steps.

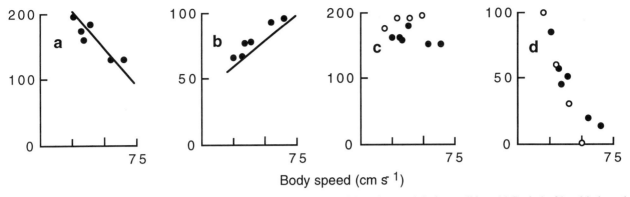

Body speed (cm s^{-1})

Figure 2. Variation of different parameters of the pigeon head-bob cycle with body speed during walking. (a) Period of head-bob cycle (ms). The regression line used in the model is shown. (b) Peak eye velocity during the thrust phase (cm s^{-1}). The line shows the predicted relationship if peak eye velocity relative to the body is 50 cm s^{-1}. (c) Duration of thrust phase (ms). (d) Duration of hold phase (ms). In (c) and (d), filled symbols are measured durations and open symbols are those predicted from the model. A good approximation to the observed variation in eye velocity over the head-bob cycle is achieved, particularly in the typical range of walking speed (20 to 40 cm s^{-1}). Data from Davies (1989) and Davies & Green (1988).

limb muscles?

3. The model: design and results

The model consists of three stages:

(1) Construction of a section through a simulated textured ground surface.

(2) Computation at regular intervals of arrays of values of retinal angular velocity as a model 'bird' walks over the simulated surface.

(3) Simulated neural operations on the array of retinal angular velocities, in parallel, by (a) the cliff edge detection system and (b) the slope detection system.

3.1 Construction of the ground surface

The section through the ground surface is represented as the heights relative to a reference value of a series of points 1 mm apart horizontally. A series of neighbouring points with the same height makes up a surface element. The lengths of elements vary randomly around a mean of 1 cm, while the differences in height between adjoining elements vary randomly with a mean which can be set at different multiples of 0.4 cm, to simulate different scales of surface texture. Cliff edges of particular heights, and constant slopes of particular angles, can be superimposed on the pattern of elements during surface construction.

3.2 Computation of retinal velocities

The aim of this stage is to compute at 10 ms intervals the angular velocities of points on the section through the ground surface, equivalent to the velocities of their images over the retina. The angular velocity $\dot{\phi}$ of a point on the ground surface is calculated from the equation

$$\dot{\phi} = v \sin^2\phi \, / \, h \tag{1}$$

where v is the velocity of the eye, h is its height relative to the point on the ground, and ϕ is the angular elevation of

the point relative to the direction of motion (see Fig. 1). Values of h are calculated assuming that the eye is 20 cm above the ground, which is a typical value for a pigeon standing upright.

In order to calculate the velocity of the eye, its variation over the head-bobbing cycle is modelled as a 'clipped sinusoid'. The first step in this model is to add a sinusoid, representing the velocity of the eye relative to the head, to a constant value of body velocity. Then, the values of eye velocity obtained are 'clipped', by setting all negative values to zero. This procedure generates realistic alternating thrust and hold phases, in which the eye moves forwards and remains still, respectively. The period of the sinusoid is derived from the regression equation of period on body velocity (see Fig. 2a). Its amplitude is taken as 50 cm s^{-1}, the value which gives the best fit to the data relating body velocity to peak eye velocity (see Fig. 2b). Using these parameters, variation in eye velocity over the head-bob cycle can be modelled accurately (see Figs. 2c and 2d).

In each cycle of the model, angular velocity is calculated at all ten retinal elevations. The eye is then advanced by the distance specified by the head-bobbing model for an interval of 10 ms, and the cycle is repeated.

3.3 Cliff edge detection system

This part of the model consists of a linear array of ten units sensitive to image motion at points 5° apart, and all tuned to the same velocity. The response of each unit is determined by the sum of excitation generated by image motion in its own receptive field, and inhibition from its immediate neighbours (see Fig. 3).

If motion-sensitive units are assumed to have receptive fields at fixed points on the retina, then the model must incorporate some way of aligning these points with angular elevations relative to the direction of travel. In other words, the optical frame of reference defined by the pole of the optic flow field (and in turn by the direction of locomotion) must be fixed relative to retinal co-ordinates. A simple way to achieve this without the need for any mechanism to

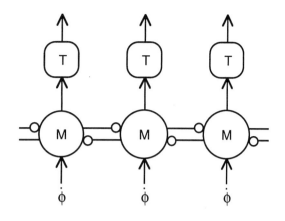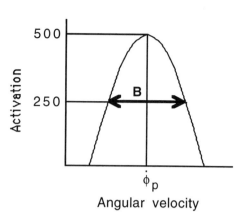

Figure 3. Left - part of the cliff edge detection system, showing three motion-sensitive units (M). The activation A of a unit depends on the angular velocity $\dot{\phi}$ in its receptive field. Units have mutually inhibitory interactions with their immediate neighbours, and the output of unit M_i is $A_i - ((A_{i+1})+(A_{i-1})/2)$. Outputs of units are fed to threshold units T. Right - the relationship between angular velocity and activation ($\dot{\phi}_p$ - peak angular velocity; B - bandwidth).

transform between co-ordinate systems is to use head and/or eye movements to bring the pole of the flow field on to a particular retinal position. This may provide an explanation for the tight linear relationship between head posture and trajectory in landing pigeons mentioned above (Green, Davies & Thorpe, 1992, 1994), which has also been observed in chicks about to jump (Green, Davies & Davies, 1994).

Some physiological justification for the lateral interactions in this part of the model is provided by the

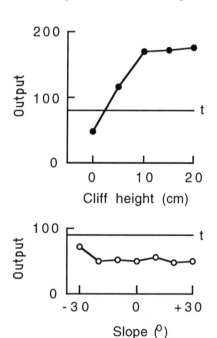

Figure 4. Outputs of motion-sensitive units in the cliff edge detection system, over a range of cliff heights and surface slopes. A threshold output t discriminates cliffs of 5 cm and above from a flat surface, and the discrimination is maintained over a range of surface slopes. (Body speed - 20 cm s^{-1}; surface texture scale - 0.4 cm; peak angular velocity and bandwidth of units - 4° s^{-1} and 2.7° s^{-1}).

existence of motion-sensitive neurons in the pigeon optic tectum with centre-surround organization (Frost, Scilley & Wong, 1981). These neurons respond maximally to image motion in opposite directions in the receptive field centre and in an area surrounding it. There are some discrepancies between the properties of these cells and those of the model units; the cells' peak responses are to stimuli moving faster than the image of the ground surface would during walking, and many give no response to stimuli moving backwards in the visual field, as the ground surface would (Frost & DiFranco, 1976). Also, it is not known whether any cells show centre-surround antagonism in stimulus speed alone, in the absence of differences in direction of motion. Even so, there may be a less well known population of tectal cells with more appropriate centre-surround interactions.

The performance of the lateral inhibition system was first tested with surfaces which were either sloped at varying angles or contained downward steps of varying heights. As a measure of model performance, the outputs of motion-sensitive units at retinal elevations of 65°, 70° and 75° were recorded. These correspond to points on the surface one footstep ahead (7-8 cm for a typical pigeon stride). As an indication of the reliability of the output as a means of detecting steps, the minimum response at any one of these elevations obtained in three approaches to a step was compared with the maximum response obtained during a test with a 1.5 m flat or sloped surface.

The results are shown in Fig. 4. With the motion-sensitive unit output threshold shown, the model is capable of discriminating cliffs of 5 cm and more from texture features on a flat surface, and this performance is not affected by slopes up to at least 30°. A second series of tests showed that this performance is maintained over a range of body speeds (see Fig. 5). On the other hand, a factor which does affect the ability of the system to discriminate steps is the texture scale of the ground surface. Fig. 6 shows the results of tests in which both cliff height and surface texture scale were varied. On the left of the figure, where cliff height is zero, are the 'false positive' responses to texture features in flat surfaces at each texture scale. Provided the scale is no

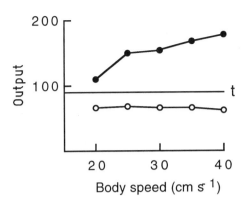

Figure 5. Outputs of motion-sensitive units in the cliff edge detection system, over a range of body speeds, to a 15 cm cliff edge (filled circles) and to a flat surface (open circles). The same threshold output t as in Fig. 4 discriminates the cliff from a flat surface at all speeds. (Surface texture scale - 0.8 cm; peak angular velocity and bandwidth of units - 5° s⁻¹ and 4° s⁻¹)

more than 0.8 cm, it is possible to discriminate cliffs of 5 cm and above from a flat surface, using the same threshold as before. With a scale of 1.2 cm, the smallest cliff which can be reliably detected is 10 cm high, while a further increase in scale to 1.6 cm prevents the detection of cliffs smaller than 20 cm.

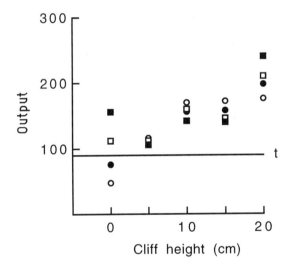

Figure 6. Outputs of motion-sensitive units in the cliff edge detection system, at different cliff heights and scales of surface texture (○ 0.4 cm; ● 0.8 cm; □ 1.2 cm; ■ 1.6 cm). The same threshold output t as in Figs. 4 and 5 discriminates cliffs of 5 cm and more, but only if the surface texture scale is less than 1.2 cm. (Body speed - 20 cm s⁻¹; peak angular velocity and bandwidth of units - 4° s⁻¹ and 2.7° s⁻¹).

The tests demonstrate that the cliff edge detection system is a robust detector of downwards steps over a wide range of body speeds and surface slopes. However, the scale of surface texture imposes a constraint on the efficiency of the system; provided their shape fits the spatial filter in the model, surface elements only a few cm in height can generate false positives. The largest such response observed was to a

surface feature 3 cm high and 1.3 cm across. Even so, this characteristic of the model may be useful in avoiding other dangerous surface features besides cliff edges; for an animal, these may include holes in which a foot could be trapped, sharp projections which could turn and damage an ankle, and so on. Perhaps the sensitivity of the cliff edge detection system to such regions of high surface curvature indicates that it could function more generally as a detector of surface features which should not be stepped on or over.

3.4 Slope detection system

The first stage in this part of the model is the same array of motion-sensitive units as in the cliff edge detection system. Each is connected to an output unit through a modifiable connection, and a feedback loop operates from the output of this second unit to the weight of the connection, to simulate adaptation of the output to a constant value of angular velocity (see Fig. 7). With the parameters used, the error signal converged to zero within 40-45 head-bob cycles when the model was run at constant speed over a flat surface.

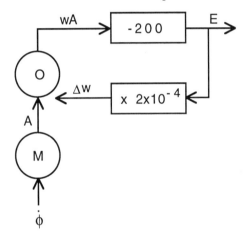

Figure 7. Part of the slope detection system, showing one motion sensitive unit (M). The activation A generated by each unit is a function of angular velocity input φ̇ (see Fig. 3, right). The weight w on the connection between M and the output unit O is modifiable. The output of O is the product of w and A, and the difference between this output and a reference value is the error signal E. The product of E and a gain factor gives Δw, the increment or decrement in w. The initial value of w in each simulation is 1.

Neurons with characteristics similar to the output units have been identified in the deep layers of the pigeon optic tectum (Woods and Frost, 1977). Over a period of 15-20 s, these cells show a decrement in response to a repeated motion stimulus of constant velocity, and the response is immediately restored to its original level by a stimulus moving along a different path across the receptive field. These properties may indicate a response to discrepancy between current and learned patterns of retinal motion, corresponding to the error signal in the model. To gain further support for the model, it would be necessary to find cells which dishabituate to a change in the speed alone of a

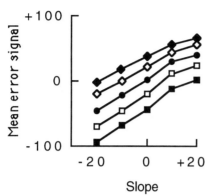

Figure 8. Error signal generated by the slope detection system over a range of slopes and body speeds (■ 20 cm s^{-1}; □ 25 cm s^{-1}; ● 30 cm s^{-1}; ◇ 35 cm s^{-1}; ◆ 40 cm s^{-1}). The error signal is a function of both these variables. (Peak angular velocity and bandwidth of motion-sensitive units - 5° s^{-1} and 4° s^{-1}).

stimulus, and also separate cell types signalling increased or decreased speed.

A further biological justification for incorporating a learning process into the model is evidence that depth perception in young birds is modifiable by experience. A number of experiments (e.g. Tallarico & Farrell, 1964; Zeier, 1970; Seitz, Seitz & Kaufman, 1973) have demonstrated that chicks reared on the deep side of a visual cliff show a reduced aversion to it in later tests. Also, normally reared chicks tested for speed of running on the deep side show habituation over a few trials (Green, Davies & Davies, 1994). As well as these results, the need to rescale depth perception with increasing eye height and body speed during growth also argues for a learning mechanism at some stage in the system.

To test the properties of the slope detection system, it was first trained at a speed of 30 cm s^{-1} with a flat, 4 m long surface with a surface texture scale of 0.4 cm. During this time, between 50 and 60 head-bob cycles occurred. Using the weights on each connection at the end of the training period, the model was next tested at a range of body

speeds over surfaces with the same texture scale but a range of slopes.

The question of interest is whether the error signal generated by the output units provides a measure of surface slope which could be used to modulate stepping. To assess this, the maximum error signal, in the elevation range 65-75°, obtained in each head-bob cycle in three tests with a 0.25 m surface, was recorded. The mean error values obtained (see Fig. 8) show that, at the original body speed in training, the error signal is modulated smoothly by slope. Note, however, that the signal is also a function of body speed; a change of speed of about 10 cm s^{-1} has the same effect on the error signal as a 20° change of slope.

Further tests were carried out to determine the sensitivity of the learning system to variation in surface texture scale. Training and testing were both at 20 cm s^{-1} body speed. As Fig. 9 shows, the relationship between slope and mean error is maintained with more roughly textured surfaces, but the variability of the error signal increases with texture scale, reducing its usefulness as a source of information to modulate stepping thrust with slope.

What is the biological significance of these results? Although the system yields an output which is a function of both slope and body speed, this may be adequate for the control of stepping. Pierotti et al (1989) obtained EMG records from the flexor and extensor muscles of the hind limbs of cats during walking on a treadmill at a range of speeds and slopes. They found that the activity of extensor muscles varied with both speed and slope, in a pattern similar to that obtained here; either increased speed or an upwards slope increased extensor activity. Although the system does not yield a representation of surface slope invariant with body speed, its output may therefore be adequate for the control of at least one parameter of muscle activity during the step cycle. The failure of the mechanism with rougher surface texture may not be biologically significant, provided that a regular step cycle does not occur in these conditions. At some point, as texture scale increases, it will be replaced by an uneven gait in which individual footholds are identified and steps are directed

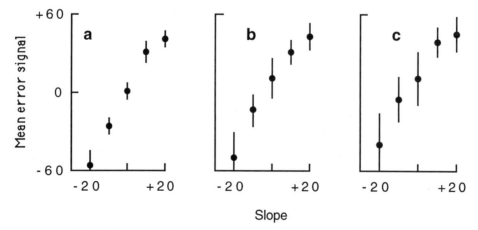

Figure 9. Error signal generated by the slope detection system over a range of slopes, at three levels of texture scale; (a) 0.4 cm, (b) 0.8 cm, (c) 1.2 cm. Vertical bars represent standard deviation of signal over approximately 12 trials. As surface texture scale increases, the error signal becomes less informative about slope. (Peak angular velocity and bandwidth of units - 4° s^{-1} and 2.7° s^{-1}).

towards them.

The parameters of the learning mechanism are largely arbitrary, and further biological evidence will be necessary to constrain the time scale over which weights of modifiable connections change. A lower limit will be imposed by the rate of growth of a young bird, and therefore of change in eye height and walking speed, while an upper limit is imposed by the need to prevent rapid re-learning of retinal velocities during a short period spent walking along a slope in a constant direction.

4. Conclusions and further development

The tests described here explore some properties of a model of the visual control of the step cycle which operates on simple motion signals in two neurally realistic ways in parallel. The results suggest that lateral inhibitory interactions within a retinal array of motion detectors can provide a means of inhibiting stepping when steep edges and possibly other dangerous surface features are approached, and that comparison of learned and current velocities can yield an output capable of modulating the activity of leg extensor muscles in relation to either walking speed or surface slope.

Although the actual outputs of the model are arbitrary, the simulation is valuable in demonstrating how variation in a range of environmental and neural parameters affects its performance. One particularly useful result is that its two sub-systems are *complementary*. The cliff edge detection system does not respond to smoothly sloping surfaces, and so a regular gait can proceed, modulated by the slope detection system. Conversely, variability in the response of the slope detection system to surface discontinuities makes it unable to operate over rough surfaces or to detect steep edges. Under these conditions, the cliff edge detection system halts the step cycle so that other patterns of locomotion, such as jumping, can be initiated. The parallel operation of these two systems may therefore provide a means of controlling locomotion in subtle ways without the need for complex metrical representations of features of the ground surface.

4.1 Towards a robot implementation

What problems would have to be solved in developing this simulation of the visual control of walking in birds for use in a robot application? The model must be extended to use as input a two-dimensional, time-varying pattern of light intensity values obtained from an on-board camera, and this development would raise two important issues for the design and performance of the model; the properties of motion-sensitive units, and the processing of a two-dimensional array of their outputs.

The simulated motion-sensitive units in the model are idealized in several ways. They are not noisy, they have point receptive fields, and their outputs are not affected by image parameters such as contrast and spatial frequency. Like biological motion detectors, an algorithm computing image motion from a camera input will give a noisy output, will have a finite receptive field, and will be sensitive to the contrast and spatial structure of the image moving through its field. The size of receptive fields in an implementation would be constrained by the minimum retinal size of images of dangerous ground features, in turn determined by their actual size and the distance at which they needed to be detected. Sensitivity of motion detectors to contrast and spatial frequency poses a more complex problem. The boundary between two regions of a flat ground surface, one in shadow and one in direct light, could yield the same output in the cliff edge detection system as a drop, because it would cause the same change in motion detector output. The same thing might happen at a boundary between two regions of a flat surface with different densities of surface markings. Empirical tests would be needed to discover how serious these problems were for a particular robot environment, and one means of solving them would be to use multiple motion-sensitive units, with varying temporal and spatial characteristics, in each region of the image. Appropriate rules for combining their outputs would allow more reliable measurement of image motion.

The change to a two-dimensional array of motion detector outputs does not affect directly the design of the slope detection system, but it requires a decision about the geometry of the lateral interactions between units in the cliff edge detection system. The simplest design would be a circular one, in which each unit received symmetrical inhibition from a ring of neighbours, but the properties of other geometries should be tested. For both systems, however, important questions would arise about the use of their outputs to control the machine's movement.

Cliff edge detection system outputs would be used from the area of the image corresponding to the ground area in which cliffs were dangerous; its width and elevation would depend on the wheelbase and the safe braking distance of the vehicle, respectively. Outputs across the whole of this region would signal an extended cliff edge ahead, and would be used to stop the vehicle, but it would also be useful to respond to local outputs signalling a small hole or sharp protrusion by steering around them. Both these aims could be achieved by using signals from each side of the midline to drive brakes on the other side of the vehicle. Similarly, in the slope detection system, asymmetrical output across the midline of the visual field would signal a smooth slope oriented across the direction of travel, which could topple the vehicle over. Independent control of gearing on the two sides of the vehicle by slope detection system outputs would turn it away from the upwards slope.

Finally, head-bobbing is a specific feature of pigeon behaviour incorporated in the model. Although a robot implementation need not 'bob' its camera, there are two reasons why this piece of biology might be worth imitating. First, it would increase the absolute values of optical velocity during the thrust phase, and so could be a useful way of increasing the reliability of motion measurements obtained from noisy detectors. Second, holding a camera still relative to the surroundings for a period in each bobbing cycle offers a short-cut to the problem of disambiguating image motion caused by the vehicle's motion and by that of objects in the surroundings.

4.2 Biological implications

Some implications of the model for further biological research have already been mentioned, but a few more are worth making in conclusion. First, the model predicts that the pigeon visual system will contain a sub-system dedicated to the processing of local, self-generated image motion. This does not fit either of the two systems distinguished by Frost et al. (1990, 1994); the analysis of local object motion in the tectofugal system and of global self-generated motion in the accessory optic system. A critical test of the model is whether a third class of neurons exist, which have appropriate properties such as small fields, responses to backwards motion at relatively slow velocities, and either habituation to stimulus speed or linear lateral inhibitory interactions.

Second, it would be valuable to have more information about the ways in which muscle activity in the hind limbs of birds is modulated in response to changes in terrain height. The pattern of muscle activity during the step cycle of birds has been analyzed (Jacobson & Hollyday, 1982), but modulation of the stepping pattern has only been studied using kinematic methods, and in the case of changes with walking speed. As speed increases, the angular excursion of the leading leg ahead of the body remains constant, while the maximum retraction of the trailing leg increases (Gatesy & Biewener, 1991). This may indicate that activity in extensor but not flexor muscles is modulated with changes in speed, but more direct evidence is needed. It will also be important to establish how muscle activity varies with changes in slope, in the same way as Pierotti et al (1989) have done for the stepping cycle of cats. These kinds of evidence will make it possible to define the critical parameters of motor activity which require control by the slope detection system.

Third, the model makes the simple assumption that in both systems the only outputs which influence locomotion are from units with receptive fields in the part of the visual field corresponding to the ground surface one stride ahead. This certainly cannot be realistic for all species, as humans can use information about surface features further ahead to arrive precisely at a target by adjusting stride length smoothly over several step cycles (e.g. Lee, Lishman & Thomson, 1982). Tests of whether birds also have this ability, and analysis of its neural control, would be important for the further development of the model.

Fourth, the mechanism of visual control involved in the slope detection system may be general across a variety of different forms of locomotion. One hint of this is provided by the fact that the close relationship between head angle and trajectory, which could serve to keep optical and retinal co-ordinate frames in register, is found both in pigeons during landing flight (Green, Davies & Thorpe, 1992, 1994) and in chicks about to jump to surfaces of varying height (Green, Davies & Davies, 1994). Another relevant finding is that the head-bobbing cycle during landing flight is tightly synchronized with wingbeat in the same way as it is with the step cycle during walking (Green, Davies & Thorpe, 1994). The slope detection system modelled here could in principle be used before landing from flight to obtain information about the height of the perch relative to the bird and so to adjust the postures of wings and tail for the correct landing trajectory. Similarly, head-bobs made before a jump

could yield information to control the force of the jump with respect to the relative height of the target surface, as they do in gerbils (Ellard, Goodale & Timney, 1984). To what extent these different locomotor mechanisms share a common means of visual control remains to be discovered.

Although so far tested in only a preliminary way, the model developed here offers ways of designing autonomous mobile robots capable of using optical information to move intelligently over rough and hilly terrain. In particular, it suggests ways that this could be achieved using fast, simple neural-like operations, without the construction of an elaborate representation of the three dimensional surroundings. The model leads to a clear series of issues to address in a robot implementation, and to a number of problems for further biological research on visuomotor organization in birds and other animals.

Acknowledgements

I am grateful to Tom Scutt and to the referees for their comments on the manuscript.

References

Beer RD, Chiel HJ, Sterling LS (1991) An artificial insect. Amer Sci 79: 444-452

Brooks RA (1991) Intelligence without representation. Artif Intell 47: 139-159

Daanje A (1951) On locomotory movements of birds and the intention movements derived from them. Behaviour 3: 48-98

Dagg AI (1977) The walk of the silver gull (*Larus novaehollandiae*) and of other birds. J Zool (Lond) 182: 529-540

Davies MNO (1989) The perception of relative movement and the control of action. Thesis, University of Nottingham, Nottingham, UK

Davies MNO, Green PR (1988) Head-bobbing during walking, running and flying: relative motion perception in the pigeon. J Exp Biol 138: 71-91

Ellard CG, Goodale MA, Timney B (1984) Distance estimation in the Mongolian gerbil: the role of dynamic depth cues. Behav Brain Res 14: 29-39

Franceschini N, Pichon JM, Blanes C (1992) From insect vision to robot vision. Phil Trans R Soc Lond B 337: 283-294.

Friedman MB (1975) Visual control of head movements during avian locomotion. Nature 255: 67-69

Frost BJ (1978) The optokinetic basis of head-bobbing in the pigeon. J Exp Biol 74: 187-195

Frost BJ, DiFranco DE (1976) Motion characteristics of single units in the pigeon optic tectum. Vision Res 16: 1229-1234

Frost BJ, Scilley PL, Wong SCP (1981) Moving background patterns reveal double opponency of directionally specific pigeon tectal neurons. Exp Brain Res 43: 173-185

Frost BJ, Wylie DR, Wang Y-C (1990) The processing of object and self-motion in the tectofugal and accessory optic pathways of birds. Vision Res 30: 1677-1688

Frost BJ, Wylie DR, Wang Y-C (1994) The analysis of motion in the visual systems of birds. In: Davies MNO, Green PR (eds) Perception and motor control in birds. Springer, Heidelberg, pp 248-269

Gatesy SM, Biewener AA (1991) Bipedal locomotion: effects of speed, size and limb posture in birds and humans. J Zool (Lond) 224: 127-147

Green PR, Davies IB, Davies MNO (1994) Interaction of visual and tactile information in the control of chicks' locomotion in the visual cliff. Perception, in press

Green PR, Davies MNO, Thorpe PH (1992) Head orientation in pigeons during landing flight. Vision Res 32: 2229-2234

Green PR, Davies MNO, Thorpe PH (1994) Head-bobbing and head orientation during landing flights of pigeons. J Comp Physiol 174: 249-256

Horridge GA (1987) The evolution of visual processing and the construction of seeing systems. Proc Roy Soc Lond B 230: 279-292

Jacobson RD, Hollyday M (1982) A behavioural and electromyographic study of walking in the chick. J Neurophysiol 48: 238-256

Laurent M, Thomson JA (1988) The role of visual information in control of a constrained locomotion task. J Mot Behav 20: 17-37

Lee DN, Lishman JR, Thomson JA (1982) Regulation of gait in long-jumping. J Exp Psychol Hum Percept Perform 8: 448-459

Lee DN, Davies MNO, Green PR, van der Weel FR (1993) Visual control of velocity of approach by pigeons when landing. J Exp Biol 180: 85-104

Pierotti DJ, Roland RR, Gregor RJ, Edgerton VR (1989) Electromyographic activity of cat hindlimb flexors and extensors during locomotion at varying speeds and inclines. Brain Res 481: 57-66

Reichardt W, Poggio T, Hausen K (1983) Figure-ground discrimination by relative movement in the visual system of the fly. Part II: Towards the neural circuitry. Biol Cybern 46: 1-30

Seitz V, Seitz T, Kaufman L (1973) Loss of depth avoidance in chicks as a function of early environmental influences. J Comp Physiol Psychol 85: 139-143

Tallarico RB, Farrell WM (1964) Studies of visual depth perception: an effect of early experience on chicks on a visual cliff. J Comp Physiol Psychol 57: 94-96

Woods EJ, Frost BJ (1977) Adaptation and habituation characteristics of tectal neurons in the pigeon. Exp Brain Res 27: 347-354

Zeier H (1970) Lack of eye to eye transfer of an early response modification in birds. Nature 225: 708-709

On Why Better Robots Make it Harder

Tim Smithers

Euskal Herriko Unibertsitatea
Informatika Fakultatea
649 Postakutxa
20080 Donostia
Espaina

Universidad del País Vasco
Facultad de Informática
Apartado 649
20080 San Sebastián
España

Email: ccpsmsmt@si.ehu.es or smithers@si.ehu.es

Abstract

In this paper I discuss something which I believe is a common, though largely unreported, experience of people who build and use real robots, but which to people who don't, can seem counter intuitive: as we build better robots they become harder to use. I use this discussion to suggest that at least some of the difficullty is a result of thinking of robots as information processing systems, and of sensors as measuring devices, in particular. As an alternative, I suggest that viewing robots and their environments as agent-environment systems, whose interaction dynamics have to be got right, is a more appropriate approach to understanding adaptive behaviour in robots and animals.

1 Introduction

Quite often, when I explain to people, who do not build robots, how difficult it can be to make the small and relatively simple robots I work with behave reliably and robustly in ordinary environments (see [Donnett & Smithers, 91], [Nehmzow & Smithers, 91], and [Nehmzow & Smithers, 92], for example) they respond by saying "Why don't you use better sensors?" Or, "Why don't you build better robots?" A related feeling is sometimes expressed by people who do build robots, or at least have done in the past, when they say "I can't do what I want to do because I need a better robot." Or, "I've given up using real robots until the technology gets better." Yet a third kind of statement that is sometimes heard goes like this: "I don't want to have to deal with all the uncertainty and unrepeatability of real robots in my investigation of adaptive behaviour." Typically these last two are offered as justification for using so called robot simulations, and assume

that the variations that do occur in real robot behaviour is something that could be made to go away, if we made better robots[1]. (Superscript numbers refer to notes at the end of the paper.)

I believe that this experience of better robots being harder to use, not easier, is a common, though largely unreported, experience amoungst people who build and use real robots, but which, as suggested above, is often counter intuitive to people who don't.

In this paper I attempt to show why the problem of making real robots behave reliably and robustly in real environments is not simply to do with the quality of the robots used, or with any inadequacy of the technology available. I do this in two parts. In the first part I present a story from the history of control and describe a problem that arose with the use of fly-ball governors as their manufacture was improved. In the second part, I use data obtained from a real robot operating in a real (though simple) environment to show that using higher resolution sensors introduces more variation into the sensor signals, not less, which in turn, can make achieving reliable and robust robot behaviour more difficult. I end by suggesting that this is a consequence of trying to understand and build robots as information processing systems, and that a more appropriate approach is to try to understand the interaction dynamics of these kinds of agent-environment systems.

2 Better Speed Regulators Worse Speed Regulation

The first widely used regulator was Jame's Watt's fly-ball governor, or centrifugal govenor[2], although many different regulation devices had been invented and used before (see [Mayr, 70]). This device was introduced in 1788 on the Boulton-Watt steam engines then built to power mills, and subsequently other factory machines. It's development and use coincided

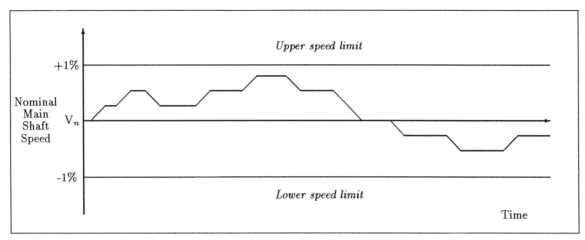

Figure 1: Speed variation in a well regulated main shaft as different machine tools are brought in and out of operation.

with the invention of an effective steam throttling valve originally intended for manual control, [Mayr, 70, page 111] and [Dickinson & Jenkins, 91, page 220], a necessary co-development to implement effective control using the fly-ball governor.

2.1 Speed Regulation in Early Machine Tools

Steam engines, and in particular those built by the Boulton-Watt company, became the main source of power in the factories of the industrial revolution in Britain. A typical arrangement involved a factory building with a steam engine installed at one end to supply power to a number of different machine tools distributed on the shop floor which occupied most of the remainer of the building. See [Kurzweil, 90, page 6] for a good illustration.

The power distribution consisted of a system of shafts, pullies, and belts. The steam engine was used to drive a main shaft running the length of the shop floor (usually some five or six meters above the ground). Each machine tool was then driven from this main shaft via a belt running down to a pully on the input shaft of the machine. To maintain a good quality of work, it was important that the speed at which each machine was driven remained constant, with only a small margin of variation. The Watt fly-ball govenor was used to "iron out" the otherwise large variations of speed which occurred due to the intermittent use of each machine: as different machines took power from the main shaft so the speed would drop, this resulted in a falling of the weights of the fly-ball governor which, in turn, resulted in a proportional openning of the steam throttle valve thus allowing more steam to the engine, and subsequently more power output on the main shaft, and a restoration to nearly the original speed[3] see figure 1.

At first, the use of the Watt fly-ball governor to regulate the speed of a set of machines tools powered by one steam engine worked well—the variation in the operating speed of each machine was kept well within acceptable limits. As manufacturing techniques improved the components of steam engines and, in particular, those for the Watt fly-ball governors, began to be made with increasing accuracy and to closer tolerances. However, rather than leading to an improvement in the operation of the machines tools—smoother and smaller speed variation—these better steam engines and, in particular, these better governors resulted in the appearance of a problem that had not occurred before. The so called *hunting problem*.

2.2 The Hunting Problem

The symptoms of the hunting problem, in this case of main shaft speed regulation, is a failure of the shaft speed to settle down to one steady speed but to continue to fluctuate up and down in a sine wave oscillation, see figure 2. This unsatisfactory behaviour is caused by the fly-ball governor first dropping thus openning the steam throttle value, which results in the engine speed increasing, but this time beyond where it is supposed to be. When the main shaft speed is too high, the fly-ball governor opens out and in turn closes the throttle value, thus reducing engine speed. In certain conditions this over correction for too slow a speed, resulting in too high a speed which is then over corrrected to produce too slow a speed again, can go on either forever, or for a long period of time before it finally dies out. When this happens the system is described as "hunting" for the correct speed.

The reason for hunting is a lack of *damping* or friction in the system. In the early speed regulated steam engines sufficient damping naturally

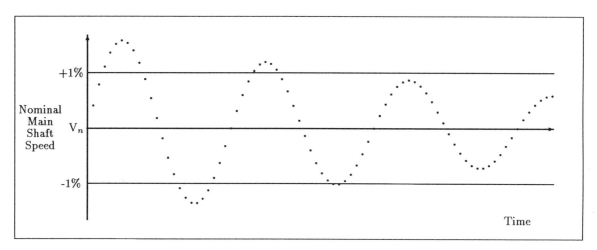

Figure 2: Hunting in an under-damped main shaft speed regulator.

existed as a result of the friction in the joints, bearings, and gears and/or pulleys of the mechanisms used. However, as the components became better made this friction was significantly reduced and the controlled system became seriously under-damped, and hunting began to be observed.

The hunting problem is not confined to the speed regulation of steam engine powered main shafts. It can occur, under certain conditions, in any feedback regulated or servo-controlled system. Today modern regulators and servomechanisms have additional components to prevent hunting from occuring under normal operating conditions—see proportional integrating derivative (PID) control in any control theory textbook[4]. In James Watt's day, however, this problem was not understood, and it became an increasingly serious one. It wasn't until a paper by James Clerk Maxwell, called "On Governors" published in 1868, [Maxwell, 68], that a mathematical treatment of these devices became available, and so enabled the hunting problem to be properly understood and effective solutions to it developed.

From this example of a problem that occurred early on in use of regulators and the beginnings of control theory, we can see that technological developments and improvements do not necessarily simply lead to better performing systems. It further illustrates that, as is typically the case, theoretical developments are what are needed to undertsand how better systems can be successfully designed and built, not just technological ones! Though modern controllers can now be used to achieve good regulation, where fly-ball govenros could not, they are more difficult to use—the gain values of the PID controllers, for example, have to be carefully set and adjusted.

We see, from this example, that though theoretical and technical developments have made it possible to design and build better regulators, they are not, in general, easier to construct and use. The same effect can, I think, be seen in other examples. It has tended to lead us to believe that the development and improvement of our theoretical and technical understanding, of how to build systems, makes their construction and operation easier. This, I believe, is an illusion: these advancements certainly enable us to design, build, and use systems that we were not previously able to construct, but they are not (in general) necessarily any easier to design and use for this. More things become possible, but they don't typically get simpler.

3   Better Sensors Worse Sensing

I now turn from an historical example to one based on data collected from a recent real robot experiment conducted at the VUB AI Lab in Brussels. This particular experiment forms part of an ongoing investigation into the dynamics of agent-environment interactions, [Smithers, 92] and [Smithers, 94], during which the sampled eight bit signals, from the five infra-red (IR) sensors on the robot used, were recorded. I first briefly describe the robot, the experiment design and setup, and data recording. I then present some of the results to illustrate the kinds of normal signal variation that can occur in this quite simple agent-environment interaction system.

3.1   The Robot and Experimental Setup

The robot used is a second generation Lego vehicle[5] (LvII). It has one-bit bumper and whisker sensors for contact detection, five eight-bit active IR sensors (all operating at the same IR and pulse frequencies) arranged in an arc from left to right across the front of the vehicle (with the centre one facing directly forward, inner side ones at 15° from forward, and outer side ones at 40° from forward), a revolution counter on the front wheel[6]

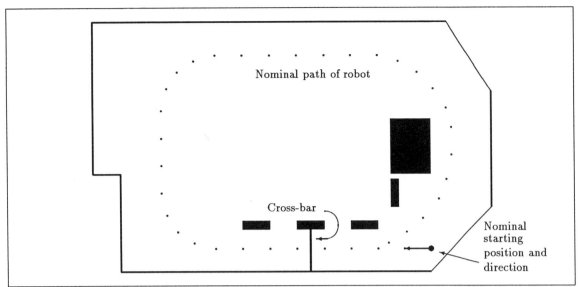

Figure 3: Schematic view of agent-environment setup used to record IR-sensor data as the LvII moves round the nominal path shown.

and a lap counter (see below). It is powered by two Lego 9v motors each supplied with 14v and controlled by a pulse-width modulation. This gives us more or less continuous variation of the power setting of each motor, and thus effective speed control and direction of the vehicle. It has a third free wheel at the front. (See [Donnett & Smithers, 91, figure 5] for an illustation of this arrangement.)

The LvII is programmed so that its default motion is to go forward in a straight line, and to use bumpers and whiskers for contact detection and IR sensors for object proximity detection in a 'don't get stuck' behaviour—do not get stuck in or trapped by things in the environment. The transfer functions, implemented by the program, between each sensor modality and motor states are dynamic (depending on recent sensor signal history), nonlinear, and independent of each other, i.e., there is no "sensor fusion" done in the program.

The experimental environment was formed by an enclosure and constructed to be a good "IR environment" so that the robot would normally not make contact with the sides of the enclosure or any of the objects within it, see figure 3. The parameters of the transfer functions, implemented by the control program, were adjusted so that, starting from the same nominal position and direction, the LvII would consistently take a route round the enclosure near the walls, passing under a cross-bar on each lap, thus triggering a sensor used to detect this event, see figure 3. Achieving this turned out to be significantly more difficult than it was for a first generation Lego vehicle (see [Donnett & Smithers, 91]) which used only three one-bit IR sensors.

Each run of the LvII consisted of ten lap counts and lasted a little over two minutes. During each run the signals from the five IR-sensors were sampled every 20 milliseconds and recorded in memory, together with the time and revolution count at the start of each lap. These data were uploaded to a host computer and stored at the end of each run. A series of nine runs were done, each of nine complete laps. The data presented here is taken from one of these runs (selected at random), with the data from the first lap discarded to avoid transients associated with the starting conditions, giving a total of eight laps.

3.2   IR-Sensor Data

Space does not allow the data for all eight complete laps to be presented. Four sets have therefore been selected (again, at random) and are presented in figures 4, 5, 6, and 7.

As can be seen from figures 4 to 7, while there is an obvious common general form, there is considerable variation in detail of the five sensor signal profiles across each of the laps shown. What is important to note here is that this detailed variation is *not* due to noise. There is, of course, noise in these signals, but it can be shown to be at least an order of magnitude smaller than the variations that can be seen here. This variation is structural and arises as a direct result of the small variations in the actual path taken by the robot on successive laps. The lap times and distances travelled, and their percentage of the average values over the eight laps (see figure captions) indicate that this variation in path is small. However, it has a large (structural) effect on the actual sensor signals generated, as can be seen.

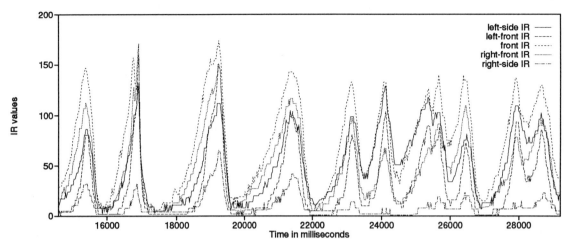

Figure 4: Lap 1/8, time=14593ms (101.48% of average), count=219, giving a distance of 9.862m (101.45% of average), and an average speed of 0.676m/s.

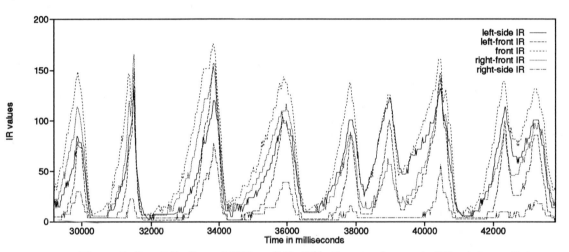

Figure 5: Lap 2/8, time=14595ms (101.49% of average), count=219, giving a distance of 9.862m (101.48% of average), and an average speed of 0.676m/s.

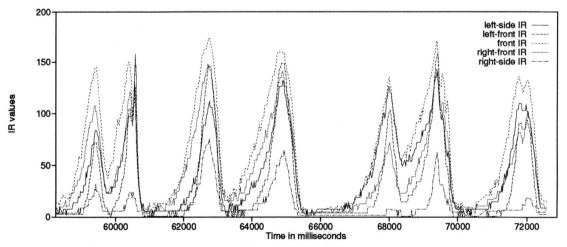

Figure 6: Lap 4/8, time=14293ms (99.39% of average), count=215, giving a distance of 9.682m (99.60% of average), and an average speed of 0.677m/s.

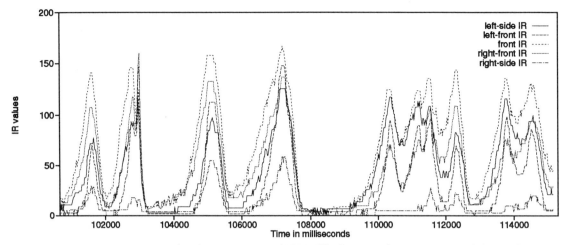

Figure 7: Lap 7/8, time=14459ms (100.55% of average), count=216, giving a distance of 9.727m (100.06% of average), and an average speed of 0.673m/s.

4   Discussion

The kind of structural variation in sensor signal profiles presented here is typical of other types of sensors used on robots, ultra-sound, and vision, for example. It can, of course, be reduced, and, at least sometimes, made effectively to go away, but only at the cost of controlling the motion of the robot so that the differences in the path taken (on each lap, in this case) become very small. This is both a difficult thing to do, and is not necessary for effective robot behaviour—the behaviour achieved is quite stable and not overly sensitive to perturbations. In other words, to reduce the sensor signal variation to a level that no longer matters—to make all the profiles effectively the same—requires much higher degrees of motion control than is necessary for the robot to get around quite well enough. This is the case in the experiment described here: the actual path taken is sufficiently close to the nominal path on each lap and sufficiently robust. To try to reduce what variation there is, to make the sensor signal profiles more similar for each lap, would take us away from the real problem of achieving reliable and robust behaviour. In fact, any attempt to make the motion control more precise simply makes the robot more sensitive to any variations that do occur, as a result of environmental perturbations. Building a controller that can deal with the effects of such perturbations requires yet further complexity, again, none of which is actually of benefit in improving the performance of the robot—which was doing perfectly well in the first place.

We have now seen two examples in which using better technology make can the problem of harder. In the first case, reducing friction in the system removed important damping effects, which then had to be put back

artificially, thus making the system more complicated and difficult to use. In the second case, increasing the resolution of the IR-sensors used, from one-bit of output to eight-bits of output, introduced more structural variation in signal profiles which, if it were to be reduced, would lead to not just a more complicated controller, but one which is likely to result in a less reliable and robust robot—since it would have to be more sensitive to such variations to reduce them.

4.1   Natural Sponges versus Natural Amplifiers

These are not two isolated examples. My claim is that this is how most of the real world works. Mechanical and electrical losses inevitable in systems built from physical media can act like sponges to soak up the variations they themselves induce in the behaviour of the system. If we construct systems from more accurate components so as to reduce losses, in an attempt to make them more energy efficient perhaps, or just to make them be 'better' systems, we can end up turning natural sponges into amplifiers of any intrinsic variations.

In this case we typically need to reintroduce the sponges somehow, which normally requires further system components, which in turn both increases the complexity of the system, and can make them harder to use successfully: as systems get more complicated they typically get harder to use. They can also become more sensitive to environmental conditions that were previously unproblematic, and often need more care in their calibration and recalibration. In general we can see that what are thought of as better systems can be worse systems as far as using them is concerned, or, more disturbing, can be less reliable and robust systems.

4.2 Sensing But Not Measuring

Are we then to conclude that increasing the accuracy of components or increasing the resolution of sensors we use on our robots is not a good idea? The answer is definately, no! Sensitivity and resolution are important in building robots. However, I want to suggest here that at least some of the difficulties experienced when using better robots are due to the approach taken to their design and use, and may thus be avoidable. In particular, I want to suggest that sensors on robots are not best understood as measuring devices, though this is how they are normally thought of. Conventionally, sensors are supposed to measure certain aspects of the environment of the robot, the distance to objects, for example: they are supposed to supply information about the state of the environment.

We can see, from the IR-sensor data presented in the previous section, that it would not be suitable to use in an attempt to acurately determine the location and direction of the robot at any particular time. There is so much structural variation in the IR sensors signals that to use them to decide what state the robot is in at any time would clearly be quite unreliable. Much too unreliable to successfully use them as measurements in some reinforcement learning scheme, or other world model-based navigation scheme, for example.

More generally, unless we introduce much better motion control into our robot, better motion control than is necessary for reliable and robust operation, and so reduce the structural variation in the sensor signals, we cannot take particular sensor signals to reliably and robustly correspond to particular robot-in-the-environment states: they cannot be taken as encoding information about the world, as is usually done. If we can't do this we can't define the reliable mappings from sensor signals to representations of robot-in-the-environment state. And, if we can't do this, we can't treat the sensor signals as measurements of anything: they simply vary in some way that depends upon the dynamics of the robot-environment interaction. Brooks, [Brooks, 91], describes similar experiences with real robots and, although he does not explicitly suggest sensors should not be treated as measuring devices, he does question the use and need of representations of the world, which require measurments in order to be built and maintained. See also, [Flynn & Brooks, 89], for further discussion and illustrations of how real robots can be made to work without trying to make sensors act as measuring devices.

4.3 Sponges, Filters, and the Right Interaction Dynamics

If the IR-sensor signals presented in section 4 are not being used as measurements what are they being used for? They are certainly used to influence the motion of the robot!

I think that a better way to view the behaviour of the LvII in its enclosure, and of agents acting in the world generally, is to consider the sensor signals as one aspect of an interaction process that is setup and maintained between the robot and its environment, and which involves other components such as the motors, control program, and physical structure of the robot. Viewed in this way, the role of sensors is to act as filters (c.f. [Wehner, 87]) on the detectable temporal changes that occur in any agent-environment interaction process, whose output is used to drive internal dynamical processes within the agent—implemented in software in the case of the LvII—which have appropriate sponge like properties to soak up unimportant variations in the filtered changes that in turn are used to influence the state of motor devices, which also have sponge and filtering properties of their own. Putting a robot together, viewed in this way, thus becomes a matter of getting the dynamics of interaction right by carefully designing, implementing, and adjusting, the filters, sponges, and internal dynamical processes, built out of both physical media, and computation.

By taking advantage of the particular properties of the physical devices used to build robots, we can, if we select and combine them well, get a lot of this filter and sponge work done intrinsically—for free. In a similar way we can also take advantage of the natural dynamics that any physical system has in getting, and keeping, the right interaction dynamics between our robot and its environment. Seen in this way, adaptive behvaiour thus becomes a problem of adjusting the filter and sponge propertise of the agent so as to maintain an effective agent-environment interaction dynamics. A good example of what, I think, can be understood as a good combination of filters and sponges in a robot control system, is Horswill's vision guided mobile robot, Poly, [Horswill, 93], which can demonstrate some relatively reliable and robust behaviour in a real world environment subject to significant variations, and which can present the robot with some unpredictable events and conditions[7].

I don't think Horswill's robot is best understood as an information processing system which uses sensors to measure aspects of its environment, and then decides what to do on the basis of this information. Treating agent-environments systems as dynamical system does not require this, see [Smithers, 94]. Mark Bickhard's interactivism model of emergent representation, [Bickhard, 93], presents an essentially similar and more thorough argument. Designing and building agent-environment systems as dynamical interaction systems which must maintain certain interaction dynamics is, I therefore suggest, a more appropriate approach to designing and building better robots, and one that does not introduce unnecessary complexity.

Acknowledgements

The work reported here was mostly carried out while the author held the SWIFT AI Chair at the VUB AI Lab, Brussels. Miles Pebody, Ian Porter, Piet Ruyssinck, and Danny Vereertbrugghen, were responsible for much of the development of the second generation Lego vehicle technology used. Anne Sjostrôm assisted in building, testing, and debugging the robot program used, and in carrying out the experiments from which the data were taken. Amaia Bernaras read and usefully commented on an earlier version of this paper. My thanks to all of them, and to two anonymous referees for their comments on the submitted draft of this paper. I am also happy to acknowledge the financial support of the University of the Basque Country for my current position, and the Faculty of Informatics, in particular, for providing my current academic home.

Notes

1. These are typically not simulations at all, not in the proper sense of the term, since they have never been validated against the robot and environment supposedly simulated. Indeed the robots and environments, mostly do not even exist, thus making any such validation impossible. What are widely referred to in the Artificial Intelligence, Artificial Life, animats, and robotics literature, as simulations, are better understood and described as computational models—often models of nonexistent robots and environments, but this is not a problem for modelling, only for simulation, which is a special type of modelling.

2. The fly-ball or centrifugal governor is so called because it uses two arms each with heavy balls attached at one end and pivoted at the other on a vertical rotating shaft. As the shaft speed increases, the balls fly out, and thus the arms swing up. As the shaft speed decreases, the balls fall in towards the shaft, and thus the arms swing down. This up and down movement of the arms is then used to open and close a value that controls the amount of steam supplied to the cylinder of a steam engine in such a way that a constant shaft speed is maintained.

3. Note that the fly-ball governor does not maintain the same speed of the main shaft as machines are brought into and out of use. It simply smooths the changes and reduces them to a minimum, given a maximum power output of the steam engine. This is because the relationship between the fly-ball governor and the throttle valve is fixed, so when a new machine is brought into use (and so draws power) the governor cannot return to exactly it's original speed since this would mean the value would be back to its original position and the amount of steam being let through

would be as it was before, which is not enough to maintain the original speed under the additional load. With a powerfull enough steam engine and a well set governor and throttle valve relationship, this difference can be kept small and within acceptable limits.

4. Note that proportional integrating derivative (PID) controllers are also able to deal with the 'steady-state' problem: the failure of the Watt fly-ball governor to maintain the same main shaft speed, only a speed near the nominal speed. This *integrating* part of the controller acts against the *derivative* part used to counteract the hunting, or 'overshoot' problem. Consequently in any application of a PID controller a compromise has to be found between the setting of the parameters for each of these opposing aspects, and this can often be difficult to do in practice.

5. Second generation Lego vehicles are essentially the same
   as first generation, see [Donnett & Smithers, 91], except that a two microporcessors architecture is used, one (a MC68HC11) to service the sensor and motor-control channels, [Vereertbrugghen, 93], and the second (a MC68340 with 0.5MByte RAM) to run the control program, together with 8 bit IR and light sensors (instead of 1 bit sensors), and a more efficient and flexible time-slicing runtime kernel, plus a number of other advanced features.

6. This uses a Hall-effect switch and six magnets placed in the front wheel with even spacing and alternating pole directions to produce three counts per complete revolution in one direction—changes in direction are detected in the program so that forward and reverse counts are maintained separately. The wheel diameter is 43mm, giving a circumference of 135.089mm, and thus a distance per wheel count of 45.03mm. Having the front wheel fixed (i.e., not a caster) means that it is always in line with the direction of motion or tangential to it. This means that, using this wheel counter, it is possible to reliably estimate the distance travelled: essentially it integrates only the forward motion of the robot, much as a planimeter does—an instrument used for measuring the area of closed plane figures, such as ship hull sections, etc.

7. Though Poly can't deal with everything that can happen. Ian was kind enough to give me a demonstration of his robot when I visited him. It happened to be one of the first warn sunny days of the year in Cambridge, so people were leaving their office doors open. This meant there were light patches on the floor which had not been there before–when Poly was being developed and tested–and these sometimes caused the

robot to get confused about where it was. The situation was not helped any by the fact that over night all the overhead lighting had been changed (for more efficient tubes) causing thr ambient light level to be a little different from before, and so affecting some of the image processing involved—a good illustration of the kinds of thing real robots have to be able to cope with.

References

[Bickhard, 93] Mark H. Bickhard, 1994. Representation Content in Humans and Machines, Journal of Experimental and Theoretical AI, vol 5, pp 285–333.

[Brooks, 91] Rodney A. Brooks, 1991. Intelligence Without Representation, Artificial Intelligence, Vol 47, no 1–3, special issue, pp 139–159.

[Dickinson & Jenkins, 91] H. W. Dickinson and Rhys Jenkins, 1981. *James Watt and the Steam Engine*, Encore Editions, London. First published 1927.

[Donnett & Smithers, 91] Jim Donnett and Tim Smithers, 1991. A Technology for Studying Inteligent Systems, in Jean-Arcady Meyer and Stewart W. Wilson (eds.), *From Animals to Animats*, proceedings of the First International Conference on Simulation of Adaptive Behaviour, The MIT Press, Cambridge, Mass., pp 540–549.

[Flynn & Brooks, 89] Anita M. Flynn and Rodney A. Brooks, 1989. Battling Reality, AI Memo 1148, MIT AI Labrotory, October 1989.

[Horswill, 93] Ian Horswill, PhD thesis, MIT AI Laboratory, 1993.

[Kurzweil, 90] Raymond Kurzweil, 1990. *The Age of Intelligent Machines*, The MIT Press, Cambridge, Mass.

[Maxwell, 68] James Clerk Maxwell, 1868. On Governors, *Proceedings of the Royal Society*, 16 (1867/68), pp 270–283. Reprinted in Richard Bellman and Robert Kalaba (eds.), *Mathematical Trends in Control Theory*, New York, 1964, pp 3-17.

[Mayr, 70] Otto Mayr, 1970. *The Origins of Feedback Control*, The MIT Press, Cambridge, Mass.

[Nehmzow & Smithers, 91] Ulrich Nehmzow and Tim Smithers, 1991, Mapbuilding using Self-Organising Networks in "Really Useful Robots", in Jean-Arcady Meyer and Stewart W. Wilson (eds.), *From Animals to Animats*, proceedings of the First International Conference on Simulation of Adaptive Behaviour, The MIT Press, Cambridge, Mass., pp 152–159.

[Nehmzow & Smithers, 92] Ulrich Nehmzow and Tim Smithers, 1992. Using Motor Actions for Location Recognition, in Francisco J Varela and Paul Bourgine (eds.), *Towards a Practice of Autonomous Systems*, proceedings of the First European Conference on Artificial Life, The MIT Press, Cambridge, Mass., pp 96–104.

[Smithers, 92] Tim Smithers, 1992. Taking Eliminative Materialism Seriously: A Methodology for Autonomous Systems Research, in Francisco J Varela and Paul Bourgine (eds.), *Towards a Practice of Autonomous Systems*, proceedings of the First European Conference on Artificial Life, The MIT Press, Cambridge, Mass., pp 31–40.

[Smithers, 93] Tim Smithers, 1993. On Behaviour as Dissipative Structures in Agent-Environment Interactions Processes, presented at the workshop *prerational Intelligence: Phenomenology of Complexity Emerging in Systems of Agents Interacting Using Simple Rules*, held at the Centre for Interdisciplinary Studies (ZiF), Bielefeld, November 22–26, 1993, as part of the Prerational intelligence Research Project.

[Smithers, 94] Tim Smithers, 1994. On Agent-Environment Systems, paper submitted to Artificial Life IV, MIT, Cambridge, July, 1994.

[Vereertbrugghen, 93] Dany Vereertbrugghen, 1993. *Design and Implementation of a Sensor-Motor Control Unit for Mobile Robots*, Licentie Thesis, AI Laboratory, Vrije Universiteit Brussel.

[Wehner, 87] Rüdiger Wehner, 1987. Matched Filters— Neural Models of the External World, *Journal Computational Physiology, A*, vol 161, pp 511–531.

Insect vision and olfaction: different neural architectures for different kinds of sensory signal?

D. Osorio[1], Wayne M Getz[2], Jürgen Rybak[3]

1. Biological Sciences, Sussex University, BN1 9QG, UK. D.Osorio@sussex.ac.uk.

2. Environmental Science, College of Natural Resources, UC Berkeley, Berkeley, CA 94720, USA. getz@nature.berkeley.edu.

3. Neurobiologie, FU-Berlin. Königin Luise Str. 28-30, Berlin 33, D-1000, Germany. rybak@castor.zedat.fu-berlin.de.

Abstract

The world is often unpredictable and complex. That the design or evolution of neural architectures for sensory perception is influenced by the structure and statistical properties of sensory signals has long been appreciated for vision (Barlow, 1981). But are similar computational strategies appropriate for all sensory worlds? To explore how the complexity and unpredictability of signals may influence computational strategies we contrast vision and olfaction; optical signals are complex but highly constrained, whilst olfactory signals generally carry less information than visual but are also less constrained and predictable. Essentially arbitrary patterns of excitation on the olfactory receptors need to be parsed and learnt, and then recognised against a complex background of smells. In insects, differences between visual and olfactory signals may have led to the evolution of different neural processing strategies, embodied in distinct neural architectures. Insect vision uses 'hardwired' neural circuits tailored to specific visual behaviours. In contrast, olfaction lacks the ordered and highly differentiated neural circuits used for vision, and may use an associative network at an early stage, to correlate arbitrary patterns of activity on the receptor array with significant stimuli such as food or danger.

1. Introduction

To control robust and reliable behaviour a sensory or perceptual system must be able to parse the limitless variety of signals that arrive on receptors. Real brains and behaviours are a familiar inspiration for the design of machines. However nature's strategies of brain design seem to vary reflecting Meyer and Juillot's (1990) observation that 'behaviour can be controlled by several different abilities and architectures'. Analogies between brains and machines range from the observation that the cerebral cortex has the features of a universal computing machine, to 'insect-like' robots with distributed special-purpose algorithms and sometimes architecture (Pitts & McCulloch, 1947; Brooks, 1991; Franceschini et al., 1992). An alternative view is that these supposed differences in biological architecture are superficial, and that common signal processing strategies are shared by different perceptual systems (Strausfeld, 1989; Konishi, 1990). An understanding of why a range of neural architectures have evolved in nature may inform us of how to build machines that operate like real animals. For example, when are 'insect-like' architectures, with stereotyped wiring between anatomically distinct neurons to be preferred to diffuse highly interconnected networks of comparatively undifferentiated neurons? Drawing on our knowledge of sensory signals and sensory processing in insects we argue that fundamentally different computational strategies are required for vision and olfaction, and that these differences are probably reflected in the brain. Likewise, design of 'animat perception' should take account of the statistics and complexities of the machine's world. Specifically tailored, or perhaps genetically evolved, algorithms may be needed for some kinds of signal, whereas other signals are so unpredictable that an associative network will be more useful.

Here we move up the visual and olfactory pathways in insects, particularly fly and honeybee. First, the signals, sensory peripheries and initial neural stages are outlined (figs. 1, 2). The inputs help define the roles of the second stages of the olfactory and visual pathways; the mushroom body and optic medulla respectively. These neuropiles are the computational powerhouses of the insect brain, containing over 75% of all its neurons, but they show striking architectural differences. In vision, outputs from the photoreceptors viewing a single point (or pixel) project to a specific column of cells in the medulla. A column

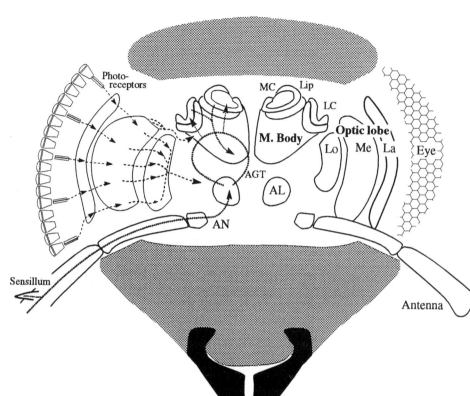

Figure 1.

Diagrammatic frontal view of a bee's head with the cuticle covering the brain cut away to reveal the main visual and olfactory pathways. Dashed lines indicate the flow of visual and dotted of olfactory signals. Odour molecules are detected by receptors in antennal sensillae which project up the antennal nerve (AN) to the antennal lobe (AL). The outputs of glomeruli in the antennal lobe project to the lips of the median (MC) and lateral (LC) calyces of the mushroom body, via the antenno-glomerular tract (AGT). Optical signals are detected by receptors which synapse in the lamina (La), the outputs of the lamina project topologically to the medulla (Me) and hence to the lobula (Lo). In bee medulla outputs also project directly to the mushroom body.

contains about 50 anatomically and physiologically distinct neurons, each with a specific role in the neural circuitry (fig. 2a). At an equivalent stage of the olfactory pathway, the mushroom-body lacks the order and neural differentiation of the optic medulla. Olfactory inputs run across an array of anatomically undifferentiated intrinsic neurons called Kenyon cells, suggesting (on anatomical grounds) that a given olfactory receptor can drive any mushroom-body intrinsic neuron (fig. 3). The architecture of the mushroom body combined with the likelihood that neural connections in the mushroom body are more plastic than those in the optic lobe, argues that input-output relations are much more flexible in this part of the insect brain than in the optic lobe.

2. Vision and the insect optic lobe

2.1 Signal Statistics & Signal Structure

Just as the sentences of a language are but a mere fraction of the utterances that the human vocal tract can produce, natural optical signals are a minute, if limitlessly variable, subset of those that are physically possible. The human brain is specialised to parse and produce natural language, and to interpret natural optical images. Constraints in natural images allow vision to recover the structure and disposition of moving or of static objects (Gibson, 1979; Marr, 1982). When the neural conventions used to model the world fail to give a veridical interpretation of a physical signal, we perceive optical 'illusions' that expose visual mechanisms or algorithms.

Vision can recover size, shape and distance, and store images, but only in a world of solid opaque objects that move coherently; it fails in a world of turbulent clouds, television 'snow', or Escher drawings. We can remember and analyse faces and expressions with exquisite skill, but a random pattern containing an equal amount of statistical information is unmemorable and meaningless.

Insects inhabit a visual world is similar to our own, and they too make use of its special properties, and experience similar optical illusions (Srinivasan, 1992). Motion vision is important for insects; visual flowfields produced by ego-motion, are used to stabilise flight, to establish the distance of surfaces, and to detect approaching obstacles or landing sites (Srinivasan, 1992; Egelhaaf & Borst, 1993). As the term flowfield implies, motion cues (e.g. direction, speed and parallax) are analysed, whereas the specific pattern is disregarded. Flowfields are usable because normally the insect alone moves while the surroundings remain static and do not change intensity. Neural algorithms used for analysing flowfields also make assumptions about spatial structure; for example, that surfaces are irregular and opaque (Egelhaaf & Borst, 1993).

Nowhere is function as clearly reflected in neural architecture as in the three ganglia of the insect's optic lobe that serve early (pixel-by-pixel) vision; the lamina, the medulla and the lobula (figs. 1,2; Strausfeld, 1976). Connections between these neuropiles have a 'neurocrystalline' precision, preserving the topological order on the retina in the neural images of the optic lobe. In the lamina and medulla together a set of some sixty

a Compound Eye & Optic Lobe

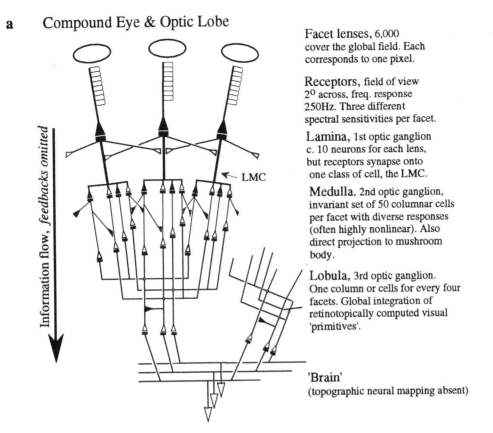

Facet lenses, 6,000 cover the global field. Each corresponds to one pixel.

Receptors, field of view 2° across, freq. response 250Hz. Three different spectral sensitivities per facet.

Lamina, 1st optic ganglion c. 10 neurons for each lens, but receptors synapse onto one class of cell, the LMC.

Medulla. 2nd optic ganglion, invariant set of 50 columnar cells per facet with diverse responses (often highly nonlinear). Also direct projection to mushroom body.

Lobula, 3rd optic ganglion. One column or cells for every four facets. Global integration of retinotopically computed visual 'primitives'.

'Brain'
(topographic neural mapping absent)

b Antennal Lobe: General organisation   Glomerular circuitry

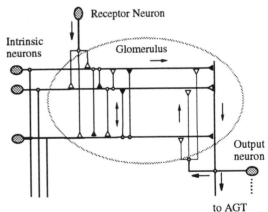

Figure 2

Diagram of neural connections in the optic and antennal lobes in the bee. The diagram for the antennal lobe is more or less complete, whereas that for the optic lobe is highly simplified.

a. Columnar connections in the optic lobe, receptor outputs from a facet drive monopolar cells (LMC's) in a lamina cartridge. These LMC's synapse upon other cells in the lamina and also project to the medulla. Medulla outputs project to the lobula where there is a columnar organisation but spatial convergence. Beyond the lobula, 'visual' areas probably lack a topological representation of visual space, except for the medulla to mushroom body projection in bees (Personal observation).

b. Left: the basic organization of the multiglomeruli model of the antennal lobe is illustrated in terms of the receptor neuron inputs, the glomeruli connected together by intrinsic neurons, and the projection neuron outputs. Right: details of the architecture of the neural network within each glomerulus and the flow of information, as indicated by the arrows.

columnar cells is repeated beneath each facet of the compound eye. Each columnar neuron is anatomically distinct and occupies a specific place in the synaptic circuitry (Shaw, 1984; Strausfeld, 1976), and probably has a distinct visual response (James & Osorio, 1994). Thus beneath the optical image on the retina is a set of sixty distinct, but interacting neural images, each at the finest possible spatial scale. The third optic ganglion, the lobula, contains a similar number of cell types to the outer two, but the structure is coarser with a column for every four facets (Strausfeld, 1976).

2.1. Compound eye and lamina: the first stages of insect vision

The compound eye of a bee or large fly comprises about 3,000 facet lenses. Each lens focuses on a coaxial set of eight or nine photoreceptor cells to give a single 'pixel' in the retinal image (but see Kirschfeld, 1967). Different receptors may be tuned to different wavelengths, in the bee about 340 nm, 440 nm and 540 nm (Menzel & Backhaus, 1991), so that each set of receptors encodes two parameters, intensity and wavelength, at one point in space. The outputs from receptors (other than so-called long visual fibres concerned with colour and UV vision) project to distinctive non-spiking cells called large monopolar cells (LMC's) in the lamina (fig. 2a). The function of the LMC's is thought to be to remove redundancy from the optical signal. Neighbouring points in visual images are highly correlated, so that data compression at an early stage optimises use of the limited bandwidth in the nervous system (Laughlin, 1987). An orderly lateral inhibitory network in the lamina, with LMC's inhibiting their nearest neighbours, achieves a high degree of data-compression (fig. 2a; temporal correlation is similarly removed by self inhibition, Shaw, 1984).

2.2 Optic medulla

The medulla is the main centre of pixel-by-pixel vision in insects. Beneath each facet of the eye the LMC's drive a column of some fifty distinct neurons in the medulla (Strausfeld, 1976), so that the receptor array is topologically mapped onto the medulla (giving about 2×10^5 medulla neurons). Whereas the visual responses of a specific anatomical class of medulla columnar neuron are highly consistent (both across the eye and between individuals), those of different cells in each column are diverse (Personal observations; James & Osorio, 1994). Some act as tuned linear filters, whereas others are highly nonlinear. Nonlinearities include rectification and adaptation (O'Carroll et al, 1992), as well as non-linear spatial interactions needed for direction selectivity (Egelhaaf & Borst, 1993).

Most medulla outputs project to the lobula, which has a similar number of columnar cell types (Strausfeld, 1976), but there is spatial convergence; a column of lobula cells repeated for every four facets in the eye. In the lobula,

widefield cells integrate signals across the visual field to abstract motion flowfields and other global features. Interestingly, in some insects including the bee a substantial number of medulla outputs run direct from the medulla to the mushroom-body (Mobbs, 1982). In contrast to the olfactory pathway (see below, fig. 3) this visual projection neurons map to the mushroom body in a way that retains the topological order of visual space (Personal observation).

The high degree of anatomical order in the optic lobes, and the constancy of cellular neuroanatomy mean that neural pathways can be traced from receptors to muscles. In flies visuo-motor pathways are known for optomotor flight control, and small object tracking. Tracking is used by males to chase females and involves a sex specific neural pathway arising from the frontal visual field (Gilbert & Strausfeld, 1992; Gronenberg & Strausfeld, 1992). The optomotor response acts to stabilise flight by abolition of rotatory (as opposed to translatory) flowfields (Milde et al., 1987; Egelhaaf & Borst, 1993).

In summary, each neuron in the visual 'front-end', the optic lobe, is genetically determined to contribute to visual behaviour in a specific way, and a great many such cells are required by insects. The optic lobe operates in a complex but rule-bound visual world, and a large 'hardwired' nervous system where each cell has a distinct function works well. Nonetheless, visuo-motor behaviour is not a simple set of reflexes, and the underlying neural circuits are not simple reflex arcs. There is feedback at every stage of the visual pathway, so, for example, motor actions might influence sensory processing. Moreover, bees learn landscapes, patterns and colours (Collett & Cartwright, 1983; Menzel & Backhaus, 1991), whilst flies show great flexibility in visuo-motor co-ordination (Wolf et al., 1992). Some learning probably takes place in the optic lobe (Dill et al., 1993).

3. Olfaction, a different world?

3.1 Olfactory signals

Unlike visual or auditory stimuli, olfactory stimuli are very noisy: they contain much less spatial or temporal information than visual stimuli. Optical signals are quantifiable in terms of amplitudes and frequencies of wave forms over time and space, and the receptive fields of associated receptors have natural metrics in terms of stimulus frequencies and amplitudes. In contrast, olfactory stimuli can be characterised only in terms of the concentrations of component odorants making up odour blends. Receptor responses may be ordinated with respect to odorant concentration (e.g. the greater the concentration the greater the response), but normally olfactory signals have no natural ordination with respect to different odorant molecules. Further air plumes that are turbulent, so that olfactory stimulation of an insect antenna may be highly variable among neighbouring sensilla, and with respect to time for a particular sensillum. The absence of a natural molecular order or spectrum for odour molecules combined with inhomogeneities of the odour plume requires specialised neural integration.

In view of the nature of olfactory signals it is perhaps not surprising that bees can be conditioned to respond to any odour that they can detect (using classical conditioning of the reflex extension of the proboscis associated with sugar water touched to the antenna). Even pheromones that normally invoke the sting reflex, and any blend of floral and pheromonal compounds will elicit the proboscis extension reflex after conditioning (Smith & Getz, 1994). This ability to learn arbitrary olfactory stimuli is in marked contrast to vision where, as we have emphasised, certain stimuli are highly salient in a specific behavioural context whilst others are not. Once learnt, the odour associated with a particular source needs to be detected and located against a background mixture or odours in the turbulent atmosphere (Hopfield, 1991).

At the coarsest level, the olfactory systems both of vertebrates and of arthropods follow the same design principles: large numbers of sensory neurons converge on several orders of magnitude fewer glomeruli – spherical regions of high synaptic density – from which neurons project to higher centres (figs. 1, 2b, 3). Pheromones, used to convey specific messages, are processed by specialised olfactory subsystems. Highly specific pheromonal receptors converge down dedicated pathways, often referred to as labelled lines, that constitute specialised olfactory processing subsystems involving macroglomeruli. Here, however, we focus on the general, nonpheromonal, odour processing subsystem where there is no equivalent of the differentiated neural pathways serving specific visual behaviours or submodalities.

3.2 Olfaction in Honeybee: Receptors and the Antennal Lobe

Olfactory receptor neurons lie in hair-like sensilla on the insect antenna (fig. 2). Each sensillum contains from two to several dozen receptors. Generalist receptors, such as those found in honeybees (Akers & Getz, 1992, 1993a) and cockroaches (Fujimura et al., 1991) respond to one or more classes of odorants, such as aliphatic alcohols, aldehydes, ketones and monoterpenes. The tuning spectrum of an olfactory neuron can be described in terms of its relative response across an array of odorant stimuli. Since no natural metrics appear to exist for characterising olfactory signals, any measured 'spectrum' is specific to the suite of odorants presented and to their individual concentrations. It is not possible to predict responses to molecules that have not been presented. Moreover the tuning spectrum generally changes with odorant concentration, perhaps due to non-linear interactions between receptor mechanisms, intra- or inter-cellularly

(Akers & Getz, 1993b). Although there is no general order or organisation in the receptors, neurophysiological data suggest that the tuning spectrum of receptor neurons in the same sensillum differ more than one would expect by assembling receptors at random (Getz & Akers, 1994a,b). Further, the response of receptor neurons is highly nonlinear. Nonlinearities arise because (i) of threshold and saturation effects, (ii) of nonlinearities in the binding dynamics of ligands (odorants or odorants bound to protein "carrier" molecules) to membrane receptor molecules, and (iii) the membranes of individual receptor neurons seem to be populated by more than one type of receptor molecule, some of which when activated (Michel et al., 1991) leading to membrane depolarisation and others to membrane hyperpolarisation. The result is that sometimes strong synergistic or strong inhibitory effects are evident in the response of olfactory receptors to mixtures of compounds. These nonlinearities can be contrasted with the highly linear behaviour of photoreceptors under normal operating conditions (i.e. one level of illumination).

3.3 Neural Circuitry of the Antennal lobe

The antennal lobe (figs. 1,2) is composed of several hundred glomeruli each of which constitute the basic functional unit for the first stage of the olfaction, as the lamina column is for vision (but c.f. Strausfeld, 1989). Although its function remains obscure considerable progress is now being made in characterising the anatomy and physiology of the insect antennal lobe (Arnold et al., 1985; Boeckh & Ernst, 1987; Boeckh et al., 1990; Flanagan & Mercer, 1989; Gascuel & Masson, 1991; Malun, 1991).

Unpublished neuroanatomical data (but see Hansson et al., 1992) suggest that olfactory receptor neurons from a single sensillum arborise in different glomeruli, but that individual olfactory receptors appear to arborise in a single glomerulus (Boeckh & Ernst, 1987; A. Brockmann, personal communication). At the same time, the group of olfactory receptor neurons arborising in the same glomerulus may share more similar response spectra than would be expected for a random selection of these olfactory neurons. Such a segregation of receptor inputs should give uniglomerular output neurons with differing responses to different odours (fig. 2b). At the same time the "across fibre" pattern of firing in these output neurons must code for the quality of the odour stimulus impinging at the periphery.

The circuitry within the glomeruli is also being unravelled (fig. 2b; Flanagan & Mercer 1989; Fonta et al., 1993). Receptor inputs synapse almost exclusively with neurons that connect several glomeruli, but are intrinsic to the antennal lobe. Somewhat surprisingly many of these neurons are GABA-ergic, and so probably inhibitory. The interglomerular neurons synapse with the output neurons that project from the antennal lobe via the lateral and median antenno-glomerular tracts (AGT's) to the

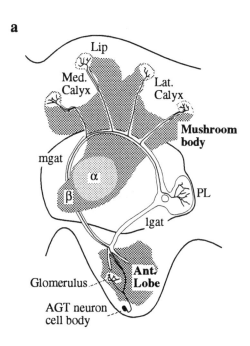

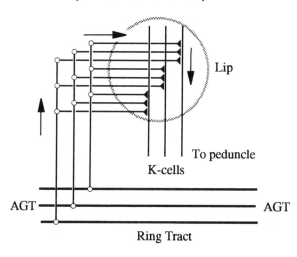

Figure 3

a. Antennal lobe to mushroom body (MB) connection in the bee. Glomerular output neurons send axons via the median and lateral antenno-glomerular tracts (m-AGT, l-AGT) to the lips of the calyces of the mushroom body. Note that the calyces are toroidal and the two sections shown here are parts of a continuous ring, throughout which the agt neurons arborise and make synaptic blebs uniformly. Kenyon cell interneurons of two classes project from the mushroom body lips to the α and β lobes of the peduncle, where they synapse upon output neurons. AGT neurons also arborise in the protocerebral lobe (PL). The outputs of the antennal lobe project to the mushroom body via the antenno-glomerular tracts (AGT's).

b. Diagram of circuitry in bee mushroom body. AGT neurons from the antennal lobe make synaptic outputs throughout the lips of the MB calyces. The MB intrinsic neurons are Kenyon (K) cells, these project from the calyces to the peduncle of the MB. The neural circuitry within the MB lips is not known, and there is no direct evidence for direct synaptic connections between AGT neurons and K-cells, (but they are highly probable). Note that K-cells are hundreds of time more numerous than the AGT inputs.

mushroom-bodies and lateral lobes of the protocerebrum (figs. 1, 2b, 3). The output neurons feedback in turn onto the interglomerular neurons (fig. 2b; Malun, 1991), to form excitatory-inhibitory feedback loops that are comparable to mitral-granule cell feedback loops in the vertebrate olfactory bulb (Freeman & Skarda, 1985; Li & Hopfield, 1989).

Besides the uniglomerular output neurons pluriglomerular projection neurons occur (Fonta et al., 1993). These neurons are not part of the computational network, but appear to be passive collectors of output that may signal the intensity of input in a pluriglomerular region of the antennal lobe (Malun, 1991). They do not appear to influence the uniglomerular projection neuron output, and may not be involved in coding odour quality.

3.4 Mushroom Bodies

The mushroom bodies receive the outputs of the antennal lobe, and so are the second stage on the olfactory pathway (figs. 1, 3). In many insects they are solely olfactory, but as mentioned above in bees they receive a large visual input (Mobbs, 1982). Very little physiological information is available about mushroom body intrinsic neurons (Menzel et al., 1994). Nonetheless, as for the medulla, neuroanatomy gives important insights into mushroom body function.

The AGT neurons almost certainly synapse onto small intrinsic neurons called Kenyon (K-) cells. The number of K-cells (1.7×10^5) is very much larger than the few hundred AGT neurons (Rybak & Eichmüller, in prep.). The AGT neurons terminate in the lips of the mushroom body calyces (fig. 3) where two of the five recognised anatomical classes of K-cell make synapses (Mobbs, 1982; Rybak & Menzel, 1993). Many or all of the AGT cells arborise throughout the target region, thus there is no anatomical evidence for segregation of outputs from the antennal lobe to specific sub-regions of the mushroom body (Menzel et al, 1994; personal observation). The K-cells project to the α and β domains in peduncle of the mushroom body from which output neurons project to various higher (or motor) centres (fig 3; Rybak & Menzel, 1993).

The lack of anatomical differentiation of K-cells in the mature mushroom body, may be reflected in its development. Insect neurons are normally derived by a stereotyped series of divisions so that each part of the nervous system contains a fixed number of cells, each with its own specific lineage. K-cells may be unique in that their stem cells (neuroblasts) divide symmetrically many times, giving rise to a large population of anatomically indistinguishable offspring (Zacharias et al., 1993).

4 Conclusions

4.1 Comparison of medulla and mushroom body

Insect brains may manifest the different needs of vision and olfaction in the architectures of the neuropiles serving the two modalities. Both the medulla and the mushroom body are second order neuropils separated from the receptors by the lamina and the antennal lobe respectively (bee mushroom bodies receive a large visual input, but this occurs at a later stage of vision). Moreover they are the largest centres of neural processing in insects, containing over 75% of all the cells in the bee's or fly's nervous system. Given these similarities the differences are striking. In the medulla anatomically identifiable columnar neurons form an invariant set of neural circuits for each point in the visual field. The principal input to a given column comes from a specific facet in the compound eye, and hence point in visual space. Thus in effect numerous separate neural images are derived from the single optical image on the retina. The mushroom body lacks such neural differentiation, it contains just five classes of Kenyon (K) cell, only two of which receive direct olfactory inputs. Owing to the geometry of the mushroom body a given K-cell can be driven by the outputs from any receptor cell or any antennal lobe glomerulus. These anatomical observations indicate that signal processing in the mushroom body relies not on pre-wired and invariant pathways, but instead on synaptic plasticity in its neural network (Menzel et al., 1994). A conjecture which is supported by the observation that genes whose products are essential for learning – and hence likely to be necessary for synaptic plasticity – in *Drosophila* are expressed in the mushroom body (Davis, 1993).

Strausfeld (1989) has taken a different view of the relationship between insect visual and olfactory pathways. He too notes that the olfactory system lacks a stage equivalent to the optic lobe, but infers that it is not needed because individual olfactory receptors act as specialised detectors so that early sensory processing is unnecessary. This interpretation may be correct for pheromones, but the broad and complex tuning of generalist olfactory receptors is at variance with Strausfeld's argument.

4.2 Comparisons with mammals

Do insects brains embody general principles of neural evolution set by fundamental constraints in signal and receptor properties? The answer to this question is not straightforward, and might appear to be 'no' because in mammals the neocortex performs most sensory processing, especially vision. Perhaps because in primates early vision is cortical Shepherd (1991) argues that analogous neural computations serve olfaction and vision, namely the abstraction of sensory 'primitives' (c.f. Marr, 1982). Why then is early pixel-by-pixel vision served by quite different neural architectures in insects and primates? (Ganglion cells with linear centre-surround receptive fields are the main outputs from the primate retina and probably comparable in function to the lamina stage of the optic lobe; Laughlin, 1987). Theory and the insect optic lobe indicate that a hardwired architecture should work well for low-level vision. Many specific algorithms for aspects of early vision, such as border detection, motion detection and stereopsis have been described (e.g. Marr, 1982; Egelhaaf & Borst, 1993). Likewise, the neural circuits of the insect optic lobe perform genetically specified neural operations giving them low-level vision comparable to our own (Strausfeld & Lee, 1991; O'Carroll, 1993; Srinivasan et al., 1993). In contrast, olfaction can make less use than vision of predetermined 'primitives' to simplify global integration of signals and more nearly resembles the later global stages than early vision (Haberly, 1985; Strausfeld, 1989; Hopfield, 1991). Thus the primate neocortex seems to perform functions such as low level vision that in insects are served by a very different neural architecture. The mammalian neocortex with its protean powers has evolved from the olfactory forebrain of primitive vertebrates (Sarnat & Netsky, 1981). Perhaps because olfaction demands a neural architecture preadapted to learning complex input patterns.

4.3 Lessons for animats

Robots or animats, like animals, must operate in an unpredictable world. Neural processing and neural architectures for perception should reflect the statistics and structure of the sensory signals. Hopfield (1991) suggests that early olfaction requires a neural network similar to that needed for higher (object) vision, in effect the early pixel-by-pixel stages of vision are useless for olfaction because the olfactory signals have little predictable structure. The olfactory system has to be prepared to learn any pattern of excitation on the receptors, to associate this with other signals (e.g. food or danger), and to recognise it, often against a complex background of other odours; to do this an associative network is necessary. However the nature and extent of the unpredictability and complexity of the various sensory worlds can vary. Whilst we have drawn attention to differences between vision and olfaction, such variations are not necessarily modality specific. For example pheromonal signals are highly predictable compared with other olfactory signals, whilst later stages of vision, especially object vision, may require processing similar to that we suggest is used at an early stage in olfaction (Hopfield, 1991). Differences in the nature of the signals encountered as much as the overall complexity of behaviour can set the computational strategy that is used. For real brains such strategy is of course reflected in the neural architecture. Likewise, the design of animat perceptual systems should take account of the world in which the machine will act, and not be taken *ad hoc* from an arbitrary biological model.

Acknowledgements.

This paper was in part written at the Neurobiology Dept, of the Free University of Berlin. D.O. and W.M.G. thank Prof. R. Menzel and Dr. W. Backhaus of the Free University of Berlin for their hospitality and support. W.M.G. also acknowledges the support of the Alexander von Humboldt Foundation. We thank P.G. Mobbs for his advice.

References

Akers RP, Getz WM (1992) A test of identified response classes among olfactory receptor neurons in the honeybee worker. *Chem Senses*, **17**, 191-209

Akers RP, Getz WM (1993a) Olfactory response characteristics and tuning structure of placodes in the honey-bee *Apis-mellifera* L. *Apidologie.* **24**, 195-217

Akers RP, Getz WM (1993b) Response of olfactory receptor neurons in honeybees to odorants and their binary-mixtures. *J Comp Physiol A,* **173,** 169-185

Arnold G, Masson C, Budharugsa S (1985) Comparative study of the antennal lobes and their afferent pathway in the worker bee and drone. (*Apis mellifica*). *Cell Tissue Res*, **242,** 593-605.

Barlow HB (1981) Critical limiting factors in the design of the eye and visual cortex. *Proc R Soc Lond B*, **212**, 1-34

Boeckh JP, Distler KD, Ernst M, Hösl M, Malun D. (199) Olfactory bulb and antennal lobe." In: Schild D (ed.) *Chemosensory Information Processing*. 201-227. Berlin: Springer-Verlag, 1990.

Boeckh J, Ernst KD (1987) Contribution of single unit analysis in insects to an understanding of olfactory function. *J Comp Physiol A*, **161**, 549-565

Brooks RA (1991) Intelligence without reason. *Proc 12th Int Conf Artificial Intelligence,* 569-595

Collett TS, Cartwright BA (1983) Eidetic images in insects: their role in navigation. *Trends in Neurosci*, **6**, 101-105

Davis RL (1993) Mushroom bodies and *Drosophila* learning. *Neuron*, **11**, 1-14

Dill M, Wolf R, Heisenberg M (1993) Visual-pattern recognition in *Drosophila* involves retinotopic matching. *Nature* **365**, 751-753

Egelhaaf M, Borst A (1993) A look in the cockpit of the fly: visual orientation, algorithms and identified neurons. *J Neurosci.* **13**, 4563-4574

Flanagan D, Mercer AR (1989) Morphology and response characteristics of neurons in the deutocerebrum of the

brain in the honeybee *Apis mellifera. J Comp Physiol A,* **164,** 483-494

Franceschini N, Pichon JM, Blanes C, Brady JM (1992) From insect vision to robot vision. *Phil. Trans R Soc B.* **337**, 283-294

Freeman WJ, Skarda CA (1985) Spatial EEG patterns, non-linear dynamics and perception: the neo-Sherringtonian view." *Brain Research Reviews* **10**, 147-175.

Fonta C, Sun XJ, Masson C (1993) Morphology and spatial-distribution of bee antennal lobe interneurons responsive to odors. *Chem Senses,* **18**, 101-119

Fujimura K, Yokohari F, Tateda H (1991) Classification of antennal olfactory receptors of the cockroach, *Periplaneta americana* L. Zool Sci , **8**, 243-255

Gascuel J, Masson C (1991) A quantitative ultrastructural-study of the honeybee antennal lobe. *Tissue & Cell*, **23,** 341-355

Getz WM, Akers RP (1994a) Honey bee olfactory sensilla behave as integrated processing units. *Behavioral and Neural Biology,* in press.

Getz WM, Akers RP (1994b) Partitioning nonlinearities in the response of olfactory neurons to binary odors. *BioSystems* in press.

Gibson JJ (1979) *The ecological approach to visual perception.* Houghton Mifflin, Boston

Gilbert C, Strausfeld NJ (1992) Small-field neurons associated with oculomotor and optomotor control in muscoid flies - functional-organization. *J Comp Neurol* **316**, 72-86

Gronenburg W, Strausfeld NJ (1992) Premotor descending neurons responding selectively to local visual-stimuli in flies. *J Comp Neurol* **316**, 87-103

Haberly LB (1985) Neuronal circuitry in the olfactory cortex: anatomy and functional implications. *Chem Senses*, **10**, 219-238

Hansson BS, Ljungberg H, Hallberg E, Lofstedt C (1992) Functional specialisation in the olfactory glomeruli of a moth. *Science*, **256**, 1313-1315

Hopfield JJ (1991) Olfactory computation and object perception. *Proc Natl. Acad Sci USA.* **88**, 6462-6466

James AC, Osorio D (1994) Characterisation of columnar neurons in the medulla of the locust's optic lobe by system identification techniques. *J Comp Physiol A*, Submitted.

Kirschfeld K (1967) Die projektion der optischen Umwelt auf das Raster der Rhabdomere im Komplexauge von *Musca. Exp Brain Res*, **3**. 248-270

Konishi M (1990) Similar neural algorithms in different sensory systems and animals. *Cold Spring Harbor Symp Quant Biol*, **50**, 575-584

Laughlin SB (1987) Form and function in visual processing. *Trends in Neurosci.*, **10**, 478-483

Li Z, Hopfield JJ (1989) Modeling the olfactory bulb and its neural oscillatory processing. *Biol Cybern.*, **61**, 379-392

Malun D (1991) Inventory and distribution of synapses of identified uniglomerular projection neurons in the antennal lobe of *Periplaneta-americana*. *J Comp Neurol,* **305,** 348-360

Marr D (1982) *Vision,* Freeman, San Francisco

Masson C, Phamdelegue MH, Fonta C, Gascuel J, Arnold G, Nicolas G, Kerszberg M (1993) Recent advances in the concept of adaptation to natural odor signals in the honeybee, *Apis-mellifera* L. *Apidologie,* 169-194

Menzel R, Backhaus W (1991) Colour vision in insects. In: Gouras P (ed) *Vision and visual dysfunction Vol. VI: The perception of colour,* pp 262-293, Macmillan, London

Menzel R, Durst C, Erber J, Eichmüller S, Hammer M, Hildebrandt H, Mauelshagen J, Müller U, Rosenboom H, Rybak J, Schäfer S, Scheidler A (1994) The mushroom bodies in the honeybee: from molecules to behaviour. *Fortschritte Zool.,* **39,** 40-46

Meyer J-A, Guillot A (199) Simulation of adaptive behaviour in animats: review and prospect. In: Meyer J-A, Wilson SW (eds), *Proceedings of the first international conference on simulation of adaptive behaviour.* pp 2-14. MIT, Cambridge.

Michel WC, McClintock TS, Ache BW (1991) Inhibition of lobster olfactory receptor cells by an odor activated potassium conductance. *J Neurophysiol,* **65,** 446-453

Milde JJ, Seyan HS, Strausfeld NJ (1987) The neck motor system of the fly *Calliphora erythrocephala.* II. Sensory organisation. *J Comp Physiol A* **160,** 225-238

Mobbs PG (1982) The brain of the honeybee *Apis mellifera* 1. The connections and spatial organisation of the mushroom bodies. *Phil Trans R Soc Lond B,* **298,** 309-354

O'Carroll D (1993) Feature-detecting neurons in dragon-flies. *Nature,* **362,** 541-543

O'Carroll DC, Osorio D, James AC, Bush T (1992) Local feedback mediated via amacrine cells in the insect optic lobe. *J Comp Physiol A,* **171,** 447-455

Pitts W, McCulloch WS (1947) How we know universals: the perception of auditory and visual forms. *Bull Math Biophys,* **7,** 89-93

Purves D, Riddle DR, LaMantia A-S (1992) Iterated patterns of brain circuitry (or how the cortex gets its spots). *Trends in Neurosci,* **15,** 362-368

Rybak J, Menzel R (1993) Anatomy of the mushroom bodies in the honey bee brain: the neuronal connections of the alpha-lobe. *J Comp Neurol,* **334,** 444-465

Sarnat HB, Netsky MG (1981) *Evolution of the nervous system,* Oxford.

Shaw SR (1984) Early visual processing in insects. *J exp Biol,* **112,** 225-251

Shepherd GM (1991) Computational structure of the olfactory system. In: Davis JL, Eichenbaum H (eds.) *Olfaction: a model system for computational neuroscience.* pp 3-41. MIT, Cambridge Mass.

Smith BH, Getz WM (1994). Non-pheromonal olfactory processing in insects. *Ann. Rev. Entomol.* **39,** 351-375

Srinivasan MV (1992) How bees exploit optic flow - behavioral-experiments and neural models. *Phil Trans R Soc Lond B,* **337,** 253-259

Srinivasan MV, Zhang SW, Rolfe B (1993) Is pattern vision in insects mediated by cortical processing. *Nature,* **362,** 539-540

Strausfeld NJ (1976) Atlas of an insect brain. Springer, Berlin

Strausfeld NJ (1989) Insect vision and olfaction: Common design principles of neuronal organization. In: Strausfeld NJ, Singh RN (eds.) *Neurobiology of sensory systems.* pp. 319-353. Plenum, New York.

Strausfeld NJ, Lee J-K (1991) Neuronal basis for parallel visual processing in the fly, *Visual Neuroscience,* **7,** 13-33

Wolf R, Voss A, Hein S, Heisenberg M (1992) Can a fly ride a bicycle? *Phil Trans R Soc Lond B* **337,** 261-269

Zacharias D, Williams JLD, Meier T, Reichert H (1993) Neurogenesis in the insect brain - cellular-identification and molecular characterization of brain neuroblasts in the grasshopper embryo. *Development,* **118,** 941-955

The Interval Reduction Strategy for Monitoring Cupcake Problems

Paul R. Cohen, Marc S. Atkin, and Eric A. Hansen
Experimental Knowledge Systems Laboratory
Department of Computer Science, LGRC, Box 34610
University of Massachusetts, Amherst, MA 01003
{cohen,atkin,hansen}@cs.umass.edu
(413) 545-3638

Abstract

Monitoring is the process by which agents assess their environments. Most AI applications rely on periodic monitoring, but for a large class of problems this is inefficient. The *interval reduction* monitoring strategy is better. It also appears in humans and artificial agents when they are given the same set of monitoring problems. We implemented two genetic algorithms to evolve monitoring strategies and a dynamic programming algorithm to find an optimum strategy. We also developed a simple mathematical model of monitoring. We tested all these strategies in simulations, and we tested human strategies in a "video game." Interval reduction always emerged. Environmental factors such as error and monitoring costs had the same qualitative effects on the strategies, irrespective of their genesis. Interval reduction appears to be a general monitoring strategy.

1 Introduction

All embedded agents must monitor. Monitoring means seeing how plans are progressing, checking how much progress has been made, finding out what time it is, updating one's location, looking for obstacles, making sure that nothing has changed unexpectedly, and so on. Monitoring has been studied to some extent by AI researchers [9, 19, 21, 22, 25, 26], indeed, the earliest work on planning for the Shakey robot emphasized monitoring [5, 6], but AI research has little to say about monitoring *strategies*, about when and how often to monitor, and how these decisions depend on the dynamics of the environment [15]. Most systems monitor periodically, although this can be wasteful of effort.

Our interest in monitoring is only partly to find efficient strategies, however. We also suspect some monitoring strategies might be very general. If they are

determined largely by environment dynamics, then we might observe the same strategies in agents as different as bumblebees, children, and simulated robots. While we cannot report anything about bumblebees, we will describe a monitoring strategy called *interval reduction* that shows up in children and adults, and was evolved by two genetic programming algorithms that produce programs to control simulated robots. We will also develop a simple statistical model of the strategy and describe the performance of a policy based on the model. All these strategies have the same general performance, but no two are identical, which prompts us to ask which is best and how close is it to optimal. To answer these questions, we develop an optimal monitoring strategy by stochastic dynamic programming. The fact that it, too, is an interval reduction strategy lends further support to our belief that interval reduction might be very general; that is, we expect it to evolve in other agents in similar environments.

2 The Cupcake Problem

In 1985, Ceci and Bronfenbrenner described a monitoring task for children that they called the *cupcake problem* [4]. Each child was instructed by an older sibling (who served as a confederate in the experiment and collected the data) as follows: "We are going to put some cupcakes in the oven and they will be done in thirty minutes. You can play PacMan while you wait, but you mustn't forget to take the cupcakes out of the oven. To help you remember, there's a clock on the wall." Cleverly, the clock was put behind the child, so the sibling could easily see when the child turned around to monitor the time. In this way, Ceci and Bronfenbrenner obtained latencies between monitoring events. For our purposes two results are notable: First, all the children monitored quite frequently for the first few minutes; Ceci and Bronfenbrenner interpret this as a period of "calibration," getting one's internal clock in synch with real time. Second, ten-year-old children monitored approximately periodically for the remainder of the trial, but fourteen-year-olds monitored infrequently after the initial calibration, and

This work was supported by ARPA/Rome Laboratory under contract #F30602-91-C-0076 and under an Augmentation Award for Science and Engineering Research Training.

increased the frequency of monitoring as the deadline approached. We call this an interval reduction strategy because the interval between monitoring events is reduced as the deadline approaches.

Cupcake problems require an agent to traverse some time or distance, at which point an event or destination is expected. If the agent quits before reaching this point or overshoots it, a penalty is incurred. Sometimes the penalties are asymmetric around the goal point; for example, a racing driver loses a race if he or she doesn't "push the envelope," but might die by pushing too far. In some cupcake problems, an agent can backtrack if it overshoots the goal; in others, particularly temporal problems, this is not an option. It is characteristic of cupcake problems that the agent cannot be sure of its location without monitoring. In spatial problems this can be due to sensor or movement errors, or to movement of the goal point itself; in temporal problems the agent's internal clock might be inaccurate. We have studied one- and two-dimensional cupcake problems. Most of the results in this paper concern the former.

3   A Strategy for One-dimensional Cupcake Problems

In a one-dimensional cupcake problem, an agent moves toward its goal along a line, and errors in the agent's estimate of its location accumulate. For instance, if you close your eyes and start walking toward a wall, you will experience uncertainty about how far you are from the wall. This is a one-dimensional problem in the sense that drift away from a line normal to the wall is negligible, and, in any case, the painful error accumulates along this line. Assume you begin with an accurate estimate of the distance to the wall. You close your eyes and begin walking. When should you look again?

To answer the question we need to model how errors in estimates of location accumulate. We assume a simple but quite flexible *binomial* model: Let G be the distance an agent must travel by taking steps of size $1 \pm d$. On each step the agent will travel $1-d$ or $1+d$ with equal probability. If the agent takes N steps it will travel $D(N)$ units of distance. The mean of $D(N)$ is N and the variance of $D(N)$ is Nd^2.[1]

If $d > 0$ and the agent aims for the goal (i.e., $N = G$) then it will overshoot the goal with probability .5. Perhaps this is satisfactory, but often the agent will want a smaller probability. Let $D(N)_{.01}$ be a distance that the agent will exceed no more than 1% of the time it moves N steps. Because the distribution of $D(N)$ is binomial with $p = .5$ we may approximate it with a normal

distribution with mean N and variance Nd^2. If we can find a value above which 2% of the distribution of $D(N)$ lies, then we can expect the agent to exceed this value in 1% of its trials: The error model is symmetric, so every extremely large value of $D(N)$ is matched by an extremely small one. We know that 2% of a normal distribution lies more than 2.05 standard deviations above its mean. Thus, if an agent travels 10 steps, $D(10)$ will exceed $10 + 2.05(\sqrt{10d^2})$ no more than one percent of the time. In general,

$$D(N)_\alpha = N + z_{2\alpha}\sqrt{Nd^2}$$

where $z_{2\alpha}$ is the number of standard deviations above the mean of a normal distribution that cuts off the highest $100\alpha\%$ of the distribution.

To ensure that an agent does not exceed the desired distance, G, with greater than $\alpha/2$ probability, we set $D(N)_\alpha = G$ and solve the previous equation for N:

$$N = \frac{2G + d^2 z_\alpha^2 - (d z_\alpha \sqrt{4G + d^2 z_\alpha^2})}{2} \qquad (1)$$

We call this policy SIR for simple interval reduction. In all our experiments, we allowed the agent to quit when it came within one unit of its destination (otherwise Zeno would have the last laugh). For example, assume $d = .5$ and the agent wants a low probability, say .01 or less, of overshooting its destination $G = 100$ units away. SIR says the agent should travel

$$\frac{(2 \cdot 100 + .5^2 \cdot 2.05^2 - (.5 \cdot 2.05 \cdot \sqrt{4 \cdot 100 + .5^2 \cdot 2.05^2}))}{2}$$

$$= 90.26$$

units before monitoring again. This, then, is how far the agent *intends* to travel, but due to accumulating errors its actual location after 90.26 steps will be something other than 90.26. Let's say $D(90.26) = 93$. Now the agent must travel seven more units to its goal, and SIR says it should go 4.76 units before monitoring again. Note, however, that the total probability of overshooting the goal, denoted α_t, is now greater than .01 because the agent has taken this bet twice, once on each move. The probability that it will *not* overshoot during m moves is $(1-\alpha)^2$, so $\alpha_t = (1 - (1-\alpha))$, which is approximately $m\alpha$ for small m. Because an agent under the control of SIR rarely monitors more than three or four times (see below) it suffices to reduce α by a factor of five, say, to ensure a desired α_t.

4   An Optimal Policy for One-dimensional Cupcake Problems

SIR is suboptimal if there are costs for monitoring and penalties for overshooting (or falling short of) the goal.

---

[1] On each step the agent goes forward one unit and then forward or backwards by d units, so $D(N) = n + d(f - (n-f)) = 2df - n$, where f is the number of times in n steps the agent travelled forward by d. The variance of $2df - n$ is $4d^2\sigma_f^2$ and because f is binomial, with variance $n/4$, the variance of $D(N)$ is Nd^2.

If monitoring costs are large and penalties small, then monitoring isn't worthwhile, but SIR will do it anyway. Unfortunately the tradeoff between monitoring costs and penalties can be played out at every place the agent might stop to monitor. In fact, deciding when to monitor is a *sequential decision problem* [24]. Finding an optimal *control policy* is also a sequential decision problem. Actions can have delayed effects that must be considered in choosing the action to take in each state, and a policy that chooses actions solely for their immediate effects may not be optimal over the long term. Monitoring problems have an additional aspect: a control action need not be taken every time a process is monitored (in cupcake problems the control action is to quit—take the cupcakes out of the oven, quit walking toward the wall). Deciding whether to act immediately or wait and monitor again with the option of acting later is a sequential decision problem because a sequence of later opportunities for acting must be considered in deciding what to do [13, 14].

Stochastic dynamic programming is a well-known optimization technique for solving sequential decision problems, but monitoring problems differ from conventional control problems in two respects: It isn't necessary to take a control action each time a process is monitored, and it isn't necessary to observe the process at each time step. The first difference is easily modeled by including a null action in the controller's action set. The second and more significant difference comes into play if monitoring incurs a cost and the controller itself must decide when to observe the state of the process.

To compute a monitoring policy as well as a control policy, the key idea is to distinguish the time steps of a sequential decision problem from its decision points (or "stages"). At a decision point, the controller observes the state of the process and makes a decision. The assumption in conventional dynamic programming is that a decision point takes place at each time-step. This assumption is relaxed when computing a monitoring policy. When the controller is responsible for deciding when to observe the state of the process, it can wait an arbitrary number of time-steps before monitoring, as determined by its monitoring policy. However, this means that the conventional payoff functions and state transition probabilities must be extended so they are defined for an arbitrary number of time steps instead of a single step. Multi-step state transition probabilities and a multi-step payoff function let the controller *project* the state of a process and the payoff it expects to receive an arbitrary number of time-steps into the future. They also add complexity to the dynamic programming search. Hansen [14] has shown that the curse of dimensionality is ameliorated if utility is assumed to be a monotonic function of monitoring interval, and he also suggests finding an acceptable but coarse-grained time interval. This sug-

gestion was tested with good results in [23].

5 Genetic Algorithm Solutions to One- and Two-dimensional Cupcake Problems

Given parameterized functions describing when to monitor next, the MON system runs a genetic algorithm to determine the best parameter values—the ones that minimize the expected cost. For the cupcake problem, the function was $N = ct + b$. Given the time t remaining till the deadline, $N = ct + b$ computes when to monitor next. When $b = 0$ and $c > 0$, the resulting strategy is a form of interval reduction called *proportional reduction*; for instance, if $c = .8$ then the strategy would always go 80% of the remaining distance before monitoring again. We call c the proportional reduction constant. If $c = 0$ and $b > 0$ then the strategy is a form of periodic monitoring. MON also learned a maximum number of times to monitor. It would quit a trial when this number was exceeded or if it went past the goal. The cost function consisted of the cost of monitoring multiplied by the number of times the agent monitored, plus the squared distance to the goal upon trial termination. This cost was also the fitness measure used by the genetic algorithm. The rest of the genetic algorithm was very basic, too. It used roulette wheel selection, fixed mutation and crossing over rates, and a population size typically around 100 [1]. MON's strategies have been tested with results shown in Table 1.

Until now we have described rather abstract one-dimensional monitoring problems. LTB is a genetic programming algorithm that evolves monitoring strategies for simulated robots in two-dimensional worlds. The programs that control all the robots' activities, including monitoring, are expressed in a language of basic effector commands such as MONITOR, MOVE and TURNRIGHT, and some control structures such as loops and simple conditionals.

The robots in LTB monitor as they approach a particular position in the map, the *goal point*, which has an obstacle on it. Their aim is to get as close to this point as possible without hitting it. They have a sensor (activated by MONITOR) that returns the distance to the goal and a command TURNTOGOAL that points them in the right direction. Since overshooting the goal point is penalized highly, this problem is in fact an *asymmetric* cupcake problem.

The version of LTB that produced the data in Table 1 represents programs as linear lists of commands, instead of the tree structures common in the Genetic Programming field [16, 17]. Crossing over simply swaps two chunks of code between two individuals; mutation changes one command into another. Since the language is relatively simple, only a few constraints are needed to keep programs legal. Tournament selection with a tour-

```
Main program:
 NOP
 NOP
 TURNTOGOAL
 MOVEQUICK
 LOOP 5 time(s):
   MOVE
   MONITOR: object_distance
   NOP
   NOP
   NOP
   NOP
   NOP
   LOOP (object_distance)/10+1 times:
     LOOP 2 time(s):
       MOVE
       NOP
       MOVE
       NOP
*reached_goal* interrupt handler:
 DISABLE: reached_goal
 NOP
 LOOP (direction)/10+1 times:
   NOP
   NOP
*object_distance* interrupt handler:
 NOP
*hit_object* interrupt handler:
 NOP
 NOP
 NOP
 IF (object_distance) <= 75 THEN STOP
 MOVEQUICK
 MONITOR: reached_goal
```

Figure 1: A proportional reduction strategy generated by LTB

nament size of two was chosen as the selection scheme, the population size was set at 1000. Since genetic algorithms are not guaranteed to produce optimal results, the system was rerun 10 times on each training problem and the best program from these 10 runs was selected as the monitoring strategy for a case.

An example for a monitoring strategy evolved by LTB is given in Figure 1. The program is the best output of LTB for a test case corresponding to $d = 1.0$, $G = 150$. The top half the code is the main body of the program; the bottom half consists of the three *interrupt handlers* corresponding to the agent's sensors; they are not used, however[2]. The program itself is quite simple: After turning itself towards the goal via TURNTOGOAL, the agent goes into a finite loop. Within this loop, it will measure the distance to the goal (MONITOR: OBJECT_DISTANCE) and then loop over this distance. Since it is executing four MOVE commands for every ten distance units, it is moving 40% of the distance remaining after each monitoring action. The proportional reduction constant is therefore $c = .4$. The program will terminate after monitoring five times. Note that there is an extra MOVE instruction within the outermost loop, so the pure propor-

tional reduction strategy will be distorted very slightly. All the other LTB programs in this study did implement proportional reduction, however.

6   Adult Human Strategies for a One-dimensional Cupcake Problem

We implemented a "video game" cupcake problem for human subjects. On the display, the subject sees a line marked with ticks at regular intervals. When a trial begins, a ball is at the leftmost end of the line. The goal is to get the ball as close as possible to the end of the line, while simultaneously minimizing the number of moves required to do it and the penalty for falling short or overshooting the end. The subject moves the ball by pointing to a tick mark with the mouse. This is equivalent to selecting N in the SIR model or the dynamic programming or genetic algorithm policies. When the subject clicks on the line, the ball travels N steps of size $1 \pm d$. The subject is then assessed the cost of monitoring and is given the opportunity to quit the trial or move again toward the goal. A trial ends when the subject decides to move no closer to the goal, or if the ball overshoots the goal. On each trial the subject is told d, the error function parameter, and also the cost of monitoring. During training the subject is told that the penalty for stopping short of the goal or overshooting the goal is the squared distance to the goal. The cost of a trial is the penalty plus the number of monitoring events. No incentives (besides pride) are provided to encourage the subjects to minimize costs. We explain to the subjects that movement errors accumulate with distance, so if d is high, aiming for the end of the line can produce big errors and penalties. We also train the subjects on as many problems as they desire before presenting them with a set of test problems.

7   Comparing Strategies

We compared humans, MON parametric functions, optimal dynamic programming policies and SIR policies on a set of one-dimensional cupcake problems. LTB programs were tested on two-dimensional versions of very similar problems. The apparatus for humans was the "video game" described earlier. MON, SIR and the optimal policies were tested in a simulator, in which each trial went as follows:

Loop

1. Monitor to find distance to the goal

   - If beyond the goal, quit; else
   - If within one unit of the goal, quit; else

2. Decide N, the number of steps to move before monitoring again.

3. Take N steps of $1 \pm d$ units

---

[2]Interrupt handlers are the mechanism by which a robot can react directly to external events. Each program contained an interrupt handler for each kind of sensor the robot had. They executed automatically when the corresponding sensor value changed.

G	mon.-cost	optimal mon's	cost	SIR mon's	cost	MON mon's	cost	%	LTB mon's	cost	human mon's	cost
20	.5	1.94	.99	2.75	1.97	1.0	4.08	84				
50	.5	1.92	1.0	2.76	1.89	1.43	1.2	90				
100	.5	2.14	1.18	3.05	2.11	1.55	1.05	67				
150	.5	2.66	1.37	3.1	2.27	1.67	1.53	84				
20	1.0	1.65	1.81	2.65	2.68	1.0	3.38	58	1.0	15.33	2.07	2.51
50	1.0	1.9	1.96	3.11	3.35	1.6	2.03	87				
100	1.0	2.22	2.25	3.11	3.52	1.46	2.7	93				
150	1.0	2.34	2.38	3.92	3.52	1.55	2.32	84	2.0	65.33	2.72	3.18
20	2.0	1.34	3.06	2.68	4.34	1.0	3.75	60				
50	2.0	1.68	3.72	2.93	4.88	1.0	7.57	42				
100	2.0	1.86	4.2	2.93	5.35	1.5	3.52	90				
150	2.0	1.82	4.12	3.08	5.89	1.69	4.56	98				
20	10.0	1.0	11.37	2.22	14.74	1.0	12.05	21			1.84	19.42
50	10.0	1.05	13.19	2.53	17.71	1.0	16.44	52				
100	10.0	1.14	15.55	2.66	19.89	1.0	24.0	65				
150	10.0	1.3	16.78	2.75	20.69	1.0	24.97	51			2.11	23.1
20	.5	3.34	1.7	3.17	3.97	2.74	3.69	98				
50	.5	3.67	1.93	3.66	4.17	2.74	4.38	93				
100	.5	4.92	2.57	3.84	7.26	3.64	4.3	100				
150	.5	4.4	2.27	3.71	8.16	3.35	5.51	97				
20	1.0	3.36	3.45	3.10	5.14	1.85	7.00	80	1.0	38.92	2.13	4.42
50	1.0	3.77	3.88	3.48	5.6	2.66	5.02	88				
100	1.0	4.5	4.54	3.67	5.71	2.28	8.43	95				
150	1.0	4.34	4.5	3.54	14.26	2.42	8.29	92	5.0	37.38	2.9	10.35
20	2.0	2.36	5.77	3.42	8.08	1.91	9.65	96				
50	2.0	3.15	6.88	3.33	9.26	2.72	8.75	98				
100	2.0	3.75	8.13	3.89	9.98	2.79	10.99	99				
150	2.0	3.56	8.53	3.68	16.28	2.47	9.89	93				
20	10.0	1.48	19.27	3.05	23.86	1.0	32.79	66			1.90	24.43
50	10.0	2.06	25.37	3.37	26.66	1.75	28.15	92				
100	10.0	2.59	30.45	3.75	34.46	1.64	29.26	67				
150	10.0	2.54	29.44	4.01	38.02	1.72	32.76	82			2.34	32.54

Table 1: The results of the cupcake experiments for all five domains; the top section is for $d = 0.333$, the bottom section for $d = 1.0$.

The three approaches differed only in how they selected N, with MON consulting its parametric equation $N = ct + b$, SIR consulting Equation 1, and the optimal approach consulting its policy. The apparatus for LTB was the two-dimensional simulated robot world, described earlier. Robots try to get as close to a point in the world as they can; bumping into it or moving past it is equivalent to running off the end of the line in the humans' video game or going beyond the goal in the simulator, above. All these conditions terminate the trial.

Trials differed in the following factors and values:

G, the initial distance to the goal. The four values of G were 20, 50, 100, 150. In the two-dimensional world, G was the length of a line between the robot's starting location and the goal object.

M, the cost of monitoring. We tried four monitoring costs: .5, 1, 2, and 10

d, the error function parameter. In pilot experiments we varied d from .2 to .5, but when we ran human subjects we discovered that these errors were too small to bother them. The current experiment is for $d = .333$ and $d = 1.0$.

The penalty function. We set the penalty to be the square of the distance between the goal and the location of the agent when it quits a trial. We tried a cubic function but it made little difference to monitoring strategies.

We did not run humans in all 32 conditions of this experiment, fearing that fatigue would affect their performance. Instead, we ran two levels of each of three factors: $M = 1, 10$, $d = .333, 1.0$, and $G = 20, 150$: Each of six subjects was tested on ten problems in each condition, for a total of 80 trials per subject. MON, SIR and the optimal policies were tested in 100 trials in each of the

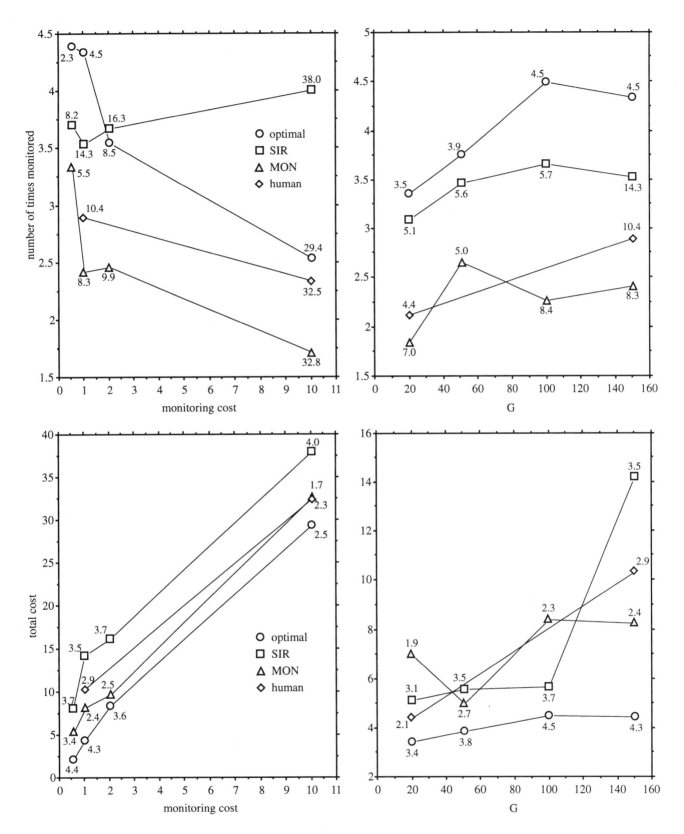

Figure 2: A selection of graphs for $d = 1.0$, illustrating data from Table 1. The graphs on the left are plotted for $G = 150$, the ones on the right for a monitoring cost of 1.0. The numbers at the nodes indicate total costs for the top graphs, and number of times monitored for the lower ones.

32 conditions. LTB was trained and tested in just four conditions. We have always had considerable difficulties getting LTB to consistently evolve monitoring strategies, even when the environment was designed in such a way that monitoring strategies were favored with higher fitness values [3].

The results of this experiment are shown in Table 1. Most data are two numbers: first, the mean number of monitoring events in a trial, and second, the mean *cost* of a trial. This cost is the number of monitoring events times the cost of monitoring, plus the penalty for falling short of the goal or overshooting it (the square of the final distance to the goal). For example, for $d = .333, G = 20, M = .5$, the optimal strategy monitors 1.94 times on average and incurrs an average penalty of .99. Data for MON include, in italics, the number of times in 100 trials that the fittest agent monitored at all during the trial. The summary statistics are based on this subset. Six trials of 448 with the human subjects were discarded because they had huge trial costs—incurred when the subjects became confused about whether a trial had ended—that skewed the means and variances.

Data from the lower half of Table 1, for $d = 1.0$, are plotted in Figure 2. The top two graphs show the average number of monitoring events plotted against G and M, respectively, and the numbers represent mean trial costs; the lower graphs show mean trial costs plotted against G and M, and the numbers represent mean monitoring incidence. Our principal observations follow:

All the agents used an interval reduction or proportional reduction strategy. The genetic algorithms, MON and LTB evolved other strategies, but they never performed as well as proportional reduction. In other words, the fitness of the proportional reduction agents was higher.

The interval reduction and proportional reduction strategies are very efficient compared to, say, periodic monitoring. Note that the optimal strategy never monitored more than five times and, averaged over all trials and conditions, it monitored 2.52 times per trial. It's easy to show that, except for very short distances, a periodic monitoring strategy will incur high penalties if it monitors as infrequently as an interval or proportional reduction strategy.

As expected, the incidence of monitoring generally decreased with M, the cost of monitoring. (The exception is SIR which doesn't take the cost of monitoring into account.) The incidence of monitoring generally increased with d, the parameter of the error function, and G, the initial distance to the goal. Note also that MON evolved a monitoring stategy least often when the cost of monitoring was high, but more often when error (D) was high. Agents monitor because they must—because error or initial distance is high.

Not surprisingly, the optimal dynamic programming strategies had the lowest trial costs in all conditions.

Individual human subjects had remarkably consistent average trial costs, yet some monitored often and others infrequently. A one-way analysis of variance showed no significant difference over subjects on mean trial cost (the means ranged from 13.62 to 18.2); but individuals differed significantly ($p < .0001$) on their mean numbers of monitoring episodes (ranging from 1.8 to 3.23 per trial). This suggests that some people kept trial costs down by monitoring relatively often and incurring small penalties, while others avoided monitoring costs and occasionally incurred large penalties.

Human trial costs were statistically indistinguishable from those of the optimal strategy when the error (d) and the monitoring cost (M) were both low. In the other six conditions, the optimal strategy outperformed humans (two-sample t tests, $p < .0001$), who tended to monitor too much when M was high and too little when M was low.

The SIR strategy paid dearly for monitoring too often. This is partly because it doesn't take M into account, partly because it treats monitoring decisions are independent. In trials with $G = 150, d = 1.0$, for example, SIR would find itself, say, six distance units shy of the goal and it would decide to move, say, four units. When the error was high it would sometimes not move at all, or might move only one unit. At this point a human will say, "I paid for a monitoring event and yet I moved no closer to my goal; I won't let that happen again. This time I will aim closer to the goal and I will just have to risk overshooting it." The optimal strategy will have compiled similar reasoning into its policy. But SIR will treat the next movement decision exactly as the previous one. We observed sequences of up to six useless or nearly useless monitoring events in a single trial.

The MON strategies don't perform well (compared with the optimal strategy) when initial distance to the goal G is low. They usually monitor just once in these conditions and they run up big penalties for overshooting the goal. It's surprising that better strategies don't evolve, given that MON is a simple parameter optimization algorithm.

The LTB strategies produce much more variable results than any others, in part because LTB robots are tested in a two-dimensional environment where they wander around instead of moving on a line toward the goal. Nevertheless, in this experiment and others, involving hundreds of trials with LTB and other genetic programming approaches to two-dimensional cupcake problems [2, 3] we have never observed a fitter strategy than interval reduction.

8   Discussion

Given the opportunity, adults and genetic algorithms will use interval reduction to solve cupcake problems. Dynamic programming tells us that interval reduction is optimal. So why is periodic monitoring, which is much less efficient, the norm?

One answer is that periodic monitoring always works, whereas interval reduction assumes that the agent monitors to find out where it is with respect to a goal. If the agent doesn't have a goal, or if the environment provides no information about it, then interval reduction won't help. Suppose your goal is to detect an event and you know the probability that it will happen in any time interval, but it happens without warning (i.e., you are monitoring a stationary Bernoulli process). If C is the cost per time unit of not detecting the event and H is the cost of monitoring for it, and p is its probability in each time unit, we can show easily that the optimal interval between monitoring is $\sqrt{2H/Cp}$. This periodic strategy is necessary because absolutely nothing is known about the event besides its probability of occurring, and nothing is learned about it by monitoring (other than whether it happened). However, if monitoring provides estimates about when or where future events will occur, then we believe periodic monitoring is inferior to interval reduction.[3]

Another answer goes like this: Periodic monitoring might be inefficient, but monitoring is free, so who cares? Monitoring is not free, of course, but in distributed architectures it can be offloaded to dedicated processors and so appears to be free. What happens when one of these processors detects something? It sends a message to other processors who must monitor their messages, or it sends an interrupt. In the first case monitoring obviously isn't free, and in the second it is bad design if the dedicated processor learns anything from its monitoring about the system's goals. Norman and Bobrow [20] show convincingly that distributed systems can avoid catastrophic failure if they adopt the *principle of continuously available output*, in effect sharing intermediate results among components. If monitoring provides information, it shouldn't be held privately by the dedicated monitoring processor, but if it is shared with other processors, they must attend to it, and monitoring is not free.

We have not found any convincing reasons to prefer periodic monitoring over interval reduction, except in situations where an agent has no goal or monitoring provides no information about progress toward the goal. Both "goal" and "progress" should be broadly construed, because the interval reduction strategy appears to be preferred in spatial and temporal domains; in one and two dimensions; when errors are due to sensor inac-

curacy or movement inaccuracy; when penalty functions are symmetric or asymmetric, continuous or discrete; by agents as diverse as humans and simple, simulated robots, evolved by genetic programming.

Acknowledgements

This research is supported by ARPA/Rome Laboratory under contract #F30602-91-C-0076 and under an Augmentation Award for Science and Engineering Research Training. The US Government is authorized to reproduce and distribute reprints for governmental purposes notwithstanding any copyright notation hereon.

References

[1] Atkin, M.S., 1991. Research Summary: Using a Genetic Algorithm to Monitor Cupcakes. *EKSL Memo #24*, Experimental Knowledge Systems Laboratory, University of Massachusetts, Amherst.

[2] Atkin, M. & Cohen, P.R., 1993. Genetic Programming to Learn an Agent's Monitoring Strategy. CMPSCI Technical Report 93-26. University of Massachusetts, Amherst.

[3] Atkin, M.S. & Cohen, P.R., 1994. Learning Monitoring Strategies: A Difficult Genetic Programming Application. *The First IEEE Conference on Evolutionary Computation*. Forthcoming.

[4] Ceci, S.J. & Bronfenbrenner, U., 1985. "Don't forget to take the cupcakes out of the oven": Prospective memory, strategic time-monitoring, and context. *Child Development*, Vol. 56. Pp. 152-164.

[5] Fikes, R., 1971. Monitored execution of robot plans produced by STRIPS. *Proc. IFIP Congress 71*, Ljubljana, Yugoslavia (August 23-28, 1971), pp. 189-194.

[6] Fikes, R., Hart, P. & Nilsson, N., 1972. Learning and executing generalized robot plans. *Artificial Intelligence* 3(4), pp. 251-188. Reprinted in: Allen, Hendler, and Tate (eds.), *Readings in Planning*, Morgan Kaufman, San Mateo, CA.

[7] Firby, R.J., 1987. An investigation into reactive planning in complex domains. *AAAI 87*, pp. 202-206.

[8] Georgeff, M. & Lansky, A., 1987. Reactive reasoning and planning. *AAAI 87*, pp. 677-682. Reprinted in: Allen, Hendler, and Tate (eds.), *Readings in Planning*, Morgan Kaufman, San Mateo, CA.

[9] Ghallab, M., Alami, R. & Chatila, R., 1988. Dealing with time in planning and execution monitoring. In:

---

[3] We have not been able to prove this as a general proposition, but we have proved it for special cases and we have the empirical evidence presented earlier.

Robotics Research: The Fourth International Symposium, ed. by Bolles and Roth, MIT Press, pp. 431-443.

[10] Goldberg, D.E., 1989. *Genetic Algorithms in Search, Optimization, and Machine Learning.* Addison-Wesley, Reading, MA.

[11] Goldberg, D.E. & Kalyanmoy, D., 1991. A Comparative Analysis of Selection Schemes Used in Genetic Algorithms, in *Foundations of Genetic Algorithms* (Gregory J.E. Rawlins ed.), pp. 69-93. Morgan Kaufman, San Mateo, CA.

[12] Hanks, S., 1990. Practical temporal projection. *AAAI 90*, pp. 158-163.

[13] Hansen, E.A., 1992. Note on monitoring cupcakes. *EKSL Memo #22.* Experimental Knowledge Systems Laboratory, Computer Science Dept., University of Massachusetts, Amherst.

[14] Hansen, E.A., 1992. Learning A Decision Rule for Monitoring Tasks with Deadlines. CMPSCI Technical Report 92-80. University of Massachusetts, Amherst.

[15] Hansen, E.A., 1994. Monitoring the execution of robot plans: A survey. In preparation for *AI Magazine.*

[16] Koza, J.R., 1992. *Genetic Programming: On the Programming of Computers by Means of Natural Selection and Genetics.* MIT Press, Cambridge, MA.

[17] Koza, J.R. & Rice, J.P., 1992. Automatic Programming of Robots using Genetic Programming. *AAAI 92*, Pp. 194-207

[18] McDermott, D., 1992. Robot Planning. *AI Magazine*, Summer 1992, pp. 55-79.

[19] Musliner, D., Durfee, E. & Shin, K., 1991. Execution monitoring and recovery planning with time. *Proceedings IEEE Seventh Conference on Artificial Intelligence Applications*, pp. 385-388.

[20] Norman, D.A & Bobrow, D.G. 1974. On data-limited and resource-limited processes. Xerox Technical Report CSL 74-2. Xerox Palo Alto Research Center.

[21] Schoppers, M., 1992. Representing the plan monitoring needs and resources of robotic systems. *Proceedings of the Third Annual Conf. on AI, Simulation and Planning in High Autonomy Systems*, pp. 182-187.

[22] Schoppers, M., 1992. Building plans to monitor and exploit open-loop and closed-loop dynamics. *Proceedings 1st International Conference on Artificial Intelligence Planning Systems*, ed. J. Hendler, pp. 204-213. Morgan Kaufman, San Mateo, CA.

[23] St. Amant, R., Kuwata, Y., & Cohen, P.R., 1993. Reactive Planning with Dynamic Programming Envelopes. CMPSCI Technical Report, University of Massachusetts

[24] Sutton, R.S., 1990. Integrated architectures for learning, planning, and reacting based on approximately dynamic programming. *Proceedings of the Seventh International Conference on Machine Learning*, pp. 216-224.

[25] Tate, A., 1984. Planning and condition monitoring in a FMS. *Proceedings of the International Conference on Flexible Automation Systems.* Institute of Electrical Engineers, London, July 1984, pp. 62-69.

[26] Wilkins, D., 1985. Recovering from execution monitoring errors in SIPE. *Computational Intelligence 1*, pp. 33-45.

Visual control of altitude and speed in a flying agent

Fabrizio Mura   **Nicolas Franceschini**

C.N.R.S/LNB Neurocybernetics study group
31, Chemin Joseph Aiguier
13402 MARSEILLE cedex 09 - FRANCE
frchini@frmop11.bitnet
fax: 33/91 22 08 75

Abstract.

A low level visual system was developed to control the altitude and speed of an artificial agent inspired by flying insects. We show that the principle of *motion vision* can be used to advantage in navigational tasks such as terrain following, cruise control and obstacle avoidance. The basic behavioural units of the agent are structured in a subsumption architecture implemented in the form of elementary distributed reflex blocks. Our multidisicplinary approach bears relevance to the field of visually guided navigation of artificial aircrafts while helping elucidate how natural flying creatures such as birds and insects have solved the control problems involved in performing visually guided navigation.

1. Introduction.

Visual perception of the environment is essential to the control of navigation in many animals such as birds, insects and fish which have to cope with a 3D environment. Vision helps these animals to regulate their course taking into account their own weight, dimensions and aerodynamic structure in spite of disturbances occurring in the surrounding medium. This situation contrasts with the world of man made mobiles, which after one century of design still require natural (human) visual system to control their navigation. Many insects have developed a robust optomotor response which allows them to maintain a course while avoiding obstacles even when they have no *a priori* knowledge of their (unstructured) environment. Several experiments have shown that in a given sensorimotor task, the wide variety of behaviours exhibited by different species of insects reflects their ability to adapt in a specific way to environmentally hostile conditions.

Our goal is to design appropriate reflex behaviours for the navigation of an "artificial flying insect", i.e. for the visual control of its flight altitude and speed. Although we are not attempting to validate any particular existing biological model, this work can be said to be an exercise in computational neuroethology [1], [4] for two reasons: first, we are applying a biological principle termed "motion parallax" that was described long ago by Helmholtz [20] (see also [17], [24]); secondly, we are using biologically inspired sensors (Local Motion Detectors or L.M.D.'s) as the basic building blocks of the visual system. Although considerable attention has focused on this type of sensor in biology, it is not commonly used for range finding in robotics [10], [19]. We denote our Artificial Insect ArIn which serves as a testbench for the study of various visually driven flight control units.

2. Reactive control.

Because flying insects use vision to control their flight and aerobatics, they constitute a rich source of inspiration for the design of visually-guided aircraft. Our multidisciplinary approach focuses on problems involving low-level, biologically inspired visual systems which are embedded in a minimalist control loop, namely one of the reflex type. The overall sensorimotor loop has the following characteristics (see figure 1):

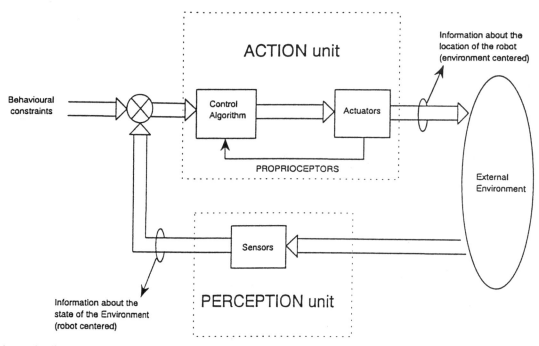

Figure 1. Schematic diagram of a basic behavioural unit. This scheme does not give any details about the subsumption of various units.

1.Tight coupling between the perception and action modules. Both have a minimal number of intermediary processing steps.

2.Output variables asynchronous with respect to the incoming sensory input.

3.No memorization of the sensors' past inputs, and hence no computational overload.

4.No symbolic higher order representation of the input to the motor units.

The processes on which the control loop is based are hardwired and the subsumption rules reflect the priorities between various loops. Approaches of this kind involving functional decomposition of elementary tasks has proven to be successful in designing autonomous land vehicles [2], [7], [27], [28].

3. Local Motion Detectors (L.M.D.'s) as smart range finders.

The compound eyes of arthropods, with their low optical resolution, are dedicated to some basic visual tasks, one of which is motion detection [11], [18], [23], [29]. Insects use their own movements in space to gather information about the external surroundings [3], [6], [25], [32], [33], [34]. Let us adapt the principle of "motion parallax" [20], [17], [24] to a terrain surveying agent. When a sighted agent moves from O to O' at speed V (fig. 2), a contrast point M

(representing the border of a physical object) successively strikes two points on its retina, the visual axes of which are separated by an angle $\Delta\varphi$. If the eye of the agent is able to measure the delay time Δt elapsing between these two excitations, it can retrieve the absolute distance D to the object:

$$D(O,M)=V.\Delta t.\sin(\varphi)/\sin(\Delta\varphi) \qquad (1)$$

We note that the speed of the agent is explicitly taken into account in the computation as a *necessary* component for measuring the perceived depth. This principle was readily used to control the steering of a *terrestrial* robot equipped with a compound eye, running at 50 cm/s in an obstacle laden environment [15], [16], [28]. Other authors have followed a similar approach [8], [30]. The use of Local Motion Detectors (L.M.D.'s) as passive range finders is all the more interesting since they can cope with an extensive range of speeds.

Furthermore, the computation of distance to object using an L.M.D. sensor does not impose any restriction on the physical nature of the obstacles (such as the inclination or the texture of their surface) since the optoelectric chain is sensitive only to the local variations in light intensity $\Delta I/I_{avg}$ i.e. to the contrast of the objects. This feature is of interest for two reasons. On the one hand, it can be used to design a geometrical model of a physical environment which is sufficiently well adapted to the low level vision process. On the other hand, this representation of the world is appropriate for simulations since we are able to reconstruct the overall shape of the obstacles by plotting the set of measurements made by ArIn during a simulation run (see figure 5b).

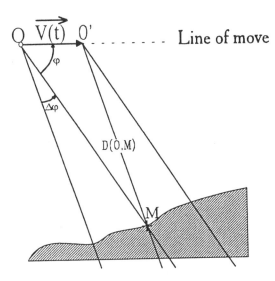

Figure 2. A Local Motion Detector (LMD) used as a "passive range finder". The LMD centered on O has two visual axes separated by $\Delta\varphi$. The movement of the LMD from O to O' at speed V yields the distance D to the contrast point M according to Equ.(1).

4. The L.M.D. eye.

The computation of the optical flow can be performed by a set of local movement detectors which process input signals from adjacent pairs of photoreceptors, the set of which form an artificial compound eye thus referred to as an L.M.D. eye. The L.M.D.s are meant to be hardwired units as in [16] and they make up the first computing layer behind the photoreceptor layer of the eye.

The non-uniform sampling strategy that was discovered in the eye of some insects, in particular flies [5], [13], was ascribed to the properties of the optic flow field [28]. A gradual increase in the angular resolution towards the frontal part of the visual field compensates for the gradual decrease in the flow field near the heading direction. For the sake of convenience, we place ourselves in a 2-Dimensional environment consisting of a vertical slice of the work space. Here again we chose a non-uniform optical gradient, but it is such that ArIn can sample a flat part of the ground in equidistant steps with full detectability over its eye (see

figure 3a). By imposing a minimal interommatidial angle of 1°, we limit the visual field and create a "blind zone" which extends down to $\varphi_0 = -24.4°$ below the horizon. The gradient is symmetrical with respect to the vertical axis and the eye has a constant radius of curvature R_{eye}. When performing a pure translation, we build up the "pie-slice" shaped detection field of the eye (figure 3b) which consists of two regions: a) the region of total detection, where any contrast point is detected by at least two optical axes, and b) the region of probable detection, where a contrast point is detected by at least one optical axis.

5. Feasibility through simulation.

The various behavioural tasks of animat ArIn are completely simulated with the contribution of three main cores: a) the optoelectrical system simulates an L.M.D. eye inspired by the compound eye of the fly where the activity of each receptor cell is fully described by optoelectric equations; b) the navigation control system combines exteroceptive and proprioceptive information, computes the outputs of the various modules, and evaluates the new state of ArIn; c) the environment, which "closes the loop" simulates a set of obstacles which are geometrically defined by the local differences in luminance.

The whole loop is controlled by two distinct temporal sequences: a) the acquisition phase is launched for a time step T during which motion detection is performed; b) at the end of the acquisition phase, the control phase instantly computes the subsequent state. The synchronized control after acquisition is not necessarily optimal because we note that the animat runs in a "motor open loop" during time T as well as a "visual open loop" during the control phase. It is more important to have a fast response of the control loop, at least fast enough to be called "real time" if it were implemented in a real robot. (As an example, response times of the order of 25 to 30 ms have been found for visuomotor control in the chasing behaviour of the male *Syritta Pipiens* [5]).

The functional principle of the Elementary Motion Detector is inspired by the model established for the fly *Musca Domestica* [14]: the optoelectric implementation developed in [16], [28] makes it possible to take into account any errors (in particular "correspondence errors") liable to occur in the real world. Consequently we are able to test the robustness of the various subsumption modules to errors resulting from the poor resolution of the eye.

6. Animat ArIn.

ArIn moves in a medium with a homogenous density where its trajectory is subject to a viscous drag and possible aerial disturbances. In the 2-Dimensional approximation, ArIn 's flight is governed by dynamic equations involving the forces of thrust and lift. The system of equations is refered to the center of gravity:

$$T - D_{fx} = m.dV_x/dt \qquad (2)$$
$$L - m.g - D_{fy} = m.dV_y/dt \qquad (3)$$

where T is forward thrust, L vertical lift, D_{fx} and D_{fy} orthogonal components of the translational drag. It is worth noting that these equations neither take into account the specific model of the system nor the way in which various forces are generated and may match the flight system of insects (frequency and amplitude of wingbeat, orientation of wingbeat plane) or artificial rotorcraft (rotor blade pitch, orientation of virtual rotation plane). Furthermore, we apply two main restrictions to our model: first, ArIn is able to change its flight direction solely by changing the lift to thrust ratio (fig.3.a). The orientation of its body remains constant during flight and any required change of flight direction is set by controlling thrust and lift independently. Secondly, ArIn's head is not free to rotate around the pitch axis and stays in a horizontal position during flight. This implies that the position of the pole of the translational optic flow is likely to vary around the eye. Theoretically, the heading direction can be internally computed using an inertial navigation system [12], [31] or by searching for the "focus of expansion" (FOE) [22] across the eye.

It is known from experiments on flies such as *Musca* [32], *Drosophila* [35], *Calliphora* [21] and other insects that changes in postural body position have a stabilizing effect on the flight course as well as producing a change in the direction of the flight course. The ArIn model shall not be based on any particular insect's flight; our goal is rather to investigate basic solutions for a flight controller using biologically inspired visual processing units for the specific tasks of controlling altitude and speed of flight.

7. Decomposition of the basic tasks.

Studies of the flight of *Musca* [32] have shown that the insects perform characteristic translatory "bouts" often followed by fast changes in orientation. Following the description of ArIn's flight mode in section 6, the useful information which is to be processed is directly available during the elementary translatory steps of the animat.

Given the behavioural nature of the task studied here, we investigate the interactions between the insect and the environment in a heuristic manner, and the various kinds of behaviour generated in a given situation are assessed qualitatively. Motor coordination between the basic behavioural units is achieved by the subsumption of elementary units in a vertical hierarchy [2], which gives the following advantages:

- Flexibility in the design of the elementary units, the inputs of which may or may not be independent. The subsumption rules define the priorities between different layers.
- Incremental and evolutive design: adding supplementary units does not alter the structures which are already in place.

We decide to decompose the visual guidance task into three main units: a. Obstacle avoidance b. Terrain following at a given altitude c. Regulation of forward speed. The definition of tasks 1. and 2. involves that they are mutually exclusive, since obstacle avoidance consists of "rejecting" any potentially hazardous obstacles from the security region. The various tasks can be described as follows:

a. Obstacle avoidance: when detecting an obstacle in direction φ_i at a distance D_i which is within a **security margin** D_{isec}:

$$D_i \leq D_{isec} \qquad (4)$$

with $D_{isec} = D_{0sec} \cdot \sqrt{(1 + i^2 . No^2)} \qquad (5)$

(N_0 is the normalized optical resolution of the L.M.D.eye ($N_0 = \tan(\Delta\varphi_{LMD}\#24)$) and D_{0sec} is the safety distance defined at -90° with respect to the horizon), ArIn generates a vertical lift equal to $L_{max}/2.[1 + (\varphi_e + \varphi_0 - \pi)/(2.\varphi_0 - \pi)]$ where φ_e is taken from $\min_i(D_i/D_i \leq D_{isec})$, φ_0 is the angle of the closest optical axis to the horizon and L_{max} is the maximal available lift.

b. Terrain following at altitude D_{0fol}: ArIn tries to maintain the set of obstacles detected at time (k-1) in its visual field at time (k) by following a predefined instruction which takes into account obstacles verifying:

$$(D_{isec} + \Delta D_{ssec}) \leq D_i \leq (D_{ifol} + \Delta D_{sfol}) \qquad (6)$$

with D_{ifol} related to D_{0fol} in the same way as in equation (5). The contribution of each obstacle to the output lift is:

$$L_{fol} = 1/\Sigma k_i.\Sigma[k_i.(1-D_i/D_{ifol})] \quad (7)$$

The constant weighting coefficients k_i are derived from the optical gradient of the eye (see figure 4) and their values are set so as to enhance the sensitivity to the obstacles detected in the anterior region rather than the posterior region. When performing terrain following at an altitude D_{0fol}, ArIn modulates its lift with the obstacles which are detected within the range $[D_{isec}+\Delta D_{ssec} ; D_{ifol}+\Delta D_{sfol}]$, where ΔD_{ssec} is the sensitivity to obstacle avoidance and ΔD_{sfol} the sensitivity to terrain following.

c. Regulation of the forward speed: the principle which is adopted for the <u>regulation of</u>

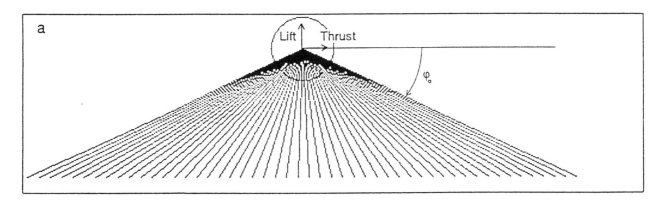

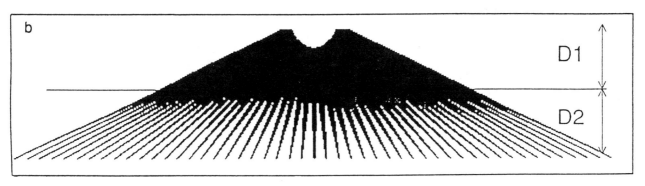

Figure 3.a: layout of the visual axes of the 2-Dimensional L.M.D. eye of ArIn surveying the terrain below. Number of facets N_f=50, number of L.M.D.'s=49, normalized resolution N_0=0.09.The closest visual axis to the horizon lies at φ_0= -24.4°. The orientation of the eye remains fixed in space (no pitching) during flight. 3.b: the region of detection of the L.M.D. eye consists of a region of total detection (D1) and a region of probable detection (D2).

<u>the forward speed</u> is as follows: ArIn modulates its forward thrust depending on the differential detection of obstacles between the anterior and posterior visual fields. This allows ArIn to modulate its forward speed in a relatively simple manner, according to the occupied space which is directly in its field of view. The forward thrust is a function of a threshold difference between average distances projected on the vertical axis:

$$T=Threshold[D_{avg.aft}-D_{avg.fore}] \quad (8)$$

with
$$D_{avg.aft}=1/N_{aft}.\Sigma_i^{ni} D_{iaft}(k).\sin(\varphi_i) \text{ if } ni\neq0$$
$$2/N_{tot}.\Sigma_i D_{iMaft}.\sin(\varphi_i) \quad \text{else} \quad (9)$$
and
$$D_{avg.fore}=1/N_{fore}.\Sigma_j^{nj} D_{jfore}(k).\sin(\varphi_j) \text{ if } nj\neq0$$
$$2/N_{tot}.\Sigma_j D_{jMfore}.\sin(\varphi_j) \quad \text{else} \quad (10)$$

and $D_i \in [D_{isec} ; D_{iM}]$
This computation is carried out regardless of the number of obstacles detected and is quite robust in the presence of any errors due to correspondence problems

in the E.M.D.'s. When no obstacles are detected in the fore region (or the aft region), distances D_{iaft} (resp. D_{ifore}) are compared to the maximum ranges D_{iMfore} (resp D_{iMaft}) since by symmetry, we have:

$$\Sigma_i D_{iMfore}.\sin(\varphi_i)=\Sigma_i D_{iMaft}.\sin(\varphi_i)=D_{0M} \quad (11)$$
$$0<i<N_{tot}/2$$

where D_{0M} is the maximum range at -90° to the heading direction.

By projecting the distances onto the vertical axis, we normalize the input values from the aft region with respect to the fore region because *a priori* neither the number of input data nor their angular positions are likely to correspond in the two regions.

For a given translation at speed V during the data acquisition cycle time T, the range D_M in the direction φ with respect to the heading direction is [26]:

$$D_M = V.T.\sin(\varphi)/\sin(\Delta\varphi) \quad (12)$$

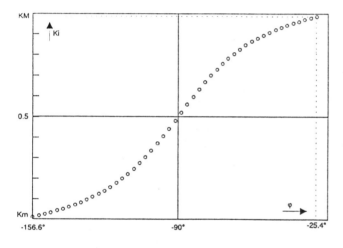

Figure 4. Distribution graph of the weighting coefficients k_i for the 49 L.M.D.'s of the terrain following eye as a function of the elevation φ of each optical axis. For the simulations $K_M=0.95$; $K_m=0.05$.

Assuming that we work at a constant T the range of vision of the L.M.D. eye is proportional to the speed of travel of ArIn. The speed regulation algorithm must actually take the range of total detection $D_M/2$ as a constraint (see figure 3b).

When ArIn is performing terrain following and detects a potentially hazardous obstacle at time (k), the forward deceleration has to be tailored to the range $D_M/2$ in order ensure avoidance at time (k+1). This imposes a limitation on the value of the deceleration

whatever the regulation of the forward speed dictates. In fact, the detection of an obstacle triggers a deceleration with a geometric constraint on the value of the computed speed. At time (k+1), for each previously detected obstacle at distance D(k), the geometrical speed constraint is:

$$V_x(k+1)>D(k)/T.\sin(\Delta\varphi)/\sin(\varphi+\Delta\varphi) \quad (13)$$

8. Simulations.

In figure 5 we present 3 simulations obtained with different constraints; the first two are unsuccessful, but in the third one, the agent succeeds in flying over a particularly hazardous terrain consisting of the crossection of an asymmetric ditch and a pole. The simulations implementing the aforementioned set of three behavioural units (see §6) lead to the trajectories shown in figures 5a and 5c. In 5a ArIn, launched at 130 cm/s, correctly follows the terrain at the preset altitude of 80 cm (TRAJ1) and its forward speed is regulated without the deceleration constraint of equation (13). In the region between A and B, the animat lifts off (because it registers a distance underestimation due to a correspondence error in the posterior part of its visual field) instead of decreasing its altitude as it would have done in order to respond to the downhill slope. The shaded area at B describes an "open loop" descent to the ground due to the fact that ArIn has detected no obstacles during the acquisition (call it a series of "No Detect" periods). As soon as visual contact is made with the wall, the forward speed is decreased to its minimal value (30cm/s) at point C. Past C, the detection of the flat piece of ground does not permit ArIn to accelerate forwards. Instead, ArIn regularly tries to come back to the terrain following altitude of 80 cm but repeatedly descends in an "open loop" whenever there is a "No Detect" period (corresponding to the subsequent shaded areas). Upon seeing the pole (to the right of figure 5a), the forward speed decreases to its minimal value (so that the range of vision is only 33.66cm) and the animat cannot avoid colliding near the top of the pole.

In figure 5c, TRAJ2 (launched at 100 cm/s) is an attempt to perform *low altitude* terrain following at only 60cm above the ground. Unlike what happened in fig. 5a there is no unexpected lift-off due to correspondence errors, but the failure of TRAJ2 is due to ArIn's inability to see directly ahead when close to the wall (this limitation results from the absence of visual axes at the front).

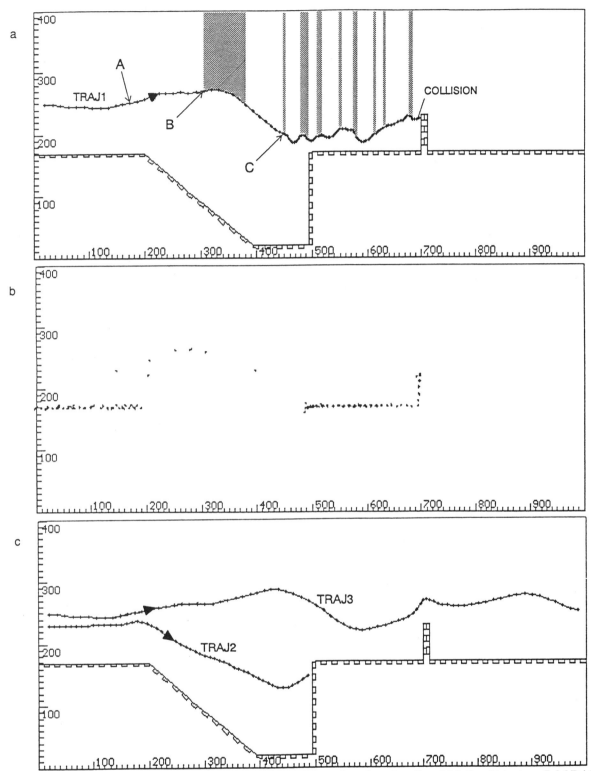

figure5: flight trajectories of the mobile agent equipped with a compound eye based on Local Motion Detectors (L.M.D.'s) and having a restricted, downward-looking field of view (see fig. 3.a). (5.a): simulation of speed regulation without any deceleration constraint at a terrain following altitude of 80 cm. The shaded areas mark the periods of "No Detect" of ArIn. (5.b): reconstruction of the environment based on the history of the visual inputs of simulation 5.a. (5.c): details of two runs, TRAJ2 with D_{0fol}=60cm and TRAJ3 with the deceleration constraint turned on (see equation (13)) and a maximum forward acceleration during the "No Detect" periods. In all three runs, T=100ms, D_{0sec}=25cm. For further details please read the text.

The lack of success of TRAJ1 and TRAJ2 tells us this much: in the context of our study, the causes of the collisions do not depend on the model of the artificial insect which is chosen, rather the bad performances of the two simulations arise each from a specific deficiency in the visual system: in the first case we have a "No Detect" problem due to the limited range of vision of the eye, whereas in the second case we have a morphological deficiency in the design of the eye.

In order to try to solve the visual "No Detect" problem we have enforced two constraints on the forward speed regulation: first of all, a limitation on the deceleration of ArIn, imposed by equation (13) and secondly a maximum forward acceleration whenever the animat is in a "No Detect" period, thereby increasing its range of vision. This leads to the successfull result of TRAJ3 which contrasts with TRAJ1 obtained with otherwise similar flight parameters (altitude following at 80 cm and initial forward speed of 130 cm/s)

9. Conclusion.

The conditions adopted for the simulation of TRAJ3 show that ArIn uses vision to overcome the severe environmental constraints imposed by a rough terrain consisting of ditches and poles, in spite of the poor angular resolution of its visual system. We have demonstrated here that it is possible for a flying agent to control its navigation solely by visual guidance with a minimalistic design strategy for the controllers: these feature simplicity of design and reactiveness based on a behavioural decomposition of the different task components. Let us recall that the kind of visual guidance dealt with here requires only passive optical detectors as frontends to E.M.D.'s, which act as "smart sensors". A reactive control loop based on the visual perception of motion turns out to be of general validity, as the distances, speed and mass of the agent can easily be scaled up without requiring any fundamental changes in the equations. The tight reciprocal interactions which are exerted between the sensory and the motor block suggest that there is a mutual reliance between the two tasks where "acting in order to perceive" becomes just as important as "perceiving in order to act".

The relative success of trajectory TRAJ3 should not let us forget that for the E.M.D. to compute the distance to obstacles, it is necessary for it to measure its own ground speed. In a simulation, the speed of travel is known but it is unlikely that insects are able to gauge the value of their speed from the motor output of their wings [29], [32]. Further control loops based on vision

therefore seem to be a compulsory addition to the above system.

Acknowledgments: We would like to thank Nicolas Martin, Roger Chagneux and Marc Boyron for fruitful comments. Thanks also to the reviewers for their helpfull suggestions on the paper. This research was supported by the Centre National de la Recherche Scientifique (C.N.R.S.), the Region Provence Alpes Côte-d'azur (P.A.C.A.), the Ministère de la Recherche et Technologie (M.R.T. Cognisciences) and the Commission of the European Communities (ESPRIT, BRA SSS 6961). F.M. was supported by a graduate fellowship from C.N.R.S. (MREN).

References

[1] R. D. BEER (1990) Intelligence as Adaptive Behavior: an Experiment in Computational Neuroethology. Perspectives in artificial intelligence. Academic Press, New York.

[2] R. BROOKS (1986) A robust Layered Control System For A Mobile Robot. IEEE journal of robotics and automation RA-2 n°1: 14-23.

[3] E. BUCHNER (1984) Behavioural Analysis of Spatial Vision in Insects. In: Photoreception and Vision in Invertebrates. Ed M. ALI, Plenum, New York pp 561-621.

[4] D. CLIFF (1990) Computational Neuroethology: a Provisional Manifesto. In Proceedings of the first international conference on Simulation of Adaptive Behaviour: From Animals to Animats p29-39.

[5] T.S. COLLETT, M. LAND (1975) Visual Control of Flight Behaviour in the Hoverfly *Syritta Pipiens* L. J. Comp. Physiol., 99: 1-66.

[6] T.S. COLLETT (1978) Peering: A Locust Behaviour Pattern For Obtaining Motion Parallax Information. J. Exp. Biol., 76: 237-241.

[7] J. CONNELL (1990) Minimalist Mobile Robotics: a Colony Style Architecture for an Artificial Creature. Academic Press, New York.

[8] D. COOMBS, K. ROBERTS (1992) 'Bee-bot':Using Peripheral Optical Flow to Avoid Obstacles in "Mobile Robots" S.P.I.E., Bellingham (USA).

[9] C. T. DAVID (1979) Optomotor Control of Speed and Height by Free Flying Drosophila. J. Exp. Biol., 82: 389-392.

[10] H.R. EVERETT (1989) Survey of Collision Avoidance and Ranging Sensors for Mobile Robots. Robotics and Autonomous systems 5: 5-67.

[11] S. EXNER (1893) The Physiology of the Compound Eyes of Insects and Crustaceans (english translation 1989 by R.C. Hardie) Springer, Berlin.

[12] G. FRAENKEL, J.W.S. PRINGLE (1938) Halteres of flies as gyroscopic organs of equilibrium. Nature, Lond. 141: 919-920.

[13] N. FRANCESCHINI (1975) Sampling of The Visual Environment by the Compound Eye of The Fly: fundamentals and Applications. In Photoreceptor Optics, Eds A. Snyder and R. Menzel, Springer, Berlin, pp 98-125.

[14] N. FRANCESCHINI, A. RIEHLE, A. LE NESTOUR (1989) Directionally Selective Motion Detection by Insect Neurons. In: Facets of Vision, Springer, Berlin, pp 360-390.

[15] N. FRANCESCHINI, J.M. PICHON, C. BLANES (1991) Real time visuomotor control: from flies to robots. IEEE Proc. Intern. Conf. Advanced Robotics, Pisa, pp 931-935.

[16] N. FRANCESCHINI, J. M. PICHON, C. BLANES (1992) From Insect Vision to Robot Vision. Phil. Trans. R. Soc. Lond. B, 337: 283-294.

[17] J. J. GIBSON (1958) Visually Controlled Locomotion and Visual Orientation in animals. British J. Psychol. 49: 182-194.

[18] K. G. GÖTZ (1969) Movement discrimination in insects. In Proceedings on Processing of Optical Data by Organisms and Machines, Academic Press, New York, pp 494-509.

[19] R. JARVIS Range Sensing for Computer Vision. In Prep.

[20] H. von HELMHOLTZ (1867) Optique Physiologique Tome II Reprinted edition 1962. London: Dover Publications.

[21] R. HENGSTENBERG (1984) Roll Stabilization During Flight of the Blowfly's Head and Body by Mechanical and Visual Cues. In Localization and Orientation in Biology and Engineering, Springer, Berlin pp 121-134.

[22] E. HILDRETH (1992) Recovering Heading for Visually Guided Navigation. Vision Res. 32:1177-1192.

[23] K. KIRSCHFELD (1976) The Resolution of Lens and Compound Eyes. Neural Principles. In: Vision Proc in life Sciences, Springer, Berlin pp 355-370.

[24] D.N. LEE (1980) The Optic Flow Field: The Foundation of Vision. Phil.Trans. R. Soc Lond. B 290: 169-179.

[25] M. LEHRER, M.V. SRINIVASAN, S. W. ZHANG, G. A. HORRIDGE (1988) Motion Cues Provide The Bee's Visual World With A Third Dimension. Nature 332: 356-357.

[26] N.MARTIN, N. FRANCESCHINI Environmental control of speed and Steering in a Sighted Mobile Robot: a bionic approach. (in prep.)

[27] M. MATARIC (1990) a Distributed Model for Mobile Robot Environment-Learning and navigation. MIT AI Lab Technical Report 1228.

[28] J.M. PICHON, C. BLANES, N. FRANCESCHINI (1989) Visual Guidance of a Mobile Robot Equipped With a Network of Self Motion Sensors. In, Mobile Robots IV S.P.I.E., 1195; Bellingham (USA) pp 44-53.

[29] W. REICHARDT (1969) Movement perception in insects . In Proceedings on Processing of Optical Data by Organisms and Machines, Academic Press, NewYork. pp 465-493.

[30] G. SANDINI, F. GANDOLFO, E. GROSSO, M. TISTARELLI (1993) Vision during Action. In Active Perception Ed Y. Aloimonos, Lawrence Erlbaum Associates, pp 151-190.

[31] B. SRIDHAR, A. PHATAK (1992) Analysis of Image Based Navigation System for Rotorcraft Low Altitude Flight. IEEE SMC, 22: 290-299.

[32] H. WAGNER (1986) Flight Performance and Visual Control of Flight of the Free Flying Housefly *Musca Domestica* L. I.Organization of the Flight Motor. Phil.Trans.R. Soc. Lond. B 312: 527-551.

[33] R. WEHNER (1981) Spatial Vision in Arthropods. In Handbook of Sensory Physiology vol VII/6C Comparative Physiology and Evolution of Vision in Invertebrates, Springer, Berlin pp 287-616.

[34] R.WOLF, M. HEISENBERG (1990) Visual Control of Straight Flight in Drosophila Melanogaster. J. Comp. Physiol. A 167: 269-283.

[35] J. M. ZANKER (1988) on the Mechanisms of Speed and Altitude Control in *Drosophila Melanogaster* Physiol. Entomol., 13: 351-361.

ACTION SELECTION
AND BEHAVIORAL SEQUENCES

What is cognitive and what is *not* cognitive?

Frederick Toates,
Biology Department,
The Open University,
Milton Keynes, UK
e-mail: F.TOATES@OPEN.AC.UK

Abstract

The ubiquitous contemporary use of the term 'cognitive' brings certain drawbacks. In the tradition of Tolman (1932), closer attention might be paid to its meaning in a way that can demarcate cognitive from non-cognitive processes. This has implications for understanding learning, motivation and behavioural hierarchies. It suggests different evolutionary pressures, reveals similarities in information processing in rats and humans and is relevant to the design of automatons.

Introduction

The term 'cognitive' is ubiquitous in behavioural science, yet there exists little consensus on its meaning. At a recent conference (note 1), cognition was used by various speakers to describe such diverse things as knowledge in rats, higher human mental processes, the control of gastric contractions in an invertebrate and the information underlying anything adaptive that any living thing, animal or plant, could possibly do. Where, at one time, a process, such as that underlying a reaction-time task, would be described in textbooks of psychology, texts now cover much the same material but packaged under a title of 'cognitive psychology' or 'cognitive science'. Even processes such as those proposed by the arch-behaviourist, Clark Hull, to underlie learning in rats are assimilated into texts under a cognitive adjective (e.g. Greene and Hicks, 1984). Some authors (e.g. Weingarten, 1984; Garcia and Garcia y Robertson, 1984) are more specific in their use of the term. They employ it only to refer to processes involving knowledge about the environment; additional, and, by implication, non-cognitive, processing (e.g. detection of energy state) is also described.

It was argued (Toates, 1994a,b) that the term 'cognitive' can only prove helpful given a definition of what is and *is not* a cognitive process. So this paper is designed to stimulate discussion by suggesting such a demarcation. This demarcation can serve to illuminate (a) the role of different evolutionary pressures underlying the emergence of different processes, (b) the interdependence between processes controlling behaviour (e.g. learning, motivation, emotion), (c) hierarchies of control and (d) similarities in behavioural processes in various species, e.g. rats and humans. Designers of automatons might profit by consideration of the demarcation in the context of the optimization of design.

The philosophy of the present paper is a direct development of the approach to animal learning of Tolman (1932). Although learning forms the basis of the present argument, the logic can be applied elsewhere, e.g. to the genetic transmission of information or developmental changes. Cognitive processes are defined here as those that involve the assimilation, storage and utilization of *knowledge*, in a way that is not linked directly to any particular behaviour. Cognition allows extrapolation beyond the sensory input and permits the maximum possible range of varied and flexible behaviour.

Within neuroscience, psychology, ethology and control theory, a number of theorists have postulated hierarchical models of behavioural control (e.g. Gallistel, 1980; Roitblat, 1991; Powers, 1973). At the lowest level in a hierarchy is the control loop involving individual motor neurons and muscle fibres. According to the logic of such hierarchies and that of the present argument, at the top level of the hierarchy would be cognitions and associated goals. That is to say, cognitions represent information at its most remote from muscular control.

Intermediate levels in the hierarchy between cognitions and motor neurons represent procedures, eg. for the well-trained rat, such things as the command to lower the lever in the Skinner box and the various possible motor acts that have been used to this end. One level in the hierarchy is sensitized or desensitized by the immediately higher level (Gallistel, 1980). In addition to modifying cognitive processes, learning can also involve changes at lower levels in the hierarchy. In some human skill learning situations, learning can be reflected at various levels in the hierarchy (discussed by Gallistel, 1980, p.112). The distinction proposed here corresponds, to a large extent, to that between declarative knowledge (cognition) and procedural learning (lower-level) (Dickinson, 1980; Squire, 1992). Some implications of this distinction are now explored.

Cognitive psychology

The hallmark of cognitive psychology is an approach to understanding mental processes that adopts computational metaphors and information processing models. Indeed, for some time now, most analogies other than computer software (e.g. hydraulic and telephone exchange models) have usually only been described in order to demonstrate how behaviour is thought *not* to be organized. However, cognitive psychology contains a paradox: whereas its brief seems all-embracing, its methods usually can illuminate only a particular, higher (mainly human) subset of processes, e.g. those involved in visual pattern and speech recognition. It brings little insight to, for example, modelling the role of hedonism in running a maze or the acquisition of phobias or taste-aversion learning. Though, arguably, some additions to the traditionally described information processing might assimilate such phenomena, so far this approach has shown little ability to come to terms with a wider range of phenomena. In the face of the rejection of S-R theories in the cognitive revolution, Furedy and Riley (1987) argue:

"....we now seem to have come to the opposing extreme view - that of an organism that is *purely* cognitive, sensitive only to propositional relationships. It is no accident that the use of the computer analogy is ubiquitous in current writings. That analogy is not influential only when specifically referred to".

In a similar vein, Maltzman (1987) argues:

"In its modern version cognitive psychology leaves the organism buried in a computer or its software as well as thoughts and expectancies. There is no connection with the biological bases of behaviour or the behaviour itself. How are the allocations of resources, subroutines, or awareness, etc translated into a GSR, action, addictions, neuroses, the release of neuropeptides, etc?".

It is hoped that the present paper will stimulate a broadening of approach within cognitive psychology.

Learning theory

Traditionally, cognitive theories of learning have been discussed in opposition to stimulus-response (S-R) theories (see e.g. Toates and Slack, 1990). In this spirit, the present author once championed the validity of a cognitive, declarative and teleological model over the S-R model (Toates, 1986; Toates and Slack, 1990). However, further reflection suggests that, in trying for an all-embracing theory, this was in some respects a false dichotomy to draw. Rather, there is evidence that, depending upon prevailing circumstances, learning can reflect a change at either a cognitive process (high level in hierarchy) or something *nearer to* an S-R link (intermediate level). Thus, external cues might present the most reliable or only *consistent* predictor (e.g. food is by the window, no matter how varied the behaviour has been), in which case, learning will take the cognitive form. Alternatively, a motor act might form the most reliable predictor (e.g. left turn, irrespective of context, leads to food), in which case this is what is learned (Tolman, Ritchie and Kalish, 1946). This might well have a cognitive aspect if, at the same time, the rat forms an expectation of the outcome of its behaviour (Cf. Bolles, 1972). However, in the terms developed here, it is seen as learning *what to do* in a given stimulus context, rather than, or in addition to, learning facts about the world.

Normally, in a stable environment and with repetition of behaviour, what is learned at one level might be entirely compatible with what is learned at another (e.g. food is by the window *and* a left turn gets there). However, under contrived laboratory conditions, learning at one level might be impossible. For instance, in a cross maze, a left turn might always lead to food, irrespective of starting point (Tolman, Ritchie and Kalish, 1946), which precludes learning by spatial cognitive cues. Conversely, in some situations, each trial might start at a different location, thus precluding learning exactly what to do and forcing reliance upon a cognitive map.

In a similar way to instrumental learning, the evidence suggests that classical conditioning can take either cognitive or non-cognitive forms and Malmo and Furedy (1993) argue against the *Zeitgeist* of an all-embracing cognitive interpretation. They refer to experiments on the conditioning of heart rate deceleration in rats that seem to fit "the classical nonteleological and non-cognitive S-R model". For subjects exposed to a classical contingency, Furedy and Riley (1987) suggest the existence of 2 distinct learning processes: (1) non-cognitive response learning (CS-CR) and (2) cognitive propositional learning. Examples of CS-CR learning include eyelid and GSR conditioning. Learning appears to occur through contiguity alone, presumably contiguity between local sensory stimulation (CS induced) and a specific efferent output (UCS induced).

Changes in weighting of levels

Given a facility for sometimes assimilating information at more than one level, should efficiency require information to be held as cognitions or procedures, or both? Should the weighting given to information at different levels change over time? It can be argued that putting weight upon information at either level has advantages and disadvantages (Cf. Toates, 1994a,b). Employing full cognitive control offers flexibility but at the price of relatively costly processing. Conversely, procedures tell the agent what to do in a way that utilizes relatively cheap processing but which offers little flexibility. If one assumes evolution to be a parsimonious selector that tends to produce an optimal solution, it is not difficult to see that learning by a combination of changes in both processes provides the best solution. In the direct context of the animal's interaction, consider those features of the environment (a) which are stable within a life-time and between generations and (b) for which a given procedural solution is adaptive. The solution can be specified in advance. In rats, an example is the relatively fixed species-specific defence reaction of freezing in response to signals of danger (Bolles, 1970). By contrast, where the environment is subject to change and thereby flexibility of interaction is needed, only full cognitive control will work.

Even in a potentially widely varying environment, within periods of the life of an individual, sufficient stability might prevail that a procedural solution could be implemented. An optimal design might permit a switch from cognitive to procedural control, corresponding to the experience of stability for a significant period. This would permit a faster reaction and free cognitive capacity for other tasks. There is evidence for such a switch. Placed at the south end of a + maze that is located in a rich environment, rats start out by learning cognitions, e.g. food is by the window. This is reflected in the flexibility of behaviour; the same goal can be approached when the rat is released from either north or south ends. However, with time, if the rat always starts from the south and hence a left turn always provides the solution, it will tend to repeat the same motor turn even if coming from the north direction and to do so leads it away from the goal (Mackintosh, 1965, 1974). So, under contrived laboratory conditions, habits can lead rats astray. Whether such errors commonly occur in a natural environment is not known. But it is clear that no one process can bring only benefits. If the rat were to retain full-strength cognitive control throughout, it might never be lead astray. However, it might risk tying up an unnecessarily large amount of specialized cognitive capacity for a routine task. Other problems might arise from a lack of cognitive capacity, such as from a failure to identify new potential predictive associations. Similarly, in a Skinner box, the rat starts learning with a representation of the expected reward forming part of the complex of causal factors that determines behaviour. However, with experience, behaviour becomes habit-like. Under some circumstances reward representation plays little role as a causal factor (Dickinson, 1985).

It is proposed that a change from cognitive to procedural control in a stable environment arises in part as a result of increased weighting of parameters lower in the hierarchy. However, it should be noted that use of a term like 'mechanistic S-R' to describe this needs qualification. For example, even very well-trained rats in a Skinner box still utilize different movements to achieve the same end point of a lowered lever (Dickinson and Balleine, 1992).

Sometimes a transfer of information can occur in the opposite direction to that just described, i.e. from procedures to cognitions. At first, such learning is unavailable to cognitive control and only becomes available with experience. An example of this is taste-aversion learning (Garcia and Garcia y Robertson, 1984): animals experiencing a distinctive taste (A) followed by gastrointestinal discomfort will reject the flavour. This is first encoded as simply a procedural change: (taste A) -> (ingest) to (taste A) -> (reject), and animals (e.g. hawks and at least one well-known experimental psychologist (Dickinson and Balleine, 1992)) will still pursue food of taste A. Only on experiencing the combination of taste and visual or other exteroceptive cues can the animal perform an extrapolation such that devaluation of the food is reflected in its cognitive, appetitive, goal-pursuit. In humans, occasionally the wrong (with respect to the true causality of the world) information, apparently assimilated at a procedural level, then becomes available at a cognitive level, as Garcia and Garcia y Robertson (1984) noted:

"If people become ill after a novel meal, they blame the food, not, for example, the new wallpaper on the dining room wall. The reaction seems cognitive and rational, but it is not. As any ship's steward knows, when the seas become stormy, the bilious voyager first blames the food, not the sea".

In humans, the affective evaluation of a previously neutral picture can be altered by following it with an affectively potent picture (Martin and Levey, 1987). They argue that "...an unmediated, non-cognitive evaluative response is elicited by evaluatively salient stimuli and transferred to contiguous neutral stimuli by the mechanism of classical conditioning". This process is non-cognitive in the sense that it occurs relatively independently of any change in the signalling properties of the first stimulus.

Central states

Researchers in the design of automatons have realized the need for a holistic approach (e.g. Brooks, 1991); that the design of one process within a system has implications for the design of others. By analogy, postulation of processes of cognitive, non-cognitive and hierarchical control has implications for theories concerning central states, variously termed motivational, emotional, affective and hedonic. Traditionally, the cognitive approach has been associated with the notion of purpose, in which motivation is seen as selecting high-level goals to be pursued flexibly. Postulation of additional and non-cognitive processes invites speculation as to how motivation interacts with procedural controls.

Cognition is not only associated with representations of the environment but also with comparisons of incoming sensory information with stored expectations (e.g. Gray, 1982). In terms of the present argument, a switch from cognitive to procedural control would correspond to a period over which both input and behavioural output match a stored expectation. It is proposed that, after finding a procedural solution, detection of disparity would cue a return to cognitive control. Some authors (e.g. Simon, 1967) would associate emotion with the disparity from expectation that triggers such a process.

The argument so far has been developed with particular reference to rats, and its exposition then allows some similarities with human information processing to be seen, as the following section shows.

Human information processing

Certain models of human information processing and behaviour are based on hierarchies similar to those deriving mainly from animal research (e.g. Baars, 1993; Norman, 1981; Reason, 1984; Shallice, 1972). Conscious processing is seen as the top level of a hierarchy of control. Reason (1984) proposes a model with a motivational aspect, termed the 'need system' which inputs to an 'intention system'. The latter is the "chief executive within the hierarchy of action control" and is directly accessible to consciousness. In turn, the intention system would take the form of a verbal tag (e.g. I must buy a paper), having at its disposal a number of automatized action schemata. For a largely automated task, within the action system, a particular action schema will be controlling the motor output.

Schneider and Shiffrin (1977) refer to *automatic processing* as being "triggered by appropriate inputs" and occurring when "stimuli are consistently mapped to responses" over a large number of trials (Schneider, Dumais and Shiffrin, 1984). It can occur even against the command of an intentional system as when one intends to dial number X but automatically dials a more familiar number Y. Shiffrin and Schneider (1977) defined an automatic process as "a sequence of nodes that nearly always becomes active in response to a particular input configuration".

What Schneider and Shiffrin term *controlled processing* (which seems to match processing involving cognitions, as employed in the present paper) is necessary for handling novel or inconsistent information. This processing probably occurs when the human has not yet been able to learn an automatic sequence. Shiffrin and Schneider (1977) argue that the price of occupying cognitive capacity is balanced by the benefits of flexibility, e.g. devising strategies in novel contexts for which no automatic sequences have been learned.

Errors have proven a valuable source of insight into the nature of hierarchies of control. Norman (1981) uses the term *capture error* to describe what occurs "....when a familiar habit substitutes itself for the intended action sequence". The principle involved is easily described "Pass too near a well-formed habit and it will capture your behaviour". Norman quotes William James' famous example:

"...very absent-minded persons in going to their bedroom to dress for dinner have been known to take off one garment after another and finally to get into bed, merely because that was the habitual issue of the first few movements when performed at a later hour".

Discussion and conclusions

This paper will surely not end controversy over where to use 'cognitive' but, at the very least, it questions the value of the promiscuous use of the term, suggests restraint and a possible demarcation. In developing theories of behaviour, controversy can polarize in a way that disguises genuine distinctions between processes. The apparent victory of cognitive psychology over behaviourism and the subsequent uncritical proliferation of 'cognitive' has involved a cost: a confusion between a school of thought and a process. It has made grey some fundamental distinctions between different processes, obscuring the fact that something like S-R links can be formed, instead of, or in addition to, cognitions. Different processes meet different adaptive considerations.

A similar argument to that made here was earlier made (Toates and Jensen, 1991; Jensen and Toates, 1993)

in connection with models of motivation. Rejection of Lorenz's model involving a hydraulic analogy came at the price of either ignoring or forcing into a straight-jacket behavioural phenomena (e.g. behaviour in the absence of tissue need) that could be explained by the Lorenz model. Furthermore, such behaviour might also be seen as the outcome of lower levels in the hierarchy gaining autonomy from higher levels (Gallistel, 1980), which would provide links with the present argument.

It would seem that a similar set of considerations applies to learning in rats and certain human performance tasks, a comparison noted by some authors but not pursued (Dickinson, 1985; Bolles, 1972; Pearce and Hall, 1980). In each case, a hierarchy of behavioural control is implicated, learning can be manifest at more than one level and one can identify top-down potentiation of relationships between a stimulus situation and behaviour such that goals are reached. Extensive repetition of a relationship between a stimulus situation and a behaviour can lead to such a strength of association that this can dominate and produce behaviour that is at odds with what would occur as a result of the same top-down potentiation in the presence of a less strong habit. In terms of a temporary insensitivity to the top-down level of the goal, an over-trained rat in a Skinner box would seem to be similar to William James' absent-minded subject.

Although rather different considerations lie behind the design of animals and automatons, none-the-less it can be useful to consider possible parallels. For animals in the wild, unlike most human artifacts, milliseconds of advantage might make the difference between life and death. Therefore, the adaptive value in finding solutions that involve rapid responses is clear. These require circumventing relatively slow and demanding cognitive processes. The solution inevitably risks the occasional wrong turn or Freudian slip. An interesting question is whether designers of automatons should allow for the occasional such slip in their designs.

Perhaps they face issues more similar to those involved in human skill learning rather than predator avoidance. A strengthening of data-driven processes with repetition is a vital part of skill learning, according to the classical analysis of Miller, Galanter and Pribram (1960). They suggest: " ... man is assumed to be capable of building up his own "instincts". Lower animals come with strategies wired in; man wires them in deliberately to serve his own purposes. And when the Plan is highly over-learned, it becomes almost as involuntary, as resistant to change depending upon its outcome, as if it were innate."

According to the argument proposed here "resistance to change" corresponds to switching to cognitive control.

NOTE 1. Conference "Cognition and evolution" held at Berder Island, France, March 1994. Copies of the author's own paper available on request.

References

Baars,B.J. (1993) How does a serial, integrated and very limited stream of consciousness emerge from a nervous system that is mostly unconscious, distributed, parallel and of enormous capacity?. In *Experimental and Theoretical Studies of Consciousness,* (eds. R.Bock and J.Marsh), Wiley, Chichester, p.282-303.

Bolles,R.C. (1970) Species-specific defense reactions and avoidance learning. *Psychological Review, 77,* 32-48.

Bolles,R.C. (1972) Reinforcement, expectancy and learning. *Psychological Review, 79,* 394-409.

Brooks,R.A. (1991) Challenges for complete creature architectures. In *From Animals to Animats,* (eds. J-A. Meyer and S.W. Wilson), The MIT Press, Cambridge, Mass., pp.434-443.

Dickinson,A. (1980) *Contemporary Animal Learning Theory.* Cambridge, Cambridge University Press.

Dickinson,A. (1985) Actions and habits: the development of behavioural autonomy. *Philosophical Transactions of the Royal Society, London,* B 308, 67-78.

Dickinson,A. and Balleine,B. (1992) Actions and responses: The dual psychology of behaviour. In *Problems in the Philosophy and Psychology of Spatial Representations.* (eds. N.Eilan, R.A.McCarthy and M.W.Brewer), Blackwell, Oxford, pp.277-293.

Furedy,J.J. and Riley,D.M. (1987) Human Pavlovian autonomic conditioning and the cognitive paradigm. In *Cognitive Processes and Pavlovian Conditioning in Humans* (ed. G.Davey), Wiley, Chichester, pp1-25.

Gallistel,C.R. (1980) *The Organization of Action: A New Synthesis.* Lawrence Erlbaum, Hillsdale.

Garcia,J. and Garcia y Robertson,R. (1984) Evolution of learning mechanisms. In *The Psychology of Learning - The Master Lecture Series* (Vol.4) (ed. B.L.Hammonds), American Psychological Association, Washington, pp.191-243.

Gray,J.A. (1982) Multiple book review of *The Neuropsychology of Anxiety: An Enquiry into the Functions of the Septo-hippocampal System. The Behavioural and Brain Sciences,* 5, 469-534.

Greene,J. and Hicks,C. (1984) *Basic Cognitive Processes.* Open University Press, Milton Keynes.

Jensen,P. and Toates,F. (1993) Who needs 'behavioural needs'? Motivational aspects of the needs of animals. *Applied Animal Behaviour Science,* 37, 161-181.

Mackintosh,N.J. (1965) Overtraining, transfer to proprioceptive control and position reversal. *Quarterly Journal of Experimental Psychology,*17, 26-36.

Mackintosh,N. (1974) *The Psychology of Animal Learning.* London, Academic Press.

Malmo,R.B. and Furedy,J.J. (1993) Settling the stimulus-substitution issue is a prerequisite for sound nonteleological neural analysis of heart-rate deceleration conditioning. *Behavioural and Brain Sciences,* 16, 392-393.

Maltzman,I. (1987) A neo-Pavlovian interpretation of the OR and classical conditioning in humans: With comments on alcoholism and the poverty of cognitive psychology. In *Cognitive Processes and Pavlovian Conditioning in Humans* (ed. G.Davey), Wiley, Chichester, pp.211-249.

Martin,I. and Levey,A.B. (1987) Learning what will happen next: Conditioning, evaluation and cognitive processes. In *Cognitive Processes and Pavlovian Conditioning in Humans* (ed. G.Davey), Wiley, Chichester, pp57-81.

Miller, G.A., Galanter, E. and Pribram, K.H. (1960) *Plans and the Structure of Behaviour.* Holt, Rinehart and Winston, New York.

Norman,D.A. (1981) Categorization of action slips. *Psychological Review,* 88, 1-15.

Pearce,J.M. and Hall,G. (1980) A model for Pavlovian learning: Variations in the effectiveness of conditioned but not of unconditioned stimuli. *Psychological Review,* 87, 532-552.

Powers,W. (1973) *Behaviour: The Control of Perception.* Wildwood House, London.

Reason,J. (1984) Lapses of attention in everyday life. In *Varieties of Attention* (eds. R.Parasuraman and D.R.Davies), Academic Press, Orlando, pp.515-549.

Roitblat,H.L. (1991) Cognitive action theory as a control architecture. In *From Animals to Animats* (eds. J-A.Meyer and S.W.Wilson), The MIT Press, Cambridge, pp.444-450.

Schneider,W., Dumais,S.T. and Shiffrin,R.M. (1984) Automatic and control processing and attention. In *Varieties of Attention* (eds. R.Parasuraman and D.R.Davies), Academic Press, Orlando, pp.1-27.

Schneider,W. and Shiffrin,R.M. (1977) Controlled and automatic human information processing: I. Detection, search and attention. *Psychological Review,* 84, 1-66.

Shallice,T. (1972) Dual functions of consciousness. *Psychological Review,* 79, 383-393.

Shiffrin,R.M. and Schneider,W. (1977) Controlled and automatic human information processing: II. Perceptual learning, automatic attending, and a general theory. *Psychological Review,* 84, 127-190.

Simon,H.A. (1967) Motivational and emotional controls of cognition. *Psychological Review,* 74, 29-39.

Squire,L.R. (1992) Memory and the hippocampus: A synthesis from findings with rats, monkeys and humans. *Psychological Review,* 99, 195-231.

Toates,F. (1986) *Motivational Systems.* Cambridge, Cambridge University Press.

Toates,F. (1994a) Animal motivation and cognition. In *Comparative Approaches to Cognitive Science,* (eds. H.Roitblat and J-A. Meyer), The MIT Press, in press.

Toates,F. (1994b) Cognition and evolution - An organization of action perspective. Paper presented at conference "Cognition and evolution", Berder Island, France, March 1994.

Toates,F. and Jensen,P. (1991) Ethological and psychological models of motivation - Towards a synthesis. In *From Animals to Animats* (eds. J-A. Meyer and S.Wilson), MIT Press, Cambridge, pp.194-205.

Toates,F. and Slack,I. (1990) Behaviourism and its consequences. In *Introduction to Psychology* (Vol. 1), (ed. I.Roth), Lawrence Erlbaum, Hillsdale, pp.250-313.

Tolman,E.C. (1932) *Purposive Behaviour in Animals and Men*. The Century Co., New York.

Tolman,E.C., Ritchie,B.F. and Kalish,D. (1946) Studies in spatial learning. II. Place learning versus response learning. *Journal of Experimental Psychology*, 36, 221-220.

Weingarten,H.P. (1984) Meal initiation controlled by learned cues: basic behavioural properties. *Appetite*, 5, 147-158.

Action-Selection in Hamsterdam: Lessons from Ethology

Bruce Blumberg
MIT Media-Laboratory
20 Ames St., E15-305
Cambridge Ma. 02139
bruce@media.mit.edu

Abstract

A computational model of action-selection is presented, which by drawing on ideas from Ethology, addresses a number of problems which have been noted in models proposed to date including the need for greater control over the temporal aspects of behavior, the need for a loose hierarchical structure with information sharing, and the need for a flexible means of modeling the influence of internal and external factors. The paper draws on arguments from Ethology as well as on computational considerations to show why these are important aspects of any action-selection mechanism for animats which must satisfy multiple goals in a dynamic environment. The computational model is summarized, and its use in Hamsterdam, an object-oriented tool kit for modeling animal behavior is briefly discussed. Results are presented which demonstrate the power and usefulness of the novel features incorporated in the algorithm.

1 Introduction

The problem of action-selection is central to the larger problem of building animats that function robustly in complex and dynamic environments. Specifically, the problem for the animat is to choose the "most appropriate" set of motor actions to perform from its repertoire of potential actions, given some set of internal needs and external stimuli. In the case of animals, "most appropriate" may be measured against some performance criteria such as maximizing their reproductive success. In the case of animats, Maes and others [Maes93, Tyrrell93, McFarland93] have discussed a variety of criteria against which the appropriateness of a set of actions might be measured.

A number of action-selection models have been proposed by ethologists [Lorenz73, Tinbergen50, Baerends76, Davey89, Dawkins76, Ludlow76,80, McFarland75, Toates83] as well as computer scientists [Maes90, Brooks86, Rosenblatt & Payton89, Tyrrell93]. The ethological models are often conceptual rather than computational models and much is left to the discretion of the reader as to how one might implement such a scheme.

With the exception of Tyrrell, the computational models proposed by computer scientists bear little resemblance to the models proposed by classical ethologists such as Baerends and Tinbergen. Nonetheless, the computational models have been used successfully in a number of applications, and their very success has called into question traditional AI approaches to planning[Maes93].

At least one researcher [Tyrrell93], however, has noted the difficulty of applying, without modification, the models of Brooks [Brooks86], Maes [Maes90], and Rosenblatt and Payton [Rosenblatt89] to the problem of modeling action-selection in animats whose behavior is to mirror that of real animals. While one may view the difficulties noted by Tyrrell as being specific to the problem of modeling animal behavior, a more serious and general concern may be lurking. Namely, previously proposed computational models of action-selection may be missing elements essential to robust action-selection in animats whose behavioral complexity (i.e. in the number of needs which must be met, and in the range of potential actions which may be taken) approaches that of real animals.

This paper presents an ethologically-inspired computational model of action-selection which improves on existing models in three areas. These include:

The Need for Greater Control Over the Temporal Aspects of Behavior

Computational models of action-selection proposed to date have difficulty providing "just the right amount of persistence". That is, it is difficult to control the temporal aspects of behavior so as to arrive at the right balance between too little persistence, resulting in dithering among activities, and too much persistence so that opportunities are missed or that the animat mindlessly pursues a given goal to the detriment of other goals. The computational model presented in this paper addresses this problem by incorporating an explicit model of inhibition and fatigue first proposed by Ludlow [Ludlow76,80]. The benefits of this approach include:

• It provides control over the level of persistence associated with an active activity, thus reducing the chances of dithering, while still allowing for opportunistic behavior.

• It provides a natural mechanism for modeling a form of time-sharing in which low priority activities are given a chance to execute despite the presence of a higher priority activity. More generally it reduces the chances of pursuing a single goal to the detriment of all others.

• It provides a robust mechanism for implementing winner-take-all arbitration among activities.

The Need for a Loose Hierarchical Structure with Information Sharing

Drawing on the tradition of hierarchical models of behavior from Ethology, Tyrrell[Tyrrell93] has convincingly made the case for computational models of action-selection which incorporate a loose hierarchical structure. However, he departs from the classical Ethological view that at any one time, only one behavior system is being expressed in the movements of the animal. He proposes a model, derived from the work of Payton & Rosenblatt [Rosenblatt89], in which all of the nodes in the hierarchy can influence the subsequent behavior of the creature.

By contrast, the computational model presented in this paper implements a winner-take-all system consistent with traditional ethological thinking, but which nonetheless allows losing activities to express their preferences in the form of recommendations to the winning activity. The winner may use these recommendations as it sees fit. The benefits of this approach include:

• It provides a mechanism for information-sharing which potentially allows the system to arrive at compromise solutions which ultimately may be more efficient for the creature, and thus avoids a potential problem associated with winner-take-all approaches.

• Relative to Tyrrell's approach, it preserves the attractive divide-and-conquer attribute of more traditional hierarchies, and thus may scale better. It is also less dependent on the careful tuning of parameters.

The Need for a Common Currency and a Flexible Means of Modeling Internal Needs and External Opportunities

The third contribution of the computational model presented here is that it explicitly includes the concepts of Releasing Mechanisms and Endogenous Variables from Ethology. It treats them as abstractions for more complicated processes and thus allows the designer to model them accordingly. Their values, however, are expressed as continuous quantities in a common currency. This is distinguished from some previous approaches which model the presence of external stimulus as a predicate [Maes90]. The benefits of this approach include:

• A natural way to model the phenomena of motivational isoclines [McFarland75,76] in which differing levels of internal motivation and external stimulus result in the same action.

• It does not require the animat designer to model all systems in a particular way, for example, as strictly homeostatic systems.

By addressing the three issues described above, we have developed an action-selection algorithm which both improves on existing algorithms and which is well suited to animats that must satisfy multiple internal needs in a dynamic and unpredictable environment.

In section 2, we discuss some lessons from Ethology and their computational implications. In particular, we focus on the importance of modeling inhibition and fatigue, the importance of hierarchical organizations of behavior with information sharing and the use of a common currency with which to express internal needs and external opportunities. The computational model is presented in section 3. We then describe Hamsterdam, a tool kit for building animated creatures which incorporates the proposed model of action-selection. In section 5 we present results which show that the algorithm does address the problems described above. We conclude with a discussion of limitations and areas for future work.

2   Lessons from Ethology and Computational Implications

2.1   The Importance of Inhibition and Fatigue

Inhibition plays an important role in ethological models of action-selection and is used to explain some of the temporal aspects of behavior. Ethologists generally agree that animals engage in one behavior at a time [Tinbergen50, Lorenz73, McFarland76, McCleery83, Toates83]. Yet animals typically do not mindlessly pursue an activity indefinitely to the detriment of other needs. Indeed, animals sometimes appear to engage in a form of time-sharing [McFarland74,93], in which low priority activities are given a chance to execute, despite the presence of an activity of higher priority. While animals typically do not dither between multiple activities they will nonetheless interrupt a behavior when another behavior becomes significantly more appropriate. Models of inhibition and fatigue are frequently used to explain these aspects of animal behavior. Thus, it is essential that an action-selection mechanism for animats include an explicit model of inhibition and fatigue.

The model used in the action-selection algorithm presented below was first proposed by Ludlow [Ludlow 76, 80]. However, our system is the first to use it in a complete action-selection algorithm.

In Ludlow's model, an activity such as feeding or drinking has a value which is based on the sum of its relevant internal and external factors less inhibition it receives from competing activities. Competing activities are mutually inhibiting, where a given activity M inhibits activity N by an amount equal to activity M's value times an inhibitory gain K_{nm}. The higher the gain, the greater the inhibition, and effectively the greater the persistence of the active activity. Ludlow's observation was that if (a) activities are mutually inhibiting, (b) the inhibitory gains are restricted to be greater than 1, and (c) the value of activities is restricted to being zero or greater, then this model would result in a winner-take-all system in which only one activity would have a non-zero value once the system stabilized. In practice we have found this to be true. It is exceedingly rare for it not to converge on a solution, particularly if the inhibitory gains are above 2.0.

An activity with a non-zero value is said to be active. In his model, there is a direct feedback loop between an activity and the endogenous factors upon which it depends so that when an activity is active, it reduces the value of those endogenous factors by some activity-specific gain times the value of the activity. In our implementation of his algorithm we relax this assumption so we can use his model in the context of a hierarchical structure. For example, the value of the feeding activity depends on the level of hunger. The feeding activity, however, includes a number of more specific activities including searching for food, handling it, and finally consuming it. It is only when the animal engages in the later activity that the level of hunger is reduced. Thus, the feeding activity relies on another activity, lower in the hierarchy, to reduce the value of one of the endogenous variables on which it depends.

An active activity will stay active until its value or the value of one of the activities with which it competes changes by an amount proportional to the inhibitory gain. For example, if eating is active, and it inhibits drinking with a gain of 2.0, the value of eating must fall to half the value of drinking before drinking will become active. The value of eating would fall, for example, in response to consuming food. Alternatively, the value of drinking would rise significantly in response to passing a water source on the way to the food.

By modifying inhibitory gains, the level of persistence of a given activity relative to those with which it competes may be adjusted accordingly. An activity associates a specific inhibitory gain with each activity it inhibits. When the gains are low, the system tends to dither between different activities with the result that the system takes longer to reach satiation levels. When gains are higher, the active activity shows more persistence with the effect that satiation is reached sooner. However, persistence comes at the expense of opportunism.

More is needed than simple inhibitory gains. Use of high gains may result in lower priority activities never becoming active. For example, feeding may always be of higher absolute priority than body maintenance, yet it is important that the creature be able to periodically interrupt searching for food so it may clean itself. As part of his model, Ludlow suggested a mechanism for modeling behavior-specific fatigue and used this, in conjunction with his model of inhibition, to implement a form of time-sharing.

In Ludlow's model, a level of fatigue is associated with every activity. The level of fatigue is influenced by a number of factors, however when an activity is active the level of fatigue increases in proportion to the activity's value (thus implementing another feedback loop), which reduces the value of the active activity over time. When the activity is no longer active, the fatigue decays toward zero, and the value of the activity rises. In his paper [Ludlow80], Ludlow uses his model to replicate some of the results of McFarland's time-sharing experiments [McFarland74].

The computational model presented below draws heavily from Ludlow's model. One important difference is that Ludlow envisioned a flat structure of competing activities all of which were mutually inhibiting. We have chosen to embed his model in a loose hierarchical organization in the spirit of Baerends [Baerends76] or Tinbergen [Tinbergen50] in which an activity competes only with a subset of the other activities, namely those at its same level in the hierarchy. We now turn to a discussion of the implications of using a hierarchical structure.

2.2 The Importance of Hierarchies with Information-Sharing

In Dawkins' view, a hierarchical structure represents one of the essential organizing principles of complex behavior [Dawkins 76] and this view is echoed by many ethologists [Lorenz73, Baerends76, Tinbergen50, Gallistel80, Davey89, Timberlake89 and McFarland75]. Baerends' model represents one example of this approach. The essential idea is that an animal is considered to have a number of activity systems, or collections of activities each organized to address a specific biological function. The activity systems are organized as loose-overlapping hierarchies. At any one time, only one system is being expressed in the movements of the animal. For example, preening and nesting represent two competing activity systems in herring gulls, each of which has a number of subordinate collections of activities such as settling, building, trimming and bathing. These in turn have motor actions associated with them. Releasing mechanisms (an abstraction for whatever perceptual process signals a biologically important object or event) and endogenous variables (hormone levels, blood sugar levels, etc.) determine in part which activity is expressed. Implicit in this model is the notion that at every level in the hierarchy, a '"decision" is being made among several alternatives of which one is chosen. At the top the decisions are very general (i.e. feed versus drink) and become increasingly more specific as one moves down a hierarchy (i.e. pounce or freeze).

A number of computational arguments have been advanced against this type of hierarchy [Maes90, Tyrrell93,93a]. As an alternative to either a totally flat distributed structure or a strict winner-take-all hierarchy, Tyrrell proposes a "free-flow hierarchy", in which all nodes in the hierarchy can influence the subsequent behavior of the animat. In this latter model, first proposed by Rosenblatt and Payton[Rosenblatt89], activities express weighted preferences for activities lower in the hierarchy and ultimately motor commands. Arbitration is ultimately done at the motor controller level when it executes the most highly preferred motor action. Tyrrell argues that free flow hierarchies avoid at least two problems associated with winner-take all hierarchies:

• In winner-take-all hierarchies information is lost at each decision point. The system is unable to arrive at compromise solutions which ultimately might be better for the creature since the preferences of losing branches are not taken into account. This problem is reduced in free-flow hierarchies since everyone gets to express their preference.

• Winner-take-all hierarchies can be structured in such a way that upper level nodes have access to all of the sensory information used by nodes beneath them in the hierarchy in order to make the right choice among alternative branches. This results in a "sensory bottleneck".

We agree with the former point, but are less convinced by the second in the case of animats driven in part by internal needs. First, following Tinbergen [Tinbergen50] and others, initial decisions among activity systems tend to be driven by internal needs with just enough sensory input to take advantage of opportunities. The sensory input relevant to a specific sub-activity within a given branch of the hierarchy is often irrelevant to the higher level decision between systems. Second, information is flowing into the hierarchy at all levels via releasing mechanisms and endogenous variables associated with different nodes in the hierarchy. Third, a winner-take-all hierarchy provides a focus of attention allowing it to avoid processing irrelevant sensory data. For example, if an animal's hormone levels are such that it has no interest in sex, there is no need to check the sensory input which is only relevant to that behavior system.

The ability of free-flow hierarchies to arrive at compromise solutions comes at the cost of complexity. In particular, the mechanism for combining preferences need to be chosen very carefully [Tyrrell93], and the performance of the system is highly dependent on careful tuning of weights. This problem is compounded by the fact that since an activity can only express its preference for a given motor command, the weight it uses to represent its preference can not be determined independent of the weights used by all other activities for that particular motor action as well as alternative motor actions. Indeed, with a pure free-flow network, one loses the attractive "divide-and-conquer" aspect of hierarchical systems. This in turn brings into question how easily such a system would scale. In addition, free-flow hierarchies do not provide the "focus of attention" described earlier, and thus irrelevant sensory data may be evaluated.

We have chosen to implement a winner-take-all hierarchical model in keeping with traditional ethological models but provide a simple mechanism for limited information sharing. In this model, there is one activity which ultimately has final say over what set of motor actions should be performed at a given instant. However, losing activities on the path to the winner may "post" recommendations for and against various motor actions. The winner has access to these recommendations, and can use them as a form of taxis, or potential modification of an underlying pattern of behavior. The key point is that the winning activity has control over how it wishes to make use of the recommendations. For example, an anti-predator system which detects the presence of a distant predator (so distant in fact, that the system is not made active) may post recommendations against movement which would bring the animat closer to the predator.

This approach reflects the ethological belief that at any one time there is one activity which is in control, presumably because it is the most important given the internal and external state of the creature. Thus, it is in the best position to decide how and when to modify its default pattern of actions so as to take the preferences of other activities into account. We can use this approach because we model activities as objects with hopefully simple, but potentially complex internal logic which "decides" what motor commands will be executed. This design provides the animat designer with the freedom to decide how a given activity makes use of recommendations from other activities.

2.3   Using a Common Currency for Endogenous Variables and Releasing Mechanisms

Internal needs and external opportunities need to be evaluated using a common currency. This idea, described by Lorenz [Lorenz73], Baerends [Baerends55] and McFarland [McFarland75,76,93] is simply that an animal's response to external stimulus depends both on the strength of the stimulus and on their internal state. This seems to imply two key points. First, a stimulus (or more precisely, the output of the releasing mechanisms) needs to be represented as a continuous quantity as opposed to a Boolean, otherwise one would not see this phenomenon. Second, some mechanism within the behavior systems of the animal is effectively combining the strengths of the relevant external and internal factors in some way. To model this properly, internal needs and external opportunities need to be expressed using a common currency.

While it is generally agreed that use of a common currency makes sense, it is less clear how the output of multiple releasing mechanisms should be combined and how external and internal factors should be combined. With respect to multiple independent external stimuli, Seitz's law of heterogeneous summation (i.e. a simple additive relationship) [Lorenz 73] may suffice for most cases. However, one simple rule may not be adequate to combine external and internal factors. McFarland [McFarland76] argues that " ...we would expect the decision criteria (shape of the isocline) for feeding to be shaped by natural selection in accordance with the animal's ecological circumstances." That is, the way that internal and external factors are combined in a given behavior system is determined by natural selection and likely to vary depending on the specific behavior system and the animal's ecological niche. As Tyrrell [Tyrrell93] points out, it is important to be able to "accommodate different rules for combination of stimuli (i.e. internal and external factors), and one should not presuppose strict summation or multiplication."

It is also important to have control over the relative ranges over which the output of specific releasing mechanisms are allowed to vary. In general, the greater the range relative to the likely range for internal factors, the greater the reactiveness of the animat with respect to the stimulus signaled by that releasing mechanism. This results in greater persistence in the presence of a given stimulus. It also means an increased likelihood of opportunistic behavior during appetitive activities associated with one behavior system when stimuli associated with another behavior system are detected.

The computational model presented in the next section reflects these considerations.

3   The Computational Model

The computational model presented below preserves the loose hierarchical structure which is implicit in the models of Tinbergen [Tinbergen50] or Baerends [Baerends76], but incorporates a modified form of information sharing via the use of recommendations. Ludlow's ·[Ludlow 76, 80]·model of mutual inhibition and fatigue is embedded in the hierarchical model, and is used to implement the winner-take-all arbitration among activities at a given level, as well as to provide added control over temporal aspects of behavior. Relevant external and internal factors are modeled using abstractions   called releasing mechanisms and endogenous variables respectively. While they may perform arbitrarily complex calculations to arrive at their value, their value is expressed in a common currency.

The essential points of the model are:

• Time is represented as discrete time-steps, where a time-step is some small fraction of a second. Action-selection is performed on each time-step.

• Activities are organized in loose overlapping hierarchies with more general activities at the top and more specific activities at the leaves. Activities correspond to nodes in a tree, and a node can have zero or more children. Action-selection is the process of determining which leaf node should be active at a given instant, starting at the root of the tree and descending downward.

• Children (i.e. all of the children activities associated with a given node) are mutually inhibiting, and only one can be active at a time. If the active activity is a leaf node, it may issue motor commands to the animat, otherwise, its children compete for control, and so on until a leaf node is reached.

• Activities compete on the basis of their value. Their value at time t is calculated using a modified form of Ludlow's model. Note while a specific function is specified for combining the output of relevant releasing mechanisms and endogenous variables, this function is intended to be activity-specific, and thus subject to modification as needed for a given activity:

$$V_{it} = Max\left[\left[(1 - f_{it}) * \left[Comb(\sum_k r_{kt}, \sum_l e_{lt})\right] - \sum_j (I_{ji} * V_{jt})\right], 0\right]$$

where:

V_{it} = value of activity i at time t.

f_{it} = level of fatigue of activity i at time t (see below).

$Comb(r, e) \rightarrow$ if$(e < 0)$ return e else return $e + r$.

r_{kt} = value of releasing mechanism k at time t where k ranges over the releasing mechanisms relevant to activity i.

e_{lt} = value of endogenous factor l at time t. l ranges over endogenous factors relevant to activity i.

• Within a collection of mutually-inhibiting activities, the system iterates until a stable solution is found in which one activity has a positive value and the value of remaining activities are within a given tolerance of zero.

• Activity specific fatigue is modeled as follows:

$$f_{it} = clamp((1 + fw_i) * f_{i(t-1)} + (V_{i(t-1)} * kf_i) - fa_i, 0, 1)$$

where:

f_{it} = level of fatigue for activity i at time t

fw_i = value - dependent rate of increase in fatigue for activity i.

kf_i = fatigue gain for activity i.

$V_{i(t-1)}$ = value of activity i at time t - 1.

fa_i = autonomous decrease in fatigue for activity i.

$clamp(a, min, max) \rightarrow$ clamp a to between min & max.

• Significant events and objects in the world relevant to a given activity are identified from sensory input by Releasing Mechanisms. The output of a given Releasing Mechanism may be the result of an arbitrarily complex calculation based on sensory input, but its value is expressed as a continuous variable clamped to a specific range. That is:

$$r_{kt} = clamp(f_k(r_{k(t-1)}, s_{kt}), min_k, max_k)$$

where:

r_{kt} = value of releasing mechanism k at time t

s_{kt} = sensory input at time t relevant to releasing mechanism k

$f_k(r_{k(t-1)}, s_{kt})$ = arbitrarily complex function of current sensor input and optionally, previous values of releasing mechanism k.

Min_k, Max_k = Min and Max of allowed range for releasing mechanism k.

• Similarly, internal state (hormonal levels, food and water levels etc.) relevant to a given activity are modeled via Endogenous Variables. Since Endogenous Variables are abstractions for the end-results of potentially complicated internal systems, the value of an Endogenous Variable may be the result of an arbitrarily complex calculation. In the default case however, its value may be calculated as follows:

$$e_{it} = e_{i(t-1)} + ea_i - \sum_h (V_{h(t-1)} * ke_h) + f_i()$$

where

e_{it} = value of endogenous variable i at time t.

ea_i = autonomous change in e_i

h = ranges over activities which affect e_i.

$V_{h(t-1)}$ = value of activity h at t - 1.

ke_h = endogenous gain associated with activity h.

$f_i()$ = arbitrary function of other factors

• An activity can depend on any number of endogenous variables and releasing mechanisms and these in turn can be shared by any number of behaviors.

• Losing activities on the path to the active activity may nonetheless post one or more recommendations. For example, in the diagram below all of the shaded nodes may post recommendations which may be used by the winning activity. A recommendation includes: the name of a motor command and a strength, where positive strength indicates a positive recommendation and a negative strength indicates a recommendation against.

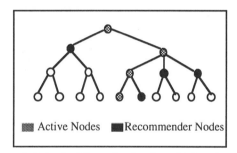

Figure 1: Behavior Hierarchy showing which nodes may issue Recommendations

• An activity at a leaf may issue one or more motor commands to the animat. What motor commands it issues depends on its function, sensory input and state, as well as on its evaluation of the recommendations which have been posted.

The model described above has been implemented as part of Hamsterdam, an object-oriented tool kit for modeling artificial animals. The next section provides a quick description of Hamsterdam.

4 Hamsterdam and Alive

Hamsterdam is an object-oriented tool kit for modeling artificial animals in a 3D simulated environment. The classes of Hamsterdam provide the generic core functionality from which a designer builds the creatures, the world in which they live, and the instruments used to gain insight into the inner state of the creatures. The creatures are modeled as autonomous creatures with a set of internal needs, a repertoire of activities which they can perform, a sensory system which allows them to sense their world, a motor system which allows them to move in the world and a behavior system which is an object-oriented implementation of the algorithm described above. Creatures do not have a

world model, nor indeed any information about the world except that which is available via their sensors. The creatures "live" in a 3D continuous world (i.e. not a grid world) populated by other creatures as well as food, water and obstacles such as walls. The system is implemented in C++ on an SGI Indigo Elan and operates in real time. Figure 2 shows the system along with a number of its gauges.

Hamsterdam has been used to model a world which includes hamsters and predators. The hamsters are very loosely modeled after real hamsters, whereas the predators are "generic". The hamster's repertoire of top-level activities (or behavior systems) includes: Foraging (finding food and carrying it back to their hoard), Feeding (finding food and eating it), Drinking (finding water and drinking it), Cleaning, Anti-Predator (avoiding and fleeing from Predators), Sleeping (finding its nest and sleeping), and Death (which occurs if eaten by the predator or if certain internal state variables exceed a given range of acceptability). Activities are organized in a loose hierarchy. For example, Feeding is a top-level activity with 3 children: Chewing, Preparing-to-Eat, and Searching-for-Food. Searching-for-Food in turn has 3 children: Wander, Avoid-Obstacles, Move-to-Food. Altogether, the activity hierarchy of the hamster includes: 55 nodes or activities, 57 releasing mechanisms, 8 endogenous variables, and 25 motor commands. The predator's repertoire is similar. The creatures sense the world by means of a sensor which shoots rays of a prescribed range and records what it finds along those rays. The creatures are physically modeled and move via motors controlled by a motor controller which accepts approximately 25 commands. A variety of gauges provide insight into why the hamster or predator is behaving as it does. An earlier version of Hamsterdam was used to demonstrate a distributed model of cooperative hunting, in which several predators effectively cooperated using a few simple distributed rules to surround and kill the hamster. Hamsterdam also formed the basis for the Alive project discussed below.

The goal of the Alive installation at Siggraph 93, was to present a virtual world in which a user could interact, in natural and believable ways with autonomous semi-intelligent creatures. The world and the creatures populating the world were built using Hamsterdam. The creatures were slightly modified versions of the hamster (the foraging behavior was modified to view the user as a potential source of food) and predator (the user was considered a predator of the predator) described above. The user was represented in the world via a virtual creature whose actions were based on what the real user was doing as sensed by a vision system. Thus, from the standpoint of the hamster and predator, the user was just another creature. Over 500 people interacted with the Alive system over the five days of the conference.

5 Results

This section uses results from Hamsterdam and Alive to demonstrate the importance of some of the ideas incorporated in the computational model.

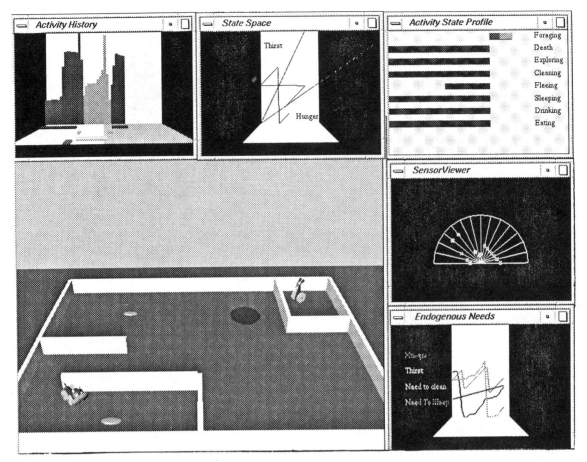

Figure 2: Screen shot of Hamsterdam. Here the hamster is engaged in foraging and is returning to its nest with food.

In the cases presented below, the hamster is in an enclosure containing food and water. To eat or drink, it must explore the enclosure until it senses the food or water, move to the appropriate resource, position its head accordingly, and then chew or drink. Thus, the various activities have the equivalent of appetitive and consumatory phases.

Figures 3 and 4 demonstrate how inhibitory gains may be used to control persistence. They present state-space diagrams [after McFarland] for hunger and thirst levels

under two different cases of inhibitory gains (low and high). The straight diagonal lines represent switching lines based on the level of inhibitory gains. The starting point for the systems is marked, and the origin represents the point of satiation for both thirst and hunger. When the gains are low, the system tends to dither between feeding and drinking with the result that the system takes longer to reach satiation levels. At higher gains, the active activity shows more persistence with the effect that satiation is reached sooner.

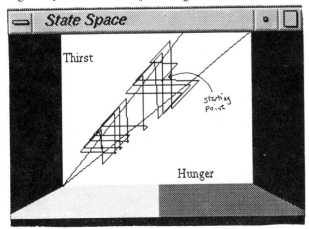

Figure 3: Low inhibitory gains encourage dithering

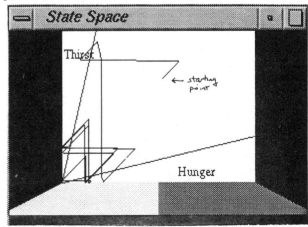

Figure 4: High inhibitory gains encourage persistence

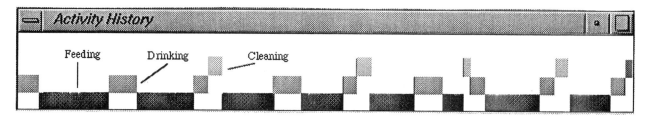

Figure 5: Use of fatigue to discourage pathological persistence

Figure 5 demonstrates the use of fatigue to discourage pathological persistence by showing the pattern of activities over time when activity-specific fatigue is included. The various blocks correspond to when a given activity is active. Feeding is represented by the black blocks, drinking by the dark gray blocks and cleaning by the lighter blocks on top. The initial level of hunger is twice that of thirst, and the need to clean is half of the level of thirst, and there is neither food nor water to be had. Without fatigue, drinking and cleaning would never become active. With fatigue, the system alternates between feeding and drinking with an occasional interruption for cleaning, even though the internal values (before fatigue) of the various activities stay unchanged. Note, additional experiments are required to demonstrate true time-sharing as defined by McFarland [McFarland74]. Nonetheless, this is an important demonstration because it shows how the system can avoid the mindless pursuit of an unattainable goal to the detriment of other goals.

Figures 6 and 7 demonstrate how adjustments to the range associated with a given Releasing Mechanism can result in opportunistic behavior. The figures show the levels of hunger and thirst over time. In both cases, the hamster starts at the same location and in the process of searching for food passes near water. In figure 6, with a lower allowed maximum for the water releasing mechanism, the hamster ignores the water until after it has eaten. When a higher value is used (figure 7), the hamster interrupts its search for food to take advantage of the water. This can be seen by comparing the respective traces of endogenous needs and noting that the level of thirst drops sooner in figure 7 than in 6.

The value of recommenders can be seen in the following experiment in which we turned off recommenders. When the move-to activity is modified so that it ignores recommendations made by the avoid activity, the hamster quickly becomes stuck oscillating between the two activities. In another experiment we turned off the anti-predator activity's ability to make recommendations when it was not active. The hamster was attacked and killed within 1600 time steps. By contrast, in the normal case the hamster manages to survive for 6400 time steps.

Performance of the algorithm has not been an issue to date since it takes less than 10ms to perform action-selection in the full behavior hierarchy of the hamster. Note, this does not include the time taken for sensors to update their state, although it does include the time taken by the releasing mechanisms to evaluate the sensor data.

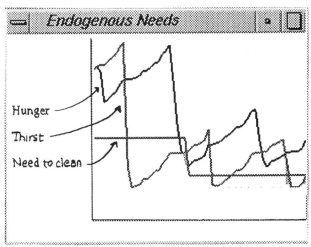

Figure 6: Low maximum allowed value for Releasing Mechanism may reduce opportunistic behavior

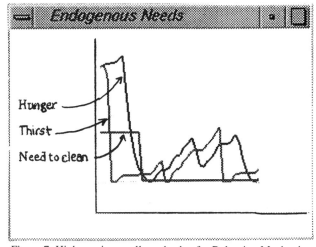

Figure 7: High maximum allowed value for Releasing Mechanism may encourage opportunistic behavior

The experience with the Alive project demonstrated that the approach described in this paper was capable of generating generally believable and robust behavior in a highly dynamic and uncertain environment and with many of the problems of real-world "sensing". People generally found the creatures' patterns of behavior and responses believable. It should be noted that the actual modifications to the hamster's behavior code to make it work in the context of the Alive project were extremely minimal.

6   Issues and areas for future work

The activity hierarchies are currently built by hand, and parameters such as inhibitory gains and rates of fatigue tuned in response to the observed behavior. As Maes points out [Maes93], this raises questions of how well the approach will scale. It should be noted that in practice parts of the hierarchy can be shared or used in multiple instances with only minor modifications. Nonetheless, more and better tools are needed, particularly to aid in finding the right values for parameters so as to achieve a given temporal pattern. Perhaps a genetic algorithm approach could prove useful, and in fact, Hamsterdam incorporates the idea of a genome which includes many of the parameters associated with the activity networks. However, no experiments have been performed, and Tyrrell had limited success using a similar approach[Tyrrell93].

Learning needs to be added and it remains to be seen how easily that can be done. However, it is believed that an ethological approach also provides a useful perspective from which to approach certain types of learning. For example, it may be possible to model "Pavlovian Conditioning" as the modification of existing releasing mechanisms or the creation of new ones, and operant conditioning as the copying (or associating) the motor patterns from one activity system into (or with) the repertoire of appetitive motor patterns of another activity system [Davey89, Timberlake89, Lorenz73]. The use of "recommenders" within the context of learning needs to be explored as well.

Even though the behavioral complexity is more complex than many of the animats described in the literature, the behavioral complexity modeled to date is still relatively simple, and it is an open question as to how well the approach will scale. We intend to investigate this issue by attempting to model a more complex creature, for example, on the order of a dog.

7   Conclusion

A computational model of action-selection has been presented, which by drawing on ideas from Ethology, addresses a number of problems which have been noted in computational models of action-selection proposed to date including the need for greater control over the temporal aspects of behavior, the need for a loose hierarchical structure with information sharing, and the need for a flexible means of modeling the influence of internal and external factors. The larger message of this paper is that in order for an animat's behavior to be natural and animal-like, we believe that incorporating some of the mechanisms proposed by Ethologists will be necessary.

Acknowledgments

The author wishes to thank Professor Pattie Maes for her many contributions to my research and this paper. Her intuition, insight, and wealth of knowledge coupled with generous amounts of patience and encouragement have been invaluable.

References

Baerends, G.,Brouwer, R. & Waterbolk H., 1955, Ethological studies on Lebistes Reticulatus,I: An analysis of the male courtship pattern. Behavior 8.

Baerends, G., 1976, On drive, conflict and instinct, and the functional organization of behavior. In: Perspectives in Brain Research 45, Corner M. & Swaab, D. eds.

Brooks R., 1986, A Robust Layered Control System for a Mobile Robot, IEEE Journal of Robotics and Automation, RA-2, April 1986.

Davey G., 1989, Ecological Learning Theory, Routledge Inc., London.

Dawkins, R. 1976, Hierarchical Organization: A Candidate principle for ethology. In: Growing Points in Ethology, Bateson P. & Hinde R. ed. Cambridge University Press.

Gallistel C., 1980, The Organization of Action: A New Synthesis, Lawrence Erlbaum , Hillsdale NJ.

Lorenz, K., 1973, Foundations of Ethology, Springer-Verlag. New York.

Ludlow, A.,1976, The Behavior of a Model Animal, Behavior Vol. 58.

Ludlow, A.,1980, The Evolution and Simulation of a Decision Maker. In: Analysis of Motivational Processes, ed. Toates, F. & Halliday, T. , Academic Press, London.

Maes P., 1990, Situated Agents Can Have Goals, In: Designing Autonomous Agents: Theory and Practice from Biology to Engineering and Back, Edited by P. Maes, MIT Press, Cambridge.

Maes, P., 1993, Modeling Adaptive Autonomous Agents, to appear in The Artificial Life Journal, Vol. 1, Numbers 1&2, Summer 1994.

McCleery, R., 1983, Interactions between Activities. In: Animal Behavior: Causes and Effects, Vol. 1, Halliday, T. & Slater P. ed., W.H. Freeman & Co., New York.

McFarland, D., 1974, Time-Sharing as a Behavioral Phenomenon. In: Advances in Animal Behavior, Vol. 5., Academic Press, New York.

McFarland, D., 1976, Form and Function in the temporal organization of behavior. In: Growing Points in Ethology, Bateson P. & Hinde R. ed. Cambridge University Press.

McFarland, D., 1993, Animal Behavior, Longman Scientific and Technical, Harlow.

McFarland, D. & Sibley, R. , 1975, The behavioral final common path, Philosophical Transactions of the Royal Society, B. 270.

Payton D., Keirsey D., Krozel J., and Rosenblatt K., 1991, Do Whatever Works: A Robust Approach to Fault-Tolerant Autonomous Control, In: Journal of Applied Intelligence, Vol. 3. 1992.

Rosenblatt K., & Payton D., 1989, A Fine-Grained Alternative to the Subsumption Architecture for Mobile Robot Control. In: Proceedings of the International Joint Conference on Neural Networks, June 1989, Washington DC.

Timberlake, W. and Lucas, G. , 1989, Behavior Systems and Learning: From Misbehavior to General Principles.

In: Contemporary Learning Theories: Instrumental Conditioning Theory and the Impact of Biological Constraints, ed. Klein S. & Mowrer, R. Lawrence Erlbaum Associates, Inc. Hillsdale NJ.

Tinbergen, N., 1950, The Study of Instinct. Clarendon Press, Oxford.

Toates, F., 1983, Models of Motivation. In: Animal Behavior: Causes and Effects, Vol. 1, Halliday, T. & Slater P. ed., W.H. Freeman & Co., New York.

Toates F. & Jensen P., 1991, Ethological and Psychological Models of Motivation: Towards a Synthesis. In: From Animals To Animats, Proceedings of the First International Conference on the Simulation of Adaptive Behavior, Edited by Meyer, J. and Wilson, S.W., MIT Press, 1991.

Tyrrell T., 1993, Computational Mechanisms for Action Selection, Ph.D. Thesis, Centre for Cognitive Science, University of Edinburgh.

Tyrrell T., 1993a, The Use of Hierarchies for Action Selection. In: From Animals To Animats, Proceedings of the Second International Conference on the Simulation of Adaptive Behavior, Edited by Meyer, J. and Wilson, S.W., MIT Press, 1993.

BEHAVIORAL DYNAMICS OF ESCAPE AND AVOIDANCE: A NEURAL NETWORK APPROACH

Nestor A. Schmajuk
Duke University
Department of Psychology: Experimental
Durham, NC 27706
U.S.A.

ABSTRACT

We present a novel, real-time two-process theory of escape and avoidance that closely integrates classical and operant conditioning processes. The model assumes that through classical conditioning animals build an internal model of their environment and that through operant conditioning animals learn alternative behavioral strategies. The internal model provides predictions of what environmental events precede other environmental events, such as the unconditioned stimulus (US). Behavioral strategies refer to the responses generated in different environmental circumstances. Whenever there is a mismatch between predicted and actual environmental events (a) the internal model is modified and (b) the behavioral strategies are adjusted. Because the warning stimulus and the US can become associated with alternative responses, animals can learn different escape and avoidance responses.

1. INTRODUCTION

Although several theories have been proposed to explain avoidance (notably Mowrer's [1947] two-factor theory, Herrnstein's [1969] one-factor theory, and Seligman and Johnston's [1973] cognitive theory), none of them was able to provide a completely successful account of the experimental data accumulated over time. Given the success of computational models in generating explicitly testable theories and offering guidance for the investigation of the physiological basis of behavior, the present paper describes avoidance in terms of a neural network.

2. THE NEURAL NETWORK

The present paper introduces a two-process neural network theory of avoidance. In simple terms, the network intimately combines classical and operant conditioning principles. The classical conditioning process involves the formation of associations between different environmental stimuli and the animal's responses with the unconditioned stimulus (US). These associations are used to predict the presence or absence of the US. Classical conditioning is regulated by the mismatch between the actual and the predicted intensity of the US: when the US is underpredicted classical associations increase, and decrease otherwise. The operant conditioning process entails the formation of associations between environmental stimuli with the escape or the avoidance response. These associations are used to select the adequate response in each case. Operant conditioning is controlled by a novel algorithm that mirrors the classical conditioning algorithm:

when the US is underpredicted operant associations decrease, and increase otherwise.

Figure 1 shows a real-time neural network that describes escape and avoidance. The network is a real-time mechanism that describes behavior as a moment-to-moment phenomenon. Nodes in the network represent neural populations, rather than individual neurons. Appendix A presents a formal description of the network as a set of differential equations that depict changes in the values of neural activities and connectivities as a function of time.

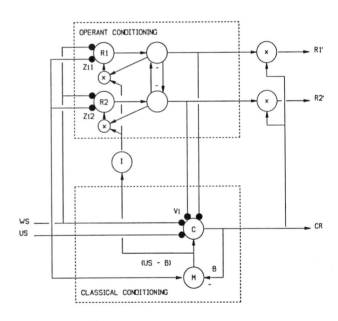

Figure 1. Neural network for escape and avoidance learning. Classical conditioning processes build an internal model of the environment used to generate predictions of the US. Operant conditioning processes establish the animal's behavioral strategy by selecting the adequate avoidance or escape responses. Mismatch between the actual and predicted intensity of the US modulates changes in both classical and operant associations. The prediction of the US also serves to regulate the strength of the operant response. WS: warning stimulus. US: unconditioned stimulus. <u>Classical conditioning</u>. CR: conditioned response. Solid circles represent V, the associations of the US, WS and Rs with the US [V(US,US), V(WS,US), V(R1,US), and V(R2,US)]. B = Σ_j V_j τ_j : Aggregate prediction of the US. <u>Operant conditioning</u>. Solid circles represent Z, the associations of WS with R [Z(WS,R1) and Z(WS,R2)], and of the US with R [Z(US,R1) and Z(US, R2)]. R1 and R2: strength of the alternative operant responses. I : neuron converting (US - B) into (B - US). R'1 and R'2: strength of the output of the operant responses.

Real-time internal representations

Environmental events are internally represented by real-time variables in the model. We assume that both the warning stimulus (WS) and the animal's responses (R) can be regarded as biologically neutral conditioned stimuli (CSs) and might become associated with the US. In addition, following Konorski (1967) we assume that the US itself has both sensory (the US as a stimulus) and emotional (the US as a biologically meaningful stimulus) representations. Hull (1951) proposed that CSs give rise to short-term memory (STM) traces, $\tau_{CS}(t)$, in the central nervous system that increase over time to a maximum and then gradually decay back to zero. Similarly, we assume that WS, US, and Rs activate different neural populations whose activity constitute respectively STM traces $\tau_{WS}(t)$, $\tau_{US}(t)$, and $\tau_R(t)$. The use of STM traces allows the model to describe paradigms, such as trace conditioning, in which the STM traces (but not the physical stimuli themselves) temporally overlap with the US. Real-time internal representations participate in two-processes, classical and operant conditioning.

Classical conditioning

The Classical Conditioning block of Figure 1 shows that node C receives inputs from the US (as a stimulus), WS, R1, and R2. Solid circles V_i represent the associations of these inputs with the US. Classical associations, regarded as a prediction of the US by the US, WS, or R, are changed according to a real-time, least mean-squares (LMS) algorithm similar to that described by Rescorla and Wagner (1972).

Node M computes the mismatch (US - B) between the actual US intensity and its "aggregate prediction", $B = \sum_i \tau_i(t) V_i$ (where $\tau_i(t)$ represents the trace of either a WS, the US, or a R). Classical associations, V_i, increase when (a) $\tau_{WS}(t)$, $\tau_{US}(t)$, or $\tau_R(t)$ is active, and (b) (US - B) is greater than zero. Classical associations, V_i, decrease when (a) $\tau_{WS}(t)$, $\tau_{US}(t)$, or $\tau_R(t)$ are active, and (b) (US - B) is less than zero. Because no learning occurs when US = B, USs, WSs, and Rs compete with each other in order to gain association with the US. When the US is predicted but is not presented, other WSs or Rs present at that time might acquire inhibitory associations with the US, i.e., predict the absence of the US. Because B is not allowed to adopt negative values, the network characterizes conditioned inhibition as not extinguishable by nonreinforced presentations of a conditioned inhibitor (see Zimmer-Hart and Rescorla, 1974). The algorithm provides real-time descriptions of classical conditioning paradigms that include acquisition and extinction of delay and trace conditioning, blocking, overshadowing, conditioned inhibition, and discrimination acquisition and reversal.

The aggregate prediction of the US, B, is interpreted as *fear* of the aversive US in the context of the model. Figure 1 shows that B is used (a) to define the strength of the conditioned response, $CR = f[\sum_i \tau_i(t) V_i]$, (b) to compute (US - B) at node M, and (c) to regulate the strength of the operant response (R1' or R2').

Operant conditioning

The Operant Conditioning block in Figure 1 shows that nodes R1 and R2 receive inputs from WS and the US (as a stimulus). Solid circles Z_{i1} and Z_{i2} represent the associations of these inputs with alternative responses R1 and R2. In Figure 1, node I inverts (US - B), computed by node M and used by the classical conditioning block, to compute (B - US), used by the operant conditioning block. Operant associations, Z_{ik}, increase when (a) $\tau_{WS}(t)$ or $\tau_{US}(t)$ are active together with $\tau_{Rk}(t)$, and (b) (B - US) is greater than zero. Operant associations, Z_{ik}, decrease when (a) $\tau_{WS}(t)$ or $\tau_{US}(t)$ are active together with $\tau_{Rk}(t)$, and (b) (B - US) is less than zero. Notice that the US and WS accrue excitatory associations with responses that gain inhibitory associations with the US, i.e., with responses, such as Ra or Re, that predict the absence of the US.

Output of nodes R1 and R2, proportional to $\sum_i \tau_i Z_{ik}$, compete to decide which alternative response will be generated. Noise is added to the intensity of each alternative response in order to provide initial random responses at the beginning of training. The response, R1 or R2, most strongly activated becomes selected and is executed by the system. This response is the one that, when fear is present, predicts the minimal amount of US (either generates the strongest prediction of the absence of the US or generates the weakest prediction of its presence). Figure 1 shows that the selected response is combined with the error signal arriving from node I to modify its association with the active $\tau_{WS}(t)$ or $\tau_{US}(t)$.

Figure 1 shows that the intensity of the selected operant response, R1' or R2', is proportional to the product of the aggregate prediction of the US, B, and the STM trace of the maximal response (R1 or R2).

3. COMPUTER SIMULATIONS

The present section contrasts experimental data with computer simulations carried out with the model presented in Figure 1. All simulations were carried out with identical parameter values presented in Appendix B.

Acquisition of Avoidance

The model can describe both delay and trace avoidance, as well as avoidance when the avoidance response is different from the escape response.

Delay Avoidance. Figure 2 shows computer simulations of acquisition of delay avoidance. During the first trials, simulations show alternated escape and avoidance responses, followed by a long period of uninterrupted avoidance behavior (over eight hundred trials). Latency time decreases over the first two hundred trials and the subject shows no sign of extinction, even after 650 trials. These simulated results are in agreement with Solomon and Wynne's (1953, 1954) data.

Panel A in Figure 2 shows that, in agreement with empirical results (Solomon, Kamin, and Wynne, 1953; Solomon and Wynne, 1954), the percentage of avoidance responses does not decrease over trials, i.e., avoidance has almost negligible extinction. This negligible extinction is explained as follows. Although protected by shorter response latencies and the inhibitory association of Ra with the US (see Soltysik, 1985), the WS-US association, and

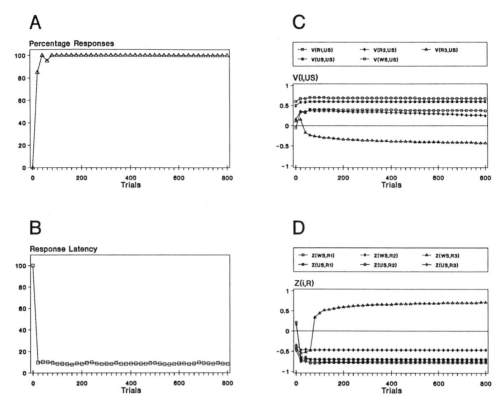

Figure 2. Delay avoidance. A: Percentage of avoidance responses. B: Response latency (number of simulated time units). C: Associations (V) of the US, WS and Rs with the US. D: Associations (Z) of WS and US with the Rs.

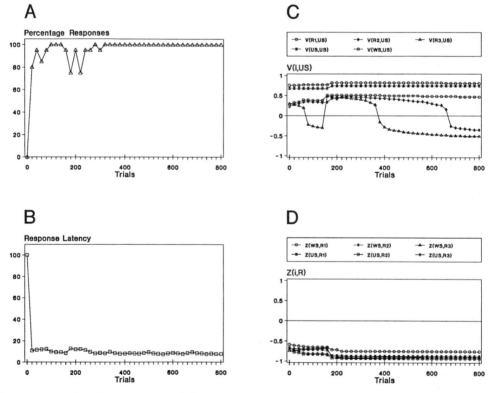

Figure 3. Different escape and avoidance responses. A: Percentage of avoidance responses. B: Response latency (number of simulated time units). C: Associations (V) of the US, WS and Rs with the US. D: Associations (Z) of WS and US with the Rs.

therefore fear, decreases over trials. As WS-US decreases, WS-Ra increases. Because the intensity of the output response is proportional to the product of the WS-US and WS-Ra associations, decreases in WS-US are compensated by increases in WS-Ra, and therefore, the percentage of avoidance responses remains constant for a long number of trials. The model's description of resistance to extinction is compatible with Baum's (1970) data, showing that response extinction is independent of fear extinction.

Panel B in Figure 2 shows that in agreement with some experimental data (e.g., Mowrer, 1947; Schoenfeld, 1950; Solomon and Wynne, 1953), response latency decreases after avoidance response is acquired. According to the model, response latency decreases because the WS-Ra association, driven by the absence of the predicted US, keeps increasing over trials. Panel C shows that in agreement with experimental results (Kamin, Brimer, and Black, 1963; Solomon and Wynne, 1953; Starr and Mineka, 1977), the WS-US association, and therefore fear, continue to gradually decrease after the animal masters avoidance. Panel C shows that whereas WS, R1, and R2 accrue a excitatory association with the US, R3 (the avoidance response, Ra) acquires a inhibitory association. Panel D shows that the WS-R3 association increases over trials.

Different escape and avoidance responses. Figure 3 shows that when Ra is different from Re, acquisition of delay avoidance proceeds at a slower pace than when Ra is identical to Re (see Figure 2). This is in agreement with Mowrer and Lamoreaux's (1946) and Bolles' (1969) results showing that, although animals can learn an avoidance response different from that required to escape the US, in most cases avoidance performance is better if the responses are identical.

At the beginning of training, the animal generates Re either in the presence of WS or the US because both WS-Re and US-Re are the dominant responses. After 25 trials, WS-Ra becomes stronger than WS-Re, and the animal correctly discriminates avoidance from escape, that is, in the presence of WS the animal avoids, and if WS is omitted, the animal escapes when the US is presented. Because it takes more trials for the animal to learn the correct discrimination, the model predicts that WS-US and US-US associations are stronger with identical avoidance and escape responses than with different ones.

Extinction of avoidance

Although in some cases avoidance might show little spontaneous extinction, avoidance can be rapidly extinguished through various alternative procedures. One procedure, called response blocking or flooding, refers to blocking the capability of an animal to generate the avoidance response without presenting the US. A second procedure consists of making the avoidance response ineffective by shocking both sides of the shuttle box. Finally, a third procedure consists of shocking the animal when it emits the avoidance response.

Blocking the avoidance response. Figure 4 shows computer simulations of blocking. During the first 200 trials, simulations show avoidance acquisition. On Trial 201, the simulated animal is presented with the WS, the avoidance response is blocked, and no US is delivered. Panel A shows that when the barrier is removed on Trial 401, the simulated animal does not generate avoidance responses. These simulated results are in agreement with Baum's (1966, 1969, 1976) and Page and Hall's (1953) data. Panel A in Figure 4 also shows simulations of the effect of reinstating an avoidance protocol on Trial 450. Panel A in Figure 4 shows that animals reacquire avoidance in few (two) shocked trials. This savings effect is based on the preserved WS-Ra association (see Panel D). This prediction of the model has not been experimentally tested.

Panel C in Figure 4 shows that on Trial 300 the WS-US association (aversion or fear to the WS) is almost entirely extinguished. According to the model, extinction of the WS-US association occurs at a faster rate than during avoidance because (a) $\tau_{ws}(t)$ is long enough to decrease its excitatory association with the US, and (b) $\tau_{R_a}(t)$ is absent and therefore does not provide protection from extinction. Based on these principles, the model is able to explain experimental data showing that weak responding (which in the model causes $\tau_{ws}(t)$ to become longer and, therefore, to decrease the WS-US association) leads to even weaker responding (Beecroft, 1967).

Shocking all responses. Figure 5 shows computer simulations of the effect of presenting the US ten seconds after the beginning of the trial, regardless of the animal's response. During the first 200 trials, simulations show acquisition of delay avoidance. From Trials 201 to 600, the animal always receives the shock US independently of the response. Panel C in Figure 5 shows that from Trial 201 to Trial 500, as all responses are shocked, WS-US and R3-US associations become excitatory. Therefore, the model explains extinction of avoidance because all responses become associated with the US and all WS-R associations become too small to activate a response (Panel D). These simulated results are in agreement with Davenport and Olson (1968) and Kamin (1957).

Panel A in Figure 5 also shows simulations of the effect of reinstating an avoidance protocol on Trial 401. Panel A of Figure 5 shows that when a normal avoidance protocol is reinstated, simulated animals do not generate any response and, therefore, avoidance is never reinitiated. This predicted behavior might be related to learned helplessness (Maier and Seligman, 1976; Overmier and Seligman, 1967; Seligman, 1975), a phenomenon by which animals exposed to an inescapable shock do not attempt to escape the shock even when later the shock becomes escapable. Panel D in Figure 5 suggests that learned helplessness is the consequence of all Z(US,Re) being very low for the system to try any response. Furthermore, Seligman and Maier (1967) reported that learned helplessness can be prevented by training the animal to escape-avoid. Panel D in Figure 5 suggests that training the animal in avoidance could immunize against inescapable shocks by increasing the value of Z(US,Re), and thereby increasing the number of inescapable trials needed to decrease Z(US,Re) to a "helpless" value.

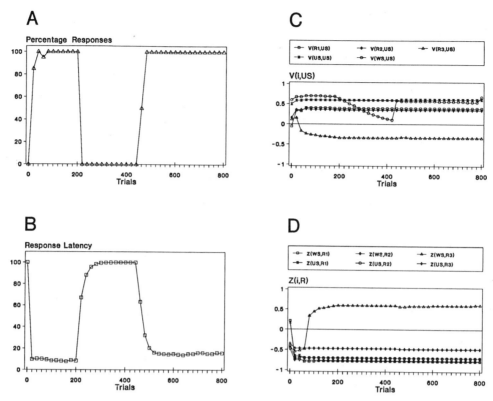

Figure 4. Blocking the avoidance response. . A: Percentage of avoidance responses. B: Response latency (number of simulated time units). C: Associations (V) of the US, WS and Rs with the US. D: Associations (Z) of WS and US with the Rs.

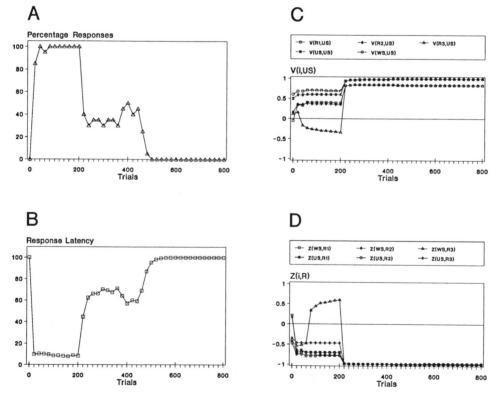

Figure 5. Shocking all responses. A: Percentage of avoidance responses. B: Response latency (number of simulated time units). C: Associations (V) of the US, WS and Rs with the US. D: Associations (Z) of WS and US with the Rs.

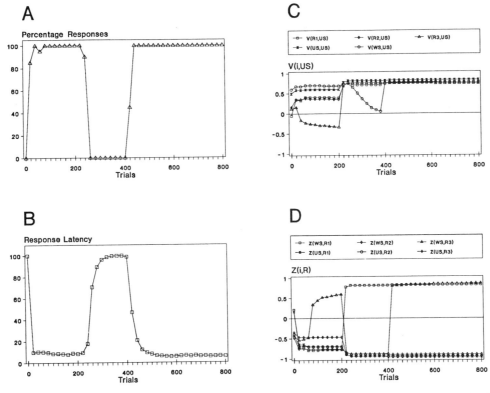

Figure 6. Shocking the avoidance response. A: Percentage of avoidance responses. B: Response latency (number of simulated time units). C: Associations (V) of the US, WS and Rs with the US. D: Associations (Z) of WS and US with the Rs.

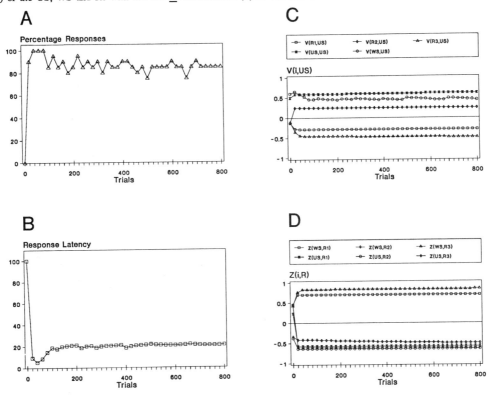

Figure 7. Extending the WS. A: Percentage of avoidance responses. B: Response latency (number of simulated time units). C: Associations (V) of the US, WS and Rs with the US. D: Associations (Z) of WS and US with the Rs.

Shocking the avoidance response. Figure 6 shows computer simulations of the effect of presenting a US only when the animal generates Ra. During the first 200 trials, simulations show acquisition of delay avoidance. From Trials 201 to 400, the simulated animal receives a US when generating Ra. From Trials 201 to approximately 320, the animal decreases its average response latency, and after that it rapidly extinguishes Ra. These simulated results are in agreement with Solomon, Kamin, and Wynne (1953). Panel A in Figure 6 also shows simulations of the effect of reinstating an avoidance protocol on Trial 401. Panel A in Figure 6 shows that animals reacquire avoidance in eight shocked trials. As in the flooding case, this savings effect is based on the preserved WS-US association. This prediction of the model has not been experimentally tested.

Panels C and D in Figure 6 show that from Trial 201 to Trial 240, WS-US increases, WS-R3 (Ra) decreases and WS-R1 and WS-R2 increase. The model explains extinction of avoidance in terms of the decrease in WS-R3 and increase in WS-R1 and WS-R2 associations. In agreement with Bolles, Moot, Grossen (1971) simulated results show that shocking the avoidance response produce faster extinction than shocking all responses.

Effects of extending the WS, terminating the WS, and classical conditioning

Kamin (1957) studied the effect that different procedures have on acquisition of avoidance. In normal avoidance, the avoidance response was followed by the immediate termination of the WS and no US was delivered on that trial. In a "terminate WS" situation, the avoidance response was followed by the immediate termination of the WS but a US was delivered to either side of the box. In an "extended WS" situation, the avoidance response prevented the US presentation but did not terminate the WS. Finally, in a classical conditioning situation, the avoidance response had no effect on either the WS duration or the delivery of the US.

Extending the WS. Figure 7 shows computer simulations of delay avoidance when the WS is not terminated even after the animal has generated the Ra. In agreement with Kamin (1957), when the WS is extended after the Ra slower acquisition and lower asymptotic levels of avoidance are attained and reinforcement is intermittently needed. This alternating behavior is explained in terms of the extinction of the aversive association between the WS and the US. Panel C in Figure 7 shows that the WS-US association extinguishes when the WS is extended. In contrast, WS-Ra is largely increased as Ra accrues an inhibitory association with the US. As mentioned, extinction of the WS-US association occurs during (a) the period when the WS is on and the US is absent, and (b) the period when WS is off but $\tau_{ws}(t)$ is still active. When the WS terminates as the animal generates Ra, $\tau_{ws}(t)$ is protected from extinction by $\tau_{Ra}(t)$ (see Equation 2 in Appendix A). By extending the WS, the value of $\tau_{ws}(t)$ is large even when the animal has avoided the US, and therefore extinction of WS-US increases, and periodical reinforcement is needed in order

to maintain the generation of avoidance responses.

Terminating the WS. Figure 8 shows computer simulations of delay avoidance when the WS is terminated after Ra but the US is still delivered. When the WS is terminated after the Ra but the US is still delivered, consistent avoidance is never attained. In agreement with Kamin (1957), simulations show alternating avoidance and escape behavior. This behavior is explained in terms of the extinction of the WS-Ra association. As mentioned, acquisition of the WS-Ra association occurs during the period when the WS and Ra are active and the predicted US exceeds the value of the actual US. When the US is delivered as the animal generates Ra, the actual US exceeds the predicted US and, therefore, WS-Ra association decreases. Panel C in Figure 8 shows that the WS-US association increased as the US is consistently presented. Panel D shows that all WS-R associations are greatly decreased.

Classical conditioning. Figure 9 shows computer simulations of delay avoidance when the US follows the WS at a fixed time interval, independently of the animal's response. When the WS is always followed by the US, consistent avoidance is never attained. Panel A shows that, in agreement with Kamin (1957), Ra increases at the beginning of training and then gradually decreases to zero. At the beginning of training, animals generate avoidance responses on a random basis, and the intensity of the responses is magnified by an increased WS-US association. As all Rs, including Ra, become increasingly aversive, the animal stops responding. This result is similar to the paradigm in which all Rs are punished, and therefore, avoidance is extinguished. Panel C in Figure 9 shows that the WS-US association increased as the US is consistently presented, as in classical conditioning. In contrast, Panel D shows that all WS-R associations are greatly decreased.

4. DISCUSSION

We present a novel, real-time two-process theory of avoidance that combines elements of classical and operant conditioning. The classical conditioning process generates associations between the WS, the US, and Rs generated by the animal with the US. Whereas WS and the US become predictors of the US, escape and the avoidance response, Re and Ra, become predictors of the absence of the US. The operant conditioning process associates WS and US with those Rs that predict the absence of the US (avoidance and escape responses). The classical conditioning process (a) provides predictions of the presence or absence of the US used by the operant conditioning process to generate WS-R associations, and (b) controls the strength of the behavior. Because the warning WS and the US can become associated with different available responses, animals can learn different escape and avoidance responses. Since the model describes behavior in real time, it is able to capture the effects of using different temporal WS and US arrangements and to describe the latency of avoidance and escape responses.

Computer simulations demonstrate that the model

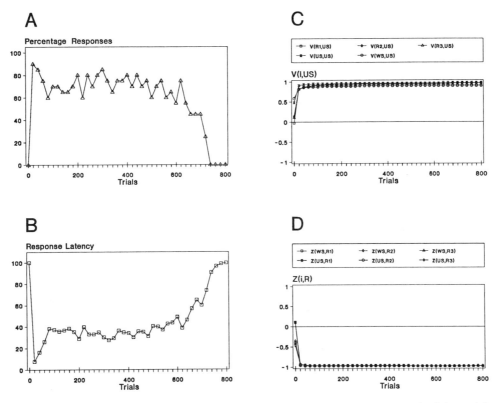

Figure 8. Terminating the WS. A: Percentage of avoidance responses. B: Response latency (number of simulated time units). C: Associations (V) of the US, WS and Rs with the US. D: Associations (Z) of WS and US with the Rs.

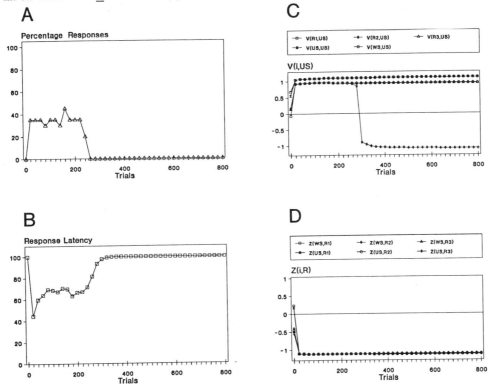

Figure 9. Classical conditioning. A: Percentage of avoidance responses. B: Response latency (number of simulated time units). C: Associations (V) of the US, WS and Rs with the US. D: Associations (Z) of WS and US with the Rs.

describes many of the features that characterize avoidance behavior: (a) fear of the US decreases as the animal masters the response, (b) techniques that decrease fear decrease, and techniques that increase fear increase, ongoing avoidance responses, (c) the amount of time needed to generate the avoidance response decreases with increasing number of trials, (d) in some situations avoidance have negligible extinction, (e) trace avoidance is less resistant to extinction than delay avoidance, (f) acquisition of trace avoidance is slower and extinction faster with increasing WS-US intervals, (g) extinction of avoidance is obtainable by blocking the animal's capability to elicit the avoidance response without delivering the US, by shocking the animal when it emits the avoidance response, or by shocking the animal whether or not it emits the avoidance response, (h) when the avoidance response terminat presentation animals show a slower acquisition and lower asymptotic levels of avoidance, (i) when the avoidance response prevents the US presentation but does not terminate the WS animals learn less than in the normal avoidance situation, (j) when the avoidance response has no effect either in the WS duration or the delivery of the US (classical conditioning) animals do not acquire consistent avoidance, and (k) the avoidance response may be different from that required to escape the US.

Ethological validity of the theory

Hull (1929) suggested that principles similar to those found in the lab may be applied to the description of how animals in the wild learn to avoid predators. According to Hull, when animals are attacked by a predator but manage to escape and survive, they learn that stimuli present at the time of the assault predict an impending aggression. Therefore, when potential preys perceive similar stimuli on future occasions, they flee to avoid the predator. Supporting Hull's view, Curio (1976) reported that predators may be effective in less than 43 % of their strikes, thereby revealing their presence and providing their prey plenty of opportunities to learn about their enemies and their circumstances. In conclusion, it is possible that animals in the wild learn to avoid predators utilizing mechanisms similar to those described in the present paper.

ACKNOWLEDGMENTS
This project was supported in part by Contract N00014-91-J-1764 from the Office of Naval Research.

APPENDIX A
A formal description of the model.

Classical conditioning process. We assume that $WS_i(t)$, $R_i(t)$, and the $US(t)$ (generically represented by $X_i(t)$) generate a STM trace, $\tau_i(t)$, according to

$$d(\tau_i(t)) / dt = - K_1 \tau_i + K_2 (K_3 - \tau_i(t)) X_i(t), \qquad [1]$$

where $- K_1 \tau_i(t)$ represents the passive decay of the STM of $WS_i(t)$, $R_j(t)$, or the $US(t)$. K_2 represents the rate of increase of $\tau_i(t)$, and constant K_3 is the maximum possible value of $\tau_i(t)$ (see Grossberg, 1975).

Changes in the association of $\tau_i(t)$ with the US, are given by

$$d(V_i(t)) / dt = K_4 \tau_i (US(t) - B(t)) (1 - |V_i(t)|). \qquad [2]$$

where $\tau_i(t)$ represents the trace of $WS_i(t)$, $R_i(t)$, or the $US(t)$. $B(t) = \Sigma_j V_j(t) \tau_j(t)$ represents the aggregate prediction of the US by all τ's active at a given time. $K_4 = K_4'$ if $US(t) > \Sigma_j V_j(t) \tau_j(t)$, $K_4 = K_4''$ if $US < \Sigma_j V_j(t) \tau_j(t)$. By Equation 2, $V_i(t)$ increases whenever $\tau_i(t)$ is active and $US(t) > \Sigma_j V_j(t) \tau_j(t)$ and decreases when $US(t) < \Sigma_j V_j(t) \tau_j(t)$. In order to prevent the extinction of conditioned inhibition or the generation of an excitatory CS by presenting a neutral CS with an inhibitory CS, we assume that when $\Sigma_j V_j(t) \tau_j(t) < 0$ then $\Sigma_j V_j(t) \tau_j(t) = 0$. The term $(1 - |V_i(t)|)$ bounds $V_i(t)$ ($-1 \leq V_i(t) \leq 1$).

Operant conditioning process. We adopt a "response-selection" view of operant conditioning by which WS or the US become associated to different alternative responses. Changes in the association of τ_i of WS_i with the R_j, are given by

$$d(Z_{ik}(t)) / dt = K_5 \tau_i(t) \tau_k(t) (B(t) - US(t)) (1 - |Z_{ik}(t)|) \qquad [3]$$

where $\tau_i(t)$ is the STM trace of $WS(t)$ or the $US(t)$, and $\tau_k(t)$ is the STM trace of the response that has the maximum output at a given time. $K_5 = K_5'$ if $US(t) < \Sigma_j V_j(t) \tau_j(t)$, $K_5 = K_5''$ if $US > \Sigma_j V_j(t) \tau_j(t)$. According to Equation 3, $WS(t)$ or the $US(t)$ become associated with $R_k(t)$ when they are active simultaneously and $\Sigma_j V_j(t) \tau_j(t) > US(t)$, and decrease if $\Sigma_j V_j(t) \tau_j(t) < US(t)$. Because WS and the US may become associated with different responses, Ra and Re might be different. More generally, the system can learn operant discriminations by generating R_1 in the presence of WS_1 and R_2 in the presence of WS_2. The term $(1 - |Z_{ik}(t)|)$ bounds $Z_{ik}(t)$ ($-1 \leq Z_{ik}(t) \leq 1$).

Performance Rules. The strength of the conditioned response is given by

$$CR(t) = f[B(t)] = f[\Sigma_j V_j(t) \tau_j(t)]. \qquad [4]$$

The strength of $R_k(t)$ is given by

$$R_k(t) = K_6 f[\Sigma_i Z_{ik}(t) \tau_i(t) + r_i(t)], \qquad [5]$$

where $f[x] = 1 / 1 + e^{-(x)}$, and $r_i(t)$ is a random number. $R_k(t)$ is always positive, even when x may vary between -1 and 1. We assume that the animal selects and tries the response with the maximum $R_k(t)$, denoted by $R_{max}(t)$, every 5 time units. When $R_{max}(t)$ is selected it activates $\tau_{max}(t)$ according to Equation 1.

The amplitude of the operant response, $R'(t)$, is given by

$$R'(t) = \tau_{max}(t) B(t), \qquad [6]$$

where $B(t) = \Sigma_j V_j(t) \tau_j(t)$. Equation 6 implies that the same operant response $R'(t)$ can be achieved by various combinations of $\tau_{max}(t)$ and $B(t)$.

Let $t_{latency}$ denote the time at which the animal crosses to the opposite side in a shuttle box and thereby avoids or escapes the shock. Then $t_{latency}$ is the earliest time such that

$$R'(t_{latency}) = \tau_{max}(t_{latency}) B(t_{latency}) \geq K_7, \qquad [7]$$

where K_7 is the threshold to escape or avoid. Equation 7 implies that latency decreases for a fast-growing $\tau_{max}(t)$ and large Bs. Because $\tau_{max}(t)$ is grows faster with increasing values of $R_{max}(t) = K_6 f[\Sigma_i Z_{ik}(t) \tau_i(t)]$, latency decreases with increasing values of $Z_{imax}(t)$ (WS-R_{max} and US-R_{max} operant associations). Also, because $B(t) = \Sigma_j V_j(t) \tau_j(t)$, latency decreases with increasing values of $V_j(t)$ (WS-US,

US-US, and R-US classical associations).

APPENDIX B
Simulation procedures and parameters

In our computer simulations, each trial is divided into 250 time units for shuttlebox avoidance and 100 time units for Sidman avoidance. Each time unit represents approximately 500 msec. At time zero, the WS is presented. If the avoidance response has not been performed after 25 time units, a shock US is applied. Three alternative responses are considered and no initial hierarchy (see Hull, 1951) is assumed, i.e. $Z_{ik} = 0$.

The parameters values used in all simulations are $K_1 = 2 \ 10^{-2}$, $K_2 = 25 \ 10^{-3}$, $K_3 = 1$, $K_4' = 1 \ 10^{-5}$, $K_4'' = 6 \ 10^{-4}$, $K_5' = 5 \ 10^{-3}$, $K_5'' = 3 \ 10^{-1}$, $K_6 = 5 \ 10^{-4}$, $K_7 = 5 \ 10^{-2}$, and $r_k = \pm \ 2 \ 10^{-4}$.

REFERENCES

Baum, M. (1966). Rapid extinction of an avoidance response following a period of response prevention in the avoidance apparatus. *Psychological Reports, 18*, 59-64.

Baum, M. (1969). Extinction of avoidance response following response prevention: Some parametric investigations. *Canadian Journal of Psychology, 23*, 1-10.

Baum, M. (1970). Extinction of avoidance responding through response prevention (flooding). *Psychological Bulletin, 74*, 276-284.

Baum, M. (1976). Instrumental learning: comparative studies. In M.P. Feldman and A. Broadhurst (Eds.), *Theoretical and experimental bases of the behavior therapies*. New York: Wiley.

Beecroft, R.S. (1967). Near-goal punishment of avoidance running. *Psychonomics Sciences, 8*, 109-110.

Bolles, R.C. (1969). Avoidance and escape learning: simultaneous acquisition of different responses. *Journal of Comparative Psychology and Physiological, 68*, 355-358.

Bolles, R.C., Moot, S.A., Grossen, N.E. (1971). The extinction of shuttlebox avoidance. *Learning and Motivation, 2*, 324-333.

Curio, E. (1976). *The ethology of predation*. Berlin: Springer Verlag.

Davenport, D.G. & Olson, R.D. (1968). A reinterpretation of extinction in discriminated avoidance. *Psychonomics Science, 13*, 5-6.

Grossberg, S. (1975). A neural model of attention, reinforcement, and discrimination learning. *International Review of Neurobiology, 18*, 263-327.

Herrnstein, R.J. (1969). Method and theory in the study of avoidance. *Psychological Review, 76*, 49-69.

Hull, C.L. (1929). A functional interpretation of the conditioned reflex. *Psychological Review, 36*, 498-511.

Hull, C.L. (1951). *Essentials of Behavior*. Westport, Connecticut: Greenwood Press.

Kamin, L.J. (1957). The gradient of delay of secondary reward in avoidance learning. *Journal of Comparative and Physiological Psychology, 50*, 445-449.

Kamin, L.J., Brimer, C.J., & Black, A.H. (1963). Conditioned suppression as a monitor of fear of the CS in the course of avoidance training. *Journal of Comparative and Physiological Psychology, 56*, 497-501.

Konorski, (1967). *Integrative activity of the brain. An interdisciplinary approach*. Chicago: University of Chicago Press.

Maier, S. F., Seligman, M. E. P., & Solomon, R. L. (1969). Pavlovian fear conditioning and learned helplessness effects on escape and avoidance behaviors of (a) the WS-US contingency and (b) the independence of the US and voluntary responding. In B. A. Campbell & R. M. Church (Eds.), *Punishment and Aversive Behavior*. New York: Appleton-Century-Crofts.

Mowrer, O. H. (1947). On the dual nature of learning--a reinterpretation of conditioning and problem solving. *Harvard Educational Review, 17*, 102-148.

Mowrer, O.H., & Lamoreaux, R.R. (1946). Fear as an intervening variable in avoidance conditioning. *Journal of Comparative Psychology, 39*, 29-50.

Overmier, J.B., & Seligman, M.E.P. (1967). Effects of inescapable shock upon subsequent escape and avoidance responding. *Journal of Comparative and Physiological Psychology, 63*, 28-33.

Page, H.A., & Hall, J.F. (1953). Experimental extinction as a function of the prevention of response. *Journal of Comparative and Physiological Psychology, 46*, 33-34.

Rescorla, R.A., & Wagner, A.R. (1972). A theory of Pavlovian conditioning: Variations in the effectiveness of reinforcement and nonreinforcement. In A.H. Black and W.F. Prokasy (Eds.), *Classical conditioning II: Current research and theory*. New York: Appleton-Century-Crofts.

Schoenfeld, W.N. (1950). An experimental approach to anxiety, escape, and avoidance behavior. In P.H. Hoch and J. Zubin (Eds.), *Anxiety*. New York: Grune and Stratton.

Seligman, M.E.P. (1975). *Helplessness: On depression, development, and death*. San Francisco: Freeman.

Seligman, M. E. P. & Johnston, J. C. (1973). A cognitive theory of avoidance learning. In F. J. McGuigan and D. B. Lumsden (Eds.), *Contemporary approaches to conditioning and learning*. Washington, D.C.: Winston-Wiley.

Seligman, M.E.P., & Maier, S.F. (1967). Failure to escape traumatic shock. *Journal of Experimental Psychology, 74*, 1-9.

Solomon, R.L., & Wynne, L.C. (1953). Traumatic avoidance learning: Acquisition in normal dogs. *Psychological Monographs, 67*, 354.

Solomon, R.L., & Wynne, L.C. (1954). Traumatic avoidance learning: The principles of anxiety conservation and partial reversibility. *Psychological Review, 61*, 353-385.

Solomon, R.L., Kamin, L.J., & Wynne, L.C. (1953). Traumatic avoidance learning: The outcomes of several extinction procedures with dogs. *Journal of Abnormal and Social Psychology, 48*, 291-302.

Soltysik, S. (1960). Studies on avoidance conditioning: II. Differentiation and extinction of avoidance responses. *Acta Biologiae Experimentalis, 20*, 171-182.

Starr, M.D., & Mineka, S. (1977). Determinants of fear over the cause of avoidance learning. *Learning and Motivation, 8*, 332-350.

Zimmer-Hart, C.L., & Rescorla, R.A. (1974). Extinction of Pavlovian conditioned inhibition. *Journal of Comparative and Physiological Psychology, 86*, 837-845.

Organizing an Animat's behavioural repertoires using Kohonen Feature Maps

Nigel Ball

Engineering Design Centre
Department of Engineering
University of Cambridge
Trumpington Street
Cambridge CB2 1PZ, UK.
e-mail - nrb@eng.cam.ac.uk

Abstract

This paper describes the simulation of an animat with a modified classifier system that represents classifier condition sets using a class of self organising neural networks known as Kohonen Feature Maps. These networks enable individual classifier selection and adaptation to be driven by an unsupervised learning mechanism . An additional competitive learning mechanism operating between classifiers produces a ranking based on feedback from the environment. These two mechanisms when coupled with a memory of goal states enable the animat to concurrently explore and exploit a problem environment. The environment simulated in this paper is Woods7 and the performance of the animat is considered in terms of number of steps to find food and the ability of the classifier population to track newly discovered food targets.

1. Classifier Systems

Classifier systems are massively parallel, message-passing, rule-based systems that learn through credit assignment and rule discovery via the application of genetic algorithms [6] . A classifier system consists of three main components - rule and message system; apportionment of credit system; genetic algorithm (G.A) The system's behaviour is governed by an external critic which embodies a specific fitness function for classifier evaluation and provides feedback to the G.A. A classifier system can be considered to be subject to extrinsic adaptation as opposed to the essentially intrinsic evolutionary processes that occur automatically as a result of the interaction of organisms with each other and their environment [5][8]. Extrinsic adaptation in this context implies that the environment imposes an order which is transferred directly onto the organism. Intrinsic adaptation implies that the organism spontaneously generates a multiplicity of internal variations in organization which exist prior to interaction with the environment. Interaction simply selects some of these variations. Extrinsic adaptation can cause difficulties for classifier systems operating in complex, multi criteria domains. These kinds of problem occur frequently in nature since decision making and autonomous learning in natural organisms requires the resolution of contradictory goals by selective attention in real time.

One approach to the application of classifier systems in more difficult domains is to reconsider the representation of the problem environment within the system [1]. If the learning problem is redefined as the incremental refinement of an (internal) world model representation, an alternate approach is to extend the classifier representation to enable environmental feedback to impinge directly upon the classifier population. This would obviate the requirement for external critic and internal credit apportionment systems and bring the system closer to the environment.

2. Kohonen Feature Maps

Topological maps are ubiquitous in the cerebral cortex of the brain and detailed maps of cortical representation patterns have been made for the areas concerned with sensory and motor input. An important organizing principle of these maps is that the placement of neurons is orderly and reflects some physical characteristic of the external stimulus being sensed. Kohonen [7] has used the concept of competitive learning to develop a unsupervised learning rule which produces topological self-organization similar to that in the brain within a single layer network called a Feature Map. The effect of the self organization process on the network is to 'tune' it to different inputs in an ordered fashion, as if a continuous map of the input data space has been formed over the network. Individual network nodes categorize the input vector space thus compressing the environmental data to a small set of archetypal vectors. This behaviour has been utilised to generate self organising classifier conditions sets in a modified classifier system known as the Hybrid Learning System (HLS) [1][2].

3. The Hybrid Learning System

The Hybrid Learning System applies a sub-symbolic, distributed data representation - the Kohonen Feature Map - to the condition sets of a classifier system to produce a hybrid that uses unsupervised learning to generate a crude

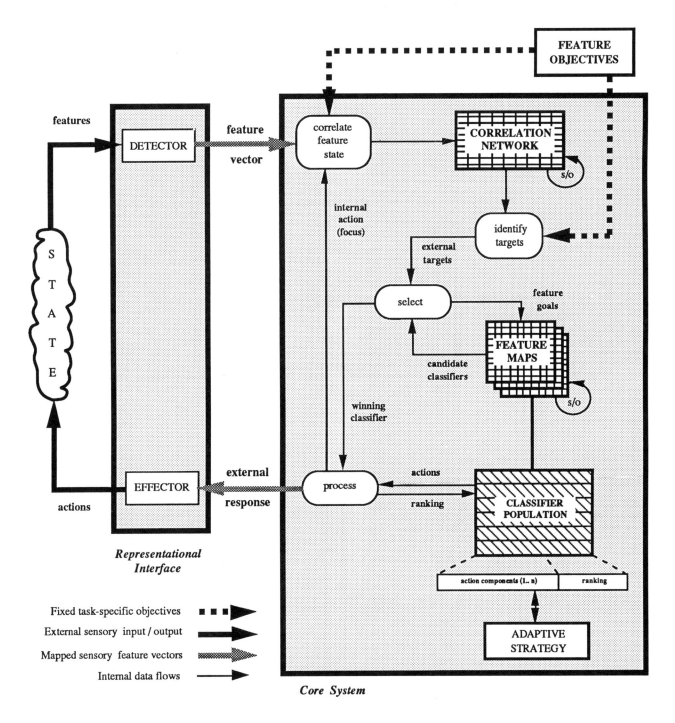

ADAPTIVE STRATEGY - application of G.A operators (based on classifier ranking)

S/O - self organization of neural networks

Figure 1. **Hybrid Learning System**

analogue of the cortical maps linking sensory input to motor output in the brain. The HLS architecture shown in figure 1 consists of two subsystems - the representational interface and the core system. The HLS model is an extension of a classifier model which allows for the encoding of multiple classifier condition/fitness values within self organizing neural network structures. The neural network subsystem is comprised of a single Feature Correlation Network (FCN) and multiple Classifier Feature Maps (CFMs). These networks are HLS's 'world model' in the form of memory (correlation network) and stereotyped

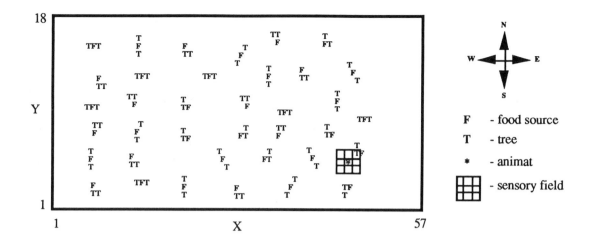

Figure 2.   **Woods7**

behaviour (feature maps). They drive the system's movements and constitute an experience-based learning system that is separate from the evolutionary learning system represented by the adaptive strategy.

CFM networks provide a low level learning capacity which enables the system to calibrate classifier behaviour independently of specific targets. The Feature Correlation Network is the system's memory of which external feature states correlate to the fulfilment of the pre-defined feature objectives. Interrogation of this memory results in the feature maps being given new feature goals at each time step. These goals combined with current state data form the input to the feature maps which are interrogated to determine the classifier most likely to produce convergent behaviour towards the given objective. Selection of a classifier results in the adaptation of the portion of the network associated with it to reflect its behaviour in terms of changes to an object's feature state. If these changes are beneficial then the classifier's condition set will become better adapted to the current scenario state and thus increase its probability of selection. Therefore frequency of selection is used as a measure of classifier fitness to drive the adaptive strategy.

Adaptation of the classifiers' condition sets reflects the system's incremental calibration of known behaviours to the problem scenario. Production of new classifiers via the adaptive strategy provides new, speculative, behaviours which may improve performance. These new classifiers are built upon the backs of previously successful ones. They displace weaker classifiers within the population and are

calibrated in their turn by the feature maps that encode their condition sets.

4. Simulating an animat in Woods7

The simulation of Wilson's Woods7 environment [11] (figure 2) illustrates the basic execution cycle of HLS. A 2D cellular environment (X,Y) with a multiple food sources (F) and trees (T) is to be explored by an animat starting at a random position with a sensory range of 1 cell. The objective of the system controlling the animat is to minimize the number of steps taken to acquire food. In this scenario the system object is configured with four features - food signal {F}, tree signal {T}, X location {X}, Y location {Y} - and eight classifiers - N, S, E, W, NE, NW, SE, SW. Feature objectives are preset on F and T (high and low) with X and Y objectives being undefined. Each time a food source is reached and food acquired (one trial), the animat is repositioned at random. A single trial has a upper bound of 41 steps (random animat movement) and a lower bound of 2.2 steps (omniscient animat).

The animat controlled by the system has to -

(1) explore the environment to locate food sources and trees.
(2) sequence classifier activation to minimize time taken to reach a food source.

4.1 System execution cycle

The basic execution cycle of the system is -

(1) detection of current feature signals {F,T,X,Y} for

all locations within sensory range of the object (fixed at a distance of 1 in this example).

(2) application of each feature signal vector { } detected in (1) onto the correlation network (using the self organizing mechanism documented in [2]).

(3) identification of external targets {X, Y} by associative lookup of preset objectives {F,T} against current state of the correlation network.

(4) selection of candidate classifiers for each external target {X, Y}.

(5) application of classifiers to problem environment to generate a new object state (in this example a single classifier is applied at each cycle).

(6) self organization of classifier feature maps based on the object state pre and post classifier application in (5).

(7) evolution and integration of new classifiers into the current population.

Steps (2), (6) and (7) constitute the learning mechanism of the system.

4.2 System performance

The behaviour of the system is shown in figures 3(a) - (d). Figure 3(a) shows the targets set by the Feature Correlation Network during the first 200 trials in terms of X/Y coordinates against time step. Figure 3(b) shows the path followed by the object to achieve the targets. Targets are of two types - fixed and derived. Fixed targets for food acquisition and tree avoidance (marked with an "*" on 3(a) and 3(b)) are specific to the Woods7 problem. The derived X and Y targets (features 2 and 3) are generated through associative lookup on the Feature Correlation Network. The target trace for X / Y in figure 3(a) is complex since each successful food acquisition (trial) results in random relocation and the correlation of new target coordinates onto the Feature Correlation Network. System performance can be measured in two ways -

(1) achievement of fixed targets

(2) tracking of derived targets.

Measure (1) relates to the effectiveness of the Feature Correlation Network in locating targets and is extrinsic to the animat. Measure (2) relates to the calibration of the animat's behavioural repertoire (which is independent of fixed targets) and is an intrinsic part of the animat. Figure 3(c) shows the performance of the animat in achieving the extrinsic target for food acquisition measured in terms of time steps per trial. Figure 3(d) shows the intrinsic performance of the classifier population in terms of tracking the derived targets generated by the Feature Correlation Network.

A number of points should be noted when considering these results -

(1) HLS does not control an omniscient animat since the Feature Correlation Network only supplies coordinates of food and trees not tree avoidance or path data (see [3] for work in this area).

(2) the performance of the system improves over time due to the discovery of new food sources and the

improved calibration of classifier feature maps.

(3) the calibration mechanism is radically different to the learning mechanisms in standard classifier systems which invalidates qualitative comparisons based on run time.(most work on woods7 has used much longer test runs (~ 8000 trials) [4] [10])

The remainder of this paper considers (3) in detail by discussing the architecture and adaptive mechanisms embedded in HLS's classifiers.

5. Architecture of Classifier Feature Maps

The architecture of the Classifier Feature Map network is shown in figure 4(a). The underlying architecture of each map is a Kohonen Feature Map [7] with extensions to node structure to enable classifier condition representation. The key parameters governing this architecture are -

(1) the dimensionality of each map (normally 2D)

(2) the size of each dimension

(3) the profile of the adaptation zone applied by an active node (see figure 4(b))

(4) the rate of habituation experienced by active nodes and its relation to local / global factors

[5] the strength of competitive connections between feature maps.

Parameters (1) - (4) are extensively discussed in the literature e.g [9]. Parameter (5) is specific to HLS and discussed in detail in [1].

One map is maintained for each feature which characterizes an object. Each classifier layer has to represent the situations in which a classifier may operate. To achieve this each node has the structure shown in figure 4(b) with two types of weights - pre-activation (state) E and post activation (goal) G. The difference between these weights encodes the behaviour of the classifier on the environmental feature represented by this feature map. The E weight is used to measure how well the classifier (corresponding to this layer) matches the current feature state, whereas the G weight is used to measure how well the classifier would match a desired goal state if activated.

5.1 Classifier activation

Selection of a classifier for a particular feature state/goal situation requires the inspection of each node within each layer of the feature map to find the best match using a Euclidean measure of distance. Actual goals are defined by the correlation network and linked with the current environment state to provide a 'match couple' vector for each feature which is applied as input data to each map node. A 'winner-take-all' strategy produces a ranked list of classifiers in order of goal convergence rate. This strategy is based on Kohonen's selection algorithm using a match measure for node i, feature f, time epoch t defined by -

$$d_i{}^C = [[G_f(t) - w_g(t)]^2 + [E_f(t) - w_e(t)]^2]^{0.5} +$$
$$K * [\sum_{h \sim f} [[G_h(t) - w_g(t)]^2 + [E_h(t) - w_e(t)]^2]^{0.5}]$$

where $d_i{}^C$ = match value of node i in layer C

E_f = state of feature f

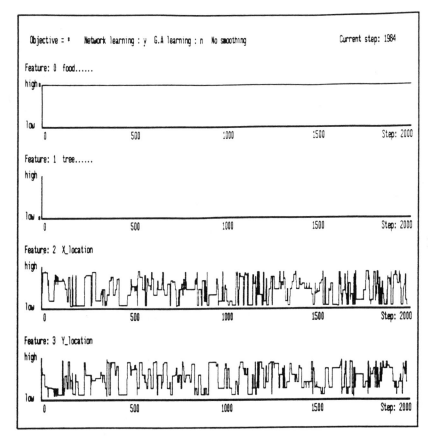

Figure 3(a). **Targets generated by**
Feature Correlation Network

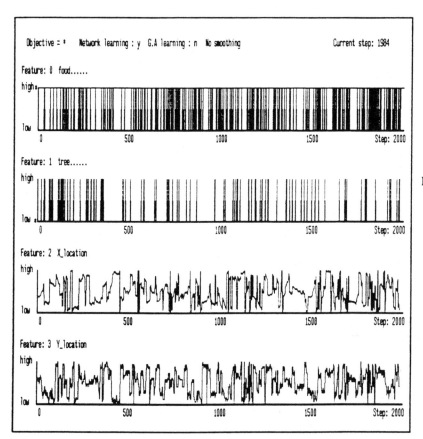

Figure 3(b). **Tracking performance of**
Classifier Feature Maps

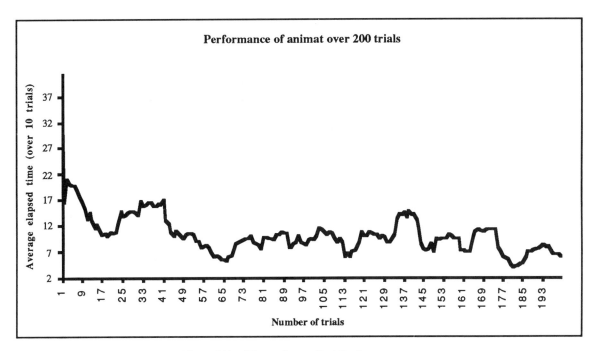

Figure 3(c). **Time taken to find food**

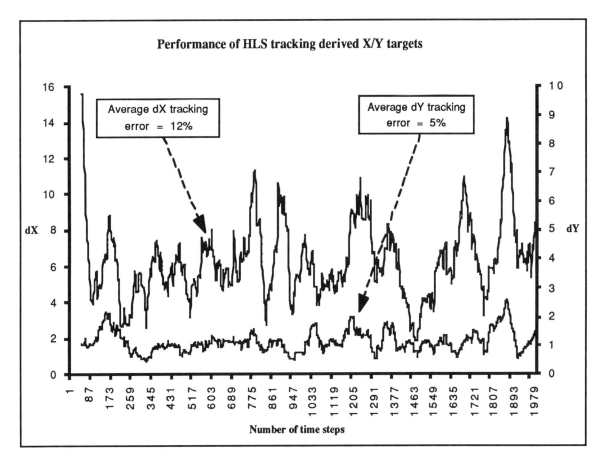

Figure 3(d). **Calibration error for X/Y features**

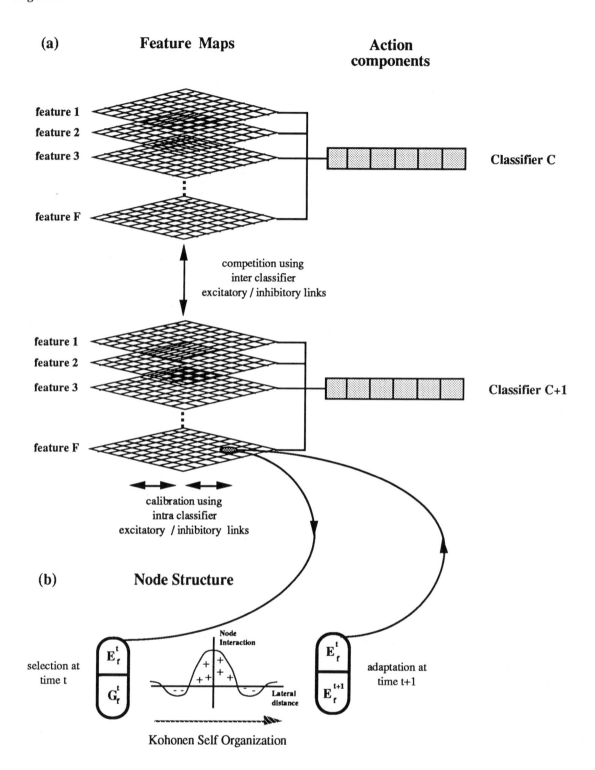

Figure 4. **HLS Classifier Architecture**

G_f = goal for feature f
w_g = node i post-activation weight (goal)
w_e = node i pre-activation weight (state)
K = constant

The winning node within a classifier layer for feature map f is -

$$d_{minC} = minimum_i[d_i{}^C]$$

The winning node across all classifier layers for feature map f is -

$$dmin = minimum_c(d_{minC} * B_i{}^C)$$

where $B_i{}^C$ = inter classifier activation of classifier C
at node i (see 5.3).

The selection process places equal emphasis on a classifier's match to the current environment state and to its potential to deliver the required convergence to the goal. This ensures that classifier layers within a feature map become sensitive to different state/goal situations and overlap in an ordered way so as to select classifiers that progressively move an object towards the goal.

5.2 Feature Map calibration

Adaptation of the feature maps occurs after the classifier has been activated and applied to the environment. At this point the new environmental state can be used to calibrate the corresponding classifier layer in a feature map in a neutral manner regardless of goal convergence or divergence. Adaptation is applied across all feature maps within the layer associated with the activated classifier. The adaptation profile is a step function approximation of the 'Mexican Hat' profile associated with Kohonen's adaptation algorithm. The centre of the profile is fixed in each feature map layer at the coordinates of the best matching node selected in the previous time step. The adaptation process within the adaptation profile at time step t+1 is defined by -

$$w_e(t+1) = w_e(t) + A_K * [E_f(t) \quad - w_e(t)]$$
$$w_g(t+1) = w_g(t) + A_K * [E_f(t+1) - w_g(t)]$$

where A_K = adaptation rate associated with the three
different profile zones -
$K= 1° =>$ excitation;
$K= 2° =>$ inhibition;
$K= 3° =>$ excitation

The size of the excitatory / inhibitory zones and their adaptive rates is subject to a decay factor proportional to the calibration of the best matched node which is independent of the final time step. This is defined at time step t as -

$$h_f = H°* [calibration_f(t+1) / calibration_f(t)]$$

where $H°$ = fixed parameter setting for each of the zones
and adaptation rates
$$calibration_f(t) = \quad [[E_f(t) - w_e(t)]^2 +$$
$$[E_f(t+1) - w_g(t)]^2 \quad]^{0.5}$$

5.3 Inter classifier competition

The adaptation process calibrates an activated classifier according to its behaviour on the (primary) feature it was selected for and for all other (secondary) features upon which it may have had an effect. However calibration alone cannot guarantee goal convergence because it cannot stimulate the potential bids of competing classifiers which may offer better performance. To do this an additional competitive mechanism is applied between classifier layers. This competition stimulates other classifiers by raising their bid potential whenever the activated classifier causes goal divergence. Competition is applied to the nearest competitor nodes j of those classifiers which were inactive at (selection) time step t. This competition at time step t+1 is defined by -

$$B_j{}^C = B_j{}^C + 1$$
if selected classifier i action produced convergence
$$B_j{}^C = B_j{}^C - 1$$
if selected classifier i action produced divergence

where $B_j{}^C$ = inter classifier activation of classifier C
at node j .

Decreasing $B_i{}^C$ increases the probability of classifier C being selected at the next selection epoch (see 5.1).

5.4 Visualizing the calibration process

The activation and calibration process for classifiers against a specific feature can be visualized by plotting each feature map node onto a 2D representation of its weight space G/E (see 5.1). Figures 5(a)-(c) are snapshots of the weight space for a single feature (Y) across all classifier layers taken at different stages during a test run in the Woods7 environment.stages. Each node on a classifier layer (01 - 08) is plotted as a single coordinate on a 2D plane defined by G (animat state at time t) and E (animat state at time t-1). The number of entries for each classifier is equal to the size of the feature map (in this case 5*5 = 25). Note - some entries share the same location and are masked in the diagrams. The activation process (5.1) generates a goal coordinate in the G/E plane with the goal state mapped onto the G-axis and current state mapped onto the E-axis. Classifiers with entries nearest this coordinate are candidates for selection. Final selection between candidates is based on the activation level B of each candidate. After activation at time t the winning classifer is calibrated (5.2) and its entries moved (by the self organizing process) in the G/E plane to reflect its actual behaviour. State at time t is mapped onto the G-axis and state at time t-1 mapped onto the E-axis. In this example all classifiers cluster along the lines G = E+1, G = E-1, G = E corresponding to a behaviour of N, S, E/W. A single classifier (N) is shown in figure 5(d).

Enabling the Genetic Algorithm (Adaptive Strategy) within HLS results in the animat generating sequences of movements by producing multi-component classifiers combining N, S, E, W actions. These classifiers move to

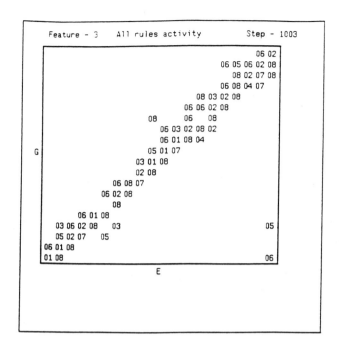

Figure 5(a). **Initial distribution of CFM nodes**
in G/E space for feature Y

Figure 5(c). **Distribution of CFM nodes after**
1000 time steps

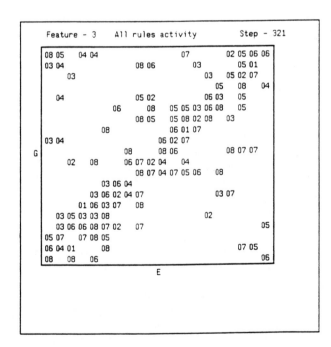

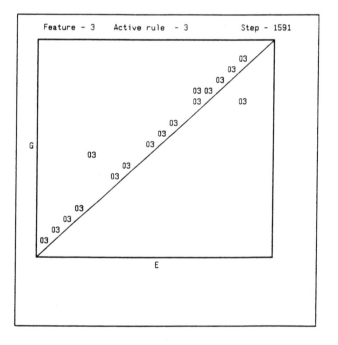

Figure 5(b). **Distribution of CFM nodes after**
300 time steps

Figure 5(d). **Distribution of CFM nodes for**
classifier ' N ' after 1500 time steps

locations further from the G/E meridan and become available for selection under the same mechanisms as for single component classifiers.

6. Conclusions

HLS's classifier feature maps represent a novel application of Kohonen Feature Maps to the active control of objects with non linear behaviour. Learning within the modified feature map is via a local learning algorithm which operates within each classifier layer (intra) and between layers (inter). The learning process calibrates classifiers according to their behaviour in the task environment as defined by the state/goal space.

HLS is now being applied to the control of line following Autonomous Guided Vehicles using infrared sensors [3] The main research focus is on quantifying the performance of classifier feature maps against increasing levels of noise on each feature detector.

References

[1] Ball N. (1991). Cognitive Maps in Learning Classifier systems. Phd dissertation, University of Reading.

[2] Ball N. & Warwick K. (1993). Using Self-Organizing Feature Maps for the control of artificial organisms. Proc. IEE, Part D, Vol 140, No.3.

[3} Ball N. (1994) Application of a Neural Network based classifier system to AGV obstacle avoidance. To be presented at IMACS Symposium on Signal Processing, Robotics and Neural Networks, Lille.

[4] Cliff D., Bullock S. (1993) . Adding "Foveal Vision" to Wilson's Animat. Adaptive Behaviour, Vol 2, No. 1, pp 49 - 72. MIT Press.

[5] Edelman G. [1988]. Neural Darwinism. Basic Books, New York.

[6] Holland J., Holyoak K., Nisbett R., Thagard P. (1986). Induction - processes of inference, learning and discovery. MIT Press.

[7] Kohonen T. (1984). Self Organization and Associative Memory. Springer Verlag.

[8] Packard N. [1988]. Intrinsic Adaptation in a Simple Model for Evolution. In Langton C. (ed) Artificial Life, Addison Wesley.

[9] Ritter H., Schulten K. (1988). Convergence properties of Kohonen's topology preserving maps: fluctuations, stability and dimesnion selection. Biological Cybernetics, 60(1):59-71.

[10] Roberts G. (1989). A Rational Reconstruction of Wilson's Animat and Holland's CS-1. In Schaffer J. D. (ed) Proc. 3rd International Conference on Genetic Algorithms, pp 317 - 321. Morgan Kaufmann.

[11] Wilson S.W. (1985). Knowledge growth in an artificial animal. In Grefenstette J. J. (ed) Proc. 1st International Conference on Genetic Algorithms, pp 16 - 23. Lawrence Erlbaum Associates.

Action Selection for Robots in Dynamic Environments through Inter-behaviour Bidding

Michael K. Sahota

Laboratory for Computational Intelligence
Department of Computer Science
University of British Columbia
Vancouver, B.C., Canada, V6T 1Z4
sahota@cs.ubc.ca

Abstract

This paper addresses the problem of action selection for an autonomous robot operating in a complex dynamic environment. We argue that other mechanisms for action selection are based on inappropriate models that do not reflect the complex dependencies of actions on the current situation. We propose the use of a simple scheme that allows task-specific behaviours to bid amongst themselves for control of the robot. Inter-behaviour bidding is not a new idea, yet previous arguments against such an approach were based on incorrect premises. Our proposal provides a weak specification of an action selection mechanism, but this allows more freedom in adapting the robot to a particular environment. Although bidding does not appear to be directly scalable to complex robots and is not intended to reflect biological systems, it does provide flexible action selection. The proposed mechanism has been tested using robots that compete in a one-on-one game of soccer.

1 Introduction

One of the goals of Artificial Intelligence is the construction of autonomous robots able to interact intelligently with their environments. Generating intelligent behaviour is the problem of getting a robot to "do the right thing" and can be reduced to the problem of selecting appropriate goals, actions, and activities. The focus of this paper is on action selection mechanisms for a robot operating in dynamic, unpredictable, and complex environments. Our attention is restricted to the adequacy of such mechanisms for building robots that are well adapted to their environment and not on their fidelity to biological organisms.

This paper is structured as follows. Section 2 discusses current approaches to action selection. Section 3 proposes the use of inter-behaviour bidding for action selection. In Section 4, the reactive deliberation architecture is introduced as a foundation for implementing inter-behaviour bidding.

Section 5 describes the experimental setup for the soccer-playing experiments that are used to verify the utility of inter-behaviour bidding. The results are presented and discussed in Section 6.

2 Approaches to Action Selection

The Good Old Fashioned AI and Robotics (GOFAIR) (Mackworth, 1993) research paradigm has shaped the area of robotics since the time of the robot Shakey (Nilsson, 1984). Some of the fundamental assumptions made of the world were that there is only one agent, that the environment is static, that actions are discrete and are carried out sequentially, and that the world can be accurately and exhaustively modeled by the robot. Under these assumptions, the problem of action selection is reduced to the problem of planning a sequence of actions that will, if executed, achieve a goal. These assumptions are invalid in complex dynamic environments where it is no longer possible to accurately predict the outcome of a sequence of actions. More recent planning-based architectures (Firby, 1992; Gat, 1992) allow for local adaptation to changes in the environment, but still commit the robot to the nearly blind pursuit of arbitrary length plans to the exclusion of alternative plans and goals.

The failure of GOFAIR has led to the development of architectures that provide a direct coupling of perception to action in order to provide highly reactive behaviour. The most notable of these is the Subsumption architecture (Brooks, 1986), where the control system of a robot is composed of a hierarchy of task-achieving behaviours in which higher levels of behaviour can subsume lower levels. The concrete-situated approach (Agre & Chapman, 1987; Chapman, 1991) formulates the control system for a robot as a collection of action proposing modules. Conflicts between proposals for external actions are resolved through a fixed priority scheme. In the situated automata approach (Kaelbling & Rosenschein, 1990), a fixed ranking of goal priorities and a set of goal reduction rules are compiled into a set of condition-action pairs so that an appropriate action can be selected at each time step. All of these approaches allow the robot to react immediately to changes in the environment, but are based on a fixed ranking of actions (or behaviours or goals). With a fixed ranking, the designer of a robot is limited in adapting the action selection mechanism since the ranking must hold over all situations.

Maes motivates the need for action selection mechanisms in complex dynamic environments (Maes, 1990). The action selection mechanism proposed by Maes is a network consisting of competence modules (actions), goals and input predicates (Maes, 1990). Activation energy flows about the network according to the dependencies and conflicts among the elements. Global parameters allow the network to be tuned to an environment; these can be learned automatically (Maes, 1991). Possible drawbacks of this mechanism are that inputs are restricted to predicates and all goals are of equal weight. The use of predicates forces potentially useful information about the environment to be discarded, while the equal weighting of goals does not reflect the likely possibility that some goals are more important than others.

A variety of computational mechanisms for action selection have been experimentally compared in a computer simulation of a zebra living on an African savannah (Tyrrell, 1993). The conclusion reached was that free-flow decision hierarchies work better than other methods principally due to their ability to combine preferences. The simulated world that was used to conduct the experiments only supported discrete actions and there is little evidence to suggest that this success extends to the continuous problem spaces that characterize robot environments. Although combination of preferences has been used for robot navigation through the concurrent enabling of multiple motor schemas (Arkin, 1990), the problem of action selection still remains for mutually exclusive actions.

A decision model for robots based on decision theory has been proposed (Kanazawa & Dean, 1989). However, it does not handle continuous variables, nor is it possible to do sophisticated spatial reasoning. A general problem with decision theory is that continuous properties must be discretized; this forces the designer of a system to abstract away (hopefully) unimportant details of the world to reduce the number of conditional probabilities to be computed. For realistic robotic environments, decision theory does not appear to be suitable; however, it motivates the approach taken in this paper where behaviours generate estimates of the utility of their actions.

3 Action Selection through Inter-behaviour Bidding

Bidding as a mechanism for action selection has been proposed as a straw man by Minsky (Minsky, 1986). He describes a central marketplace where *mental proto-specialists* compete for control of an agent. Each proto-specialist represents a different goal (e.g. eat, drink, sleep) and generates a bid based on the internal urgency of the goal. He argues that this approach is bound to result in unstable behaviour, but this conclusion is reached since actions in his proposal are based only the urgencies of the goals and not the current situation. In our approach, bids are based on both the importance of the goal *and* the current situation, so the objections raised are invalid. A comparison of action selection mechanisms (Tyrrell, 1993) showed that bidding systems can provide adequate performance in a simulated environment when the current situation is not ignored.

We propose the use of concurrently active modules called *behaviours* that represent the goals of the robot and are analogous to Minsky's mental proto-specialists. Each behaviour evaluates the world and performs whatever planning is needed to fully describe the action it wants to perform. A bid is produced by each behaviour that is an estimate of how beneficial it would be for the behaviour to gain control of the robot. The behaviour with the highest bid gains control of the robot's effectors. In this way, the putatively most appropriate behaviour, and hence action, is determined in a distributed manner without a central decision maker. Some examples of behaviours are: shoot ball, defend goal, go to midfield, clean floor, and deliver mail.

Semantics

It is useful to think of the semantics of a bid as an estimate of the expected utility of an action given the current world state and any computations (planning) the behaviour has performed. Currently, the criteria for generating the bids are hand coded and tuned so that the most appropriate behaviour is active in each situation. This approach requires the designer of a system to explicitly state the conditions under which certain behaviours are suitable and favourable. A simplified version of this appears in reactive architectures where there is a fixed ranking that holds under all conditions in the environment.

Learning

It is possible to design and implement a learning system that would generate appropriate bids. The bid for each behaviour is a function of several variables: the internal importance of the goal, sensed values of the environment and internal computations. Given a fixed set of inputs with these attributes, appropriate bids could be learned. For example, neural networks are good for approximating nonlinear multivariable functions. However, the training set may be difficult to generate for dynamic domains.

Starvation and Stability

There are two issues that must be addressed by any arbitration mechanism: starvation and stability. Starvation occurs when a behaviour should gain control but does not. This can be avoided by making behaviours "impatient" so that bids that increase with time until the behaviour gains control. A system is unstable if it alternates between two behaviours without accomplishing the goal of either one. Behaviours that have actions that terminate may bias their bid upward to reflect the fact that they are closer to completing the action. This prevents the system from alternating between two different behaviours without accomplishing either objective. Behaviours that select nonterminating activities may have to incorporate a "boredom" component so that if they have control for a long period of time, they get bored and reduce their bid to allow other behaviours to gain control.

Modularity

The principle advantage of action selection through behaviours is modularity. Since bids are calibrated to an external measure of utility, behaviours can be added, modified or deleted without changing the bidding criteria of the established system. Behaviours are independent, so they can have different representations and approaches to generating actions. For instance, a behaviour could incorporate a traditional planner and generate a bid that reflects the utility of the current step of the plan. Another advantage is that behaviours can be run concurrently on different processors (instead of timesharing a single processor), thus improving the speed of the system.

Negotiation

In our approach, there is no negotiation between behaviours, unlike in systems such as contract nets (Smith, 1980) and other Distributed Artificial Intelligence approaches. As a result, it is not possible to combine the preferences of multiple behaviours; this remains an open problem. However, negotiation is inconsistent with the semantics of a bid as an estimate of utility.

Psychology

Action selection mechanisms based on bidding are referred to as *drives* or *simple motivational competition* in psychological literature (McFarland, 1985). We make no claims of biological relevance of our proposal, since we are interested in generating intelligent behaviour in robots, and not in reproducing natural behaviour.

4 Reactive Deliberation

The proposed mechanism for action selection described in the previous section is embedded in a robot architecture called *reactive deliberation*. This architecture is intended to combine responsiveness to the environment with intelligent decision making (Sahota, 1993; Sahota, 1994). Even deliberation must be to some extent reactive to respond to changes in the environment. Although the name is apparently an oxymoron, it is consistent with Artificial Intelligence nomenclature (cf. Reactive Planning).

Under reactive deliberation, the robot controller is partitioned into a deliberator and an executor; the distinction is primarily based on the different time scales of interaction. Informally, the deliberator decides what to do and how

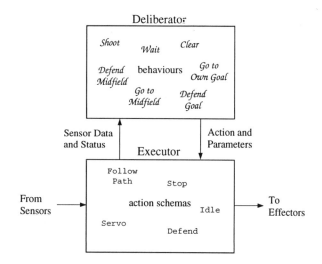

Figure 1 The Reactive Deliberation Controller

to do it, while the executor interacts with the environment in real-time. These components run asynchronously to allow the executor to interact continuously with the world and the deliberator to perform time consuming computations. A structural model illustrating the partition with examples can be seen in Figure 1. The deliberator is responsible for generating a single action, whereas other planning-based architectures generate a complete plan (i.e. sequences of actions). This distinction helps focus the deliberative activities on the immediate situation.

The executor is composed of a collection of action schemas. An *action schema* is a robot program that interacts with the environment in real-time to accomplish specific actions. Only one action schema is enabled at a time and it interacts with the environment through a tight feedback loop. The active schema receives run-time parameters from the deliberator that fully define its activity.

The deliberator in reactive deliberation is composed of behaviours. A *behaviour* is a robot program that computes an action that may, if executed, bring about a specific goal. Behaviours propose actions whereas action schemas perform actions. Each behaviour must perform the following: 1) select an action schema, 2) compute run-time parameters for the schema (plan the action), and 3) generate a bid describing how appropriate the action is.

In our current implementation, behaviours generate bids as real numbers in the range (0,10). The bids are simple algebraic formulas that are easily computed. Each behaviour has a basic bid that is modified through the addition and subtraction of weighted factors that depend on the environment and the results of motion planning. Complex conditions in the environment, such as the distance of the ball from one's home goal, are converted to factors in the range (0,1). One exception is path plans that are converted to factors based on the log of the expected travel time.

At this stage, only a very coarse estimate of utility is being generated. Even with complete information, computing the utility of actions in the world is difficult. Something like a calculus for spatial reasoning is needed to extract useful information from the world. An example of a question that is difficult to answer is, "Can the other player shoot the ball at my net in the next few seconds?"

Reactive deliberation is not a panacea for robotic architectural woes. A further disclaimer is that it is an incomplete robot architecture since it focuses on the issues related to dynamic domains and ignores a number of issues such as perceptual processing and the development of world models. The proposal is orthogonal to those issues. However, it makes explicit the need to evaluate the actions and goals of the robot at a rate commensurate with changes in the environment.

5 Soccer-Playing: An experiment with robots

The reactive deliberation architecture has been used to construct the controller for a soccer-playing robot. Soccer has a number of features that make it an interesting domain for experiments with autonomous robots. Robot agents are embodied and are situated in an unfolding game with neutral, friendly, and hostile agents. They must act in real-time to accomplish tasks in a unpredictable and dynamic environment. One advantage of the soccer domain is that there are objective performance criteria; the ability to score and prevent goals and the overall score of the game allow explicit comparisons of alternative controller designs.

A facility called the Dynamite testbed has been designed to provide a practical platform for testing theories in the soccer domain using multiple mobile robots (Barman *et al.*, 1993a; Barman *et al.*, 1993b). It consists of a fleet of radio controlled vehicles that perceive the world through a shared perceptual system. In an integrated environment with dataflow and MIMD computers, vision programs can monitor the position and orientation of each robot while planning and control programs can generate and send out motor commands at 60Hz. This approach allows umbilical-free behaviour and very rapid, lightweight fully autonomous robots.

The mobile robot bases are commercially available radio controlled vehicles. We have two controllable 1/24 scale racing-cars, each 22 cm long, 8 cm wide, and 4 cm high excluding the antenna. The testbed (244 cm by 122 cm in size) with two cars and a ball is shown in Figure 2. The cars have each been fitted with two circular colour markers allowing the vision system to identify their position and orientation. The ball is the small object between the cars.

A feature of the Dynamite testbed is that it is based on the "remote brain" approach to robotics. The testbed avoids the technical complexity of configuring and updating on-board hardware and makes fundamental problems in robotics and artificial intelligence more accessible. We have elected not to get on-board the on-board computation bandwagon, since the remote (but untethered) brain approach allows us to focus on scientific research without devoting resources to engineering compact electronics.

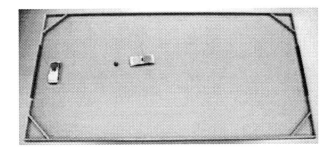

Figure 2 Robot Players on the Soccer Field

A physics-based graphics simulator for the Dynamite world is also available for testing and developing reasoning and control programs.

6 Results and Evaluation

Several controllers based on reactive deliberation have been implemented to allow robots to compete in complete one-on-one games of soccer (Sahota, 1993). Current functionality includes various simple offensive and defensive strategies, motion planning, ball shooting and playing goal. The robots can drive under accurate control at speeds up to 1 m/s, while simultaneously considering alternate actions. We have produced a 10 minute video that documents these features.

As documented in (Sahota, 1993), a series of experiments, soccer games, called the Laboratory for Computational Intelligence (LCI) Cup were performed using the Dynamite testbed. The most elaborated reactive deliberation controller competed with subsets of itself to provide, through the scores of the games, an objective utility measure for some of the architectural features of reactive deliberation and the behaviour themselves. Through the results of the LCI Cup the importance of modifying goals in response to changes in the environment has been shown. Further, the results demonstrate that the architectural elements in reactive deliberation are sufficient for real-time intelligent control in dynamic environments.

The bidding functions for the behaviours have been adapted to the environment through an iteration cycle with observations of partial soccer games followed by incremental changes. A useful abstraction that helps determine how to adjust them is *routines* of action from the concrete-situated approach (Agre & Chapman, 1987). The idea here is that the agent (or robot) interacts with the environment in a routine or typical way. One routine in soccer is: clear the ball, go to midfield, shoot, etc. In the case of soccer-playing, the construction of successful robots does involve careful attention to patterns of activity. This is an emergent (and surprising) result of the soccer-playing experiments.

Bidding works reasonably well for the limited environment and task domain of one-on-one soccer. One problem is that it is not that easy in practice to add new behaviours. The reason for this is that a bid in any reasonably complex domain such as soccer is a function of many variables, and accurately specifying bids that are hyper-volumes in this high-dimensional space is difficult. As mentioned previously, noticing routines of activity can help with this. In conclusion, bidding is effective in real environments, but the difficulty in tuning individual behaviours suggests that this approach is not scalable to complex systems.

7 Conclusions

A robot controller for soccer-playing experiments has been constructed using a behaviour-based bidding mechanism that is part of the reactive deliberation architecture. Its effectiveness has been demonstrated through a tournament of one-on-one soccer games using autonomous mobile robots. The advantage of this approach is that the bidding mechanism is flexible and can be adapted to the environment with the potential extension to automatic learning. Further, the use of behaviours allows modular changes, multiple representations and parallelism. The disadvantages of this approach are that it does not appear to be directly scalable to larger systems and that it does not allow the combination of the preferences of different behaviours.

Acknowledgments

I am grateful to Rod Barman, Keiji Kanazawa, Stewart Kingdon, Jim Little, Alan Mackworth, Dinesh Pai, Heath Wilkinson and Ying Zhang for help with this. This work is supported, in part, by the Canadian Institute for Advanced Research, the Natural Sciences and Engineering Research Council of Canada and the Institute for Robotics and Intelligent Systems Network of Centres of Excellence.

References

Agre, P., and Chapman, D. 1987. Pengi: An implementation of a theory of activity. In *AAAI-87*, 268–272.

Arkin, R. 1990. Integrating behavioural, perceptual, and world knowledge in reactive navigation. In Maes, P., ed., *Designing Autonomous Agents: Theory and Practice from Biology to Engineering and Back*. M.I.T. Press. 105–122.

Barman, R.; Kingdon, S.; Little, J.; Mackworth, A. K.; Pai, D.; Sahota, M.; Wilkinson, H.; and Zhang, Y. 1993a. Dynamo: real-time experiments with multpile mobile robots. In *Proceedings of Intelligent Vehicles Symposium*, 261–266.

Barman, R.; Kingdon, S.; Mackworth, A.; Pai, D.; Sahota, M.; Wilkinson, H.; and Zhang, Y. 1993b. Dynamite: A testbed for multpile mobile robots. In *Proceedings IJ-CAI—93 Workshop on Dynamically Interacting Robots*, 38–45.

Brooks, R. A. 1986. A robust layered control system for a mobile robot. *IEEE Journal of Robotics and Automation* RA-2:14–23.

Chapman, D. 1991. *Vision, Instruction, and Action*. MIT Press.

Firby, R. J. 1992. Building symbolic primitives with continuous control routines. In *First International Conference on Artificial Intelligence Planning Systems*, 62–69.

Gat, E. 1992. Integrating planning and reacting in a heterogeneous asynchronous architecture for controlling real-world mobile robots. In *AAAI-92*, 809–815.

Kaelbling, L. P., and Rosenschein, S. J. 1990. Action and planning in embedded agents. In Maes, P., ed., *Designing Autonomous Agents: Theory and Practice from Biology to Engineering and Back*. M.I.T. Press. 35–48.

Kanazawa, K., and Dean, T. 1989. A model for projection and action. In *IJCAI-89*, 49–54.

Mackworth, A. 1993. On seeing robots. In Basu, A., and Li, X., eds., *Computer Vision: Systems, Theory, and Applications*. World Scientific Press. 1–13.

Maes, P. 1990. Situated agents can have goals. In Maes, P., ed., *Designing Autonomous Agents: Theory and Practice from Biology to Engineering and Back*. M.I.T. Press. 49–70.

Maes, P. 1991. Learning behaviour networks from experience. In *Proceedings of the First European Conference on Artificial Life*. M.I.T. Press.

McFarland, D. 1985. *Animal Behaviour*. Longman.

Minsky, M. 1986. *The Society of Mind*. Simon & Schuster Inc.

Nilsson, N. 1984. Shakey the robot. Technical Report 323, SRI International. Collection of Earlier Technical Reports.

Sahota, M. K. 1993. Real-time intelligent behaviour in dynamic environments: Soccer-playing robots. Master's thesis, University of British Columbia.

Sahota, M. K. 1994. Reactive deliberation: An architecture for real-time intelligent control in dynamic environments. In *Proceedings of AAAI-94*. Forthcoming.

Smith, G. 1980. The contract net protocol: High-level communication and control in a distributed problem solver. *IEEE Transactions on Computing* 29(12).

Tyrrell, T. 1993. *Computational Mechanisms for Action Selection*. Ph.D. Dissertation, Edinburgh University.

MOTIVATION AND EMOTION

A Hierarchical Classifier System Implementing a Motivationally Autonomous Animat

Jean-Yves Donnart and Jean-Arcady Meyer

Groupe de BioInformatique

Ecole Normale Supérieure, CNRS-URA 686

46, rue d'Ulm 75230 Paris Cedex 05, France

(donnart@wotan.ens.fr - meyer@wotan.ens.fr)

Abstract

This work describes a control architecture based on a hierarchical classifier system. This architecture, which uses both reactive and planning rules, implements a motivationally autonomous animat that chooses the actions it will perform according to the expected consequences of the alternatives. The adaptive faculties of this animat are illustrated through various examples.

1 Introduction

The behavior of an animat is adaptive to the extent that this behavior allows the animat to "survive," that is to maintain its *essential variables* within their *viability zone*, even when confronted with a changing environment ([Mey91a]). According to present knowledge on animal behavior ([McF93], [Mel94]), it may be supposed that several complementary components or mechanisms can be called upon in the design of an adaptive animat. Besides the fact that it would appear necessary to equip the animat with sensors and actuators and to interconnect these through an equivalent to an appropriate nervous system, further adaptive properties can be gained from the use of a memory, a motivational system and a planning system. Likewise, it may prove effective to hardwire some components or mechanisms, while leaving others free to change in the course of a learning process. The work described in this paper puts these ideas into practice and begins by describing the architecture of an animat with adaptive capabilities that depend, among other things, on a hierarchical classifier system. These capacities are illustrated in the specific context of a navigational task. The architecture's main functionalities are then compared with a variety of creations or propositions arising out of ethology, computer science, and robotics. It turns out that it implements a *motivationally autonomous system* as described by McFarland and Bösser ([McF93]); it accordingly has the potential to exhibit, at least to a certain degree, the adaptive properties of the most advanced animals.

2 The Architecture

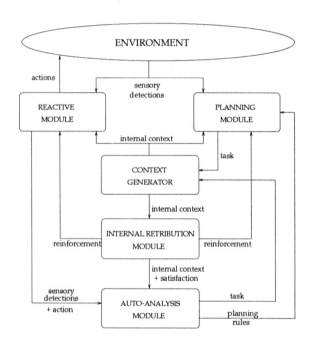

Figure 1: The architecture

In its current configuration, the architecture proposed here enables an animat to navigate from one point to another in a two-dimensional environment that may contain assorted materials, and obstacles in particular. A variety of possible generalizations of this implementation, capable of conferring on the animat many additional adaptive abilities, are in the process of realization and will be dealt with in this text. The animat is equipped with three proximate sensors that keep it informed of the presence or absence of material elements in front of it, 90° to its right, or 90° to its left. It is also able to estimate the spatial coordinates of the position it is located in and the direction of a goal to be reached in each of the eight sectors of the space surrounding it. Lastly, it is capable of moving straight ahead, 90° to its right, or 90° to its left. This architecture, which relies upon a hierarchical classifier system ([Hol86]), is organized into five modules - a reactive module, a planning module, a context generator, an internal retribution module and an auto-analysis module (Figure 1).

2.1   The Reactive Module

This module consists of a series of rules - or classifiers - that allow the animat to react to incoming sensory information from the environment as well as to the internal context generated by the context generator. In the current configuration, the internal context is the direction of the current goal. The reactive rules take the form:

If *<sensory information>* and *<direction of current goal>* then *<action>*

For example, rule *R1 :* 100|001 ==> 01 can be activated when the animat becomes aware of the presence of a material element in front of it, but not on either side (information coded by "1", "0" and "0"), and when the direction of the current goal is 45° to its right (direction "001"). If this rule is actived, the animat performs an elementary displacement 90° to its right (action "01"). An internal strength - which will be discussed later - is associated with each rule of the reactive module, as is a prediction of the consequences of the corresponding action. This prediction is learned incrementally and describes how the animat's position changes when the rule is applied. For instance, the prediction $X := X + 1$, $Y := Y$ will be associated with rule *R1*.

To each pair of conditions on the *<sensory information>* and the *<direction of current goal>* correspond, at any point in time, three rules capable of being triggered, each of which is associated with one out of the three possible actions. The choice of which rule is actually actuated is effected probabilistically, on the basis of the respective strengths of the three rules involved. In the current version of the system, there are $8 * 8 * 3 = 192$ possible rules. These rules are all created when the system is initialized and charged into the reactive module, which does not change in size as long as the system is in operation. The strengths of each rule are all initialized to a given value and are subsequently modified by learning. In the future, a genetic algorithm ([Hol86]) will be used in the interest of discovering more general rules.

2.2   The Planning Module

This module is made up of another series of rules, that allow it to decompose a task[1] into a sub-task accord-

---

[1] In AI, this type of decomposition is classically called problem decomposition. Wilson ([Wil87]) discusses a decomposition of behavior modules. The term task appears more general and is derived from robotics terminology ([Alb81]).

ing to current sensory information. These rules take the form:

If *<sensory information>* and *<current task>* then *<new current task>*

Sensory information is provided by the sensors and comes from the environment. It consists of information supplied by the proximate sensors and of the animat's coordinates and current orientation. As explained below, the *<current task>* is the one registered at the top of the pile of tasks governed by the context generator. The current task is used as an internal context which contributes to the triggering of the planning rules. The *<current task>* and the *<new current task>* are each coded at present as a pair of coordinates. Later, they will be described in a more general form.

Thus, the rule *P1 :* 000|5, 1|001|3, 0; 3, 5 ==> 5, 1; 5, 2 can be activated at point 5,1 (in (x,y) spatial coordinates) if the animat is headed in a north-easterly direction (coded by "001"), if it perceives no material element ahead or on either side of it (coded by "0", "0" and "0"), and if its current task is to reach the point with coordinates 3,5 when starting at point 3,0. If this rule is activated, the new task, which involves reaching point 5,2 from point 5,1 will be placed on top of the context generator pile.

With each rule of the planning module are associated two strengths - one local, the other global - the evaluation of which will be explained later. The local strength is used to determine the probability of triggering a rule whose condition part matches the current situation. When the system is initialized, the planning module is empty. During operation, this module can dynamically acquire rules - generated by the auto-analysis module - or lose rules - according to how the global strengths of these rules evolve. The size of the planning module thus varies over time, though it cannot exceed a preestablished upper limit.

2.3   The Context Generator

The context generator consists essentially of a pile of tasks the top of which represents the current task of the system. New tasks are added to the pile either by the planning module, as just seen, or by the auto-analysis module, when an obstacle is detected. This latter case occurs when the presence of an obstacle prevents the action judged to be the most conducive to reaching the goal associated with the current task from being fully applied. An obstacle can be detected in two ways:

1) When a rule is triggered by the reactive module and the results obtained are not those expected (a situation designated as failure).

2) When the system can predict that a rule will lead to failure if it is applied.

For example, rule $R2$: $100|110 ==> 00$ - that stipulates that, in the presence of a material element situated in front of the animat (coded by "1", "0" and "0") and of a goal situated 45° to its left (direction coded by "110"), it should proceed straight ahead (action coded by "00") - may have been triggered because it presented the strongest strength at a given moment. This rule predicts that $X := X$ and $Y := Y + 1$. However, because the material element is actually an obstacle, Y cannot change. The obstacle is therefore recognized as such by the auto-analysis module, which generates a general subtask. This *"skirting around the obstacle"* task is to go beyond the line which lies perpendicular to the direction of the animat and passes through the point where the obstacle has been detected (Figure 2a). This task is coded by the pair $<$*coordinates of the point*$>$ $<$*direction vector of the straight line to be crossed*$>$ and is registered at the top of the pile of the context generator.

The context generator also includes an algorithm that transforms the current task, situated at the top of its pile, into a goal, then supplies the direction of this goal to the reactive module. In the case of a task posted by the planning module, the corresponding goal is simply described by the coordinates of the point to be reached. In the case of a task posted by the auto-analysis module, the goal is described by the coordinates of the projection of the animat's current location on the straight line to be crossed. This projection, and accordingly the corresponding direction information, varies whenever the animat moves.

An *emergent functionality* ([Ste91]) of the internal dynamics of the system, and more particularly of the context generator, is to enable the animat to skirt around the obstacles it encounters. In fact, if we reexamine the Figure 2a example, when the obstacle is detected at point 1, the task of having to go beyond the straight line $\delta 1$ is placed on top of the current task - which corresponded to the goal direction $d0$ - and the current goal becomes the point marked with a "?" on the figure, in direction $d1$. Since rule $R2$ cannot be applied, the animat chooses to apply another, causing it, for example, to move towards the left. After this displacement, the animat arrives at point 2. The current goal, with which direction $d2$ is associated, becomes that in Figure 2b but the pile of tasks doesn't change.

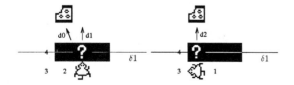

Figure 2: a / b

At point 2, if the learning has progressed sufficiently,

the best action the animat can perform consists in progressing to the right in order to move in direction $d2$. As this action is not possible, it chooses to move forward. After arriving at point 3, the current goal becomes that of Figure 3a, in direction $d3$. This time, the best rule can be applied: the animat turns right and reaches the current goal. The task associated with $\delta 1$ is erased, and the animat can resume pursuing the goal of direction $d4$ (Figure 3b).

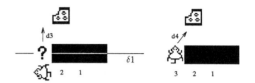

Figure 3: a / b

Following this reasoning, had the animat encountered an obstacle perpendicular to the preceding, preventing it for example from reaching point 3, this obstacle would have been detected as the preceding one had been. This is because the forward action, judged to be the best since turning right was already forbidden, has become impossible. In that case, the task of having to go beyond the line $\delta 2$ would have been placed on top of the task associated with $\delta 1$. The animat would thus have been directed successively through points 3 and 4 (Figure 4). At 4, it would have been able to turn right and reach point 5, where the task linked with $\delta 2$ would have been erased. Likewise, the task linked with $\delta 1$ would in turn have been erased at point 9.

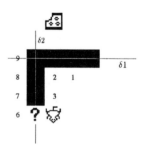

Figure 4:

In more complex situations, it can happen that the animat, seeking to attain the current goal, will erase a task placed farther down than the current task in the pile. In this case, all the tasks situated above the erased task are also erased, as they were generated for the sole purpose of executing this task and no longer have any justification. It will be shown later on that such mechanisms enable the animat to skirt around obstacles and to extricate itself from dead-ends with arbitrarily complicated shapes.

2.4   The Internal Retribution Module

The retribution module works through a process of reinforcement which causes the strengths of the rules of the reactive and planning modules to change.

Within the reactive module, this reinforcement takes place each time a rule is used. It depends on the *satisfaction* of the animat, that is, on an estimation of the success with which this rule brought the animat closer to, or took it farther from, the current goal:

$$S(R, u + 1) = (1 - \alpha) * S(R, u) + \alpha * satisf$$

$$satisf = \frac{dist\_goal(u) - dist\_goal(u - 1) + max\_dist}{max\_dist * 2}$$

where
S (R, u) : strength of rule R after u triggers
S (R,0), α, max_dist : parameters of simulation
dist_goal(u) : estimated distance to the current goal.

In the present version of the system, distances are calculated exactly. However, distance information does not need to be very accurate because it is used merely as a heuristic for triggering good reactive rules, which are not necessarily optimal. It is the role of the planning module to orient the reactive module towards a near optimal path, by means of the internal context.

A failure can occur when the action of a rule is executed. For instance, going forward when there is an obstacle in front of the animat is impossible. In that case, the strength of the rule will be reset to zero.

The rules of the planning module are characterized by two strengths: a local strength and a global strength. The local strength evaluates the usefulness of decomposing a task into a sub-task proposed by the rule. The global strength, on the other hand, detects and suppresses the rules which are unlikely to be used by the system.

To calculate the local strength of a rule *P1* that decomposes, for example, a task *T* - such as that of going from i to f - into a sub-task *T1* - such as that of going from j to k - the retribution module evaluates the average cost of all the paths tested by the animat which enable it to reach f from i without resorting to decomposition. In the present version of the system, this cost, denoted by *AC (T)*, is a average of the lengths of the paths expressed in terms of the number of elementary displacements they contain. *AC (T)* is evaluated incrementally:

$$AC(T, u + 1) = (1 - \alpha) * AC(T, u) + \alpha * C$$

where
u : number of times that task T was accomplished
C : cost of the u+1th path
α : parameter.

The retribution module also evaluates the average cost of all the paths joining i to f and using rule *P1*, that is, that reach k from j:

$$AC(P1, u + 1) = (1 - \alpha) * AC(P1, u) + \alpha * C1$$

C1 is computed when task *T* is erased, with the cost *C* of the path covered being divided among all the rules *P1*, *P2*, ... which decomposed *T*. This succession of rules is thus memorized, and a *profit sharing* algorithm ([Gre88]) is called on to manage the corresponding retributions. In these conditions, the local strength of *P1* is given by:

$$LS(P1, u + 1) = \frac{AC(T, u)}{AC(P1, u)}$$

The shorter the paths joining i to f and passing through j and k have turned out to be on average than the paths joining i to f by way of other paths the stronger this strength is.

Each time a task generated by the planning module is at the top of the context generator pile, the planning module can decide whether or not to decompose this task and to trigger one of various decomposition rules *P1*, *P2*, ... it contains. These rules have been created by the auto-analysis module from salient states detected in the environment, as will be explained later. The decision to decompose is then made on the basis of a probabilistic choice depending on the local strength of each rule (a local strength of 1 being assigned to the non-decomposition option), weighted by an exploration-exploitation coefficient. The role of this coefficient is to modify, in the course of operation, the probability that the system will apply rules with a high local strength. Its value is constant for the time being; it could subsequently be modified according to the progress of the simulation.

It is clear that, whatever the local strength of rules *P1*, *P2*,... that decompose task *T*, these rules are unlikely to be triggered if task *T* itself is unlikely to be posted on the context generator pile. The global strength of each rule allows this type of situation to be detected and the less useful rules to be eliminated whenever the size of the planning module exceeds the maximum permissible threshold. The global strength of *P1* that decomposes *T* into *T1* is given by:

$$GS(P1) = LS(P1) * GS(T)$$

GS (T) is the average of the global strengths of all the rules P liable to post T on the context generator pile, this average being calculated incrementally:

$$GS(T, u + 1) = (1 - \alpha) * GS(T, u) + \alpha * GS(P, u)$$

When the system is initialized, a principal task *PT* - for example, going from point 3,0 to point 3,5 - is assigned to the animat, and the corresponding global strength *GS (PT)* is set arbitrarily at 1000. Under these conditions, if task T happens to be generated only rarely, its global strength will be weak, as will be those of all the rules that decompose T.

2.5 The Auto-Analysis Module

Besides its role in the characterization of obstacles, the analysis module is used to detect recursively the *salient states*[2] of the environment. To accomplish this, the module calculates, from the satisfaction of the animat after each completed action, the variation of this satisfaction between two successives actions. In positions where the corresponding gradient is positive, the analysis module detects *satisfaction states*, which are added to the departure and arrival states of the path in question. These satisfaction states are only detected when the pile contains a "skirting around the obstacle" task.

The recursive process effected by the analysis module applies first of all to the path actually travelled by the animat, then to the successive fictitious paths that can be abstracted from the satisfaction states detected on these paths. Such a process is thus a consequence of the metaphor which conceives planning as a series of "thought experiments". When the path obtained by direct connection of the satisfaction states detected on the preceding path generates the same sequence of satisfaction states, the recursion is stopped, and the last satisfaction states discovered are recognized as salient states.

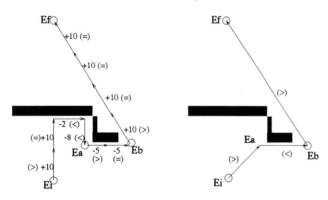

Figure 5: Satisfaction states: Numerical values indicate the satisfaction brought by each action. >, < and = symbols indicate the sign of the satisfaction gradient.

Thus, in the case of Figure 5, the animat has accomplished ten actions in order to reach state Ef from state Ei, while simultaneously skirting around an obstacle. The gradient of satisfaction is positive at Ea and Eb during a "skirting around" task, and the analysis module accordingly generates four satisfaction states: Ei, Ef, Ea and Eb. At the next stage, the satisfaction gradient as-

sociated with each fictitious action, which makes it possible to progress from one satisfaction state to the next, is computed. Ea can then be eliminated, as the gradient is negative between Ea and Eb. Because no other satisfaction point can be eliminated along the path directly connecting the three remaining states with one another, the recursive process stops at this stage, and the analysis module recognizes and memorizes three salient states: Ei, Ef and Eb, each characterized by its coordinates, by the sensory information obtained by the animat at this point, and by the corresponding orientation of the animat.

The salient states are then used to generate planning rules. Thus, at the conclusion of the path described on Figure 5, the two rules $P1$ and $P2$ that decompose path Ei-Ef into Ei-Eb and Eb-Ef:

$P1$: $000|3, 0|000|3, 0, 3, 6 ==> 3, 0, 6, 3$
$P2$: $010|6, 3|000|3, 0, 3, 6 ==> 6, 3, 3, 6$

are created and input to the planning module. The advantage of the redundancy in the description of these rules is to make it possible to recognize the salient states, even when there are imprecisions in the coordinates, or in the sensory information, or in the animat's orientation, or when the animat reaches one of these points with a new orientation.

A current weakness of the model is that absolute (x, y) coordinates are used to code the tasks. In the future, the position and the direction of each salient state will be calculated relatively to the position of the previous salient state of the plan. A "relative-position estimator", analogous to the one used by Kuipers [Kui93], will allow the animat to navigate from one salient state to another. Also, a more general description of salient states will be sought by means of a genetic algorithm.

3 Operation of the System

The following examples describe the results obtained in the instance of an animat moving in a square environment.

Figures 6, 7 and 8 illustrate the capacities of the animat, when learning only reactive rules, to skirt around obstacles of various shapes and to adapt to changing circumstances. The path on Figure 6 is the one obtained after 50 iterations - that is, after 50 experiments during which the animat has reached the goal when starting from the initial state - in an environment containing a dead-end. Path 7 is the one obtained when the dead-end is replaced by a double spiral, after five additional iterations in this new environment. Path 8 is the one obtained when the double spiral is replaced by an arc after a single additional iteration.

---
[2]In a purely navigational task, one could have used the word "landmarks" instead. We prefer to refer to "salient states" as our approach aims at solving more general tasks.

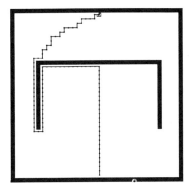

Figure 6: The dead-end environment

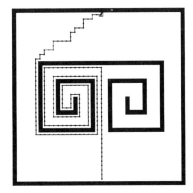

Figure 7: The double spiral environment

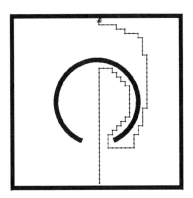

Figure 8: The arc environment

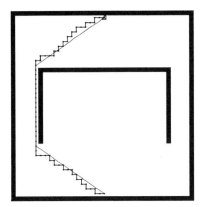

Figure 9: Plan abstracted in the dead-end environment, and a path obtained when using this plan

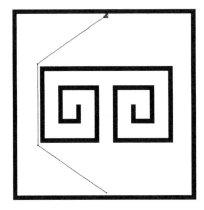

Figure 10: Plan abstracted in the double spiral environment

Figures 9 and 10 show what salient states and what corresponding action plan are found in the environments with a dead-end and with a double spiral, using the reactive paths from Figures 6 and 7. In both cases, it is apparent that the original task is decomposed into three sub-tasks and that the plan which is thus abstracted from the actual paths is simple because it depends on the convex envelope of the obstacles, rather than on the complexity of these obstacles.

A path following the new plan is also shown in Figure 9. The three planning rules which define this plan are successively triggered, activating the three corresponding sub-tasks. At its starting point, the animat has used the first salient point as a subgoal, and when it arrived at this point, it used the second salient point as another subgoal. The planning module influenced the activation of the reactive rules in order to generate a shorter path to the goal.

Figures 11, 12 and 13 illustrate the decomposition of a plan into three hierarchical levels. The plan in Figure 11 is obtained from a path generated when using reactive rules only. When this plan is carried out, it is seen that the necessity of avoiding an obstacle yields a path that defines new salient states and that new sub-tasks are superimposed on the preceding (Figure 12). Likewise, when this new plan is put into effect, a third level of sub-tasks appears (Figure 13). Beyond this third level, the paths travelled no longer involve the avoidance of obstacles, and the corresponding plan does not result in additional decompositions.

Figure 11: Plan level 1

Figure 12: Plan level 2

Figure 13: Plan level 3

Figures 14 to 16 illustrate the fact that the system retains several plans in its memory and that it is continually updating the local and global strengths of the rules of the planning module. It consequently follows that it can rapidly switch from one plan to another, or create

new plans, as a function of the new obstacles appearing in the environment.

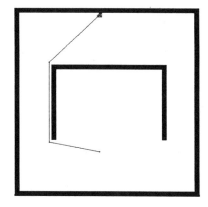

Figure 14: The best plan : iteration 15

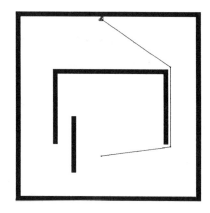

Figure 15: The best plan : iteration 22

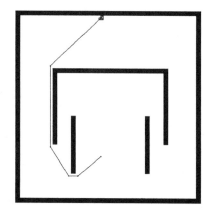

Figure 16: The best plan : iteration 38

Thus, after 15 iterations in the environment depicted on Figure 14, the animat has memorized two plans for avoiding the dead-end. The best plan is shown on Figure 14, while the less effective one is shown on Figure 15. If, at iteration 16, a new obstacle is added to the environment along the animat's optimum path, this obstacle is avoided, and the corresponding plan is modified accordingly. However, as the cost of this modified plan exceeds the cost of the second plan stored in the memory, this second plan is the one most likely to govern the animat's path from the 22th iteration on. Likewise, introducing a new obstacle into the environment at the 30th iteration gives the advantage once again to the modified version of the first plan (Figure 16). It is thereby seen that the animat is capable of altering its plans as a reaction to modifications in its enviroment.

4   Related Research

As compared with related computer or robotics approaches, the architecture proposed here displays certain distinguishing characteristics.

Where learning is concerned, this architecture makes it possible to avoid the problem of the "two-platform station" described by Westerdale ([Wes89]) as applied to traditional classifier systems. In these systems, a single rule can be rewarded at times and punished at others, according to the corresponding context. Here, the context of use is expressly taken into account and is used to distinguish the rules. Likewise, the problem of the "temporal credit assignment" ([Sut91]), inherent to traditional classifier systems when a large number of rules have been involved in the acquisition of a reward, is eliminated here because the strength of each reactive rule is updated after its utilization, thanks to the management of an internal reward. This, however, is not at all the case with the local strength of the planning rules. Nevertheless, the corresponding profit sharing plan concerns only a given level of planning and therefore calls on only a small number of rules, in agreement with the logic envisaged by Wilson ([Wil87]) for the bucket brigade algorithm ([Hol86]).

The architectures described by [Wil87], by [Shu91] and by [Col93a] also rely on hierarchical classifier systems, but only the first - which is a theoretical construction and has not yielded any concrete application - might implement a planning process. Nevertheless, Wilson does not specify how the corresponding tasks and sub-tasks could be identified by the system. Likewise, though the architecture proposed by Colombetti and Dorigo provides for a classifier system to coordinate the actions proposed by two other classifier systems, the hierarchical relationships are predetermined by the programmer. On the contrary, in the present work, the hierarchical relationships among tasks are dynamic because they are generated internally on the basis of the experience gained by the animat.

As to planning, the architecture used here does not call on any predefined operators for decomposing problems

into sub-problems, for the purpose of generating a plan which would then be executed ([Nil80]). Such a practice, which implies that planning precedes acting, has shown itself to be singularly ineffective ([Bro91]). Conversely, here, acting precedes planning, and the latter does not depend on predefined operators, but rather is abstracted from the paths actually travelled. The plans thus elaborated are initially quite general and are based on a small number of rules - thereby reducing the cost of learning, as was just mentioned. These plans are refined as needed. They are not executed mechanically by the animat, but instead are used as one ressource among others to decide which action to perform ([Agr88], [Suc87]). The organization of these plans thus appears as an emergent property, arising from the interactions between the animat and its environment and elicited by the animat's needs. Lastly, the value of these plans is continually reevaluated, which confers considerable adaptive faculties on the system.

Albus ([Alb81]), too, described a hierarchical architecture able to decompose a complex task into a series of sub-tasks, then into a series of elemental moves, then into a series of motor drive signals which actuate observable behavior in a robot. However, although Albus describes how such architecture relates to a general theory of intelligence ([Alb91]), he doesn't state how the corresponding hierarchy might be dynamically generated, nor how it could be modified according to the robot's needs and to the environmental conditions encountered.

In comparison with the literature on animal behavior, the architecture proposed here implements a *motivationally autonomous agent* ([McF93]). In everyday language, the term motivation is used to describe the experience of desiring to act in particular ways in order to achieve certain ends. As Toates ([Toa86]) argues, a motivational system is one that selects a goal to be pursued and organizes the animal's commerce with it. Current research on the relationships between motivations and behavior focus on the notions of motivational space and motivational state ([McF85]). The motivational state of an animal at any particular time depends on its physiological or internal state, on the cue state arising from its perception of the external world, on the consequences of its current behavior and on the expected consequences of its future behavior. Such a motivational state can be portrayed as a point in a motivational space, the axes of which are the animal's important motivational stimuli, such as an energy level or the odor of food. As a consequence of the animal's behavior, the motivational state changes, and the corresponding point describes a trajectory in the motivational space. Such displacements are monitored by sensors that relay nervous messages to the brain. They are also calibrated in terms of their estimated contribution to the animal's fitness ([Hou76], [McF81]). Then a decision is made about which behavior to perform. If this decision doesn't take into account the expected consequences of the alternatives, the animal behaves like a *motivated automaton*, otherwise it behaves like a *motivationally autonomous agent* ([McF93]). To do so, the animal requires knowledge of the probable consequences - or expected utility - of its acts. In other words, it must have some memory of the past consequences of similar activities, and it must be capable of planning - i.e. it must use some form of cognition. Furthermore, as Dennett ([Den83]) pointed out, it must want something, it must have goals[3].

The animat described here displays all these characteristics. Indeed, the behavior, or the action, it performs at any instant depends both on sensors and on what was called here the internal context. This context actually includes the goals that the animat has selected and that it seeks to achieve. There is nothing to prevent this context from subsequently taking into account other information about the internal state of the animat. The animat's goals are generated by an explicit planning process, and the strength of the rules memorizes the consequences of the various choices that the animat has made in the past. These consequences are actually evaluated in terms of their aptitude in bringing the animat nearer its goal; they may later depend on an appropriate utility function. It will be noted in passing that McFarland and Bösser do not specify how the weighting coefficients associated with the different actions can induce the animal to choose one action when pursuing one goal and another action when pursuing another goal. Here, this problem is solved by the fact that the actions performed depend on the internal context and accordingly on the current goal.

This latter point is likewise to be compared with the hypothesis proposed by Wilson ([Wil91]) according to which the most efficient systems would be those that "convert every frequently encountered important situation to one of 'virtual stimulus-response' in which internal state (intention, memory) and sensory stimulus together form a compound stimulus that immediately implies the correct next intention or external action". As Wilson remarks, such an hypothesis is compatible with the observation that, "in animals and people, even complex behavior, if frequent and important enough, tends to become reflexive". It should also be related with the distinction between "interpreted" and "compiled" knowledge of the standard AI ([Lai86]).

In comparison with other approaches aimed at including a motivational system in the architecture of an animat ([Bee90], [Cec93], [Gab93], [Hal91]), this approach is the only one that incorporates a planning process which, as seen previously, substantially enhances the adaptive faculties of the animat. It would accordingly seem that, in the continuum described by McFarland and Bösser ([McF93]) which distinguishes motivated automata from motivationally autonomous agents, these other approaches tend to be situated in the former category, while the present approach would belong to the latter.

It is moreover clear that the animat's *behavioral sequences* described here are not random, which could be demonstrated using the same methods that ethologists do ([Gui86]). These sequences are organized according to the animat's goals, so that a given action tends preferably to be followed by one action in the context of a particular goal and by another action in the context of a different goal. Such an organization is by no means arbitrary but rather tends to maximise the utility function, contrary, for instance, to what is learned in Colombetti and Dorigo ([Col93b]). Nor is it determined once and for all, and it does not preclude reacting opportunistically to the surprises of the environment.

5   Conclusion and Ongoing Research

The architecture described in this text is that of a motivationally autonomous agent. It accordingly could prove useful in reproducing at least certain adaptive abilities of the most advanced animals, that have amply proven their aptitude to survive in more or less predictible and more or less threatening environments.

This work continues in three directions. The first aims at adapting this architecture to an actual robot and to the corresponding constraints. The second aims at improving the present implementation by managing other motivations and other actions - such as eating, drinking, or exploring the environment. Another improvement will allow the animat to generalize the knowledge it acquires - in order notably to permit the animat to avail itself, in new contexts, of isolated actions or behavioral sequences which proved useful in the context in which they were learned. Finally, the third direction seeks to demonstrate the generality of the approach described here by applying the corresponding architecture to various planning problems like those of the *block-world* ([Nil80]).

References

[Agr88]   Agre, P.E. and Chapman, D. (1988) "What are Plans for ?" *MIT Dept. of Computer Science, Tech. Rep. 1050*

[Alb81]   Albus, J.S. (1981) "Brains, behavior and robotics." *Byte Books.*

[Alb91]   Albus, J.S. (1991) "Outline of a Theory of Intelligence." *IEEE Trans. Syst. Man and Cybernetics. 21, 3, 473-509.*

---

[3]In other words, the animal must be goal-achieving and goal-seeking. Whether his behavior is goal-directed or intentional is another issue ([Den83], [McF89]).

[Bee90]   Beer, R.D. (1990) "Intelligence as Adaptive Behavior: an Experiment in Computational Neuroethology." *Academic Press.*

[Bro91]   Brooks, R.A. (1991) "Intelligence without representations." *Artificial Intelligence 47, 139-159.*

[Cec93]   Cecconi, F. and Parisi, D. (1993) "Neural networks with motivational units." *In [Mey93].*

[Col93a] Colombetti, M. and Dorigo, M. (1993) "Learning to Control an Autonomous Robot by Distributed Genetic Algorithms." *In [Mey93].*

[Col93b] Colombetti, M. and Dorigo, M. (1993) "Training Agents to Perform Sequential Behavior." *Adaptive Behavior. Under Press.*

[Den83]   Dennett, D. (1983) "Intentional Systems in Cognitive Ethology: the 'Panglossian paradigm' defended." *Behavioral and Brain Science. 6, 343-390.*

[Gab93]   Gabora, L.M. (1993) "Should I Stay or Should I Go: Coordinating Biological Needs with Continuously-updated Assesments of the Environment." *In [Mey93].*

[Gre88]   Grefenstette, J.J. (1988) "Credit Assignment in Rule Discovery Systems Based on Genetic Algorithms" *Machine Learning 3, p225-245.*

[Gui86]   Guillot, A. (1986) "Revue générale des méthodes d'étude des séquences comportementales." *Etudes et analyses comportementales. 2(3): 86-106.*

[Hal91]   Halperin, J.R.P. (1991) "Machine Motivation" *In [Mey91b].*

[Hol86]   Holland, J.H. (1986) "Escaping Brittleness: The Possibilities of General-Purpose Learning Algorithms Applied to Parallel Rule-Based Systems" *Machine Learning: An Artificial Intelligence Approach II.*

[Hou76]   Houston, A. and McFarland, D. (1976) "On the measurement of motivational variables." *Animal Behavior. 24, 459-475.*

[Kui93]   Kuipers, B. and al. (1993) "The Semantic Hierarchy in Robot Learning" *Robot Learning, Kluwer Academic Publishers.*

[Lai86]   Laird, J.E. and al. (1986) "Chunking in Soar." *Machine Learning. 1, 11-46.*

[McF85]   McFarland, D. (1985) "Animal behaviour. Psychobiology, ethology and evolution." *Longman Scientific and Technical.*

[McF89]   McFarland, D. (1989) "The teleological imperative." *In Montefiore and Noble (Eds). Goals, No Goals and Own Goals. Unwin-Hyman.*

[McF93]   McFarland. D. and Bösser, T. (1993) "Intelligent Behavior in Animals and Robots." *The MIT Press/Bradford Books.*

[McF81]   McFarland, D. and Houston, A. (1981) "Quantitative Ethology: the State-Space Approach." *Pitman.*

[Mel94]   Mel, B.W. (1994) "Animal Behavior in Four Components." *In Roitblat and Meyer (Eds). Comparative Approches to Cognitive Science. The MIT Press/Bradford Books. Under Press.*

[Mey91a] Meyer, J.A. and Guillot, A. (1991) "Simulation of adaptive behavior in animats: review and prospect." *in [Mey91b].*

[Mey91b] Meyer, J.A. and Wilson, S. (Eds) (1991) "From Animals to Animats" *Proceedings of the 1st Int. Conf. on Simulation of Adaptive Behavior. The MIT Press/Bradford Books.*

[Mey93]   Meyer, J.A., Roitblat, H.L. and Wilson, S. (Eds) (1993) "From Animals to Animats 2." *Proceedings of the 2nd Int. Conf. on Simulation of Adaptive Behavior. The MIT Press/Bradford Books.*

[Nil80]   Nilsson, N.J. (1980) "Principles of Artificial Intelligence." *Palo Alto , Calif: Tioga Pub. Co.*

[Shu91]   Shu, L. and Schaeffer, J. (1991) "HCS: Adding Hierarchies to Classifier Systems." *Proceedings of the 4th Int. Conf. on Genetic Algorithms.*

[Ste91]   Steels, L. (1991) "Towards a Theory of Emergent Functionality." *in [Mey91b].*

[Suc87]   Suchman, L.A. (1987) "Plans and Situated Actions: The Problem of Human-Machine Communication" *Cambridge University Press.*

[Sut91]   Sutton, R.S. (1991) "Reinforcement Learning Architectures for Animats" *in [Mey91b].*

[Toa86]   Toates, F.M. (1986) "Motivational systems." *Cambridge Univ. Press.*

[Wes89]   Westerdale, T.H. (1989) "A Defense of the Bucket Brigade" *Proc. of the 3rd Int. Conf. on Genetic Algorithms.*

[Wil87]   Wilson, S.W. (1987) "Hierarchical Credit Allocation in Classifier System" *in IJCAI 87.*

[Wil91]   Wilson, S.W. (1991) "The animat path to AI" *in [Mey91b].*

Using Second Order Neural Connections for Motivation of Behavioral Choices

Gregory M. Werner

Artificial Intelligence/Artificial Life Laboratory
Department of Computer Science
UCLA, Los Angeles, CA 90024
gwerner@cs.ucla.edu

Abstract

We introduce a novel behavioral choice mechanism that makes a response to a particular type of stimulus more likely, instead of making a specific action more likely as other methods do. This method allows opportunistic behavioral choice, compromise choices of actions when given several different goals, and simultaneous execution of multiple actions. It is computationally and conceptually simple, and avoids several shortcomings common to other mechanisms. We show that it fulfills most requirements of an action selection mechanism.

1 The Action Selection Problem

A fundamental problem for an animal or robot is to determine what action it should take given information from the environment, its internal motivational state, and its memory of past events.

The ultimate goal of action selection for animals is to maximize the number of copies of their genes in the environment. They can accomplish this goal by keeping themselves alive, by reproducing, and by helping other copies of their genes (their relatives) to do the same.

For a robot, the action selection problem entails maintaining the safety of the robot while pursuing the goals that the robot has been assigned.

This is a difficult problem because a wide range of information must be processed in real time, and one or a small set of possible actions must be chosen from many possibilities.

2 Requirements for an Action Selection Mechanism

A number of capabilities are important for an action selection algorithm. Tyrrell (1993b) has enumerated many of these features. We present the most important of these

features below. We also present several additional requirements that we feel are necessary for such a mechanism, namely the abilities to execute parallel actions, to change choices through learning, to produce directly usable output signals, the use of environmental stimuli with motivational inputs, and the ability for the design to be easily extended.

2.1 Deals with all subproblems

The mechanism should allow decisions to be made on all types of actions. The method should be general enough that only one type of action selection mechanism is sufficient for the overall functioning of the agent.

2.2 Exhibits persistence

The agent should continue with consummatory behaviors (those that directly help the agent, such as eating, drinking, and mating) even when a physical need has been reduced to a point when there are other needs that are greater. Since getting into a position to execute other consummatory actions requires time, this time must be taken into account when deciding what to do. For example, it would be undesirable to move back and forth between food and water instead of simply eating until satiated and then drinking until satiated.

2.3 Prioritizes according to current needs

Actions should be prioritized according to the strength of a need for a type of consummatory behavior. For instance, the thirstier an agent becomes, the more likely it should be to look for water. The overall relative importance of a behavior should also play a role in prioritization. A moderate need for food might outweigh a strong desire for shade, for example.

2.4 Prefers consummatory over appetitive actions

Actions that actually achieve goals (consummatory) should be favored over those that simply move the agent into a state where a goal is more likely to be achieved (appetitive). For example, it is more important to eat than to move toward food when hungry.

2.5 Allows contiguous action sequences

The mechanism should allow a sequence of behaviors to be chosen that will accomplish some goal. The decision mechanism should remember what problem it is solving and continue solving it. It should avoid doing only the first step in several competing sequences of actions and thus getting nowhere.

2.6 Interrupts if necessary

If the agent is working on a sequence of actions, it must be able to interrupt the sequence in order to pursue a line of action that has become more important than the one it was originally working on. If a predator appears while the agent is moving toward some food, the agent should abandon food seeking and begin to avoid the predator.

2.7 Exhibits opportunism

The agent should execute consummatory actions unrelated to the action sequence it is currently working on if such actions become unexpectedly possible. If some food unexpectedly appears while the agent is moving toward water, the agent should move out of its way to obtain the food if it can be done easily.

2.8 Uses all available information

The agent often has access to different streams of information that are pertinent for different needs, e.g. location of a predator, food, and water. All of this information should be used in action selection even if only some of it is directly relevant to the agent's most pressing need, e.g. food. In this manner, preferences for different actions can be combined so that the action that best takes care of all of the agent's needs is chosen. For instance, an agent that sees a predator next to food while water lies in a different direction should go toward the water even though it is more hungry than thirsty. This capability would be absent if seemingly irrelevant information (i.e. the perception of a predator by a hungry agent in the example) is indiscriminately discarded or ignored.

2.9 Has real-valued sensors

Binary sensors require that information be discarded. This information is potentially important for decision making. Real values keep all information that may prove to be relevant. Among other things, this allows compromised choices and blends of actions to be selected.

2.10 Allows parallel actions to be executed

Agents should be able to walk and chew gum at the same time. If actions do not share a common motor pathway (i.e. they don't directly interfere with each other like talking and eating do, for example), and they both will

improve the state of the agent, they should both be carried out at the same time.

2.11 Is easily extensible in design

To be useful in engineering, the mechanism should allow new actions to be added to the behavioral repertoire of the agent without entirely reworking the priorities of other actions.

2.12 Allows choices to be changed through learning

Experience in particular environments can be used to optimize the performance of the decision maker. Ideally, the agent can learn to choose more appropriate actions if its innate behaviors are found to be inappropriate.

2.13 Produces directly usable output signals

Ultimately decisions made by an action selection mechanism must be converted to actions. A mechanism that produces signals that actually control these actions is preferable to one that requires additional processing on the signals to actually drive behavior.

2.14 Doesn't act solely based on internal motivations in absence of environmental stimuli

It is undesirable to produce an action based only on desire to fulfill a need, even if there is nothing in the environment to act upon. For example, hunger alone should not trigger eating actions when there is no food in the environment to be eaten.

3 Other Approaches

Tyrrell extensively compared a number of action selection algorithms and found that his (Tyrrell, 1993a) modification of Rosenblatt and Payton's (1989) method was most successful at choosing actions that led to survival in a simulated environment. This method is quite successful--it features many strengths from our aforementioned list. We compare our approach with Tyrrell's since it outperformed all other mechanisms tested.

Tyrrell's mechanism, however, exhibits several shortcomings. First, it doesn't actually produce signals directly usable by effectors. It is designed to produce priorities for a set of actions and then a separate mechanism chooses which action has the highest activation and executes this action. The separate winner-take-all mechanism it requires is itself difficult to design if a neural mechanism is used. Issues such as what the agent should be doing as the winner take all network settles to a solution arise.

Second, Tyrrell's mechanism allows no principled way to select concurrent actions. The previously mentioned winner-take-all mechanism would also have to determine which actions could be executed concurrently and what the threshold should be for more than one action to be chosen.

Thirdly, its hierarchical structure produces a problem of double-counting motivation from higher levels. For example, activation from an "avoid predators" system node may flow into subsystem nodes for running toward shelter and running away from the predator. This activation may then be added back together in a "move north" unit. The tendency to move north has been doubly activated by one source of information. This type of problem emerges whenever subsystems activated by the same system node both activate the same low level actions.

Finally, its drive mechanism simply multiplies the current need for something by the strength of the sensory signal from the environment for something that satisfies that need. This precludes having a simple mechanism for prioritizing specific needs according to their importance. For example, it is not easy to make food seeking behavior more important than shade seeking behavior. To get around this problem, Tyrrell introduces arbitrary maximums for overall activation into subsystems. It would be preferable to somehow explicitly weight these needs.

We developed a new behavioral choice mechanism to address some of these weaknesses.

4   Principle for proposed mechanism

In typical action selection mechanisms, the motivations directly drive the motor activities. These mechanisms use drives to make specific actions more likely by adding some drive value to the possibility that the agent will produce a specific action.

The problem with this approach is that an action should not be made more likely without knowing that there is something in the environment that should be acted on. That is, we don't want to make a specific action more likely. Instead, we want to make a response to a particular type of stimulus more likely.

Our mechanism makes specific actions more likely by making the agent pay more attention to inputs that drive behaviors that satisfy needs. Neural connections between sensors and actions that help satisfy particular needs are strengthened proportionally to the need for those behaviors. The result is that the agent's overall behavior is driven by its strongest connections--those that will satisfy the current needs of the agent.

For example, a hungry agent responds more vigorously to food than if it is not hungry. But, in the absence of food, it will not produce food-homing or eating actions. This corresponds to selective attention that is paid mainly to the types of inputs that are currently important to the agent.

5   Architecture

We propose an action selection mechanism that addresses shortcomings in Tyrrell's model, and has other desirable features as well. There are several components to this behavioral choice mechanism.

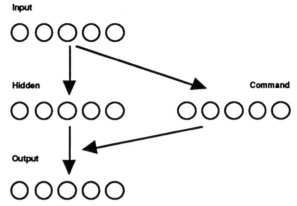

Figure 1. Neural Architecture of Selection Mechanism.

5.1   Environmental Inputs

The environmental inputs in the input layer provide information about the outside world. It includes real-valued sensors for touch, sound, and smell. Each input unit has an activation between 0 and 1. Touch sensors are binary; their activation is 1 if touching something, 0 otherwise. Sound and smell sensors respond proportionally to the logarithm of the strength of the input to which they are tuned. This is important because they are presented with signal strengths spanning several orders of magnitude in the simulated environment.

5.2   Internal State Inputs

The state inputs in the input layer provide information about the internal state of the agent. Sensors indicate the energy level of the agent, the amount of damage to it, etc. The activation of these inputs is proportional to the difference between the current state of the animal and the satiation point for the animal.

5.3   Hidden layer

The hidden layer allows an arbitrary mapping from input to output in the behavior of the agent. These units use a standard sigmoid squashing function common in connectionist models:

$$output = \frac{1}{1+e^{-activation}}$$

Where needed, the hidden layer is augmented with inhibitory cross connections that accentuate the differences in inputs on the left and right sides of the body.

5.4   Output layer

The output layer drives the actual motor behavior of the agent. Activation in this layer causes the movement of specific actuators. Movements are proportional to the activation of the units. The same squashing function is used for the output units as is used for the hidden units.

The strength of the connections between input and hidden, and hidden and output units encode which motor actions should be chosen given a particular set of input conditions. For example, connections between food smell and movement units cause the agent to move toward food.

5.5 Command layer

The command layer determines the priority for different actions to be executed. To prioritize actions, command units have connections that modify the connections between other units. They receive activation from the input layer and activate gating connections that connect to other connections leading to the output layer. These gating connections are second-order (multiplicative). The activation across each connection to the output layer is multiplied by the gating strength that the particular connection receives from the command layer.

$$gating\_strength = \frac{10^{2g(c-0.5)}}{10}$$

In this equation, g is the strength of the connection from the command unit to the gated connection and c is the activation of the command unit.

The activation of a particular command unit is proportional to the current necessity for a particular action to be executed. For example, the greater the activation of a "Find Food" neuron, the higher the gating strength becomes. This, in turn, strengthens the connection between food sensors and output units that cause the agent to move toward food.

The strength of the gating connection from the command unit to the connection that is gated represents the overall importance of that particular action. This connection strength determines amount of change caused by the activation of the command neuron. For example, being very hungry has a greater affect on the behavior of an agent than being very tired, because the gating strength (g) from the find food unit is greater than that from the rest unit. Otherwise, an agent that was tired and hungry might rest until it starved to death.

The strength of the connections between input and command units determine what to look for in the input conditions when deciding what to do. For example, a connection from a hunger sensor to the find food command neuron causes the agent to start prioritizing food finding when the agent gets hungry.

5.6 A sample network

We show here a very simple example of the mechanism being used to prioritize water seeking and food seeking behaviors. For clarity, many units, including all hidden units have been omitted.

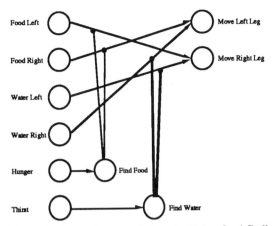

Figure 2. A sample network for prioritizing food finding and water finding behaviors. Arrowheads are regular additive connections. Filled-in circles are gating connections. The relative strength of a connection is indicated by the width of the line.

The units on the left side of figure 2 are inputs. The first four inputs sense information from the environment. For example, "Food Left" represents the sensor that smells food in the left nostril of the agent. The final two inputs, "Hunger" and "Thirst," provide the network information on the internal state of the agent.

The "Move Left Leg" and "Move Right Leg" units constitute the output layer. If these units have the same activation, the agent will move directly forward. Higher activation in one will cause the agent to turn as it moves. Crossed connections from the food and water sensing neurons cause the agent to generally move toward food and water (Braitenberg, 1984).

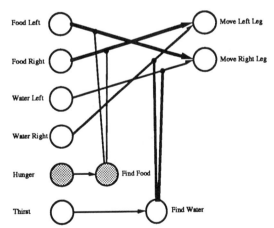

Figure 3. The hunger input unit becomes active and activates the "Find Food" command unit. This unit, in turn, strengthens the connections that cause the agent to move toward food.

The "Find Food" and "Find Water" units make up the command layer. When they are active, they modify the strength of the connection they are attached to. The connections from the "Find Water" command neuron are stronger than those from the "Find Food" neuron because in the current environment water-finding is generally more important.

When the "Find Food" command unit is activated by the "Hunger" input (Figure 3), it strengthens the connections leading from the food smell inputs. This causes the agent to be more sensitive to food than to water and it will preferentially move toward food (if it is present) until its hunger level goes down.

If the agent becomes slightly thirsty (Figure 4), the thirst input will activate the "Find Water" command neuron. Since the gating connections from this neuron are stronger than those from the "Find Food" neuron, the weights from the water sensors to the movement motor neurons become stronger than those from the food sensors to the motor neurons, and the agent will tend to move toward water, even if food is closer.

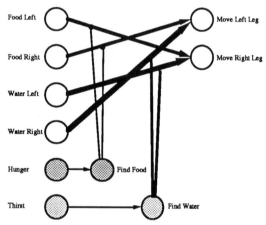

Figure 4. The thirst input unit becomes slightly active and activates the "Find Water" command unit. This unit, in turn, strengthens the connections that cause the agent to move toward water. The command unit's effect on the weights is greater than that of the "Find Food" unit because its gating connections are stronger.

5.7 Connection weights

We start off our agents with engineered weights, but then to evolve the weights we create genes that map into our neural networks. By then setting populations of these neural networks loose, we can evolve better neural networks than we can design, but also gain the huge time advantage of not having to evolve the whole neural architecture and set of weights from scratch--a prospect that is nearly impossible for complex behavior.

6   Task environment

We have created a simulated environment called BioLand in which we can test agent designs. Several of the definitive features of BioLand are included below. See Werner and Dyer (1994) for more details.

6.1   Real Space

Unlike many of the grid-based environments used in similar experiments, our environment allows agents to move in real space. Inputs to the agents are gradients. This allows us to do away with the grid-like object detectors that cannot be scaled up for a large number of object types or a large retina.

6.2   Gradients of Sound and Smell

Each type of object in the environment has a distinctive smell. Each action produced by an agent also has a distinctive sound. The strength of these sounds is proportional to how vigorously the agent is carrying out a particular action. In addition, agents can produce volitional signals, the strength of which is under their control. The strength of sounds and smells diminishes with the square of the distance from the source:

$$perceived\_strength = \frac{actual\_strength}{distance^2}$$

Each agent has two ears and two nostrils. These are full of sensors that respond to specific sound frequencies and smell types. Sensors on the agents respond to these signals by assuming activations proportional to the logarithm of the strength of the signal. By comparing the strength of sounds and smells on each side of the body, a neural network can localize the sources of these gradients.

6.3   Multiple Species

The environment supports multiple species of agents, each of which can only reproduce by mating with other agents of the same species. Species have different physical characteristics, capabilities, and neural networks that produce their behavior. Agents may move, produce volitional sounds, eat, drink, and mate. They use combinations of these primitive actions to find mates, communicate, avoid obstacles and predators, find food, etc.

6.4   Emergent evaluation function

No evaluation function is used. Animals reproduce when they survive and successfully mate.

6.5   Neural net development

When two agents mate, an offspring is produced using a combination of the parents' genes to determine the structure of its neural network.

Two chromosomes are used to encode the neural network. The first chromosome is a series of triples used to encode the normal connections. The first element of the triple is the unit a particular connection starts from. The second is the unit the connection goes to. The third is the strength of the connection.

The second chromosome shares the same triple structure, except that the destination of each connection represented is another connection instead of a unit. These are axoaxonal (gating) connections.

6.6 Design and evolution

To avoid a very long wait for basic behavior to evolve, we hand code the original genes so that the behavior of the agents allows them to survive and generally exhibit the behavior we want them to. Evolution from this starting point optimizes this design and can add additional useful behavior.

7 Task

The task we chose for our agents was that of staying alive and reproducing. A successful agent is one that maximizes the number of copies of its genes in the population.

The specific subproblems that the agents face include: eating food, drinking water, avoiding predators, and avoiding obstacles and edges.

Successfully accomplishing these subgoals requires that:
1. Multiple goals are worked on simultaneously.
2. Competing goals are prioritized.
3. Internal and external information trigger actions.
4. Short sequences of actions are used to accomplish goals.

While we set up the original neural architecture of the agents, we used a genetic algorithm to optimize the actual weights chosen for each of the connections. The behavior of the unevolved networks is good, but the GA allows us to tweak specific preferences so that the agents are well adapted to the specific environment we place them in.

After approximately 50 generations, (there are not explicit generations in the simulation) the agents exhibit well-adapted behavior and their genes are not noticably changing.

8 Resulting behavior

Our agents evolved to successfully survive in the simulated environment. We present here an example of agent behavior that we observed.

The agent is originally more hungry than thirsty (Figure 5), so it moves toward food sources, even though they are more distant than water sources--it persists in its pursuit of food, even when distracted by water. In this case, the water sources are not so close that the agent can opportunistically get a quick drink without going far out of its way.

The agent approaches the food, slows down, and eats (Figure 6). A hidden unit calculates the distance to the food and inhibits movement as the agent gets very close to the food. It also excites the eating motor neuron. The agent

prefers eating, a consummatory action, over moving toward food, an appetitive action. Note that all of these behaviors are gated by axoaxonal connections. If the agent was not hungry, none of these behaviors would take place.

Figure 5. Beginning of a sequence of actions.

Figure 6. The agent moves to a nearby plant and eats it.

Figure 7. The agent eats a second, nearby plant.

The agent is now more thirsty than hungry (Figure 7), but there is food nearby and its hunger is not completely satisfied, so it takes the opportunity to eat the other nearby plant.

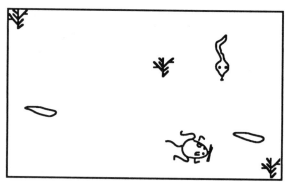

Figure 8. The agent eats a plant that it stumbles across.

Now the agent's thirst is so strong that it outweighs the close proximity of yet another food source, so the agent moves toward the water source (Figure 8). Along its way to the water, the agent senses a predator near its path. It changes its trajectory so as to keep a safe distance from the predator--it interrupts its sequence of actions to pursue a different sequence. Its new path is a compromise between safety and speed. Along its new path is a food source. It opportunistically stops and eats it.

Figure 9. The agent gets a drink.

Finally (Figure 9), the agent approaches the water, slows down, and drinks.

9 Fulfillment of requirements

We evaluated the performance of the mechanism using our original list of requirements.

9.1 Deals with all subproblems

The mechanism is general enough to be used for all decisions made by an agent.

9.2 Exhibits persistence

The agent continues consummatory behavior even when a need has been reduced to a point where there are other needs that are greater. This is because the sensory input to the agent is proportional to the inverse of the square of the distance to the object being sensed. This causes nearby objects to be more important in behavioral selection than distant objects, unless the internal motivation to approach

the distant objects is much stronger than for the close objects.

9.3 Prioritizes according to current needs

Actions are prioritized in proportion to the deficit below total satiation. Weights that cause particular actions to be selected are strengthened by command neurons proportionally to the needs that the actions help to satisfy.

9.4 Prefers consummatory over appetitive actions

Consummatory actions inhibit the appetitive actions that lead to them. This ensures that actions that achieve goals are preferred over those that are precursors to them. For example, eating inhibits movement so that the agent doesn't have to eat while moving past food.

9.5 Allows contiguous action sequences

The mechanism correctly produces sequences of appetitive actions that lead to consummatory actions.

9.6 Interrupts if necessary

The sudden appearance of a nearby predator causes the agent to abandon the sequence of actions that it was pursuing and move away from the predator.

9.7 Exhibits opportunism

The sudden appearance of something to be consumed causes the agent to interrupt what it was doing and to go a short distance out of its way to consume the item.

9.8 Uses all available information

Since this model is a neural network, all information available at the input level remains in the system to be used for preference combination and compromises. Preferences and sensory input are combined so that agents choose actions which, while not optimizing behavior for a specific goal, do optimize the overall behavior of the agent.

9.9 Has real-valued sensors

The sensors used are floating-point and the information they provide allows the agent to determine the distance and direction of an object, as well as the identity of the object.

9.10 Allows parallel actions to be executed

Actions that are not on the same behavioral final path (those that don't directly interfere with each other) may all be selected at the same time. So, for example, the agent can produce signals while moving. Inhibitory connections that are explicitly added between actions can preclude parallel actions if they are not desired.

9.11 Is easily extensible in design

Adding new behavior requires the addition of new command neurons and the appropriate output units. The weights between the new units can then be set without resetting all of the other weights in the architecture.

9.12 Allows choices to be changed through learning

This mechanism should allow learning, but the capability has not yet been added. Reinforcement learning can be applied to the weights of gating connections from the command layer in order to learn priorities for different actions.

9.13 Produces directly usable output signals

The mechanism produces output signals that may be directly interpreted by effectors to produce the agent's behavior. No selection mechanism is required to interpret the output and actually select the behavior to be performed.

9.14 Doesn't act solely based on internal motivations in absence of environmental stimuli

Since our mechanism chooses behavior by strengthening connections from environmental inputs, it has no effect on behavior if there is nothing sensed in the environment to act upon.

10   Future work

We plan to do the following:
1.   Test the usefulness of this behavioral choice mechanism in real robots.
2.   Run a head-to-head test against Tyrrell's modified hierarchical decision maker.
3.   Add reinforcement learning to the choice mechanism.

We also solicit competing behavioral choice mechanisms to compete with ours in a battle to the death (to extinction).

11   Conclusions

We present a mechanism for behavioral choice that has a number of desirable features. It is computationally simple, deals with all types of subproblems, persists at following a task once it is started but interrupts it if necessary, is opportunistic, prefers consummatory over appetitive actions, allows compromise in choices of actions, combines preferences flexibly, and allows the choice of parallel actions.

The mechanism presented features several advantages over Tyrrell's behavioral choice mechanism. It allows multiple actions to be performed simultaneously, produces directly usable outputs, and because of its non-hierarchical

design, similar in flavor to Maes (1989, 1991), does not suffer from motivational double-counting effects.

We combine this basic framework with Genetic Algorithms to optimize the specific parameters of the mechanism, thus allowing us to produce more intelligent behavior than other techniques have allowed us to produce.

Acknowledgments

Thanks to Ruth Liow and two anonymous reviewers for valuable comments and suggestions.

References

Agre, P. & Chapman, D. (1987). Pengi: An implementation of a theory of activity. In: *Proceedings of the Sixth National Conference on Artificial Intelligence*, Morgan Kaufmann.

Beer, R. (1990). *Intelligence as Adaptive Behavior: an Experiment in Computational Neuroethology*. Academic Press.

Braitenberg, V. (1984). *Vehicles: Experiments in Synthetic Psychology*. MIT Press.

Maes, P. (1989). How to do the right thing. *Connection Science*, 1, 291-323.

Maes, P. (1991). A bottom-up mechanism for behavior selection in an artificial creature. In: *From Animals to Animats: Proceedings of the First International Conference on Simulation of Adaptive Behavior*, (J.A. Meyer & S. W. Wilson, eds.), MIT Press.

Rosenblatt, K. J., & Payton, D. W. (1989). A fine-grained alternative to the subsumption architecture for mobile robot control. In Proceedings of the IEEE/INNS International Joint Conference on Neural Networks, Washington, DC.

Tyrrell, T. (1993a). *Computational Mechanisms for actions selection*. Unpublished doctoral thesis, Centre for Cognitive Science, University of Edinburgh, Scotland.

Tyrrell, T. (1993b). The Use of Hierarchies for Action Selection. *Adaptive Behavior*, 1:4, 387-420.

Werner, G. M. and Dyer, M. G. (1994). BioLand: a Massively Parallel Simulation Environment for Evolving Distributed Forms of Intelligent Behavior. In: Hiroaki Kitano (ed.) *Massively Parallel Artificial Intelligence*. AAAI/MIT Press.

INTERNAL WORLD MODELS
AND COGNITIVE PROCESSES

Spatial Learning and Representation in Animats

Tony J. Prescott

Artificial Intelligence Vision Research Unit,
Sheffield University,
Sheffield S10 2TN,
United Kingdom.

Telephone +44 742 826547
Fax +44 742 766515

Email: T.Prescott@aivru.sheffield.ac.uk

Abstract

Animat AI has generally emphasised learning of a *dispositional*, or task-specific nature over that of a *representational* or task-independent kind. However, many animals are capable of both forms of learning, and, in particular, exploit representational learning to construct spatial knowledge that allows efficient and flexible navigation behaviour. The focus on building versatile *mobile* robots may therefore force the development of representational learning systems in animat AI. This paper considers the navigation problem and argues against the view that qualitative spatial representations, encoding principally topological relations, may necessarily be simpler to construct, store, or use than more quantitative models. It further argues against constructing a unified or global representations of space suggesting instead that knowledge should be distributed between multiple, partial, local models encoding complimentary constraints which can be combined at run-time to address a specific navigation task.

1. Learning in natural systems

Research in psychology suggests that underlying a large number of observable phenomena of learning and memory, there are two broad clusters of learning processes[1].

First, there are the *dispositional* learning processes involved in habit formation, the acquisition of motor skills, and certain forms of classical and instrumental conditioning. These processes involve incremental adaptation and do not seem to need attention or awareness. Learning is generally task-specific in that it is driven by a significant outcome in the form of a positively or negatively reinforcing event. Further, it does not seem to require or involve the acquisition of knowledge about the causal processes underlying the task that is solved.

Second, there are the *representational*[2] learning processes involved in acquiring knowledge about the relationships between events (stimuli or responses). For instance, that one event follows another (causal knowledge), or is close to another (spatial knowledge). These forms of learning appear to be have more of an all-or-none character, and may require attentional resources. They are also not directly involved in generating behaviour, and need not be acquired with respect to a specific task or desired outcome. The knowledge acquired can support both further learning or decision-making through inference.

Lesion studies with animals and patterns of learning impairment in human amnesiacs indicate that in mammals this second style of learning relies on specific medial-temporal structures in the brain, in particular, the hippocampus. In contrast the simpler associative forms of learning underlying habit and skill acquisition are not affected by damage to this brain region, but appear instead to be supported by neural systems that evolved much earlier. This view is supported by observations that all vertebrates

---

[1]For reviews of this extensive literature see [15, 43, 46].

[2]The terms *dispositional* and *representational* have been suggested by Thomas [47] and Morris [29] to refer to these two clusters of learning/memory processes.

and most invertebrates show dispositional learning abilities, whereas representational learning styles have evolved primarily in higher vertebrates coinciding with increased brain-size.

2. The Animat approach

The shared interest in adaptive systems, between psychologists and ethologists, on the one hand, and Artificial Intelligence researchers and roboticists on the other, has recently seen the development of a new inter-disciplinary research field. The common aim of 'Animat' (simulated animal) (Wilson [51]) research is to understand how autonomous agents—animals, simulated animals, robots, or simulated robots—can survive and adapt in their environments, and be successful in fulfilling needs and achieving goals.

Some important themes in much of this work (see, for instance [28]) are as follows: control in the agent is not centralised but is distributed between multiple task-oriented modules; there is minimal reliance on internal world models and on reasoning or planning processes; instead there is an emphasis on the role of the agent's interaction with its environment in driving the selection and performance of appropriate, generally reflexive, behaviours; perception is targeted at acquiring task-relevant information rather than delivering a general description of the current state of the perceived world .

The animat approach is thus in good accord with dispositional learning approaches (such as reinforcement learning) to the adaptation of behavioural competences. In view of the aim of building complete intelligent systems in an incremental, and bottom-up fashion this is wholly consistent with the earlier observation that learning in simpler animals is principally of a dispositional nature. However, the development of this research paradigm is already beginning to see the need for some representational learning. One reason for this is the emphasis on mobile robotics as the domain of choice for investigating animat AI.

3. Navigation as a forcing domain

The fundamental skill required by a mobile agent is the ability to move around in the immediate environment quickly and safely, this will be referred to here as *local navigation* competence. Research in animat AI has had considerable success in using pre-wired reactive competences to implement local navigation skills (e.g. [3, 10, 45]). The robustness, fluency, and responsiveness of these systems have played a significant role in promoting the animat methodology as a means for constructing effective, autonomous robots. The possibility of acquiring adaptive local navigation competences through reinforcement learning has also been investigated and has been advanced as an appropriate mechanism for learning or fine-tuning such skills [31, 40].

However, a second highly valuable form of navigation expertise is the ability to find and follow paths to desired goals outside the current visual scene. This skill will be referred to here as *way-finding*. The literature on animal spatial learning differentiates the way-finding skills of most invertebrates and lower vertebrates, from those of higher vertebrates (birds and mammals). In particular, it suggests that way-finding in most invertebrates is performed primarily by using path integration mechanisms and compass senses and secondarily by orienting to specific remembered stimulus patterns [49, 50][4-6]. This suggests that these animals do not construct models of the spatial layout of their environment and that consequently, their way-finding behaviour is relatively inflexible and restricted to homing or retracing familiar routes[3]. In contrast, higher vertebrates appear to construct and use representations of the spatial relations between locations in their environments (see, for example, [13, 32, 33, 35]). They are then able to use these models to select and follow paths to desired goals. This form of spatial learning is often regarded as *the* classic example of a representational learning process (e.g. [43]).

This evidence has clear implications for research in animat AI. First, it suggests that systems employing minimal representation and reactive competences could support way-finding behaviour similar to that of invertebrates[4]. Second, however, the acquisition of more flexible way-finding skills would appear to require representational learning abilities—this raises the interesting issue of how control and learning architectures in animat AI should be developed to meet this need.

---

[3]Gould [14] has proposed a contrary view that insects do construct models of spatial layout however, the balance of evidence (cited above) appears to be against this position.

[4]In particular it should be possible to exploit the good odometry information available to mobile robots.

4. How should space be represented?

In keeping with the animat approach it would seem reasonable to require the *on-line* acquisition of appropriate spatial knowledge, and the use of representations that are simple to construct and use, cheap to store, and support a 'graceful degradation' of performance when confronted with unreliable sensory data. What forms of representational learning might satisfy these criteria?

Some recent research on robot way-finding has sought to address this challenge by advocating a substantial change in the character of the systems under investigation. Specifically, the emphasis of 'classical' AI methods on detailed path-planning using metric models of the environment (e.g. [8, 11, 16, 24, 41, 48]) has been rejected by some researchers in favour of the use of more 'qualitative' methods and models (e.g. [10, 17-19, 21-23, 25, 26, 30]). In these systems metric modelling and wayfinding is often regarded as supplementary to a core level of navigation skill based, primarily, on representations of topological spatial relations. This approach has, as part of its motivation, the perceived inadequacies of classical systems which are regarded as over-reliant on accurate sensing and detailed world models. It is suggested that such systems are both too 'brittle' in the face of degraded or missing sensory information, and too costly in terms of the computational and memory resources they require.

A second motivation for investigating topological spatial models is research on human way-finding. Much of this literature follows a theory originating with Piaget [36] that human spatial knowledge has a hierarchical structure and is acquired through a stage-like process. Specifically, Piaget, and later Siegel and White [44], have argued that a fundamental stage in the acquisition of spatial knowledge is the construction of qualitative models of the environment from more elementary sensorimotor associations. This representation is then gradually supplemented by distance and direction information to form a more detailed quantitative map. An important element of this theory is the view that a primarily topological representation can support robust way-finding behaviour in everyday environments. Computational models inspired by the human way-finding literature have been described by Leiser [22] and by Kuipers [18-21]. The latter in particular has developed a number of robot simulations of considerable sophistication and detail based on the hypothesis of a hierarchical representation of spatial knowledge. The following extract serves to illustrate this theoretical position, which has been influential in other recent work on robot way-finding (e.g. [23]):

"There is a natural four-level semantic hierarchy of descriptions of large-scale space that supports robust map-learning and navigation:

1. *Sensorimotor:* The traveller's input-output relations with the environment.

2. *Procedural:* Learned and stored procedures defined in terms of sensori-motor primitives for accomplishing particular instances of place-finding and route-following tasks.

3. *Topological:* A description of the environment in terms of fixed entities, such as places, paths, landmarks, and regions, linked by topological relations such as connectivity, containment and order.

4. *Metric:* A description of the environment in terms of fixed entities [...] linked by metric relations such as relative distance, relative angle and absolute angle and distance with respect to a frame of reference.

In general, although not without exception, assimilation of the cognitive map proceeds from the lowest level of the spatial semantic hierarchy to the highest, as resources permit. The lower levels of the cognitive map can be created accurately without depending greatly on computational resources or observational accuracy. A complete and accurate lower level map improves the interpretation of observations and the creation of higher levels of the map." ([21], p. 26)

In many respects this view is highly acceptable, for instance, the proposal that spatial knowledge is organised in distinct components encoding separate forms of constraint is a welcome contrast to the traditional approach of unitary global models. However, there are several implications of this view that are open to question. First it is important to ask in what sense the organisation of spatial knowledge should be viewed as hierarchical rather than heterarchical; second, to what degree global models, such as those described for the topological and metric levels, are required (as opposed to multiple overlapping local models); and finally, whether the emphasis on geometric content as the main distinguishing factor between models is correct.

Some of these issues can be highlighted by contrasting the literature on human way-finding with much of the research from the wider field of animal navigation.

In particular, this latter evidence suggests a discontinuity between procedural knowledge and the use of map-like metric spatial representations [13, 32, 33].

For instance, in contrast to an incremental hierarchy, O'Keefe [32, 33] has argued that there are two fundamentally independent navigation systems used by mammals including man. The first of these, which he calls the *taxon* system is supported by route-like chains of $stimulus \times action \rightarrow stimulus$ associations. Each element in such a chain is an association that involves approaching or avoiding a specific cue, or performing a body-centred action (generally a rotation) in response to a cue. Taxon strategies therefore have a similar nature to the procedural knowledge in the second level of Kuipers hierarchy. O'Keefe's second system, called the *locale* system, is, however, a 'true' mapping system in that it constructs a representational model describing the $stimulus \rightarrow stimulus$ metric spatial relations between locations in the environment. Evidence for the existence of this system and its independence from taxon strategies consists of both observational and laboratory studies of animal behaviour, and neurophysiological studies suggesting that different brain structures underlie the two systems.

Although the highest level of Kuipers' hierarchy can be identified with O'Keefe's locale system the former suggests a continuity—with assimilation of information onto 'weaker' representations to generate the metric model, whereas the latter stresses the discontinuity and apparent autonomy of the two alternative mechanisms. A further difference is that O'Keefe's theory bypasses the level of the topological map, if such a map exists it is as an abstraction from the full metric representation—this contrasts with Kuipers view in which the topological model is simpler and comes first.

Gallistel [13], who provides an extensive review of research on animal navigation, also concludes that animals make considerable use of metric data for navigation. Like O'Keefe he also proposes a modular and autonomous

mapping system that stores a *metric* representation of spatial layout[5].

5. Topological and/or Metric Modelling?

The nature of the spatial relations encoded by a world model determines the type of navigation behaviour that can be supported. Procedural (or route) knowledge can only support movement along segments of known paths. Knowledge of the topological layout of the environment gains the navigator the ability to identify suitable sub-goals, and generate and follow novel routes between locations. However, because this knowledge is limited to knowing the connectivity of places navigation is constrained to using known path segments between adjacent sub-goals. A navigator with a topological map who enters unfamiliar territory can explore new paths and construct new map knowledge but cannot engage in goal-directed movement to target sites. The ability to determine short-cut or straight-line routes across un-explored terrain requires knowledge of higher-order spatial relations. Where such behaviours are observed in animals this is usually taken as strong evidence for the use of a metric model. That such skills would be very useful to an animal or robot is undeniable giving a strong incentive for constructing and using knowledge of this type.

Given the value of metric knowledge is there a justification for constructing, as the first or only form of spatial representation, models encoding weaker geometric constraints? One possible argument for such a view is the idea that a topological model could be constructed without the need to detect higher-order relations. Mathematically topological geometry is simpler and more basic than metric geometry—it requires fewer axioms. However, this mathematical simplicity perhaps belies the real difficulties of constructing topological knowledge in the absence of metric knowledge. I have argued elsewhere [39] that such a model is in general realisable only if the agent has sensory abilities that can be relied on to give accurate identification and re-identification of most locations (henceforth *place identification*), and that in practice this may require vision

---

[5]O'Keefe and Gallistel agree on the existence of a separate metric mapping system but largely disagree on the relative importance of dead reckoning and environmental fixes in constructing the map. This debate will be considered further below.

skills capable of object recognition or, at least, of very robust visual pattern matching[6]. This fits uneasily with the bottom-up bias of Animat AI, and, indeed, with the current perceptual abilities of animat-style robots. Many systems currently use local sonar patterns to characterise different places. However, this sort of local geometry information is not likely to be sufficiently distinctive to allow the disambiguation of similar places. For this reason sonar patterns are often supplemented by odometry information in order to make the place identification task feasible (e.g. [25]). This need to exploit metric knowledge (albeit of a rough and ready kind) demonstrates the difficulty of topological mapping with non-visual sensory data[7].

The use of some approximate metric knowledge in model-building introduces the possibility that such information might be computed and exploited in constructing representations, but might not actually be explicitly recorded or used for way-finding. Given the advantages that metric knowledge of any sort can endow the main justification for this proposal must be that the cost or complexity of building (or using) such representation would outweigh its usefulness. This supposition, which may stem from the perceived weaknesses of some existing metric-based systems, may, however, be premature. A distinctive characteristic of much research in quantitative model-building has been an emphasis on combining all available information into a unique *global model*. One aim of this paper is to suggest that it is perhaps this characteristic, rather than the use of quantitative information, that has

contributed to the inflexibility and over-sensitivity to measurement error observed in some existing systems.

6. Constructing metric models

The task of building a representation of an environment that encodes distance and direction requires that places are located with respect to common coordinate frames. The coordinate frames most directly available are *egocentric*, that is, they are defined by the navigator's instantaneous position and orientation in space. However, to construct a useful model, observations from different view-points must be integrated into representations with respect to environment-centred or *allocentric* frames. That is egocentric relations must be transformed to give allocentric spatial relations.

The arguments that metric models are more complex or expensive to construct and use than more qualitative ones, generally concern the difficulties of obtaining accurate distance information (or failing that, dealing with noisy information), and the resource demands of the need for continuous transformations between egocentric and allocentric frames. However, there are representations and mechanisms that may overcome some of these objections. Specifically, distributed representations have been proposed [23, 38] in which the environment is represented using multiple models based on coordinate frames defined by distinctive local landmarks.

Two landmarks are sufficient to define a two-dimensional coordinate frame (three for 3D), however, coordinate transformations based on such frames require non-linear computations (trigonometric functions and square-roots) and further require that an arbitrary ordering of the reference points is remembered in order to specify a unique coordinate frame. However, as Zipser [52] has pointed out, if a further landmark is used to define each local frame then all the transformation calculations become linear. In [38, 39] I have described a simulation based on this proposal in which the positions of salient goals are stored with respect to the two-dimensional co-ordinate frames[8] defined by groups of three local landmarks. Multiple local frames are represented in a connectionist network in which the task of determining direction or route information to a desired goal is performed

---

[6]Some recent work on metric-free topological map-building for robot navigation has recognised this need for powerful visual processing e.g. [17].

[7]The problem of constructing a topological map are eased considerably by introducing additional constraints to the map-building process. One possible constraint is to limit the behavioural repertoire of the robot. One way this might be achieved is to force the robot to maintain a travel-path that follows object boundaries [25, 30]. This constraint of 'wall-following' limits the connectivity of the resulting topological graph and reduces the number of true choice points (i.e. vertices in the graph of degree>2). This eases the tasks of segmenting the environment (into the regions that form graph vertices) and of place identification, and also avoids the need to represent places that lack distinctive local features. This approach has lead to some successes in building way-finding systems for indoor autonomous robots, however, it also has an obvious cost—open spaces will be poorly represented in the map and movement will be more rigidly limited to a small set of paths.

---

[8]These coordinates are, strictly speaking *affine* rather than metric, however, sssuming that the agent detects metric egocentric spatial relation according to some calibrated Euclidean measure, metric relations—direction and distance—will be recoverable from a stored affine model.

by a parallel, 'spreading activation' search. The computations required to construct these representations from (noisy) egocentric metric data require only linear mathematics (indeed a simple 'perceptron'-like learning rule will suffice) and have memory requirements roughly proportional to the number of goal-sites and landmarks stored. While following a planned route the system can also exploit run-time error-correction by incorporating egocentric fixes on sighted landmarks. This makes the route following system highly robust to noise in the representation or perceptual system.

In contrast to approaches in which the goal is to construct a permanent 'map' of environmental layout (in which position errors are minimised or explicitly modelled) this approach builds no long-term static representation of global spatial relations. Instead the store of knowledge concerning a specific goal or landmark is distributed across a number of local models in the network allowing the constraint information to be combined at run-time for any given task. Methods for combining different constraints using Kalman filtering techniques are currently being investigated.

7. A 'multiple schemata' view

This last section is an attempt to set out a perspective on the acquisition of representations of space. In contrast to Kuipers' hierarchical approach in which global topological and metric models are constructed, it proposes a heterarchy of local models in which the geometric distinction is only one among a number of characteristics identifying complimentary representational forms. Following Michael Arbib [1, 2], I call this a 'multiple schemata' view.

Arbib has proposed the use of the term *schemata* to describe active representational systems or "perceptual structures and programs for distributed motor control" ([1] p. 47). In the context of constructing and using models of space he suggests—

"The representation of [...] space in the brain is not one absolute space, but rather a patchwork of approximate spaces (partial representations) that link sensation to action. I mean '*partial*' and '*approximate*' in two senses: a representation will be *partial* because it represents only one small sample of space (...), and it will be *approximate* in that it will be based on an incomplete sample of sensory data and may be of limited accuracy and reliability. I will suggest that our

behaviour is mediated by the interaction of these partial representations: both through their integration to map ever larger portions of the territory relevant to behaviour, and through their mutual calibration to yield a shared representation more reliable than that obtained by any one alone." ([2] p. 380)

In the specific context of cognitive maps, he also suggests that:

"There is no reason, in general, to expect the system to use Euclidean space or Cartesian coordinates for such a map. Rather, the system needs a whole array of local representations that are easily interfaced and moved between." ([1] p. 47).

The view advocated here is, I hope, in close accord with these ideas.

Spatial information can be picked-up through multiple sensory modalities in a number of different guises and forms. This information may describe spatial relations upto any level of geometric richness (topological—metric) it may also be anywhere on a scale from precise to vague. Each piece of information can be viewed as supplying a potential constraint that can assist navigation.

I propose that the critical distinction with regard to different forms of constraint information has less to do with the geometric content of the knowledge and more with *the process by which that knowledge is derived*. For instance, metric information derived from odometry is (to a large extent) independent from metric information determined by perceived distance and direction to identifiable salient landmarks. These two forms of quantitative knowledge thus provide constraints that are complimentary because they derive from *different sensory modalities*. Multiple constraints can also be obtained from within a single sensory modality by observing *different environmental cues*. For instance, the observed position of a single distant landmark (such as the sun) gives a direction constraint that is essentially independent from spatial localisation with respect to local landmarks. Indeed, different individual landmarks or landmark groups can supply separate constraints as has been demonstrated in [23, 38]. Finally, relatively independent constraints can arise within a modality by reference to the same external cues but by employing *different computational mechanisms*. It is in this sense, perhaps, that the distinction between different geometries may be most relevant. For instance, the visual characteristics of landmarks might be used to construct knowledge of topological relations that is largely independent of the mechanisms that extract distance or direction from the visual scene.

To the extent that different constraints are independent two constraints will clearly be much more powerful than one, three more than two, etc. It therefore seems reasonable to suggest that an agent should seek to detect and represent a number of independent or near independent constraints that describe the spatial relations between important places.

The emphasis of a multiple schemata approach is not on constructing unified representations such as topological or metric maps but rather on establishing multiple complimentary spatial descriptions. Each schema should exploit a different combination of *cues, channels,* and *mechanisms* to instantiate a set of environmental spatial relations. Thus, there will overall, be a number of relatively distinct path-ways through which knowledge is acquired. This suggests a heterarchy of models (as opposed to a hierarchy), with some, but not all, schemata sharing common sources and resources. At any time an agent should exploit the knowledge in several schemata to support its current navigation task. Although some tasks may require the temporary creation of a unified model (drawing a graphical map of the environment might constitute such a task) in general the underlying representations can remain distinct allowing the reliability of each source of information to be assessed at run-time.

Way-finding should exploit acquired schemata via *arbitration* procedures which decide on the basis of the content and accuracy of each active model the extent to which it should contribute to the decision process. This arbitration could be carried out through some fixed subsumption mechanism whereby, for instance, knowledge determined from large-scale metric relations could override taxon (route-following) strategies. Alternatively a more sophisticated system would seek to combine the constraints afforded by multiple schemata by weighting them according to their perceived accuracy or reliability. In this way, reliable identification of a highly distinctive landmark might override estimates of spatial position or orientation determined by some metric reckoning process.

These ideas are currently being investigated with respect to the distributed coding system described in [38, 39] (and, briefly, above). If a specific location is encoded by two separate schemas based on non-overlapping landmark triples then these would constitute relatively independent constraints. To the extent that landmark sets do overlap they will obviously be less independent, but will nevertheless encode partially distinct constraint information.

However, the idea of multiple schemata also generalises to encompass different coding systems. For instance, representations based principally on direction sense and odometry could be constructed which would provide a modality-independent source of information from the landmark-based coding.

An obvious argument against a multiple schemata view is that acquiring and storing spatial knowledge is not without cost. It makes demands on attention, processing and memory (there are really separate costs associated with detecting constraints, storing them, retrieving them, and combining them!). One defence against this argument is the relative independence between different schema which will allow parallel processing to be exploited to a considerable extent. A second possibility, which is rarely explored in research with artificial animats, is that the amount of resources devoted to a given location (i.e. the number of constraints stored) may vary according to the subjective importance of being able to relocate that place or reach it quickly. We could expect, for instance, that an animal's home or nest (or a robots power source) would have the highest priority and that therefore 'homing' might be the most robustly supported way-finding behaviour.

A multiple schemata view can help in understanding the evolution of way-finding competence in animals, and may also provide support for the essentially pragmatic approach of Animat AI. In the case of the former, O'Keefe's [32] separate taxon and locale systems (which follows a very long line of research into response vs. place knowledge in animal navigation, see Olton [34, 35]) can be viewed as a distinction along these lines. However, there also seems to be a reasonable case for breaking up the 'locale' system into multiple schemata, for instance, models derived from odometry and direction senses [13, 27] and those derived principally from codings with respect to distinct local landmark groups [32].

In robotics this view suggests the abandonment of theoretical pre-conceptions about the priority, or lack of it, of different forms of geometric knowledge. It further implies that the 'brittleness' of classical approaches arises not so much from the emphasis on metric modelling but from the search for an accurate unified metric model.

Much existing work is compatible with this approach. In addition to Michael Arbib's work on schema theory [2] much work in psychology (e.g. [42]) and AI (e.g. [23]) shares similar objectives. Work in animal navigation that specifically fits this research theme has been performed by Poucet et al. (e.g. [7, 37]), Collett et al. [9] and Etienne et al. (e.g. [12]). To end this paper I would therefore like to draw upon a couple of examples from this work.

Etienne et al. [12] report that hamsters have effective dead reckoning skills which are sufficient to relocate their nest in darkness. However, in lighted conditions hamsters were found to orient primarily using visual information about local landmarks. In conflict situations, where a landmark (a single light spot) was rotated relative to the learned position, the hamsters homed using either the landmark information or their dead-reckoning sense. When the visual information and dead reckoning produced highly divergent paths dead reckoning was used, however, with smaller discrepancies visual information took priority over path integration. Etienne et al. also report that the dead-reckoning sense was more precise when used to return to the nest than when used to locate a secondary feeding site. This suggests that a dead reckoning way-finding schema maybe more available for homing than for general path-finding.

Experiments by Collett et al. [9] with gerbils suggests that these animals may encode goal positions (buried sunflower seeds) in terms of individual visible landmarks by using some form of direction sense. For instance, in one experiment gerbils were trained to locate a food cache at the centre of an array of two landmarks. When the distance between landmarks was doubled the gerbils searched at two sites each at the correct distance and orientation to one of the landmarks rather that at the centre of the two locations (as some theories of a landmark 'map' might predict). In a further experiment the gerbils were trained to go to a goal-site at the centre of a triangle of three landmarks. During testing the distance of one landmark to the centre was doubled, Collett et al. report that the animals spent most of their search time around the place specified by the two landmarks, ignoring the one that broke the pattern. They interpreted this result in the following way:

> "The gerbil is thus equipped with a useful procedure for deciding between discrepant solutions. When most of the landmarks agree in specifying the same goal, with just a few pointing to other sites, the chances are that the majority view is correct and that the additional possibilities result from mistakes in computation or from disturbances to the environment." ([9] p. 845).

Collett et al. are therefore suggesting that this multiple encoding of landmark-goal relations by hamsters occurs to provide the system with robustness. In other words, they advocate something like a multiple schemata system and give a clear example of the ability of such a hypothesis to generate interesting and testable predictions.

8. Conclusions

This paper has argued that the problem of representation for animat spatial learning may be best approached by discarding the goal of a complete global model of the environment in favour of the use of multiple, partial local models encoding complimentary constraints. This approach, I believe, has a resonance with the general ethos of animat research that opposes the need for representation for its own sake (which has often seemed to be the goal of classical AI) and is against a strong distinction between model and mechanism. This view constitutes a theoretical position that has as yet only been partly explored in simulation, it is thus proposed as a hypothesis which awaits evaluation through the construction of genuine way-finding robots.

Acknowledgements

The author is grateful to John Mayhew for advice and comments. This research was funded by the Science and Engineering Research Council.

References

1.   Arbib, M.A. (1989). *The Metaphorical Brain*. New York: Wiley and Sons.

2.   Arbib, M.A. (1990). Interaction of multiple representations of space in the brain, in *Brain and Space,* J. Paillard, Editor. Oxford University Press: Oxford. p. 380-403.

3.   Brooks, R.A. (1989). "Robot beings". in *International Workshop on Intelligent Robots and Systems*. Tsukuba, Japan.

4.   Cartwright, B.A. and T.S. Collett (1979). "How honeybees know their distance from a nearby visual landmark". *Journal of Experimental Biology.* **82**: p. 367-72.

5.   Cartwright, B.A. and T.S. Collett (1983). "Landmark learning in bees: experiments and models". *Journal of Comparative Physiology A.* **151**(4): p. 521-544.

6.   Cartwright, B.A. and T.S. Collett (1987). "Landmark maps for honeybees". *Biological Cybernetics.* **57**: p. 85-93.

7.   Chapuis, N., C. Thinus-Blanc, and B. Poucet (1983). "Dissociation of mechanisms involved in dogs' oriented displacements". *Quarterly Journal of Experimental Psychology.* **35B**: p. 213-219.

8.   Chatila, R. (1986). "Mobile robot navigation: space modelling and decisional processes". in *3rd International Symposium on Robotics Research.* . MIT Press.

9.   Collett, T.S., B.A. Cartwright, and B.A. Smith (1986). "Landmark learning and visuo-spatial memory in gerbils". *Journal of Comparative Physiology A.* **158**: p. 835-51.

10.   Connell, J.H. (1990). *Minimalist Mobile Robots.* Perspectives in Artificial Intelligence, Boston: Academic Press.

11.   Crowley, J.L. (1985). "Navigation for an intelligent mobile robot". *IEEE Journal of Robotics and Automation.* **1**(1): p. 31-41.

12.   Etienne, A.S. (1992). "Navigation of a small mammal by dead reckoning and local cues". *Current Directions in Psychological Science.* **1**(2): p. 48-52.

13.   Gallistel, C.R. (1990). *The Organisation of Learning.* Cambridge, MA: MIT Press.

14.   Gould, J.L. (1986). "The locale map of honeybees: do insects have cognitive maps?". *Science.* **232**: p. 861-63.

15.   Hintzman, D.L. (1992). "Twenty-five years of learning and memory: was the cognitive revolution a mistake". in *Fourteenth International Symposium on Attention and Performance.* Michigan. Bradford Books.

16.   Iyengar, S., *et al.* (1985). "Learned navigation paths for a robot in unexplored terrain". in *2nd Conference on Artificial Intelligence Applications.*

17.   Kortenkamp, D., *et al.* (1991). "A scene-based multi-level representation for mobile robot spatial mapping and navigation". *IEEE transactions on robotics and automation.*

18.   Kuipers, B. (1982). "The "map in the head" metaphor". *Environment and behaviour.* **14**: p. 202-220.

19.   Kuipers, B. and Y.T. Byun (1991). "A robot exploration and mapping strategy based on a semantic hierarchy of spatial representations". *Robotics and Autonomous Systems.* **8**, also in *Towards Learning Robots,* W.Van de Welde (ed.), MIT Press 1993.

20.   Kuipers, B. and Y.T. Byun (1987). "A robust, qualitative method for robot exploration and map-learning". in *Proceedings of the Sixth National Conference on AI (AAAI–87).* St. Pauls, Minneapolis. Morgan Kaufmann.

21.   Kuipers, B. and T. Levitt (1988). "Navigation and mapping in large-scale space". *AI Magazine.* (Summer 1988): p. 25-43.

22.   Leiser, D. and A. Zilbershatz (1989). "The traveller: a computational model of spatial network learning". *Environment and behaviour.* **21**(4): p. 435-463.

23.   Levitt, T.S. and D.T. Lawton (1990). "Qualitative navigation for mobile robots". *Artificial Intelligence.* **44**: p. 305-360.

24.   Lozano-Perez (1983). "Spatial-planning: a configuration space approach". *IEEE transactions on computers.* **C-32**(2): p. 108-121.

25.   Mataric, M.J. (1990). "Navigating with a rat brain: A neurologically-inspired model for robot spatial representation". in *From Animals to Animats: Proceedings of the First International Conference Simulation of Adaptive Behaviour.* Paris. MIT Press.

26.   Mataric, M.J. (1992). "Integration of representation into goal-driven behaviour-based robots". *IEEE Transactions on robotics and automation.* **8**(3): p. 304-312.

27.   McNaughton, B.L., L.L. Chen, and E.J. Markus (1991). "Landmark learning and the sense of direction - a neurophysiological and computational hypothesis.". *Journal of Cognitive Neuroscience.* **3**(2): p. 192-202.

28.   Meyer, J. and A. Guillot (1990). "Simulation of adaptive behaviour in animats: review and prospect". in *From Animals to Animats: Proceedings of the First International Conference Simulation of Adaptive Behaviour.* Paris.

29.   Morris, R.G.M. (1990). "Toward a representational hypothesis of the role of hippocampal synaptic plasticity in spatial and other forms of learning". *Cold Spring Harbor Symposia on Quantitative Biology.* **55**: p. 161-173.

30.   Nehmzow, U. and T. Smithers (1990). "Mapbuilding using self-organising networks in "really useful robots"". in *From Animals to Animats: Proceedings of the First International Conference Simulation of Adaptive Behaviour.* Paris.

31. Nehmzow, U., T. Smithers, and B. McGonigle (1992). "Increasing behavioural repetoire in a mobile robot". in *From Animals to Animats: Proceedings of the Second International Conference on Simulation of Adaptive Behaviour.* Honolulu, USA.

32. O'Keefe, J. (1990). The hippocampal cognitive map and navigational strategies, in *Brain and Space,* J. Paillard, Editor. Oxford University Press: Oxford.

33. O'Keefe, J.A. and L. Nadel (1978). *The Hippocampus as a Cognitive Map.* Oxford University Press.

34. Olton, D.S. (1979). "Mazes, maps, and memory". *American Psychologist.* **34**(7): p. 583-596.

35. Olton, D.S. (1982). Spatially organized behaviours of animals: behavioural and neurological studies, in *Spatial Abilities: Development and Physiological Foundations,* M. Potegal, Editor. Academic Press: New York.

36. Piaget, J., B. Inhelder, and A. Szeminska (1960). *The Child's Conception of Geometry.* New York: Basic Books.

37. Poucet, B., C. Thinus-Blanc, and N. Chapuis (1983). "Route planning in cats, in relation to the visibility of the goal". *Animal Behaviour.* **31**: p. 594-599.

38. Prescott, A.J. (1993). "Building long-range cognitive maps using local landmarks". in *From Animals to Animats: Proceedings of the Second International Conference on Simulation of Adaptive Behaviour.* Honolulu, USA.

39. Prescott, A.J. (1993). *Explorations in Reinforcement and Model-based Learning.* Phd thesis. University of Sheffield, UK.

40. Prescott, A.J. and J.E.W. Mayhew (1992). "Obstacle avoidance through reinforcement learning". in *Advances in Neural Information Processing Systems 4.* Denver. Morgan Kaufman.

41. Rao, N., N. Stoltzfus, and S. Iyengar (1988). "A retraction method for terrain model acquisition". in *IEEE International Conference on Robotics and Automation.* .

42. Scholl, M.J. (1992). "Landmarks, places, environments: multiple mind-brain systems for spatial orientation". *Geoforum.* **23**(2): p. 151-164.

43. Sherry, D.F. and D.L. Schacter (1987). "The evolution of multiple memory systems?". *Psychological Review.* **94**(4): p. 439-454.

44. Siegel, A.W. and S.H. White (1975). The development of spatial representations of large-scale environments, in *Advances in Child Development and Behaviour,* H.W. Reese, Editor. Academic Press.

45. Soldo, M. (1990). "Reactive and preplanned control in a mobile robot". in *IEEE Conference on Robotics and Automation.* Cincinnati, Ohio.

46. Squire, L.R. (1992). "Memory and the Hippocampus: A synthesis from findings with rats, monkeys and humans". *Psychological Review.* **99**(2): p. 195-231.

47. Thomas, G.J. and P.S. Spafford (1984). "Deficits for representational memory induced by septal and cortical lesions in rats". *Behavioural Neuroscience.* **98**: p. 394-404.

48. Turchan, M. and A. Wong (1985). "Low-level learning for a mobile robot: Environment model acquisition.". in *2nd Conference on Artificial Intelligence Applications.*

49. Wehner, R. (1983). Celestial and terrestrial navigation: human strategies - insect strategies, in *Neuroethology and Behavioural Physiology,* F. Huber and H. Markl, Editor. Springer-Verlag: Berlin.

50. Wehner, R. and R. Menzel (1990). "Do insects have cognitive maps?". *Annual Review of Neuroscience.* **13**: p. 403-14.

51. Wilson, S.W. (1990). "The animat path to AI". in *From Animals to Animats: Proceedings of the First International Conference on the Simulation of Adaptive Behaviour.* Paris.

52. Zipser, D. (1986). Biologically plausible models of place recognition and place location, in *Parallel Distributed Processing: Explorations in the Micro-structure of Cognition, Volume 2.,* J.L. McClelland and D.E. Rumelhart, Editor. Bradford: Cambridge, MA. p. 432-70.

Location Recognition in Rats and Robots

William D Smart

Computer Science Department

Box 1910

Brown University

Providence, RI 02912-1910

United States

wds@cs.brown.edu

John Hallam

Department of Artificial Intelligence

University of Edinburgh

5 Forrest Hill

Edinburgh

United Kingdom

john@aifh.ed.ac.uk

Abstract

Location recognition is an important skill in both animals and mobile robots. The ability to adapt to different environments, learning to orient oneself in them and navigate purposefully around them is a necessity for any autonomous agent. We summarise some previous work exploring location recognition in both rats and mobile robots and present the results of new experiments with a mobile robot which draw on this work and exhibit rat-like performance in a location recognition task. Based on our experiments, we offer some suggestions to account for observations made during location recognition studies with rats.

1 Introduction

Location recognition is an important skill in both animals and mobile robots. The ability to adapt to different environments, learning to orient oneself in them and navigate purposefully around them is a necessity for any autonomous agent. In this paper we summarise some previous work exploring location recognition in both rats and mobile robots and present the results of new experiments which draw on this work and show that rat-like performance in a location recognition task is possible using topological mapping techniques.

It is thought that rats encode navigation information mostly in terms of their movements in the world, using this to build some form of cognitive map of their environment [Cheng 86, Margules & Gallistel 88]. This theory has much in common with the approach reported in [Nehmzow et al 91], where a mobile robot uses information about its movements to construct topological maps of its environment in order to perform location recognition. They both use information derived from the motion of an agent to build topographic maps of an environment which are subsequently used in location recognition and navigation tasks.

In this paper, we present the results of a set of experiments which attempt to embody the theories of rat navigation and location recognition presented in [Cheng 86]. We compare our results with a mobile robot to those reported with rats and draw parallels between them and offer possible explanations for some of the observations made in [Cheng 86].

2 Rats and Robots

In this section, we describe some of the previous work on which this paper builds, summarising the results of location recognition experiments with both rats and robots. We also outline the methods used to achieve the results presented in section 3 of this paper.

2.1 Rats

In [Cheng 86], Cheng describes a series of experiments carried out with rats to determine the cues which they use to perform location recognition. In all of the reported experiments, the rats were placed in a rectangular enclosure, shown the position of some food and allowed to wander around the enclosure. After a short while, they were removed from this enclosure and placed in another identical one, where some more food was buried at the same relative location as in the first enclosure. Their task was to locate and dig for this food, based on what they remembered of the location of the previous food source. There were no cues external to the enclosure for the rats to use (such as overhead lights) and the change of enclosures ensured that aids such as scent marking could not be used.

In the first experiment, the walls of the enclosure were all black and there were distinct features at each of the corners[1]. Since the enclosure was rectangular (and hence exhibited half-turn symmetry) any purely geometric description of a point, p, was also a description of another point, p', diametrically opposite p. The results of this experiment were that most of the rats either dug for the food at the correct location or at a location diametrically opposite from the correct one, with almost equal probability. This indicated that the rats were using purely geometrical information to perform location recognition and largely ignoring the featural cues provided. In an attempt to determine if featural information would be used if the features were more obvious, one of the long walls of the enclosure was made white and the experiment repeated. Very similar results were obtained, again suggesting that featural information is very much secondary to geometric information.

In a further attempt to measure the use of featural information, food was placed in one corner of the enclosures and the featural information at that corner and the one diametrically opposite was removed. This meant that since the correct location and the one diametrically opposite it now had the same geometric descriptions and the same local features, to correctly disambiguate the correct location, the rat had to use non-local featural information (that is, features from the points before or after the target corner). Three points emerged from this experiment. Featural information was used under certain circumstances, geometric location recognition was preferred when possible and the rats seemed to need *local* featural information to disambiguate locations and did not use global features.

In the final experiment reported, the features were rearranged between the learning and searching phases. The features local to the location of the food, however, were unaltered. The result of this experiment added support to the theory that the rats were using mostly geometrical information, supplemented by local featural information when performing location recognition.

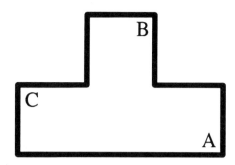

Figure 1: A typical enclosure.

To summarise, Cheng suggests that rats encode the position of locations in terms of geometric properties of their environments, with additional featural information near the target used to supplement this representation. This featural information is very much secondary to the geometric information and serves to help disambiguate locations which are geometrically similar. Global features do not seem to be used by rats although these might seem a useful source of information for navigation.

2.2 Robots

Location recognition by a mobile robot in a simplified enclosure was investigated as part of the "Really Useful Robots" project at the University of Edinburgh. One particular set of experiments, reported in [Nehmzow *et al* 91], dealt with a small mobile robot wall-following around an enclosure, recording information about its movements for use in location recognition experiments on a workstation. This information, in the form of direction-duration pairs (*e.g.* (forward 5)) was used to train a series of Kohonen-style self-organising feature maps (SOFMs) [Kohonen 88][2]. Seven such feature maps were used, each trained using input vectors constructed from different numbers of direction-duration pairs. For example, one network was trained with vectors constructed from the two most recent pairs, another with vectors built from the four most recent pairs, and so on. This scheme was inspired by a theory of low-level visual processing described in [Marr & Hildreth 80] and attempted to take into account the inherently multiscalar nature of this type of location recognition. That is to say that, depending on the geometry of the enclosure, different locations need different numbers of direction-duration pairs to uniquely identify them. For example, in Figure 1, a robot moving anti-clockwise needs only

---

[1]These features covered several modalities (tactile, visual and olfactory) to ensure that the rats were able to easily discriminate between them.

[2]It should be remembered that although this work is described as if it were fully implemented on a mobile robot and although the direction-duration pairs were collected on a real robot running round an enclosure, the SOFMs were actually implemented off-line on a workstation.

one direction-duration pair to identify location A, since it is the only place which is at the end of a long straight wall. However, location B needs seven pairs to uniquely identify it (long wall, left turn, short wall, left turn, short wall, right turn, short wall) otherwise it may be confused with location C.

There are two stages to the experiment, learning and searching. In the learning phase, the robot trains its SOFMs with incoming data on its motions and, at the end of this phase, is instructed to "remember" a location by storing the activation values of the SOFMs at that point. The second phase involves the robot again wall-following around the enclosure, this time comparing the activation values generated by the incoming motion data looking for a match with the stored values and hence arrival at the "remembered" location.

Once the SOFMs were trained with a few circuits worth of direction-duration pairs the activation patterns of all seven networks for a particular location were stored. The robot then started round the enclosure again from a randomly chosen location, constructing input vectors from the incoming direction-duration pairs and comparing the activation patterns generated against the stored patterns. When a new pattern came within a specified threshold distance of one of the stored patterns, the corresponding network signalled that it recognised the current location as the one which was remembered. When all seven of the networks signalled in this way at the same time, the robot stopped and announced that it had reached the remembered location.

A success rate of approximately 90% is reported in [Nehmzow *et al* 91] for this approach, with the system never "recognising" a wrong location. That is, all failures were because *no* location was recognised, not because a wrong one was identified erroneously.

As an extension to this scheme, we implemented a similar system on a small mobile robot. The system was the same as described above except for the following points. The matching scheme for the SOFMs was made much less computationally expensive, necessary to enable to system to run in real-time on the limited resources of the robot. Also, less SOFMs were used and the requirement that all of them should signal recognition was relaxed, so that only a sequential subset of specified size had to agree[3]. This is closer to the scheme described in [Marr & Hildreth 80] for visual processing, which requires that only two adjacent channels (equivalent to SOFMs in this case) must agree for recognition to be achieved.

Our system, more fully described in [Smart & Hallam 94], achieved comparable results to those reported in [Nehmzow *et al* 91], with slightly over

---

[3]For example, in a system with five networks trained on one to five direction-duration pairs respectively, three might be required for recognition. In this case, networks 1, 2 and 3; or 2, 3 and 4; or 3, 4 and 5 would have to agree for the system to signal recognition.

	% correct	% rotational	% miss
Rats 1	47	31	22
Rats 2	44	25	31
Robot	63	8	29

Table 1: Average correct recognitions, rotational errors and other errors (after [1]).

90% recognition. It operated in real-time on a fully autonomous mobile robot, providing further validation for the ideas behind the earlier system and also generalising the work presented there.

3 New Results

It has been suggested that rats form topological maps of their environment based on geometric relationships and their own movements for use in navigation [Margules & Gallistel 88]. The observations of Cheng, reported in [Cheng 86], seemed to exhibit some similarity to our experiences with location recognition in mobile robots. To further explore this, a set of experiments, based on those described in [Cheng 86] were carried out with a mobile robot and SOFMs implemented on a workstation.

The robot was programmed to wall-follow in a simplified environment and record its actions in terms of direction-duration pairs, as in [Nehmzow *et al* 91]. A rectangular enclosure was constructed and data for approximately fifty circuits were gathered. These data formed the basis of our experiments, which were carried out subsequently on a workstation.

A system of four SOFMs was implemented, as described above. The SOFMs were repeatedly trained on vectors constructed from two, four, six and eight direction-duration pairs respectively. These feature maps were trained on data from four circuits of the enclosure and then tested on eight further circuits. For each set of input vectors generated during the test phase, the system attempted to match each to one of the "remembered" locations. The average success rates of the individual SOFMs, along with results for similar experiments from [Cheng 86] are shown in Table 1.

The data in Table 1 refer to the first two experiments from [Cheng 86], described above (normal and enhanced featural data) and the results gathered from our own experiments. The results of our experiments are qualitatively similar to those in [Cheng 86], with most of the "recognised" locations being correct and of the mistakes made, a disproportionate number were at the diametrically opposite location. The high percentage of correct identifications is most likely an artefact of the robot used to gather the data. When wall-following inside an enclosure, the path which the robot takes is not necessarily the

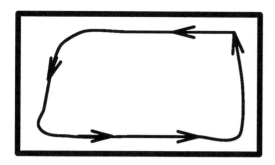

Figure 2: A possible path for a robot.

two	% correct	% rotational	% miss
no features	77	10	13
local features	82	7	11
global features	85	5	10
three	% correct	% rotational	% miss
no features	97	2	1
local features	99	0	1
global features	100	0	0

Table 3: Results from the full recognition system.

	% correct	% rotational	% miss
no features	63	8	29
local features	67	3	30
global features	69	0	31

Table 2: Results of adding featural information.

same as that followed by the walls. It may, for example, turn well before a certain corner because it can detect the approaching wall at a greater distance than any of the others, causing the path to become non-rectangular (see Figure 2).

In the robot used to gather data, infra-red proximity sensors were utilised for wall-following, so it is possible that some of the walls produced a higher return signal, leading to earlier detection and turning. This would lead to a less symmetrically shaped enclosure (from the robot's point of view) and hence less ambiguity in locations specified by geometric data alone. The sensors of rats, however, are more robust, both visually and in other modalities and processing and are more likely to follow a path which is closer to the true shape of the enclosure when wall-following.

Cheng suggests that local featural information is used by rats as part of their location representation and that this is "glued on" to the geometric representation. In accordance with this, we generated simulated features for each of the four walls and corners of the enclosure. Each side and corner had its own unique feature and these were appended to the vectors used to train the SOFMs. Two cases were considered, local features, where only the feature at the current location is added, and global features, where the feature local to *each* direction-duration pair is added to the representation. The results of these experiments are given in Table 2.

As suggested by Cheng, the addition of local featural information allows the discrimination between correct locations and their diametrical opposites. Further, the results show that the addition of global featural informa-

tion enhances the location recognition capabilities of the system more than local information does. It should be noted that the addition of featural information only reduces the number of rotational errors and that the number of "background" errors remains more or less constant. This confirms that the featural information takes a secondary role in the recognition task and it is the geometric information that dominates. In this system, this is due to the representations used. Each direction-duration pair is encoded as 16 bits and each feature is only 8 bits. In the case of local features, this means that the ratio of geometric to featural information is between 4:1 and 16:1 and for global features it is 2:1. This may indicate a qualitatively similar weighting scheme in the rat navigation system, explaining the preference for geometric information.

The data presented above were for the individual SOFMs. When the entire system was used for recognition, as described in section 2.2, performance improved but still followed the same general pattern, with the addition of featural data reducing the number of rotational errors, while leaving other errors largely unaffected. The results for the full recognition system are presented in Table 3. The entries "two" and "three" refer to the system requiring two or three sequential SOFMs to agree for recognition to occur.

The last experiment performed used data which included the generated features for training the SOFMs but them went on to test the recognition with data including randomly generated features. This simulated the "feature sensor" of the robot returning random values to explore the importance of correct featural information. The results are summarised in Table 4 (again these are averages for the individual SOFMs, not for the whole system).

When the local features are added in this case, they serve mostly as noise in the input to the SOFMs since there is only a one-in-eight chance of the random feature being the same as the correct feature for any given point. As expected, the number of correct recognitions and rotational errors drops, with a resultant increase in erroneous identifications. When global features are added,

	% correct	% rotational	% miss
no features	63	8	29
local features	58	6	36
global features	51	3	46

Table 4: Corrupted featural information.

the signal-to-noise ratio for the SOFMs drops even more, with predictable results. Note that the drop in signal-to-noise ratio is greater for global features than for local features and this is reflected in the greater number of errors for global features than for local ones.

4   Conclusions

The results presented above agree closely with those reported in [Cheng 86] and add support to Cheng's theories of rat navigation. In particular they show that the idea of having local featural information "glued on" to a geometric representation is feasible and, indeed, gives qualitatively similar results to those observed with rats.

But why are only local features used when global ones seem to give better results? Global featural information gives better results than local features do, but involves a heavier computational overhead, increasing the size of the representation by up to 50% in our implementation. In all systems, there is a trade-off between performance and efficiency and it may be that the environments in which rats generally find themselves are irregular enough that the inclusion of local features is sufficient for most location recognition tasks. Generally speaking, the more irregular an environment is, the less geometric information needed to uniquely specify a location. The rectangular enclosure used in these experiments is an extreme case of regularity which would rarely be found in a rat's natural habitat[4].

The preference for geometric information may also be a product of the availability of features in the natural world. When a rat moves about there is always reliable information available about these movements (from the rat's own propriocentric sensors). It may not always be possible to discern external features properly. By using local features while performing location recognition, the rat gains some ability to disambiguate locations which are geometrically similar without being too adversely affected if the features are absent or corrupted. The use of global featural information, although adding more in the ideal case, suffers to a greater extent when the incoming information is not ideal, as can be seen from the results presented above.

We can conclude from our experiments that Cheng's

theories, expressed in [Cheng 86], are a valid explanation of how rats might perform location recognition, showing an implemented system building a form of cognitive map produces qualitatively similar results to those in [Cheng 86].

Acknowledgements

The work described in this paper was done mostly in the Intelligent Sensing and Control lab of the Department of Artificial Intelligence at the University of Edinburgh and we would like to thank all the support staff there who kept the robots going through the experiments. We would also like to thank Joanna Bryson and Gerry Lacey for their comments and criticism of early drafts of this paper.

References

[Cheng 86] Ken Cheng. A purely geometric model in the rat's spatial representation. *Cognition*, 23:149–178, 1986.

[Kohonen 88] Teuvo Kohonen. *Self-Organisation and Associative Memory*. Springer-Verlag, second edition, 1988.

[Margules & Gallistel 88] J Margules and C R Gallistel. Heading in the rat: Determination by environmental shape. *Animal Learning and Behaviour*, 16:404–410, 1988.

[Marr & Hildreth 80] David Marr and Ellen Hildreth. Theory of edge detection. *Proc. R. Soc. London*, 207:187–217, 1980.

[Nehmzow et al 91] Ulrich Nehmzow, Tim Smithers, and John Hallam. Location recognition in a mobile robot using self-ordering feature maps. In G Schmidt, editor, *Proceedings of the International Workshop on Information Processing in Autonomous Mobile Robots, Munich, Germany*, pages 267–277. Springer-Verlag, March 1991.

[Smart & Hallam 94] William D Smart and John Hallam. Location recognition with self-ordering networks. In *Proceedings of the IMACS – IEEE/SMC International Symposium on Signal Processing, Robotics and Neural Networks (SPRANN '94), Lille, France*, 25–27 April 1994.

---

[4]Certainly in the habitat in which they evolved, if not now, when many rats live in the regular confines of basements and attics.

Emergent Functionality in Human Infants

Julie C. Rutkowska
School of Cognitive & Computing Sciences
University of Sussex
Brighton BN1 9QH, U.K.
julier@cogs.susx.ac.uk

Abstract

Criticisms of behavior-based robotics that demand sensory and motor connections with the environment be supplemented by concepts and representations (viewed as models substituting for the environment) are questioned by analysis of early human abilities. Animat models based on 'emergent functionality' converge with an independently motivated model of the human infant, and infant performance on tasks requiring 'anticipation' (a proposed upper boundary for situated behavior-based systems) suggests emergent functionality appropriately characterizes initial mechanisms and is advantageous developmentally, supporting preadaptation without rigid predetermination. Principles of 'serendipity' and 'scaffolding' are outlined, which govern transactions between phylogenetically determined mechanisms and the environment to support ontogenetic change.

1 Animats, human infants and situated action

Reservations about the animat direction in contemporary behavior-based robotics often center on the kinds of (seemingly lowly) real-life creatures from which it draws inspiration (e.g. crickets are implemented (Webb, 1993), hoverflies simulated (Cliff, 1990) and so forth). Kirsh's (1991) sceptically titled paper 'Today the earwig, tomorrow man?' is representative of the view that artificial creatures such as Brooks's (1986, 1990, 1991a & b) exploratory robots are unlikely to scale up even to everyday human activities such as collecting used drinks containers or making tea. Sooner rather than later, the argument generally goes, sensory and motor connections with the environment will need to be supplemented with concepts and representations, viewed as models that substitute for things in the environment and support environment-independent thought processes.

Such conclusions are questioned in this paper, which is concerned with animat work's potential significance for human abilities. It focuses on understanding a real-life creature of special relevance to this endeavour: the human infant. Rather than trying to understand cognition by working bottom-up on the evolutionary scale, this approach works bottom-up on the human developmental path. It assumes that the way infant abilities function and change can make a non-trivial contribution to understanding how evolution 'designed' humans to work as embodied, situated agents, and to an alternative to traditional 'between the ears' ideas of what it is to have a mind.

A core concept in recent computational work that endorses a decentralized, situated approach to the mind is 'emergent functionality'. This encompasses the notions that complex abilities can be shown to emerge indirectly from the operation of independent, seemingly simple components, without the hierarchical control that typifies traditional AI planning systems; and that it is the interplay between those components and the environment that underwrites their functionality (e.g. Maes, 1990; Steels, 1991). How applicable are such ideas to human functioning? I shall suggest that they are useful in at least 3 ways. First, theoretical analysis reveals interesting convergences between animat models based on this approach and an independently motivated model of the human infant (Section 2). Second, emergent functionality may offer an appropriate characterization of the infant's initial mechanisms, providing a better explanation of behavioral data that have been thought to require precocious 'goals' and 'anticipation' (Section 3). Finally, emergent functionality is developmentally advantageous and helps to clarify the process through which novel abilities are acquired (Section 4).

2 Action and emergent functionality

In my view, infant abilities are best understood in terms of action, broadly defined as purposive transformation of the environment, and computational concepts – of the right kind – offer the best route to understanding action systems (Rutkowska, 1991, 1993b). A functional decomposition of the infant as an action system that can begin accounting for infant performance and the possibility of developmental change requires 4 main components. The subject contributes: perceptual processes that make explicit potentially usable information; behavioral processes that transform structures of the environment; and action programs. In this scheme, both perceptual and behavioral components are envisaged as based on preadapted modular capacities, and as having their own computational principles of operation independent of the action program level (both probably implementing some version of constraint analysis by parallel processing). The final major component is contributed by the embedding environment in which the subject is situated.

In so far as it contributes effectively to predicting typical successes and errors in infant performance, a good candidate for ideas about organization of the perceptual component has proved to be Marr's (e.g. 1982) computational decomposition of preattentive low-level vision into independent algorithms for constructing a range of descriptions in representational formats that make explicit universal information about the physical world. For example, Marr's proposal for a $2\frac{1}{2}$-D sketch, which describes input in terms of depth and orientation of patches of visible surface plus discontinuities in these properties, could fit well into the organization of infant prehension. Infants have been found to reach for segmented surfaces whose boundaries are specified by separation in depth and/or by motion, rather than for the nearer or smaller of two objects (von Hofsten & Spelke, 1985). And they cease reaching for an object if this segmentation is disrupted by placing it directly onto a larger one (Wishart & Bower, 1985).

Even newborns provide evidence of well-defined movement patterns that can provide the causal basis of overt behavior, such as reaching of hand and arm (von Hofsten, 1984), hand-to-mouth movements (Butterworth & Hopkins, 1988) and stepping/kicking leg movements (Thelen, 1984). The overall architecture of this component remains less well understood than low-level vision. In this context, however, it is interesting to note principles recently suggested from neuroscience by Giszter and colleagues (Giszter, 1993; Giszter, Mussa-Ivaldi & Bizzi, 1993). Their work concerns what kind of (neurally based) computation underlies voluntary movements, which depend on activating muscles to produce the forces needed to implement limb movement(s) with prespecified direction, amplitude and velocity. It suggests this transformation is based on vectorial combination of motor outputs across different regions of a 'map' of limb postures ('convergent force fields', located spinally in the frog). These combinations yield a repertoire of motor patterns that is exhibited not only via experimental microstimulation but also in natural behaviors, supporting the view that they are behavior primitives which can be activated by other neural processes to serve as building blocks for the construction of more complex behaviors.

'Action programs' here do not imply traditional programs with rules specifying the selection and activation of individual muscles (not least because a lower-level virtual machine structure offers a more plausible solution to the degrees of freedom problem, e.g. as suggested above by Giszter et al.'s scheme). What is intended are virtual and modifiable structures that govern the generation and coordination of perceptual and behavioral processes. An initial repertoire of basic programs may be very simple, looking like little more than S-R connections. However, viewing action programs in terms of procedural computational notions, such as pattern matching and pattern-directed invocation of procedures (including behavioral procedures), permits openness to development through changing program structure in ways that cannot be captured by chaining of S-R connections. This model is sympathetic to Russian activity theory's emphasis on reflexes being elementary actions not elements of action (Sokolov, 1993).

Finally, transactions with the environment are essential to understanding the successful functioning of the subject's contributions to action, since it relies heavily on an externalization of processing (supported by behavior's dual status as both program-governed procedure and spatio-temporally constrained movement) that is scaffolded by regularities in environmental structures and processes. 'Action' is a useful organizing construct, but it does not reside in any 'bit' of this system (certainly not in isolated behavioral procedures governed by action programs, or in the movement processes that are generated when those procedures are invoked). Likewise, no isolated component corresponds to the infant's 'knowledge' of the world, which is distributed through the operation of this pragmatic system. Although this model exploits classical 'symbolic' ideas about computation, the way they are used converges with current 'anti-symbolic' (sometimes 'anti-computational') emergent functionality approaches. Both perspectives share cognitivism's general commitment to a kind of systematic explanation in which abilities emerge from properties of a system's functional components; their structure; and organized cooperative interaction between components that cannot play their functional role without each other (Haugeland, 1978). However, they differ from traditional AI cognitivism by extending this systematic explanation, redrawing the boundaries of computation and cognition to encompass the necessary role of environmental components.

More specific convergences between this scheme for infant action and emergent functionality models can be highlighted by considering the example of Brooks's (1986, 1990, 1991) subsumption architecture for behavior-based robotics. This decomposes a situated system into a number of simple task-achieving behaviors, each of which links sensory and motor capacities so as to be (ideally) capable of independent interaction with properties of its embedding environment in a purely reactive way. What robot-controlled interaction there is between task-achieving behaviors is unlike the traditional selection and ordering in response to an explicit goal-directed plan. Instead, layered control is achieved by first engineering the lowest level task-achieving behavior, then adding another to this foundation, and so on (cf. the notion of 'terminal addition' of new structures or stages in orthodox evolutionary theory). A robot that 'explores' a real-world environment is designed by layering task-achieving behaviors such as (Level 0) 'do not come into contact with other objects', (Level 1) 'wander aimlessly without hitting things' and (Level-2) 'visit interesting places' (e.g. corridors of free space detected by sensors). Higher levels operate in parallel with lower ones, but are wired up so that they can sometimes subsume their functioning. For instance, they may be empowered to suppress and replace a lower layer's normal data input, as when Level 1's 'avoid' module takes over Level 0's 'runaway' input to the 'turn' module connected to the robot's motors.

Despite apparent conflict between this robotics example's emphasis on special-purpose 'wires' and 'wiring' and the computational 'virtual machine' talk of the infant action scheme, their organization shares 3 important features.

Firstly, the overall structure of both models carves up vertically rather than horizontally. Neither model fits the traditionally clear AI decomposition into a series of processing components between sensors and actuators, devoted in turn to perception, modelling, planning, task execution and motor control. The idea of multiple action programs, which may (at least initially in development) attempt to operate independently of one another, converges with that of multiple task-achieving behaviors.

Secondly, in neither model is there a central place where an exhaustive, general-purpose description of 'the' world is delivered to serve as a basis for planning what behavior(s) to execute. The action-based infancy model explicitly questions Fodor's (1983) claims that the computational role of preadapted perceptual processes is to provide an 'input' to 'central' processes that are engaged in the fixation of propositional beliefs about the world that can be 'true' or 'false' (see e.g. Rutkowska, 1991, 1993b).

It is assumed that infants' engagement with physical objects neither requires nor involves the construction of an 'integrated object description' (i.e. a computational symbol structure that brings together a range of properties and explicitly represents them as applicable/relevant to the object concerned). Instead, preattentive vision provides multiple descriptions of objects and events, and even descriptions that seem impoverished from the viewpoint of objective definitions of 'objectness' may be di-

rectly exploited by action programs to support viable transactions with the environment. For example, infant action appears capable of using directionally selective visual elements, which play a role in the construction of Marr's crudest 'primal sketch' description, to support avoidance behavior towards approaching objects. Marr (1982) notes how motions of corresponding points on the two retinas away from the nose could be pre-wired to provide a crude detector for 'looming' (i.e. symmetrical expansion of a bounding optical contour centered at the mid-point of the visual field, which generally specifies an object approaching on a 'hit' course). Infants have no need of a central belief that a unitary, constant object is moving towards them. Indeed, studies show that they will attempt to 'avoid' film of a continuously expanding object, even if it changes shape during this time (Ball & Vurpillot, 1981).

Finally, for both the infancy scheme and subsumption architecture, the function of the system's components is not intrinsic but is determined by the role that they are playing in the system as a whole, including its supporting environment (see Rutkowska (1993a & b) for discussion of behavior-based ideas of 'representation' and 'meaning' in this vein). In infants, the 'looming' example noted above illustrated how directionally selective visual elements can acquire the function of indicating an approaching object for the infant from the way they are selectively used by an action program to generate viable (avoidance) behaviour in the human environment of evolutionary adaptedness. (Such elements may be exploited by other species to support different purposes.) Animat design can be thought of as simulating this kind of evolutionary adaptedness. A sonar pattern associated with free space does not indicate or 'mean' anything in isolation. But it can be viewed as acquiring the function of indicating a place to explore for the animat from the way it is used in the animat-environment system of which it is a component, i.e. from being wired into a task-achieving behavior that successfully embeds the animat in its environment.

Likewise, different action programs can invoke the same infant movement patterns to attain distinct outcomes. Even a typically infantile motor pattern like the tonic neck reflex has been shown to turn up as a functional component of some adult sporting activities (Keele, 1982). In the animat case, different layers of the subsumption architecture are capable of exploiting the same motor capacities. Whether the creature's overt behavior is 'wandering' or 'exploring' is determined by the task-achieving behavior in which it is embedded, not by the movements executed.

These organizational principles have important implications for explanations of early abilities, and for understanding their developmental possibilities.

3   Anticipation and control

The question of whether empirical studies of infants offer support for emergent functionality has not been asked directly, but it can be approached by evaluating evidence for the converse viewpoint: that explicit goals and hierarchical control underlie successful infant activities. This issue is equally relevant to demarcating the competence boundaries of emergent functionality systems. Traditional developmental evidence for goals and so forth highlights tasks that are believed to involve anticipation, i.e. seeking and reaching the end/outcome of an activity sequence ahead of the environmental conditions that are normally associated with it. And anticipation has been considered an obvious upper boundary or cut-off point for the abilities of situated behavior-based systems in general (Kirsh, 1991). If we look at the treatment of 'anticipation' in typical developmental tasks - visual search and manual prehension - infants' initial performance on them reveals interesting similarities. These suggest that both tasks are open to explanation in terms of an action-based model of ability, and compatible with emergent functionality notions.

Observations of infants' visual tracking purport to test infants' search for objects, and to assess if their behavior is controlled by an object concept. They derive from Piaget's (1955) views of the nature of knowledge, which see representation of the 'goal of action' as notably absent at birth, developing around the final quarter of the first year of life. The infant is presented with a moving object, part of whose path is hidden by an occluder. It is assumed that an infant who sees the object disappear from view will look to the opposite edge of the occluder, just as or before the object comes back into view, provided s/he 'believes' that the object continues to exist; i.e. 'out of sight' is not 'out of mind'. Kirsh's (1991) critique of Brooks's creatures makes very similar assumptions; he proposes anticipation as the boundary beyond which they will need concepts. When 'egocentrically perceptible cues' are no longer available to support appropriate task-achieving behaviors operating in their usual reactive mode, concepts can 'licence inferences'.

Data revealing successful anticipation on visual tracking tasks is taken by most contemporary researchers as evidence, contra Piaget, for a precocious object concept. However, if we go beyond simply recording whether or not 3-, 6- and 9-month-old infants are looking at the 'right' place before the object comes back into view, then early success is not what it seems (see Rutkowska (1993b) for a fuller account). Using ethological techniques to classify observed performance into behavior patterns, each composed of a distinct sequence of head-eye movements and fixation locations during the object's disappearances, reveals that the behavior pattern that sometimes leads 3-month-olds to be looking at the object's reappearance point, as if in 'anticipation', is quite

different from that used by 9-month-olds to attain the same outcome.

3-month-olds simply continue tracking as the object disappears from view, sometimes stopping part way along the occluder, but sometimes tracking as far as the reappearance end. By way of contrast, 9-month-olds characteristically pause as the disappearance occurs, then make a single head and eye movement to fixate the opposite side of the occluder, waiting there until the object comes into view. This and other aspects of the data suggest that 3-month-olds' behavior is not wired up to 'search' for objects that disappear (even if they sometimes happen to 'find' them). Their continued tracking is precisely that: failure to alter ongoing behavior in response to altered environmental circumstances. In particular, although continued tracking looks like functionally adequate search for the unseen object, its frequency declines with age, rather than increasing as that interpretation would predict. Furthermore, 6-month-old subjects exhibit less of either form of 'successful' anticipation than their younger and older counterparts, but they do more often show a behavior pattern involving backtracking: the infant continues tracking as the object disappears, as if about to anticipate, but then turns head and eyes sharply back to fixate the object's disappearance point. This is a strange observation, since backtracking is generally used as a criterion of the infant having noticed some change in the (re)appearing object (e.g. of identifying features), looking back to the disappearance point where s/he last saw the original object that s/he is supposedly searching for. Here, however, a single object moving at constant speed is involved, and has generally not returned to view before the infant turns back.

Such observations suggest that anticipation governed by some kind of infant search mechanism is not present until the second half of the first year. This task does not initially constitute a problem from the infant's viewpoint. Infants start out equipped with an action program that coordinates visible object movement with a straightforward behavioral procedure for tracking visible objects. For behavior to change when the situation changes, i.e. the object disappears, the infant must attend to the new perceptual information, and 'redescribe' the situation to invoke alternative behavioral procedures. If this new information is available to the infant system only preattentively, and not yet salient at the action program level, two behavioral possibilities are likely: do nothing when the situation changes, i.e. look away; or maintain the current action-based interpretation, i.e. continue tracking. These are, in fact, the two behavior patterns most characteristic of 3-month-olds.

The fact that backtracking is replaced by increasingly persistent attention to the disappearance point, in its clearest form yielding a 'cat and mousehole' behavior pattern throughout the object's period of invisible movement, suggests the 6-month-old is just beginning to attend to the characteristic perceptual pattern ('kinetic occlusion') associated with the object's disappearance. Initially, infants' backtracking is not motivated by failure to find the object. Rather, it is a typical 'growth error', i.e. the infant's performance appears to get worse from an observer's viewpoint but marks developmental advance in terms of the infant's changing action-based representation of the situation.

Prehension directed at visible objects looks a very different task, but the notion of anticipation also plays a key role in ideas about the mechanisms involved. An influential analysis due to Bruner (1968, 1973) sees the infant's developmental task as attempting to order preadapted motor components into a functional sequence of reaching, grasping, retrieving and finally manipulating/mouthing a viewed object. This, he proposed, is achieved through experience that must be controlled from the outset by an intention. Bruner relates this to the idea of goal-directed hierarchical control, which he considers necessary for serial-ordering of component behaviors. A clear example of how this is purportedly revealed is that infants of 10-weeks-old onwards are assumed to open the mouth as they view and attempt to reach for an object, as if in anticipation of getting it to the mouth, despite top-level reaching being unlikely until around 20-weeks. The open mouth is said to serve a 'place holding' function, externally marking the predetermined 'goal' to which the selection (and initially unsuccessful execution and ordering) of preadapted component behaviors is directed.

Observations of infants from 12- to 22-weeks-old fail to support these proposals (Rutkowska 1992). Noticeable mouth opening around 12 to 16 weeks is almost invariably the concomitant of enthusiastic vocalization or yawning. As infants' prehensile abilities develop, silent mouth opening is regularly seen, but not before or during reaching attempts. It is characterized by hand contact clearly preceding mouth opening. Figure 1 shows a typical sequence at 20 weeks.

It is plausible that vision elicits reaching; getting hands to an object elicits attempts at contact; and contact elicits hand-to-mouth movements. There seems no necessity to assume these perception-behavior pairings are initially coordinated within a higher-order control structure. Their serial ordering can just as well emerge from the way each individual component is preadapted to interact with a typical environment of physical objects.

In neither visual tracking nor prehension is it necessary to propose that early infant activity is goal-governed, i.e. controlled by a representation of the end/outcome that it achieves. However, it looks as if it is so controlled. And developmentally later forms of control appear to exhibit genuine features of anticipation, as in 9-month-olds'

Figure 1: Anticipatory mouth opening follows manual contact at 20 weeks.

prompt movement from an object's disappearance point to where it will reappear, and their preadjustment of hand shape and grip on approaching objects of different shape and weight. The final section of this paper considers how best to characterize the behavioral processes that relate these qualitatively distinct levels of functioning.

4   Naturally engineered change

How are transactions between phylogenetically determined initial mechanisms and the environment engineered to guide ontogenetic change? The context(s) and form(s) of feedback that define the space in which developmental mechanisms operate impose important constraints on how those mechanisms need to work. Attempts to construct animats through genetic algorithms that evolve a functional architecture, or which aim to incorporate learning mechanisms, come up against a concern familiar from work on isolated unsituated neural networks: just what kind of 'supervision', if any, is appropriate and necessary? Network training by feedback about discrepancy between actual and designer-desired output has been thought totally unrealistic (Partridge & Paap, 1988), but so has spontaneous undirected learning (Minsky & Papert, 1988). Looking at what goes on in natural human development can be useful here, since we can assume that whatever processes have evolved can be expected to work reliably.

In traditional AI approaches, learning is generally defined in terms of change that is adaptive because it improves a system's ability to do a task better next time round (e.g. Simon, 1983); and considered unnaturally difficult unless the subject knows the goal in advance (Mitchell, 1983). Neither of these assumptions fits the preceding account of young infants' development on (what are for them) novel tasks; and they make it difficult to see where novel abilities and goals might come from. Two notions are important to clarifying the form of subject-environment interplay through which these originate: 'serendipity' and 'scaffolding'.

4.1   Serendipity

'Serendipity' is defined as accidental, fortunate discovery. It marks the fact that the fit between infant activity and environmental structure recurrently leads to viable outcomes that are not motivated by implicitly or explicitly represented plans or goals on the part of infant mechanisms. There is nothing 'wired up' in the infant to connect context and behavior, even at the reactive level of perception-behavior pairs designed for that outcome, such as a basic action program or Brooksian task-achieving behavior. Instead, what may look like purposive or intentional activity can initially be grounded in one-off local exchanges between infants' perceptual and

physical-motor capacities and environmental structure. These constitute a temporary form of emergent functionality that has the potential to become a more permanent adaptive change. Examples are provided by the typical infancy tasks discussed above.

On the tracking task, infants were not initially searching for the out-of-sight object. To be doing that, they needed to learn about the relationship between the object's disappearance and reappearance. Initially, the spatio-temporal structure of environmental events involving the object's movement, disappearance, invisible movement and reappearance is crucial to generating the illusion of search/anticipation, 'selecting' the preadapted infant perceptual and motor capacities that are exhibited, and determining the order in which they occur. Anticipation develops from concatenation of two initially independent processes: novel attention to the object's kinetic occlusion; and turning (necessarily in the direction of its unseen movement) to (re)fixate the object. Repetition of this serendipitous sequence establishes the developmental space within which turning to (re)fixate can become search and anticipation, as it is embedded in a new action program coordinating it with attention to kinetic occlusion. This offers an example of new behavioral procedures being constructed from old movement primitives, with reactive head and eye movements, initially employed for turning to look at movement in the periphery of the visual field, becoming prospective 'search'.

In the case of prehension, similar transitions occur. Movements that initially emerge from the reciprocal fit between infant and object are first seen in a tentative form, but quickly start to look like infant-controlled behaviors. For example, even the youngest infants exhibit a type of ballistic forward-swiping movement, which sometimes makes brief contact with the object. This may be a form of early reaching, but it generally results in object contact only to the extent that the object's size and location provide physical support for the infant's hand. Around 20 weeks of age, when controlled visually guided reaching is coming to the fore, this more primitive swiping does not disappear. Rather, it is often converted into repeated vigorous slapping of objects, which infants appear to find extremely gratifying. Again, local yet replicable transactions support potentially more permanent instances of novel functionality, including re-use of preadapted motor patterns in new behavioral procedures.

Even behaviors with apparently obvious functionality may initially be flexible and play an exploratory role. For example, Figure 1 illustrated how infants attempt to get just about anything with which their hands establish contact into the mouth, even improbably large objects. And other body parts, especially feet, may become a focus of interest and of potential object-directed activity, depending upon their 'fit' to object properties. Figure 2 shows how a small object may not facilitate foot-object contact, but larger ones do: when their size and location mesh with the infant's physical structure, the feet are enabled to lead the hands in object contact.

Such developments may parallel evolutionary examples of changing functionality of physical-motor processes, such as breathing and panting, which initially supported respiration, eventually being used by some animals in temperature regulation (Satinoff, 1978). They suggest that emergent functionality may not only offer an appropriate organizing principle for early performance, it may be advantageous developmentally. A key benefit would be to underwrite preadaptation without rigid predetermination. Emergent functionality is said to serve a system well 'when there is a lot of dependence on the environment and it is difficult to foresee all possible circumstances in advance' (Steels, 1991, p. 459). Such arguments are directed at established systems, but they are equally applicable to developing systems that are capable of flexibility in the face of variable or altered environments. Interactions between preadapted abilities of such a system and the environment in which it finds itself could enable it to 'tune in' perceptual-behavioral coordinations previously found useful in evolution, and sequences of such coordinations, if their viability is confirmed by the individual's experience. Novel coordinations could be established in the face of altered environmental conditions and/or properties of the subject (e.g. physical-motor disabilities).

4.2 Scaffolding

Infant-environment exchanges that are serendipitous from the perspective of infant mechanisms may nevertheless be predictable when the whole infant-environment system is considered. Strongly constrained knowledge structures are sometimes assumed to be predetermined because they appear to be acquired effortlessly, rapidly and universally, without formal tuition; and to exhibit mapping from a wide range of experience to a narrow range of outcome structures (see e.g. Keil, 1981). However, 'scaffolding' illustrates that informal tuition may be ubiquitous and play a significant role in restricting the infant's range of experience in the service of 'spontaneous' natural acquisitions. It can be thought of as a form of supervised learning that exploits temporarily engineered emergence of function to support permanent adaptive change.

Scaffolding involves more able humans manipulating the infant's transactions with the environment so as to foster novel abilities (e.g. Wood, Bruner & Ross, 1976). Key features of this process are distraction reduction and marking a task's critical attributes. Especially important in terms of the preceding discussion are reduction of the number of degrees of freedom in the target task and enabling the subject to experience the end/outcome of a

Figure 2: At 18-20 weeks feet become a focus of interest and can implement object-directed activity, provided object size offers appropriate support.

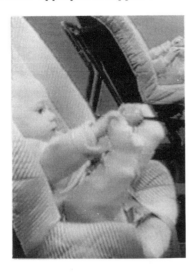

sequence of activity before they are cognitively and/or physically capable of seeking and attaining it for themselves.

A clear example is offered by Valsiner's (1987) analysis of how infants learn to handle utensils and acquire the eating rules of their culture. Properties of the infant, especially perceptual capacities and motor control, and of the environment, play an essential role. But most significant is the way adults structure the environment so as to constrain the relation between the sensory-motor possibilities of the infant and features of the environment (by analogy with Waddington's metaphor for ontogenesis, Valsiner calls this 'social canalization'). The feeding environment is arranged to discourage 'inappropriate' behavior, and to encourage activities that infants are capable of performing but would not usually exhibit at mealtimes.

Narrowing down the infant's zone of free movement is important. In European cultures, the high-chair with tray (and often straps) fixes the infant at the adult's level, and acts as a constraining device on free movement, keeping the infant in the meal-situation and excluding escape from the zone of potential action. Other inappropriate behaviors that remain possible, such as chucking food around, are discouraged and/or attempts made to limit the damage by covering surrounding areas. Special utensils support gradual approximation to appropriate adult activity, while restricting and/or eliminating possibilities of the adult equipment, e.g. cup-like juice-feeders, with spouts to restrict spillage, and forks with blunt, rounded prongs that eliminate stabbing potential. The infant's progress is from completely adult-controlled activity, such as being fed (often forcibly) with a spoon, to infant-controlled activity.

Such scaffolding is also evident in adult intervention in infant locomotion (e.g. support for walking), and in prehension, where attention management, bringing objects within grasping distance and limiting frustration engendered by motor immaturity may all be important.

Scaffolding is generally viewed as a social process, but it can be suggested that infants are designed to exploit similar principles in their spontaneous untutored/unsupervised transactions with the physical world. For example, on the visual tracking task we can note two aspects of scaffolding in the infant-environment system. One is the way the spatio-temporal properties of environmental events 'elicit' sequences of processing that are initially unrelated as far as infants' permanent mechanisms for interacting with the environment are concerned. In general, serendipitous features of the infant's causal embedding in the physical environment operate to reduce the number of degrees of freedom for action, enabling infants to experience 'successful' outcomes that they could not attain through planned, goal-governed action. Also notable is how attention might be limited to critical task

attributes, if not by social means. Even in the relatively impoverished laboratory context, how do particular environmental features, such as the object's kinetic occlusion, come to be attended to and connected by infants' action mechanisms to anticipatory (re)fixation behavior? One way of achieving this is through inbuilt subject processes that impose spatial and temporal restrictions on what connections can be established, and which may be evidenced by the well-known limits on infant conditioning. This is not to say that infant development can be reduced to conditioning, but such processes may play an important role by supporting self-generated marking of salient task attributes in novel contexts.

5   Conclusions

The notion of emergent functionality can prove useful to our understanding of human development in two ways: to characterize infants' initial mechanisms and temporarily engineered infant-environment transactions that generate the space for permanent adaptive changes.

Such developments need not take the subject beyond the boundaries of situated, behavior-based mechanisms. The anticipatory behavior of 9-month-old infants in the visual tracking context, for example, does not require mechanisms that involve concepts or images of invisibly moving objects. The action program that they construct is more akin to a novel task-achieving behavior, exploiting environmental regularities to support behavioral prediction of future events. Turning to a location to look for an object that is seen to disappear from view is a form of situated inference (Barwise, 1987), whose validity relies on predictable continuation of the environmental context that gave rise to it. Prazdny (1981) offers a range of interesting ideas about how such performance could be implemented in a computational system that relies heavily on procedures for exploiting changing perceptual information to control behavior (see Rutkowska (1993b) for discussion of this form of 'procedural representation').

A key issue, beyond the scope of this paper, is to clarify what kind(s) of internal structures and processes could 'fix' recurrent patterns of viable activity as stable adaptive changes, abstracting novel perceptual and motor variables from a range of local problem solutions to make them explicit at the action program level of control.

Acknowledgements

I am grateful to the SAB94 referees for their helpful comments on content and organization.

References

[1] Ball, W. and Vurpillot, E. (1981) Action and perception of displacements in infancy. In G.E. Butterworth (ed.) *Infancy and Epistemology*. Harvester.

[2] Barwise, J. (1987) Unburdening the language of thought. *Mind and Language,* **2,** 82-96.

[3] Brooks, R. (1986) A robust layered control system for a mobile robot. *IEEE Journal of Robotics and Automation,* **RA 2,** 14-23.

[4] Brooks, R. (1990) Elephants don't play chess. In P. Maes (ed.) *Designing Autonomous Agents.* Bradford/M.I.T. Press.

[5] Brooks, R. (1991) Intelligence without representation. *Artificial Intelligence,* **47,** 139-160.

[6] Butterworth, G.E. and Hopkins, B. (1988) Hand-mouth coordination in the newborn baby. *British Journal of Developmental Psychology,* **6,** 303-314.

[7] Bruner, J.S. (1968) *Processes in Cognitive Growth: Infancy.* Clark University Press.

[8] Bruner, J.S. (1973) Organization of early skilled action. *Child Development,* **44,** 1-11.

[9] Cliff, D. (1991) The computational hoverfly. In J.-A. Meyer and S.W. Wilson (eds.) *From Animals to Animats: Proceedings of the first international conference on the simulation of adaptive behavior.* Bradford/M.I.T. Press.

[10] Fodor, J.A. (1983) *The Modularity of Mind.* Bradford/M.I.T. Press.

[11] Giszter, S. (1993) Modelling spinal organization of motor behaviors in the frog. *Proceedings of the Second European Conference on Artificial Life,* Vol. **1,** 379-390.

[12] Giszter, S., Mussa-Ivaldi, A. & Bizzi, E. (1993) Convergent force fields organized in the frog's spinal column. *Journal of Neuroscience,* **13,** 467-491.

[13] Haugeland, J. (1978) The nature and plausibility of cognitivism. *Behavioral and Brain Sciences,* **1,** 215-260.

[14] Keele (1982) Learning and control of coordinated movement patterns. In J.A.S. Kelso (ed.) *Human Motor Behavior.* Lawrence Erlbaum.

[15] Keil, F.C. (1981) Constraints on knowledge and cognitive development. *Psychological Review,* **88,** 192-227.

[16] Kirsh, D. (1991) Today the earwig, tomorrow man? *Artificial Intelligence,* **47,** 161-184.

[17] Maes, P. (1990) Situated agents can have goals. In P. Maes (ed.) *Designing Autonomous Agents.* Bradford/M.I.T. Press.

[18] Marr, D. (1982) *Vision.* Freeman.

[19] Minsky, M.L. and Papert, S.A. (1988) *Perceptrons.* 2nd edition. M.I.T. Press.

[20] Mitchell, T.M. (1983) Learning and problem solving. *Proceedings of the Eighth International Joint Conference on Artificial Intelligence,* Vol. **2.**

[21] Partridge, D. and Paap, K. (1988) An introduction to learning. *Artificial Intelligence Review,* **2,** 79-102.

[22] Piaget, J. (1955) *The Child's Construction of Reality.* Routledge and Kegan Paul.

[23] Prazdny, S. (1981) A computational study of a period of infant object concept development. *Perception,* **9,** 125-150.

[24] Rutkowska, J.C. (1991) Looking for constraints in infants' perceptual-cognitive development. *Mind and Language,* **6,** 215-238.

[25] Rutkowska, J.C. (1992) Early prehension intention. Paper presented at the BPS Developmental Section Annual Conference, Edinburgh, 5-8 September.

[26] Rutkowska, J.C. (1993a) Ontogenetic constraints on scaling up sensory-motor systems. *Proceedings of the Second European Conference on Artificial Life,* Vol. **2,** 970-979.

[27] Rutkowska, J.C. (1993b) *The Computational Infant: Looking for Developmental Cognitive Science.* Harvester Wheatsheaf.

[28] Satinoff, E. (1978) Neural organization and evolution of thermal regulation in animals. *Science,* **201,** 16-22.

[29] Simon, H.A. (1983) Why should machines learn? In R.S. Michaelski, J.G. Carbonell and T.M. Mitchell (eds.) *Machine Learning,* Vol. **1.** Morgan Kauffman.

[30] Sokolov, A. (1993) Action in Russian activity theory and ecological psychology. Paper presented at the International Society for Ecological Psychology Workshop, 'The Primacy of Action'. Manchester, 13-15 December.

[31] Steels, L. (1991) Towards a theory of emergent functionality. In J.-A. Meyer and S.W. Wilson (eds.) *From Animals to Animats: Proceedings of the first international conference on the simulation of adaptive behavior.* Bradford/M.I.T. Press.

[32] Thelen, E. (1984) E. (1984) Learning to walk: ecological demands and phylogenetic constraints. In L.P. Lipsitt and C. Rovee-Collier (eds.) *Advances in Infancy Research,* Vol. **3.** Ablex.

[33] Valsiner, J. (1987) *Culture and the Development of Children's Action.* Wiley.

[34] von Hofsten, C. (1984) Developmental changes in the organization of prereaching movements. *Developmental Psychology,* **20,** 378-388.

[35] von Hofsten, C. and Spelke, E. (1985) Object perception and object-directed reaching in infancy. *Journal of Experimental Child Psychology,* **114,** 192-212.

[36] Webb, B. (1993) Modelling biological behavior or 'dumb animals and stupid robots'. *Proceedings of the Second European Conference on Artificial Life,* Vol. **2,** 1090-1103.

[37] Wishart, J. and Bower, T.G.R. (1985) A longitudinal study of the development of the object concept. *British Journal of Developmental Psychology,* **3,** 243-259.

[38] Wood, D., Bruner, J.S. and Ross, G. (1976) The role of tutoring in problem-solving. *Journal of Child Psychology and Psychiatry,* **17,** 89-100.

Connectionist Environment Modelling In A Real Robot

William Chesters and Gillian Hayes

Department of Artificial Intelligence, University of Edinburgh
5 Forrest Hill, Edinburgh EH1 2QL, Scotland
031-650 3079 & 3082 Fax: 031-225 9370
{williamc,gmh}@uk.ac.ed.aifh

Abstract

This paper describes some experiments with an adaptive controller, based on multi-layer perceptrons, which tries to solve a simple reinforcement learning task for a real robot vehicle. One neural network (the 'model') is trained to predict how the robot's sensor readings will change if it performs a given action; another learns, with the aid of the model, to evaluate sensory states according to how close the robot is to receiving a reward when it experiences them. Two kinds of model which exploit context information were evaluated in robot runs, as well as a 'flat' (memoryless) model. The results confirm that backprop can provide the learning mechanism needed to solve simple adaptive control tasks, and point up some problems which will need to be addressed before it can help with more complicated skills.

1. Introduction

Nearly all robot learning experiments have been implemented in computer simulations. This paper describes an attempt to implement a simple reinforcement learning architecture, based on multi-layer perceptrons, in a real robot.

The core of the controller is an adaptive world model, which tries to predict what will happen at the next time-step if the robot performs a particular action. In many simulated learning experiments, the robot has easy access to information (such as its location)

isomorphic to the space of different situations it might be in—its world has no 'hidden state'. A real robot, especially when it has only a few simple sensors at its disposal, must take account of circumstances which are not made explicit in its sense vector. This paper examines in particular two simple ways to give the world model some memory so that it can exploit context information in making its predictions: the use of a 'history' which tells the model what happened at the previous time step, and the incorporation of recurrent 'context' units into the model network. Both history and context models, as well as memory-less 'flat' models, were evaluated in experiments in which the robot was let loose in the arena with an initially untrained controller and allowed to learn what it could.

2. The Robot And Its Task

2.1. The Arena

The idea is for a robot vehicle to learn to find its way across a simple pen to some 'food', marked by a patch of black paper taped to the floor, while not bumping into the walls—see figure 1. The lamp is there to induce a light gradient across the pen, which it is intended that the robot learn to use to guide it to the food.

2.2. The Robot

The robot is constructed out of Technical Lego™. It carries ten simple sensors. Two microswitches on the vehicle's forward bumper detect collisions with the

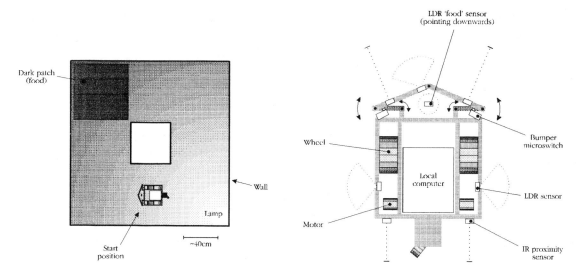

Figure 1. The arena and the robot

walls. Four infra-red proximity sensors (IRs) report objects in their field of view; their range readings are non-linear and rise sharply as the robot approaches an obstacle, until they saturate at about 25cm. The ones pointing roughly north-west and north-east serve to warn the robot of impending collisions, while the ones pointing backwards are mounted so as to saturate when the robot is actually in contact with a wall, or nearly so. Four wide-field (~70°) light-dependent resistors (LDRs) read the light intensity ahead, to the left and right, and underneath the vehicle; they give the robot the means to observe the light gradient at the bottom of which the food is placed. All sensors are normalised to read between 0 and 1.

By turning its two main drive wheels together or separately, the robot can support a limited repertoire of four actions: move ahead 30cm or astern 20cm, and turn left or right through 60°.

2.3. Reinforcement

A reward accrues whenever the robot is positioned on the food (whenever the light level measured by the ventral LDR drops below a threshold, indicating that it is looking at the black paper), and a penalty when it is jammed up against a wall (the bumper is depressed or the rear IRs are triggered). Most of the time, the robot receives no feedback.

$$\text{reinf } v = \begin{cases} 0 & \text{if } v[\text{bumper or rear IR}] > 0.75 \\ 1 & \text{if } v[\text{ventral LDR}] < 0.15 \\ undef & \text{otherwise} \end{cases}$$

2.4. The Controller

The controller comprises two MLPs (multi-layer perceptrons), called the **model** and the **heuristic**, and a procedure for choosing an action at each step, called the **policy**. The **model** aims to foresee what will happen if the robot carries out a particular action; the **heuristic** rates sense states according to how near the food they indicate the robot to be; and the **policy** draws on the two nets in choosing the best action to perform. The nets are trained using the backpropagation algorithm.

Model

The **model** is trained at step $t+1$ to map the sense readings from step t (v_t), and the action that was performed (a_t), to the new sense readings. It is also allowed some context information (c_t), which is updated at each step according to one of the rules discussed below.

$$\textbf{model}\ c_t\ v_t\ a_t \rightarrow v_{t+1}$$
$$c_{t+1} = \textbf{update}\ c_t\ v_t$$

Simply training a feedforward network to predict the sense vector a robot will see next, given its current sense vector and the action it intends to perform, will not in general do. This is because in the real world—as opposed to experimental simulations such as that presented in Sutton 1990—the sense data available to the robot do not map one-to-one onto its state with respect to the world[1]. The problem is particularly acute if the robot has only a few simple sensors: it might be possible for insects, with vast amounts of information coming in from their eyes, to use reactive strategies such as they are reputed to employ; but if one is trying to employ sparse data effectively to solve a simple task—or rich data to solve a complex task—then some kind of memory is called for.

Williams 1990 suggests three classes of solution to this problem[2]. Two involve the use of "tapped delay lines" to make information about the past available to the model in the most direct way; but he comes down firmly on the side of the third, "radical" approach: the use of partially recurrent networks. In this paper, simple implementations of both ideas are evaluated.

Heuristic

The purpose of the **heuristic** is to interpolate between the sparse positive (non-*undefined*) readings provided by **reinf**. It is not trained directly on sensor readings, but rather indirectly using the **model**, in a series of pseudo-experiences. Broadly, it is taught to value a state at the value of the best state the robot thinks it can reach in one step starting there, scaled down by a constant discount rate: reinforcement is attenuated backwards along (supposed) robot trajectories[3].

Each pseudo-experience proceeds as follows. A state[4] s is picked (generated) at random, and the **policy** procedure is asked what the robot would do if it found itself in that situation. Then the **model** determines what state s' the robot would get into as a result of the chosen action, and the **reinf** oracle (or failing that the **heuristic**) provides a value for the new state. Finally the **heuristic** is 'backpropped' to rate s like s', but scaled down. Symbolically

$$\textbf{heuristic}\ s \rightarrow \frac{\textbf{eval}\ (\textbf{newState}\ s\ (\textbf{policy}\ s))}{\text{step penalty}}$$

where **eval** supplies the best known (pseudo-) reinforcement for a given state (c, v)

$$\textbf{eval}\ (c, v) = \begin{cases} \textbf{reinf}\ v & \text{if defined} \\ \textbf{heuristic}\ (c, v) & \text{otherwise} \end{cases}$$

and **newState** is just a wrapper for **model** which works on states rather than sense vectors:

$$\textbf{newState}\ (c, v)\ a = (\textbf{update}\ c\ v, \textbf{model}\ c\ v\ a)$$

By a process of relaxation, the **heuristic** comes to learn a function satisfying its recursive training equation and the boundary conditions provided by the **reinf** oracle.

Policy

Actions are chosen stochastically, the likelihood that a particular action will be performed in a particular state being proportional to its predicted payoff. That is to say, the **model** is used to predict what new experience will result from each of the four possible actions; these supposedly neighbouring experiences are then evaluated according to the reinforcement rule (for collisions or 'found the food' states) or using the **heuristic** (for other states); and these values are used as weights in deciding what to do.

Actually, there is a further twist in that the action weightings are scaled by an action-specific constant;

---

[1]We ignore completely the issues that arise when things in the world are allowed to change.
[2]See also Hertz, Krogh & Palmer 1991, p. 176ff.

[3]Compare, for instance, Sutton 1990.
[4]i.e., context-sense vector pair

and zero reinforcement predictions are adjusted upwards.

$$P\left[\text{policy } b = a\right] = \frac{\text{wgt } b\ a}{\sum_{x \in action} \text{wgt } b\ x}$$

where *action* = { *forward, backward, left, right* }, and

$$\text{wgt } b\ a = (\max \{ \text{ eval (predict } b\ a), .05 \}) \times \text{pref } a$$

$$\text{pref}\begin{array}{l} forward \\ backward \\ left \\ right \end{array} = \begin{array}{l} 1.0 \\ 0.5 \\ 0.6 \\ 0.6 \end{array}$$

The point of incorporating an element of randomness into the policy is to ensure that the robot explores its environment thoroughly (by a kind of random walk) and doesn't get into a rut. Occasionally, for instance, it comes to believe that going forwards *always* results in a collision, and for a while it will avoid that action entirely[5]. But it will eventually move forwards anyway—simply because it tries even things it thinks are stupid sometimes (note the forcing of zero reinforcement predictions to 0.05)—and then its overly pessimistic theory will be disconfirmed.

The point of the preferences is just to keep the robot moving forward and speed up its exploration of the arena (recall too that the robot moves further in response to a *forward* command than it does in response to a *backward*).

2.5. Incremental Learning

It is generally held that backprop works best when it is given a sequence of training pairs selected at random from a representative body of data. The data collected by a robot and used to train the **model** network is, by contrast, likely to be biased, because its character will tend to change slowly as the robot moves around. On the face of it, it appears to be necessary to buffer a lot of experiences as a pool from which randomized samples may be selected; and that is potentially expensive if the environment is complicated[6].

The technique investigated as a way of circumventing this problem is based on the idea that a network can be used as a device for regenerating something like the training data that went into its construction. If a randomly chosen vector r could plausibly have been an input vector in the previous training data[7], then applying the network to r ought—to the extent that the network has been satisfactorily trained—to yield the corresponding output vector. So we should have a fair substitute for a library of training data available to us, at the cost only of storing an old version of the network.

When a new training pair (u, v) comes in for network N,

```
make a copy of the network as it is now (call it N₀)
repeat learnings times
    backprop N to associate u with v
    repeat rememberings times
        pick a vector r at random
        let s be the output to which N₀ maps r
        backprop N to associate r with s
```

The idea is to use the training data regenerated from the old network N_0 as a constraint to ensure that new mappings don't obliterate important old ones.

It is clearly desirable to run through enough r vectors ('old training pairs') to cover a significant proportion of N's input space—otherwise there is no reason to suppose that interesting old mappings will be protected—and for a medium-sized network, this is going to mean rather many ('*rememberings*'). There is then a real danger that the new data will simply get lost in amongst them, and will not have the desired

---

[5]If the robot gets stuck in the confined space between the central obstacle and one of the outer walls, it can even come to learn that it will be penalised whatever it does. In this situation it shows no systematic preference for any particular action beyond that introduced by its built-in **preference** scalars. This behaviour is somewhat similar to what psychologists call 'learnt helplessness'.

[6]But see Myers 1992 on the subject of "attention-directed buffering".

[7]This will not always be the case, because the encoding of the robot's sensor data is redundant. What is the **model** to make of a random pseudo-sense vector which includes a bumper switch reading of 0.37, when the only values encountered in its training data are 0 and 1? It would be easy to generate only legal pseudo-sense-vectors, but for the experiments described below, purely random vectors were used.

Table 1. Summary of collision avoidance performance

Type of model	Learnings, Rememberings	Steps to plateau*	Collisions thereafter†	Number of robot runs	Steps per run
Flat	1, 0	50	44%	10	300
	10, 60	50	26%	10	300
History	7, 40	50	24%	10	300
Recurrent	–	450	26%	5	700

*The number of robot steps needed on average for the controller to reach its best performance (in multiples of 50)
†The proportion of robot steps (after the controller's performance had flattened off) at which a collision occurred

influence, which is why the procedure is repeated several times ('*learnings*').

3. Modelling

The robot has two goals set for it through the **reinf** function: it is supposed to avoid obstacles, and find the food. Obstacle avoidance can be learnt by attending to the IR and bumper sensors, and the 'characteristic timescale' is short: actions have immediate large effects on these sensor readings, and feedback from **reinf** is received straight away. To learn to find the food, on the other hand, the robot needs to model the effect of its actions on the LDR readings, which change gradually as it moves around, and reinforcement is delayed (so that guidance from the **heuristic** is needed). We consider the two problems separately.

3.1. Obstacles

Some experiments with driving the robot manually demonstrated that (at least) the following fairly stable phenomena were there to be learnt:

(1) moving forwards, left or right when already jammed head-on against a wall (or backwards when jammed tail-on) does not change anything

(2) moving backwards always releases the bumpers, and reduces the forward IR readings; driving forwards always reduces the rear IR readings to near their minimum

(3) moving forwards when both the forward IRs are strongly activated often results in a forward collision: these sensors were in fact

carefully placed so that this would in general (if the robot was not approaching a wall at a shallow angle) be true

(4) backing away from a forward collision, and then immediately moving forwards, results in another collision (because the robot moves further in response to a *forward* command than it does for a *backward*)

(5) moving forwards three times is quite likely to run the robot against a wall (because the arena is fairly cramped)

Obviously some context information beyond the bare v_t and a_t is required for the **model** to be able to spot the last two situations. All three kinds of **model** (flat, history and recurrent) were tried out in robot runs; the results are summarised in table 1.

'Flat' Models

A 'flat' **model**[8] which makes no use of context information can learn (1), (2) and (3) within forty to 100 steps. It does not automagically generalise 'correctly': for instance, most head-on collisions are characterised by both bumper switches and both forward IRs being activated simultaneously, and when the net is first presented with a situation in which perhaps only one side of the bumper is depressed, or only one or neither of the IRs is triggered, it does not correctly predict the result of moving forwards (namely, continued collision). And not surprisingly, given that its training data is presented in a most un-

---

[8]Flat **model** nets have 14 inputs (for ten sensors plus a one-out-of-four encoded action), 14 hidden units and ten outputs (for ten sensors).

random order, a flat **model** has trouble remembering everything it learns. For instance, if the robot happens to spend some time in 'free space' out of contact with the walls of the arena, it can learn that the bumper switches are *never* quite activated[9]. If learning is disabled at any time, the **model** will most likely be frozen in a version which fails in some class of situations; with learning enabled, it only needs a few steps to re-learn (for instance) about (1), and the overall behaviour of the robot is reasonably satisfactory.

The 'incremental learning' technique does go some way to alleviating the **model**'s forgetfulness. When ordinary backprop is used (*learnings* = 1, *rememberings* = 0), the robot needs a lot of reminding about how to avoid walls, and ends up jammed against them (receiving negative reinforcement) at 44% of the steps. With *learnings* = 10 and *rememberings* = 60 this figure drops to 26%. Of course, this improvement is achieved at the cost of a sixhundredfold increase in computation. For comparison, with an untrained **model** the robot suffers collisions at 78% of the steps. The **model** requires about 50 steps to achieve its best performance.

Flat **models** are limited in what they can learn by their lack of memory, and this causes the robot to do stupid things, such as backing off from a wall and then immediately driving forwards into it again (cf. (4)). If the **model** is to make helpful predictions in these cases, it needs some context information.

'History' Models

Perhaps the simplest form of context information is a history of what the robot has recently seen—Williams 1990's "tapped delay line" on the **model**'s input. Here we consider only one-step histories: in the notation of this paper,

$$c_t = v_{t-1} \; @ \; a_{t-1}$$

(@ means concatenation). The **model**[10] should now be able to make an appropriate warning prediction in situation (4), since it knows that the robot's last action was to move backwards from a collision.

In fact, history **models** do often learn about (4). They also tend to believe (fairly enough) that moving forwards twice results in the forward IRs being activated, as well as making an actual collision fairly likely[11] (compare (5)).

The robot performed very slightly better with a history **model** than with a flat one, spending 24% of its time up against walls when *learnings* = 7 and *rememberings* = 40. Although the extra information available to history **models** did allow them to make better predictions when they were working well, they were somewhat more prone to forgetting than the *learnings* = 10, *rememberings* = 60 flat **models**. The history **models**' larger input space should mean that more *rememberings* are needed for the 'incremental learning' technique to have a beneficial effect, but because they are quite a lot bigger than flat **models**, with 1064 weights as opposed to 360, they consume that much more CPU time per backprop pass, and it proved impractical to make robot runs with higher settings. As before, performance flattened out after 50 steps or so.

Recurrent Models

To extend a history-based context further back into the past would quickly become expensive (especially if the robot had higher-bandwidth sensors at its disposal). A tidier solution is to let the net develop a rolling context representation of its own,

---

[9]Although real bumper switch readings can only ever take the values 0 and 1, the **model** is free to predict any value in between. If its prediction exceeds 0.75, then it is treated as an 'on' by the **reinforcement** function and hence by the **policy**.

[10]History **models** have 28 inputs (twice as many as flat **models**), 28 hidden units and ten outputs.

[11]Although real bumper switch readings are always 0 or 1, the **model** can predict that the next reading will be anywhere between 0 and 1; what tends to happen is that 'risk factors' such as moving forwards, having moved forwards at the last step, or activated forward IRs all push up the predicted bumper readings, so that when several such factors come together, the prediction will pass the threshold beyond which negative reinforcement applies. MLPs are inherently prone to this kind of interpolation: if they can't say for sure whether the reading will be 0 or 1, they have to predict a weighted average in order to get the expected error down. Compare Elman 1990.

along the lines of an Elman or Jordan net[12]. A recurrent model was implemented with context units updated according to the rule

$$c_{t+1} = 0.5\ c_t + 0.5\ hidden_t$$

—a weighted sum of the current context and the current activations of the net's hidden units. The context units have (modifiable) connections to the net's hidden units, just like the input units. With suitable weights, as Elman 1990 points out, the model can in principle have an indefinitely long memory, encoded compactly in a way tailored to its task; and partially recurrent nets have indeed been found to learn such encodings for themselves in a wide variety of simulations.

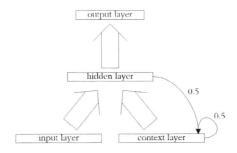

Figure 2. A recurrent model

With a recurrent model[13], the robot spent 26% of its time stuck against obstacles. It did not require the use of 'incremental learning' to achieve these results, so that although recurrent models take 450 or so steps before they start performing at their best—as opposed to 50 for both the incrementally-learned models—they use up less computer time along the way. The greater the overlap in the network's input between two situations with different outcomes, the more likely it is that weight adjustments appropriate for one are necessarily going to interfere with the net's response in the other, and so a context memory that distinguishes between situations better than the bare sense vector will have the desirable side-effect of rendering the model more stable. Interestingly, recurrent models only started outperforming *learnings* = 1, *rememberings* = 0 flat models after about 250 steps, presumably because

[12]See for instance Hertz, Krogh & Palmer 1991 pp. 179ff.

[13]Recurrent models have 14 inputs like flat models, 14 hidden units with 14 context units, and ten outputs.

the changing 'meanings' of the context units interfere with the conclusions the net might draw from the sense vector alone.

Recurrent models do generally learn about situation (4), but not about (5), perhaps because the fairly low momentum parameter on the context units (0.5) means that their weights would have to be set quite sensitively to implement a suitable memory that extended over the necessary three steps. Of the various models tested, recurrent models seemed to make the best predictions when they were working well, but they were more prone to forgetting (and subsequent painful periods of relearning) than non-recurrent models with incremental learning.

3.2. Light Levels

If it is to find the food efficiently, the robot is ultimately going to have to learn how the ventral light levels it observes change in response to its actions as it moves around, so that it can find its way down the light gradient; the following regularities were found to hold most of the time, although not as robustly as those relating to obstacles ((1)–(5)):

(6) if the robot moves forwards twice in row (and does not run into a wall in the process), there is a consistent trend in the ventral light level—if it goes (e.g.) up after the first step, it will go up after the second as well

(7) if it is brighter on the right than on the left, then turning to the right and moving forwards will increase the ventral light level (and vice versa)

Direct Prediction

Modelling absolute light levels with a sequentially trained net was attempted but proved impossible. The likely reason for this was that they change rather slowly, so that models of every kind could simply keep predicting a constant

$$(\text{model } c_t\ v_t\ a_t)[\text{ventral LDR}] = k \approx v_{t+1}[\text{ventral LDR}]$$

which floats up and down as the network is trained on each new sense vector. At each particular step, the prediction is more or less right, but if one presents the model with a historical or hypothetical situation, it will in general make a very poor prediction.

$$(\textbf{model } c_x \ v_x \ a_x)[\text{ventral LDR}] = k$$
$$\neq v_{x+1}[\text{ventral LDR}]$$

Providing the **model** with context information does not help: if a network can substantially reduce its cost function by outputting a constant, it won't learn anything more sophisticated.

Generous use of 'incremental learning' (with *learnings* = 3 and *rememberings* = 100) did make a **model** trained on recorded data learn, after several thousand steps, a function whose peaks and troughs matched those of the input light levels, but whose overall range was only about a fifth as great.

Randomised Training Data

A history **model** trained on data recorded from a robot run and presented to it in random order learned something much more like an identity function:

$$(\textbf{model } c_t \ v_t \ a_t)[\text{ventral LDR}] \approx v_t[\text{ventral LDR}]$$
$$\approx v_{t+1}[\text{ventral LDR}]$$

But it did not learn to predict the small changes which need to be controlled if the robot is to find its way down the light gradient, perhaps because they were not large enough to cause big errors and force the net to take account of them.

Predicting Differences

The LDR data has a small, fast component—because every time the robot moves, the readings change slightly—but it also has a large, slow component caused by the robot's gradual semi-random walk around the arena between light and dark areas. A sequentially trained **model** will not capture regularities whose characteristic timescale is longer than a few steps; but there is an easy way to tease the two components apart and isolate the fast one: get the **model** to predict the *difference* between this reading and the coming one, rather than its absolute value. It is after all the light *gradient* in which we would like the **model** to interest itself.

0.5 was added to the difference targets to fit them into the net's [0, 1] output range; they were also scaled

up by a constant m to fill the whole interval rather than clustering around the middle:

$$\textbf{model } c_t \ v_t \ a_t \rightarrow m \ (l_{t+1} - l_t) + 0.5$$

where l_t is the vector of light readings from v_t. The particular action taken by the robot now has a strong effect on the signal the **model** is trying to predict.

Nevertheless, flat, history and recurrent **model**s all failed to predict light level changes accurately. They always picked up on just one salient fact about the data—that if the readings are very high, they are likely to fall, and vice versa—and learned to map even moderately high (low) readings to negative (positive) changes, while ignoring other regularities, including (6) and (7). This looks to be a case of unwanted interpolation: the net will naturally tend to 'generalise' the rule "if the reading is very high, it will fall" to "the higher the reading, the more it will fall". Initially, this is not a bad way to get the cost function down. But then it seems the net is unable to make further progress, perhaps because it cannot incrementally mutate this generalised rule into a more discriminating one—it is stuck in a 'local maximum'.

4. Conclusions

The controller described in this paper did learn to reduce the number collisions suffered by the robot. The versions with flat, history and recurrent **model**s were all about equally effective, though for different reasons. The recurrent **model** was computationally the cheapest, since the others required time-consuming 'incremental learning' to perform at their best; but it needed more physical robot steps before it began to work well.

There is an irreducible minimum of bumps which the robot cannot be expected to foresee; but others would be avoidable if the **model** was less prone to forget what it had learnt. 'Incremental learning' is of only limited help here.

One way to solve the forgetting problem would be by selective buffering of experiences for later reference as training data for the model. In general, though, buffering (like 'incremental learning') is incompatible with the use of adaptive context representations such as those developed by recurrent models, because there is no 'neutral language' in which to store the buffered experiences' contexts. If it is known that the context information is largely determined by the preceding n readings leading up to it, then a library of n-step sequences will serve. But systems capable of supporting the acquisition of significant skills will probably have to maintain a hierarchy of contexts at different timescales, and it is not clear how buffering can be integrated into such a scheme.

The **models** were less successful at capturing how the light levels around the robot varied as it moved around its pen. Sequentially trained **models** would predict accurately neither absolute readings (because of the forgetting problem) nor differences between successive readings (because of over-generalisation or interpolation); randomly trained **models** would not take account of the small action-dependent component of the signal, for reasons unknown. (This modelling failure meant that the **heuristic** could not be trained to guide the robot to the food.) If backprop nets are to learn (with or without buffering) to model awkward data such as the LDR readings discussed above, they are going to need some help from signal preprocessing.

The problem of over-eager interpolation is perhaps inherent in any adaptive learning device which works by composing continuous functions; it might be possible to find an alternative cost function which penalised persistent small systematic errors as much as occasional big surprises, and discouraged the net from quickly landing itself with a simple, but dead-end, solution.

Acknowledgments

The authors would like to thank Edinburgh University, the Department of AI, and particularly everyone in the workshop for help with the hardware. William Chesters was supported by a SERC Advanced Studentship, and currently holds a Research Studentship; he would like to thank SERC.

References

Elman 1990. *Finding Structure in Time*, in *Cognitive Science* **14**, pp. 179–211.

Hertz, Krogh & Palmer 1991. *Introduction to the Theory of Neural Computation*, Addison-Wesley.

Miller, Sutton & Werbos (eds.), 1990. *Neural Networks for Control*, MIT Press.

Myers 1992. *Delay Learning in Artificial Neural Networks*, Chapman & Hall.

Sutton 1990. *First Results with Dyna*, in Miller, Sutton & Werbos 1990, p. 179.

Williams 1990. *Adaptive State Representation and Estimation Using Recurrent Connectionist Networks*, in Miller, Sutton & Werbos 1990, p. 97.

A Hybrid Architecture for Learning Continuous Environmental Models in Maze Problems

A. G. Pipe[1], T. C. Fogarty[2], A. Winfield[1]

1 Intelligent Autonomous Systems Group
Faculty of Engineering

2 Bristol Transputer Centre
Faculty of Computer Science & Mathematics

University of the West of England
Coldharbour Lane, Frenchay, Bristol BS16 1QY
United Kingdom

email ag_pipe@csd.uwe.ac.uk

Abstract

We present three variants of a hybrid architecture, each of solves mazes with large search spaces. All three learn continuous valued internal models of the environment through interaction with it, however the power and scope of the model increases with each architecture so as to better exploit knowledge gained through exploration. They each employ a Genetic Algorithm (GA) to search & optimise each movement. The GA fitness function is supplied by a Radial Basis Function (RBF) Neural Network which acts as an Adaptive Heuristic Critic (AHC) of the GA's actions. Over successive trials the V-function is learned, a mapping between real numbered positions in the maze and the value of being at those positions. Through experimentation we found that our architectures were quite robust in solving the environmental problems which we set. We found that despite our efforts to separate the roles of exploration and exploitation they were nonetheless subtly and multitudinously linked in these respects.

1. Background

Much work has been done in attempting to solve problems which involve goal oriented movements through an unknown or uncertain environment. Such problems are typified by, though not restricted to, mobile robots navigating through 2-dimensional maze-like environments. Much work has been done, embracing a wide range of disciplines. Recently the techniques of Temporal Difference learning, Neural Networks, Genetic Algorithms and "Holland" style Classifier Systems have all been brought to bear with promising results, some researchers using more than one technique to build hybrid systems as we have done here.

The use of Temporal Difference (TD) reinforcement learning algorithms [Barto et al 1989] in action/critic architectures such as the Adaptive Heuristic Critic (AHC) [Sutton 1984, Werbos 1992] and in Q-learning [Watkins 1989], both of which are "on-line" approximations to Dynamic Programming [Barto et al 1991], have shown great promise when applied to maze problems where an agent, such as a mobile robot, attempts to establish an efficient path to a goal state by interaction with its environment.

1.1 TD learning with Neural Networks

A good representative example of work in this area has been conducted by Long-Ji Lin. As part of his PhD thesis [Lin 1993] he presented an excellent comparison of these two learning algorithms for two classes of maze solving problem. He used feedforward, and later recurrent, Multi-Layer Perceptron (MLP) Neural Networks to store information about the states (ie. positions) in the maze. For example in the case of AHC the Neural Network learns the V-function, an arbitrarily non-linear mapping between state inputs and the value of being at that state. In the case of Q-learning the analogous Q-function learned by the Neural Network represents the multi-output mapping between being at a state and the value of each possible movement from that state. In each case embedding TD learning in the Neural Network learning algorithm results in the V- or Q-function being modified after each interaction with the environment (ie. a movement for maze problems) so that it eventually reflects the "true" function for those areas which have been visited to date.

It is typical of published work to date in this field [eg. Sutton 1991, Lin 1993, Roberts 1993] that mazes are discretized by dividing the area into a number of states on an equally spaced 2-dimensional grid. It is also typical to restrict the possible actions from any state to a small set. For example in Lin's earlier work only movements to the nearest neighbouring states are allowed, and in later work [earlier & later both in Lin 1993] six possible actions are available from a set of discretized rotations or linear fixed sized movements. These restrictions allow the use of simple search strategies, such as "random walk" or, in Lin's case, a "Stochastic Action Selector" which chooses a movement by "noisy auction" using the V- or Q-values of the available states or state/action pairs as appropriate.

Whilst these problem domains are useful ones in which to establish the efficacy of a learning algorithm they result in some serious limitations for the many "real world" applications where there is a higher requirement for movement accuracy. Let us consider a simple illustrative example. We wish to allow a mobile robot to explore a 10 metre by 10 metre environment, which contains obstacles unknown to it at the outset, in order to reach a "goal" position. We require its movements to be resolved to an accuracy of approximately 1 centimetre, a not unreasonable requirement for this type of problem. The obstacles consist of four randomly placed packaging boxes approximately 250 centimetres on each side. The accuracy requirement causes us to use a 1000 X 1000 grid to represent the agent's model of the environment, resulting in 1 million states. The obstacles will be quite sparse in this state space and clearly any "nearest neighbours" action policy will be highly restrictive, leading to a rather laborious exploration of the environment, particularly in the open spaces between obstacles.

If we open up the problem a little and allow the set of possible actions from a state to be linear movements to any other state in the maze then straight line traversals of the open spaces become possible in one movement, thus obviating the need for "close quarters" exploration in those areas which do not require it. However, although this is clearly a very desirable property for the agent to possess, its task of effective exploration at each new position becomes much harder. "Random walk" is prey to all the criticisms levelled at it, for example from the Genetic Algorithm community, if the maze is large enough.

If we open up the problem still further we could effectively circumvent our accuracy requirement altogether and allow movements in the maze to be expressed as real valued numbers. We could choose to view our model of this environment as either having states of a size set by the floating point number resolution of the computer we are using or, in the limit, as a continuous environment.

As Lin points out towards the end of his PhD thesis [Lin 1993], it is fortuitous that a Neural Network representation of the V- or Q-functions can make the switch from a discrete input space to a continuous one relatively effortlessly, whereas by contrast a tabular representation cannot. However the question of how to efficiently explore such an environment remains open.

1.2 TD learning with "Holland" style Classifier Systems

Gary Roberts [Roberts 1993] has reconstructed Wilson's Animat (WA) [Wilson 1985, Roberts 1989, Roberts 1991], and his experimental environment "WOODS7" in order to compare the performance of the traditional "bucket brigade" reinforcement learning algorithm of "Holland style" Classifier Systems [Booker et al 1989] with Q-learning in a Classifier System. The overall goal in the "WOODS7" environment is survival rather than reaching a particular position, the various rewards/punishments being food, enemies etc. However the agents designed to solve these problems clearly have much in common with conventional maze solving agents. In both of Roberts' architectures the Classifier System creates rules (and chains of rules) for movement which result in increased chances of survival. A Genetic Algorithm (GA) operates on the rule set, displacing weak rules with new ones evolved from the strong rules. The reinforcement learning algorithm increases the strengths of good rules after interaction with the environment.

This work provokes some interesting considerations of the level of abstraction of knowledge which may be gained through interaction with a particular environment since, at least potentially, situation dependent rather than state dependent rules may be learnt. However the problem of searching large or continuous search spaces is not the emphasis of this work and is not addressed, again the action set is small.

1.3 Evolving Neural Network Controllers

Genetic Algorithms (GAs) have been used in evolving Neural Network controllers. Two approaches have been popularly adopted, either each member of the GA population represents a complete Neural Network [Cliff et al 1992], or the GA is used to replace the Neural Network learning algorithm [Belew et al 1990].

Of greater interest here is the approach adopted by Cliff, Husbands & Harvey [Cliff et al 1992]. They have proposed a method by which the number of neurons in a Neural Network and their connection scheme can be encoded into the chromosomes of a Genetic Algorithm (GA) to evolve controllers for simple "sighted" mobile robots. The type of Neural Network used is simple, the connections are either unity weighted or infinitely inhibitory, however the neurons are real valued. The resulting architectures may be arbitrarily complex in terms of the number of hidden neurons and recurrency in the connectivity. To date publications cover evolving robots in simulated environments where the task is to avoid colliding with the walls in a cylindrical environment.

Although there appears to be much promise in this research direction no on-line learning component for an individual agent has been included in this work as yet. It remains at present an essentially off-line method where populations of complete controllers are "tried out" in the environment, with their good features being retained in the following generation of controllers, ie. no alterations to the controller are made during its interaction with the environment.

2.   Introduction

In this paper we present the results of an attempt to develop a learning architecture with distinct exploration and exploitation parts, but with strong interaction between the two. It follows three distinct phases, the main changes at each phase being the nature and completeness of the agent's internal model of the environment. All three variants of the basic architecture have the same overall structure as described below.

A Genetic Algorithm (GA) is used directly as the main exploring part of the agent and a Radial Basis Function (RBF) Neural Network is used to store the knowledge gained from exploration. It acts as an Adaptive Heuristic Critic (AHC), using a Temporal Differences (TD) learning algorithm to learn the V-function as the search progresses.

Each GA population member consists of an (x,y) coordinate position in the maze. At each "movement time step" the GA is restarted with a fresh population and with the entire maze at its disposal searches for the "best next movement", any straight line traversal of the maze from the current position to the (x,y) coordinate defined by a GA population member, on a "move-&-return" basis. Lamarckian interactions with the environment occur during the search, ie. the GA population members which result in maze collisions are modified to the (x,y) coordinates of the collision and fed back into the population. The fitness function used to rate GA population members is supplied by the RBF Neural Network, which performs a mapping between a given continuous real valued (x,y) coordinate input and a measure of "value" for that position as its output, ie. the V-function as described above.

This process continues through the normal process of multiple GA generations until either the population has converged or a maximum number of generations has been reached. The highest rated population member is then used to make a movement to the next position in the maze. After this has happened a Temporal Difference algorithm is executed on the RBF network to change the V-function's shape. Changes are made in the regions of the maze surrounding the movements made so far in the current trial by distributing a discounted reward or punishment back to them. The amount of this reward/punishment is simply derived from the value of the V-function at the new position. For example if the V-function value at the new position is 255.5 and the value at the previous position was 180.5 then some proportion of the difference (75.0) is added to the previous position's value. According to a simple variant of the standard TD algorithm [Sutton 1991], this process is "daisy-chained" back through time until a "horizon" of backward time steps is reached.

The processes described above are then repeated from the new position in the maze until the goal position is reached. This completes one trial. The RBF Neural Network thus acts as an Adaptive Heuristic Critic (AHC) of the GA's every attempt to explore the maze. It learns a V-function which reflects the true value of being in those regions of the maze which have so far been visited, refining the accuracy of the function after every movement in every trial of the maze. Knowledge of the maze is embodied in the Neural Network and all that is inherited in successive trials is the new RBF network weight vector.

In the following sections we first describe the common elements to each of the three architectures developed, then go on to describe the essential features which differentiate each of them along with pertinent experimental results. We then discuss some points arising from the experiments and conclude.

3.   The Maze Problem

Our maze is set on a unit square. In order to test our architectures, we simplified the environmental model by scaling down the resolution of movements in this square from full floating point resolution to fixed 9-bit accuracy, ie. the minimum movement size was 1/512. From the perspective of the GA the maze therefore appears as a 512 X 512 square grid, ie. 262144 states. This retains the property of a large search space, but simplifies both modelling of the environment and the required complexity of the GA.

The action space is therefore large but discrete, however the environmental model learned by the agent, the Neural Network **V-function**, maps **real numbered input coordinates** in the unit square to a real numbered V-output.

A number of straight line obstacles impede the agent's path from start to goal position. An example may be seen in figure 2, where the agent starts in the top left-hand corner and finishes in the bottom right.

4.   Genetic Algorithm

Each GA population member is made up of an x-coordinate and a y-coordinate. These are absolute coordinates rather than being relative to the present position purely for computational ease. In all three architectures each GA population member is therefore an 18-bit integer made up of a 9-bit x-coordinate and a 9-bit y-coordinate. Before use as (x,y) coordinates in the maze each population member is scaled to the unit square.

Though large for maze problems this is quite a small search space for contemporary GAs. A simple implementation was therefore used with a population of 40 individuals. The number of generations is 20. The selection method is "Roulette wheel". Crossover and mutation are both 2-point, one in the x-coordinate and one in the y-coordinate. At each new generation the fittest individual from the previous generation is inherited unchanged.

Every time the GA is re-initialized one member of its population is the goal position. Obviously this results in immediate convergence when an unimpeded path to the goal state is possible. This is a representative example of one way in which *a priori* knowledge may be incorporated into the system. If the knowledge is in the form of rules, then the result of applying those rules may be used to seed the initial GA population with "good guesses" as to the correct movement. In this case the rule is "its always worth trying a direct movement to the goal position", obviously a good rule for large search spaces relatively sparsely populated with obstacles.

5.   Neural Network

A Neural Network has a number of advantages over tabular methods for storing the V-function. Firstly the function learned is **continuous** in the input space. Secondly a certain amount of data compression can be achieved, though this is variable dependent upon network type.

We chose a gaussian Basis Function RBF Neural Network of the standard form [eg. Poggio & Girosi 1989, Sanner & Slotine 1991] rather than the global learning Multi-Layer Perceptron (MLP) used by Long-Ji Lin [Lin 1993] since this class of Neural Network has certain advantages for real time control applications. Firstly since passes of the learning algorithm affect only weights in the local region the problem of "knowledge drift" in other unrelated parts of the input space is avoided. Secondly learning time for these types of networks can be orders of magnitude faster with no local minima to get stuck in. Most importantly however the characteristic of "local generalisation" which this Neural Network type possesses means that changing the V-function mapping at one point in

the input space has a tendency to modify the local region to a gradually diminishing degree as distance from this point increases. This property is very useful here in extracting as much knowledge as possible from each movement through the maze. It translates roughly as, for example, "if a position is a good one then the immediate region around it will also be good".

Since the RBF network is intended to reflect the value of states in the maze it can be used as a second way to incorporate *a priori* knowledge possessed by the agent before the search begins via off-line pre-training. In this case we assume that the agent knows its position in the maze at all times and where the goal position is. The Basis Function centres of the Neural Network were off-line trained with a smoothly reducing function of the Euclidean distance from the goal state. This affects the whole search policy. We borrow terminology from traditional AI in saying that this initiates a "depth first" attitude to searching rather than a "width first " policy which would be initiated by off-line training with, say, equal values everywhere except at the goal state.

6.   Temporal Difference Learning

The V-function network was modified after each movement using a simple Temporal Differences (TD) algorithm, according to the following update rules;

$$V_{t-1} = V_{t-1} + TDRATE ((V_t - PUNISH) - V_{t-1})$$

for the movement prior to the current one then;

$$V_{t-i} = V_{t-i} + TDRATE (V_{t-i+1} - V_{t-i})$$

for i = 2 to HORIZON

Where; V_t = V-function output at time step t; TDRATE = Temporal Difference learning rate between 0 and 1; PUNISH = a small punishment to encourage exploration; HORIZON = TD scope.

If the new value for a V-function output becomes negative it is bounded to zero. The PUNISH factor was included to counteract limit cycles and/or stationary behaviour. Under these circumstances the value of those states will incur a penalty at each time step, thus resulting in the agent eventually breaking out into new areas of the maze.

7.   The EXP1 Model

In this first architecture, at each generation of the GA, Lamarckian interaction with the environment occurs for each population member wherein the "suggested" new position is tried out on the maze by making the movement and then returning. If a collision with an obstacle or a wall occurs then that population member is modified to be the coordinates of the collision. The fitness function used to rate each member of the GA population is supplied by the RBF Neural Network at the position of the collision.

7.1 Experiments & Results

Many experimental runs were undertaken, here we give a representative set only. The following maze, GA, Neural Network and TD learning parameters pertain to the results given below.

Maze: (10,10) is the starting position (the top left corner in figure 1) and (400,400) is the goal position. Maximum fitness at the goal position is 512. Other off-line trained initial fitnesses calculated by;

$$Fitness_{ij} = 512 \times \left(1 - \left(\frac{\sqrt{(cx_i - goalx)^2 + (cy_j - goaly)^2}}{max.distance} \right) \right)$$

GA: Crossover prob. = 0.9, mutation = 0.01.

RBF: 64 Basis Function centres on each axis, ie. 8 minimum size maze movements between each centre.

TD: TDRATE = 0.6, PUNISH = 50.0, Horizon = 20

Figure 1 illustrates the results of the first trial from start to goal position. It shows only the final move made from each position in the maze to the next, ie. the GA's "move-and-return" tests are not illustrated. EXP1 took 465 moves to find the goal position. This trial covered most difficult parts of the maze.

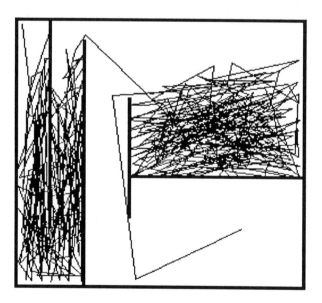

Figure 1

At first glance the exploration looks somewhat random. However closer investigation reveals an interplay between the GA search, TD learning and off-line pre-training of the V-function network. Although it is difficult to see in figure 1 because of later movements, initial negotiation of the first "corridor" is relatively quick since the V-function off-line pre-training matches the direction in which movement should proceed. However the second "corridor" is counter to this and involves much local movement whilst the fitness landscape is devalued through TD learning. This eventually involves revisiting the first "corridor" for a while since this looks more favourable than reaching the top of the second "corridor". After this the shape of the off-line trained V-function results in EXP1 getting stuck in the trap posed by the horizontal obstacle. Again much local movement is required to devalue the initial pre-trained landscape in this area before a path to the goal is discovered. Movements in the top right-hand quadrant follow a rough semicircle of gradually increasing radius until the area is left altogether. Not surprisingly the final part of the route is completed quickly because again it is well matched to the off-line pre-trained V-function values, the final move being quickly dictated by the GA's "seed" of a direct move to the goal as previously described.

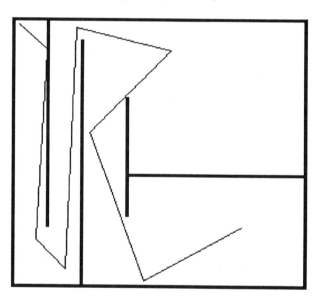

Figure 2

In the next 9 runs the number of moves required to complete the maze reduced more or less smoothly from 73 to 8, mostly spent investigating some small area missed by GA searches in the previous trials or staying still whilst the worth of a position was devalued through the TD learning PUNISH factor. By the 5th trial the top right hand quadrant of the maze ceased to be of any interest to EXP1. Figure 2 shows the 10th trial. From this trial onwards EXP1's path was stable taking 8 direct moves to the goal. These moves were mirrored by stable "peaks" in the fitness landscape presented by the V-function Neural Network.

We induced a limited form of time variance in the environment by opening up a more direct path at the bottom of the second vertical obstacle. In this case EXP1 immediately explored it, discovering the quicker route in one trial. We also tested the GA performance against a random search by setting the number of generations to zero, ie. the population was randomly initialized only. Under these circumstances, with all other factors the same as before, the random search started with a lower number of movements to solve the maze but convergence was much slower and the best solution it discovered consisted of 18 moves, though this was not a stable state.

8. ALICEI (Adaptive Learning In Continuous Environments 1)

EXP1 modifies its V-function to reflect "good" and "bad" places to be in the maze, but it does not build up a sense of which movements between "good" places are possible and which are not, ie. no internal model of the positions of the obstacles is acquired. It is left to interaction with the environment for each population member at each generation of the GA from each new position to eliminate impossible moves from the current place in the maze. Although this elimination typically occurs quite quickly in the first few generations of each GA run, leaving the GA with a population of "possible moves" to evolve, clearly a real mobile robot would expend a large amount of time testing all moves suggested by the GA during its convergence.

ALICEI incorporates a second "collision" model to store the boundaries of obstacles. This model is bit-mapped with the maze. At the outset it is initialized to zero everywhere, ie. no obstacles are known. Subsequently, when a collision occurs that position in the model becomes non-zero.

The GA driven search for the next movement is modified to include this second model as described below. At each GA generation all the population members are tested against the collision model as if they were real movements in the maze, ie. model collisions modify the population members and their fitnesses according to the V-function output at that position. The resulting fittest member is evaluated on the real maze for fitness and collision. If it collides then it is modified accordingly and the collision model is updated. If no collision occurs at this first evaluation on the real maze then the next GA generation begins. If a collision occurs then the fittest individual is again selected from the population and tested against the real maze. This process continues until a collision free test occurs. This whole process is continued in the ensuing GA generations until the population is converged or the maximum number of generations is reached.

8.1 Experiments & Results

ALICEI was tested against the same maze as EXP1, with all other RBF Neural Network, TD learning and GA parameters unchanged. The overall results were, not surprisingly, very similar in terms of final moves made from each position and the way in which the maze was investigated at each trial. ALICEI took 509 moves on the first trial, reducing steadily to a stable 9 moves by the 7th trial.

Figure 3

However an analysis of the number of interactions with the real maze on successive trials, also not surprisingly, yields a very differing picture between the two architectures. EXP1 requires 40 "move-and-return" evaluations at each of 20 generations, ie. 800 evaluations, to establish each movement in the maze. By contrast on the first trial ALICEI required, for example, an average of only 29 real maze interactions over the first 60 moves. By the 7th trial interactions with the real maze were much lower than this.

ALICEI's collision model after the 7th trial is illustrated in figure 3. Obviously this map is only partially complete, reflecting the areas which were tested during the 7 trials.

9. ALICEII

ALICEI's collision model is a discrete one, it will not scale well. If the number of states in the maze becomes very large or, more generally, the environment is continuous valued then it is unusable. It is also somewhat inelegant to have two internal models present in the agent. Consequently ALICEII incorporates the collision model into the continuous mapping of the RBF Neural Network V-function as described below. V-function fitness values for non-obstacle areas of the maze are already restricted to positive values increasing from zero. Allocating negative values to areas which contain obstacles is a convenient way of combining the two models. An alternative method of combination could have been to add a second output to the RBF Neural Network. However ALICEII utilises the former method.

The search method is quite similar to that found in ALICEI, except that model collisions are evaluated by determining whether a GA population member under test specifies a movement from the current position which traverses a negative valued area of the V-function.

9.1   Experiments & Results

ALICEII was tested against the same maze as EXP1, with all other RBF Neural Network, TD learning and GA parameters unchanged. Under these circumstances although it always satisfactorily solved the maze over repeated trials it occasionally became stuck during a trial inside an "imaginary" box because the local generalisation of the RBF Neural Network was too wide for the characteristics of the maze, with its relatively narrow "corridors". In this case becoming stuck was not an insurmountable problem because redistribution of fitness in the V-function during the next trial always allowed ALICEII to remove or avoid them and complete the maze. However this may not hold in all scenarios. The density of Radial Basis Functions was doubled on each axis which removed this problem but resulted in a more laborious search in early trials since the generalisation in open spaces was more local than necessary.

The overall results were however, again not surprisingly, very similar in form to ALICEI in terms of final moves made from each position and the way in which the maze was investigated at each trial. Figure 4 shows a 3-dimensional illustration of the fitness landscape, ie. the V-function, after the 3rd trial of the maze. It gives only an approximate idea of the view which ALICEII has of its environment since it has been inverted to make the "valleys" into "ridges" and scaled to enhance visibility.

10.   Discussion

We found all three architectures presented here were fairly robust to changes in value of the many parameters in the system, such as number of RBF centres, TD learning rate, PUNISH & HORIZON values, GA population size & number of generations, mutation and crossover probabilities etc. Most changes induced a more or less efficient search or

affected the convergence behaviour over successive trials rather than resulting in incorrect behaviour. There seemed to be two distinct behaviours, first a strongly investigative mode in which large parts of the states space are searched, and then a stable TD reinforced mode which persists until some time variance in the environment occurs.

Although it is claimed in this paper's introduction that the GA performs the exploration whilst the Neural Network performs exploitation, clearly this is an oversimplification. The GA uses knowledge gained to date in searching from the current position in the maze at each new generation. The TD learning algorithm presented here clearly shapes the form of exploration because of the PUNISH factor for stationary or cyclic behaviours and any off-line training which is done. In ALICEI & II interactions between the GA and the environmental model greatly affect the characteristics of the GA's convergence.

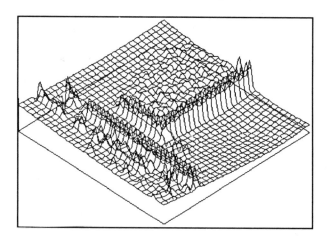

Figure 4

Factors such as Neural Network RBF density and radius will clearly affect the accuracy and local generalisation of the V-function in both approximation and convergence, as will TD learning rate and the size of the punishment factor. However they all affect exploration as well as exploitation. For example a coarse distribution of wide radius RBFs will result in a correspondingly coarse search policy and resultant model of the V-function.

In the "Holland" style Classifier Systems described above [Roberts 1993] the GA and TD learning act in an indirect way in evolving and reinforcing the population of rules in the system. However there are some clear analogies between their on-line interactions and those found here. By contrast the evolved Neural Networks of Cliff et al [Cliff et al 1992] use the GA in an off-line way with the GA performing both exploration of the solution space and exploitation between generations in the traditional GA manner.

11.   Conclusions and Further Work

Our principal aim was to construct architectures for agents capable of investigating maze-like problems where the environment was characterised by a large discrete search space or, in the limit, a continuous real valued one. We have gained some measure of success in this. However although ALICEII's environmental model is continuous real valued in the input space, our action space is still discretized. Although the Genetic Algorithm can be modified and constrained to search real numbered spaces, this is not its natural territory. We would like to pursue the use of an Evolutionary Strategy [Back & Schwefel 1993] which has been specifically designed for searching such environments.

We were also interested in observing the roles of exploration and exploitation in an agent's on-line learning about these kinds of environments. We have found that despite our attempts to separate these roles our architectures are subtly and multitudinously linked in these respects. However, more experimental and analytical work needs to be done here to fully characterize the situation.

The RBF Neural Network used here is based on a regular array of Basis Functions, as are most such networks. However there is no fundamental reason why this should be the case. It would be beneficial, for example to introduce additional small radius Basis Functions at points of collision with obstacles in the environment so as to better map the sharply changing V-function in these areas whilst retaining a generally coarser distribution in other areas. In fact there is no reason why distribution and radius should not be variable from one Basis Function to another, these factors being incorporated into the learning algorithm.

In comparing these architectures with others in the field we find some interesting analogies with Classifier System based agents and would like to conduct an experimental comparison between them.

References

Back T., Schwefel H-P., 1993, 'An Overview of Evolutionary Algorithms for Parameter Optimization', Evolutionary Computation Vol.1 Num.1, pp1-23

Barto A. G., Bradtke S. J., Singh S. P., 1991, 'Real-Time Learning and Control using Asynchronous Dynamic Programming', Dept. of Computer Science, University of Massachusetts, USA, Technical Report 91-57

Barto A. G., Sutton R. S., Watkins C. J. C. H., 1989, 'Learning and Sequential Decision Making', COINS Technical Report 89-95

Belew R. K., McInerney J., Schraudolph N. N., 1990, 'Evolving Networks: Using the Genetic Algorithm with Connectionist Learning', University of California at San Diego, USA, CSE Technical Report CS90-174

Booker L. B., Goldberg D. E., Holland J. H., 1989, 'Classifier Systems and Genetic Algorithms', Artificial Intelligence 40, pp.235-282

Cliff D., Husbands P., Harvey I., 1992, 'Evolving Visually Guided Robots', University of Sussex, Cognitive Science Research Papers CSRP 220

Lin L., PhD thesis, 1993, 'Reinforcement Learning for Robots using Neural Networks', School of Computer Science, Carnegie Mellon University Pittsburgh, USA

Poggio T., Girosi F., 1989, 'A theory of Networks for Approximation and Learning', MIT Cambridge, MA, AI lab. Memo 1140

Roberts G., 1993, 'Dynamic Planning for Classifier Systems', Proceedings of the 5th International Conference on Genetic Algorithms, pp.231-237

Sanner R. M., Slotine J. E., 1991, 'Gaussian Networks for Direct Adaptive Control', Nonlinear Systems Laboratory, MIT, Cambridge, USA, Technical Report NSL-910503

Sutton R. S., 1984, PhD thesis 'Temporal Credit Assignment in Reinforcement Learning', University of Massachusetts, Dept. of computer and Information Science

Sutton R. S., 1991, 'Reinforcement Learning Architectures for Animats', From Animals to Animats, pp288-296, Editors Meyer, J., Wilson, S., MIT Press Reinhold, Ed. White D. A., Sofge D. A.

Watkins C. J. C. H., 1989, PhD thesis 'Learning from Delayed Rewards', King's College, Cambridge.

Werbos, P. J., 1992, 'Approximate Dynamic Programming for Real-Time Control and Neural Modelling', Handbook of Intelligent Control: Neural, Fuzzy, and Adaptive Approaches, Van Nostrand Reinhold, Ed. White D. A., Sofge D. A.

A PLACE NAVIGATION ALGORITHM BASED ON ELEMENTARY COMPUTING PROCEDURES AND ASSOCIATIVE MEMORIES

Simon BENHAMOU[+], Pierre BOVET[*] & Bruno POUCET[+]

[+]C.N.R.S.-L.N.C., F-13402 Marseille cedex 20
[*]F.P.S.E., Université de Genève, CH-1227 Carouge
e-mail: simon@lnf.cnrs-mrs.fr

Abstract

Place navigation refers to the ability of an animal to process the location-based (site-dependent) information to return to a given goal. The algorithm we developed to account for this ability in mammals is based on the angular information provided by both the bearings and angular sizes of landmarks. It is implemented by a system which combines elementary computing procedures and two types of simple associative memory networks. One type of network enables the animal to learn how the environmental perspective changes when it makes a one-step translation in any direction whereas the other type enables the animal to learn how the currently experienced panorama is oriented in relation to an overall reference direction. This system highlights the fundamental role of exploration of the environment prior to place navigation, and assigns specific functions to hippocampal place cells and postsubicular head-direction cells which have been found in mammals.

1. INTRODUCTION

Mammals are able to process the location-based (site-dependent) information provided by the spatial layout of landmarks to navigate towards a goal whose location is memorized exocentrically in relation to the same landmarks (e.g. Sutherland & Dyck 1984; Collett & Cartwright 1986; Collett 1987). Neurobiological evidence provides some hints as to how this ability is implemented by the brain. As a matter of fact, electrophysiological studies relevant to the analysis of the neural correlates of mammals' spatial behaviour demonstrated the existence of neurons located in the hippocampus, called place cells, whose firing depends on the animal's current location in relation to the spatial layout of landmarks, whatever the direction faced (review in Muller *et al.* 1991). Furthermore, neurons located in the postsubiculum (a cortical area close to the hippocampus), called head-direction cells, fire as a function of the absolute orientation of the head in relation to the spatial layout of landmarks, whatever the animal's location (Taube *et al.* 1990a,b). At the neural level, absolute head orientations are therefore coded by specific postsubicular firing patterns just as places are coded by specific hippocampal firing patterns.

The place navigation algorithm we developed aims to specify the way a mammal may process location-based information to navigate towards a goal. It is biologically plausible because it relies on the existence of both place cells and head-direction cells. This algorithm is based on the angular information provided by both the head-referred bearings and angular sizes of landmarks, which can be easily determined from the animal's current location at the retinal level, rather than on Euclidean metric distances, which are not definitely used by mammals (see Poucet 1993).

2. CONCEPT OF PANORAMA

By integrating the rotations of eyes, head, and whole body, the animal interlinks the various "local views" available at a given location into a "panorama" which constitutes a form of place representation (Poucet 1993). The panorama which defines a given place is assumed to be self-coded in terms of both the vertical angular sizes [L] (above the horizon line) and the relative bearings λ_r of landmarks L as perceived from this place. The vertical angular sizes, which will be referred to simply as angular sizes, are relevant because numerous landmarks have a striking vertical dimension when perceived by a terrestrial animal moving on a roughly horizontal two-dimensional space. The relative bearings of the landmarks in a given panorama are encoded as angular deviations from a single arbitrary origin, called local (place-dependent) reference direction (LRD), which is specific to this panorama. As a working rule, the head-referred value Φ_h of the LRD is expressed as the vectorial angular mean of the head-referred bearings λ_h of the landmarks L weighted by their angular sizes [L] (Fig. 1). Relative bearings are then computed as the differences between the head-referred bearings and the LRD:

$$\lambda_r = \lambda_h - \Phi_h$$

By construction, relative bearings therefore depend on the panorama but not on the head orientation.

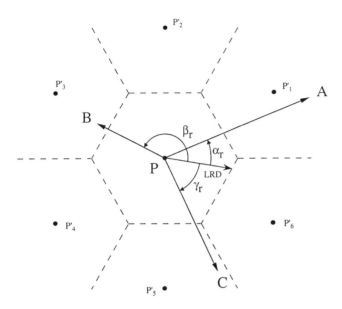

Fig. 1. Determining the LRD of place P as the vectorial angular mean of the bearings (arrow directions) of the landmarks (A, B, and C) weighted by their respective angular sizes (arrow lengths). Greek letters stand for relative bearings of landmarks. Places are assumed to be regular hexagons (see text).

Panoramas which are different enough to be discriminated make it possible to structure the space as a mosaic of adjacent places. A place is therefore defined as a small area within which the animal experiences a specific panorama. The particular local view seen by the animal specifies the orientation of its head in relation to the current panorama. For convenience, all places are assumed to have the same size and to be shaped like regular hexagons. Consequently, any place is contiguous with six other places. The possible locations of the animal, the goal and landmarks are restricted to the place centres. The animal can therefore move at each step in one of six directions labelled j (60° apart from each other), from the current place P to one of the six adjacent places P'_j.

Given the retinal resolution of many mammals, the model animal is assumed to measures angular sizes and head-referred bearings to the nearest 1°. Then, about 2000 adjacent places can be discriminated on the basis of their respective panoramas in an environment comprising 10 randomly located landmarks.

3. PLACE NAVIGATION ALGORITHM

When the animal is at any place, it experiences a specific panorama, independently of its current orientation, and recalls the panoramas corresponding to each of the six adjacent places (see next section). The direction of the animal's next step is then derived from the discrepancies between the panoramas of the six adjacent places and the goal panorama.

The measurement of the discrepancy between any panorama corresponding to a given place P and the goal panorama is based on Carnot's formula about ordinary triangles:

$$S_L{}^2 = R_L{}^2 + 1 - 2.R_L.\cos(\lambda_a - \lambda^*_a)$$
$$\text{with } S_L = PG/LG \text{ and } R_L = LP/LG$$

where PG, LP and LG are the distances between place P, goal G, and a given landmark L, and λ_a and λ^*_a are the absolute bearings of the landmark L as perceived from place P and goal G respectively, i.e. referred to an overall (place-independent) reference direction (ORD; see Fig. 2). The discrepancy between the two panoramas is defined as

$$D = (\Sigma S_L{}^2)^{1/2}$$

for all landmarks L which are perceived from both place P and goal G.

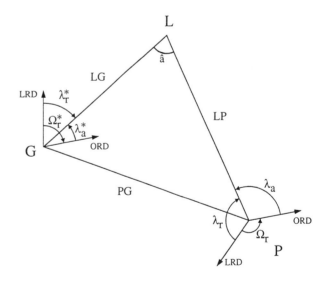

Fig. 2. Spatial relationships existing between place P, goal G and a given landmark L. Relative bearings (λ_r and λ^*_r) are referred to the LRD, whereas absolute bearings (λ_a and λ^*_a) are referred to the ORD. The values of the ORD (Ω_r and Ω^*_r) are referred to the LRD. The angle in L is equal to the difference between the absolute bearings ($\hat{a} = \lambda_a - \lambda^*_a$).

Importantly, the animal is not assumed to compute the distances between any landmark L and place P (LP) or goal

G (LG). Indeed, the ratio $R_L = LP/LG$ is derived directly from the angular sizes [L]* and [L] of landmark L as perceived from goal G and place P, respectively:

$$R_L = \tan([L]^*) / \tan([L])$$

Because most mammals seem unable to use a compass, the ORD should be supplied by the spatial layout of landmarks, and its specific value at any place, Ω_r referred to the LRD (Ω_r^* at the goal), should be learned during exploration of the environment (see next section). The absolute bearings of a given landmark L as perceived from place P and goal G are therefore expressed as

$$\lambda_a = \lambda_r - \Omega_r \qquad \lambda_a^* = \lambda_r^* - \Omega_r^*$$

The algorithm presupposes that the angular sizes [L]* and absolute bearings λ_a^* of landmarks L as perceived from the goal are stored in a long-term memory, so that they can be recalled at any time.

Whatever its current place P, the animal estimates the goal direction as the vectorial angular mean of the directions j of the six adjacent places P'_j weighted by the inverse of the discrepancies D'_j between their respective panoramas and the goal panorama. The animal then efficiently navigates to the goal by moving at each step in the direction j which is the nearest to (i.e. less than 30° from) the locally estimated goal direction (Fig. 3).

This process is repeated until the goal has been reached, i.e. until the current and the goal panoramas are identical (D=0).

The efficiency of the algorithm depends on the accuracy with which the discrepancies D and D'_j are computed. Computer simulations showed that the algorithm is robust to approximation errors. Indeed, even if the value of the ORD is estimated only to the nearest 15°, the animal reaches the goal along a path with a length equal to or slightly greater than the shortest one (Fig 4).

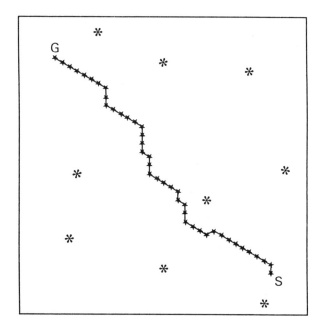

Fig. 4. Example of a path from a starting place S to a goal G. The animal navigates step by step by processing the location-based information supplied by nine discriminable landmarks (labelled with large stars). The places crossed by the animal are labelled with small stars. Actual path length: 41 steps; Shortest possible length: 40 steps.

4. IMPLEMENTATION

The implementation of the place navigation algorithm involves two phases: exploration, during which information is collected and memorized, and navigation, during which information is retrieved and used. The directions of the six places P'_j adjacent to the current place P are labelled j; conversely, the direction of the current place P from any adjacent place P'_j is labelled i, with i=j+3 modulo 6 and j=i+3 modulo 6 (directions i and j are opposite).

4.1. Exploration

Exploration is an iterative process (Fig. 5). When the animal was at the previous place P'_j, it experienced a specific panorama defined by the angular sizes $[L]'_j$ and

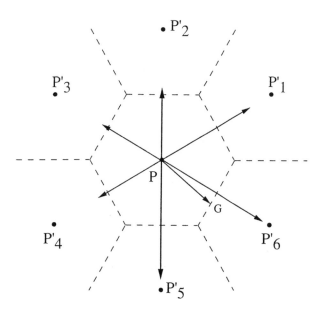

Fig. 3. Determining the direction of the goal from the current place P as the vectorial angular mean of the directions of the six adjacent places P'_j (arrow directions) weighted by the inverse discrepancies between their respective panoramas and the goal panorama (arrow lengths). In this example, the animal will move to the adjacent place P'_6 whose direction is the nearest to the estimated goal direction (G).

relative bearings $\lambda'_{r(j)}$ of landmarks L. The ORD had been transferred to place P'_j during the previous step and mnesically associated with the panorama as an angular value $\Omega'_{r(j)}$ referred to the LRD.

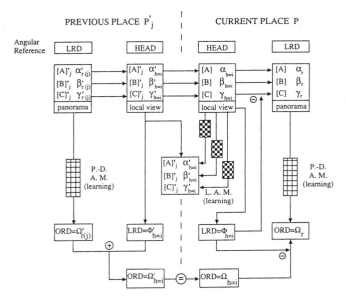

Fig. 5. Exploration process from the previous place P'_j (one of the six adjacent places) to the current place P in an environment comprising 3 landmarks (A, B and C: Letters between square brackets stand for angular sizes; Greek letters stand for bearings).

The animal then chose one of the six possible directions i, and moved from the previous place P'_j to the current place P along a one-step translation. When leaving place P'_j, it saw a particular local view, in which head-referred bearings have specific values $\lambda'_{h=i}$ and the LRD has the head-referred value $\Phi'_{h=i}$. The head-referred value of the ORD was then computed as

$$\Omega'_{h=i} = \Omega'_{r(j)} + \Phi'_{h=i}$$

When arriving at place P, the animal is still facing the same absolute direction. According to the one-step translation, it sees a new local view defined by specific values of angular sizes [L] and head-referred bearings $\lambda_{h=i}$ of landmarks L. First at all, the previous values of the angular size [L]$'_j$ and head-referred bearing $\lambda'_{h=i}$ of each landmark L are mnesically associated with the current ones ([L] and $\lambda_{h=i}$) by means of a specific "Landmark Associative Memory" (LAM; see next section). This type of memory enables the animal to learn how the environmental perspective changes when it makes a one-step translation.

Thereafter, the head-referred value of the LRD of the current panorama $\Phi_{h=i}$ is determined and the local view is converted into a self-coded (head orientation-independent)

panorama by computing the relative bearings of the landmarks from their head-referred bearings:

$$\lambda_r = \lambda_{h=i} - \Phi_{h=i}$$

As the animal moves in the same absolute direction when leaving the place P'_j and arriving at the place P, the head-referred value of the ORD does not change:

$$\Omega_{h=i} = \Omega'_{h=i}$$

The animal can then easily determine the value of the ORD referred to the LRD of the current panorama:

$$\Omega_r = \Omega_{h=i} - \Phi_{h=i}$$

The ORD is thus transferred from the previous place P'_j to the current place P. Its value Ω_r referred to the LRD is then mnesically associated with the current panorama by means of the "Place-Direction Associative Memory" (PDAM; see next section). In this way, the animal can learn how the current panorama is oriented in relation to the ORD.

4.2. Navigation

Like exploration, navigation is an iterative process (Fig 6). When the animal is at the current place P, it experiences a specific panorama defined by the angular sizes [L] and relative bearings λ_r of landmarks L. The informational content of the panorama is used in two ways.

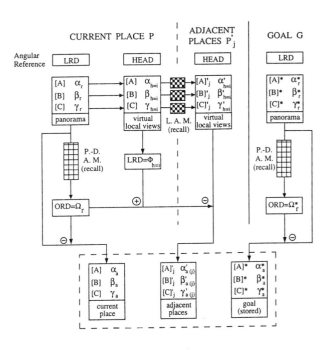

Fig. 6. Navigation process: determining to which adjacent place P'_j to move from the current place P in order to approach the goal. Same symbols as in Fig. 5.

On the one hand, it activates the PDAM, making it recall the value Ω_r of the ORD referred to the LRD (see next section). The absolute bearings of landmarks as perceived from the current place P are then computed as:

$$\lambda_a = \lambda_r - \Omega_r$$

On the other hand, the informational content of the panorama enables the animal to have access to the six virtual local views, defined by the angular sizes [L] and head-referred bearings $\lambda_{h=i}$, corresponding to what it would see if it oriented its head in each of the six possible directions i.

Each virtual local view, involving a particular head-referred value $\Phi_{h=i}$ of the LRD, activates the specific LAMs (one LAM per landmark). These memories recall the angular sizes and head-referred bearings $\lambda'_{h=i}$ of landmarks [L]$'_j$ defining the virtual local view the animal would see by looking towards the current place P from the adjacent place P$'_j$ located behind the animal (j=i+3 modulo 6; see next section). The absolute bearings of landmarks as perceived from adjacent places P$'_j$ are then computed as:

$$\lambda'_{a(j)} = \lambda'_{h=i} - \Phi_{h=i} - \Omega_r$$

When the animal was at the goal, the value Ω^*_r of the ORD, referred to the LRD of the goal, was mnesically associated with the goal panorama ([L]*; λ^*_r). The absolute bearings of landmarks as perceived from the goal G were computed as:

$$\lambda^*_a = \lambda^*_r - \Omega^*_r$$

As specific values of the goal ([L]*; λ^*_a) are stored in a long-term memory, they can be recalled at any time.

The animal computes the discrepancy D between the current panorama and the goal panorama, as well as the discrepancies D$'_j$ between the panoramas of the adjacent places and the goal panorama, since the bearings of the landmarks as perceived from the goal, the current place and the adjacent places, are all referred to the ORD. It can therefore use the place navigation algorithm to reach the goal.

5. ASSOCIATIVE MEMORY NETWORKS

The adaptive neuromimetic networks we developed are just simple technical means of modelling the Landmark Associative Memories (LAMs) and the Place-Direction Associative Memory (PDAM) required to implement the place navigation algorithm. These networks are in no way intended to represent what actually occurs in the nervous system. Although hippocampal place cells and postsubicular head-direction cells might be involved in actual associative memories (see Discussion), it would be

extremely hazardous to seek for any correspondence between the formal and actual neurons.

Both LAM and PDAM comprise only two layers. All the units in the input layer are connected to all the units in the output layer by means of adaptive connections, as in most neuromimetic models (see Anderson & Rosenfeld 1988). The activity level of any output unit Y_m depends on the linear combination of the activity levels of all the input units X_n weighted by the corresponding connection weights W_{nm} (i.e. the sum $\Sigma_n W_{nm}.X_n$; see Kohonen, 1984).

In both LAM and PDAM, the input layer is made of directionally tuned units: each input unit is activated if and only if a specific value of the head-referred (LAM) or relative (PDAM) bearing of a given landmark is experienced, and its activity level is proportional to the angular size of the landmark. The output layer is made of binary units: the activity level of any output unit Y_m is equal to 1 if the sum $\Sigma_n W_{nm}.X_n$ is greater than a given threshold, otherwise it is equal to 0 (heaviside function).

During learning (exploration), the appropriate activity levels Z_m that output units should produce are determined by the particular local view seen by the animal leaving the previous place (LAM) or by the particular value of the overall reference direction which is transferred to the current place (PDAM). The differences Z_m-Y_m are used to modify the matrix of connection weights W_{nm}.

5.1. Landmark Associative Memory

The LAM specific to a given landmark L is designed to recall the change in the head-referred bearing $\lambda_{h=i} - \lambda'_{h=i}$ (which is easier to manage than the value $\lambda'_{h=i}$ itself: see below) that the animal would perceive if making a one-step translation (no rotation) to the current place P from any adjacent place P$'_j$, and the angular size [L]$'_j$ that it would perceive from this place, in response to the current head-referred bearing $\lambda_{h=i}$ and angular size [L].

The structure of the LAM and the learning rule are simple. They are based on elementary geometrical considerations about any one-step translation:

(1) The landmark L remains in the same visual hemi-field (left or right) from the start to the end of the step. Its apparent rotation is always clockwise in the right hemi-field and counterclockwise in the left hemi-field: the change in the head-referred bearing is always positive if head-referred bearings are measured from front to back, whatever the side involved.

(2) The magnitude of the change in the head-referred bearing $\lambda_{h=i} - \lambda'_{h=i}$ (ranging from 0 to 60°) and the previous angular size [L]$'_j$ (ranging from 0 to 90°) are decreasing functions of the distance to the landmark L, and therefore increasing functions of the current angular size [L]. The exact function specifying how the change in the head-referred bearing and the previous angular size vary

with the current angular size depends on the current head-referred bearing.

Consequently, the input layer encodes the current head-referred bearing, measured from front to back, in only one (not specified) visual hemi-field. Only the one input unit tuned to the currently perceived value $\lambda_{h=i}$ is activated, and its activity level is proportional to the current angular size [L]. The output layer is divided into two parts. One part encodes the change in the head-referred bearing $\lambda_{h=i} - \lambda'_{h=i}$, whereas the other part encodes the previous angular size $[L]'_j$ (Fig. 7). The value of each of these two parameters is expressed as the number of active units in the corresponding part of the output layer. In this aim, all the output units are threshold responsive: in each part of the output layer, the most responsive unit is activated as soon as the angular value to be coded reaches 1°, a slightly less responsive unit is activated as soon as this value reaches 2°, and so on.

	x_0	0	0	0	0	0	1/68	1/78	1/78	1/90	1/90	0
	x_{30}	1/70	0	0	0	0	1/70	1/70	0	0	0	0
	x_{60}	1/59	1/68	1/78	1/78	0	1/68	1/68	1/78	1/78	0	0
	x_{79}	1/62	1/62	0	0	0	1/62	0	0	0	0	0
	x_{90}	1/70	1/70	1/70	1/70	0	1/70	1/70	1/70	0	0	0
	x_{101}	1/62	1/62	1/62	0	0	1/62	1/62	0	0	0	0
	x_{120}	1/59	1/59	1/68	1/68	1/78	1/59	1/59	1/68	1/68	1/78	0
	x_{139}	1/62	1/62	0	0	0	1/62	1/62	1/62	0	0	0
	x_{150}	1/70	1/70	1/70	1/70	0	1/70	1/70	1/70	1/70	1/70	0
	x_{161}	1/62	0	0	0	0	1/62	1/62	1/62	1/62	0	0
	x_{180}	0	0	0	0	0	1/59	1/59	1/59	1/68	1/68	1/78

Y_1	Y_{12}	Y_{20}	Y_{23}	Y_{31}	Y_1	Y_{60}	Y_{63}	Y_{69}	Y_{72}	Y_{80}
Y_{11}	Y_{19}	Y_{22}	Y_{30}	Y_{60}	Y_{59}	Y_{62}	Y_{68}	Y_{71}	Y_{79}	Y_{90}

CHANGE IN H-R. BEARING	PREVIOUS ANGULAR SIZE

OUTPUT LAYER

Fig. 7. Structure of a LAM. For convenience, this network is built for an animal which explored only the 37 places surrounding a given landmark: only a small fraction of the input units (11/181) can therefore be activated, and numerous output units are connected to input units with the same weights. The values of connection weights indicated in the matrix are computed for an input activity level X_n equal to the angular size (expressed in degrees) of the landmark whose height is set to 5 times the distance between two adjacent place centres. H-R (head-referred) bearings are measured from front to back.

In both parts of the output layer, each unit is activated ($Y_m = 1$) if and only if the sum $\Sigma_n W_{nm}.X_n$ is greater than 1 (otherwise $Y_m = 0$). During the exploration phase, the values of change in head-referred bearing and of the previous angular size are used to specify which units in each part of the output layer should be active ($Z_m = 1$) or inactive ($Z_m = 0$). The weights W_{nm} of the connections between the active input unit and all the output units which should be but are not active ($Z_m - Y_m = 1$) become equal to a value slightly greater than $1/X_n$, whereas the weights W_{nm} of the connections between the active input unit and all the output units which should not be but are active ($Z_m - Y_m = -1$) become equal to 0. The sum $\Sigma_n W_{nm}.X_n$ thus become slightly greater than 1 for all the output units which should be active. None of the other connection weights are modified.

This simple learning rule causes connection weights to be all the lower as the responsiveness of the corresponding output units is low. When the animal has explored sufficiently its environment, perceiving at least once all the possible head-referred bearings and angular sizes of each landmark, the corresponding matrix of connection weights becomes fully operational. The animal does not need to visit all the places: the space around each landmark is radially equivalent in six directions, so that what the animal learns in 1/6 of the environment about this landmark can be used in the other 5/6.

During navigation, the number of active units in the two parts of the output layer in response to a given virtual local view ([L]; $\lambda_{h=i}$) corresponds to the change in the head-referred bearing $\lambda_{h=i} - \lambda'_{h=i}$ that the animal would perceive if making one step to the current place P from the adjacent place P'_j, and to the angular size $[L]'_j$ it would perceive from this place. By considering all the available landmarks together, the animal can therefore determine the virtual local view corresponding to each of the six adjacent places.

5.2. Place-Direction Associative Memory

The PDAM is designed to recall the value Ω_r of the ORD referred to the LRD of any learned panorama when this panorama is currently experienced. Contrary to the LAM, there is no geometrical considerations making it possible to determine the connection weights directly. Learning therefore proceeds more slowly by trial and error.

The input layer is divided into as many parts as there are available landmarks (one part per landmark). Each part (a ring of 360 units) of the input layer encodes the relative bearing of a given landmark. Only the one input unit which is tuned to the current value of the relative bearing λ_r of the corresponding landmark L is activated in each part of the input layer, whatever the animal's current place, and its activity level X_n is proportional to the angular size [L] of the landmark. The output layer (a ring of 360°/15° bin = 24 units) encodes the ORD referred to the LRD of the current place. Any output unit is activated ($Y_m = 1$) if and only if the sum $\Sigma_n W_{nm}.X_n$ is strictly greater than 0. After learning, only the one output unit which corresponds to the appropriate value of the ORD is activated when the animal is at a given place (Fig. 8).

During the continuous exploration of the environment, the ORD is transferred from place to place, and its value Ω_r is referred to the LRD of the current place.

This value is used to determine which output units should be active or inactive ($Z_m=1$ or $Z_m=0$; only one output unit at once is allowed to be active). The learning obeys the rule of Widrow & Hoff (1960) or delta rule (Rumelhart *et al.* 1986). According to this rule, the change V_{nm} in weight W_{nm} of the connection between any input unit (activity level X_n) and any output unit (activity level Y_m) is given by $V_{nm}=X_n.(Z_m-Y_m)$. In the present study, most of the input units are not activated ($X_n=0$) when the animal experiences a given panorama (only one unit in each part of the input layer is active at once). Consequently, only a very small fraction (1/360) of the whole matrix of connection weights is possibly updated when the animal is at any given place.

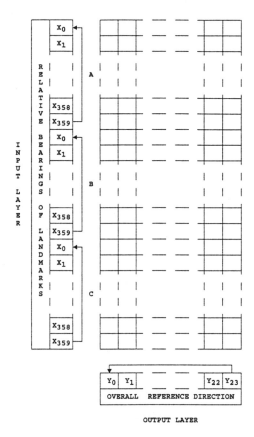

Fig. 8. Structure of the PDAM. For convenience, this network is built for an environment comprising only three landmarks (A, B, and C). The input layer is a series of rings of units (one ring per landmark) and the output layer is also a ring of units. All rings start from the same angular origin (LRD).

If all the places in the environment can be distinguished on the basis of the relative bearings only (i.e. without taking the angular sizes into account), the connection weights converge progressively to values causing the network to recall the appropriate value of the ORD at any place as the animal repeatedly visits each place

during exploration (otherwise, the network recalls the same value at all the places where place discrimination requires the angular sizes, whatever the appropriate value of the ORD). The place area should therefore be large enough (given the number of available landmarks) to enable the animal to discriminate between places using the relative bearings only.

The learning speed was studied using computer simulations involving 10 environments, each encompassing 1951 hexagonal places fields and comprising 10 randomly located landmarks. The height of the landmarks was set to 5 times the distance between any two adjacent place centres. The number of places at which the network was able to produce the appropriate output was determined after each visit to the whole environment (i.e. after all 1951 places had been successively visited). This network turned out to be able to recall the appropriate value of the ORD at all the places in the environment in response to their corresponding panoramas after 10.2 ± 2.5 visits, but the output of the network is already appropriate at $97.6\%\pm0.8\%$ of the places after only 5 visits.

6. DISCUSSION

The place navigation algorithm developed in this paper is based on the angular information provided both by the bearings and angular sizes of landmarks. It is implemented by a system which combines elementary computing procedures and two types of simple associative memory network. As the goal location is memorized in the form of an exocentric coding whereas perceiving the environment and performing actions must be carried out from the egocentric animal's point of view, this system works mainly as a two-way converter of frames of reference. Place (or location-based) navigation is complementary to vector (or route-based) navigation, which involves the goal location being memorized in the form of an egocentric coding (a vector specifying the head-referred direction of the goal and its distance from the animal) updated by processing route-based (site-independent) information (see Benhamou *et al.* 1990).

The importance of vestibular inputs in place navigation has been underlined by Semenov & Bures (1989) and McNaughton *et al.* (1991). In our model, vestibular and other kinesthetic inputs generated by locomotion are required to determine whether the apparent rotation of landmarks is due to the animal's own rotation on the spot or to a purely one-step translation. The absence of rotation input, causing the postsubicular head-direction cells to continue to produce the same specific firing pattern, informs the animal that it is still facing the same absolute direction (so that the head-referred value of the ORD does not change). Actual movements combine rotations and translations simultaneously rather than alternately, and the vestibular system is not very accurate. Fortunately, our place navigation algorithm is particularly robust against approximation errors as to the ORD: it is able to work well even if this direction (which is primarily referred to the head orientation) is estimated only to the nearest 15°.

In line with O'Keefe & Nadel (1978), many authors have attributed a cognitive mapping function to the hippocampus. Our model shows that possessing a cognitive map (stricto sensu) is not necessary to perform accurate place navigation: the animal was not assumed to know anything about the geometrical relationships between the goal location, its own current position, and the landmark locations. In our view, hippocampal place cells do not map space, but learn to respond to specific panoramas whatever the particular limited local view to which the animal is currently exposed (this nevertheless involves a high level of neural integration). The specific firing patterns of hippocampal place cells might be fed into a place-direction associative memory, whereas postsubicular head-direction cells might produce specific firing patterns depending on the angular deviations between the outputs of this associative memory and the head orientation. Furthermore, the hippocampal place cells might be also involved in the input and output of landmark associative memories. The actual neurobiological structure of these two types of associative memory still remains to be established.

REFERENCES

Anderson J.A. & Rosenfeld E. 1988. *Neurocomputing*. Cambridge (Mass.): MIT press.

Benhamou S., Sauvé J-P. & Bovet P. 1990. Spatial memory in large scale movements: efficiency and limitation of the egocentric coding process. *J. Theor. Biol.* 145, 1-12.

Collett T.S. 1987. The use of visual landmarks by gerbils: reaching a goal when landmarks are displaced. *J. Comp. Physiol.* A 160, 109-113.

Collett T.S., Cartwright B.A. & Smith B.A. 1986. Landmark learning and visuo-spatial memories in gerbils. *J. Comp. Physiol.* A 158, 835-851.

Kohonen T. 1984. *Self-organization and associative memory*. Berlin: Springer-Verlag.

McNaughton B.L., Chen L.L. & Markus E.J. 1991. Dead-reckoning, landmark learning and the sense of direction: a neurophysiological and computational hypothesis. *J. Cognit. Neurosci.* 3, 190-202.

Muller R.U., Kubie J.L., Bostock E.M., Taube J.S. & Quirk G.J. 1991. Spatial firing correlates of neurons in the hippocampal formation of freely moving rats. In: *Brain and space* (ed. J. Paillard) pp. 296-333. Oxford: Oxford University Press.

O'Keefe J. & Nadel L. 1978. *The hippocampus as a cognitive map*. Oxford: Oxford University Press.

Poucet B. 1993. Spatial cognitive maps in animals: new hypotheses on their structure and neural mechanisms. *Psychol. Rev.* 100, 163-182.

Rumhelhart D.E., Hinton G.E. & Williams R.J. 1986. Learning internal representations by error propagation. In: *Parallel distributed processing*, vol. 1 (ed. D.E. Rumhelhart & J.L. McClelland) pp. 318-362. Cambridge (Mass.): MIT press (reprinted in Anderson & Rosenfeld, 1988).

Semenov L.V. & Bures J. 1989. Vestibular stimulation disrupts acquisition of place navigation in the Morris water tank task. *Behav. Neural Biol.* 51, 346-363.

Sutherland R.J. & Dyck R.H. 1984. Place navigation by rats in a swimming pool. *Can. J. Psychol.* 38, 322-347.

Taube J.S., Muller R.U. & Ranck J.B. 1990a. Head-direction cells recorded from the postsubiculum in freely moving rats. I. Description and quantitative analysis. *J. Neurosci.* 10, 420-435.

Taube J.S., Muller R.U. & Ranck J.B. 1990b. Head-direction cells recorded from the postsubiculum in freely moving rats. II. Effects of environmental manipulations. *J. Neurosci.* 10, 436-447.

Widrow B. & Hoff M.E. 1960. Adapting switching circuits. In: *IRE WESCON Convention record,* pp. 96-104. New-york: IRE (reprinted in Anderson & Rosenfeld, 1988).

Self-organizing topographic maps and motor planning

Pietro Morasso and Vittorio Sanguineti
Department of Informatics, Systems, and Telecommunications
University of Genova, Italy
Via Opera Pia 11A, I-16145 Genova, Italy
E-mail: morasso@dist.unige.it, sangui@dist.unige.it

Abstract

The topic of interest is the coordination of multiple joints and, in particular, the motor and task planning processes which are capable to transform a concise motor intention into a detailed activation flow. We propose to look at this topic as a *pattern completion* problem, driven by a *selective attention* paradigm. We investigate self-organizing topographic maps for addressing both elements and we focus our attention on perfectly-topology preserving maps, based on competitive learning at the level of both the input weight vectors and the lateral connectivity. We show how an internal representation of Euclidean space can emerge from this process and we discuss a general way of linking self-organizing maps with cellular automata, demonstrating its usefulness for carrying out pattern completion tasks.

Topic areas: Motor control; neural networks; emergent structures; internal world models.

1   Introduction

Since movements with multiple joints imply sensory-motor patterns in different spaces, early experiments on trajectory formation addressed the question of the coordinate system in which motor plans are formulated and initiated. Is this space, that we may call the *planning space*, the *proprioceptive* space of joints and muscles or the *exteroceptive* space related to distal actions of the end-effector?

Experiments on reaching [6] hinted that planning might occur in exteroceptive coordinates because exteroceptive descriptions appear to be more invariant than the proprioceptive ones. Of course, this is not a proof that planning always takes place in such a way and, in fact, other experiments [4] were reported in which invariant features at the proprioceptive level were detected. However, the fact remains that the CNS seems to be able, at least in some circumstances, to formulate motor plans in terms of an abstraction (the exteroceptive space with Euclidean metric) without any direct sensory-motor connection to it: There are indeed no *Euclidean* sensory or motor channels and, in particular, the typical exteroceptive sensory channels (vision, audition, or even olfaction) do not give any hint of *Euclideanism*. The vestibular system is somehow an exception but it is unlikely to play a significant role in planning.

Thus it seems fair to conclude that motor planning cannot be a direct, although non-linear, sensory-motor transformation but it requires at the same time two different crucial skills: (i) the ability to build an internal abstract representation of external space and (ii) the possibility to mix it, in a task-dependent way, with more concrete representations directly linked with the sensory channels. In a sense, this is also a definition of the (fuzzy) borderline between sensory-motor reflexes and motor plans: the latter imply an intermediate and internal level of representation which can be *cognitively penetrable* whereas, in the former case, there is just a multi-level transformation of input patterns into output patterns. The borderline, however, is fuzzy as an effect of learning because overtrained movements can end-up incorporating previous planning components as mere processing levels (no more cognitively penetrable) in newly acquired reflex behaviours.

If there is not a unique space in which motor coordination is carried out, then the planning system must be *neutral* in the sense that it must have representations of sensory-motor patterns in all different spaces. We also wish to distinguish two different planning levels:

- a **motor planning** level, where complete sensory-motor patterns in different spaces are represented, and

- a **task planning** level, for selecting (during movement preparation time and/or run-time) which pattern components are *the input*, which ones are *the output*, and also for setting up a *metric* in the input-output transformation.

There is no need to assume any kind of hierarchical relation between the two levels: The former one can be considered to have a function of *pattern completion* and the latter a function of *selective attention*. The two functions are complementary and are just two aspects of the same dynamical process.

Another important aspect of (motor and task) planning is its *ecological* nature because the consequence of a plan is behavior, which implies the complex interaction of an active agent with its environment; this interaction is characterized by well structured albeit extremely complex patterns of action/reaction, efference/reafference. The traditional symbolic approach to robotic planning is defeated by the *frame problem*, i.e. the difficulty of maintaining in an explicit form valid internal representations of the world necessary for decision making because any action changes the state of the world in ways which cannot be predicted explicitly. The emphasis on the ecological nature of behavior, on the contrary, is based on the observation [1] that a behaving robot or animal has the possibility of extracting a rich repertoire of sensory-motor invariances from the flow of sensory-motor patterns and this is the powerful substrate for a sub-symbolic approach to planning.

It is also appropriate to note the apparent discrepancy between the notion of planning to be developed in the following sections and the one usually implied in the robotics and artificial intelligence literature, which is typically concerned with what we may call the *exogenous* aspects of planning: the problem of finding a sequence of steps capable of reaching a goal state, given an initial state of the world, the problem of decomposing a difficult plan into a number of sub-plans with suitable sub-goals, the problem of re-planning in case of failure, etc. In fact, we shall mainly focus our attention on the *endogenous* components of planning, such as building and maintaining *maximally coherent* sensory-motor representations in order to support selective attention and pattern completion of concise task specifications.

In particular, we wish to address the following points: (i) the emergence of an internal representation of Euclidean space as a self-organized data compression/dimensionality reduction mechanism, (ii) the process of self-supervised learning (circular-reaction) for capturing sensory-motor invariants and thus building a distributed representation of the task space, and (iii) the implementation of plans as navigation processes in such a space. The modelling tools that we intend to use for this purpose are derived from the large class of self-organizing maps [3] because, in general, these models are compatible with self-supervised learning and the Hebb's rule, typical of all *SOM* models, is biologically plausible. In particular, the specific *SOM* models that we propose for motor/task planning are characterized by their ability of adapting to the hidden structure of the input-output patterns (a concept, as explained in the following, of *perfect topology preservation*) and carry out pattern completion by means of a local computation scheme which exploits the learned topology of the map and implements a process of gradient-descent in a *task-dependent potential*

field.

2 Self-organizing exteroceptive map

In this section, we show how a Euclidean internal representation of external space can emerge from the self-supervised learning of a sensory map which integrates exteroceptive afferences from different modalities, such as vision and audition. A generic *SOM* can be treated as a graph $\mathcal{G}$ as follows (see figure 1):

- $\mathcal{G} = (\mathcal{N}, \mathcal{A})$

- $\mathcal{N} = \{\mathcal{N}_i = 1, 2, ... m\}$ is a set of neurons

- $\mathcal{A} = \{a_{ij};\ \ i, j = 1, 2, ... m\}$ is the connection matrix ($a_{ij} = 1$ if $\mathcal{N}_i$ and $\mathcal{N}_j$ are connected and $a_{ij} = 0$ otherwise).

- The neurons in the map are activated by a common input vector $\mathbf{x} \in \mathcal{M}^k \subset \mathcal{R}^n$ which is defined in an n-dimensional *embedding space* but is actually varying in a lower-dimensional *curvilinear manifold* ($k < n$).

- Each neuron $\mathcal{N}_i = (\tilde{\mathbf{x}}_i, u_i)$ is characterized by two quantities: the center of its receptive field $\tilde{\mathbf{x}}_i \in \mathcal{R}^n$ (also called a prototype vector) and an activation level u_i, usually normalised in the $0 - 1$ range, which is determined by an activation function $u_i = u_i(\mathbf{x})$.

- The prototype vectors are learned with the Hebbian rule

$$\Delta\tilde{\mathbf{x}}_i = \eta(\mathbf{x} - \tilde{\mathbf{x}}_i)u_i(\mathbf{x}) \qquad (1)$$

where the input patterns $\mathbf{x}$ are sampled from a source characterized by an (unknown) probabilistic distribution $p(\mathbf{x})$, with its support on the (unknown) manifold $\mathcal{M}$.

SOM models differ mainly for the connectivity pattern and the activation function[1]. For example, the standard Kohonen maps have a fixed connectivity (typically a 2D regular lattice) which guarantees some degree of topology preservation but only in some cases. On the contrary, for multi-sensory data fusion we need *perfect* topology preservation, a concept which has been recently formalized by Martinetz [5]. This requires to use Hebbian learning in two ways:

- A competition among weights according to the equation above, with an activation function which is a decreasing function of the dissimilarity between the input pattern $\mathbf{x}$ and the receptive field center $\tilde{\mathbf{x}}_i$.

---

[1]In our studies, we used a softmax function which is a normalized Gaussian $u_i(\mathbf{x}) = g_i(\mathbf{x}) / \sum_j g_j(\mathbf{x})$, with $g_i(\mathbf{x}) = exp(-\|\mathbf{x} - \tilde{\mathbf{x}}_i\|^2 / 2\sigma^2)$. It is a normalized function in the sense that the activation pattern over the whole map is a partition of unity: $\sum_i u_i(\mathbf{x}) = 1$.

- A competition among connections, which consists, for each input pattern, of selecting the two most responding neurons and incrementing the corresponding connection strength against a general decay term.

At the end of training, the database of prototype vectors or *codebook* $\mathcal{C} = \{\tilde{\mathbf{x}}_i; \ i = 1, ...m\}$ tesselates the input manifold $\mathcal{M}$ into m Voronoi hyper-polygons
$$\mathcal{V}_i = \{\mathbf{x} : \|\mathbf{x} - \tilde{\mathbf{x}}_i\| < \|\mathbf{x} - \tilde{\mathbf{x}}_j\|, \forall j\}$$
$$\mathcal{M} = \cup_{i=1}^{m} \mathcal{V}_i$$
which are approximately equi-probable, under the input distribution, as a consequence of the competition among weights. The competition among connections guarantees a perfect topology preservation in the sense that it generates a subset of the Delaunay triangulation (induced Delaunay triangulation, as defined by [5]) compatible with the topology of the manifold: $a_{ij} = 1$ if and only if the corresponding Voronoi polygons are *neighbors* in $\mathcal{M}$. From the biological point of view, the underlying hypothesis is that the formal neuron $\mathcal{N}_i$ is representative of cortical microcolumns in association areas of the cerebral cortex. The learning procedure described above suggests a mechanism for shifting the receptive field centers of the columns and, at the same time, strengthening/weakening their lateral connections.

2.1 Estimation of the map dimensionality

After training the map with the extended competitive technique explained above, the dimensionality of the underlying manifold is implicitly encoded by the connectivity pattern of the map. How can it be recovered (or discovered)? Although the learned tessellation is generally irregular, the theory of regular high-density tessellations in high-dimensional vector spaces is useful for attempting a heuristic answer to the question. The theory is concerned with the problem of packing the largest number of equal hyper-spheres in a given hyper-volume. In particular, a useful notion is that of *osculating* or *kissing* number, i.e. the maximum number of hyperspheres which are touched by a given sphere in a dense regular packing. This number c has been found exactly only in a limited number of dimensions, but it can be evaluated numerically for all the other dimensions; in any case, it grows quickly with the number n of dimensions[2].

In the case of regular lattices extended indefinitely, it is immediate to observe that the osculating number is coincident with the number of connections of each node of the Delanay triangulation induced by the distribution

---

[2]In one dimension, there is only one type of regular lattice, with $c = 2$. In 2 dimensions, the densest lattice is exagonal and $c = 6$. In 3 dimensions, the densest lattice has $c = 12$ and after that the first regular lattice to be well understood is in 8 dimensions (Gosset lattice), which has $c = 240$. Another quite remarkable structure is found in 24 dimensions (Leech lattice) which has $c = 196560$: lower dimensional lattices can be considered as sections of the Leech lattice, whereas the geometry of higher dimensional lattices is still poorly understood.

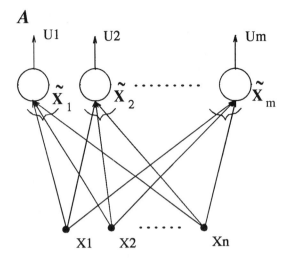

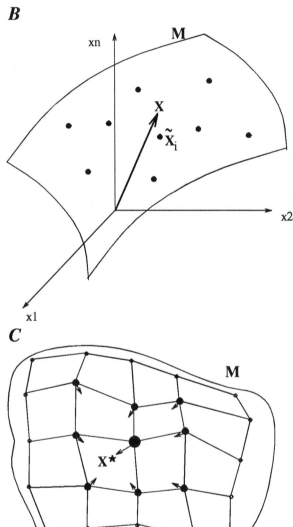

Figure 1: SOM. A: architecture; B: relation to the input manifold; C: Hebbian learning

of sphere centers. With non-regular lattices we cannot say anything rigorously, but we wish to propose the following

conjecture: *unless the lattice is not too irregular, the average connectivity of the Delaunay triangulation, which is a side-effect of the self-organization process, is a good indicator of the dimensionality of the underlying manifold.*

2.2 Emergence of an Euclidean representation of exteroceptive space

The explicit estimation of the dimensionality of the map is a natural self-organizing mechanism for discovering the topology of the exteroceptive sensory space and thus building an internal representation. In the spirit of *circular reaction* [8], we may assume that an input stimulus, with varying position P in the external space generates a multi-sensory array vector $\mathbf{x}$ with visual and acoustic components. In many cases, this stimulus is generated actively by the agent when watching his hand in motion and listening to the sounds determined by impacts with environment (see figure 2). The embedding space of $\mathbf{x}$ is high-dimensional but the physical process which originates the visual-acoustic patterns is obviously characterized by a 3-dimensional geometry and this *hidden* or implicit regularity is automatically detected by the self-organization process. Thus, we may expect that, on average, each node will be attributed 12 links, structuring the map as a 3-dimensional manifold.

Remarkably, this internal representation of the Euclidean space does not need any kind of abstract systems of coordinates but is based on the topology of the pattern of connectivity of the map of neurons, i.e. an analogical type of representation. An interesting side-effect of this mechanism is that it does not need to be spatially uniform; rather, the spatial resolution will tend to follow the non-uniformity of the probabilistic distribution of the input patterns, a typical behavior of all *SOM* models which well mirros the amplification phenomena know in different topographic maps of the cerebral cortex.

2.3 Self-organization and cellular automata

A self-organized map with a perfectly topology preserving pattern of connectivity is an ideal substrate for carrying out complex computational tasks in an analogic way, in the spirit of cellular automata. Cellular automata [2] are distributed dynamical systems in which space, time, and state variables are discrete. CAs are characterized by regular lattices of equal computing elements with a deterministic and local interaction rule. A SOM can be treated as a CA by extending the computational features of each processing element, necessary for supporting competitive learning, with local interaction rules

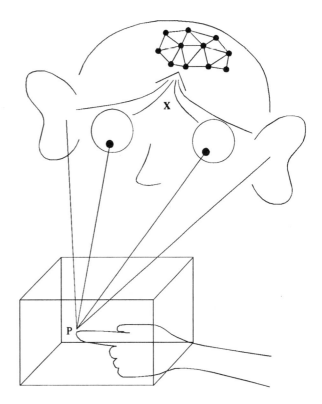

Figure 2: Schematic representation of circular reaction, with emergence of an internal representation of external space.

which may support "interesting" computational processes at the map level. Differently from standard CAs, in the CA derived from a SOM (we may call it *self-organized cellular automaton*) the lattice of computing elements is not regular and externally imposed but is the result of a learning process. Moreover, interesting computations in the specific context of motor/task planning are likely to require continuous and not discrete state variables[3]. Among the many problems which can be solved by such a hybrid (neural + cellular) architecture, here we focus on the following: distributed gradient descent.

Distributed gradient descent.
On the trained map, any given pattern $\mathbf{x}$ is represented by a *population code* $\mathcal{P}$, which is a set of active neurons clustered around the *winner*: $\mathcal{P} = \{\mathcal{N}_i; i \in \mathcal{I}(i_{win})\}$, where $i_{win} = argmin_i \|\mathbf{x} - \tilde{\mathbf{x}}_i\|$ and $\mathcal{I}(i)$ is the set of neighbors of $\mathcal{N}_i$ on the map.

From $\mathcal{P}$ it is possible to recover the pattern as follows: $\mathbf{x} \approx \sum_i \tilde{\mathbf{x}}_i \, u_i$. For gradient descent, the problem consists of distributing on the map a penalty function or potential $\varepsilon = \varepsilon(\mathbf{x})$ and then driving the population code $\mathcal{P} = \mathcal{P}(t)$ of the current pattern $\mathbf{x} = \mathbf{x}(t)$ through the map, following the gradient of ε until equilibrium is reached. In

---

[3]CAs with continuous state variables are more appropriately named *coupled map lattices* [2].

terms of CA dynamics, $\mathcal{P}$ can be considered as a *soliton* and thus the problem is to express a local interaction rule of the general type $z_i(t+1) = f(\{z_j(t); j \in \mathcal{I}(i)\}$ which moves the soliton along the gradient. ($z_i(t)$ is a local state vector for neuron $\mathcal{N}_i$ and $f(\cdot)$ is the local iterative map.)

Let us suppose that the potential function is sampled for the values of the argument which correspond to the prototype vectors and such samples are made available to each processing element of the map: $\{\tilde{\varepsilon}_i = \varepsilon(\tilde{\mathbf{x_i}}); \ i = 1, 2, ...m\}$.
Elsewhere [7], we showed that this problem can be solved by integrating over time the following equation:

$$\frac{d\mathbf{x}}{dt} = \eta \sum_i (\mathbf{x}(t) - \tilde{\mathbf{x}}_i) \ \tilde{\varepsilon}_i \ u_i(t) \qquad (2)$$

where $u_i(t) = u_i(\mathbf{x}(t))$ is computed using the softmax activation function.

This is not a local interaction with implicit recurrent connections. The non-locality is determined by several elements: (i) the definition of the softmax function (the normalization factor is extended to all the units of the map), (ii) the computation of the output pattern $\mathbf{x}$ (which requires to know the activation level of all the units; this is a global feedback from the output of the map to the input of each unit), and (iii) the dynamic computation itself, which requires a bank of integrators outside the map.

The locality problem can be overcome, as explained in the following, with an approximate algorithm which exploits the knowledge about tessellation of the workspace into Voronoi domains $\mathcal{V}_i$, one around each prototype vector $\tilde{\mathbf{x}}_i$.

- First of all, we need to locally code the population code of a map. For this purpose, we can simply use two bits of information for each cell: b_i and s_i. The former one denotes the current *winner* in the map and the latter one identifies the first neighbors of the winner. Remarkably, the identification of the winner (and as a consequence of its neighbors) does not require a global search but can be decided locally, as stated in the following lemma:
  Lemma: *In a self-organized map with perfect topology preservation and localized population code, the winner is identified by the fact that its activation level is higher than that of all its neighbors.*

- The population code is assumed to be limited to the immediate neighborhood of the winner and this requires to slightly modify the activation function:

$$u_i = u_i(\mathbf{x}) = \frac{g_i(\mathbf{x})}{\sum_{j \in \mathcal{I}(i)} g_j(\mathbf{x})(b_j + s_j)} \ (b_i + s_i) \qquad (3)$$

where $\mathcal{I}(i)$ is the set of direct neighbors of neuron $\mathcal{N}_i$. In this way, only the winner and its immediate neighbors have non-zero activation for each time instant, but still we keep the total activation equal to 1.

- The current winner ($b_i = 1$) can estimate locally $\mathbf{x}$ and $\dot{\mathbf{x}}$, without any global operation:

$$\mathbf{x} = (\sum_{j \in I(i)} \tilde{\mathbf{x}}_j u_j) b_i \qquad (4)$$

$$\dot{\mathbf{x}} = \eta (\sum_{j \in I(i)} (\mathbf{x}(t) - \tilde{\mathbf{x}}_j) \tilde{\varepsilon}_j u_j(t)) \ b_i \qquad (5)$$

The two vectors are passed by the winner to its neighbors in order to allow them to update their activation values.

- In conclusion, the local rule computes for each time step the following quantities ($b_i, s_i, u_i, \mathbf{x}, \dot{\mathbf{x}},$) and then propagates the state of the cell from time t to time $t + 1$: $\mathbf{x}(t+1) = \mathbf{x}(t) + k \ \dot{\mathbf{x}}(t) \longrightarrow u_i(t+1)$.

The CA-like implementation of gradient descent is attractive because it is biologically plausible, due to the locality of connections, and it exploits in a very natural way the topological knowledge which is an intrinsic fall-out of self-supervised learning in the real-world.

As regards the specific problem of the internal representation of external Euclidean space, a distributed gradient descent process could be used for the generation of virtual trajectories. Suppose that, in a target-reaching problem, the distributed potential is monotonically related to the distance from a "target". Then, gradient-following will generate a trajectory to the target. Interestingly, the shape of the trajectory can be controlled by means of modifications of the potential function $\varepsilon = \varepsilon(\mathbf{x})$: an isotropic or radially symmetric function will tend to generate straight trajectories, whereas a non-isotropic function will curve the trajectory in many possile ways. If we look at gradient descent as a mechanism for finding the shortest path to a target, compatibly with given constraints, then the choice of the potential function is equivalent to the choice of a metric in the motor space and trajectory formation is the process of computing geodesics in that space.

3 Self-organizing proprioceptive map

The purpose of a self-organizing proprioceptive map is to establish an internal topographic representation of articular and muscular variables as the exteroceptive map is meant to build an internal representation of the external space. The map can be trained by an agent in a self-supervised way by generating spontaneous movements appropriately distributed over the whole workspace and detecting the consequent (coherent) sensory-motor vectors $\mathbf{y} \in \mathcal{M}^r \subset \mathcal{R}^l$, where $\mathcal{R}^l$ is the embedding space with a large number of articular and muscular components and $\mathcal{M}$ is the underlying manifold of much lower dimensionality, although probably larger than the dimensionality of the corresponding manifold in the exteroceptive space ($k < r << l$). Of course, we know such a dimensionality, which is equal to the number of mechanical degrees of freedom, but we do not need to assume that this knowledge is available a priori to the brain. Rather, we can expect that the self-organization process, already described in the previous section, is able to discover it and embody it in the topology of connections.

The result of learning is a network $\mathcal{G}_p = (\mathcal{N}_p, \mathcal{A}_p)$ which contains a database or codebook $\mathcal{C}_p = (\tilde{\mathbf{y}}_i; \ i = 1, 2, ...m)$ and a pattern of connectivity $\mathcal{A}_p$. Each vector prototype of the codebook is a concise representation of a specific configuration of the body-part represented in the map and thus the codebook can be considered as a distributed and analogic *body-schema* [7]. Similarly to the exteroceptive map $\mathcal{G}_e$ discussed in the previous section, also for the proprioceptive map $\mathcal{G}_p$ we can define interesting computational tasks such as gradient descent in a task-related potential field. For example, we can designate a target point in the proprioceptive space and distribute a potential function on the map monotonically related to the "distance" from that point. The output of such a process has an obvious relevance for motor planning: it gives coordinated patterns of muscle-contractions and, at the same time, it predicts the consequent patterns of joint rotations. These patterns are represented in a distributed way by means of an island of activation (population code $\mathcal{P}_p(t)$), travelling over the map. A CA-like mechanism can implement it in a distributed way by means of local interactions, consistently with what was said in the previous section.

3.1 Selective attention and pattern completion

What we further need is a method for integrating articular/muscular patterns with abstract representations of exteroceptive space. This can be obtained by linking the two maps, $\mathcal{G}_e$ and $\mathcal{G}_p$, by means of suitable cross-connections, learned during the same process of self-supervised learning of coherent sensory-motor patterns which builds $\mathcal{G}_e$ and $\mathcal{G}_p$ in the first place. A plausible model could use the same mechanism of competition among weights, mentioned in the previous section. As a result of this, we may expect that in general redundant systems, there will not be a one-to-one connection: each neuron in $\mathcal{G}_p$ will be linked with one neuron in $\mathcal{G}_e$, but neurons in $\mathcal{G}_e$ will be linked with many neurons of $\mathcal{G}_p$ (this set of neurons share the same position of the end-effector or, more abstractly, define the null-space of the exteroceptive/proprioceptive mapping).

The purpose of the cross-connections, together with appropriate processing, is to keep the two maps in register, i.e. to guarantee that for each time instant the two

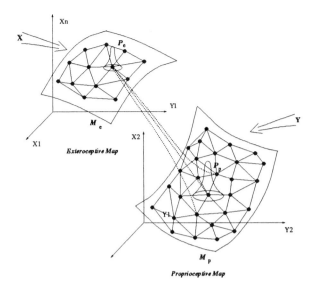

Figure 3: Interaction of an exteroceptive and proprioceptive map.

population codes, $\mathcal{P}_e(t)$ and $\mathcal{P}_p(t)$, are compatible. In particular, we may think of a mutual attractor dynamics: whatever happens in one map is reflected in the other as an attractive field towards a situation of compatible population codes. This kind of dynamic invariance can be expressed by means of mutual potential fields: each neuron in one map transmits to the cross-connected neuron(s) in the other map a penalty value inversely related to its activation level. Thus, if the population code in one map moves under the action of a task-related potential field, then the mutual field forces the population code in the other map to follow (see figure 3).

For example, in the simple case of a reaching movement, we may assume that the task specifies a target in the exteroceptive space and this is transformed (with a mechanism which is outside the present modelling framework) into a distribution of potential values in the $\mathcal{G}_e$. Following the gradient, $\mathcal{P}_e$ (limited to a small cluster of neurons) starts moving towards the target and it is reflected onto a much larger cluster of neurons in $\mathcal{G}_p$ due to redundancy. However, the current proprioceptive state, coded by $\mathcal{P}_p$, automatically restricts the cluster and drives the musculo-articular patterns along a path, compatible with the exteroceptive path. The indeterminacy is implicitly solved by gradient-descent process which always chooses the shortest path in relation with the current state and the shape of the potential field.

In the previous example, the *input* is the target (defined in the exteroceptive space) and the *output* is a flow of musculo-articular patterns (defined in the proprioceptive space). But we are not restricted to this: We can define *targets, obstacles* and other significant *cognitive objects* in both spaces, alternatively or simultaneously, and the global dynamics will attempt to complete the plan in a way which is most consistent with the expressed set of constraints. What we called selective attention is the preparation process of distributing on the two maps potential functions which capture the essential aspects of a task.

We conclude this section by noting a degree of similarity between our modeling framework, in which we attempt to learn and represent not a specific input-output transformation but a whole family of it, and the one proposed by [9] in his model PSOM (Parametric Self-Organized Map). A difference is that his operator of selective attention is a projection operator while, in our case, it has to do with the choice of a potential field.

4   Conclusions

The purpose of this paper was to outline a computational framework which could possibly support the coordination of multiple joints in a sufficiently flexible and general way. The kind of complexity which is addressed is far from both the peripheral and the cognitive processes but somehow is able to understand the "language" of both of them. Thus, we think we outlined the associative functions which might underly sensory-motor coordination.

References

[1] J.J. Gibson. *The perception of the visual world.* Houghton Mifflin, Boston, 1950.

[2] H. Gutowitz. *Cellular automata, theory and practice.* The MIT Press, Cambridge, USA, 1991.

[3] T. Kohonen. Self organizing formation of topologically correct feature maps. *Biological Cybernetics,* 43:59–69, 1982.

[4] F. Lacquaniti, C. Terzuolo, and P. Viviani. *Acta Psychologica,* 54:115–130, 1983.

[5] T. Martinetz. Competitive hebbian learning rule forms perfectly topology preserving maps. In S. Gielen and B. Kappen, editors, *International Conference on Artificial Neural Networks,* pages 427–434, London, September 1993. Springer-Verlag.

[6] P. Morasso. Spatial control of arm movements. *Exp. Brain Res.,* 42:223–227, 1981.

[7] P. Morasso and V. Sanguineti. Self-organizing body-schema for motor planning. *J. Motor Behavior,* 1993.

[8] J. Piaget. *The origin of intelligence in children.* Norton, New York, 1963.

[9] H. Ritter. Parametrized self-organizing maps. In S. Gielen and B. Kappen, editors, *Proceedings of the International Conference on Artificial Neural Networks,* pages 568–575, Amsterdam, September 1993. Springer-Verlag.

The Effect of Memory Length on the Foraging Behavior of a Lizard

Sharoni Shafir and Jonathan Roughgarden
Department of Biological Sciences
Stanford University, Stanford, CA 94305-5020
sharoni@ecology.stanford.edu, rough@pangea.stanford.edu

Abstract

A technique is proposed for measuring the time-frame of past experiences over which a real or artificial animal bases its decisions. Simulations were motivated by the foraging ecology of the neotropical lizard genus *Anolis*. Lizards foraged according to a simple decision rule that determined whether insects that appeared at different distances from the lizard's perch were pursued or ignored. Different individuals were provided with different memory lengths. The cutoff radius beyond which insects were not pursued more closely approached the optimal cutoff radius for lizards with longer memories than for those with shorter memories. However, lizards with shorter memories adjusted their cutoff radius more quickly than those with longer memories when insect abundance changed. The adjusted cutoff radius began to stabilize at its new value precisely the number of episodes following the change in insect abundance equal to the lizard's memory length. This pattern held for different memory lengths and insect abundances. It is suggested that measuring how long it takes an animal to begin stabilizing its behavior may be an effective technique for determining memory length.

1   Introduction

An animal (real or artificial) can only learn from experience if it remembers past events. The optimal relative weighting of past and present events depends on the manner in which the environment is changing [14, 7]. But the cost to the animal, in terms of a measurable currency of reproductive fitness, of having suboptimal memory is difficult to assess from general models. In a previous paper we used simulations to evaluate the effect of memory length on fitness, measured as the number of days it takes a female to produce an egg [11]. The model was motivated by the foraging behavior of *Anolis* lizards, a large neo-tropical genus for which extensive ecological data are available. Here, we present simulations that could be used to assess the memory length employed by a "flesh and blood" foraging lizard.

2   A Lizard's Dilemma

Trunk-ground anoles "sit-and-wait" on the bottom of tree trunks and scan the ground below them. When an insect appears nearby, they dart in pursuit, then return to their perch. To maximize rate of net energy intake a lizard should chase close insects and ignore distant insects, because chasing an insect that is a short distance away is energetically less expensive and takes less time than chasing one that is farther away. The lizard must determine what is the cutoff radius beyond which it should not pursue prey.

2.1   The Theoretical Solution

The cutoff radius that maximizes rate of net energy intake, E/T, depends on the abundance of insects in the environment. When insects are rare the optimal cutoff radius is greater than when insects are abundant. In a simple environment with one insect type, the cutoff radius, r_c, that maximizes the long-term rate of net energy intake is:

$$r_c = \frac{-\frac{2(e_p-e_w)}{\pi ae} + \left(\frac{3ev}{2\pi ae} + \sqrt{\left(\frac{3ev}{2\pi ae}\right)^2 + \left(\frac{2(e_p-e_w)}{\pi ae}\right)^3}\right)^{2/3}}{\left(\frac{3ev}{2\pi ae} + \sqrt{\left(\frac{3ev}{2\pi ae}\right)^2 + \left(\frac{2(e_p-e_w)}{\pi ae}\right)^3}\right)^{1/3}} \quad (1)$$

where a is the abundance of prey in units of prey per m^2 per time, e is the insect's energy content, e_w is the energy expended per time while sitting perched and looking for prey, e_p is the energy expended per time while pursuing a prey item, and v is the lizard's speed. The derivation of this solution can be found in [10], where the model is also extended to multiple prey types, and to prey that can escape.

2.2   The Problem of Attainability

One of the main criticisms of optimal foraging theory is that attaining the optimal strategy is often well beyond an animal's cognitive abilities [8]. It is quite inconceivable that a lizard could solve cubic equations and calculate cube roots.

Genetic programming is one approach that has been successful in demonstrating how an animal with limited computational abilities could evolve a foraging strategy that is close to the optimal one [6]. Another approach, that is discussed here, is developing simple rules-of-thumb that an animal could follow and that yield close to optimal behavior.

A growing body of experimental evidence suggests that many animals have a concept of number, time, space and rate, and that they can perform abstract operations isomorphic to addition, subtraction, and division [3, 4]. A simple decision rule proposed by Roughgarden [10] requires a lizard no more than the ability to perform such basic operations. In simulations, the average rate of net energy intake of a lizard that follows this rule and that remembers all its prey encounters indefinitely into the past seems to converge on the maximum possible rate.

A lizard need not have a very large memory size to approach the maximum possible energy yield. Gains diminish steeply with increased memory. A lizard that can remember only ten past insect appearances can adapt its foraging behavior to be almost optimal and gain a three-fold increase in fertility compared to a lizard with no memory [11].

2.3 A Rule of Thumb

When the nth insect appears in the lizard's field of vision the lizard is assumed to make two calculations. It calculates what its long-term mean E/T would be if it pursued the insect ($E/T_p^{[n]}$), and what it would be if it ignored the insect ($E/T_i^{[n]}$). It chooses the option that yields the higher rate.

The net energy intake from the previous m ($m \geq 1$) insect appearances, E^m, is

$$E^m = \sum_{j=1}^{m}(e^{[n-j]} - t_w^{[n-j]}e_w - t_p^{[n-j]}e_p), \quad (2)$$

and the total duration of the previous m insect appearances, T^m, is

$$T^m = \sum_{j=1}^{m}(t_w^{[n-j]} + t_p^{[n-j]}) \quad (3)$$

where t_w is the time waiting for an insect to appear since the last insect appeared, and t_p is the time to pursue the insect and return to the perch. The expected long-term mean E/T is the net energy intake in the past plus the net energy gain (or loss) from pursuing or ignoring the present insect, divided by the total time past plus the time of waiting for the present insect or of waiting and pursuing it. The equations are the following:

$$(E/T)_p^{[n]} = \frac{E^m + e^{[n]} - t_w^{[n]}e_w - t_p^{[n]}e_p}{T^m + t_w^{[n]} + t_p^{[n]}}, \quad (4)$$

and

$$(E/T)_i^{[n]} = \frac{E^m - t_w^{[n]}e_w}{T^m + t_w^{[n]}}. \quad (5)$$

Memory is treated as a window of the last m insect appearances. The larger m is, the greater is the weight given to past episodes relative to the present one. For the special case of $m = 0$, E^m and T^m equal zero.

A memory window results in a step-function weighting of the past. Different weighting functions (e.g. [13, 5]) could be incorporated into the model as a better understanding of lizard memory is gained.

3   Determining a Lizard's Memory Size

In the field, one can measure the distance at which prey are pursued (e.g. [1]) and determine the cutoff radius, r_c, which is the maximum distance a lizard will pursue prey of a specific type. Ideally, this r_c could be compared to that of simulated lizards having different memory lengths, and the best fit would reveal what was the memory length used by the real lizard. Such a method, however, would be very sensitive to the value of the model parameters used in the simulations. Also, since incremental gains in performance decrease steeply with additional memory [11], such a method would not be useful if memory length were not very small.

The technique we propose here involves tracking how a lizard changes its r_c in response to a changing environment. We simulate lizards with different memory lengths, and calculate what their r_c is when they are foraging in a stable stochastic environment. Then the environment is changed, and we monitor how r_c changes. Results of simulations of lizards with different memory lengths can be compared to how real lizards adapt their foraging distance to changes in insect abundance, in order to find the best memory length match.

Setting $(E/T)_p^{[n]}$ equal to $(E/T)_i^{[n]}$, and solving for $t_p^{[n]}$, provides the maximum time of pursuit, $t_{p,max}^{[n]}$, that would still make an insect be worth pursuing,

$$t_{p,max}^{[n]} = \frac{e^{[n]}(T^m + t_w^{[n]})}{E^m - t_w^{[n]}e_w + e_p(T^m + t_w^{[n]})}. \quad (6)$$

Half of $t_{p,max}^{[n]}$ is the time it takes to reach an insect that is at r_c. Multiplying this time by the lizard's speed yields the maximum radius to which an insect should be pursued,

$$r_c^{[n]} = \frac{vt_{p,max}^{[n]}}{2}. \quad (7)$$

4   Simulation

All the lizards foraged according to the decision rule described above (section 2.3), and were naive about the state of the environment at the beginning of each simulation, $E^{[0]} = T^{[0]} = 0$. Values for the parameters used in the model were based on available physiological and ecological data that are presented in [10].

We endowed individuals with a fixed memory length of between 0 and 100 last insect appearances (episodes), and calculated $r_c^{[n]}$ for each individual every 5 insect appearances. Insects were 2 mm long, representing a typical ant or a small fly. The lizard could see insects that appeared up to 12 meters away, within 180° in front of it. At the beginning of each simulation insects appeared at a rate of 5 per m^2 per hour. After the 125th insect the abundance was increased to 10, 20, or 40 per m^2 per hour. A simulation ended when a lizard had encountered a total of 250 insects. Each simulation of a lizard with a particular memory length was repeated 400 times for each of the three environments.

5   Results

The optimal cutoff radii in the simulated environments were 6.81, 5.75, 4.79 and 3.95 meters, for insect abundances of 5, 10, 20 and 40 insects per m^2 per hour, respectively. These radii are represented by dashed horizontal lines in Figure 1. When insect abundance was stable, r_c of lizards with longer memories asymptoted at values closer to the optimal r_c than that of lizards with shorter memories. When insect abundance changed, however, it took more time for lizards with longer memories to asymptote at the new r_c.

Figure 1. The cutoff radius, r_c, up to which a lizard foraging according to the rule of thumb would pursue an insect if it remembered the previous 0 (a), 1 (b), 10 (c) or 100 (d) episodes. Insect abundance during the first 125 episodes was 5 insects per m^2 per hour. After the 125th episode insect abundance changed to 10 (open circles), 20 (closed circles) or 40 (diamonds) insects per m^2 per hour. Each data point is the mean r_c of 400 individuals at a particular episode in a particular environment. Standard errors were too small to be shown in the figure. Since insect abundance was the same during the first half of all the simulations, only one set of data points is shown (open circles, episodes 0 - 125). Horizontal dashed lines represent the optimal cutoff radius for insect abundances of 5, 10, 20 and 40 insects per m^2 per hour, from greatest to smallest radius, respectively.

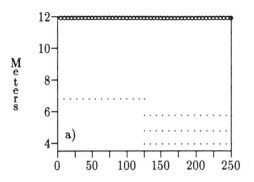

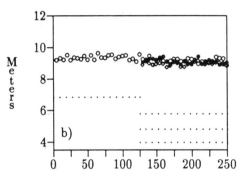

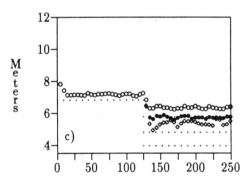

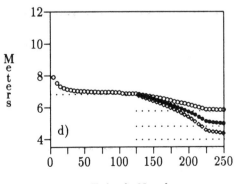

Episode Number

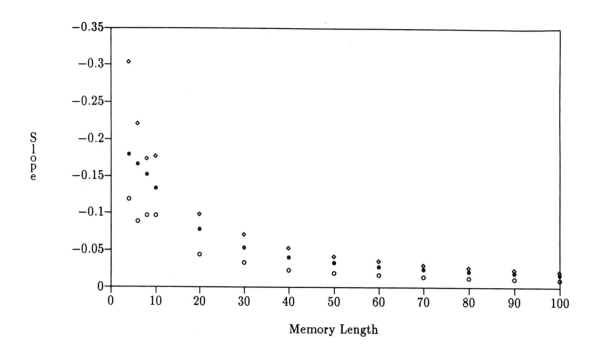

Figure 2. The rate of change (meters per episode) of the cutoff radius, r_c, following an increase in insect abundance. Insect abundance changed from 5 insects per m^2 per hour to 10 (open circles), 20 (closed circles) or 40 (diamonds) insects per m^2 per hour. Each data point is the mean rate of change of r_c of 400 individuals with a particular memory length.

With no memory, a lizard would pursue prey up to 11.94 meters (Fig. 1a); the energetic cost of pursuing farther prey was greater than the energy that could be assimilated from a 2 mm insect. With a memory of just one previous episode, a lizard greatly reduced the maximum distance it would pursue an insect (Fig. 1b). A memory of 10 episodes allowed a lizard to forage close to optimally when insect abundance was low. But as insect abundance increased, the difference between the lizard's r_c and the optimum increased (Fig. 1c). A memory of 100 episodes sufficed for a lizard to adjust its foraging distance close to the optimum within ecologically realistic insect abundances (Fig. 1d).

The r_c changed most quickly from when the environment changed until exactly m episodes later. This was most noticeable with the larger memory lengths. For $m = 10$ or 100, for example, a sharp change of slope occured at 10 or 100 episodes after the insect abundance was increased (Figs. 1c and 1d, respectively). For a particular memory size, the abrupt change in the rate at which r_c approached its asymptotic value occured at precisely the same point regardless of the value of the new insect abundance.

We calculated the rate of change of r_c during the period of greatest change by dividing the difference between r_c in episode 125 and r_c in episode $125 + m$ by m.

Figure 2 shows the mean values of these slopes in the three simulated environments. Lizards with longer memories changed their r_c more slowly than lizards with shorter memories. The difference in the slopes was especially pronounced for memory lengths of up to about 30. The rate of change of r_c was greater when the difference in insect abundance between the first and second environments was greater.

6   Discussion

The simulations illustrate the tradeoff between the ability to forage more efficiently in a stable environment by making decisions based on more distant events, and the ability to adapt more quickly to a changing environment by considering only more recent events. For example, by the 10th insect appearance after the rate of insect appearance increased, the cutoff radius to which lizards with a memory of 10 previous episodes would chase prey was closer to the optimal value than that of lizards that remembered the previous 100 episodes. But after about the 75th insect after the environment changed, the r_c of lizards with the longer memory was closer to the optimum than that of lizards with the shorter memory.

For a particular complex environment the optimal memory size could be estimated by comparing the fitness of individuals with different memory lengths that forage in that environment, as we have done for a stable environment [11].

The main finding of the simulations presented here is that r_c began to stabilize precisely m episodes after insect abundance changed, where m is the number of past insect appearances that a lizard remembered. This pattern is similar to that predicted by Cowie and Krebs [2] for the patch giving-up time of a bird with a fixed memory window.

The manner in which r_c changes in response to a change in insect abundance suggests a technique for measuring the number of past episodes that real lizards incorporate into making foraging decisions. The rate at which insects appear and the distance to which a lizard pursues prey could be measured. Then insects abundance could be increased by adding insects around the lizard's perch. The time it takes the lizard to stabilize on a new critical foraging radius, and the rate at which the lizard changes its foraging radius, would reflect how far back it remembers when adapting its foraging strategy. We are currently conducting such field experiments. Earlier work revealed that anoles do learn to modify their foraging behavior based on past experience [12].

Measuring the time between when the environment changes until behavior begins to stabilize in the new environment, and the rate at which the behavior changes, may be an effective technique for assessing the time frame over which an animal or a robot bases its decisions. This approach complements others that have been applied successfully in studying foraging behavior. Observed behavior can be compared to results of simulations of animals with different memory lengths to find the best match [9], or the behavior at the nth episode of different animals that foraged in similar environments that only differed m episodes previously can be compared to determine if that n^{th} minus m episode affected the animals' decisions at the nth episode [13]. The most effective method for determining the memory length employed by an organism in a particular situation would depend on the characteristics of the system studied.

Acknowledgments

This research was supported by a grant from Interval Research Corporation.

References

[1] D. J. Bullock, H. M. Jury, and P. G. Evans. Foraging ecology in the lizard *Anolis oculatus* (Iguanidae) from Dominica, West Indies. *Journal of Zoology (London)*, 230:19–30, 1993.

[2] R. J. Cowie and J. R. Krebs. Optimal foraging in patchy environments. In R. M. Anderson, B. D. Turner, and L. R. Taylor, editors, *Population Dynamics*, pages 183–205. Blackwell Scientific Publications, Oxford, 1979.

[3] C. R. Gallistel. Animal cognition: the representation of space, time and number. *Annual Review of Psychology*, 40:155–189, 1989.

[4] C. R. Gallistel. *The Organization of Learning*. MIT Press, Cambridge, 1990.

[5] A. Kacelnik and R. Krebs. Learning to exploit patchily distributed food. In R. M. Sibly and R. H. Smith, editors, *Behavioural Ecology: Ecological Consequences of Adaptive Behaviour*, pages 189–205. Blackwell Scientific Publications, Oxford, 1985.

[6] J. R. Koza, J. P. Rice, and J. Roughgarden. Evolution of food-foraging strategies for the caribbean *Anolis* lizard using genetic programming. *Adaptive Behavior*, 1:171–199, 1992.

[7] J. M. McNamara and A. I. Houston. Memory and the efficient use of information. *Journal of Theoretical Biology*, 125:385–395, 1987.

[8] G. J. Pierce and J. G. Ollason. Eight reasons why optimal foraging theory is a complete waste of time. *Oikos*, 49:111–118, 1987.

[9] L. Real, S. Ellner, and L. D. Harder. Short-term energy maximization and risk-aversion in bumble bees: A reply to Possingham et al. *Ecology*, 71:1625–1628, 1990.

[10] J. Roughgarden. Anolis *Lizards of the Caribbean: Ecology, Evolution, and Plate Tectonics*. Oxford University Press, Oxford, In Press.

[11] S. Shafir and J. Roughgarden. The effect of memory length on individual fitness in a lizard. In R. Belew and M. Mitchell, editors, *Plastic Individuals in Evolving Populations*. In Press.

[12] S. Shafir and J. Roughgarden. Instrumental discrimination conditioning of *Anolis cristatellus* in the field with food as a reward. *Caribbean Journal of Science*, In Press.

[13] I. A. Todd and A. Kacelnik. Psychological mechanisms and the Marginal Value Theorem: dynamics of scalar memory for travel time. *Animal Behaviour*, 46:765–775, 1993.

[14] L. A. Zhivotovsky, A. Bergman, and M. W. Feldman. A model of individual behavior in a fluctuating environment. In R. Belew and M. Mitchell, editors, *Plastic Individuals in Evolving Populations*. In Press.

CHARACTERIZATION OF ENVIRONMENTS

The blind breeding the blind:
Adaptive behavior without looking

Peter M. Todd, Stewart W. Wilson
The Rowland Institute for Science
100 Edwin H. Land Boulevard
Cambridge, MA 02142 USA
ptodd@spo.rowland.org
wilson@smith.rowland.org

Anil B. Somayaji
Department of Mathematics
MIT
Cambridge, MA 02139 USA
somayaji@mit.edu

Holly A. Yanco
MIT AI Lab
545 Technology Square
Cambridge, MA 02139 USA
holly@ai.mit.edu

Abstract

Sensors and internal states are often considered necessary components of any adaptively behaving organism, providing the information needed to adapt a creature's behavior in response to conditions in its external or internal environment. But adaptive, survival-enhancing behavior is possible even in simple simulated creatures lacking all direct contact with their environment -- evolutionarily shaped blind action may suffice to keep a population of creatures alive and reproducing. In this paper, we consider the evolution of the behavioral repertoires of such sensor-less creatures in response to environments of various types. Different spatial and temporal distributions of food result in the evolution of very different behavioral strategies, including the use of looping movements as time-keepers in these otherwise cognitively-challenged creatures. Exploring the level of adaptiveness available in even such simple creatures as these serves to establish a baseline to which the adaptive behavior of animats with sensors and internal states can be compared.

1 Introduction

Adaptive behavior is usually thought of as behavior that can change in response to conditions in an organism's external or internal environment, with the result that the organism's survival is enhanced. As Meyer and Guillot (1991, p. 2) have put this, "In a changing, unpredictable, and more or less threatening environment, the behavior of an animal is adaptive as long as the behavior allows the animal to survive." Almost universally, sensory systems are assumed to be the organism's link with conditions in its external environment, allowing it to respond adaptively to the situation in which it finds itself. Adaptive behavior can also be generated as a consequence of internal conditions, as Meyer and Guillot point out; homeostatic mechanisms that sense an organism's internal state with reference to some desired fixed point can cause behavior that will lead to a return to

that fixed point. These sorts of adaptive responses to environmental conditions, the kinds of things that nervous systems and computer circuits do, form the basis of research on adaptive behavior. Without some way of knowing what's out (or in) there, without knowledge of the prevailing conditions to which behavior *should* adapt, how can there be any adaptive behavior?

In this paper, we construct a series of "changing, unpredictable, and more or less threatening environments" populated by simple simulated creatures that have *no* sensors nor internal states, and yet still manage to survive and prosper in their worlds. Through our simulation system, *SPO* (*S*imulation of *P*rimitive *O*rganisms), we demonstrate that, at least according to the definition given in the previous paragraph, adaptive behavior *is* possible without any knowledge of the environment. True, the behavior of any individual creature is fixed throughout its lifetime and does not change in response to any internal or external stimuli, so that in the strictest sense the use of the term "adaptive" is arguable. But the creatures still behave in a way particularly suited to the environment they inhabit, so that we may say that their behavior is at least "adapted," if not adaptive.

In actuality, the behaviors of the creatures in the SPO system *do* change over time in response to the environment -- but only *between* individual lifetimes, rather than within them. Instead of shaping behavior through the adaptive processes of development, learning, or sensor-guided action, all of which bring about changes in the behavioral responses of an individual, we employ only the adaptive process of evolution, which brings about changes in the aggregate behavioral responses of a population of individuals. The individuals in our system each act blindly in their world (surrounded by a population of other simultaneously-acting individuals), choosing randomly according to some unchanging weighted probability distribution among a small set of actions, including eating, moving, and reproducing. Individuals who find and eat the food-energy in their world can survive and produce slightly modified offspring, while those that run out of energy will die. Over the course of time, the evolutionary process of descent with modification and selection through competition will result in a gradual tuning of the behavioral repertoires of individuals in the population. After this adaptive process has run long enough, the behaviors of individual creatures will be adapted to their particular environment.

One of the simplest ways to show that the behavior of these creatures is indeed adapted to their particular environment is to evolve several populations under *different* environmental conditions, and look for evidence that the final adapted behaviors differ as well. This is the approach we take here, constructing a variety of very simple environments, each of which is composed solely of some pattern of food placed at various locations in a square grid. The spatiotemporal structure of these environments is determined by a small set of parameters that control food growth and distribution. We then investigate how different environmental structures lead to the evolution of different adapted behavioral strategies in individual creatures. We are also interested in discovering what environmental differences do *not* lead to differences in evolved behaviors -- that is, the structural invariances that the adaptive process of evolution ignores. Separating aspects of environmental structure into those that matter for the creatures (e.g., the distribution of food in the world) and those that do not (e.g., the color of the food) is of central importance both in applying the results of this work to understanding natural systems, and in designing adaptively behaving artificial systems in light of the critical features of their operating environments.

This work thus fits into the general research program of characterizing the important features of environment structure in terms of the adaptive behavior they elicit, as outlined in Todd and Wilson (1993). By beginning with the simplest possible form of adaptive (or adapted) behavior, that of blind stateless creatures, we can establish a baseline against which the adaptiveness of sensors and internal state or memory systems will be much clearer in comparison. In the rest of this paper, we cover the results of this first foray in this research direction, beginning in the next section with a discussion of similar work on environment/creature simulations. In section 3, we present the way the world works, and the various parameters that control environment structure in this system. Section 4 covers the types of actions that creatures can perform, and the way they are chosen amongst at each time-step. In section 5, we present the results of many runs of this system, first discussing the process of adaptation of the behavioral repertoires over time (in section 5.1), and then going into more detail on the nature of the final adapted behavior patterns themselves (in section 5.2). Finally, in section 6, we draw conclusions and indicate the next steps to be taken with this work.

2 Past Work

Before going into the details of our system, it is important first to review the design and goals of recent related work on the simulation of creatures behaving in more or less naturalistic environments. Most of the systems surveyed here use "gridworld" environments composed of a square grid of locations (rather than continuous-space models) that can contain various objects in addition to the creatures. This overview should make apparent how our system differs in motivation and emphasis from past work.

Among systems that use gridworlds to model animats (artificial creatures) interacting with an environment, a significant number place only one creature in an environment at a time. The environment defines a fitness function that is used for some sort of genetic search over the space of possible behaviors of individual creatures. Systems of this type include Wilson's original animat (1985), the Genesys/Tracker system (Jefferson et al., 1992), Floreano's (1993a) work on nest-based foraging strategies, the work of Parisi, Nolfi, and Cecconi (1992) and Todd and Miller (1991a,b) on neural network-controlled creatures that evolve learning abilities, and Cecconi and Parisi's (1993) neural networks with motivational units. In AntFarm (Collins & Jefferson, 1992a), and Koza's (1992) ant colony simulations, ants within a given colony interact; however, the ants in each colony have a single common genome, and selection occurs between these single genomes based on the fitness of each colony determined in isolation. All of these systems differ from ours in that multiple creatures with different behaviors never interact in a common world, and as a result much of the richness of both social behavior and the effects of whole populations on a shared environment is left out.

The RAM system (Taylor et al., 1989) is notable in having the potential to model arbitrary interactions between multiple animals in a gridworld by representing each part of the system as a distinct computer program. The modeller chooses what features are relevant and hand-codes programs that embody them, as the model itself has almost no predetermined "biological smarts." For instance, reproduction must be explicitly written into each program. In contrast, all of the behavior of creatures in our SPO system is determined solely by evolution; if a creature never specifically chooses to reproduce in our system (in this case by having too low an evolved probability of randomly selecting the reproduction action), it will die (or live) childless.

Many gridworlds that allow multiple creatures to interact have been constructed with the goal of illustrating certain kinds of interactions between creatures or certain kinds of system dynamics. Ackley and Littman (1992) focus on the relation between learning and evolution. Bedau and Packard (1992) create a simple system with which they study measures of evolutionary activity. Werner and Dyer (1992, 1993) explore systems that illustrate specific kinds of communication and herding activity. Floreano's (1993b) shared environment research examines the differences in behavior that occur when creatures can or cannot sense each other. This work in particular bears on our current interest in the effects of multiple creatures in a commonly grazed environment, but his methods are quite distinct and his system starts at a higher level of behavioral (and sensory) complexity. Each of these systems comes much closer to the work we describe here, but all differ in being set up to explicate some particular form of behavior. Our approach instead is to build in the possibility of evolving a wide set of different types of behaviors, and then manipulate general features of environment structure to see what types of behaviors actually do evolve as adaptive.

Packard's (1989) work on intrinsic evolution shares similar motivations with ours, striving for simplicity in order to bring a variety of basic evolutionary questions to the forefront. Some of the main differences are that his creatures are born a lot smarter (they know how to find food) and have significant sensory input, and only a few types of food distribution and growth are examined. Littman (1992) has approached the problem of characterizing environments in terms of behavioral capabilities by expanding on Wilson's (1991) scheme for classifying environmental indeterminacy, and he has recently explored half of the problem we pose here, analyzing the goal-seeking abilities of agents with no memory or internal state, only current sensation (Littman, in press). Mason (1993; Erdmann and Mason, 1988) has discussed the other half of the equation, designing state-guided robots that have no sensors. Other more recent projects by Yeager (1994) and Grant (1993) and the LEE system of Menczer and Belew (in press) introduce rich creature simulation environments in which a variety of behaviors can evolve. But each come with predetermined decisions about the cognitive, sensory, and memory abilities of the creatures involved and the structures of the environments in which they live. The SPO system, of course, also makes such choices about the evolvable capabilities of the simulated creatures, but at what we hope is a lower level of complication (if not also sophistication), more appropriate for the kind of study we are undertaking here into the simplest forms of blind adaptive behavior evolved across a range of environments.

3 The World

We begin the exploration of the evolution of sensor-less, stateless behavior in response to environmental structure with the creation of the environments themselves. The world our creatures inhabit is at present a very simple (and commonly used) one, a two-dimensional 64x64 grid of distinct square locations, toroidally connected at opposite edges so that movement wraps around and nobody will fall off. Any number of creatures can occupy any of the 4096 locations in the world. The only other type of object found in the world is food, which can also be present in different locations in varying amounts. ("Food" is equivalent to energy, the common currency in the world, which creatures absorb through eating, use up in all their activities, and die without.) The only direct control we have over their environment is the spatial and temporal distribution of the food they encounter.

There are an endless number of ways to parameterize the possible patterns of food distribution over space and time in our simple world. We have started with just a few parameters that are particularly salient and more or less clearly connected to patterns of plant growth in natural environments (see e.g. Barbour, Burk, & Pitts, 1987; Bell, 1991). First of all, we specify the maximum overall density of food in the world -- that is, the percentage of locations in the world in which food can be present simultaneously. If food is distributed purely randomly in the world with a given density (as it is in many of the experiments described in this paper), then the density also determines how far on average a creature will have to travel from one food-bearing location before encountering another.

The pattern over time with which food regrows determines its temporal distribution. We control this aspect of the environment with two parameters. First, there is a food regrowth delay, that specifies how long a just-grazed location will remain empty (food-less) before food can regrow there. Where the maximum food density specifies how far a creature must go to find food, the regrowth delay specifies

how long a creature must wait at a given location before food reappears there. Once food can sprout again in a given empty location, the second parameter -- the food regrowth rate -- says how much food energy will be added to this location at each time-step, that is, how fast the food-plants (re)grow.

Food does not go on growing indefinitely in a given location in this world -- we also specify a maximum amount of energy per location (that is, maximum food-plant "size"). This maximum food amount can be specified directly, but we usually use a more indirect computation of this parameter, instead specifying the desired energy "flux" in the world -- that is, the average amount of energy appearing over all locations in the world and across all time-steps. Say for instance that we have two environments in which food regrows instantly (zero regrowth delay) to a level of 2.0 units of energy. In one case, we specify a maximum food density of 100%, so that there are 2.0 units of energy everywhere in the world. In the second case, we specify a maximum food density of 50%, so that half of the locations have 2.0 units of energy, and half have 0.0 units. Thus, in the second environment, we have the same maximum food amount per location, but only half as much energy is ever available for the population of creatures, and this can seriously affect their livelihood. We would like to have two environments with different densities (and other parameters) that can support the *same* numbers of creatures, by having the same *average* amount of energy per location per time-step. If we want 2.0 units of energy per location per time-step in the 50% density environment, we can achieve this by doubling the maximum food amount that can grow at each location.

The same thing applies if we have a food regrowth delay. For instance, in an environment with 100% food density and 1 time-step regrowth delay, food appears only half as often (every second time-step), so to give this environment an equal energy flux, we again have to double the maximum food amount used in the zero delay case. The energy flux can thus be computed as

$$energy\_flux = food\_max\_amount * food\_max\_density \, / \, (1 + regrowth\_delay)$$

Since the energy flux is what is critical for maintaining creature populations in the world, rather than the maximum food amount per location, we can set the energy flux and then switch around the above equation to compute the maximum food amount from the flux and the density and delay parameters. Again we set the food regrowth rate to be equal to the maximum food amount per location, so that food regrows to its full level as soon as it can.

4 The Creatures

As we described in our original statement of this research program (Todd & Wilson, 1993), we are interested in the evolution of three components of behavior in response to different environment structures, namely action, sensation, and memory. Only the first, action, is actually necessary for behavior, and indeed adaptive behavior. That is, creatures need not be able to sense nor remember anything about their world (or themselves) in order to behave adaptively in it, provided the world is generous and benign enough. Simply performing different actions with certain probabilities can suffice for survival and reproduction. There are probably no creatures alive today that adhere to this strategy -- the competitive real world is probably no longer kind enough to allow such blind-faith behavior, if it ever was -- but it is possible that such mindless action could play a part in earlier periods of the evolution of life, terrestrial or otherwise. (In any case, the simple creatures we simulate here could be likened to nothing more complicated than a primitive unicellular organism; even plants have more sensory abilities and behavioral options than the individuals in the SPO system!) And since such unguided action is the logically simplest case we can construct, it is sensible to begin here in our exploration of the evolution of adaptive behavior. Once we have established this base-level state, it will also be much easier to show clearly the adaptiveness of evolved sensors and memory systems in comparison.

4.1 Action types

There are only four kinds of actions that we allow these first simple creatures to perform. To absorb the food-energy in their environment upon which they subsist, the creatures can eat; to travel from location to location in search of new food, the creatures can move; to populate the world with more of their own kind, the creatures can split; and to pass time until conditions have changed (or maybe not changed), the creatures can sit and do nothing. We will discuss each of these in greater detail.

The only way that creatures can get the energy they need to live is to absorb it from the environment through eating, and the only option available to them for eating at present is the food-plants growing in the world. Plants can only be consumed whole in these worlds; thus, if there are multiple creatures all trying to eat at one particular food-bearing location, only one of the creatures actually succeeds in eating, and it alone will get all the food-energy in that location, while all the others get no new energy. The winning creature -- the one that gets to eat -- is chosen randomly from among all the contenders attempting to eat in a location. The winning creature's own internal energy is incremented by the amount of food-energy in the location, and the location's food-energy is set to zero, ready to sprout again after the specified regrowth delay.

Creatures might not need to move about in their environment in order to survive -- if they are lucky enough to be born on a food-growing location, they might be able to get by with just sitting and eating their whole lives -- but since movement is the basis of all outwardly observable behavior, without it we would end up with very dull creatures. The creatures in SPO can move one location at a time in one of the four orthogonal directions in the square grid. Movement is relative to the current heading of the creature, so that an individual does not choose to move north, south, east, or west, but rather forward, backward, left, or right. Every move-action resets the current heading to make the creature face the direction it is going to move (e.g. if the creature chooses to move backward, it first turns around and then moves one step *forward* in that new heading). This heading-relative movement has implications for the creatures' behavior, as we will see in section 5.2.

The ultimate arbiter of what behavior patterns have been adaptive in a given environment is those creatures that are still around populating the environment after a suitable length of time. This could be accomplished simply by filling the world with randomly generated creatures and seeing who remains after the selective filtering process of death weeds out the maladaptive ones. But to enable powerful evolutionary search through behavior-space by means of small adjustments to existing behavior patterns, we need replication with modification. In SPO, we allow the creatures to reproduce by asexual splitting, which creates a modified copy of the "parent" individual and divides that individual's current energy equally between it and its new "offspring." The newborn is placed in the same location as the original splitting creature, and they go on to lead separate lives from that instant. The modifications in the newborn consist of rare changes in the probabilities of choosing the various actions in the creature's behavioral repertoire, as will be described in the next section on action selection. (The mutation rate -- the chance that any given action probability will be replaced with a completely new probability value -- is 0.05 throughout the runs described here.) This results in an individual who will behave slightly differently from the parent it split off from, allowing evolution to search behavior-space appropriately.

Finally, we allow creatures to do nothing in a particular time-step, just sit and wait for the moment to pass. In this way, creatures can "travel" through time in the same way they can traverse space, and the two are separable (at least insofar as sitting merely covers time, not space -- movement at present crosses both time and space simultaneously, since it takes time to move a given distance). We hope that including this ability will allow interesting aspects of the duality of space and time in these environments to manifest themselves in the behaviors of the creatures.

Every action a creature performs has energetic side-effects determined by the bioenergetic characteristics of the world (see Todd & Wilson, 1993; Menczer and Belew, in press, present another approach). Each type of action uses up a certain amount of energy; varying these action-costs across different worlds can yield very different behavioral repertoires, as we will discuss in section 5.2. Beyond these action-costs, some actions can further increase or decrease an individual's energy. Successful eating attempts increase the individual's energy by the amount of food-energy absorbed from the current location, while splitting cuts the individual's energy in half. Thus energy flows into the simulated world through food growth, continues into creatures when they eat, and flows back out of the creatures by being burned up through the actions they perform. Since creatures currently die only when they run out of energy, no energy-filled carcasses ever end up in the world -- dead creatures just disappear.

4.2 Action selection

Since our very simple creatures have neither sensors nor memories or internal states to distinguish any location from any other or any time-step from the rest of eternity, there is not much they can use to decide what actions to perform at a given instant. In fact, all they *can* use is the roll of a die --

they select among all the possible actions randomly. But the die can be weighted, with different probabilities (all summing to 1.0) assigned to each of the seven possible actions (move forward, backward, left, or right, eat, split, or sit). It is these probabilities, distinct in each individual creature, that determine the makeup of their behavioral repertoire, and allow them to behave more or less adaptively in response to the different environments they live in.

Each creature therefore has an internal list of seven probabilities for selecting among the seven possible actions. These probabilities remain constant during the creature's lifetime. When a creature splits, it is these probabilities that are modified slightly in the newborn offspring. At every time-step, each creature chooses one action at random according to its own internal probability distribution, and then performs that action. These probability distributions are thus all we can look at to assess the behavioral repertoire of the creatures in our evolving populations, but this situation has the advantage of allowing us a very easy and straightforward way of analyzing what is happening in the world. In contrast, trying to make sense of the behaviors of a population of sensing, remembering, and acting neural network-based simulated creatures is a far more daunting proposition. And as we will see in the next section, even so simple a behavioral repertoire as this set of seven actions weighted relative to each other can still lead to some interesting evolved results.

5 Results

We have currently implemented the SPO system on a 4096-processor 7 MHz Connection Machine 2 (CM2), using the *Lisp data-parallel language. Each processor maintains one location in the world (hence the current 64x64 size), as well as one or more creatures (which may be located anywhere in the world). The simulation churns along at a rate of about five time-steps per second for a population of up to 16,000 creatures. We have watched the evolution of these simple creatures in a wide variety of environments (in the hundreds of different settings to date) created with the parameters described in section 3. In this section, we first describe a typical run embodying general features, and then discuss some of the trends in the evolved behavior patterns that appear with changing parameter settings and a few of the more peculiar behaviors we have encountered.

Each run is begun the same: first, the world is populated with food as described in section 3. Then, to create the initial population, we generate 500 creatures with random action probability distributions and place them randomly across the world. Each creature is started off with an arbitrary 20.0 units of energy, to give everybody an equal foot in the door for survival. This initial population gives the evolutionary process a variety of starting points to begin working from in parallel, and allows multiple possible behavioral strategies to appear simultaneously and compete with each other for domination. In this way, the final population may come represent the most successful -- the most adaptive -- of several contending patterns of behavior. Once we first populate the world, the only way new creatures can be introduced after this is through the splitting actions of the creatures themselves.

5.1 Adapting over a typical run

The evolutionary course through which a population's behaviors adapt to the environment contains several common features across different environmental structures. Figure 1 shows aspects of a typical run of a population of creatures evolving in a simple environment over 20,000 time-steps. In this environment, we have specified a maximum food density of 40%, and a food regrowth delay of 4 time-steps, giving abundant food that takes a bit of time to reappear. The energy flux for the world is 0.6 units per location per time-step. These three parameters combine to give a maximum amount of food per location of 7.5 units of energy (which regrows all at once after the regrowth delay).

The first thing that happens as the initial random creatures begin to act in their environment can be seen in Figure 1a: the population size shoots up from its starting point of 500 to a high of 1645 by time-step 7. This is because the initial population contains a large number of creatures with very high probabilities of splitting, so that's what they do, resulting in a miniature population explosion. But since reproducing is basically *all* that these prolific creatures do, they soon run out of energy and die, and the population crashes over the next 70 time-steps to a low of about 300 individuals. From that point on, though, the successful creatures begin to make their presence felt, as they responsibly move about their world, eat, and only very occasionally have offspring. The population grows steadily over the next 800 time-steps, reaching a high of 2188 at time-step 1949 (Figure 1b), and then gradually falling to a relatively stable plateau of about 1600 creatures. (If we continue to run this world past 20,000 time-steps, little changes.) This initial population explosion followed by a rapid collapse and slower rebuilding is seen in the majority of runs. The final population size reached, though, depends greatly on the exact structure of the environment.

The reason for this population size growth pattern can be seen in Figures 1c and 1d, showing the average action probability distributions over time. (In each figure, "e" represents percentage of action devoted to eating, "m" is the combined movement percentage, "s" is splitting percentage, and "n" is sitting/do-nothing percentage.) In the initial population, all of the actions are performed about equally, meaning that splitting will make up about 14% (1/7th) of all behavior. Now every time a high-splitting-probability creature splits, it creates an additional new creature that also is likely to have a high splitting probability, so that very rapidly, the probability of splitting increases in the population. By the tenth time-step, 30% of all behavior is splitting. This rampant reproduction cannot be maintained for long -- even these simulated creatures must stop to eat -- and the splitting rate rapidly falls off as the hyper-splitters fall dead from exhaustion (or at least lack of energy).

The percentage of time spent splitting in fact continues to drop steadily over the course of evolution, eventually reaching a low of 0.17% by time-step 20,000. This is accounted for largely by the fact that relatively few of the creatures in the population ever bother to split at all -- the majority of them have a 0% chance of splitting. Indeed, only 175 out of the total 1609 creatures at time-step 20,000 can split. This means that most of the creatures spend their

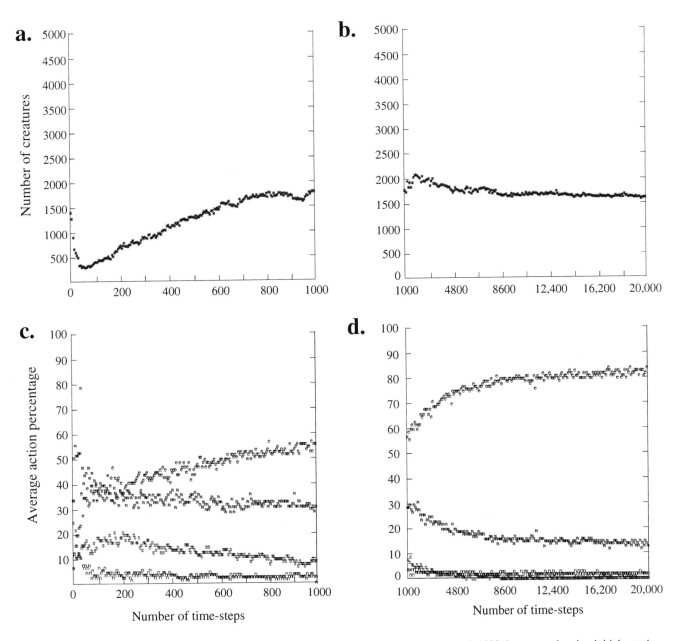

Figure 1. Population features evolving over time in a single typical run. a. Population size from 0-1000 time-steps showing initial population explosion, decline, and slow regrowth. b. Population size from 1000-20,000 time-steps showing eventual stable plateau. c. Proportions of different actions at each time-step averaged across the entire population, from 0-1000 time-steps. From top to bottom (at right edge), "e" represents average percentage of individuals eating, "m" represents combined movement percentage (in all four directions), "s" represents splitting (reproduction), and "n" represents sitting/doing nothing. d. Proportions of different actions, from 1000-20,000 time-steps.

time just eating and occasionally moving, building up greater and greater amounts of energy, reaching an average energy per creature of over 7800 units by the end of this run. This effectively makes these non-splitting creatures immortal, a situation that can lead to such dire consequences as the eventual end of all evolution (as described in Todd, 1993).

In place of the disappearing likelihood of splitting, though, another action must increase in likelihood (since the creatures always select *something* to do at each time-step,

even if it is just sitting still). Eating takes up the slack from the decreasing splitting, growing constantly after its initial low probability. In fact, the percentage of time creatures spend eating on average rises at the expense of *all* of the other actions. Eating beats out the combined movement percentage (the sum of movements in each of the four directions) to become the most popular action shortly after 100 time-steps. This all-important activity continues to rise until it plateaus around 83% by time-step 16,000.

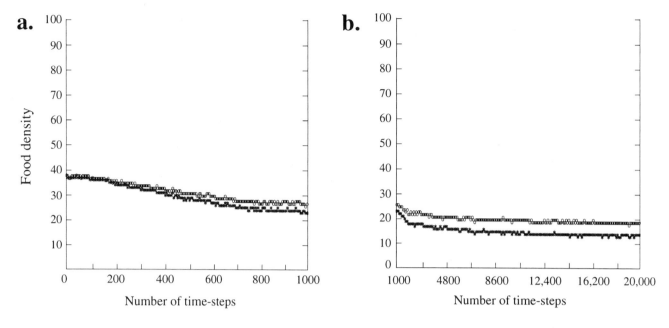

Figure 2. Environmental changes occuring over time in a single typical run. a. Food density in percent of locations containing food-plants at each time-step from 0-1000; the upper line ("o"s) shows density after food regrowth, while the lower line ("*"s) shows density before regrowth. b. Food density from 1000-20,000 time-steps showing eventual leveling off and large difference before and after regrowth.

The combined movement probability begins very high (since it subsumes four different actions, or 4/7th of the total initial probability distribution), but it quickly falls off. It remains a useful action in this environment, though, leveling at around 14%. (In other environments, as we will see, movement is a much less adaptive behavior, and ends up at much lower levels.) The amount of time spent moving in each of the four directions is not evenly distributed, however, as we will see in the next section -- interesting patterns emerge. Finally, the sit (do nothing) action proves relatively pointless in this environment, rapidly falling to about 2.5% usage. This is still much higher than the final splitting percentage, though, indicating that just sitting still is not as risky a proposition -- and thus not as strongly selected down -- as is losing half of one's energy to a new (and competing!) offspring.

These patterns of evolution of the average behavioral repertoire are fairly representative of the range of runs we have performed. (Since the action probability distribution seems to have become more or less stable by 15,000 time-steps, we use this as the length of the runs in the remainder of this paper.) Using averages, though, can hide multiple strategies existing within a single population, a concern to which we will return in the next section; but often the populations that evolve are fairly homogeneous, with one particular behavioral pattern winning out over time.

Other things are afoot in the world besides behaviors changing, however. As the population of creatures adapts to the environment and comes to contain more individuals with behavioral repertoires better tuned to the world they encounter, the world itself changes as well, owing solely to the actions of the creatures. This can be seen in Figure 2, which shows the density of food in the world over time. Two lines are plotted in both panes (Figures 2a and 2b); the

bottom one ("*"s) shows the percent of food-bearing locations after the population has grazed, while the top one ("o"s) shows the percent of food-bearing locations after food has regrown in the world. Remember that the maximum food density in this particular environment is 40% -- but as can be seen, this value is never actually reached, even following regrowth, after the initial planting of food. The reason for this is the long regrowth delay (4 time-steps), which keeps much of the world infertile for much of the time, so that the maximum food density never can actually regrow. As soon as some of the locations regrow, the creatures graze them down again, keeping the entire percentage low. This in turn has an impact on the future evolution of the creatures themselves, limiting their numbers and probably making movement in search of the sparser food locations more adaptive.

This is a very different situation from simulation systems that run single creatures in their own worlds to test out their adaptiveness. In those cases, each creature experiences the same type of environment over the entire course of evolution, and they become better and better adapted (one hopes) to that fixed environment over evolutionary time. In our situation, though, the environment we initially specify is quite different from the picked-over world the creatures end up making for themselves -- they must evolve to a moving target, because the world itself changes over evolutionary time as well. This complicates our task in analyzing evolution in response to environments, but it also makes the model more realistic.

But the creatures never eat *all* of the food at a given instant; as can be seen in Figure 2b, even after 20,000 time-steps the grazing creatures leave behind food in about 14% of the locations (out of about 20% of locations that regrow each time-step). This is because there are too few creatures in the final population to graze everywhere. The 1600 creatures in the population at 20,000 time-steps in fact end up only occupying 29% of the locations in the world. The creatures are relatively well dispersed, though, as there are only an average of 1.36 creatures per occupied location, compared to the stack of 2.3 per location that occurs at time-step 10 (right after the initial population explosion, when many creatures and their offspring are sitting on the same spot).

5.2 Adapted behavior patterns and trends

The typical run just discussed shows that the behavioral repertoires of creatures are changed over time through the simulated evolutionary process -- but are the creatures actually adapted to their particular environment? Or are we just witnessing the unwinding of some general dynamic process independent of the pattern of food distribution in the world? The most direct way to answer this question is to vary the structure of the environment, and see whether or not the evolved behaviors also change as a result. We have varied the maximum food density, the food regrowth delay, the average energy flux per location per time-step, and the cost of movement relative to the costs of the other actions, and have found that the behavioral strategies evolved do in fact change significantly in response. This indicates that the challenges of different types of environments are best (most adaptively) met by different probability distributions of blind actions. In this section we briefly discuss some of the major trends we see as we vary the environmental parameters, and a few of the adaptational oddities that pop up.

The most significant trends we find as the environments change are in the big-ticket actions, the ones that creatures spend most of their time doing: moving and eating. Holding other parameters constant, the rate of movement in general increases both as the density of food increases, and (independently) as the food regrowth delay increases. The former result is a bit counter-intuitive: why should creatures move *more* when food is denser, that is, closer together? In such environments, it should take *less* movement to find the next fertile food spot. But this is probably just why more movement *is* possible in such environments -- there is far less risk to it, because food is likely to be encountered soon. In low-density environments, moving randomly in the way these creatures are restricted to may take them a very long time to stumble from a location where there is certain to be more food growing -- if they just wait long enough -- to another similarly good oasis, and the possibility of starving on the way is great. In high-density environments, this risk is much reduced, and creatures can afford to allot more of their time to movement from one food-bearing location to another nearby.

As regrowth delay increases from 0 (instant regrowth on the next time-step), again so does the percentage of time spent moving. If food is certain to reappear immediately at your current location, there is little incentive to move from there in hopes of finding another place to eat; but if food won't grow back for some time, wandering away in search of more might be reasonable. This seems to be what the creatures do. But still, why should they give up a good thing if they begin at a food-growing location? If we look

carefully at the distribution of individual movement types the creatures are using, it appears that they do *not* simply abandon the location where they begin -- instead, the loop back to it after some delay! Analyzing the possibilities, it is clear that only movement solely in direction 0 -- straight ahead -- takes creatures ever further away from their starting point. Repeated movements in direction 1 -- turn right and move forward -- bring a creature back to where it started in four moves, as does movement in direction 3 (looping leftwards instead), while movements in direction 2 -- turn around and move forward -- bring it back in two moves. So if food regrows after a short delay, moving in short two-step loops with direction 2, interspersed with eating, may match the temporal distribution of food most appropriately. If food takes quite a bit longer to regrow, moving in longer four-step loops could be more adaptive.

Remarkably, this pattern is indeed borne out in the data: for instance, in the run described in the previous section, with regrowth delay of 4 time-steps, at the end of 15,000 time-steps of evolution we get 1% of the population only moving in direction 0 (straight ahead), 29% of the population only moving in direction 2 (two-step loops), and 21% of the population either moving only in direction 1 or only in direction 3 (four-step loops) -- the rest of the population (49%) has some mixed movement strategy (or no movement). When we look at regrowth delay of 2, the emphasis on two-step loops is even greater, with 32% of the population moving only in direction 2, and just 14% moving in only direction 1 or 3. In contrast, when we change the regrowth delay to 12, these values become rougly inverted: we get 7% movement in direction 0 only, 17% in direction 2 only, and 40% in direction 1 or 3 only, showing that four-step loops have now become much more prevalent, and are therefore probably more adaptive and more often selected for. (Movement only in direction 0 increases as we continue to raise the regrowth delay, showing that the creatures eventually start to give up on the looping strategy when the delays between food reappearances are too large.) Thus, even these extraordinarily simple creatures are able to invent a behaviorally-based clock to adaptively time their behaviors in response to the structure of the environment, something we were quite surprised to find. (Of course, these timers are not *that* useful, in some sense, because the creatures don't really know when to start them, nor when to stop them, nor even how to keep them running -- everything is done probabilistically, and a rogue "sit" action coming in the middle of a four-step loop could throw off the timing of the entire sequence, for instance. Only through the use of internal states can such timers be made more accurate.)

The percentage of time spent trying to eat basically follows trends opposite to those for movement, falling with both increasing food density (because it is less necessary) and increasing regrowth delays (because it is useful less often). Splitting and doing nothing both remain quite low-percentage actions in most worlds, splitting because it is a very costly act, and sitting because it does not offer much positive return (why sit when one can try to eat instead, since both have the same energy cost in this case?). All of these trends are modified somewhat by the cost of movement relative to the costs of the other actions, but basically they are just scaled up or down in magnitude, and the direction of change remains the same. For instance, when we run another world like the one described in the previous section, but this time movement costs only 0.1 unit of energy instead of 0.5 (i.e., it costs one-fifth of what all the other actions cost), after 15,000 time-steps creatures spend about 27% of the time moving and 72% of the time eating (compared to 14% and 83% respectively above). When movement costs 1.0 unit of energy (twice the other action costs), these values change to 8% moving and 88% eating, reflecting the fact that it's cheaper to attempt to eat than to move. Finally, in an extreme case, when movement costs *nothing* (0.0 unit of energy), creatures switch to spending 74% of their time skidding joyfully around their frictionless air-hockey world, and only pausing to try to grab a mouthful of food 25% of the time.

Despite these general trends, there are still occasions at particular parameter settings when very curious behavioral strategies appear and take over the population. For instance, with movement cost of 1.0, food density of 10%, and regrowth delay of 2 time-steps, we find great variation in the kinds of strategies that different populations (on different runs of the system) converge upon, indicating different "species" of creatures. One particularly odd species spends 32% of its time just sitting in place (with 18% movement and 50% eating), far higher than any other population ever encountered. In another case, with food density 5% and regrowth delay of 1 time-step, one species spends 38% of its time splitting, again an unheard-of figure. The reasons for these strange strategies are being investigated, as well as their prevalence at other parameter settings. It is possible that they are very rare but widespread, and only occasionally take over an entire population (indeed, we find considerable variation in many evolved populations -- convergence is often not attained so long as splitting continues). The extent of speciation in general, and how much within-population variation is hidden by our use of behavioral repertoire averaging, remains to be explored. But the fact that multiple behavioral strategies can be found for dealing with certain kinds of environments, and the peculiarity of some of these solutions, further indicates the extent to which the behaviors of individual creatures have been adapted to the particular situations they evolve in.

6 Conclusions and Further Directions

Despite the simplicity of our simulation model for the evolution of behavior in blind, amnesic creatures, we have found a surprising amount of richness in the results. The behaviors of creatures are adapted by evolution over time to the particular spatiotemporal structure of food growth in their environment. Even in creatures with nothing else to do but sit, eat, move about, and reproduce in the dark, unexpectedly sophisticated strategies emerged, like the use of movement-based time-keeping to deal with temporal delays in the world. Sensors, internal states, and memory systems are thus clearly unnecessary for at least the grossest level of adapted behavior.

But such enhanced information-gathering abilities will obviously help, and that is the direction we are heading in with the SPO research program. The next step is to add food-detecting sensors which can focus at any relative posi-

tion in the world, to investigate the particular deployment of sensors that prove adaptive in different types of environments. Furthermore, in keeping with the philosophy that every action must be chosen by the creature (and not by some external system bias), we want to let sensation itself be a selectable action, so that creatures will "have their eyes shut" unless they specify otherwise, rather than always having a constant stream of input data impinging on them from ever-active sensors. Monitoring the pattern of "eye-opening" will also allow us to get a better handle on just when creatures need to use sensory input, in a way that is impossible with constantly-sensing creature models.

After this, we will add internal state (memory) systems that allow creatures to "look back in time" at the state of a particular world location in the past (e.g. whether or not it held food four time-steps ago), in a manner analogous to the way their sensors look "across" time to locations that will take several time-steps into the future to reach. In this way, we hope to explore both the temporal and spatial aspects of environmental variation and behavioral responses to them more accurately. But before these enhancements, we will continue to establish the baseline of adaptive behavior capable in sensor-less, memory-less creatures of the kind described here, showing that adaptive behavior *is* possible without looking.

References

Ackley, D., and Littman, M. (1992). Interactions between learning and evolution. In C.G. Langton, C. Taylor, J.D. Farmer, and S. Rasmussen (Eds.), *Artificial life II* (pp. 487-509). Reading, MA: Addison-Wesley.

Barbour, M.G., Burk, J.H., and Pitts, W.D. (1987). *Terrestrial plant ecology,* 2nd ed. Mcnlo Park, CA: Benjamin/Cummings.

Bedau, M.A., and Packard, N.H. (1992). Measurement of evolutionary activity, teleology, and life. In C.G. Langton, C. Taylor, J.D. Farmer, and S. Rasmussen (Eds.), *Artificial life II* (pp. 431-461). Reading, MA: Addison-Wesley.

Bell, W.J. (1991). *Searching behaviour: The behavioural ecology of finding resources.* London: Chapman and Hall.

Cecconi, F., and Parisi, D. (1993). Neural networks with motivational units. In J.-A. Meyer, H.L. Roitblat, and S.W. Wilson (Eds.), *From animals to animats 2: Proceedings of the Second International Conference on Simulation of Adaptive Behavior* (pp. 346-355). Cambridge, MA: MIT Press/Bradford Books.

Collins, R.J., and Jefferson, D.R. (1992). AntFarm: Towards simulated evolution. In C.G. Langton, C. Taylor, J.D. Farmer, and S. Rasmussen (Eds.), *Artificial life II* (pp. 579-601). Reading, MA: Addison-Wesley.

Floreano, D. (1993a). Emergence of nest-based foraging strategies in ecosystems of neural networks. In J.-A. Meyer, H.L. Roitblat, and S.W. Wilson (Eds.), *From animals to animats 2: Proceedings of the Second International Conference on Simulation of*

Adaptive Behavior (pp. 410-416). Cambridge, MA: MIT Press/Bradford Books.

Floreano, D. (1993b). Patterns of interactions in shared environments. In *Pre-proceedings of the Second European Conference on Artificial Life,* Brussels, Belgium, May 1993.

Grant, W. (1993). *Artificial life worlds as discovery environments for learning.* Talk presented at the Artificial Life III Workshop, Santa Fe, NM.

Jefferson, D., Collins, R., Cooper, C., Dyer, M., Flowers, M., Korf, R., Taylor, C., and Wang, A. (1992). Evolution as a theme in artificial life: The Genesys/Tracker system. In C.G. Langton, C. Taylor, J.D. Farmer, and S. Rasmussen (Eds.), *Artificial life II* (pp. 549-578). Reading, MA: Addison-Wesley.

Koza, J.R. (1992). Genetic evolution and co-evolution of computer programs. In C.G. Langton, C. Taylor, J.D. Farmer, and S. Rasmussen (Eds.), *Artificial life II* (pp. 603-629). Reading, MA: Addison-Wesley.

Littman, M.L. (1992). An optimization-based categorization of reinforcement learning environments. In J.-A. Meyer, H.L. Roitblat, and S.W. Wilson (Eds.), *From animals to animats 2: Proceedings of the Second International Conference on Simulation of Adaptive Behavior* (pp.). Cambridge, MA: MIT Press/Bradford Books.

Littman, M.L. (in press). Memoryless policies: Theoretical limitations and practical results. In J.-A. Meyer, P. Husbands, and S.W. Wilson (Eds.), *From animals to animats 3: Proceedings of the Third International Conference on Simulation of Adaptive Behavior.* Cambridge, MA: MIT Press/Bradford Books.

Mason, M.T. (1993). Kicking the sensing habit. *AI Magazine, 1,* 58-59.

Erdmann, M.E., and Mason, M.T. (1988). An exploration of sensorless manipulation. *IEEE Journal of Robotics and Automation, 4,* 369-379.

Menczer, F., and Belew, R.K. (in press). Latent energy environments. In R.K. Belew and M. Mitchell (Eds.), *Plastic individuals in evolving populations.* Reading, MA: Addison-Wesley.

Meyer, J.-A., and Guillot, A. (1991). Simulation of adaptive behavior in animats: Review and prospect. In J.-A. Meyer and S.W. Wilson (Eds.), *From animals to animats: Proceedings of the First International Conference on Simulation of Adaptive Behavior* (pp. 2-14). Cambridge, MA: MIT Press/Bradford Books.

Packard, N.H. (1989). Intrinsic adaptation in a simple model for evolution. In C.G. Langton (Ed.), *Artificial life* (pp. 141-155). Redwood City, CA: Addison-Wesley.

Parisi, D., Nolfi, S., and Cecconi, F. (1992). Learning, behavior, and evolution. In F.J. Varela and P. Bourgine (Eds.), *Towards a practice of autonomous systems: Proceedings of the First European Conference on Artificial Life.* (pp. 207-216). Cambridge, MA: MIT Press/Bradford Books.

Taylor, C.E., Jefferson, D.R., Turner, S.R., and Goldman, S.R. (1989). RAM: Artificial life for the exploration of complex biological systems. In C.G. Langton (Ed.), *Artificial life* (pp. 275-295). Redwood City, CA: Addison-Wesley.

Todd, P.M. (1993). Artificial death. In *Pre-proceedings of the Second European Conference on Artificial Life,* Brussels, Belgium, May 1993.

Todd, P.M., and Miller, G.F. (1991a). Exploring adaptive agency II: Simulating the evolution of associative learning. In J.-A. Meyer and S.W. Wilson (Eds.), *From animals to animats: Proceedings of the First International Conference on Simulation of Adaptive Behavior* (pp. 306-315). Cambridge, MA: MIT Press/Bradford Books.

Todd, P.M., and Miller, G.F. (1991b). Exploring adaptive agency III: Simulating the evolution of habituation and sensitization. In H.-P. Schwefel and R. Maenner (Eds.), *Proceedings of the First International Conference on Parallel Problem Solving from Nature* (pp. 307-313). Berlin: Springer-Verlag.

Todd, P.M., and Wilson, S.W. (1993). Environment structure and adaptive behavior from the ground up. In J.-A. Meyer, H.L. Roitblat, and S.W. Wilson (Eds.), *From animals to animats 2: Proceedings of the Second International Conference on Simulation of Adaptive Behavior* (pp. 11-20). Cambridge, MA: MIT Press/Bradford Books.

Werner, G.M., and Dyer, M.G. (1992). Evolution of communication in artificial organisms. In C.G. Langton, C. Taylor, J.D. Farmer, and S. Rasmussen (Eds.), *Artificial life II* (pp. 659-687). Reading, MA: Addison-Wesley.

Werner, G.M., and Dyer, M.G. (1993). Evolution of herding behavior in artificial animals. In J.-A. Meyer, H.L. Roitblat, and S.W. Wilson (Eds.), *From animals to animats 2: Proceedings of the Second International Conference on Simulation of Adaptive Behavior* (pp. 393-399). Cambridge, MA: MIT Press/Bradford Books.

Wilson, S.W. (1985). Knowledge growth in an artificial animal. In J.J. Grefenstette (Ed.), *Proceedings of an International Conference on Genetic Algorithms and their Applications* (pp. 16-23). Pittsburgh, PA: Carnegie-Mellon University.

Wilson, S.W. (1991). The animat path to AI. In J.-A. Meyer and S.W. Wilson (Eds.), *From animals to animats: Proceedings of the First International Conference on Simulation of Adaptive Behavior* (pp. 15-21). Cambridge, MA: MIT Press/Bradford Books.

Yeager, L. (1994). Computational genetics, physiology, metabolism, neural systems, learning, vision, and behavior or PolyWorld: Life in a new context. In C.G. Langton (Ed.), *Artificial life III* (pp. 263-298). Reading, MA: Addison-Wesley.

Memoryless policies: theoretical limitations and practical results

Michael L. Littman

Brown University / Bellcore
Department of Computer Science
Brown University
Providence, RI 02912-1910
mlittman@cs.brown.edu

Abstract

One form of adaptive behavior is "goal-seeking" in which an agent acts so as to minimize the time it takes to reach a goal state. This paper presents some theoretical and empirical findings on algorithms that devise goal-seeking behaviors for "memoryless" agents who base their behavioral decisions solely on current sensations. The basic results are that (1) the general problem of finding good deterministic memoryless policies is intractable, however, (2) simple branch-and-bound heuristics can be used to find optimal memoryless policies extremely quickly for some established example environments.

1 Introduction

This paper looks at a class of behaviors, or policies, that can be called "memoryless" since action decisions are made solely on this basis of the agent's current sensation. In nature, it would seem that memoryless behavior makes little sense. What organism would possibly ignore recent events in deciding how to act? Research on artificial agents, however, is more apt to focus on memoryless policies, which are better understood and more easily studied than general forms of policies. This is not just because memoryless policies are simpler, they are also quite powerful. In the class of *Markov* environments, in which sensations completely determine underlying state, it is always possible to find a deterministic memoryless policy that is optimal; no other behavioral strategy is superior.

The study of Markov decision processes by the operations research community (e.g., [9, 4]) and more recently by reinforcement learning researchers (e.g., [1]) has yielded deep insights and efficient algorithms for finding optimal memoryless policies in Markovian environments. It is natural to ask whether similar results can be obtained for the non-Markovian case in which an agent's sensations do *not* give it complete information about its current state.

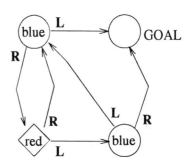

Figure 1: A sample environment.

This paper begins with a warning. When we leave the realm of Markovian environments, finding good deterministic memoryless policies (even for a very weak definition of "good") is intractable. This result holds even in the case when a complete map of the environment is available to the agent for preprocessing; the more realistic case in which the adaptive agent begins with no model is therefore even harder. It then goes on to ignore this warning and describes branch-and-bound heuristics for finding not just good, but optimal, policies in the case where the model is given and discusses the successful application of these heuristics to several example environments.

2 Definitions and Notation

In this paper, an environment is defined by a finite set of *states*, S, *actions*, A, *sensations*, X, and *goal-states*, G. A *transition function*, $T : S \times A \rightarrow S \cup G$, specifies how the agent's state changes in response to each action. A *perception function*, $O : S \rightarrow X$, specifies how each state is perceived by the agent—different states might give the same sense impression. This paper assumes that T and O are deterministic functions although most of the results easily extend to the probabilistic case. Note that this definition of an environment is more restrictive than the standard one in which a reward function generalizes the notion of goal-states. Nevertheless this formulation is fairly popular and simplifies the present discussion.

The agent is an independent entity whose task is to generate actions which bring it to a goal-state from some unknown initial state. The agent's *policy*, or behavior, is the function that maps its sensory history and internal state to actions. Figure 1 illustrates an environment with 3 states, 2 distinct sensations ("red" and "blue") and two actions ("L" and "R"); in this environment, an example policy that uses memory is: "If sense red: do L then R. If sense blue: do R and if that doesn't take me to the goal, do R then L." This form of policy is atypical since it makes use of sequences of actions but it is still well-defined since all decisions are made on the basis of past or present sensations.

A *memoryless policy*, $P : X \rightarrow A$, returns an action based solely on the current sensation; for instance: $P_1(\text{red}) = L$, $P_1(\text{blue}) = R$. The set of all memoryless policies for an environment is finite since there are $|A|^{|X|}$ different ways to specify this mapping. We'll call P *satisficing* if, independent of initial state, an agent following P is guaranteed to reach the goal. The policy P_1 above is satisficing whereas $P_2(\text{red}) = R$, $P_2(\text{blue}) = R$ is not; the agent would never reach the goal from the upper left state.

The performance of a policy is measured by its *total steps to goal*: the sum, over all possible initial states, of the number of steps an agent with that policy would take to get to a goal. An alternate definition of a satisficing policy, therefore, is one whose total steps to goal is finite. In the sample environment, the performance of P_1 is 6 total steps to goal. An *optimal* policy is one that achieves the minimum total steps to goal. The unique optimal memoryless policy for the sample environment is $P_3(\text{red}) = R$, $P_3(\text{blue}) = L$ that takes 5 total steps to reach the goal. This paper is concerned with finding optimal memoryless policies. The problem of finding more general optimal policies is addressed by research on *partially observable Markov decision processes* [6, 2] and is even harder in some sense although the policies are typically of higher quality.

We can also distinguish policies as to whether they are *deterministic* or *probabilistic*. The intractability arguments of the next section only apply to deterministic policies, which consistently choose the same action when faced with the same sensation. Probabilistic memoryless policies are quite interesting since almost any such policy will the satisficing. They seem not to improve performance in the specific example environments addressed here so this paper focuses on only deterministic policies. Note that for probabilistic policies or transitions functions, the performance measure is the total *expected* steps to goal. A model-free learning algorithm for this class of policies has been proposed recently [10].

3   NP-completeness results

Work in the area of NP-completeness tells us that there is a set of very natural decision problems—problems that require a yes/no response for each input—for which there is no known efficient algorithm but that if an algorithm is found for any *one* of them, then there are efficient algorithms for *all* of them. This section proves that finding satisficing deterministic memoryless policies is one such NP-complete problem. (For more on NP-completeness, see [3].)

3.1   Reduction

Consider the following decision problem: "Given an environment, is there some satisficing deterministic memoryless policy for it?" That is, is there some way to assign actions to sensations so that the goal is eventually reached from every initial state? The complete set of states, actions, and sensations, as well as the transition function, perception function and definition of the goal states are all provided as input.

We can show that this decision problem is NP-complete by proving that it satisfies two conditions. First, it is in NP, meaning that it is solvable quickly after "guessing" a short verification string. Second, it is NP-hard, meaning an efficient solution to this problem would give us an efficient solution to some other NP-complete problem.

To see that it is in NP, consider that if we could guess a satisficing policy we could verify that it is satisficing by doing a graph search as follows. The graph is built from a description of the environment and looks like Figure 1 except all links that are not used by the policy are deleted. It is then easy to determine whether every state reaches the goal, that is, whether the guessed policy is satisficing, by traversing the graph from all initial states.

The proof that the problem is NP-hard depends on a reduction from the classic NP-complete problem 3-CNF-SAT. A boolean formula is in 3-CNF if it is made up of a conjunction of clauses, each of which is a disjunct of triples of variables and complements of variables. The bottom of Figure 2 gives an example 3-CNF formula. A formula is in 3-CNF-SAT if it is in 3-CNF and there is *some* assignment of truth values to the variables such that the formula evaluates to **true**. The example formula is in 3-CNF-SAT since ($x_1 = $ **true**, $x_2 = $ **true**, $x_3 = $ **false**, $x_4 = $ **false**, $x_5 = $ **true**) is a satisfying assignment.

We can show that any 3-CNF formula can quickly be turned into an environment that has a satisficing policy if and only if the corresponding 3-CNF formula is satisfiable. Hence, a fast solution to the problem of whether or not a satisficing policy exists for a given environment would give a fast solution to 3-CNF-SAT and therefore to all NP-complete problems.

The top of Figure 2 shows the environment corresponding to the example 3-CNF formula. The environment is constructed in very tight analogy to the formula: the 12 literals become 12 non-goal states; the 5 variable names become 5 sensations; the two truth values (**true** and **false**) become the two actions; the 4 clauses become 4 levels in the environment; and finally, an assignment becomes a policy. The transitions in the environment are constructed so that satisfying a variable brings the agent closer to the goal.

To show that this construct is a proper reduction we need to demonstrate two things: that a satisfying assignment yields a satisficing policy and the converse. A satisfying assignment is one that makes at least one variable or complement in every clause **true**; by construction, an agent following a policy from any state on a given level of the environment advances to the next level if and only if that happens. Therefore, given a satisfying assignment, the agent will reach the goal from every state—we have a satisficing policy.

The converse is straightforward also. A satisficing policy will bring the agent to the goal from all states including those in the leftmost level. But the only way the agent can advance from one level to the next is if the corresponding clause is satisfied by that assignment. Since the agent advances through all the levels and arrives at the goal, all clauses must be satisfied, so a satisficing policy gives us a satisfying assignment.

This shows that we can rephrase any 3-CNF-SAT problem as an equivalent satisficing environment problem and that the question "Is there a satisficing deterministic memoryless policy for a given environment" is NP-complete.

3.2 Corollaries

There are several immediate and important corollaries. The first is that the corresponding optimization problem, "Find the optimal deterministic memoryless policy," is NP-hard. If we could solve this problem for a given environment, we would know instantly whether or not that environment had a satisficing deterministic memoryless policy: if and only if the total steps to goal for the optimal policy is finite.

Another corollary is that the result still holds for more general environments such as those with probabilistic transition or perception functions, and those in which the agent is given some fixed amount of short-term memory. It also holds under more restricted conditions, as when we consider only environments that can be represented by planar graphs (like most grid-world environments), or when the question of the existence of a satisficing policy pertains to only a selected subset of initial states. All these results follow directly from the reduction presented above.

Since the problem of finding optimal deterministic memoryless policies is NP-hard, there is reason to be-

lieve that any algorithm for solving it must enumerate all possible policies and take the best one. For even moderate-sized environments, this brute-force approach will take a very long time since there are $|A|^{|X|}$ distinct policies.

4 Branch-and-bound heuristics

In spite of its intractability, the problem of finding an optimal deterministic memoryless policy is an interesting and important one. This section introduces several heuristics that can be used to guide the search for optimal memoryless policies. They have been applied to a number of environments including one well-known environment for which the optimal memoryless policy was previously unknown.

Branch-and-bound algorithms systematically search the space of all solutions and use information about partial solutions to exclude entire regions of the search space. The critical component takes a partial solution, in this case, a policy that covers some subset of the sensations, and finds a *lower bound*, which is a level of performance that no completion of that policy can beat. If the lower bound for a given partial policy is worse than an *upper bound* that some other policy is known to achieve, then it is useless to extend that partial policy further. If not, each extension of that partial policy can be considered in turn.

A collection of branch-and-bound heuristics can be used to decide which extensions to pursue first and how to search for good upper bounds, which allow more of the space to be excluded quickly. The next section discusses one approach to finding good upper bounds.

4.1 Finding upper bounds: A hill-climbing approach

In the context of the current problem, an upper bound is simply the total steps to goal for the best known policy. The strategy adopted in this work for finding good policies is to consider small changes to known policies and to "hill-climb" to locally optimal policies. This approach, which bears some relation to Howard's policy iteration [4], is not guaranteed to find optimal policies in non-Markovian environments but empirically often does.

The algorithm takes an existing policy and considers changing the action associated with a single sensation chosen at random. The resulting policy is evaluated and if the change results in an improvement, it is kept and the revised policy adopted. Otherwise, it is discarded and some other change is considered at random. The algorithm continues making local changes until it can be shown that every local change would result in an inferior policy.

When such a local minimum is reached, the algorithm generates a new policy at random and again proceeds to

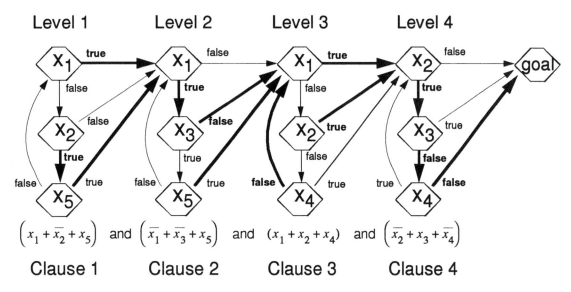

$$\left(x_1 + \overline{x_2} + x_5\right) \quad \text{and} \quad \left(\overline{x_1} + \overline{x_3} + x_5\right) \quad \text{and} \quad \left(x_1 + x_2 + x_4\right) \quad \text{and} \quad \left(\overline{x_2} + x_3 + \overline{x_4}\right)$$

Clause 1   Clause 2   Clause 3   Clause 4

Figure 2: A 3-CNF formula and its corresponding environment.

search for a local minimum. The total steps to goal for the best policy discovered this way is used as an upper bound for the branch-and-bound algorithm described in the next section.

This hill-climbing algorithm is extremely practical because the performance of deterministic policies acting in deterministic environments can be computed very rapidly. This work utilized a dynamic programming algorithm for computing the total distance to goal for all states in $O(|S||A|)$ time.

4.2 Finding lower bounds: Using complete information

In addition to upper bounds, the algorithm needs a way to bound the fewest total steps to goal that could be achieved by any extension of a given partial policy. This way, futile regions of the search space can be avoided.

A partial policy defines an action choice for some sensations, but leaves others unspecified. The lower bound algorithm takes such a partial policy as input and must then respond to the following request: "If we considered all possible ways of completing the given partial policy, tell me a level of performance which none of these completed policies can surpass."

Two extreme lower bound algorithms are: (1) always return zero, and (2) exhaustively try all possible extensions and return the performance of the best one. Both of these are lower bounds, but the first one is too weak a bound though easily computed and the second is perfect but too expensive.

Linear programming [7] forms the basis of a sophisticated method for computing lower bounds for this problem, but this section presents a simpler and faster algorithm which seems to give bounds that are just as good.

Consider an agent, such as one in a Markovian environment, that has complete information as to its state at all times and uses that information to minimize its total steps to goal. Certainly no memoryless agent could surpass this level of performance, since the memoryless agent would be restricted to perform the same action from all states with the same sensation. The performance of this *omniscient* agent is a lower bound on the performance of the optimal memoryless policy.

This idea can be extended to partial policies as follows. Imagine that our omniscient agent is obligated to behave according to the partial policy from all states with sensations covered by the policy, but from other states it is unconstrained and performs actions that minimize its total steps to goal. Since, over the unconstrained states, it uses information unavailable to a memoryless agent to optimize its behavior, its performance is a lower bound on the performance of any completion of that partial policy. Returning to the environment of Figure 1, the partial policy $P(\text{red}) = \text{L}$ is assigned a lower bound of 4 by this method since an omniscient agent could choose a different action in each of the two "blue" states.

Lower bounds can be computed particularly quickly for deterministic policies in deterministic environments by a backwards breadth first search in $O(|S||A|)$ time. This makes the algorithm practical for even moderate-sized to large environments.

4.3 Branch-and-bound heuristics

The optimal memoryless policies reported here were computed using the following branch-and-bound algorithm. The algorithm first executes the upper bound algorithm of Section 4.1 to identify a reasonable policy. It next enumerates the set of all sensations and sorts it in order of increasing ambiguity such that sensations that correspond to a large number of states appear first and those corresponding to a small number last. In the sample environment, then, "blue" would be listed before "red." Then an empty partial policy is generated to start things off.

The algorithm decides how to extend the current partial policy by removing the first sensation in the sorted list and generating a set of $|A|$ candidate partial policies by extending the current policy with each possible action for the selected sensation, such as $P_x(\text{blue}) = \text{R}$ and $P_y(\text{blue}) = \text{L}$. Lower bounds for each of these policies are generated using the algorithm from Section 4.2, yielding 6 for P_x and 5 for P_y here, and all of those worse than the upper bound are discarded because they correspond to decisions that are guaranteed to lead to suboptimal policies.

The other candidates are then considered in order, starting from the least lower bound and heading towards the largest, e.g., P_y before P_x. Extensions are computed and evaluated recursively using the method from the previous paragraph. If, at any time, the current partial policy is complete (i.e., assigns an action to every sensation) then the current lower bound is also an upper bound and we have found a policy that achieves the lower bound. The new upper bound is substituted for the old one and the process continues with the tighter bound.

When all avenues have been explored, the policy corresponding to the final upper bound is in fact the optimal policy and the process terminates. The basic structure of the algorithm is a generic branch-and-bound routine with the addition of two important heuristics: (1) consider the sensations from most to least ambiguous, and (2) branch on the smaller lower bounds before the larger ones. These heuristics seem to be very well-suited to the problem of finding optimal deterministic memoryless policies, as demonstrated by the results in the next section.

5   Empirical results

This section describes three environments developed by other researchers and uses the techniques from the previous section to find optimal memoryless policies for them.

5.1   Wilson's woods7

Wilson's woods7 environment [13] consists of an 18 by 58 cell toroidal grid on which an agent can wander to any of its eight neighboring cells in a single step. Non-empty cells contain "trees" which block motion and "food" which serves as the goals. An omniscient agent with complete information about its state can reach a goal from each initial state in turn in a combined total of 2038 steps. However, agents are not given information about their position and can only see the contents of the

# of times discovered	steps to goal
310	2895
389	2896
58	2961
73	3012
100	3032
29	3079
14	3080
27	3118

Table 1: Upper bounds found for Wilson's woods7

eight cells surrounding them.

With 933 states, 92 distinct sensations, and 8 actions, woods7 can be considered a moderate-sized environment. Littman [5] examined the resources an agent would need to achieve optimal performance in woods7. At the time, the best known memoryless policy (Class 1 agent) took a total of 3412 steps to reach the goal from all states which is an average of 3.66 steps to goal or 0.27 goals per step. This policy was found by running the Q-learning algorithm [12] many times and keeping the best policy found.

Table 1 summarizes 1000 runs of the upper bound algorithm from Section 4.1 on this environment. The best policy, taking a total of 2895 steps to goal or 3.10 steps per goal on average, can be shown to be optimal in just 15 seconds on a SPARC 10 by the branch-and-bound algorithm. Starting with no *a priori* upper bound, the algorithm finds the optimal policy in less than 45 seconds: recall that this effectively involves a search of $|A|^{|X|} = 1.2 \times 10^{83}$ policies. An optimal policy is shown in Figure 3 with goals shown as O's and trees as X's. Arrows indicate the actions taken from each state in the environment by an optimal policy.

There is an astonishing difference in terms of performance and computation time between the branch-and-bound procedure and Q-learning. This comparison is not entirely fair though since the Q-learning does not use a model and is only intended to work in Markovian environments. Nonetheless, the branch-and-bound algorithm *guarantees* optimality and runs quickly.

5.2   Sutton's gridworld

A classic example from the reinforcement learning literature is Sutton's gridworld [11], depicted in Figure 4.

In the figure, empty squares represent individual states, X's impassable walls, and O the goal state. Only the four principal compass directions are permitted as actions and in Sutton's work, each state is completely distinguishable from every other state giving an optimal performance of 404 steps from all initial states or an av-

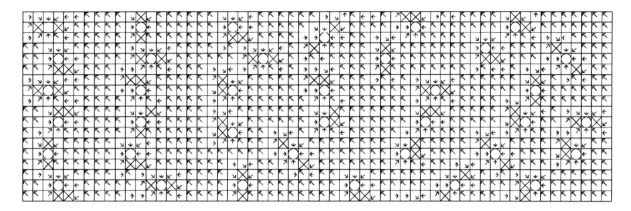

Figure 3: An optimal memoryless policy for Wilson's woods7.

# of times discovered	steps to goal
676	416
153	428
25	430
121	432
23	444
1	458
1	∞

Table 2: Upper bounds found for Sutton's gridworld

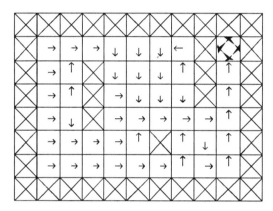

Figure 4: An optimal memoryless policy for Sutton's gridworld.

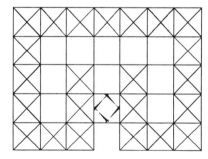

Figure 5: McCallum's maze.

erage of 8.78 steps to goal.

This section considers the variation where an agent can only distinguish a state on the basis of its 8 immediate neighbors just as in woods7. This leads to an environment with 46 states, 30 distinct sensations, and 4 actions.

Table 2 summarizes 1000 runs of the upper bound algorithm on this environment. The environment is simpler than woods7 in terms of total states, actions, and sensations and has a total of 1.2×10^{18} distinct policies. However, the paths required are significantly longer and this adds to the complexity.

The best policy listed in the table has a performance of 416 total steps to goal and the branch-and-bound algorithm finds this optimal level of performance from scratch in less than half a second. A policy achieving this bound is shown in Figure 4. An interesting aspect of this policy is the choice of leftward action in the corner just to the left of the goal. This decision is chosen because the sensation of "three walls to your right" is ambiguous and an upward action is the most sensible one for that sensation. This makes it impossible for the agent to select a downward action in the corner and a slightly twisty policy is the result. Nonetheless, there is no way for a memoryless policy to untwist the path without worsening performance.

5.3 McCallum's maze

McCallum [8] studied an environment for which no satisficing deterministic memoryless policy exists. It is depicted in Figure 5.

Once again empty squares represent individual states, X's impassable walls, and 0 the goal state. Only the four principal compass directions are permitted as actions and the sensation associated with a given state is determined by the set of directions in which the agent can move from that state.

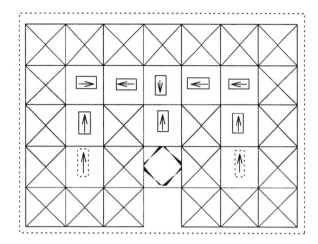

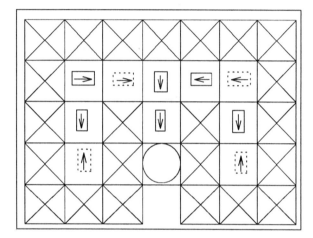

Figure 6: An optimal policy with memory for McCallum's maze.

The environment, therefore, consists of 10 states, 6 sensations, and 4 actions. An agent with perfect information can reach the goal in a total of 39 steps from all initial states. No deterministic memoryless policy can do nearly this well because either choice for the sensation that says "you can go left or right from here" leads to a non-satisficing policy for either the left half or the right half of the maze.

It is possible, however, to move from memoryless policies to a very simple form of memory. In particular, we can change the state, action, and sensation sets to consist of duplicate copies of each where the action set becomes: "go up, remember 0", "go up, remember 1", "go right, remember 0", "go right, remember 1", etc., and the normal sensations and states are augmented with the remembered bit from the previous action. The result is a little like the agent tying and untying a piece of string around its finger.

The optimal policy for the resulting environment has a performance of 43 total steps to goal and is shown in Figure 6. Actions are drawn in a box which indicates

whether the agent is to remember a zero (dashed box) or a one (solid box). The mazes themselves are similarly drawn in boxes to indicate whether they correspond to the behavior for memory 0 (dashed, on top) or 1 (solid, on bottom). An agent starting from the lower left-hand state with an initial memory of "0" (the agent is always given memory "0" to start) will move up remembering "0", then up remembering "1", then right remembering "1" (it is in the bottom maze now), then right remembering "0", down remembering "1", and down to the goal. This is the shortest possible path from that initial state and it is worth noting that it passes through three ambiguous states including two that share a sensation and yet are handled differently by the policy.

In this case, the extra memory bit serves to remind the agent of the direction it came from when entering a corridor. The same function could have been served by providing the agent with the additional input of its last action or by changing the definition of the environment so that an agent's body has some directionality. The memory-bit approach, however, is purer in that the agent can define for itself how to organize its short-term memory.

For McCallum's maze, one bit of memory is sufficient to give optimal performance, making it is an $h = 1$-environment [5]. This means that even with additional bits of memory, no better policy can be found. But what of Wilson's woods7 and Sutton's gridworld? Does adding additional bits of memory allow for better policies in these environments?

For Sutton's gridworld, we can answer "yes." The techniques of this paper, applied to the gridworld with 1 bit of memory, yield an optimal policy with a performance of 408 total steps to goal. However, the branch-and-bound algorithm is not able to solve the woods7 problem with one bit of memory given many hours of computer time. New heuristics will probably be needed to solve these problems efficiently.

6   Conclusions

This paper conveys a mixed message. In general, memoryless policies are a sensible approach to behavior in reinforcement learning environments but we must be wary of *deterministic* memoryless policies since deciding whether any such policy can be used to reach a specified goal state from a specified initial state in a non-Markovian environment is NP-complete. On the other hand, a simple hill-climbing algorithm finds excellent policies and a branch-and-bound algorithm can quickly prove these policies optimal in many cases.

There are a large number of related issues that deserve more attention. The algorithms in this paper are model-based in that they require detailed information about the underlying environment to work. Model-free methods, such as Q-learning [12] do not require such detailed information and are therefore more appropriate as on-line learning algorithms. These methods can also be quite effective for this problem.

Some environments, such as McCallum's maze, cannot be solved by any deterministic memoryless policy. For these environments, it may be possible to derive probabilistic memoryless policies that perform well. A preliminary algorithm has found probabilistic policies with expected total steps to goal of 80.30 for the maze, 2986.10 (apparently close to optimal) for woods7, and 416.00 (optimal) for the gridworld. This class of policies seems quite promising.

Lastly, the issue of finding short term memory based strategies for non-Markovian environments is extremely intriguing and some of the insights from this paper can be brought to bear on this problem.

Acknowledgments

Thanks to David Ackley, Avrim Blum, Justin Boyan, Bill Cook, Leslie Kaelbling, Andy Kaplan and Jak Kirman, for ideas and suggestions.

References

[1] A. G. Barto, R. S. Sutton, and C. J.C.H. Watkins. Learning and sequential decision making. Technical Report COINS Technical Report 89-95, Department of Computer and Information Science, University of Massachusetts, Amherst, MA, 1989.

[2] Anthony R. Cassandra, Leslie Pack Kaelbling, and Michael L. Littman. Acting optimally in partially observable stochastic domains. In *Proceedings of the Twelfth National Conference on Artificial Intelligence*, Seattle, WA, 1994.

[3] M. R. Garey and D. S. Johnson. *Computers and intractability: A guide to the theory of NP-completeness.* Freeman, San Francisco, CA., 1979.

[4] Ronald A. Howard. *Dynamic Programming and Markov Processes.* The MIT Press, Cambridge, Massachusetts, 1960.

[5] Michael L. Littman. An optimization-based categorization of reinforcement learning environments. In I. H. Meyer, H. Roithlat, and S. Wilson, editors, *From Animals to Animats: Proc. Second International Conference on Simulation and Adaptive Behavior.* MIT Press, 1992.

[6] William S. Lovejoy. A survey of algorithmic methods for partially observable markov decision processes. *Annals of Operations Research*, 28:47–66, 1991.

[7] D. G. Luenberger. *Introduction to Linear and Nonlinear Programming.* Addison-Wesley, Reading, Massachusetts, 1973.

[8] R. A. McCallum. Overcoming incomplete perception with utile distinction memory. In *Proceedings of the Tenth International Conference on Machine Learning*, pages 190–196, Amherst, Massachusetts, 1993. Morgan Kaufmann.

[9] S. M. Ross. *Introduction to Stochastic Dynamic Programming.* Academic Press, New York, 1983.

[10] Satinder Pal Singh, Tommi Jaakkola, and Michael I. Jordan. Model-free reinforcement learning for non-markovian decision problems. In *Proceedings of the Machine Learning Conference*, 1994. To appear.

[11] R. S. Sutton. Integrated architectures for learning, planning, and reacting based on approximating dynamic programming. In *Proceedings of the Machine Learning Conference*, 1990.

[12] C. J.C.H. Watkins. *Learning with Delayed Rewards.* PhD thesis, Cambridge University, 1989.

[13] Stewart W. Wilson. Knowledge growth in an artificial animal. In *Proceedings of the First International Conference on Genetic Algorithms and Their Applications*, pages 16–23, Hillsdale, NJ, 1985. Lawrence Erlbaum Associates.

LEARNING

A COMPARISON OF
Q-LEARNING AND CLASSIFIER SYSTEMS

Marco Dorigo[+],[*] and Hugues Bersini[*]

[*] IRIDIA - Université Libre de Bruxelles
Avenue Franklin Roosevelt 50, CP 194/6, 1050 Bruxelles, Belgium
bersini, mdorigo@ulb.ac.be

[+] Progetto di Intelligenza Artificiale e Robotica
Dipartimento di Elettronica e Informazione, Politecnico di Milano
Piazza Leonardo da Vinci 32, 20133 Milano, Italy
dorigo@elet.polimi.it

Abstract

Reinforcement Learning is a class of problems in which an autonomous agent acting in a given environment improves its behavior by progressively maximizing a function calculated just on the basis of a succession of scalar responses received from the environment. Q-learning and classifier systems (CS) are two methods among the most used to solve reinforcement learning problems. Notwithstanding their popularity and their shared goal, they have been in the past often considered as two different models. In this paper we first show that the classifier system, when restricted to a sharp simplification called *discounted max very simple classifier system* (D_{MAX}-VSCS), boils down to tabular Q-learning. It follows that D_{MAX}-VSCS converges to the optimal policy as proved by Watkins & Dayan (1992), and that it can draw profit from the results of experimental and theoretical works dedicated to improve Q-learning and to facilitate its use in concrete applications. In the second part of the paper, we show that three of the restrictions we need to impose to the CS for deriving its equivalence with Q-learning, that is, no internal states, no don't care symbols, and no structural changes, turn out so essential as to be recently redis-covered and reprogrammed by Q-learning adepts. Eventually, we sketch further similarities among ongoing work within both research contexts. The main contribution of the paper is therefore to make explicit the strong similarities existing between Q-learning and classifier systems, and to show that experience gained with research within one domain can be useful to direct future research in the other one.

1. Introduction

Reinforcement Learning (RL) is a class of problems in which an autonomous agent acting in a given environment improves its behavior by progressively maximizing a function calculated just on the basis of a succession of scalar responses (rewards or punishments) received from the environment. No complementary guidance is provided for helping the exploration/exploitation of the problem space, and therefore the learning agent can rely only on a trial-and-error strategy. Q-learning (Watkins, 1989) and classifier systems (CSs) (Booker, Goldberg, Holland, 1989) have been separately proposed as two general frameworks for treating reinforcement learning problems. Despite their shared goal, only a few researchers (Sutton, 1988; Twardowski, 1993; Roberts, 1993; Wilson, 1994) have discussed the relationship between them, and they are largely regarded as different approaches.

We believe that the reason for this situation is to be found in their different origins. Although Samuel's (1959) work on learning the game of checkers appears to be a common inspiration, Q-learning and temporal differences (TD) methods originated from the behaviorist and cybernetic tradition of cognitive science, paying large attention to neural networks, control theory, and ethology; on the other hand, the CS found its origin back in the symbolic and AI roads of cognitive science, more focused on rule-based systems and symbolic types of representation, reasoning and learning. Indeed, there are some clear indications of these different backgrounds in, for instance, the use of neural networks (or any numerical type of classifier) to attack the issue of generalization for Q-learning and TD, while relying on don't care symbols in CSs. In the field of process control, we observe today a similar kind of convergence between two types of methods, likewise having the two behaviorist and symbolic distinct origins: neural networks and fuzzy systems (Bersini and Gorrini, 1993). A second reason for this situation is that while the Q-learning algorithm is the heart of the first reinforcement strategy to be compared, the bucket brigade (BB) algorithm (Holland, 1980), that is the counterpart of Q-learning in the CS framework, is only a component of the CS, making its restricted analysis harder to achieve.

In this paper our objective is to underline the strong similarities between not only the original CS and Q-learning, but also between ongoing research being developed in the two respective communities. This objective will be pursued in four successive steps.

First, a radical simplification is achieved on the CS in order to obtain a primitive version of it called Very Simple CS (VSCS). This is very easily derived when complying with four restrictions: (i) classifiers have one condition and one action; (ii) the message list has length one and contains only messages coming from the environment, that is there are no internal messages; (iii) the don't care symbol is not used in the classifier coding; (iv) the classifier set is complete, that is all state-action pairs (classifiers, in CS jargon) are covered, and therefore no genetic search is necessary.

Second, we will show the equivalence of a slightly modified version of the just derived VSCS, called Discounted Max VSCS (D_{MAX}-VSCS), with Watkins' original Q-learning algorithm. The first good new of this equivalence is immediate: all the theoretical studies developed around the convergence proofs of Q-learning can be likewise applied to the D_{MAX}-VSCS. Also all the experimental works aiming at making possible the use of Q-learning for real applications can be of interest for CS users.

Third, three of the restrictions we need to impose to Holland's original presentation of the CS for showing the equivalence with Q-learning might be regarded as an impoverishment and all three turn out so essential as to be recently rediscovered and reprogrammed by Q-learning adepts. They are on one hand the presence of hidden state and don't care symbols in the coding of the agent, points (ii) and (iii) above, and on the other, point (iv), the existence of a double level plasticity that we will call *parametric* and *structural* plasticity.

The internal states provide the system with a short term memory capacity which allows the agent to decide its actions not only on the basis of its current perceptions, but also as a consequence of its past perceptions and actions. This interesting CS feature has been integrated in Q-learning by people like Lin and Mitchell (1992), Whitehead and Lin (1994), Chrisman (1992) and McCallum (1993). The presence of don't care symbols allows the agent to generalize a certain action policy over a class of environmental states with an important gain in learning speed by data compression: a key requirement in any trial-and-error based learning strategy. This generalization capacity has been investigated by Q-learning users either by means of NN (Lin, 1992) or by statistical clustering techniques (Mahadevan and Connell, 1992).

The double level plasticity, *parametric* and *structural*, whose biological inspiration is largely discussed in (Farmer, 1991) and (Bersini, 1993; Bersini and Varela, 1994), refers to the strong adaptive capacity of a system which automatically adjust its numerical parameters with the simultaneous possibility to modify the structure of the system by the generation of new agents. For example, parametric plasticity accounts for changes in the classifiers strengths, in the

actions Q-values, or in the NNs synaptic weights; on the other hand, structural plasticity accounts for new actions in Q-learning, new neurons in a NN, new classifiers in CSs, or other structural modification of the system like a finer division of the state space. The double level plasticity leads to an acceleration of the reinforcement learning discovery of good policies in large problem spaces. This acceleration is obtained by a simultaneous search of a satisfying minimal structural representation of the problem space and, within this minimal representation, the discovery at a computationally reduced cost of the optimal solution. In addition, it makes the system exhibit a larger degree of adaptivity thus escaping from the brittleness of classical AI methods.

Fourth, since the original proposals of both methods, a lot of developments have been carried out in the two communities with astonishing resemblance; examples are hierarchical task decomposition and the fuzzification of the methods. The main contribution of this paper is to make explicit the strong analogy between Q-learning and CSs so that experience gained in one domain can be useful to guide future research in the other.

The paper is organized as follows. In Section 2 we present VSCS and D_{MAX}-VSCS, and we compare D_{MAX}-VSCS to Q-learning. In the second part of the paper we continue our comparative analysis of CSs and Q-learning approaches to reinforcement learning. We compare extensions of the VSCS model, i.e. the original Holland's CS obtained again by replacing the four constraints, with currently investigated extensions to the basic Q-learning[1] model. In Section 3 we discuss hidden state and short-term memory. Section 4 is devoted to the problem of generalization. In Section 5 we discuss parametric and structural plasticity. Finally, in Section 6 we conclude with a brief overview of current research topics.

2 . The very simplified classifier system and Q-learning

A very simple CS complies with four restrictions: (i) classifiers have one condition and one action, (ii) the message list (ML) length is constrained to one: $|ML|=|ML_e|=1$ where the subscript e denotes the fact that the ML slot is reserved for environmental messages, (iii) classifiers are symbols on $\{0,1\}^*$, that is, no don't cares (#s) are allowed, and finally (iv) the classifier set contains one copy of all the possible classifiers (state-action pairs), and therefore there is no need to use the genetic algorithm to modify the covering of the state space.

Constraint (ii) says that only one message is possible at each time step, and that this message comes from the sensors (this is often called an environmental message and

---

[1] In this paper we follow the following convention: (i) basic Q-learning is Watkin's Q-learning (1989) in tabular form; (ii) the classifier system, is Holland's CS (Booker, Goldberg, Holland, 1989).

represents the state of the environment as perceived by the agent). Constraint (i) is in some way connected to (ii) because it would make no sense to have more than one condition when there is a single slot on the message list. Constraint (iii) removes the machinery which CSs use to generalize. Constraint (iv) allows a one-to-one correspondence between classifiers and Q-learning state-action pairs. The VSCS algorithm which results from these restrictions is given in Fig.1.

Initialization
   Create a classifier for each state-action pair;
   t:=0;
   Set $S_t(c_c, a_c)$, the strength at time t of
   classifier c, to an initial value;
              {c_c is the condition part of classifier
              c, while a_c is its action part}.
Repeat for ever
   Read(m) {*m is the sensor message*};
   Let M be the matching set;
   Choose the firing classifier c ∈ M, with a
   probability given by $S_t(c_c, a_c) / \sum_{d \in M} S_t(c_d, a_d)$;
   Change classifiers strength according to the
   implicit bucket brigade;
   t:=t+1;
   Execute(a_c);

Figure 1. *The very simple classifier system. The implicit bucket brigade is explained in the text.*

In VSCS the equation which rules the change in strength of a classifier c is the following:

$$S_{t+1}(c_c, a_c) = (1-\alpha) \cdot S_t(c_c, a_c) + R + \alpha \cdot S_{t+1}(c_d, a_d) =$$
$$S_t(c_c, a_c) + \alpha \cdot \left(\frac{R}{\alpha} + S_{t+1}(c_d, a_d) - S_t(c_c, a_c) \right) \quad (1)$$

where $S_{t+1}(c_c, a_c)$ is the strength of classifier c at time $t+1$, conditions are called c and actions a, and subscripts c and d identify the classifiers to which conditions and actions belong (e.g., c_d is the condition part of classifier d). Equation (1) essentially says that, each time a classifier is activated its strength changes, and that this change amounts to the algebraic sum of outgoing payments (the $-\alpha$ times strength component), environmental rewards, and ingoing payments. The VSCS reinforcement algorithm is the same as the reinforcement algorithm used in Wilson (1985) except that to create the parallel with Q-learning only one classifier is reinforced on each time-step. Wilson's algorithm was termed the 'implicit bucket brigade' in Goldberg (1989). The sense of the word 'implicit' is that there is no direct connection between a classifier activated at time t and one activated at time $t+1$. In the standard bucket brigade a

classifier activated at time $t+1$ is, most of the times[2], activated by messages sent by a precise set of classifiers at time t. Conversely, this is never the case in the implicit bucket brigade, as there are no internal messages. In the implicit bucket brigade a classifier activated at time $t+1$ implicitly owes its activation to the previously active classifiers, as they were the cause[3] for the new environmental message.

If we now consider 1-step Q-learning, the equation which rules the change of the Q-value for the state-action pair (x,a) is

$$Q_{t+1}(x,a) = (1-\alpha) \cdot Q_t(x,a) + \alpha \cdot \left(R + \gamma \cdot \underset{b}{\text{MAX}} Q(y,b) \right) =$$
$$Q_t(x,a) + \alpha \cdot \left(R + \gamma \cdot \underset{b}{\text{MAX}} Q(y,b) - Q_t(x,a) \right) \quad (2)$$

where y is the state obtained when executing action a in state x. In both equations R is the external reward.

We can continue our analogy noting that, in the constrained CS we have chosen to deal with, the condition part c_c of classifier c represents the state of the system, and its action part a_c represents the action. That is, in the analogy with Q-learning we have $c_c \Leftrightarrow x$, $a_c \Leftrightarrow a$, and $c_d \Leftrightarrow y$. If we substitute x and y in the corresponding symbols of equation (1), we obtain

$$S_{t+1}(x,a) = S_t(x,a) + \alpha \cdot \left(\frac{R}{\alpha} + S_{t+1}(y,b) - S_t(x,a) \right) \quad (3)$$

where $b = a_d$. This is the VSCS rule for changing strengths of state-action pairs.

Remembering that $Q(x,a)$ represents the value of action a in state x and that action a in state x causes the system to move to state y, while in the bucket brigade $S(x,y)$ represents the strength of the rule which, if activated, causes a state transition from state x to state y, we obtain D_{MAX}-VSCS changing formula (3) to meet formula (2). This is easily done if we observe that the two formulas, (2) and (3), differ only in the way the error part is computed, and in particular:

(i) Q-learning evaluates the next state y by choosing the value of the best action in the next state, while in VSCS it is evaluated by the strength of the state-action pair actually used,

(ii) in VSCS the evaluation of the next state is not discounted, that is, it is not multiplied by γ.

Regarding point (i), in a companion paper (Bersini, Nowé, Caironi, Dorigo, 1994) we have proposed a generalization of formula (2), which allows the definition of a more general class of RL algorithms. An original aspect of the general-

---

[2] Also in the standard bucket brigade it can happen that a classifier is activated by an environmental message, and therefore the standard bucket brigade contains the implicit bucket brigade as a special case.

[3] They are the only cause in static environments, one of the causes in dynamic environments.

ization we propose is the use of a *next state evaluation* (NSE) operator which generalizes the MAX operator. We experimented with different values for NSE; among them we tried the ACT operator, which corresponds to using the Q-value of the move actually chosen, as it is done by the BB of formula (3). Experimental results have shown that this choice gives rise to a worse performance than with the MAX operator, but that it does not seem to affect the convergence properties of the algorithm.

With respect to the discounted nature of the algorithm (i.e., $\gamma < 1$), this is usually justified (Schwartz, 1993) by Q-learning adepts with the need to guarantee the boundness of the final expected value of an action. This can be guaranteed either by the presence of a reachable absorbing state in the problem state space or, in the absence of such a state, by $\gamma < 1$ (see Watkins and Dayan, 1992; Tsitsiklis, 1993; Schwartz, 1993; for a more formal analysis of this issue). However, apart from these theoretical considerations, it can be very useful in practice, even in presence of a reachable absorbing state, to choose either $\gamma < 1$ or $\gamma = 1$, depending on the problem nature. When the problem relates to a path minimization (like the maze problem), $\gamma < 1$ is highly desirable, since in that case the final expected cost will be as big as the number of steps to reach the goal. On the contrary, in problems in which a possible solution is a cyclic behavior, like the cart-pole, $\gamma = 1$ is an interesting option, since all the Q-values in that case converge towards a same value, and therefore the probability of falling in a cycle is considerably increased (see Twardowski (1993) for an experimental confirmation).

Our comparison of the Q-learning algorithm with the CS approach has made clear that the CS is a much more complex model than Q-learning. It is interesting that most of the researchers which have been studying Q-learning were unsatisfied with it in ways that led them to generalizations which were already present in the original CS model. In the following of this paper we will try to discuss some of these similarities.

3. Hidden state and short-term memory

In this section we consider the implications of removing the first two constraints on our VSCS; that is, classifiers have more than one condition[4], but still one action, and the message list has extra slots beside the one for the external message. This new kind of CS, which we call VSCS-M (VSCS with memory), although still less general than Holland's original CS, is more powerful than VSCS in that it allows the system, at least in principle, to have short-term memory and to solve therefore hidden-state problems.

---

4   It can be shown that while moving from one to two conditions increases the representational power of a rule based system, all formalisms with two or more conditions are, from a representational power point of view, equivalent.

In the Q-learning community a similar direction was taken by Lin and Mitchell (1992) in their work on Q-learning with recurrent networks. To compare the two approaches we refer to Fig.2. In Fig.2a are shown those components of a VSCS-M which are interesting for our comparison. In particular, it should be noted that the message list comprises the following.

(i)   One slot for the external message; we call this ML_e, and we have $|ML_e|=1$.

(ii)   One slot for the action message. This is the message which causes the action; appending it on the message list gives the system a one-step memory. We call this ML_a, and we have $|ML_a|=1$.

(iii) The rest of the list is for internal messages; we call this ML_i, and we have $|ML_i|=n-2$.

As we said, the CS of Fig.2a has two new characteristics: classifiers have two conditions, and all three kinds of messages are matched against classifiers in the classifier set. (Matching classifiers produce two kinds of messages: (i) internal messages, which are appended to ML_i, and action messages which, after entering a probabilistic conflict resolution module, are reduced to a single winning message. This winning message, beside causing an action to be performed, is also appended to ML_a.)

Lin, in his neural net implementation of Q-learning (Lin, 1992), uses a feedforward neural net for each action. Each net receives as input a message, which is the equivalent of the environmental message in CSs, and proposes an action with a given strength. Thereafter, an action is chosen with a probabilistic choice which resembles the one going on in the conflict resolution module of CSs.

Consider now the recurrent architecture of Fig.2b; a similar architecture was proposed by Lin and Mitchell (1992). Feedback connections link the hidden units and the output unit to the input units. It is clear that, at least from a functional point of view, hidden units and feedback connections play the same role of internal messages and of the message appended to ML_a respectively.

4. Generalization

To be a viable tool for real world applications, reinforcement learning techniques need effective methods to partition the state-action space. This point has been the subject of research by both the CSs and the Q-learning communities. In this section we briefly discuss the role of don't cares (see constraint (iii) in Section 1), and the correspondent machinery found in Q-learning research.

In CSs generalization has been addressed by the use of the don't care (#) operator. A classifier attribute occupied by a don't care is considered to be irrelevant, and it is therefore by means of don't cares that generalization over classes of equivalent state-action pairs is achieved.

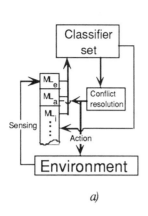
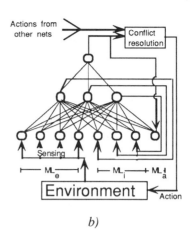

a)   *b)*

Figure 2. *A comparison of VSCS-M with recurrent-net Q-learning.*
  a) VSCS-M, the CS with constraints only on the use of # symbols and on the complete covering of the
    state-action space.
  b) Q-learning augmented with recurrent neural nets.

However, it is still an open problem how to develop set of rules which can effectively exploit this generalization possibility (so called default hierarchies, in which general rules cover default situations, and specialized rules are activated by exceptions, see Riolo, 1987; 1989). Moreover, CSs are inherently discrete systems (although fuzzy-CSs have been proposed to deal with continuous valued inputs and outputs, see (Valenzuela-Rendón, 1991; Bonarini, 1993)), which makes it difficult to achieve the kind of generalization in which a similar input should cause a similar output. This is more easily achieved in Q-learning systems enriched by neural nets, like Lin's system (1992).

Observing reinforcement learning algorithms, we are in presence of the two traditional and opposite ways to obtain partitions of the input space: bottom-up and top-down (Mitchell, 1982). In the bottom-up approach, the input space is initially very fine grained, and the partitions are created by clustering together input regions showing similar properties. In the top-down approach, the initial input space is uniformly coded and is progressively subdivided in finer parts. The bottom-up type of generalization has been investigated by Q-learning users following two approaches. The first one is the already cited approach of Lin (1992), who uses a neural net for each action. In the second, proposed by Mahadevan and Connell (1992), state-action points are clustered using statistical clustering methods. Since top-down methods amount to a progressive structural modification of the problem space, they will be discussed in the next chapter.

5. The double plasticity

In this section we discuss the last constraint we introduced to get VSCS, that is constraint (iv) of Section 1, regarding the coverage of state-action space. Q-learning and CS are both concerned with populations of agents which collec-

tively achieve a certain objective: they are adaptive and distributed types of control. Holland's biological inspiration, that is ecosystems and genetic mechanisms, led him to address structural plasticity by the GA. However, an ecosystem does not perform any kind of distributed control; instead, each individual selfishly tries to survive in an environment constituted by the other individuals. A perhaps more adequate biological inspiration could have been the immune system in which new cells are produced at a very high speed (Bersini, 1993; Bersini and Varela, 1994) to improve the capacity of the system to achieve, as a whole and in an adaptive way, its vital functions. We hypothesize that, when interested in the collective performance of a system, its structural adjustments should aim at compensating for the current weakest parts of the system. This is in contrast with Holland's GA approach in which the generation of new actors is biased towards the best ones.

In CS, the GA is responsible for two types of structural changes, depending on whether it applies to the condition or to the consequent part of the classifiers: a change in the coding of the state space and a change in the set of actions. These two types of changes have also been investigated in the Q-learning community, but within the "collective and compensatory" perspective just presented. Aware of the exponential dependency of the search duration with respect to the size of the state-action space, different methods have been proposed in order to progressively divide the space so to obtain a final solution in the smallest possible space. Chapman and Kaelbling's G-algorithm (1991) recursively splits the state space using statistical measures of differences in reinforcements received. Munos, Patinel and Goyeau (1994) make a similar recursive splitting of the state space following a different criterium. They split an action-state pair if the action acting in that particular state presents variations of great amplitude, indicating that the reinforcement received by that action is highly fluctuating and then requires a subdivision of the state (a similar approach was taken by Dorigo, 1993, in his CS called ALECSYS). This is typical of a mechanism which, contrary to GA, focuses on the current unsatisfactory part of the system to guide its improvement by a structural addition.

Regarding the action part, Bersini (1993) has implemented an adaptive control strategy in which the adaptation relies on the parametric and structural types of change occurring at different time scales (the inspiration is the immune system two-level adaptive strategy). First, the Q-learning tries to find for each state the best actions among a preliminary set of actions (the same in each state) during a certain number of Q-learning iterations. Then, after a certain number of steps, new actions are recruited in the states in which the current actions show bad Q-values as compared to other actions acting in the same state or actions acting in neighboring states. The new actions are selected so as to be the opposite of bad ones they replace (for instance *move left* instead of *move right* or a negative value instead of a positive one) and they are given the Q-value of the best action already present in the state (so that new actions are immediately tested). Q-learning is then activated again on the basis of the new set of actions.

6. Conclusions

We have seen that D_{MAX}-VSCS and Q-learning share

* the class of problems to which they are applied,
* the apportionment of credit mechanism.

We have also seen that both models are subject to research directed to enrich them with more powerful capabilities to make them useful for real world applications. These

researches bring the D_{MAX}-VSCS back to its original form, namely Holland's CS; on the other hand, Q-learning is being enriched by functionally similar mechanisms. We have seen that the CS model is an inherently discrete model (but see Valenzuela-Rendón (1991), and Bonarini (1993) for fuzzy implementations of the CS), while Q-learning can smoothly go from the discrete implementation (e.g., Watkin's tabular Q-learning or other more efficient kinds of discrete partition of the state space like Chapman and Kaelbling (1991) or Munos et al. (1994)), to continuous neural net implementations. Regarding generalization capabilities the two models have followed rather different directions, with CSs using don't cares symbols, and Q-learning a whole set of different techniques. Both have tackled the short-term memory problem with functionally similar mechanisms: internal messages in CSs, recurrent nets in Q-learning.

Finally, both have proposed the idea that to build working systems it could be useful to use a *divide and conquer* approach, in which the global task is decomposed into many simpler tasks which are then used as modules of a designed architecture. This can be found in the work of Dorigo and Schnepf (1993), Dorigo (1992), Dorigo and Colombetti (1994), Colombetti and Dorigo (1992), for CSs, and in the work of Lin (1993), Dayan and Hinton (1992), and Mahadevan and Connell (1992), for Q-learning. In all these works the proposed architecture is a hierarchic architecture in which simple tasks are learned by reinforcement learning and coordination is designed (in Dorigo's and Lin's work also coordination is learned).

Finally, in Table 1 we summarize the characteristics of the two models as discussed in the paper.

Table 1. *Characteristics of the two models as discussed in the paper*

	Classifier system	Q-learning
Discrete representation	Holland's style CS	Tabular Q-learning
Continuous representation	Fuzzy CS	Q-learning with neural nets
Short-term memory	Internal messages	Recurrent neural nets
Generalization	Don't cares	Neural nets Statistical clustering
Double plasticity	Genetic algorithm plus bucket brigade	Incremental net division New action recruitment G-algorithm Partitioned Q-learning
Hierarchy	Explicitly designed with learning of both basic tasks and coordination (Dorigo and Colombetti, 1994)	Explicitly designed with learning of both basic tasks and coordination (Lin, 1993)

References

Bersini H., 1993. Immune network and adaptive control. *Toward a Practice of Autonomous Systems - Proceedings of the First ECAL*, Varela and Bourgine (Eds.), 217–225, MIT Press.

Bersini H. and Gorrini V., 1993. FUNNY (FUzzY or Neural Net) methods for adaptive process control. *Proceedings of EUFIT '93*, ELITE Foundation, Aachen, Germany, 55-61.

Bersini H. and Varela F., 1994. The immune learning mechanisms: Recruitment reinforcement and their applications. *To appear in Computing with Biological Metaphors*, R. Patton (Ed.), Chapman and Hall

Bersini H., Nowé A., Caironi P.V.C., Dorigo M., 1994. A family of reinforcement learning algorithms. *Tech. Rep. IRIDIA/94-1*, Université Libre de Bruxelles, Belgium.

Bonarini A., 1993. ELF: Learning incomplete fuzzy rule sets for an autonomous robot. *Proceedings of EUFIT '93*, ELITE Foundation, Aachen, Germany, 69–75.

Booker L., Goldberg D.E., and Holland J.H., 1989. Classifier systems and genetic algorithms. *Artificial Intelligence*, 40, 1-3, 235–282.

Chapman D. and Kaelbling L.P., 1991. Input generalization in delayed reinforcement learning: An algorithm and performance comparison. *Proceeding of the Twelth International Joint Conference on Artificial Intelligence (IJCAI-91)*, 726–731.

Chrisman L., 1992. Reinforcement learning with perceptual aliasing: The perceptual distinction approach. *Proceeding of the Tenth National Conference on Artificial Intelligence* (AAAI-92), 183–188.

Colombetti M. and Dorigo M., 1992. Learning to control an autonomous robot by distributed genetic algorithms. *Proceedings of From Animals To Animats, Second International Conference on Simulation of Adaptive Behavior (SAB92)*, Honolulu, 305–312, Bradford Books, MIT Press.

Dayan P. and Hinton G.E., 1992. Feudal reinforcement learning. In C.L. Giles, S.J. Hanson and J.D. Cowan (Eds), *Advances in Neural Information Processing Systems 5*, 271-278. San Mateo, CA, Morgan Kaufmann.

Dorigo M., 1992. ALECSYS and the AutonoMouse: Learning to control a real robot by distributed classifier systems. *Technical Report No.92-011*, Politecnico di Milano, Italy.

Dorigo M., 1993. Genetic and non-genetic operators in ALECSYS. *Evolutionary Computation*, 1, 2, 151–164, MIT Press.

Dorigo M. and Colombetti M., 1994. Robot shaping: Developing autonomous agents through learning. *Artificial Intelligence, to appear.*

Dorigo M. and Schnepf U., 1993. Genetics-based machine learning and behavior-based robotics: A New Synthesis. *IEEE Transactions on Systems, Man, and Cybernetics*, 23, 1, 141–154.

Farmer D. 1991. A Rosetta Stone to connectionism. *In Emergent Computation*, Forrest S. (Ed.) MIT Press.

Goldberg D.E. 1989. *Genetic algorithms in search, optimization, and machine learning.* Addison-Wesley.

Holland J.H., 1980. Adaptive algorithms for discovering and using general patterns in growing knowledge bases. *International Journal of Policy Analysis and Information Systems*, 4, 2, 217-240.

Lin L-J., 1992. Self-improving reactive agents based on reinforcement learning, planning and teaching. *Machine Learning*, 8, 3-4, 293–322.

Lin L-J., 1993. Hierarchical learning of robot skills by reinforcement. *Proceedings of 1993 IEEE International Conference on Neural Networks*, IEEE, 181–186.

Lin L-J. and Mitchell T.M., 1992. Memory approaches to reinforcement learning in non-Markovian domains. *Tech.Rep. CMU-CS-92-138*, Carnegie Mellon University, Pittsburgh, PA, May 1992.

Mc Callum R.A., 1993. Overcoming incomplete perception with utile distinction memory. *Proceedings of the Tenth International Conference on Machine Learning*, Morgan Kaufmann, San Mateo, CA, 190–196.

Mahadevan S. and Connell J., 1992. Automatic programming of behavior-based robots using reinforcement learning. *Artificial Intelligence*, 55, 2, 311–365.

Mitchell T.M., 1982. Generalization as search. *Artificial Intelligence*, 18, 2, 203-226.

Munos R., Patinel J. and Goyeau P., 1994. Partitioned Q-learning. *Proceedings of From Animals To Animats, Third International Conference on Simulation of Adaptive Behavior (SAB94)*, Brighton, United Kingdom, August 8–12, 1994.

Riolo R.L., 1987. Bucket Brigade performance: II. Default hierarchies. *Proceedings of the Second International Conference on Genetic Algorithms*, J.J. Grefenstette (Ed.), Lawrence Erlbaum, 184–195.

Riolo R.L., 1989. The emergence of default hierarchies in learning classifier systems. *Proceedings of the Third International Conference on Genetic Algorithms*, J.D. Schaffer (Ed.), Morgan Kaufmann, 322–327.

Roberts G., 1993. Dynamic planning for classifier systems. *Proceedings of Fifth International Conference on Genetic Algorithms*, Morgan Kaufmann, San Mateo, CA, 231–237.

Samuel A.L., 1959. Some studies in machine learning using the game of checkers. *IBM Journal on Research and Development*, 3, 210–229. Reprinted in E.A. Feigenbaum and J.Feldman (Eds.) *Computers and thought.* New York: McGraw-Hill.

Schwartz A., 1993. A reinforcement learning method for maximizing undiscounted rewards. *Proceedings of Tenth*

International Conference on Machine Learning, Morgan Kaufmann, San Mateo, CA, 298–305.

Sutton R.S., 1988. Learning to predict by the methods of temporal differences. *Machine Learning*, 3, 1, 9–44.

Tsitsiklis J.N, 1993. Asynchronous stochastic approximation and Q-learning. *Internal Report from Laboratory for Information and Decision Systems and the Operations Research Center, MIT.*

Twardowski K., 1993. Credit assignment for pole balancing with learning classifier systems. *Proceedings of Fifth International Conference on Genetic Algorithms*, Morgan Kaufmann, San Mateo, CA, 238–245.

Valenzuela-Rendón M., 1991. The fuzzy classifier system: A classifier system for continuously varying variables. *Proceeding of the Fourth International Conference on Genetic Algorithms*, Morgan Kaufmann, San Mateo, CA, 346–353.

Watkins C. J. C. H., 1989. Learning with delayed rewards. *Ph. D. dissertation*, Psychology Department, University of Cambridge, England.

Watkins C. J. C. H. and Dayan P., 1992. Technical Note: Q-learning. *Machine Learning*, 8, 3-4, 279–292.

Whitehead S.D. and Lin L.J., 1994. Reinforcement learning in non-Markov environments. *Artificial Intelligence*, to appear.

Wilson S.W., 1985. Knowledge growth in an artificial animal. *Proceedings of the First International Conference on Genetic Algorithms and their Applications*, J.J. Grefenstette (Ed.), Lawrence Erlbaum, 16–23.

Wilson S.W., 1994. ZCS: a zeroth level classifier system. *Evolutionary Computation*, MIT Press, to appear.

Paying Attention to What's Important: Using Focus of Attention to Improve Unsupervised Learning

Leonard N. Foner
MIT Media Lab
20 Ames St, E15-305
Cambridge, MA 02139
foner@media.mit.edu

Pattie Maes
MIT Media Lab
20 Ames St, E15-305
Cambridge, MA 02139
pattie@media.mit.edu

Abstract

Adaptive autonomous agents have to learn about the effects of their actions so as to be able to improve their performance and adapt to long term changes. The problem of correlating actions with changes in sensor data is $O(n^2)$ and therefore computationally infeasible for any non-trivial application. We propose to make this problem more manageable by using focus of attention. In particular, we discuss two complementary methods for focus of attention: *perceptual selectivity* restricts the set of sensor data the agent attends to at a particular instant, while *cognitive selectivity* restricts the set of internal structures that is updated at a particular instant. We present results of an implemented algorithm, a variant of the *schema mechanism* [Drescher 91], which employs these two forms of focus of attention. The results demonstrate that incorporating focus of attention dramatically improves the tractability of learning action models without affecting the quality of the knowledge learned, at the relatively small cost of doubling the number of training examples required to learn the same knowledge.

1 Introduction

Autonomous agents have to learn about their environment so as to improve (because user programming has its limitations) and adapt (because things change). Several learning methods for autonomous agents have been proposed, in particular reinforcement learning [Sutton 91] [Kaelbling 93], classifier systems [Holland 86] [Wilson 85], action model learners [Drescher 91] [Maes 92] and mixed methods [Sutton 90] [Booker 88]. No matter which of these algorithms is used, a learning agent will have to correlate some number of sensory inputs with some number of internal structures in an attempt to extend its knowledge. This is conceptually a cross-product problem: each sensory bit should be correlated in some fashion with each already-built internal structure. As the number of sensory bits or the number of internal structures grows, the work required to perform this correlation grows approximately as $O(n^2)$.

Most unsupervised learning algorithms attempt to learn all that there is to know about the environment, with no selectivity. They flail about, often at random, attempting to learn every possible fact. It takes them far too long to learn a mass of mostly-irrelevant data. For example, [Drescher 91] introduces an algorithm for building successively more powerful descriptions of the results of taking particular actions in an unpredictable world. However, his algorithm scales poorly, and hence is unsuitable for realistic worlds with many facts, given the current state of computational hardware. Since its running speed decreases as more is learned about the world, the algorithm eventually becomes unusably slow, just as the agent is learning enough to make otherwise useful decisions.

A real creature does not do this. Instead, it uses different focus of attention mechanisms, among others *perceptual selectivity* and *cognitive selectivity*, to guide its learning. By focusing its attention to the important aspects of its current experience and memory, a real creature dramatically decreases the perceptual and cognitive load of learning about its environment and making decisions about what to do next. This research uses similar methods of selectivity to build a computationally tractable, unsupervised learning system that might be suitable for use in an autonomous agent that must learn and function in some complex world.

This paper presents an algorithm for learning statistical action models which incorporates perceptual and cognitive selectivity. In particular, we implemented a variation on Drescher's *schema mechanism* and demonstrate that the computational complexity of the algorithm is significantly improved without harming the correctness of the action models learned. The particular forms of perceptual and cognitive selectivity that are employed represent domain-independent heuristics for focusing attention that potentially can be incorporated into any learning algorithm.

The paper is organized as follows. Section 2 discusses different notions of focus of attention, concentrating on heuristics for perceptual and cognitive selectivity. Section 3 describes the algorithm implemented and the microworld used. Section 4 elaborates on the experimental results obtained. Section 5 lists some shortcomings and discusses future extensions. Finally, section 6 discusses related work.

2 Focus of Attention Methods

2.1 Introduction

To ease its learning task, an agent can employ a range of methods for focus of attention. It can be selective in terms of what sensor data it attends to as well as what internal structures it considers when acting and learning. These forms of focus of attention are termed *perceptual* and *cognitive selectivity* respectively. They are illustrated by the left and right braces respectively in Figure 1 below, and discussed in more detail in the following sections.

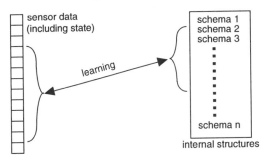

Figure 1. Sensory (left) and cognitive (right) pruning.

Along another dimension, there is a distinction between *domain-dependent* and *domain-independent methods* for focus of attention. Domain-independent methods represent general heuristics for focus of attention that can be employed in any domain. For example, one can attempt only to correlate events that happened close to one another in time. Domain-dependent heuristics, on the other hand, are specific to the domain at hand. They typically have been preprogrammed (by natural or artificial selection or by a programmer). For example, experiments have shown that when a rat becomes sick to its stomach, it will assume that whatever it ate recently is causally related to the sickness. That is, it is very hard for a rat to learn that a light flash or the sound of a bell is correlated to the stomach problem because it will focus on recently eaten food as the cause of the problem [Garcia 72]. This demonstrates that animals have evolved to pay attention to particular events when learning about certain effects.

Finally, the focus mechanism can be *goal-driven* and/or *world-driven*. Focus of attention in animals is both strongly world- and goal-dependent. The structure of the world determines which sensory or memory bits may be "usually" ignored (e.g. those not local in time and space), while the task determines those which are relevant some of the time and not at other times. For example, when hungry, any form of food is a very important stimulus to attend to.

The results reported in this paper concern world-dependent, but goal-independent, as well as domain-independent cognitive and sensory selectivity. Such pruning depends on constant properties of the environment and common tasks, and does not take into account what the current goal of the agent is. The methods can be applied to virtually any domain. While it is true that, in complex worlds, goal-driven and domain-dependent pruning is quite important, it is surprising how much of an advantage even goal-independent pruning can convey. Goal-driven and domain-dependent strategies for focus of attention are briefly discussed in the future research section.

2.2   Perceptual selectivity

Perceptual selectivity limits what stimuli might possibly be attended to at any one time, which puts limits on what might be learnable at that time. For example, a real creature would not pay attention to every square centimeter of its skin and try to correlate every nerve ending therein to every possible retinal cell in its eyes at every moment. Consequently, it might never learn some peculiar correlation between a particular patch of skin and a flash of light on some part of its retina, but presumably such correlations are not important to it in its natural environment.

Obvious physical dimensions along which to be perceptually selective include *spatial* and *temporal* selectivity. The universe tends to be spatially coherent: causes are generally located nearby to their effects (for example, pushing an object requires one to be in contact with it). Further, many causes lead to an observable effect within a short time (letting go of an object in a gravity field causes it to start falling immediately, rather than a week later). Real creatures use these sorts of spatial and temporal locality all the time, often by using eyes that only have high resolution in a small part of their visual field, and only noticing correlations between events that take place reasonably close together in time. While it is certainly *possible* to conceive of an agent that tracks every single visual event in the sphere around it, all at the same time, and which can remember pairs of events separated by arbitrary amounts of time without knowing a priori that the events might be related, the computational burden in doing so is essentially unbounded.[1] The algorithm discussed in section 3 implements temporal selectivity as well as spatial selectivity to reduce the number of sensor data that the agent has to correlate with its internal structures (see Figure 1 above). Note that the perceptual selectivity implemented is of a "passive" nature: the agent prunes its "bag of sensory bits," rather than changing the mapping of that bag of bits to the physical world by performing an action that changes the sensory data (such as changing its point of view). The latter would constitute active perceptual attention.

2.3   Cognitive selectivity

Cognitive selectivity limits what internal structures are attended to at any given moment.

Notice that for any agent that learns many facts, being cognitively selective is likely to be even more important than being perceptually selective, in the long run. The reasons for this are straightforward. First, consider the ratio of sensory to memory items. While the total number of possible sensory bits is limited, the number of internal structures may grow without bound. This means that, were we to use a strategy which prunes all sensory information and all cognitive information each to some *constant fraction* of their original, unpruned case, we would cut the total computation required by some constant factor—but this factor would be much larger in the cognitive case, because the number of facts stored would likely far outnumber the number of sensory bits available.

Second, consider a strategy in which a *constant number* of sensory bits or a *constant number* of remembered facts are attended to at any given time. This is analogous to the situation in which a real organism has hard performance limits along

---

1. Many algorithms for learning from experience employ an extreme form of temporal selectivity: the agent can only correlate events that are "one timestep" apart.

both perceptual and cognitive axes; no matter how many facts it knows, it can only keep a fixed number of them in working memory. In this case, as the internal structures grow, the organism can do its sensory-to-memory correlations in essentially constant time, rather than the aforementioned $O(n^2)$ time, though at a cost: as its knowledge grows, it is ignoring at any given time an increasingly large percentage of all the knowledge it has.

Compromise strategies which keep growth in the work required to perform these correlations within bounds (e.g., less than $O(n^2)$), yet not give in completely to utilizing ever-smaller fractions of current knowledge (e.g., more than $O(1)$) are possible. One way to compromise is to use the current *goal* to help select what facts are relevant; such *goal-driven pruning* will be discussed later. Since generally only a small number of goals are likely to be relevant or applicable at any one time (often only one), this can help to keep the amount of correlation work in bounds.[2]

Similarly, one can use the world or sensor data to restrict the number of structures looked at (as is the case in the algorithm described in this paper). Not all internal structures are equally relevant at any given instant. In particular, internal structures that refer neither to current nor expected future perceptual inputs are less likely to be useful than internal structures which do. This is the particular domain-independent, goal-independent, world-driven heuristic for cognitive selectivity which is employed in the algorithm described in the next section. Again, in real creatures domain-dependent and goal-driven cognitive selectivity play a large role too. For example, the subset of internal structures that are considered at some instant is not only determined by what the agent senses and what it expects to sense next, but also by what it is "aiming" to sense or not sense (i.e., the desired goals). Goal-driven and domain-dependent solutions to cognitive selectivity are discussed in the future research section.

3   Improving learning via focus

3.1   The agent and its environment

This research started with an existing learning algorithm [Drescher 91], and added a focus of attention mechanism, as described below, to make learning faster (requiring less computation per timestep). While Drescher's original work does include a concept similar to both tactical and strategic goals, his system does not exploit goals to guide the learning process. Further, it has no perceptual selectivity (apart from a narrow temporal selectivity), and assumes that every sensory bit might be useful all the time.[3] This approach leads to a theoretically "pure" result, but one which is difficult to use in a real application, and somewhat implausible in describing how real organisms learn.

Drescher is interested in Piagetian modeling, so his microworld is oriented towards the world as perceived by a very young infant (less than around five months old). The simplified microworld (which is shown below) consists of a simulated, two-dimensional "universe" of 49 grid squares (7 by 7).

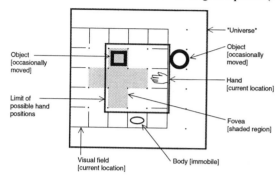

Figure 2. The domain microworld.

Each square can be either empty or contain some object. Superimposed upon this universe is a simulated "eye" which can see a square region 5 grid squares on a side, and which can be moved around within the limits of the "universe." This eye has a "fovea" of a few squares in the center, which can see additional details in objects (these extra details can be used to differentiate objects enough to determine their identities). The universe also consists of a "hand" which occupies a grid square, and can bump into and grasp objects. (The infant's arm is not represented; just the hand.) An immobile "body" occupies another grid square.

Every sensory item is represented in the simulation as a single bit. In Drescher's original algorithm, there is no grouping of these bits in any particular way (e.g., as a retinotopic map, or into particular modalities); the learning algorithm sees only an undifferentiated "bag of bits."

The "facts" learned by this system are what Drescher calls **schemas**. They consist of a triple of **context** (the initial state of the world, as perceived by the sensory system), the **action** taken on this iteration, and **result** (the subsequent perceived state), which maps actions taken in a particular configuration of sensory inputs into the new sensory inputs resulting from that action. A typical schema might therefore be, "If my eye's proprioceptive feedback indicates that it is in position (2,3) [*context*], and I move my eye one unit to the right [*action*], then my eye's proprioceptive feedback indicates that it is in position (3,3) [*result*]." Another typical schema might be, "If my hand's proprioceptive feedback indicates that it is in position (3,4) [*context*], and I move it one unit back [*action*], I will feel a touch on my mouth and on my hand [*result*]" (this is because the hand will move from immediately in front of the mouth to in contact with the mouth). Notice that this latter

---

2. Another way to compromise might be to investigate much more of memory when other demands on the agent's time are minimal, essentially doing as much extra work as possible when the opportunity presents itself. Such an agent might "dream" in an attempt to piece together old, probably-irrelevant facts and recent data to build new facts, but only do this when it is not otherwise engaged in performing useful work.

3. With one very small exception, as follows. The last action taken is itself represented in the bits given to the learning algorithm (since any new schema created to represent the results of the action just taken will be a schema mentioning that action, and no other). Since *only* the last action taken is so represented to the learning algorithm, *only* the last action taken is attended to when attempting to correlate actions with their results. All other sensory inputs (e.g., proprioceptive, visual, etc) are attended to whether or not they have changed recently.

schema is *multimodal* in that it relates a proprioceptive to a tactile sense; the learning mechanism and its microworld build many multimodal schema, relating touch to vision, vision to proprioception, taste to touch (on the mouth), graspability to the presence of an object near the hand, and so forth. It also creates *unimodal* schemas of the form illustrated in the first schema above, which relates proprioception to proprioception.

A schema is deemed to be *reliable* if its predictions of (**context, action, result**) are accurate more than a certain threshold of the time. A schema maintains an *extended context* and an *extended result* which keep statistics for every item not yet present in the context or result so as to detect candidates for spinning off a new schema. If we already have a reliable schema, and adding some additional sensory item to the items already expressed in either its context or its result makes a schema which appears that it, too, might be reliable, we *spin off* a new schema expressing this new conjunction. *Spinoff schemas* satisfy several other constraints, such as not ever duplicating an existing schema, and may themselves serve to be the basis for additional spinoffs later.

The behavior of the world is allowed to be nondeterministic (e.g., actions may sometimes fail, or sensory inputs may change in manners uncorrelated with the actions being taken), and each schema also records statistical information which is used to determine whether the schema accurately reflects a regularity in the operation of the world, or whether an initial "guess" at the behavior of the world later turned out to be a coincidence.[4]

The possible sensory inputs consist of all bits arriving from the "eye," proprioceptive inputs from eye and hand (which indicate where, relative to the body, the eye is pointing or the hand is reaching), tactile inputs from the hand, and taste inputs from the mouth (if an object was in contact with it). The "eye" reports only whether an object (not *which* object, only the presence of one) is in a grid square or not, except in its central fovea, where it reports a few additional bits if an object was present. The "infant" does *not* have a panoramic knowledge of all 49 squares of the universe at once; at any given instant, it only knows about what the eye can see, what the hand is touching, or what the mouth is tasting, combined with proprioceptive inputs for eye and hand position. In particular, certain senses, viewed unimodally, are subject to perceptual aliasing [Whitehead and Ballard 90]: for example, if a schema mentions only a particular bit in the visual field, without also referring to the visual proprioceptive inputs (which determine where the eye is pointing), then that schema may be subject to such aliasing. Similarly, any schema mentioning any visual-field sensory item that is not in the fovea may alias different objects, since the non-foveal visual field reports only the presence or absence of an object in each position, rather than the exact identity of the object in question. In Drescher's original implementation, the system spent most of its time (a fixed 90%) taking random actions and observing the results. The remaining 10% of its time was spent

taking actions which had led to some reliable outcome before, to see if actions could be combined.[5]

3.2 The work of learning

Given the action model learning algorithm described above, at each clock tick, we must first update various statistics reflecting what just happened; this is the "perception" part of the learning algorithm, and a focus mechanism must dictate which sensory item numbers to pay attention to ($Stat_i$), for which schema numbers ($Stat_s$). Second, we must decide whether to spin off a new schema; this is the "learning" part of the algorithm, and here the focus mechanism dictates which item numbers to check for reliability ($Spin_i$) for which schema numbers ($Spin_s$). Thus, our choice of these four sets of numbers determines which sensory items and schemas are used in either updating our perception of the world, or deciding when a correlation has been learned. $Stat_i$ and $Stat_s$ determine the perceptual selectivity, while $Spin_i$ and $Spin_s$ determine the cognitive selectivity.

	Statistics	**Spinoffs**
Which items?	$Stat_i$	$Spin_i$
Which schemas?	$Stat_s$	$Spin_s$

The algorithm does the vast majority of its work in two inner loops (one for updating statistics, reflecting what is currently perceived, and one for deciding whether to spin off new schemas, reflecting learning from that perception). The number of items or schemas selected at any given clock tick determines the amount of work done by the learning algorithm in that tick. Thus, if $Work_{Stat}$ is the work done during the statistical-update part of the algorithm (e.g., perceiving the world) of any one clock tick, and $Work_{Spin}$ is similarly the amount of work done in deciding which spinoff schemas to create, then the work done during either one is the product of the number of items attended to and the number of schemas attended to, or:

$$Work_{Stat} = \|Stat_i\| \bullet \|Stat_s\|$$
$$Work_{Spin} = \|Spin_i\| \bullet \|Spin_s\|$$

This means that the total work per step (clock tick) is simply the sum of these individual pieces, and that the total work over many steps is simply the sum of the work during the individual steps:

$$Work_{Step} = Work_{Stat} + Work_{Spin}$$

$$Work_{Total} = \sum_{steps} Work_{Step}$$

Thus, the behavior of $Work_{Step}$ over time tells us how well the algorithm will do at keeping up with the real work, e.g., how fast it slows down as the number of iterations, hence schemas, increases.

A way of evaluating the utility of various algorithms is to examine the amount of work performed per schema (either reliable schemas or all schemas; the former being perhaps the more useful metric):

$$Work_{Step}SchemaRel = \frac{Work_{Step}}{SchemaRel_{Step}}$$

---

4. We ignore here the details of the statistical mechanism that keeps the algorithm from being fooled by mere coincidence; see the marginal attribute mechanism of [Drescher 91].

---

5. See the composite action mechanism of [Drescher 91].

which is simply the amount of work performed during some steps divided by the number of reliable schemas generated by that work.[6] A similar definition for total schemas over total work is straightforward.[7]

An algorithm which determines these choices is thus described by the pairs $<<Stat_i, Stat_s>, <Spin_i, Spin_s>>$; we will call each element a *selector*.

A little more terminology will enable us to discuss the actual selectors used. $Schema_{max}$ is the number of schemas currently learned. $Item_{max}$ is the number of sensory items. $Item_n$ is the value of sensory bit n, and $Item_{n,t}$ is the value of that item at some time t. $SchemaDep_sOn_i$ denotes some schema s which is dependent upon (e.g., references in its context or result) some item i.

3.3   The basic learning algorithm

In Drescher's basic algorithm, every possible sensory bit *before* an action taken by the "infant" was correlated with every possible sensory bit *after* the action, for *every* schema that has been created so far. In other words, $Stat_i$ and $Spin_i$ use the selector **all item numbers**, or **AIN**:

$$AIN = \{n \mid 0 \leq n \leq Item_{max}\}$$

and $Stat_s$ and $Spin_s$ use the selector **all schema numbers**, or **ASN**:

$$ASN = \{n \mid 0 \leq n \leq Schema_{max}\}$$

This means that the basic algorithm does a tremendous amount of work in the two $n \times m$ inner loops, where n is the size of the set of items in use, $\|AIN\|$, and similarly m is the size of the set of schemas in use, $\|ASN\|$. Hence,

$$Work_{Stat} = Work_{Spin} = \|AIN\| \bullet \|ASN\|$$

It can eventually learn a large number of facts about the world in this way, but it runs slowly, and becomes increasingly slow as the number of known facts increases.

3.4   The focused algorithm

Various pruning techniques help a great deal over the basic approach. The most successful of the approaches, which we shall call the *focused* approach, takes the following tack:

- *Perceptual selectivity.* When updating statistics, only consider sensory items which have changed very recently (last two clock ticks) and only in schemas which make predictions about those items.

- *Cognitive selectivity.* When deciding whether to spin off (make a new fact), only consider sensory items which

have changed in the last clock tick, and only consider schemas which have had their statistics changed in the last clock tick (such schemas can only have had their statistics changed if they themselves made predictions involving sensory items which themselves have changed).

Put more precisely, the items used were as follows. $Stat_i$ used the **all changed items in history**, or **CINIH** selector (where the word "history" refers to a timeline of prior events, of some chosen length, and in this case of length 2),

$$CINIH_H = AIN \cap \{\exists (0 < T \leq H) \mid Item_{n,t} \neq Item_{n,t-T}\}$$

while $Spin_i$ used a specialization of this, in which the history is only the very last event, which we shall call the **changed item numbers**, or **CIN**, selector for compactness:

$$CIN = AIN \cap \{Item_{n,t} \neq Item_{n,t-1}\} = CINIH_1$$

Similarly, the schemas used were as follows. Consider the set **all bare schemas**, or **ABS**, which consists only of schemas which make no predictions about anything (there is one of these per action at the start of any run, and no other schemas; this is the root set from which new schemas which predict correlations between actions and sensory inputs may be spun off):

$$ABS = ASN \cap \{\forall (0 \leq i \leq Item_{max}) \mid \neg SchemaDep_nOn_i\}$$

To define $Stat_s$, we add to these **schemas dependent upon changed items**, to get:

$$ABSPSDUCI = ABS \cup \{SchemaDep_nOn_{i \in CIN}\}$$

This selector is a special case of the more general one (which uses an arbitrary-length history), in that it uses a history of length 1. The general case, of course, is:

$$ABSPSDUCIIH_H = ABS \cup \{SchemaDep_nOn_{i \in CINIH_H}\}$$

Finally, $Spin_s$ is defined as schemas with recently updated statistics, or

$$SWRUS = ASN \cap \{SchemaDep_nOn_i \mid (i \in CIN)\}$$

Adding these changes amounts to adding some simple lookup tables to the basic algorithm that track which items were updated in the last clock tick, and, for each item, which schemas refer to it in their contexts or results, then using these tables to determine which sensory items or schemas will be participants in the statistical update or spinoffs. Such tables require a negligible, constant overhead on the basic algorithm.

The perceptual and cognitive strategies above place a high value on novel stimuli. Causes which precede their effects by more than a couple of clock ticks are not attended to. In the world described above, this is perfectly reasonable behavior. If the world had behaviors in it where more prior history was important, it would be necessary to attend further back in time to make schemas which accurately predicted the effects of actions.

These particular strategies also place a high value on a very specific spatial locality. Even sensory items that are very near items which have changed are not attended to. Since this microworld only has objects which are one bit wide, and the actions which involve them are, e.g., touch (which requires contact), this is the right strategy. [8]

---

6. Note a peculiar detail here. It is possible for a schema that was formerly thought to be reliable to be later decided to be unreliable. This could happen if the world has changed in the meantime, or if some not-very-correct correlation happened often enough to push the schema over the arbitrary threshold from not being considered reliable to being considered reliable, and then later data pushed the schema's reliability back down. Hence, it is possible for the number of reliable schemas to *decrease* during a single step, and this is not an altogether infrequent occurrence. This means that, while the *average* of $Work_{Step}SchemaRel$ is positive, the instantaneous value might be negative if $Step$ is a single step or a small number of steps.
7. Since the *total* number of schemas (as opposed to *reliable* schemas) can never decrease, this number must always be nonnegative.

```
                        (-vp02&vp12)/eyer/vp22
                        (-vp10&-vf33)/eyef/-vf33         (-vp10&-vf33)/eyef/-vf33
                                                                                   (-vp11&-vf33)/eyer/-fovf01        (-vp11&-vf33)/eyer/-fovf01
                                                                                   (-vp11&-vf33)/eyer/-fovf23        (-vp11&-vf33)/eyer/-fovf23
                                                                                   (-vp11&-vf33)/eyer/-vf23          (-vp11&-vf33)/eyer/-vf23
(-vp11&-vf33)/eyer/vf33
(-vp12&-vf20)/eyer/vf33
                        (-vp12&-vf34)/eyef/-vf33         (-vp12&-vf34)/eyef/-vf33
                                                                                   (-vp12&vf22)/eyel/vp12            (-vp12&vf22)/eyer/vp12
                        (-vp20&-vf23)/eyef/-fovf01       (-vp20&-vf23)/eyef/-fovf01
                        (-vp20&-vf23)/eyef/-fovf23       (-vp20&-vf23)/eyef/-fovf23
```

Figure 3. A tiny chunk of a 5-way comparison of generated schemas. Five columns of schemas, sorted alphabetically by their printed representations, are shown here side-by-side, horizontally aligned. Small holes are fine, but large holes could indicate a potentially missing class of schemas.

The computational complexity of the two $n \times m$ inner loops is reduced by these selectors as follows:

$$Work_{Stat} = \|CINIH_2\| \bullet \|ABSPSDUCI\|$$
$$Work_{Spin} = \|CIN\| \bullet \|SWRUS\|$$

In any run which generates more than a trivial number of schemas or has more than a handful of sensory bits, this is a dramatic reduction in the complexity, as shown in Figure 4 on the next page.

4 Results

4.1 Evaluation of the learning

A crucial question that must be addressed concerns what the system learns, and whether these focus of attention mechanisms impair that learning in any way. After all, one way to decrease the work of learning would be to simply ignore the world completely—but the resultant gain in speed could hardly be said to be worthwhile, because nothing would be learned.

4.1.1 Were enough correct schemas learned?

The schema system generates thousands of schemas in runs of reasonable duration, for instance, runs of ten or twenty thousand iterations have generated over 7000 schemas. How is one to know what all of these facts really represent? The state of the knowledge base is critically dependent upon prior knowledge: a more-detailed schema can only be generated from a less-detailed one, so any change in the learning mechanism which changes which schemas are generated leads to rapidly-diverging sets of generated schemas. While all may say *approximately* the same thing, the fine details of exactly which facts are learned will tend to be different. It would be possible to run enough iterations so that almost every possible fact that *is* true about the microworld could be *learned* to be true, but this is an unreasonably large amount of computation (the total number of learned schemas plotted over time appears to have an asymptote at least in the tens of thousands of schemas, even for this simple world).

4.1.1.1 Manual evaluation methods

Manual inspection of the schemas generated by these runs was employed as a first cut at establishing that alternative focus mechanisms were not preventing the learning of crucial

facts, and tools were developed for examining how many schemas, representing what general categories of facts (e.g., unimodal visual field, multimodal across various modalities, etc) were being learned. By comparing rough totals of different types of generated schemas, one assurance that nothing critical was being left out could be obtained.

Another manual method of checking the results employed *n*-way comparisons of the generated schemas themselves. The **(context, action, result)** triple of each schema can be represented relatively compactly in text (ignoring all the statistical machinery that also makes up a schema); by sorting the schemas generated in any particular run into a canonical order, and then comparing several runs side-by-side, one can gain an approximate idea of how different runs fared. Figure 3, at the top of this page, demonstrates a tiny chunk from a 5-way comparison of a certain set of runs, in which 5 somewhat-different runs were compared for any large, overall changes to the types of schemas generated.

4.1.1.2 Automatic evaluation methods

Manual methods are tedious and error-prone. Furthermore, the underlying reason that an agent learns is to aid it in the pursuit of its goal. This means that a sensible evaluation strategy is to ask if the agent has, indeed, learned enough to accomplish goals that it was unable to accomplish before learning.

A simple way to establish what the agent knows is therefore to use the generated schemas as parts of a plan, "chaining" them together such that the result of one schema serves as the context of the next, and to build these chains of schemas until at least one chain reaches from the initial state of the microworld to the goal state. If we can build at least one such chain, we can claim that the agent "knows" how to accomplish the goal in that context; the shortness of the chain can be used as a metric as to "how well" the agent knows.[9] For this task, the schemas to be used should be those deemed "reliable," e.g., those which have been true sufficiently often in the past that their predictions have a good chance of being correct. Simply employing *all* schemas, reliable or not, will lead to many grossly incorrect chains.

At the start, no facts about the world are known, hence no chain of any length can be built. However, after a few thousand schemas are built (generally between 1000 and 5000), most starting states can plausibly chain to a simple goal state,

---

8. Selectors which attended to the unchanged items in a spatial "halo" around changed items were found to be less efficient, in terms of work per reliable schema, than the selectors described here. A different microworld (such as one with spatially larger objects, or different types of actions available to the agent) might require selectors that attended to a wider radius of (unchanged) sensory items around items which actually changed, in which case such "haloing" would be necessary to reliably learn the effects of actions.

---

9. Note that the small size of the microworld and the small number of actions possible at any given timestep mean that even a random walk through state space has a significant chance of accomplishing the goal, if we are willing to wait long enough; hence, a path which is *close to optimal*, rather than one which exists at all, should be our metric for whether learning has succeeded.

Algorithm				Learning			Work required			Facts per work unit		
Spinoff selectors		Statistic selectors		Schemas			Inner loops (x10^6)			Reliable schemas over		
Items	Schemas	Items	Schema	Total	Rel	T/R	Spin	Stat	Both	Spin	Stats	Both
AIN	**ASN**	**AIN**	**ASN**	**1756**	**993**	**1.77**	**533**	**533**	**1066**	**1.9**	**1.9**	**0.9**
AIN	ASN	CINIH	ABSPSDUCI	1135	403	2.82	398	12	410	1.0	33.6	**1.0**
AIN	ASN	AIN	ABSPSDUCI	1110	518	2.14	391	55	446	1.3	9.4	**1.2**
CIN	**ASN**	**AIN**	**ASN**	**1693**	**948**	**1.79**	**44**	**524**	**568**	**21.5**	**1.8**	**1.7**
CIN	**SWRUS**	**AIN**	**ASN**	**1395**	**791**	**1.76**	**2**	**463**	**466**	**316.4**	**1.7**	**1.7**
CIN	ABSPSDUCI	AIN	ASN	1622	924	1.76	15	510	525	61.6	1.8	**1.8**
CIN	ASN	AIN	ABSPSDUCI	1110	506	2.19	33	54	87	15.3	9.4	**5.8**
CIN	ABSPSDUCI	AIN	ABSPSDUCI	1110	506	2.19	10	54	64	50.6	9.4	**7.9**
CIN	ABSPSDUCI	CINIH	ASN	1366	643	2.12	13	64	77	49.5	10.0	**8.4**
CIN	ASN	CINIH	ABSPSDUCI	1136	399	2.85	34	12	46	11.7	33.3	**8.7**
CIN	**SWRUS**	**AIN**	**ABSPSDUCI**	**1102**	**498**	**2.21**	**1**	**53**	**54**	**415.0**	**9.4**	**9.2**
CIN	SWRUS	CINIH	ASN	1353	688	1.97	2	64	66	275.2	10.8	**10.3**
CIN	ABSPSDUCI	CINIH	ABSPSDUCI	1136	399	2.85	10	12	22	40.7	33.3	**18.3**
CIN	**SWRUS**	**CINIH**	**ABSPSDUCI**	**1134**	**398**	**2.85**	**1**	**12**	**13**	**331.7**	**33.2**	**30.2**

**Figure 4. Various selectors versus number of schemas and total computation, for 5000 iterations.
Bold lines are discussed in section 4.2 (below); the acronyms for the algorithms are defined in sections 3.2-3.4.**

such as centering the visual field over the hand, in a close-to-optimal number of steps.

Given this mechanism, how well did the focus of attention mechanisms fare? Quite well. In general, given the same approximate number of generated schemas, both the basic and focused approaches cited above learned "the same" information: they could both have plausibly short chains generated that led from initial states to goals. Both the chaining mechanism described above, and manual inspection, showed no egregious gaps in the knowledge or particular classes or types of facts that failed to be learned.

As shown in Figure 4 above, and explained in section 4.2 below, the focused approach tended to require approximately twice as many timesteps to yield the same number of schemas as the unfocused approach. This means that a real robot which employed these methods would require twice as many experiments or twice as much time trundling about in the world to learn the same facts. However, the reduction of the amount of computation required to learn these facts by between one and two orders of magnitude means that the processor such a robot must employ could be much smaller and cheaper—which would probably make the difference between having it onboard and not. This is even more compelling when one realizes that these computational savings get bigger and bigger as the robot learns more facts.

4.1.2 Were any incorrect schemas learned?

The existing statistical machinery of the schema mechanism goes to great pains to avoid being fooled by occasional coincidence. Only if some change in the state of the world is positively correlated with an action more often than it is negatively correlated, and only if we have seen enough instances of both the event happening after some specific action and the event *not* happening in the absence of the action, *and* if the event is unexplainable by any other schemas, will the mechanism conclude that the action is truly the cause of the event. (Further explanation is beyond the scope of this paper; see the marginal attribution mechanism in [Drescher 91].)

Because of this, the only way that any learning algorithm which uses this system could learn "incorrect" facts (e.g., correlations that do not, in fact, reflect true correlations in the world) would be to systematically exclude relevant evidence that indicates that a schema that is thought to be reliable is in fact unreliable. No evidence of this was found in spot checks of any test runs. It is believed (but not proved) that none of the algorithms here can lead to such systematic exclusion of relevant information: the mechanism may miss correct correlations (such is the tradeoff of having a focus of attention in the first place), but it will not miss only the correlations that would tend to otherwise invalidate a schema thought to be reliable.

4.2   Comparison of the strategies

The table above presents partial results from several runs with different choices of selectors. Only the most salient combinations of selectors were included in this table. Of those, the rows in boldface will be discussed below; the non-boldfaced rows are included to give a feel for how different choices can influence the results.

The results in this table were all produced by runs 5000 iterations long. Similar runs of two or three times as long have produced comparable results.

The first four columns of the table show the particular selectors in use for any given run; the top row shows those selectors which correspond to the basic (Drescher) algorithm, while the bottom row shows the most highly-focused algorithm, as described in section 3.4 above.

The table is sorted in order by its last column, which shows number of *reliable* schemas generated during the entire 5000-iteration run, divided by the amount of total work required. For conciseness, we shall call the value in this column β, which is defined as:

$$\text{Facts per work unit} = \beta = \frac{SchemaRel_{Total}}{Work_{Total} \times 10^{-6}}$$

where the multiplication by 10^{-6} is simply to normalize the resulting numbers to be near unity, given the millionfold ratio between work units and number of schemas generated.

The bold rows in the table show successive changes to the selectors used, one at a time. The top row is the basic algorithm, which shows that about a billion total inner loops were required to learn 1756 schemas, 993 of which were reliable, which gives a β of 0.9.

Note that, because the world is stochastic (for example, the two "inanimate" objects occasionally move from one square to a neighboring square, approximately every few hundred clock ticks), one might imagine that there would be variance in the number and reliability of schemas generated between two runs, even if they use the same strategy. In fact, this is true, but the variance is quite low: out of a run of two or three thousand schemas with the same strategy and different seeds for the random number generator (hence different random behaviors in the world), the difference in the number of schemas generated is generally less than ten. In other words, the number of schemas generated is usually within 1% between runs using the same algorithm. Further, the types of schemas generated also match each other quite closely, as determined by *n*-way comparisons between runs, using the techniques discussed in section 4.1.1.1 above. (The exact schemas generated will, of course, be different, as discussed in section 4.1.1.)

Let us examine changes to the selectors for spinoffs, which determine the cognitive selectivity, or what is attended to in learning new schemas from the existing schemas. When we change $Spin_i$ from **AIN** to **CIN**, the amount of work drops by about a factor of two, while the number of generated schemas barely decreases. This means that virtually all schemas made predictions about items which changed in the immediately preceding clock tick (e.g., that corresponding to the action just taken), hence looking any further back in time for them costs us computation without a concommittant increase in utility.

Changing $Spin_s$ from **ASN** to **SWRUS**, given that $Spin_i$ is already using the selector **CIN**, yields a small improvement in β (not visible at the precision in the table), and also a small improvement in the ratio of reliable to total schemas. (Were $Spin_i$ not already **CIN**, the improvement would be far more dramatic, as demonstrated in runs not shown in the table.) Note, however, the enormous decrease in the amount of work done by the spinoff mechanism when $Spin_s$ changes from **ASN** to **SWRUS**, dropping from 10% of $Work_{Total}$ to 1%.

Next, let us examine the effects of perceptual selectivity. Changing $Stat_s$ from **ASN** to **ABSPSDUCI** increases β by a factor of 5.4, to 9.2, by decreasing the amount of work required to update the perceptual statistics by almost an order of magnitude. In essence, we are now only bothering to update the statistical information in the extended context or extended result of a schema, for some particular sensory item in some particular schema, if the schema depends upon that sensory item.

Finally, examine the last bold row, in which $Stat_i$ was changed from **AIN** to **CINIH**. β increases by a factor of 3.2, relative to the previous case, as the amount of statistical-up-

date work dropped by about a factor of four. We are now perceiving effectively only those changes in sensory items which might have some bearing in spinning off a schema which already references them.

Note that each successive tightening of the focus has some cost in the number of schemas learned in a given number of iterations. This means that, e.g., a real robot would require increasingly large numbers of experiments in the real world to learn the same facts. However, this is not a serious problem, since, given the focus algorithm described here, such a robot would require only about twice as many experiments, for any size run, as it would in the unfocused algorithm. This means that its learning rate has been slowed down by a small, roughly constant factor, while the computation required to do the learning has dropped enormously.

5   Discussion and Future Work

Even though it shows promising results, the algorithm discussed above only represents a small piece of the puzzle. Several major topics deserve further attention if this research is to grow into a more complete model describing focus of attention's role in learning by an autonomous adaptive agent; some of these are being addressed in current work.

1. The work reported above demonstrates that large savings can be obtained even if goals are not incorporated into the mechanism of focus of attention. A real creature has short-term *goals*, which not only inform its choice of actions, but also help it to decide what is worth learning about. These short-term goals (such as individual steps toward feeding: searching for food, cleaning the food, etc) are usually inspired from long-term goals or *drives* (such as trying to keep its level of hunger low). We intend to expand the model discussed above to include goal-based, domain-independent heuristics for focus of attention. In particular, we will experiment with the agent also attending to the sensor data related to the goal (and active subgoals) and the internal structures that refer to the goal or active subgoals. Even though this would make the agent attend to more items at one time than is currently the case, we hope to prove that this will improve the overall learning rate for learning "the facts that matter" (i.e., how to achieve the goals).

2. The work reported above does not deal with domain-dependent perceptual and cognitive attention. As was already mentioned in section 2, it is evident that in nature, creatures have an innate bias towards certain sensor data or certain internal structures given a goal (drive) and current state [Garcia 72].

3. The model of perception in the above model is narrow-minded. The set of sensor data that the agent tries to correlate with its actions is taken as a given. The system does not couple learning about actions with learning about perception. It does not *learn* what to pay attention to or learn that more features should be paid attention to. Ideally, an agent would create new features and categories to perceive the environment based on whatever categories its goals and environment require.

4. Another way in which the model presented above is naive about perception is that perception is modeled as a pure

feed-forward process. Given a particular gaze, resulting in a particular image, the model dictates which sensor items to prune. We will have to take this further and consider a model in which the agent can actively seek out the sensor data that it considers "relevant" at some point in time (i.e., relate this to work in active perception [Aloimonos 93]).

6   Related Work

A typical agent in the world cannot perceive every part of the world at once, nor should it—even "perceiving" without "learning" is expensive if the agent must perceive everything. However, not perceiving the whole world at once can lead to a phenomenon that [Whitehead and Ballard 90] calls *perceptual aliasing*, in which different world states can appear identical to the agent, and which causes most reinforcement learning mechanisms to perform poorly or not at all. Both they and [Woodfill and Zabih 90] propose systems which combine selective visual attention (which is used to "ignore" certain parts of the world at certain times) with special algorithms to attempt to overcome the aliasing problem.

[Kaelbling and Chapman 90] propose a technique (the G algorithm) for using statistical measures to recursively subdivide the world known by an agent into finer and finer pieces, as needed, making particular types of otherwise intractable unsupervised learning algorithms more tractable. One could view that as an example of perceptual selectivity: the agent gradually increases the set of state variables that are considered, as needed, when selecting actions and learning (updating statistics).

[Chapman 90] describes a system that uses selective visual attention to play a video game. Even though the principles described are general, the particular methods used by his agent are very domain-dependent (they are specific to the particular problems his agent faces). Chapman is less concerned with how focus of attention and learning correlate. Instead he focuses on how to reduce the problem of perception and the inferencing problem by the use of visual routines.

Finally, all classifier systems have a built-in mechanism for generalizing over situations as well as actions and thereby perform some form of selective attention. In particular, a classifier may include multiple "don't care" symbols which will match several specific sensor data vectors and actions. This makes it possible for classifier systems to sample parts of the state space at different levels of abstraction and as such to find the most abstract representation (or the set of items which are relevant) of a classifier that is useful for a particular problem the agent has. [Wilson 85] argues that the classifier system does indeed tend to evolve more general classifiers which "neglect" whatever inputs are irrelevant.

It should be mentioned that the methods described in the core of this paper are likely to be applicable to many other machine learning systems. While Drescher's schema system keeps exhaustive statistics and is thus easy to adapt in the manner shown, *any* agent that tries to correlate its actions with results must keep around *some* sort of statistics regarding those results from which to learn, even if they are only available for the instant of perception, and those stored statistics are candidates for pruning. Further, any such agent must

somehow perceive the world, and its sensory inputs are likewise candidates for pruning.

For example, the particular "best" strategies chosen here (bottom line of Figure 4) are likely to be available to most learning systems operating in a discrete microworld. They require being able to keep track of which sensory items have changed recently, and which facts depend upon (e.g., make predictions concerning) those items. This does not seem an insurmountable obstacle for many possible algorithms. It is even possible that particular algorithms which do not possess absolute knowledge about, for example, which sensory items are mentioned in any given learned fact (such as the hidden nodes of a neural net) might nonetheless be able to yield a probabilistic estimate of how likely it is that some particular part of the internal knowledge base might depend on a particular sensory input. If so, such algorithms might also allow cognitive pruning to take place.

7   Conclusion

Trying to learn every possible fact about the world, without reference to the utility of those facts or the cost in computational power to acquire them, is a self-defeating strategy that leads to systems that require too much computation and which run too slowly to function adequately in the real world or on real tasks. Selective perceptual attention and selective access to relevant memories can be used to reduce the perceptual and cognitive load for agents that have to learn from experience. We have implemented an algorithm for learning action models which incorporates a domain-independent set of heuristics for focus of attention. Experimental results have demonstrated that this algorithm is significantly more computationally tractable than its non-focused counterpart and that it still is able to learn correct knowledge that is relevant. However, it should be remembered that such focus, as in real animals, amounts to an engineering tradeoff: in this case, it took approximately twice as many interactions with the world to learn the same number of facts.

Acknowledgments

[Ramstad 92] provided an initial implementation part of the algorithm described in [Drescher 91] for use on a sequential architecture computer. Though the first author has subsequently completely rewritten that implementation, and simultaneously extended for the purposes of this research, it served as a jumping-off point for that later work.

References

Yiannis Aloimonos, editor, *Active Vision*, Lawrence Erlbaum Associates, Inc., 1993.

Lashon Booker, "Classifier Systems that Learn Internal World Models," in *Machine Learning Journal*, Volume 1, Number 2,3, 1988.

David Chapman, *Vision, Instruction, and Action*, MIT TR-1204 (doctoral thesis), April 1990.

Gary Drescher, *Made Up Minds: A Constructivist Approach to Artificial Intelligence*, MIT Press, 1991.

J. Garcia, B. K. McGowan, and K. F. Green, "Biological constraints on conditioning," in *Biological Boundaries of Learn-*

ing, edited by M. E. P. Seligman and J. L. Hager, Appleton-Century-Crofts, New York, 1972., pp. 21-43.

John H. Holland, "Escaping Brittleness: the Possibilities of General-Purpose Learning Algorithms applied to Parallel Rule-Based Systems," in *Machine Learning, an Artificial Intelligence Approach, Volume II*, edited by R.S. Michalski, J.G. Carbonell and T.M. Mitchell, Morgan Kaufmann, 1986.

Leslie Pack Kaelbling, *Learning in Embedded Systems*, MIT Press, 1993.

Leslie Pack Kaelbling and David Chapman, "Learning from Delayed Reinforcement in a Complex Domain," Teleos TR-90-11, December 1990.

Pattie Maes, "Learning Behavior Networks from Experience,' in *Toward a Practice of Autonomous Systems, Proceedings of the First European Conference on Artificial Life*, edited by F.J. Varela and P. Bourgine, MIT Press/Bradford Books, 1992.

Robert Ramstad, *A Constructivist Approach to Artificial Intelligence Reexamined* (MIT combined Bachelor's and Master's thesis, 1992).

Rich S. Sutton, "Integrated Architectures for Learning, Planning and Reacting based on Approximating Dynamic Programming," in *Proceedings of the Seventh International Conference in Machine Learning*, Austin, Tx, June 1990.

Rich S. Sutton, "Reinforcement Learning Architectures for Animats," in *From Animals to Animats, Proceedings of the First International Conference on the Simulation of Adaptive Behavior*, edited by Meyer J.-A. & Wilson S.W., MIT Press/Bradford Books, 1991.

Steven Whitehead and Dana Ballard, "Active Perception and Reinforcement Learning," submitted to the Seventh International Conference on Machine Learning, Austin, TX, June 1990.

Stewart W. Wilson, "Knowledge Growth in an Artificial Animal," in *Proceedings of the First International Conference on Genetic Algorithms and their Applications*, edited by Greffenstette, Lawrence Erlbaum Associates, 1985.

John Woodfill and Ramin Zabih, "An Architecture for Action with Selective Attention," submitted to AAAI-90.

Learning Efficient Reactive Behavioral Sequences
from Basic Reflexes
in a Goal-Directed Autonomous Robot

José del R. MILLÁN
Institute for Systems Engineering and Informatics
Commission of the European Communities. Joint Research Centre
TP 361. 21020 ISPRA (VA). ITALY
e-mail: jose.millan@cen.jrc.it

Abstract

This paper describes a reinforcement connectionist learning mechanism that allows a goal-directed autonomous mobile robot to adapt to an unknown indoor environment in a few trials. As a result, the robot learns efficient reactive behavioral sequences. In addition to quick convergence, the learning mechanism satisfies two further requirements. First, the robot improves its performance incrementally and permanently. Second, the robot is operational from the very beginning, what reduces the risk of catastrophic failures (collisions). The learning mechanism is based on three main ideas. The first idea applies when the neural network does not react properly to the current situation: a fixed set of basic reflexes suggests where to search for a suitable action. The second is to use a resource-allocating procedure to build automatically a modular network with a suitable structure and size. Each module codifies a similar set of reaction rules. The third idea consists on concentrating the exploration of the action space around the best actions currently known. The paper also reports experimental results obtained with a real mobile robot that demonstrate the feasibility of our approach.

1 Introduction

In this paper, we investigate how a *goal-directed autonomous mobile robot* can rapidly *adapt its behavior* in order to navigate efficiently in an unknown indoor environment. Efficient navigation strategies are common in animals (see Gallistel (1990) for a review) and are also critical for autonomous robots operating in hostile environments.

In the case of unknown environments, a common approach to control of autonomous mobile robots is that of *reactive* systems (e.g., Brooks, 1986; Connell, 1990; Schoppers, 1987). However, there exist two reasons to prefer a robot that acquires automatically the appropriate navigation strategies. First, a learning approach can considerably reduce the robot programming cost. Second and most importantly, pure reactive controllers may generate inefficient trajectories since they select the next action as a function of the current sensor readings and the robot's perception is limited.

Autonomous robots can adapt to unknown environments in two ways. The first one is to acquire a *coarse global map* of them. This map is made out of landmarks and is built from sensory data. Then, planning takes place at an abstract level and all the low level details are handled by the reactive component as the robot actually moves (e.g., Connell, 1992; Mataric, 1992; Miller & Slack, 1991). The second adaptive approach is to learn directly the appropriate *reactive behavioral sequences* (e.g., Lin, 1991; Millán, 1992; Millán & Torras, 1992; Mitchell & Thrun, 1993).

While we agree that global maps are very helpful for navigation, we believe that the addition of learning capabilities to reactive systems are sufficient to allow a robot to generate efficient trajectories after a limited experience. This paper presents experimental results that support this claim: a real autonomous mobile robot equipped with low-resolution sensors learns efficient goal-oriented obstacle-avoidance reactive sequences in a few trials.

This paper describes TESEO, an autonomous mobile robot controlled by a neural network. The neural controller maps the current perceived situation into the next action. A situation is made of sensory information coming from physical as well as virtual sensors. This neural network offers two advantages, namely good generalization capabilities and high tolerance to noisy sensory data. TESEO improves its performance through *reinforcement learning* (Barto et al., 1983; Barto et al., 1989; Sutton, 1984; Watkins, 1989; Williams, 1992) and adapts itself permanently as it interacts with the environment. An important assumption of our approach is that the robot receives a reinforcement signal after performing every action. Thus TESEO's aim is to learn to perform those actions that optimizes the total reinforcement obtained along the trajectory to the goal. Although this assumption is hard to satisfy in many reinforcement learning tasks, it is not in the case of goal-directed tasks since the robot can easily evaluate its progress towards the goal at any moment.

A second assumption of our approach is that the goal location is known. In particular, the goal location is specified in relative cartesian coordinates with respect to the starting location.

TESEO overcomes three common limitations associated to basic reinforcement connectionist learning. The first and most important one is that reinforcement learning might require an extremely long time. The main reason is that it is hard to determine rapidly promising parts of the action space where to search for suitable reactions. The second limitation is related to the first one and concerns the inability of "monolithic" connectionist networks —i.e., networks where the knowledge is distributively codified over all the weights— to support incremental learning. In this kind of standard networks, learning a new rule (or tuning an existing one) could degrade the knowledge already acquired for other situations. Finally, the third limitation regards the robot's behavior during learning. Practical learning robots should be operational at any moment and, most critically, they should avoid catastrophic failures such as collisions.

2 Experimental Setup

The physical robot is a wheeled cylindrical mobile platform of the *Nomad 200* family (see Figure 1). It has three independent motors. The first motor moves the three wheels of the robot together. The second one steers the wheels together. The third motor rotates the turret of the robot. The robot has 16 infrared sensors and 16 sonar sensors that provide distances to the nearest obstacles the robot can perceive, and 20 tactile sensors that detect collisions. The infrared and sonar sensors are evenly placed around the perimeter of the turret. Finally, the robot has a *dead-reckoning* system that keeps track of the robot's position and orientation.

As stated before, the connectionist controller uses the current perceived situation to compute a *spatially continuous action*. Then, the controller waits until the robot has finished to perform the corresponding motor command before computing the associated reinforcement signal and the next action. We will describe next what the input, output and reinforcement signals are.

The input to the connectionist network consists of a vector of 40 components, all of them real numbers in the interval [0, 1]. The first 32 components correspond to the infrared and sonar sensor readings. In this case,

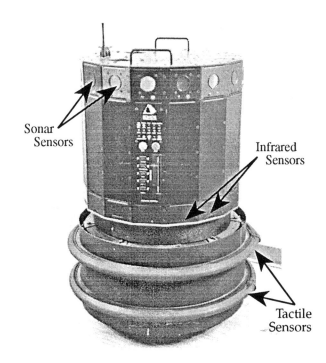

Figure 1. The Nomad 200 mobile robot.

a value close to zero means that the corresponding sensor is detecting a very near obstacle. The remaining 8 components are derived from a virtual sensor that provides the distance between the current and goal robot locations. This sensor is based on the dead-reckoning system. These 8 components correspond to a *coarse codification* of an inverse exponential function of the virtual sensor reading. The main reason for using this codification scheme is that, since it achieves a sort of interpolation, it offers three theoretical advantages, namely a greater robustness, a greater generalization ability and faster learning.

The output of the connectionist network consists of a single component that controls directly the steering motor and indirectly the translation and rotation motors. This component is a real number in the interval [−180, 180] and determines the direction of travel with respect to the vector connecting the current and goal robot locations. Once the robot has steered the commanded degrees, it translates a fixed distance (10 inches) and, at the same time, it rotates its turret in order to maintain the front infrared and sonar sensors oriented toward the goal.

It is worth noting that a *relative codification* of both the physical sensor readings and the motor command enhances TESEO's generalization capabilities.

The reinforcement signal is a real number in the interval [−3, 0] which measures the *cost* of doing a particular action in a given situation. The cost of an action is directly derived from the task definition, which is to reach the goal along trajectories that are sufficiently short and, at the same time, have a wide clearance to the obstacles. Thus actions incur a cost which depends on both the step clearance and the step length. Concerning the step clearance, the robot is constantly updating its sensor readings while moving. Thus the step clearance is the shortest distance provided by any of the sensors while performing the action.

Finally, TESEO has a low-level asynchronous emergency routine to prevent collisions. The robot stops and retracts whenever it detects an obstacle in front of it which is closer than a safety distance.

3   The Reinforcement Approach

TESEO's learning task is to associate with every perceived situation the action that optimizes the total reinforcement in the long-term (i.e., from the moment this action is taken until the goal is reached). To solve it, TESEO uses two different learning rules, namely *temporal difference (TD) methods* (Sutton, 1988) and *associative search (AS)* (Barto et al., 1983; Sutton, 1984; Williams, 1992). TD methods allow TESEO to predict the total future reinforcement it will obtain if it performs the best currently known actions that take it from its current location to the goal. AS uses the estimation given by TD to update the situation-action mapping, which is codified into the neural network.

In Section 1 we mentioned that TESEO seeks to satisfy three learning requirements, namely quick convergence, incremental improvement of performance, and collision avoidance. TESEO uses three main ideas to cope with these requirements. First, instead of learning from scratch, TESEO utilizes a fixed set of *basic reflexes* every time its neural network fails to generalize correctly its previous experience to the current situation. The neural network associates the selected reflex with the perceived situation in one step. This new reaction rule will be tuned subsequently through reinforcement learning. Basic reflexes correspond to previous elemental knowledge about the task and are codified as simple reactive behaviors (Brooks, 1986). As the actions computed by the neural controller, the reflexes determine the next direction of travel which is followed a fixed distance while the robot rotates its turret. Each reflex selects one of the 16 directions corresponding to the current orientations of the infrared and sonar sensors. We have chosen this fixed set of directions because they are the most informative for the robot in terms of obstacle detection. It is worth noting that, except in simple cases, these reflexes alone do not generate efficient trajectories; they just provide acceptable starting points for the reinforcement learning algorithm to search appropriate actions. Integrating learning and reaction in this way allows TESEO to focus

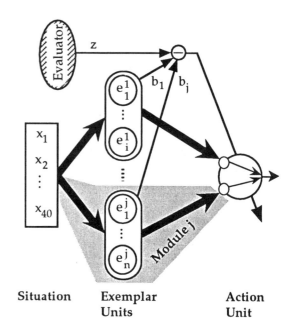

Figure 2. Network architecture.

on promising parts of the action space immediately and to be operational from the very beginning.

Second, TESEO utilizes a *resource-allocating procedure* to build automatically a *modular network* with a suitable structure and size. Each module codifies a *consistent set of reaction rules*. That is, each module's rules map similar sensory inputs into similar actions and, in addition, they have similar long-term consequences. This procedure guarantees that improvements on a module will not negatively alter other unrelated modules.

Finally, TESEO explores the action space by concentrating the search around the best actions currently known. The width of the search is determined by a *counter-based scheme* associated to the modules. This exploration technique allows TESEO to avoid experiencing irrelevant actions and to minimize the risk of collisions.

4   Network Architecture

The controller is a modular two-layer network (see Figure 2). The first layer consists of units with *localized receptive fields*. This means that each of these so-called *exemplars* represents a point of the input space and covers a limited area around this point. The activation level of an exemplar is 0 if the perceived situation is outside its receptive field and it is 1 if the situation corresponds to the point where the exemplar is centered. The second layer is made of one single stochastic linear unit. There exists a full connectivity between the two layers of units. The jth module consists of the exemplars $e_1^j, \ldots, e_n^j$ and their related links.

Actions are computed after a *competitive process* among the existent modules: only the module that best classified the perceived situation propagates the activities of its exemplars to the output unit. The winning module, if any, is that having the highest active exemplar. In the case that no exemplar matches the perceived situation, then the basic reflexes are triggered and the current situation becomes a new exemplar. Section 6.2 provides more details about the resource-allocating procedure. Thus, in order to improve its reactions to a particular kind of situations, TESEO needs just to fit the size or to tune the weights of the module that covers that region of the input space.

As pointed out before, the modules are not predefined, but are created dynamically as TESEO explores its environment. Every module j keeps track of four adaptive values. First, the expected total future reinforcement, b_j, that the robot will receive if it uses this module for computing the next action. Second, the width of the receptive fields of all the exemplars of this module, d_j. Third, a counter that records how many times this module has been used without improving the robot's performance, c_j. Fourth, the prototypical action the robot should normally take whenever the perceived situation is classified into this module, pa_j. There are as many prototypical actions as reflexes. Thus the first one is the direction of the front infrared and sonar sensors — i.e., a deviation of 0 degrees from the vector connecting the current and goal robot locations—, the second one is 22.5 degrees, and so on. Section 6.2 explains how pa_j is initially determined and evolves.

Finally, after reacting, the *evaluator* computes the reinforcement signal, z, as specified in Section 2. Then, if the action was computed through the module j, the difference between z and b_j is used for learning. Only the weights of the links associated to the winning module j are modified.

5 Action Unit

As illustrated in Figure 3, the action unit's output is a prototypical action pa plus a certain variation s that depends upon the location of the perceived situation in the input subspace dominated by the module that classifies the situation. Normally, the prototypical action is that of the winning module.

As any other reinforcement system, TESEO needs to explore alternative actions for the same situation in order to discover the best action. However, this exploration is not conducted upon the whole action space, but it is performed around the best actions currently known. Since each action is the sum of two components, pa and s, the exploration mechanism works on each of them separately. This exploration mechanism depends on c_j, the counter associated to the winning module.

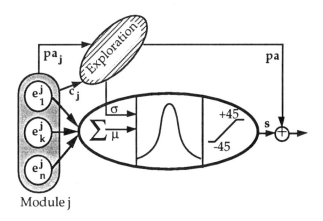

Figure 3. The action unit.

The action unit transforms the contributions of the winning module j as follows. On the one hand, the exploration mechanism uses pa_j and c_j to compute the prototypical action, pa, around which to select the output. On the other hand, the activation levels of $e_1^j, \ldots, e_n^j$ as well as c_j determine the deviation, s, from pa. Thus TESEO will perform an action which is located in the interval $[pa - 45, pa + 45]$. That is, TESEO will only explore actions between pa and its four neighboring prototypical actions (two to the left and two to the right).

The exploration mechanism selects pa from the prototypical actions associated to all the modules that classify the perceived situation. That is, if the situation is located in the receptive field of one of the exemplars of the module m, then pa_m is a candidate. The selection is as follows. If c_j is not divisible by, say, 3 then it chooses pa_j, the prototypical action of the winning module. Otherwise, it chooses the prototypical action associated to the module m with the best expected total future reinforcement, b_m. The basic idea behind this exploration mechanism is that the winning module could well benefit from the knowledge of neighboring modules.

Concerning the computation of s, an effective way of implementing exploration techniques in continuous domains is to use a *stochastic* process that selects with higher probability the best currently known value. This process controls separately the location being sought (*mean*) and the breadth of the search around that location (*variance*). The computation of s is done in three steps.

The first step is to determine the value of the stochastic process' parameters. The mean μ is a weighted sum of the activation levels of the exemplars:

$$\mu = \sum_{k=1}^{n} w_k^j a_k^j, \tag{1}$$

where w_k^j is the weight associated to the link between e_k^j and the action unit, and a_k^j is the activation level of e_k^j. The variance σ is proportional to c_j. The basic idea is that the more times the module j is used without improving the performance of TESEO, the higher is σ.

In the second step, the unit calculates its *activation level* l which is a normally distributed random variable:

$$l = N(\mu, \sigma). \qquad (2)$$

In the third step, the unit computes s:

$$s = \begin{cases} 45, & \text{if } l > 45, \\ -45, & \text{if } l < -45, \\ l, & \text{otherwise.} \end{cases} \qquad (3)$$

6 Learning

There are four basic forms of *learning* in the proposed architecture. The first regards the *topology* of the network: initially, there exist neither exemplars nor, consequently, modules and the resource-allocating procedure creates them as they are needed. The second kind of learning concerns *weight* modification. The third type of learning is related to the update of the b_j values and is based on TD methods. Finally, the fourth consists on the adaptation of the other three adaptive parameters associated to every module j, namely d_j, c_j and pa_j.

6.1 Temporal Difference Methods

Every value b_j corresponds to an estimate of the total future reinforcement TESEO will obtain if it performs the best currently known actions that take it from its current location (whose associated observed situation is classified into the jth module) to the goal.

Consequently, the value b_j of the module j should be equal to the sum of the cost z of reaching the best next module i plus the value b_i:

$$b_j = \max_{y \in Actions} (z) + b_i. \qquad (4)$$

During learning, however, this equality does not hold for the value b_j of every module j because the optimal action is not always taken and, even if it is, the value b_i of the next module i has not yet converged.

A way of improving the quality of b_j is to use the simplest TD method, i.e. TD(0). This procedure works as follows. If the situation perceived at time t, $\mathbf{x}(t)$, is classified into the module j, and after performing the action $\mathbf{y}(t)$ the next situation $\mathbf{x}(t+1)$ belongs to the module i, and the reinforcement signal —or cost— is $z(t+1)$, then:

$$b_j(t+1) = b_j(t) + \eta * \left[z(t+1) + b_i(t) - b_j(t) \right]. \qquad (5)$$

Note that even if the robot reaches the module i at time $t+1$, the value $b_i(t)$ is used to update b_j. This makes sense, since the module i could be the same as the module j.

η controls the intensity of the modification, and it takes greater values when TESEO behaves better than expected than in the opposite case. These two values of η are 0.75 and 0.075, respectively. The rationale for modifying less intensively b_j when $z(t+1)+b_i(t)-b_j(t) < 0$ is that this error is probably due to the selection of an action different from the best currently known one for the module j.

The problem is for TESEO to figure out $b_i(t)$ when the next situation $\mathbf{x}(t+1)$ does not match any stored exemplar. In this case, b_i is estimated on the basis of the distance from the next location to the goal and the distance from the next location to the perceived obstacles in between the robot and the goal.

Finally, the value b_j of every module j observed along a path taking to the goal is also updated in reverse chronological order. To do that, TESEO stores the pairs $\langle j(t), z(t+1) \rangle$, where $j(t)$ indicates the winning module at time t. Then, after reaching the goal at time $n+1$ and updating the last value $b_{j(n)}$, the value $b_{j(n-1)}$ is updated, and so on until $b_{j(1)}$. As Mahadevan and Connell (1992) point out, this technique only accelerates the convergence of the value b_j of every module j —especially if it classifies situations far from the goal—, but does not change the steady value of b_j.

6.2 When to Learn

Let us present now the three occasions in which learning takes place. The first of them arises during the classification phase, whereas the other two happen after reacting.

1. if the perceived situation is not classified into one of the existent modules —i.e., no exemplar matches it—, **then** the basic reflexes get control of the robot, and the resource-allocating procedure creates a new exemplar which is added either to one of the existing modules or to a new module.

The new exemplar has the same coordinates as the perceived situation. That is, both represent the same point of the input space. The weight of the link from this exemplar to the action unit is initially set to zero and evolves through reinforcement learning.

The new exemplar is added to one of the existing modules if its receptive field overlaps the receptive fields of the module's exemplars and the selected reflex is the same as the module's prototypical action. The first condition assures that every module will cover a closed input subspace.

If any of the two conditions above is not satisfied, then the new exemplar is added to a new module. This module consists initially of the exemplar and its associated connections. Concerning the four parameters associated to this new module v, they are initially set to the following values: b_v is estimated as when no module classifies the perceived situation (see Section 6.1), d_v equals 0.5, c_v equals 0, and pa_v is the selected reflex.

2. if (i) the perceived situation is classified into the module j, **and** (ii) $z(t+1) + b_i(t) - b_j(t) \leq k_z$, where k_z is a constant, **then** (i) the exemplars of that module, $e_1^j, \ldots, e_n^j$, are modified to make them closer to the situation, (ii) the weights associated to the connections between the exemplars and the action unit are modified using reinforcement learning, (iii) b_j is updated through TD(0), **and** (iv) d_v, c_v, and pa_v are adapted.

The coordinates of the kth exemplar, e_k^j, are updated proportionally to how well it matches the situation:

$$\phi_k^j(t+1) = \phi_k^j(t) + \epsilon * a_k^j(t) * \left[\mathbf{x}(t) - \phi_k^j(t)\right], \quad (6)$$

where ϕ are the coordinates of the exemplar and ϵ is the learning rate. In the experiments reported below, the value of ϵ is 0.1.

Simultaneously, the connections from the exemplars $e_1^j, \ldots, e_n^j$ to the action unit are updated so as to strengthen or weaken the probability of performing the action just taken for any situation in the input subspace dominated by the module j. The intensity of the weight modifications depends on the relative merit of the action, which is just the error provided by the TD method. Thus, the AS reinforcement learning rule is:

$$w_k^j(t+1) = w_k^j(t) + \alpha * \left[z(t+1) + b_i(t) - b_j(t)\right] * e_k^j(t), \quad (7)$$

where α is the learning rate, and e_k^j is the eligibility factor of w_k^j.

The eligibility factor of a given weight measures how influential that weight was in choosing the action. In our experiments, e_k^j is computed in such a manner that the learning rule corresponds to a *gradient ascent* mechanism on the expected reinforcement (Williams, 1992):

$$e_k^j(t) = \frac{\partial lnN}{\partial w_k^j}(t) = a_k^j(t)\frac{l(t) - \mu(t)}{\sigma^2(t)}, \quad (8)$$

where N is the normal distribution function in (2). The weights w_k^j are modified more intensively in case of *reward* —i.e., when TESEO behaves better than expected— than in case of *penalty*. These two values of α are 0.2 and 0.02, respectively. The aim here is that TESEO maintains the best situation-action rules known so far, while exploring other reaction rules.

Finally, the adaptive parameters are also updated differently in case of reward than in case of penalty. In case of reward, d_j is increased by 0.1, c_j is initialized to 0, and if the output of the action unit, $pa + s$, is closer to

a prototypical action other than pa_j, then pa_j becomes this new prototypical action. In case of penalty, c_j is increased by 1 and d_j is decreased by 0.1 if it is still greater than a threshold k_d.

3. if (i) the perceived situation is classified into the module j, **and** (ii) $z(t+1) + b_i(t) - b_j(t) > k_z$ **then** (i) the topology of the network is slightly altered, **and** (ii) d_j is updated.

If the total future reinforcement computed after reacting, $z + b_i$, is considerably worse the expected one, b_j, this means that the situation was incorrectly classified and needs to be classified into a different module. In order for TESEO to classify this and other very similar situations into a different module the next time they will be perceived, the resource-allocating procedure modifies the network topology. Simultaneously, d_j is decreased by 0.1 if it is still greater than a threshold k_d.

The resource-allocating procedure creates a new exemplar, e_u, that has the same coordinates as the perceived situation, but it does not add it to any module. The next time this situation will be faced, e_u will be the closest exemplar. Consequently, no module will classify the situation and the basic reflexes will get control of the robot. Then, the resource-allocating procedure will add e_u either to one of the existing modules or to a new module as described in point 1 above.

This means that our architecture classifies situations, in a first step, based on the similarity of their input representations. Then, it also incorporates task-specific information for classifying based on the similarity of reinforcements received. In this manner, the input space is split into *consistent* clusters since a similar total future reinforcement corresponds to similar suitable actions for similar situations in a given input subspace.

7 Experimental Results

The environment where TESEO has to perform its missions consists of a corridor with offices at both sides. In one of the experiments TESEO is asked to go from inside an office to a point in the corridor. The first time it tries to reach the goal it relies almost all the time on the basic reflexes which make TESEO follow walls and move around obstacles. As illustrated in Figure 4, in the first trial, TESEO enters into a dead-end section of the office (but it does not get trapped into it) and even it collides against the door frame because its sensors were not able to detect it. Collisions happened because the frame of the door is relatively thin and the incident angles of the rays drawn from the sensors were too large resulting in specular reflections.

Thus this task offers three learning opportunities to TESEO. The first and simplest one is to tune slightly certain sections of the trajectory generated by the basic reflexes. The second opportunity consists in avoiding

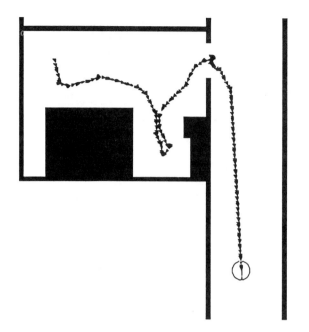

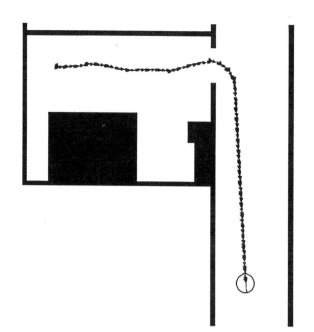

Figure 4. The environment and first trajectory generated for a starting location within the office. Note that TESEO has some problems in going through the doorway.

Figure 5. Trajectory generated after travelling 10 times to the goal.

dead-ends or, in general, in not following wrong walls. The third and most critical opportunity arises in very particular occasions where the robot collides because its sensors cannot detect obstacles.

TESEO solves all these three learning subtasks *very rapidly*. It reaches the goal efficiently and without colliding after travelling 10 times from the starting location to the desired goal (see Figure 5). The total length of the first trajectory is approximately 13 meters while the length of the trajectory generated after TESEO has learned the suitable sequence of reactions is about 10 meters.

This experiment was run several times. TESEO learned the suitable motor skills after, at most, 13 trials.

Finally, Figure 6 depicts instances of the reaction rules learned. For every location considered (little circles) the move to be taken by the robot is shown. The figure shows that TESEO generates solution paths from any starting location inside the room. This experiment indicates that TESEO exhibits *good generalization abilities*, since it can handle many more situations than those perceived during the learning phase.

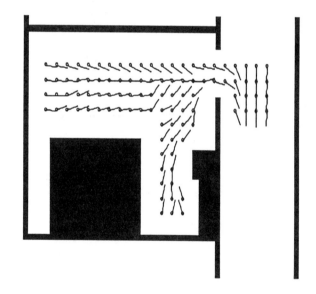

Figure 6. Generalization abilities: Situation-action rules applied for a sample of locations within the office and the first part of the corridor.

8 Related Work

The architecture we have described in this paper bears some relation to a number of previous works.

Some researchers have recently shown the benefits of letting the robot learn automatically the appropriate

reaction rules. Berns et al. (1992) use Kohonen maps (Kohonen, 1988) to split the sensory input space into clusters, and then associate an appropriate action to every cluster through reinforcement learning. Their architecture maps all the situations of a given cluster to a single action, and classifies situations solely by the similarity of their representations. Lin (1991) combines reinforcement connectionist learning and teaching to reduce the learning time. In this framework, a human teacher shows the robot several instances of reactive sequences that achieve the task. Then, the robot learns new reaction rules from these examples. The taught reaction rules help reinforcement learning by biasing the search for suitable actions toward promising parts of the action space. In our approach, the basic reflexes play the same guidance role (but it does not require a human teacher). Mitchell and Thrun (1993) integrate inductive neural network learning and explanation-based learning. The domain theory is previously learned by a set of neural networks, one network for each discrete action the robot can perform. As Mitchell and Thrun's domain theory, our basic reflexes also represent prior knowledge about the task; however, they are much more elemental and are used in a different way.

Our approach is also related to the Dyna integrated architectures introduced by Sutton (1990) and further extended by Lin (1991, 1992) as well as Peng and Williams (1993), among others. Roughly, Dyna uses planning to speed up the acquisition of reaction rules through reinforcement learning. Dyna also learns a global model of the task on which it plans.

Jacobs et al. (1991) and Singh (1992) have also described modular neural networks that learn to decompose a given problem into distinct subtasks and assign each of them to the appropriate module. The allocation of input patterns to modules is done by a specific gating module. Jacobs et al.'s approach has been developed in the framework of supervised learning, while Sing's approach is intended for reinforcement learning systems. Mahadevan and Connell (1992) also extend the basic reinforcement learning framework by combining several modules, each one specialized on solving a particular subtask. They adopt the *subsumption architecture* (Brooks, 1986) to develop their agent. In all the three cases the number of modules is predefined.

9 Discussion

In this paper we have shown how to improve the initial performance of a basic reactive controller through reinforcement connectionist learning. The main benefits of our learning robot's architecture are: rapid acquisition of efficient reactive sequences, self-adaptation, incremental learning, high tolerance to noisy sensory data, good generalization abilities, and the robot is operational from the very beginning.

However, the current implementation of our approach suffers from one main limitation, namely it requires a reliable *odometry system* that keeps track of the robot's relative position with respect to the goal. The version of the robot used during the experiments cannot detect the goal, and so the odometry system is totally based on dead-reckoning.

In all the experiments we have carried out so far, dead-reckoning from the robot's wheel encoders has proven sufficient to reach the goal. As long as the dead-reckoning system's estimation of the position of the robot does not differ greatly from the actual one, the connectionist controller is still able to produce correct actions. However, dead-reckoning will probably be insufficient in more complicated missions requiring long travels and many turns.

A way of improving the reliability of the odometry system is to equip the robot with sensors especially designed to detect the goal. For example, the goal could be a modulated light beacon and the robot could have infrared sensors. Thus TESEO will initially rely on the dead-reckoning system such as it does now. Then, at the moment it detect the goal, it will use the beaconing system. We are currently working on this new implementation.

Acknowledgements

I gratefully acknowledge the contributions of Carme Torras to the ideas presented here. I thank Aristide Varfis for helpful discussions. This research has been partially supported by the ESPRIT Basic Research Action number 7274.

References

Barto, A.G., Sutton, R.S., & Anderson, C.W. (1983). Neuronlike elements that can solve difficult learning control problems. *IEEE Transactions on Systems, Man, and Cybernetics*, **13**, 835–846.

Barto, A.G., Sutton, R.S., & Watkins, C.J. (1989). Learning and sequential decision making. Technical Report 89-95, Dept. of Computer and Information Science, University of Massachusetts, Amherst.

Berns, K., Dillmann, R., & Zachmann, U. (1992). Reinforcement-learning for the control of an autonomous mobile robot. *Proc. of the IEEE/RSJ International Conference on Intelligent Robots and Systems*, 1808–1815.

Brooks, R.A. (1986). A robust layered control system for a mobile robot. *IEEE Journal of Robotics and Automation*, **2**, 14–23.

Connell, J.H. (1990). *Minimalist Mobile Robotics: A Colony-Style Architecture for an Artificial Creature*. San Diego, CA: Academic Press.

Connell, J.H. (1992). SSS: A hybrid architecture applied to robot navigation. *Proc. of the IEEE International Conference on Robotics and Automation*, 2719–2724.

Gallistel, C.R. (1990). *The Organization of Learning*. Cambridge, MA: MIT Press.

Jacobs, R.A., Jordan, M.I., Nowlan, S.J., & Hinton, G.E. (1991). Adaptive mixtures of local experts. *Neural Computation*, **3**, 79–87.

Kohonen, T. (1988). *Self-Organization and Associative Memory*. Second Edition. Berlin: Springer-Verlag.

Lin, L.-J. (1991). Programming robots using reinforcement learning and teaching. *Proc. of the 9th National Conference on Artificial Intelligence*, 781–786.

Lin, L.-J. (1992). Self-improving reactive agents based on reinforcement learning, planning and teaching. *Machine Learning*, **8**, 293–321.

Mahadevan, S. & Connell, J. (1992). Automatic programming of behavior-based robots using reinforcement learning. *Artificial Intelligence*, **55**, 311–365.

Mataric, M.J. (1992). Integration of representation into goal-driven behavior-based robots. *IEEE Transactions on Robotics and Automation*, **8**, 304–312.

Millán, J. del R. (1992). Building reactive path-finders through reinforcement connectionist learning: Three issues and an architecture. *Proc. of the 10th European Conference on Artificial Intelligence*, 661–665.

Millán, J. del R. & Torras, C. (1992). A reinforcement connectionist approach to robot path finding in non-maze-like environments. *Machine Learning*, **8**, 363–395.

Miller, D.P. & Slack, M.G. (1991). Global symbolic maps from local navigation. *Proc. of the 9th National Conference on Artificial Intelligence*, 750–755.

Mitchell, T.M. & Thrun, S.B. (1993). Explanation-based neural networks learning for robot control. In C.L. Giles, S.J. Hanson, and J.D. Cowan (eds.), *Advances in Neural Information Processing Systems 5*, 287–294. San Mateo, CA: Morgan Kaufmann.

Peng, J. & Williams, R.J. (1993). Efficient learning and planning within the Dyna framework. *Adaptive Behavior*, **1**, 437–454.

Schoppers, M.J. (1987). Universal plans for reactive robots in unpredictable environments. *Proc. of the 10th International Joint Conference on Artificial Intelligence*, 1039–1046.

Singh, S.P. (1992). Transfer of learning by composing solutions of elemental sequential tasks. *Machine Learning*, **8**, 323–339.

Sutton, R.S. (1984). Temporal credit assignment in reinforcement learning. Ph.D. Thesis, Dept. of Computer and Information Science, University of Massachusetts, Amherst.

Sutton, R.S. (1988). Learning to predict by the methods of temporal differences. *Machine Learning*, **3**, 9–44.

Sutton, R.S. (1990). Integrated architectures for learning, planning, and reacting based on approximating dynamic programming. *Proc. of the 7th International Conference on Machine Learning*, 216–224.

Watkins, C.J. (1989). Learning with delayed rewards. Ph.D. Thesis, Psychology Dept., Cambridge University, England.

Williams, R.J. (1992). Simple statistical gradient-following algorithms for connectionist reinforcement learning. *Machine Learning*, **8**, 229–256.

The Importance of Leaky Levels for Behavior-Based AI

Gregory M. Saunders, John F. Kolen, and Jordan B. Pollack

Laboratory for Artificial Intelligence Research

Computer and Information Science Department

The Ohio State University

Columbus, Ohio 43210   USA

saunders@cis.ohio-state.edu

kolen-j@cis.ohio-state.edu

pollack@cis.ohio-state.edu

Abstract

From the many possible perspectives in which an agent may be viewed, behavior-based AI selects observable actions as a particularly useful level of description. Yet behavior is clearly not structure, and anyone using behavior-based constraints to construct an agent still faces many implementational roadblocks. Such obstacles are typically avoided by adopting a finite state automaton (FSA) as a base representation. As a result, potential benefits from alternative formalisms are ignored. To explore these benefits, our work adopts a multilevel view of an agent: behaviors and FSAs are but two of many levels of description. We still focus on behaviors for the expression of design constraints, but we avoid using FSAs as an implementation. Our particular agent, Addam, is comprised of a set of connectionist networks, a substrate which promotes the automatic design of subsumptive systems. Moreover, the implementational choice has important behavioral consequences – some complex behaviors emerge due to interactions among networks and need not be specified explicitly. In this way, the underlying layers *leak* into one another, each affecting the others in subtle and desirable ways.

1 Introduction

Historically, AI has viewed agents from the Knowledge Level (Newell, 1982), in which an individual is characterized by its knowledge, goals, and rationality.[1] The abstract nature of this level has been called into question from many different directions: e.g., connectionism (Hinton et al., 1986; McClelland et al., 1986), situated action (compare Vera and Simon, 1993, with Agre, 1993), the observers' paradox (Kolen and Pollack, 1993, to appear), and others (e.g., Searle, 1993). Most recently, those studying the simulation of adaptive behavior have stressed that intelligence should not be viewed simply as knowledge and goals held together with procedural glue; there is much to learn from studying intelligence through self-sufficient agents competent to exist in the world (Meyer and Guillot, 1991; Wilson, 1991).

Yet we often forget that agents can be viewed at multiple levels of description, and as Chandrasekaran and Josephson (1993) point out, there is no single level of description which captures all aspects of an agent's behavior. To borrow their example, a simple coin sorter can be described as an abstract machine which classifies coins based on their weight and diameter, but if a lever jams, then the physical nature of the device becomes particularly important. Chandrasekaran and Josephson propose that agents be described by a set of "leaky levels," where each level of description contributes to the overall story of agent behavior, but the total picture arises due to the way the various levels interact.

The lesson is an important one, but it fails to address an important question: How does the recognition of multiple levels of description help one to implement an intelligent agent? In particular, how should one approach the task of constructing an agent which satisfies multiple behavioral constraints?

Brooks (1986, 1991) proposes an interesting answer to this question. Rather than observing a set of behavioral constraints and reasoning "The agent must have functional modules for perception, planning, etc.," one can remain more faithful to the actual observations by constructing an agent which satisfies the first behavioral constraint, and then incrementally adding layers of structure to satisfy the remaining constraints sequentially. This behavior-based stance removes

---

1. While none of these terms is ever rigorously defined, knowledge is the set of "beliefs" of the agent, a goal is a desired state (of the world, for instance), and the principle of rationality stipulates that an agent will use its knowledge to accomplish its goals.

a large bias on the part of the designer: modules arise from directly observable constraints on behavior rather than functional constraints implicit in the mind of the designer.

Unfortunately, Brooks does not go far enough. After performing a behavioral decomposition to define the functionality of a layer, he then proceeds to design a set of finite state automata (FSAs) to implement that layer. Yet, this is precisely the type of functional decomposition he warns against (Brooks, 1991, p. 146). One might appeal to learning to avoid performing this functional decomposition by hand, but current work in automating behavior-based design focuses instead on learning the interactions between preexisting behavioral modules (e.g., Maes, 1991).

We feel that the reliance upon designed modules arises from choosing FSAs as the level in which to implement subsumptive systems; in particular, from the arbitrary ways in which FSAs interact. Brooks achieves modularity through task-based decomposition of complex behavior into a set of simpler behaviors. In his system, for example, layer 0 implements obstacle avoidance and layer 1 controls wandering. Activity in layer 1 suppresses the activity of layer 0, and yet obstacles are still avoided because *layer 1 subsumes the obstacle avoidance behavior of layer 0*. In order to avoid duplication of lower layers as subparts of higher layers, he allows the higher layers to randomly access the internal components of any lower level FSAs. This fact, combined with multiple realizability of layers forces us to question Brooks' design methodology: development of single layer competence, freezing it, and then layering additional competencies on top of the first. If layer 0 can be realized equally well by method M_1 or M_2, then under Brooks' methodology we will not know until layer 0 is fixed which methodology's internal modules better facilitate the design of layer 1.

Furthermore, Brooks fails to limit the suppression and/or inhibition which may occur between layers, so that a higher-level may randomly modify a lower-level's computation. This unrestricted suppression/inhibition combined with the unrestricted access problem described above permit complicated interactions among layers. In Brooks' case, careful design keeps the interactions under control, and the resulting behavioral modules perform well together. For evolving subsumptive systems, however, such design-space freedom must be limited.

In this paper, we present an alternative approach to subsumptive learning. Recognizing the multitude of formalisms with which to describe behaviors (Chandrasekaran and Josephson, 1993), we explore the merits and drawbacks of adopting a connectionist implementation for our layers.[2] As will be discussed below, our version of subsumption replaces Brooks' FSAs with feedforward networks and additional circuitry, combined so that each module in a hierarchy respects

the historical prerogatives of those below it, and only asserts its own control when confident. Given this basic architecture, we demonstrate how multiple behavioral constraints can be translated into network-level constraints. Finally, we discuss the importance of the connectionist substrate for the implementation of leaky levels which produce emergent behavior in an agent.

2 Additive Adaptive Modules

Our control architecture consists of a set of Additive Adaptive Modules, instantiated as *Addam*, an agent which lives in a world of ice, food, and blocks. To survive in this world, Addam possesses 3 sets of 4 (noisy) sensors distributed in the 4 canonical quadrants of the plane. The first set of sensors is tactile, the second olfactory, and the third visual (implemented as sonar that passes through transparent objects). Unlike other attempts at learning that focus on a single behavior such as walking (Beer and Gallagher, 1992), we chose to focus on the subsumptive interaction of several behaviors; hence, Addam's actuators are a level of abstraction above leg controllers (similar to Brooks, 1986). Thus, Addam moves by simply specifying δx and δy.

Internally, Addam consists of a set of feedforward connectionist networks, connected as shown in Figure 1. The 12 input lines come from Addam's sensors; the 2 output lines are fed into actuators which perform the desired movement (δx, δy). Note that we desire δx, $\delta y \in (-1, 1)$ so that Addam may move in the positive or negative direction. Initially, we implemented desired movement as a single scalar value, but this proved inadequate. It did not permit zero as a stable output as the network outputs tended to saturate with training. We then switched to a difference scheme in which the actual movement control was the difference between two outputs ($+\delta x$ and $-\delta x$). This configuration allows the system to stably learn and generate positive and negative movement, as well as no movement at all.

Addam controls its movements as follows. First, the 12 sensors are sampled and fed into layer 0, placing its suggestion for δx and δy on the output lines. Layer 1 combines these same 12 sensor readings with the sum squared output of layer 0, calculates its suggestions for δx and δy, and adds these to the output lines. Layer 2 works similarly, and the final δx and δy values are translated automatically to motor controls which move Addam the desired amount and direction.

Note that we could have avoided feeding the sum-squared activation line into each module M_i by gating the output of M_i with the sum-squared line. We did not do this because our architecture is more general; gating can be learned as one of many behaviors by each M_i. Our goal was to have each module decide *for itself* whether it should become active – had we used gating, this decision would have been made by M_i's predecessors.

---

2. Cliff (1991) makes a similar proposal from the context of computational neuroethology, but does not offer an implementation.

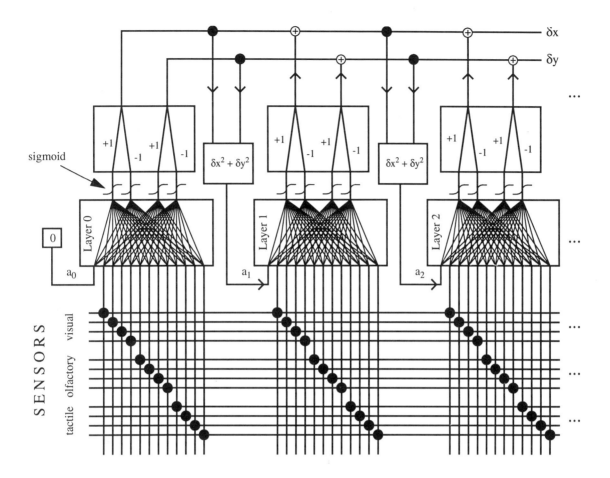

Figure 1: Addam's internal architecture. Each module possesses only limited information about the activity of its predecessors. Layer 1 receives only the sum-squared activation of layer 0, implemented as a_1. Similarly, layer 2 monitors the activity of its predecessors through a single input a_2. Through training, each layer learns to exert control only when relevant based on the current sensors, and when none of its predecessors is active.

Instead of lumping Addam with other subsumptive systems, we prefer to identify our architecture as *preemptive*. The modules are prioritized such that the behaviors associated with the lower levels may take precedence over those associated with the higher levels. Prioritization is reflected both architecturally as well as functionally. Architecturally, a lower level provides its outputs to higher levels. Functionally, higher-level modules are trained to relinquish control if a lower-level module is active. For example, suppose that layer 0 behavior is to avoid predators, and layer 1 behavior is to seek out food. In the absence of any threatening agents, layer 0 would remain inactive and layer 1 would move Addam towards food. However if a predator suddenly appeared, layer 0 would usurp control from layer 1 and Addam would flee.

Earlier we criticized Brooks' method of subsumption for two of its freedoms: unrestricted access by one layer to another's internal state, and unrestricted modulation of a lower-layer's computation by suppression/inhibition from a higher-layer. Neither problem is present in Addam. A higher

layer has access only to the sum-squared output of all previous layers, and any preemption of layer i results from a single real value (a_i). This eliminates the methodological problem with multiple realizability: the input a_i to a layer depends only on *what* is computed below, not on *how* it is being computed.

A few more things should be noted about Addam's architecture. First, it has no internal state (or equivalently Addam's entire state is stored external to the agent in the environment, as in Simon, 1969). Second, a few of Addam's connections are fixed a priori. (The changeable connections are those in the boxes labelled layer 0, 1, and 2, above.) This minimal structure is the skeleton required for preemption, but it does not assume any prewired behaviors.

Finally, we should acknowledge the similarity of Addam's internal structure to the cascade correlation architecture of Fahlman and Lebiere (1990). There are several important differences, however. First, our system is comprised of several cascaded *modules* instead of cascaded *hidden units*. Second, Fahlman and Lebiere's higher-level hidden units

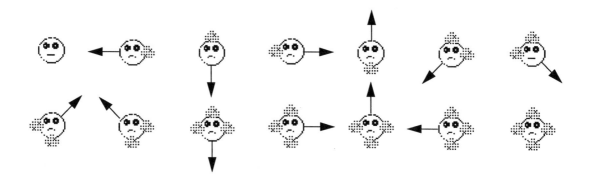

Figure 2: Training scenarios for level 0 behavior, along with desired responses. Circles denote patches of ice. The scenarios capture a range of situations; from each, Addam's target response moves it away from the ice.

function as higher-level feature detectors and hence must receive input from all the preceding hidden units in the network. This can lead to a severe fan-in problem. Due to the preemptive nature of our architecture, higher-level modules need only know if any lower-level module is active, so they require only a single additional input measuring total activation of the previous modules. Third, Fahlman's system grows more hidden units over time, correlating each to the current error. The nodes of our architecture are fixed throughout training, so that modularity is not achieved by simply adding more units. Finally, there is a difference in training: Fahlman gives his network a single function to learn, whereas our system attempts to learn a series of more and more complex behaviors. (More on this below.)

3 Training Addam

As mentioned above, Addam's environment consists of three types of objects: ice, food, and blocks. Ice is transparent and odorless, and is hence detectable only by the tactile sensors. Blocks trigger both the tactile and visual sensors, and food emits an odor which diffuses throughout the environment and triggers the olfactory sensors. Addam eats (in one time step) whenever it comes into contact with a piece of food.

Addam's overall goal is to move towards food while avoiding the other obstacles. This makes training problematic – the desired response is a complex behavior indexed over many environmental configurations, and yet we do not wish to restrict the possible solutions by specifying an entire behavioral trajectory for a given situation. Beer and Gallagher (1992) attempted to solve this problem by using genetic algorithms, which respond to the agent's overall performance instead of to any particular movement. We take a different approach, namely, we train Addam on *single moves* for a given number of scenarios, defined as one particular environmental configuration. Under this methodology, the *extended moves* which define Addam's behavior emerge from the complex interactions of the adaptive modules and the environment.

Training begins with level 0 competence, defined as the ability to avoid ice. The training scenarios are shown in Figure 2, along with the desired response for each scenario. Module 0 can successfully perform this behavior in about 600 epochs of backpropagation (adjusted so that the fixed +1/-1 connections remain constant), and the connections of this module are then frozen.

We next train Addam on level 1 behavior, defined as the ability to move towards food, *assuming no ice is present*. Once again, training is problematic, because there are a combinatorial number of environmental configurations involving food and ice. We solve this problem as follows. First, we define 14 scenarios as above, but with food replacing ice. This defines a set S of {(SensorValues, MoveToFoodOutput)} pairs. Note that this does not define a value for a_1, the activation of the system prior to module 1. (See Figure 1.) Instead of forcing module 1 to recognize the presence of ice, we assume that module 0 is doing its job, and that when ice is present a_1 will be $\gg 0$. This allows us to define a training set T for level 1 behavior by prepending the extreme values of a_1 to the SensorValues in S, thus doubling the number of configurations instead of having them grow exponentially:

T={ {(0-SensorValues, MoveToFoodOutput)},
    {(1-SensorValues, ZeroOutput)} }

Thus layer 1 (which is initially always active) must learn to suppress its activity in cases where it is not appropriate.

After level 1 competence is achieved (about 3500 epochs), a training set for level 2 competence (avoid blocks) is obtained in a similar manner. Note again that this avoids the combinatorial explosion of specifying the many possible combinations of ice, food, and blocks. Level 2 competence is achieved in about 1000 epochs.

4 Results

Once Addam was trained, we placed it in the complex environment of Figure 3. Its emergent behavior is illustrated in the top half of the figure, where the small dots trace out Addam's path. Each dot is one time step (defined as one applica-

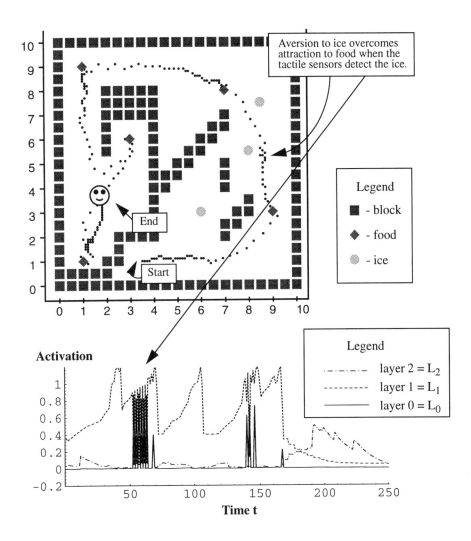

Figure 3: Addam's emergent behavior in a complex environment. The dots in the upper figure trace Addam's path as it moves through the environment in search of food. The graph shows the activity of each of Addam's layers over time.

tion of the trained network to move one step), so the spacing indicates Addam's speed.

Addam begins at (3.5, 1) touching nothing, so its tactile sensors register zero and layer 0 is inactive. The olfactory sensors respond slightly to the weak odor gradient, causing a slight activation of layer 1, disabling the block-avoidance behavior of layer 2. Thus we observe a constant eastward drift, along with random north-south movements due to the noise inherent in the sensors. As Addam approaches the food, the odor gradient increases, the olfactory sensors become more and more active, and layer 1 responds more and more strongly. When the random noise becomes negligible at about (6.5, 1), Addam speeds up and reaches the food, which is consumed.

Subsequently, Addam detects the faint odor of another piece of nearby food, and once again layer 1 controls its movement. However, at about (9, 5.5) Addam's tactile sensors detect the presence of a piece of ice, activating layer 0,

and usurping control from layer 1. In other words, Addam's aversion to ice overcomes its hunger, and it moves southeast. After "bouncing off" the ice, the tactile sensors return to zero, and layer 1 regains control, forcing Addam back towards the ice. This time it hits the ice just a little farther north than the last time, so that when it bounces off again, it has made some net progress towards the food. After several attempts, Addam successfully passes the ice and then moves directly towards the food.

To reach the third piece of food, Addam must navigate down a narrow corridor, demonstrating that its layer 1 behavior can override its layer 2 behavior of avoiding blocks (which would repel it from the corridor entrance). After finishing the last piece of food, Addam is left near a wall, although it is not in contact with it. Thus both the tactile and olfactory sensors output zero, so both layers 0 and 1 are inactive. This allows Addam's block avoidance behavior to become activated. The visual sensors respond to the open area to the north, so Addam slowly makes its way in that direction. When it reaches the middle of the enclosure, the visual sensors are balanced and Addam halts (except for small random movements based on the noise in the sensors).

The bottom half of Figure 3 shows the activation of each layer i of the system (where the activation of layer i is $\|(\delta x, \delta y)_i\|$, the norm of layer i's contribution to the output lines). L_0 is generally quiet, but becomes active between time $t=52$ and $t=64$ when Addam encounters an ice patch, and shows some slight activity around $t=140$ and $t=168$ when Addam's tactile sensors detect blocks. L_1 ("approach food" behavior) is active for most of the session except when preempted by the "avoid ice" behavior of L_0, as between $t=52$ and $t=64$. The 5 peaks in L_1's activity correspond to Addam's proximity to the 5 pieces of food as it eat them; when the last piece of food is consumed at $t=164$, L_1's activity begins to decay as the residual odor disperses. Finally, we see that L_2 ("avoid blocks" behavior) is preempted for almost the entire session. It starts to show activity only at about $t=160$, when all the food is gone and Addam is away from any ice. The activity of this layer peaks at about $t=190$, and then decays to 0 as Addam reaches the center of its room and the visual sensors balance.

5 Remarks

The behavior of Chandrasekaran and Josephson's coin sorter is best described by appealing to multiple levels of behavior (Chandrasekaran and Josephson, 1993). Addam is best described in a similar way. At one level, it is an agent which exhibits only three behaviors: avoid ice, go to food, and avoid blocks. But the underlying connectionist levels leak through in the complex interaction that allows Addam to navigate around the ice in Figure 3. Had Addam been implemented as a set of FSAs, such complex behavior would not have emerged; it would have required explicit design (Cariani, 1989). Similarly, had preemption been absolute, Addam would have become stuck at the ice as module 0 and module 1 alternately controlled the agent's behavior.[3]

This performance benefit of simplified subsumption is complemented by a benefit in training. As mentioned above, Brooksian FSAs are difficult to train because of the complicated ways in which they may interact. Our connectionist networks, on the other hand, permit a host of training algorithms. In fact, the work of Beer and Gallagher (1992) or Maes and Brooks (1990) is really complementary to ours, for although Addam's modules were instantiated with feedforward networks trained by backpropagation, they could have

just as easily been trained by either genetic or correlation algorithms.

Our work also sheds light on the issue of neural network representations for agents. Collins and Jefferson (1991) explored such representations, but found them lacking because of their inability to shift behavior based on changing inputs. Preemption offers one way in which these shifts may be obtained.

One drawback, or at least cause for concern, with our method of preemption arises from the way in which the structural modules were defined. First, as with Brooks' subsumption, we used a behavioral decomposition to define the number of modules, and second, we assumed a fixed network architecture for each module. Angeline (1994) has explored how modularization can arise without a behavioral decomposition, and elsewhere, we have explored how the structure of a module (i.e., number of hidden units and network connectivity) can arise from an evolutionary program (Saunders, Angeline, and Pollack, 1994).

Many of the problems of training behavior-based systems stem from the failure to recognize the multiplicity of levels in agents. We whole-heartedly agree with Brooks that the level of behaviors is particularly useful for the expression of design constraints. The level of FSAs may also be useful for refining the behavioral description. Yet, in the context of evolving agents, the network level is more appropriate. Our connectionist approach maintains the benefits of subsumption: a behavior-based view, incremental construction of the agent, and distributed control. But, in addition to the performance and training benefits described above, the neural network substrate offers a many-to-many mapping between structure and behavior: a single module can affect multiple behaviors, and a single behavior can arise from the interaction of multiple modules. Chandrasekaran and Josephson proposed such leaking from a philosophical point of view; here we have shown how leaking occurs naturally and aids performance in an evolved connectionist system.

Acknowledgments

This research has been partially supported by Office of Naval Research grants N00014-93-1-0059 and N00014-92-J-1195. We thank Pete Angeline for his help in an earlier version of this work.

References

Agre, P. E. (1993). The symbolic worldview: Reply to Vera and Simon. *Cognitive Science*, 17(1):61–69.

Angeline, P. J. (1994). *Evolutionary Algorithms and Emergent Intelligence*. Ph.D. thesis, The Ohio State University, Columbus, Ohio.

Beer, R. D. and Gallagher, J. C. (1992). Evolving dynamical neural networks for adaptive behavior. *Adaptive Behavior*, 1(1):91–122.

---

3. This also illustrates how our work differs from other methods of connectionist modular control (e.g., Jacobs, Jordan, and Barto, 1990), which adopt a negative view of the interactions between modules. In fact, some work along these lines explicitly focuses on training away such interactions (Nowlan and Hinton, 1991).

Brooks, R. A. (1986). A robust layered control system for a mobile robot. *IEEE Journal of Robotics and Automation*, 2(1):14–23.

Brooks, R. A. (1991). Intelligence without representations. *Artificial Intelligence*, 47:139–159.

Cariani, P. (1989). *On the Design of Devices with Emergent Semantic Properties*. Ph.D. thesis, State University of New York at Binghamton.

Chandrasekaran, B. and Josephson, S. G. (1993). Architecture of intelligence: The problems and current approaches to solutions. *Current Science*, 64(6):366–380.

Cliff, D. (1991). Computational neuroethology: A provisional manifesto. In Meyer, J. A. and Wilson, S. W., editors, *From Animals to Animats: Proceedings of the First International Conference on Simulation of Adaptive Behavior*, pages 29–39, Cambridge. MIT Press.

Collins, R. J. and Jefferson, D. R. (1991). Representations for artificial organisms. In Meyer, J. A. and Wilson, S. W., editors, *From Animals to Animats: Proceedings of the First International Conference on Simulation of Adaptive Behavior*, pages 382–390, Cambridge. MIT Press.

Fahlman, S. E. and Lebiere, C. (1990). The cascade-correlation architecture. In Touretzky, D. S., editor, *Advances in Neural Information Processing Structures 2*, pages 524–532. Morgan Kaufmann.

Hinton, G. E., McClelland, J. L., and Rumelhart, D. E. (1986). Distributed representations. In Rumelhart, D. E. and McClelland, J. L., editors, *Parallel Distributed Processing: Explorations in the Microstructure of Cognition*, Volume 1: Foundations, pages 77–109. MIT Press, Cambridge, MA.

Jacobs, R. A., Jordan, M. I., and Barto, A. G. (1990). Task decomposition through competition in a modular connectionist architecture: The what and where vision tasks. *Cognitive Science*, 15:219–250.

Kolen, J. F. (In press). The observers' paradox: The apparent computational complexity of physical systems. *Journal of Experimental and Theoretical Artificial Intelligence*.

Kolen, J. F. and Pollack, J. B. (1993). The apparent computational complexity of physical systems. In *Proceedings of the Fifteenth Annual Conference of the Cognitive Science Society*, pages 617–622, Hillsdale, NJ. Erlbaum Associates.

Maes, P. (1991). The agent network architecture. In *AAAI Spring Symposium on Integrated Intelligent Architectures*, March.

Maes, P. and Brooks, R. A. (1990). Learning to coordinate behaviors. In *Proceedings of the Eighth National Conferences on AI*, pages 769–802.

McClelland, J. L., Rumelhart, D. E., and The PDP Research Group (1986). *Parallel Distributed Processing: Explorations in the Microstructure of Cognition*, Volume 2: Psychological and Biological Models. MIT Press, Cambridge, MA.

Meyer, J. A. and Guillot, A. (1991). Simulation of adaptive behavior in animats: Review and prospect. In Meyer, J. A. and Wilson, S. W., editors, *From Animals to Animats: Proceedings of the First International Conference on Simulation of Adaptive Behavior*, pages 2–14, Cambridge. MIT Press.

Newell, A. (1982). The knowledge level. *Artificial Intelligence*, 18:87–127.

Nowlan, S. J. and Hinton, G. E. (1991). Evaluation of adaptive mixtures of competing experts. In Lippmann, R., Moody, J., and Touretzky, D., editors, *Advances in Neural Information Processing Systems 3*, pages 774–780. Morgan Kaufmann.

Saunders, G. M., Angeline, P. J., and Pollack, J. B. (1994). Structural and behavioral evolution of recurrent networks. In *Advances in Neural Information Processing 7*. Morgan Kaufmann.

Searle, J. (1992). *Rediscovery of the Mind*. MIT Press, Cambridge, MA.

Simon, H. A. (1969). *Sciences of the Artificial*. MIT Press.

Vera, A. H. and Simon, H. A. (1993). Situated action: A symbolic interpretation. *Cognitive Science*, 17(1):7–48.

Wilson, S. W. (1991). The animat path to AI. In Meyer, J. A. and Wilson, S. W., editors, *From Animals to Animats: Proceedings of the First International Conference on Simulation of Adaptive Behavior*, pages 15–21, Cambridge. MIT Press.

A Topological Neural Map for On-line Learning: Emergence of Obstacle Avoidance in a Mobile Robot

Philippe Gaussier   Stephane Zrehen
Laboratoire de Microinformatique
EPFL-DI
CH-1015 Lausanne, SWITZERLAND

EMail : zrehen or gaussier @lamisun.epfl.ch
Tel: ++ (41)(21) 693 52 64
Fax: ++ (41)(21) 693 5263

Abstract

In this paper, we present an experiment of emergent behavior learning with neural networks. Such a choice is inspired by biological systems where solutions to behavior emergence obviously exist. The aim of this first experiment is to get the mobile robot Khepera to learn how to avoid collisions in walls through its experience.

We show that traditional neural algorithms are inadequate for plausible behavior learning. We present a novel architecture and two combined algorithms that lead to the desired result. In particular, a new kind of topological map is presented in detail. Khepera learns how to solve the conflict between two contradictory behaviors: moving forward and avoiding obstacles, with the help of a pain signal. Unforeseen abilities such as getting out of a dead-end also emerge.

1. Introduction

Our long term goal is to design an autonomous mobile robot with its own internal motivations such as hunger, pain, pleasure that develops cognitive abilities. For instance, it should be able to avoid obstacles, locate food and find short ways to get back to it without relying on an a priori map of the external world. The robot should find its own solutions to the problems, without any help of an external expert guiding its decisions. This research aims at finding a general method that allows artificial systems to "survive", where "survival" means satisfying a constraint linked to finding solutions to different tasks.

This poses a challenge to classical Artificial Intelligence (AI) techniques that rely on symbolic representations of the outside world, as they suppose that the world can be perfectly modeled. In case of an unknown world, complete knowledge of the possible situations and of the behavior to adopt is impossible. Moreover, such AI systems also rely on absolute confidence of the lower levels (sensors, effectors) which is extremely costly to obtain.

Thus, prior symbolic representations of the outside world should be excluded from our developments: the whole knowledge the robot would have about its environment should exclusively come from its own experience.

Our approach takes the coupling of actions and perceptions via the interactions with the outside world as a basis for developing cognitive capacities for artificial organisms (Stewart, 1991; Maturana &Varela, 1987). One should not consider autonomous agents as input-output machines, but rather as dynamic systems that can keep internal coherence while being perturbed by the outside world.

This view implies that the observed behaviors of a mobile robot should emerge as the effect of the interactions between the robot and the environment on its internal structure. If the robot, equipped with sensors and effectors, is also provided with the adequate control procedures, interesting or "intelligent" behaviors might emerge. This interpretation should be left to the observer *a posteriori*. The main point is that the behavior -- that might be judged as intelligent -- should not be programmed. This typically appears with Braitenberg's first vehicles (Braitenberg, 1986), where the control procedures, simple as they are, give rise to very interesting behaviors. Nevertheless, the behavior repertoire of these machines is very limited and they are not adaptive. Learning procedures should be added in order to magnify this repertoire, and to provide autonomous agents with adaptation capacities.

This paper will first analyze the general problem posed to Khepera[1]. Traditional neural approaches will be analyzed and their drawbacks pointed out. We will then present our own control architecture and algorithms. In particular, we introduce a new kind of binary topological map. The final experiment shows that this neural network allows Khepera to solve a conflict problem: it learns when to use its built-in reflex of

---

[1]Khepera is the robot designed by F. Mondada at the LAMI-EPFL (Mondada et al, 1993)

moving forward with a local associative procedure, and when to avoid obstacles with a global reinforcement rule. Both learning schemes, together with the organization of the topological map, are performed simultaneously. It also happens that unforeseeable interesting behaviors emerge after some time : Khepera is able to escape from a dead-end, and it chooses the turning direction that minimizes the trajectory when it meets an obstacle.

2. Presentation and Analysis of the Problem

The natural choice for commanding a mobile robot is the sense-think-act scheme. We use a mechanism inspired from generalized Darwinism (Edelman, 1987), (Changeux, 1985), based on the principle of diversity generation and selection. Our choice is derived from the works by Hecht-Nielsen (Hecht-Nielsen, 1987) on the network architecture, by Linsker on competitive hierarchical networks (Linsker, 1986) and by Grossberg on Adaptive Resonance Theory (ART) (Carpenter&Grossberg, 1987). In our model, neurons in Winner-Take-All groups or topological maps are associated in a hierarchical structure. Noise is added to the neuron output function to allow diversity and choice in the case of neurons with the same activation.

Darwinism cannot be applied between two different levels of a system. The structure must be frozen at some point to apply selection to the next level. Therefore, it is necessary to have hard-wired reflexes to learn the next level of behavior. Then selection can be applied to those emerging behaviors, with the help of a very simple selection tool. In fact, without a "go-forward" reflex, the robot might as well choose to remain still or turn on place, as these behaviors avoid contact with the walls and thus pain.

We take a very simple neural coding of the reflex: only the "Forward" cell receives an unconditional afference (Figure 2), which is activated when there is no collision. This leads to a natural forward movement when it is possible. But this tendency can be overcome, if other afferences are stronger than this one.

2.1. Why Use Neural Networks ?

Our choice for neural networks is motivated by their generalization capacities, as well as their resistance to noise and contradictions. Such features are very precious for controlling a real mobile robot which is to operate in real-world situations. Furthermore, as they are directly inspired from animal whose behavior is controlled by neurons, a global solution to the behavior emergence problem can be expected to come from such tools.

There are mainly two kinds of learning rules for artificial neural networks: supervised and unsupervised. The former (Rumelhart et al., 1986) requires the existence of an explicit evaluation function that can be computed at any time step and a learning rule to adapt the weights accordingly. Supervised learning implies an external expert who guides learning, which makes it a bad candidate for designing an autonomous machine. We will examine in the following paragraph why also unsupervised learning, as occurs in Kohonen maps, is not practical (Kohonen, 1982).

In order to design a completely autonomous machine, several aspects of neural network research need to be tackled together: self-organization according to environment-driven stimuli, architecture of the network and a scheme for choosing among all possible behaviors.

Our goal is to combine such facets of learning to solve the general problem of behavior emergence. Our solution is to define a general neural architecture with its associated algorithms. Our approach can also be seen as a new technique of incremental programming.

2.2. Why Design New Algorithms and Architectures ?

Kohonen maps have been used for localization of the robot in its environment (Nehmzov & Smithers, 1991). But learning in such topological maps requires a separation between the learning and utilization phase. While a similar process may happen in biological systems such as building of somatotopic maps, it cannot be used for higher level applications where the environment is changing : when a new learning example is presented to a Kohonen map, all learning has to be done over again. It is thus impossible to make a gradual learning and to question decisions in a systematic way. Obviously, most learning in living systems does not start from scratch when a new item is encountered: this leads us to reject that algorithm.

Therefore, it is necessary to design a network that can learn incrementally, without prior knowledge of the training set. Since the environment is subject to change, there should be no difference between learning and utilization.

However, the information provided by topological maps is precious, especially when implemented in real systems: their main feature is that two close stimuli should produce close activity patterns in the map (Figure 1). Also when real sensors are used, noise should not perturb the resulting activities of the network. Close situations should be coded on nearby neurons (Edelman & Weinshall, 1991; Zipser, 1985). This justifies the use of a new kind of topological maps which are not fraught with the difficulties mentioned above. The algorithm we use will be detailed in 3.2.

Coding a special situation on certain neurons of a topological map does not enable the robot to adopt a particular behavior. In this experiment, the aim is to learn how to avoid collisions into walls. Therefore, we need a learning procedure that enables the robot to choose from all sensorial situations the movements that do not cause it to collide into a wall. We use for this level a Winner Take All and Hebbian learning modulated by a pain signal.

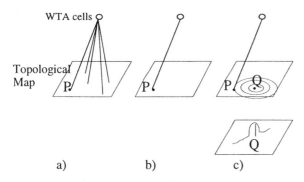

Figure 1: Usage of the topological map
a: Each neuron on the WTA receives afferences from all cells on the map. b: P is the winner. Only this weight is modified by reinforcement learning. c: When a new stimulus is presented to the map, Q is the winner. The activity in the WTA decreases with the map distance between Q and P.

3.   The Neural Architecture

At this stage, the whole navigation process is discrete. Weights are initialized at random values. Then, at each time step, the following processes take place in order:

1   Sensory information is collected
2   A decision is made, a movement is performed
3   A pain signal is computed and possibly perceived by the network.
4   Synaptic weights are adapted.

Movements are chosen among three possibilities: turn left, turn right, go straight ahead, each of them of a fixed quantity.
The global architecture of our neural system is depicted in Figure 2.

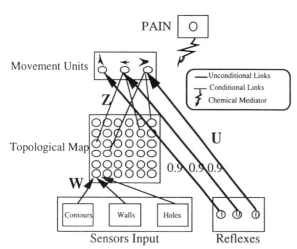

Figure 2 : The Neural Network Architecture
Data from the infrared sensors are pre-processed in the "Sensors Input" box. The pre-processing is shown on Figure 3 and explained in 3.1.

Two neural groups are used: one topological map that codes sensorial input and a Winner-Take-All (WTA) group that decides what movement to make.

The topological map is a Probabilistic Topological Map (PTM) (Gaussier&Zrehen, 1993). It gets rough information from the infrared sensors only. The detail of the pre-processing is explained in 3.1.

The PTM learning algorithm, i.e. adaptation of the synaptic weights - called W weights - between the input and the neurons of the map will be explained in 3.2.

The WTA group receives input from a Reflexes box and from all cells of the topological map. The go-forward reflex is represented in a neural fashion: three neurons are used, each in state 0 (for the turning movements) or 1 (for the forward movement). The activity they produce in the WTA is their own activity weighted by the weights U. These weights are unmodifiable, and the stimulus is called unconditional after Pavlov. On the contrary, links between the topological map and the WTA - called Z weights - must be adapted afterwards, in function of the pain signal.

This architecture is well adapted to the defined task: with the appropriate learning rule on the Z weights, it is possible to avoid making movements that cause pain when a similar situation has been met before. The one we use is inspired by Barto's reinforcement learning (Barto, Sutton & Anderson, 1983), and is described in 3.3.

If more complex tasks are to be performed, such as learning how to act when new sensors are added to the system, a new box can be added to the system in a subsumption fashion (Brooks, 1986), with links to the WTA group.

3.1. Input Representation

The input we use are the result of a pre-processing of the value of the sensors. Those are integers, ranging from 0 (for a distance > 5 cm) to 1023 (approximately 2 cm). For more technical details, see (Mondada 1994). The map needs binary input values and a dynamic of distances between inputs that is large enough. Therefore, we extracted three eight-dimensional binary vectors from the data (See Figure 3). The first is made of the contours of the sensors' patterns [Marr, 1980]. Those contours are computed with a three-neighbor edge extraction mask. The second called "Holes" has a value of 1 when the corresponding sensor is close to zero and 0 otherwise. The third set called "Walls" has a coordinate of 1 when the corresponding sensor is above 500 and 0 otherwise. The three different input types are normalized over three to get activities between 0 and 1. This representation is extremely redundant, and that helps palliating the small number of sensors. Situations that seem close to the observer of the robot do code on close cells on the map.

Contour extraction is known to happen in mammals retina (Hubel & Wiesel, 1977), while the "walls" and "holes" can be seen as an over-simplification of the

OFF-Center and OFF-Surround cells also found in mammals retina.

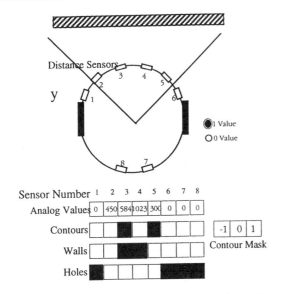

Figure 3 : Sensory Representation from the sensors

3.2. The Probabilistic Topological Map (PTM)

This was first proposed by Gaussier (Gaussier, 1992) as a support of the model of Burnod's cortical column (Burnod, 1989). The details and proofs of its functioning can be found in (Gaussier&Zrehen, 1993). Here, we only indicate the global principle (Figure 5).

Probabilistic Topological Map

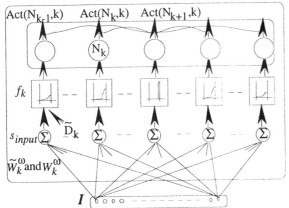

Figure 5: The different stages of the PTM

As mentioned in 2.2., we need an unsupervised learning algorithm that makes no distinction between learning and utilization, and that does not need to know in advance the whole training set. In order to obtain an immediate topology preserving mapping, the desired neuron activation by an input pattern *I* is forced and we maintain a continuity on the map by allowing the coding

of the intersection of two learned patterns between their maximally responding cells (Figure 4).

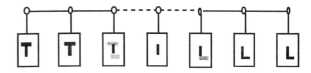

Figure 4: Coding of patterns on the map. *Straight lines represent neighbohood relations in the map: the intersection "I" of two patterns "T" and "L" is coded on the neuron located at an intermediate neuron on segment TL.*

We consider the activity of neuron N_k under presentation of binary input vector *I* at time t. The algorithm comes in four stages:

> i) Present an input vector *I* to the map
>
> ii) Find the winner cell N^*, i.e. the map cell with highest activity. The similarity between *I* and the weight vector is first computed and the real neuron activity is processed trough an activation function f_k with variable selectivity $\tilde{D}_k(t)$.
>
> iii) Diffuse the winner activity on the map according to a diffusion function.
> $$D_k(t) = D_k(N_k, N^*) = exp\left[-u.\,d_{map}^2(N^*, N_k)\right]$$
>
> iv) If $D_k(t) - \tilde{D}_k(t) > v$ (the vigilance parameter) enable learning on the map:
>
> a- Adapt the weights according to a probabilistic law that matches the diffusion function $D_k(t)$
>
> b- Increase the selectivity $\tilde{D}_k(t)$ of the activation function of each modified neuron else do not learn

The diffusion function is chosen as a Gaussian function (Seibert & Waxman, 1989) of fixed width which depends only on the map distance between the winner and other neurons (Figure 6).

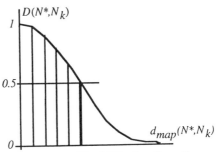

Figure 6 : The Diffusion Function

Its action is meant to model the effect of lateral coupling of the winner with its neighbors: it makes them learn the input pattern, with an effect that decreases with distance. The goal of the synaptic weight adaptation rule is to get the weights create an activity under presentation of the same input which is close to the value of the diffusion function. In order to limit the size of the bubbles around a winner, the diffusion is stopped below 50%.

Thus, after presentation of an input, all neurons around the winner have a given diffusion value. We assimilate certainty of knowledge to closeness to the winner and denote by $\tilde{D}_k(t)$ the maximal value of the diffusion in N_k's history at time t. This factor is essential in the definition of the activation functions:

$$f_k[x](t) = \tilde{D}_k(t) \exp\left[-\frac{1}{2\sigma}\left(\frac{1-x}{1-\tilde{D}_k(t)-\varepsilon}\right)^2\right]$$

where σ is a width parameter and ε a small factor meant to avoid a division by zero for the winner. σ must be tuned to control the location of neurons coding new input. This expression defines a family of functions: f_k's narrowness and height decrease with $d_{map}(N^*, N_k)$ (Figure 7).

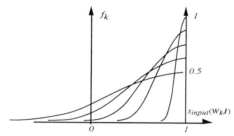

Figure 7: A Family of activation functions.
Their maximum is equal to the maximal value of the diffusion in the neuron's history.

The activity in neuron N_k under presentation of binary input vector I is measured as follows:

$$Act(N_k, I) = f_k\left[s_{input}(W_k, I)\right] + noise, \text{ where}$$

$$s_{input}(W_k, I) = \frac{\sum_{\omega=1}^{P} V_k^\omega . I_\omega}{S} + \frac{\sum_{\omega=1}^{P} \overline{W}_k^\omega . \overline{I}_\omega}{P-S} \quad if \tilde{D}_k < 1$$

$$s_{input}(W_k, I) = \frac{\sum_{\omega=1}^{P} V_k^\omega . I_\omega}{\sum_{\omega=1}^{P} V_k^\omega} + \frac{\sum_{\omega=1}^{P} \overline{W}_k^\omega . \overline{I}_\omega}{\sum_{\omega=1}^{P} \overline{W}_k^\omega} \quad otherwise$$

where W_k is N_k's weight vector and

$$\begin{cases} \overline{W}_k^\omega = 1 - W_k^\omega \\ \overline{I}_k^\omega = 1 - I_k^\omega \end{cases} \text{ and } V_k^\omega = W_k^\omega + \alpha \cdot \tilde{W}_k^\omega$$

$\tilde{W}_k$ is the vector derived from W_k whose components $\tilde{W}_k^\omega$ are equal to 1 when W_k^ω has been reinforced more than once and 0 otherwise. The term $\alpha \tilde{W}_k$ is intended to allow a continuity between coded patterns on the map: its use allows the coding of the intersection of two already coded patterns at the middle of the neurons coding each pattern. f_k is N_k's activation function meant to avoid forgetting learned patterns and to avoid abusive learning. P is the dimension of the input space and S is the presumed number of ones of the input vector (it is a constant value). The case $\tilde{D}_k = 1$ allows a different normalization for the winners and the other neurons. It is necessary to avoid indecision when several patterns with a common intersection have been coded.

We have introduced a vigilance parameter $v \in [0, 1]$ meant to prevent saturation of the map. It is used in the following way: if under presentation of a new input, the proposed winner is close to a previous winner, then the new pattern is very likely to belong to the same category as the previous one. In that case it is not necessary to learn the new input, unless a negative reinforcement signal comes from the upper level.

The initialization of all parameters is the following:

$$\forall k, \omega, W_k^\omega = noise, \tilde{W}_k^\omega = 0, \tilde{D}_k(t=0) = noise$$

Admitting that input I is presented at time t and that the neurons' parameters are modified at time t+1 and that random is a random number between 0 and 1, the adaptation rule writes:

If $D_k(t) - \tilde{D}_k(t) > 0$ then
If random $< D_k(t)$ then
adapt N_k's weight W_k:
-   $W_k^\omega(t+1) = I^\omega$
-   If $I^\omega = 1$ and $W_k^\omega(t) = 1$
then $\tilde{W}_k^\omega(t+1) = 1$.
Else $W_k^\omega(t+1) = W_k^\omega(t)$
Modify N_k's selectivity parameter:
$\tilde{D}_k(t+1) = D_k(N^*, N_k)$

Those features are very precious for our robot : input vectors are met all the time. When they are close to some situation already encountered, they get coded on nearby cells. When they are completely different, they get coded far away on the map. In any case, when an input is presented, an activity bubble appears in the map, as for Kohonen maps.

However, the organization is only local, and new input tend to be coded at the outer limit (where D=50%) of previous bubbles. This results in a progressive organization of the map which gives account for the continuity of the input patterns recorded as the robot wanders (Figure 8).

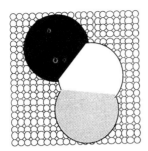

Figure 8: Progressive organization of the PTM. *The three different colors correspond to three bubbles of input presented at successive times t=0,t=1,t=2*

3.3. Reinforcement Learning

This procedure conditions entirely the robot's behavior: learning of those weights is modulated by the pain signal. The philosophy of this process is very simple: if the chosen action in a given sensory situation caused pain, then the link between that situation and the resulting action should be inhibited. If it caused pleasure, it should be reinforced. If no pleasure and no pain happened, then it should slightly be reinforced. Since the sensorial situations are represented as an activity pattern on the map, these rules can be expressed as a special Hebbian learning:

$$Z_{jk}(t+1) = Z_{jk}(t) +$$
$$\eta \left(\frac{1 - 2.Pain}{3} \right). T\left[D_k(t)\right]. H_j(t),$$

where

$$H_j(t) = \sum_k Z_{jk}.D_k(t) + S_j U_j$$

where k indexes the cells of the topological map and j the WTA cells. S_j is the unconditional stimulus and U_k the unmodifiable weight. $D_k(t)$ is the diffusion value on neuron N_k due to the winner at time t. T is a threshold function that allows learning on the only interesting map cells, e.g., those with a high activity. We have : $\eta < 1/2$, and Pain = -1, 0, 1. We can choose to adapt the weights of the map cells whose activity is above a high threshold, so that only the cells of the map responsible for the action have their influence modified. This learning scheme converges very fast, as will be seen in 4.

3.4. The Pain Function

This function determines entirely the behavior of the robot. For reasons of simplicity, we choose to use the same function for pain and pleasure. Pain is here the contrary of pleasure. Pain occurs when the final position of the robot corresponds to a collision (Pain=1). Pleasure

occurs when the initial position corresponds to a collision and the final does not (Pain=-1). These two cases allow a selection of the right associations between a sensory situation and one of the three possible movements. When there is no collision at initial and final positions, Pain = 0. This case allows an automatic association between the reflex and the sensory situations that let it be chosen without harm.

The choice of such a simple function helps to understand the influence of that parameter on the general behavior. It is the only parameter of the control system where the designer can inject his interpretation of the world. However, the resulting behavior is not programmed as such: it is due to the internal structure of the neural architecture, and to the interactions with the outside world.

All neurons in this system have noise added to their output to help choice in cases of equality. The range of noise could be also modulated by the pain signal, thus allowing to try more easily a new solution in order to get out of a painful situation.

4. Experimental Results and Analysis

In order to illustrate the convergence properties of the whole neural network, we launched the robot in an arena, where obstacles can be introduced or removed. This makes a good field to study how the robot learns not to collide with obstacles. The rotation angle is set around 30°, and the forward step to about 1.5 cm, that is half the sensors range. Figures 9 to 14 illustrate the two experiments that were done with the robot. It was launched in the arena. After a few steps, it finds itself with the wall on its left; it goes over in the arena, keeping the wall on its left (Figure 12a, 9), and turning right before or after bumping on the wall. After around 400 steps, collisions almost disappear (Figure 11): the robot has learned to associate each sensory situation it has met with the "right turn" movement. If we then take the robot and turn it so that the wall is on its right (Figures 12b, 10), after a few steps, it starts turning left, and avoids bumping in the same way it did before.

After those two experiments, the robot is now placed in an arena loaded with new obstacles (Figure 12c). Here it then takes an "eight" trajectory, turning right when the wall is on the left, and left when it is on the right. This shows that it has learned the right associations for all the sensory situations and that it has not forgotten anything. Thus, Khepera exhibits a kind of "intelligent" behavior at this stage, as its ability of turning in the "good" direction had not been decided in advance. It could indeed always turn in the same direction as well, say left, until it does not collide anymore, whatever the initial position towards the wall.

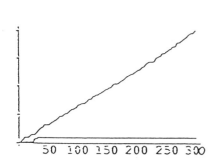

Figure 9 : Wall on the Left. *The higher curve represents the cumulated number of right-turns*

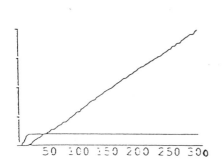

Figure 10 : Wall on the Right. *The higher curve represents the cumulated number of left-turns*

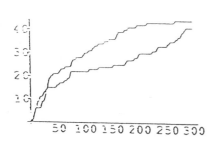

Figure 11: Cumulative number of bumps vs. time. *The higher curve is for the first experiment: wall on the left. The other for the second.*

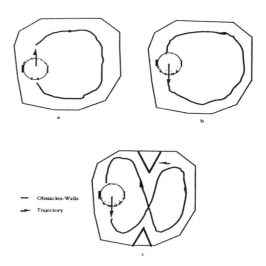

Figure 12: Different trajectories of the robot, depending on the initial situation.

With the same learning procedure, Khepera also shows an ability of getting out of a dead-end (Figure 13). This apparently easy problem happens to be interesting because it shows a second-order learning capacity: in a dead-end, each movement leads to pain, therefore escaping from it shows may imply the choice of a sequence of actions, while no device is here to remember sequences.

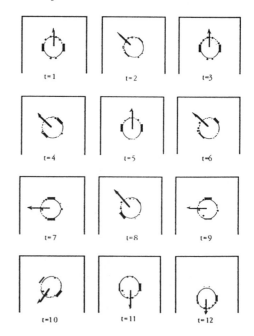

Figure 13 : A typical succession of positions of Khepera in a dead-end. *More oscillations usually happen, but the general pattern is always similar to this one.*

This happens through multiple right-left oscillations. As each movement leads to pain, inhibition rises (par. 3.3) and that leads to choosing another movement at some point. Therefore, a sequence right-left-right may take place until either right-left-left or right-right-left appears. This allows the robot to move of one increment of angle and start the same procedure again. This process can take long, depending mostly on the learning rate, but it always ends up with a solution: the robot privileges one direction and uses it each times it gets close to a dead-end (but not inside) that resembles the one where he did its learning. The choice of two successive movements in the same direction can happen at different times.

This is another example of behavior that could indeed be hard-wired as a reflex but that can be learned.

Figure 14 shows the different sensorial patterns learnt by the neurons of the map.

5. Conclusion and Future Work

We have successfully designed a neural network that allows our robot to exhibit a behavior which has not been programmed. Our neural architecture proves to be very effective in several ways:

- No idealization of the sensors or of the outside world was needed. The primitives extracted from the infrared sensors are very robust to noise, and lend themselves extremely well to neural processing.
- No pre-analysis of the sensors is needed: the meaning of the sensory situations appears through the robot's experience. There is no grounding problem as the designer's role is not to interpret a priori the meaning of those situations.
- The topological map is organized while the behavior is emerging. This happens very fast (around 20 steps), if it is to be compared with Kohonen maps which generally need some 10,000 steps before organization appears.

Another striking feature of this architecture is that it was used exactly as such for a totally different application: recognition of visual scenes (Gaussier&Cocquerez, 1992). This leads us to think that this type of architecture might serve as a building block for more integrated tasks.

From a cognitive point of view, Khepera has learned to overcome its natural tendency to go forward. In other words, it has learned when not to use its reflexes, which might be considered as a first step toward intelligence. One might argue that such a basic reaction as turning right when there is an obstacle on the left is hard-wired in many animals (Braitenberg, 1986). This is also true of the right attitude to adopt in a dead-end: turn in the same direction until space in front is free. What we showed is that those behaviors can be learned from such a simple Pain function as the one we used. Such learning might then be used to learn more complex behaviors, by Pavlovian conditioning of reflexes .

Current research explores how to integrate the robot's movements, in order to make navigation possible. Sensors fusion will also be studied, with CCD cameras as eyes for the robot. The architecture is perfect for such subsumption-like evolution of robot behaviors (Brooks, 1986). New information can be added to the network, by adding a box and connecting it to the right cells. If the new box is removed, only the new ability is lost, while the rest remains reliable.

6. Acknowledgments

This research is supported by the Swiss National Fund's PNR 23 program.

We would like to thank Francesco Mondada for designing the robot, and for his precious help during this research, and the French Ministry of Foreign Affairs who allowed Ph. Gaussier to make his civil service at the LAMI.

7. References

Barto A.G., Sutton R.S., & Anderson C.W. (1983). Neuronlike Adaptive elements that can solve difficult learning control problems. *IEEE Transactions on Systems, Man, and Cybernetics* **SMC-13**, 5, pp834-846.

Braitenberg V. (1986). Vehicles : Experiments in synthetic psychology, MIT Press, Cambridge.

Brooks R.A. (1986). A robust layered control system for a mobile robot. *IEEE Journal of Robotics and Automation* **RA-2**, 14-23.

Burnod Y. (1989). An adaptive neural network : The cerebral cortex, Masson, Paris.

G.A. Carpenter & S. Grossberg (1987) "Invariant Pattern recognition and recall by an attentive self organizing ART architecture in a nonstationary world", *Proceeding of Neural Network,* vol 2, p 737-745

Changeux J.-P. (1985). Neuronal Man : The Biology of Mind, Oxford University Press, Oxford.

Edelman G. (1987). Neural Darwinism : The Theory of Neuronaˡ Group Selection, Basic Books, New-York.

Edelman S. & Weinshall D. (1991). A Self-Organizing Multiple View of 3D Objects. *Biological Cybernetics* **64**, pp209-219.

Gaussier P. (1992). Doctoral Thesis. Paris XI - Orsay.

Gaussier P. , Cocquerez, J.-P.(1991), *Neural Networks For Complex Scene Recognition: Simulation Of A Visual System With Several Cortical Areas*, in Proceedings of IJCNN, Baltimore, Vol. 3, pp. 233-259.

Gaussier P. Zrehen S. The Probabilistic Topological Map (PTM): a self organizing and fast learning neural map that preserves topology, Submited to *Neural Networks*

Hecht-Nielsen R. (1987). Counterpropagation Networks. *Applied Optics* **26**, 23, pp4979-4984.

Hubel D. & Wiesel T. (1977). Functional architecture of macaque monkey visual cortex. *Proceedings of the Royal Society* **198**, Ferrier Lectures, pp1-59.

Kohonen T. (1982). Self-organized formation of topologically correct feature maps. *Biological Cybernetics* **43**, 59-69.

Linsker R. (1986). From basic network principles to neural architectures : emergence of spatial-opponent cells. *Proc. Natl. Ac. Sci.* **83**, 7508-7512.

Mondada F., Franzi E, Ienne P. (1993) Mobile Robot miniaturization: A tool for investigation in control algorithms, *Proceedings of Third International Symposium on Experimental Robotics*, Kyoto, In Press

Mondada F. (1994) Khepera user's manual, Khepera Support Team, Lausanne.

Nehmzov U. & Smithers T. (1991). Using Motor Actions for Location Recognition. *In proceedings of First European Conference on Artificial Life*, Paris, Varela F.J. & Bourgine P. eds. , pp. 96-104. MIT Press.

Rumelhart D.E. et al. (1986). Parallel Distributed Processing, MIT-Press, Cambridge.

Seibert M. & Waxman A.M. (1989). Spreading Activation Layers, Visual Saccades, and Invariant Representations for Neural Pattern Recognition Systems. *Neural Networks* **2**, pp9-27.

Stewart, J. (1991) Life=Cognition: The epistemological and Ontological significance of Artificial Life, *proccedings of SAB 91 Paris,* Bourgine P. & Varela F. eds, MIT Press, pp 475-483

Zipser D. (1985). A Computational Model of Hippocampal Place Fields. *Behavioral Neuroscience* **99**, 5, pp1006-1018.

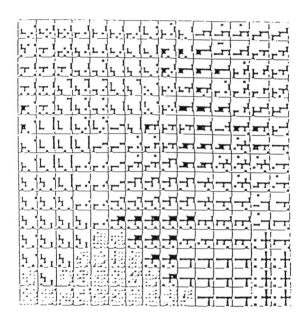

Figure 14: Patterns learned by the topological map.

Each neuron's weight is represented as a square. All squares are disposed in the two-dimensional array fashion that represents the map. Inside each square, the weight components are represented as an array of black or white small squares.

Reinforcement tuning of action synthesis and selection in a 'virtual frog'.

Simon Giszter
E25-526 MIT,
Dept. Brain and Cognitive Science, MIT,
Cambridge MA 02139 USA
E-mail giszter@ai.mit.edu

Abstract:

Maes networks have been used for action selection for adaptive behavior in several contexts. Coupled to force-field primitives they can simulate several aspects of frog reflex behaviors. A scheme for reinforcement based tuning of such a situated Maes-type network, operating for action synthesis and selection using force-field mechanisms is presented. The scheme attempts learning in a context of concurrent actions and environmental dynamics which cause severe credit assignment problems. The a priori rationale and advantages and disadvantages of this new learning scheme are discussed in the context of an analysis of Maes networks. Tests of learning using this scheme are applied to networks which were previously hand coded to perform a simulation of a frog wiping behaviors. Experiments with the learning scheme show the tuned networks improved considerably, the networks often altered qualitatively, and were able to remove irritants in as little as half the time of the original hand coded networks.

1 Introduction

This article introduces a novel scheme for learning more effective weights in a Maes network for action selection (Maes 1989). The Maes networks have been used to simulate frog spinal behaviors (Giszter 1993). Spinal reflex behaviors can be improved with practice even in spinal cords isolated from the brain. Learning in the frog spinal cord reflex responses has been demonstrated (Franzisket, 1963). The Maes networks that have been used in simulations of the frog act on their environments in a manner which differs radically from most action selection networks. The network 'actions' are in the simulations presented here are the activation of force-field primitives in the motor system of a limb (see Bizzi et al.,1991, Giszter 1993, Giszter et al., 1993, Mussa-Ivaldi et al. 1994). These force-field primitives are summed in the limb, using a simple vector summation mechanism for command fusion. The net force-field in the limb resulting from this fusion drives motion of the limb and its interaction with the environment. The actual effect of an action selection in the Maes network may thus be dependent on the context of other concurrent actions, and the limb state. This framework for connecting the network to the environment thus provides severe credit assignment problems for a learning scheme. However it also leads to very robust and flexible limb behavior (Mussa-Ivaldi and Giszter, 1992).

Maes 1993 outlines several areas of interest in design and understanding of adaptive autonomous agents. The current 'virtual frog' model and proposed learning scheme together provide information in several of these areas of interest: (1) they provide a scheme for low level command fusion (vector summation of force-field primitives), (2) they examine mechanisms for synthesis of hybrid actions from a few primitives using this command fusion, (3) they examine learning in the context of such multiple concurrent actions and their synthesis.

The learning scheme to be presented here is based on intermittent reinforcement of the network. Reinforcement follows the successful event. The successful event is the end result of an action chain, in which selection of a series of several weighted concurrent actions may also be necessary for success. The learning scheme here uses spreading 'reinforcement activation' distributed from the executing action modules to determine which network weights or links should be adjusted, and by how much. Adjustments thus occur in connections that are remote from the executing modules, but which are nonetheless important in activating the executing module. Experiments with the scheme show it is a viable approach to improving performance of a Maes behavior selection network in some circumstances.

2 Motivation:

Recent work in the frog spinal cord suggests that the actions of the frog may result from the combination of a small number of vector-field primitives by vector summation (Bizzi et al. 1991, Giszter et al. 1993, Mussa-Ivaldi et al. 1994). See figure 1. Theoretically, these primitives might be combined by descending systems in constructing plans (Mussa-Ivaldi and Giszter 1993) or by spinal pattern generators and

action selection systems for reflex actions (Giszter 1993), or by both concurrently. See figure 2. It has been shown that the spinal cord systems can learn, even in isolation from the brain (Franzisket, 19). Thus, learning in models of reflex organization should be feasible if they represent a reasonable approximation to the animal.

3 The Maes action selection network:

The Maes network is designed to choose primitive actions from a repertoire. Each action is associated with a node. The network uses a vector of conditions abstracted from the environment to determine the dynamic behavior of the network and the selection process. The basic Maes network design and operation can be summarized succinctly in a few rules. Each node controlling an action has a vector of conditions (which are a subset of the total conditions) must all be true for the action to execute. A node with all such preconditions true is termed 'executable'. Action nodes are 'non-executable' until their vector of

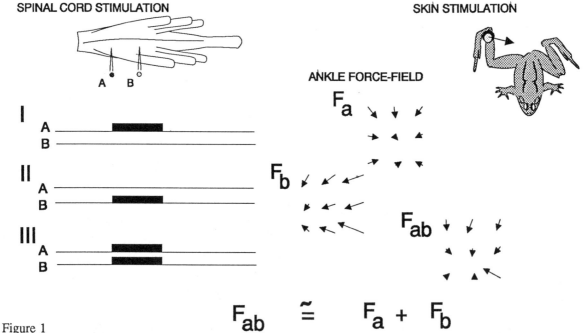

Figure 1

Summation of spinal primitives. These are the biological results motivating the simulation are presented here. Spinal cord stimulation in the frog reveals a small number of force-field primitives. These can be combined by vector summation. They also closely resemble the force-fields elicited in reflex responses. These primitives can be summed simply: Fab due to stimulation condition III (electrode A and B together) can be viewed as the vector sum of Fa (field due to electrode A alone) and Fb (field due to electrode B alone). See Bizzi et al. 1991 and Mussa-Ivaldi et al. 1994 for details. This mechanism provids a powerful means of control of multi-joint limb behavior.

preconditions are all true. Action nodes execute if they are both executable, and have activation above a threshold value. Conditions that are true (ON) pass activation directly to any action nodes for which they are a precondition. In addition the network of has an internal dynamics due to activation passing among nodes. This internal dynamics occurs through three link types. The link type and the behavior of the links are determined by the relations of conditions to action nodes (or action-modules). Given a set of pre-conditions and action results (setting of conditions by actions) the architecture and basic behavior of the network is defined.

Internal connections or links between action-modules consist of three types:
1: Predecessor links exist to any action-modules expected to make a precondition true. One link for each module exists for each precondition affected. Predecessor links are active only if the associated condition is untrue (OFF).
2: Successor links exist to each action-module expected have a precondition enabled by the action-module execution. One link to each module exists for each precondition affected. Successor links are active only if the associated condition is untrue (OFF), and the source node is executable.

I Field Approximation Models   II Behavioral / recurrent models

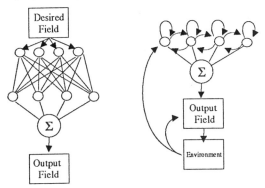

Figure 2
Two frameworks for viewing how the nervous system uses force-field primitives. (I) Top down: planning approximation using force-field primitives (see Mussa-Ivaldi and Giszter 1993) (II) Bottom up: dynamic recurrent networks for local reflex control and reactive agent framework using force-field primitives (Giszter 1993). It is almost certain the living spinal cord must somehow accommodate and integrate processes in both these frameworks.

3: Conflictor links exist that inhibit action-modules that would make a precondition untrue if they executed. Predecessor links are active only if the associated condition is true (ON).
Thus one link of each type can pass from module to module for each condition the modules have in common.

The net effect of the rules for link construction and operation, as given above, can be summarized in the following way: In a given environment, which determines a particular state of the condition vector **C**, the internal dynamics of network behavior due to links (or connections) among action modules, can be characterized as a linear system **A**. [This is provided no action-module's activation saturates.] The activation in each time step is also incremented due to inflow from the conditions vector **C**. This may be calculated as the result of a matrix **B** acting on **C**.

The energy vector **E** composed of each action-modules activation each time step is given by:

$$E(t+1) = A.E(t) + BC \tag{1}$$

The matrix **A** is square, of dimensions n by n, where n is the number of action modules, and consists of entries A_{ij}. Elements on the diagonal are 1 (or < 1 for a decay process at each action-module). Each A_{ij} is composed of the sum of the active predecessor, successor and conflictor links in the network that operate between action-module i and j. In principle each link can have a different strength s. Thus:

$$A_{ij} = \sum_k s_k \, G_k(C, P_i, P_j, R_i, R_j) \tag{2}$$

Index k runs over the size of condition vector **C**. P_x is the precondition vector of module x, R_x is the effect of module x. $G_k(C, P_i, P_j, R_i, R_j)$ is the operation of the set of rules for successor, predecessor and conflictor links and node executable status stated above, which govern whether a type of link exists, and whether a link is active. It is particularly important to note that given a particular state of **C**, equation (2) is fixed and thus the A_{ij} are all determined, and thereby equation (1) is also fixed.

The matrix **B** consists of a matrix n by r, of entries B_{pq} where n is the number of action-modules and r the length of condition vector **C**.

Execution of an action(s) and alteration of the condition vector, switches the system from dynamics $\mathbf{A_0}$ determined by $\mathbf{C_0}$ to a new dynamics $\mathbf{A_1}$ determined by $\mathbf{C_1}$. There may be up to 2^r such linear systems determined by the rules specified by Maes among which a Maes system may switch.

Thus, to summarize, the network, (as implemented here) can be seen as a set of linear systems with transitions between systems

occurring on changes in the condition vector. The action(s) chosen depends on when an executable action-module's activation crosses its threshold. This in turn depends on the vector of action-module states on entering, or switching to, the current linear system. This can be better understood with the simple concrete example shown in figure 3A. This represents a network with 3 actions (A,B,C) and 4 conditions (1,2,3,4). Node A requires condition 1 be true in order to be executable, B requires 2, and C requires 3 and 4 respectively. (This is tabulated in the "Propos'n" column). Action A turns 2 on. Action B turns 3 on and 4 off. Action C turns 1 on. (This is tabulated in "Result of" column). Thus the links in the table at upper right ("S link", "P link", and "C

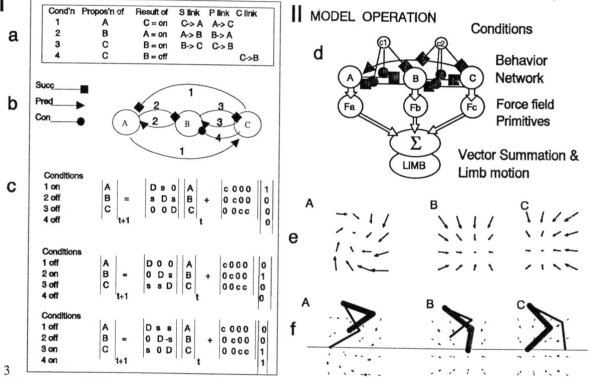

Figure 3

A sample Maes network. (I) A network of 3 actions and 4 conditions. (a) The number of conditions and the proposition list and result list of the action nodes determine the links and link structure diagrammed below in (b). The conditions vector may have 16 different states (2^4). (b) The link connectivity is drawn as a graph below. (c) The dynamics associated with 3 of these 16 different condition states are written out in full below the network diagram. (II) (d) The Maes network of part I is shown used to drive a set of 3 force field primitives. The detailed link structure of (b) is ommitted for clarity. The integration of the network with the force-field primitive system is shown. The Maes network selects force-field primitives that are combined by vector summation to drive the limb. Thus action node A controls primitive FA. When A executes, the force-field controlled by FA is summed with other executing primitives. The magnitude of FA is proportional to the amount of above threshold activation of action node A. (e) The 3 primitives' force-fields, and (f) examples of their kinematic actions in pure form are shown. In each case, barring serious obstacles, the force-fields will bring the linkage from the lightly drawn position (or any other location) to the heavily drawn position. The path taken will depend on the interactions of starting location, force-field strength, limb dynamics and external constraints such as interaction with a surface.

link" columns are created). This leads to the network diagrammed below. The condition vector in this system can have 2^4 states of which 3 are shown. For each of these three states a linear system summary of the network dynamics is shown. It is assumed every link has the same strength s, and conditions pass energy c when true. In the first panel of matrix equations, only condition 1 is ON and only A is executable (condition 1 = 1). Thus S link A-> B is active. P link B-> A is active. P link C-> B is active. Diagonal elements D represents the dissipation of activation energy each cycle. Activation feeds from condition 1 to A as given by the matrix of strength to the right.

The goal of a reinforcement learning scheme is to determine an optimum or near optimum action selection policy. The switching mechanism, and the parameters of the individual linear systems determined by the network, (which are of course not independent from one another), determine the action policy implemented by the network.

The modelling used here placed the Maes type of action selection network in control of a set of vector field primitives. These primitives could be combined by summation to drive a linkage as described in the next section. Figure 3 B gives the basic scheme for driving vector field primitives with the Maes network and a diagram of the ways field activation by the three actions in the simple example might operate.

4 The spinal behavior model in summary:

The model used here (designed to simulate frog spinal cord) consists of four components: (1) a simple sensory system (2) an action selection network (3) an effector system (4) an environment:

(1) The sensory system consisted of 5 skin regions. Stimuli applied to regions caused activation of propositions in the action selection network. Stimuli could be removed from the skin regions by appropriate motions of the effector limb in the environment. The limb must hit the stimuli with the last link (or tool), on one side of

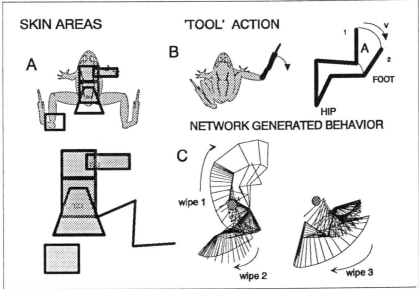

Figure 4

The 'Virtual frog' model in detail. A Skin areas where stimuli are applied, and the correspondence to frog body structure are shown. Five areas are designed to represent body regions. These regions are 'wiped' by motions of the simulation (three link) limb's last link. (B) The tool corresponds to the length of the distal joints of the frog limb from ankle down. Clockwise motions (1->2) cause wiping. Anticlockwise motion (2->1) is ineffective. Thus a wipe from position 1 to position 2 would cover area A. Effectiveness of the wipe is proportional to velocity of motion from posture 1 to 2. (C) Examples of model responses from the basic (untrained) simulation are shown. The simulation can generate different versions of the same response (wipe 2 and wipe 3), and different wipe types (wipe 1 vs. 2 and 3). The system chooses, switches, and blends of responses. The choice of these depend on stimulus numbers, locations and network state on stimulus application. This leads to variable but effective behaviors.

the link only. Effectiveness in removing stimuli depends on velocity of contact of the tool on the stimulus. This is diagrammed in figure 4.

(2) The action selection network is a Maes network (see Maes , 1989). This was modified to allow concurrent behaviors, behavioral intensity, and exclusions among behaviors as described in Giszter 1993. This network generates to activation parameters for force-field primitives in the effector system. The network is described in detail in the preceding section and in Giszter
1993 In the original Maes network, activation could be normalized each iteration. In this study, there was no normalization, but absolute activation of a single action-module could not exceed a given value (i.e. saturation was possible).

(3) The effector system consisted of a set of force-field primitives which represent actions of different muscle combinations in the limb. Each primitive could be summed with others by simple vector summation (Bizzi et al. 1991). The net (summed) force-field provided a specification of the force generated at the end-point for any limb position. This force was used to drive a limb motion. Limb motions in the environment can remove stimuli.

(4) The environment provides stimuli and removes them on appropriate impacts by the leg. This is diagrammed in figure 4. The network and effector used here provided the basic functionality described in Giszter 1993, 1994. Stimuli in any location were eventually removed by the limb. A sequence of 500 trial stimuli provided a baseline performance of mean time and variance in time to remove a stimulus prior to training.

Hand constructed versions of this network were able to replicate several aspects of frog wiping behaviors including switching and blending of different forms, stimulus removal and the transition zone phenomena described in the biological literature. The goal of this study was to improve the performance of such a hand-constructed network by using a reinforcement scheme for learning better link strengths in the context of the structure defined by Maes formulation.

5 Problems posed by the situated model network

Problems of training the situated 'frog' system outlined above are numerous. The most severe of these are: (1) Several concurrent actions may be needed for success. (2) Success may require a sequence of actions of which only the last is rewarded (3) Several stimuli interact in concurrent applications, so successful sequences and network dynamics depend on both stimuli. (4) Modification of the dynamics can be achieved in several ways. Consider equation (1). Sites of modification which allow 'tuning' of the network dynamics, but do not alter the basic structure of the network (i.e. the preconditions or results of action-modules, or number of conditions) are either the strengths of links s_k in matrix **A** or the entries of matrix **B**, that pass activation from conditions to nodes. This paper examines learning of the link strengths alone (matrix **A** not **B**).

If each action can be assessed for success, at each instance, the learning scheme of Maes 1992 is appropriate. However, the work here describes a network embedded in a second layer of dynamics, due to the vector primitives through which it acts. This additional layer does not allow a simple assessment of performance.

6 The learning scheme:

Examining equation (1) above, we would like the linear system that is operating at the execution of a successful action (receiving reinforcement), to change as follows: (1) decrease the time to execution of successful actions and (2) increase the domain of action-module state space in which the correct action execution is reached. There are difficulties in this approach however. Ideally we need to do this with minimal interference in the effectiveness of the other sets of linear systems specified by the network that also participated in sequences that lead to correct actions. Additionally, execution of an action too soon may fail in a complex dynamic environment. Presumably, however, there may often be local regions of the action-module state space in which performance can be improved. One approach to learning with minimum alteration of other behaviors could be to act only on connections to or from the executing action-modules (Maes 1992).

The switching system among the set of linear systems is determined by the action-module precondition lists, and for the purpose of this presentation considered fixed.

The activation leading to execution of the action(s) that were successful depended both on the connection matrix **A**, and the activation vector **E**. Particular patterns of links in the network were most instrumental in activating the successful action depending on E and A. These links in particular should be increased. Other links although large and experiencing strong flow, might contribute nothing. For example the network might be divided into two portions which are unconnected although operating concurrently. The action executed in one sub-network owes nothing to the connectivity and activation flow in the other. To deal with this, but still reinforce remote links which are important the following scheme is proposed:

The approach used here concentrates on the update of the link strengths of the matrix **A** : i.e. changes to each s_k. The method uses a separate learning pass following each successful action. This pass operates as follows. The first step is to inject 'reinforcement activity' into the executing modules, and zero reinforcement activity in all others. This is then propagated through the network in reverse to the normal flow, in a manner analogous to backpropagation. Each iteration of the learning response the reinforcement-activation is decremented by each action-module. The decrement is in proportion to the ratio of the action-module's normal (non-reinforcement) activity to the highest normal activity of an action-module through out the network. The cumulative flow through each connection is then used to update the connection using a simple delta rule.

Thus at time t_0 reinforcement activation $Z(t_0)$ is injected into the network at executing action modules. The flow of activation is reversed and thus depends on the transpose of matrix **A**. Each time step reinforcement activation is also decremented by a fraction, by diagonal matrix **D**.

$$Z(t+1) = D.(Z(t) + A^T Z(t))$$

(3)

The diagonal entries of **D**, D_{ii} , are the activation of action module i divided by the activation of the maximally activated module. Thus each D_{ii} <=1.0 The goal of the matrix **D** is to allow longer persistence of reinforcement in highly activated action-modules, but to gradually drain activity from the network.

Each link passes reinforcement, but also integrates and saves the flow of reinforcement activation at each time step. After a success, reinforcement is injected into network of equation (3) at the executing nodes alone, and then allowed to flow according to equation (3) for some number of time steps (20 in the experiments described below). The network is then stopped and each link is updated based on its saved measure of cumulative reinforcement flow through the link ('F' below) using a delta rule. i.e.

$$s_k \text{ (new)} = s_k(\text{old}) + d \ (F - s_k(\text{old}))$$

(4)

The goal of the scheme is to distribute small changes through all the relevant connections and in proportion to the connections importance in the activation of executing modules, but decremented with distance from the executing modules. It is hypothesized this may minimize the disturbance to other behaviors by localizing increasing change only in relevant links. The remainder of the network is very slightly degraded by the same reinforcement. Each link strength is slightly decreased. It is thus important that all behaviors occur sufficiently often on the average to maintain their performance.

7 Learning experiments

The scheme was examined by applying sequences of 500 to 1000 stimuli in simulations. Learning performance was assessed in two slightly different networks, the second network had a starting performance about equal to the best trained performance of the first. Initial link strengths were uniformly 0.001. With these initial link strengths the B matrix of equation 1 dominated the network dynamics. Experiments were performed first with no learning to obtain a baseline, and then with learning of two different rates (delta d= 0.01, and 0.1). In a set of runs stimuli were applied either in a cyclic pattern in each skin region in succession throughout the trials or were applied randomly. Performance was measured as the time to removal of a stimulus. Thus, lowered time represents improved performance. Stimuli were presented every 500 time units regardless of success or failure of removal and persisted in the simulation until removed. On removal of a stimulus the network received reinforcement and updated links as described above. Reinforcement was associated with a decrease in stimuli not the absolute removal of stimuli. Reinforcement accumulation in links was run for 20 time steps.

8 Results

The two different networks both exhibited tuning of performance with learning. Performance was improved in both random and cyclic stimulus presentations. Both parametric and nonparametric tests showed the performance was improved significantly. Mean time to stimulus removal improved from 630 to 330 time units in one network over 500 trials, and from 300 to 200 in the second more efficient network over 999 trials. Two sample t tests comparing learned and untrained performance showed significance at $p<0.0001$. It could be seen that the final systems differed qualitatively from the initial unlearned systems. Final connections strengths differed considerably from those at the outset. All strengths began at 0.001. Some strengths went to close to zero (0.000001) while others were increased to 1. The operation of the learning scheme is expected to force a links weight to a maximum value or to extinction depending on the average flow accumulation in the link over time. Stability of the delta rule normally derives from a gradient descent process moving the weights to an equilibrium or

fixed point. In the system presented here the (not infrequently) intrinsically unstable dynamics of the excited network are the source of the changes of delta. Thus links may sometimes only become fixed in becoming extinguished. More precisely, the ideal Maes action selection system may often comprise sets of matrices A and B of equation (1) and with characteristic equations of roots outside the unit circle (i.e. unstable). This may make the update rule unstable depending on the patterns of reinforcement. In the simulations here, learning showed a step-like improvement with regions of noisy and poor performance between long slowly improving plateaus. Presumably the slowly decreasing plateau of each step represents gradual speedup and improvement using a particular set of stable state space trajectories and switches. These may be rearranged in each noisy phase into a new stable set, as a new link is added or extinguished. The effect of the reinforcement was to make the influence of the matrix A of equation 1 on network dynamics become stronger and more focussed with learning. It was observed that cyclic presentation of stimuli to a network resulted in final networks of sparser strong connections in the A matrix than did random presentation of stimuli. These networks trained with cyclic stimuli also exhibited a stereotyped response pattern phasclocked to the stimulus cycle and order.

9 Discussion

The work here represents a highly focussed use of reinforcement learning. A spreading activation mechanism is used for distributing 'reinforcement activation', following which a simple delta rule is applied. This scheme is used to tune a Maes-type action-selection network. Previous learning schemes for Maes behavior networks (Maes 1992, Maes and Brooks 1990, and see Maes 1994) have assumed agents have full knowledge of the results of executed actions. Actions in these frameworks were not concurrent. Learning was all local to the connections of an executed action and its sequential predecessor and successor actions. The learning scheme proposed here differs from these previous learning schemes for Maes networks in several ways. These differences are motivated by the way the Maes networks that are examined here have been used in simulations of frog spinal behavior. The differences in approach between this work and Maes 1992 are due to qualitative differences between the embedding, environment and action systems of the Maes networks used in this and previous frog simulations , as compared to Maes 1992 . These differences in embedding provide different opportunities and constraints for learning schemes (see Kaelbling 1993). In the simulations described here, network generated 'actions' cannot be simply or directly associated with results or probability of results. In a sense, the network 'actions' here are once removed from the direct actions of Maes (1992). Success is a result of an ongoing dynamical interaction with the limb state and other concurrent actions and their strengths. Successes are achieved intermittently. Hertz, Krogh and Palmer (1991) have divided reinforcement learning problems into three classes: Class I, reinforcement is constant for a given action in a given environment, Class II, the environment is stochastic, but reinforcement probability is stationary, Class III reinforcement depends on past history of the environment and there are thus both temporal and structural credit assignment problems. As a reinforcement learning problem, learning in the simulated frog is of Type III in the Hertz, Krogh and Palmer classification.

The learning scheme presented here has several shortcomings. Reinforcement dynamics are frequently not stable, and the network reinforcement behavior can thus cause links to become unstable, increasing without bound unless restricted to a range (0 to 1 here).

The scheme here has no 'unlearning' mechanism at present in the absence of reinforcement. When reinforcement occurs, some 'forgetting' occurs by decreasing strengths in the less active links. If the network enters a state in which all actions, or a class of actions, are unsuccessful and thus not reinforced, it could thus get stuck and never return to successful domains. A measure of bootstrap and exploration for learning is provided by the B matrix of equation 1 which might sometimes obviate this problem.

Nonetheless, repetition and reinforcement of a particular task could lead to destruction of previously successful response sequences implemented by the network in other tasks. Speed up of responses may not always be adaptive although it is implicitly assumed so here. The learning scheme in its present form has no ability to use information about the network's history, using only a 'snapshot' at execution. The activation from conditions (matrix B) although a possible site for learning, is fixed through time.

Finally, the alternative 'structural' learning methods are ignored: there is no way of altering the precondition vectors of each action-module, and thereby modifying the control of switching among systems, the number of systems, and number of adjustable parameters in the systems that comprise the action selection policy implemented by the network. Future work will address these issues.

Despite criticisms above, this preliminary study does show the feasibility of reinforcement tuning of Maes networks with very intermittent reinforcement feedback. The learning scheme did not disrupt the network dynamics severely in the experiments described here, and in fact improved performance. The use of cumulative flow of activity in each link is pseudo-Hebbian. Biological implementation of the scheme proposed here is not implausible. The dynamics of the Maes scheme has similarities to pattern generator networks.

Both the network type or system used in action selection and their embedding in environmental dynamics are likely to determine what learning methods are feasible. Similarly, particular learning schemes, action-selection systems and their embedding in a particular dynamics must also both constrain exploration of different network designs by genetic algorithms, or evolution in biological systems. How these all interact and co-evolve is an important and poorly understood question. This paper has suggested and presented a first examination of a reinforcement scheme for the Maes action-selection network, which could also be biologically plausible.

Acknowledgements: I would like to thank Pattie Maes, Bruce Blumberg, Pushpinder Singh and Terrence Sanger for helpful discussions at various stages. This work was done in part during participation in the Univ Bielefeld ZIF for the Study of Prerational Intelligence.

References:

Barto AG, Sutton RS and Watkins CJCH (1991) Learning and sequential decision making. In Learning and Computational Neuroscience, eds M Gabriel and JW Moore. Cambridge, MIT Press.

Bizzi E, Mussa-Ivaldi FA, Giszter SF (1991) Computations underlying the execution of movement: a novel biological perspective. Science 253: 287-291.

Franzisket L (1963) Characteristics of instinctive behaviors and learning in reflex activity of the frog. Animal Behavior, 11:318-324.

Giszter SF (1993) Behavior networks and force fields for simulating spinal reflex behaviors of the frog. Second Intl. Conf. on the Simulation of Adaptive Behavior, ed Meyer J-A, Roitblat HL, and Wilson SW, MIT Press, Cambridge MA.

Giszter SF, Mussa-Ivaldi FA, Bizzi E (1993) Convergent force fields organized in the frog spinal cord. J.Neurosci. 13(2): 467-491.

Giszter SF (1994) Conceptual issues in frog wiping behavior. To appear in : Handbook of Brain Theory and Modeling ed. M. Arbib (forthcoming).

Grossberg S (1980). How does the brain build a cognitive code? Psych Rev 87: 1-57

Hertz J, Krogh A and Palmer RG (1991) Introduction to the theory of neural computation. VolI in Santa Fe Institute studies in the sciences of complexity. Addison-Wesley

Jordan MI (1989) Serial Order: A Parallel distributed processing approach. In Advances in Connectionist theory: Speech, eds JL Elman and DE Rumelhart. Hillsdale: Erlbaum.

Kaelbling LP (1993) Learning in embedded systems. MIT Press/Bradford Books.

Klopf AH (1982) The hedonistic neuron: A theory of memory, learning and intelligence. Washington: Hemisphere.

Klopf AH Morgan JS and Wheeler SE (1993) Modeling nervous system function with a hierarchical network of control systems that learn. Second Intl. Conf. on the Simulation of Adaptive Behavior, ed Meyer J-A, Roitblat HL, and Wilson SW, MIT Press, Cambridge MA.

Lin LJ and Mitchell TM (1993) Reinforcement learning with hidden states. Second Intl. Conf. on the Simulation of Adaptive Behavior, ed Meyer J-A, Roitblat HL, and Wilson SW, MIT Press, Cambridge MA.

Maes P (1989) The dynamics of action selection. Proc IJCAI -89 Conf Detroit

Maes P (1991a) Situated agents can have goals. In: Designing Autonomous Agents ed. Maes P. pp.49-70 MIT/Elsevier.

Maes P (1991b) A bottom up mechanism for behavior selection in an artificial creature. In: From Animals to Animats: Proc. First Intl.Conf on Simulation of Adaptive Behavior. ed Meyer J-A and Wilson SW., pp. 238-246

Maes P (1992) Learning behavior networks from experience, In: Toward at practice of Autonomous Systems, Proceedings of the First European Conference on Artificial Life, ed. FJ Varela and P Bourgine, MIT Press/ Bradford Books.

Maes P (1994) Modeling Adaptive Autonomous Agents. Artificial Life Journal, Vol 1 MIT Press (in press).

Maes P and Brooks RA (1990) Learning to coordinate behaviors, Proc AAAI-90, Boston 1990.

Mussa-Ivaldi, F.A. and Giszter S.F. (1992). Vector field approximation: a computational paradigm for motor control and learning. Biol. Cybern. 67:491-500.

Mussa-Ivaldi FA, Giszter SF and Bizzi E. (1994) Proc Nat Acad. Sci. (submitted)

Tesauro G (1986) Simple Neural models of Classical Conditioning. Biological Cybernetics 55, 187-200.

Sutton RS and Barto AG (1991) Time derivative models of Pavlovian reinforcement. In Learning and Computational Neuroscience, eds M Gabriel and JW Moore. Cambridge, MIT Press.

Achieving Rapid Adaptations in Robots by Means of External Tuition*

Ulrich Nehmzow* and Brendan McGonigle

Laboratory for Cognitive Neuroscience at the Department of Psychology
University of Edinburgh
GB - Edinburgh EH8 9LE
e-mail:B.O.McGonigle@ed.ac.uk

*Department of Computer Science
University of Manchester
GB - Manchester M13 9PL
e-mail:u.nehmzow@cs.man.ac.uk

Abstract

Experiments with the *Edinburgh R2* mobile robot
are presented that show how robots can be *taught*
to accomplish various different tasks, without
the need for re-programming the controller, and
without using self-tuition.

In an externally supervised teaching process —
not unlike the process of "shaping" known in
animal learning — the robot acquires competences such as obstacle avoidance, contour following, box pushing, phototaxis or route learning
(mazes). The learning is fast.

1 Introduction

It has been shown that competences fundamental to
robot control, such as obstacle avoidance or contour following can, in behaviour-based robotics, be achieved
through the interaction of independent, so-called behavioural modules ([Malcolm *et al.* 89, Brooks 85]).
The question of how to re-combine and orchestrate several of those fundamental competences in order to syn-
thesize new, more complex global behaviours is as yet
an unresolved problem. The experiments presented here
show one way to approach this: the *Edinburgh R2* mobile robot acquires fundamental motor competences, *as
well as* combinations of them, through an externally supervised learning process.

This method of providing external feedback to
accelerate a learning process is known as "shaping" in the field of animal learning, but is as yet
relatively rarely used in robotics (see, for example, [Colombetti & Dorigo 93, Shepanski & Macy 87]).
Rather, the predominant methods used for controller
design have rested either on complete knowledge installation (an approach we consider unsuitable for
all but the most basic behaviours), or self-tuition.
The latter involves *autonomous* acquisition of task-
achieving competences, and has successfully been used
to accomplish tasks such as obstacle avoidance and
contour following ([Nehmzow *et al.* 89, Nehmzow 91]),
box pushing ([Mahadevan & Connell 91]), leg coordination ([Maes & Brooks 90]) or phototaxis ([Kaelbling 90,
Colombetti & Dorigo 93]).

The advantage of providing external feedback (shaping) is, firstly, the considerable acceleration of the learning process. The fundamental robot behaviours described in this paper, for example, are all acquired in
a couple of learning steps, taking less than a minute in
real time; more complex behaviours such as maze learning are still obtained in tens of learning steps. Secondly,
one and the same robot can be used for a number of
different tasks, without any alteration to its control program or control parameters, merely using the training
process to define the robot's behaviour.

---

2   Experimental Setup

The experiments described in this paper were conducted using an R2 mobile robot, the *Edinburgh R2*, shown in figure 1.

Figure 1: The *Edinburgh R2*

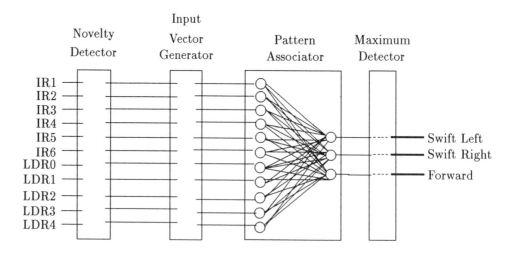

Figure 2: Controller structure

The robot has two differentially driven wheels, which allow the robot to move in any direction and perform turns on the spot. The robot's maximum speed is $40cm/s$, however the speed travelled at in the experiments described here does not exceed $8cm/s$. Its sensors comprise eight infrared sensors (IRs), which are used for obstacle detection and approximate range sensing (three range bins), six light-sensitive sensors based on passive light dependent resistors (LDRs), which are usually used for orientation and navigation, and five bumper sensors. The arrangement of the infrared and light sensors is shown diagrammatically in figure 3. The robot also has a gripper, which was not used for the experiments reported here.

2.1 Controller Architecture

The controller used for the experiments described here is shown in figure 2.

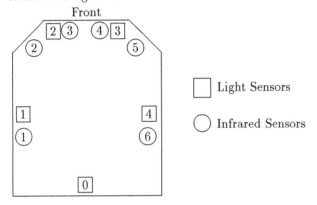

Figure 3: Sensor arrangement in the *Edinburgh R2*

Motor actions of the robot are associated with sensor signals by means of an artificial neural network (described in more detail later in this paper). Sensor signals, coming from both the infrared and the light sensors, are used as input to the network. The responses of the robot to each particular sensory stimulus — i.e. the motor actions performed by the robot — are stored as associations in the network: the three output nodes of the network stand for three distinct motor actions of the robot (swift left turn, swift right turn, and forward motion).

2.2 Representation of Network Input Space

A fresh input vector is generated whenever the novelty detector of the controller detects that either the general heading of the robot has changed[1] or the sum of all

---

[1] This can be done measuring the robot's orientation with respect to a distant light source, using the light sensors.

current IR readings differs by more than the numerical value of 2 from the previous one. If neither of these conditions apply, no input vector is generated and the robot continues performing the action it is currently performing.

Once an input vector is generated, it is fed into the artificial neural network serving as associative memory. The input vector contains information from both the obstacle detecting and range sensing infrared sensors, as well as from the orientation sensing light sensors. It is shown in figure 4.

Figure 4: Input vector used

Each of the infrared sensors of the Edinburgh R2 returns a numerical value between '0' ('nothing detected') and '3' ('object seen at close range' — about 15 cm in the case of a white wall). Light sensors return numerical values between '0' (total darkness) and '255' (very bright). The sensor are adjusted such that '128' is returned for average lighting conditions in our laboratory. The six values of all front-facing and side-facing infrared sensors form the first part of the input vector, the five values coming from light sensors the second part.

As these sensors respond to different environmental stimuli, and furthermore return numerical values of different orders of magnitude, both components of the input vector have to be balanced to avoid a bias towards one or the other component (i.e. *sensor fusion* has to be performed). Here, this is accomplished by first normalising the six-element long vector containing infrared sensor information, then normalising the five-element long vector containing information from the light sensors, and then normalising the eleven-element long overall input vector.

2.3 Representation of Network Output Space

The artificial neural network used as an associative memory is a *Pattern Associator* ([Rumelhart & McClelland 86, Kohonen 88]). It has eleven input units and three output units. A unique compound motor action is assigned to each of the three output units: swift left turn (i.e. left motor turning backwards, right motor turning forwards), swift right turn and forward motion. The action associated with the most excited output cell is the action performed by the robot at any one time. As input vectors change, due to changing stimuli from the environment, different excitation patterns will develop in the output layer of the associative memory, resulting in different motor actions performed by the robot.

2.4   Teaching Procedure

2.4.1   The Associative Memory

The central element of the controller shown in figure 2, the Pattern Associator (see figure 5), is a two-layer artificial neural network that is taught by *supervised* learning.

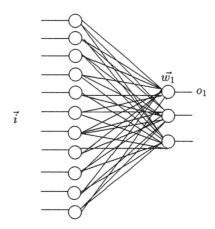

Figure 5: Schematic diagram of Pattern Associator

The output o_j of each output unit j of the network is computed as the dot product of input vector $\vec{i}$ and weight vector $\vec{w_j}$:

$$o_j(t) = \vec{i}(t) \cdot \vec{w_j}(t) \qquad (1)$$

2.4.2   Teaching the Network

Training a Pattern Associator is done in a supervised way, i.e. a teaching signal, signifying the desired output vector $\vec{\tau}$, given a particular input vector $\vec{i}$ is provided from outside. In work reported elsewhere ([Nehmzow 91, Nehmzow *et al.* 93]) such teaching signals were generated internally by the controller, using so-called *instinct rules*; in the experiments described here, however, they are provided externally by the experimenter: by covering or uncovering the upward facing light sensor of the robot positive or negative feedback respectively can be provided. As long as the upward facing light sensor of the robot is covered, the robot's actions are assumed to be correct, as soon as negative reinforcement is given by uncovering the upward facing light sensor, the robot cycles through its repertoire of three motor actions until positive reinforcement is given again, signifying that the correct motor action for a particular sensory stimulus is performed.

Equation 2 shows the update rule used in the Pattern Associator, indicating how weight vector $\vec{w_j}$ of output unit j is changed in each learning step, given the desired output τ_j of unit j and the actual output o_j of unit j. η is the learning rate, a parameter that influences the speed of learning. Its value is typically chosen between 0.2 and 0.7.

$$\vec{w_j}(t+1) = \vec{w_j}(t) + \eta \cdot (\tau_j(t) - o_j(t)) \cdot \vec{i}(t) \qquad (2)$$

Compared to other network paradigms, for example multi-layer Perceptrons, this type of network has the advantage to learn extremely fast (one-shot learning in most cases) — an advantage that is vital to applications in robotics as certain fundamental functions (such as obstacle avoidance) need to be acquired rapidly, because the robot's safe operation depends on them. However, Pattern Associators can only learn linearly separable functions, i.e. functions like "exclusive OR" cannot be learned perfectly. For those functions the network settles in the minimum energy state, resulting in the robot always making *one* mistake first. So far, however, we have not encountered real-world applications that require the acquisition of input-output mappings that are not linearly separable, so that this shortcoming has not been a problem in our particular case.

3   Experiments

The robot uses both infrared (i.e. obstacle detecting) sensors and light (i.e. direction detecting) sensors, and has the choice of three distinct motor actions (swift left turn, swift right turn and forward movement). Virtually all combinations of associations between sensor input and motor output can be taught.[2] To demonstrate this, we have taught the robot a number of competences, emphasizing those competences that are typically required for robot operation in office-like environments. These comprise fundamental behaviours such as avoiding obstacles (to ensure safe operation), following contours, complex routes, and orientation (i.e. competences related to navigational tasks), or moving objects (material handling). These experiments are described below. For all experiments the very same controller was used, no programming, nor adjustment of parameters, nor any change other than erasing the artificial neural network before teaching a new task were performed.

3.1   Obstacle Avoidance

It is obvious that no higher level tasks can be accomplished by the robot if safe operation is not guaranteed. Obstacle avoidance is fundamental to this. We therefore trained the robot to avoid obstacles first.

When facing open space (i.e. neither of the IR sensors detects anything) the robot was given positive reinforcement, likewise for turning left whilst facing an object on its right hand side, and for turning right when facing an object on the left hand side. After three learning steps, one for each of the aforementioned constellations, the Edinburgh R2 had acquired an obstacle avoidance behaviour. The teaching process takes under one minute.

3.2   Box Pushing (Object Following)

Object following displays the robot's ability to react to sensor stimuli in a dynamically changing environment; we trained the robot to push a cardboard box, as an example of an object following competence (the function of following an object moved by the robot is equivalent to that of following an object moved by an external power source). Figure 6 shows this experiment: whenever the box moves out of the center of the robot, the robot adjusts it course and steers back towards the box.

Object following behaviour is achieved in four learning steps. Positive reinforcement needs to be given twice for moving forward when facing an object straight ahead, and once each for the appropriate turns when facing objects on the left hand side or right hand side, respectively.

3.3   Wall Following

Route following is the most reliable method of navigation, used widely in the animate world (e.g. rodents). Following contours, such as walls, is one instance of route following, and relevant for navigational tasks of a robot.

The robot can be taught to stay within a given range of distances to objects on its side (either left or right), and to move ahead at the same time if the space in front is obstacle-free by giving positive reinforcement whenever the robot is in the 'correct' distance to the wall (approx. 20 cm in this case), and by positively reinforcing moves towards the wall or away from the wall whenever the robot is too far away or too close respectively.

Four teaching steps were necessary to acquire the wall following competence, two for the 'move forward' situation and one each for the 'turn away' and 'move closer' situation. Again, this teaching process requires less than one minute in real time.

---

[2]With the restriction mentioned in section 2.4.1, that the learned function has to be linearly separable.

Figure 6: Object following, here: box pushing.

Figure 7: The Edinburgh R2 in the Route Following Experiment.

3.4 Phototaxis

Like contour following, orientation is indispensible for successful navigation. Insects, for example bees and ants, use the position of the sun for orientation, birds are able to sense the earth's magnetic field ([Waterman 89]).

Like insects, the robot uses external light sources for orientation. It can be taught to move towards a light source (phototaxis), or away from it (negative phototaxis). This is achieved in four learning steps, taking under one minute in real time: twice giving positive reinforcement for a forward movement whilst facing the light source, once giving positive reinforcement for a right turn whilst seeing the light on the right hand side, and once similarly for the light source on the left hand side. To achieve negative phototaxis, four teaching steps are required as well, obviously positive reinforcement is then given for movement *away* from the light source.

4 Re-combination of Basic Behavioural Components

Using the same teaching process, the *Edinburgh R2* can be taught to acquire more than one of the above mentioned competences at the same time. This leads to more complex behaviours.

4.1 Phototaxis and Obstacle Avoidance

After the robot has acquired the phototaxis competence (section 3.4), it can be taught to avoid obstacles (section 3.1) as well. This requires a further two learning steps, one to associate objects on the left hand side with a right turn, and one to associate objects on the right hand side with a left turn. The ability to move towards a light source is not lost by this.

If no further teaching is used, the robot will, however, repeatedly turn towards and away from an obstacle that is placed exactly in the path towards the light source, until small fluctuations make the robot pass the object. This problem can be alleviated by further teaching (see section 4.2).

4.2 Obstacle Avoidance, Phototaxis and Wall Following

Using the fundamental competences of obstacle avoidance (section 3.1), phototaxis (section 3.4) and wall following (section 3.3), the robot can also be taught to learn routes through simple mazes, such as the one shown in figure 8. This is an example of an acquired navigational competence.

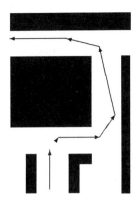

Figure 8: A three-junction maze

This maze contains three T-junctions, which means the robot has to associate the sensory stimuli perceived at each of the three junctions with either a left or a right turn, as well as those stimuli perceived in corridors (of whatever heading) with a forward movement. Whilst moving through the maze, walls must be avoided at all times, so that maze learning involves both obstacle avoidance and direction-oriented movement. Figure 7 shows the robot negotiating the maze.

To achieve route learning in mazes, more learning steps than in the examples previously given are necessary. Firstly, this has to do with the fact that the robot has to acquire both the obstacle avoidance and wall following competences, *and* has to learn the correct turns at junctions. Secondly, *sensor fusion* becomes important: directional information (coming from the light sensors) has to be combined with object information (coming from the infrared sensors), in order to negotiate the maze successfully. In our implementation, sensor fusion occurs in the construction of the input vector (see section 2.2), and in the artificial neural network itself.

In order to learn the path shown in figure 8, the robot needs about five presentations of the whole route through the maze. This means that about thirty to fifty learning steps are required, in real time this takes about ten minutes.

The complexity of mazes learnable by the robot depends, on the one hand, on the robot's sensors and sensory stimuli perceived at different junctions. If distinct junctions give rise to identical sensory stimuli, only one and the same action at these distinct junctions can be learned. Secondly, the capacity of the network (see [Hertz *et al.* 91] for more details) influences the maximum complexity of a learnable maze. More research is necessary to address the latter point conclusively.

5   Summary and Conclusion

In experiments with the *Edinburgh R2* mobile robot we have shown that it is possible to teach robots fundamental competences such as obstacle avoidance, contour following, phototaxis or object following, as well as more complex combinations of these (such as phototaxis *and* obstacle avoidance, or route learning in mazes).

The teaching process used is similar to a method known as "shaping" in the field of animal learning: through external feedback, given by the experimenter, the robot acquires the effective associations between perceived sensor signals and desired motor responses.

Learning these task-achieving competences is very fast, in the experiments presented here the robot acquires fundamental competences such as obstacle avoidance or contour following in a couple of learning steps, taking under one minute of real time; more complex capabilities such as maze learning are acquired in tens of learning steps.

Acknowledgements

The research reported here was conducted in Edinburgh and supported by the MRC, grant number G9110835 ("Cognitive Modelling and the Design of Artifically Intelligent Systems", principal investigators Dr. Brendan McGonigle and Professor Mark Lee, Computer Science, National University of Wales at Aberystwyth).

We thank Claudia Nehmzow for helpful comments on earlier versions of this paper.

References

[Brooks 85] Rodney Brooks, *A Robust Layered Control System for a Mobile Robot*, MIT AI memo 864, 1985.

[Colombetti & Dorigo 93] M. Colombetti & M. Dorigo, *Robot Shaping: Developing Situated Agents through Learning*, International Computer Science Institute, Berkely, Technical Report no. 40, April 1993.

[Hertz *et al.* 91] John Hertz, Anders Krogh and Richard Palmer, *Introduction to the Theory of Neural Computation*, Addison Wesley, 1991.

[Kaelbling 90] Leslie Kaelbling, *Learning in Embedded Systems*, Stanford Technical Report TR-90-04, June 1990.

[Kohonen 88] Teuvo Kohonen, *Self-Organization and Associative Memory*, 2nd edition, Springer Verlag 1988.

[Maes & Brooks 90] Pattie Maes and Rodney Brooks, *Learning to Coordinate Behaviours*, Proc. AAAI 1990.

[Mahadevan & Connell 91] Sridhar Mahadevan and Jonathan Connell, *Automatic Programming of Behaviour-Based Robots using Reinforcement Learning*, Proc. AAAI 1991.

[McGonigle 91] Brendan McGonigle, *Incrementing Intelligent Systems by Design*, in J.A. Meyer & S. Wilson (eds.), *From Animals to Animats*, MIT Press 1991.

[Malcolm *et al.* 89] Chris Malcolm, Tim Smithers and John Hallam, *An Emerging Paradigm in Robot Architecture*, in T. Kanade, F.C.A. Groen and L.O. Hertzberger (eds.), *Intelligent Autonomous Systems 2*, Amsterdam 1989; ISBN 90-800410-1-7.

[Nehmzow *et al.* 89] Ulrich Nehmzow, John Hallam and Tim Smithers, *Really Useful Robots*, in T. Kanade, F.C.A. Groen and L.O. Hertzberger (eds.), *Intelligent Autonomous Systems 2*, Amsterdam 1989; ISBN 90-800410-1-7.

[Nehmzow 91] Ulrich Nehmzow, *Experiments in Competence Acquisition for Autonomous Mobile Robots*, PhD thesis, Edinburgh University, 1991.

[Nehmzow *et al.* 93] Ulrich Nehmzow, Tim Smithers and Brendan McGonigle, *Increasing Behavioural Repertoire in a Mobile Robot*, in J.A. Meyer, H. Roitblat and S. Wilson (eds.), *From Animals to Animats 2*, MIT Press 1993.

[Waterman 89] Talbot H. Waterman, *Animal Navigation*, Scientific American Library, W.H. Freeman, 1989.

[Rumelhart & McClelland 86] David Rumelhart, James McClelland and the PDP Research Group, *Parallel Distributed Processing*, Vol. 1, p.61, MIT Press 1986.

[Shepanski & Macy 87] J.F. Shepanski & S.A. Macy, *Manual Training Techniques of Autonomous Systems Based on Artificial Neural Networks*, Proc. IEEE First Intern. Conf. on Neural Networks, San Diego 1987.

Two–Link–Robot Brachiation with Connectionist Q-Learning

Fuminori Saito

saitoo@mein.nagoya-u.ac.jp

Toshio Fukuda

fukuda@mein.nagoya-u.ac.jp

Department of Mechano–Informatics and Systems
School of Engineering, Nagoya University
Furo–cho, Chikusa–ku, Nagoya 464–01, JAPAN

Abstract

This paper describes a connectionist Q-learning method for behavior learning of real robotic systems which require continuous input–output representation. The proposed method is applied to the approaching control of a two–link brachiation robot. The robot performs trial motions with a heuristic sequence generator and explores state space near objective states. It stores novelty sequences of experiences encountered in the trial phase and they are used to obtain a utility function which is represented by a CMAC. A simulation result is presented to show the fundamental ability of the proposed method.

1 Introduction

Q-learning[10] is one of the reinforcement learning methods, which has recently been paid much attentions, and some researchers have applied to the learning control of robotic systems (for example [2][4][11]). In the previous studies, the states and the actions are treated as being discreat. However when we should control more realistic robots, they often require continuous control inputs and their states should be represented as continuous variables. In this paper, we discuss the Q-learning method for learning control of real robotic systems. In the proposed method, the Cerebellar Model Arithmetic Computer (CMAC)[1], which is one of the connectionist model, is employed to represent nearly continuous inputs and outputs. Generally, in the course of reinforcement learning such as Q-learning, the most common difficulty is the requirements of large amount of trials to learn behavior of a system, so that we also discuss the methods to effectively utilize experiences obtained through actual trials. The proposed connectionist Q-learning is applied in simulations to the two–link brachiation robot, which we have been investigatedsaitoo94a.

1.1 Brachiation as an example of dynamic behavior

"Brachiation" is the locomotion style of long–armed apes, which move from branch to branch using their arms

Figure 1: Brachiation of a gibbon

Figure 2: The experimental model of a two–link brachiation robot

as shown in Fig. 1. The authors have investigated the robot to brachiate in order to develop a robot which performs such dynamic motions like animals. Recently we have developed a two–link brachiation robot shown in Fig. 2 which has only one input for moving at the joint between the links, although it has two degrees of freedom, and we experimentally achieved its continuous locomotion with employing a heuristic motion generation method[5][7].

When we humans and animals perform complex motions such as walking, they can be divided into fundamental units of actions. For instance, walking can be divided into "an action to sustain the body", "an action to stretch out a free leg", "an action to swing arms", "an action to control pitching and rolling", "an action to find obstacles", and so on. In this work, we consider behaviors as such fundamental units of actions. Complex motions can be realized with a sequential and/or parallel combination of such behaviors. We consider that brachiation is consisting of a behavior to control its swing amplitude, a behavior to approach its free arm to the target branch, a behavior to position its hand to the target with high gain feedback control, and so on. In [6] we discussed learning of the amplitude control behavior, and in this work we will describe learning of the approaching behavior.

In [7], we have discussed the heuristic motion generation method and applied the method to the generation of the input sequence for the approaching motion of the developed two–link robot, and we have confirmed through experiments that the heuristic method can generate adequate input sequences for given targets. However, all the memorized result obtained in the course of this learning is the time sequence of the input which is specific for the target given to learn. Therefore if the position of the target changed, the sequence of the result becomes meaningless data, and the robot should generate another sequence from scratch, so it is important to retain experience in some form to avoid long trial phase. The method proposed in this paper allows the robot to learn motions not only in the form of time sequences but in the form of a utility network, which is to represent mapping from each state to the optimal actions during the heuristic motion generation process. If the robot could learn this utility space precisely, it means that it had built an optimal feedback controller from experiences.

2   The Heuristic Sequence Generator

Reinforcement learning methods progress very slowly if the learning agent can obtain reinforcements infrequently. To provide trial motions around desired states, we employ a heuristic sequence generator described in this section, which is the improved method of the heuristic learning used in [7]. First, an input sequence is represented by a spline function which interpolates several given points. (Though in the case of multi–input systems, a control input to a robot is a vector sequence, here we address only a scalar sequence to simplify the discussion. It can easily be extended to the description for multiple input systems.) In Fig. 3, we call the points composing the sequence *control points*. In learning process, the sequence is applied to activate the robot and obtains the performance evaluation denoted by E, which is determined according to the control objective. In the previous algorithm[8], the positions of the control points are changed upward and downward sequentially and repeatedly from the first point to the last one, and the modification which leaded to a better result is repeated several times. However it is rather slow process, because the changes of the points which may never bring better results are always performed when their turns came.

The new algorithm described here chooses the change of the sequence according to the probabilities obtained

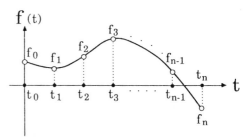

Figure 3: Formation of $f(t)$ generated by the heuristic method using spline function curve

from the recent statistics of the evaluation improvements. The algorithm of the new heuristic sequence generation is listed in table 1. Here the points which compose the best sequence obtained so far are denoted by $f^* = [f_0, f_1, \ldots, f_n]$ and the evaluation obtained with the sequence is denoted by E^*. A change given to the sequence, which we call *heuristics step*, is denoted by $h_i = [h_{i0}, h_{i1}, \ldots, h_{in}]$. In the simplest case, the heuristics steps are provided to change each point upwards and downwards with a certain step Δf, such as

$$h_1 = [\Delta f, 0, 0, \ldots, 0],$$
$$h_2 = [0, \Delta f, 0, \ldots, 0],$$
$$\ldots$$
$$h_{n+1} = [0, 0, \ldots, \Delta f],$$
$$h_{n+2} = [-\Delta f, 0, \ldots, 0],$$
$$\ldots$$
$$h_{2n+2} = [0, 0, \ldots, -\Delta f].$$

The heuristics step can also be given intuitively. For example, if we know that the optimal input sequence will bias positively or negatively, the generation will progress faster if we give positive or negative changes to all the control points. In this case, however, it would be better to provide a condition for each h_i such as $\sum_{j=0}^{n} |h_{ij}| = \Delta f$ in order to avoid drastic change of the subsequent motion.

In order to select one of heuristics steps, which seems to lead to better performance judging from the recent experience, the probabilities p_i to select h_i are calculated according to the Boltzmann probabilities. When E_i denotes a difference between the maximum evaluation obtained during the trial with a sequence changed by h_i, E^* denotes the currently best evaluation and $\overline{\Delta E_i}$ denotes a cumulative mean of the changing ratio of E, $(E_i - E^*)/E^*$, the probability p_i is calculated as:

$$p_i = \exp(\overline{\Delta E_i}/T) / \sum_{i=0}^{n} \exp(\overline{\Delta E_i}/T). \quad (1)$$

Each time when a trial is performed with h_i, $\overline{\Delta E_i}$ is updated successively according to the following formula:

$$\overline{\Delta E_i} \leftarrow \left((E_i - E^*)/E^* + \beta \zeta_i \overline{\Delta E_i}\right)/(1 + \beta \zeta_i), \quad (2)$$
$$\zeta_i \leftarrow 1 + \beta \zeta_i, \quad (3)$$

Table 1: The algorithm of the heuristic sequence generation method

---

1. Initialize all the $\overline{\Delta E_i} = 0$ and $\zeta_i = 0$. Give initial values to f^* (for example $f^* = [0, 0, \ldots, 0]$) and obtain E^* by performing a trial with the initial sequence f^*.

2. Calculate all the probabilities p_i of Eq. 1 and select one of heuristics steps h_i according to the probabilities.

3. Perform a trial motion with the sequence composed by $f^* + h_i$ and obtain the best evaluation E_i in the trial motion.

4. Update $\overline{\Delta E_i}$ and ζ_i.

5. Go back to 2 until the robot can obtain a satisfactory motion.

---

where ζ_i is cumulation number and β is a decaying factor. In order to forget $\overline{\Delta E_i}$ of non–selected heuristics steps as f^* changes, because the informations may become obsolete for new f^*, $\overline{\Delta E_i}$ and ζ_i for non–selected heuristics steps are changed when the f^* is renewed, namely when $E_i - E^*$ is positive value, as follows:

$$\overline{\Delta E_i} \leftarrow \beta \, \zeta_i \, \overline{\Delta E_i} / (1 + \beta \, \zeta_i) , \quad (4)$$

$$\zeta_i \leftarrow 1 + \beta \, \zeta_i . \quad (5)$$

All of $\overline{\Delta E_i}$ and ζ_i are initially zero. If necessary, the temperature T should be controlled adequately with a method such as simulated annealing to avoid local minima.

3 Q-Learning with CMAC

Q-learning is one of reinforcement learning techniques and we obtain mapping from states to optimal actions with this method. The utility to perform action u in state x is represented by $Q(x, u)$, which is called Q-value. Lin[4] applied backpropagation multilayered neural networks in the framework of Q-learning and demonstrated his method with a task like a survival game. By employing connectionist networks rather than using pure tables, experiences can be generalized to the states near experienced states. Also it is a merit that connectionist networks can represent continuous input–output functions.

In this paper, we apply the CMAC connectionist model. Although the CMAC has an ability to generalize data, it is fundamentally a table–lookup method, therefore it can memorize more accurate data than other connectionists such as backpropagation neural networks. Moreover it can memorize additional information to show how much it learned concerning with each state, and we can distinguish well–learned and poorly–learned state region. The outputs of a CMAC are not precisely continuous, because it quantizes the input space before mapping to

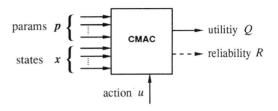

Figure 4: Inputs and outputs of a utility network

the weight table, however if a CMAC is structured with small quantization, it can represent sufficiently smooth functions.

3.1 The structure of the CMAC utility network

In order to deal with various control objectives of a behavior, we include objective parameters in the arguments of the utility function. Here the parameter is denoted by p, which we call a *behavioral parameter*. In the case of brachiation, it is the desired amplitude for the amplitude control behavior and the target position for the approaching and grip position feedback behaviors. Hereafter the utility function is denoted by $Q(p, x, u)$ including the behavioral parameter. The CMAC is structured as shown in Fig. 4 in order to represent this Q-value. Inputs are behavioral parameters, p, and states, x, and a control variable, u, and a output is a utility of the input u. The utility network learns $Q(p, x, u)$, namely utility estimation of the action u ($u_{min} \leq u \leq u_{max}$) at states x and params p, employing a Q-learning rule. Each weight of CMAC has an additional information to store a count of updation of the weight. This value is used to estimate the reliability of a CMAC's output. Here we define the reliability as

$$R = 1 - \exp(-c/a) , \quad (6)$$

where c is a mean of updation counters of weights which are summed to calculate the output and a is a positive constant.

This reliability measure is based on updation count of the weights, therefore it has no meanings if nothing useful experiences are taught and counters are updated. The counter should be incremented only when the CMAC is learning useful experiences. Therefore in our method, they are updated only during experience sequence replay phase described in the section 4.

3.2 The learning equation and the action policy

We define an *experience* as a quintuple (p, x, u, y, r), which means when a behavior agent performed an action u at a state x, the state has changed to y at next sampling time and the agent received a reinforcement signal r during the transition under condition of a behavioral parameter p. When the experience at the state y was (p, y, u', z, r'), the Q-learning updation rule of the

TD(λ) version [3] [9] is

$$Q(p, x, u) \leftarrow Q(p, x, u) + \alpha\Delta \ , \qquad (7)$$

$$\Delta = r + \gamma\{(1 - \lambda)\max_{v \in U} Q(p, y, v)$$
$$+ \lambda(Q(p, y, u') + \Delta')\} - Q(p, x, u) \ , \qquad (8)$$

where Δ' is the updation error Δ at state y, γ is a discount factor, λ is a parameter for TD (temporal-difference) method and α is a learning rate for the C-MAC. In the case of on–line learning and at the first experience presentation of off–line learning, λ should be zero because Δ' cannot be obtained.

We define the policy to derive actions from the utility such as

$$u_p(p, x) = \arg\max_{u \in U} Q(p, x, u) \ , \qquad (9)$$

which is the action with the highest Q-value. Though the control variable u is continuous, actually it is quantized by the CMAC, therefore $U = \{u_i \mid u_{min} \leq u_i \leq u_{max}, i = 1, ..., n\}$, so that (9) means to derive one of the central values of the quantization.

4   Experience Sequence Replay

For the sake of the best utilization of experiences, which cost to obtain through actual actuation, Lin [4] has used a method called experience replay. Much like this method, we process the learning procedure with two phases: the phase to actuate the actual robot with storing sequences of novelty experiences (without learning), and the phase to replay the stored experience sequences to process relaxation planning. (Experiences are replayed as a sequence in our method). These two phases are repeated with an adequate ratio.

First, we define a novelty measure of a experience just as the updation error, Δ, in (8), because if Δ is large, it means that the agent does not know much about the learning space around the experience, and if Δ is small, the agent need not know more about the experience.

The actuation phase is processed as follows. While the actuation, the behavior agent is always keeping a sequence of the recent experiences in a FIFO (First In First Out) buffer of a certain length. When the behavior agent encountered a novel experience, it copies the contents of the FIFO buffer to an experience sequence storage, which we call ESS, with storing Δ_s, which is the largest Δ in the sequence. The behavior agent judges that the experience is a novelty when the current Δ is grater than one of Δ_s of stored sequences. The size of a ESS is determined adequately enough to keep sufficient experience sequences, and if it is fully used, the sequence with the smallest Δ_s will be deleted.

The replay phase is processed as follows. The experience sequence which has the largest Δ_s among the stored sequences is picked up and the experiences contained in it are replayed in backward order in time, from the new

experience to the old one. Replaying in the backward order will propagate utility values faster than in the forward order [3]. The largest Δ during the replay of the sequence is newly stored as Δ_s, and the sequence has chances to be replayed again.

Finally, in actual systems, it is not ensured that the utility networks can learn all of the presented experiences, which may involve error and noise. Therefore two rules are made for replaying.

- If the total number of times of replaying the same sequence exceeded given maximum times, the sequence is deleted from the ESS.

- If the same sequence was continuously replayed more than given maximum times, the next novelty sequence is replayed during given penalty times.

5   Simulation

5.1   Structure of a utility network

The inputs for the utility network are r_x and r_y that are the relative distance of the target from the holding bar as a behavioral parameters, $\theta_1, \theta_2, \dot{\theta}_1$, and $\dot{\theta}_2$ as states, and u as a control variable. All of the inputs are squashed into values from -1 to 1 by a linear function in the case of the control variable, and by a sigmoid function in other cases. Then the squashed variables are uniformly quantized into 40 in the case of u and 50 in other cases, and the weight activation band widths are let be 3 quantized values in the case of u and 8 in other cases. The output is calculated by adding 15 weights. The total weight space is hashed randomly into 100 thousand weights.

5.2   Heuristic performance evaluation function

The performance evaluation function used for the heuristic sequence generation should be determined so that the robot should be leaded to the control objective. The control objective in this work is to approach a grip to a target bar in order to catch it. Obviously, for achieving the objective, the relative distance and the relative velocity between the grip and the target bar should be small. When C_D denotes the relative distance and C_V denotes the relative velocity, we define an evaluation function C as follows:

$$C = k_D C_D + k_V C_V. \qquad (10)$$

The coefficients k_D and k_V are for normalizing the terms with respect to each desired value. The evaluation value for the heuristic sequence generation E is calculated by squashing the inverse of C such as

$$E = 1 - \exp(-a/C). \qquad (11)$$

In simulations, the parameters are let be $k_D = 33$ [1/m], $k_V = 3.3$ [sec/m] and $a = 1$.

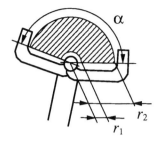

Figure 5: The catchable area of the grip

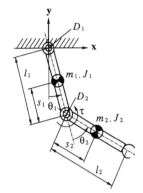

Figure 6: The simulation model

5.3   Reinforcement function

A positive unit reinforcement signal is produced when the robot succeeded to catch its target. In simulations, we judge that it succeeded to catch the target when the target bar resided within the catchable area ($r_1 = 0.01$ [m], $r_2 = 0.09$ [m] and $\alpha = 160$ [deg]) of its grip in Fig. 5 for 0.05 [sec].

5.4   Learning process

Simulations are carried out with the Runge–Kutta method of 0.01 [sec] step. The control sampling step, Δ_t, is a double of the simulation step. A set of learning consists of an actuation phase of 50 [sec] and a replay phase of 50 times, and totally six learning sets are carried out. The length of a heuristic input sequence is 1.4 [sec] and it is composed by 10 points. The Δf for heuristics steps is 1.5 [Nm]. The temperature T in (1) is constantly 0.01 and decaying factor β in (2) and (3) is 0.7. The maximum length of a experience sequence is 1.4 [sec] and a ESS has space to hold 300 sequences. The maximum total replay of a sequence is 30 times, and the maximum continuous replay times of a same sequence is 5 and if it exceeded, 10 times penalty was given.

The output, u, is filtered for realistic simulations to provide torque considering the characteristics of the actuator by limiting the value within ± 10[Nm] and its differential value within ± 50 [Nm/sec]. Physical parameters of the simulation model in Fig. 6 are determined such as masses of links $m_1 = m_2 = 2$ [kg] and their moments

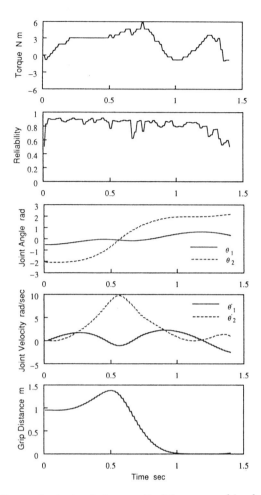

Figure 7: A simulation result of the approaching behavior control using a obtained utility network

of inertia $J_1 = J_2 = 0.2$ [kg m^2], lengths $l_1 = l_2 = 0.5$ [m] and $s_1 = s_2 = 0.25$ [m], damping coefficients $D_1 = 0.1$ and $D_2 = 0.5$ [N m / (rad sec)]. Learning parameters in (8) are determined such as $\alpha = 0.3, \gamma = 0.995$ and $\lambda = 0.3$. A parameter a for calculation of reliability in (6) is determined as 100. As we used one–byte counter for weight updation, c is up to 255 and hence R is up to 0.922 in this simulation. In this work, we use the reliability measure only to confirm the progress of learning procedure of the utility network.

5.5   Results

We show the result of a fundmental simulation: behavior learning from fixed initial state to a fixed desired state. The initial state is given such that the robot is catching bars with a distance of 0.5 [m] and the target bar is positioned at 0.5 [m] forwards.

Figures 7 and 8 show a control result using a CMAC utility network trained with experience sequences obtained from the heuristic sequence generation process.

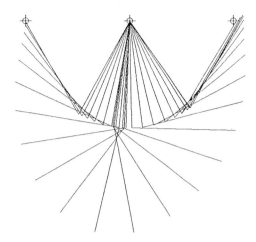

Figure 8: A stick diagram of the simulation result (0.05 [sec] step)

The utility network has learned near optimal control actions, and the robot achieved the state, in which it can obtain a reinforcement, at 1.15 [sec]. From the reliability measure, we can estimate how the CMAC has learned utilities along the approaching motion. Occasionally the reliability became relatively low value and the torque changed abruptly at the time, for example at 0.66 [sec]. This happened because the utility network has not yet learned well around these states. A few more set of learning covered such holes and smoother torques were obtained.

6 Discussion

Although what the heuristic sequence generator learns are only time sequences of control inputs, the CMAC utility network represents "good" inputs with respect to the state space of the robot which is independent of time. Therefore, if we can put the robot into already learned states, the robot can be "absorbed" to its control objective. The robot should acquire a lot of experiences to expand this absorption region by repeating trials with changing a variety of parameters such as the heuristics steps, the initial states and the behavioral parameters. In order to make sure of the potential of the proposed method, we have to further study to provide such a variety of experiences for the robot.

Another hopeful idea to fully utilize the experiences is "experience evaluation with multiple objectives". When a robot is performing trial motions for a certain control objective, even if the obtained result would be a failure for the objective, it might be a worthy experience for another objective. To utilize such experiences, each experience is evaluated with many behavioral parameters and if it found to be a novelty experience for some behavioral parameter, the experience sequence should be stored and replayed afterwards.

7 Conclusions

A method based on connectionist Q-learning for learning behaviors of real robotic systems has been shown and applied to the approaching control of a two–link brachiation robot. In this method, while the robot is performing trial motions with a heuristic sequence generator in order to explore the state region near objective states, it stores novelty sequences of experiences encountered in the trial motions. The stored experience sequences are employed to obtain utility functions which is represented with one of connectionist models, CMAC. In the simulation we have confirmed that the proposed learning scheme has desirable abilities.

References

[1] James S. Albus. *Brain, Behaviour, and Robotics*, pages 139–179. BYTE Books, Peterborough, NH, 1981.

[2] Jonathan H. Connell and Sridhar Mahadevan. Rapid task learning for real robots. In Jonathan H. Connell and Sridhar Mahadevan, editors, *Robot Learning*, chapter 5, pages 105–139. Kluwer Academic Publishers, 1993.

[3] Long-Ji Lin. Programming robots using reinforcement learning and teaching. In *Proceedings, Ninth National Conference on Artificial Intelligence (AAAI-91)*, pages 781–786. American Association for Artificial Intelligence, 1991.

[4] Long-Ji Lin. Self–improving reactive agents based on reinforcement learning, planning and teaching. *Machine Learning*, 8(3/4):69–97, May 1992.

[5] Fuminori Saito and Toshio Fukuda. Brachiation robot. In *IEEE International Conference on Robotics and Automation Conference Video Proceedings*, 1993.

[6] Fuminori Saito and Toshio Fukuda. Learning architecture for real robotic systems — Extension of connectionist Q–learning for continuous robot control domain. To appear in *Proceedings of IEEE International Conference on Robotics and Automation*, 1994.

[7] Fuminori Saito, Toshio Fukuda, and Fumihito Arai. Swing and locomotion control for two–link brachiation robot. In *Proceedings of IEEE International Conference on Robotics and Automation, vol. 2*, pages 719–724, 1993.

[8] Fuminori Saito, Toshio Fukuda, and Fumihito Arai. Swing and locomotion control for a two–link brachiation robot. *IEEE Control Systems Magazine*, 14(1):5–12, February 1994.

[9] Richard S. Sutton. Learning to predict by the methods of temporal differences. *Machine Learning*, 3:9–44, 1988.

[10] C.J.C.H. Watkins. *Learning from Delayed Rewards*. PhD thesis, University of Cambridge, England, 1989.

[11] Steven Whitehead, Jonas Karlsson, and Josh Tenenberg. Learning multiple goal behavior via task decomposition and dynamic policy merging. In Jonathan H. Connell and Sridhar Mahadevan, editors, *Robot Learning*, chapter 3, pages 45–78. Kluwer Academic Publishers, 1993.

An Architecture for Learning to Behave

Ashley M. Aitken

AI Laboratory, School of Computer Science & Engineering,
University of New South Wales, Box 1 PO Kensington,
Sydney NSW 2033, Australia
ashley@cse.unsw.edu.au

Abstract

The SAM architecture is a novel architecture, based on the gross structure and function of the cerebral neocortex, for combining unsupervised learning modules. When used as the high-level behavioral mechanism of an agent, the architecture enables the agent to learn the functional semantics of its high-level motor outputs and sensory inputs, and to acquire high-level and complex behavioral sequences by imitating other agents (learning by 'watching', or learning from a coach). This form of learning involves the agent attempting to produce motor sequences that recreate the sensory sequences it has been repeatedly exposed to. The architecture should scale well to multiple motor and sensory modalities, and to cope with more complex behavioral requirements. Finally, insofar as it is based on the architecture of the cerebral neocortex, the SAM architecture may also help to explain several features of the operation of the cerebral neocortex.

Introduction

To adapt and survive in a *realistic environment* (Booker, 1991) agents require a number of different behavioral and learning strategies (Lorenz, 1978; Meyer & Guillot, 1990). Some agents behave predominantly according to *reflexes* or *fixed action patterns* (Beer, 1990; Braintenberg, 1984). Others include more complex and flexible but still *instinctive behaviors* or *learning programs* (Gould, 1982). Finally, some agents (for example, those animals with cortical structures) are also capable of learning and executing *complex behavioral sequences*. In fact, this ability to *learn to behave* in a complex manner is arguably one of the most important facets of higher intelligence.

The SAM (Sensory-Association-Motor) architecture is a novel architecture designed to enable an agent to learn to behave. The architecture combines unsupervised learning modules in a triangular and hierarchical fashion. It enables an agent to learn how to control its motor systems to produce desired sensory states, and then to learn and execute complex behavioral sequences. Although the components of the SAM architecture are unsupervised learning modules, the architecture learns by 'watching' and attempting to mimic a coach. The coach provides sensory sequences (often through performing the desired motor sequence him- or herself). The architecture adapts to produce motor sequences to reproduce those sensory sequences it was repeatedly exposed to. This can be contrasted with learning from a supervisor who directly provides correct motor response sequences for particular sensory input sequences.

The SAM architecture enables an agent to learn and execute *complex behavioral sequences*; that is, behavioral sequences that are extended and highly context dependent. An extended behavioral sequence is one that consists of a sequence of actions and not simply a single response to a stimulus. A context dependent behavioral sequence is one that is constructed as the behavior proceeds and in response to sensory inputs and context, rather than simply being 'read' out of memory. The extended and context dependent nature of these behavioral sequences makes an agent's behavior more adaptive and less stereotypical than traditional planned action sequences. The ability to learn and reproduce such complex behavioral sequences seems to be a unique characteristic of higher intelligence.

What type of human behavior is representative of these complex behavioral sequences? Language is perhaps the best (although admittedly a very high level) example of learned human behavior. To some degree, a great deal of language is almost scripted in its regularity and predicability, and yet it is also very highly context dependent. As a particular example, consider human greetings, the rapport between two people as they meet - "Hello Geoff." "Hello Mary." "How are you today Geoff?" "Fine, and you?" "Oh, I can't complain." .... Although such greetings are complex sequences of context dependent behavior, they are also often quite predictable in their regularity. Like other behavioral traits they are also often learnt by children from their parents or peers. Perhaps, in some sense, the process of conscious 'logical' thought may also be a learnt behavior. Behavior that is learnt by way of its public expression in language and logical processes.

In general, learning the type of complex behavioral sequences described above is a slow process. It takes a large number of exposures to learn the required sensory sequences and to learn the motor sequences that will recreate these sensory sequences. On the other hand, as a result of this, the behavior is remembered for a long time. The slow rate of learning enables an agent to still be flexible and learn new behavioral sequences, while maintaining a certain stability and conservatism with its current behavioral repertoire. For example, it takes years to learn a language but fortunately it also takes years to forget it. This form of learning should be contrasted with one-shot associative memory where only one or a small number of exposures is required to learn something. This distinction is somewhat akin to the contrast between procedural and episodic forms of memory. Although this one-shot type of memory is certainly important, and would nicely compliment the slower learning of complex behavioral sequences, it is not considered here.

A notably successful architecture for constructing agents that produce complex behavior in an 'unprogrammed' fashion is the *subsumption architecture* (Brooks, 1986, March). The subsumption architecture employs a vertical decomposition (with horizontal slices) of an agent's behavior into tasks. The higher-level behavioral mechanisms control the lower level mechanisms, as well as producing behavior themselves. If an agent employs a subsumption architecture it is possible to consider the lower-level behavioral mechanisms as part of an *extended environment* for the higher-level behavioral mechanism (see Fig. 1). In this way the lower-level mechanisms can be factored out into the environment allowing one to focus on the higher-level mechanism. In doing this however, it is

important to remember that inputs and outputs from the higher-level behavioral mechanism do not necessarily correspond to inputs and outputs of the agent.

Now the precise problem tackled here can be made clear — *how can a high level behavioral mechanism, with no a-priori representations or control information, learn the functional semantics of its high-level motor outputs and sensory inputs, and acquire and execute complex behavioral sequences?* This paper suggests a solution to this problem by presenting an architecture based upon the structure and function of the cerebral neocortex (Eccles, 1984; Szentagothai, 1975). The solution builds upon the hypothesis that "... the cortex is nothing but a mixer of information for the purpose of discovering and recording correlated activity ..." (Braitenberg, 1982).

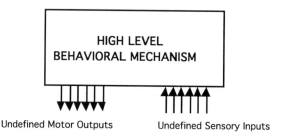

Figure 2. A black-box view of a high-level behavioral mechanism. How does it learn the meaning of its inputs, the effect of its outputs, and appropriate behavioral sequences?

The high-level behavioral mechanism does not assume any specific a-priori 'labelling' of the input and output lines with their functional semantics (although it may assume some gross specification of groups of inputs and outputs). For example, in the human visual cortex it is unlikely that each thalamic afferent is 'labelled' beyond the fact that it is from the visual system. This has its advantages and disadvantages. On the negative side, as the architecture cannot assume any labelling of the input and output lines, it must itself learn their semantics. On the positive side, the architecture does not require that specific input or output lines be connected to specific sensors or effectors, which can make construction simpler for complex sensory and motor systems. Similarly, the high level behavioral mechanism places only gross constraints on the behaviors that will be learnt and executed (as seems to be the case for the cerebral neocortex (Sur, Garraghty, & Roe, 1988)). The particular behaviors that are learnt and executed depend upon the behavioral sequences it is exposed to. For example, the human neocortex places constraints on the type of languages that it can learn but not on the particular language or the set of utterances.

Neural networks (Rumelhart, McClelland, et al., 1986a; Rumelhart, McClelland, et al., 1986b) have provided an interesting and powerful paradigm for constructing learning machines. However, most contemporary neural network architectures are not modular (in that there is no general method to combine them to form larger systems), use

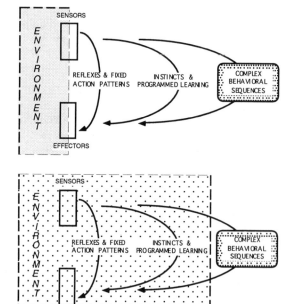

Figure 1. Brooks' creatures employ a range of behavioral mechanisms by way of a subsumption architecture (top). It is possible to consider the lower level behavioral mechanisms as a part of an extended environment for the higher level (bottom).

supervised learning rules, and are predominantly used for spatial pattern processing. Modularity and unsupervised learning are essential to enable neural networks to scale to larger applications (Murre, 1992). Recent work has sought to find useful modular, but still supervised, learning architectures (Jacobs & Jordan, 1991; Nowlan & Hinton, 1991). There has been research into unsupervised learning modules, for example (Carpenter & Grossberg, 1988; Murre, 1992), but little emphasis has been placed on a general architecture for combining these modules. *The SAM architecture is a general and extendible architecture for combining unsupervised learning modules to learn complex behavioral sequences.*

Neural networks for temporal pattern processing have predominantly used *time-delay lines* and standard layered networks (for example, see Waibel (Waibel, 1989)), or *recurrent networks* (for example, see Elman (Elman, 1990)). Although both of these approaches have had considerable success they have both primarily employed error-backpropagation from desired output states to train the network. For an agent this assumes the teacher knows the motor representations of the student and is quite unreasonable (particularly for high-level behavioral mechanisms). The SAM architecture employs unsupervised learning modules with a coach who provides the sensory sequences which result from the desired behavior. In this way the agent and coach need not share similar motor or even sensory representations (although some commonality of 'sensory view' and 'motor control' of the world is assumed). This relates more closely to the human situation wherein we are instructed, for example, in learning to speak, by the sensory consequences of the speech rather than by the motor states.

Finally, before the architecture is outlined in detail, it is important to make clear that the use of the terms 'sensory inputs', 'motor outputs', and 'behavioral sequences' is not meant to suggest that full sensory-motor control and all behavior is necessarily learnt and produced by this method alone. For example, when motor control is discussed in the architecture it only relates to the high-level motor command sequences. It does not necessarily include feed-back control, for example. In mammals, structures responsible for such mid-level processing are found in the mid- and lower brain, and, in particular, in the cerebellum. A large amount of research has been done on this level of motor control (Albus, 1971; Neilson, Neilson, & O'Dwyer, 1992). The aim here is not to supplant this research but to suggest a mechanism that could sit on top of these other control systems and provide higher-level behavioral directives.

This paper presents an outline and discussion of the SAM architecture and learning paradigm. In section 1, a specification of the requirements and operation of the building blocks of the architecture, the SAM modules, is presented. In section 2, the paper introduces the basic SAM architecture - the Sensory-Association-Motor triangle. In section 3, the paper discusses how the architecture can learn the semantics of its sensory inputs and motor outputs. In section 4, it is shown how the addition of SAM modules can enable the system to learn more complex behavioral sequences. In section 5, the paper discusses in more detail the general idea of learning by imitation, and the nature of processing in the SAM architecture. To finish this section, it is suggested how this architecture may provide a few hints to assist in our understanding of the operation of the cerebral neocortex. Finally, the paper finishes with a summary, and brief discussion of future work.

1. The SAM Module

The building blocks of the SAM architecture are *unsupervised learning modules*. The primary requirement of these modules is that they detect and represent correlations, or more precisely coincident activity, in their inputs. If all, or a subset, of the inputs to a SAM module are correlated, that is, if they are repeatedly active at the same time, and there is representational space, the module will detect and represent this correlation. The module is also required to be tolerant to noise, and to ignore random inputs.

The SAM module is inspired by the representational fields, or perhaps even by entire areas, of the cerebral neocortex. The cerebral neocortex is composed of a number of interconnected cortical areas (Brodmann, 1909) (defined by structural and functional differences). The cortical areas themselves are composed of a large number of cortical columns (defined by the termination zones of intracortical efferents). Cortical areas define representational fields (Kaas, 1987) for the inputs they receive. The most familiar being the field representing possible oriented line-segment at locations in the visual field, which is found in the visual cortex (Hubel & Wiesel, 1977).

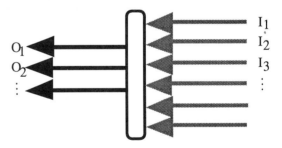

Figure 3. A representative SAM module. In this case there are a number of input streams I_1, I_2, I_3, ... and a number of output streams O_1, O_2, ... Each input (and the output) stream can contain a single input (output) line, or a number of input (output) lines affording more complex symbolic or sub-symbolic representations.

Learning in the SAM module is correlation-based (that is, Hebb-like (Hebb, 1949)). The output state is a stochastic function of the vector of inputs. For any input vector, a distribution across the possible output states is formed (as a function of the input vector). The output state is then chosen according to this distribution. After the output state is chosen the distribution is updated so that later the correlated inputs in this input vector will be more likely to cause the same output state. Competition for representational space ensures that correlations subsequently unrepresented in the inputs will eventually be replaced by more prevalent correlations.

Consider some simple demonstrative examples of learning in a SAM module. If a SAM module has three inputs and the inputs are all random the output from the SAM module will similarly be random. If two of the inputs are random, but one has a number of particularly frequent inputs, the SAM module will detect and represent these particular inputs by particular output states. If the simplified input sequence represented in Table 1 is repeatedly presented to the SAM module, it will detect and represent the correlation between I_1 and I_2, that is when $I_1 = A$, most likely $I_2 = B$, whereas I_3 is uncorrelated with I_1 and I_2. The correlation in the inputs can be written as follows $(A,B,*)$ where the star represents a *don't care* or random input. If the SAM module represented this correlation by output state R say, the classifier rule could be written as $(A,B,*) \rightarrow R$.

Apart from the above requirements, the SAM architecture is independent of the exact nature of the modules. This research considers two types of modules. The first, is neural model based upon extended BCM (Bienenstock-Cooper-Munro) neurons (Aitken, 1993; Bear & Cooper, 1990) with lateral inhibition amongst the neurons to provide competition for representation. The second, is a symbolic module that uses explicit classifier rules. The neural module benefits from emergence of representations and generalisation of behavior, whereas the symbolic module is simpler to implement and analyse. In some sense, the module is required to perform something similar to principal component analysis (PCA) on the sequence of inputs it receives (Oja, 1982; Softky & Kammen, 1991). Other modules, in particular, Rubner's hierarchical network (Rubner & Schulten, 1990), CALM (Murre, 1992), Linsker's layers (Linsker, 1988) and ART (Carpenter & Grossberg, 1988, March), may also provide the required functionality.

2. The Basic SAM Architecture

The SAM architecture, in its simplest form, consists of three unsupervised learning modules with feed-forward and feed-backward connections between them (see Fig. 4). The sensory module (S) also receives sensory inputs from the extended environment (ξ). The motor module (M) also produces motor outputs which effect the extended environment (ξ). The remaining module that neither

directly receives sensory inputs nor directly produces motor outputs is an example of an association module (A). Each module can be considered independently — at any time step, it receives inputs from other modules (and in the case of the sensory module from the extended environment) and produces an output state (which in the case of the motor module is sent to the extended environment).

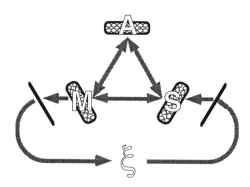

Figure 4. The basic SAM architecture.

The SAM architecture is based on the gross architecture of the cerebral neocortex. Cortical areas are also commonly labelled sensory or motor cortex depending on whether they receive inputs from the sensory systems (commonly by way of the thalamus) or send outputs to the motor systems. The other areas, which do not directly receive sensory inputs or send motor outputs are labelled association cortex. Cortical areas are also bi-directionally connected — if a cortical area sends outputs to another cortical area it also receives inputs from that cortical area. It is also well known that sensory areas are directly interconnected with motor areas as well as being indirectly interconnected through association areas.

Unlike most other classical or neural network architectures, the SAM architecture relies on the *closing of the loop* between motor outputs and sensory inputs by way of the extended environment to define the functional semantics of its motor outputs and sensory inputs (see Fig. 5). Consider, for example, if the loop was open, the motor outputs would have no effect on the sensory inputs and thus all the modules will receive only random input patterns (as a result of their stochastic firing) and there will be no significant learning (since learning requires correlations). However, if the loop is closed, the motor outputs effect the environment and subsequently the sensory inputs. It is the correlations between the motor outputs and their sensory consequence that initiates significant learning in the SAM

I\t	0	1	2	3	4	5	6	7	8
I_1	X	A	X	A	A	J	A	O	A
I_2	M	B	A	B	B	T	S	O	B
I_3	J	D	F	Z	A	N	T	O	K

Table 1. Listing of inputs (I) to a SAM module over a small number of time steps (t). The shaded inputs highlight the correlation between $I_1 = A$ and $I_2 = B$, whereas I_3 appears to be uncorrelated.

architecture. Kuperstein (Kuperstein, 1988) uses a similar *circular reaction* to train a simulated robot arm to reach in space.

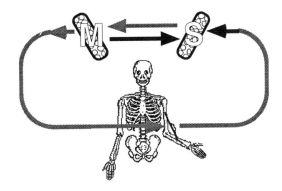

Figure 5.   Closing the loop. Sensory modules detect correlations in the motor outputs and the sensory inputs. Effective motor sequences cause correlated sensory sequences. Clearly, this is a highly schematized diagram - for any reasonable control of an elbow a much more complex control system is required.

3.   Learning to Act and Perceive

Learning begins in the SAM architecture with random explorations of the motor space due to the stochastic output of the motor module - much like an infant's random movements or babblings.   Consider firstly, a system consisting only of a sensory and motor module.   When the motor module execute an *effective motor sequence* the sensory module detects and represents the correlation between the motor states and the sensory inputs (see Fig. 5). An effective motor sequence is simply a motor sequence that causes a tangible sensory consequence (compare, in mammals for example, an ineffective random firing of muscle fibres with a progressive firing of muscle fibres - the former would produce little, if any, action whereas the latter would cause a physical action and sensory consequence). The SAM architecture is in effect learning the primitive motor command sequences and their sensory consequences, it is labelling the motor outputs and sensory inputs, *it is learning to act and to perceive*.   Note that at a much higher level the sensory consequence

Table 2 demonstrates an example of when this learning would occur with a hypothetical and simplified sequence of motor states.   During the random exploration of the motor

space the motor module will most likely happen upon small effective sequences of motor states (in this case, the sequence A,B,C).   These motor sequences cause a correlated sensory consequence as a result of their effect on the environment.   As the table shows, the output from the motor module and the sensory consequence of the motor sequence will be correlated .   At this time the sensory module will begiin to detect and represent these correlations.   This is the first component of the learning in the SAM architecture.

Significantly then, in the SAM architecture *the sensory modules detect and represent correlations between the motor states and the sensory inputs*.   This is in contrast to the traditional view of sensory processing, particularly in the mammalian sensory neocortex, where it has been assumed that sensory areas directly represent sensory inputs (not the correlations between the sensory inputs and the motor states).   Interestingly, there may be some physiological evidence for this view in the relationship between whisker sweeps and the spatio-temporal properties of receptive fields found by Nicolelis et al. (Nicolelis, Luiz, & Lin, 1993) in simultaneous recording from multiple neurons in rats.   A qualitatively similar effect is expected in the SAM architecture where changes in motor states (sweeping of the whiskers) would introduce different motor inputs to the sensory areas and thus alter receptive field profiles.   Note, however, that if one was only 'looking' for sensory representations (without considering motor states) that is what would be found (even within the SAM framework).

Whereas the first component of learning in the SAM architecture occurs in the sensory module, the second component occurs in the motor module.   As the sensory module learns correlations between the motor states and the sensory inputs (the sensory consequences of previous motor states) it will become correlated with the motor module.   In a Hebbian fashion, the correlation between the output state of the motor module (as it randomly explores the motor space) and the sensory module (as a result of effective motor sequences) will make it more likely that the state of the sensory module will initiate the same motor state in the future.   Consider again the example of Table 2.   After the sensory module has detected and represented the correlation between B and E(A).   When the motor module is in state C, the sensory module will consistently be in the representational state <B,E(A)>[1].   As a result of the Hebb-

---

[1]The notation <x,y,...,z> is used to denote the state of a module representing the correlation of x, y, ..., and z on

S \ t	0	1	2	3	4	5	6	7	8
M	A	B	C	X	M	A	B	C	J
E	Z	E(A)	E(B)	E(C)	Y	M	E(A)	E(B)	E(C)

Table 2.   Listing of inputs to the *sensory module* resulting from random expiration of motor space.   M = motor input to sensory module (= state of motor module);   E = extended environment input to sensory module (= effect of previous motor output on extended environment) across a sequence of time steps.   The shaded columns show correlations that will be represented by the sensory module.

like learning in the motor module it will subsequently become more likely to produce motor state C when the sensory module is in the state <B,E(A)>. In this way the motor module is learning appropriate motor responses to sensory states to continue the effective motor sequences, which in turn makes production of the effective motor sequences more likely.

4. Learning to Behave

Learning to behave is a more complex and less constrained task than learning to act and perceive. It is generally not feasible to use random exploration of the motor space to learn complex behavioral sequences. The space of behavioral sequences is usually too large and there are too many behavioral sequences to choose from. Once the SAM architecture has learnt to act and perceive it learns more complex behavioral sequences by imitation[2]. Unlike most supervised learning architectures, the SAM architecture learns by exposure to the sensory consequences of desired motor sequences rather than exposure to the desired motor sequences themselves. The problem for the SAM architecture then is to construct motor sequences that will reproduce the desired sensory sequence. The SAM architecture is learning how to produce a sensory sequence rather than learning a particular motor sequence.

The learning occurs when the agent is repeatedly exposed to sequences of sensory inputs. These can naturally be thought of as the sensory consequences of another agent's motor sequences (see Fig. 6). The learning occurs as a result of sensory sequences pushing the sensory module through a sequence of states and, as a result of the learnt correlations between the motor module and the sensory module (recall the second component of learning in the SAM architecture), the motor module through the appropriate motor sequence for the production of the sensory sequence. The learning of complex behavioral sequences relies heavily on the fact that the required elementary effective motor sequences have been learnt previously. The repeated exposure to sensory sequences essentially joins up these sequences of elementary behaviors to form the more complex behavioral sequences. Eventually, initiation of the sensory sequence can cause the entire motor sequence to be reproduced.

Learning of complex sequences can however be problematic in that they may overlap or share primitive effective sequences. How can the architecture discriminate and learn overlapping behavioral sequences? The SAM architecture solves this problem by employing association modules to provide distinguishing context within the overlapping sequences. Consider now adding to the initial sensory and motor modules an association module. The association module forms bi-directional connections with

---

the inputs to that module.

[2]Imitation as a form of learning is well known in psychology (Weinsheimer, 1984) but relatively neglected in machine learning.

both the sensory and the motor modules to form the basic SAM triangle (see Fig. 4). Initially, when the sensory and motor modules are uncorrelated, the inputs to the association module will also be uncorrelated. Hence, the association module will not represent any correlations and its output will also be uncorrelated. However, as discussed above, when executing a behavioral sequence the sensory and motor modules become correlated, the association module will detect and represent these correlations. Similarly, when the association module's state becomes correlated with the sensory and motor modules, these modules will also detect and incorporate this correlation. The association module then provides the context that signals the motor and the sensory modules to distinguish particular behavioral sequences. In this way multiple overlapping behavioral sequences may be learnt.

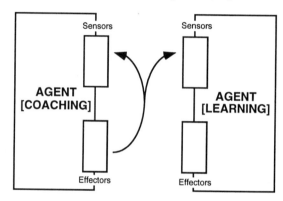

Figure 6. Learning by Imitation. The teacher (or coach) provides the desired sensory sequences (most commonly as a result of his or her own motor sequences). In this way the teacher is not required to know the agent's sensory or motor representations.

One association module can only provide one level of contextual information to influence the sensory and motor modules. What if higher level contextual information is required to further distinguish complex behavioral sequences — to provide the context for the context, so to speak. It is possible to extend the basic SAM architecture (as described above) to incorporate higher levels of contextual information. This is achieved by the addition of more association modules. Conceptually this can be understood by regarding the standard association module as a higher level 'motor' module — since its state will effect the sensory module (by way of the standard motor module and the extended environment). It is then possible to add an extra higher-level association module connected to the sensory module and the standard association module (the additional association module on the right-hand side in Fig. 7). A similar extension can also be made on the motor side of the basic sensory-association-motor triangle (the additional association module on the left-hand side in Fig. 7). With multiple association modules the system can capture and perform more complex behavioral sequences - the association modules allow the architecture to capture the higher-level correlations in the behavior and to use these correlations as context to reproduce the behavior at a later stage.

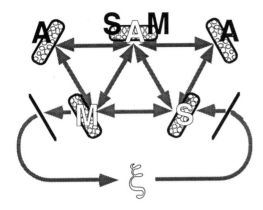

Figure 7. The extended SAM architecture. By considering the standard association module as a higher-level 'motor' module it is possible to add an extra higher-level association module on the right-hand side. Similarly, by considering the standard association module as a higher-level 'sensory' module it is possible to add an extra, higher-level, association module on the left-hand side.

To this point the discussion has only considered one sensory module and one motor module representing one sensory modality and one motor modality. An agent will most likely have multiple sensory and motor modalities. The modularity of the SAM architecture suggests it will scale well to multiple sensory and motor modalities and more association modules. In this situation the SAM hierarchy could become much more complex, and there may not even be individual SAM hierarchies, but rather an interweaving of the separate hierarchies. In the neocortex for example, the likelihood of finding independent SAM hierarchies for each sensory-motor pair is small. Instead it is more likely that there exists a complex hierarchy of interconnections between areas that follows the general pattern and operation as described above. With multiple sensory, motor and association modules the SAM architecture can learn and execute much more complex behavioral sequences. In particular, different sensory modalities can provide contextual information for the behavior in other modalities.

5. Further Discussion

Although this paper focuses on learning by imitation (learning by 'watching', or learning from a coach) it is not necessarily the only form of learning possible within the SAM architecture. Reinforcement learning (Sutton, 1991) could be included in the SAM architecture by using a critic's evaluation to modify the learning rates of all or some of the modules and hence to 'direct' the learning. When the critic recognises efficacious states (of the environment with respect to the agent) it can increase the learning rate of appropriate SAM modules and hence learn the current sequence faster. On the other hand, when the critic

recognises undesirable states it can decrease the learning rate of the appropriate SAM modules and hence slow the learning of the current sequence. In the cerebral neocortex, the diffuse thalamo-cortical connections are well situated to effect such a modulation of learning.

Another important factor that may discriminate the behavioral sequences learnt by the SAM architecture is that the agent's behavior is also controlled by lower-level behavioral mechanisms. As the SAM architecture sits on top of a layered architecture (much like the neocortex sits on top of the mid- and lower brain in mammals) it operates with and through the lower levels. At times these lower levels may independently cause behavioral sequences and *blinker* what behavioral sequences the SAM architecture observes and learns. In a sense this is still learning by imitation but in this case the coach is internal to the agent. These behaviors may extend from simple reflexes to complex instinctive behavioral sequences. For example, the reflex circuits that are responsible for withdrawing a hand from a hot stove would blinker what behaviors the neocortex 'sees'; that is, the neocortex would not 'see' many behavioral sequences where the hand remained on the stove. Hence, it is unlikely that the neocortex would produce a behavior to put a hand on a hot stove.

To describe his work with recurrent networks Elman (Elman, 1989) proposes an intriguing *combination lock metaphor* wherein the inputs to his network need to go through a certain sequence of states (ie a combination) to unlock the appropriate output. Here the metaphor is extended to portray the SAM architecture as a system learning behavioral sequences as it is pushed through the 'combination' of states. Later, an appropriate initiating input sequence can unlock these behaviors. For example, a human can be exposed to many behavioral sequences and later, when initiated reproduce these behaviors. One of the benefits of a neural SAM module is that the behavioral sequences don't need to exactly match — spatially or temporally — every time as a combination does. The neural network approach provides the ability to generalize, that is, to respond to unseen input sequences with appropriate behavioral sequences. In this way an agent's behavior becomes a collage of complex, overlapping, and contextual, behavioral sequences.

The representations in the association modules of the SAM architecture can be considered as abstractions of the combined state of the sensory and motor modules. Traditionally, the process of abstraction in intelligent agents, and in particular in the brain, has been portrayed as proceeding in stages from inputs, to more abstract representations, and then to even more abstract representations. In this case abstraction can be thought of as occurring 'horizontally' along the input-output or sensory-motor axis — and so here it is called *horizontal abstraction*. In horizontal abstraction, it is the sensory states that are being increasingly abstracted. The difficulty with this is form of abstraction is that, in itself, it is not sufficient for intelligent behavior. A more abstract representation of the inputs is still just a representation of the inputs. Horizontal abstraction in the end can only go so far.

The SAM architecture makes explicit the notion of *vertical abstraction*. This is abstraction that can be thought of as occurring 'perpendicular' to the input-output or sensory-motor axis (see Fig. 8). Abstraction proceeds from the bottom up this axis. Unlike the case of horizontal abstraction, vertical abstraction is an abstraction of sensory-motor (or higher level association) states. This solves the problem of horizontal abstraction going nowhere. Vertical abstraction of sensory-motor states can proceed as high as necessary, each level representing new correlations, not just a more abstract representation of inputs. These vertical abstractions can then be employed directly in the operation of the agent as top-down contextual information.

Figure 8. *1. Horizontal vs Vertical Abstraction.* Abstraction is traditionally horizontal, that is of purely sensory states and occurs along the input-output or sensory-motor axis. Vertical abstraction (as depicted here) is of sensory-motor states and occurs along an axis 'perpendicular' to the input-output or sensory-motor axis. *2. Sensory and Motor Symmetry.* Correlations are detected and represented symmetrically up the SAM hierarchy. Top-down contextual information flows symmetrically back down the SAM hierarchy.

Another interesting feature of the SAM architecture is the symmetry between the sensory and motor sides of processing. Traditionally, again, processing has been portrayed as progressing from inputs to outputs. If any information did flow back to the input processing it was often an asymmetric component tacked on to the system. In the SAM architecture, detecting and representing correlations in the sensory and motor (and higher association) modules is a bottom-up process. Using the high-level contextual information to effect the lower level sensory and motor (and lower association) modules is a top-down process. The flow of information down the SAM hierarchy is just as symmetrical as the flow of information up the SAM hierarchy; that is, the high-level contextual information effects the sensory modules just as much as it does the motor modulese. In this way the SAM architecture

makes the provision of contextual information to the sensory modules to assist in recognition of sensory inputs just as important as the provision of contextual information to the motor modules for the production of motor outputs. The symmetry is a natural part of the SAM architecture.

Finally, insofar as the SAM architecture is inspired by the mammalian cerebral neocortex it also provides a model (perhaps even a preliminary step towards a theory) of the operation of the cerebral neocortex. As such, it also hints at a possible explanation for a number of clinical findings about the cerebral neocortex. Here, we discuss briefly two such findings and possible explanations within the SAM architecture and learning paradigm. Firstly, from behavioral studies of young children, Karmiloff-Smith (Karmiloff-Smith, 1987;; Karmiloff-Smith, 1992) has suggested that cognitive abilities develop in a layered fashion. Extending this idea, Clark and Karmiloff-Smith (Clark & Karmiloff-Smith, 1993) have suggested that 'true cognizers' employ a process of representational redescription (RR) wherein implicit procedural skills are spontaneously rerepresented as explicit symbolic knowledge so that they can be applied in a broader context.

Learning in the SAM hierarchy also occurs in a somewhat layered fashioned. It is only when the sensory and motor modules (or association modules) become correlated, that is, when a behavior is learnt, that the (higher-level) association modules form a more abstract representation of the (lower-level) behavior. In this way, learning in the SAM architecture proceeds up the SAM hierarchy only as the lower-level behaviors are learnt. At present, no clear mechanism can be suggested for how the SAM architecture can reapply such abstract representations of behavior to other situations in a similar way to the reapplication of symbolic knowledge. However, one possibility is that this reapplication is a result of generalisation — not of the behavior itself, but of the application of the abstraction to other behaviors. Rather than the sensory to motor module map being generalized, it is the application of the context information from the association module (to the motor and sensory modules) which is generalized. Thus, the SAM architecture may offer a little hint at how the neocortex rerepresents, and uses these new representations.

The second hint the SAM architecture possibly gives regarding the operation of the cerebral neocortex relates to the amount of activity in cortical areas (which roughly map to SAM modules). Recent anecdotal experiments indicate that experts tend to use less cortical activity than novices on similar tasks. Begley (Begley, Wright, Church, & Hager, 1992) found that scans of the brain activity of video game players demonstrated that brain activity decreased as the player became more skilled at the game. The brain of a novice displayed much more activity even though it was operating less effectively than the expert. In the SAM architecture this could possibly be explained by their being more correlated activity in the modules of experts because they have learnt the required behavior. The different modules would be, to a great degree, in synchrony - the expected sensory consequences in-line with the actual sensory consequences. On the other hand, in the novice player there will be little synchrony in the activity - there will be great mismatch between the expected sensory consequences of a motor sequence and the actual sensory consequence. Similarly, for the novice, there will be few representations formed in the association modules and the behavior will be chosen without appropriate contextual guidance from the association modules. All this may lead to extra activity in the modules of the novice as the architecture 'searches' for correlations to represent, and later guide, behavior.

Summary and Future Work

In summary, the SAM architecture provides a method for combining unsupervised learning modules to allow an agent to learn the functional semantics of its high-level sensory inputs and motor outputs, and to learn and execute complex behavioral sequences. The SAM architecture learns complex behavioral sequences by a combination of random exploration of the motor space and imitation of observed sensory sequences (that is, by finding the correct motor sequences to reproduce observed sensory sequences). The fact that the architecture does not assume any predefined semantics of specific inputs and outputs should make the construction of agents with large and complex sensory and motor systems simpler. Also, as a result of learning by imitation, the coach need not share, or even know, the motor or sensory representations used by the agent. The SAM architecture is inspired by the anatomy and physiology of the cerebral neocortex and as such also provides a model for, and possible explanation of, cortical operation.

Future work includes, an investigation of the relationship between the number of modules, their interconnection, and the complexity of the behavioral sequences that can be learnt and executed; a consideration of the semantics of the higher association modules (on the motor and the sensory side); an investigation of how best to integrate a number of different sensory and motor modalities and their association modules; an investigation of the interconnection of the representational fields (and cortical areas) in the mammalian cerebral neocortex (Van Essen & Maunesll, 1983) to see if there is any more clear anatomical evidence for the SAM hierarchy; further simulations of the SAM architecture to investigate Begeley's finding of a relationship between cortical activity and skilled behavior; and to consider further the representational redescription hypothesis with respect to the SAM architecture.

Finally, the most radical and beneficial changes to the behavioral capabilities of animals seems to have arisen from the evolution and expansion of the cerebral neocortex (Rakic, 1988) in the mammalian brain. If the neocortex evolved to sit on top of the brain to detect correlations and to provide context in the execution of complex behavioral sequences, perhaps it is time to consider adding something similar to the SAM architecture on 'top' of our most successful animats.

References

Aitken, A. M. (1993). Preliminary Aspects of the SAM theory of the Cerebral Neocortex. In *Proceedings of the Second Australian Cognitive Science Conference (CogSci-93)* (pp. 104-106).

Albus, S. A. (1971). A Theory of Cerebellar Function. *Mathematical Biosciences*, 10, 25-61.

Bear, M. F., & Cooper, L. N. (1990). Molecular Mechanism for Synaptic Modification in the Visual Cortex: Interaction between Theory and Experiment. In M. A. Gluck & D. E. Rumelhart (Eds.), *Neuroscience and Connectionist Theory* (pp. 65-94). Hillsdale, N.J.: Lawrebce Erlbaum Associates.

Beer, R. D. (1990). *Intelligence as Adaptive Behavior: An Experiment in Computational Neuroethology*.

Begley, S., Wright, L., Church, V., & Hager, M. (1992, June 9). Mapping the Brain. *Bulletin (with Newsweek)*, p. 76 - 80.

Booker, L. B. (1991). Instinct as an Inductive Bias for Learning Behavioral Sequences. In J.-A. M. Meyer & S. W. Wilson (Eds.), *From Animals to Animats* (pp. 230-237). Cambridge, MA: Bradford Book, The MIT Press.

Braintenberg, V. (1984). *Vehicles : Experiments in Synthetic Psychology*. Cambridge, Massachussetts: The MIT Press.

Braitenberg, V. (1982). Outline of a theory of the cerebral cortex. In L. M. a. S. Ricciardi A.C. (Ed.), *Biomathematics in 1980* (pp. 127-132). Amsterdam: North-Holland.

Brodmann, K. (1909). *Vergleichende Localisationslehre der Grosshirnrinde in Ihren Prinzipien Dargelstellt auf Grund des Zellenbaues (Principles of comparative localization in the cerebral cortex presented on the basis of cytoarchitecture)*. Lepzig: Barth: Barth Publishing.

Brooks, R. A. (1986, March). A Robust Layered Control System For A Mobile Robot. *IEEE Journal Of Robotics And Automation, RA-2*(1), 14-23.

Carpenter, G. A., & Grossberg, S. (1988, March). The ART of Adaptive Pattern Recognition by a Self-Organizing Neural Network. *IEEE Computer*, 77-88.

Clark, A., & Karmiloff-Smith, A. (1993). The Cognizer's Innards: A psychological and philosophical perspective on the development of thought. *Mind and Language*.

Eccles, J. C. (1984). The Cerebral Neocortex : A Theory of Its Operation. In E. G. Jones & A. Peters (Eds.),

Cerebral Cortex (pp. 1-36). New York, New York: Plenum Press.

Elman, J. (1989, August). *Representation and Structure in Connectionist Models* (CRL Technical Report 8903 No. CRL Technical Report 8903). University of California, San Diego.

Elman, J. L. (1990). Finding Structure in Time. *Cognitive Science*, 14, 179-211.

Gould, S. J. (1982). Darwinism and the Expansion of Evolutionary Theory. *Science*, 216, 380.

Hebb, D. O. (1949). *The Organization of Behavior*. New York: Wiley.

Hubel, D. H., & Wiesel, T. N. (1977). Functional Architecture of Macaque Monkey Visual Cortex. *Proc. R. Soc. Lond. B.,* 198, 1-59.

Jacobs, R. A., & Jordan, M. I. (1991). A competitive modular connectionist architecture. In R. P. Lippmann, J. E. Moody, & D. S. Touretzky (Eds.), *Advances in Neural Information Processing Systems* 3 (pp. 767-73). Morgan Kaufmann Publishers.

Kaas, J. H. (1987). The Organization of Neocortex in Mammals: Implications for Theories of Brain Function. *Ann. Rev. Psychol.,* 38, 129-151.

Karmiloff-Smith, A. (1987, April). Beyond Modularity: A Developmental Perspective On Human Consciousness.

Karmiloff-Smith, A. (1992). *Abnormal Phenotypes and the Challenges They Pose to Connectionist Models of Development* (Technical Report No. PDP.CNS.92.7). MRC Applied Psychology Unit, Cambridge, England.

Kuperstein, M. (1988). Neural Model of Adaptive Hand-Eye Coordination for Single Postures. *Science*, 239, 1308-1311.

Linsker, R. (1988, March). Self-organization in a perceptual network. *IEEE Computer*, p. 105-117.

Lorenz, K. Z. (1978). *The Foundations of Ethology*. New York: Springer-Verlag.

Meyer, J.-A., & Guillot, A. (1990, September 24-28). *From animals to animats: everything you wanted to know about the simulation of adaptive behavior*

Murre, J. M. J. (1992). *Learning and categorization in modular neural networks*. Hillsdale, NJ: Lawrence Erlbaum.

Neilson, P. D., Neilson, M. D., & O'Dwyer, N. J. (1992). Adaptive Motor Control: Applications to Disorders of Motor Control. In J. J. Summer (Ed.), *Approaches to the study of motor control and learning* (pp. 495-548). Amsterdam: North Holland.

Nicolelis, M. A. L., Luiz, B. A., & Lin, R. C. S. (1993). Distributed Spatiotemporal Properties of Networks of Neurons in the Ventral Posterior Medial Thalamus of Awake Rats. In J. M. Bower (Ed.), *Computation and Neural Systems*. Washington, D.C.

Nowlan, S. J., & Hinton, G. E. (1991). Evaluation of Adaptive Mixtures of Competing Experts. In R. P. Lippmann, J. E. Moody, & D. S. Touretzky (Eds.), *Advances in Neural Information Processing Systems* 3 (pp. 774-80). Morgan Kaufmann Publishers.

Oja, E. (1982). A Simplified Neuron Model as a Principal Component Analyzer. *Journal of Mathematical Biology*, 15, 267-273.

Rakic, P. (1988). Specification of Cerebral Cortical Areas. *Science*, 241(8 July), 170-6.

Rubner, J., & Schulten, K. (1990). Development of Feature Detectors by Self-Organization: A Network Model. *Biological Cybernetics*, 62, 193-199.

Rumelhart, D. E., McClelland, J. L., and the PDP Group, P. R. (1986a). *Parallel Distributed Processing : Explorations in the Microstructure of Cognition; Vol. 1: Foundations*. Cambridge: The MIT Press.

Rumelhart, D. E., McClelland, J. L., and the PDP Group, P. R. (1986b). *Parallel Distributed Processing : Explorations in the Microstructure of Cognition; Vol. 2: Psychological and Biological Models*. Cambridge: The MIT Press.

Softky, W. R., & Kammen, D. M. (1991). Correlations in High Dimensional or Asymmetric Data Sets: Hebbian Neuronal Processing. *Neural Networks*, 4(3), 337-347.

Sur, M., Garraghty, P. E., & Roe, A. W. (1988, 9 December). Experimentally Induced Visual Projections into Auditory Thalamus and Cortex. *Science*, 242, 1437-1441.

Sutton, R. S. (1991). Reinforcement Learning Architectures for Animats. In J.-A. M. Meyer & S. W. Wilson (Eds.), *From Animals to Animats* (pp. 288-96). Cambridge, MA: Bradford Book, The MIT Press.

Szentagothai, J. (1975). The "Module-Concept" in Cerebral Cortex Architecture. *Brain Research*, 95, 475-96.

Van Essen, D. C., & Maunesll, J. H. R. (1983). Hiearchical organization and functional streams in the visual cortex. *Trends in Neurosciences*, 6, 370-375.

Waibel, A. (1989). Modular Construction of Time-Delay Neural Networks for Speech Recognition. *Neural Computation*, 1, 39-46.

Weinsheimer, J. (1984). *Imitation*. London: Routledge & Kegan Paul.

REINFORCEMENT LEARNING FOR HOMEOSTATIC ENDOGENOUS VARIABLES

Hugues Bersini

IRIDIA - Université Libre de Bruxelles
Avenue Franklin Roosevelt, 50
CP 194/6
1050 Bruxelles
Belgium
bersini@ulb.ac.be

Abstract

This paper experimentally shows how an autonomous agent can learn to interact with a complex environment so as to maintain endogenous variables in a given bounded zone. Three key notions which, although have been studied in depth when regarded separately, have not received sufficient attention when integrated in a same modeling, they are: endogenous variables, homeostasis and reinforcement learning. All along the paper, a little computer simulation is presented in which an agent wandering in a grid world (cluttered with static or dynamic objects), and endowed with local perception mechanism, has to eat when hungry, have sex (with similar agents) when being short of and escape predators when facing them. Results indicate high sensitivity to the type of reinforcement policy, to the completeness of the perception and the complexity of the environment.

1. Introduction

The work described in this paper intends to join in one instance of simulated autonomous agent three key notions which, although have been largely investigated when taken separately, have not received sufficient attention when integrated in a same modeling: endogenous variables, homeostasis and Reinforcement Learning (RL). Endogenous variables capture information related to the internal state of the agent, state influenced both by the agent's perceptions and actions but in now way to be restricted to them. In substance, they are additional influences which allow to differentiate the effect of similar perception input on the resulting agent's action. For instance, thirsty any biological entity will react differently when facing water that when satiated. The existence of these variables is a fundamental sign of the strong "emancipation" of biological creatures

with respect to their environmental pressure. They constitute an important type of cognitive intermediates in between the sensory and motor poles of the behavioral loops.

These endogenous variables can be associated with internal goals or basic motivations: "being thirsty", "hungry", emotional states: "being afraid", "happy", physiological states: "stress", "fatigue", expectation about next environmental input, current hypothetical mental schema ... They need not to be confused with another type of internal variables receiving today an increasing attention by researchers in RL, and which are akin to a form of short-term memory [8] [9] [11] [13] allowing the agent to decide its action not only on the basis of its current perception but also of its past perceptions and actions. The reason to label these new variables "endogenous" instead of "internal" is indeed to stress their radical difference with variables coding the agent's perceptions and actions both in the present and the past. The nature of these endogenous variables together with computer simulations in which they appear will be the object of the next section. From now on the state of an agent will be obtained by grouping its perception input with values taken by its endogenous variables.

In the model to be described, these endogenous variables learn to obey homeostatic constraints namely to be maintained within pre-determined boundaries called "viability" or "viable" zone. This type of constraint is far from being original and has been deeply discussed in many fields: systemic, biology, ethology, psychology, process control, economy, artificial life, autonomous robotics, etc. like the third section will show. Only the effect of the agent's actions can keep these endogenous variables within their viability zone. For instance, the "thirsty" behavior might be dependent on an homeostatic endogenous variable which when getting close to its inferior threshold forces the agent to look for water so as to bring back the variable far from this threshold. One can easily imagine the "action selection" problem induced by a multi-objective situation i.e. maintaining several of these endogenous variables, dependent on the same set of actions, within their respective viability zone. Looking for food or for sex or escaping from a predator will keep the associated variables within their specific zones but at the same time will increase the risk of the agent's lost by the impossibility of keeping the "thirst associated" variable within its viability domain. When facing the delicate problem posed by discovering a satisfactory action policy keeping simultaneously all the variables viable, a learning mechanism turns out to be the only alternative.

Indeed the third key aspect of the model is the use of a reinforcement learning strategy namely Watkin's Q-learning to discover a sequence of actions which allows the agent to remain viable the longer the better despite the strong constraints exerted by the environment and by the agent's own endogenous variability. In contrast with toy applications like the traditional maze problem [18], here the presence of RL appears unavoidable since any strategy leading to a continuous viability (and which, if known initially, could be taught to the agent in a supervised way) is hard to determine a priori. All along the paper, a little computer simulation is presented in which an agent wandering in a grid world (cluttered with static or dynamic objects), and endowed with local perception mechanism, has to eat when hungry, have sex (with similar agents) when being short of and escape predators when facing them. Sections four and five will present how the Q-learning is applied in the model and the different results achieved when using various forms of reinforcement, when varying the quality of the perception and increasing the complexity of the environment. This toy simulation will help to present better the three aspects whose conjoined presence is the main message of this work. Since the general type of problem exemplified by this simulation encompasses more engineering applications such as viable process control and the design of autonomous robot, showing that a reinforcement learning algorithm performs well despite the problem intrinsic difficulty can encourage the introduction of these notions as well as the use of RL in these engineering contexts.

2. Endogenous Variables

Let's our simulated agent be one of the frogs moving in the simulated ecosystem shown in fig.1 in company with three types of entity: other frogs they can copulate with, falcons they need to avoid and pears they can eat. Our simulated world is a two-dimensional grid in which each of the three possible entities occupies one cell (the dimension of the grid is 20 X 25 cells). Two types of environment are considered: 1) a static one where only one of the frogs, the one which learns, moves and all the remaining frogs, falcons and pears are motionless, and 2) a dynamic one where all the frogs can

move and learn, the falcons move randomly and the pears disappear when eaten to re-appear afterward in a random location on the grid. A frog can perceive its local environment in two different ways like indicated in fig.2.

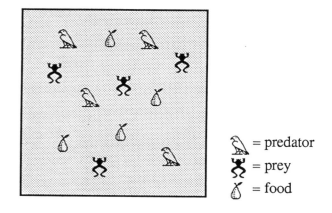

= predator
= prey
= food

Figure 1: The simulated environment

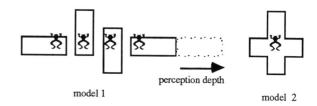

model 1   perception depth   model 2

Figure 2: The agent's perception

On the left (model 1 perception) the frog can only perceive the content of the neighboring cell in its moving direction (four possible contents by cell: nothing, a frog, a falcon or a pear) and then 16 possibilities (4 direction x 4 entities) in all. On the right the frog has a far better perception and can simultaneously perceive the content of the four neighboring cells and then 256 possible states (4 entities $^{4\ directions}$) in all. Moreover, the perception can vary in depth, the depth being, for each of the four directions, the number of cells whose content can be examined by the frog. For both models, the result of the perception in any direction is the content of the closest cell containing an entity different than nothing (if any). Obviously as the final section will show, the quality of the perception (model 2 and great depth) significantly influences the learning performance. As regards the actions, the frog can only make the classical one-cell move in the four directions (then just four actions).

So far the problem would be classical in its form and similar to a large amount of animat experiments [18] [23] : 256 perception-based different states and for each state, a slow learning process which aims at selecting the best action out of the four possible moves so as to maximize an expected utility function computed over a certain temporal horizon (like for instance the number of pears eaten). Now the description of the frogs will be enriched by adding two endogenous variables in the coding of their states: an energy-variable Xe and a sexual-variable Xs, which both can take integer values in a [0,99] interval, and are divided in 5 intervals of length 20. Accordingly, the perception-based states will be added with 25 possible endogenous states. The energy and sexual variables will simultaneously decrease by one at each time step. The energy variable will decrease by 40 when meeting a falcon. The sexual variable will reach back its superior threshold 99 when encountering another frog, and the energy variable similarly by eating a pear.

The presence of endogenous variables in the description of an agent is an important step on the road to increase the agent's autonomy, since its behavior will no longer depends only upon its perception but will largely be influenced by the state of its endogenous variables. The addition of these endogenous variables makes the resulting system to some extent similar to the sensory-motor based systems which incorporate internal goals units, like the Maes' action network [14] and Gabora's modulatory architecture [10] in which the action to be selected depends on the current goals being activated. It is also similar to Cecconi and Parisi's neural network [7] which includes motivational units in the input layer. Again, according to their activation, these units induce different behaviors in response to the same perceptions. However although these units can take numerical values in a continuous interval, they don't present the kind of homeostatic property described in the next section, since the nature of their influence is in no way related to their position in a given bounded zone, and their are not subject to any self-maintaining goal.

3. Homeostasis

The notion of "homeostasis" has been widely commented in the ethological literature (see Toates [19] and McFarland [15]) to describe variables whose temporal dynamics must be such as to guarantee their keeping within pre-determined boundaries. Since exceeding these boundaries will result either in a large discomfort or in the death of the agent, actions are taken to prevent these variables to depart from the set-value. In the systemic literature Ashby [2] is responsible for a similar notion: "*In the living organisms, the scale of values is usually related to their essential variables -- those fundamental variables that must be kept within certain physiological limits if the organism is to survive. Other organizations also often have their essential variables: in an economic system , a firm's profit is of this nature, for only if this variable keeps positive can the firm survive*".

Kauffman in a paper entitled "Principles of Adaptation in Complex Systems" [12] talks the matter over: "*Ashby's Design for a Brain is delightful, elegant, extremely clear and simple, reflecting very great care on the author's part. He sets himself the task of attempting to capture the central problem of adaptation in a system with many interacting parts ... He conceives of a system and an environment which are mutually coupled. He supposes that the system + environment, hereafter written "System" is deterministic. If released from any initial state, it will flow to an attractor and remain there. The critical idea is to suppose that a subset of the system's variables are essential variables, which must be maintained within certain bounds. For example, the critical variables might be physiological ones, such as blood glucose, body temperature, etc. For an autopilot-airplane system, the essential variables might be those characterizing straight and level flight. From the idea of essential variables which must be kept in bounds, it follows that the System after reaching an attractor, either does or does not keep the essential variables within bounds. Ashby's next essential is simple: If the System on the attractor keeps the essential variables in bounds, change nothing. Don't fix it if it ain't broke. But if the essential variables are not in bounds, then make a jump change in one of the parameters in the system. This may alter the state transitions in the system, hence alter the basins of attraction.... If the new attractor is successful in boxing the essential variables, stop changing the parameters. If not, make another step change, at random, in some other parameter. Keep making random changes in parameters, until a parameter setting is found such that the System keeps its essential variable in bound*".

In a very similar vein but in a more theoretical way, J-P. Aubin [3], in the adaptive process control theory framework, addresses the question of learning how to keep a given process within a viability domain. The problem is to find a regulation map which maps any state of the process to a subset of control actions which are viable in the sense that the process remains within the viability domain subsequent to the application of the control action. Since this regulation map is in general a multivalued mapping, a further selection policy has to be provided such as for instance control action with minimal norm, or looking for solutions complying with the inertia principle (i.e. keep the control constant as long as the viability of the system is not at stake). The classical control of the cart-pole is a good illustration of a viable control, where the objective is to keep the pole infinitely balancing (see [5] [6]). J-P. Aubin has constructed a complete mathematical framework in order to formalize the notion of viability in control theory (the design of control laws for nonlinear processes with state constraints) and its possible exploitation for macrosystems arising typically in economics, biology and complex engineering process.

In [5] [6], it is discussed how such constraint of viability might relax the objective to follow a referential trajectory for processes either too complex or interacting with an open, hard to formalize and unpredictable environment. While smoothing classical engineering objectives which are more inclined to optimize than to keep viable, this constraint fits better the objective of reliability and safety which are generally stated by the establishment of a bounded zone for essential variables of the process. In theoretical biology, Varela et al [21] attempt a connection between their study of the immune network and a related notion of viability. They identify a viable immune network as, roughly speaking, a non-collapsing (all the species concentration going to 0) and non-diverging (at least one species growing infinitely) network. Their advocated viewpoint demands to move beyond the immune system as a basic defense system essentially shaped by its external interactions, to one where the internal self-consistency is the central issue.

In the SAB community, it is quite intriguing to see that despite the emphasis on such aspect laid from the very beginning by Meyer and Guillot who recalled the Ashby's essential variables and labeled adaptive an animat which cannot transgress viability boundaries [16], homeostasis has received very scarce attention in the following conferences (except some sketchy remarks by Tyrrel and Mayhew [20] and Pfeifer and Verschure [17]). Although the profits gained by these ideas of homeostasis and viability in ethology, biology, economy, process control, etc. are today largely recognized, only recently sharp connections have been done with autonomous robot design. Arkin [1] states that for robots to be truly autonomous, they must be not just capable of intelligent action but also be self sustaining. *"A robot must be able to recognize its own needs as to fuel, component failure, and self-preservation in general .... The premise is forwarded that many aspects of self-preservation can be implemented by taking advantage of a control system analog of the endocrine system in mammals whose biological function is to maintain internal self-consistency of the organism (homeostasis) .... Since it is a fundamental goal of robotics to put intelligent machines in places where it is hazardous for humans to venture, autonomous robots must have this ability to discern their own internal states and alter their plans in a manner consistent with their own survival"*.

Coming back to our computer experiments, fig.3 shows how the two endogenous variables can take values in two different zones: a non-viable one $0 \leq Xe, Xs \leq 19$ and a viable one $20 \leq Xe, Xs \leq 99$. Initially the frog moves randomly with at each move a decrement of the endogenous variables: $Xe(t+1)=Xe(t)-1$ and $Xs(t+1)=Xs(t)-1$. When a frog meets another frog: $Xs(t+1)=99$ and when a frog meets a pear $Xe(t+1)=99$. When a frog meets a falcon: $Xs(t+1)=Xs(t)-40$. Now a frog, in order to keep viable, has to maintain these two endogenous variables in the viable

zone, something which is not guaranteed at all (as we will see later) if the moves are selected randomly.

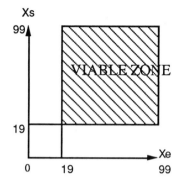

Figure 3: The Viable Zone

In consequence, the moves have to be selected in an improved way. Looking carefully at the problem, it is not, in contrast with the maze type of problem largely treated by the RL researchers, easy to find such a selection policy just by a simple observation. A basic difficulty, as the experimental results will shown, is that trying to satisfy the two constraints in a separate way leads to unsatisfactory solutions. Since there is naturally a compromise to find out between the two endogenous needs (actions need to be selected according to their simultaneous effects on the two needs), and because the way to find this compromise grows in difficulty with the complexity of the environment: dynamic rather than static, incomplete perception etc. finding the action policy by gradual learning turns out to be the only alternative, and it is the object of the next section.

4. Q-learning for the Homeostatic Endogenous Variables

Reinforcement Learning (RL) concerns a family of problems in which an agent acting in a given environment aims at improving its behavior i.e. maximizing the cumulative outcome of its actions just on the basis of poorly informative responses coming from the environment. Together with Holland's Bucket Brigade and Sutton's Temporal Difference methods, Watkin's Q-learning succeeds to evaluate actions which affect the environment response not only at the successive time step but over a temporal horizon. The agent learns a good action policy on the basis of a recursive measure available at the immediately following time step and which, through the recursive iteration, will finally evaluate the goodness of an action by estimating its effects on the overall temporal horizon. Q-learning learns to select, for each state (perceptual + endogenous states), which action to execute so that, at the end of the actions sequence, the selected action policy maximizes a utility function computed over the full sequence. Right now Q-learning has been abundantly analyzed in the literature [22] [4] [18] both in an experimental and in a more theoretical vein [22].

One basic problem when using Q-learning, and so it is in our little computer experiment, is how to determine a reinforcement measure received by the agent as a feedback of its action. Since the objective for the learning frog is to maintain its endogenous variables in their viable zone the longer the better, the type of reinforcement measure to be chosen should reflect this objective. Three possible measures of reinforcement have been tested:

Reinforcement of type 1: A positive reinforcement r=+1 is received by an action if, when following its execution, the updated endogenous variables are above 75:

- r=+1 if $\forall$ Xe(t) and Xs(t), both Xe(t+1) and Xs(t+1)>75

- a negative reinforcement r=-1 is received if Xe(t+1) or Xs(t+1) < 19

The reason for this new threshold: 75, above the viability threshold 20, for the attribution of positive reinforcement is that the agent must be able to move in search of frogs and pears, while staying viable. For this measure of reinforcement, the value 75 was among several attempts the most satisfactory one in terms of the quality of the discovered solution.

Reinforcement of type 2: A positive reinforcement r=+1 is received whenever a frog meets another frog or a pear. Again a negative reinforcement is given when transgressing the viability zone

Reinforcement of type 3: A positive reinforcement is received when meeting another frog or a pear, and the value of the reward depends on the endogenous current need. The idea is very simple: the stronger the need to be satisfied sexually or energetically the greater the value of the received reinforcement because the stronger should be the motivation to look for sources of reward.

- if Xe(t+1) = 99 and Ie being the value of the interval containing the current Xe(t) (Ie= 0,1,2,3 or 4) then: r=(4 - Ie)/4

- if Xs(t+1) = 99 with Is here again = 0,1,2,3 or 4 then r=(4-Is)/4

Again a negative reinforcement is given when transgressing the viability zone.

In the last section, the effect of choosing one among these three possibilities will be experimentally tested and discussed.

5 . The Final Algorithm

In general the category of problems which includes the application presented in this paper can be characterized by five functions as illustrated in fig.4.

Let's designated by W(t) the external world at time t and X(t) the endogenous variables:

I(t) = PER (W(t))   I(t) is the perception achieved by the agent

X(t+1) = END (X(t),W(t),A(t))   A(t) is the actions executed by the agent

A(t) = ACT (X(t),I(t))   ACT is the action selection policy

R(t) = REW (X(t), I(t))   R(t) is the reinforcement received by the agent

W(t+1) = WOR (W(t), A(t))   How the world evolves in response to the actions

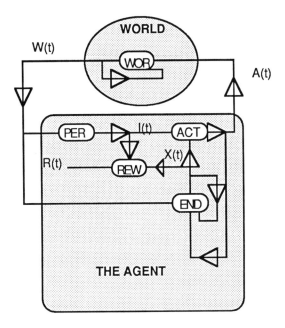

Figure 4: The General Framework

A classical problem of adaptive control is described by the evolution in time of the state variables (the END function) of a process in response to a control action A(t) and perturbed by an environmental noise W(t). On the other hand, the standard sensory-motor agent treated in the RL literature is obtained by suppressing the endogenous variables and then by eliminating the function END. Therefore the family of problems represented in fig.4 and characterized by the five functions is large enough to encompass both adaptive process control and the learning of autonomous robot.

For our little application, the final algorithm is:

```
Initialize Q-values ;
    ∀ Xe(t), Xs(t) and I(t), Q(Xe,Xs,I) = 0;
Initialize Xs (0) and Xe (0) = random in [0,99]
LOOP:
        - I(t) = Perception-state out of x,y: the coordinates
          of the agent
        - Establish the new frog state: (Xe(t), Xs(t), I(t))
        - Select the next action (a Boltzman type of
          selection has been used (see Sutton [18]))
        - Move the frog accordingly --> x(t+1) and y(t+1),
          being the new position on the grid
        - Xe, Xs <---- Xe-1, Xs-1, decrement the
          endogenous variables
    If:
        - the new position contains a pear: Xe <-- 99
        - the new position contains a frog: Xs <-- 99
        - the new position contains a falcon: Xe <-- Xe-40
        - the new position content is nothing: move the
          frog in that position
    ENDIF
        - I(t+1) = Next perception-state out of the new
          coordinates x(t+1), y(t+1)
        - Establish the new frog state: (Xe(t+1), Xs(t+1),
          I(t+1))
        - Calculate the reinforcement r
        - Update the Q-values with Q-learning:
          Q(Xe(t),Xs(t), I(t))<--(1-α)Q(Xe(t),Xs(t), I(t))
              + α (r+γMax(Q(Xe(t+1),Xs(t+1), I(t+1)))
ENDLOOP
```

6. The Results

All the results are summarized in the five diagrams of fig.5. In each diagram, the x-axis indicates the simulation time, from 0 to 200000 time steps. In the y-axis, the life-rate(t) is plotted as a function of the number of simulation steps. The life-rate is given by:

$$life\_rate(t) = (life\_time(t) - life\_time(t-10000))/10000$$

where the life_time(t) is the number of time steps the learning frog succeeds to stay viable from time 0 until the present time t. Thus the life_rate indicates the fraction of time the frog succeeds to stay viable during a given period of 10000 time steps. A perfectly adapted frog should have its life_rate equal to 1 (scaled to 100 in the graphs).

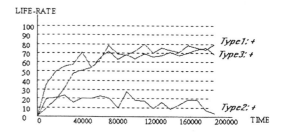

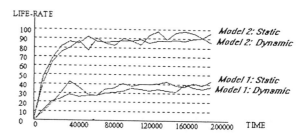

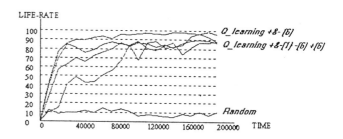

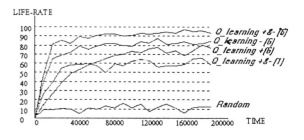

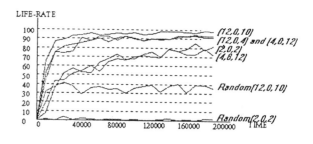

Figure 5 a,b,c,d,e: Simulation results obtained by varying the reinforcement measures, the models of perception and the environment complexity.

In the third diagram, you can see the bad performance achieved by a non-learning frog which makes a random selection of which direction to move (the curve labeled "random", its life_rate is maintained around 0.1) as compared with a learning frog which slowly reaches nearly maximal level of viability. Each diagram allows to compare the effect of choosing among various types of environment, various models of perception and various types of reinforcement.

The first diagram shows the difference in performance obtained by the three types of reinforcement policy explained in section 4. For this simulation, the environment is dynamic, all the frogs are learning (and one of them is being plotted), they are 5 pears and no falcon. Reinforcements of type 2 don't work at all. The frog satisfies exclusively one need or the other but does not discover any compromising strategy. In this particular case, it aims only at binding to other frogs and don't care about its energy variable. Since meeting another frog gives a positive reward, one very satisfactory strategy is to try to encounter as many frogs as possible. Nothing in the attribution of the reinforcement pushes the frog to simultaneously care for its two endogenous variables and the reinforcement to be received is not an explicit function of the position of the endogenous state in the viability zone. Reinforcement of type 1 and 3 work in a much more satisfactory way. The best results are obtained with the first type of reinforcement which better fits the objective to really maintain the two variables simultaneously viable, since positive reinforcement is given as long as both variables remain in their viability zone.

The second diagram shows a result which could has been expected. The action policy obtained on the basis of the more informative perception (model 2 described in section 2) is always better (both for the static environment and for the dynamic one) than the policy found with the less complete one (model 1). With the restricted perception, the results although improved on the non-learning case are far from satisfactory. Clearly a "partial observability" does not allow to discriminate between two external situations at which associated action should be distinct. The environment becomes non-markovian for the frog and Q-learning is not expected to work for such problems. In the third diagram, the environment has been kept static with here again 5 frogs and 5 pears but only one frog is moving and learning. The number in bracket indicates the perception depth discussed in section 2. "+" indicates the presence of positive reinforcement and "-" negative ones. The best result is obtained with a deep perception (although no real information is provided on the distance) and the presence of positive together with negative reinforcements. Restricting the reinforcement to be exclusively positive or negative and

degrading the perception lead to the discovery of less viable strategies. The fourth diagram shows how the difference between the strategies just discussed increase when switching from a static environment to a dynamic and thus more difficult one (in which the 5 frogs are moving irregularly and the pears disappear to re-appear in random location).

In a large part of our simulations with dynamic environment, all the 5 frogs were allow to learn. Interestingly enough in environment including multiple adaptive agents, collective phenomena occur, the less surprising being the formation of clusters of frogs moving together so as to be prompt at satisfying their sexual need. In addition, from each frog point of view, the learning progressively becomes easier since the other frogs behavior become less random and more predictable. Totally random environment is by principle impossible to interact with since no regularity can be captured on which to base and to decide a strategy of actions. Thus making all the frogs learning together allows simultaneously the emergence of collective phenomena such as grouping of frogs, and to make the environment faced by each frog more regular with consequence to facilitate their learning (which is highly sensitive to the "predictability" of what is perceived).

The last diagram again shows the effect of varying the environment complexity on the quality of the action policy to be learned. The three numbers in bracket represent: [the number of frogs, the numbers of falcons, the number of pears]. For all cases, the learning algorithm was run with the best options: positive + negative reinforcement and model-2 perception with depth 6. As expected the greater the number of pears and frogs, the easier to survive in the resulting ecosystem. With the most prodigal environment: 12 frogs and 12 pears, although worse than the learned policy (close to the optimal value reached by immortal frogs), the random choice of actions gives already better results than if less sources of reward existed. The introduction of eight falcons which randomly wander in the environment degrades the frogs viability.

7. Conclusions

This paper experimentally shows how an autonomous agent can learn to interact with a complex environment so as to maintain endogenous variables within given bounds. The learning is of reinforcement type and the best version is for the agent to be positively rewarded as long as staying more than viable i.e. with its endogenous variables above a threshold greater than the viable one, and punished when transgressing the viability zone. Expected sensitivity of the learned action policy to the "informativeness" of perception and the complexity of the environment has also been experimented. Homeostasis is a well known and well described notion in various scientific fields and its integration in animat simulation and in the design of autonomous agent was a natural attempt. Nevertheless it does not appear in related works including endogenous variables in which the connection between the action and these variables is pre-defined [10] [14] [7]. In these works, these endogenous units just serve to trigger associated actions: "drink" when unit "thirsty" is on, and "eat" when unit "hungry" unit is on. Here, not only the agent learns to eat when hungry, but also "how much hungry" must it be to look for food, and finally to organize its actions so as to maintain a satisfactory balance between all its endogenous needs.

The family of problem including the one presented here is general enough to encompass more engineering type of applications such as maintaining viable or safe complex processes subject to unpredictable environmental noise or guaranteeing the self-preservation of autonomous robots acting in rough environments. However in order to use such learning mechanisms for these more engineering applications, further questions would need to be addressed among which : how to represent these applications through the five functions given in section five, the definition of viability domains related to more real-life problems (the meaning of viable and not viable for those problems), the nature of the reinforcement for these problems, more sophisticated viability domains like several disconnected ones, the performance of RL as a function of the environment predictability and complexity, the scalability of this approach for continuous environments and continuous actions.

Acknowledgments

I would like to thank Laurent Couteau for his precious computer simulation work.

References

[1]   Arkin, R.C., 1992. Homeostatic Control for a Mobile Robot: Dynamic Replanning in Hazardous Environments - In *Journal of Robotic Systems* 9 (2), pp. 197-214.

[2]   Ashby, W.R, 1954. *Design for a brain* - 2nd imp. Chapman & Hall, London.

[3]   Aubin, J.P., 1991. *Viability Theory* - Systems & Control: Foundations and Applications, Birkhäuser.

[4]   Barto, A.G., Bradtke, S.J. and S.P. Singh, 1993. Learning to Act using Real-Time Dynamic Programming - CMPSCI *Technical Report* 93-02.

[5]   Bersini, H.,1992. Reinforcement and Recruitment Learning for Adaptive Process Control - In *Proceedings of the 1992 IFAC/IFIP/IMACS on Artificial Intelligence in Real Time Control* pp.331-337

[6]   Bersini, H. and F. Varela, 1994. The Immune Learning Mechanisms: Recruitment Reinforcement and their applications" in *Computing with Biological Metaphors* - Chpaman and Hall - R. Patton (Ed.)

[7]   Cecconi, F. and D. Parisi, 1993. Neural networks with motivational units. In Meyer, J.A. , Roitblat, H.L and S.W. Wilson (eds) - *From animals to animats 2 - Proceedings of the Second International Conference on Simulated Adaptive Behaviour* - MIT Press - pp. 346-355.

[8]   Chrisman, L., 1992. Reinforcement learning with perceptual aliasing: The predictive distinctions approach. In *Proceedings of the 11th National Conference on Artificial Intelligence*, pp. 183-188. AAAI Press/The MIT Press.

[9]   Dorigo, M. and H. Bersini, 1993. A Comparative Analysis of Q_Learning and Classifiers Systems. *IRIDIA Technical Report* - 93-21.

[10]   Gabora, L.M, 1993. Should I Stay or Should I Go: Coordinating Biological Needs with Continuously-updated Assessments of the Environment - In Meyer, J.A. , Roitblat, H.L and S.W. Wilson (eds) - *From animals to animats 2 - Proceedings of the Second International Conference on Simulated Adaptive Behaviour* - MIT Press - pp. 156-162.

[11]   Holland, J.H., 1980. Adaptive algorithms for discovering and using general patterns in growing knowledge bases. *International Journal of Policy Analysis and Information Systems*, 4, 2, pp 217-40.

[12]   Kauffman, S.A. 1989. Principles of Adaptation in Complex Systems - In *Lectures in the Sciences of Complexity - SFI Studies in the Sciences of Complexity* - D. Stein (Ed.) - Addison Wesley.

[13]   Lin, L-J. and T.M. Mitchell, 1992. Memory approaches to reinforcement learning in non-Markovian domains. *Tech.Rep. CMU-CS-92-138,* Carnegie Mellon University, Pittsburgh, PA, May 1992.

[14]   Maes, P. 1990. Situated Agents Can Have Goals - In *Robotics and Autonomous Systems* 6 , Elsevier Science Publishers B.V. (North-Holland) - pp. 49-70.

[15] Mc Ferland, D.J. 1974. *Motivational control systems analysis*. Academic Press.

[16] Meyer, J-A. and A. Guillot, 1991. Simulation of Adaptive Behaviour in Animats: Review and Prospect - In Meyer J-A and S.W. Wilson (eds.) *From animals to animats - Proceedings of the 1st International Conference on Simulation of Adaptive Behavior* - The MIT Press - pp. 2-14.

[17] Pfeiffer, R.   and P.   F.M.J.Verschure, 1993. Designing efficiently navigating non-goal-directed robots - In Meyer, J.A. , Roitblat, H.L and S.W. Wilson (eds) - *From animals to animats 2 - Proceedings of the Second International Conference on Simulated Adaptive Behaviour* - MIT Press - pp. 31-39.

[18] Sutton, R.S. Integrated architectures for learning, planning and reacting based on approximating dynamic programming. In *Proceedings of the Seventh International Conference on Machine Learning*, pp. 216-224, San Mateo, CA, Morgan Kaufman.

[19] Toates, F. 1986. *Motivational Systems*. Cambridge University Press, Cambridge.

[20] Tyrell, T. and J. E.W. Mayhew, 1991. Computer Simulation of an Animal Environment - In Meyer J-A and S.W. Wilson (eds.) *From animals to animats - Proceedings of the 1st International Conference on Simulation of Adaptive Behavior* - The MIT Press - pp. 263-272.

[21] Varela, F., V. Sanchez and A. Coutinho (1989) Adaptive strategies gleaned from immune networks, in B. Goodwin and P. Saunders (Eds.), *Evolutionary and epigenetic order from complex systems: A Waddington Memorial Volume*. Edinburgh U. Press

[22] Watkins, C. J. C. H., and P. Dayan, 1992. Technical Note: Q-learning. *Machine Learning*, 8, 3-4, 279–292.

[23] Wilson, S.W., 1987. Classifiers systems and the animat problem. *Machine Learning*. 2, pp.199-228.

An Architecture for Representing and Learning Behaviors by Trial and Error

Pascal BLANCHET

CRIN-CNRS / INRIA Lorraine

BP 239, 54506 VANDOEUVRE-les-NANCY Cedex, FRANCE

E-mail: blanchet@loria.fr

Abstract

We propose an architecture for representing and learning behaviors by trial and error. This architecture is a network of automata which is dynamically built while the system evolves in its environment. It is presented as an alternative to rule based systems which learn through temporal differences algorithms. This system learns sequences of perceptions instead of perception-action rules. These sequences represent rules of the environment, and can also be considered as production rules. The learned sequences are used for learning other sequences. An induction mechanisms is applied to produce general sequences from the different trials of the system. Different experiments has been carried out, including a block manipulation task which is described at the end of this paper.

1. Introduction

The question we are interested in, is the one of learning through interaction with the external world in a way that is as close as possible to human's one. In this paper, we focus on the following problem: given an environment with fixed rules, some goals, an input device, and a set of actions, how can a system learn by trying actions and receiving a positive feedback only when it reaches one of its goals?

The difficulty of such a problem is that the actions of the system are not always followed by an external feedback indicating whether it was good or not. The system must learn to estimate the utility of its actions from the feedback received occasionally, when a goal is achieved. This problem has been addressed with encouraging performances through Temporal Differences algorithms (TD) [11][12]. But these algorithms are limited to the task of learning reactive behaviors in markovian environments (i.e. environments where each state transition entirely depends on the current state). The problem of learning more complex tasks, through the same kind of interactions, remains unsolved.

A well known approach to this problem is the classifier system approach (CS) proposed by Holland [5]. CS are production systems which can support both knowledge representation [2], and rule acquisition through TD algorithms combined with genetic algorithms (GA). The utility of the rules created by GA is evaluated by the bucket brigade algorithm. Theoretically, any representation could be built by GA. But practically, problems occur when one tries to make CS learn a task which needs a short term memory of two consecutive states [10].

Despite the problems encountered by CS, it seems that a system capable of learning in real-world situations should also have the capability of learning through TD-like algorithms together with the capability of representing complex knowledge. But, of course, many other characteristics should be added to this same system to make it really work. Our work is an attempt to develop an architecture which must satisfy a set of competences that we think necessary for an animat. The competences we have taken into acount are the following ones:

1) Learning rules with as few trials as possible: we suppose that in any environment there may exist many rules which can be learned by simple memorization and induction algorithms. These ones must be learned with few trials.

2) Consuming as few memory as possible: When a rule is never used it must be removed. When a task has been completly learned, only the usefull rules must remain in memory.

3) Learning the effect of actions on the environment together with their utility: When the effects of the rules are known, they can be used for planing tasks.

4) Learning more than reactions to the current state: sometimes the condition which ensures the succes of an action depends on a short sequence of several consecutive states intead of the single previous state.

The reasons for these choices can be discussed by comparison with other related approaches.

Several works only focus on the problem of learning the effect of actions on the environment, such as the connectionist system SLUG proposed by Mozer and Bachrach [8]. Other systems, such as the one studied by Moore and Atkeson [7], can use what they have learned about the effect of their actions, in order to chose the best possible action in each state. For each triple (i,a,j), the system learns the probability that state i is followed by state j after the execution of action a. This knowledge provides a way to compute the utility of each state i. As a matter of fact, the utility is related to the probability of reaching a goal state g with a sequence of actions starting from i.

In the previous work, the system learns rules concerning transitions between states of a finite-state environment. But in real world problems any single state may be characterized by too numerous parameters, and the number of possible states can be considered as infinite compared to the memory capacity of our machines. An animat should be able to learn general rules concerning transitions between large classes of external states. Besides, in order to make the best use of its limited memory, it should also be able to select what is important to be learned and what can be neglected.

A system which consumes little memory in regard to the impressive results it obtains in the field of TD learning, is the one proposed by Tesauro [11] for learning to play backgammon. It is a neural network which learns to associate each state of the game to the probability of wining when this state has been observed. This system has the important generalization capabilities of perceptrons. Classes of states can be associated to the same probability.

The constraints in game playing problems are not the same as the ones encountered by animats in natural environments. One difference is that the goals of an animat may change. In a game, the final goal is fixed once for all. Therefore, it seems important for an animat to be able to use what has been learned for a particular goal, to solve other goals. This is not possible when the system only learns to associate states to the probability of reaching a fixed goal state. It seems more adequate to learn the effect of an action, then to decide if this effect is good with regard to the current goal.

Our work is also related to several other approaches, whose common goal is to explore the possibilities of representing and learning knowledge with connectionist architectures using complex automata [1][3][9]. Most of these works are inspired from the biological model proposed by Y. Burnod [6]. In this model the cortical column is presented as a complex automaton which relates perceptions to actions and goals. It is also the role of the automaton we have used in our system.

The following sections describe the architecture and the learning algorithms that we have used. The system has been applied to several learning problems, one of which is described at the end of this paper. This experiment is a block manipulation task which is similar to the one studied by Whitehead and Ballard [13].

2. Sequences of perceptions vs condition-action rules

We explain here the kind of representation we have used to take into account the following constraints :
- the same structure represents prediction rules together with production rules,
- the condition parts of rules can be sequences of states,
- rules concern classes of states instead of single states.

2.1 Perceptions and actions

Let S be the set of all possible states of the environment where the system evolves. The time dimension is a discrete sequence of instants. The state of the environment at time t is given by $s(t) \in S$.

Let F be the set of binary feature-detectors which constitutes the perceptual device of the system. Each detector of F represents a particular property of the environment, it takes the value 1 (active) when the feature is observed, and 0 (inactive) otherwise. $P(S)$ and $P(F)$ are the sets of parts of S and F. $f(t)$ is the set of feature detectors activated at time t. Each element of $P(F)$ can be related to an element of $P(S)$. For each $f_i \in P(F)$, we define $E(f_i) \in P(S)$ as the set of external states which activate every detectors of f_i. The application E satisfies the following rule :

$$f_1 \subseteq f_2 \Rightarrow E(f_2) \subseteq E(f_1)$$

We call A the set of actions that the system can execute in order to modify the current state of the environment. We consider that the execution of an action is also a property of the external environment. In order to detect the execution of an action $a \in A$, F contains an *action-detector* d_a which takes the value 1 at time $t+1$ if and only if a is executed at time t. There is one action-detector for each action in A.

2.2 Rule representation

A production (and prediction) rule r is represented by a couple of sets of feature-detectors:

$$r = (f_1, f_2),$$

where $(f_1, f_2) \in P(F) \times P(F)$. f_1 is the condition part of the rule. It is satisfied when the state of the environment belongs to $E(f_1)$. If f_2 contains one action-detector d_a (f_2 could contain several action-detectors but we have only worked with rules containing one action), then the action part of the rule is a, the action which is detected by d_a. We say that a is the action of f_2. If there is no action-detector in f_2, the action of f_2 is the *empty action*, the action which has no effect on the environment.

When (f_1, f_2) is interpreted as a production rule, it corresponds to the rule:

$$E(f_1) \rightarrow a$$

which means that a must be executed at time t if $s(t) \in E(f_1)$.

When it is interpreted as a prediction rule, it corresponds

to the rule :

$$E(f_1) \to_a E(f_2)$$

which means that if $s(t) \in E(f_1)$ then $s(t+1) \in E(f_2)$ if a is executed at time t. In other words, the effect of action a when every detectors of f_1 are activated, is the activation of every detectors of f_2. (Though the execution of a occurs at time t, the activation of d_a occurs at $t+1$. As a matter of fact, d_a is one of the effects of a).

2.3 Sequences of perceptions

Since a rule can be represented by a sequence of two perceptions, it seems natural to consider how longer sequences of perceptions, such as $(f_1,..., f_n)$, should be treated.

Let a_i be the action of f_i. In term of production device, $(f_1,..., f_n)$ means that for each i, $1 < i \leq n$, a_i must be executed at time t if for each j, $1 \leq j < i$, we have $s(t-j) \in E(f_{i-j})$. In fact, the sequence represents a set of production rules whose conditions are sequences of classes of states. If we used a more classical notation to represent these rules, the sequence $(f_1, ..., f_n)$ could be represented by this set of rules :

$$(E(f_1)) \to a_2$$
$$(E(f_1), E(f_2)) \to a_3$$
$$...$$
$$(E(f_1), E(f_2), ... , E(f_{n-1})) \to a_n$$

where a condition $(E(f_1),..., E(f_j))$ defines the *sequence of classes of states* which must be observed before triggering the action.

In term of prediction device, $(f_1, ..., f_n)$ means that if for each j, $1 \leq j < i$, we have $s(t-j) \in E(f_{i-j})$, and if a_i is executed at time t, then we will have $s(t) \in E(f_i)$. It defines a set of prediction rules:

$$(E(f_1)) \to_{a2} E(f_2)$$
$$(E(f_1), E(f_2)) \to_{a3} E(f_3)$$
$$...$$
$$(E(f_1), E(f_2), ..., E(f_{n-1})) \to_{an} E(f_n)$$

It is clear that such sequences can be used to deal with non-markovian environment where the condition of a prediction may depend on a succession of several states. But they can be useful also in markovian environment, if the perceptual device of the system is incomplete, so that the perception of one state is not sufficient to predict the next one.

3 An overview of the learning strategies

3.1 Learning markovian decision tasks in a finite-state environment.

In such an environment, it is possible to learn for each triple $(i,a,j) \in S \times A \times S$, the probability that $s(t) = j$ when $s(t-1) = i$ and action a is applied. The notation q^a_{ij} is used for this probability. Each q^a_{ij} can be estimated with the trials made by the system. Once the system has an estimation of each q^a_{ij}, it can estimate the *reward-to-go* from each state i (i.e. the utility of state i), if the reward associated to each goal state is known (Moore & Atkeson, 1993):

$$J_i = r_i + max_{a \in actions(i)}(\gamma \times \sum_{j \in succ(i, a)} q^a_{ij} \times J_j) \quad (1)$$

where J_i is an estimation of the optimal reward-to-go from state i, r_i is the reward associated to state i (for example *100* for a goal state and *0* for any other state), $succ(i,a)$ is the set of states which has already been observed after using the action a in state i. γ is a discount factor which is usually a little bit lower than *1*. This formula gives at the same time the best action to use when the state i is observed : it is the one which gives the maximum value.

3.2 Utility of sequences of perceptions

In our approach, the value q^a_{ij} has no reality since the system can only identify classes of states through its set of feature detectors F. The probabilities that the system will have to learn, concern transitions from an element of $P(F)$ to another one, with a given action. Such a probability value must be associated to each element of a sequence. For the sequence $r = (f_1, f_2, ..., f_n)$, we can define q_i as the probability to observe $s(t) \in E(f_i)$ when for each j, $1 \leq j < i$, there is $s(t-j) \in E(f_{i-j})$ and when a_i, the action of f_i, is executed at time $t-1$. It is the probability of the prediction

$$(E(f_1), E(f_2), ..., E(f_{i-1})) \to_{ai} E(f_i)$$

There exists too many sequences of perceptions to learn these probabilities for every one of them. The system has to chose which sequence must be treated.

Despite this limitation, the utility (the expected reward-to-go) of a class of states can be computed with almost the same formula, except this important difference: the summation over the successors of a sequence cannot be used, since these successors are not necessarily independent. Therefore, when there are several classes of successors, the utility should be approximated with the *min* operator instead of the Σ operator. In fact we have treated the problem of multiple successors in a particular way (as it is discussed in subsection 4.4).

Another difference concerns the discount factor and the reward associated to the goal states. We fix them to *1*, and we compute independently the expected reward-to-go and the distance of a state from the goal. There is no discount factor like in equation (1), which enables the utility value to take into account the distance to the goal together with the probability to reach it.

For example, if the expected reward-to-go in $E(f_n)$ is J_n, we simply compute the expected reward-to-go in $E(f_i)$ as:

$$J_i = q_{i+1} \times ... \times q_n \times J_n$$

or

$$J_i = q_{i+1} \times J_{i+1}$$

and if D_n is the distance of $E(f_n)$ to a goal state (according to the experiments of the system), then

$$D_i = (n-i) + D_n$$

or

$$D_i = 1 + D_{i+1}$$

We have made this choice because it is important in our algorithm to make the difference between rules which *always* work and rules which *often* work. In a deterministic environment, the first ones are real knowledge about the environment, while the second ones must be considered as short term solution until more reliable knowledge is discovered.

In this approach, the rules that have a utility value below *1* are essentially used to «guide» the system when it learns: they are used as *counter-examples*.

3.3 Induction of sequences

The system uses an induction mechanism in order to create general sequences from its experimentations. In supervised learning problems the systems have to build general representations of given concepts from subsets of examples. The simplest induction mechanism consists in eliminating the features which are not in every examples. The final representation of the concept only keeps the common features of all the examples. The same induction mechanism can be applied to build general sequences.

Let r_1 and r_2 be two sequences of length n. We define the generalization of r_1 and r_2 as the sequence r_3

$$r_1 = (f_{11}, f_{12}, ..., f_{1n}),$$
$$r_2 = (f_{21}, f_{22}, ..., f_{2n}),$$
$$r_3 = (f_{31}, f_{32}, ..., f_{3n})$$
$$\text{with} \quad f_{3i} = f_{1i} \cap f_{2i}$$

The problem is to know which couples of sequences must be generalized. We cannot generalize r_1 with r_2, if their actions are different. It would create a sequence with an empty action part, which is generally less useful than two sequences with real actions.

We distinguish two reasons for applying generalization to sequences:

a) discovering the general effect of a given action in a given context :

given $f_1, ..., f_{i-1} \in P(F)$ and $a \in A$, find $f_i \in P(F)$ so that if a is executed at time t-1 and $\forall\, j \in \{1, ..., i-1\}$, $s(t-j) \in E(f_{i-j})$ then $s(t) \in E(f_i)$

b) discovering the minimal condition in which a given action produces a given effect :

given $f_i \in P(F)$, and $a \in A$, find $(f_1, ..., f_{i-1}) \in P(F)^{(i-1)}$ so that if a is executed at time t-1 and $\forall\, j \in \{1, ..., i-1\}$, $s(t-j) \in E(f_{i-j})$ then $s(t) \in E(f_i)$, and $\forall\, (h_1, h_2, ..., h_{i-1})$ if $\exists\, k \in \{1, ..., i-1\}$, $h_k \subset f_k$, then $\exists\, t$ which verifies
  - $\forall\, j \in \{1, ..., i-1\}$, $s(t-j) \in E(h_{i-j})$,
  - a is executed at time t-1
  - $s(t) \notin E(f_i)$.

If a solution exists to the question (a), it is

$$f_i = \bigcap_{t \in Ta} f(t)$$

where Ta is a set of instants so that $t \in Ta$ if a is executed at t-1 and $\forall\, j \in \{1, ..., i-1\}$, $s(t-j) \in E(f_{i-j})$.

A similar method can be applied to find the solution of question (b) when this solution is unique, and when we know its maximal length (the length is the number of successive perceptions). If the maximal length is i-1, the solution is $(f_1, ..., f_{i-1})$, where

$$f_j = \bigcap_{t \in Tb} f(t-j)$$

where $t \in Tb$ if a is executed at time t-1 and $s(t) \in E(f_i)$.

In a goal directed learning problem, the question (b) is the more useful. It is necessary to know what is the minimal condition for a given action to produce a given goal or subgoal. The role of the induction mechanism we have used is to find this solution.

The problem of the length of the solution is treated in the following manner. The first hypothesis is that the length is *1* (the first induction steps are applied to single perceptions). Then if no solution is discovered, the hypothetical length becomes 2, and the system applies induction to sequences of two successive perceptions. The length can grow until a limit, fixed to 5 in our experiments.

When several solutions exists for (b), this induction algorithm can produce *over-generalized* rules. Such rules may fail when the system tries them. Then, they are used as *counter-examples*, in order to prevent the system from creating other rules, more general than these counter-examples.

3.4 An overview of the learning algorithm

At the beginning, the system only knows how to recognize goal states. It contains a set of goal perceptions g_1, g_2, ..., $g_m \in P(F)$ so that $E(g_1) \cup E(g_2) \cup ... \cup E(g_m)$ is the set of goal states.

The system randomly tries its actions until a goal state is recognized. If t_1 is the instant at which this event occurs $(s(t_1) \in E(g_i))$, the system memorizes the sequence of perceptions

$$(f(t_1\text{-}1), f(t_1)).$$

This new sequence is associated to the goal g_i which has just been recognized. The sequence is considered as a production rule by the system :

if $s(t) \in f(t_1\text{-}1)$, the action of $f(t_1\text{-}1)$ must be executed.

We say that this sequence is a *method* of the goal g_i. If this method is efficient (if its execution is often followed by the recognition of g_i) then $f(t_1\text{-}1)$ is considered as a new goal (a subgoal). It means that new methods are created and associated to it, each time $s(t) \in f(t_1\text{-}1)$.

The efficiency of each sequence is updated after each trial according to the success or failure of its action.

When a new sequence r_2 is about to be created for a goal g, the system checks if g already has an efficient method r_1 which uses the same action as r_2. If it is true, a general sequence r_3 is created by the induction mechanism described in the previous section.

r_3 will be associated to g as one of its methods. But before, the system checks if g has not an inefficient method, more specific than r_3, and containing the same action. If such a sequence exists, r_3 is destroyed, since it cannot be efficient if a more specific sequence is not.

Several criteria control the memorization process, so that new sequences are created only when it is necessary. For example, if r_3 is efficient, the system will never associate a method r_4 to g, if r_4 is less general than r_3.

Because of this criterion, it occurs that, after several memorization and generalization steps, no more methods needs to be associated to a given goal. The system stops learning for such an easy goal.

For a more difficult goal g (if the system always needs to memorize new sequences), the length of the methods which are associated to g, is increased. For example, if the

$s(t_i) \in E(g)$, the sequence

$$(f(t_i\text{-}2), f(t_i\text{-}1), f(t_i))$$

is memorized and associated to g. This sequence defines two production rules, one of which takes into account two successive states of the environment.

In order to save memory, the old sequences which are never used are periodically removed to make room for new ones. The «age» of a sequence is the number of time steps from its creation, or from its last successful execution.

4 The associative architecture

4.1 The units

The sequences of perceptions contained in the memory of the system are represented by sequences of automata (or internal units). We call U the set of internal units contained in the memory. A sequence of perceptions is represented by a sequence of units:

$$r = (c_1, c_2, ..., c_n)$$

where each c_i is an internal unit which contains the following parameters :

- a goal flag	$gf(c_i) \in \{ 0, 1 \}$
- a utility value	$u(c_i,t) \in [0,1]$
- a probability of succes	$p(c_i) \in [0,1]$
- a number of success	$nsuc(c_i) \in \aleph$
- a number of trials	$ntry(c_i) \in \aleph$
- a distance to a goal	$dist(c_i) \in \aleph$
- an age	$age(c_i) \in \aleph$
- a learning number	$nlearn(c_i) \in \aleph$
- a learning length	$llearn(c_i) \in \aleph$
- an activity value	$act(c_i,t) \in \{ 0, 1 \}$
- a global activity value	$gact(c_i,t) \in \{ 0, 1 \}$
- a contextual activity	$cont(c_i,t) \in \{ 0, 1 \}$

The feature detectors are also represented by units. But these ones are more simple. A feature detector $d \in P(F)$ has only an activity value $act(d,t) \in \{ 0, 1 \}$.

Each internal unit is connected to several other units and feature detectors. Each unit c_i can be associated to

- a set of feature detectors	$f(c_i) \in P(F)$
- a successor	$succ(c_i) \in U$
- a predecessor	$pred(c_i) \in U$
- a subgoal	$sg(c_i) \in U$
- a set of methods	$m(c_i) \subset U$

The sequence of perceptions represented by r is $(f(c_1), ..., f(c_n))$.

The goals of the system are represented by a set of units with a goal flag set to 1. If $gf(c) = 1$, c is a goal unit, and $E(f(c))$ is a set of goal states.

4.2 The links

The feature detectors are associated to internal units through a particular kind of links called *instantaneous links* (because they propagate the activity of the feature detectors instantaneously to the internal units).

In order to represent the sequences of perceptions, the internal units are linked together through *sequential links*. In the sequence r, there is a sequential link between each couple (c_i, c_{i+1}), and we have

$$\begin{aligned} &succ(c_i) = c_{i+1} \\ \text{and}\quad &pred(c_{i+1}) = c_i \\ \text{and}\quad &succ(c_n) = nil \\ \text{and}\quad &pred(c_1) = nil \end{aligned}$$

The last unit of each sequence is associated to a subgoal unit (a unit which has a maximal utility value, this definition includes goal units). The subgoal of c_n, $sg(c_n)$, is associated to c_n through a *hierarchical link*. Each subgoal may be associated to several units. The set of units which are associated to a subgoal g is called $m(g)$. We have

$$sg(c) = g \Leftrightarrow c \in m(g)$$

A sequence which terminates by $c \in m(g)$ is a method of g.

The figure *1* illustrates the kind of network we can build with such constituents.

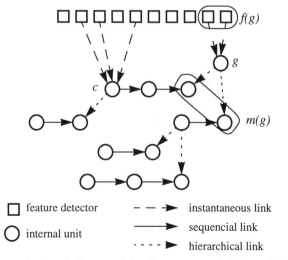

Figure 1: A typical connectivity (for a matter of clarity, only the instantaneous links of c and g has been drawn).

4.3 The algorithm

This section gives a step by step description of the algorithm.

0) The programmer gives a set of units g_1, g_2, ..., g_m so that $E(f(g_1)) \cup E(f(g_2)) \cup ... \cup E(f(g_m))$ is the set of goal states. No units are associated to the goal units ($pred(g_i) = succ(g_i) = sg(g_i) = nil$, $m(g_i) = \varnothing$). The goal flags of the goal units are set to 1 ($gf(gi) = 1$). The other parameters of gi are initialized as follows: $p(g_i) = 0$, $nlearn(g_i) = 0$, $llearn(g_i) = 2$. The remaining parameters are computed while the system is running.

The programmer also defines the size of the memory (the maximum number of units, $MaxUnits$), and the *age limit* after which a unit must be destroyed ($AgeLimit$).

1) Compute the activity values of every feature detector, according to the current state of the environment.

2) Compute the different activity values of each internal unit c

$$\begin{aligned} &act(c,t) = min_{d \in f(c)} (act(d,t)) \\ &gact(c,t) = cont(c,t\text{-}1) \times act(c,t) \\ &cont(c,t) = gact(pred(c),t) \end{aligned}$$
with $\quad gact(nil,t) = 1 \text{ (by convention)}$

3) Increase the age of each unit, and clear the memory

if $gf(c) = 0$ then $age(c) = age(c) + 1$
if $gact(c_{best},t) = 1$ then $age(c_{best}) = 0$

if $age(c) > AgeLimit$ then destroy c
if $Card(U) > MaxUnits$ then
destroy the oldest units so that $Card(U) \le MaxUnits$.

4) Evaluate the unit c_{best} ($c_{best} = nil$ at the beginning)

$$\begin{aligned} &ntry(c_{best}) = 1 + ntry(c_{best}) \\ &nsuc(c_{best}) = nsuc(c_{best}) + gact(c_{best},t) \\ &p(c_{best}) = nsuc(c_{best}) / ntry(c_{best}) \end{aligned}$$

5) Compute the utility values of each units:

if $gf(c) = 1$ then $u(c,t) = 1$
else if $succ(c) = nil$ then
   $u(c,t) = u(sg(c)) \times (1\text{-}gact(sg(c),t))$
else $u(c) = p(succ(c)) \times u(succ(c)) \times (1\text{-}gact(succ(c),t))$

6) Compute the distance to the goal:

if $gf(c) = 1$ then $dist(c) = 0$
else if $succ(c) = nil$ then $dist(c) = dist(sg(c))$

else $dist(c) = 1 + dist(succ(c))$

7) Choose the best unit (c_{best}) :

Let *Umax* be the set of units which verify:
$$c \in Umax \Leftrightarrow cont(c,t) \times u(c,t) \times p(c) = \\ max_{b \in U}(cont(b,t) \times u(b,t) \times p(b))$$

The set of units which can be executed is *Ubest*, which is given by:

$$c \in Ubest \Leftrightarrow c \in Umax \text{ and } dist(c) = min_{b \in Umax}(dist(b))$$

The system chooses c_{best} in *Ubest*, so that the condition of c_{best} is the most general as possible (the number of feature detectors associated to its predecessors is minimal). Then a random value *rv* is taken in [0,1]. If $u(c_{best}) \times p(c_{best}) < rv$, then $c_{best} = nil$ (the choice is rejected, and a random action will be executed).

8) Learn new sequences

Let *Ulearn* be the set of units to which new methods will be associated:
$c \in$ *Ulearn* if and only if
  - $gact(c,t) = 1$
  - $u(c,t) = 1$
  - $gf(c) = 1$ or ($succ(c) = c_{best}$ and $succ(c) \neq nil$)
for each c in *Ulearn*
  { create a set (*Snew*) of new sequences }
  $Snew = \varnothing$
  for $i = 2$ to $llearn(c)$
    create a sequence of units $(c_1, ..., c_i)$
    so that $f(c_j) = f(t-(i-j))$
    and add it to *Snew*
    for each b in $m(c)$
      if $p(b) = 1$ and if the action of $f(b)$ is the same as the action of $f(c_i)$ then create the sequence
      $h = (h_1, ..., h_i)$ with $f(h_j) = f(c_j) \cap f(pred^{(i-j)}(b))$
      and add h to *Snew*.
      (if $pred^{(i-j)}(b) = nil$ then $h_j = nil$)
    end { for each b }
  end { for i }
  { associate the useful sequences of *Snew* to $m(c)$ }
  for each r in *Snew*
  $r = (r_1, ..., r_k)$
  if $\exists b$ in $m(c)$ so that
    - $p(b) = 1$
    - $\forall i \in \{1, .., k\}$, $f(pred^{(k-i)}(b)) \subseteq f(r_i)$
  or
  if $\exists b$ in $m(c)$ so that
    - $p(b) < 1$

  - $\forall i \in \{1, .., k\}$, $f(r_i) \subseteq f(pred^{(k-i)}(b))$
  then destroy r
  else add r_k to $m(c)$
end { for each r }
$nlearn(c) = nlearn(c) + 1$
if $nlearn(c) = 3 \times llearn(c)$ and $nlearn(c) < 6$ then
    $nlearn(c) = 0$, $llearn(c) = 1 + llearn(c)$
end { for each c }

Each unit r_i of each new sequence r is initialized with the following values: $p(r_i) = 1$, $gf(r_i) = 0$, $llearn(r_i) = 2$, $nlearn(r_i) = 0$, $age(r_i) = 0$.

9) Execute the action
  if $c_{best} = nil$, execute a random action,
  else
  if $\exists d_a$ an action-detector so that $d_a \in f(c_{best})$ then execute the action corresponding to d_a,

10) update the state of the environment according to the executed action, and return to step *1*.

4.4 Improvements

As it is described here, the system could not learn a problem where the same action in the same condition may have different benefic effects. As a matter of fact, each unit represents the effect of its execution: the set of feature detectors which must be activated after its execution. If this set is not always activated, the unit will have a low probability of success ($p(c)$), even if another goal or subgoal is recognized at each failure.

This problem is easy to solve with a slight modification of step *4*:

if $\exists c \in U$ so that
    $gact(c) = 1$, $u(c,t) = 1$ and $dist(c) \leq dist(c_{best})$

then $nsuc(c_{best}) = 1 + nsuc(c_{best})$
else $nsuc(c_{best}) = gact(c_{best},t) + nsuc(c_{best})$

The drawback of this solution, is that once this rule is applied, the unit c_{best} does not represent a rule of the environment anymore. But in all the experiments we have done, this problem occurs only for a minority of units.

5 The experiments

5.1 The problem

This system has been applied to several different problems (see [4] for their complete description). The experiment described here is a simulation of a cube manipulation task. It is similar to the experiment described by Whitehead & Ballard [13]. The system must pick up a green cube among four cubes of different colors. The cubes are randomly stacked on a table so that the green cube can be under several other cubes. In such a case, the system must unstack several cubes before accessing the green one. There is a hand which can be moved laterally on the left or on the right. It can also be moved vertically to take or put one cube on the table or on a stack.

There is an active visual device which can be used to focus on a particular cube. Most of the perceptions are relative to the focus: the position of the hand, the number of cubes above the focus, and the position of other cubes.

In order to find a cube with a particular color, there is an action which selects the desired color. When a color is selected, the position detectors react to this color.

Finally, the problem is to learn to select the green color, to move the focus on a green cube, to unstack the cubes above the green one, and to take the green cube (figure 2).

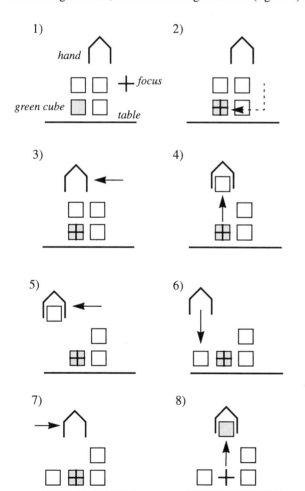

Figure 2: The system focuses on the green cube (step *2*, actions *MFB* and *MFR*), then it uses its hand to unstack it (step *3* to *8*, actions *ML, TAKE, ML, PUT, MR, TAKE*).

For this task, the system has forty-three feature detectors, including eleven action-detectors:

- *P0, P1, ... P10* detect the position of the hand relatively to the focus (*P5* is active when the focus and the hand are vertically aligned)
- *N0, N1, N2, N3* detect the number of cubes above the focus.
- *D0, D1, ..., D8* detect the position of the selected color from the focus point. *act(D0,t) = 1* when the color is in the focus. The others detect the color in each of the height surrounding directions.
- *SR, SG, SB* detect the selected color (red, green or blue).
- *HR, HG, HB* detect the color of the cube in the hand.
- *HC, HN* detect the state of the hand: *HC* when it contains a cube, *HN* otherwise.
- *MR* and *ML* detects the execution of the right and left move.
- *TAKE* and *PUT* are the action-detectors of the elementary actions *take* and *put*.
- *MFL, MFR, MFA, MFB* are the action-detectors of the focus movements: left, right, above, or below.
- *ASR, ASG, ASB* are the action-detectors of the color selections.

Two goals are given to the system:

a) the *focus-goal*: to focus on the green cube,
b) the *take-goal*: to take this cube.

They are represented by two goal-units. The *focus-goal* unit is associated to *D0* and *SG*. The *take-goal* unit is associated to *HG*. We can consider these two goals as two macro-actions: *focus-on-green-block* and *take-green-block*. The condition for the second one is the detection of the first one.

5.2 The results

The learning experiment consists in presenting a pile of blocks and waiting until the system takes the green cube, before presenting a new pile. The performance of the system is the number of actions used to get the green cube. As we can see in figure *3*, for the first piles, the system may use several hundred of random actions (sometimes more than one thousand) before taking the desired cube. After the *359*th pile, this number is definitely below *30*. This is the last time a new sequence is created. As a matter of fact, our system learns a new method only when it is not already in its memory. Since the environment is quite simple, and because the system has some generalization capabilities, the set of necessary methods is rather small.

The system learns a complete representation of the problem using a network of *148* cells and *904* links, with no redundance nor useless methods (other methods are destroyed). The *359* first problems are solved with a total of *18742* actions. As we can see on the curve, this last problem corresponds to an isolated peak. There are isolated peaks because the system cannot learn to solve a situation before it faces it for the first time. Since some situations are less frequent than others, the system may a great number of problems before facing a new one which does not match its knowledge.

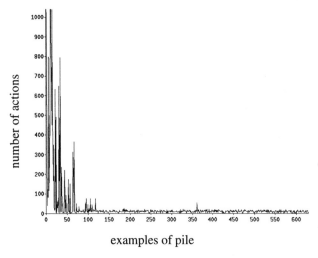

Figure 3: Number of actions used to get the green block for each example of stack.

As it was predictable, the system almost learns the whole set of methods which are necessary solve the *focus-goal*, before starting to learn methods for the *take-goal*. Once it focuses on the green cube, it starts using random actions to unstack it. Then, it often occurs that one of these random actions removes the focus from the green cube. Therefore, the system must solve the *focus-goal* again. When the *focus-goal* has enough methods, the bad effect of a random action is immediately canceled by one of them. Therefore, the only actions which have a real effect are the ones concerned with the *take-goal*. The learning rate is increased by the cooperation of the goals.

An interesting result is that the system learns long methods (with three units) to «refocus» on the green cube. As a matter of fact, when the system focuses on the green cube (which means that the selected color is green and that the position information is *D0*), and randomly chose the action which selects the blue color, it looses the information about the position of the green cube (while it get information about the position of the blue ones). But with a long method, it is possible to «remember» that before selecting the blue color the green cube was in focus. In this case a simple selection of the green color is sufficient to focus on the green cube again. Here is one of the methods which has been learned:

$$(\{D0, SG\}, \{ASB, SB\}, \{ASG, SG, D0\})$$

D0 and *SG* represent the *focus-goal*. The whole sequence

means that if the selection of the blue color occurs while the focus is on the green cube, then the execution of the green color selection, *ASG*, will be followed by the *focus-goal*.

This method which is only used to «refocus» on the green cube, is no more necessary once the system has learned every unstacking methods. It is thus forgotten several hundred time steps after the last time the system has learned a sequence.

It is difficult to compare our system to the one used by Whitehead and Ballard: the perceptual and action devices are very different. They use a rule based system which maps perceptual states to actions. It does not create general rules. But its active perceptual device provides implicit generalization of external states. Their system learns to solve *95%* (with less than *30* actions) of the presented pile of blocks after about *400* examples.

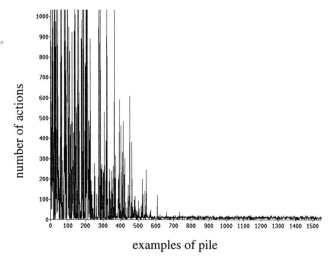

Figure 4: Performance curve in the second environment.

A second experiment has been carried out, with a slight change in the environment, so that longer methods are necessary to solve the *take-goal*. The problem is the same except that the table is smaller than in the previous experiment. For example, the green cube can be near the right border of the table, so that it is impossible to put a cube on its right side. In such a case, the action which moves the hand on the right is inhibited. Since the same problem occurs on the other side of the table, the system cannot learn an efficient method to put the block on the right side of the green cube. Moreover, there is no detector in the perceptual device to indicate whether there is room or not, on the right or on the left side of the focus. Then, the only solution is to learn a long method. The method learned by the system consists in trying to move the hand on one side, and if the action had no effect, to move the hand on the other side. Here is the method:

$$(\{HC, P5\}, \{HC, P5, MR\}, \{HC, P4, ML\})$$

HC indicates that the hand holds a cube, *P5* that the hand is vertically aligned with the focus point. *MR* and *ML* are the right and left move of the hand. *P4* indicates that the hand is on left side of the focus. The second perception, *{HC, P5, MR}*, indicates that the hand is at the same position after using *MR*. The third perception indicates that the hand is on the left side of the focus after using *ML*. To summary, this sequence means that if the left move has no effect then the right move will have. The first two units are necessary to detect the fact that the left move has no effect.

The results of this experiment are shown in figure *4*. The system stops learning after *731* problems. They are solved with a total of *103844* actions. The number of units remaining in the memory is *218*. There is *856* links. The number of actions decreases more slowly than in the previous experiment, but the convergence time is not prohibitive. It seems that learning methods with three units is not a so hard problem in this environment. But this is not true for methods with large number of units. As a matter of fact, a method can be learned only if the system can do it a first time. The probability of generating randomly a particular sequence of *3* or more actions in a particular context, may be very low if the number of actions is high. Then we cannot expect such a system to learn very long methods in a reasonable time. Despite this limitation, the experiments have shown that the capability of learning sequences with more than two units may be useful. The algorithm we propose has no problem to discover them when they are necessary.

6 Conclusions

We have described a reactive system which can learn a representation of the deterministic environment where it evolves. The behavior is represented as a succession of goals and subgoals related by sequences of perceptions representing the rules which must be used in order to get from one subgoal to another. The sequences represent the effect of their actions in the environment, and they concerns classes of sequences instead of single states. The system is also capable of learning rules which take into account successions of states. This seems to be more difficult in classifier systems [10].

The limits of the learning capabilities of our system can be characterized. Let us remember that it can learn to solve a subgoal only if it can be reached by few actions from a previous subgoal. Since a subgoal is represented by a set of feature detectors, the system can learn a given task if every property of each subgoal is detected by one the given detectors. This capability is not sufficient for learning complex tasks such as those addressed by symbolic systems. But many improvement can be done from this first version of the architecture. One idea consists in using the sequences for planning tasks. We could also try to adapt the system to real world data, using perceptron learning rule instead of classical induction.

An important observation is that it is necessary to give *a priori* goals to the system when it has to learn a non-trivial task. It is not realistic to expect such a system to learn only one complex final goal, since the system begins to learn only when this goal is observed. Thus, it seems that an animat should have many *a priori* goals such as focusing on objects, touching objects, grasping objects, moving objects... The robot would have to learn to solve these goals before trying to use them as macro-actions to solve a more complex problem.

References

[1] F. Alexandre, F. Guyot, J.P. Haton, Y. Burnod : «The Cortical Column: A New Processing Unit for Multilayered Networks», Neural Network, vol. 4, pp. 15-25, 1991.

[2] R.K. Belew, S. Forrest : «Learning and Programming in Classifier Systems», Machine Learning, vol. 3, number 2/3, October 1988.

[3] D. Béroule : «Guided Propagation Inside a Topographic Memory», IEEE First International Conference On Neural Networks, pp. 469-476, vol. 4, San Diego, California, June 21-24,1987.

[4] P. Blanchet : «Une architecture connexionniste pour l'apprentissage par l'expérience et la représentation des connaissances», Thèse de Doctorat de l'Université d'Orsay, December 1992.

[5] L. B. Booker, D.E. Goldberg, J.H. Holland : «Classifier Systems and Genetic Algorithms», Artificial Intelligence, vol. 40, number 1-3, pp. 235-282, Sept. 1989.

[6] Y. Burnod : «An adaptative neural network : the cerebral cortex», Masson, Paris, 1989.

[7] A. W. Moore, C. G. Atkeson: «Prioritized Sweeping: Reinforcement Learning With Less Data and Less Time», Machine Learning, vol. 13, pp. 103-130, 1993.

[8] M.C. Mozer, J. Bachrach: «SLUG : A connexionist Architecture for Inferring the Structure of Finite-State Environments», Machine Learning, vol. 7: 139-160, 1991.

[9] M. Roques, D. Béroule : «Strategies of Unsupervised Learning for Parallel Parsing Architecture», IJCNN, Seatle, July 1991.

[10] G.G. Robertson, R.L. Riolo : «A tale of two Classifier Systems», Machine Learning, vol. 3, pp. 139-159, 1988.

[11] G. Tesauro : «Practical Issues in Temporal Difference Learning», Machine Learning, vol. 8, pp. 257-277, 1992.

[12] R. S. Sutton : «Learning to predict by Temporal Differences», Machine Learning, vol. 3, pp. 9-44, 1988.

[13] Steven Whitehead, Dana H. Ballard : «Learning to Perceive and Act by Trial and Error», Machine Learning, vol 7, number 1, pp. 45-83, 1991.

A Distributed Adaptive Control System for a Quadruped Mobile Robot

Bruce L. Digney and M. M. Gupta

Canadian Department of National Defence, DCIEM Robotics Laboratory,
1133 Sheppard Ave West, North York, Ontario, M3M 3B9, CANADA,
and the University of Saskatchewan, Saskatoon, Saskatchewan.
E-mail: digney@dretor.dciem.dnd.ca

Abstract

In this research, a method whereby reinforcement learning can be combined into a behavior based control system is presented. Behaviors which are impossible or impractical to embed as predetermined responses are learned through self-exploration and self-organization using a temporal difference reinforcement learning technique. This results in what is referred to as a distributed adaptive control system (DACS); in effect the robot's artificial nervous system. A DACS was developed for a simulated quadruped mobile robot and the locomotion and body coordination behavior levels were isolated and evaluated.

1 Introduction

Although conventional control and artificial intelligence researchers have made many advances, neither ideology seems capable of realizing autonomous operation. That is, neither can produce machines which can interact with the world with an ease comparable to humans or at least higher animals. In responding to such limitations, many researchers have looked to biological/physiological based systems as the motivation to design artificial systems. As an example are the behavior based systems of Brooks [1] and Beer [2]. Behavior based control systems consist of an interacting structure of simple behavior modules. Each module is responsible for the sensory motor responses of a particular behavioral level. The overall effect is that higher level behaviors are recursively built upon lower ones and the resulting system operates in a self-organizing manner. Both Brooks' and Beer's systems were loosely based upon the nervous systems of insects. These artificial insects operated in a hardwired manner and exhibited an interesting repertoire of simple behaviors. Although this approach has been successful it is obvious that many situations exist where predetermined solutions are impossible or impractical to obtain. It is subsequently proposed that by incorporating learning into the behavior based control system, these difficult behaviors could be acquired through self-exploration and self-learning.

Complex behaviors are usually characterized by a sequence of actions with a critical error signal (success or failure) only known at the end of that sequence. Thus the required learning mechanism must be capable of both reinforcement learning as well as temporal credit assignment. Incremental dynamic programming techniques such as Barto and Sutton's [3] temporal difference (TD) appear to be well suited to such tasks. Based upon their previous adaptive heuristic critic [4], TD employs adaptive state and action evaluation functions to incrementally improve its action policy until successful operation is attained. The incorporation of TD learning into behavior based control results in a framework of adaptive behavior modules (ABMs) which is referred to here as a distributed adaptive control system (DACS). The remainder of this paper is concerned with a brief description of the DACS and ABMs, and implementation of the interacting behavioral levels of locomotion and body coordination on a simulated quadruped mobile robot. Other levels such as global navigation, task planning and task coordination are implemented and discussed by Digney [5] [6].

2 Adaptive Behavior Modules

2.1 Introduction

Within a behavior based control system each individual behavioral level is established through connections to the environment via sensors and actuators or to other behaviors via command signals. The individual behavioral levels of a DACS are established in a similar manner. Sensory connections are used to establish the system state, goal state, and the sensory based reinforcement vectors. Command and reinforcement connections are used to connect individual ABMs into the DACS's framework. The system state vector contains the responses of sensors which establish the system state of the behavioral level. The goal state vector contains the responses of sensors which define system state locations or transitions which may be of use to higher behavioral levels. The sensory based reinforcement vector contains the responses from sensors monitoring the condition of the robot's components that might be damaged by the actions or inactions of that behavioral level. A generic adaptive behavior module is shown in Figure 1.

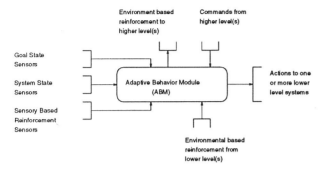

Figure 1: Adaptive Behavior Module.

2.2 Sensory Connections

For a given adaptive behavior module operating within a DACS at behavioral level m, the groups of sensory systems establishing the goal state, G^m, the system state, S^m, and the sensory based reinforcement vector, F^m, are established as follows:
For the goal state:

$$G^m = \left[\ w_g^0, \quad \cdots \quad w_g^n, \quad \cdots \quad w_g^{N_g} \ \right] \qquad (1)$$

where w_g^n are the sensors or the sensor preprocessing systems describing the goal state, and N_g is the number of sensors describing the goal state.
For the system state:

$$S^m = \left[\ w_s^0, \quad \cdots \quad w_s^n, \quad \cdots \quad w_s^{N_s} \ \right] \qquad (2)$$

where w_s^n are the sensors or the sensor preprocessing systems describing the system state, and N_s is the number of sensors describing the system state.
For the sensory based reinforcement:

$$F^m = \left[\ w_f^0, \quad \cdots \quad w_f^n, \quad \cdots \quad w_f^{N_f} \ \right] \qquad (3)$$

where w_f^n are the sensors or the sensor preprocessing systems describing the sensory feedback, and N_f is the number of sensors describing the sensory feedback.

Although these sensory connections establish the behavioral level of the ABM, they do not contribute any predetermined knowledge or external direction regarding the discovery and the learning of its skills and behaviors.

The DACS configuration requires that the attainable goal states of all of the lower level ABMs become valid commands for use by the higher level ABMs to which the lower level ABMs are connected. This currently requires the quantization of goal and system state spaces. Once quantized, the realizable goal and system states are effectively coarse coded into the following distinct states.

For convenience, in the derivations to follow, the distinct goal and system states of are represented as simply

$$g^m = \left\{ \ 0, \quad 1, \quad \cdots, \quad g^m, \quad \cdots, \quad g_{max} \ \right\} \qquad (4)$$

$$s^m = \left\{ \ 0, \quad 1, \quad \cdots, \quad s^m, \quad \cdots, \quad s_{max} \ \right\} \qquad (5)$$

where s^m is a realizable system state and g^m is a realizable goal state of the adaptive behavior module, m.

The maximum number of realizable goal states, g_{max} and system states, s_{max}, depends upon the physical capabilities of the robot and the particular environmental setting in which it operates.

2.3 Reinforcement and Command Connections

The command and reinforcement signals provide communication between the components of the DACS framework. It is through these connections that ABMs control lower level ABMs and actuators systems and, in turn, receive feedback from those lower level systems. These feedback reinforcements allow each ABM to influence other ABMs and are essential for learning, adaption and self organization.

2.3.1 Goals and Command Signals

The valid commands available for use by each ABM are determined by the realizable goal states of all lower level systems to which it is connected. For any particular adaptive behavior module, m, connected within a DACS hierarchy, the commands, c^m, that can be requested of it by higher level ABM(s) are established by the ABM's currently valid goal states

$$c^m = \left\{ \ g^m \ \right\} \qquad (6)$$

In the course of performing command c^m, module m issues action(s), a^m, which in turn become commands to lower level systems (either ABMs or actuators). The general form of this action vector is

$$a^m = \left[\ c^{o_0}, \quad c^{o_1}, \quad \cdots, \quad c^{o_j}, \quad \cdots, \quad c^{o_J} \ \right] \qquad (7)$$

where o_j are the lower level modules connected to module m and J is the number of lower level systems connected to the module m.

2.3.2 Reinforcement Signals

As the system makes the transition to a new state, three reinforcement signals are experienced: goal based, r_g^m, environment based, r_e^m, and sensory based, r_f^m. These reinforcements are combined to form an overall indicator of the difficulty, productivity or non-productivity resulting from that system state transition. This total reinforcement will be used later in Section 2.5 for incrementally evolving the system state evaluation functions.

Goal Based Reinforcement   Goal based reinforcement provides the reinforcement signal required to drive the adaptive behavior module, m, towards the commanded goal state and is defined as

$$r_g^m = \begin{cases} 0 & \text{if } g^m = c^m \\ -R_g & \text{otherwise} \end{cases} \qquad (8)$$

where g^m is the current goal state, c^m is the commanded goal state and R_g is a positive constant.

The goal based reinforcement signal can be considered the core reinforcement signal as it defines the objective of the ABM while all other reinforcements can only modify how the ABM accomplishes that objective.

Sensory Based Reinforcement   Sensory based reinforcement can be thought of as being analogous to pain and is included to condition the robot to avoid dangerous situations. Sensory based reinforcement originates from sensors monitoring components of the robot which might be damaged by the actions or inactions of the robot. In general, the total sensory based reinforcement for behavioral level m is expressed in the form of the scalar product between the sensory system's responses and a weighting vector

$$r_f^m = -(F^m \cdot R^m) \qquad (9)$$

where

$$R^m = \begin{bmatrix} R_f^0, & R_f^1, & \cdots, & R_f^n, & \cdots, & R_f^{N_f} \end{bmatrix} \qquad (10)$$

and where R^m is the vector of reinforcement values associated with the sensory based reinforcement vector, F^m.

Environmental Based Reinforcement   Environmental reinforcement reflects the difficulty experienced by the lower level systems, o_j, while performing the actions issued to them by the higher level module, m. Essentially, the environmental based reinforcement signal is the summation of all the reinforcement signals encountered by all of the lower level ABMs and actuator systems below that particular ABM. The incorporation of environmental reinforcement allows the learning mechanism to not only learn skills and behaviors, but to learn how to perform them in an efficient manner.

For an adaptive behavior module, m, connected to J lower level systems, the environmental reinforcement is the summation of all the reinforcements encountered by the lower level systems to which the ABM is connected by command signals

$$r_e^m = \sum_{j=0}^{J} r_c^{o_j} \qquad (11)$$

where $r_c^{o_j}$ is the reinforcement encountered performing the command by module o_j.

Two types of lower level systems are considered in this paper. Considered first as lower level systems are other ABMs whose actions are a multi-step adaptive process. These lower level ABMs have operating characteristics which evolve over time and whose performance depends upon each ABM's level of convergence. Considered second are the actuators whose actions are a single step non-adaptive process and whose performance is constant. By constant it is meant that the DACS has no control over the operating characteristics of the actuators, but that the actuators are still susceptible to externally originating malfunctions and changes.

For a multi-step adaptive system from the lower level ABM, o_j, the command reinforcement, $r_c^{o_j}$, is the summation of the total reinforcement over all the steps required to perform that command. For a command requiring K steps, the command reinforcement is

$$r_c^{o_j} = \sum_{k=0}^{K} r_t^{o_j}(k) \qquad (12)$$

where k is the step index, K is the total number of steps required and $r_t^{o_j}$ is the total reinforcement encountered by adaptive behavior module o_j.

For a non-adaptive actuator system the command reinforcement is simply the difficulty, as determined by some performance criteria, that the actuator encounters while performing the command. This criteria may represent the power consumed or some other relevant quantity required to perform the command.

2.4   Combining Reinforcement Signals

The three reinforcement signals will affect the operations of each individual ABM as well as that of the overall DACS framework. These three reinforcements signals: goal, environmental and sensory based, are combined into a total reinforcement signal, r_t^m. This combination is a simple summation of the functions of the three reinforcement signals

$$r_t^m = f_g^m(r_g^m) + f_f^m(r_f^m) + f_e^m(r_e^m) \qquad (13)$$

where f_g^m, f_f^m and f_e^m are scaling functions.

The functions of Equation (13) are used to scale the reinforcement signals. The relative scaling between reinforcement signals can be used to define the operating characteristics of the robot. For example, placing a high value on goal based reinforcement will result in a machine that will achieve its goal with little regard for safety or efficiency. On the other hand, placing a high value on environmental reinforcement will cause the robot to operate in the least energy expending manner with little regard for safety or achieving the goal.

2.5   Learning Mechanism

The learning mechanism employed within the adaptive behavior module utilizes an incremental dynamic programming technique. Other reinforcement learning systems using such techniques are Temporal Difference (TD) and Q-learning which have been developed by Barto, Sutton and Watkins [3]. The fundamental principle in incremental dynamic programming based learning systems is the use of adaptable state and action evaluation functions to incrementally refine an initially random action policy to one which operates successfully.

The Temporal Difference (TD) algorithm as developed by Barto [7] learns by adjusting state and action evaluation functions and then uses those evaluations to select an optimum action policy. It can be shown that the action policy can be determined directly from a single evaluation function of action-state pairs, say $Q_{s,a}$, similar to that described by Barto [7]. Given the system at state s, the action taken, a^*, is the action which satisfies

$$\max_a \{ Q_{s,a} + \zeta \} \Rightarrow a^* \qquad (14)$$

where ζ is a random valued function.

In Equation (14), $Q_{s,a}$ and ζ can be thought of as the goal driven and exploration driven components of the action policy respectively. Taking the action a^* results in the transition from state s to state v and the incurring of a total reinforcement signal r_t. The action dependent evaluation function error is obtained by modifying the TD error equation and is

$$e = \gamma \cdot Q_{virtual} - Q_{s,a^*} + r_t \qquad (15)$$

where $Q_{virtual}$ is the virtual state evaluation value of the next state v and γ is the temporal discount factor.

If action, a^*, does not achieve the desired goal, the virtual state evaluation is

$$Q_{virtual} = \max_a \{ Q_{v,a} \} \qquad (16)$$

It is easily seen that $Q_{virtual}$ becomes the minimum action dependent evaluation function of the new state, v, (remember the evaluation functions are negative in sign) and in effect corresponds to the action most likely to be taken when the system leaves state v.

If the action, a^*, achieves the desired goal, the virtual state evaluation is

$$Q_{virtual} = 0 \qquad (17)$$

This provides relative state evaluations and allows for open ended or cyclic goal states. This is illustrated by considering that for cyclic goals, it is the dynamic transitions between states that constitutes a goal state and not simply the arrival at a static system state(s).

The error is used to adapt the evaluation functions according to the LMS rule

$$Q_{s,a=a^*}(k+1) = Q_{s,a=a^*}(k) + \eta \cdot e \qquad (18)$$

where η is the rate of adaption and k is the index of adaption.

As the evaluation function converges, the goal driven component begins to dominate over the exploration driven component. The resulting action policy will perform the command in a successful and efficient manner.

In general, an adaptive behavior module will be capable of performing more than a single command. For an adaptive behavior module, m, capable of c_{max} commands, the vector of evaluations functions, $Eval^m$ is

$$Eval^m = \begin{bmatrix} Q_{s,a}^0 \\ \vdots \\ Q_{s,a}^c \\ \vdots \\ Q_{s,a}^{c_{max}} \end{bmatrix} \qquad (19)$$

Each element of the $Eval^m$ contains the evolving evaluation function and the action policy required for the performance of all the realizable skills.

3   Distributed Adaptive Control Systems

Using the ABM as the primary adaptive element, a distributed adaptive control system can be developed. Figure 2 schematically illustrates the DACS as being loosely divided into a hierarchy of interacting behavioral levels. At the highest behavior level the desired goals are specified using an externally supplied favorable goal based reinforcement signal. At the lowest level are the actuators which interact with the environment and ultimately perform these high level goals. It is the responsibility of the DACS to learn all the intermediate skills and behaviors. These intermediate behavior levels are combined in a recursive manner to form increasingly more complex behaviors. Such complex behaviors cannot be realized using a single adaptive sensory-response coupling but require interaction between two or more behavioral levels. Figure 2 also shows the conceptual reinforcement signal flow directions. Environmental based reinforcement originates at the actuators and flows upward toward the highest behavioral level. Sensory based reinforcement originates at all behavioral levels and again flows upward towards the highest behavioral level. Goal based reinforcement can be thought of as originating at the highest behavior level and flowing downward throughout all of the branches of the DACS where it competes with the other reinforcements signals to influence the operating characteristics of each individual behavioral level.

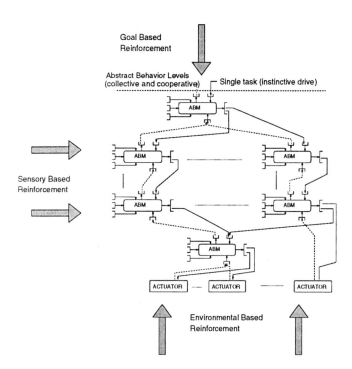

Figure 2: Schematic of Typical DACS.
Note: Reinforcement originations and flow directions indicated by large arrows.

Changes and malfunctions can confront the robot and its DACS at any behavioral level. To what extent the adaptive framework is affected depends upon the severity of the change. Two categories of change are defined: severe and non-severe. If adaption within the ABM at the behavioral level of the change's origin is adequate for recovery, a non-severe change is said to have occurred. If the adaption of higher level(s) is required for recovery, a severe change is said to have occurred.

The instinctive drive of a robot is specified at the highest behavioral levels of the DACS and establishes the purpose of the robot. For an instinctive drive, this system state transition is externally specified as being desirable and resulting in a favorable goal based reinforcement signal. This reinforcement signal will condition the DACS to perform the desired tasks. At each of the interacting behavioral levels it is left to the adaptive behavior modules within the DACS to learn the skills and behaviors necessary to fulfill this instinctive drive.

4   DACS for a Quadruped Mobile Robot

4.1   Robot Configuration

To investigate the capabilities of the distributed adaptive control system the simulated quadruped mobile robot shown in Figure 3 was used. The robot was equipped with all the actuator and sensory systems required for successful operation. It had moveable legs and

a hopper through which it could load and transport substances. If controlled properly, these actuators would be adequate for the performance of its intended tasks as well as its survival. The robot was capable of perceiving its external world using visual, sonar and tactile sensors as well as monitoring its own internal states. At the chosen level of abstraction the robot model neglected dynamics and the sensors and actuators were assumed ideal, although in other work [5] a tolerance to non-ideal sensors and actuators was demonstrated.

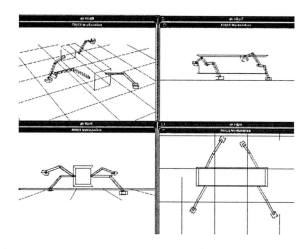

Figure 3: Simulated Robot.
Note: External sensors and actuators are not shown.

A DACS was developed for the robot which was then given an open-ended task embedded as an instinctive drive. The robot was externally rewarded whenever it eradicated an undesirable substance from its world. Once the robot was placed inside the simulated three dimensional world it was left to develop skills and behaviors as it interacted with its environment.

4.2   DACS Configuration

The DACS used to control the robot is shown schematically in Figure 4. It consists of six adaptive behavior modules distributed over the behavioral levels of locomotion (LM), body coordination (BC), local navigation (LN), global navigation (GN), task planning (TP) and task coordination (TC). The robot's actuators for its leg and loading mechanisms are shown at the bottom of that hierarchy. Figure 4 shows only the command and reinforcement signal paths between behavioral levels. In this paper only the interacting behavioral levels of locomotion and body coordination will be investigated and discussed.

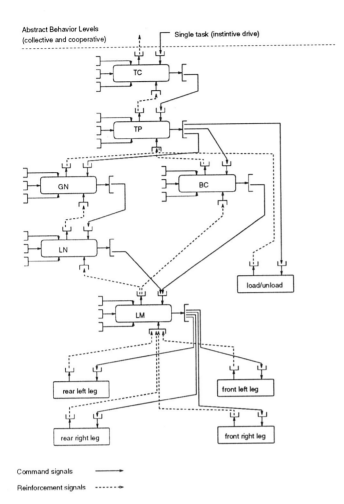

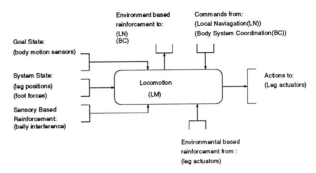

Figure 5: Locomotion ABM.

changes of the robot's body orientation that can be realized using the given locomotion system. These changes in body orientation are determined by the internal body orientation sensors and are assembled into the goal state vector

$$G^{LM} = \left[\begin{array}{c} [\quad w_g^{trans}(x), \quad w_g^{trans}(y), \quad w_g^{trans}(z) \quad] \\ w_g^{rot}(x), \quad w_g^{rot}(y), \quad w_g^{rot}(z) \quad] \end{array} \right]$$
(20)

where $w_g^{trans}(axis)$ and $w_g^{rot}(axis)$ measure the translational and rotational movements, respectively and $axis$ can be any one of the three principle axes, x, y or z.

Command Signal   For a robot in this environmental setting it is easily seen that the realizable goal states that will eventually be discovered will include forward, right turn, left turn and backward. The possible commands for use by higher behavioral levels are then

$$c^{LM} = \left\{ \begin{array}{ll} 0 & \text{forward} \\ 1 & \text{left turn} \\ \vdots & \vdots \\ c_{max} & \text{all possible modes} \end{array} \right.$$
(21)

System State Vector   Each leg is equipped with sensors for measuring the forces on each foot and the positions of each leg. These sensor responses are assembled into the system state vector

$$S^{LM} = \left[\begin{array}{c} [\quad w_s^{f_{vertical}}(leg_0) \quad \cdots \quad w_s^{f_{vertical}}(leg_3) \quad] \\ [\quad w_s^{f_{horizontal}}(leg_0) \quad \cdots \quad w_s^{f_{horizontal}}(leg_3) \quad] \\ [\quad w_s^{p_{vertical}}(leg_0) \quad \cdots \quad w_s^{p_{vertical}}(leg_3) \quad] \\ [\quad w_s^{p_{horizontal}}(leg_0) \quad \cdots \quad w_s^{p_{horizontal}}(leg_3) \quad] \end{array} \right]$$
(22)

where $w_s^{f_{dir}}(leg_n)$ and $w_s^{p_{dir}}(leg_n)$ are the leg force and position sensors, respectively.

Sensory Based Reinforcement Vector   The sensory based reinforcement originates from the body interference sensors. In particular, the belly of the robot is expected to be the fragile component at this behavioral level and a sensory based reinforcement from the body

Figure 4: DACS for a Single Quadruped Robot.
Note: Dashed lines represent environmental based reinforcement signals and solid lines represent command signals. A single goal state is defined as an instinctive drive at the highest behavior level.

4.3   Locomotion (LM)

4.3.1   Description

Although not the most efficient method of locomotion, walking provides many interesting and challenging problems for the proposed learning and adaptive systems. Quadruped walking requires the learning of complex actuator sequences in the midst of numerous false goal state locations and modes of failure. Quadruped locomotion particularly exploits the temporal credit assignment and cyclic goal capabilities of the adaptive behavior module. Shown in Figure 5 is the locomotion ABM with its sensory, reinforcement and motor action connections.

4.3.2   Sensory and Inter DACS Connections

Goal State Vector   The achievable goal states of the locomotion ABM are determined by the possible interference sensor, I_{belly}, is specified to protect it. This belly sensor detects any potentially damaging forces on the belly of the robot. The sensory system's response is

$$w_f^{I_{belly}} = \begin{cases} 0 & \text{if } I_{belly} = 0 \quad \text{Non-damaging} \\ +1 & \text{if } I_{belly} > 0 \quad \text{Damaging} \end{cases} \quad (23)$$

and the sensory reinforcement vector is

$$F^{LM} = \begin{bmatrix} w_f^{I_{belly}} \end{bmatrix} \quad (24)$$

Action Signal The locomotion action vector contains the command signals sent to each of the robot's leg actuators and is

$$a^{LM} = \begin{bmatrix} c^{leg_0}, & c^{leg_1}, & c^{leg_2}, & c^{leg_3} \end{bmatrix} \quad (25)$$

where the commands possible at each leg are

$$c^{leg_n} = \begin{cases} v_{ex} & \text{Extend vertical} \\ v_{rt} & \text{Retract vertical} \\ h_{ex} & \text{Extend horizontal} \\ h_{rt} & \text{Retract horizontal} \\ h & \text{Hold} \end{cases} \quad (26)$$

4.4 Body Coordination (BC)

4.4.1 Description

The body coordination ABM utilizes the goal states of the lower level locomotion ABM. The gaits of the locomotion ABM become the valid the commands to be used by the body coordination ABM. These movements are referenced relative to some goal substance location and are usually performed in the vicinity of local features.

When a substance of interest enters the robot's local sensor range it is the responsibility of the body coordination ABM to coordinate the body movements in such a way as to perform the commands requested of it. These commands are established by the goal state vector and are expected to include moving the robot into loading position or moving it away from the target substance. The body coordination ABM with the appropriate sensory, reinforcement and action connections is shown in Figure 6.

Body coordination is an intermediate behavior level which does not interact with the world directly, but indirectly through the locomotion ABM. At this behavioral level the complexity of the skills capable of being learned in this hierarchical structure becomes evident.

4.4.2 Sensory and Inter DACS Connections

Goal State Vector The goal states of the body coordination ABM are established by the proximity sensors which detect whether or not the substance is close

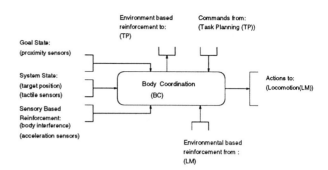

Figure 6: Body Coordination ABM.

enough for it to be loaded, w_g^{load} or if the substance is out of local sensor range, w_g^{lose}. The goal state vector is then

$$G^{BC} = \begin{bmatrix} w_g^{load}, & w_g^{lose} \end{bmatrix} \quad (27)$$

Command Signal For the goal state vector of Equation (27) it is obvious that only two possible goal states exist. These states are referred to as capture and avoid. The possible commands for the body coordination ABM which are usefull to higher behavioral levels are then

$$c^{BC} = \begin{cases} 0 & \text{Capture} \\ 1 & \text{Avoid} \end{cases} \quad (28)$$

System State Vector The body coordination system state is defined by the local sensor system (sonar) and the tactile sensors surrounding the robot. What is referred to as sonar is considered to be a sensory system capable of detecting a target substance and responding with the particular area of the receptive field that the target occupies. The tactile sensor system is comprised of eight sensors capable of distinguishing three types of local terrain features. These tactile sensors used here are a whisker contact type and are capable of detecting changes, which correspond to local features, in the ground surface surrounding the robot. Their sensory response, $f_{tactile}$, is in the form of high and low surface level signals, but for convenience they are referred to as rocks and holes. The system state vector for the body coordination ABM is then

$$S^{BC} = \begin{bmatrix} \begin{bmatrix} w_s^{sonar}(0, 0), & \cdots, & w_s^{sonar}(range, dir), \end{bmatrix} \\ \begin{bmatrix} w_s^{tactile}(0), & \cdots, & w_s^{tactile}(dir), \end{bmatrix} \end{bmatrix} \quad (29)$$

where $w_s^{sonar}(range, dir)$ is the response of the receptive field area determined by its distance from the robot, $range$, and direction, dir, and $w_s^{tactile}(dir)$ is the response of the tactile sensor corresponding to the direction.

Sensory Based Reinforcement Vector For the body coordination ABM, the components considered to be in danger are the body and the internal components of the robot. The body is in danger from colliding with hard surfaces and is protected by sensory based reinforcement signals from the side interference sensors, I_{side}. The internal workings are in danger from excessive accelerations and are protected by sensory based reinforcement signals from the acceleration sensors, a_{quad}.

The interference sensors, I_{side}, detect damaging forces on the sides of the robot and respond as follows

$$w_f^{inter}(side) = \begin{cases} 0 & \text{if } I_{side} = 0 \text{ No damage} \\ 1 & \text{if } I_{side} > 0 \text{ Damage} \end{cases} \quad (30)$$

where

$$side = \begin{cases} 0 & Front \\ 1 & Right \\ 2 & Rear \\ 3 & Left \end{cases} \quad (31)$$

The purpose of the robot's internal acceleration sensors is to supply sensory based reinforcement signals which conditions the DACS to avoid dangerous accelerations by avoiding whatever situations are found to cause them. For example, such accelerations may occur when the robot falls either down a cliff or into a hole. This sensor is described in Equation (32).

$$w_f^{a_{quad}} = \begin{cases} 1 & \text{if } a_{quad} > a_{max} \\ 0 & \text{if } a_{quad} < a_{max} \end{cases} \quad (32)$$

where a_{quad} is the robot's acceleration and a_{max} is the maximum allowable acceleration.

The sensory based reinforcement vector is then

$$F^{BC} = \left[\begin{array}{c} [\ w_f^{inter}(front), \ \cdots, \ w_f^{inter}(side)\ ] \\ [\ w_f^{a_{quad}}\ ] \end{array} \right] \quad (33)$$

Action Signal   The action vector is simply the currently realizable commands of the locomotion ABM.

$$a^{BC} = \left[\ c^{LM}\ \right] \quad (34)$$

5 Simulation and Results

5.1 Locomotion

5.1.1 Physical Constraints and Assumptions

The responsibility of the locomotion ABM was to learn the actuator sequences which enabled the robot to operate using all of the realizable gaits. Quadruped locomotion over a solid surface involved both balance and movement in the desired direction. The robot was assumed to be balanced, with its body free of contact with the surface of the world when a straight line could be drawn between any two legs in contact with the ground that

passed through the robot's center of gravity. In effect, at least two diagonally opposite legs had to be in contact with the ground at the same time for the robot to be balanced. In this simulation, the quadruped mobile robot was assumed to be moving if all the legs in contact with the ground were applying forces such that their collective effort resulted in the desired motion of the robot body. No movement occurred if any leg was applying a force that opposed the desired motion and a reinforcement of R_{high} was then sent from that actuator. R_{nom} and R_{high} reinforcements resulted from the normal and restricted or over-extended leg actuator movements, respectively. Sensory based reinforcement was used to condition the robot to walk in a safe manner. When operating on a solid surface, the safety of the robot required that the robot move with its body free of the ground. Hence, any resulting gaits which the robot learned had to also suspend and balance the robot above the ground. The body interference sensor on the belly of the robot supplied R_{high} sensory based reinforcement when it was in contact with a damaging surface and 0 when the robot was safely suspended.

5.1.2 Results

The locomotion ABM quickly discovered and learned gaits. Initially, the leg movements were random as the robot began exploring both its own internal operating characteristics and its external surroundings. As the locomotion ABM gained experience, four realizable gaits emerged. Once the robot had mastered all of its realizable gaits, an internal malfunction was introduced. This malfunction specifically involved the disabling of the horizontal actuator on a single leg. Effectively, the robot was then capable of only supporting itself and incapable of applying any horizontal forces with that disabled leg. After a short period of adaptation the robot recovered and had re-learned all the gaits and transitions. If the malfunction had rendered the robot incapable of a previously learned gait, adaption of higher behavioral level(s) would have been required and a severe change would have occurred.

Figure 7 shows the total reinforcement signal experienced during the initial learning and recovery from this malfunction. The vertical axis of this performance curve shows the unscaled total reinforcement occurring for each successful step taken and the horizontal axis indicates the number of steps taken. In this plot the robot was alternating between gaits at ten step intervals. This allowed for transitions between gaits to be learned and investigated as well. Gait learning was evident in the rapid improvement section of Figure 7, while the section of slower improvement was where the gait transitions were learned.

The converged leg sequence for the intact forward gaits is shown in Figure 8. Considering the end of the robot

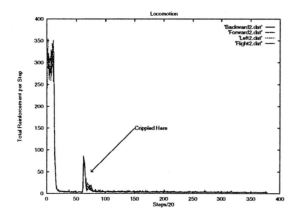

Figure 7: Performance of the Locomotion ABM.

closest to the reader as the front, leg_0, leg_1, leg_2 and leg_3 are the right front, left front, left rear, and right rear legs, respectively. The actuator extensions, v_{ex} and h_{ex}, resulted in downward and forward movements of a leg, respectively. The actuator retractions, v_{rt} and h_{rt}, resulted in upward and backward movements of the leg, respectively. The intact forward gait's command and reinforcement signals are listed in Table 1.

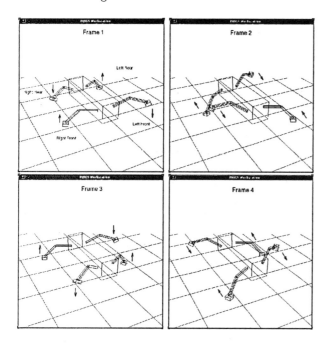

Figure 8: Leg Sequence of Locomotion ABM: *Forward*
Note: Action sequence, frame 1, 2, 3, 4, 1, $\cdots$.

5.2   Body Coordination

5.2.1   Physical Constraints and Assumptions

Once a substance was detected within range of the local sensor system, it became the responsibility of the

Table 1: Command Sequence: *Forward Gait.*

Frame	Actions				Reinforcements		
k	c^{leg_0}	c^{leg_1}	c^{leg_2}	c^{leg_3}	r_e	r_g	r_s
1	v_{rt}	v_{ex}	v_{rt}	v_{ex}	R_{nom}	R_g	0
2	h_{ex}	h_{rt}	h_{ex}	h_{rt}	R_{nom}	0	0
3	v_{ex}	v_{rt}	v_{ex}	v_{rt}	R_{nom}	R_g	0
4	h_{rt}	h_{ex}	h_{rt}	h_{ex}	R_{nom}	0	0

body coordination ABM to coordinate the robot's actions such that useful behaviors resulted. These behaviors included the learning of movement sequences to either capture or avoid the target substance.

Contact of the robot body with a rock was considered damaging and undesirable. Any such contact was detected or felt by the body interference sensors and resulted in a R_{high} sensory based reinforcement signal. Furthermore, the presence of a rock physically prevented further motion in that direction. Contact with a hole was also considered undesirable and resulted in R_{high} sensory based reinforcement from the internal acceleration sensors. However, the robot could continue on and traverse the hole, whereas it could not continue through a rock.

5.2.2   Results

When considering the two realizable behaviors of avoid and capture, it was seen that the capture behavior required the learning of the most challenging and interesting movement strategies, while the avoid behavior simply resulted in the robot scurrying away from the target. Therefore, the more difficult capture behavior was chosen to be examined in detail. To make this behavior even more difficult, the robot was considered permanently incapable of performing the backward gait.

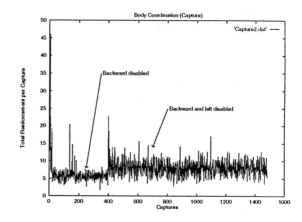

Figure 9: Performance of the Body Coordination ABM.

The performance of the robot at learning the capture behavior is shown in Figure 9. The vertical axis shows the un-scaled total reinforcement encountered per target capture and the horizontal axis indicates the current capture attempt. This plot shows initial poor performance which eventually improved to some optimum performance. In addition to having the backward gait disabled, the robot then had its left turn gait disabled. The body coordination ABM then relearned the capture behavior with only the forward and right turn gaits available. Initially the robot wandered around unproductively, hitting rocks and going through holes. Eventually a safe, efficent and productive capture behavior was learned as indicated in Figure 10 and Table 2.

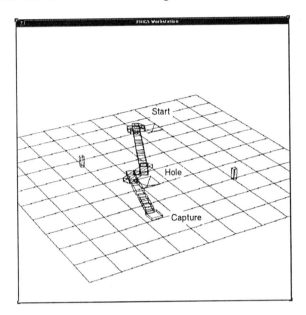

Figure 10: Capture Behavior. Note: Rocks are represented by tall blocks, holes by inverted pyramids, targets by flat plates and the moving robot by the sequence of long blocks.

Table 2: Command Sequence: *Final Capture Behavior*.

Step k	Actions c^{LM}	Reinforcements			Comments
		r_e	r_g	r_s	
1	*left*	R_{nom}	R_g	0	In line with target
2	*forward*	R_{nom}	R_g	0	Contacts hole
3	*right*	R_{nom}	R_g	0	Turns to avoid hole
4	*forward*	R_{nom}	R_g	0	Goes around hole
5	*left*	R_{nom}	R_g	0	In line with target
5	*forward*	R_{nom}	R_g	0	Target close
6	*forward*	R_{nom}	0	0	Target captured

6 Conclusions

The research described in this paper was initiated to realize a higher level of autonomy in robotic and control systems. This resulted in an intelligent robot capable of autonomously learning tasks bounded by its sensory and physical capabilities. This increase in autonomy was attained by the incorporation of biological and physiolog-

ical motivated learning and adaption schemes within the robot's control system rather than by simply increasing the amount of predetermined and embedded information. The robot learned what it needed during operation and was not burdened by, or limited to the predetermined actions and responses of its designers.

It is conceded that the level of abstraction used in these simulations is a significant departure from reality. These simplifications were necessary for these preliminary investigations. Current work in continuous state and actions spaces, emergent structures, robot conditioning and implementation on a real robot has all grown out of these preliminary studies.

References

[1] Brooks, R. (1986), A Robust Layered Control System For A Mobile Robot, *IEEE Journal of Robotics and Automation*, Vol. 2, no. 1, pp. 14-23.

[2] Beer, R.D., Chiel, H.J., and Sterling, L.S., (1990), A Biological Perspective on Autonomous Agent Design, *Robotics and Autonomous Systems*, Vol. 6, pp. 169-186.

[3] Barto, A.G., Sutton R.S. and Watkins C.H. (1989), Learning and Sequential Decision Making, *COINS Technical Report*.

[4] Barto, A.G., Sutton, R.S., and Anderson, C.W. (1983), Neuronlike Adaptive Elements That Can Solve Difficult Learning Control Problems, *IEEE Transactions on Systems, Man, and Cybernetics SMC-13*, pp. 834-846.

[5] Digney, B.L. (1994) Emergent Intelligence in A Distributed Adaptive Control System. *Ph.D. Thesis*, University of Saskatchewan, Saskatoon, SK, CANADA.

[6] Digney B. L., (1993) A Distributed Adaptive Control System for a Quadruped Mobile Robot, *IEEE Conference on Neural Networks*, San Francisco, March 1993, pp. 144-150.

[7] Barto, A.G., Bradtke S.J., and Singh S.P. (1991), Real-time Learning and Control Using Asynchronous Dynamic Programming, *University of Amherst Technical Report 91 - 57*.

Reinforcement learning with dynamic covering of state-action space : Partitioning Q-learning

Rémi Munos[1&2] and **Jocelyn Patinel**[1]

(1) CEMAGREF, Artificial Life and Artificial Intelligence Laboratory
Parc de Tourvoie, B.P. 121, 92185 Antony Cedex, FRANCE
Tel : (33-1) 40 96 61 21   Fax : (33-1) 40 96 60 80
E-mail : rm@cemagref.fr
(2) DASSAULT-AVIATION, DGT-DEA-IA2
78, Quai Marcel Dassault, 92214 Saint-Cloud, FRANCE
Tel : (33-1) 47 11 54 38   Fax : (33-1) 47 11 52 83

Abstract

This paper presents a reinforcement learning algorithm : "Partitioning Q-learning", designed for generating an adaptive behavior of a reactive system with local perception in a complex and changing environment. This algorithm includes two dynamics : the learning dynamics based on the Q-learning and Bucket Brigade algorithms, and the structural dynamics (the partitioning of regions of the state-action space) that modelizes the acquisition of expert knowledge. The combination of these two dynamics intends to solve the problem of the combinatory explosion of the number of qualities to be estimated (the generalization problem), by dividing the state-action space into a minimal number of homogeneous regions using the formalism of Classifier Systems. This algorithm is applied to the simulation of a reactive robot which tries to cut weeds and to avoid plants in a cultivated field.

Introduction

We consider a reactive system built with a set of simple rules, i.e. a Classifier System (see [Goldberg,1989]), which tries to solve an adaptive task defined in terms of reinforcement. The adaptation consists of two dynamical processes :
- the *learning dynamics* : for a given set of rules (which defines a covering of the state space), it modifies the parameters according to reinforcements from the environment.
- the *partitioning dynamics* : it starts with a general, non relevant set of rules (knowledge of a novice) and builds an accurate and relevant one (knowledge of an expert) through a selection-specialization process (which specializes general rules leading to heterogeneous reinforcements).
These two dynamics are called *Partitioning Q-learning* (see [Munos, 1992]).

The rules selected are the ones which extract relevant information among all the available and lead to good reinforcement. They emerge and acquire significance in the environment thanks to reinforcement.

Section 1 deals with learning dynamics. It introduces Q-learning [Watkins,1989], its limitation due to the combinatory explosion of the number of qualities to be estimated in non-simple applications, and some ways to overcome this problem. The Bucket Brigade algorithm and its similarities with Q-learning are presented. Our solution : "Partitioning Q-learning", which takes advantage of both algorithms, uses a covering of the state-action space with a minimal number of homogeneous regions, using the formalism of Classifier Systems.
Section 2 is about partitioning dynamics. It explains which classifiers are specialized and how.
Section 3 presents an application of Partitioning Q-learning to the simulation of an autonomous robot moving around in a cultivated field and trying to cut weeds while avoiding plants.

Previous related work

The reinforcement learning algorithms described in this paper originate from the neurophysiological models of pavlovian conditioning (see for example Sutton and Barto (1990) who describe the Rescola-Wagner model [Rescola and Wagner,1972] as a time derivative theory of reinforcement). In the field of Genetic Algorithms, this led to the Bucket Brigade algorithm in Classifier Systems (see [Goldberg,1989] and [Wilson and Goldberg,1989]). Closely related to the control theory, Barto, Sutton and Anderson (1983) defined a reinforcement learning algorithm using both an evaluation function (Adaptive Critic Element) and a control unit (Associative Search Element). Watkins (1989) proposed the Q-learning algorithm as an alternative which uses only one structure : the quality function (estimating the state-action pairs). These algorithms are forms of Temporal Differences methods (see [Sutton,1988]).

A limitation of Q-learning is the increase of the learning time with the size of the state-action space. Many attemps to speed up Q-learning have been proposed (see [Kaelbling,1993] for a review). One way is to build a world model : Dyna-Q [Sutton,1990] appoximates the world dynamics in order to learn from hypothetical experiences. Lin (1992) uses past experiences to do an "experience replay" in a neural network structure. Moore (1991) uses Variable Resolution Dynamic Programming for generating mental trajectories and defining a variable resolution state space. McCallum (1992) diffuses qualities according to transitional proximity in state space.

Another possible approach is to reduce the number of evaluated parameters in Q-learning, either by estimating the quality function with neural networks (see for example [Lin,1992]) or by clustering states of homogeneous qualities. Whereas Mahadevan and Connell (1991) aggregate individual states into statistical clusters, our method in this paper is to partition large regions into specialized ones according to some reinforcement dissimilarity criterion. Tan (1991) uses cost-sensitive Q-learning, that is cost-effective sensing features of the external world are selected in order to build a consistent internal state representation. The application of a new sensor is similar to our specialization operator, but Tan's criterion differs from ours in that it is based on the application cost of a sensor.

In the later discussion, we compare our work with the one of Chapman and Kaelbling (1991) which is closely related.

1. Learning dynamics

1.1 Reinforcement learning

Reinforcement learning is a learning process inspired by experimental psychology which applies when the amount of available information is poor : a qualitative evaluation (called reinforcement or reward) of some states of the system. The objective of learning is to build an optimal policy given the available information, i.e. a mapping from each situation to an action so as to optimise a function of obtained reinforcements during sequences of actions (and thus solve the temporal credit assignment problem [Sutton,1984]).

To reach this goal, the system has to mix an exploration phase of its environment, in order to build an evaluation function that gives the long-term expected reinforcement, and an exploitation phase which optimise obtained reinforcements by choosing at each time the action leading to the state of highest evaluation.

1.2. Introduction to Q-learning

1.2.1. Caracteristics of the Q-learning algorithm :

Q-learning is a reinforcement learning algorithm created by Watkins (1989) which uses one structure : the quality function.

Let X be the state space of the system and A its action space. A *policy* is a mapping from X to A. A *trajectory* is a sequence of states followed by the system. The aim of learning is the building of a policy that optimises reinforcements obtained along trajectories. To reach this goal, the system associates a value (called quality : $Q_{\mathbf{x},a}$) to each state-action combination $\mathbf{x}, a$; this value has to be estimated and represents the long-term discounted expected reinforcement when the system is in state $\mathbf{x}$ and does action a. The value $Q_{\mathbf{x},a}$ should be the sum of the reinforcement obtained by doing action a and the discounted best quality $Q_{\mathbf{y},b}$ of the resulting state $\mathbf{y}$:

$$Q_{\mathbf{x},a} \text{ "should be" } \gamma.Q_{\mathbf{y},b} + r(\mathbf{x}, a)$$

where γ is a discount factor ($0 \le \gamma < 1$) which lessen the weights of later rewards with respect to immediate ones in order that qualities take reinforcement delay into account. When the system has learned such an evaluation function, it can run along optimal trajectories by choosing the action of best quality at each time.

1.2.2. Learning rule

Suppose that the system is in state $\mathbf{x}$. Choosing action a may be :
- deterministic : a is such that

$$Q_{\mathbf{x},a} = \max_{a' \in A} Q_{\mathbf{x},a'}$$

- probabilistic (in order to improve the exploration of the environment) : a is chosen with a probability function of $\{Q_{\mathbf{x},a'}\}_{a' \in A}$, for example, with a Boltzmann distribution :

$$P(a \mid \mathbf{x}) = \frac{e^{\beta.Q_{\mathbf{x},a}}}{\sum_{a' \in A} e^{\beta.Q_{\mathbf{x},a'}}}$$

Then the system goes to a new state $\mathbf{y}$ and gets a reinforcement r from the environment.
The modification law of the quality is :

$$Q_{\mathbf{x},a} \leftarrow Q_{\mathbf{x},a} + a \, (\gamma Q_{\mathbf{y},b} - Q_{\mathbf{x},a} + r)$$

where a is the learning rate, g the discount factor and b is the action of best quality in state $\mathbf{y}$:

$$Q_{\mathbf{y},b} = \max_{b' \in A} Q_{\mathbf{y},b'}$$

1.2.3. Limitations and improvement of Q-learning

This algorithm is very efficient when the state-action space and the number of intermediate states before getting a reinforcement are small. Unfortunately, the increasing of the size of the state-action space (and thus the number of qualities to be fixed) leads to a learning time too high to allow the processing of non-simple applications. There are several ways to overcome this limitation, whose common idea is to make some assumption on the smoothness of the quality function in order to reduce the number of parameters.

One possible approach is to code the evaluation function in a neural network (See [Lin,1992]). Either a single network maps the inputs $(\mathbf{x},a)$ to the qualities $Q_{\mathbf{x},a}$ or several networks, one for each action a, map the inputs $\mathbf{x}$ to the qualities $Q_{\mathbf{x},a}$. This may reduce the number of parameters but a new problem arises : we need to make some a-priori hypotheses about the regularities of the quality function in order to choose the appropriate structure of the neural networks.

Another appoach is to work on a variable resolution state space (see for example [Moore,1991], [Chapman and Kaelbling,1991], [Mahadevan and Connell,1991]). Our work uses this idea for partitioning the state-action space : we assign a quality to a region of the state-action space rather than to each state, thus reducing the number of values to be fixed. Besides, the partitioning is dynamic : the subsets are built and modified continuously in order to enclose states whose expected reinforcements are similar.

We choose to represent these regions within the formalism of classifier systems and so we establish a connection between the Q-learning and the Bucket Brigade algorithms.

1.3. Classifier Systems and the Bucket Brigade algorithm

1.3.1. Characteristics of classifier systems

The Bucket Brigade is a reinforcement learning algorithm which is generally used within the framework of classifier systems (see [Goldberg,1989], [Holland,1985], [Wilson and Goldberg,1989]).

A classifier system consists of a set of reactive rules (classifiers) of the following type :

Rule R_i : if state $\mathbf{x}$ belongs to subset X_i

then do action a.

where $\mathbf{x}$ is the current state (or message) of the state space X $(=\{0,1\}^n)$, a is the action (of action space A) which modifies the current state, X_i is the set of the states which match the conditional part of rule R_i, written $c_1c_2...c_n$ with c_k Œ $\{0,1,\#\}$:

$$X_i = \{ (x_1,x_2,...,x_n) \in X \text{ s.t. } x_k = c_k \text{ if } c_k = 0 \text{ or } 1\}$$

For example, condition 10#0# defines subset : {10000, 10001, 10100, 10101}. Besides, a strength (or fortune) f_i is attributed to R_i.

It is useful to represent state and action in the same space. So we define $Z = X \times A$ the state-action space, and $Z_i^a = (X_i,a)$ the region defined by R_i. For our problem, space X

represents the perceptive space of a robot. So, for each action a, we need to have a covering of (X,a) by the regions $\{Z_i^a \}_i$ so that in any state, at least one rule of each action can be applied.

1.3.2. Bucket Brigade algorithm

The environment provides the system with some perceptive data, which define state $\mathbf{x_1}$. Among all rules that match $\mathbf{x_1}$: $\{R_i / \mathbf{x_1} \in X_i\}$ the system chooses one, say R_1 (either in a deterministic way : the one of highest strength, or in a probabilistic way, for example with a Boltzmann distribution). R_1 leads to action a_1 whose effect is to move the system into a new state $\mathbf{x_2}$. The action brings a reinforcement r from the environment (equal to zero if there is no reinforcement). Then, in the same way, rule R_2 is chosen.

The law for the modification of the classifier strengths f_1 and f_2 is :

$$f_1 \leftarrow f_1 + c.(f_2 + r)$$
$$f_2 \leftarrow f_2 - c.f_2$$

(Rule R_2 pays a fraction c of its fortune to R_1 to "thank" it for giving R_2 a message it has dealt with).

The idea which has motivated the elaboration of this law is that the system should be able to anticipate rewards (by assigning credit upon sequences of actions) ; this is very close to the aim of Q-learning, i.e. the building of a long-term expected reinforcement function.

Remark : the Bucket Brigade algorithm presented here slightly differs from the one defined in [Goldberg,1989] in that, in this version, only one classifier (instead of every classifier matching a given message) pays a fraction of its fortune at a time. Besides, here, there are no internal messages.

1.4. Partitioning Q-learning

1.4.1. Connection between Bucket Brigade and Q-learning

Let us consider the strength modification of R_2, resulting of two consecutive modifications when the system applies the sequence of rules $R_1 R_2 R_3$ (doing actions a_1 and a_2 and obtaining reinforcements r_1 and r_2) :

First modification :

$$f_1 \leftarrow f_1 + c.(f_2 + r_1)$$
$$f_2 \leftarrow f_2 - c.f_2 \qquad \text{after choosing } R_2$$

then:
$$f_2 \leftarrow f_2 + c.(f_3 + r_2)$$
$$f_3 \leftarrow f_3 - c.f_3 \qquad \text{after choosing } R_3$$

The resulting modification of f_2 is :

$$f_2 \leftarrow f_2 + c.(f_3 - f_2 + r_2)$$

which is very similar to the Q-learning modification rule without the discount factor γ.

Partitioning Q-learning takes some advantages of both Q-learning and Classifier Systems :

- it uses a covering $\{Z_i{}^a\}$ of the state-action space, like Classifier Systems, in order to reduce the huge number of qualities to be estimated in Q-learning,
- it includes a discount rate γ so that qualities converge towards an evaluation function that takes reward delay into account.

The linking of these two learning algorithms may be useful to the theory of Bucket Brigade (by transposing theoretical analysis already available in Q-learning, see [Watkins and Dayan,1992], [Dayan,1992], [Saurel,1992]) as well as to the application of Q-learning (which suffers from slow convergence in non-trivial problems).

1.4.2. Partitioning Q-learning

Here are the characteristics of the learning dynamics of Partitioning Q-learning : X is the state space, A is the action space and $Z = X \times A$ is the state-action space. $\{X_i\}_{i \in I}$ are subsets of X with $I = \cup I_a$ where I_a is the set of indices i of rules R_i whose action is a.

For all $a \in A$, let : $Z^a = (X, a)$ and region $Z_i^a = (X_i, a)$.

We suppose further that $\{Z_i^a\}_{i \in I_a}$ covers Z^a.

Rule i is defined by the region $Z_i{}^a$ and is attributed a strength f_i and means : *if $x \in X_i$ then do action a*.

When the system is in $x \in X_i$ and does action a according to rule i, it moves to y and gets a reinforcement r. Then, the strength modification law is :

$$f_i \;\text{''}\; f_i + \alpha \;(\gamma f_{\mathbf{max}} - f_i + r)$$

with :
- f_i the strength attributed to rule R_i.
- $f_{\max}$ the maximum, for all actions b, of strengths f_j attributed to rules R_j whose regions Z_j^b include (y, b) :

$$f_{\max} = \max_{b \in A,\, j \in I_b \,\text{s.t.:}\, (y, b) \in Z_j^b} (f_j)$$

The efficiency of the learning dynamics depends on the subdivision of Z^a into regions $Z_i{}^a$ for all a, which has to be minimal and regroup states of homogeneous evaluation.

The subdivision process has to be dynamical so that it allows an adaptation to the environment. This leads to the partitioning dynamics explained in the next section.

2. Partitioning dynamics

We have a set of rules defining a covering of the state-action space. These rules are regularly modified by a selection-specialization process which creates and eliminates some of them according to some criterions. This dynamics intends to modelize a cognitive process that ensures the transition from novice to expert knowledge.

2.1. Specialization operator

We need to partition our state-action space into homogeneous regions of the largest possible size, so that the number of qualities (or strengths) to be estimated should be minimum. In particular we need a criterion allowing us to determine which regions have to be divided.

2.1.1. Specialization criterion

In order to obtain homogeneous regions we subdivide the most heterogeneous ones, i.e. those whose action induces variable rewards in time. Thus we choose as criterion a pseudo standard deviation of the long-term expected rewards obtained by applying a rule.

$$Criterion = \frac{1}{n} \sum_{i=1}^{n} \left[\gamma . f_{\max}(t_i) + r(t_i) - \gamma . f_{\max}(t_{i-1}) - r(t_{i-1}) \right]^2$$

where $t_0, t_1, ..., t_n$ are the successive times when the considered rule has been used during the training period. The choice of the rules to be specialized is made according to a Boltzmann probability distribution upon this criterion (note that a single rule can be chosen several times, and specialized in different ways).

2.1.2. Validation of the specialization : the selection operator

The partitioning of the space leads to a thiner and thiner partition, thus multiplying the number of regions. Yet we wish to reduce this number at a minimum ; we therefore need a mecanism to regroup resembling regions and to eliminate unnecessary subdivisions. This is realized by a unique mechanism : the selection operator.

After a number of iterations of the learning algorithm sufficient to give reliable values of the qualities for a given covering, a selection is made among the rules : a rule is kept only if there is not any "more general" rule (i.e. defined by a region including the one of the less general rule) of higher strength.

Remark : the specialization operator can generate rules that apply to a region of the state space that is never encountered by the system during the learning period. These rules are eliminated by the selection operator.

Once selection has been made, a new specialization process applies to the remaining rules.

2.2. Application to the classifier systems

2.2.1. Specialization of a rule

Let us consider that the rule : *# 1 # # 0 => action a* of strengh f (called "mother rule") has been chosen according to the criterion. Specialization consists in selecting one of the # (for instance the second one) and replacing it by all possible symbols (i.e. 0 and 1). We thus obtain two new rules ("daughter rules") :

 # 1 1 # 0 => action a   ;   strengh f
 # 1 0 # 0 => action a   ;   strengh f

The new rules keep the same action and the same strength as their mother. They will be in competition with their mother, which is kept, and with other rules able to apply in the same situations, but with different actions.

2.2.2. Geometric interpretation : trees of rules

We can visualize the progressive partitioning of the state-action space as the construction of a tree whose nodes are the rules and whose branches are the specialization links. Since rules keep the same action through specialization, there is one independant tree for each possible action : one tree represents one covering of Z^a. The root of the tree for an action a (##### => a) is the most general rule ; it is always kept so that in any situation all the actions are theoretically possible. The first level nodes (issued from a specialization of the root) have $(n-1)$ # where n is the number of # in the root. A node of level m has $(n-m)$ #. A node of level n is entirely specified. See *figures 1a & 1b*. A level corresponds to a degree of specialization. We therefore have built a system starting with a general and approximative set of rules (which cannot distinguish among situations leading to different reinforcements), as is the knowledge of a novice, and acquiring more and more specialized and relevant rules : the knowledge of an expert.

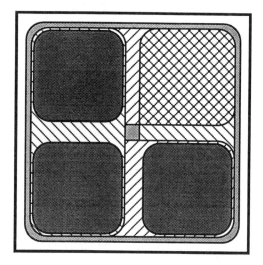

Figure 1b :
The covering of the state space by regions according to the tree of rules defined in figure 1a. The darker the region, the more numerous the rules covering it.

Remark : It is the whole set of rules which constitutes, by their interactions, the knowledge of the system ; it is generally not possible to interpret one rule in isolation.

3. Numerical simulations

3.1. Application to the simulation of an Animat

3.1.1. The environment and the task

We use our algorithm to train a simulated autonomous robot both in a structured environment and in an unstructured one.

The environment is a cultivated field, discretized into squares containing either a plant P, a weed W or nothing N. The robot itself occupies four squares. The task of the robot consists in weeding the field, thus the environment transmits to the robot a positive reinforcement (+1) for each W-square being run over, a small negative one (-0,2) for each N-square and a strong negative one (-6) for each P-square. The content of a square becomes N after the robot has run over it. The *structured environment* (see *figure 2a*) is characterized by the regular spacing of plant rows and by the constant distance between two plants on the same row. Weeds are distributed according to a probability distribution taking into account the distance from the plants (there are more weeds close to the plants). The field is of infinite dimensions : only a window centered on the robot is defined at any time ; it is permanently regenerated every time the robot moves. On the contrary, in the *unstructured environment* weeds and plants are distributed randomly.

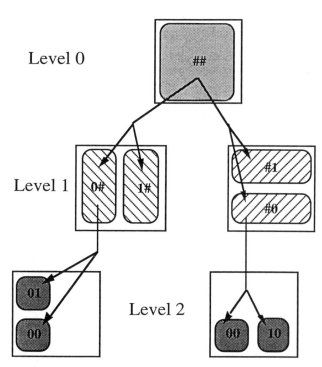

Level 0

Level 1

Level 2

Figure 1a :
Visualization of the regions of the state space where a rule can apply. The result of the specialization operator is to split a region into two smaller ones.

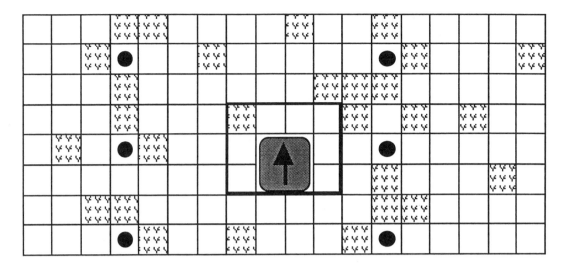

Figure 2a : The robot in the structured environment. The figure shows a portion of the infinite field.
Black circles represent the plants and the other pattern the weeds.

3.1.2. The robot

The robot is 2x2 square large and has a defined orientation (among 4 possible). Its perceptive capacities are local : it is able to see 8 adjacent squares (two on the left, four in front of him, two on the right) so state-space X is the perceptive space : $\{P, W, N\}^8$. These are the squares into which it can enter in one step. See *figure 2b*. The perception will be compared with the conditional part of the rules in order to determine which ones can be applied.

Remark : as the complete state of the system robot-environment is hidden from the robot, we consider the perception as the state of the system, for our dynamics.

The robot can move in five different ways corresponding to the action part of the rules : forward (F), in diagonal towards left (FL), towards right (FR), turn left (L) and turn right (R).

3.1.3. Definition of our classifiers

In our simulation, the bits c_k of the conditional part of the classifiers (see § 1.3.1) can take the values #, P, W or N. When a rule is specialized 3 daughters are consequently created and the state space is then split in three. The action space A is $\{F, FL, FR, L, R\}$.

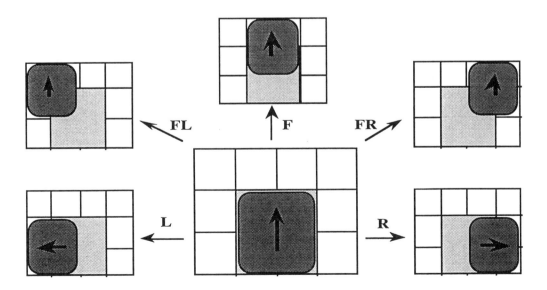

Figure 2b : The 2x2-square robot, its 8-square vision and the resulting position and orientation for the 5 possible actions.

3.2. The simulations

3.2.1. Parameters

-Structured environment : plant rows are 9 columns apart, plants are 3 lines apart, the probability of having a weed inside the plant rows is 0.7, adjacent to the rows : 0.4, elsewhere : 0.1. Globally the weeds' proportion in the field is 21%, the proportion of plants is 4%. The probabilities are chosen in order to depend on the alignment structure so that the robot can exploit it. The weeds must not be too numerous if we want to be able to judge the efficiency of the robot's strategy.

-Unstructured environment : the plants and weeds are distributed randomly, the proportions are the same as before : 21% weeds and 4% plants.

-Learning : the parameters of the learning dynamics are $\alpha = 0.1$ and $\gamma = 0.8$ for the structured environment and g = 0 for the unstructured one (indeed there can be no anticipation when the features are distributed randomly because of the local perception).

- The simulation starts with the set of all 0-level and 1-level rules (having n # and $(n-1)$ #) and all possible actions (5 + 8 x 3 x 5 = 125 rules). The maximal number of rules allowed in our classifier system is 400. The number of steps of the learning dynamics between two selection-specialization processes is 5000.

-The probabilistic choice of the rules to be executed and specialized is done according to Boltzmann distributions. For the choice of the rule to be applied, the temperature $(T=1/\beta)$ decreases regularly each time the selection-specialization operator is applied.

3.2.2. Results

We evaluate the performance of the robot by two measures : the average number of weeds cut in one move (NbW) and the average number of plants cut in one move (NbP). These figures have to be compared with the estimated performance of a robot choosing its actions randomly, going in diagonal all the time ("straight") and with the human (optimal ?) performance (it is indeed possible to pilot the robot from the keyboard, with the same local vision as the robot).

We have plotted the performance of our robot during learning for the first 5000x20 steps. See *figures 3a & 3b*. (each value of the curves is an average computed on 500 steps). The results at the end of this period and after setting to 0 the temperature of the choice of the action to be applied, are given in the following table.

3.3 Analysis of performances

(see table 1 & figure 3)

Unstructured environment : the decrease of the average number of plants cut (NbP) towards 0 shows that the partitioning dynamics leads to rules which take into account the relevant input (vision) bits. Besides, the average number of weeds cut (NbW) reaches the human optimal performance.

Structured environment : NbW is not significantly higher than in the unstructured environment, whereas a human performes much better using his knowledge of the weeds distribution. *Figure 3c* shows the performance of a robot with a 12-square vision (the 4 additional squares being ahead of the robot) making the anticipation easier : NbW is slightly higher in this case (0.91) but this is still not enough to conclude that the robot has learnt the regularity of the environment. This may be because our local vision system does not allow an easy detection of field regularities. An internal message coding the orientation of the robot might facilitate the task.

Note that the learning time of the 12-square vision simulation is the same as that of the 8-square vision though the state space is 3^4 (= 81) times larger.

Environment	Structured				Unstructured			
Strategy	Random	Straight	Partitioning Q-learning	Human	Random	Straight	Partitioning Q-learning	Human
NbP	0.07	0.11	**0.002**	0	0.07	0.08	**0.003**	0
NbW	0.33	0.59	**0.88**	0.98	0.33	0.59	**0.87**	0.87

Table 1 : quantitative results for various strategies and environments.

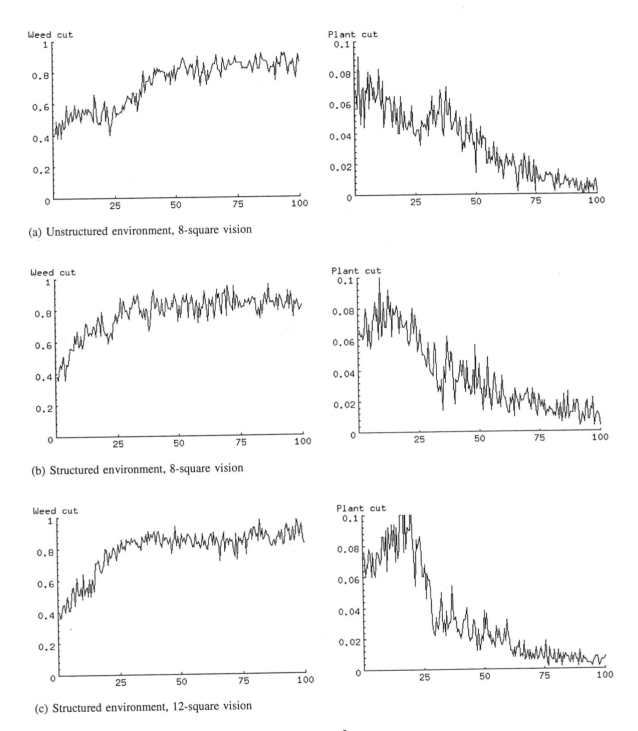

(a) Unstructured environment, 8-square vision

(b) Structured environment, 8-square vision

(c) Structured environment, 12-square vision

Figure 3 : Average number of weeds and plants cut for 100×10^3 steps

4. Discussion and conclusion

The emergent rules

None of the initial rules leads to an homogeneous reinforcement because they consider at most 1 square (they contain n or (n-1) #) and the robot runs over at least 2 squares every iteration (3 squares for actions FL and FR).
We observe that, thanks to the partitioning dynamics, rules that take into account the squares into which the robot moves appear ; theses rules have a constant reinforcement over time.

Comparison with the work of Chapman and Kaelbling (1991)

They propose an algorithm (G-learning) that attempts to solve the "input generalisation problem" for the Q-learning algorithm which rests basically on the same principles as our Partitioning Q-learning : they use a splitting of the state space into subblocks, generated by specifying input bits into 0 or 1.

However the criterion used to split the state space is different and much more complex than ours. Whereas they use a criterion based on a statistic test that gives a relevance value for each bit of each block and allows them to choose directly which bit to split on, we use an incrementally calculated criterion to select regions that need to be specialized and the bit on which the partition is made is randomly chosen.
Our method generates useless splits but these are later pruned by the selection operator. This method allows the system to modify the covering of the state-action space when the environment changes.

Besides, the undisputable advantage of splitting on the relevant bit is hindered by the need to collect a huge number of values to insure that the normallity assumption can be made, and by the need to store in memory all the experience of the system. Moreover, in order to obtain reliable values for the relevance test, they have to separate the learning into two phases : the qualities estimation phase and the bit relevance statistics collection phase.
On the contrary, our criterion is updated every iteration and does not need to keep any value in memory. In fact their criterion may be worthier when handling inputs with a large number of bits. However we partially solve this problem by allowing more than simply two values for our input "bits".

As the authors acknowledge, the main shortcoming of their algorithm is that they are compelled to « throw away all experience accumulated thus far on each split » as all the qualities (and bit relevance statistics) have to be reset when a block is split. This is because they split the state space and then try all actions on the obtained subblocks : this is how we started to design our specialization operator i.e. we generated daughter rules with all possible actions. This allowed for a faster and larger exploration by the system but, as there was no more link between the mother and the daughters, we could not transmit the strength of the mother to them. To allow a true competition among all the rules, we were compelled to turn all the strengths to zero. Thus each time the selection-specialization operator was applied, the system was totally reset with a new set of rules, having lost all its learned performance. Then we found that keeping the same action as the mother when generating daughter rules, thus building one independent partition for each possible action, allows us to have *a continuous and therefore faster learning.*

The main contribution of this work is the general-towards-specialized approach using the standard deviation reinforcement criterion which speeds up the convergence of the learning dynamics and never needs the storage of all the qualities (in opposition to the clustering approach). Besides the selection-specialization operator used here allows the system to have a continuous performance, thus enabling it to adapt itself to a changing environment while continuing to perform efficiently. Finally, the use of the classifier systems formalism allowed a connection between the Q-learning and Bucket Brigade algorithms to be made.

Acknowledgments

We would like to thank the persons who contributed to this work by their relevant advices and through numerous discussions : Paul Bourgine, Pascal Goyaux and Olivier Higelin of the AL & AI Lab, CEMAGREF.

References

[Barto et al.,1983] A.G. Barto, R.S. Sutton, C.W. Anderson. *Neuronlike elements that can solve difficult learning control problems.* IEEE Transactions on Systems, Man and Cybernetics, 13, (p. 835-846).

[Chapman and Kaelbling,1991] D. Chapman, L.P. Kaelbling. *Input Generalisation in Delayed Reinforcement Learning : an Algorithm and Performance Comparisons.* Proceedings of IJCAI-91.

[Dayan,1992] P. Dayan. *The convergence of TD(λ) for general λ.* Machine Learning, vol 8, 341-362.

[Goldberg,1989] D.E. Goldberg. *Genetic Algorithms in search, optimization, and machine learning.* Addison Wesley.

[Holland,1985] J.H. Holland. *Properties of the bucket brigade algorithm.* Proceedings of the First International Conference on Genetic Algorithms and Their Applications. Pittsburgh, PA : Lawrence Erlbaum.

[Kaelbling,1993] L.P. Kaelbling. *Learning in Embedded Systems.* A Bradford Book, MIT Press, Cambridge, MA.

[Lin,1992] L.J. Lin. *Self-Improving Reactive Agents Based on Reinforcement Learning, Planning and Teaching.* Machine Learning, 8, 293-321.

[Mahadevan and Connell,1991] S. Mahadevan, J. Connell. *Automatic programming of behavior-based robots using reinforcement learning.* Artificial Intelligence 55, 311-365.

[McCallum,1992] R.A. McCallum. *Using Transitional Proximity for Faster Reinforcement Learning.* Technical report, Departement of Computer Science, University of Rochester.

[Moore,1991] A.W. Moore. *Variable Resolution Dynamic Programming : Efficiently Learning Action Maps in Multivariate Real-valued State-spaces.* Proceedings of the eighth International Workshop on Machine Learning, 333-337.

[Munos, 1992] R. Munos. *Algorithmes Génétiques et Apprentissage par renforcement.* Rapport DEA Sciences Cognitives. CEMAGREF.

[Rescola and Wagner,1972] R.A. Rescola, A.R. Wagner. *A Theory of Pavlovian Condidtioning : Variations in the Effectiveness of Reinforcement and Non-Reinforcement.* Classical Conditioning II : Current research and theory. New York : Appleton-Century-Crofts.

[Saurel,1992] P.Saurel. *Q-learning et apprentissage par renforcement.* Rapport de DEA Sciences Cognitives. CEMAGREF.

[Sutton and Barto,1990] R.S. Sutton, B.G. Barto. *Time-Derivative Models of Pavlovian Reinforcement,* in book : Learning and Computational Neuroscience : Foundations of Adaptive Networks, M. Gabriel and J. Moore, MIT Press Cambridge, MA.

[Sutton,1984] R.S.Sutton, *Temporal Credit Assignment in Reinforcement Learning.* PhD thesis, University of Massachusetts, Amherst, MA.

[Sutton,1988] R.S.Sutton, *Learning to predict by the methods of Temporal Differences.* Machine Learning, 3, 9-44.

[Sutton,1990] R.S.Sutton, *Integrated Architectures for Learning, Planning, and Reacting based on approximating Dynamic Programming.* Proceedings Seventh International Conference on Machine Learning, Austin, TX, 216-224.

[Tan,1991] M. Tan. *Cost-Sensitive Reinforcement Learning for Adaptative Classification and Control.* Proceedings of Ninth National Conference on Artificial Intelligence, AAAI , MIT Press.

[Watkins,1989] C.J.C.H. Watkins. *Learning from Delayed Rewards.* PhD thesis, Kings's Colledge, Cambridge.

[Watkins and Dayan,1992] C.J.C.H. Watkins, P. Dayan. *Q-learning.* Machine Learning, vol 8, 279-292.

[Wilson and Goldberg,1989] S.W. Wilson, D.E. Goldberg, *A critical review of classifier systems.* In Schaffer, Proceedings of the Third International Conference on Genetic Algorithms. Morgan Kaufmann.

The Five Neuron Trick: Using Classical Conditioning to Learn How to Seek Light

Tom Scutt

Artificial Intelligence Group
Department of Psychology
University of Nottingham
Nottingham NG7 2RD
tws@psyc.nott.ac.uk

Abstract

This paper describes how a simple Braitenberg light-seeking vehicle can be extended by the addition of a single facilitatory interneuron so that it *learns* how to use its wheels in order to move towards the light. The original Braitenberg vehicle can be thought of as having four neurons (two sensory, two motor). Even this simple circuit produces surprisingly complex behaviour when situated in the real world. However, the circuit is "hard-wired", and so cannot adapt to the environment. Normal methods of learning in neural networks usually require some training signal, and are therefore unsuitable for adaptive networks in autonomous robots. This paper shows that, by using model neurons which are far more physiologically accurate than conventional models, and simple learning mechanisms (i.e. habituation, classical conditioning), a single additional neuron can produce an *adaptive* light-seeking vehicle. The circuit which produces this behaviour can be considered as "soft-wired"—that is, there is an inbuilt "goal" which is achieved in an adaptive manner. This suggests that by taking principles from invertebrate neurophysiology, and building very simple artificial networks which use these principles, we will gain insight into how to solve the "bootstrapping" problem of intelligence in autonomous robots.

1 Introduction

Work on situated systems has shown that even the simplest of systems can show interesting emergent behaviour when placed in the real world. Even when the system is placed in a fairly simple, *simulated* environment we may still be surprised by its behaviour. Researchers like Brooks (1991) and Braitenberg (1984) have demonstrated the power of *synthesising* such systems by building up simple circuits or behaviours.

However, the problem with synthetic AI is that we are tempted into building systems from scratch. But we can build all sorts of abstract systems that have nothing whatsoever to do with existing creatures. If we do not have a strong physiological basis for our synthetic systems then we run the risk of a) never stumbling across a really intelligent system, or b) creating an artificially intelligent system which sheds no light at all on how animal intelligence

works. By lowering the level of our analysis, from behaviour to biology, we make sure that our synthetic activities have a sound basis in fact. So, analysis is important, but by analysing neurophysiology, we are less open to problems of interpretation and the over-complication which seem to go along with representational views of cognition.

Although Braitenberg based his work on sound neurophysiological principles, it suffered from the problem that it existed only as a series of "thought experiments"—that is, Braitenberg did not actually build the models that he described, even in simulation. The problem with thought experiments is not that they fool us; it is rather that they often *underestimate* the complexity of behaviour of even the simplest of systems when placed in a suitably complex environment.

Recently, there has been a surge of interest in the area known as computational neuroethology (Cliff, 1991). Researchers such as Beer *et al.* (1989) have built systems based on actual invertebrate neural circuitry, and tested these systems, both in simulation and embedded in the real world on autonomous robots. In general, their work is exemplary; both in showing how a particular neural circuitry can give rise to a particular behaviour and in drawing heavily from real neurophysiology. However, if we are to truly *understand* the way in which each neuron and its interactions contributes to behaviour (and this is vital if we are building systems incrementally), then perhaps we need to look at a level even lower than the "artificial cockroach". We also need to understand how such systems can adapt to their environment rather than being "hard-wired".

This paper begins by briefly examining one of the simplest "interesting" neuronal circuits—a four neuron system which steers towards light—and shows that it has emergent properties that are not immediately obvious. A model for small systems of neurons is then outlined. This model is more neurophysiologically accurate than conventional PDP networks, and also exhibits the simple forms of learning found in invertebrate systems. It is shown that the addition of a single neuron to the light-seeking system is all that is necessary to produce an adaptive system which *learns* how to use its wheels in order to find light. Finally, suggestions are made as to how this research will be extended, and the implications for adaptive autonomous robot design.

2 Light-Seeking Vehicles

In the second chapter of his classic book *Vehicles* (1984), Braitenberg describes a vehicle with two light sensors connected to two motors which navigates towards light (figure 1). On a flat plain with a light source, the sensor nearest the source receives more light, thus sending a stronger signal to the motor on the opposite side of the vehicle, turning it towards the light. What is not stated in the book (and is not apparent to many who have read it) is the emergent property that such a vehicle will avoid obstacles between it and a light source because of shadows occluding the light sensors. This shows the danger of "thought experiments".

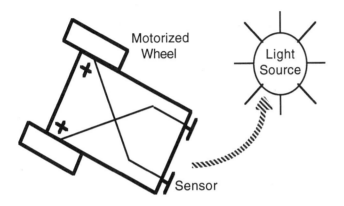

Figure 1: A Braitenberg light-seeking vehicle.

The basic Braitenberg vehicle[1] we built consisted of two photo-receptors and two motorised wheels attached to a Lego chasis[2]. It was simply hard wired so that the more light that fell on the receptor, the faster the opposite wheel went. As predicted, the vehicle avoided an object placed between it and a light source. During the first day of testing, increasingly complex patterns of objects were placed between the vehicle and the light to test the limits of its light-seeking. In the end, there were so many interposing objects that it appeared there was no light at all visible from a "vehicle's-eye-view". There seemed to be no way that the vehicle would even move, never mind steer a path to the light. But the vehicle *did* start to move—away from the objects and towards the wall. It then drove along the edge of the wall, slowly gaining speed until it had passed all the objects; then it turned and drove straight into the light! What we the experimenters had failed to realise, was that the skirting board was painted with gloss white paint, and this was reflecting the light. "Solving" a problem in this way—

by completely *avoiding* it—is not an option for systems in closed-world simulations; but this is exactly the sort of behaviour that is desirable if a system is be viewed as having intentional states rather than hard-wired goals.

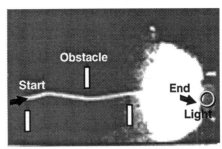

Figure 2: A light-seeking vehicle entering from the left steers its way past three obstacles to get to the light.

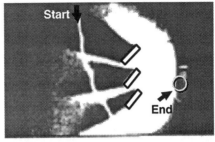

Figure 3: A vehicle entering from the top of the picture is perturbed, but not fooled, by the small gaps between obstacles.

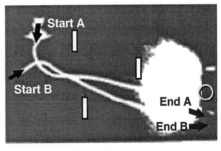

Figure 4: Vehicle A at top left of picture is 'stranded' in the shadow cast by an obstacle. It is 'rescued' by following the tail lights of B (entering left).

Figures 2-4: These figures show photographs of the trails left by the tail lights of light-seeking vehicles. Unfortunately, the glare from the floor near to the main light source makes it difficult to see the trails of the vehicles as they approach the source. Location of the lamp (circle), obstacles (rectangles), and the start and end positions of the vehicles (arrows) are overlayed on the photographs for clarity.

The more formal experiments conducted since have used a camera on open shutter to record the motion of these vehicles, mainly in a situation where there are a number of objects between the vehicle and the light source. The vehicles have an onboard light source which produces an image of the vehicle's path on the photograph. Unless indicated otherwise, objects were videotapes (18.5cm x 10.5cm) covered in black paper. The light source was a 100w bulb used in an 'Anglepoise' desk lamp, placed so the centre of the bulb was as close to the floor as possible (about 8cm). The vehicles were attached to an external power supply. Human intervention was occasionally required to ensure that the trailing power lead did not become tangled around objects or the vehicle itself.

---

[1]This vehicle was designed and built by Giles Mayley at Southampton University.

[2]Two years after this Lego vehicle was built I found out that Edinburgh University had been using Lego vehicles for teaching and research purposes for a number of years (e.g. Donnett and Smithers, 1990). This is the only paper I have come across which has noted the obstacle avoidance behaviour of simple Braitenberg vehicles.

As can be seen from figures 2 and 3, these simple vehicles are adept at object avoidance, and can even engage in a certain degree of what we might consider "social interaction" (figure 4) if we didn't know better! However, it does not feel like a great deal has been acheived by building a hard-wired system such as this (even if it is capable of surprising us occasionally). What is needed is some kind of adaptive system. The first step towards this is to regard the circuit as a very simple neural network, with two sensory and two motor neurons. The learning paradigms typically used in PDP research will be of little use because they require some training signal (in this case, telling the motor neurons what they *should* be doing). This is inappropriate for an autonomous vehicle, missing as it does the "crucial aspect of ... real-time, closed-loop, goal-seeking interactions between a (biological or synthesized) learning system and its environment" (Klopf *et al.*, 1992), and also goes against the need for neurophysiological realism discussed earlier. Instead we need to use networks that incorporate learning techniques which are actually found in simple animals.

3   Object-Oriented Modelling of Small Systems of Neurons

The model used here for simple neural systems has been detailed in previous papers (Scutt & Damper 1991, 1992). Almost all attempts to model neural and brain function have fallen into one of two categories: "artificial neural nets" using (typically) large numbers of simple but densely-interconnected processing elements, or detailed physiological models of single neurons. By contrast, the model outlined here functions at a level between these two extremes. It is apparent that the power of real neural networks as information processors arises as a product of complexity at both the network and the neuron level. In this model, individual neurons are considered at the level of membrane potential[3]; this allows outputs from the model to be compared directly with physiological data obtained in intracellular recording. An object-oriented programming (OOP) language has been used to produce a model where networks, neurons and synapses are represented as objects. The program has been tested by modelling the learning and behaviour of the gill-withdrawal reflex in the marine snail *Aplysia* (Hawkins et al., 1983; Hawkins and Kandel, 1984). Results show good agreement with physiological data. In particular, the simple forms of learning underlying this behaviour have been successfully modelled.

The object-oriented programming methodology is, in many ways, an obvious choice for neural modelling (Scutt and Damper, 1992). Objects are semi-autonomous units which have their own internal mechanisms (constructed by pieces of code known as 'methods'), and which send and receive messages. Thus, there is a natural mapping from object to neuron. However, there are other less obvious benefits which suggest OOP as a very suitable choice for modelling neuronal systems.

The benefits of using an object-oriented language are two-fold. First, there is the OOP property of *polymorphism*. Not all neurons are identical—especially in small neural systems. It is important to allow heterogeneity. However, it is also important that a synapse can send a message to another object without having to work out the type of the recipient. Polymorphism allows us to treat our units in this way as 'black boxes', despite the fact that there is a variety of ways in which they may deal with messages.

The second benefit of OOP is the ability for objects to *inherit* properties from other objects. This means that it is easy to define more physiologically exact neurons in terms of simpler neurons. In fact, the system allows a typical connectionist threshold unit as the most basic type of object (in this case, a *neuron* object). More complex neurons inherit certain properties from this object (e.g. the fact that it has weighted connections to other objects) but will also have additional new properties (for instance, such features as pacemaker activity and synapse-on-synapse connections have been added without difficulty).

Now we can show that the property of inheritance makes the realisation of this structure very easy. We appreciated early on in our research that there are also strong correspondences between neurons and synapses. For example, neurons have a variable membrane potential which tends to a resting position at a rate which depends on the time constant of the neuron; synapses have a variable 'weight' that tends to a resting position at a rate dependent on the synapse's recovery parameter. Both of these properties can be inherited from a common ancestor object. There are also correspondences in structure between the different levels. For instance, a network consists of a number of methods which each determine what the network actually does, plus the *neuron* objects which make up the network. Similarly, a neuron has its own internal processes, plus a number of *synapse* objects. In our model, all objects inherit these properties from a basic *meta* object. Thus, there is self-similarity at all levels.

3.1 Learning

As well as featuring heterogenous neurons, the model also allows different types of synapse, corresponding to different forms of synaptic modification. Three simple forms of learning are simulated by the model: *habituation* (where the weight of a synapse is lowered by repeated firing), *sensitisation* (where activity in a neuron increases the strength of the synaptic connection between two other neurons—see figure 5), and *classical conditioning* (similar to sensitisation, but dependent on the target synapse having been recently active).

Habituation is programmed into the neuronal circuit simulation by the three parameters *base-level*, *dynamic-level* and *recovery*. *Base-level* is the "normal" weight of the synapse and is a constant. *Dynamic-level* holds the present synaptic strength and is variable during the program's run. *Recovery* is a constant (within each synapse) which determines how quickly *dynamic-level* returns to *base-level*. If a synapse is of a habituating type, then the *dynamic-level*

---

[3]Thus, the model neurons produce spikes, unlike those in conventional PDP networks.

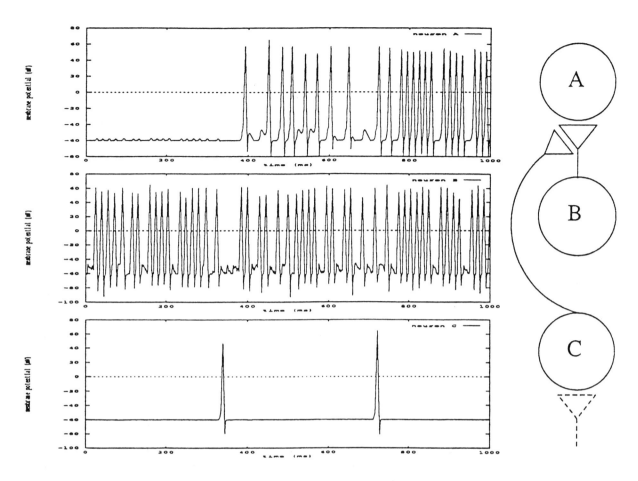

Figure 5: An example of output from the neuronal model showing sensitisation. Sporadic firing in neuron **B** produces one-for-one EPSPs in neuron **A**. Neuron **C** is a facilitatory interneuron which makes synapse-on-synapse connections with the synapse between **B** and **A**. Spikes generated by **C** facilitate an increase in weight of the connection from **B** to **A**.

of the synapse is lowered every time it is fired; but this effect diminishes with time (depending on the value of *recovery*).

The sensitising synapse uses the same parameters as are used in the habituation routines in order to simulate the Ca^{++} influx associated with sensitisation (also known as *presynaptic facilitation*). The major difference is one of addressing. In the case of habituation, if synapse i of neuron A (i.e. synapse A_i) fires, it transmits a signal to neuron B and the weight of A_i is changed. With sensitisation, however, if A is a facilitatory interneuron, then the synapse A_i will not connect onto a neuron; but onto another synapse—B_j. When synapse A_i fires, it increases the *dynamic-level* of B_j. The program works out the pointer for this "indirect" addressing when the network file is loaded and the objects constructed.

Conditioning uses a similar routine to sensitisation, but the strength of the facilitation depends on the length of time since the target synapse last fired. The facilitatory effect is strongest when this period is approximately half a second.

As with habituation, the value of *recovery* (of the target synapse, in this case) determines how quickly the effects of sensitisation or conditioning wear off.

4 An Adaptive Light-Seeking Vehicle

As an example of how we can go forward from neurophysiology to synthesise systems with interesting behaviour, the network model described above has been used to consider the Braitenberg vehicle in terms of real neurons. The simple vehicles described earlier can be modelled using just four neurons (two sensory, and two motor). But our experience with modelling learning in *Aplysia* led us to ask the question of how the hard-wired architecture of this vehicle could be altered so as to produce a "soft-wired" version, which learned how to use its wheels so as to steer towards light. The answer is that a single facilitatory neuron, making synapse-on-synapse connections to the synapses from sensors to motors, allows the vehicle to learn (via classical conditioning and habituating) how to turn towards light (figure 6).

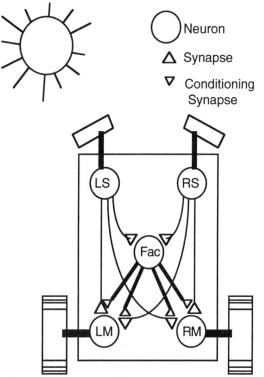

Figure 6: The Five Neuron Trick: The two sensory neurons (LS & RS) have connections to both of the motor neurons (LM & RM), and also connect to the facilitatory interneuron (Fac). This in turn makes (conditioning) synapse-on-synapse connections to the four (habituating) synapses between sensory and motor neurons. This vehicle adapts in a way that makes it light-seeking.

To explain: the vehicle is connected up completely neutrally, with connections of equal strength going from each sensory neuron to both of the motor neurons—these are"noisy habituating" synapses which have a probability of firing proportional to the membrane potential of their parent neuron, and their weight decreases slightly each time they fire. The facilitatory interneuron makes conditioning synapse-on-synapse connections with all four of the sensory to motor synapses. Now, in the figure the light is on the vehicle's left. This means that the two synapses made by the LS neuron are more likely to fire than the ones made by the RS neuron. The two synapses made by the left sensor are both equally likely to fire. However, because of their "noisy" nature they will not necessarily fire at the same time. If the left hand synapse fires (the straight connection), then the vehicle will turn away from the light. This means that the facilitatory neuron (which receives input from both light sensors) is less likely to fire, and the strength of the left hand synapse will not be increased (in fact it will decrease slightly because of the effects of habituation). If, on the other hand, the right hand synapse fires (the crossed connection), then the vehicle will turn towards the light, the facilitatory neuron is likely to fire, and the strength of the right-hand synapse will be increased due to the effects of classical conditioning (which greatly outweigh the slight habituation). The system as a whole is riddled with "noise", and there is a delicate balance between the antagonistic effects of habituation and conditioning. However, a system which is originally wired up neutrally (it will move faster in lighter areas, but the direction of movement is essentially random), will gradually adapt so that its crossed connections become stronger (due to the effects of conditioning), while the straight connections become weaker (because of habituation). The five-neuron vehicle therefore effectively builds itself the circuit shown earlier in figure 1. This system has been tested in a simple situated environment of a single light source and two obstacles. Figure 7 shows the path of an initially neurtrally wired vehicle. It is clear that there is some adaptation going on. Figure 8 shows the path of a vehicle which has already been "in the world" for several minutes and has thus adapted to a light-seeking configuration.

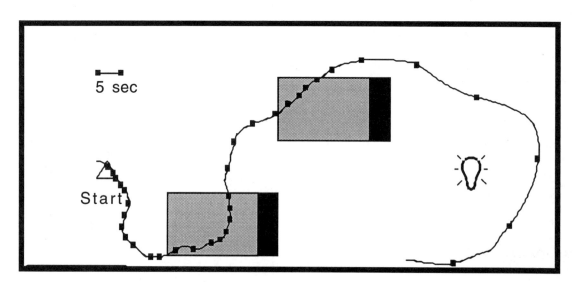

Figure 7: A "new-born" vehicle (neutrally wired) enters the world. After several minutes it begins to show signs of light-seeking. Shaded areas show shadows behind objects.

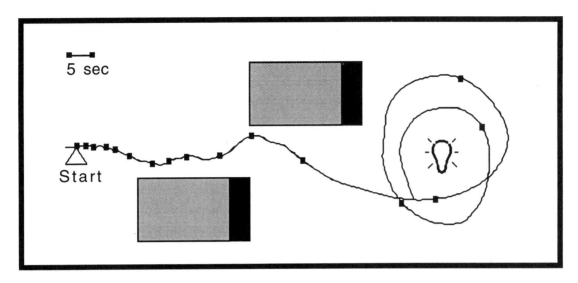

Figure 8: A vehicle which has already been adapting for some time shows light-seeking and dark-avoidance.

During the running of these simulations it became clear that nearly all of the adaptation was taking place at the borders between light and shadow. This is because it is at these boundaries where turning one way (toward the light) will result in reinforcement while turning the other (into the shadow) results in none. In fact, the vehicle never learns in an environment where there are no objects—again proving the point that a complex environment is a help rather than a hinderance.

So, the five neuron vehicle is a soft-wired version of the original light-seeking Braitenberg vehicle. Its "goal" is the same, but the wiring adapts to acheive this goal. Even if we were to take the two light sensors and cross them over, the vehicle would still go towards the light. This suggests that the benefits brought by synaptic plasticty come fairly cheaply (i.e. in this case the addition of a single neuron).

5 Conclusions

It has been show that the simple forms of learning present in invertebrate systems can be of great use in designing situated autonomous robots. The problem of how to give a system goals without resorting to external intervention has been solved. The goal of the system is still determined by its initial wiring, but the way that this goal is acheived (and the *effective* wiring of the network) is determined by the manner in which the system adapts to its environment. The model could be extended further to give a clearer picture of this. Imagine a five neuron vehicle modified so that it contains an additional sensory neuron which is heat sensitive (figure 9).

This vehicle uses heat sensory neuron to drive the facilitatory interneuron. This means the connections from light sensory neurons to wheels would be reinforced by an increase in heat. This vehicle would adapt differently in different environments. If the heat sources in its world were naked flames, then the crossed connections would become

reinforced—as in the five neuron vehicle. But in a world in which matt black radiators were the major sources of heat, the vehicle would learn to avoid light (or seek darkness) and the straight connections would be strengthened. Thus the vehicle would learn how to use information about light in order to seek out warm places.

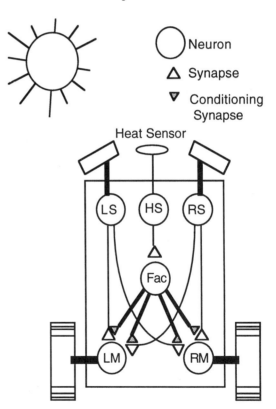

Figure 9: A six neuron vehicle that learns how to seek heat using light information. HS is a sensory neuron tuned to heat.

The vehicles outlined here adapt most quickly in noisy, complex environments. Using "soft-wired" goals avoids the need to pre-configure a system for a particular environment. It remains to be seen to what degree these simple forms of learning can be combined to give more sophisticated adaptive behaviours.

References

BRAITENBERG, V. (1984) *Vehicles*. MIT Press

BEER, R.D., CHIEL, J. & STERLING, L.S. (1989) "An artificial insect", *American Scientist*, **79**, 444-452.

BROOKS, R.A. (1991) "Intelligence without representation", *Artificial Intelligence* 47, 139-159.

CLIFF, D.T. (1991) "Computational neuroethology: a provisional manifesto", *Proceedings of the First International Workshop on the Simulation of Adaptive Behaviour: From Animals to Animats*, 29-39.

DONNETT, J. & SMITHERS, T. (1991) "Lego vehicles: a technology for studying intelligent systems", *Proceedings of the First International Workshop on the Simulation of Adaptive Behaviour: From Animals to Animats*, 540-549. MIT Press.

HAWKINS, R.D., ABRAMS, T.W., CAREW, T.J. & KANDEL, E.R. (1983) "A cellular mechanism of classical conditioning in *Aplysia*: activity-dependent amplification of presynaptic facilitation", *Science*, **219**, 400-405.

HAWKINS, R.D. & KANDEL, E.R. (1984) "Is there a cell-biological alphabet for simple forms of learning?", *Psychological Review*, **91**, 375-391.

KLOPF, A.H., MOGAN, J.S. & WEAVER, S.E. (1992) "Modelling nervous system function with a hierarchical network of control systems that learn", *Proceedings of the Second International Workshop on the Simulation of Adaptive Behaviour: From Animals to Animats 2*, 254-261.

SCUTT, T.W. & DAMPER, R.I. (1991) "Computational modelling of learning and behaviour in small neuronal systems", *Proceedings of International Joint Conference on Neural Networks, Singapore*, 430--435.

SCUTT, T.W. & DAMPER, R.I. (1992) "Object-oriented modelling of small neuronal systems", *AISB Quarterly*, **80**, 24-33

Adaptation in dynamic environments through a minimal probability of exploration

Gilles Venturini

Equipe Inférence et Apprentissage
Laboratoire de Recherche en Informatique, bat. 490
Université de Paris-Sud
91405 Orsay Cedex, FRANCE.
email: venturi@lri.lri.fr

Abstract

In this paper, we consider the problem of an autonomous learning agent that evolves in a dynamic environment which may undergo unseen variations over time. One way to adapt the agent strategy to these variations is to perform a minimal rate of exploration, i.e. testing another strategy than the current best one. Classifier systems can deal with such problem but they cannot guarantee easily a fixed minimal rate of exploration. The presented algorithm called Agil is an extension of a simple classifier where a clear difference is made between exploration and exploitation. This is done by modifying the strength computation scheme and the decision procedure used in classifier systems. The new decision procedure takes into account a rule optimality measure which is based on a process similar to simulated annealing, and can decrease the rate of exploration from a value $P_{exploinit}$ to $P_{explomin}$ with a speed λ.

Agil is applied to the F_6 learning task where the problem to be learnt is inverted during the experiment. It is also applied to a problem in autonomous robotics where engine failures can occur. This system proves to be useful in dynamic environments.

1 Introduction

The environment of an autonomous robot is usually dynamic, which means that it may undergo variations over time. These variations may be important enough to disable the robot's strategy for dealing with the problem to solve. Among these variations, some are easy to perceive by the robot, because it has sensors or programmed mechanisms to detect several varying features of the environment. In this case, the robot can "easily" adapt its strategy to the new environment because it knows that something has changed and how it has changed, like in (Grefenstette and Ramsey 1992). Some other variations may be difficult to perceive because the robot has not been designed initially to deal with such variations, and it may not have the appropriate sensors or detection mechanisms that allows it to detect these variations and adapt its behavior to the new environment, like in (Sutton 1990). For instance, we consider in this paper a simulated autonomous moving robot that must reach a target in an unknown environment with obstacles. The robot and the environment models may undergo variations of the two kinds mentioned. For instance, if the robot has telemeters to sense obstacles, then the appearance of an obstacle with a new shape is easy to perceive. If the robot has no sensors or detection mechanisms for engine failures, then such a variation is difficult to detect. This robot can be viewed as an animal looking for food in a changing environment.

Let us now suppose that the robot has learnt a control strategy C that is efficient for the current environment. The only way the robot can detect variations that are difficult to perceive, is to test sometimes a different strategy C', just in case the environment has changed and C' has become more efficient than C. Therefore, the robot or animal must solve the exploration versus exploitation (EVE) dilemma: it must apply the current efficient strategy C (exploitation) as often as possible to solve efficiently its problem in the current environment, but it must also sometimes apply a different strategy C' with unknown efficiency (exploration) to possibly adapt its behavior to an environment change.

Thus, an important aspect of the EVE dilemma for this problem is that the robot must maintain a minimal probability of performing an exploration. Only a minority of learning systems have the required abilities (like incrementality, autonomy and adaptability) to deal with dynamic environments and with variations in the problem to solve. Among these systems, several reinforcement learners have these abilities, like Qlearning

(Watkins 1989), Dyna (Sutton 1990) or classifier systems (CS) (Holland 1986). Qlearning and Dyna can easily guarantee a minimal rate of exploration for every situation encountered because these systems keep an exhaustive list of environment situations (they do not generalize) and an exhaustive list of actions for every situation. For a situation S, these systems can sometimes apply another action that the best observed action (see for instance the changing world experiment performed in (Sutton 1990)). However, these systems have rarely been studied in dynamic environments that undergo variations over time like in (Sutton 1990) or (Lin 1991).

CS also have basic random procedures for applying other actions than the current best one (Wilson 1985 and 1987) (Booker 1989) (Goldberg 1990). Some studies like (Holland and Reitman 1978) (Zhou and Grefenstette 1989) (Goldberg 1990) show that classifier systems can deal with dynamic environments.

However, the next section shows that CS cannot guarantee easily a given minimal rate of exploration. Thus, section 3 describes an extension of a simple CS (called Agil) where the EVE dilemma is solved explicitly with a controllable strategy that can guarantee a minimal probability $P_{explomin}$ of exploration. Section 4 describes some results of Agil on the F_6 learning task with variations, where we show that without a minimal exploration probability, Agil cannot adapt itself to the variation. The robot problem previously mentioned is also used to demonstrate Agil ability to adapt the robot behavior to an engine failure and to deal with obstacles that appear or disappear randomly.

2   Classifier systems and the EVE dilemma

We consider a simple model of CS (no message list and instant reward) inspired from Boole (Wilson 1987a) or Gofer-1 (Booker 1989). A CS is a rule system which, in our example, controls the robot behavior. Each rule has the form "If Set of situations Then Action". Each situation is represented as a fixed length binary message. The set of situations in the left part of a rule is represented by a fixed length pattern using the $\{0, 1, \#\}$ alphabet, where $\#$ replaces either 0 or 1. The right part of a rule is also a binary message with fixed length. Each rule R is numerically evaluated by its strength $s(R)$ which is computed with the reward the rule gets from the environment. A simple CS uses the following algorithm:

1. Perceive the current situation S,

2. Among the rules that matches S, choose one rule R to apply with a probability:

$$\frac{s(R)}{\sum_{R' \ matches \ S} s(R')}$$

3. Apply the action proposed by R and compute a reward r,

4. Update $s(R)$: $s(R) \leftarrow (1 - \alpha)s(R) + \alpha r$,

5. Possibly, use the genetic algorithm to learn new rules,

6. Goto 1.

In this algorithm, one can notice that no difference is made between exploration and exploitation: the same probability distribution is used for all the rules. However, it is possible to make this distinction: exploration consists in applying a rule with an unknown strength (with the aim of evaluating this strength), and exploitation consists in applying a rule with a known and high strength. Thus, one first extension to perform is to make a distinction between rules with evaluated strength and rules with non-evaluated strength. This has been done in Agil by modifying the strength computation scheme common to the bucket brigade algorithm (BBA) (Holland 1986) and to the profit sharing plan (PSP) (Grefenstette 1988).

A second issue is that the probability distribution used in CS does not guarantee easily a minimal rate of exploration. We would like to explicitly maintain a probability $P_{explomin}$ of exploration for every situation S that the system encounters. Ranking techniques would not be useful for this purpose because applying a low strength rule is not necessarily an exploration (newly created rules may not have a low strength). Thus, a second extension to perform consists in modifying the step 2 of the precedent algorithm, such that the decision procedure takes into account exploration and exploitation.

Finally, we would like the CS to perform more exploration at the beginning of the learning process than at the end. More precisely, for every situation S, the probability of performing an exploration should decrease from a value $P_{exploinit}$ to $P_{explomin}$, with a speed of convergence λ that can be controlled. Furthermore, when a variation has been detected, this probability of exploration should go up on again in order to start a new learning process for situation S, and should converge on again to $P_{explomin}$. This may happen several times during the system lifetime.

An alternative to the roulette wheel selection of step 2 in the precedent algorithm consists in using the variance sensitive bidding described in (Goldberg 1990). When the reward variance of a given rule is high then the CS may apply other rules with a higher probability. Detecting variations in such a way is interesting but however, this technique has the same drawbacks as the roulette wheel: no difference is made between exploration and exploitation, and a given minimum of exploration cannot be guaranteed precisely.

3 AGIL

We present now the four mechanisms that enables Agil to maintain a fixed minimal rate of exploration.

3.1 Making a difference between exploration and exploitation

This first step consists in making a distinction between exploration and exploitation. For this purpose, the BBA/PSP strength computation scheme is modified in order to make a difference between rules with evaluated strength and rules with non-evaluated strength, and also to solve the problem of initial strength in CS. Intuitively, the strength of a rule R is evaluated when R has been sufficiently applied and has received enough reward values such that its strength is relevant statistically. To implement this idea, the strength of a rule R is computed in two steps. The first step consists in computing a relevant initial value of $s(R)$ using the N first rewards R gets:

$$s(R) = \frac{1}{N} \sum_{i=1}^{N} r(i)$$

where $r(i)$ denotes the ith reward R gets. The second step consists in updating this strength value with the BBA/PSP scheme and with $\alpha = \frac{1}{N+1}$:

$$s(R) \leftarrow (1 - \alpha)s(R) + \alpha r$$

This two-step computation can be represented and computed in the same way as the BBA/PSP, but with a varying α:

$$s_{i+1}(R) \leftarrow (1 - \alpha(i))s_i(R) + \alpha(i)r(i)$$

where $s_i(R)$ denotes the rule strength value at its ith application and where:

$$\alpha(i) = \frac{1}{i+1}, \; for \; i \leq N$$

$$\alpha(i) = \frac{1}{N+1}, \; for \; i > N$$

During the first step, $s_i(R)$ is equal to:

$$s_i(R) = \frac{1}{i} \sum_{j=1}^{i} r(j)$$

which is the mean of the i first rewards R gets. At the end of this first step ($i = N$), the CS is sure that R has been applied at least N times and that $s(R)$ is a relevant estimation of R mean reward. Thus, when $i \geq N$, R is said to be evaluated.

The second step uses the standard BBA/PSP scheme because this scheme is necessary to follow the variations

of the mean reward. However, the standard BBA/PSP has the drawback of giving a high importance to the initial strength value of R which may not be relevant because R has never been applied.[1] This is not the case here, because the initial value is $s_N(R)$ which is relevant because it was computed from the N first rewards of R.

The value of N may be computed according to R generality $g(R)$ (number of # in R left part). One possible relation between N and $g(R)$ could be :

$$N = 2^{g(R)}$$

A smaller constant than 2 can be chosen. N may also depend on background knowledge, like noise level in the rewards.

With this new principle, when several rules can be applied to a given situation, it is possible to distinguish between exploration and exploitation: if an evaluated rule with high strength is chosen, then an exploitation will occur. If an non-evaluated rule is chosen, then an exploration will occur. The problem now is how to handle the tradeoff between exploration and exploitation. Intuitively, it seems sensible to do more exploration at the beginning of the learning process, where the CS needs a lot of different experiences to learn, than at the end, where the CS has learnt optimal rules. However, CS do not provide such kind of information: it is difficult to know whether the learning process is at its beginning or its end (a technique like "solution count" used in (Wilson 1987a) cannot be generalized here). Thus, the next step consists in computing for every rule R a measure of its optimality, denoted by $opt(R)$. Then, the rule optimality will be used in the decision procedure (step 2 in the CS algorithm), following the principle "the more optimal a rule is, the more often it should be exploited (and applied)".

3.2 Rule optimality

The optimality $opt(R)$ of any rule R in the population is initially equal to 0 when this rule is created. Then, once R is evaluated, $opt(R)$ may increase using some principles of simulated annealing. Let us suppose that a second rule R' has just been evaluated (it has received exactly N rewards). Agil is going to use R' to possibly increase $opt(R)$ and will possibly delete R'. For this purpose, R' is compared to R: if R and R' are close to each other, and if R is better than R', then $opt(R)$ is incremented by one and R' is deleted (in fact, before being deleted, R' is also used to possibly increase the optimality of other rules in the population). Now we must explain the meaning of "close to each other" and of "better than".

Two rules R and R' are close to each other whenever $R \subset R'$ or $R' \subset R$. For instance, $R \subset R'$ means that

---

[1]This initial strength value is usually computed from the parent strength values as in (Wilson 1987a).

R' matches all the binary messages matched by R. For example, the following inclusion holds:

$$(01\#\#\# \rightarrow 000) \subset (0\#\#\#\# \rightarrow 011)$$

In other words, R and R' are close to each other when R is a kind of super-concept or sub-concept of R'.

Then, a rule R is better than a rule R' whenever $s(R) > (1 - \epsilon)s(R')$ where ϵ is a constant used to deal with noise in the rewards. Thus, the strengths of R and R' must be evaluated (relevant strength values), otherwise this test may result in a biased comparison. In this paper, we have omitted other information that are used in Agil for comparing rules. For instance, when R and R' have equal strength, then R is better than R' only if R is more general than R'.

If the rule R is really optimal, then $opt(R)$ is going to increase because all the generated rules that are close to R will be less efficient than R (or equally efficient and less general than R). This process is similar to simulated annealing because it uses a comparison between two solutions and it decreases a temperature like coefficient (the inverse of $opt(R)$). This simulated annealing process works in parallel because one rule R' can be used to update the optimalities of other evaluated rules in the population that are close to R'.

When a comparison between a rule R and R' has been won by R, then R' can be deleted. In this case, R' is really useless because there exists in the population at least one rule R which is either more general and more efficient than R', or more specific and more efficient than R'.

When no rule R in the population is better than R', then R' is kept in the population. In this case, R' may be more efficient or more general for the situations it matches than the other rules in the population. Several extensions could be performed at this level. For instance, if R' is better than a rule R, the optimality of R could be decreased, or R could be deleted. In its actual version, Agil only increases the rules optimalities. Rules that are no more optimal because of a variation will be deleted using a different process described in section 3.5.

Section 3.4 shows that this optimality computation is sensitive to the rules generated by the genetic algorithm (GA).

3.3   Decision procedure

This procedure can now use the information previously described (like the difference between exploration and exploitation, and the rule optimality) in order to solve explicitly the EVE dilemma and to maintain a minimal rate of exploration. For this purpose, let M denote the set of rules that match the current situation S. This set can be split into two subsets: M_e denotes the set of evaluated rules, M_{ne} the set of non-evaluated rules. M_e can be on again split into two subsets: M_e^+ denotes

the rules with high strength and generality. M_e^- denotes the other rules of M_e. To build M_e^+, we firstly consider the rule of M_e which has the highest strength denoted by S^*. Then, among the rules of M_e with a strength greater than $(1-\epsilon)S^*$, the rules with the highest generality form the set M_e^+.

The system can now choose between exploitation (applying a rule of M_e^+) or exploration (applying a rule of M_{ne}). Applying a rule of M_e^- would consist in revising the strength of a low or medium strength rule in case it has changed, and is also considered as exploration. This kind of exploration can be useful for dealing with temporary variations (see section 3.5). Before we explain how the decision procedure works, let us define for every rule R the probability $P_{explo}(R)$ of applying another rule than R:

$$P_{explo}(R) = max(P_{explomin}, P_{exploinit} - \lambda opt(R))$$

where $P_{exploinit}$ is the initial probability of exploration, $P_{explomin}$ is the minimal probability of exploration, and where λ is the speed of convergence of $P_{explo}(R)$ from $P_{exploinit}$ to $P_{explomin}$. Thus, the more optimal a rule is, the lower is the probability of applying another rule.

Then, the decision procedure works as follows: a rule R is selected randomly and uniformly in M_e^+. This rule R is thus an efficient one according to the system. With a probability $1 - P_{explo}(R)$, R is triggered (exploitation). Else, with a probability $P_{explo}(R)$, a rule R'' is randomly selected in $M_{ne} \cup M_e^-$ (exploration) and is triggered.

With this process, the minimal rate of exploration is guaranteed for every situation S because for any rule R, $P_{explo}(R)$ is greater than $P_{explomin}$, and provided that for every situation S there exists a rule to explore (M_{ne} is not empty). This last condition is fulfilled thanks to the genetic algorithm described in the next section.

3.4   Triggering the genetic algorithm

To ensure that $M_{ne} \neq \emptyset$, the principle of triggering the GA is used as in (Booker 1989). Here, this technique is adapted to our problem, and the GA is used to generate new rules whenever $M_{ne} = \emptyset$, or more generally when $|M_{ne}| < mrex$. $mrex$ is the minimal number of rules to explore for every situation, and is given by the user. Any newly created rule is inserted in the population at its first step of evaluation, and applying such a rule consists in exploration.

The GA uses standard operators like mutation or crossover, but also specialization or generalization (Antonisse and Keller 1987). It selects rules only in the set M_e and it does not duplicate rules in the population (this is not necessary any more). It produces one offspring rule at a time.

The GA plays an important role in Agil because the generated rules, once evaluated, are used to update the rules optimalities. If for instance the GA always generates the same rule, then the optimalities may be irrelevant. Fortunately, thanks to the GA randomness, this case does not occur in practice.

3.5 Algorithm

The new algorithm that results from the mechanisms described in this paper is the following one:

1. Perceive the current situation S,

2. Among the rules that match S, select one rule R in M_e^+. With a probability $1 - P_{explo}(R)$, choose definitively R (exploitation), else, with a probability $P_{explo}(R)$, choose a rule R'' in $M_{ne} \cup M_e^-$ (exploration or revision). Let R' denote the chosen rule.

3. Apply the action proposed by R' and compute a reward r,

4. Update the strength of R' using the two-step procedure. If R' has just been evaluated, then compare R' to the other rules in the population and possibly update the rules optimality.

5. If $|M_{ne}| < mrex$, then use the genetic algorithm to learn new rules,

6. Possibly, delete rules with a low internal utility,

7. Goto 1.

The rule population is initially empty. When a new situation appears, Agil may create some rules that matches the current message like in Boole or Gofer-1. Thus, the system performs initially only exploration.

Step 6 consists in deleting rules which are not useful to the system. This concerns rules which are redundant and specific, and more generally, rules which are not optimal. For this purpose, Agil computes an internal measure of rule utility, which is a measure of how often an evaluated rule R belongs to the sets M_e^+ for the situations it matches. This measure is computed in a similar way as the rule strength described previously, but with a different reward, called internal reward. For a given situation S, this reward equals 1000 for rules of M_e^+, and it equals 0 for rules of M_e^-. A rule can be deleted if it belongs to the sets M_e^- for a given proportion of matched situations. Also, this allows Agil to manage a dynamic population size, and to tell the user when the maximum allocated size is exceeded. Agil can tell which rules are important in the system behavior according to their utility measures.

In the case of a variation in a given situation S, the previously optimal rule (denoted by R^*) will belong more and more often to M_e^- because its strength will be decreasing or because other rules may get higher rewards. In such cases, other rules, possibly new ones, with smaller optimalities will enter M_e^+. Thus, without deleting R^*,

Agil will perform more and more exploration. If the variation lasts only a short time, then R^* may come back in M_e^+ because when Agil performs exploration it may also apply a rule of M_e^-, and may thus apply R^* and give it an opportunity to increase its strength on again. But if the variation lasts for a longer and maybe infinite time, then the internal utility of R^* may fall below the minimum utility threshold, which results in R^* elimination. If a newly evaluated rule replaces R^* in M_e^+, then Agil will perform exploration with a probability of $P_{exploinit}$ because a newly evaluated rule has an optimality of 0. If this new rule is optimal, then the probability of exploration will converge on again towards $P_{explomin}$ and Agil will be adapted on again to the new environment in situation S. Many such processes occur in parallel for all the situations encountered.

The main parameters of this algorithm are $P_{explomin}$, $P_{exploinit}$, λ and $mrex$. These parameters are explicit. Some other points where omitted in this paper, like a short term memory that deals with "painful actions", and like dealing with background knowledge. Agil also uses explicit heuristics for many of its behaviors that deal with adaptation. For instance, when a situation does not occur anymore, Agil may forget the corresponding rules when they have not been used during T cycles.

The complexity of Agil is however greater than for a standard CS because the precedent step 4 introduces in the worst case an $o(|pop|^2)$ operation where $|pop|$ denotes the population size. However, the average case is not that severe because the rule comparison is not called at every cycle and it only involves a small fraction of the population (the rules that have just been evaluated) and not systematically all the population.

4 Experiments

4.1 F_6 multiplexor with variations

The F_6 learning task has been used as a benchmark in several studies like (Wilson 1987a) (Booker 1989). It consists in learning a boolean function of 6 bits to 1 bit. For this task, the perception is a 6 bits message and the action is a 1 bit message. F_6 is defined as follows: the two first bits of the input vector are used to address one of the four remaining bits, and the function output is equal to the value of the addressed bit. For instance, we have $F_6(001000) = 1$ and $F_6(111000) = 0$. Let us define the function $\bar{F}_6$ by the binary complement of F_6. When an input message is presented to the CS, the system decides what is the function output for this vector. If the output proposed by the CS is correct, then the system receives a 1000 reward, else it receives a 0 reward. This learning task thus requires incrementality and reinforcement learning.

In this experiment, Agil is going to learn the F_6 problem during 20000 cycles (i.e. 20000 vector

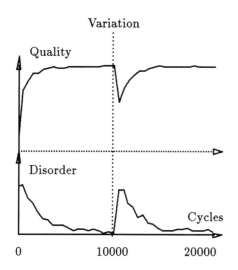

Figure 1: Agil quality and disorder when learning the $F_6/\bar{F}_6$ problem.

presentations), and then the problem is changed to $\bar{F}_6$ for the next 20000 cycles. Agil is not told about this variation.

At every cycle, it is possible to measure the quality and disorder of Agil as described in (Venturini 1991). The quality measure is the mean reward Agil gets during the previous 50 cycles. The disorder measure is simply an estimation of the exploration rate of Agil. This rate can be computed as the mean of a binary variable which, for a given cycle, is equal to 1 if the system performs an exploration, or 0 if it performs exploitation. This rate is computed also on the previous 50 cycles.

Agil learning time T_L is the number of cycles necessary for reaching a quality of 97.3% before the variation takes place (this value is used to compared Agil to other systems like Boole). The adaptation time T_A is the number of cycles needed to recover a quality of 97.3% after the problem variation. All results were averaged on 10 experiments. With $P_{exploinit} = 50\%$, $\lambda = 0.5\%$ and $mrex = 10$, Agil obtains the following results with different values of $P_{explomin}$:

$P_{explomin}$	T_L	T_A	Final des.
0 %	8810	>20000	0.2%
0.5 %	9490	7590	1%
1 %	9230	8690	1.6%
2 %	7860	7880	2.8%

"Final des." is the final disorder at the end of the experiment (40000 cycles). The final disorder is roughly equal to $P_{explomin}$, which shows that Agil behavior can be easily controlled.

Agil can learn initially F_6 for all four values of $P_{explomin}$, and obtains comparable results to Boole or Gofer-1. However, the dynamic population of Agil never

exceeded 130 rules, instead of 200 and 400 for Gofer-1 and Boole, and Boole needed 12000 cycles for the same task (Wilson 1987b).

For $P_{explomin} > 0$, Agil is able to adapt the rules to the variation. The adaptation time are equal to or even smaller than the learning times, which is due to the fact that a correct rule of F_6 can be directly changed into a correct rule of $\bar{F}_6$ by a single bit mutation.

For $P_{explomin} = 0$, the exploration probability is too small to enable Agil to adapt successfully the rules to the variation. It seems also that a low minimum rate of exploration (0.5%) is enough to ensure adaptation to the new problem.

The graph on figure 1 shows the system disorder and quality for this problem with $P_{explomin} = 2\%$ (however, the variation took place after 10000 cycles instead of 20000 in order to get a more readable graph). When the variation occurs, the quality decreases because the system is not adapted any more. The exploration rate increases because Agil replaces the rules in the M_e^+ sets. Then, the quality increases and the exploration rate decreases because Agil has learnt new rules with an increasing optimality.

4.2   Simulated autonomous robotics

In this experiment, an autonomous moving robot must reach a target in an environment with obstacles. It can perceive the obstacles with 8 telemeters, the target distance and direction, and also its speed. The robot perception is encoded as a 10 bits message. The first 8 bits are used to encode the telemeters and the target direction. Telemeter 1 is supposed to be always pointing in the target direction (the robot has a rotative head). If telemeter i detects an obstacle, then the ith bit of the message is equal to 1, else it is equal to 0. The 2 remaining bits are used to encode the robot speed.

The robot can move in one of the 8 directions but has inertia (the trajectories are smooth). An action is thus a 3 bits message telling in which direction to go.

To evaluate the interest of an action, a reward is computed as the robot-target distance variation that occurs when the action is performed. The closer the robot gets to the target, the higher is the reward. When an obstacle has been hit, then the reward is set to a low value.

A trial consists in letting the robot reach the target from a distant position. At the end of each trial, the environment is modified by adding or removing randomly some obstacles. Thus, some situations may appear or disappear, which results already in a highly dynamic environment. Furthermore, after performing 400 such trials, the robot commands are inverted in order to simulate an engine failure for the last 400 trials. When the robot wants to go forward, it is going backward.

For this problem, the system parameters are

Figure 2: Trajectory example for the first trial.

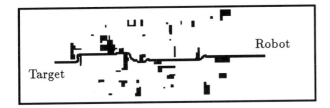

Figure 3: Trajectory example after 100 trials.

$P_{exploinit} = 50\%$, $P_{explomin} = 0.5\%$, $\lambda = 1\%$ and $mrex = 5$. Initially, the robot trajectories look like the one represented in figure 2 because the robot has no initial strategy. Then after 100 trials, which corresponds to 6 hours of simulated real time or 20000 CS cycles, the robot has learnt roughly 500 rules that result in trajectories as represented in figure 3. For instance, the robot has learnt one very general rule :

$$0\#\#\#\#\#\#\#\# \rightarrow 000$$

which means "If the target direction is free (and whatever is around the robot and whatever the speed is), then go in the target direction". The robot strategy can be globally summarized as "going in the free direction which is the closest to the target direction". The robot may thus get very close to some obstacles provided that it does not hit them, as can be seen in figure 3. The trajectories are thus locally optimal. The robot may escape from simple "C-like" obstacles provided that they are not too deep.

It is also possible to measure the system disorder (exploration rate) and quality as described previously. The quality and disorder graphs of figure 4 are more noisy than those of the F_6 learning task. Firstly, this graph was generated for only one run. Then, the obstacles are generated randomly, and sometimes a difficult obstacle appears, and disappears only several trials later. Such difficult obstacles are for instance mazes that would require a more planned strategy to be avoided. These obstacles create important local minima in the robot-target distance. If the environment is static, the graphs are comparable to those of figure 1.

After the variation, Agil needs about 200 trials to recover from the engine failure and to invert all the

actions, which corresponds to 11 hours of simulated time or 40000 CS cycles. This adaptation time is longer than the learning time because starting the adaptation process from an empty strategy is easier than from a false strategy. Here, single bit mutations are not as useful as for the previous experiment. Also, as explained in the following, the robot inertia makes exploration of new actions more difficult.

This learning task differs from and is more difficult than the previous F_6 one for several reasons. Firstly, because of the robot inertia and the environment randomness, the robot behavior is not deterministic and the rewards may have a high variance. For instance, if exploitation consists in going straight forward for a while, then a single exploration that would command the robot to go backward would have almost no effect because of inertia. Thus the reward associated to this exploration may have a high variance. This also makes adaptation more difficult because other actions than the current best one may seem to have the same effects. The randomness of the environment may cause also several difficulties. As mentioned previously, some local minima may appear which Agil cannot avoid easily. Secondly, the obstacles boundaries may become extremely noisy, and some very small obstacles of a few pixels only may appear. These obstacles may not be perceived by the robot which may hit them. This may result for instance in penalizing a good rule. Therefore, the parameter ϵ of Agil was set to 0.05 in order to deal with these sources of noise. Also, the rewards are not binary anymore and may have at least 6 different levels that correspond to the possible robot movements and obstacle hits. Two optimal actions in different situations, like going around the corner of an obstacle or going straight forward when there is no obstacle, may get different reward level. Thus the rule strengths cannot indicate directly which rules are important in the population, while the internal utility defined previously can.

Another important difference comes from the fact that the probabilities of the encountered situations are not uniform and depend on the environment and also on the robot behavior. For instance, if the robot has learnt some rules that deal with a difficult but very rare situation, the robot may forget these rules after a while, and may learn them on again when the same situation appears again. Also, these probabilities vary over time. For instance, initially the robot encounters many different situations, but when it has learnt a good strategy, the set of situations reduces very much. Thus, it has to forget the rules that have become useless because the corresponding situations do not occur anymore.

The Agil approach to robot learning can be compared with other studies in reinforcement learning. As mentioned already, the robot strategy here is a reactive one which gives a clear advantage to Dyna for instance

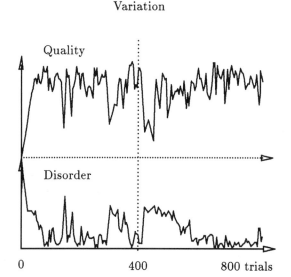

Figure 4: Agil quality and disorder when solving the task in simulated robotics.

(Sutton 1990) which performs planning. However, Dyna does not generalize and must use an exhaustive list of environment situations. Also, the environment used in Sutton's paper is only submitted to a simple variation. The robot described here is in some way similar to the Spanky robot studied in (Kaelbling 1991). The interval estimation algorithm can probably deal with this problem if it is stationary. This algorithm does not generalize, and as far as we know it has not be tested in dynamic environment. Also, like Agil, it does not deal with delayed rewards. In several other studies also, the environment is stationary (Millan and Torras 1991) (Dorigo and Sirtori 1991). Many efficient algorithms exist in moving robotics that learn behaviors from an interaction with the environment, but they usually assume that the environment and robot models are stationary, like for instance (Iyengar et al. 1985) or (Faverjon and Tournassoud 1987).

5   Conclusion

We have presented an extension of a simple classifier system that can solve explicitly the exploration versus exploitation dilemma. The first extension has consisted in making a difference between exploration and exploitation by using a new strength computation scheme. Then, the decision procedure was modified in order to take into account this difference, and also a rule optimality measure that is computed using a simulated annealing like process. The resulting algorithm can control explicitly the tradeoff between exploration and exploitation according to the parameters given by the user. It has been applied to different problems where adaptability is an important property. A minimal

exploration probability was necessary for adapting the system behavior to variations in the environment.

However, several limitations remain. Firstly, we have supposed that the reward was not delayed, which is a strong assumption that could be certainly removed by using the profit sharing plan for instance and by updating the rule strengths only when the reward is available.

Then, if we consider the range of possible variations in a dynamic environment, totally unseen variations (that needs an exploration mechanism) is the worst possible case. For other kinds of variations that can be perceived more easily, a minimal exploration probability is certainly not the best mechanism for adapting the system behavior. In this case, some detection mechanisms could be used, like detecting variations in the rewards (Goldberg 1990). Also, we have studied only sudden changes in the environment, and not other kind of variations like gradual changes, or incremented problems like in (Zhou and Grefenstette 1989). A comparison with Boole or Gofer-1 in changing environments would also be interesting in order to compare Agil with related adaptive algorithms.

We would also like to find some biological clues for solving the EVE dilemma. For instance, it would be interesting to look for biological experiments, where an animal have to solve a given problem, and where this problem is modified over time. In such an experiment, it could be possible to measure the animal disorder and quality on a small set of situations, and to see how it solves the EVE dilemma, and for instance, what minimal exploration probability it applies, like it has been done for Agil.

References

Antonisse H.J. and Keller K.S. (1987), Genetic operators for high level knowledge representations, Proceedings of the Second International Conference on Genetic Algorithms, 1987, J.J. Grefenstette (Ed.), LEA Pub, pp 69-76.

Booker L.B. (1989), Triggered rule discovery in classifier systems, Proceedings of the third International Conference on Genetic Algorithms, 1989, J.D. Schaffer (Ed.), Morgan Kaufmann, pp 265-274.

Dorigo M. and Sirtori E. (1991), Alecsys: a parallel laboratory for learning classifier systems, Proceedings of the Fourth International Conference on Genetic Algorithms, R.K. Belew and L.B. Booker (Eds), Morgan Kaufmann, pp 296-302.

Faverjon B. and Tournassoud P. (1987), The mixed approach for motion planning: learning global strategies from a local planner, Proceedings of the

Tenth International Joint Conference on Artificial Intelligence 1987, J. McDermott (Ed), pp 1131-1137, Morgan Kaufmann.

Goldberg D.E. (1990), Probability matching, the magnitude of reinforcement, and classifier system bidding, Machine Learning 5, pp 407-425.

Grefenstette J.J. (1988), Credit assignment in rule discovery systems based on genetic algorithms, Machine Learning 3, pp 225-245.

Grefenstette J.J. and Ramsey C.L. (1992), An approach to anytime learning, Proceedings of the Ninth International Workshop on Machine Learning 1992, D. Sleeman and P. Edwards (Eds), Morgan Kaufmann, pp 189-195.

Holland J.H. and Reitman J.J. (1978), Cognitive systems based on adaptive algorithms, Pattern-directed Inference Systems, D.A. Waterman and F. Hayes-Roth (Eds), Academic Press.

Holland J.H. (1986), Escaping brittleness: the possibilities of general-purpose learning algorithms applied to parallel rule-based systems, Machine Learning: an AI approach, volume 3, R.S. Michalski, T.M. Mitchell, J.G. Carbonell and Y. Kodratoff (Eds), pp 593-623.

Iyengar S.S., Jorgensen C.C., Rao S.V.N. and Weisbin C.R. (1985), Learned navigation path for a robot in unexplored terrain, IEEE Second Conference on Artificial Intelligence Applications 1985, pp 176-183.

Kaelbling L.P. (1991), An adaptable mobile robot, Proceedings of the first European Conference on Artificial Life 1991, F.J. Varela and P. Bourgine (Eds), MIT press/Bradford Books, pp 41-47.

Lin L.J. (1991), Self improvement based on reinforcement learning, planning and teaching, Proceedings of the Eight International Workshop on Machine Learning 1991, Morgan Kaufmann, pp 323-327.

Millan J.R. and Torras C. (1991), Learning to avoid obstacles through reinforcement learning, Proceedings of the Eigth International Workshop on Machine Learning 1991, L.A. Birnbaum et G.C. Collins (Eds), Morgan Kaufmann, pp 298-302.

Sutton R.S. (1990), Integrated architectures for learning, planning, and reacting based on approximating dynamic programming, Proceedings of the Seventh International Conference on Machine Learning 1990, B.W. Porter and R.J. Mooney (Eds.), pp 216-224, Morgan Kaufmann.

Venturini G. (1991), Characterizing the adaptation abilities of a class of genetic based machine learning algorithms, Proceedings of the first European Conference on Artificial Life 1991, F.J. Varela and P. Bourgine (Eds), MIT press/Bradford Books, pp 302-309.

Watkins C.J.C.H. (1989), Learning with delayed reward, PhD thesis, Cambridge University, Psychology Department.

Wilson S.W. (1985), Knowledge growth in an artificial animal, Proceedings of an International Conference on Genetic Algorithms, J.J. Grefenstette (Ed.), LEA Pub, pp 16-23.

Wilson S.W. (1987a), Classifier systems and the animat problem, Machine Learning 2, pp 199-228.

Wilson S.W. (1987b), Quasi-Darwinian Learning in a Classifier System, Proceeding of the Fourth International Workshop on Machine Learning 1987, P. Langley (Ed), 59-65, Morgan Kaufmann.

Zhou H. H. and Grefenstette J.J. (1989), Learning by analogy in genetic classifier systems, Proceedings of the third International Conference on Genetic Algorithms, 1989, J.D. Schaffer (Ed.), Morgan Kaufmann, pp 291-297.

EVOLUTION

Integrating Reactive, Sequential, and Learning Behavior Using Dynamical Neural Networks

Brian Yamauchi[1,3] and Randall Beer[1,2]

Department of Computer Engineering and Science[1]
Department of Biology[2]
Case Western Reserve University
Cleveland, OH 44106

Navy Center for Applied Research in Artificial Intelligence[3]
Naval Research Laboratory
Washington, DC 20375-5000

yamauchi@alpha.ces.cwru.edu
beer@alpha.ces.cwru.edu

Abstract

This paper explores the use of dynamical neural networks to control autonomous agents in tasks requiring reactive, sequential, and learning behavior. We use a genetic algorithm to evolve networks that can integrate these different types of behavior in a smooth, continuous manner. We apply this approach to three different task domains: landmark recognition using sonar on a real mobile robot, one-dimensional navigation using a simulated agent, and reinforcement-based sequence learning.

A novel feature of the learning aspects of our approach is that we assume neither an a priori discretization of states or time nor an a priori learning algorithm that explicitly modifies network parameters during learning. Instead, we expose dynamical neural networks to tasks that require learning and allow the genetic algorithm to evolve network dynamics that generates the desired behavior.

1. Introduction

Animals and robots need many different types of behavior to operate effectively in a dynamic environment. Consider, for example, an animal that needs to forage for food and return that food to its nest. As it explores its environment, it needs to react to any threats or obstacles that it encounters. When it finds food, it needs to remember the way back to its nest. Finally, it needs to learn the location of the food source and remember how to return, so that it can come back for more. So, in order to forage effectively, such an animal would require the capability for reactive and sequential behavior, as well as the ability to learn from experience. Similar capabilities would be required for a planetary rover collecting rock samples and returning those samples to its lander, or a mobile robot retrieving objects in an office environment.

Of the three types of behavior mentioned above, reactive behavior has been the primary focus of most autonomous agents research. The capability to react to the immediate situation *is* of central importance to an agent that must operate in an unpredictable world, but other capabilities are important as well. Agents also need the capability to perform sequences of activities, where each action may depend not only on the agent's current perceptions, but previous perceptions and actions as well. This broad category spans a wide range of behavior -- from stereotyped sequences where each action depends only on the previous action, to recognition tasks where an agent must make a decision based upon sequences of perceptions, to spatial navigation where an agent's motions depend not only on previous motions but also on landmarks and goals in the environment, to reinforcement learning where an agent's actions are shaped by the degree to which they elicit a reward. The common quality that these different behaviors share is their requirement that the agent be able to integrate perceptions over time into some form of internal memory, and that the agent be able to use this memory to modify its actions.

Most attempts to combine sequenced and learned behavior with reactive behavior have assumed a sharp division between the components that are reactive and those that are in charge of sequencing or learning. In animals, however, such divisions are far less distinct. For example, the boundary between instinctual and learned behavior is a fuzzy one -- instincts can be modified by learning, and learning often takes place within a limited range of possible behaviors. This provides organisms with the ability to learn what they need to learn within their lifetimes, but also with the innate behaviors that have been evolved over previous generations -- and a continuum of intermediate behaviors that exhibit varying degrees of plasticity. We would like to give robots the same capability that animals possess to integrate reactive, sequential, and learned behavior in a manner that is smooth and continuous.

In animals, *all* behavior is evolved behavior -- including behavior that incorporates learning -- and this idea has motivated the research described in this paper. In this research, we explored the possibilities for using genetic algorithms to evolve dynamical neural networks that are capable of performing tasks that require both sequential behavior and learning.

A unique aspect of our approach is that the processes of sequencing and learning are internalized in the activation dynamics of the individual networks. No external algorithm is used to modify network weights during an agent's lifetime. Instead, perceptions integrated over time modify the internal state of the network, and these changes modify the dynamical behavior of the network and the agent that it controls.

Previous research in our group (Beer & Gallagher, 1992) has shown that dynamical neural networks can be evolved for tasks requiring reactive behavior and simple sequential motor control, but there are a number of open questions regarding the applicability of this approach to learning tasks. How general is this approach? Can neural networks use internal state to integrate perception? What types of sequential behavior can be generated? What types of learning?

In order to investigate these questions, we applied this approach to three different types of tasks: landmark recognition, one-dimensional navigation, and sequence learning. These tasks fall at very different points in the continuum of behavioral plasticity defined above, but they all share a requirement for agents that can use previous perceptions and actions to modify their behavior. In this paper, we describe these tasks, the methods used to evolve solutions, and the results obtained. Finally, we summarize with our conclusions about the strengths and weaknesses of this approach.

2. Methods

2.1 Dynamical Neural Networks (DNNs)

In the experiments described in this paper, we employed continuous-time recurrent neural networks whose behavior is governed by a system of differential equations of the following form:

$$\frac{dv_i}{dt} = \frac{1}{\tau_i}\left(-v_i + \sum_j w_{ij}f(v_j) + \sum_j s_{ij}I_j\right)$$

where v_i is the voltage of neuron i, τ_i is the time constant of unit i, w_{ij} is the weight of the connection from neuron j to neuron i, I_i is the input from sensor i, and s_{ij} is the weight of the connection from sensor j to neuron i.

The firing rate of neuron i is given by the sigmoid function $f(v_i) = (1 - e^{(t_i - v_i)})^{-1}$ where t_i is the threshold of neuron i.

2.2 The Genetic Algorithm

A real-valued genetic algorithm with a modular encoding scheme was used to search the parameter space of the above dynamical neural networks. Network parameters were encoded as a vector of real numbers, with the time constant, bias, sensor weights and incoming connection weights for each neuron represented as an indivisible unit for the purposes of crossover. This modular encoding is motivated by our belief that a neuron's intrinsic parameters and input weights form a useful building block that would not be preserved by a more conventional binary coding of parameters which allowed crossover to occur at arbitrary points.

The initial population was typically produced by randomly selecting a real value for each parameter of each network with a uniform probability distribution over the range of allowable values. The fitness of each individual in the population was then evaluated in simulation. An agent controlled by each network was run through a series of test trials, and the average score on these trials was used as the network's fitness.

Once fitness scores were assigned to all individuals in the population, a new population was generated. Individuals were selected for reproduction with a probability proportional to their fitness. If crossover did not occur, a single parent was randomly selected. If crossover did occur, two parents were randomly selected and a crossover point x was randomly chosen. The child then received the parameters for neurons 1 through x from its first parent and the parameters for the remaining neurons from its second parent.

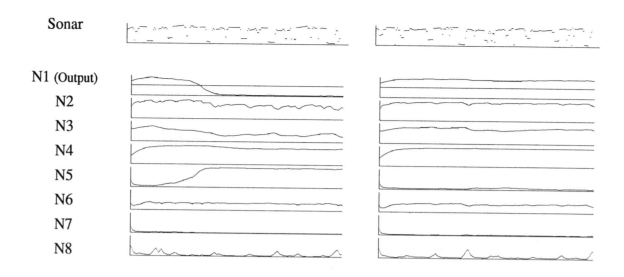

Figure 1: Behavior of landmark recognition network on (a) a landmark 1 trial (left), and (b) a landmark 2 trial (right). The top trace shows the sonar sensor input. The remaining traces show the neuron outputs. The first neuron is the classifier neuron.

Regardless of whether or not crossover occurred, there was a small probability (mutation rate) that any particular parameter of the child would be mutated. When mutation occurred, a new value was randomly chosen for the parameter to be mutated with a uniform probability distribution over the range of allowable values.

3. Landmark Recognition

3.1 Task

In reactive tasks, an agent's actions are determined by its immediate perceptions, but many other types of tasks require that an agent integrate those perceptions over time before it can decide what action to take. Consider the task of landmark recognition. The identity of the landmark may determine which way the agent should move. If the agent can identify a landmark based on perceptions received at a single moment in time, it can make a reactive decision about which way to move. However, if a single set of perceptions is not sufficient to identify the landmark, the agent will need to collect sensory information over time as, for example, it views the landmark from different directions, and eventually the agent needs to reach a decision based on the time-varying pattern of sensor data that it has received. For this reason, we chose the landmark recognition task to investigate whether dynamical neural networks can be evolved for tasks requiring the integration of perceptions over time.

For these experiments, we used a Nomad 200 mobile robot in an indoor environment. The task consisted of

identifying one of two landmarks based on the time-varying sonar signals received as the robot circles the landmark. The focus of this research was on the ability of the neural network to perform the recognition task itself, rather than on the integrated control of the robot, so a simple behavior-based control system was used to allow the robot to find a wall and follow the wall counterclockwise around the perimeter of the room. The range signals received from the single sonar on the left side of the robot were used as the single input to the network. After integrating this information over a period of time, the robot was required to identify this landmark as one of two possible landmarks. Landmark 1 consisted of a long rectangle formed from two crates pushed together. Landmark 2 consisted of two squares formed from the same two crates separated by a distance of one crate width. Since a single sonar reading is not sufficient to differentiate between these two landmarks, the robot needed to use information in the temporal sequence of sonar returns in order to perform this task.

3.2 Methods

An eight-neuron dynamical neural network was evolved to solve this task. All of the neurons in this network received input from the left side sonar sensor. Neuron 1 was designated the output unit, and its firing rate $f(v_o)$ was treated as the network's output. After a fixed period of time (45 seconds of simulator time, corresponding to 135 seconds of time for the real robot), the output of neuron 1 was examined and used to classify the landmark. An output of less than 0.5 identified the landmark as landmark

1. An output of 0.5 or greater identified the landmark as landmark 2.

A population of 100 networks was evolved in simulation with a crossover rate of 0.5 and a mutation rate of 0.025. Six test trials were run for each individual in each generation -- three trials on landmark 1 and three trials on landmark 2. In each trial, the agent was started at a random position and orientation in the environment and allowed to run for a fixed length of time .

The score for each trial was computed as follows:

$$score = \begin{cases} 1 - f(v_0) \text{ for landmark } 0 \\ f(v_0) \quad \text{ for landmark } 1 \end{cases}$$

The average of these test scores was used as each network's fitness value, and the genetic algorithm was applied to evolve populations that maximized this fitness function.

3.3 Results

After 15 generations, a network was evolved that was capable of recognizing these landmarks in simulation. This network was then transferred to the real mobile robot, where it was able to correctly classify landmarks in 17 out of 20 test trials. The network correctly identified landmark 1 in all 10 out of 10 trials, and it correctly identified landmark 2 in 7 out of 10 trials.

The top track in Figure 1a shows the sonar input that the agent received during a trial with landmark 1. Since the output of the sonar sensor is inversely proportional to the range reading, a high output indicates a nearby obstacle (the landmark) while a low output indicates a distant obstacle (the walls of the room). The remaining tracks in Figure 1a show the corresponding neuron outputs for this trial. The first of these tracks shows the firing rate for the output neuron, with the central horizontal line indicating a firing rate of 0.5. A neuron firing rate below this line indicates the agent is currently identifying the landmark as landmark 1 -- while a neuron firing rate above this line indicates that the agent is identifying the landmark as landmark 2. The identification made at the end of the trial is the one used for classification and scoring purposes. In this trial, the agent starts out by identifying the landmark as landmark 2, but after circling the landmark it changes its identification to landmark 1, and this remains unchanged for the duration of the trial. Figure 1b shows the sonar sensor output that the agent received during the trial with landmark 2 along with the corresponding neuron firing rates. Again the agent starts out by classifying the landmark as landmark 2, but in this case, the classification remains the same, even after the agent has circled the landmark.

We also investigated the application of dynamical neural networks to two other mobile robot tasks: predator avoidance and reactive navigation. For predator avoidance, DNNs were evolved to allow a robot to escape from moving pursuers while avoiding static obstacles. For reactive navigation, a hand-designed DNN was used in combination with algorithms for detecting static and cyclic behavior to allow a robot to navigate to a destination while avoiding obstacles. Further details about these tasks can be found in Yamauchi (1993).

4. One-Dimensional Navigation

4.1 Task

The results from the landmark recognition task showed that dynamical neural networks could be evolved to integrate sensory perceptions over time to arrive at a decision. The next question we explored was whether DNNs could integrate the ability to make decisions based on learning with the ability to control the motor behavior of an autonomous agent.

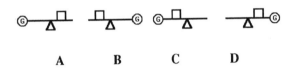

Figure 2: Environments for the navigation task. The triangle represents the agent, the circle represents the goal, and the rectangle represents the landmark. The landmark-far environments (A and B) are on the left, and the landmark-near environments (C and D) are on the right.

We chose the simplest possible continuous environment for our first experiments in this domain, a one-dimensional continuum along which the agent could move in either direction. Each environment contains a goal and a landmark. At the start of each trial, the agent is positioned in the center of the continuum, and the goal is positioned randomly at either the left end or the right end. In landmark-far environments (Figures 2A and 2B), the landmark is located on the opposite side of the agent from the goal. In landmark-near environments (Figures 2C and 2D), the landmark is located on the same side of the agent as the goal.

The agent possesses a landmark sensor and a goal sensor. Both of these provide only proximal information. The agent is treated as a point body and can only detect the landmark or the goal when it is directly in contact.

The agent's task is to learn, over a series of successive trials, whether the current environment is landmark-far or landmark-near, and then to reach the goal. Each trial lasts

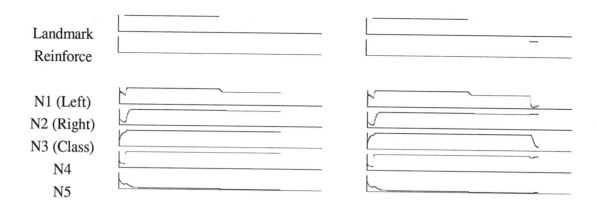

Landmark

Reinforce

N1 (Left)

N2 (Right)

N3 (Class)

N4

N5

Figure 3: Behavior of the classifier network on (a) a landmark-near, goal-left trial (left) and (b) a landmark-far, goal-right trial (right). The upper two traces describe the landmark sensor input and the reinforcement sensor input. The remaining traces show the neuron outputs. The first two neurons are the left and right motor neurons. The third neuron is the classifier neuron.

until either the agent reaches the goal, the agent reaches the non-goal end of the continuum, or the time limit (1000 timesteps) is exceeded. If the agent reaches the goal, it receives reinforcement for 50 timesteps. If the agent does not reach the goal -- because it went to the wrong end or because it ran out of time -- then it does not receive any reinforcement, but the network is updated for 50 timesteps without any input.

In this task, as in many more complex tasks, the elements of reactive behavior, sequential behavior, and learning are all closely related rather than separated by sharp boundaries. Agents need to react to their perception of the landmark, but this action must be part of a sequence that will lead the robot to the goal. Since the goal location is randomly chosen, the agent cannot simply move left or right and expect to find the goal. In addition, the agent cannot search both the left and right ends of the continuum, because the trial ends as soon as the agent touches either end. As a result, the agent needs to learn the type of environment in which it is situated, based upon its perceptions of the landmark and the goal. Since the agent never perceives the landmark and the goal at the same time, it must integrate its perceptions over time in order to determine the position of the goal relative to the landmark. Once it has learned the environment type, it can then use the perception of the landmark in each individual trial to guide it toward the goal.

4.2 Methods

Attempts to evolve a single network capable of solving the entire task were unsuccessful, so a modular, incremental approach was used instead. The network architecture contains three separate subnetworks: one for goal-seeking behavior in landmark-far environments, one for

goal-seeking behavior in landmark-near environments, and one for environment classification. Each of these subnetworks was evolved separately, then the three networks were assembled into an integrated system. The classifier network controls the agent during the first trial in each environment. At the end of the trial, the classification output determines which of the other two networks is used to control the agent for the remaining trials.

Each subnetwork consisted of a five-neuron, fully-interconnected DNN. All of these subnetworks have a sensor input for landmark detection and two motor outputs -- a left motor neuron and a right motor neuron. In addition, the classifier network has a sensor input for reinforcement, and a classification output used to determine the environment type. All of the neurons in all of the networks receive inputs from all of the available sensors.

The agent's velocity is equal to the difference in output between the left and right motor neurons: $dx/dt = f(v_R) - f(v_L)$, where x is the agent's current location, dx/dt is the agent's velocity, $f(v_R)$ is the output of the right motor neuron, and $f(v_L)$ is the output of the left motor neuron. The classification of the environment is landmark-far if the output of the classification neuron at the end of the trial is less than 0.5, and landmark-near otherwise.

Both of the goal-seeking networks were evolved using similar methods. A population of 1000 networks was evolved with a crossover rate of 0.5 and a mutation rate of 0.025. For each generation, each network was run for two trials -- one with the goal left, and one with the goal right. The landmark-far network was evolved exclusively in landmark-far environments, and the landmark-near network was evolved exclusively in landmark-near environments. The performance of a network on a given trial was 1 if the goal was reached and 0 if the goal was not reached. The fitness of a network was equal to its average performance over both trials.

The classifier network was evolved to identify the environment type in a single test trial. In each generation, each network was run on four separate trials. These trials covered all of the possible combinations of environment type and goal location: landmark-far/goal-left, landmark-far/goal-right, landmark-near/goal-left, and landmark-near/goal-right. The performance of the network was equal to the error between the optimal classification (0 for landmark-far, 1 for landmark-near) and the actual classification output at the end of the trial:

$$P = \begin{cases} f(v_C) & for\ landmark-far \\ 1-f(v_C) & for\ landmark-near \end{cases}$$

where P is the network's performance and $f(v_C)$ is the network's classification output. The fitness of each classifier network was equal to its average performance over all four test trials.

4.3 Results

Networks were successfully evolved for all three of these tasks. One of the networks in the initial population for the landmark-far goal-seeking task was able to find the goal for both the goal-left and goal-right trials. Initially, this network moves left for a short period of time (not far enough to contact a left-side landmark), then it starts moving right. If the agent *does* encounter the landmark, then it reverses direction again, moving left until it reaches the goal (Figure 2A). If the agent does *not* encounter the landmark, then it continues moving right until it reaches the goal (Figure 2B).

After two generations, a network was evolved to solve the landmark-near goal-seeking task. This network starts moving right until it has moved far enough to encounter a right-side landmark, if one exists. If it does *not* encounter a right-side landmark, then it reverses direction and moves left until it reaches the goal (Figure 2C). If it *does* encounter the landmark, the it continues moving right until it reaches the goal (Figure 2D).

After five generations, a network was evolved that could correctly classify all of the trials in both of the environment types. Figure 3a shows the sensor and neuron traces for a landmark-far trial where the goal is located on the right (Figure 2B). Figure 3b shows the sensor and neuron traces for a landmark-near trial where the goal is located on the left (Figure 2C). In landmark-far environments, the landmark is located on the opposite side of the environment from the goal, and in landmark-near environments, the landmark is located on the same side of the environment as the goal -- so in both cases, the landmark will be located to the left of the agent.

The network starts with its classification output high, and its left motor output higher than its right motor output, so the agent moves left until it encounters the landmark. At this point, the landmark sensor becomes active, and the left and right motor outputs both increase to roughly equal levels, but the right output is actually slightly higher, so the agent moves right slowly. When the agent moves past the right edge of the landmark, the landmark sensor becomes inactive, the left output drops slightly, and the agent moves right at a somewhat faster rate of speed. In the trial shown in Figure 3a, the goal was located on the left so the agent never reached the goal, and its classification output remained high, identifying the environment as landmark-near. In the trial shown in Figure 3b, the goal was located on the right, so the agent was reinforced when it reached the goal, and its classification output went low, identifying the environment as landmark-far.

If the landmark had been on the right side of the agent instead, then the agent would not have reversed direction, and would have continued moving until it reached the left edge of the environment. In a landmark-near environment, a right landmark means that the goal is located on the right, so the agent will not be reinforced, and will continue to generate a high classification output, identifying the environment as landmark-far. In a landmark-far environment, a right landmark means that the goal is located on the left, so the agent *will* be reinforced, and will change its classification output to identify the environment as landmark-near.

Thus, the classifier network can correctly identify all four possible combinations of environment type and goal location. This network was then integrated with the two goal-seeking networks to create a system that could navigate to the goal in all four cases.

5. Sequence Learning

5.1 The Task

The results from the one-dimensional navigation task demonstrated that a dynamical neural network could control an autonomous agent and integrate perceptions over time to learn the identity of an environment, and that based on this identification, one of two other DNNs could be used to control the agent appropriately for that environment. The next question we addressed was whether this selection process could be internalized. Instead of using the output of one network to activate or deactivate others, could a single network switch between several different modes of behavior based on what it learned about its environment?

Consider a rat attempting to navigate a maze. As it traverses a maze, it is presented with a series of choice points at variable intervals of time. Each time it reaches an intersection, it must choose to go either left or right. While each intersection may be partially distinguished by

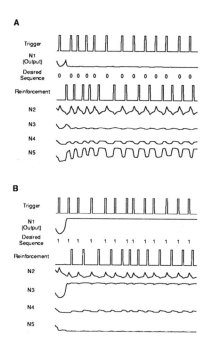

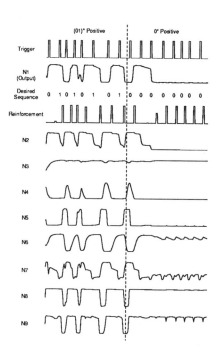

Figure 4: Behavior of the one-bit sequence learning network on (a) a 0* positive trial and (b) a 1* positive trial.

Figure 5: Behavior of the two-bit sequence learning network on a (01)* positive trial followed by a 0* positive trial.

perceptual cues, such as visual appearance or smell, in general perceptual information will be insufficient to uniquely determine the appropriate action. Instead, the rat must integrate these partial perceptual cues with its previous decisions in that run in order to determine the most appropriate action. Furthermore, in order to learn its way through new mazes, a rat must also be capable of learning new decision sequences. If we idealize the decision trigger from the environment as a binary input and the decision to be made as a binary choice, then the sequential learning problem becomes the problem of learning to generate a particular sequence of binary digits in response to a sequence of environmental triggers occurring at variable intervals of time.

In the sequence learning task, the network is required to generate one of a set B of possible sequences based on environmental reinforcement. The reinforcement of a given decision was delayed by a variable amount of time, but always occurred before the next environmental trigger. Thus, while the network could not rely upon receiving reinforcement at a fixed point in time, we did not address the general problem of delayed reinforcement. If a sequence repeats with a period *n*, then we will refer to it as an *n*-bit sequence learning task. For example, using regular expression notation, a maze for which the path to the goal consisted of alternating left and right turns would pose a two-bit sequence learning task of the form (01)* or

(10)* depending upon whether 0 or 1 was the correct decision for the first intersection.

Fully interconnected dynamical neural networks with two inputs, one binary (the trigger) and one continuous (the reinforcement signal), and one continuous output (the decision) were employed. The decision trigger input I_1 normally had a value of 0. At variable intervals of time, however, the environment signaled that a decision must be made by setting I_1 to 1 for 10 time steps. The time interval between triggers was drawn from a uniform probability distribution over the range [10,40] time steps. By convention, neuron 1 always served as the output of the network. For the duration of a trigger, the output of neuron 1 was compared to the corresponding bit in the desired sequence.

Following a decision trigger, reinforcement was presented for a fixed duration of 10 time steps with a delay uniformly distributed over the range [10,40] time steps. For a given stimulus and response, the reinforcement is:

$$R = 1 - \frac{1}{end-start} \int_{start}^{end} |p - f(v_1)|$$

where R is reinforcement signal, p is the desired output, $f(v_1)$ is the firing rate of the output neuron, and start and end are the starting and ending times of the stimulus input The interval between the presentation of the reinforcement signal for the networks response to one trigger and the next trigger was uniformly distributed over the range [10,40] time steps.

The overall performance of the network on a given trial is given by:

$$P = 1 - perf_{base} - \frac{1}{n} \sum_{i=1}^{n} R_i$$

where P is the performance value, $perf_{base}$ is the the base performance (usually the performance score expected from a random or constant output), n is the number of stimuli in the trial, and R_i is the ith reinforcement signal. Performance scores of less than zero were treated as zero.

The results of these experiments are summarized below. A more detailed treatment can be found in Yamauchi and Beer (1994).

5.2 One-Bit Sequence Learning

In our first learning experiment, we sought to evolve five-neuron networks that could learn to generate the set of one-bit sequences B = {0*, 1*} based on environmental reinforcement. The learning problem here is relatively simple -- the network must utilize the reinforcement signal in order to determine which constant output state to adopt. Two experiments were run on a population of 1000 networks for 500 generations, with a crossover rate of 0.3, a mutation rate of 0.01, and $perf_{base}$ set to 0.5. Both experiments consisted of four trials.

In the first experiment, networks were evaluated on two 0* positive and two 1* positive trials. The behavior of one network is shown in Figure 4. This network initially adopts an output state of 0. If this output is reinforced, then it remains in this state as long as it is reinforced (Figure 4a). If, however, this output is not reinforced, then the network adopts an output of 1 and then remains in this state permanently (Figure 4b). Using the techniques of dynamical systems theory, we were able to analyze the behavior of these networks in terms of fixed point and limit cycle attractors. This analysis is described in Yamauchi and Beer (1994).

5.3 Two-Bit Sequence Learning

In our second set of learning experiments, we sought to evolve dynamical neural networks that could learn to generate the set of sequences B = {0*, 1*, (01)*, (10)*} based on environmental reinforcement. Unfortunately, attempts to directly evolve such networks were unsuccessful. However, we were able to produce solutions to this problem using an incremental approach.

First, we evolved five-neuron networks that could learn to generate the more limited set of two-bit sequences {(01)*, (10)*}. We already have five-neuron networks that

can learn to generate the sequences 0* and 1* from our previous experiments. Then, we seeded a population with ten-neuron networks formed by fully interconnecting {0*, 1*} one-bit sequence learning networks with {(01)*, (10)*} networks and evolved this population on the full two-bit sequence learning task, with the output neuron of the {0*, 1*} network serving as the output neuron for the composite network. Two such experiments were run on a population of 1000 networks for 500 generations, with a crossover rate of 0.3, a mutation rate of 0.002 and $perf_{base}$ set to the average performance of each generation.

The behavior of one solution to the full two-bit learning task is shown in Figure 5. Note that this particular network made use of only nine of its neurons. Figure 5 shows this network on a (01)* positive trial followed by a 0* positive trial. After receiving one low reinforcement following its output of near 1 during the first trigger, the network locks into the (01)* sequence. When the pattern of reinforcement changes from (01)* positive to 0* positive after eight triggers, it takes the network three trigger-reinforcement pairs before it successfully makes the transition to 0*. Part of this delay is due to the fact that the networks output of 0 on the ninth trigger is fortuitously reinforced because 0* and (01)* share the same next bit. It is not until the tenth trigger that a low reinforcement following an output of 1 signals that a switch in behavior is necessary. This network is also capable of learning the other two two-bit sequences, 1* and (10)*.

5.4 Three-Bit Sequence Learning

In our final set of learning experiments, we sought to evolve networks that could learn the set of three-bit sequences B = {(011)*, (101)*, (110)*} based on environmental reinforcement. All of the members of this particular set are related by a phase shift. A population of 1000 ten-neuron networks was evolved, and after 700 generations, with a crossover rate of 0.3. a mutation rate of 0.002, and $perf_{base}$ set to 0.666, a network was evolved that was capable of successfully learning all three sequences.

6. Related Work

Many researchers have used genetic algorithms to evolve autonomous agents, and a few researchers have evolved recurrent neural networks capable of reactive behavior. Jefferson and Collins evolved agents capable of following a fixed trail (Jefferson, et al. 1992) and performing reactive foraging (Collins & Jefferson, 1991). Beer and Gallagher (1992) evolved agents capable of chemotaxis and legged locomotion. Cliff, Harvey, and Husbands (1993) evolved a network capable of using vision to center a simulated robot in a cylindrical environment. What makes our work different from these research efforts is that we evolve agents that can not only react to their environment, but also integrate information over time to modify their future behavior. Ackley and Littman (Ackley & Littman, 1992) combine evolutionary techniques with reinforcement learning by evolving an evaluation network that modifies the weights on an action network, based on the amount of reinforcement received. The primary differences between our work and theirs are that they use a separate learning algorithm (an extension of back-propagation) to modify weights during learning, and that both the world state and agent actions are discretized in their simulation.

Much research has been done in the area of reinforcement learning. Our work differs from traditional approaches (for example, Sutton, 1988; Kaelbling, 1993), in several fundamental ways. In traditional approaches, both world states and agent actions are assumed to be discrete in both space and time, while in our experiments, continuous perceptions and actions occurred in continuous space (for the navigation and landmark recognition tasks) and continuous time (for all tasks). In traditional approaches, a learning algorithm is used to adjust parameters that allow the agent to learn from experience. In our approach, the genetic algorithm is used to adjust parameters between generations, but no external algorithm is used to adjust parameters during an agent's lifetime. Instead, the internal dynamics of the neural network are used to integrate the perceptions of the agent, and to determine the agent's actions based upon these perceptions.

Some work has also been done in combining reinforcement learning with the techniques from behavior-based robotics. Maes and Brooks (1990) have used reinforcement learning to learn to coordinate the activity of hand-designed behaviors for legged locomotion. Mahadevan and Connell (1990) have used reinforcement learning to learn reactive behaviors in a system where the behavior decomposition and arbitration was designed by hand. Our work differs not only in the control mechanism (dynamical neural networks vs. finite-state behaviors), but more fundamentally, in the use of network dynamics rather than an external learning algorithm to allow the agent to learn from experience. Maes (1992) has also used reinforcement-based weight adjustment in a network of behaviors to learn behavior selection. Our work is similar in using internalized, distributed learning, but different in that our learning emerges directly from neuron activation dynamics, while Maes' algorithm is based upon statistics accumulated from the co-activation of behavior nodes. In addition, the individual behaviors in Maes' network are hand-designed, while the behaviors in our networks are evolved.

7. Conclusions

The principal aim of this research was to determine whether dynamical neural networks could provide an effective control mechanism for integrating reactive, sequential, and learning behavior in autonomous agents. In order to investigate this question, we attempted to evolve DNNs that could solve tasks involving landmark recognition, one-dimensional navigation, and sequence learning.

In the landmark recognition task, networks were evolved that could learn the identity of different landmarks based on time-varying sonar input on a real mobile robot. In the one-dimensional navigation task, networks were evolved that could learn the relationship between a landmark and the goal, then use this relationship to guide the agent to the goal. In the sequence learning task, networks were evolved that could learn to generate different sequences of output based on the reinforcement received.

Our primary conclusion, based on the results from these experiments, is that dynamical neural networks can provide a means of integrating reactivity, sequencing, and learning within a single control system.

In addition, we also conclude that genetic algorithms provide a means of generating these networks, at least for simple problems. The primary limitation that we encountered was one of scaling -- *not* in the DNNs themselves, but in the time required for the genetic algorithm search.

One way to deal with the scaling problem is to use a modular approach. In this approach, small networks are evolved to solve subtasks, and then these networks are assembled to solve the entire task. A good problem decomposition can minimize the amount of search that the genetic algorithm needs to perform, and in some cases (such as the landmark-far goal-seeking task) even random generation combined with a single round of selection can find solutions. The results from the two-bit sequence learning task and the one-dimensional navigation task indicate that this approach can be used to build networks that can perform tasks that would otherwise present scaling problems.

Acknowledgments

This work was supported in part by grant N00014-90-J-1545 from the Office of Naval Research. The robot experiments were performed at the Navy Center for Applied Research in Artificial Intelligence at the Naval Research Laboratory.

References

Ackley, David and Michael Littman (1992). Interactions between learning and evolution. In *Artificial Life II,* Chris Langton, et al., eds. Redwood City, CA: Addison-Wesley.

Beer, Randall and John Gallagher (1992). Evolving dynamical neural networks for adaptive behavior. *Adaptive Behavior*, Vol. 1, No. 1.

Cliff, Dave, Inman Harvey, and Phil Husbands (1993). Explorations in evolutionary robotics. *Adaptive Behavior*, Vol. 2, No. 1.

Collins, Robert and David Jefferson (1991). Representations for artificial organisms. In *From Animals to Animats: Proceedings of the First International Conference on Simulation of Adaptive Behavior*, Cambridge, MA: MIT Press.

Jefferson, David, Robert Collins, Claus Cooper, Michael Dyer, Margot Flowers, Richard Korf, Charles Taylor, and Alan Wang (1992). Evolution as a theme in artificial life: the Genesys/Tracker system. In *Artificial Life II,* Chris Langton, et al., eds. Redwood City, CA: Addison-Wesley.

Kaelbling, Leslie (1993). *Learning in Embedded Systems.* Cambridge, MA: MIT Press.

Mahadevan, Sridhar and Jonathan Connell (1990). Automatic programming of behavior-based robots using reinforcement learning. Research Report RC16359, IBM Research Division, Yorktown Heights, NY.

Maes, Pattie (1991). "Learning behavior networks from experience", *Towards a Practice of Autonomous Systems: Proceedings of the First European Conference on Artificial Life*, Francisco Varela and Paul Bourgine, eds., Cambridge, MA: MIT Press.

Maes, Pattie and Rodney Brooks (1992). Learning to coordinate behaviors. In *Proceedings of the Eighth National Conference on AI*, San Mateo, CA: Morgan Kaufmann.

Sutton, Richard (1988). Learning to predict by the method of temporal differences. *Machine Learning*, Vol. 7, pp. 227-252.

Yamauchi, Brian (1993). Dynamical neural networks for mobile robot control. NRL Memorandum Report AIC-033-93, Naval Research Laboratory, Washington, DC.

Yamauchi, Brian and Randall Beer (1994). Sequential behavior and learning in evolved dynamical neural networks. *Adaptive Behavior,* Vol. 2, No. 3.

Seeing The Light: Artificial Evolution, Real Vision

Inman Harvey and Phil Husbands and Dave Cliff

School of Cognitive and Computing Sciences
University of Sussex, Brighton BN1 9QH, UK
`inmanh or philh or davec@cogs.susx.ac.uk`

Abstract

This paper describes results from a specialised piece of visuo-robotic equipment which allows the artificial evolution of control systems for visually guided autonomous agents acting in the real world. Preliminary experiments with the equipment are described in which dynamical recurrent networks and visual sampling morphologies are concurrently evolved to allow agents to robustly perform simple visually guided tasks. Some of these control systems are shown to exhibit a surprising degree of adaptiveness when tested against generalised versions of the task for which they were evolved.

1 Introduction

In previous papers (see e.g. [1]) we have discussed our reasons for adopting an evolutionary methodology for the design of control systems for mobile robots using low-bandwidth vision for simple navigational tasks. We also discussed what class of control systems are appropriate for evolutionary development, proposing dynamic recurrent real-time (artificial) neural networks as one strong contender.

The evolutionary process, based on a genetic algorithm [3], involves evaluating, over many generations, whole populations of control systems specified by artificial genotypes. These are interbred using a Darwinian scheme in which the fittest individuals are most likely to produce offspring. Fitness is measured in terms of how good an agent's behaviour is according to some evaluation criterion. The work reported here forms part of a long-term study to explore the viability of such an approach in developing interesting adaptive behaviours in visually guided autonomous robots, and, through analysis, in better understanding general mechanisms underlying the generation of such behaviours.

In this paper we present results from experiments in which visually guided behaviours are artificially evolved in the real world. As far as we know, this is the first time this has been achieved.

2 From Simulation to Reality

The experiments described in earlier papers [1] used simulations of a round two-wheeled mobile robot with touch sensors and just two visual inputs — simulated photoreceptors, with (genetically specified) angles of acceptance, and of eccentricity relative to the frontal direction of the robot. The environment was a simulated circular arena, with black walls and white floor and ceiling; ray-tracing techniques allowed the calculation of visual inputs. Success was reported in evolving control systems (and visual morphologies) which allowed the robot to reach the centre of the arena.

These early experiments were intended to test the plausibility of our approach. However, the simulated visual environment was very simple and it was noted that computational costs would increase dramatically as the visual environment became more complex. Indeed, even ignoring computational costs, the plausible modelling of visual inputs in such circumstances is highly problematic. Hence plans were made to perform the whole evolutionary process with a real robot, moving in the real world, and without recourse to simulated vision.

Artificial evolution in the real world requires equipment which allows the automatic evaluation of very large numbers of robot control systems. With navigation tasks, it is useful to have the position and orientation of a robot continually available to an overseeing program responsible for scoring candidate control systems. Of course, this information should not be available in any way to the individual robot control systems. Automatic re-positioning of the robot at fixed or random positions for the start of each trial is also desirable. Rather than imposing a fixed visual sampling morphology, we believe a more powerful approach is to allow the visual morphology to evolve along with the rest of the control system. This establishes a further desired property of the experimental setup.

One solution might involve the parallel evaluation of populations of control systems using a large number of mobile robots, radio links, recharging stations, and the like. In this paper we describe a much cheaper, shorter term, solution we have developed using a specialised piece of visuo-robotic equipment — the gantry-robot.

Figure 1: *The Gantry viewed from above. The horizontal girder moves along the side rails, and the robot is suspended from a platform which moves along this girder.*

3   The Gantry-Robot

3.1   Introduction

The gantry-robot can be thought of as occupying a position partway between a physical mobile robot with two wheels and low-bandwidth vision, and the simulation thereof. The robot is physically built, cylindrical, some 150mm in diameter, and moves in a real environment — the term 'robot' is here used to refer to that part which moves around and has the sensors mounted on it. Instead of two wheels, however, the robot is suspended from the gantry-frame with stepper motors that allow translational movement in the X and Y directions, relative to a co-ordinate frame fixed to the gantry (see Figure 1). The maximum X (and Y) speed is about 200mm/s. Such movements, together with appropriate rotation of the sensory apparatus, can be thought of as corresponding to those which would be produced by left and right wheels. The visual sensory apparatus consists of a CCD camera pointing down at a mirror inclined at 45° to the vertical (see Figure 2). The mirror can be rotated about a vertical axis so that its orientation always corresponds to the direction the 'robot' is facing. The visual inputs undergo some transformations en route to the control system, described in detail below. The hardware is designed so that these transformations are done completely externally to the processing of the control system. If all the transformations made on the sensory inputs and the motor outputs accurately reflected the physics of a real mobile robot, then, in principle, a control system successfully evolved on the gantry could be transplanted to a mobile robot with two genuine wheels, and with photoreceptors instead of the vision system described below. Such a transplantation has not been attempted, and is not a prime concern of our present work with this apparatus. Indeed, there are current limitations, discussed later, which would probably hinder it. Despite this, the experiments discussed here can be considered as having conditions comparable in complexity and difficulty to those met by a free-running mobile robot; our aim is a fairly general investigation of the artificial evolution of sensorimotor control systems. Of course, the optic array available to the robot is now the real thing.

The control system for the robot is a recurrent dynamic neural net, genetically specified, and in practice simulated on a fast personal computer, the 'Brain PC'. During each robot trial this PC is dedicated solely to running the neural net simulation. It receives any changes in visual input by interrupts from a second dedicated 'Vision PC'. A third (single-board) computer, the SBC, sends interrupts to the Brain PC signalling tactile inputs resulting from the robot bumping into walls or physical obstacles. The only outputs of the control system are motor signals specified by values on particular nodes of the neural network; these values are sent, via interrupts, to the SBC, which generates the appropriate stepper motor movements on the gantry.

Thus all interactions between the three computers used (Brain PC, Vision PC and SBC) are mediated by interrupts (see Figure 3); and the overall system is deliberately designed so that these interrupts, although inherently asynchronous and unpredictable, are nevertheless sufficiently infrequent for them not to clash with the intrinsic timescales of the neural network, vision and stepper motor processing.

This setup, with off-board computing and avoidance of tangled umbilicals, means that the apparatus can be run continuously for long periods of time – making artificial evolution feasible. A top-level program automatically

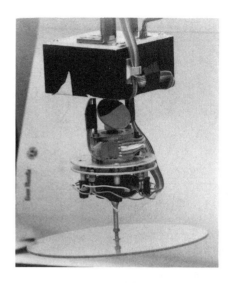

Figure 2: *The gantry-robot. The camera inside the top box points down at the inclined mirror, which can be turned by the stepper-motor beneath. The lower plastic disk is suspended from a joystick, to detect collisions with obstacles.*

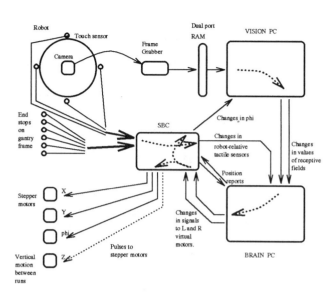

Figure 3: *The different rôles of the Vision computer, the Brain computer and the SBC.*

evaluates, in turn, each member of a population of control systems. A new population is produced by selective interbreeding and the cycle repeats.

3.2   The Vision System

Continuous visual data is derived from the output of a small monochrome CCD camera. With a wide-angle (about 40°) fixed-focus lens about 6mm in diameter, this is housed in a box facing vertically downwards onto the angled mirror of the robot. The CCD produces composite video output of some 1 volt peak to peak, with a video bandwidth of 4MHz. A purpose-built Frame-Grabber transfers a 64×64 image at 50Hz into a high-speed 2K CMOS dual-port RAM, completely independently and asynchronously relative to any processing of the image by the Vision PC.

We advocate an incremental evolutionary approach, progressing from the simple to the complex. In keeping with this philosophy, current experiments use very low bandwidth vision. This implies sub-sampling the image produced by the camera. Rather than imposing a fixed way of sampling the image, we allow this to evolve along with the neural networks. This is achieved by genetically specifying the size and position of visual receptive fields. These are circular patches within the visual field of the camera (see Figure 4). Up to 256 such receptive fields can be specified with, to 8-bit accuracy: the diameter of the field; and the polar coordinates of the centre of the field relative to the centre of the camera's field of view. The angle of acceptance of the CCD camera (via the mirror) is about 60°; the maximum angle of acceptance of a receptive field is about 16°, and its maximum angle of eccentricity off the cameras visual axis is about 22°.

To calculate the signal from such a field, the average is taken of 25 pixels in the camera image scattered across the appropriate area. In this way a value (4 bits) can be calculated for each receptive field at least as fast as the camera image is updated. The only visual inputs available to the genetically designed robot control system are such scalar values.

The Vision PC is dedicated solely to processing the camera output to calculate the visual signals from the receptive fields. At the beginning of a set of trials for a particular robot, the genetic specification for the visual morphology (positions and sizes of receptive fields) is passed to this PC. During each trial, whenever the orientation of the robot changes (the full circle is discretized into 96 orientations) a single byte is sent to the Vision PC from the SBC specifying the new orientation. Whenever the visual input to any of the receptive fields changes in value (scaled in the range 0 to 15) then the details of such a change are sent as single-byte interrupts to the Brain PC.

3.3   The Brain PC

This is a 66MHz 486 PC which has two separate groups of tasks to do at different times. Firstly, the Genetic Algorithm (GA) code is run on this machine. Reproduction, crossover and mutation are performed here in between generations, and at the start of a set of trials for each robot architecture the specification of the visual morphology is transmitted to the Vision PC. As with most GAs, however, the amount of time spent running the genetic machinery is trivial compared with the time spent running the evaluations, and this latter constitutes the second group of tasks.

During an individual evaluation, the Brain PC is ded-

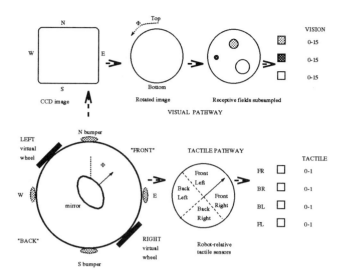

Figure 4: *A schematic of the sensory pathways, visual and tactile, from the gantry-robot hardware at bottom left through to the nodes of the neural network on the right.*

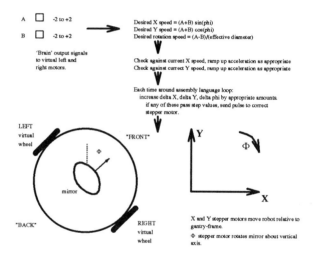

Figure 5: *The conversion from the motor outputs signalled by the neural network to the stepper motor movements which move the gantry-robot.*

icated to running a genetically specified neural network for a fixed period. At intervals during an evaluation, a signal is sent from the Brain PC to the SBC requesting the current position and orientation of the robot. These are used in keeping score according to the current fitness function. At the end of a run, a byte sent from the Brain PC to the SBC requests the return of the robot to the 'origin' of the gantry. The Brain PC receives signals, to be fed into the neural net, representing sensory inputs from the Vision PC and the SBC. The only signals that the Brain PC sends out indicate changes in values of the left and right virtual motors of the robot. These values, which are restricted to integers from -2 to 2, are passed on as single-byte interrupts to the SBC (see Figure 5).

3.4   The SBC

The SBC is a minimal 16 bit 68000 system with 256K of RAM and 128K of ROM, running at 10MHz. It has memory mapped ports that connect it to the Vision PC, the Brain PC and the various switches and motors attached to the gantry. The SBC does all the transformations between hardware-relative and robot-relative signals, plus some housekeeping.

Occasional interrupts from the Brain PC will notify new values of the desired speeds of the virtual left and right wheels. These are translated into desired speeds in the gantry X and Y directions, and desired angular velocity of the mirror. The SBC also keeps track of the current position and orientation of the robot. Instantaneous changes in desired speed cannot be translated directly into instantaneous changes in stepper motor pulse frequency, due to the momentum of the masses these motors must move. Hence speeds are ramped up relatively slowly towards the desired speed — from zero to full speed in about 2 seconds — decelerations are ramped down rather more swiftly. As the mirror is so light, such ramping was not deemed necessary for rotation — with unexpected side-effects described below.

Signals from end-stops for maximum movement along the gantry-frame, and signals from the touch-sensors on the robot, are also processed by the SBC. A plastic disc in the horizontal plane is suspended on a joystick vertically below the robot(see Figure 2). This detects contacts, on each of 4 sides of the robot (in gantry-relative coordinates). The SBC converts these into robot-relative directions.

4   The robot dynamics

Some issues relating to the physical dynamics have already been mentioned; the ramping up and down of stepper motor movements broadly (and perhaps inaccurately) relates to the momentum of a freely mobile wheeled robot.

With the present setup, on collision with a wall, all further movement into the wall is prevented, as is any translational movement along the wall. Hence, of any desired robot motion, only that component perpendicularly away from the wall is allowed, until contact with the wall is lost. Angular velocity that attempts to turn the robot further in towards the wall is ineffective.

One puzzling phenomenon often observed, particularly in initial randomly generated populations, was that of a robot turning on the spot in a noisy fashion. On reflection, this turned out to be an artefact of the way translational momentum had been implemented in the SBC code, but without angular momentum. This clearly showed how the virtual physics as currently implemented does not accurately reflect the real physics of a free mobile robot.

5   Visual Limitations

The visual inputs are currently subject to various limitations which are worth noting. Firstly, the lower part of the robot body is supported from the upper half with two thin vertical bolts, which come into the field of view when the mirror is facing towards them. These appear as dark bars 2 to 3 pixels wide on the CCD image, and affect the values of any receptive fields sampling from this area. In principle this could directly provide visual information for two fixed directions for the robot to 'face'. In addition, these bars tend to occlude any distant target used in navigation trials. For our early crude experiments this may not be too significant, but it certainly will matter when finer resolution is needed, and these bars produce greater effects than background noise levels. In future work we intend to fit a new head on the gantry which overcomes this problem.

Secondly, the fact that the mirror turns in discrete jumps, of 3.75^o at the moment, means that either the angles of acceptance of the receptive fields, or alternatively the horizontal angle subtended by any significant visual features, should be somewhat greater than 3.75^o. This could be overcome with a finer resolution motor.

Thirdly, the visual inputs are naturally noisy (see section 6.2). The natural variation in daylight, as day progresses into night, causes particular problems. When the gantry was exposed to such variation, it was discovered that evolved systems that worked well in the daytime did not work well under artificial light alone at night-time, and vice versa. Our individual robot systems were evaluated over a period of perhaps 3 minutes only, and hence it is no surprise that robustness against such longterm variations was not achieved. Since the recognition of this problem the gantry has been largely shielded against daylight variations. We intend soon to deliberately vary lighting conditions *within* each robot trial, to try to achieve robustness against such variations.

6   Preliminary Experiments

The following sections describe some initial simple experiments we have carried out, mainly to ascertain how well our methods cope with the move from simulations to the real world. We have begun by exploring primitive visually guided behaviours in static environments, concentrating on target approaching. However, as we shall see, some of the evolved control systems showed surprising degrees of adaptiveness when tested on more general versions of the task they were evolved for.

6.1   Networks and Genotypes

In all of the experiments reported here we used the same networks and genetic encoding schemes as in our earlier simulation work (for full details see [1]). This was mainly because we have a detailed understanding of their properties and wanted to see how well they transferred to real world tasks. However, they are the simplest, and we believe least powerful, of the classes of networks and genetic encodings we advocate, and we are currently exploring more sophisticated methods. Briefly, the evolutionary algorithms search concurrently for a network architecture and visual morphology capable of generating behaviours resulting in a high score on an evaluation function that implicitly describes a visually guided task. This is achieved by using a genetic algorithm acting on pairs of 'chromosomes' encoding the network and visual morphology of a robot control system. One of the chromosomes is a fixed length bit string encoding the position and size of three visual receptive fields as described above. The other is a variable length character string encoding the architecture of the control network. Each net has a fixed number of input nodes and output nodes, one input for each visual receptive field and one for each of the four tactile sensors described earlier. There are four output nodes, two for each 'virtual motor'. The output signals of these pairs are subtracted to give motor signals in the range [-1,1]. The genotypes encode for a variable number of hidden units and for a variable number of unrestricted excitatory and inhibitory connections between the nodes.

The model neurons use separate channels for excitation and inhibition. Real values in the range [0,1] propagate along excitatory links subject to delays associated with the links. The inhibitory (or veto) channel mechanism works as follows. If the sum of excitatory inputs exceeds a threshold, T_v, the value 1.0 is propagated along any inhibitory output links the unit may have, otherwise a value of 0.0 is propagated. Veto links also have associated delays. Any unit that receives a non zero inhibitory input has its excitatory output reduced to zero (i.e. is vetoed). In the absence of inhibitory input, excitatory outputs are produced by summing all excitatory inputs, adding a quantity of noise, and passing the resulting sum through a simple linear threshold function, $F(x)$, given below. Noise was added to provide further potentially interesting and useful dynamics. The noise was uniformly distributed in the real range [-N,+N].

$$F(x) = \begin{cases} 0, & \text{if } x \leq T_1 \\ \frac{x-T_1}{T_2-T_1}, & \text{if } T_1 < x < T_2 \\ 1, & \text{if } x \geq T_2. \end{cases} \tag{1}$$

The networks' continuous nature was modelled by using very fine time slice techniques. In the experiments described in this paper the following neuron parameter setting were used: N=0.1, T_v=0.75, T_1=0.0 and T_2=2.0. The networks are hardwired in the sense that they do not undergo any architectural changes during their lifetime, they all had unit weights and time delays on their connections.

6.2 Experimental Details

In each of the experiments a population size of 30 was used with a genetic algorithm employing a linear rank-based selection method, ensuring the best individual in a population was twice as likely to breed as the median individual. Each generation took about 1.5 hours to evaluate. The most fit individual was always carried over to the next generation unchanged. A specialised crossover allowing small changes in length between offspring and parents was used [1]. Mutation rates were set at 1.0 bit per vision chromosome and 1.8 bits per network chromosome.

With the walls and floor of the gantry environment predominantly dark, initial tasks were navigating towards white paper targets. In keeping with the incremental evolutionary methodology, deliberately simple visual environments are used initially, as a basis to moving on to more complex ones. Illumination was provided by fluorescent lights in the ceiling above, with the gantry screened from significant daylight variations. However, the dark surfaces did not in practice provide uniform light intensities, neither over space nor over time. Even when the robot was stationary, individual pixel values would fluctuate by up to 2 units, on a scale of 0 to 15. Varying illuminance of different parts of the walls provided potential visual information, other than the targets specifically displayed.

6.2.1 Big Target

In the first experiment, one long gantry wall was covered with white paper, to a width of 150cm and a height of 22cm; the mirror on the robot, which effectively determines the position of the visual inputs, came about 2/3 of the way up on this white wall. The evaluation function $\mathcal{E}_1$, to be maximised, implicitly defines a target locating task, which we hoped would be achieved by visuomotor coordination:

$$\mathcal{E}_1 = \sum_{i=1}^{i=20} Y_i \qquad (2)$$

where Y_i are the perpendicular distances of the robot from the wall opposite that to which the target is attached, sampled at 20 fixed time intervals throughout a robot trial which lasted a total of about 25 seconds. The closer to the target the higher the score. For each robot architecture 4 trials were run, each starting in the same distant corner, but facing in 4 different directions; these directions were approximately in 4 different quadrants, to give a range of starts facing into obstacle walls as well as towards the target. As the final fitness of a robot control architecture was based on the *worst* of the 4 trials (to encourage robustness), and since in this case scores accumulated monotonically through a trial, this allowed later trials among the 4 to be prematurely terminated when

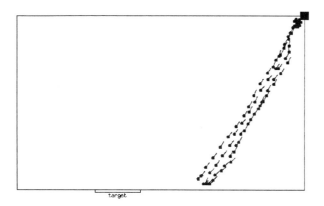

Figure 6: *From those evolved for the first task, this is the behaviour of the one best at the 2nd evaluation function. The dots, and trailing lines, show the front of the robot, and its orientation. Coarsely sampled positions from each of 4 runs are shown, starting in different orientations from the top right corner.*

they bettered previous trials. In addition, any control systems that had not produced any movement by 1/3 of the way into a trial was aborted and given zero score.

Two runs starting from a random initial populations made little progress after 15 generations. For reasons described in Section 9, we then tried starting from a converged population made entirely of clones of a single randomly generated individual picked out by us as displaying vaguely interesting behaviour (but by no means able to do anything remotely like locate and approach the target). In two runs using this method very fit individuals appeared in less than 10 generations. From a start close to a corner, they would turn, avoiding contact with the walls by vision alone[1]. The best would rotate on the spot until the target was in their visual field and then move straight towards it, stopping when they reached it.

6.2.2 Small Target

The experiment continued from the stage already reached, but now using a much narrower target (22cm) placed about 2/3 of the way along the same wall the large target had been on, and away from the robot's starting corner (see Figure 6), with evaluation $\mathcal{E}_2$:

$$\mathcal{E}_2 = \sum_{i=1}^{i=20} (-d_i) \qquad (3)$$

where d_i is the distance of the robot from the centre of the target at one of the sampled instances during an evaluation run. Again, the fitness of an individual was set to the worst evaluation score from four runs with starting

---

[1]They were forced into this by a software error, only discovered later, which meant that all the tactile sensors were turned off. This made this initial task far harder than we had intended.

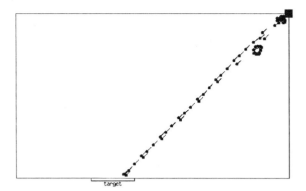

Figure 7: *Behaviour of the best of a later generation evolved under 2nd evaluation function. Format as in previous Figure.*

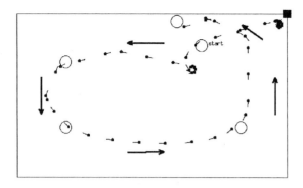

Figure 8: *Tracking behaviour of the control system that generated the behaviour shown in previous Figure. The unfilled circles show the position of the target at a number of points on its path (starting position indicated). The arrows roughly indicate the path of the target.*

conditions as in the first experiment. The initial population used was the 12th generation from a run of the first experiment (i.e. we incrementally evolved on top of the existing behaviours). The behaviour of the best of this initial population is shown in Figure 6. Interestingly, this was not the best at the previous task – that individual did very poorly on the new task.

Within six generations a network architecture and visual morphology had evolved displaying the behaviour shown in Figure 7. This control system was tested from widely varying random starting positions and orientations, with the target in different places, and with smaller and different shaped targets. Its behaviour was general enough to cope with all these conditions for which it had not explicitly been evolved.

For comparison a second evolutionary run using $\mathcal{E}_2$ throughout was undertaken; this time $\mathcal{E}_1$, and the big target, were not used as a stepping stone. The run started from the same initial converged population as was used for the first task. High scoring individuals emerged after 15 generations. When tested on more general versions of the task they performed much worse than the best of the incremental run. This result is suggestive, but we do not have enough data to be able to report anything statistically significant about the advantages of doing incremental evolution at this low-level of task.

6.2.3 Moving Target

Following a moving target can be thought of as a generalised version of static target approaching. Hence we tested a number of the evolved small target locators with a white cylinder (of similar width) substituted for the target; this was pushed around the gantry area in a series of smooth movements. The tracking behaviour of the control system that generated the behaviour shown in Figure 7 is illustrated in Figures 8 and 9. To understand how this was achieved, we analysed it.

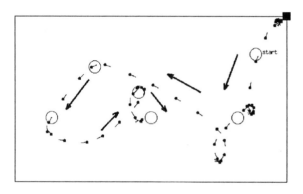

Figure 9: *Further tracking behaviour of the control system that generated the behaviour shown in previous Figure.*

7 Control System Analysis

In [4] it is shown in detail how evolved control systems of the type developed here can be analysed in terms of network dynamics and the way in which the visual morphology couples the control system with the environment. It was shown how the active part of the network can be characterised in terms of major feedback loops and visual pathways. The active part of the network that generated the behaviours shown in Figures 7, 8 and 9 is shown in Figure 10, and its coupled (evolved) visual morphology is shown in Figure 12. On analysis it was seen that in this control system only receptive fields 1 and 2 are involved in generating visually guided behaviours.

Only a brief description can be given here of the workings of the network. Due to the same software error mentioned earlier in relation to the tactile sensors, unit 5 (one of the tactile input units) acts as a source of noise over the range [0,0.25]. This unintended property of the unit has been exploited by evolution to produce a tightly self-regulating system. Unit 5 feeds into the two coupled

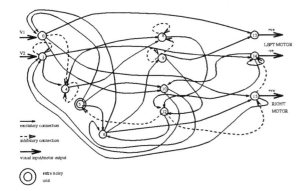

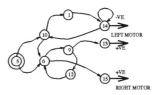

Figure 11: *Subnetwork responsible for rotations in absence of visual input.*

Figure 12: *The large dotted circle indicates the extent of the entire visual field available via camera and mirror. The smaller circles indicate the relative positions and sizes of the genetically specified visual receptive fields (no. 3 is not used).*

Figure 10: *Active network of the best tracker. V1 and V2 are visual inputs from receptive fields 1 and 2.*

feedback loops shown in Figure 11. It can be shown that the resulting subnetwork is responsible for generating a noisy turn on the spot behaviour when visual inputs to receptive fields 1 and 2 (*v1* and *v2*) are both low (the robot is facing a dark object). When *v1* is low and *v2* is very high, unit 1 self-inhibits and the same rotational behaviour follows. When *v1* is low and *v2* is medium high the robot rotates in a medium radius circle. When *v1* is high a straight line motion follows. Due to inhibition between motor signals this straight line motion is maintained as long as *v1* remains high, irrespective of *v2*. The basic behaviour generated then, is to rotate until the white target is within receptive field 1, and then to move in a straight line as long as the target remains within the field. If the target is lost, the robot rotates until the target is again within the field of receptor 1 and straight line motion is resumed.

Further, it can be shown that in the task it was evolved to perform (small target location) this system's particular visual morphology (especially the position of field 2) was able to exploit various other visual features in the environment to ensure a rapid fixation on the target. The behaviour generated when *v2* was medium high and *v1* was low was particularly important in providing the system with surprisingly smooth tracking abilities with the moving target. Other systems tested had evolved to be too fragilely adapted to the particular task they were evaluated for; they made a lot of use of visual features other than the intended target. Consequently, when started from different positions, or with the moving target, they tended to chase reflected light spots on the walls! Clearly, great care must be taken in setting up the tasks and environments in order to get behaviour of the required robustness and generality. At the same time, it was encouraging to find a number of instances of evolved control systems that were far more general and robust than might have been expected from the evaluation function used.

8 Rectangles and Triangles

A further experiment will be very briefly described here. Two white paper targets were fixed to one of the gantry walls; one was a rectangle 21cm wide and 29.5cm high, the other was an isosceles triangle 21cm wide at the base and 29.5cm high to the apex. The robot was started at four positions and orientations near the opposite wall such that it was not biased towards either of the two targets. The evaluation function $\mathcal{E}_3$, to be maximised, was:

$$\mathcal{E}_3 = \sum_{i=1}^{i=20} [\beta(D_{1_i} - d_{1_i}) - \sigma(D_{2_i}, d_{2_i})] \qquad (4)$$

where D_1 is the distance of target-1 (in this case the triangle) from the gantry origin; d_1 is the distance of the robot from target-1; and D_2 and d_2 are the corresponding distances for target-2 (in this case the rectangle). These are sampled at regular intervals, as before. The value of β is $(D_1 - d_1)$ unless d_1 is less than some threshold, in which case it is $3 \times (D_1 - d_1)$. The value of σ (a penalty function) is zero unless d_2 is less than the same threshold, in which case it is $I - (D_2 - d_2)$, where I is the distance between the targets; I is more than double the threshold distance. High fitnesses are achieved for approaching the triangle but ignoring the rectangle. It was hoped that this experiment might demonstrate the efficacy of concurrently evolving the visual sampling morphology along with the control networks.

After about 15 generations of a run using as an initial population the last generation of the incremental small target experiment, fit individuals emerged capable of approaching the triangle, but not the rectangle, from each of the four widely spaced starting positions and orientations. The behaviour generated by the fittest of these control systems is shown in Figure 13. When started

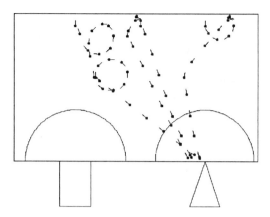

Figure 13: *Behaviour of a fit individual in the two target environment. The rectangle and triangle indicate the positions of the targets. The semi circles mark the 'penalty' (near rectangle) and 'bonus score' (near triangle) zones associated with the fitness function. In these 4 runs the robot was started directly facing each of the two target, and twice from a position midway between the two targets; once facing into the wall and once facing out.*

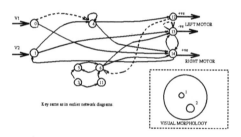

Figure 14: *Active part of the control system that generated fit behaviour for the rectangle and triangle experiment. Visual morphology shown inset.*

from many different positions and orientations near the far wall, this controller repeatedly exhibited very similar behaviours to those shown.

The active part of the evolved network that generated this behaviour is shown in Figure 14. The evolved visual morphology for this control system is shown inset. Only receptive fields 1 and 2 were used by the controller.

Whereas the fit control systems for the previous experiments only made use of one visual receptive field at a time, this one used two simultaneously. The visual morphology/networks evolved such that robots rotated on the spot when both visual inputs were low (this is effected by the subnetwork made from nodes 3, 5, 6 and 11). When the signal from receptive field 1 (v_1) is high but that from receptive field 2 (v_2) is low, the connection from unit 0 to unit 14 generates a rotational movement.

When v_1 and v_2 are both medium high, the inputs from unit 1 to units 12 and 13 tend to cancel each other out whereas unit 14 is strongly activated, again resulting in a rotational movement. When v_1 and v_2 are both high, the inhibitory links from unit 0 to unit 4, and from unit 13 to itself, come into play. This just leaves unit 14 active and rotation follows. If v_1 is high but v_2 low, similar behaviour ensues. However, if v_2 is high and v_1 is low, units 12 and 14 (via 4) are active and unit 13 is inhibited. Hence straight line motion is produced. The active receptive fields were so arranged to result in the robot tending to accurately fixate on the the triangle and moving in a straight line towards it. It would often fixate on the edge of the rectangle but as it moved towards it both visual signals would go high, resulting in a rotation towards the triangle. As the robot moved towards the triangle with only v_2 high, the looming target would cause v_1 to go high. However, the (evolved) layout of the receptive fields relative to the geometry of the triangle meant that the ensuing rotational movement very rapidly sent v_1 low while v_2 remained high, and the robot carried on moving towards the triangle usually only slightly deflected from its original path. When it reached the target, depending on its orientation, the robot either stopped or slowly rotated away from the triangle and then looped back towards it. These results illustrate that tasks such as these can be achieved with extremely minimal vision systems and very small networks.

9   An Initially Converged Population

Whereas Genetic Algorithms (GAs) are normally used to search high-dimensional spaces, the modified form of GAs, 'SAGA' [2], employed here uses a genetically largely converged population, and in effect searches a relatively local space of adaptations to the current population; artificial evolution is treated as exploration, driven largely by mutation, rather than search. The population is maintained at some fairly high degree of convergence by the balance between mutation and selection. For a continuing sequence of experiments, with tasks of added complexity, the starting point in each case is the population that succeeded before, but there are different choices for the very first population.

One could start with a randomly generated population (i.e. their genotypes are randomly generated from valid symbols), which would be the normal GA technique. But often in a normal GA problem, different parts of the genotype contribute semi-independently to the evaluation function, and through the Schema Theorem [3] progress of some sort can be made from such a random start. In our case, however, the genotypes describe control systems which in turn generate behaviour, with no simple correlation between the genotypes and the behaviour; which means that, at least with encodings like the one used here, two different genotypes which both produce promising behaviour will, on recombination, almost always produce a genotype with near-average performance — i.e. useless performance. It is only once the population has largely converged — as advocated with SAGA [2] — that recombination is likely to be useful.

For this reason, from a start with a randomly generated population, the early stages will do no more than allow some early promising candidate to dominate the population. In which case we can speed up the process, and help give some desired initial direction, by ourselves observing the first random population, choosing by eye the most promising, and seeding the next generation with clones of this one. Thereafter the population settles down to its asymptotic degree of genetic convergence from above, rather than from below. For the experiments reported here, an initial randomly generated population of size 30 was judged by eye on the intuitive criterion of 'interesting' behaviour. Two members displayed forward-moving behaviour, which altered in character when the white target was within view of the visual system, and one of these two was selected. The informal criterion of 'interestingness' allowed a clear choice, whereas the 'official' evaluation function used thereafter did not give clear preferences on this initial random population, as the scores it gave there were dominated by noise. This use of different evaluations over time is completely consonant with the underlying philosophy of this approach, that of human-directed evolution of the robots.

As has already been mentioned, the successes we have had with initially converged populations are from too small a sample of experiments to have any statistical significance. It should also be noted that the genetic encoding scheme plays an important role in determining how effective crossover is in early generations.

10   Future Work

Encouraged by the initial results with the gantry apparatus we intend to start using it in more complex experiments. In these we intend to use networks with much richer intrinsic dynamics, and more sophisticated genotype to phenotype developmental processes allowing a less restricted open-ended evolutionary process. We will explore behaviours in cluttered and dynamic environments and under changing lighting conditions.

Evaluations with the gantry using a real optic array take less than one order of magnitude longer than the early simulations we did using ray-tracing in a very simple environment. But whereas ray-tracing simulations rapidly scale up in computational requirements as the environment is made more complex, with the gantry there is no such constraint.

11   Conclusions

This paper has described a specialised piece of visuo-robotic equipment allowing us to evolve visually guided agents in the real world. It has reported on work that has demonstrated that our methods developed using simulation experiments have transferred to the real world. We have been able to evolve robust visually guided behaviours with very small populations in very few generations, even though the visual signals in the real world are far more noisy than in our simulations; this is in contrast to the difficulties experienced by others using evolutionary techniques, but with different control system building blocks [5]. A number of our evolved control systems showed interesting levels of adaptation when tested on generalised versions of the task they were evolved for, even though they use only one or two visual receptive fields and a very small network. We have demonstrated the efficacy of concurrently evolving the visual morphology along with the control networks. We find it promising that we have obtained interesting results with a simple type of network and an unsophisticated genetic encoding. Particularly since we regard both of these as being among the least powerful of the classes of networks and genetic encodings we advocate.

Acknowledgements

We thank Tony Simpson, Martin Nock, Jerry Mitchell and Harry Butterworth for engineering design and construction work on the gantry. The work was funded initially by a University of Sussex research development grant, and continuing research is now funded by the UK Science and Engineering Research Council.

References

[1] D. Cliff, I. Harvey, and P. Husbands. Explorations in evolutionary robotics. *Adaptive Behavior*, 2(1):71–104, 1993.

[2] I. Harvey. Evolutionary robotics and SAGA: the case for hill crawling and tournament selection. In C. Langton, editor, *Artificial Life III, Santa Fe Institute Studies in the Sciences of Complexity, Proc. Vol. XVI*, pages 299–326. Addison Wesley, 1993.

[3] J. Holland. *Adaptation in Natural and Artificial Systems*. University of Michigan Press, Ann Arbor, USA, 1975.

[4] P. Husbands, I. Harvey, and D. T. Cliff. Circle in the round: State space attractors for evolved sighted robots. *Robotics and Autonomous Systems*, forthcoming.

[5] C. Reynolds. An evolved, vision-based model of obstacle avoidance behavior. In C. Langton, editor, *Artificial Life III, Santa Fe Institute Studies in the Sciences of Complexity, Proc. Vol. XVI*. Addison Wesley., 1993.

Evolution of Corridor Following Behavior in a Noisy World

Craig W. Reynolds

Electronic Arts
1450 Fashion Island Boulevard
San Mateo, CA 94404, USA
telephone: 415-513-7442 / fax: 415-571-1893
creynolds@ea.com
cwr@red.com

Abstract

Robust behavioral control programs for a simulated 2d vehicle can be constructed by artificial evolution. Corridor following serves here as an example of a behavior to be obtained through evolution. A controller's fitness is judged by its ability to steer its vehicle along a collision free path through a simple corridor environment. The controller's inputs are noisy range sensors and its output is a noisy steering mechanism. Evolution determines the quantity and placement of sensors. Noise in fitness tests discourages brittle strategies and leads to the evolution of robust, noise-tolerant controllers. Genetic Programming is used to model evolution, the controllers are represented as deterministic computer programs.

1 Introduction

Designing reactive controllers for autonomous agents can be a challenging task. For increasingly complex behavior, building controllers by hand becomes prohibitively difficult. As suggested in [Cliff 1993b], a promising alternative is to *evolve* the controllers, using their ability to perform the desired behavior as a measure of *fitness*. In these experiments, *corridor following* behavior is used as a simple test case, representative of the more complex behaviors to which this approach might eventually be applied.

Previous work [Reynolds 1993b] has shown that the Genetic Programming Paradigm [Koza 1992] can be used to automatically create control programs which enable a simple moving 2d vehicle to avoid collisions with obstacles by mapping sensory input (range data) into motor output (steering action). In those experiments all fitness tests were identical. As a result, the control programs evolved to use *brittle* strategies. Their success was like a "house of cards" which stands only until anything changes.

In the absence of variability in fitness testing, evolution will discover solutions that capitalize on the deterministic, precisely repeatable nature of the fitness tests. Evolved controllers will come to depend on utterly insignificant coincidental properties of the vehicle's sensors, its actuators, and their interaction with the environment.

The current work concerns an approach to avoiding this brittle behavior and seeks to evolve robust, general purpose control programs for the corridor following problem. Determinism is removed from fitness testing by injecting noise into the system. This noise will tend to "jiggle" coincidental

relationships between elements of the system and so tend to discourage evolution from capitalizing on them. A house of cards cannot be built on a shaky table.

The controllers evolved in this work are computer programs composed of basic arithmetic operations, conditionals, and a function to aim and read a nonlinear proximity sensor. The number and orientation of sensors are determined through evolution of control programs. On each simulation step control programs read their sensors and compute a steering angle. The vehicle always moves forward at a constant rate, so steering is its only means of avoiding collision.

These experiments have produced robust control programs capable of corridor following behavior in the presence of noise. Figure 1 shows some examples of successful behavior.

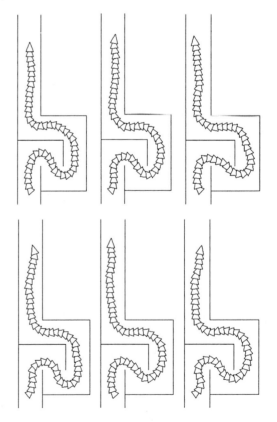

Figure 1: Several collision-free runs.

2 Related work

An early series of experiments [Reynolds 1993b] used Genetic Programming to create reactive controllers for a similar obstacle avoidance task. The fitness test employed a single, precisely repeatable simulation-based fitness test. This allowed evolution to take the easy path to discover a program which only solved this one specific control task. There was no incentive, no survival advantage, to find a controller that could generalize. As a result, the evolved controllers were "brittle" and could not solve similar but slightly different problems.

Subsequent experiments [Reynolds 1994a] attempted to use noise to promote robust solutions to the corridor following task, but were unsuccessful. The most significant difference between those experiments and these is the addition of a syntactic constraint to the sensor-reading function. In the earlier work, the control program could rotate its sensors relative to the vehicle. In the current work, the sensors are fixed to the vehicle during its run. Sensor orientation is still subject to change by the action of evolution.

Closely related to these experiments is the work of the Evolutionary Robotics Group at the University of Sussex. While using a different model of evolution (SAGA [Harvey 1992]) and a different model of controller architecture (dynamic, recurrent neural nets [Cliff 1993a], [Cliff 1993b], and [Harvey 1993]) they have investigated closely related problems in evolution of robotic controllers. They were the first to document the beneficial role of noise in the evolution of robust robotic controllers. The general approach used here, of evolving stimulus-response behavior based on simulated performance using simulated perception inside a closed simulated world, was originally inspired by [Cliff 1991a] and [Cliff 1991b]. The specific technique used here, of taking the "worst of four noisy trials" came directly from [Harvey 1993] and [Cliff 1993a].

The experiments reported here have much in common with some of Koza's work, particularly the evolution of behaviors such as "wall following" and "box pushing" as reported in [Koza 1992]. See also Simon Handley's GP robotics work [Handley 1994].

The evolution of robust controllers is related to the larger problem of generalization in evolutionary computation. This issue of generalization is an active area of research in many branches of evolutionary computation. In GP, see for example [Tackett 1994] on the evolution of generality in a classification problem, and [Kinnear 1993] on generalization in sorting.

Earlier work on obstacle avoidance behavior based on remote (distal) sensors (as opposed to touch sensors) for vehicles moving at "moderate speed" can be found in [Reynolds 1987], [Reynolds 1988], [Mataric 1993] and [Zapata 1993], among many others.

A classic reference on controllers and behaviors for this class of *vehicle* is [Braitenburg 1984] which is highly recommended.

3 Vehicle

The design of the simulated vehicle used in these experiments is kept intentionally vague and abstract. It could equally well represent an animal as a wheeled or legged robotic vehicle. The intent is to gloss over the low level details of locomotion and to concentrate instead on the more abstract issues of "steering" and "path determination." (Not "path *planning,*" since these reactive controllers neither plan nor learn.) In order to survive, the controllers need only steer along a clear pathway while avoiding contact with the danger region surrounding it. The skill involved is similar to that required by a squirrel running along a tree branch, or by an automobile's driver, negotiating through a narrow alley.

The control programs evolved by Genetic Programming represent the vehicle's "thought process" for a single simulation step. During fitness testing, the evolved program is run at each time step of the simulation. Using its sensors, the program inspects the environment surrounding the vehicle from its own point of view (that is, relative to the vehicle's local coordinate space), performs some arithmetic and logical processing, and decides how to steer (adjust the heading of) the vehicle. The value returned by the control program is interpreted as a steering angle. The vehicle then automatically moves forward by a constant amount (half of its body length). The fitness test continues until the vehicle takes the required number of steps (50), or until it collides with one of the obstacles. The raw fitness score for each corridor run is the number of steps taken divided by the maximum number of steps, producing a normalized score between 0 and 1, with 1 being best.

These vehicles have a fixed minimum turning radius because the maximum per-simulation-step turn is limited to ±0.05 revolutions (18 degrees or 0.31 radians). This limitation implies a minimum turning circle which is somewhat larger than the width of the corridors of the obstacle course. As a result, the vehicle cannot spin in place, it cannot turn around in the corridor, and its only choice is to travel along the corridor.

Limiting turning radius produces a model of a vehicle moving at "moderate" speed. This qualitative description is intended to capture a relationship between the vehicle's momentum and its available turning acceleration. At "low" speed a vehicle has relatively little momentum, in a single time step it might be able to bring itself to a stop, or make an abrupt change of heading. At moderate speed momentum begins to dominate acceleration and changes of heading require many time steps. In this speed regime, maneuvers are less abrupt and paths tend to curve more gently, producing a motion more like running than crawling.

4 Corridor and Fitness Testing

The training environment used in these experiments was designed to test a control program's ability to follow a corridor, and to quickly reject those which are completely unsuited to the task. This approach allows the majority of the computational effort to go into testing higher fitness individuals. A fitness function based on this kind of simulation has the desirable property that execution time is roughly proportional to the individual's fitness.

Figure 2 shows the corridor and an series of increasingly successful runs. The vehicle is initialized in the center of the corridor and pointing toward one wall or the other. Initial random headings range from 0.1 to 0.15 revolutions (36 to 54 degrees) off of the corridor's midline. If a controller turns continuously (see Figure 2(a)) or does not steer at all (see Figure 2(b)), it will run into a wall almost immediately. To survive more than a few steps the controller must develop the skill of sensing and turning away from a glancing collision so it can proceed down the corridor. To reach higher fitness levels the vehicle must be able to safely negotiate U-turns in both directions, right-angle turns in both directions, and long straight corridors.

In the early stages of evolution most of the controllers are quite inept and so incapable of following the corridor for long. During this stage it is important to notice and encourage progress, no matter how slight. In the initial population only a few controllers can take more than one or two collision-free steps so the scoring system must differentiate between degrees of ineptness, as illustrated in Figure 2. Later in the run some controllers will have progressed to the point where they can occasionally make a collision-free run through the corridor. At this stage the point of fitness testing begins to be reliability. One way to address this is to look at the controller's performance on a series of corridor runs. These considerations lead to the following scheme for each fitness trial: the controller is allowed to make a run through the corridor, if no collisions occur it is allowed to make another run, and so on up to a

maximum of 16 runs. This creates a selection pressure for controllers to be able, at least occasionally, to make it all the way through the corridor so as to have a chance at another run. This approach also serves to further focus effort on promising controllers: we don't even bother with a second trial unless the controller has "proven" itself worth on the first trial.

The scores of all runs of a trial (up until the first collision) are weighted and summed. The first collision-free run is worth 1/2, the second is 1/4, and so on. Figure 3 shows the cumulative fitness assigned to a controller based on the number of collision-free runs. This weighting scheme captures the idea of an open-ended reliability rating, but is probably not significant now that tournament selections is being used and all that matters is fitness rank. Monotone functions do not alter rank.

An obstacle course used in earlier experiments had a longer straight-away before and after the first turn. This arrangement seemed to promote premature convergence, particularly in small populations. Some individuals would discover how to make it to the first turn (and sometimes past it) but they would then so dominate the population that diversity would be lost and the population would never discover how to get around the second turn. In the subsequent experiments described here these problems were addressed in two ways. First, the long straight-aways were moved from the beginning of the course to the end. This

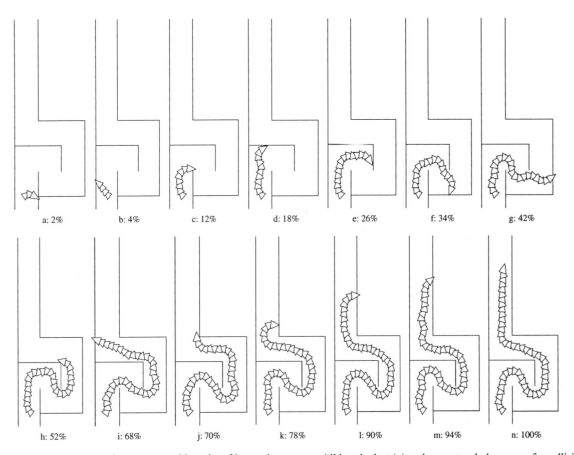

Figure 2: An assortment of runs, arranged in order of increasing scores. All but the last (*n*) end prematurely because of a collision.

forced the turning problem to be addressed sooner, and weeded out the non-turners sooner. Second, the entire obstacle course was mirrored at random about the axis of the first corridor. This procedure ensured that evolving controllers could turn equally well in both directions and so prevented convergence towards right-turners.

Because the training corridor is laid out on a grid, it has some built-in regularities. The passageway has uniform width throughout. All walls meet at right angle corners. Presumably evolution will construct controllers which depend on these regularities. That is, in the absence of counter-examples, it will assume that all corridors are the same width. A different kind of training environment may be required to evolve controllers capable of following irregular corridors.

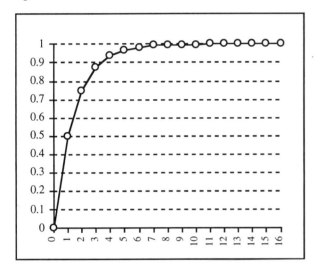

Figure 3: Fitness versus number of sequential collision-free runs through the corridor.

5 Genetic Programming Considerations

The technique used to evolve computer programs in this work is known as Genetic Programming and was invented by John Koza. The best reference on this technique and its application is [Koza 1992]. While often used as a generational technique, it is also possible to combine Genetic Programming with Steady State Genetic Algorithms [Syswerda 1989], [Syswerda 1991] as described in [Reynolds 1993a].

A very brief description of Steady State Genetic Programming (SSGP) follows. First a population of random programs is created and fitness tested. (In these experiments the population consisted of 2000 to 10000 programs.) Thereafter SSGP proceeds by: (1) choosing two *parent* programs from the population, (2) creating a new *offspring* program from them, (3) fitness testing the new program as described in the previous section, (4) choosing a program to remove from the population to make room, and (5) adding the new program into the population. The parent programs are chosen in a way that favors the more fit while not totally ignoring the less fit, thus balancing *exploration* of the whole gene pool with *exploitation* of the champions. In these experiments this choosing is done using *tournament selection*

with k=7, that is: seven individuals are chosen from the population at random, and the most fit of those seven is selected as the winner. The recombination of two parents to form a new offspring is accomplished by the Genetic Programming crossover operator. GP crossover is a little like "random cut and paste" but is done in a why that guarantees the new program's syntactic correctness.

Selecting a program to remove from the population could be done by using inverse tournament selection: taking the least fit of seven randomly chosen programs. However the greedy nature of SSGP, combined with the noisy fitness testing used in these experiments, leads to the possibility of a mediocre-but-lucky program receiving an undeservedly high fitness and going on to dominate the population. To combat this possibility a modified removal policy was used in these experiments: half the time inverse tournament selection was used, the other half of the time an individual was selected for removal at random (without regard to fitness). Hence all programs, even the best one, had a certain small but non-zero possibility of being removed at each SSGP step. This tended to ensure that the population could not stagnate with a collection of mediocre-but-lucky programs, winning strategies were continually being retested.

Because steady state genetic computation proceeds individual by individual, there is no demarcation of generations. However it is often convenient to describe the progress or length of a SSGP run in terms of "generation equivalents:" processing as many new individuals as there are programs in the population.

Applying Genetic Programming to a problem requires specifying several parameters such as the genetic population size and the fitness function (both described above). In addition we must specify the *functions* and *terminals* that define the language in which evolved program will be expressed. In these experiments the terminals were simply random floating point numbers. The function set consisted of:

The first three are the standard Common Lisp function for addition, subtraction, and multiplication. The % and iflte are standard GP functions [Koza 1992]: % is "protected divide" (returns zero when denominator is zero), and iflte is an arithmetic conditional (if A is less than or equal to B, then C, else D). abs is the standard Common Lisp function for absolute value.

The look-for-obstacle function is specific to the obstacle avoidance problem. It takes a single numeric argument which represents an angle relative to the current vehicle heading. Angles are specified in units of *revolutions*, a normalized angle measure: 1 revolution equals 360 degrees or 2π radians. look-for-obstacle points its sensor in the given direction and returns a measure of obstacle proximity. In this implementation, the range is computed by performing a 2d ray-tracing operation on the obstacles.

The Genetic Programming substrate used here, and the application-specific functions for the simulation, were originally developed on Symbolics Lisp Machines. For the current series of experiments, the software was ported to Macintosh Common Lisp (version 2.0p2) and was run on Macintosh Quadra 950 workstations. In this implementation, an average fitness test (composed of up to 64 corridor runs) in run z6 took about 65 seconds to perform.

6   Results

Three runs will be discussed in this section. One uses fixed sensor positions, the other two allow the sensor placement to evolve. The genetic population size and upper limit on evolved program size also differ between the runs:

run:	population:	sensors:	program size limit:
z4	10000	fixed	50
z6	2000	variable	35
z7	10000	variable	35

Run "z4" used a fixed-sensor model. The vehicle was defined to have exactly nine sensors, spaced 1/16 of a revolution (22.5 degrees) apart across the vehicle's front. (If the vehicle's heading is "north," this would correspond to placing sensors at compass points: W, WNW, NW, NNW, N, NNE, NE, ENE, and E.) In Genetic Programming terms, this was implemented by adding a set of nine sensor-reading functions to the GP function set. For comparison with the other two runs described below, this fixed sensor model could also have been implemented by restricting the argument to look-for-obstacle to be one of the nine numeric values (3/4, 13/16, 7/8, 15/16, 0, 1/16, 1/8, 3/16, 1/4). In this model, the evolved control programs would call various sensor-reading functions, perform some arithmetic and logical processing, and return a steering angle. Evolution could not alter the sensor placement, it could only select which sensors to use, and how to combine their readings.

This formulation of the corridor following turned out to be very easy. So much so that the GP system almost solved it by random search. The initial generation of a GP run corresponds to random search over the space of programs (subject to the limitation of size, function set, and terminal set which are parameters to GP). During the initial generation of 10000 random programs for run "z4," the best program had a fitness of 76.5%. This value represents better performance than evolved in any of the previous variations of this problem as reported in [Reynolds 1994a], even though this program was found by random search before the beneficial effects of evolution were applied to the population. During the third generation equivalent (around individual number 35000) of run "z4" it began to attain best-of-population fitness scores above 99%.

Figure 5 summarizes the z4 population's fitness distribution over time. It shows a time series of discrete fitness histograms portrayed as a bilinear surface. The population's progress towards increasing fitness over time can be seen. Dominating this landscape are fin-shaped features probably caused by two artifacts of the fitness function. The corridor is a series of turns, most runs end at a turn, so scores tend to

be clumped at certain values. Then as described in Figure 3, this distribution is repeated at half scale, at quarter scale, and so on for additional runs.

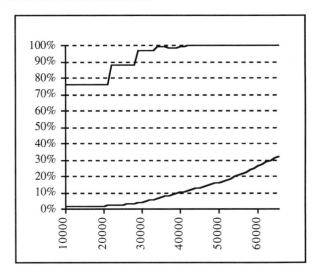

Figure 4: Fitness plots for run z4.
(best-of-population and population average)

Koza has described what he calls the "lens effect," [Koza 1994] the way in which every representation alters the difficulty of a given problem. Koza explores the lens effect by looking at the distribution of fitness values found during random search through the specified program space. In those terms, it appears that the fixed sensor representation of the corridor following problem is a "lens" that makes the problem quite easy to solve. An analysis of fitness distribution in the initial generation of these three runs can be found in [Reynolds 1994b]. By that metric it appears that the fixed sensor representation is easier than the variable sensor representation, which is in turn easier than the original "roving" sensor representation of [Reynolds 1994a].

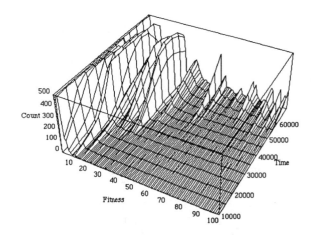

Figure 5: Fitness histograms of run z4 over time.

While not the best-of-run, one high scoring (99.82%) and compact (size 15) controller which caught the author's eye was this elegant three sensor design that appeared during the fourth generation-equivalent (individual number 46515, see Figure 6). It is shown here hand-simplified down to size 7:

```
(% (- (obs-3/16) (obs-13/16))
   (- (obs-15/16) 2.5))
```

This program works by comparing the proximity of obstacles (walls) at relative headings of ±3/16 (the expression `(- (obs-3/16) (obs-13/16))` returns a value between -1 and 1 which indicates relative lateral proximity), then scales that value down by dividing it by a number ranging between -2.5 and -1.5 which is related to the obstacle proximity at a heading of -1/16. This appears to increase the rate of turn as to the amount of free space "ahead" decreases.

The controllers evolved in run z4 were both more and less complicated than the individual discussed above. Many were variations on the same theme: divide the relative lateral proximity by a sensor-dependent scalar, most varied only in the form of modulation. At the end of the run, after about 6.5 generation equivalents, there were two individuals who tested at 100% fitness. After simplification by hand, they were of size 5 and 33:

```
(% (- (obs-3/16)
      (obs-13/16))
   -1.995)

(% (- (obs-3/16)
      (obs-13/16))
   (- (abs (iflte (obs-15/16)
                  0.0
                  (+ (obs-3/16)
                     (obs-7/8)
                     (obs-15/16))
                  (* (* (iflte (obs-1/8)
                               (obs-0)
                               (obs-1/8)
                               0)
                        (iflte (obs-3/16)
                               (- (obs-1/8)
                                  (obs-3/16))
                               (obs-7/8)
                               0)
                        (obs-13/16)
                        0.5)
                     (obs-0)
                     (obs-1/8)
                     0.2)))
      2.0))
```

Based on those results, run z6 was designed to test whether evolution could correctly determine quantity and placement of sensors in addition to determining how to combine the various sensor readings into a correct steering angle. The approach was to restrict the argument to `look-for-obstacle` to be a number. That is, each call to `look-for-obstacle` has a constant numeric argument representing a certain angle. Any number is allowed, but more complicated expressions, particularly those involving additional calls to `look-for-obstacle` are not allowed. When a new program is created (randomly or by crossover) it is checked to ensure that arguments to `look-for-obstacle` are each numeric constants. When non-constant arguments are found, they are replaced by a random number between 0 and 1. As a result, each call such as `(look-for-obstacle 0.17)` corresponds to a sensor fixed at an arbitrary angular offset

from the vehicle's heading. In this way, sensor *morphology* can evolve in parallel with the processing needed to map sensor data into a steering signal.

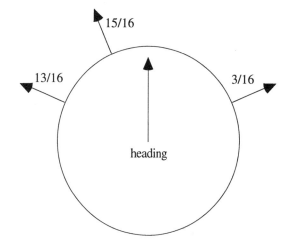

Figure 6: Sensor morphology of individual z4-46515.

Sensors pointing in certain directions (such as directly ahead) are presumably more relevant to corridor following than sensors pointing in other directions (such as directly behind). Therefore certain sensors, represented as code fragments, will tend to increase the fitness of programs in which they appear. This is known as the *constructional fitness* of the code fragment [Altenberg 1994]. Programs containing the more useful sensor-defining fragments will have a survival advantage, and so those fragments will tend to proliferate in the population. In this way the evolutionary process decides which sensor directions are most useful for solving the corridor following problem.

On the tenth generation equivalent of run z6, the best-of-population individual has a fitness of 98.03%. This run developed a rather elaborate *hitch-hiking intron*[1] that has spread throughout the population, so while the best-of-population individual is almost as large as it can be (size 34), most of its genetic material is irrelevant. After removing the irrelevant *intron wrapper* this size 10 program remains:

```
(* (look-for-obstacle 0.13)              A
   (look-for-obstacle 2.0)               B
   (- (look-for-obstacle 0.81)           C
      (look-for-obstacle 0.17)))         D
```

While based on a slightly different approach, this program shares certain features of the program from run "z4" analyzed above. Specifically, the subtraction (on lines C and D) is computing the same sort of lateral proximity measure by taking the difference between a left pointing sensor

---

[1] By analogy with its usage in biological genetics, the term *intron* is used in GP to refer to code that is included in an evolved program but which does not contribute to the program's action or result. An intron is part of the genotype but not of the phenotype. When an intron becomes structurally associated with a highly fit code fragment, the intron can hitch-hike and so proliferate through the population. In the case of run z6, essentially all programs had a large no-op conditional wrapped around the active code.

and a right pointing sensor. In fact the left sensor used is essentially identical to the left sensor used in the "z4" program. The pair of sensors used here are not quite symmetrically placed: +0.17 revolutions on the right and -0.19 on the left. The lateral proximity value is then scaled down by multiplication by two numbers each of which are between 0 and 1. The sensor specified on line B points directly ahead (2.0 revolutions is the same angle as 0 revolutions) and the sensor on line A points 0.13 revolutions (47 degrees) to the right. Hence the lateral proximity signal is reduced as the obstacle-free path, either ahead or to the right, increases.

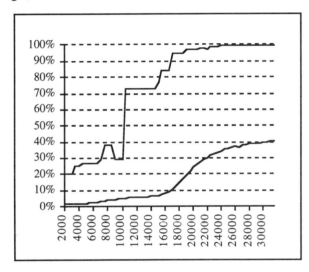

Figure 7: Fitness plots for run z6.
(best-of-population and population average)

Essentially all of the high-fitness individuals in run z6 use this same basic framework, within which there are a few variations of the sensor placement. For example the best-of-population individual at 21600 is identical except that it uses the values 0, 2.0, 0.82, and 0.17 (on lines A, B, C, and D, respectively). Effectively it has become a three sensor design, since both forward-pointing sensors are at the same angle. It is almost exactly symmetrical, which seems appropriate for its task.

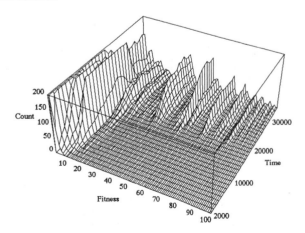

Figure 8: Fitness histograms of run z6 over time.

Run z6 found what might be regarded as a competent controller, but one that is clearly less than perfect. To attain 100% fitness in these experiments, a controller must be able to execute 64 (16 times 4) consecutive perfect runs through the corridor, for a total of 3200 correct steps. The best-of-generation fitness in z6 was always below 100%. This implies that the failure rate for these controllers is at least once in 64 runs. To put this in perspective, imagine a human driver who averages one collision every 64 automobile trips! While there is clearly room for improvement in the controllers from run z6, there is also evidence that the population became converged and would be unable to progress any further.

Another run was attempted to duplicate and hopefully surpass the results of z6. Run "z7" was identical to z6 except that the population was increased by a factor of five to 10000. Unfortunately the run appeared to "top out" running out of steam perhaps because the population converged too rapidly on an inferior strategy. See Figure 9. After about 8.5 generation equivalents, the best of population was stuck at 40% and population average was leveling off at 15%. This outcome demonstrates that evolutionary computation is a stochastic technique, and not all runs succeed. There are suggestions that most reliable way to use computational resources is to use a series of many smaller runs in place of a single large run.

7 Conclusions

These results indicate that behavioral control programs can be evolved using Genetic Programming and a noisy simulation-based fitness test. The solutions discovered by this process are simple and robust. It appears that noise in fitness testing discourages strategies that are brittle, opportunistic, or overly complicated. The only solutions that can survive noisy fitness testing are compact and robust.

8 Future Work

As corridor following behavior developed in these experiments it became clear that *reliability* is a difficult property to measure. While competent behavior clearly arose, it is hard to measure just how robust and how reliable these controllers are. If we wanted to measure the reliability of a human automobile driver, what would be the criterion? Would we count the number of collisions over a long period of time, say a year? How would we differentiate between all of the individuals who had zero collisions? Is a year a long enough test period, and if not, how long are we willing to wait for an answer? All of these same issue come up in trying to rate the reliability of the corridor following controllers evolved here. A topic of future study will be to determine the most efficient techniques for testing reliability.

The competent behavior evolved in these experiments represented a breakthrough after a long series of unsuccessful experiments in applying very similar GP techniques to the same problem. The fact that a seemingly tiny change in the GP representation (restricting the argument of look-for-obstacle to be a constant) made a huge difference in the difficulty of the problem is a tantalizing result which deserves further study. What does this say about the problem domain? What does it say about Genetic Programming? How can we characterize this representational difficulty, and how can we avoid it in the future? Some first thoughts are explored in [Reynolds 1994b].

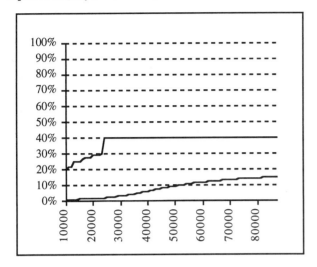

Figure 9: Fitness plots for run z7 (best-of-population and average-of-population).

Acknowledgments

This work was supported by Electronic Arts. The author wishes to thank his supervisor Steve Crane and Vice President of Technology Luc Barthelet, for allowing blue-sky research to coexist with product development. Thanks to John Koza and James Rice for advice. Thanks to "assistant GP guy" Emmanuel Berriet for providing extra CPU cycles. Special thanks to my wife Lisa and to our first child Eric, whose gestation corresponded with this paper's.

References

Altenberg, L. (1994) The Evolution of Evolvability in Genetic Programming, in *Advances in Genetic Programming*, K. E. Kinnear, Jr., Ed. Cambridge, MA: MIT Press.

Braitenburg, V. (1984) *Vehicles*, MIT press, Cambridge, Massachusetts.

Cliff, D. (1991a) Computational Neuroethology: A Provisional Manifesto, in *From Animals To Animats: Proceedings of the First International Conference on Simulation of Adaptive Behavior* (SAB90), Meyer and Wilson editors, MIT Press, Cambridge, Massachusetts.

Cliff, D. (1991b) The Computational Hoverfly; a Study in Computational Neuroethology, in *From Animals To Animats: Proceedings of the First International Conference on Simulation of Adaptive Behavior* (SAB90), Meyer and Wilson editors, MIT Press, Cambridge, Massachusetts.

Cliff, D. (1993a) P. Husbands, and I. Harvey Evolving Visually Guided Robots, in *From Animals to Animats 2: Proceedings of the Second International Conference on Simulation of Adaptive Behavior* (SAB92), Meyer, Roitblat and Wilson editors, MIT Press, Cambridge, Massachusetts, pages 374-383.

Cliff, D. (1993b) I. Harvey, and P. Husbands, Explorations in Evolutionary Robotics, *Adaptive Behavior* 2(1), pages 73-110.

Collins, R. J. (1992) *Studies in Artificial Evolution*, Ph.D. thesis, University of California at Los Angeles..

Handley, S. (1994) The Automatic Generation of Plans for a Mobile Robot via Genetic Programming with Automatically defined Functions, in *Advances in Genetic Programming*, K. E. Kinnear, Jr., Ed. Cambridge, MA: MIT Press.

Harvey, I. (1992) Species Adaptation Genetic Algorithms: The Basis for a Continuing SAGA, in *Toward a Practice of Autonomous Systems: Proceedings of the First European Conference on Artificial Life*, Varela and Bourgine editors, MIT Press/Bradford Books, pages 346-354.

Harvey, I. (1993) P. Husbands, and D. Cliff, Issues in Evolutionary Robotics, in *From Animals to Animats 2: Proceedings of the Second International Conference on Simulation of Adaptive Behavior* (SAB92), Meyer, Roitblat and Wilson editors, MIT Press, Cambridge, Massachusetts, pages 364-373.

Kinnear, K. E. Jr. (1993) Generality and Difficulty in Genetic Programming: Evolving a Sort, in *Proceedings of the Fifth International Conference on Genetic Algorithms*, S. Forrest, Ed San Mateo, CA: Morgan Kaufmann, pages 287-294.

Koza, J. R. (1992) *Genetic Programming: on the Programming of Computers by Means of Natural Selection*, ISBN 0-262-11170-5, MIT Press, Cambridge, Massachusetts.

Koza, J. R. (1994) *Genetic Programming II: Scalable Automatic Programming by Means of Automatically Defined Functions*, MIT Press, Cambridge, Massachusetts (in press).

Mataric, M. J. (1993) Designing Emergent Behaviors: From Local Interactions to Collective Intelligence, in *From Animals to Animats 2: Proceedings of the Second International Conference on Simulation of Adaptive Behavior* (SAB92), Meyer, Roitblat and Wilson editors, MIT Press, Cambridge, Massachusetts, pages 432-441.

Ngo, J. T. (1993) and J. Marks, Spacetime Constraints Revisited, Proceedings of SIGGRAPH 93 (Anaheim, California, August 1-6, 1993), in *Computer Graphics Proceedings*, Annual Conference Series, 1993, ACM SIGGRAPH, New York, pages 343-350.

Reynolds, C. W. (1987) Flocks, Herds, and Schools: A Distributed Behavioral Model, in *Computer Graphics*, 21(4) (SIGGRAPH '87 Conference Proceedings) pages 25-34.

Reynolds, C. W. (1988) Not Bumping Into Things, in the notes for the SIGGRAPH '88 course *Developments in Physically-Based Modeling*, pages G1-G13, published by ACM-SIGGRAPH.

Reynolds, C. W. (1993) An Evolved, Vision-Based Behavioral Model of Coordinated Group Motion, in *From Animals to Animats 2: Proceedings of the Second International Conference on Simulation of Adaptive Behavior* (SAB92), Meyer, Roitblat and Wilson editors, MIT Press, Cambridge, Massachusetts, pages 384-392.

Reynolds, C. W. (1993) An Evolved, Vision-Based Model of Obstacle Avoidance Behavior, in *Artificial Life III*, Santa Fe Institute Studies in the Sciences of Complexity,

Proceedings Volume XVI, C. Langton, Ed. Redwood City, CA: Addison-Wesley.

Reynolds, C. W. (1994a) Evolution of Obstacle Avoidance Behavior: Using Noise to Promote Robust Solutions, in *Advances in Genetic Programming*, K. E. Kinnear, Jr., Ed. Cambridge, MA: MIT Press.

Reynolds, C. W. (1994b) The Difficulty of Roving Eyes, in *Proceedings of the IEEE World Congress on Computational Intelligence*, IEEE (in press).

Syswerda, G. (1989) Uniform Crossover in Genetic Algorithms, in *Proceedings of the Third International Conference on Genetic Algorithms*, pages 2-9, Morgan Kaufmann Publishers.

Syswerda, G. (1991) A Study of Reproduction in Generational and Steady-State Genetic Algorithms, in *Foundations of Genetic Algorithms*, G. J. E. Rawlins, Ed. San Mateo, CA: Morgan Kaufmann, pages 94-101.

Tackett, W. A. (1994) and A. Carmi, The Donut Problem: Scalability, Generalization, and Breeding Policy in the Genetic Programming, in *Advances in Genetic Programming*, K. E. Kinnear, Jr., Ed. Cambridge, MA: MIT Press.

von Neumann, J. (1987) Probabilistic Logics and the Synthesis of Reliable Organisms from Unreliable Components, in *Papers of John von Neumann on Computing and Computer Theory*, W. Aspray and A. Burks Eds. Cambridge, MA: MIT Press.

Zapata, R. (1993) P. Lépinay, C. Novales, and P. Deplanques, Reactive Behaviors of Fast Mobile Robots in Unstructured Environments: Sensor-based Control and Neural Networks, in *From Animals to Animats 2: Proceedings of the Second International Conference on Simulation of Adaptive Behavior* (SAB92), Meyer, Roitblat and Wilson editors, MIT Press, Cambridge, Massachusetts, pages 108-115.

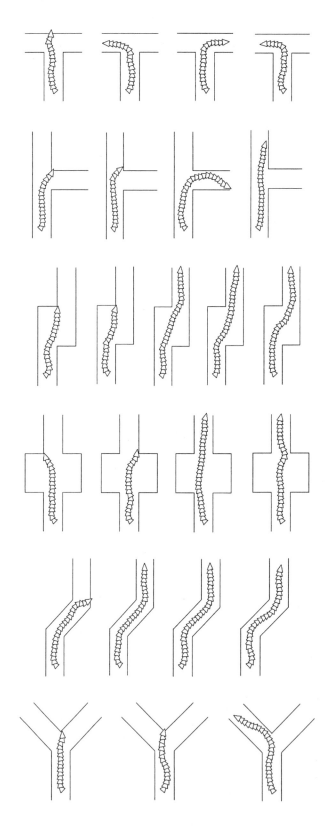

Figure 10: some tests of generalization. Controllers evolved in runs z4 and z6 have been placed in corridors containing novel features. Corridors used in their evolution had only right angles, were of constant width, and contained no branch points.

Protean Behavior in Dynamic Games:
Arguments for the co-evolution of pursuit-evasion tactics

Geoffrey F. Miller and Dave Cliff
School of Cognitive and Computing Sciences
University of Sussex, BRIGHTON BN1 9QH, U.K.
Email: geoffm, davec@cogs.susx.ac.uk

Abstract

Animals often chase each other about. These pursuit-evasion contests require the continuous dynamical control of complex sensory-motor behavior, and give rise to some of the most common and challenging co-evolutionary arms races in nature. This paper argues for the importance and fruitfulness of studying pursuit-evasion scenarios using evolutionary simulation methods. We first review the biological ubiquity of pursuit-evasion contests and the *protean* (adaptively unpredictable) behavior that often evolves in evasion strategies (e.g. when prey zig-zag to evade predators). We then review the *differential game theory* relevant to analyzing pursuit-evasion games, including the proven optimality of *mixed strategies* (corresponding to protean behavior) in many such games. Previous simulation work on evolving pursuit-evasion tactics is also reviewed. Following this, we describe results from some initial experiments that extend previous work in evolutionary robotics to explore the co-evolution of pursuit and evasion tactics in populations of simulated robots. We conclude with some possible scientific implications and engineering applications.

1 Introduction

Contests of pursuit and evasion are among the most common, challenging, and important adaptive problems that confront mobile animals, and are some of the most important potential applications for robots and other artificial autonomous agents. In a typical contest of this sort, a predator chases a prey animal around until the prey is eaten or the predator gives up. More symmetrically, two members of the same species may fight over a territory or resource, alternating between attack and defense tactics analogous to pursuit and evasion tactics. Pursuit and evasion behaviors, like attack and defense behaviors, tend to co-evolve against one another, resulting in some of the most intense and sustained evolutionary arms races in nature. Although pursuit-evasion (P-E) contests have been relatively neglected in research on the simulation of adaptive behavior, they have five major features that render them interesting and relevant.

First, pursuit and evasion strategies require highly robust forms of adaptive behavior and have particularly important fitness consequences. Animals that pursue or evade must maintain complex sensory-motor coordination with respect to both a physical environment and a hostile animate opponent. Pursuit-evasion contests also require continuous, real-time, dynamical control, in the face of an opponent that will ruthlessly exploit any delay, uncertainty, or error. Natural or artificial behavior-control systems that are slow, brittle, easily confused, or error-prone do not survive long in P-E scenarios. For these reasons, traditional artificial intelligence methods may prove particularly poor as models of P-E behaviors, and newer reactive, behavior-based, bottom-up approaches (e.g. [32]) may prove particularly apt.

Second, pursuit and evasion strategies evolve against one another in an ongoing, open-ended, frequency-dependent way, so P-E contests often give rise to co-evolution within or between species. Because P-E scenarios may be the simplest and most common cases of behavioral co-evolution, their investigation may illuminate behavioral arms races in general (see [23]). Such sustained co-evolution reinforces all of the challenges discussed in the previous paragraph: temporary adaptive advantage is continually eroded under co-evolution as new tactics arise. Co-evolution probably drives the evolution of both special perceptual capacities to entrain, track, and predict animate motion, and special motor capacities to generate complex, robust, unpredictable behavior [40]. Understanding both motion perception and motor control may thus depend on appreciating the role of P-E contests in behavioral evolution.

Third, P-E contests have received serious attention from at least three scientific disciplines: behavioral biology, neuroethology, and game theory. Animal behavior studies have revealed the ubiquity and importance of P-E tactics, anti-predator behaviors, and fighting skills [14]. The centrality of such behaviors is revealed by the fact that P-E games are the most common form of animal play behavior; such play facilitates learning sensory-motor coordination through "developmental arms races" between play-mates. Neuroethology (e.g. [6]) has spent much effort understanding neural systems for pursuit ("approach") and evasion ("avoidance"), including: explorations of specific circuits for rapid startle and escape behaviors (e.g. [7]); the role of the (very fast) tectospinal pathway in mediating pursuit behaviors in vertebrate predators such as salamanders, frogs, cats, and owls (e.g. [2]); and the specific attunement of sensory cells to patterns of animate motion relevant to pursuit and evasion (e.g. [3]). Game theorists have also studied P-E contests intensely for several decades, because of their importance in tactical air combat (e.g. telling pilots how to evade guided missiles) and other military applications (see [55]). "Differential game theory" [27] has developed a vocabulary for analyzing the structure and complexity of P-E games, and a number of formal results concerning optimal strategies for particular P-E games. We review the relevant animal behavior studies and game theory at length in the next sections.

Fourth, P-E contests are of considerable theoretical interest because they give rise to several unique behavioral phenomena. They are the simplest situations that can favor "protean" (adaptively unpredictable) behavior, as when prey animals zig-zag unpredictably to escape predators (see e.g. [8, 14]). Further, because effective pursuit may often require prediction and 'mind-reading', while effective evasion may require the use of unpredictable or deceptive tactics [14], such contests raise issues of signaling, communication, and tactical deception [38], and may provide a natural bridge from the evolution of basic sensory-motor control to the evolution of social psychology and 'Machiavellian intelligence' [5, 38].

Fifth, the study of P-E behaviors has many scientific implications and practical applications. A better understanding of the evolutionary, behavioral, and cognitive dynamics of P-E contests would have wide implications for animal behavior, neuroethology, comparative psychology, and evolutionary psychology [40]. Better methods for evolving P-E behaviors would have many applications in robotics, video games, virtual environments, and any other technology where real or simulated mobile agents come into behavioral conflict with other agents.

Because P-E contests are a major new area of investigation for simulation of adaptive behavior, which we hope will excite much further research, this paper lays out the biological and game-theoretic foundations in some detail: this is essentially a position paper. We are currently conducting experiments that extend previous work in evolutionary robotics [10] to investigate: (1) whether co-evolution between simulated robots engaged in P-E contests can lead to the more and more complex pursuit and evasion tactics over generations; (2) whether the use of continuous recurrent neural networks as control systems allows the emergence of more interesting and dynamic perceptual, predictive, pursuit and evasion abilities; and (3) whether the incorporation of random-activation units in the control system allows the evolution of adaptively unpredictable tactics. Section 5 discusses some prelim-

inary results. For a longer version of this paper, with a more extensive bibliography, see [39]. For a more detailed discussion of our methods and results, see [11].

2   Biological foundations

2.1   The generality of pursuit-evasion problems

We use the term "fitness affordances" (FAs) to denote things that have particular statistically expected consequences for the fitness (survival or reproduction) of organisms of a particular age, sex, condition, and species [37, 40, 50]. Positive FAs such as food, mates, shelter, or offspring have a positive expected effect on the replication of one's genes; negative FAs such as poisons, predators, parasites, and physical dangers have a negative expected effect. FAs are objective features of the environment insofar as their potential fitness effects exist regardless of whether the organism facing them knows or cares of their existence, but FAs are relational insofar as their biological significance exists only in relation to organisms with particular modes of survival and reproduction (e.g. what is food to one species is poison to another in a perfectly objective and yet perfectly relational way). Most FAs are spatially localized (at some scale), and only impose their fitness effects on organisms immediately present.

Mobility allows animals to actively approach and exploit positive FAs, and to actively avoid negative FAs. But very often, FAs are themselves mobile animals with their own fitness interests, which may turn the problem of approach into a problem of pursuit, or the problem of avoidance into one of evasion. Whenever there are recognized conflicts of interest over fitness effects between mobile animals, we may predict manifest conflicts of movement. If the conflict of movement is sustained across some expanse of space and time, there is a P-E conflict. Thus, interactions between two mobile agents that have conflicting expected fitness effects creates a pursuit problem for one agent and an evasion problem for the other.

The above scenario, where the roles of pursuer and evader are pre-determined by the FA relationships, and fixed for the duration of the interaction, could be called an asymmetric P-E contest. More symmetric sorts of P-E contests can unfold when similar animals both seek access to a positive FA, such as a territory or resource, that is worth more if enjoyed alone. Animals of the same species often fight over food, nest sites, and mates. In symmetric contests, the roles of pursuer and evader can switch back and forth rapidly as the animals take offensive or defensive roles. In both symmetric and asymmetric contests, the immediate behavioral conflict can result in a co-evolutionary arms race between pursuit and evasion tactics, if the agent-types in question encounter each another with reasonable frequency and with significantly opposed fitness consequences across generations.

2.2 Biological observations

Pursuit is fairly simple: animals are usually observed to move towards the remembered, observed, or predicted location of the target. Evasion is more complex. For example, animal escape behavior in asymmetric P-E contests generally breaks down into three phases: (1) directional fleeing if a predator (or other negative, mobile FA) is threatening but still distant; (2) erratic zig-zagging if the predator begins catching up; and (3) convulsive 'death-throes' if caught. Directional fleeing is about as simple as directional chasing, but the last two tactics, zig-zagging and convulsing, are examples of a more interesting type: protean behavior.

Animals generally evolve perceptual and cognitive capacities to entrain, track, and predict the movements of other biologically-relevant animals such as prey, predators, and potential mates [40]. Such predictive abilities mean that unpredictable behavior will inevitably be favored in many natural P-E situations. For example, if a rabbit fleeing from a fox always chose the single apparently shortest escape route, the very consistency of its behavior would make its escape route more predictable to the fox, its body more likely to be eaten, its genes less likely to replicate, and its fitness lower. Predictability is punished by hostile animals capable of prediction. This is the basic logic behind the theory of protean behavior: the effectiveness of almost any behavioral tactic can be enhanced by endowing it with characteristics that cannot be predicted by an evolutionary opponent [14]. An arms race between perceptual capacities for predicting animate motion, and motor capacities for generating protean behavior, will generally result from evolutionarily recurring P-E contests [40].

Along with directional fleeing, protean escape behaviors are probably the most widespread and successful of all behavioral anti-predator tactics, being used by virtually all mobile animals on land, under water, and in the air. Driver and Humphries [14] review examples from hundreds of species, including humans. Predators can also exploit unpredictability to confuse prey, as when weasels do "crazy dances" to baffle the voles they stalk.

Even if erratic zig-zagging fails, another form of proteanism, convulsive behavior, may succeed. Sudden, unpredictable, vigorous "death-throes", alternating with puzzling passivity ("playing dead") is often effective at allowing prey to escape from predators [14]. Adaptive convulsions can also occur in more abstract state-spaces, as when cuttlefish and octopi undergo rapid color changes to defeat the search images (perceptual expectations) of their predators. Additional confusion effects may arise from group flocking and mobbing behaviors that include unpredictable movements, complex motion dynamics, and confusing coloration (zebra stripes or shiny scales on fish). Unpredictability can also be exploited by divergence between individuals, as when animals within a species evolve "aspect diversity" (polymorphic coloration or behavior) through "apostatic selection" that favors low-frequency traits (e.g. because predators' use of search images penalizes common appearances). Indeed, apostatic selection may be a general feature of P-E arms races: novel and unexpected tactics may be favored at a variety of levels.

Co-evolution itself can be viewed as a P-E contest, operating between lineages rather than between individuals. From this perspective, sexual recombination makes sense as a protean strategy which unpredictably mixes up genes so as to "confuse" pathogens [22]. Indeed, this proteanism argument is one of the leading explanations for the the evolution of sex [45]. Despite proteanism's importance, it has been long overlooked in biology, because complex order rather than useful chaos was assumed to be the defining feature of Darwinian adaptations.

3 Game-theoretic foundations

3.1 Differential pursuit-evasion game theory

Game theory [44] is concerned with the formal analysis of situations called "games" where: (1) players can choose different strategies that determine their actions under particular conditions; (2) conditions and outcomes unfold through the interactions of the players' strategies; and (3) players have preferences among outcomes, i.e. payoffs exist. In brief, players are agents that can make choices, implement strategies, and receive payoffs.

Traditional game theory focused on games with discrete moves (e.g. chess), but in the 1950s, Isaacs (e.g. [27]) wondered whether game theory could be used to model P-E situations such as aerial combat, where moves unfold continuously over time. Isaacs had two basic insights. First, P-E contests do require game theory rather than simple optimality theory, because the optimal pursuit strategy for one player (e.g. a guided missile) depends on the evasion strategy adopted by the other player (e.g. an aircraft), and vice-versa. This chicken-and-egg problem is precisely what game theory is good at analyzing. Second, the continuous nature of P-E contests can be modeled using differential equations that specify how state conditions (such as player positions and velocities) change incrementally as a function of players' strategies and previous state conditions: pursuit and evasion moves become continuous trajectories through a state-space. Isaacs [27] developed the "Tenet of Transition" which specifies that players must optimize (find the minimax solution for) the transitions between states leading towards a goal-state, which can be represented as optimizing the temporal derivatives of the relevant state variables. For example, pursuers try to minimize the time until capture and evaders try to maximize it. Applying the tenet of transition, pursuers at each moment in time should try to maximize the rate of their instantaneous approach towards the capture-state, and evaders should try to minimize it. If a solvable set of differential equations can be written that specify the continuous effect of strategies on state-conditions, then the optimal pursuit and evasion strategies can be found by applying the tenet of transition. Isaacs's ideas have proven enormously fruitful: Rodin's [46] recent bibliography of P-E differential game theory contains about 1200 entries, and theoretical results are often used in practical situations such as design of military aircraft control systems.

Differential P-E games are defined by a set of controls (what each player can do), a set of dynamics (that maps from the control variables onto the state variables of the game, and from state variables at one moment in time to the next moment), and a set of termination conditions (state conditions that determine when successful capture or evasion happens). For example, in a classic case analyzed by Berkovitz [4], a pursuer and an evader move with equal and constant speed in a plane, and control the direction of their velocity vector (which thus becomes their control variable). These two velocity vectors give rise to a system of first-order differential state equations that determine how the players move over time. The pursuer wants to minimize time to capture the evader and the evader wants to maximize time until capture, with capture defined as proximity within some small distance. Both players know the present state of the game (e.g. both of their positions and velocity vectors) but at each time-point they make separate and simultaneous decisions about what to do next. The available strategies are therefore functions that map from current states of the game (i.e. the positions and velocity vectors of both players) onto velocity-vector decisions about what direction to move next. In all differential games, strategies determine trajectories through the relevant state-space; in P-E games, strategies determine trajectories through physical space. From each player's perspective, the game becomes a problem of optimal spatio-temporal control with respect to the opponent and the environment. Indeed, control theory can be viewed largely as the solution of one-player differential games [28]; differential game theory addresses the more complex multi-player cases.

In classic "asymmetric" games (e.g. missile vs. aircraft), the roles of pursuer and evader are pre-determined and fixed. But in "symmetric" games (e.g. aircraft vs. aircraft), both players can collect payoffs for successful pursuit and successful evasion. Symmetric P-E contests have been analyzed as "two-target games" [18, 36]. The symmetric contests in our initial experiments (see [11]) resembled the sort of two-target aerial combat games that have been subject to intense game-theoretical analysis for several decades (see [21] for review).

3.2   The optimality of mixed strategies

The key to formal analysis in game theory is for games to be reduced from descriptive form (e.g. rules and heuristics) or "extensive form" (i.e. decision-tree form) to "normal form" (i.e. a joint payoff matrix that lists game outcomes given all possible strategies for all players). Some games in normal form have "minimax solutions" (a.k.a. "saddle points") that minimize each player's expected loss regardless of what the opponent does to maximize their expected gain; minimax solutions, if they exist, are jointly optimal for rational players. In games of perfect information, players are precisely and continuously aware of all moves made by other players, so that deception, confusion, and uncertainty are impossible. All games of perfect information have one or more saddle points corresponding to "pure" deterministic optimal strategies (though finding them may often be difficult, as in chess).

However, games of imperfect information (e.g. games where deception is possible) may have multiple saddle points or no saddle points. In such cases, "mixed strategies" (probability distributions across pure strategies) may be optimal. Perhaps the most important result from [44] was that every two-player, zero-sum game of incomplete information with multiple saddle points has an optimal strategy that is mixed rather than pure:

> "One important consideration for a player in such a game is to protect himself against having his intentions found out by his opponent. Playing several different strategies at random, so that only their probabilities are determined, is an effective way to achieve a degree of such protection. By this device the opponent cannot possibly find out what the player's strategy is going to be, since the player does not know it himself. Ignorance is obviously a good safeguard against disclosing information directly or indirectly." [44, p.146]

The logic of mixed strategies is simple. If a player's choice sometimes remains unknown to others after the move is made, the game is one of imperfect information. This can result from the move being hidden, or the other players' sensors being insufficient to register all moves with complete accuracy. Typically, games lose their saddle points when they are no longer games of perfect information, such that the first player's minimax solution does not correspond to the second player's minimax solution. For example, the popular children's game Rock, Paper, Scissors involves a circular pattern of dominance among the pure strategies (Rock beats Scissors, Scissors cut Paper, Paper smothers Rock), so there is no saddle point, and one's optimal (minimax) strategy against a rational opponent is to choose each move with one-third probability. In general, mixed strategies randomize moves to confuse opponents and keep them guessing.

(But the task of determining the optimal mixed strategy is usually very difficult for games with many pure strategies and complex interactions.)

Because many P-E games are games of incomplete information with multiple saddle points, mixed strategies have often proven useful in such games. Mixed strategies are optimal for a P-E game with rectilinear movement on a planar grid [15]. In some more complex continuous cases, the optimal strategies for both pursuer and evader are also mixed. Important recent work in this area has been by Forte and Shinar (e.g. [16, 49]); they showed that in aerial combat scenarios, mixed strategies yielded much better performance than any previously known guidance law, and did so for both pursuers and evaders. Such game-theoretic results support the protean behavior hypothesis of Driver and Humphries [14] that erratic zig-zagging by animals is truly stochastic behavior that derives its utility from its unpredictability. We might expect then that in any P-E game with incomplete information and complex dynamics, unpredictable pursuit and evasion strategies will evolve.

Evolutionary game theory [33] has also recognized the optimality of mixed strategies in many contests between animals. Animals can be considered players in the game-theoretic sense because they make choices, implement behavioral strategies, and receive fitness payoffs contingent on their interactions with other animals' strategies. Mixed strategies can be implemented as behavioral polymorphisms across individuals in a population or as protean behavior within each individual. However, evolutionary game theory has focused mostly on single-step games (such as sex-ratio determination or the Hawk-Dove game: see [33]) and discrete-step games (such as the iterated prisoner's dilemma). The literature on differential P-E games has been strangely overlooked despite its obvious relevance to predator-prey interactions and territorial fights, so the importance of protean evasion behavior has been neglected. Dynamic programming methods (e.g. [25, 26]) may prove more useful in analyzing P-E contests, since they can optimize stochastic dynamic strategies, even in two-player games (e.g. [9]). However, such methods require the specification of a fairly well-defined strategy set, and Miller [41] has argued that genetic algorithms can evolve strategies in a more open-ended fashion than dynamic programming. Evolutionary game theory and dynamic programming should prove useful adjuncts to differential game theory as ways of analyzing simple P-E conflicts, but the next section suggests that simulated evolution may be required to deal with complex cases.

3.3   Reasons to simulate pursuit-evasion games

Games are characterized by various dimensions of complexity: (1) the number of players, ranging from one-player cases (covered by control theory) to classic two-player cases to more difficult multi-player cases; (2) the number of moves, ranging from "static" games of one discrete move per player (e.g. Rock, Paper, Scissors) to games with multiple discrete moves per player (e.g. chess), to differential games with continuous moves (e.g. air combat); (3) the payoff structure, with zero-sum games usually simpler than non-zero-sum games; (4) the information structure, with games of complete information much simpler than games of incomplete information. Moreover, in differential games with continuous dynamics, the complexity and noisiness of the dynamics has a major influence on the tractability of the game. Anything that complicates the differential state equations complicates the game analysis. Finally, formal application of game theory requires the complete specification of a strategy space. Such a complete specification may not be possible if the strategies are emergent properties of human heuristics, animal brains, or evolved robot control systems. These problems suggest that differential P-E games are difficult to analyze even under the best circumstances, and that the introduction of realistic complexity renders most of them formally intractable.

To avoid these complexities, differential game theory usually assumes that the P-E game is one of perfect information between two players with fixed and predetermined roles (one "pursuer" and one "evader"), deterministic dynamics and constant speeds, and a zero-sum payoff structure. Mathematically adept researchers can relax one or two of these assumptions at a time to derive results for special and simplified cases, but relaxing all the assumptions at once makes the game hopelessly complex. Some recent work attempts to analyze more difficult asymmetric and symmetric games with noise-corrupted environments [54], uncertain environments [13], or uncertain dynamics [17]. Yet even with bounded uncertainties in dynamics, the classical game-theoretic concepts of optimality, value, and saddle point may be irrelevant [17]. P-E games that cannot be reduced to differential state-space equations cannot be analyzed using the traditional methods of differential game theory. For example, without a linear and deterministic mapping from control to state variables (e.g. from a player's sensors to its effectors), it is impossible to construct tractable differential equations that relate player strategies directly to changes in the game's state-space.

Another important assumption, very rarely mentioned in game theory, is that strategies can be implemented instantaneously, without time-lags, computational costs, or speed-accuracy trade-offs. That is, decision dynamics are assumed to be much faster than behavioral dynamics. For real animals and robots, this assumption is unrealistic. Indeed, the basic assumption in game theory that unpredictability is only useful given incomplete information assumes that decision-making happens so much faster than action, that the dynamics of information-processing are irrelevant to the dynamics of action. But if we view both cognition and action as dynamical processes operating on similar time scales [40], then the utility of unpredictability becomes more apparent. The terms "perfect" and "imperfect" information conflate the objective information structure of the game (e.g. the state-information available in the world) with the sensory and information-processing capacities of the players. If the latter are limited, then confusion, uncertainty, deception, and protean behavior may prove relevant even if the objective information structure of the game is "perfect".

In recognition of these problems, some game theorists have recently shifted to numerical and simulation methods to derive near-optimal strategies for more complex P-E games (e.g. [29, 47]). For example, [47] used artificial intelligence (AI) methods to simulate players in an air combat maneuvering scenario. But such methods for controlling autonomous agents tend to become hopelessly slow as the dynamics of agents and environments become more complex and noisy. We need simulation methods that yield reactive, robust, dynamic P-E strategies, rather than slow, brittle, hand-designed AI systems.

Differential game theory provides a framework for describing the important features of P-E contests, and a set of normative results concerning optimal strategies in simple cases. However, it cannot generally provide optimal strategies for realistically complex P-E problems, nor can it show how strategies can be implemented in a real control system subject to limited sensory capacities, sensory and motor noise, component failure, and constraints on processing speed and accuracy. Evolutionary simulation methods can fulfill these goals and can complement game-theoretic approaches, because adaptive P-E strategies can be evolved in contest scenarios that defy formal analysis. Others have recognized this, and so we next review previous simulation work related to P-E issues.

4 Review of Related Simulation Work

Themes of pursuit and evasion are implicit in much of the recent work in artificial life and simulation of adaptive behavior. Classic problems of obstacle avoidance and of foraging and navigation can be viewed as degenerate special cases of evasion and pursuit, respectively, with the "opponents" consisting of inanimate, non-moving obstacles, food items, or other goal objects. Much of the work on simulation of collective behavior involves issues of dynamical interaction with other agents that may be similar to the those arising in P-E contests. For example, the cooperative behaviors of following, flocking, and aggregation are similar to pursuit behaviors; others such as dispersion and collision-avoidance are more similar to evasion behaviors. (But note that selection for cooperation rarely favors deception or protean behavior.)

Previous simulation work has examined the origins and effects of P-E tactics with neither player evolving

or with one player evolving; these will be reviewed in order (we are not aware of any prior work with both players co-evolving.) Given very simple, fixed rules for individual movement, Schmieder [48] examined the different P-E dynamics that result when a number of simulated males and females are attracted or repulsed by one another with varying strengths, and with varying degrees of mutual knowledge about one another's movements. Some artificial life simulations have successfully used pre-programmed predators that impose selection for simple evasion behaviors (e.g. [1, 51]).

Grefenstette's [19, 20] SAMUEL system, resembling a classifier system, evolved robust rule-based strategies for simulated agents with noisy, coarse-grained sensors and effectors, including both effective evasion rules given one or two pre-programmed pursuers (in the 'predator-prey' problem), and effective pursuit rules given a randomly moving evader (in the 'cat-and-mouse' problem). However, SAMUEL uses high-level sensory input (e.g. direct heading, bearing, speed, and range information), symbolic condition-action rules operating in discrete time-slices (e.g. 2 to 20 decisions per contest), and fairly domain-specific genetic operators (such as Lamarckian rule deletion, generalization, and specialization).

Koza's [30, 31] genetic programming work includes the widest array of P-E simulations. His Pac-Man scenario [31] required both evasion (of pre-programmed "monsters") and pursuit (of sluggishly moving "fruit"); control systems evolved through genetic programming that were capable of prioritizing these activities appropriately. Some evolved Pac-Man controllers were skillful enough to eat the monsters after eating a special "pill" that made the monsters vulnerable, so to some extent the roles or pursuer and evader could be switched in this scenario. Koza [31] also investigated the evolution of P-E strategies in Isaacs' [27] "squad car game", where a police squad car pursues a slower pedestrian evader on a discrete grid. Most relevantly, Koza [30] used genetic programming to evolve LISP S-expression controllers for both players in a differential P-E game. His game had pre-determined and fixed roles for pursuer and evader, constant speeds for both agents, and perfect information. Agents were randomly placed in a planar world, controlled their directions (velocity vectors) based on simple inputs concerning the current heading of the opponent, and received fitness payoffs for effective pursuit or evasion. This game has a single optimal pursuit strategy (move directly towards the evader) and a single optimal evasion strategy (move directly away from the pursuer). Given an optimal evader as the "environment", genetic programming was successful in evolving a near-optimal pursuer within a few generations (e.g. 51 generations of 500 individuals each); likewise, near-optimal evaders evolved given fixed optimal pursuers as the environment. However, Koza's P-E game was very simple: it required mapping a single input (current angle of opponent) onto a single output (direction to move in), given perfect information and trivial movement dynamics, and it had a known optimal solution from differential game theory. Co-evolution between pursuer and evader did not occur. Nevertheless, Koza's work represents an important fore-runner and inspiration for our research.

Aside from explicit P-E research, some simulated evolution has demonstrated the adaptiveness of mixed strategies and protean behavior. Koza [31] used genetic programming to evolve random-number generation programs under "entropy-driven evolution"; this direct selection for randomness is analogous to the indirect selection for unpredictable evasion that occurs in P-E contests. Other simulation work has shown the utility of co-evolution in evolving strategies for game-like interactions. Work by Hillis [23] on the co-evolution of sorting strategies and test sets can be viewed as an abstract version of a one-play P-E contest, in which the sorting strategies 'pursue' optimal sorts while the test sets 'evade' the strengths of particular sorting algorithms. Co-evolution has also been used successfully in Holland's [24] ECHO system, Koza's [30, 31] genetic programming research, and J. H. Miller's [43] work on the iterated prisoner's dilemma. This previous work on evolving pursuit and evasion strategies, together with Koza's demonstration of entropy-driven evolution through selection for randomness, and demonstrations of co-evolution by Hillis and others, gave us hope that a co-evolutionary P-E scenario could lead to the evolution of protean behaviors.

5   Experimental Methods and Results

In previous work on evolutionary robotics [10], Cliff *et al.* have used simulated evolution through natural selection to design sensory and control systems capable of guiding simulated robots to perform simple homing and guidance tasks. Here, as a natural extension to this work, we increase the number of agents in the world from one to two, and set up a fitness function that rewards hostile pursuit and effective evasion.

To limit computational costs, the full 3-D simulation system employed in [10] was simplified to yield a 2-D 'flatland' simulation; nevertheless, both time and space were still modeled as continuous values. Visual sensing was modeled using computer graphics techniques, with visual sensors (e.g. number, placement, and angular sensitivities of 'eyes') evolving under genetic control. All agents had the same motor system (2 wheels) and kinematics, which were modeled as differential-drive steering systems. The faster an agent moved, the larger its minimum turning radius became. All agents had the same visual appearance with distinguishable head and tail ends, so an agent could in principle detect whether its opponent was oriented towards or away from it.

Since P-E games unfold in continuous space and time

as an interplay between each agent's continuous dynamical trajectory, rather than as a series of discrete, alternating moves, we preferred to use agent control systems based on dynamical, recurrent neural networks, rather than controllers with discrete condition-action rules, such as classifier systems (e.g. [52]), LISP S-expressions [30], or deterministic finite-state automata [12]. Our agents' control systems are genetically-specified continuous-time noisy recurrent neural networks with heterogeneous time-constants, modeled using numerical approximation techniques with the same very short time-slice interval (Δt) as was used for resolving sensor and motor responses. The networks can, to a good approximation, generate continuous output based on continuous input, and have intrinsic dynamics that can be used to guide complex adaptive behavior.

In each P-E contest, a pair of individuals are placed at random on the planar surface, each moves as directed by its evolved control system based on its visual input, and each amasses fitness points for effective pursuit and/or effective evasion, depending on the fitness function. Because contest outcomes are noisy, each individual takes part in a number of contests (typically 8 or 16) to determine overall fitness. Elitist rank-based reproduction, with crossover and mutation, are used to form the next generation.

We have implemented two types of simulation. In inter-population asymmetric P-E co-evolution, a 'pursuer' population is selected for pursuit ability (like a predator species), and co-evolves against a second, reproductively separate 'evader' population, which is selected for evasion ability (like a prey species). In intra-population symmetric P-E competition, individuals in a single population compete against each other and are selected for both pursuit and evasion abilities using a single zero-sum evaluation function. The following discussion considers this latter case, which we expected to be easier, but which proved quite tricky.

We found that many of our intra-population zero-sum evaluation functions, which were designed to reward both pursuit and evasion capacities in the same individual, resulted in pseudo-cooperative solutions, such as: (1) both competitors turning away from each other and running off at full speed; (2) both competitors turning to face each other and then shutting down all motor activities, resulting in an indefinite face-off; or (3) both competitors turning to face each other and then accelerating to a high-speed collision. In most evaluation functions we have examined, the first two outcomes appear to be strong attractors, and the second two are perhaps evolutionarily stable strategies. These outcomes, and the difficulty of constructing fitness functions for intra-population co-evolution, are discussed further in [11].

In co-evolution based on zero-sum contests within populations, there are further problems in measuring real performance increases in the population, because average population fitness will necessarily hover around zero. Figure 1 (solid line) shows the fitness score of the best individual (highest average score over 16 trials) in the population at the end of each of 300 generations. These results do not appear promising: despite selecting for *higher* scores (i.e. maximizing), fitness rapidly falls towards zero and stays there for the duration of the experiment. However, when the best individual from each generation is tested against the best individual in the original random population of generation 0 (Fig. 1, broken line), it is clear that improvement has occurred. This improvement rapidly approaches an asymptote (within 10 generations), and is largely due to genetic convergence (this experiment was performed with a high selection pressure and a relatively low mutation rate). Despite the apparent asymptote, scores vs. the best individual from generation 300 (Fig. 1, dotted line) indicate that beneficial mutations continue to occur: e.g. at generations 70 and 202; after each such mutation, performance reaches a significantly higher plateau; see [11] for further details.

By analogy, ancient predators may have caught ancient herbivores only half the time, and modern cheetahs may catch modern gazelles only half the time, but modern cheetahs would catch ancient herbivores very efficiently. To register progress in zero-sum co-evolutionary situations, we need to explicitly test individuals against their ancestors (or the ancestors of their competitors).

6   Conclusions

Pursuit and evasion behaviors are common because conflicts of interest over approach and avoidance are common, and they are difficult because dynamic, stochastic, continuous-space, continuous-time, zero-sum games are difficult. This paper has argued that the exploration of P-E contests is the next logical step in the simulated evolution of adaptive behavior. Such contests introduce many complexities, such as co-evolution, protean behavior, dynamical behavior, and collective movement patterns. We conclude by examining the engineering and scientific benefits of pursuing rather than evading these complexities.

Many traditional robot control tasks are degenerate special cases of P-E problems: collision-avoidance is evasion of non-moving obstacles, goal-directed navigation and homing behavior are pursuit of a non-moving target region, and grasping can be pursuit of a non-moving target object. Clearly, the avoidance, pursuit, or manipulation of active mobile agents radically increases the difficulty of such tasks, and their robust solution may require co-evolutionary design methods, where robot control systems evolve against pursuer or evader agents. Even where a robot's operating environment is expected to contain only static or passively moving objects, co-

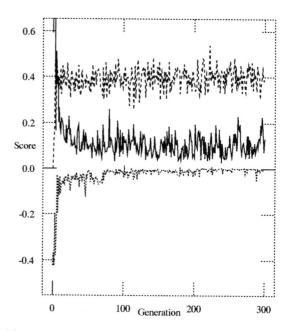

Figure 1:   Scores from zero-sum P-E intra-population co-evolution. Solid line: score of best individual in generation when tested against a random selection of other individuals in that generation (peak value is 1.16 at generation 1). Broken line: score of best individual in generation when tested against best individual from generation 0. Dotted line: score of best individual in generation when tested against best individual in generation 300. All points are averages of 16 trials.

evolution of grasping and movement tactics against animate opponents might increase the robustness, speed, smoothness, and generality of control systems, because the opponents would evolve to exploit any instabilities or weaknesses in the control system. For example, a legged robot that is harried by a hostile predator that keeps trying to trip it up will probably evolve more robust walking abilities than one that merely clambers over passive obstacles. Any real robot that operates in public spaces that contain potentially hostile (or merely clumsy and curious) agents, such as children, dogs, or Luddites, must have escape and evasion abilities at least as effective as those of the average house pet. The co-evolution of evasion tactics through interaction with simulated animal, human or vehicle pursuers may help to solve this potentially catastrophic problem. Pursuit and evasion capacities have other obvious applications in computer animation, video games, and virtual environments, aside from less savory military uses.

The scientific benefits of a better understanding of pursuit and evasion would extend to game theory, animal biology, evolutionary psychology, and neuroethology. Implications also arise for our understanding of the general relationship between agents and environments. For those seeking a general theory of environmental complexity (e.g. [53, 50]), the addition of animate agents capable of unpredictable pursuit and evasion in the environment represents a significant conceptual challenge. For example, an environment that contains creatures with continuous-time dynamical recurrent networks as their control systems would be difficult to model as an environmental finite state machine, as proposed in [53]. As in sexual selection [37, 42] and other forms of "psychological selection" [38, 40], P-E contests break down the distinction between environment complexity and agent complexity, because agents become the most important selective forces in each other's environments.

Acknowledgements:

Miller's research was supported by NSF-NATO Post-Doc Fellowship RCD-9255323 and NSF Research Grant INT-9203229. Thanks to Inman Harvey, Alasdair Houston, Phil Husbands, Peter Todd, and an anonymous reviewer for useful comments and criticisms.

References

[1] D. Ackley & M. Littman. Interactions between learning and evolution. In C. G. Langton *et al.*, eds, *Artificial Life II*, pp. 487–509. Addison-Wesley, 1992.

[2] B. Alstermark, *et al.* Effect of different spinal cord lesions on visually guided switching of target-reaching in cats. *Neurosci. Res.*, 5(1):63–67, 1987.

[3] M. A. Arbib & A. Cobas. Schemas for prey-catching in frog and toad. In [35, pp.142–151], 1991.

[4] L. D. Berkovitz. Two person zero sum differential games: An overview. In J. D. Grote, ed, *The theory and application of differential games*, pp. 12–22. D. Reidel, 1975.

[5] R. Byrne & A. Whiten, eds. *Machiavellian intelligence: Social expertise and the evolution of intellect in monkeys, apes, and humans.* Oxford U. Press, 1988.

[6] J. Camhi. *Neuroethology: Nerve cells and the natural behavior of animals.* Sinauer, 1984.

[7] J. Camhi. Invertebrate neuroethology: Escape behavior in the cockroach and distributed neural processing. *Experientia (Basel)*, 44(5):401–408, 1988.

[8] M. R. A. Chance & W. M. S. Russell. Protean displays: a form of allaesthetic behavior. *Proc. Zoological Soc. of London*, 132:65–70, 1959.

[9] C. W. Clark & R. C. Ydenberg. The risk of parenthood I. General theory and applications. *Evolutionary Ecology*, 4(1):21–34, 1990.

[10] D. Cliff, I. Harvey, & P. Husbands. Explorations in evolutionary robotics. *Adaptive Behavior*, 2(1):73–110, 1993.

[11] D. Cliff & G. F. Miller. The co-evolution of pursuit-evasion tactics in simulated robots. Cognitive Science Research Paper, University of Sussex, 1994. In Preparation.

[12] R. J. Collins & D. R. Jefferson. Representations for artificial organisms. In [35, pp.382–290], 1991.

[13] M. Corliss, G. Leitmann, & J. M. Skowronski. Adaptive control for avoidance or evasion in an uncertain environment. In [55, pp.1-11], 1987.

[14] P. Driver & N. Humphries. *Protean behavior: The biology of unpredictability.* Oxford U. Press, 1988.

[15] A. Ermolov, B. Kryakovskii, & E. Maslov. Differential game with mixed strategies. *Avtomatika i Telemekhanika*, 47(10):1336–1349, 1986.

[16] I. Forte & J.Shinar. Improved guidance law design based on the mixed-strategy concept. *J. of Guidance, Control, and Dynamics*, 12(5):739–745, 1989.

[17] E. Galperin & J. Skowronski. Pursuit-evasion differential games with uncertainties in dynamics. In [55, pp.13-35], 1987.

[18] W. Getz & M. Pachter. Two target pursuit-evasion differential games in the plane. *J. Optim. Theory Applic.*, 34:383–404, 1981.

[19] J. J. Grefenstette. The evolution of strategies for multiagent environments. *Adaptive Behavior*, 1(1):65–89, 1992.

[20] J. J. Grefenstette, C. L. Ramsey, & A. C. Schultz. Learning sequential decision rules using simulation models and competition. *Machine Learning*, 5(4):355–381, 1990.

[21] W. Grimm & K. Well. Modelling air combat as differential game: Recent approaches and future requirements. In *Proc. 4th Int. Symp. Differential Games and Applications*, pp. 1–13. Springer, 1991.

[22] W. D. Hamilton, R. Axelrod, , and R. Tanese. Sexual reproduction as an adaptation to resist parasites: A review. *Proc. Nat'l Acad. Sciences (USA)*, 87(9):3566–3573, 1990.

[23] W. Hillis. Co-evolving parasites improve simulated evolution as an optimization procedure. *Physica D*, 42:228–234, 1990.

[24] J. Holland. Echo: Explorations of evolution in a miniature world. In C. G. Langton *et al.*, eds, *Artificial Life II*. Addison-Wesley, 1992.

[25] A. Houston & J. McNamara. Singing to attract a mate: A stochastic dynamic game. *J. Theoretical Biology*, 129:57–68, 1987.

[26] A. Houston & J. McNamara. A framework for the functional analysis of behavior. *Behavioral and Brain Sciences*, 11(1):117–164, 1988.

[27] R. Isaacs. *Differential games.* John Wiley, 1965.

[28] R. Isaacs. The past and some bits of the future. In J. D. Grote, ed, *The theory and application of differential games*, pp. 1–11. D. Reidel, 1975.

[29] B. Jarmark. On closed-loop controls in pursuit-evasion. In [55, pp.157-166], 1987.

[30] J. Koza. Evolution and co-evolution of computer programs to control independently-acting agents. In [35, pp.366-375], 1991.

[31] J. Koza. *Genetic Programming: On the programming of computers by means of natural selection.* MIT Press, 1992.

[32] P. Maes, ed. *Designing autonomous agents: theory and practice from biology to engineering and back.* MIT/Elsevier, 1990.

[33] J. Maynard Smith. *Evolution and the theory of games.* Cambridge U. Press, 1982.

[34] J.-A. Meyer, H. L. Roitblat, & S. W. Wilson, eds. *Proc. Second Int. Conf. Simulation of Adaptive Behavior (SAB92)*, MIT Press/Bradford Books, 1993.

[35] J.-A. Meyer & S. W. Wilson, eds. *Proc. First Int. Conf. Simulation of Adaptive Behavior (SAB90)*, MIT Press/Bradford Books, 1991.

[36] A. Merz. To pursue or to evade that is the question. *J. Guidance, Control, and Dynamics*, 8:161–166, 1985.

[37] G. F. Miller. *Evolution of the human brain through runaway sexual selection: The mind as a protean courtship device.* PhD thesis, Stanford University Psychology Department, 1993.

[38] G. F. Miller. Psychological selection in primates: The evolution of adaptive unpredictability in competition and courtship. In A. Whiten & R. W. Byrne, eds, *Machiavellian Intelligence II*. In Press.

[39] G. F. Miller & D. Cliff. Protean behavior in dynamic games: Arguments for the co-evolution of pursuit-evasion tactics. Cognitive Science Research Paper 311, University of Sussex, 1994.

[40] G. F. Miller & J. J. Freyd. Dynamic mental representations of animate motion: The interplay among evolutionary, cognitive, and behavioral dynamics. Cognitive Science Research Paper 290, University of Sussex, 1993. Submitted for journal publication.

[41] G. F. Miller & P. M. Todd. Let evolution take care of its own. *Behavioral and Brain Sciences*, 14(1):101–102, 1991.

[42] G. F. Miller & P. M. Todd. Evolutionary wanderlust: Sexual selection with directional mate preferences. In [34, pp.21–30], 1993.

[43] J. H. Miller. The co-evolution of automata in the repeated prisoner's dilemma. Report 89-003, Santa Fe Institute, 1989.

[44] J. von Neumann & O. Morgenstern. *Theory of games and economic behavior.* Princeton U. Press, 1944.

[45] M. Ridley. *The red queen: Sex and the evolution of human nature.* Viking, 1993.

[46] E. Y. Rodin. Pursuit-evasion bibliography, version 2. *Computers and Mathematics with Applications*, 18(1-3):245–320, 1989.

[47] E. Y. Rodin, *et al.* Artificial intelligence in air combat games. In [55, pp.261-274], 1987.

[48] R. W. Schmieder. A knowledge-tracking algorithm for generating collective behavior in individual-based populations. In *Pre-proceedings Second Euro. Conf. Art. Life*, pp. 980–989, 1993.

[49] J. Shinar, I. Forte, & B. Kantor. Mixed strategy guidance (MSG) - a new high performance missile guidance law. In *Proc. 1992 Amer. Control Conf. (Vol. 2)*, pp. 1551–1555. American Automatic Control Council, 1992.

[50] P. M. Todd & S. W. Wilson. Environment structure and adaptive behavior from the ground up. In [34, pp.11–20], 1993.

[51] G. M. Werner & M. G. Dyer. Evolution of herding behavior in artificial animals. In [34, pp.393–399], 1993.

[52] S. W. Wilson. Classifier systems and the animat problem. *Machine learning*, 2:199–228, 1987.

[53] S. W. Wilson. The animat path to AI. In [35, pp.15–21], 1991.

[54] Y. Yavin. A stochastic two-target pursuit-evasion differential game with three players moving in a plane. In [55, pp.141-149], 1987.

[55] Y. Yavin & M. Pachter, eds. *Pursuit-evasion differential games.* Pergamon Press, 1987.

Automatic Creation of an Autonomous Agent: Genetic Evolution of a Neural-Network Driven Robot

Dario Floreano
Laboratory of Cognitive Technology
AREA Science Park
Trieste, Italy
dario@psicosun.univ.trieste.it

Francesco Mondada
Laboratory of Microcomputing
Swiss Federal Institute of Technology
Lausanne, Switzerland
mondada@di.epfl.ch

Abstract

The paper describes the results of the evolutionary development of a real, neural-network driven mobile robot. The evolutionary approach to the development of neural controllers for autonomous agents has been successfully used by many researchers, but most -if not all- studies have been carried out with computer simulations. Instead, in this research the whole evolutionary process takes places *entirely* on a real robot without human intervention. Although the experiments described here tackle a simple task of navigation and obstacle avoidance, we show a number of emergent phenomena that are characteristic of autonomous agents. The neural controllers of the evolved best individuals display a full exploitation of non-linear and recurrent connections that make them more efficient than analogous man-designed agents. In order to fully understand and describe the robot behavior, we have also employed quantitative ethological tools [13], and showed that the adaptation dynamics conform to predictions made for animals.

1 Introduction

A mechanical device that can operate without being attached to a power supply or an external computer is not necessarily an autonomous robot. Although this may be an additional desirable feature, autonomous robots are rather identified by their ability to adapt to an environment by finding optimal solutions, develop a suitable control system, define their own goals, and, possibly, perform some self-monitoring [19]. All these capabilities cannot be pre-defined, but should rather emerge from the interaction between the robot and its own environment. A possible solution for building autonomous systems consists in using simple components and primitive structures for the control system; in this case, articulated and complex behaviors would be the spontaneous result of the interactions among all these parts through a process of self-organization guided by a continuous exchange of information with the environment. Major steps in this direction have already been taken. Brooks's subsumption architecture [4] is indeed a case of constructive, bottom-up approach toward building autonomous robots that display emergent behaviors. His approach consists of providing the robot with a set of simple behaviors; further behavior-modules can be added on the top of these primitives and connected to them via simple excitatory or inhibitory links. A similar approach has been formulated by Steels [19], who is pursuing the goal of building intelligent agents by focusing on action-centered skills, autonomy, behavior-oriented decomposition, emergent functionality, and layered architectures. In a more general context, Maes [11] has tried to define the theory, methodology, and goals of a new Behavior-Based Artificial Intelligence, as contrasted to the Knowledge-Based Artificial Intelligence. Beside these solutions, some other researchers have fulfilled the requirements of learning and adaptation by employing various sorts of neural networks to control a robotic system [2], [20]; whether pre-wired or plastic, these neural controllers exhibit characteristics of generalization, flexibility, robustness, and, possibly, plastic adaptation. All these features are indeed important prerequisites of autonomous agents. A somehow different step toward design automatization of autonomous robots is taken by those researchers that try to evolve the robot control system. Rather than starting from a designed solution, they describe the primitives of the robot in the form of an artificial chromosome, build many of these chromosome with some random arrangement of the genes, test the control system generated with every chromosome on a robot, select and reproduce only those chromosomes that guarantee the robot a better fitness according to some survival criterion; this process is repeated until the average population performance is good enough or some mutant with exceptional characteristics is born. Although the evolutionary procedure [9], [7] is well known to a vast community of researchers, it is not a straightforward task to apply it to real robots, as we will see later. Our work concerns the evolution of a neural-network-controlled mobile robot. What is really important in our experiments is that the whole evolutionary process takes places *entirely* on a real robot without human intervention. Before going into the description of our results and the following discussion, let us stress two points that we think to be of general relevance, namely the choice of a neural architecture and the role of simulations versus real implementations.

2   Neural Architectures

Artificial neural networks seem to us to be particularly good candidates for the control system of artificial autonomous agents because they possess many desirable features required by the principles of autonomy in real environments (see also [8]). Let us list some of these properties.

- Neural networks are flexible. The ability to learn enables dynamic adaptation of robot behavior to changes in the environment. Even when the synapses are not modifiable, a neural network still exhibits a reasonable degree of flexibility, i.e., it is able to produce appropriate behaviors in response to a range of possible variations of the physical stimulation.

- Artificial neural networks are robust: missing links or malfunctioning of some hardware components do not strongly impair the robot's behavior.

- A neural network deals with the micro-structure of the robot: this means that it can either shape its own structure to exploit at its best the sensory-motor features of the robot [5], or actively select and use only those sensors and motors that are best suited for performing the task [16].

- The well known tolerance to noise (in some cases noise enhances performance [17], or is an essential component for learning, such as in self-organizing neural networks) makes them good candidates for mediating between physical sensors and actuators with intrinsic noise.

- If we do not put limits to the network architecture, and thus have recurrent and lateral connections, and non-linear transfer functions, we have a potentially powerful device that could cope with the temporal structure and complex mappings required by real-world operations.

Finally, artificial neural networks are well-suited structures also for artificial evolution. Small changes in a neural network usually correspond to small changes in its behavior, at least for feed-forward architectures. Genetic algorithms find their way toward a maximum by sampling new solutions obtained by random combinations and mutations, and thus take advantage of the intrinsic "gradualism" of the neural network structure.

3   Simulation versus Implementation

There is currently a hot debate among people trying to understand and reproduce intelligent agents, that could be stated as follows: "Is the simulation a powerful enough tool to draw sound conclusions, or should a theory or an approach be tested on a real agent, i.e., a robot¿' Although both numerical simulations and physical implementations have their own merits in different fields of research, the issue becomes important when we investigate autonomous and intelligent agents. Let us examine in more detail the respective advantages and drawbacks of these two methodologies in our particular case. It is usually argued that computer simulations are fast. High performance serial machines and massively parallel computers nowadays are powerful tools for the virtual reproduction and analysis of complex-system dynamics. In a few days of computation the scientist can reproduce birth and death of whole populations of organisms (see, e.g., [1]). But this holds only to a limited level of sophistication. It is still much faster to have a real camera acquiring images from a real world than simulating the world, the camera, and the image acquisition process (see [8]). This is not a problem of "bottlenecks", but it is due to the fact that enormous calculations are sometimes necessary for simulating a very trivial [1] physical phenomenon, partly because computers are general-purpose machines whereas natural devices are "dedicated hardware". Another common belief is that computer simulations are cheaper. The researcher may think that it is worth exploring a hypothesis or a new algorithm by computer simulations before investing money and time in a robot. Although this may be true in many situations, in some cases it is not. It all depends on the degree of plausibility and "reality" of the simulation. If the standard is intended to be high, then it is very likely that it will involve one or more specialized programmers on the project for many months. Sometimes, this may cost more than building, purchasing, or modifying real robots. It is widely accepted that numerical simulations allow complete control and record of all the variables; it is thus possible to replicate results, analyze phenomena, accelerate or slow down processes. This is certainly true. But why should we have complete control over an autonomous agent? After all, an artificial agent will never be truly autonomous while there is an umbilical chord that limits its field of action Autonomous agents living within a computer are limited by the necessarily-predefined number of experiences and levels of interactions with the environment. If we are to build intelligent autonomous agents, then we will have to

---

[1] Here "trivial" is meant in a naive sense, as opposed to number of processes or complexity of the dynamics involved

give up -sooner or later- with the obsession of controlling and replicating every possible accident. Computer simulations are still a powerful tool for our research. They provide a viable solution for experimenting non-existing devices or non feasible (with physical tools) hypotheses about the nature and characteristics of artificial agents. "Life as it could be" is indeed one of the major topics of Artificial Life [10], a field of investigation that much inspires research in autonomous agents. Computers leave us free to use our imagination and test the most bizarre hypotheses to recreate new autonomous organisms living and behaving within worlds with different physical laws. However, when we simulate something we must always be aware that we are putting some constraint somewhere at some level. It is not anymore the real world that we are dealing with. And this may be a crucial point when trying to create an autonomous system. By definition, an autonomous agent itself will define the level of interaction with its own environment and alone will choose the relevant information to take into consideration. If we are to restrict at some point the range of available possibilities, we may hamper or greatly reduce the potentiality of our agent. One of the strongest critics made against the simulative approach is that numerical simulations do not consider all the physical laws of the interaction of a real agent with its own environment, such as mass, weight, friction, inertia, etc. Although this may be questionable, it is certainly true that simulations do not take into account Murphy's Laws, such as malfunctioning, component failures, and consumption that govern both artificial and biological organisms. Finally, a real danger with computer simulations is that it cannot be guaranteed that a transfer to the implementation phase will be smooth, if feasible at all. But, let us imagine this to be possible. Who will guarantee to us, then, that the robot is actually doing what it was doing in the simulations? How to compare precise numerical values with behavioral data collected in a noisy world? This is especially important for those researchers who develop the control system of the robot with a computer simulation, and then "inject" the resulting "brain" into the processor of their physical agent and leave it free to move. The analysis and discussion of the reasons why one method should be preferred over the other may take much longer; here, we have only tried to outline a few important topics that we felt relevant for our methodology.

3.1 Evolutionary Development of a Physical Robot

But, for what concerns our specific research, there is a more compelling question. Why are several groups working on simulations, but it is hard -or even impossible- to find cases of generational development of populations of real robots, that is, robots that must survive in a real world on the basis of some fitness criterion, where only the fittest can mate and reproduce through a generational and cyclic process? We believe that the reason is not the cost and waste of material (not fitted robots), or difficulties with the mating procedure, but it is rather based on the construction principles of robots. Most of the available robots are not suited for evolution, in terms of mechanical robustness, design concepts, and automatic evaluation of the robot performance:

- Evolution (Genetic Algorithms) takes a long time; it may require hours, days, weeks, or even months, of continuous functioning of the hardware. Most of available robots tend to break down in these conditions and are not capable of self-repair, as biological organisms often do.

- The common philosophy underlying the construction of robots designed for operating in autonomy dictates that many precise and sophisticated sensory devices should be mounted on the main board. The mechanical solutions for moving around and performing other actions are taken either from well established engineering solutions (three wheel synchronous drive, for instance), or from successful biological organisms (stick insects, ants, etc.). This leads to the construction of complex, highly structured, and fragile mechanisms. For this reason, such robots would easily get trapped in corners and local minima during the first generations of the evolutionary process. Whereas there is no reason in principle why the evolutionary technique should not be applicable to complex robots (and indeed it will have to, at least to some extent), it is definitely true that biological evolution did not start with a structured and sophisticated body coupled with a virtually non-existing brain. Evolutionary studies have shown that there is a gradual co-evolution of body and "mind" in biological organisms. Thus, either we start with a robot designed with new principles (simple components and geometry, robust and reliable hardware, only necessary and elementary sensors and actuators), or we provide a complex robot with a set of "basic instincts" (but which?) and let evolution work on higher control structures. We have chosen the first approach because we consider it to be chronologically and logically the first thing to try, and also because the second solution, although viable in principle, may still be problematic at this stage.

- In order to get a sensible behavior out of a *tabula rasa* (whatever type of architecture we use), Genetic Algorithms require a fitness function, i.e., a survival criterion against which each individual of the population is tested. As long as the artificial agent is a virtual entity within a computer it is fairly easy to precisely evaluate its performance. However, when the agent takes form into a physical and mobile body free to wander in our world, automatic fitness evaluation becomes a non-trivial task. We will take into consideration this issue in a later section.

4   Navigation and Obstacle Avoidance

Because of all the reasons outlined in the section above, we were not certain that the evolutionary approach would have worked with a real robot. Mainly, we did not know how to assess and compare the results that we could have obtained with this approach. Thus, we have decided to start from a classic task, a sort of exercise and test for all people working with mobile robots. The robot had to learn to move in an environment and avoid obstacles. For its simplest formulation, there is already a well-known, optimal, and simple distributed solution for this task: the Braitenberg's vehicle [3], with which we have compared our results. Thus, we have put our robot in an arbitrary environment, set a few parameters concerning the fitness function and the network structure, and let it free to evolve. We have run this experiment many times in order to obtain reliable data and draw sound conclusions. Each time, we have kept track of a some relevant variables during the evolutionary process, analyzed the best organisms, and compared the solutions obtained by evolution with those designed by man.

4.1   Experimental Setup

The robot employed in our experiments is Khepera, a miniature mobile robot [14]. Khepera has many of the characteristics required by the evolutionary approach to autonomous robots. It has a circular shape (Figure 1), with diameter of 55 mm, height of 30 mm, and weight of 70 g, and is supported by two wheels and two small Teflon balls.

The wheels are controlled by two DC motors with incremental encoder (10 pulses per mm of advancement of the robot), and can move in both directions. The simple

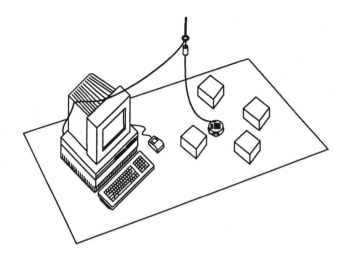

Figure 2: Operating methodology.

geometrical shape and the motor layout allow Khepera to potentially negotiate any type of obstacle and corner. These characteristics, together with many other mechanical solutions, have resulted in a robot that has continuously and reliably operated for weeks and weeks, most of the time crashing into walls and obstacles (due to the functioning principles of Genetic Algorithms). In the basic configuration used here, the robot is provided with eight Infra-Red proximity sensors. Six sensors are positioned on one side of the robot (front), the remaining two on the other side (back). A Motorola 68331 controller with 256 Kbytes of RAM and 512 Kbytes ROM manages all the input-output routines and can communicate via a serial port with a host computer.

Because of its size and design principles, Khepera is well-suited for laboratory experiments. Its communication protocol can exploit all the power and disk size available in a workstation by letting high-level control processes (genetic operators, neural network activation, variables recordings) run on the main station while low-level processes (sensor-reading, motor control, and other real time tasks) run on the on-board processor (Figure 2).

We have adopted this solution for our experiments. Khepera was attached via a serial port to a Sun SparcStation 2 by means of a lightweight aerial cable and specially designed rotating contacts. In this way, while the robot was running, we could keep track of all the populations of organisms that were born, tested, and passed to the genetic operators, together with their "personal life files". At the same time, we could also take advantage of specific software designed for graphic visualization of trajectories and sensory-motor status while the robot was evolving. Skeptics should not consider this methodology as an attempt on the very hearth of autonomy: as stated in the very beginning of this paper, running with

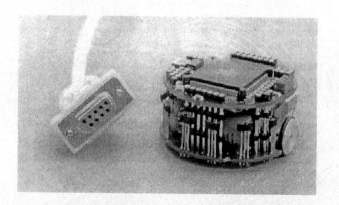

Figure 1: Khepera, the miniature mobile robot.

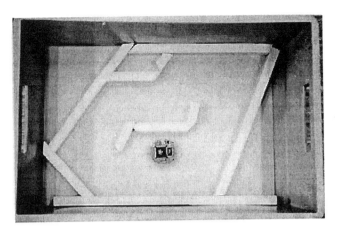

Figure 3: Environment of the experiment.

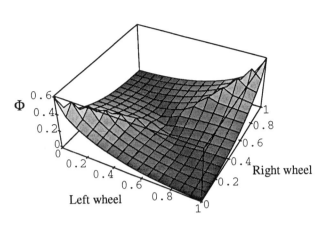

Figure 4: Function surface for i = 0.4. Wheel speed values have already been transformed into positive range where 0.5 is the point of direction inversion. Please note that this is not a full picture of the fitness function maximized by the genetic algorithm, which is instead n-dimensional (n = number of neural network free parameters). Furthermore, it does not take into account the physical characteristics of the environment.

its own batteries is only an optional feature of an autonomous agent. For what concerns Khepera, the robot is not aware of where its own "brain" is located, and this is indeed not important in this experiment of navigation and obstacle avoidance. However, it should be noted that the software that implements the genetic development of neural networks [6] could be slimmed down and downloaded into the robot processor.

The robot was put in an environment consisting in a sort of circular corridor whose external size was approx. 80x50 cm large (Figure 3). The walls were made of light-blue polystyrene and the floor was a gray thick paper. The robot could sense the walls with the IR proximity sensors. Since the corridors were rather narrow (8-12 cm), some sensors were slightly active most of the time. The environment was within a portable box positioned in a room always illuminated from above by a 60-watt bulb light. A serial cable connected the robot to the workstation in our office, a few rooms away from it. Our goal was to develop a robot that could learn to maximize some sort of exploration measure while accurately avoiding all the obstacles on its way. This statement was also the base for the fitness criterion used in the experiments. One of the desirable features of autonomous robots is the independence from an external operator, also during the development process of the control system. This would mean that the performance criterion for an autonomous agent should rely solely on a set of variables that can be measured within the frame of interaction between the robot and the environment. If this constraint is satisfied, we achieve a practical advantage, because the robot could eventually learn to operate in any environment by a continuous self-assessment of its own performance without external controllers. Hence, our fitness criterion Φ was function of three variables, directly measured on the robot, as follows,

$$\Phi = V\left(1 - \sqrt{\Delta v}\right)(1 - i) \qquad (1)$$

$$0 \leq V \leq 1$$
$$0 \leq \Delta v \leq 1$$
$$0 \leq i \leq 1$$

where V is a measure of the average rotation speed of the two wheels, Δv is the algebraic difference between the signed speed values of the wheels (positive is one direction, negative the other) transformed into positive values, and i is the activation value of the proximity sensor with the highest activity. The function Φ has three components: the first one is maximized by speed, the second by straight direction, and the third by obstacle avoidance. Since the robot has a circular shape and the wheels can rotate in both directions, this function has a symmetric surface with two equal maxima, each corresponding to one motion direction (Figure 4).

The evolutionary training was a standard genetic algorithm as described by Goldberg [7] with fitness scaling and roulette wheel selection, biased mutations [15], and one-point crossover (experiment parameters are given in the Appendix). The neural network architecture was fixed and consisted of a single layer of synaptic weights from eight input units (clamped to the sensors) to two output units (directly connected to the motors)

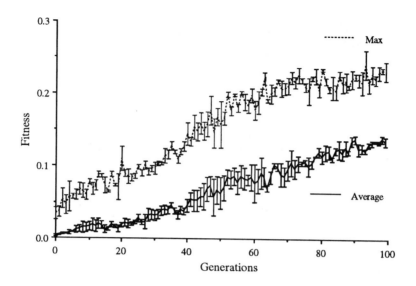

Figure 5: Population average fitness and best individual fitness at each generation. Values are averaged over three runs (S.E. displayed).

with mobile thresholds, logistic activation functions, and discrete-time recurrent connections only within the output layer. Given the small network size, each synaptic connection and each threshold was coded as a floating point number on the chromosome [21]. Each individual of a population was in turn decoded into the corresponding neural networks, the input nodes connected to the robot sensors, the output nodes to the motors, and the robot was left free to move for a given number of steps (motor actions) while its performance Φ was automatically recorded. Each motor action lasted 300 ms. Between one individual and the next, a pair of random velocities was applied to the wheels for 5 seconds. This procedure was aimed at limiting the artifactual inheritance of particular locations between adjacent individuals in the populations.

4.2   Results

Khepera genetically learns to navigate and avoid obstacles in less than 100 generations (Figure 5), each generation taking approximatively 39 minutes. However, around the 50th generation the best individuals already exhibit a near to optimal behavior. Their navigation is extremely smooth, they never bump into walls and corners, and try to keep a straight trajectory. This allows them to perform complete laps of the corridor without turning back. These results are highly reliable and have been replicated in many runs of the experiment.

It is interesting to analyze a single run of the evolutionary development of Khepera by looking at the values of the three fitness components for the best individuals

in the population at each generation (Figure 6).

During the initial generations the best individuals are those that move straight at very low velocities (about 2 mm/s). High oscillations of the sensory component indicates that they cannot yet discriminate between walls and empty spaces: it is still much up to individual "luck" (starting location) to avoid crashing into an obstacle. Most of the remaining individuals in the initial generations spend their life by rotating in place. Maximizing the fitness function Φ means to find a balance among the three components because none of them can assume the maximum value without lowering one of the other two. A stable balance is found around the 50th generation. In the remaining 50 generations the robot increases only the global motion speed. However, the global speed never reaches the maximum value (80 mm/s), not even when the evolutionary process is continued until the 200th generation. For all the best individuals, the robot speed peaks at 48 mm/s when positioned in zones free of obstacles. This self-adjustment of the maximum cruising speed has an adaptive meaning. Since sensors and motors are updated only every 300 ms and many passages in the environment are rather narrow, if Khepera had moved faster it would have often crashed into walls without the possibility to detect them. Thus, the system has adapted its own behavior to the physical characteristics of its own sensory system and of the environment where it lives. We have tested some of the best individuals of the last generations in new environments with a variety of objects (differing in shape, color, texture, and light absorbency) and new light conditions (full sunlight, new rooms with different artificial light). We have

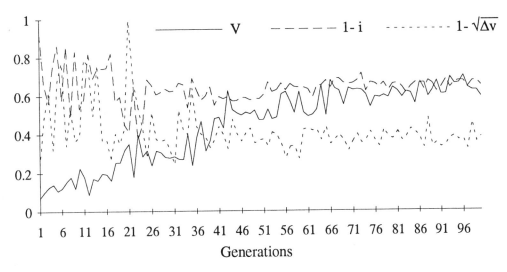

Figure 6: Fitness components values for the best individual of each generation. V is maximized by robot velocity; $1-i$ is maximized by obstacle avoidance; $1 - sqrt(\Delta v)$ is maximized by straight trajectory.

also tested the best individuals with other robot bodies (same model, but obviously with slight variations of the sensor responses). In all these cases Khepera navigates successfully without touching any of the objects and trying to keep a straight trajectory. All the individuals tested show a preferential turning direction which solely depends on the initial conditions of the evolutionary run (initial weight values, interaction with the environment), but they can turn in both directions when required by the environment.

4.3 Discussion

A basic characteristic of autonomous systems is the ability to self-regulate their own behavior in order to maximize the probability of survival and reproduction. In this sense adaptation is function of the interaction between two variables, the physical properties of the environment and the characteristics of the organism's body. The success of any plan, strategy, or single action, depends not only on the affordances of the environment, but also on the capacity to detect them and adequately respond. In nature we can observe a continuous evolutionary co-adaptation of body structures and behavioral repertoire. Although we cannot yet expect changes in the hardware structure of an autonomous robot, still we should observe self-selection of the behavioral strategies that exploit at best the physical features of the robot's body and sensory-motor apparatus. We have already seen an example of such a behavioral adaptation in the case of the speed self-regulation of our robot. Another significant example of autonomous adaptation is given by the direction of motion.

Khepera has a perfectly circular and symmetric body

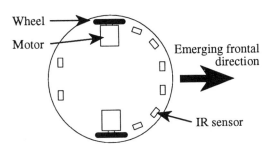

Figure 7: IR sensors and motors layout in Khepera. Diameter size is 55 mm, maximum speed in either direction is 80 mm/s.

shape and the wheels can rotate at equal speeds in both directions. In terms of pure kinematics, thus, it is logical to expect that the robot will equally move in either direction, depending on initial internal and external conditions. However, in all our experiments, early during the evolution the robots develop a frontal direction of motion that corresponds to the side with more sensors (Figure 7). The development of this frontal direction of motion allows the robot to face obstacles with the side that provides a finer resolution and a larger visual angle. Those individuals that move "backward" are very likely to get stuck in convex and sharp corners or fail to detect a lateral collision with a wall; hence, they disappear very soon from the population. (Analogous phenomena of behavioral adaptation to the visual configuration of a simple simulated organism have been shown by [5].) However, rear sensors do not go out of use. The neural networks of the best individuals of the final generations still make use of that information to change trajectory if

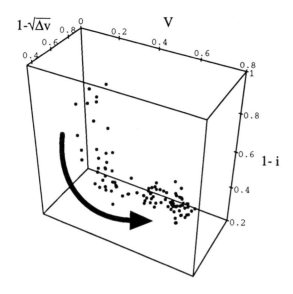

Figure 8: State-space representation of the adaptation process. Each dot is the state of the best individual of a generation. The arrow shows the direction of motion during evolution. The dots concentrate in a sub-space indicated by the arrow tip in the last 20 generations. Axes range spans from 0 to 1 (only covered space is shown in the picture).

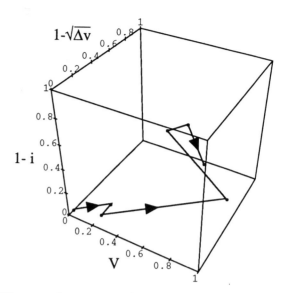

Figure 9: State-space representation of the behavior of the best individual of the last generation, when pulled apart from its equilibrium state.

something is approaching the robot from the back. As for any dynamic system, also in the case of evolved robots it is important to understand and try to describe the state-transition phase. But an autonomous system is not completely controllable and observable [12]. This holds also for our robot, both because the dynamics and results of the evolutionary process cannot be controlled, and because the inner functioning of the neural network, as we will see later, is not linear and each state depends upon a previous history of states. However, as in the case of animals, the activity of an autonomous agent depends on the state of the agent itself, such as its level of energy, the perception of the environment, and the memory of previous states. This analysis yields to the construction of an n-dimensional state space, where the axes are provided by n state variables considered. This "state-space approach" has been used in ethology [13] to describe animal behavior in quantitative terms, and can be applied also to our agent. We can describe our agent as a point in a three dimensional space given by the values of the three fitness components and monitor its change in time.

Figure 8 is a state-space plot of the best individuals of each generation during evolution. The adaptation process is described by a reduction of oscillations and by a gradual displacement toward a sub-region of this space. This region of the adaptation space is compact and bounded, and represents the stability conditions of the system [12] that satisfy the survival criterion.

Our system is asymptotically stable because, when disturbed (by the recombination and mutation operators during the last 20 generations), it tends to stay within the same adaptation zone. This holds also when we analyze the behavior of a single individual. If we disturb the system by pulling it away from its equilibrium state, it will tend to return and stay in its original state (Figure 9). This analysis may be carried further on along the lines of the "Adaptation Theorem" of Sibly and Mc-Farland [18], but there is not space enough here (we will consider this issue in further detail with more complex examples of evolved behaviors in another paper). A final consideration is deserved by the comparison between our agent and a distributed Braitenberg's vehicle designed to go straight and avoid obstacles. Braitenberg's vehicle (which has been implemented on Khepera too) is a linear reactive system that, basically, when some sensors are activated, gives more energy to the ipsilateral motor and inhibits the controlateral one. The pattern of synaptic connections is symmetrical about the front axis. This very simple system is very efficient, but is gets stuck as soon as two symmetric and controlateral sensors become equally activated. In this case the total amount of energy given to each motor is equal and tends to 0. Instead, our agent has developed a pattern of synaptic connections similar to Braitenberg's vehicle, but it has also accurately exploited the recurrent connections at the output layer and the non-linearities embedded in the activation functions. The best individuals of the last generations never get stuck in such cases because the state of the motors is not uniquely defined by the current state of the sensors, but also by the previous history of actions.

5   Conclusion

We have described and analyzed a working example of an artificial autonomous agent. Our robot satisfies most of the basic criteria that underlie the definition of autonomous agents. Through the evolutionary process Khepera has automatically and autonomously developed the optimal distributed control system to survive in the environment where it has been placed. The role of the human experimenter has been indeed rather small, specifically limited to formulate only the survival criterion and the global structure of the net. We have neither pre-designed the behaviors of the robot, nor have intervened during evolution. The robot itself and alone has developed -starting from a sort of *tabula rasa* - a set of strategies and behaviors as a result of the adaptation to the environment and its own body. Despite its simple components and the simple survival criterion, it is difficult to control and predict the robot behavior, due to the non-linearities and feedback connections exploited for optimal navigation and obstacle avoidance. We have tried to describe our agent's behavior with quantitative ethological tools, and we have also showed two emergent phenomena such as speed self-regulation and frontal direction. Our current work is aimed at using the same approach in more complex environments where the fitness criterion is not anymore fixed by the experimenter, but is the natural and logical result of the interaction between the physical characteristics of the robot and the type of environment. We have already obtained new significant results where homing for battery recharge is purely an emergent behavior. These data make us confident in thinking that our approach is a valid methodology for automatically creating complex autonomous agents. Future work will enable evolvability and more flexibility (through a major adherence to biological plausibility) in the neural network structure and will employ learning during life as well.

Appendix

Genetic algorithm parameters:

Population size	80
Generation number	100
Crossover probability	0.1
Mutation probability	0.2
Mutation range	±0.5
Initial weight range	±0.5
Final weight range	Not bounded
Life length	80 actions
Action duration	300 ms

Acknowledgments

We would like to thank Edo Franzi and André Guignard for the important work in the design of Khepera. Dario Floreano has been partially supported by the Italian National Research Council, grant n. 92.01065.PF67 (co-ordinator W. Gerbino). Francesco Mondada has been partially supported by the Swiss National Research Foundation (project PNR23).

References

[1] D. H. Ackley and M. L. Littman. Interactions between learning and evolution. In C.G. Langton, J.D. Farmer, S. Rasmussen, and C. Taylor, editors, *Artificial Life II: Proceedings Volume of Santa Fe Conference*, volume XI. Addison Wesley: series of the Santa Fe Institute Studies in the Sciences of Complexities, 1991.

[2] R. D. Beer and J. C. Gallagher. Evolving dynamical neural networks for adaptive behavior. *Adaptive Behavior*, 1:91–122, 1992.

[3] V. Braitenberg. *Vehicles. Experiments in Synthetic Psychology*. MIT Press, Cambridge, MA, 1984.

[4] R. A. Brooks. Intelligence without representation. *Artificial Intelligence*, 47:139–59, 1991.

[5] D. T. Cliff and S. G. Bullock. Adding "foveal vision" to Wilson's animat. Technical report CSRP 263, University of Sussex, School of Cognitive and Computing Sciences, December 1992.

[6] D. Floreano. Robogen: A software package for evolutionary control systems. Release 1.1. Technical report LabTeCo No. 93-01, Cognitive Technology Laboratory, AREA Science Park, Trieste, Italy, 1993.

[7] D. E. Goldberg. *Genetic algorithms in search, optimization and machine learning*. Addison-Wesley, Reading, MA, 1989.

[8] I. Harvey, P. Husbands, and D. T. Cliff. Issues in evolutionary robotics. In J. Meyer, H. L. Roitblat, and S. W. Wilson, editors, *From Animals to Animats II: Proceedings of the Second International Conference on Simulation of Adaptive Behavior*, Cambridge, MA, 1992. MIT Press-Bradford Books.

[9] J. H. Holland. *Adaptation in natural and artificial systems*. The University of Michigan Press, Ann Arbor, 1975.

[10] C. G. Langton. Preface. In C.G. Langton, J.D. Farmer, S. Rasmussen, and C. Taylor, editors, *Artificial Life II: Proceedings Volume of Santa Fe Conference*, volume XI. Addison Wesley: series of the Santa Fe Institute Studies in the Sciences of Complexities, 1991.

[11] P. Maes. Behavior-based artificial intelligence. In J. Meyer, H. L. Roitblat, and S. W. Wilson, editors, *From Animals to Animats II: Proceedings of the Second International Conference on Simulation of Adaptive Behavior*, Cambridge, MA, 1992. MIT Press-Bradford Books.

[12] D. J. McFarland. Autonomy and self-sufficiency in robots. AI-Memo 92-03, Artificial Intelligence Laboratory, Vrije Universiteit Brussel, Belgium, 1992.

[13] D. J. McFarland and A. Houston. *Quantitative Ethology: the state-space approach.* Pitman Books, London, 1981.

[14] F. Mondada, E. Franzi, and P. Ienne. Mobile robot miniaturization: A tool for investigation in control algorithms. In *Proceedings of the Third International Symposium on Experimental Robotics*, Kyoto, Japan, 1993.

[15] D. Montana and L. Davis. Training feed forward neural networks using genetic algorithms. In *Proceedings of the Eleventh International Joint Conference on Artificial Intelligence*, San Mateo, CA, 1989. Morgan Kaufmann.

[16] S. Nolfi. Genotypes for neural networks. In M. A. Arbib, editor, *The Handbook of Brain Theory and Neural Networks.* MIT Press, Cambridge, MA, 1993.

[17] S. Nolfi, D. Parisi, and R. Pedone. How noise helps generalization in feed-forward networks. In E. R. Caianiello, editor, *Parallel Architectures and Neural Networks: Proceedings of the 6th Italian Workshop on Neural Networks*, Singapore, 1992. World Scientific P.

[18] R. M. Sibly and D. J. McFarland. A state-space approach to motivation. In D. J. McFarland, editor, *Motivational Control Systems Analysis.* Academic Press, London, 1974.

[19] L. Steels. Building agents out of autonomous behavior systems. In L. Steels and R. Brooks, editors, *The "artificial life" route to "artificial intelligence". Building situated embodied agents.* Lawrence Erlbaum, New Haven, 1993.

[20] P. F. M. J. Verschure, B. J. A. Kröse, and R. Pfeifer. Distributed adaptive control: The self-organization of structured behavior. *Robotics and Autonomous Agents*, 9:181–96, 1992.

[21] X. Yao. A review of evolutionary artificial neural networks. *International Journal of Intelligent Systems*, 4:203–222, 1993.

The Effect of Parasitism on the Evolution of a Communication Protocol in An Artificial Life Simulation

Phil Robbins

School of Computing and Information Technology
University of Greenwich
Wellington Street
London
SE18 6PF
U.K.

p.robbins@greenwich.ac.uk

Abstract

The introduction of parasites is shown to improve the performance of an artificial life simulation in which a common mate-finding communication protocol is evolved. Improvements in mating frequency are obtained by (separately) introducing two different types of parasite. Adaptation to the presence of the parasites induces the emergence of more efficient mating protocols. The results presented here suggest that the insights that research into natural parasites provide can be utilised in evolutionary programming.

1 Introduction

Evolutionary programming techniques (such as genetic algorithms [Holland 1975], genetic programming [Koza 1992] and evolution programs [Michalewicz 1992]) are becoming more widely used as we attempt to solve problems which are highly complex, or whose solutions are not fully known or understood in advance.

The objective of this paper is to demonstrate that substantial improvements in the results obtained from evolutionary programming can be obtained by introducing parasites into the system.

An artificial life simulation in which a population evolve a common communication protocol to assist in the problem of mate-finding, as addressed in [Werner and Dyer 1990] and [Ono and Rahmani 1993], is described. In separate sets of experiments, two very different classes of parasite are introduced into the simulation. In each case the mating protocols evolved were substantially more effective than those evolved in simulations where there were no parasites. The additional evolutionary pressure exerted by the parasites provides motivation for the evolution of more efficient mating protocols.

2 Natural Parasites

There are many definitions of parasitism. In this work I subscribe to the broad definition of a parasite as an entity that benefits from a close association with another creature (the host), whilst the host in some way suffers as a result of the association. The parasite may or may not be dependant on the host. The association may last for the whole of the parasite's life, for one of the parasite's life stages, or for a shorter time.

Section 2.1 is intended to illustrate how widespread and how fundamental are the effects of parasitism on natural evolution. Sections 2.2 and 2.3 describe the two classes of parasite which are the models upon which the artificial parasites used in the simulation are based.

2.1 Effects of Parasitism in Natural Evolution

Parasitism is a major driving force in evolution. The majority of species occurring in nature are parasitic, and free-living (non-parasitic) organisms typically host several individuals of several parasite species [Schmidt 1989], [Halliday 1993].

The population growth of host organisms can be checked by disease in the form of parasites [Mielke 1989]. Parasites and their host species co-evolve, each driving the other to further evolve in a natural arms race [Dawkins 1976]. Parasites can directly affect the behaviour of their host for their own benefit [Moore 1983], extending the effect of their phenotype beyond their physical bodies [Dawkins 1982]. Sexual reproduction may have evolved as a response to parasitism [Zuk 1984]. The extravagant secondary characteristics displayed by some species (such as the large and brightly coloured tails of male peacocks) may have evolved to signal to prospective mates that the animal is resistant to parasites[1] [Hamilton and Zuk 1982]. The parasitic species may itself evolve to actively enhance the secondary characteristic to improve its own chance of transmission [Cronin 1991].

2.2   *Intraspecific Satellite Parasites*

A parasite of the same species as the host is known as an intraspecific parasite. A satellite parasite is one that positions itself spatially close to the host.

The male field cricket exemplifies this class of parasite [Cade 1979]. Males who possess a territory signal their presence to females by rubbing their wings together. But other male crickets (the satellite parasites) lay in wait near to the caller (the host). The satellite parasites do not signal, but hope to intercept and mate with females who have been attracted by the call of the host. The cost of this association to the host can be two-fold. Firstly he has expended the energy to signal. Secondly his calling may also attract the parasitic tachnid fly which lays its larvae into the body of the male cricket, eventually resulting in the cricket's death.

Satellite parasitism of this type does not appear to be genetically determined, but is rather an opportunistic behaviour pattern. It has been observed that the same animal may take on the rôles of parasite and of host at different times in its life.

2.3   *Interspecific Endoparasites*

Interspecific parasites are not of the same species as the host (this is most often the case in nature). Endoparasites live within the host. The best known example of an interspecific endoparasite is the tape worm, which lives within the gut of its host.

3   Previous Research Involving Artificial Parasites

[Hillis 1990] reported the successful application of artificial parasites in improving the quality of the sorting networks discovered by simulated evolution. The objective was to define sorting networks that would sort 16 inputs with the least number of comparisons. The parasites genomes contained test cases against which the population of sorting networks fitness values were evaluated. Fitness for the parasites was calculated according to how poorly the network population as a whole performed against the test cases contained in the parasite's genotype. The parasites and the sorting networks were allowed to co-evolve. The parasite population discouraged the host population from

settling at local optima, because the parasite population would evolve to reduce the fitness of the host population in that region of solution space. The host population would therefore further evolve. Thus waves of epidemic and immunity were observed. The best network that evolved without parasites required 65 exchanges. The best network discovered with parasites required only 61 exchanges. For this 16 input problem, the best solution ever discovered required exactly 60 comparisons.

Parasitism emerged, without being explicitly programmed in Tierra [Ray 1990]. Tierra is a simulation designed to parallel the Cambrian explosion in which the diversity of life on Earth increased dramatically in a relatively short period of time. A self-replicating program was allowed to reproduce and evolve. A complex series of symbioses followed, starting with parasites that were unable to reproduce in isolation, but which could reproduce by using the code contained within other, non-parasitic, population members. Later, hyper-parasites (which parasitise parasites) and social hyper-parasites (which can only reproduce when part of a group) were observed.

4   The Babel Animal System

4.1   *Babel Animals and their Environment*

Babel animals inhabit a toroidal world which is implemented as a square four-connected two-dimensional array. Time in this world is divided into days. Each day the list of inhabitants is traversed, and each inhabitant is given the opportunity to take some action. A full day is deemed to have passed when the entire population has been processed in this manner.

The environment can support a fixed number of babels. When a babel is born, the least fit[2] member of the population must die to maintain the population level. This is the only circumstance in which a babel animal can die.

4.1.1 *Babel Chromosomes and Communication Protocol*

Babel animals evolve a common communication protocol to aid in mate-finding. Two babel animals can only mate if they are on the same square. An effective communication protocol enables the (immobile) mature female babel to guide the (blind) mature male babel to her.

Each babel has two chromosomes, known as the messages chromosome and as the interpretations chromosome. These chromosomes are encodings of look-up

---

[1]Infestation by parasites would hinder the ability of the animal to express the secondary characteristic to the full.

[2]Fitness is discussed in section 4.1.3.

tables which dictate the babel animal's communication protocol.

The values of the genes stored within the chromosomes are generated randomly at the start of the simulation. When two animals mate, a child animal is born, and the chromosomes of the child are created by applying straightforward crossover and mutation operators to copies of the chromosomes of the parents [Goldberg 1989]. In this way, combinations of genes are passed on to descendant babels with a probability relative to the effectiveness of the mating protocol that they represent.

Mature female babels can see in each direction for a distance of two squares. This region is her territory. When a mature female babel sees a mature male she notes his relative position and his current direction, uses this information to index into the data stored in her messages chromosome, and emits a message dictated by that entry in the chromosome. A message is an integer in the range zero to seven. A mature male babel who is in receipt of a message uses the message number to index into the data stored in his interpretations chromosome, and acts according to the instruction found there. There are four instructions that can be stored in a gene within the interpretations chromosome, namely "move forward in the direction you are currently facing", "turn 90 degrees left", "turn 90 degrees right", and "stand still[3]".

Each Babel animal has one of each type of chromosome, but these have a sex-limited effect. A female's actions are only affected by the messages chromosome, and a male's actions are only affected by the interpretations chromosome.

4.1.2 The Babel Animal Life Cycle

Female and male babel animals go through different life stages in their development. The female life cycle is described first:-

Immature - When a female is born she begins her immature stage. The immature female usually moves one square per day in whatever direction she is facing. However, there is a seven per cent chance that she will randomly change her direction and turn either right or left.

The immature stage lasts for ten days, after which the immature female moves into her nesting stage.

Nesting - The nesting female's movement is the same as that of the immature female. But once she has moved, she looks to see if there are any mature females within four squares in any direction. If there are not, the nesting female changes her status to mature, otherwise she retains the nesting status[4].

Mature (female) - A female in her mature stage cannot move, but she can see two squares in all directions (her territory). If a mature male babel animal is within this range, she emits a message as described in section 4.1.1. above. If there are more than one mature male in her territory, the female will emit the sound applicable to the closest male, but all the other males within her territory will receive it.

When a mature male lands on the square occupied by the mature female the couple reproduce and then the female goes into her resting stage.

Resting - The resting female is disinterested in males, emits no signals, and will not mate. She is mobile in this stage, and moves in the same way as an immature female. The resting stage lasts for ten days, after which she begins another nesting stage.

The male life cycle is as follows:-

Juvenile - When a male baby is born, he starts his juvenile life stage. During this stage he moves around in the same way as an immature female. He does not listen for female signals, and, even if he happens to chance upon a mature female, he does not mate. At the age of six days, the juvenile male becomes mature.

Mature (male) - Each day the male checks to see if he has heard a sound emitted by a female. If he has, he looks up in his interpretations chromosome what action to take on receipt of the message and then acts accordingly, as described in section 4.1.1. above. If, however, the male has already spent 20 consecutive days listening to female messages, he will ignore the message and move forward one square.

If the mature male has not received a message, he will move in the normal way.

When a mature male lands on a square occupied by a mature female the couple reproduce, and then the male moves into disinterested mode.

---

[3]The "stand still" message interpretation is clearly of no use to a couple of babel animals trying to mate. However, such a message was included in [Werner and Dyer 1990] and [Ono and Rahmani 1993], and was originally implemented in the babel animals for the sake of comparison. [Koza 1992] states that the inclusion of some additional functions (over and above the minimal function set required to solve a problem) can improve performance in certain systems. Investigation of the precise effect of the "stand still" message in this system has not yet been undertaken.

---

[4]This is so that the territories of mature females cannot overlap.

Disinterested - A disinterested male does not respond to messages, and does not mate even if he happens by chance to land upon a square occupied by a mature female. The movement characteristics of the disinterested male are identical to those of the juvenile male. After being disinterested for five days, the male reverts to the mature stage.

4.1.3 Measure of Babel Animals' Fitness

At birth, a babel is given a fixed number of fitness points (in the program runs described in this paper, the initial fitness value was set to 2000). Each day that passes, one point is subtracted from the animal's fitness.

The babels' relative fitnesses are important because the babel with the lowest fitness dies when a child is born (see section 4.1).

4.2   Babel Animal Simulations

All of the results presented in this paper are the average of eight separate runs, each with a population of 100 babels living in a 50x50 world. In each case the simulation was allowed to run for 10,000 (babel) days. In the graphs reproduced as Figure 1 to Figure 5, the abscissa represents the number of days passed, and the ordinate represents the number of matings in the last 250 days.

4.2.1 Babel Animal Control Experiments

Three control experiments were conducted.

Firstly, communication between the babel animals was disallowed, so that the number of matings that would occur by chance could be recorded. Between 140 and 150 matings per 250 days occurred.

Secondly, an optimal mating protocol was hard-wired into the code and the number of matings was again recorded. In this case there were on average between 350 and 355 matings per 250 days.

Finally the babels were allowed to return to their "natural" state in which the communication protocol evolves by natural selection. At the start of the runs when the genes were random, the evolving population mated less frequently than they would have by chance. But from 2,500 days onwards the mating protocol had increased in efficiency so that mating is effected more frequently than by chance alone. The number of matings settled to around 270 to 300 per 250 days.

The results from these runs are plotted in Figure 1.

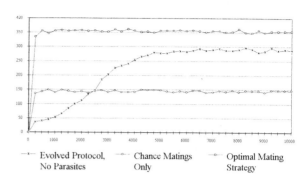

Figure 1 - Control Experiment Results

5   Artificial Parasites in the Babel System

Two types of parasite were introduced into the babel system. These experiments are described in the following two sections.

5.1   Babel Animals and Intraspecific Satellite Parasites

Intraspecific satellite parasites, modelled on the natural parasites described in section 2.2, were introduced into the babel world. These were in the form of females who, if they could not find a suitable nesting place after searching for ten days, would settle in the territory of an established mature female, in the hope of "stealing" a male who is on his way to mate with the host female. When such a male lands on the parasite female, the couple mate, and the male assumes the disinterested mode and wanders off. The parasite thereby gains the mating at the expense of the host who had incurred the cost of locating a suitable territory and guiding the male towards her.

The introduction of these parasites increased the selective pressure on the population to evolve an efficient common mating protocol, in which the females guide their mates to them by the shortest route, thereby minimising the chance of their being waylaid by parasite females.

Figure 2 shows the average number of matings per 250 day period in populations which contained satellite female parasites (the number of matings with no parasites is also shown for comparison). The number of matings is comparable between the runs with and without parasites up until around day 5,500. But then the frequency of matings in the runs with no parasites stopped increasing, whereas the frequency of mating in the runs with the intraspecific parasites continued to increase until it reached the 330 to 340 matings per 250 days level.

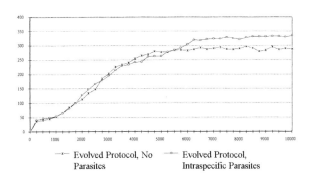

Figure 2 - Intraspecific Parasite Results

Figure 3 shows the total number of matings per 250 day period (parasitic and non-parasitic females) in this simulation, plotted against the number of matings in which the female was *not* parasitic. It can be seen that the high number of matings is not simply due to the matings with parasitic females.

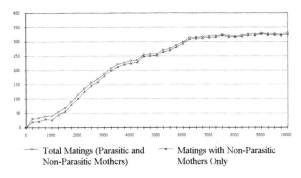

Figure 3 - Parasitic and Non-Parasitic Matings

The number of matings with parasitic females (per 250 day period) is plotted in Figure 4. The frequency of matings with parasitic females decreases as the communication protocol improves because the males move more directly to the square occupied by the signalling female, thus decreasing the probability of encountering a satellite female parasite.

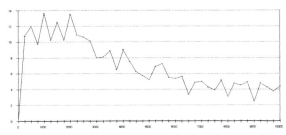

Figure 4 - Total Number of Matings with Parasitic Females

5.2 Babel Animals and Interspecific Endoparasites

Interspecific endoparasites, similar to the naturally occurring parasites described in section 2.3, were introduced into the babel world.

Each day that a mature male is within the territory of a mature female, there is a chance of his picking up a parasite. The probability increases with the number of consecutive days that the male has been within the female's territory according to the following formula:-

$$0 < d < 9, \quad p = (2d^3) / 3000$$

$$9 <= d, \quad p = 0.66$$

where d = no. of days spent in female territory

and   p = probability of being infected

A babel can be infected by at most 20 parasites at any one time. The cost to the babel of being infected is that each parasite that the babel is carrying has a probability of 0.05 (per day) of taking a fitness point away from the host.

A parasite may be transmitted to a new host when its current host (of either sex) reproduces. There is a 0.20 probability that the parasite will be transmitted to the offspring (vertical transmission). If vertical transmission does not take place, then there is a 0.40 probability that the parasite will be transmitted to the other parent (horizontal transmission). A parasite can only die when its host dies.

The parasite population does not evolve. The parasites' behaviour and effect are entirely dictated by the above rules.

The average number of matings per 250 day period over eight runs of the simulation is plotted in Figure 5, and the number of matings obtained when the simulation was run with no parasites is also shown for comparison. The graph shows that the runs with parasites converged more quickly, and to more efficient protocols, than did the runs with no parasites.

The parasites increase the selective pressure to evolve a more efficient communication protocol. Male babel animals which spend longer than necessary in the female's territory acquire more parasites. Their offspring become less fit as they inherit some of the parents' parasites. A female with a poor protocol may be infected horizontally by her mates.

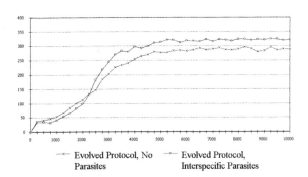

-×- Evolved Protocol, No   -∘- Evolved Protocol,
    Parasites   Interspecific Parasites

Figure 5 - Interspecific Parasite Results

6   Discussion and Conclusion

The babel populations in simulations in which parasites were present attained more efficient communication protocols than those which were not exposed to parasites. This is due to the increased evolutionary pressure which the parasites apply to the babels.

Parasitism is a major driving force in natural evolution. The results of the experiments described in this paper suggest that parasitism can provide additional motivation for our evolutionary programs to achieve more efficient and effective results .

A potential problem with the introduction of parasites to artificial evolutionary systems is the resulting increase in the complexity of the simulation, in that it will not always be possible to foresee the effect of the parasites on the host population. Also the parameters controlling the reproduction, transmission and virulence of the parasites may require careful fine tuning. It would, however, almost certainly be possible to evolve suitable values for these parameters.

Use of evolutionary programming techniques is becoming more common as we attempt to solve problems which defy traditional design methods (because the solutions are highly complex or cannot be specified in advance). But we should not lose sight of the fact that evolution is not a perfect optimisation process [Mayr 1983]. We should therefore not expect our evolutionary programs to be perfect optimisers either [DeJong 1985]. Furthermore, programs run on finite machines within finite amounts of time. Artificial parasitism, by increasing the evolutionary pressure in our programs, may help us to obtain solutions that are more effective than would have otherwise been possible given these constraints.

The problem of the evolution of a communication protocol for mate-finding, as used for the practical part of this work, is a relatively simple optimisation problem. It will be interesting to see if the introduction of parasites into more complex simulations reinforces the encouraging results described here.

Acknowledgements

I would to thank Janet Lovell for her stimulating discussion and constructive criticism.

References

Cade, W. (1979). The Evolution of Alternative Male Reproductive Strategies in Field Crickets. In Blum, M and Blum, NA, editors, *Sexual Selection and Reproductive Competition in Insects.* London, Academic Press.

Cronin, H. (1991). *The Ant and The Peacock.* Cambridge, Cambridge University Press.

Dawkins, R. (1976). *The Selfish Gene.* Oxford, Oxford University Press.

Dawkins, R. (1982). *The Extended Phenotype.* Oxford, Oxford University Press.

DeJong, K (1985). Genetic Algorithms: A 10 Year Perspective. *Proceedings of the First International Conference on Genetic Algorithms.* 1985. 169-177.

Goldberg, D. (1989). *Genetic Algorithms in Search, Optimisation and Machine Learning.* Reading, Massachusetts, Addison Wesley.

Halliday, T. (1993). Evolutionary Ecology. In Skelton, P, editor, *Evolution: A Biological and Palaeontological Approach.* Wokingham, Addison Wesley.

Hamilton, W. and M. Zuk. (1982). "Heritable True Fitness and Bright Birds: A Role for Parasites?" *Science.* 218(Oct 22, 1982): 384-387.

Hillis, WD. (1990). Co-Evolving Parasites Improve Simulated Evolution as an Optimization Procedure. *Artificial Life II - Proceedings of the Workshop on the Synthesis and Simulation of Living Systems Held February 1990 in Santa Fe, New Mexico.* 313-324.

Holland, JH. (1975). *Adaptation in Natural and Artificial Systems.* Cambridge, Massachusetts, MIT Press.

Koza, J. (1992). *Genetic Programming: On the Programming of Computers by Means of Natural Selection.* Cambridge, Massachusetts, MIT Press.

Mayr, E. (1983). How to Carry Out the Adaptationist Program. *American Naturalist.* 121:324-334.

Michalewicz, Z. (1992). *Genetic Algorithms + Data Structures = Evolution Programs.* Berlin, Springer-Verlag.
Mielke, H. (1989). *Patterns of Life.* Boston, Unwin Hyman, Inc.

Moore, J. (1983). Parasites That Change the Behaviour of Their Host. *Scientific American.* 250(5): 82-89.

Ono, N. and A. Rahmani. (1993). Self-Organisation of Communication in Distributed Learning Classifier Systems. In *Artificial Neural Nets and Genetic Algorithms.* 1993. 361-367.

Schmidt, G. and L. Roberts. (1989). *Foundations of Parasitology.* St. Louis, Missouri, Times Mirror/Mosby College Publishing.

Ray, TS. (1990). An Approach to the Synthesis of Life. *Artificial Life II - Proceedings of the Workshop on the Synthesis and Simulation of Living Systems Held February 1990 in Santa Fe, New Mexico.* 371-408.

Werner, G. and M. Dyer. (1990). Evolution of Communication in Artificial Animals. *Artificial Life II - Proceedings of the Workshop on the Synthesis and Simulation of Living Systems Held February 1990 in Santa Fe, New Mexico.* 659-687.

Zuk, M. (1984). A Charming Resistance to Parasites. *Natural History.* 4: 28-34.

COLLECTIVE BEHAVIOR

Towards Robot Cooperation

David McFarland

Department of Zoology
and Balliol College
Broad Street
Oxford, OX1 3BJ

Abstract

This paper describes how cooperative behaviour proper, as opposed to collective behaviour, can be achieved in robots without it being explicitly programmed into the robot brain. An artificial ecosystem is described in which robots cooperate in maintaining both their short term and long term energy supply. The cooperative behaviour requires communication, but much of this is emergent rather than being pre-engineered.

Keywords: cooperation, communication, ecosystem

1. Introduction

The aim of this paper is to report on a framework that has been set up in the laboratory to study cooperative behaviour in self-sufficient robots. In the long term we may expect to see such robots deployed in real life situations, such as pollution patrol, sewer inspection, etc. To be self-sufficient a robot must not enter into irrecoverable debt of any vital resource. In some field situations this could be achieved only through robot cooperation. The laboratory study is intended to reflect, in a simplified version, some of the problems that are likely to arise in the field. This paper reports on the first phase of a multi-phase study.

Cooperative behaviour proper is to be distinguished from collective behaviour. The latter is found in many insect species which have an unusual genetic makeup. Many insects have a haplodiploid mode of sex determination, in which fertilised eggs produce females and unfertilised eggs produce males. A consequence of this is that females are more closely related to their sisters than they are to their own daughters, and a female is more likely to contribute genes to the next generation by rearing a sister than by rearing a daughter. The result is the evolution of species with sterile female castes and a tight colonial organisation centred on a single fertile female (Wilson, 1975). These eusocial insects include all the ants and termites, and the more highly organised bees and wasps. It is these insects that have been chosen as models of collective behaviour in artificial agents.

Eusociality is quite different from the type of social behaviour normally found in vertebrates. The behaviour of a eusocial insect depends upon carefully designed rules, but the social behaviour of a vertebrate individual involves much more complex communication and cooperation. The essential difference between eusocial behaviour and vertebrate social behaviour is that the latter is based on individual (genetic) self-interest, whereas the best-interest of a sterile eusocial animal will often be to aid particular types of relative (such as the queen).

Cooperative behaviour proper inevitably involves communication, but such communication is not always straightforward. From the point of view of evolutionary theory, it is clear that it will not always be the best strategy for an animal to 'honestly' inform another individual about its true motivational state or about what it is likely to do next. Such behaviour would be a form of altruism, and a population of honest animals is always open to invasion by dishonest cheaters. In any complex communications situation, there are always a number of design opportunities that are open to exploitation by mutants.

The design opportunities that present themselves to an evolving communications system can usefully be summarised in terms of Hamilton's (1964) classification of social behaviour in general, shown in Figure 1.

| | | CHANGE IN RECEIVER'S FITNESS | |
		increase	decrease
CHANGE IN SIGNALLER'S FITNESS	increase	**mutuality**	**deceit**
	decrease	**eavesdropping**	**spite**

Figure 1: Classification of communication based upon Hamilton's classification of social interactions in general.

Mutuality occurs when both signaller and receiver benefit from the interaction. *Deceit* occurs when the signaller's fitness increases at the expense of the receiver's. *Manipulation* by receivers can occur when the receiver obtains information about the signaller, against the interests of the signaller. For example, the courtship display of a male may attract rivals who may steal copulations from females attracted to the display. This form of manipulation has been called *eavesdropping*. The situation in which an animal reduces its own fitness in the process of harming another animal has been called *spite*. (Hamilton, 1964). It is important to remember that these terms, borrowed from everyday language, are names of evolutionary strategies, and have nothing to do with the motivation of the individual.

2. Animal cooperation

In true symbiosis, or *mutualism*, both species benefit and communication usually occurs between them. For example, the honey badger (*Mellivora capensis*) lives in symbiosis with a small bird called the honey guide (*Indicator indicator*). When the bird discovers a hive of wild bees, it searches for a badger and guides it to the hive by means of a special display. Protected by its thick skin, the badger opens the hive with its large claws and feeds on the honeycombs. The birds feed upon the wax and bee larvae, to which it could not gain access unaided. If the honey guide cannot find a badger, it may attempt to attract people. The natives understand the bird's behaviour and follow it to the hive. It is an unwritten law that the bird be allowed to take the bee larvae.

Courtship requires cooperation. In a typical vertebrate courtship the male approaches the female, advertising his suitability by various displays. Initially, the female is usually coy. She needs to assess the male's suitability to father her offspring. The male persists, sometimes in the face of rivalry from other males. Eventually, the female decides that a particular male is acceptable. The two now have to cooperate in mating. For this they have both to know what to do, and to communicate effectively so that their behaviour can be synchronised.

The courtship process may be likened to baton-passing in a relay race. The donor approaches the recipient, making sure that it is a recipient of the correct type (i.e. a female that is reproductively receptive). The donor communicates with the recipient - "Please take my baton?". The recipient, before agreeing, needs to check that the donor is OK, and is offering a desirable baton. So the recipient may initially say "no thanks", or "not yet". The donor persists. Once the recipient has agreed to take the baton, this readiness is communicated to the donor. From this point on, both donor and recipient must cooperate in passing the baton. Both have a self-interest in ensuring that the pass goes smoothly. The donor has identified a desirable recipient, and has invested time and energy in salesmanship. The recipient, initially sales-resistant, has finally decided to accept (or sometimes not to accept) the baton, because it is worth having.

In the evolution of baton passing behaviour there is considerable scope for deceit. It may be of advantage to the donor to exaggerate the desirability of the baton. It may be of advantage to the recipient to discriminate different types of donor sales-talk, and to discount certain types. It may even be of advantage to the recipient to pretend to be interested in the baton in order to find out more about the donor. In the study of cooperation in animals there is a large amount of evolutionary theory of the type outlined above (e.g. Axelrod, 1984; Trivers, 1985). This type of theory is also relevant in robotics.

3. Robot cooperation

The design of communication systems, whether by natural selection, or by man, should be viewed in terms of the ultimate payoff. In the case of animals the ultimate payoff is to maximise inclusive fitness by means of some evolutionary strategy. In the case of systems designed by man it is to maximise profitability by means of some marketing strategy (McFarland, 1991; McFarland and Bosser, 1993). In the case of animal courtship, the ultimate payoff can be characterised in terms of the male and female evolutionary strategies (with respect to courtship) as indicated in Figure 2.

	DESIGN PAYOFF/ EVOLUTIONARY STRATEGY	TASK	COMPETING MOTIVATIONAL SYSTEMS
MALE	maximise baton pickup by female	persuade female to pickup batons	courtship, baton deposition
FEMALE	choose best male	assess and test male without losing good sperm opportunities	coyness, cooperation
ROBOT DONOR	maximise baton use by recipient	pass baton to good recipient	advertise, pass baton/ retain baton
ROBOT RECIPIENT	maximise baton use	receive only good batons	detect donors, assess donors accept/reject baton

Figure 2: Analysis of behavioural transactions

In the case of a baton-passing robot, the design payoff would be to maximise some function of the use of the baton, as indicated in the figure.

The task facing the individual male is to persuade the female to pick up his batons without too much cost to himself. The task facing the individual female is to assess the male and test him (by prolonging the courtship), without losing an opportunity to obtain a sperm from a good male. Similarly, we can think of the tasks facing a baton-passing robot (Fig. 2). The task facing the donor is to pass the baton to a good recipient, while that facing the recipient is to receive only good batons.

In motivational terms, as outlined above, the male has to achieve a good balance between courtship (long enough to be effective, but not so long as to be exhausting), sperm deposition (when to do it), and other activities such as predator avoidance, feeding etc. For the female there is a motivational conflict between coyness (sales-resistance) and cooperation in sperm transfer. Similarly, we may imagine that a donor robot has motivation to advertise the baton, to pass the baton, or to retain the baton if the recipient seems unsuitable or uncooperative. The recipient robot has motivation to look out for donors, to assess donors when detected, and to accept or reject donors (Figure 2).

Suppose we imagine a baton passing exercise for robots. The baton does not have to be a small object, but may be a fixed resource, or a desirable place. Imagine two or more robots, suitably equipped, put in a situation where they must compete for environmental resources. The robots are completely autonomous and self-sufficient and depend upon the resources for their viability. Matters are so arranged that it is of longterm advantage to each robot to cooperate with others. Such cooperation can be achieved through a suitable communication system, designed along ethological lines.

To be more specific, we imaging two lightweight robots, each of which can be a donor or a recipient. Each plays one role at a time. The robots depend for their survival on a common energy resource in the form of a nest in which on-board batteries can be recharged. When in the nest the robot is playing the donor role, because it can give up its place to the other robot, the recipient. The donor advertises its presence in the nest by emitting a bright light, which is an aid to the recipient in finding the nest.

Why should the donor robot on the nest indulge in apparently altruistic behaviour by advertising the whereabouts of the nest and thus making it easier for the other robot to find? Longterm survival of the donor is promoted by giving up the nest to a worthwhile recipient, because recipient will aid donor (by advertising) when roles are reversed. If the recipient is allowed to die, then the donor will be on its own, and will have to find the nest without aid (i.e. by expensive random search). A worthwhile recipient is one that really needs the energy.

4. Robot Reality

We imagine a scenario in which one robot helps another out of self-interest. To translate such a scenario into reality we have to take account of the robots' ecological situation. In real life, sometime in the future, autonomous robots will be sent out to accomplish tasks in the real world. Their ecological situation will be similar to our ecological situation. In the meantime, to effectively study robot cooperation in the laboratory, we have to construct a closed robot ecology, in the laboratory.

In the AI Laboratory, at the VUB in Brussels, Luc Steels and I have devised a closed robot ecology in which there in a single system battery that has a constant unalterable rate of energy inflow. In the absence of any robots there is a constant rate of outflow of energy due to a number of lamps that are housed in boxes in the robot arena. In the absence of any robots, the system is in balance, the rate of outflow of energy equalling the rate of inflow.

Once we introduce robots that recharge at the nest, then the rate of outflow of energy is potentially increased because energy is drained from the system battery when robot batteries are recharged. To keep the system in balance, the robots have to turn of the lamps in the arena. This they can do by knocking on the boxes in which the lamps are housed. The robots thus have two main tasks: (1) to recharge their on-board batteries from time to time, (2) to reduce energy waste in the ecosystem. They accomplish the first task by seeking the nest, and they accomplish the second task by "gardening", i.e. seeking out lamp boxes and extinguishing the lamps.

The lamps are, in effect, parasites that feed upon the energy in the ecosystem. Even when a lamp has been extinguished by a robot, it gradually regrows to its former energy-dissipating magnitude. So the robot "gardening" task is never ending. They must keep eradicating the parasites to maintain sufficient energy in the ecosystem for recharging their own batteries.

Matters are so arranged that one robot cannot survive alone. A single robot cannot do "gardening" quickly enough to prevent a drain on the energy in the ecosystem, and it cannot find the nest often enough to recharge its on-board batteries. The presence of another robot is a help, because the other robot helps with the gardening, and when one robot is on the nest it emits a bright light that aids the other robot in finding the nest. Thus it is in the long-term interest of one robot to keep the other alive.

As in animals, each robot communicates with the other out of self interest. The donor (on the nest) has an interest in keeping the recipient alive, and the recipient has an interest in gaining access to the nest. In both cases this self-interest must be translated into motivation, as illustrated in Figure 3.

ROBOT ROLE	DESIGN PAYOFF	TASK	MOTIVATION TO
Donor	Maximise longterm survival	give up nest to worthwile recipient	recharge, garden
Recipient	Maximise short-term survival	obtain nest with least energy cost	search, home-in, garden

Figure 3: Analysis of robot self-interest.
The robots are hermaphrodite, i.e. each can be donor or recipient.

The donor has motivation to recharge its batteries (otherwise it would not be on the nest). It also has some level of motivation to extinguish lamps (gardening). The recipient has motivation to gain access to the nest (by random search or by homing-in on the donor's advertising signal) and to garden. These motivational variables will be closely related to the state of the batteries and the state of the robot's individual gardening memory. Thus, as in animals, the motivation to perform particular activities relates to fundamental state variables.

Once the recipient arrives at the nest some cooperation is required if the donor is to give up its place for the recipient. In motivational terms there are four main possibilities (for an animal example see Niebuhr and McFarland, 1983). (1) The donor has little motivation to remain on the nest (because its batteries are nearly recharged), and the recipient has strong motivation to gain access to the nest. In this case the donor is likely to give up the nest readily, because its own self-interest is outweighed by the interest is has in the welfare of the recipient. (2) The donor has little motivation to remain on the nest, but the recipient also has low motivation to gain the nest. What happens here may hinge on the exact details of the communication between the two, but the final outcome is of little consequence. (3) The donor has strong motivation to remain on the nest, because it needs to recharge its batteries, and the recipient has little motivation to gain the nest. Although the recipient may put in a request, this is certain to be refused, and no nest exchange will take place. (4) The donor has strong motivation to remain on the nest and the recipient also has strong motivation to gain the nest. Here we have a *bargaining* situation, in which two contestants are competing for a divisible resource. Each would like a larger share than the other is willing to grant, yet both would prefer to share the resource rather than allow negotiations to break down. This type of situation is well known in evolutionary theory (e.g. Maynard Smith, 1982). Much depends on whether there is complete or incomplete information available to both parties (Selten, 1975). In the case of robot communication, much will depend upon the communication and physical abilities of the robots. Such questions as - is all communication honest? can one robot push the other? - must be answered at the design stage. It may well be that the robots can learn, can calculate, or can be aggressive. Whatever the design outcome, it must conform to the basic evolutionary strategy that is relevant to the situation. Otherwise the situation will not be behaviourally stable, robots will die, and the system of cooperation will collapse. The onus is on the designer to make sure that, whatever ploys the robots can produce, the system as a whole is ecologically stable.

The present state of play with the real robots is that the robot on the nest turns on a bright light, which enables the other robot to find the nest by phototaxis (for robot details see Steels, 1994). On approaching the occupied nest the incoming robot emits a sound signal which is a true and honest indication of its on-board battery state. If the robot on the nest does nothing then it will be pushed off the nest by the incoming robot. If the robot on the nest does not "want" to be displaced from the nest then it simply turns off the bright advertising light, thus preventing the other robot from finding the nest by phototaxis.

In this way we have designed a straightforward, honest, communication system. The incoming robot effectively requests entry to the nest by signalling its on-board battery state. The resident robot effectively signals "yes come in" or "no go away" by controlling the nest light. Note that the communication between the two robots is not explicit and pre-engineered. Much of the communication is an emergent property of the situation.

Note that we assume honest signalling for the time-being, but the best recipient strategy may be to exaggerate energy need and so obtain possession of the nest in anticipation of real need. While the best donor strategy may be to discount the urgency of the request and turn off the nest-light to see what the other robot does. At present the robots are incapable of learning, but in future experiments we plan to see if the robots can learn the relevant deceitful strategies.

Acknowledgments

The author is grateful for support given by I.R.S.I.A. - I.W.O.N.L. Research in Brussels, and the AI Lab of the V.U.B., Brussels

References

Axelrod, R. (1984) *The evolution of cooperation.* New York, Basic Books, Inc.

Hamilton, W.D. (1964) The genetical theory of social behaviour (I and II) *J. Theoret. Biol.* 7:1-16; 17-32.

Maynard Smith, J. (1982) *Evolution and the Theory of Games.* Cambridge University Press.

McFarland, D. (1991) What it means for robot behaviour to be adaptive. *From animals to animats.* (eds) J. Meyer and S. W. Wilson. MIT Press, Cambridge, Mass.

McFarland, D. and Bosser, T. (1993) *Intelligent Behavior in Animals and Robots.* MIT Press.

Niebuhr, V. and McFarland, D. (1983) Nest-relief behaviour in the herring gull. *Anim. Behav.,* 31. 701-707.

Selten, R. (1975) Bargaining under incomplete information - a numerical example. In Becker, O. and Richter, R. *Dynamische Wirtschafts-Analyse.* 203-232.

Steels, L. (1994) A case study in the behavior-oriented design of autonomous agents. (submitted to SAB94)

Trivers, R. (1985) *Social Evolution.* The Benjamin-Cummings Publishing Company, Inc. Menlo Park.

Wiley, R.H. (1983) The evolution of communication: information and manipulation. In T.R. Halliday and P.J.B. Slater (eds) *Animal Behaviour: 2 communication.* Oxford, Blackwell.

Wilson, E.O. (1975) *Sociobiology.* The New Synthesis. The Belknap Press of Harvard University Press: Cambridge, Mass.

A case study in the behavior-oriented design of autonomous agents.

Luc Steels

Artificial Intelligence Laboratory
Vrije Universiteit Brussel
Pleinlaan 2, B-1050 Brussels, Belgium
E-mail: `steels@arti.vub.ac.be`

Abstract

The paper documents a case study in the design and implementation of a robotic multi-agent system. It illustrates known design guidelines, namely that the physics of the environment must be exploited, that behavior is the result from the interaction dynamics between the agent and the environment, and that emergent behavior can and must be utilised whenever possible. But the case study also challenges certain views, such as the subsumption architecture, the need for an action selection mechanism, the goal-oriented design methodology dominating the literature on planning, and the algorithmic style of writing control programs. Alternatives are explored in the form of a cooperative, parallel, behavior-oriented design.

1 Introduction

An autonomous agent is a physical system that has its own resources to operate independently in a dynamically changing real world environment. The resources include energy, computational power, sensors, actuators, and body parts. A multi-agent system is an ecosystem in which two or more autonomous agents cooperate. The paper describes an experiment exploring cooperation in multi-agent systems. The experiment focuses on individual cooperation, such as found between two birds that are rearing young, rather than societal cooperation as observed in insect societies. Instead of taking a knowledge-oriented approach, in which the agents make models of each other and negotiate through explicit natural language-like communication, we explore a behavior-oriented approach [11] in which cooperation is forced upon the agents by the environment and emerges from the activities of individual agents. McFarland [7] has defined the biological background and motivation for the experiment.

Designing autonomous agents and multi-agent systems is notoriously difficult. The paper intends to illustrate a set of design guidelines about which there seems to be a consensus in the field [2]: (a) exploit the physics, (b)

exploit the interaction dynamics between the agent and the environment, and (c) use emergent behavior when possible. It also illustrates some novel principles (see [10] for a more extensive discussion): (a) use a cooperative as opposed to a subsumption architecture, (b) use parallelism as opposed to action selection, (c) perform a behavior-oriented as opposed to goal-oriented design, and (d) view control programs as dynamical systems.

The first part of the paper describes the main characteristics of the experiment. The second part describes the realisation in terms of physical robots. The final part discusses the design guidelines explored in the experiment.

2 The experiment

The agents used in the experiment are relatively small robotic agents (30 x 10 cm and 20 cm high). They are equipped with sensors, motors, rechargeable batteries, a central processor in the form of a small PC-like computer, and a sensory-motor board to offload most of the sensor and actuator processing from the main processor. Prototypes of the agents have been built using $Lego^{TM}$-technology (figure 1) (as in [4] or [3]). A more robust version of the agents, which can operate for days in a row, is currently under construction.

The first two characteristics of the experiment center around a single agent operating in an environment in which it can gather energy but also benefits from weakening competition for the same energy. The remaining characteristics have been chosen to bring in a multi-agent perspective.

[1] An agent can recharge itself.

The primary goal of an autonomous agent is to sustain itself. This implies at least that the agent has at all times enough energy to keep on functioning. Each agent has therefore a set of batteries and the capability to recharge itself. The environment contains a charging station with two disks mounted on poles (figure 2). The agent has two charging rods sticking out, one at the top and one at the bottom. When these charging rods make contact with the disks, current is drawn and the battery starts charging. There is a continuous supply of energy to the

Figure 1: Prototype of robotic agents used in the experiment. The body has been built with LegoTechnics^{TM}. The main processor is a pocket PC computer inserted in the robot body.

Figure 2: The complete ecosystem consists of two or more agents, obstacles, a charging station and boxes with lamps mounted in them.

whole system.

[2] There is competition for energy in the form of additional lights.

There are lamps which are in competition for the overall energy available in the ecosystem. The lamps are mounted in boxes installed in the environment (figure 2). They draw current from the same total energy source as the charging station. Lights can be diminished by an agent as it knocks repeatedly against the box in which the lamp is mounted. Lights regenerate slowly after they have been dimmed. There are additional obstacles in the environment which do not act as competitors for energy but need to be avoided by the robot as it is seeking out box-lights. Energy stored in the charging station is drained, if all lamps are fully on. Hence it is in the interest of the agent to move away from the charging station to dampen the box-lights.

The boxes as well as the charging station must be detectable by the agent. The charging station emits blue light and the boxes emit yellow light. The agent performs phototaxis using photosensors mounted on the left and right sides of the body. They are covered with filters to be only sensitive to yellow or blue light.

[3] There is an opportunity for cooperation between agents.

Obviously it would be beneficial for the agent which is recharging, if there were another agent weakening the competition for the available energy. So there is an opportunity for cooperation. While one agent recharges, the other one seeks out boxes and pushes against them to dim the lights. In a first series of experiments we use two agents, but a larger group is planned.

[4] One agent cannot survive.

The agents can cooperate but they are also in competition and can potentially exploit each other. One agent may stay on the charging station while the other agent dims the lights, eventually running out of energy. To avoid this situation, the experiment is set up in such a way that one agent cannot survive on its own. Consequently it is in its own interest to let the other agent occasionally get on the charging station. Each agent has the capability to emit sound and to perceive sound through a microphone. Using this capability an agent can indicate that it needs to be on the charging station.

[5] A balance must be sought between egoism and altruism.

An agent can help another agent get to the charging station by turning additional light on, so that the other agent has better chances to reach the charging station through phototaxis. On the other hand, when an agent does not want another agent to come nearer (and thus risk that it will be pushed out) it can turn off the light on the charging station, thus hiding the charging station for the approaching agent. This way an agent can help another agent find the charging station, and behave "altruistically", but it should at the same time worry about its own self-preservation and so occasionally behave "egoistically".

These five characteristics in many ways parallel similar situations in nature. Seeking out the charging station can be compared to foraging, charging to feeding, and damping the box-lights to anti-parasitic behavior. There is in addition the kind of cooperation we find between individual animals, such as between two birds that are keeping eggs warm on a nest and occasionally have to go out for food [6]. These situations have been well studied in ethology and part of the case study is to make explicit

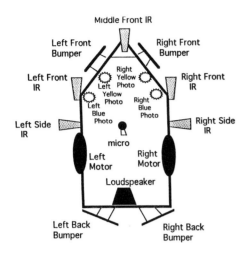

Figure 3: Hardware layout of the robot used in the experiment. The sensors are two pairs of photosensitive sensors, 6 infrared sensors, 4 bumper sensors, a loudspeaker, and a sensor measuring the energy level in the battery. The actuators are a left and right motor and a loudspeaker.

comparisons with known properties of animal behavior [7].

3   The behavior systems

The robot used for the experiment has the hardware characteristics outlined in figure 3. We use a dynamical systems approach to the programming of the behavior systems using a programming language PDL designed for this purpose [9]. The C-based implementation of PDL is used. PDL supports a set of quantities (such as RightFrontIR for the measured reflection of infrared reflection or WeakenCompetitor for the 'drive' to seek out competitors). The quantities are frozen at the beginning of a time cycle. The value of a quantity q can then be obtained by the form `value(q)`. Various processes can add to the value of the quantity at the next time cycle. This is done using the procedure call `AddValue(q, v)` which adds the value v to the quantity q. At the end of the cycle, each quantity takes on the sum of all the added values. The new values are sent off to the actuators and new sensory quantities are read in. The PC-compatible processor used in the experiment is able to execute 20 cycles per second for the complexity of the programs discussed in this paper. Integer arithmetic is used for processor efficiency reasons. The range of values for sensors and actuators is between 0 and 255.

3.1   Overview of Behaviors

A behavior-oriented design starts by identifying desirable behaviors and then seeking the subset for which behavior systems need to be developed. In the present case the following behavior systems are needed:

- Forward movement: The robot moves forward at a default speed.

- Touch-based obstacle avoidance: The robot touches an obstacle, retracts and turns away.

- Smooth obstacle avoidance: The forward path deviates as the robot comes in the neighborhood of an obstacle.

- Blue phototaxis: The robot is attracted to blue light.

- Halt while recharging: The robot stands still as it is drawing current from the charging station.

- Yellow phototaxis: The robot is attracted to yellow light.

The behavior systems realizing these behaviors in interaction with the environment are all active in parallel. Several of these behaviors will not be observed together because they contradict each other. For example, retraction (in touch-based obstacle avoidance) contradicts moving forward. The regulation which behavior is visible depends mostly on the environment as perceived by the sensors. An exception is the choice between blue and yellow phototaxis for which a motivational system is used, as explained later.

The different behaviors implement the various functionalities (translated to goals in classical AI) needed in the experiment. For example, blue phototaxis implements 'go to charging station', assuming that blue light is mounted on the charging station. Sometimes a functionality emerges from the interaction of different behaviors. For example, yellow phototaxis together with touch-based obstacle avoidance implements 'dim out competing light' in the presence of a box with a light mounted in it. Blue phototaxis together with touch-based obstacle avoidance implements 'drive into the charging station' in the presence of the charging station. A major point of this paper is that the design of the mechanisms should not focus on functionalities (and definitely not on goals) but on behaviors.

The rest of this section documents the different behavior systems. For some behavior systems, minor details have been left out due to space limitations.

3.2   Forward movement

Forward movement is implemented through a stabiliser [10] which adds or subtracts part of the difference between the current speed and the default speed. As a result speed always moves progressively back to the default. The default speed may be different for the left and right motors because motors are not necessarily equal. In the present case the default is set at 150.

define DefaultRightSpeed 150
define DefaultLeftSpeed 150
AddValue(LeftSpeed, −(LeftSpeed − DefaultLeftSpeed)/10;
AddValue(RightSpeed, −(RightSpeed − DefaultRightSpeed)/10;

3.3   Touch-based Obstacle Avoidance.

Two behavior systems (in parallel) ensure the obstacle avoidance competence. The first one is based on the bumper sensors. The second one uses the infrared sensors. Infrared-based obstacle avoidance is more efficient because it avoids bumping into obstacles, but it is less reliable because infrared reflection gives only approximate information about the presence of obstacles. Obstacles sensed in the back should also be avoided because occasionally the robot may bump into obstacles as it is moving backwards or it may have to move away when another object hits the back.

Touch-based obstacle avoidance is accomplished through a disturber [10] which increases speed in the opposite direction and causes a rotation away from the touch location (to the left when touched left and to the right when touched right). On robots with translation and rotation motors, touch-based obstacle avoidance would be implemented by influencing the speed of the translation and rotation motors. In the present case, we have a right and left motor so rotation is implemented by introducing a difference between the right and left motor speeds.

The influence from touch-based obstacle avoidance on the motor speed must be sufficiently strong to make the effect of normal forward movement ineffective. In a cooperative architecture, the forward movement behavior system remains active at all times. In a subsumption architecture, the obstacle avoidance behavior system would inhibit the forward movement behavior system.

define Retract; 300; *defineDeltaRetract*; 100
define Jump 200; *define DeltaJump*; 200
/ ∗ 1. When left front bumper touched ∗ /
AddValue(LeftSpeed, −Retract ∗ LeftBumper);
AddValue(RightSpeed, −(Retract + DeltaRetract)
| ∗ LeftFrontBumper);
/ ∗ 2. When right front bumper touched ∗ /
AddValue(LeftSpeed, −(Retract + DeltaRetract)
| ∗ RightFrontBumper);
AddValue(RightSpeed, −Retract ∗ RightFrontBumper);
/ ∗ 3. When left back bumper touched ∗ /
AddValue(LeftSpeed, Jump ∗ LeftBackBumper);
AddValue(RightSpeed, (Jump + DeltaJump)
| ∗ LeftBackBumper);
/ ∗ 4. When right back bumper touched ∗ /

AddValue(LeftSpeed, (Jump + DeltaJump)
| ∗ RightBackBumper);
AddValue(RightSpeed, Jump ∗ RightBackBumper);

Side effects:

[1] The inverse translation progressively decreases because the forward movement behavior system brings the speed back to the default.

[2] When the robot is touched in the front and the back simultaneously, it will not make any change in movement because the influences cancel each other out.

Figure 4 illustrates this behavior. We see that there is indeed backward movement and a turning away to the left. The figure is taken with a camera from the top of the robot arena. A lamp is mounted on the robot and the trace is produced by filtering the images coming from the camera in real time.

3.4   Smooth Obstacle Avoidance.

Smooth obstacle avoidance is implemented by the creation of a repelling force field, similar to a potential field [1], based on the measured infrared reflection. This influences the motor dynamics in such a way that when the infrared sensors on the left side (LeftFrontIR and LeftSideIR) are low (meaning obstacle approaching), there is a turning away to the right and when the infrared sensors on the right side (RightFrontIR and RightSideIR) are low, there is a turning away to the left. Low MiddleFrontIR causes inverse translation.

AddValue(LeftSpeed,
| value(RightFrontIR)/2 + value(MiddleFrontIR) +
| value(RightSideIR)/4 − value(LeftFrontIR)/2
| − value(LeftSideIR)/4 − IRBackground);
AddValue(RightSpeed,
| value(LeftFrontIR)/2 + value(MiddleFrontIR) +
| value(LeftSideIR)/4 − value(RightFrontIR)/2
| − value(RightSideIR)/4 − IRBackground);

IRInfluence is equal to the normal background infrared so that there would be no impact from IR-based obstacle avoidance unless the perceived IR is different from normal IRBackground.

Figure 4 illustrates this behavior. We see that the robot now turns away from the wall instead of bumping against it.

As with many sensors, there is a need for adaptive behavior. When there are a lot of obstacles in the environment, there is so much infrared reflection that the agent will move away from the area. This is like us being blinded by light to which our eyes adapt by letting less light onto the retina. A similar mechanism has been introduced that brings down the amount of IR that has been emitted, and brings it back up when relatively little IR is perceived.

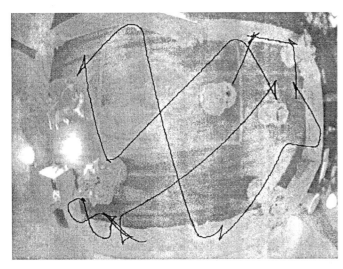

Figure 4: Touch-based obstacle avoidance and infrared-based obstacle avoidance. Both are executed in parallel with forward movement. After a period, the robot moves away from an object it senses through the infrared sensors instead of bumping into it.

3.5 Blue phototaxis (Attraction to the charging station)

Phototaxis is achieved by the creation of an attracting force field which influences the motor speed dynamics so that the robot turns right when there is less blue light on the left side and left when there is less blue light on the right side. The deviation is determined by subtracting the left and right yellow photosensor quantities and multiplying by a parameter which determines the weight of the influence.

$AddValue(RightSpeed, PhotoFactor *$
$|\quad (value(BluePhotoLeft) - value(BluePhotoRight));$
$AddValue(LeftSpeed, PhotoFactor *$
$|\quad (value(BluePhotoRight) - value(BluePhotoLeft));$ Side effects:

[1] A regular zig-zag behavior is typically observed (see figure 3.7). This zig-zag behavior is not explicitly programmed (for example by specifying that there must be for a while forward movement then left turn to a certain angle, then again forward movement, etc.) but follows from the interaction between the agent's internal dynamics and those of the environment, in particular the changing position of the agent with respect to the charging station.

[2] The robot will end up between the walls of the charging station (and thus ready for charging) due to the interaction between the obstacle avoidance and phototaxis behaviors (figure 3.7). As the robot is attracted to the light, it moves in on the charging station. If it bumps into the side of the charging station, it will move backwards and then try again. This is a very clear ex-

ample of an emergent functionality from the viewpoint of the total system. The parking behavior has not been programmed explicitly (although it could be), but it nevertheless occurs reliably.

3.6 Halt while recharging.

Recharging takes place when the robot is located in between the two disks of the charging station and when current is flowing to the batteries to recharge them. Recharging starts up automatically as soon as the charging rods mounted at the top and bottom of the robot make contact. EnergyInflow is not directly sensed, but the robot can determine the EnergyAvailability. The quantity EnergyInflow is then based on comparing the change of EnergyAvailability over a time period. The EnergyInflow is a function of the energy available in the charging station and the energy already stored in the batteries. As batteries near completion, less energy is drawn.

The robot must not move forward when energy is flowing in. We therefore need an additional influence on the motor speed related to the availability of energy determined by testing whether there is a positive rate of change in the battery charge.

$AddValue(RightSpeed,$
$|\quad - (DefaultRightSpeed * EnergyAvailability);$
$AddValue(LeftSpeed,$
$|\quad - (DefaultLeftSpeed * EnergyAvailability);$

Side effects:

[1] As the robot is charging, the batteries will become fuller and less energy will be drawn from the charging station. EnergyInflow will decrease and the default forward movement influence on the motor speeds will take over. Consequently the robot will leave the charging station.

[2] If the available current is reduced as a result of competition from the box-lights, EnergyAvailability decreases. If competition for the energy from the lights increases, less current will be available from the charging station and EnergyInflow decreases. As a result, the robot will automatically leave the charging station.

3.7 Yellow phototaxis (seek out boxes) and revised blue phototaxis.

A motivation is an internal state which is a function of sensed aspects of the environment and the internal state of the robot. It influences the occurrence of certain behavior by being a parameter to the dynamics. Motivations can either be explicit quantities, or, the quantities influencing the motivation can be directly used in the dynamics of behaviors which are sensitive to the motivation. We need two motivations in the present case: (1) A motivation for energy (comparable to hunger in ani-

450   Luc Steels

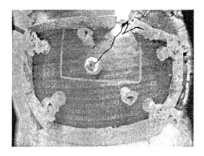

Figure 5: The figure shows phototaxis towards the light source mounted on top of the charging station. A characteristic emergent zig-zag behavior is observed. Notice also the parking behavior which emerges from phototaxis and touch-based obstacle avoidance.

mals). This motivation should increase as the amount of energy available in the robot decreases. (2) A motivation to avoid energy drain. This motivation should increase if the amount of energy available from the charging station is low and a charging robot is still in need for more energy.

The energy motivation is directly determined by the availability of energy, measured and translated to the quantity EnergyDebt. This should play a role in the strength with which the phototaxis behavior occurs. The EnergyDebt decreases due to charging. The motivation to stop the drain is more complex. It should be a function of the energy debt in the batteries and the energy inflow. It should strengthen (yellow) phototaxis behavior and decrease as the agent manages to put out the box-lights.

First the blue phototaxis behavior is extended to become sensitive to energy availability:

    AddValue(RightSpeed, PhotoFactor *
| (value(BluePhotoLeft) − value(BluePhotoRight))
| /EnergyDebt);
AddValue(LeftSpeed, PhotoFactor *
| (value(BluePhotoRight) − value(BluePhotoLeft))
| /EnergyDebt);

EnergyDrain is a motivational quantity, regulated as follows:

    AddValue(EnergyDrain, EnergyDebt * EnergyAvailability);
AddValue(EnergyDrain,
| YellowPhotoLeft * YellowPhotoRight *
| (LeftBumper + RightBumper));

The EnergyDrain quantity is then used in determining the tendency for going towards the boxes and dim out the lights:

    AddValue(RightSpeed, PhotoFactor *
| (value(YellowPhotoLeft) − value(YellowPhotoRight))
| /EnergyDrain);
AddValue(LeftSpeed, PhotoFactor *
| (value(YellowPhotoRight) − value(YellowPhotoLeft))

| /EnergyDrain);

Side effects:
[1] As the robot is attracted to the yellow light, there is enough momentum that it will bump into the box, thus causing the light to be dimmed. The bumping causes touch-based obstacle avoidance and therefore retraction, but because the is still causing phototaxis, a second approach takes place, etc.

[2] Bumping stops when there is no longer yellow light emmitted by the lamp associated with the box. It also stops when the EnergyDrain quantity has become so low that infrared-based obstacle avoidance becomes stronger.

4   Discussion

The complete ecosystem with all the behaviors described in the paper has been implemented and has been demonstrated to operate. The system works with one agent as well as two. Observers unfamiliar with the design interpret the behavior as cooperative although no explicit cooperation has been programmed. Extensions of the behavioral repertoire have been designed and implemented so that agents can engage in communication and explicitly 'decide' to leave the charging station as a response to a request from another agent. This leads to a more efficient exploitation of the available energy. These extensions will be discussed in another paper.

The case study illustrates some of the design guidelines published earlier [2]:

- *The physics of the agent and the ecosystem is exploited.* For example, the momentum from forward movement enforced by yellow phototaxis causes the robot to bump into a box and thus dim the light. There is no 'dim the light' behavior system needed.

- *The total design exploits the interaction between internal and external dynamics.* For example, when the agent is charging there will be internally an increase in energy and when the competition from the lights increases there will be a decrease in energy at the charging station. The agent does not model these physical processes but its internal dynamics (e.g. as in the halting behavior system) is in concordance with it.

- *Emergent behavior is explored whenever possible.* For example, there is no explicit parking behavior. It emerges from the interaction between blue phototaxis and obstacle avoidance.

The case study also explores some novel design principles:

[1] *We use a cooperative as opposed to a subsumption architecture.* Our approach has been to progressively consider different behaviors, each time adding more

mechanisms to achieve more competence. This methodology has been recommended by several researchers, in particular Brooks [2]. But we see additional behavior systems cooperating rather than subsuming existing behavior systems. A particular behavior system may never inhibit the in- or outflow of information to another behavior system and the effects of different behavior systems are always summed. In this sense, the architecture is a cooperative as opposed to a subsumption architecture.

[2] *We use parallelism as opposed to action selection.* Many researchers assume that the overall activity of the agent has to be split up into different, mutually exclusive actions and that consequently there is an action selection mechanism necessary which selects what action is the most appropriate at a particular point in time [5]. Instead, we work from the hypothesis that behavior systems exert a continuous influence on the actuators by a large set of parallel processes. The influences are summed. As observers we sometimes see only one action and not others but this is the consequence of properties in the environment. For example, retraction and turning away, which is part of touch-based obstacle avoidance, will not be visible if there are no obstacles. However, the action of doing obstacle avoidance is never explicitly selected. It is always there. The same is true for all the other 'actions' observable in the experiment.

[3] *We perform a behavior-oriented as opposed to a goal-oriented design.* There is a long tradition in AI to perform design by identifying goals, identifying actions that can satisfy those goals, and by then refining the analysis in terms of preconditions and postconditions. Existing planning systems all operate with this abstraction. Also in more recent work on reactive agents, a goal-oriented analysis has been proposed [8]. Instead we use a behavior-oriented design approach. The different needed observable behaviors are identified. These behaviors have as a side effect that certain goals will be achieved (if one insists on a goal-oriented analysis). For some behaviors, a behavior system is developed which establishes the desired behavior in continuous interaction with the environment. This behavior system is integrated with already existing behavior systems (to ensure that the mutual influences are compatible) and it is always active.

[4] *Control programs are based on dynamical systems as opposed to algorithms.* There are no sequential steps, control flow in the form of goto's, conditional statements, timers, etc. Instead each behavior system establishes a continuous link between a set of quantities and a set of other quantities.

The case study demonstrates that all these design principles lead to robust working systems. Larger scale experiments are needed to see whether they scale up and whether additional design guidelines are desirable.

5   Acknowledgement

The experiment discussed in this paper is a team effort at the VUB AI Lab. David McFarland has played a crucial role to make the experiment in tune for ethology. Several engineers and computer scientists have participated in the design of the hardware of the robot and the ecosystem. The most important role in hardware construction has been played by Danny Vereertbrugghen. Filip Vertommen has been responsible for the PDL version used in the experiment. Peter Stuer has been the principal designer for the behavior systems and the global ecosystem. Geert Machtelinck has made important contributions to the specific behavior systems reported in this paper. Research has been funded by the ESPRIT basic research project SUBSYM (particularly some of the early hardware development) and by the Belgian Government IUAP Centre of Excellence grant to the VUB AI lab.

References

[1] Arkin, R. (1989) Motor Schema based mobile robot navigation. Int. Journal of Robotics Research. Vol 8, 4 p. 92-112.

[2] Brooks, R. (1991) Intelligence without reason. Proceedings of IJCAI-91. Morgan Kaufmann, San Mateo Ca. p. 569-595.

[3] Jones, J.L. and A.M. Flynn (1993) Mobile Robots. Inspiration to implementation. A.K. Peters, Wellesley Ma.

[4] Donnett, J. and T. Smithers (1990) Lego Vehicles: A Technology for studying intelligent systems. In: Meyer, J-A., H.L. Roitblatt, and S.W. Wilson (1993) From Animals to Animats2. Proceedings of the Second International Conference on Simulation of Adaptive Behavior. MIT Press/Bradford Books, Cambridge Ma. p. 540-569.

[5] Maes, P. (1989) The Dynamics of Action Selection. In: Proceedings of the 11th International Joint Conference on AI (IJCAI 89) Morgan Kaufmann, Pub. Los Altos. p. 991-997.

[6] McFarland, D. (1990) Animal behaviour. Oxford University Press, Oxford.

[7] McFarland, D. (1994) Towards Robot Cooperation. [submitted to SAB1994].

[8] Nilsson, N. (1994) Teleo-reactive programs for robot control. In: Journal of AI Research. [to appear]

[9] Steels, L. (1992b) The PDL reference manual. VUB AI Lab memo. 92-5.

[10] Steels, L. (1993) Building Agents with Autonomous Behavior Systems. In: Steels, L. and R. Brooks (eds.) (1993) The 'artificial life' route to 'artificial intelligence'. Building situated embodied agents. Lawrence Erlbaum Associates, New Haven.

[11] Steels, L. (1994) The artificial life roots of artificial intelligence. Artificial Life Journal, Vol 1,1. MIT Press, Cambridge.

Learning to Behave Socially

Maja J Mataric

MIT Artificial Intelligence Laboratory

545 Technology Square #721

Cambridge, MA 02139

phone: (617) 253-8839

fax: (617) 253-0039

email: maja@ai.mit.edu

April 10, 1994

Abstract

Our previous work introduced a methodology for synthesizing and analyzing *basic behaviors* which served as a substrate for generating a large repertoire of higher–level group interactions (Matarić 1992, Matarić 1993). In this paper we describe how, given the substrate, agents can learn to behave *socially*, i.e. to maximize average individual by maximizing collective benefit. While this is a well–defined problem for rational agents, it is difficult to learn in situated domains. We describe three sources of reinforcement and show their necessity for learning non–greedy social rules. The learning strategy is demonstrated on a group of physical mobile robots learning to yield and share information in a foraging task.

1 Introduction

Our previous work focused on analyzing and synthesizing complex group behaviors from simple social interactions between individuals (Matarić 1992, Matarić 1993). We introduced a methodology which involved designing a collection of *basic behaviors* which served as a substrate for a large repertoire of higher–level interactions. In this paper we describe how agents can extend the basic repertoire in order to learn to behave *socially*.

The importance of social behavior needs no elaboration. Social rules, from the simplest traffic protocols to the most complex ethical constructs, minimize conflict and optimize global efficiency. Consequently, social rules are a natural part of any society, and the acquisition of those rules is an important aspect of adaptive behavior. This paper will describe how social learning, a fundamental form of adaptive group behavior, can be used for acquiring social rules.

1.1 Social Learning

Social learning is the process of acquiring new behavior patterns in a social context, by learning from conspecifics. Also called *observational learning*, social learning is ubiquitous in nature (McFarland 1985, McFarland 1987) and the propensity for it appears to be innate. Animals imprint, mimic, and imitate adults of their own kind instinctively, often without obtaining direct rewards or even successfully achieving the goal of the behavior (McFarland 1985, Gould 1982). A crucial form of learning during development, social learning remains an important aspect of social interaction throughout an animal's life.

Observational learning is a phylogenetically old method of adapting behavior. It has been found in some invertebrates (Fiority & Scotto 1992), in many birds (Moore 1992), aquatic mammals (Mitchell 1987) and of course primates and humans. In all cases, it is a faster and more efficient form of acquiring new behaviors than its traditional classical conditioning counterpart. Imitation of conspecifics is easier than general imitation and mimicry, but animals, and some birds (Moore 1992), are capable of both.

Social learning includes learning *how* to perform a behavior, through imitation, and *when* to perform it, through social facilitation. *Imitation* is defined as the ability to observe and repeat the behavior of another animal or agent. It is one of the principal modes of acquiring new patterns of behavior. True imitation is distinct from mimicry and social facilitation. *Mimicry* is the ability to repeat some aspects of the behavior of another agent, without having the imitator understand the goal of the behavior or of the internal state of the agent being imitated (Tomasello, Kruger & Rather 1992).

Social facilitation refers to the process of selectively expressing a behavior which is already a part of the animal's species–specific repertoire. Birds pecking at milk bottle caps in order to drink the milk inside (Davis

1973, McFarland 1985), and eating more in groups then when alone (McFarland 1987) are both examples of social facilitation in which the animals are not learning any new behavior but only responding to a releaser (Davis 1973).

Some previous work has addressed the problem of learning behavior selection (e.g. (Maes & Brooks 1990)) and we have also demonstrated an algorithm for learning higher-level group behaviors by selecting among basic primitives (Mataric 1994). Unlike previous work, this paper focuses on learning social rules, i.e. behaviors that do not produce immediate payoff for the agent but benefit the group as a whole. Game theory has dealt extensively with related problems (for example see Axelrod (1984), Kraus (1993) and Durfee, Lee & Gmytrasiewicz (1993)) but exclusively in the domains with rational agents capable of correctly evaluating the utility of their actions and strategies. In contrast, we are interested in finding out what is required for learning social strategies in situated agent domains where, due to incomplete or nonexistent world models, inconsistent reinforcement, noise and uncertainty, the agents cannot be assumed to be rational. In general, systems treated by game theory are usually simpler and more cleanly constrained than those found in biology and thus those that motivate this work.

The first section of the paper describes the key issues in interference as the underlying motivation behind social rules. The next section puts forth the notion of prototypical social states which effectively prune the space of social interactions. The following part of the paper postulates the key sources of reinforcement in social learning. The reminder of the paper describes the robot experiments used to test the proposed theory as applied to learning social rules. The last part of the paper summarizes current conclusions and outlines continued experimental work.

2   Interference and Conflict

Although not universally accepted, a popular theory postulates that social interactions are evolutionarily beneficial because social structure minimizes interference and maximizes benefit of the group as a whole, presumably in terms of reproductive success.

Interference, then, is any influence that opposes or blocks the agents' goal-driven behavior. In societies consisting of agents with similar goals, interference manifests itself as competition for shared resources. In diverse societies, where agents' goals differ, more complex conflicts can persist between agents, including undoing of each other's work, deadlocks, and oscillations.

Two functionally distinct types of interference are relevant to this work: interference caused by multiplicity, which we will call *resource competition*, and interference caused by goal-related conflict, which we will call *goal competition*. Resource competition includes any interference resulting from multiple agents competing for common resources, such as space, food, and information. This type of interference causes the decline in performance in multi-agents systems as more agents are added. It is also the primary impetus for social rules.

While resource competition is simply caused by physical coexistence, and can thus exist in any multi-agent system, goal competition only applies to systems with heterogeneous agents. Functionally different agents can create lasting interference over conflicting goals. An agent can undo the work of another not out of immediate need for the resources but due to some higher-level goal such as, for instance, establishing dominance.

Goal competition is studied primarily by the Distributed AI community (Gasser & N. Huhns 1989). The approaches usually involve predicting other agents' goals and intentions, thus requiring agents to maintain models of each other's internal state (e.g. Huber & Durfee (1993), Miceli & Cesta (1993)). Such prediction abilities require computational resources that do not scale well with increased group sizes. In contrast, our work deals with homogeneous societies in which social rules are shared by all individuals. Consequently, only resource competition, and social rules aimed at minimizing it, are relevant and will be addressed.

2.1   Individuals vs. Groups

Social rules that minimize interference among agents attempt to direct behavior away from individual greediness and toward global efficiency.[1] Greedy individualist strategies perform poorly in group situations in which resource competition is inevitable and not correctly managed, since resource competition grows with the size of the group.[2] Not all group dynamics fall into this category. For example, some tasks allow for efficient greedy strategies in which agents specialize by task division, as demonstrated by Deneubourg, Goss, Pasteels, Fresneau & Lachaud (1987). In contrast, this work focuses on tasks and solutions in which the agents cannot specialize, and instead must find means of optimizing their activity within the same task by developing social rules.

In such situations, agents must give up individual optimality in favor of collective efficiency. At least in theory, it is in the interest of each of the individuals to obey social rules, since on the average their individual efficiency will be improved as well. However, since the connection between individual and collective benefit is not always direct, the problem of learning social rules is a difficult one.

Outside game theory, this problem has been addressed in the filed of Artificial Life at the genetic learning level. Genetic algorithm allow generations of agents with differ-

---

[1] Global efficiency can, in a cultural context, be elevated to "the common good."

[2] The rate of growth is determined by the properties of the particular system.

ent social rules to be tried out, mutated, and recombined, in order to find the best fit (for example, see MacLennan (1990) for a strategy for evolving communication, and Chris Langton (1989) for related work).

The work presented in this paper is fundamentally different because it addresses the problem learning of social rules by each of the individuals during their lifetime and within the context of a task, in this case foraging. It is aimed at loosely modeling higher animals rather than insects that are preprogrammed with the appropriate social strategies. Consequently, it cannot directly assume social rules and build them in, but rather it must deal with tradeoffs in individual versus global efficiency and incorporate those appropriately into the on-line real-time learning strategies.

3 Prototypical States in Social Interaction

Animal interactions are largely ritualized and drawn from a small social repertoire. In theory, the number of possible social situations among multiple agents is prohibitively large, especially since it grows with the size of the group. In practice, however, the rules of social behavior are quite independent of exact group size. Specifically, only a few classes of group sizes and prototypical relations among agents are relevant for any given type of interaction.

The canonical form of social relation is the *dominance hierarchy* or *pecking order*, ubiquitous in animal societies, from hermit crabs and chickens to primates and people (Chase 1982, Chase & Rohwer 1987). Besides mating, the majority of animal social interaction focuses on establishing and maintaining pecking orders (Cheney & Seyfarth 1990). Although no directly derivable evolutionary benefit has been proven, hierarchies certainly serve to ritualize and thus simplify social interactions.

While dominance hierarchies are a prevalent social structure and simplify social interaction, we are interested in learning social rules that are not directly embedded into a dominance structure, but instead need to be derived by the agent based on its interactions with others and its effectiveness at its tasks over time.

Besides by dominance hierarchies, animal social interactions can be classified into one-on-one, one-to-few, and one-to-many[3], with the first two being by far the most prevalent. The work described in this paper will use the group size classification to prune the state space of social interactions, and focus on learning social rules that are applied in one-on-one and one-to-few interaction classes. In particular, we will work on yielding rules for one-on-one motion conflicts, and communication rules for one-to-few interaction. We will postulate that learning social

rules for such interactions requires specific types of social reinforcement, as described in the next section.

4 Social Reinforcement

Social settings offer a plethora of information useful for learning. The relevance of conspecifics' behavior is recognized in biology by the innate propensity for social learning. For instance, young animals copy the behavior of an adult automatically, often without any direct reward (Gould 1982). Furthermore, behavior of peers is also copied, especially if it leads to a reward. This type of social behavior results in the development of culture in the form of behavior patterns that are passed on through generations. In a well known example, monkeys repeatedly discovered washing potatoes and separating dirt from seeds (McFarland 1985).

Observed behavior of conspecifics can serve as negative as well as positive reinforcement. For example, animals quickly learn not to eat food that has had a poisonous effect on others, or to avoid people if others have been hunted by them (Davis 1973, Gould 1982, McFarland 1987). Vicarious punishment and vicarious reward are both effective, although less so then their direct counterparts. In a sense, vicarious learning is a means of distributing trials over multiple agents so that one agent need not perform then all. As long as the experience of an agent is "visible", it can serve as a source of vicarious learning trials for others.

Evidence from ethology guides us to derive three forms of reinforcement involved in social learning. The first type is the individual perception of progress relative to the current goal. This type of reinforcement is inherent in any learning task, but its availability varies depending on the specific agent and environment. In most tasks, the agent can maintain some measure of progress[4] that is critical for efficient learning.

The second type of reinforcement comes from observing the behavior of conspecifics. Similar behavior in a peer is considered to be a source of positive reinforcement. Although this in itself does not constitute a reliable reinforcement signal, coupled with a direct estimate of progress toward the agent's particular goal, it can provide useful feedback for the agent.

Finally, the third type of reinforcement is that received by conspecifics. Interestingly, using this type of information does not require the agent to model another agent's internal state. Since the agents belong to a homogeneous society in which they obey consistent social rules, any reward or punishment received by a conspecific would have been received by the agent itself in a similar situation. Consequently, vicarious reinforcement is a useful learning signal.

---

[3]Where "many" is bounded by the sensing and communication range.

[4]Most tasks do not resemble maze learning where the only reward is found at the goal.

Figure 1: Each robot consists of a differentially steerable wheeled base, and a gripper that can grasp and lift objects. The robots' sensory capabilities include piezo-electric bump and gripper sensors, infra-red sensors for collision detection, proprioceptive sensors for maintaining drive and gripper-motor current, voltage, and position, and a radio transmitter for communication and absolute positioning.

We postulate that all three of the above described forms of reinforcement are necessary for learning social rules. Individual reinforcement is not sufficient because it, by definition, maximizes individual benefit. Since the kind of rules we are interested in learning do not immediately and directly benefit the individual and, in some cases, even have a delaying effect on its individual reinforcement, then cannot be learned with such reinforcement alone.

Observing other agents' behavior helps the learning because it gives the impetus to the agent to try behaviors that do not immediately benefit it. Repeating the behavior of others enforces multiple trials of an otherwise rare social behavior, so more stable reinforcement is received. Although observing other agents' behavior clearly encourages exploration in the group and thus speeds up learning, it still cannot induce individual agents to behave in ways that will reduce their reinforcement.

How can a society develop social rules based on individual learning, i.e. without some centrally imposed arbiter? It can be accomplished if the agents are able to estimate other agents' reinforcement and their individual reinforcement is positively correlated with their conspecifics. In short, what is good for one, is good for another, at least indirectly. This simple model allows for learning a variety of powerful social rules which minimize interference and maximize group benefit.

To test this hypothesis, we have designed a collection of experiments on situated agents (mobile robots) learning to yield and communicate, in order to become more globally efficient at foraging, their high-level task. The next section describes the experimental environment.

5   The Robots

The experimental environment to be described is designed for performing a variety of group behavior experiments. It has been used for verifying work on basic behaviors as well as for demonstrating an algorithm for accelerated situated learning (Mataric 1994). It allows for implementing various interactions between robots capable of communicating with each other, and sensing and manipulating objects.

The experiments are conducted on a collection of up to four R2 mobile robots. The robots are fully autonomous with on-board power and sensing. Each robot consists of a differentially steerable wheeled base and a gripper that can grasp and lift objects. The robots' sensory capabilities include a piezo-electric bump sensor strip around the base for detecting collisions, another strip inside each finger of the gripper for detecting the grasping force, and a set of infra-red (IR) sensors: two on the inside of the fingers for detecting graspable objects, and ten more for obstacle avoidance: a set of eight sensors around the top of the robot, and one more on each gripper tip (see Figure 1).

In addition to the described external sensors, the robots are also equipped with proprioceptive sensors supplying battery voltage and current information, sensors for drive motor current, and shaft encoders in the gripper motors for maintaining position and height information.

Finally, the robots are equipped with radio transceivers, used for determining absolute position and for inter-robot communication. Position information is obtained by triangulating the distance computed from synchronized ultrasound pulses from two fixed base stations. Inter-robot communication consists of locally broadcasting 6-byte messages at the rate of 1 Hz. The radios are particularly useful for transmitting any information that could not be reasonably sensed with the available on-board sensors, such as the external state of other robots (i.e. holding "food", finding home, etc.), which is required for social learning.

The robots are programmed in the Behavior Language, a parallel programming language based on the Subsumption Architecture (Brooks 1990, Brooks 1987). Their control systems are collections of parallel, concurrently active behaviors.

6   The Learning Environment

In order to make the learning task realistic, we tested the learning algorithms on robots situated in a foraging task, having a common higher-level goal of collecting "food" and taking it home during the "day" and sleeping at home at "night." Thus, the robots' world is a confined area which contains a fixed home region shared by all robots, and scaled so as to accommodate them, i.e. large enough for all of them to "park" for the night, with some

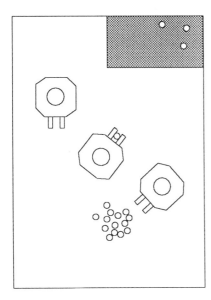

Figure 2: The experimental area in which the learning task was conducted. The home region is shaded. Pucks are clustered. The relative sizes of the environment and the robots are shown to scale.

reasonable amount of maneuvering (figure 2).

Food is clustered in a single location in the workspace. The clustered nature of the food certainly has an effect on what the optimal set of strategies will be for the collection task. We chose the single cluster arrangement for two reasons. First, clustering food gives incentive for the agents to cooperate and exchange information. If food were randomly scattered around the environment, there would be no point to communicating and social rules could be reduced to avoidance. Second, clustering food reduces the overall duration of each experimental run because the agents need to spend much less time looking for it. The complexity of the learning task is not diminished, but finite resources such as battery power are conserved by designing the experiment so as to maximize the relevance of the robots' interactions.

For the same reason, the chosen workspace is small enough to result in frequent interaction and interference between the robots in order to make learning possible.

The experimental environment is meant to loosely resemble a society that spends its days foraging (or hunting and gathering) by making repeated trips to a resource-rich area, getting the food, and taking it home. At fixed periods (meant to resemble night time), the society gathers at home and rests. Foraging activities resume at the beginning of each day.

7 The Learning Task

The task consisted of learning two social rules: 1) yielding and 2) communicating puck location. Sincy the rules

are not symmetric, they translate into four behaviors, two per social situation. Yielding consists of learning when to on one side give way and on the other keep going. Sharing information consists of learning when to broadcast position information when when to receive and store it.

The social rules are expressed within the robots' natural habitat and the context of their usual routines, in this case foraging. The foraging context was chosen because our previous work (Matarić 1992, Matarić 1993) provided the basic behavior repertoire to which social rules could easily be added. The built-in foraging behavior consists of a finite state controller which, in response to mutually-exclusive conditions consisting of internal state, activates appropriate basic behaviors from the robots' repertoire. The conditions include externally-triggered events, such as getting close to another robot or finding a puck, and internally-generated events, such as the the onset of night time, indicated by the internal clock. Basic behaviors include avoidance, dispersion, searching for pucks, picking up pucks, homing, and sleeping. Our earlier work has shown how foraging itself can be learned (Matarić 1994). This work demonstrates how it can be improved with social rules.

It is important to note that the alternative to behaving socially is not behaving randomly, but behaving greedily.[5] Thus, this learning task is realistic and difficult, since each agent is biased toward its built-in instinctive greedy and individualistic behavior which guarantees survival.[6]

In order to learn social rules, the behavior repertoire must include the appropriate social behaviors: yielding, proceeding, broadcasting, listening & storing, and observing & remembering, so that these behaviors would be tried and eventually have their conditions learned. Most of the above active behaviors did not require adding new abilities to the robots, since they already contained the necessary actions for each: yielding consists of stopping and waiting, and proceeding consists of going on with the current behavior. Non-active behavior requiring observation and storage were added exclusively for the social learning algorithms, but are based on the existing mechanism for sending and receiving messages already used for communicating positions of neighbors. The job of the learning algorithm was to correlate appropriate conditions for each of these behaviors in order to optimize the higher-level behavior, i.e. to maximize received reinforcement.

If this learning task could be set up as a simple search in the space of possible strategies, with highest reward for the strategies that result in highest efficiency of foraging, then it could be simply solved using game-

---

[5] Greediness is often the basis of antisocial behavior.

[6] No interpretation of basic human nature is implied or intended. Tendency toward friendliness can also be built-in but is not the goal of this experiment.

theoretic strategies that derived tit–for–tat related so-lutions. However, in the described domain, the agents cannot simply "search" the condition–behavior space be-cause they cannot directly and completely control events in the world. Instead, the world is stochastic, noisy and uncertain, and in particular it is made more complex by the presence of other learning agents. However, it is exactly their presence and the ways in which they inter-act that constitute relevant conditions for learning social rules.

We postulate the following three types of social knowl-edge and related reinforcement as necessary for learning the proposed social rules:

1. direct reinforcement,

2. observation of the behavior of other agents,

3. observation of reinforcement received by other agents.

The next section describes how this reinforcement was formally implemented.

8   Implementing Social Reinforcement

The learning algorithm produces and maintains a total order on the appropriateness of social behaviors asso-ciated with every condition, expressed as $A(c, b)$. As described earlier, the matrix of $A(c, b)$ values is not pro-hibitively large, since the number of relevant social con-ditions and behaviors is relatively small. The values in the correlation matrix fluctuate over time based on the received reinforcement, but the learning algorithm is ex-pected to converge on a stable ordering. At each point in time the value of $A(c, b)$ is the sum of all past rein-forcement R:

$$A(c, b) = \sum_{t=1}^{T} R(t)$$

The implementation of direct reinforcement is straightforward. A progress monitoring behavior con-stantly compares the agent's current state with its im-mediate goal. Whenever it detects progress (whether in terms of reaching a subgoal, as in the case of finding food, or in terms of diminishing the distance toward the goal, as in the case of going home), it gives a small reward to the most recently active social behavior.[7] Analogously, whenever a regress from the goal is detected, a small punishment is delivered. Formally:

$$D(t) = \begin{cases} m & \text{if progress is made} \\ n & \text{if regress is made} \\ 0 & \text{otherwise} \end{cases} \quad m > 0, \quad n < 0$$

---

[7]Note that only *social* behaviors are reinforced, since only social rules are being learned.

This algorithm is guaranteed to keep the learning sys-tem from settling in local minima, since the system con-tinuously adapts the correlation values with each re-ceived reinforcement. The algorithm relies on estimat-ing progress at least intermittently. If progress mea-surements are not available, and the reward function is an impulse at goal only, then the algorithm reduces to one–step temporal differencing (Sutton 1988), which has been proven to converge, however slowly. Given that most environments are not of this kind, this algorithm is bound to work faster. It has been successfully used to acquire the basic, greedy strategy for individual foraging (Mataric 1994).

The motivation for using progress estimators (also called internal critics) rather than a delayed reinforce-ment algorithm such as Q-learning comes from the non-Markovian uncertainty and inconsistency properties of the group situated agent domain. The reasoning is de-scribed in detail in Mataric (1994) but in short, progress estimators provide unbiased, principled reinforcement which is not so delayed as to become useless in a dy-namic environment.

Observational reinforcement, i.e. reinforcement for re-peating another agent's behavior is delivered in a similar form:

$$O(t) = \begin{cases} o & \text{if repeated observed behavior} \\ 0 & \text{otherwise} \end{cases} \quad o > 0$$

An agent receives positive reinforcement if it repeats the behavior it has most recently observed next time it finds itself in the same condition, unless it has already recently performed that behavior. $O(t)$ has a tempo-ral component. It expires after a fixed time so that the agent, in effect, forgets what it last saw if it has not seen it recently. This feature eliminates some cyclic behav-ior patterns between multiple learning agents observing each other.

Finally, vicarious reinforcement, i.e. reinforcement re-ceived based on that received by other agents, is delivered in the following form:

$$V(t) = \begin{cases} v & \text{if vicarious positive reinforcement} \\ w & \text{if vicarious negative reinforcement} \\ 0 & \text{otherwise} \end{cases}$$
$$v > 0, \quad w < 0$$

Vicarious reinforcement delivers a form of "shared" re-inforcement to all agents involved in a local social inter-action. By spreading individual reward or punishment over multiple agents, it serves to extend individual bene-fit beyond a single agent. As a consequence, the amount of reward received for social behaviors over time out-weighs that received for greedy strategies.

The complete reinforcement function then, is the sum of the subset of social reinforcement being used in the given learning experiment. Specific examples are given in the next section.

9   Learning Experiments

In a typical learning experiment all of the agents are endowed with identical basic behaviors and the social learning reinforcement function. They are started out from home at a beginning of a "day" and go about their foraging task as usual. The social learning algorithm is activated whenever an agent finds itself:

1. near a large amount of food away from home,

2. receiving an agent's message,

3. within observing range of another stopped agent,

4. within observing range of another moving agent,

5. within interference range of another stopped agent,

6. within interference range of another moving agent.

These conditions are specified by the designer in order to speed up the learning. They could be learned using one of the available statistical methods for state generalization (for example, Chapman & Kaelbling (1991) and Mahadevan & Connell (1991)) but the process could take almost as long as the social learning and is likely to suffer from sensory errors.

The first condition enables learning to communicate about sharable resources such as food. The last two conditions are based on two distance thresholds established a priori: $\delta_{observe}$ and $\delta_{interfere}$. In the basic foraging behavior, the presence of another agent within $\delta_{interfere}$ triggers avoidance. In the social learning algorithm, a social behaviors is attempted as an alternative.

Whenever an event occurs that makes one of the above conditions true, the current behavior the agent is executed is terminated and appropriate social reinforcement is delivered. Then, a new behavior is selected using the following strategy:

1. choose a recently observed behavior, if appropriate,

2. choose an untried social behavior,

3. choose the best behavior,

4. choose a random behavior (5% probability)

Given their confined physical work area, the agents interact enough to generate a plethora of events enabling social conditions. Consequently, we can observe learning in real time over the period of minutes.

10   Preliminary Results

As mentioned previously, the basic learning algorithm has been tested and shown to work both theoretically and practically, and the results are described in detail in Matarić (1994). Within an average fifteen minute trial

Condition	Behavior
finding food	broadcast
receiving a message	store location
near a stopped agent	proceed
near a moving agent	store behavior
too near a stopped agent	proceed
too near a moving agent	yield

Figure 3: The condition–behavior pairings of the desired social policy.

run the robots were able to learn foraging by learning to select appropriate individual behaviors for each state. The algorithm, however, did not allow for learning social rules, which is why social reinforcement was introduced.

We tested the following reinforcement functions:

1. $A_d(s, b, T) = \sum_{t=1}^{T} D(t)$

2. $A_{do}(s, b, T) = \sum_{t=1}^{T} (\alpha D(t) + \beta O(t))$

3. $A_{dov}(s, b, T) = \sum_{t=1}^{T} (\alpha D(t) + \beta O(t) + \gamma V(t))$

Weighting factors in learning rules are usually ad hoc. Our approach uses a simple scheme in which direct progress is weighted the highest, while observation-induced experience and vicarious reinforcement are weighted less. In the second set of experiments listed above we used:

$$\alpha + \beta = 1 \ and \ \alpha > \beta$$

In the third set we used:

$$\alpha + \beta + \gamma = 1 \ and \ \alpha > \beta \ and \ \beta = \gamma > \gamma$$

The relative effectiveness of the three reinforcement types was evaluated based on the portion of the social rule policy the algorithms learned. Figure 3 shows the condition–behavior pairings of the desired social policy.

The evaluation metrics used to compare the results of the different reinforcement were:

1. the percentage of the optimal social strategy the agents managed to learn,

2. the relative amount of time required to learn it.

Relative rather than absolute time is used because the duration of any learning run varies depending on the arrangement of the agents and the temporal distribution of their interactions. Consequently, exact time to convergence is not a valid evaluation metric in an event–driven situated environment of the kind we are using. Relative average time, on the other hand, gives us a measure of comparative effectiveness of different algorithms.

As a control experiment, we tested the performance of a pre-programmed foraging behavior that contained the

Reinforcement	Performance
$A_d(s, b, T)$	does not converge
$A_{do}(s, b, T)$	does not converge
$A_{dov}(s, b, T)$	converges

Figure 4: Comparative performance of different reinforcement functions.

Condition	Behavior
near a stopped agent	proceed
too near a stopped agent	proceed
receiving a message	store location
near a moving agent	store behavior
too near a moving agent	yield
finding food	broadcast

Figure 5: The Relative difficulty of each condition–action pair, in increasing order.

desired social rules, and compared it to the base case foraging. Not surprisingly, groups using social rules always outperformed groups with only greedy individual strategies. Thus, we were convinced that incentive for learning social rules did exist, and it was then a matter of finding out which reinforcement strategy makes it learnable in the given environment.

Figure 4 shows preliminary convergence results. Convergence is defined as learning the complete social policy. The results shown above are averaged over multiple trials and are qualitative because insufficient trials were run to perform accurate statistical analysis. However, results from the performed trials were consistent in that the first two strategies never converged, and learned only a very small part of the policy. The third strategy converted in all sufficiently long trials, i.e. some trials required up to 20 minutes to converge. Trial duration was not an issue in case of the other two reinforcement strategies, as they did not improve over time and uniformly failed to converge regardless of experiment duration.

Duration of learning was a direct effect of using physical hardware to run the learning experiments, since the domain was ridden with unavoidable intermittent error and noise. For instance, agents did not always behave consistently due to their inability to accurately sense external state. Such unavoidable (and undetectable) errors generated "unintentional deserters" in that robots experiencing sensor error (and in some cases radio transmission delay in communication) occasionally failed to behave socially. We found that these effects did not disable the learning algorithm, although they did slow it down, as described above. The basic learning algorithm is designed to adapt throughout the lifetime of an agent so learning does not suffer long–term consequences from intermittent errors.

In terms of speed of learning, the social condition–behavior pairs consistently ranked in the following increasing order of difficulty, as shown in figure 10. This ordering directly reflects the immediacy of the reward associated with each social behavior. The rules that produce the most immediate reward were learned the fastest. The social rule of sharing information about food was by far the hardest to learn, as the benefit to the agent had the least direct payoff. Consequently, it required multiple instances of observational reinforcement, which insti-

gated exploration of the behavior. If after attempting it, the agent could not received immediate vicarious reinforcement since other agents, who received the message, had not always learned to store and use the information, thus receiving positive reinforcement and passing it on to the agent who originally broadcast the information. This effect could be eliminated if agents were learning from experts, but we were interested in having social rules emerge in a homogeneous group.

The proposed observational and vicarious reinforcement strategies, coupled with direct reinforcement, were effective in enabling the learning of social rules, but their effectiveness varied depending on the rule being learned. This is not unexpected, since some rules are certainly harder than others. However, the difficult of certain learning problems, such as particularly altruistic social rules, indicates that those are best learned genetically. Data from biology seems to support this intuition, since animals do not appear to learn altruism toward their kin but instead are endowed with it (McFarland 1985).

All of the presented results are preliminary, and are only a glimpse at the wide variety of social rules that can be learned, and forms of social reinforcement that are worth exploring. In order to properly evaluate our theories, we are currently implementing a battery of tests which will produce an amount of learning data that allows us to draw conclusions that are statistically significant.

11   Summary and Continuing Work

This work has focused on learning social rules in situated multi–agent domains. We have studied the difficulty of learning behaviors which do not have direct benefit to the agent and therefore are in contradiction with its basic, greedy, survival instincts. We postulated three types of reinforcement that are useful and possibly necessary for learning such social rules. We then tested this postulate by applying an already effective situated learning algorithm to the social learning problem by adding the proposed types of reinforcement to it. We demonstrated the algorithms by implementing them on a group of four autonomous mobile robots capable of communication and cooperation and given the task of learning yielding and sharing information.

We are interested in expanding this work in a number of directions. In particular, it would be interesting to consider variations on the learning experiments, such as a gathering task with multiple food and home regions, in order to study what kinds of specializations emerge between agents and how those affect the resulting social rules. We would also like to test the presented social reinforcement strategies on quite different types of tasks in order to see how general they are. Another area we are interested in exploring is learning to distinguish what aspects of the situation (state) are relevant, in the context of learning relevant group sizes and dominance hierarchies. If this turns out to be difficult to learn it will give us an idea of what types of biases may be genetically programmed.

The work we have presented is very much in progress. The data for comparison and evaluation of the different learning strategies is still pending and is being gathered gradually. A full statistical analysis of a complete set of experiments is in order and is in preparation. We believe that the presented preliminary results give us new insight into how difficult certain types of social learning may be and how we may go about synthesizing it on artificial agents in order to study biological mechanisms of interaction and social learning.

Acknowledgements

The author wishes to thank Simon Goss and an anonymous reviewer for detailed helpful comments on an earlier draft of this paper.

The research reported here was done at the MIT Artificial Intelligence Laboratory. Support for this research was provided in part by the Jet Propulsion Laboratory contract 959333 and in part by the Advanced Research Projects Agency under Office of Naval Research grant N00014–91–J–4038.

References

Axelrod, R. (1984), *The Evolution of Cooperation*, Basic Books, New York.

Brooks, R. A. (1987), A Hardware Retargetable Distributed Layered Architecture for Mobile Robot Control, *in* 'IEEE International Conference on Robotics and Automation', Raleigh, NC, pp. 106–110.

Brooks, R. A. (1990), The Behavior Language; User's Guide, Technical Report AIM-1127, MIT Artificial Intelligence Lab.

Chapman, D. & Kaelbling, L. P. (1991), Input Generalization in Delayed Reinforcement Learning: An Algorithm and Performance Comparisons, *in* 'Proceedings, IJCAI-91', Sydney, Australia.

Chase, I. D. (1982), 'Dynamics of Hierarchy Formation: The Sequential Development of Dominance Relationships', *Behaviour* **80**, 218–240.

Chase, I. D. & Rohwer, S. (1987), 'Two Methods for Quantifying the Development of Dominance Heirarchies in Large Groups with Application to Harris' Sparrows', *Animal Behavior*.

Cheney, D. L. & Seyfarth, R. M. (1990), *How Monkeys See the World*, The University of Chicago Press, Chicago.

Chris Langton, e. (1989), *Artificial Life*, Addison-Wesley.

Davis, J. M. (1973), Imitation: A Review and Critique, *in* Bateson & Klopfer, eds, 'Perspectives in Ethology', Vol. 1, Plenum Press.

Deneubourg, J. L., Goss, S., Pasteels, J. M., Fresneau, D. & Lachaud, J. P. (1987), 'Self-Organization Mechanisms in Ant Societies, II: Learning in Foraging and Division of Labor', *From Individual to Collective Behavior in Social Insects* **54**, 177–196.

Durfee, E. H., Lee, J. & Gmytrasiewicz, P. J. (1993), Overeager Reciprocal Rationality and Mixed Strategy Equilibria, *in* 'Proceedings, AAAI-93', Washington, DC, pp. 225–230.

Fiority, G. & Scotto, P. (1992), 'Observational Learning in Octopus vulgaris', *SCI* **256**, 545–547.

Gasser, L. & N. Huhns, e. (1989), *Distributed Artificial Intelligence*, Pitman, London.

Gould, J. L. (1982), *Ethology; The Mechanisms and Evolution of Behavior*, W. W. Norton & Co., New York.

Huber, M. J. & Durfee, E. H. (1993), Observational Uncertainty in Plan Recognition Among Interacting Robots, *in* 'Proceedings, IJCAI-93 Workshop on Dynamically Interacting Robots', Chambery, France, pp. 68–75.

Kraus, S. (1993), Agents Contracting Tasks in Non-Collaborative Environments, *in* 'Proceedings, AAAI-93', Washington, DC, pp. 243–248.

MacLennan, B. J. (1990), Evolution of Communication in a Population of Simple Machines, Technical Report Computer Science Department Technical Report CS-90-104, University of Tennessee.

Maes, P. & Brooks, R. A. (1990), Learning to Coordinate Behaviors, *in* 'Proceedings, AAAI-91', Boston, MA, pp. 796–802.

Mahadevan, S. & Connell, J. (1991), Automatic Programming of Behavior-based Robots using Reinforcement Learning, *in* 'Proceedings, AAAI-91', Pittsburgh, PA, pp. 8–14.

Mataríc, M. J. (1992), Designing Emergent Behaviors: From Local Interactions to Collective Intelligence, *in* 'From Animals to Animats: International Conference on Simulation of Adaptive Behavior'.

Matarić, M. J. (1993), Kin Recognition, Similarity, and Group Behavior, *in* 'Proceedings of the Fifteenth Annual Conference of the Cognitive Science Society', Boulder, Colorado, pp. 705–710.

Matarić, M. J. (1994), Reward Functions for Accelerated Learning, *in* 'Proceedings, Eleventh International Conference on Machine Learning (ML-94)'.

McFarland, D. (1985), *Animal Behavior*, Benjamin Cummings.

McFarland, D. (1987), The Oxford Companion to Animal Behavior, *in* 'Oxford, University Press'.

Miceli, M. & Cesta, A. (1993), Strategic Social Planning: Looking for Willingness in Multi-Agent Domains, *in* 'Proceedings of the Fifteenth Annual Conference of the Cognitive Science Society', Boulder, Colorado, pp. 741–746.

Mitchell, R. W. (1987), A Comparative-Developmental Approach to Understanding Imitation, *in* Bateson & Klopfer, eds, 'Perspectives in Ethology', Vol. 7, Plenum Press.

Moore, B. R. (1992), 'Avian Movement Imitation and a new Form of Mimicry: Tracing the Evolution of a Complex Form of Learning', *Behavior* **122**, 614–623.

Sutton, R. (1988), 'Learning to Predict by Method of Temporal Differences', *The Journal of Machine Learning* **3**(1), 9–44.

Tomasello, M., Kruger, A. C. & Rather, H. H. (1992), 'Cultural Learning', *to appear in The Journal of Brain and Behavior Sciences*.

Signalling and Territorial Aggression: an investigation by means of synthetic behavioural ecology

Peter de Bourcier and Michael Wheeler
School of Cognitive and Computing Sciences
University of Sussex, BRIGHTON BN1 9QH, U.K.
E-Mail:peterdb@cogs.susx.ac.uk, michaelw@cogs.susx.ac.uk

Abstract

Intra-specific aggressive signalling is an adaptive behaviour which occurs throughout the animal kingdom. But the scientific understanding of such signalling is incomplete, partly because the relevant ecological factors are hard to isolate in highly complex natural environments. We perform a series of experiments in which populations of simulated animals (animats), with idealized sensory mechanisms, are placed in a simulated world in which there are aggressive confrontations over food. An individual animat's behaviour is determined by relatively simple relationships between the sensory information that it can pick up from its environment (including information about food and other animats) and its internal states (energy, hunger and aggression). When animats can sense the resource holding potential of other individuals within sensory range, there is evidence of a simple form of territoriality. To this ecological context, we introduce the signalling of aggressive intentions, and the possibility that some agents will be dishonest. Our analysis of subsequent experiments, in which we gradually increase the cost — in energy terms — of producing such signals, provides qualitative evidence that the handicap principle, according to which higher costs enforce honesty, can be applied to multi-agent, territorial situations. We conclude with a discussion of the scope and implications of our results.

1 Background and Rationale

Autonomous agent researchers interested in the issue of communication have tended to concentrate on the emergence of complex co-operative behaviours from simple signalling interactions between individuals (e.g., [11, 19]). This emphasis on 'acting together' is, of course, valuable and unsurprising, given the theoretical and practical benefits to be gained from the development of co-operative group-behaviour in populations of autonomous robots. But, in the natural world, communication for co-operation is just one possibility. Not all naturally-occurring communication-scenarios involve agents who are on 'the same side.' The paradigmatic cases of 'non-co-operative' communication occur in confrontations between aggressors (or between an aggressor and its chosen opponent), where the selfish goal of each participant is the personal control of some resource (e.g. a food supply or a mate).

In intra-specific aggressive encounters, the incidence of unrestrained, potentially damaging battles is relatively low [21]. Instead of all-out battles, such confrontations tend to revolve around 'ritualized' displays or signals which allow the contestants to conclude matters without the need for physical combat [6, 17]. Intra-specific aggressive communication evolves if, in conflict situations between members of a particular species, it is beneficial for a signalling animal to have an adversary make predictions about that signaller's subsequent behaviour [15]. Thus such signalling-behaviours are genuinely adaptive when, in a hostile, uncertain environment, their deployment increases the survival and reproductive prospects of the signalling animal via a net benefit gained through the responses of receivers.

However, the scientific account of biological signalling is incomplete. In a recent paper [13], Grafen and Johnstone conclude that the "existing body of [biological signalling] theory is probably too simple to be applied convincingly to any empirical example" (p.249). In part, at least, this 'gap' between our theoretical models and our empirical observations is due to our still limited understanding of the roles played by the ecological contexts in which the mechanisms for the production and receiving of signals have developed (cf. [9, 14, 29]). With this in mind, the investigation described in this paper can be conceptualized as an experiment in synthetic behavioural ecology, or 'SBE' for short (cf. the closely related concepts of 'synthetic ethology' [18] and 'computational neuroethology' [2, 4].) Our aim was to mount a qualitative investigation of the logic of aggressive signalling by allowing existing work in theoretical biology, ethology and behavioural ecology to inform the construction of a simple (although not trivial) simulated eco-system populated by artificial animals — henceforth *animats* [27] — who are competing for limited supplies of food. We create an ecological situation on the basis of which a minimal form of territoriality can be seen to emerge. Aggressive signalling is then introduced to this simple ecological context.

At the outset, we must stress that there is no suggestion that the SBE approach provides any easy answers to the difficult problems faced by biologists in this area. However, we hope that SBE will contribute to the debate. It is pitched at an intermediate level between, on the one hand, abstract theories based on mathematical models and, on the other hand, empirical observations in complex environments. All processes of scientific modelling make simplifying assumptions. In our SBE-model, perception and action, and the demands of the environment are highly idealized. In the context of adaptive behaviour research, these simplifications allow us to move more rapidly in the desire to confront artificial analogues of natural problems. But we remain fully aware of the limitations of minimally complex simulations [3, 5]. We discuss this question in section 6. Our claim is merely that SBE provides a new way of asking old questions and, in time, has the potential to find some new questions to ask.

2   Biological Context

Before we describe the simulation itself, we use this section to present the theoretical framework for the experimental model. All the key terms are defined, and our investigation is placed in context by means of a review of the debate in the biological literature over aggressive signalling. Of necessity, this review is brief and selective.

Aggression can be defined as the disposition to fight more intensely or for longer [24]. We treat aggression not as an end in itself, but as an adaptive phenomenon, the purpose of which is to win or defend a resource [10]. Aggressive signalling and aggressive communication occur in this context.

To ensure the basic applicability of our model, meanings were needed for the terms 'signalling' and 'communication' which were suitable within both SBE and real ethological/ecological situations. We adopted the following definitions: Consider two individuals, X and Y. A behaviour performed by X counts as a *signal* to Y when

1. the function of X's behaviour, explained in an evolutionary or intentional context, is to change the behaviour of Y, and

2. X's behaviour affects Y's dispositions to behave via Y's sensory mechanisms, and not by physical force. (This prevents the situation where one animal shoves another from counting as an example of signalling behaviour.)

So *communication* has taken place (in the relevant direction) when Y perceives, via its sensory mechanisms, the signalling behaviour of X, and that behaviour influences Y's disposition to behave. (We take these definitions to be equivalent to those offered in [21], and in the spirit of those adopted in [10].)

In the study of aggressive interactions, Parker [20] introduced the concept of an animal's 'resource holding potential' (RHP). This is defined by Maynard Smith [22] as "a measure of the capacity of an individual to hold a resource, which can be increased, if at all, only with a substantial cost in fitness" (p.2). Examples of RHP would include size and fighting ability. Signals which are biologically correlated with RHP have been dubbed *assessment signals* [25]. Such signals cannot be faked and are, therefore, reliable. But are all signals so reliable? In particular, should an animal be expected reliably to signal its 'intentions' — its local strategy for action from any specific moment until the end of the conflict?

Initially, game-theoretic models of biological signalling (e.g., [22]) supported the prediction that, in aggressive communications, animals should not be expected honestly to signal their intentions. The reasoning was that honest signalling of intentions was an evolutionarily unstable strategy. (An evolutionary stable strategy — 'ESS' — is a strategy which, when adopted by most members of a population, means that that population cannot be invaded by a rare alternative strategy [23].) A species adopting the honest signalling of aggressive intentions would not be stable against invasion by a mutant which consistently signalled the maximum commitment to an escalation of conflict, whatever that mutant's actual intentions. (For the remainder of this paper, we refer to such creatures as *bluffers.* If, in some population, signal A is usually followed by some action, *AA*, then any individual which gives A but does not intend to perform *AA* is a bluffer — cf. the notion of 'lying' in [22].)

As an alternative to the 'no signalling of intentions' view, Zahavi [28, 29, 30] offered the *handicap principle*, according to which the reliability of intention-signals could be increased if the animal, in some way, had to invest in those signals. The idea is that a signal which is 'wasteful' of energy is reliably predictive of the possession of energy, and hence enforces honesty [12]. Only if intention-signals were relatively 'cost-free' would they be open to exploitation by bluffers. Of course, all signals cost the signaller *something* in effort required to transmit information in an environment; but that is not the relevant cost. Reliable signals of aggressive intent must be more costly in fitness terms than they strictly need be merely to communicate unambiguously the information at issue. Moreover, the costs involved must be differential in that giving some signal indicating the intent to escalate to a particular level will be proportionally more costly to a weak individual than to a strong one. Zahavi's principles have received support from formal models developed within the game-theory paradigm [10, 12].

Territoriality provides a common context in which aggressive encounters occur, no matter what the specific function (e.g., feeding or reproduction) of a particular instance of territorial behaviour. Following Davies and Houston [8], we define a *territory* as "a more or less exclusive area defended by an individual or group" (p.148). Territories are not necessarily 'permanently fixed' in space. 'Floating territories' consist of well-defined defended areas which nevertheless fluctuate, sometimes because the substratum on which the animal depends moves (e.g., bitterlings who lay their eggs in the mantle cavities of live mussels), but sometimes even given a fixed substratum (e.g., ovenbirds, whose floating territories change from day to day, and even from hour to hour) [26].

The defence of a territory can involve an animal in dangerous border skirmishes. However, some territorial creatures evolve capacities for both the sending and the receiving of signals. As in the non-territorial case, these adaptations tend to result in a decrease in the frequency of unrestrained battles. But does the move to *territorial* aggression change the rules of the game, so to speak? McGregor [14] argues that because territorial signalling has evolved in the context of networks of many signalling and receiving individuals, territoriality provides a prime example of a context to which the standard theoretical models of dyadic aggressive communication are inapplicable. The reasons advanced for this are as follows:

1. Communication-behaviours geared towards territorial defence are often between neighbours. They are repeated interactions between individuals who, the evidence suggests [14], can identify each other. The standard models do not account for the effects of reidentifications, e.g., a difference in response based on whether the territory holding receiver has identified a neighbouring territory holder signalling from within its own boundaries, or a stranger signalling from that same spatial location.

2. At least some territorial animals appear to show the ability to estimate how far away a signaller is by means of signal amplitude and/or signal degradation. McGregor argues that such abilities can be used by a receiver in the territorial context to decide whether or not a signaller is inside or outside that receiver's territory.

3. In cases of long-range signalling, the multiple-agent context raises the possibility that a particular signal or interaction will be 'overheard' by another animal, and the information contained therein used by that 'eavesdropper' in its own interests.

Our experiment in SBE takes place against the background described in this section. We have used insights from the work described to guide the development of our model. But our results — described in later sections — also allow us to comment on the issues raised by the body of work in the biological sciences.

3   Experimental Model

We now describe the basic animat-environment system employed in our simulations. This initial model, in which there is no signalling of intentions, produces the results discussed in section 4. The crucial extension to the model, as far as the investigation of honest aggressive signalling is concerned, is introduced in section 5.

Our animats 'perceive' and 'act' in a two-dimensional, non-toroidal simulated world, 1000 by 1000 units square. (Each animat is round and 25 units in diameter.) The decision to make the environment non-toroidal is indicative of the fact that we were originally attracted to the issue of aggressive behaviour by Lorenz' seminal work on aggression in coral fish [17]. Many of the observations made by Lorenz were based on the behaviour of coral fish in captivity, i.e., fish tanks — clear cases of non-toroidal worlds. However, this feature of our SBE-environment does not mean that the system bears no relation to any naturally-occurring eco-system. There are often environmental borders which place restrictions on how far animals can/will travel (primarily changes of habitat); our simulation merely reflects this fact.[1]

The world is effectively continuous. This is in contrast to the cellular environments originally favoured in simulations such as [27], in which an animat occupies one cell on a rectangular grid, and moves from cell to cell. Discrete cellular environments, whilst useful, introduce severe limitations into the dynamics of perception and action [3, 5].

In our simulation, an animat's environment consists of food, plus other animats of the same species.[2] Each animat may move in any one of 36 directions corresponding to a full circle in 10 degree divisions about its current position. Movement takes place in response to sensory information gleaned from the environment via two sensory modalities. Both senses are distal, but have different ranges. The first — which we think of as idealized 'vision' — provides information about other animats, and has a range of 350 units. The second — which we think of as idealized 'olfaction' — provides information about food,

---

[1]Historical anecdote: The influence of Lorenz' coral fish studies is also to be found in the fact that, when we began our work, we referred to the animats as 'the fish.' We toyed with the idea of calling them 'aquamats' for 'artificial aquatic animals' — apologies to Stewart Wilson — but decided against it when the simulation developed further and became less maritime.

[2]For the purposes of this paper, we hold that members of the same species are identified purely by phenotypic similarity in sensory-motor capacities.

and has a range of 100 units. The visual system (figure 1) is simulated using ray-tracing graphics, and is based on a 36-pixel eye providing information in a full 360 degree radius around the animat. The value of each pixel is a real number in the range 0 to 1, and corresponds to the proportion of that pixel's receptive field containing other animats. The olfactory system employs principles similar to those used for vision, the only difference being that food particles are treated as point sources.

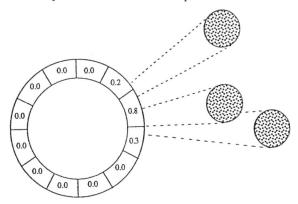

Figure 1: The animats' visual system illustrated, for clarity, with a 12 pixel 360 degree eye rather than the 36 pixel 360 degree eye which was actually used in the model. If a more distant animat within visual range is partly obscured by a nearer animat, only the non-obscured part of that more distant individual will have an effect on the pixel value for that direction.

To create the initial environment, 'food' is introduced into the world in the form of randomly distributed food particles, each carrying an energy value. An animat 'eats' any food particle on which it lands, and the energy value of the particle is then transferred to the animat, incrementing that animat's energy level. If an animat lands on more than one particle of food at a time, its intake is restricted to one unit. In order to replenish the resource, new food particles are added to the world (again with random distribution) at each time-step. The number of new particles to be added is set by the user, but the resource is 'capped' so that the food supply is never more plentiful than at the beginning of the run.

The initial population is created by placing a number of animats at randomly chosen positions in the world (figure 2). Each individual begins life with the same energy level. But animats lose energy in a number of different ways. If an animat's energy level sinks to 0, then that creature is deemed to have died. Under these circumstances, it is removed from the world. Energy is lost for the following reasons:

1. *Being Alive:* At each time-step, a small 'existence-cost' is deducted from the energy level of each surviving animat.

2. *Movement:* When an animat moves in any one of the

36 possible directions, it incurs a movement-cost. If an animat's chosen direction of movement is blocked by the edge or the corner of the world, then no move is made and no movement-cost is deducted from its energy level.

3. *Reproduction:* If an animat becomes very strong (has a high energy level), then it will 'asexually reproduce.' The offspring — an only child placed randomly in the world — is given the same initial energy level as each member of the population had at the start of the run, and the corresponding amount of energy is deducted from the parent. (So, as well as being decreased by deaths, population size can increase.)

4. *Fighting:* Fights occur when animats touch. Such 'physical' combat results in a large reduction in the energy levels of the participants.

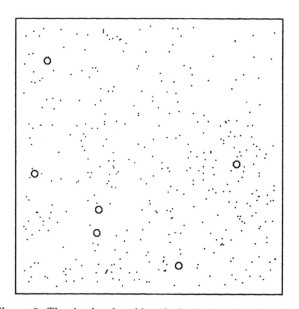

Figure 2: The simulated world at the beginning of a typical run. The particles of food are shown as dots, and the animats are shown as circles. Both food particles and animats are placed randomly.

Due to the relatively hostile nature of the ecological niche, food-finding is an essential task. To encourage this behaviour, each animat has a hunger-level — its desire to move towards food — which, at any time step, is the difference between the maximum individual energy level possible (= value at which reproduction takes place), and that animat's current energy level.

Given the fact that the food supply is limited, the members of the population are in intra-specific competition for access to the available resources. Each animat has a level of aggression which controls its general disposition to approach and to attack other individuals in its visual field. Each animat's aggression varies dynamically as a function of individual energy level and recent individual history. If a particular animat moves in an aggressive manner (i.e., directly towards another individual) its level of aggression is reduced by an amount proportional to the previous value. This prevents aggressive animats from chasing less aggressive members of the population all over the world, only to commit eventual suicide through exhaustion.[3] A non-aggressive movement results in an increment to an animat's aggression-level, by an amount corresponding to a small proportion of that individual's energy level. The net effect of all this is that an animat with a high energy level can regain a high aggression-level quite soon after an aggressive encounter. For a low-energy individual, the process will take longer, meaning that weaker individuals are less likely to involve themselves in potentially fatal, premature battles.

This model of aggression is not equivalent to the controversial Lorenzian account, according to which aggression is essentially a 'spontaneous appetite' which inevitably finds expression [1, 17, 26]. An animat's disposition to respond aggressively towards other animats increases with time in the absence of aggressive encounters. (There is some evidence for this tendency in certain animals, e.g., Siamese fighting fish [16].) But our animats do not 'actively seek fights' and the disposition to behave aggressively does not inevitably 'find expression.' For any particular animat, the stimulus provided by a second animat within visual range is required to trigger aggressive behaviour. In the natural world, a particular aggressive encounter may well have a context-sensitive mixture of positive and negative consequences for the likelihood of subsequent aggressive behaviours [16], but this complexity is beyond the scope of the current simulation.

At each time-step, the direction in which each animat will move is calculated using the following probability equation:

$$p(d) = \frac{h.s(d) + a.v(d) + t(o).v(o) + c}{\sum_{i=1}^{36}(h.s(d_i) + a.v(d_i) + t(o_i).v(o_i) + c)}$$

where $p(d)$ is the probability that the particular animat will move in the direction d; h is the animat's hunger-level; $s(d)$ is the value returned by the olfactory system in direction d; a is the animat's aggression-level; $v(d)$ is the value returned by the visual system for direction d; o is the direction 180 degrees off d — i.e., in the opposite direction to d; $t(o)$ is the threat that the animat perceives from other animats from the opposite direction to d — what information constitutes the 'perceived threat'

varies according to the scenario — see later sections; $v(o)$ is the value returned by the visual system in the opposite direction to d; and c is a small constant which prevents zero probabilities.

The basic effects of this equation, for some animat F, are :-

- If there are no other animats in F's visual field, and no food within F's olfactory range, then F will make a random movement.

- If F can sense food, and F is hungry, then the probability of F moving in the direction of that food is proportional to F's degree of hunger.

- If there are other animats in F's visual field, then the probability that F will move in the direction of another animat is proportional to F's aggression-level. But F is also likely to move in the opposite direction (away from the other animat) with a probability proportional to the threat which F perceives from that animat. So, for example, if F is averagely aggressive, and perceives another animat as being a threat, then F is more likely to retreat rather than to attack, whilst, if F is very aggressive, and perceives the other animat as posing little threat, then F is more likely to attack than to retreat.

4   Scenario 1: Territoriality

In the first scenario, the animats are able to sense directly the energy levels of other individuals within visual range; that is, the level of threat emanating from a particular direction is determined by the energy levels of the potential adversaries who are visible in that direction. Because the cost of fighting is a large deduction in energy level, the animats pick up values which are correlated with — and therefore reliable indicators of — RHP. This is equivalent to each animat producing assessment signals at no cost to fitness.

The values of the various parameters were set (largely as a result of trial and error) as follows: initial supply of food = 400 particles; initial size of population = 6; initial energy level = 300; energy level at which reproduction takes place = 1000; initial hunger level = 700; initial level of aggression = 500; energy value of 1 particle of food = 45; rate of food replenishment = a maximum of 16 particles per time-step; existence-cost = 1; movement-cost = 3; cost of fighting = 100 units of energy per time-step of fight; cost of making an aggressive movement = one-tenth of previous aggression-level; increment to aggression-level after a non-aggressive movement = an amount corresponding to one-hundredth of current energy level; constant preventing zero probabilities = 1.

The qualitative behaviour of the population of animats, over time, can be divided into two qualitatively distinct phases. For the parameter-settings detailed above,

---

[3]In the interests of increased biological realism, when an animat makes an aggressive movement, its aggression-level should be lowered only if its potential opponent retreats. We intend to incorporate this modification into our simulation when the work is extended further.

these behavioural phases were observed in every run, no matter what the (randomly chosen) starting positions of the various animats — the members of the initial population and the subsequent offspring — or the (randomly chosen) distribution of food.

1. *Settling Down:* During this first phase, there is no stable global structure to the patterns of interactions between the animats. It is relatively common for the observer to witness pursuit-style interactions in which a stronger, aggressive individual chases a weaker, more timid, retreating individual through the world (figure 3).

2. *The Development of Structured Interactions:* Eventually the interactions develop a discernible global pattern. This phase is characterized by the fact that individual animats tend to move around within more or less exclusive areas which they will defend against intruders or potential intruders.

We feel confident in calling the behaviours exhibited during the second phase *territorial*. Two distinct types of low-level aggressive encounter punctuate the overall stability: *border skirmishes* in which one animat moves aggressively in order to chase away an approaching intruder (figure 4), and *oscillatory behaviours* in which two well-matched animats move back and forth, as if respecting some mid-placed border between their respective domains (figure 5). It is also possible for the interactions to settle into a highly stable, global pattern in which individuals move within entirely exclusive areas. These equilibrium states feature very few radical movements by neighbouring individuals (figure 6). We have observed stable patterns in worlds with up to 8 concurrently existing individuals. The birth of a new individual tends to destabilize matters until a new equilibrium emerges.

We do not claim that the interactions in our simulation display the richness evident in most naturally-occurring territorial behaviour. For instance, our animats do not mark their domains in the style of dogs. Nevertheless, it is significant that global dynamics of a distinctly territorial nature can arise on the basis of locally defined relationships between resource-distribution, the survival needs of individuals and idealized perception. Notice that the observed behaviour cannot be analysed entirely non-territorially, either as simply the stronger animats chasing away any weaker animat which comes towards them, or as something like 'individual distance fighting' [7]. The defence-behaviour is correlated with the distribution of food. If an individual finds itself in an area with a relatively poor supply of food, it will not only tend to wander away from that area, but also will be less likely to defend the patch against potential intruders. So the territories, such as they are, are essentially individual feeding-grounds. These can sometimes take the form of floating territories (see section 2). In a speculative frame of mind, we believe that general principles similar to the ones adopted in this system may have the potential to account for territorial behaviour in some creatures, such as certain species of fish.

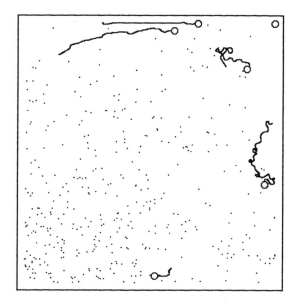

Figure 3 — Pursuit: The displays in figures 3-6 show the final position of each animat at the end of the selected time intervals, together with trails of each animat's movements during that period. The trace above shows 64 frames of movement captured during the first phase of a run from the first scenario. A pursuit can be seen in the behaviour of the two animats at the top of the world.

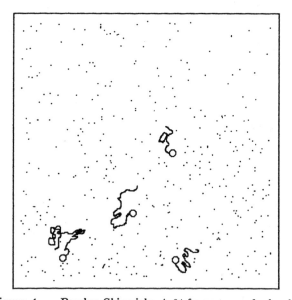

Figure 4 — Border Skirmish: A 64 frame trace of a border skirmish occurring during the second phase of a run from the first scenario. A strong animat in the bottom left hand corner has its territory momentarily violated by an intruder from the centre of the world. The defending animat makes an aggressive move towards the intruder, which retreats.

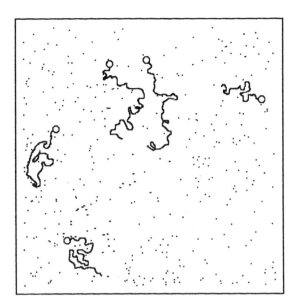

Figure 5 — **Oscillatory Behaviour:** A 128 frame trace of oscillatory behaviour during the second phase of a run from the first scenario. The two well-matched neighbours in the top-middle tend to oscillate in time with each other, apparently about some mid-placed boundary.

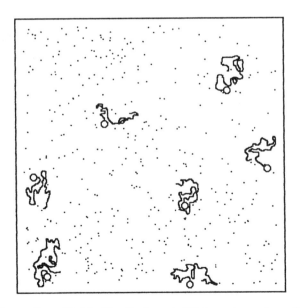

Figure 6 — **Stable Territories:** A 128 frame trace, from the second phase of a run from the first scenario. The seven animats have formed a stable pattern of behaviour in which there are no aggressive encounters.

The minimalist nature of our approach means that our animats do not build maps of their domains of influence or, indeed, have any objective record of where they are, or where they have been. In fact, in this eco-system, there are no fixed environmental landmarks, the identification of which would enable the animats to make such decisions. One possible tactic would be for an animat to calculate its coordinate position in relation to the edges of the world. But such a tactic is impossible in this simulation, because the visual system employed does not allow the animats to see the edges of the world. In any case, such a calculation would require each animat to possess sophisticated processing mechanisms, the like of which we have excluded from our model.[4]

5 Scenario 2: Testing the Handicap Principle

At the next stage of the investigation, we introduced the signalling of aggressive intentions. The aim was to test whether or not the handicap principle would hold in the simulated ecological context of minimal territoriality through aggressive competition for food.

The animat visual systems are now 'retuned' so that they pick up not the RHP of an animat within range, but a value indicating, to the perceiver, a visible animat's aggression-level, i.e., its disposition towards fighting. Here we make an important simplifying assumption. We assume that the animats' perception-action systems are no longer responsive to indicators of RHP, but now react solely to aggression-signals. Such signals (which now provide the threat-values for the movement equation) are displays for which the signalling animats have to pay a cost via a deduction from their energy levels. This cost increases as the value of the aggression-value signalled increases, so that it costs more in energy to make a more aggressive signal. (As what is being signalled is supposed to be an indicator of willingness to fight, a disposition which will vary dynamically over time, it is appropriate that what is taxed is the capacity to wage battle which, in this model, is correlated directly with energy. Costs paid in natural environments may be more complex although some notion of an 'appropriate link' still seems to apply [9].)

In our scenario, individuals produce signals indicating aggressive intent whenever they can see another animat. Some individuals — *truth-tellers* — always signal a value which accurately reflects their aggression-level, and they pay the corresponding cost in energy. However, we also introduce other individuals — *bluffers* — who sometimes 'lie' by signalling an aggression-level higher than

---

[4]Although some animals may (possibly) possess internally stored maps and objective personal records, we are far from convinced that anything like a majority do. We certainly did not want to make such an assumption at the outset, given the rationale of our investigation.

that which they actually possess. The exact value of the signal is chosen, at random, from a value somewhere between their true aggression and an upper bound (here 500 units above actual aggression). Bluffers pay the cost appropriate for the aggression-level signalled. In our experiments, bluffers lie, on average, for fifty percent of the time, and individuals always produce offspring who adopt the parental strategy i.e., bluffers produce bluffers.

The experimental method adopted was to create an initial population made up of equal numbers of truth-tellers and bluffers. The relative adaptive success of truth-tellers and bluffers was then assessed by recording, as the scenario unfolded through time, the total energy present in the two groups — including any offspring. (At time = 0, the total energy levels will, of course, be equal.) The control-parameters described in section 4 were set at the same values for the second set of experiments as were used in the first, and the same movement equation was used. Once again the food particles, the members of the initial population, and any offspring were placed randomly. The cost of signalling (units of energy deducted per unit of aggression signalled) is set at the start of each run.

The second scenario exhibited qualitatively similar global dynamics as were observed in the first scenario (the phase 1 to phase 2 transition), but with fewer prolonged pursuits. The two distinct phases of behaviour continued to occur in every run, no matter what the cost of signalling. (The only exception is when the cost of signalling is increased to such an extent that both truth-tellers and bluffers quickly die out.) On the basis of this ecological situation, we set about testing the handicap principle.

Experiment 1: Low Signalling-Cost: The cost of aggressive signalling was set very low — 0.0001 units of energy deducted per unit of aggression signalled. We allowed that there must be *some* cost in energy involved in transmitting such a signal at all. The results of one representative run are shown in figure 7. It is clear from this graph of total energy against time, that in this specific run, bluffers outperformed truth-tellers. The energy level of the bluffing group quickly rises above that of the truth-telling group, and, apart from one period (approx. t = 300 to t = 450), during which the bluffers were losing their relative advantage, that superiority is maintained until the truth-tellers die out (total energy = 0). The *qualitative aspects* of this result were in evidence in *all* runs based on such a low cost of signalling. These results indicate that, *in this simple eco-system*, if there is a very low cost to signalling aggressive intentions, honest signalling of aggressive intentions is not an ESS, as a truth-telling population could be invaded by a bluffing mutant. Honesty is not the best policy.

Experiment 2: Medium Signalling-Cost: The cost of aggressive signalling was set to 0.003 units of energy deducted per unit of aggression signalled. Figure 8 shows the results of one representative medium-cost run. In this case, the overall similarity in the energy-histories of the truth-telling and bluffing groups suggests that, despite occasional periods of divergence, the two groups are coexisting and surviving equally well in the environment.

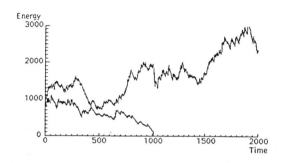

Figure 7 — Low Cost Signalling: The total energy levels of the two groups are plotted against time. The upper plot represents the bluffers, whilst the lower represents the truth-tellers.

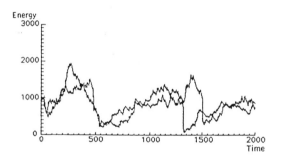

Figure 8 — Medium Cost Signalling: The two total-energy plots tend to be very close together.

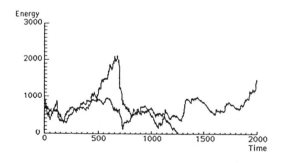

Figure 9 — High Cost Signalling: The upper plot represents the total-energy of the truth-telling group, whilst the lower represents that of the bluffers.

Experiment 3: High Signalling-Cost: The cost of aggressive signalling was set to 0.006 units of energy deducted per unit of aggression signalled. Figure 9 shows the results of one representative high-cost run. Now, with a higher signalling cost, the truth-tellers are the dominant group. It is no longer beneficial to bluff, because the energy-cost incurred through such behaviour is prohibitive. Although the traces are less distinct during the earlier stages of the run than in the low-cost case, truth-tellers generally maintain an advantage in terms of relative total-energy possessed by the two groups. The bluffers eventually die out, leaving the world to the truth-tellers. The same qualitative pattern was observed in all runs which featured this high-level of cost. This indicates that, in this eco-system, if a higher cost has to be paid to signal aggressively, the honest signalling of intentions is an ESS. Thus a high cost to signalling appears to enforce honesty, in exactly the way that Zahavi originally predicted, and the handicap principle seems to have been vindicated.

6 Discussion

As stressed at the beginning of this paper, we have undertaken our experiment in SBE with our eyes wide open to the potential shortcomings of simulated environments. But without wishing to claim, for one moment, that the issues raised in our simple eco-system are the same as those faced in natural environments, we have several good reasons to claim that our model avoids some of the most serious criticisms of such work, such as those levelled in [5]. We have not used a coarse cellular grid as the space in which our animats perceive and act. Our animats expend energy as they act, and hence need access to food-resources in order to survive. So we have not assumed that our animats can act without using up their available energy, or exist without replenishing that energy. Moreover, the animats we have described are not solitary foragers. Each individual exists in an environment in which the dynamics are made relatively complex by the behaviour of other animats. For these reasons, we have some confidence that our results will generalize to other synthetic eco-systems.

We have shown by empirical demonstration that results qualitatively similar to those predicted by Zahavi's handicap principle can emerge in a simple eco-system populated by individuals whose aggression-levels vary dynamically over time as a result of their food-intake and activity. The continuous variation in degrees of 'hawkishness' and 'dove-ishness' exhibited by each individual increases the complexity of the ecological niche, as do the continuous variation in degree of bluffing, and the probabilistic nature of the behaviour. The logic of aggressive communication, as identified in dyadic confrontations, carries over into this multi-agent environment in which a minimal form of territorial behaviour is common. And

although we hesitate to draw too wide a conclusion, such a result tends to suggest that McGregor's claim — that the territorial context affects, fundamentally, the logic of such interactions — may be premature. Of course, McGregor's observations were based on a more complex territoriality. For example, we have not allowed for the reidentification of individuals. However, our animat's visual system does provide an implicit distance estimate of sorts; within certain limits, nearer individuals will produce a higher pixel value for the relevant direction, and values in a larger number of pixels. Also notice that the behaviour of an animat which 'oversees' a battle will be affected by that battle's outcome. For instance, an averagely aggressive animat which is within visual range of a fight will tend to pursue the weaker or less aggressive of the two combatants in the aftermath. Whilst this behaviour is indicative of quite complex multi-agent dynamics, we do not claim that it is equivalent to the 'overhearing' of signalling interactions.

There are myriad ways in which this work can be extended. The general habitat, the communication-mechanisms, and, hence, the resulting territoriality, need to be made more complex to produce more penetrating insights. In addition, we need to carry out an analysis of the changes which occur in the global ecological dynamics when we vary parameters other than the cost of signalling. But we believe that our minimal beginnings may have opened-up another space in which fruitful interactions between the biological sciences and the adaptive behaviour community can take place.

Acknowledgements

Peter de Bourcier is supported by the States of Jersey Education Committee. Michael Wheeler is supported by British Academy award no. 92/1693. Many thanks to Dave Cliff, Inman Harvey, Phil Husbands and Geoffrey Miller for valuable discussions during the preparation of this paper. We would also like to thank our anonymous reviewers for their helpful comments and suggestions.

References

[1] J. Archer. *The Behavioural Biology of Aggression.* Cambridge University Press, Cambridge, 1988.

[2] R. Beer. *Intelligence as Adaptive Behaviour: An Experiment in Computational Neuroethology.* Academic Press, San Diego, California, 1990.

[3] R. Brooks. Artificial life and real robots. In F. J. Varela and P. Bourgine, editors, *Toward a Practice of Autonomous Agents: Proceedings of the first European Conference on Artificial Life*, pages 3–10, Cambridge, Massachusetts, 1992. MIT Press / Bradford Books.

[4] D. Cliff. Computational neuroethology: a provisional manifesto. In J.-A. Meyer and S. W. Wilson, editors, *From Animals to Animats: Proceedings of the First International Conference on Simulation of Adaptive Behaviour*, Cambridge, Massachusetts, 1991. M.I.T. Press / Bradford Books.

[5] D. Cliff and S. Bullock. Adding "foveal" vision to Wilson's animat. *Adaptive Behaviour*, 2:49–72, 1993.

[6] T.H. Clutton-Brock and S.D. Albon. The roaring of red deer and the evolution of honest advertisement. *Behaviour*, 69(145-170), 1979.

[7] P. J. Conder. Individual distance. *The Ibis*, 91:649–55, 1949.

[8] N.B. Davies and A.I. Houston. Territory economics. In J.R. Krebs and N.B. Davies, editors, *Behavioural Ecology — An Evolutionary Approach*, chapter 6, pages 148–169. Blackwell, Oxford, second edition, 1984.

[9] M. Stamp Dawkins. Are there general principles of signal design? *Philosophical Transactions of the Royal Society: Biological Sciences*, 340:251–255, 1993.

[10] M. Enquist. Communication during aggressive interactions with particular reference to variation in choice of behaviour. *Animal Behaviour*, 33:1152–1161, 1985.

[11] S. Goss, J.L. Deneubourg, R. Beckers, and J.-L. Henrotte. Recipes for collective movement. In *Proceedings of the Second European Conference on Artificial Life*, pages 400–410, 1993.

[12] A. Grafen. Biological signals as handicaps. *Journal of Theoretical Biology*, 144:517–546, 1990.

[13] A. Grafen and R.A. Johnstone. Why we need ESS signalling theory. *Philosophical Transactions of the Royal Society: Biological Sciences*, 340:245–250, 1993.

[14] P.K. Mc Gregor. Signalling in territorial systems: a context for individual identification, ranging and eavesdropping. *Philosophical Transactions of the Royal Society: Biological Sciences*, 340(1292):237–244, 1993.

[15] D.G.C. Harper. Communication. In J.R. Krebs and N.B. Davies, editors, *Behavioural Ecology — An Evolutionary Approach*, chapter 12, pages 374–397. Blackwell, Oxford, 3rd edition, 1991.

[16] R. A. Hinde. *Animal Behaviour — a Synthesis of Ethology and Comparative Psychology*. McGraw-Hill, London and New York, 2nd edition, 1970.

[17] K. Lorenz. *On Aggression*. Methuen, London, 1966.

[18] B. MacLennan. Synthetic ethology: an approach to the study of communication. In C.G. Langton, C. Taylor, J.D. Farmer, and S. Rasmussen, editors, *Artificial Life II. SFI Studies in the Science of complexity*, volume X, pages 631–658. Addison-Wesley, 1991.

[19] M.J. Mataric and M.J. Marjanovic. Synthesizing complex behaviors by composing simple primitives. In *Proceedings of the Second European Conference on Artificial Life*, pages 698–707, 1993.

[20] G.A. Parker. Assessment strategy and the evolution of fighting behaviour. *Journal of Theoretical Biology*, 47:223–243, 1974.

[21] M. Ridley. *Animal Behaviour: a concise introduction*. Blackwell Scientific Publications, Oxford, England, 1986.

[22] J. Maynard Smith. Do animals convey information about their intentions? *Journal of Theoretical Biology*, 97:1–5, 1982.

[23] J. Maynard Smith. *Evolution and the Theory of Games*. Cambridge University Press, 1982.

[24] J. Maynard Smith and D.G.C. Harper. The evolution of aggression. *Philosophical Transactions of the Royal Society*, 319:557–570, 1988.

[25] J. Maynard Smith and G.A. Parker. The logic of asymmetric contests. *Animal Behaviour*, 42:159–175, 1976.

[26] E. O. Wilson. *Sociobiology: The New Synthesis*. Harvard University Press, Cambridge, Massachusetts, 1975.

[27] S. W. Wilson. Knowledge growth in an artificial animal. In J. J. Grefenstette, editor, *Proceedings of an International Conference on Genetic Algorithms and their Applications*, pages 16–23, Pittsburg, PA and Hillsdale, New Jersey, 1985. Lawrence Erlbaum Associates.

[28] A. Zahavi. Mate selection — a selection for a handicap. *Journal of Theoretical Biology*, 53:205–214, 1975.

[29] A. Zahavi. The cost of honesty (further remarks on the handicap principle). *Journal of Theoretical Biology*, 67:603–605, 1977.

[30] A. Zahavi. The fallacy of conventional signalling. *Philosophical Transactions of the Royal Society: Biological Sciences*, 340:227–230, 1993.

Integration of Reactive and Telerobotic Control in Multi-agent Robotic Systems

Ronald C. Arkin and Khaled S. Ali

Mobile Robot Laboratory

College of Computing

Georgia Institute of Technology

Atlanta, GA, USA 30332-0280

e-mail: arkin@cc.gatech.edu, kali@cc.gatech.edu

Abstract

Multi-agent schema-based reactive robotic systems are complemented with the addition of a new behavior controlled by a teleoperator. This enables the whole society to be affected as a group rather than forcing the operator to control each agent individually. The operator is viewed by the reactive control system as another behavior exerting his/her influence on the society as a whole. Simulation results are presented for foraging, grazing, and herding tasks. Teleautonomous operation of multi-agent reactive systems was demonstrated to be significantly useful for some tasks, less so for others.

1 Introduction

Reactive multi-agent robotic societies can be potentially useful for a wide-range of tasks. This includes operations such as foraging and grazing (e.g., [1,9,6]) which have applicability in service (vacuuming and cleaning), industrial (assembly) and military (convoy and scouting) scenarios.

Although promising results have been achieved in these systems to date, purely reactive systems can still benefit from human intervention. Many purely reactive systems are myopic in their approach: they sacrifice global knowledge for rapid local interaction. Global information can be useful and it is in this capacity that a teleoperator can interact with a multi-agent control system.

A related problem in teleoperation is that a human operator is potentially overwhelmed by the large amount of data required to control a multi-agent system in a dynamic environment. This phenomenon is referred to as cognitive overload. The approach described in this paper provides a mechanism to significantly reduce the teleoperator's cognitive and perceptual load by allowing the reactive system to deal with each robot's local control concerns. Two principal mechanisms to achieve this are by allowing the operator to act either as a constituent behavior of the society or to allow him/her to supervise the societal behavioral sets and gains, acting only as needed based upon observable progress towards societal task completion.

In this research, the teleoperator is allowed to control whole societies of agents; not one robot at a time, but rather controlling global behavior for the entire multi-agent system. This is a straightforward extension of our work in both multi-agent robotic systems [1] and teleautonomy [2]. The end product is a simple way for a commander to control large numbers of constituent elements without concern for low-level details (which each of the agents is capable of handling by themselves). In essence, the teleoperator is concerned with global social *strategies* for task completion, and is far less involved with the specific behavioral tactics used by any individual agent.

2 Single agent teleautonomous control

Our previous results [2] in the integration of reactive and telerobotic control in the context of single agents provide the basis for our extension of this concept into multi-agent societies. In this earlier work we have shown that a teleoperator can interact with a reactive robot in at least two different ways:

- **Teleoperator as a schema**: Here the human acts as an additional behavior in the already existing collection of behaviors that are active within the robot. Using a schema-based methodology [3], each active behavior contributes a vector that is related to the agent's intentions - such as to get to a particular object, not crash into something, etc. The teleoperator's intentions are introduced at the same level - as another schema contributing forces in the same manner as all the other behaviors do.

- **Teleoperator as a supervisor**: In this case, the teleoperator changes the behavioral settings of the robot as it moves through the world, essentially changing its "personality". For example, the robot can become more aggressive by increasing its attraction towards a desirable object or decreasing its repulsion from obstacles.

In schema-based reactive control [3], each active behavior (schema) provides its own reaction to the environment by creating a vector response to a specific perceptual stimulus. The entire set of vector outputs created by all active schemas is summed and normalized and then transmitted to the robot for execution. No arbitration is involved, rather a blending of all active concurrent behaviors occurs. The system at this level is completely reactive, not retaining knowledge of the world or the agent's past performance.

3   Multi-agent Teleautonomous Control

Our laboratory is conducting extensive research in multi-agent robotic systems [1,4,5] both in simulation and on our 3 Denning Mobile Robots. Robotic systems are specified as a finite state acceptor that specifies the behavioral (schema) assemblages [7,8] and the transitions between them. An example state machine for a foraging task appears in Figure 1. In this figure there exist three distinct high-level behavioral states for each agent:

- *Wander* - which consists of a high gain and long persistence **noise** schema that is used to produce wandering while having moderate inter-robot repulsion to produce dispersion coupled with significant obstacle repulsion (**avoid-static-obstacle** schemas).

- *Acquire* - which consists of using a **move-to-goal** schema to move towards a detected or reported attractor (depending on the communication strategy used [4]) with a reduced inter-robot repulsion to allow for multi-robot convergence on attractors and continued obstacle avoidance (again provided by the **avoid-static-obstacle** schema). A small amount of **noise** is still injected into the system to facilitate navigation [3].

- *Deliver* - which occurs after acquisition of the attractor and results in delivery of the object back to home base by one or more agents. The same behaviors are used as in the *acquire* state with the goal location now being the home base.

Space prevents a full discussion of the mechanisms for reactive multi-agent control. The interested reader is referred to [1,4] for more information.

3.1   Implementation

In the results presented below, teleoperation is implemented as an additional schema in the system (the teleoperator as a schema approach). Based on the

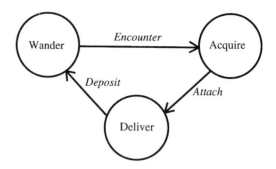

Figure 1: Behavioral States for Foraging Task

instructions of a human agent, the **teleautonomy** schema contributes a vector in the same way as do the other schemas, such as **move-to-goal** or **avoid-static-obstacle**. Unlike the other schemas, however, which produce different vectors for each robot, the **teleautonomy** schema produces the same output for all of the robots. Thus, if the human agent tells the robots to go north, then all the robots receive the same instructions. The vector produced by the **teleautonomy** schema is summed with the vectors produced by the other schemas in each agent to produce a combined vector which determines the overall direction and rate of travel of the robot. In this way, the robots use environmental knowledge provided by the human agent in conjunction with their other goals, such as not to collide with obstacles or each other, rather than having the teleoperator's goals completely override the robots' other behaviors.

The human agent has control over both the direction and magnitude of the vector produced by the **teleautonomy** schema. The operator uses an on-screen joystick (via a mouse) to provide input to the **teleautonomy** schema.

3.2   Simulation Environment

The system is tested on a graphical simulation environment prior to its port to our Denning robots. The objects represented in the simulation environment include robots, obstacles, and attractors. Each robot's trail is depicted by a broken line. Every robot uses the same set of behaviors (a homogeneous society), but the sensory input for each is different, depending on the robot's location within the environment. The robots can sense objects within a certain radius around them. They have the ability to distinguish whether a sensed object is an obstacle, another robot, or an attractor.

The agents have a limited form of communication between themselves. A robot is capable of communicating its current behavioral state or the location of an attractor that it is acquiring or delivering [4]. The communication is simulated by using shared memory. Each agent only looks at this shared memory when there is no attractor within its sensing range.

In tasks that require the movement of attractors, more than one robot is allowed to contribute to the transport of the object at the same time. The net effect of this cooperation is simulated by having the robots move the attractor farther during each time unit if there are more robots carrying it. The distance traveled while carrying an attractor is determined by the mass of the object and the number of robots carrying it.

3.3 Tasks

The use of teleoperation in multi-agent systems was tested for three different tasks. The tasks were foraging, grazing (vacuuming), and herding the robots into a pen. In all three tasks, a teleoperator provided input at his own discretion.

In the foraging task, the robots wander around looking for attractors. When a robot finds a target object, it communicates its location to the other agents while simultaneously moving to acquire it. After its acquisition, the robot carries the attractor back to a home base, then deposits it, and finally returns back to the task of searching for more attractors. If a robot cannot detect an attractor within its sensory radius, it checks to see if any other agent has communicated the location of another candidate goal object. If so, then the robot proceeds to acquire it.

In the grazing task, the robots are placed in an environment studded with obstacles. Initially, all of the floor that is not covered with obstacles is considered "ungrazed". Each section of the floor that is ungrazed is treated as if it had a a large number of distributed attractors on it. That is, a robot can sense an ungrazed section of floor from a distance, and it can also communicate the presence of an ungrazed section of the floor to the other robots. When an agent passes over an ungrazed region it becomes grazed (clean). The task is completed when a certain percentage of the floor, specified in advance, has been grazed. The robots normally wander randomly until an ungrazed floor area is detected.

In the herding task, there is a pen with an opening formed of obstacles in the simulation environment. All the agents are initially outside of the pen. The robots remain in the *wander* state for the duration of the run and wander aimlessly in random directions. The robots are repulsed by the obstacles and the other robots. The task is to get all of the robotic agents inside the pen at the same time.

4 Results

For the foraging and grazing tasks, tests were conducted that compared the total number of steps taken by the robots to complete the tasks with and without the help of a teleoperator. For the herding task, no comparison

could be made between teleoperation and no teleoperation, because the likelihood of all the robots wandering into the pen by themselves at the same time is virtually nil. Interesting information was gained about this task nonetheless.

4.1 Foraging Results

In the tests conducted for the foraging task, three robots were used to gather six attractors. The density of obstacles in the environment was 10%. The total number of steps required to finish the task was measured both with and without a teleoperator. If teleoperation is used wisely, it can significantly lower the total number of steps required to complete the task by greatly reducing the time spent in the *wander* state (i.e., the number of steps that the robots spend looking for attractors). If none of the agents currently sense an attractor, then the teleoperator can assist by guiding the robots in one's direction. However, once the robots can sense an attractor, the teleoperator should stop giving instructions, unless the instructions are to deal with a particularly troublesome set of obstacles. In general, the robots perform more efficiently by themselves than when under the control of a teleoperator if the agents already have an attractor in sight. The human's instructions tend to hinder the robots if they are already moving to acquire or return an attractor. Indeed, when teleoperation is used at all times, the overall number of steps required for task completion often increases when compared to no teleoperation at all. However, if the human only acts to guide the robots toward an attractor when none are currently detected, significant reductions in time for task completion are possible. The average over several experimental runs of the total number of time steps required for task completion when teleoperation was used in this manner was 67% of the average task completion time when no teleoperation was used.

An example trace of a forage task without teleoperation is shown in Figure 2(a). Another trace of the same forage task with a human teleoperator helping the robots find the attractors when they did not have one in sensing range is shown in Figure 2(b). The robots all started at the home base in the center of the environment. In the run without teleoperation, the robots immediately found the two closer attractors at the lower right. Then they quickly found the two closer attractors at the upper right. At this point, the robots did not immediately detect the remaining two attractors. Two of the three agents proceeded by chance to the left and upper left sides of the environment, wandering unsuccessfully while seeking an attractor. Eventually, the other robot found the attractor in the lower right corner, and the other two robots moved to help with its return. After delivering it to the home base, the robots wandered again for a while without finding the last attractor. Finally, the last attractor was detected and successfully delivered to home base. In the same world with the help of a human teleoperator, the two protracted periods of wandering while searching for attractors are avoided. This indicates the types of environments where the use of teleoperation for the forage task is most beneficial. The greatest benefit from teleoperation can be seen when there are one or more attractors that are far from both the home base and the start locations of the robots. Typically, this is when the robots do not sense the target objects without wandering for a while.

4.2 Grazing Task Results

For the grazing task, five robots were used. A sample run of a grazing task is shown in Figure 3. In this case, the robots performed poorly when a large amount of teleoperation was involved. Teleoperation only proved useful when the robots had difficulty in locating a section of ungrazed floor. When the robots had already detected an ungrazed area, they performed better without any input from the teleoperator. The agents' performance degraded considerably, often taking several times longer to complete the task, if teleoperation was used when a robot had already located an ungrazed floor area. Moreover, since remaining untreated areas tend to be clustered together in large patches, the agents typically do not need to spend long periods of time looking for another ungrazed spot (which is opposite the case of the foraging task discussed above). Therefore, the use of teleoperation did not help significantly with the grazing task. When teleoperation was used solely to help the robots find ungrazed floor area when they were not already cleaning, only a 4% improvement in average task completion time performance was observed when compared to not using teleoperation. Thus, when used wisely, teleoperation helped somewhat but not to a large extent.

4.3 Herding Task Results

For the herding task, five robots were herded into a pen that was 36 units long by 18 units wide, with a 12 unit long door in one of the longer sides. All of the robots started at one spot on the side of the pen with the door. In most test runs, the teleoperator encountered no difficulty with this task. He was able to herd the robots into the pen without problems. In some of the test runs, there were a few minor difficulties, such as robots wandering back out of the pen after having been herded in. However, the teleoperator was still able to complete the task without much frustration and in a reasonable amount of time. The results of a test run for the herding task are shown in Figure 4.

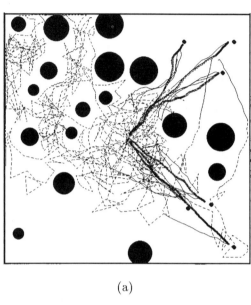

(a)

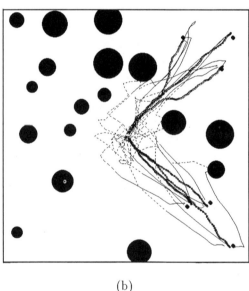

(b)

Figure 2: Foraging task.
(a) Without Teleoperation (b) With Teleoperation

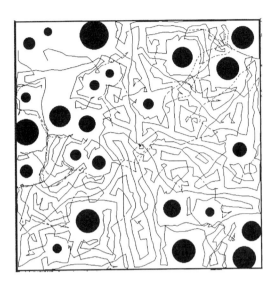

Figure 3: Grazing Task

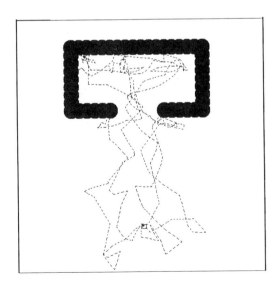

Figure 4: Herding task

5   Analysis

Some conclusions can be ascertained from the studies conducted thus far. It should be remembered, however, that these are preliminary studies, and there are many variables that have not yet been explored. For instance, we intend to explore the effects of teleoperation while varying the number of robots for a particular task, to study the role and impact of different inter-agent communication methods on teleoperation, and to conduct an analysis of what types of environments teleoperation is most suited for.

The use of the **teleautonomy** schema in conjunction with the robots' other behaviors proved particularly effective for the foraging task, while being less so for the grazing task. Herding the robots into a pen was also feasible using this method. During foraging, the best results were observed when teleoperation was used only to guide the robots in the direction of an attractor if one had not been previously sensed. For the grazing task, teleoperation was not significantly better than no teleoperation, although minor improvements were observed. The best results were again seen when teleoperation was used in guiding the robots towards dirty areas that were outside the sensor (or communication) range of the agents.

Two conceivable improvements can be implemented for the herding task regarding teleoperation. The first is to allow the teleoperator to turn off the input from the teleoperation schema for specific robots but not for others, allowing the operator to concentrate on the outside robots without worrying what effects his actions will have on robots already inside the pen. The other improvement is to allow the teleoperator to completely stop a robot's movement when it is inside the pen. In this way, the output of the teleoperation schema could be thought of as producing a vector that nullifies the vectors produced by the robot's other schemas. However, both of these strategies involve producing different output for the **teleautonomy** schema for different robots. This means that the teleoperator would have a greater burden, defeating the purpose of this research in reducing the cognitive workload.

Another important point is that if the teleoperator is given unrestricted control of the magnitude of the vector produced by the teleoperation schema, it is possible for the teleoperator to force a robot to collide with obstacles and other robots. The teleoperator must be careful when increasing the gain of the **teleautonomy** schema so that this does not occur. It can be a delicate task to override the output of the **noise** schema, which is necessary to cause the robots to quickly move in a particular direction, while not overriding the **avoid-static-obstacle** behaviors.

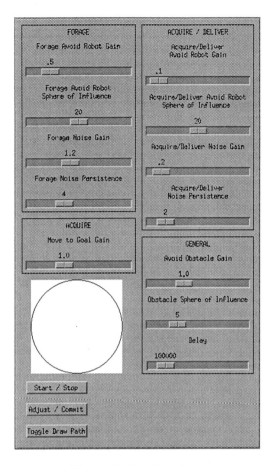

Figure 5: User interface

6   Summary

A method by which multi-agent reactive robotic societal task execution can be influenced via human intervention has been demonstrated. This has been shown for a range of tasks including: improving the efficiency of foraging behavior; limited impact on improving grazing (vacuuming) activity; and the ability to congregate agents in a small confined area (herding) under human guidance.

The next phase of this research has involved extending the simulations to include the second type of teleoperation described in Section 2. We have recently developed an interface, shown in Figure 5, that allows the teleoperator to act as both a schema and as a supervisor of schema parameters. The next step is to port the results of this simulation onto our multi-agent robotic testbed consisting of three Denning Mobile Robots. An additional aspect of future research might involve the generation of an additional autonomous agent (e.g., another more informed robot) that could ultimately supplant some of the activities of the teleoperator.

Acknowledgments

Support for this project is provided by the National Science Foundation under grant #IRI-9100149 and the Office of Naval Research/Advanced Research Projects Agency (ARPA) Grant #N00014-94-1-0215. The authors would also like to thank Tucker Balch for his role in developing the simulation software used in this research.

References

[1] Arkin, R.C., "Cooperation without Communication: Multi-agent Schema Based Robot Navigation", *Journal of Robotic Systems*, Vol. 9(3), April 1992, pp. 351-364.

[2] Arkin, R.C., "Reactive Control as a Substrate for Telerobotic Systems", *IEEE Aerospace and Electronics Systems Magazine*, Vol. 6, No. 6, June 1991, pp. 24-31.

[3] Arkin, R.C., "Motor Schema-Based Mobile Robot Navigation", *International Journal of Robotics Research*, Vol. 8, No. 4, August 1989, pp. 92-112.

[4] Arkin, R.C., Balch, T., and Nitz, E., "Communication of Behavioral State in Multi-agent Retrieval Tasks", *Proc. 1993 IEEE International Conference on Robotics and Automation*, Atlanta, GA, May 1993, Vol. 3, pp. 588-594.

[5] Arkin, R.C. and Hobbs, J.D., "Dimensions of Communication and Social Organization in Multi-Agent Robotic Systems", *From animals to animats 2: Proc. 2nd International Conference on Simulation of Adaptive Behavior*, Honolulu, HI, Dec. 1992, MIT Press, pp. 486-493.

[6] Brooks, R., Maes, P., Mataric, M., and More, G., "Lunar Base Construction Robots", *IEEE International Workshop on Intelligent Robots and Systems (IROS '90)*, pp. 389-392, Tsuchiura, Japan, 1990.

[7] Lyons, D.M., and Arbib, M.A., "A Formal Model of Computation for Sensory-Based Robotics", *IEEE Transactions on Robotics and Automation*, Vol. 5, No. 3, June 1989.

[8] MacKenzie, D. and Arkin, R.C., "Formal Specification for Behavior-based Mobile Robots", *Mobile Robots VIII*, Boston, MA, Nov. 1993, pp. 94-104.

[9] Mataric, M., "Minimizing Complexity in Controlling a Mobile Robot Population", *1992 IEEE International Conference on Robotics and Automation*, Nice, pp. 830-835.

MINIMEME : Of Life and Death in the Noosphere

Stéphane BURA

LAFORIA - IBP - UPMC - Case 169
4, Place Jussieu 75252 PARIS CEDEX 05, FRANCE
E-mail: bura@laforia.ibp.fr

Abstract

This paper deals with artificial animals able to communicate beliefs about their environment's properties to each other. In order to study the relations existing between the information exchanged and the emergence of behaviors or organizations, we propose a model called MINIMEME. This model exploits Dawkins' paradigm stating that ideas, or *memes*, can be compared to parasites infecting their host and trying to duplicate themselves in other hosts' memories.

MINIMEME models the interactions occurring between the world of the memes and the animal societies. It is shown that some ecological concepts can be applied to memes, as if they wcrc some kind of *animats*, and how these concepts relate to the simulated animals. The way this model can be used as a tool to help objectively qualifying emergent behaviors in simulated societies is then discussed.

1. Introduction

How does adaptive behavior in animal societies relate to the information exchanged between its members ? What is the impact of a communication protocol on the organization of such societies ? If we make the hypothesis that the animals we study have a very limited cognitive capacity, how do new rules governing the working of their societies emerge ? That is, what can be considered a "good idea" by a society already following a set of rules and how does change occur ?

What is a good idea ? Rather that computing the efficiency of a given set of rules, we will adopt in this paper the approach proposed by Richard Dawkins in [Dawkins 76]. According to Dawkins, a good idea is a successful idea, an idea that is believed by a great number of individuals.

These ideas, or *memes*, are reproduced (or reproduce themselves, according to Dawkins's anthropomorphic formulation[1]) from one memory to another, acting like parasites in their hosts.

This paper will propose a simple model of the interactions occurring between the world of the memes and the animal societies. We will see that we can apply some ecological concepts to memes, as if they were some *animats*, and examine the kind of relations existing between the different levels of the simulation. Then, we'll consider how this model can be a tool to help qualifying emergent behaviors in simulated societies.

2. MINIMEME

The MINIMEME system [Bura 93][Bura 94] is composed of two parts : the environment and the animats which may change with each simulation and the meme level, or noosphere, which keeps the same structure and rules in all the simulations.

2.1. The noosphere

Dawkins defines a meme as a transmittable cultural unit or an imitation unit. If we generalize, he says that any idea capable of transmitting itself from one person to another, of replicating itself, is a meme. In MINIMEME, we'll only consider memes that define a behavior. These memes can be "executed" by their hosts to produce an effect (e.g., movement, sustenance, nest building techniques...). In order to be successful and continue to exist, a meme must satisfy three conditions :

---

[1] Even if this anthropomorphic approach has been much debated in the past, some of its terminology will be used in this paper for the sake of simplicity. Memes have no real *will* to reproduce themselves, their hosts just communicate them to new hosts, following strict rules.

- It must find at least one host, that is an individual who keeps it in his memory.

- As the meme defines a behavior, the execution of this behavior must not endanger the host's life, at least not before the meme has been able to reproduce itself.

- The meme must be able to resist the attack of concurrent memes in the meantime.

There are two kinds of concurrent memes for a given meme. Either a concurrent meme contains information pertaining to the same behavior as the attacked meme and attempts to replace it (because a host can't believe two incompatible memes), or the meme is about another behavior but takes up enough memory space to prevent the acquisition of new memes. For MINIMEME's animats, memory is a finite resource and each meme has a certain size, thus limiting the number of memes a given animat can hold.

The sum of the memories of all the animals in the system constitutes a space called the *noosphere* [Morin 91]. Memes inhabit the noosphere as animats inhabit the simulated environment.

2.2. How do memes evolve

To simulate the ability of the memes to conquer a part of the noosphere, we'll use two parameters for each meme : *change*, which is a measure of the meme's propensity to mutate or to succumb to other memes' attacks, and *proselytism*, which quantifies the meme's aggressiveness, i.e., the probability that it will try to reproduce itself. These parameters take real values in [0,1], a new meme receiving random values. Thus, a successful meme has, for all its instances in the noosphere, a high mean *proselytism* and a low mean *change*.

As we'll see later, it is noteworthy that these parameters don't take into account the ability of the meme to keep his host alive.

The change and proselytism parameters evolve according to simple rules. This evolution takes place at the end of a system cycle, which is described in details in the following section.

First, a *satisfaction* function is evaluated for each host. This function depends on the kind of simulation ran. It may involve an estimation of the correct accomplishment of a task, state variables in the host (is it hungry, ill...), constraints applying to the host, etc. If the host is satisfied, it increases the proselytism of each of its memes by 25% and decreases their change by the same amount. Conversely, if the host is not satisfied, it decreases its memes' proselytism and increases their change.

Then the memes may mutate and reproduce themselves. A mutation occurs when a random draw in [0,1] gives a number lower than the meme's change. The nature of this mutation is simulation dependent. Both change and proselytism are assigned random values for the new meme. If the meme didn't mutate and if another random draw is lower than its proselytism, replication may take place. A random number of individuals are chosen among the host's neighbors (i.e., the ones it can communicate with) and the meme is proposed to each of them. A potential host can resist taking the meme only if either it has not enough memory left or it already has an incompatible meme. In the latter case, a new random draw is made and if the result is higher than the attacked meme's change, it stays in the host's memory, repelling the attacking meme. If a meme tries to "infect" a host that already possesses it, the host's meme is reinforced (its change is decreased and its proselytism increased).

It is a easy way to model that satisfied hosts tend to hold on their ideas and spread them around, while unsatisfied hosts are more prone to change theirs or to accept new ones.

Figure 1 - Replication of the "Drink coffee" meme. As it is incompatible with the "Drink liqueur" meme (in this example), it replaces the attacked meme.

This mechanism governing the evolution of the memes is the same for all the simulations made with MINIMEME. The only characteristics to be defined for a given simulation are :

- The satisfaction criterion for the hosts;
- The nature of the mutations each meme can undergo;

- The "range" of the communication between hosts or, more precisely, how to find the "neighbors" of a given host (e.g., in the same room/cell, along a pheromone trail...). This range may be infinite if there are no limitations regarding communication.

This last characteristic is very important because of the relation between the two levels of the simulation. In this first version of MINIMEME, the hosts can learn new memes only by interacting with each other. The reproduction of memes is thus limited to a "conversion" process (as shown in figure 1). Many other ways of transferring a meme exist (imitation, coding a meme in the environment...) and they'll be the object of future studies.

3. Grazers

The "grazers" system will help to understand the relationship between the population of animats and its noosphere and how these animats adapt their behavior to environmental constraints using memes.

As shown in the previous section as in [Dawkins 76] and [Morin 91], the evolution in the noosphere involves a positive feedback mechanism. The more instances a meme has in the noosphere, the better it is able to reproduce itself. As acquired behaviors can only be chosen among existing memes, the replication process will assure the durability of the dominant meme (or group of memes). Likewise, a mutated "deviant" meme (incompatible with the dominant memes) will find it very difficult to spread in the noosphere, because the majority memes reinforce themselves.

From a systemic point of view, it means that the noosphere stops evolving and has reached a dynamic equilibrium. The capacity to recognize such states is fundamental when one works with Artificial Life systems. The study of the noosphere's population gives precious information concerning the system's global behavior.

The grazers example has been chosen because it is simple, using few animats and only one family of memes, but nonetheless produces complex trajectories. Furthermore, it allows us to observe the relationship between animats' survival and memes'. Lastly, the simulations made with this system converge very quickly toward a dynamic equilibrium (several hundred cycles at most).

3.1. Defining the grazers

This example deals with the emergence of a stable territorial distribution of animats subjected to various environmental constraints. As we'll see this distribution depends on the stability of the noosphere.

While the rules governing the noosphere are immutable, the animats and their environment can change according to the kind of simulation chosen.

Here, the environment is made up of four identical territories having the same *carrying capacity*. The carrying capacity is the maximum number of *grazers* that can find sustenance in this territory during each cycle.

A grazer is a very basic animat that can't do much. It can only move from one territory to another and communicate with the other grazers in the same territory. There are twelve grazers in the system, each being defined by its position, its energy and the contents of its memory.

The position of a grazer is one of the four territories. Even if the territories have a carrying capacity, there is no upper limit to the number of grazers a given territory can hold. The original position of a grazer is chosen at random.

The energy of a grazer is an integer from 0 to 5. A new-born grazer gets the maximum energy. This energy is decreased by 1 when the grazer can't eat and increased by the same amount (up to the maximum) when it finds food. Movement costs energy too (1 point if the grazer changes its position) as do predators attacks (2 points; cf. last experiment). When its energy reaches 0, a grazer dies. It is then replaced by a new grazer whose memory is initialized. This allows to keep the size of the noosphere constant[2]. A new-born grazer automatically receives a new meme, either learnt from one of its neighbors or randomly generated if the grazer is alone in its territory.

The memes used in this simulation all belong to the same family. They are all beliefs about the optimal density of grazers per territory. There are ten different memes corresponding to densities from one to ten grazers per territory. Each grazer knows one of these memes and only one (they are all incompatible). At the beginning of each cycle,

---

[2] Indeed, this choice has an impact on the working of our system. The death of hosts generally means the disappearance of the noosphere. The size of the studied population being so small, this rule (akin to some kind of birth control) is used. A future version of this simulation may use memes to regulate births over a larger population.

a grazer checks if the density in his own territory is equal to the optimal value it seeks. If this isn't the case, the grazer moves to the best territory according to its meme. For instance, a grazer with a meme whose value is 5 will seek a territory populated by 4 other grazers. A meme is mutated by randomly increasing or decreasing its value for the optimal density by one.

It is worth noting that grazers do not arbitrarily favour less populated territories when they move. Again, a grazer believing that the best density is 5 would choose randomly between territories holding 3 or 5 other grazers if none held four. Apart from the rules governing the memes evolution, there are no cognitive apriorisms.

Lastly, a grazer can only communicate with other grazers in the same territory and it is satisfied only if its energy is at its maximum.

3.2. The system's cycle

The simulations use a discreet time, each cycle consisting of four phases.

• Action phase : Each animats executes its meme. For the grazers, it means checking the position's density and possibly moving. The grazers are sorted by increasing energy, so that the "fittest" act last. This way they suffer less from the perturbations caused by the movement of the other grazers.
• Environment phase : This phase is significant only during the last experiment involving predators (q.v.).
• Feeding phase : Now sorted by decreasing energy, the grazers eat. A territory can only feed as many grazers as its carrying capacity. If there are grazers in excess, only the stronger get to eat (to emphasize the effects of overpopulation, the food is not split between them all).
• Meme phase : The evolution of the noosphere takes place during this phase. Each grazer tests its satisfaction (is its energy at its maximum ?) and possibly communicate with some of the other grazers in the same territory.

4. Experimenting with the grazers

Three experiments involving different environmental conditions have been run. For each experiment, a hundred simulations have been made. A simulation was stopped when the distribution of memes in the noosphere had stayed

unchanged for 100 consecutive cycles[3] or if it had run for 1000 cycles. Most of the simulations (76%) lasted less than 300 cycles and only 2% failed to yield a dynamic equilibrium before the 1000th cycle.

The parameters for the three experiments were :

• Just enough food : In this experiment, the carrying capacity of the territories is 3, which means that there is just enough food in the system to feed all the grazers (4 x 3 = 12). The optimal distribution for the grazers is three individuals per territory (3-3-3-3). This distribution is said to be optimal for the grazers because, after a certain time, it leads to the satisfaction of all of them.
• Too much food : The carrying capacity is raised to 4 for each territory. The environmental constraint being relaxed, an optimal distribution for the grazers consists of groups of zero to four individuals per territory.
• Too much food with predators : The carrying capacity is still 4, but territories holding less than four grazers during the *environment phase* of the cycle are attacked by predators. Each of the grazers in the attacked territories loses 2 energy points. There is only one optimal distribution consisting of four grazers per territory (4-4-4-0, one territory remaining empty).

The system being fully defined, we may try to predict its behavior[4]. Apparently, MINIMEME is controlled by a simple negative feedback loop : when a meme that is not adapted to the environmental constraints "infects" some hosts, their energy soon decreases and the meme mutates or is replaced by another meme (because its *change* increases greatly). Even if the meme resists, its hosts will die and, in the end, a more suited meme will take its place in the reinitialized memories. Thus this system seems bound to lead to the optimal distribution for the grazers.

---

[3] Further experiments lasting several thousand cycles have shown that once a state of dynamic equilibrium had been reach in the noosphere, the system didn't evolve anymore. A stray "deviant" meme could appear in particular instances (because of the randomness of the process), but the system would then quickly return to its previous state (in a few cycles).

[4] According to Assad and Packard [Assad & Packard 92], identifying the degree of deductibility of a system is a mean to qualify emergent behavior.

4.1. Just enough food

The colonization of the noosphere by memes producing the optimal distribution can effectively be observed in some simulations (Figures 2 and 3).

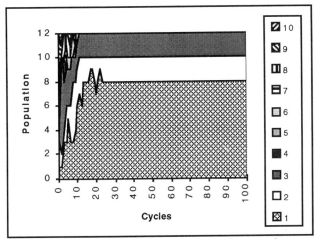

Figure 2 - Distribution of the memes in the noosphere. Just enough food. The carrying capacity is 3. (Example 1) The equilibrium is reached before the 30th cycle, lea-ving only "1", "2" and "3" memes in the noosphere.

Figure 2 shows the distribution of the memes in the noosphere during the simulation. The vertical space allotted to each meme is a measure of how many grazers hold it in their memories. Thus, at the 50th cycle, the "1" meme has eight hosts and the "2" and "3" memes have two hosts each. The "X" meme means "The density in my territory should be X."

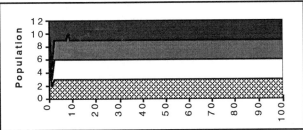

Figure 3 - Distribution of the population in the four territories. Just enough food. (Example 1) After the 10th cycle, each territory holds three grazers

Figure 3 shows the distribution of the grazers among the different territories (each color corresponding to a territory). For instance, at the 9th cycle (small peak), the first and second territories hold three grazers, the third four and the last two (a 4-3-3-2 distribution).

Memes with a value higher than 3 disappear quickly from the noosphere. Because a grazer seeks the territory with the density closest to the value of its meme, the "1" and "2" memes have the same effect than the "3" meme, once the 3-3-3-3 distribution is reached. Grazers distribute themselves evenly in the four territories, they are all satisfied and they don't have to spend their energy to move. The mean change for all the memes diminishes quickly while the mean proselytism reaches its maximum (around the 30th cycle).

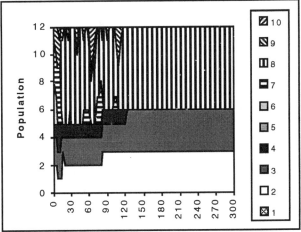

Figure 4 - Distribution of the memes in the noosphere. Just enough food. The carrying capacity is 3. (Example 2) Even if the "2" and "3" memes are still present, the "8" meme has six hosts.

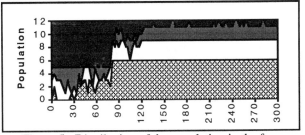

Figure 5 - Distribution of the population in the four territories. Just enough food. (Example 2) The grazers distribution oscillates between 6-3-3-0 and 6-3-2-1.

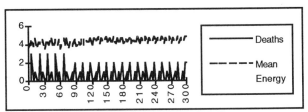

Figure 6 - Death rate (for each cycle) and mean energy. Just enough food. (Example 2)

Yet, in the same conditions, the grazers may fail to reach their optimal distribution. In the second example (Figure 4), even if the "2" and "3" memes are still present, curiously the "8" meme is persistent. This is curious because, as we can see in the figures 5 and 6, the distributions it causes (6-3-3-0 and 6-3-2-1) provokes an increase in the death rate of grazers. Nonetheless, some "8" memes have managed to get a low change and a high enough proselytism to survive and be replicated. What happens is the following self-catalytic phenomenon : memes with a high value provoke the gathering of their hosts. In such a milieu, they reinforce each other and their replication is made easier. **Thus, a meme that kills its host can survive in the noosphere and even become dominant.**

Of course, this requires special conditions (there are seven grazers in the same territory at the beginning of the simulation and a large proportion of high value memes), but it must nonetheless be taken into account.

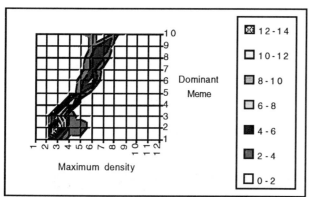

Figure 7 - "Just enough food" Synthesis. (100 simulations) The carrying capacity is 3. The values shown are the number of couples (density / meme) in all the simulations once equilibrium has been reached.

Figure 7 synthesizes the results of the 100 simulations made with these parameters. It shows the number of instances of each couple (dominant meme / maximum density). The dominant meme in a simulation is the one taking up the largest space in thenoosphere, once the equilibrium is reached. The maximum density is the number of grazers in the most populated territory, once the equilibrium has been noted. The reason for the size of this area is that some distributions of the grazers are note stable (as in example 2 above). Nonetheless, the peaks allow us to identify easily the possible states of dynamic equilibrium for this system and their relative frequencies.

In this first experiment, 45% of the simulations generate a maximum density of 3 or 4, 40% of 5 or 6, the last 15% giving higher densities.

4.2. Too much food

In this second experiment, the carrying capacity is raised to four. The excess food, diminishing the death rate, has two consequences. If the memes with a value smaller than 5 predominate in the noosphere, a stable optimum distribution is soon obtained (4-4-4-0 or 3-3-3-3 distributions). If this is not the case, the self-catalytic effect is accentuated as shown by figure 8. The synthesis (Figure 9) reveals that most of the simulations (66%) lead to an equilibrium situated far from the optimum distributions for the grazers. Relaxing the environmental constraints only speeds up the action of the high value memes.

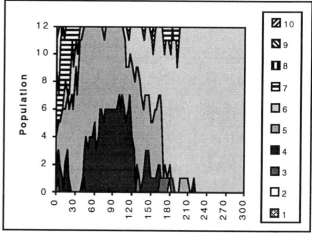

Figure 8 - Distribution of the memes in the noosphere. Too much food. The carrying capacity is 4. A majority of "5" and "6" memes soon produces a 6-6-0-0 distribution of the grazers.

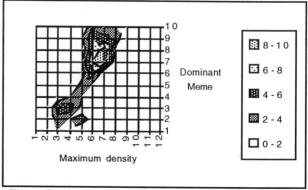

Figure 9 - "Too much food" Synthesis. (100 simulations) The carrying capacity is 4. Most of the results are far from the optimum densities (3 and 4).

4.3. Too much food with predators

In order to make life harder for both the grazers and the memes, predators are put into the system. As they attack the territories holding less than four grazers, the optimum distribution becomes 4-4-0-0. In the simulation described in figures 10 and 11, a high value meme ("8") quickly overtakes the other memes. By the 100th cycle, it has conquered the noosphere and caused all the grazers to gather in one territory. But this meme is so "unfit" (the death rate is too high in the main territory and the few grazers that leave it are attacked by predators), that it is soon rejected by the system. The meme's *change* raises rapidly, provoking its mutation, and its *proselytism* diminishes so that it is unable to stop his fall. This doesn't mean that the "4" meme (which would lead to the optimum distribution) takes over. The perturbations caused by two "less unfit" memes ("5" and "6") are not important enough to prevent them from surviving.

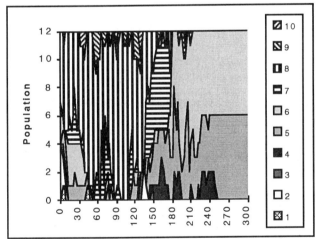

Figure 10 - Distribution of the memes in the noosphere. Too much food with predators. The carrying capacity is 4. Rise and fall of the "8" meme which fails to survive even after having conquered the whole noosphere.

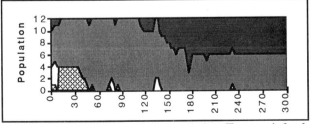

Figure 11 - Distribution of the population. Too much food with predators. A stable 6-6-0-0 distribution appears around the 240th cycle.

It is worth noting that the self-catalytic process observed in the previous experiments can be stopped. In fact, instead of a simple loop based on negative feedback, we have two intertwined processes in MINIMEME. As we've seen, memes' duplication is essentially controlled by positive feedback and shapes the animats' societies. But the environment, through the animats, can regulate the self-catalytic process, exposing "dangerous" memes.

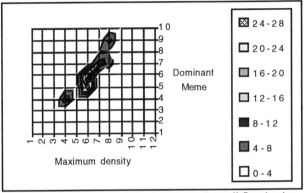

Figure 12 - "Too much food with predators" Synthesis. (100 simulations) The carrying capacity is 4. Notice the co-evolution of high value memes and the "4" meme (the absolute maximum density is eight).

Survival is nonetheless possible for killing memes ("9" in 10% of the simulations) as show in figure 12. However, it requires the parallel evolution of memes that keep them in check. In all the simulations of the peak in (density 8 / "9" meme), the last four grazers are hosts to the "4" meme. It is essential if they are to avoid the overpopulated territory, thus not upsetting its fragile balance. The co-evolution of two antagonistic memes allows the survival of one of them. This can be compared to the way a co-evolving parasite improves the evolution of a given species [Hillis 91].

5. Qualifying emergent behavior

Structures and global behaviors emerge from simulations, identified as macro-level properties of micro-level rules [Ferber & Drogoul 92][Bura & al 93]. Functionalities emerge from complex systems [Steels 92], as do functional dependencies or global properties [Bourgine & Varela 92]. It is hard to characterize emergence in Artificial Life systems when there are so many definitions for it. But it is generally accepted that emergence implies a certain degree of surprise, an intrinsic difficulty to predict the behavior of a system [Langton & al 92][Assad & Packard 92].

Does this apply to the system's programmer or to a naïve observer ? Can we only observe emergent behaviors in systems complex enough to confuse even their makers ?

The main problem is objectivity for, most of the time, we know what we want to see emerge or what the system is capable of[5]. Much work has already been done concerning the objective qualification of emergent properties, either by looking for asymptotic functions [Steels 92] or identifying *clues* for cooperative behaviors [Miriad 92].

Using memes, as is MINIMEME, can take objective observation of a system a step further. In order to survive and become dominant, a meme must modify the hosts' environment so that its replication becomes easier. Conversely, we've seen that the environment constraints the kind of memes that may get a "niche" in the noosphere. To sum it up, **a successful meme is an idea about the system that became a property.** If the memes are varied and their possible combinations numerous, the evolution of the system should be hard to predict. Moreover, results don't need to be interpreted to find *what* has emerged as one has only to look at the composition of the noosphere. Thus, we can reasonably say that the behavior of the hosts, too, emerge as the memes transform the system and find niches in the noosphere.

Because the memes' evolution mechanism is very simple, it doesn't really compare with the way real ideas evolve. For instance, some ideas need only a small group of hosts and should decrease their proselytism once they've found it. Future work may involve "meta-memes" governing this evolution, as well as the notion of *schemes* or groups of memes that get replicated together.

References

[Assad & Packard 92] Andrew M. Assad & Norman H. Packard 1992. "Emergent colonization in an artificial ecology". In [Bourgine & Varela 92].

[Bourgine & Varela 92] Francisco J. Varela & Paul Bourgine 1992. "Toward a practice of autonomous systems", MIT Press.

[Bura 93] Stéphane Bura 1993. "MINIMEME, la mémoire collective d'un système multi-agents".

Actes de la Journée Multi-Agents du PRC-IA, Montpellier, 1993.

[Bura 94] Stéphane Bura 1994. "De la vie et la mort dans la noosphère". Actes des Journées de Rochebrune, "Autonomie et interactions fonctionnelles". A paraître.

[Bura & al 93] Stéphane Bura, France Guérin-Pace, Hélène Mathian, Denise Pumain, Lena Sanders 1993. "Multi-agents systems and the dynamics of a settlement system". In "Proceedings of Simulating Societies '93" Nigel Gilbert.

[Dawkins 76] "The Selfish Gene", Richard Dawkins 1976, Oxford University Press.

[Ferber & Drogoul 92] Jacques Ferber & Alexis Drogoul 1992. "Using Reactive Multi-Agent Systems in Simulation and Problem Solving". In "Distributed Artificial Intelligence: Theory and Praxis" N.M. Avouris & Les Gasser.

[Hillis 91] Daniel W. Hillis, "Co-Evolving Parasites Improve Simulated Evolution as an Optimization Procedure". In [Langton & al 91].

[Langton & al 91] "Artificial Life II" Christopher G. Langton, Charles Taylor, J. Doyne Farmer, Steen Rasmussen, Addison-Wesley.

[Miriad 92] Miriad, "Approcher la Notion de Collectif", Actes de la Journée Multi-Agents du PRC-IA, Nancy, 1992. (Article Collectif de l'équipe MIRIAD, LAFORIA, Université Paris VI).

[Morin 91] Edgar Morin, "La méthode - 4. Les idées - Leur habitat, leur vie, leurs moeurs, leur organisation", 1991, Seuil.

[Steels 92] Luc Steels 1992. "Toward a theory of emergent functionality". In "Simulation of adaptive behavior: From animals to animats" Jean-Arcady Meyer & Stewart W. Wilson.

---

[5] This doesn't mean that collective sorting, for instance, doesn't "emerge" from robot ants' interactions. The surprise in this case comes from the lack of complexity in the animats. It's a kind of top-down approach to emergence.

Learning Coordinated Motions in a Competition for Food between Ant Colonies

Masao KUBO Yukinori KAKAZU

Department of Precision Engineering,
Hokkaido University
N-13,W-8, Sapporo 060,JAPAN
TEL:(+81)-11-706-6445 FAX:(+81)-11-736-3818 e-mail: kubo@hupe.hokudai.ac.jp

Abstract

In this study, a simple and powerful methodology for realizing a distributed and autonomous system is proposed. Usually, *Multi Agent Systems* have difficulty in generating actions that will be suitable taken in their totality, and which we should refer to here as *Coordinated motions*. The proposed methodology improves a colony's total activity through an individual learning process for each agent by Stochastic Learning Automaton (SLA). We propose a Game, similar to football, called The Competition for Food between Ant Colonies. By applying such system to an dynamic changeable environment, we will demonstrate its adaptability. This ability should be evaluated solely through its solution-reaching capability against a highly changeable environment. This game environment serves sufficiently as a complex and changeable environment. By the winning rate of the Competition, the suitability of the coordinated motions is demonstrated.

1. Introduction

In this paper, we would like to propose a Multi-Agent System(MAS) which agents acquire appropriate coordinated motions by on-line learning mechanism. For its evaluation of our MASes, we compare theirs adaptability on changeable environment through our game, a competition for foods between ant colonies. By this evaluation methods as winning rates of 2- players game, MASes total adaptability and self-organization ability may be speculated.

In the recent decade, many researchers have studied the MAS. MAS is consisted of agent which is a solver, MAS solve problems by the self-organization of its agents. By this parallelism and self-organization ability, MAS is expected to be one of the problem solver with fast and robustness against changeable problem environment. Usually, the agent can only solve more primitive problems by itself, then agents must do coordinately for more complex problem solving. Then the MAS's total ability is depended on its agents's self-organization speed and fitness against their problem.

Generally, we cannot describe the rule or regulation about the self-organization against all possible problems. Then in this, we propose the acquisition of this rules by on-line learning using reinforcement learning(SLA). In SLA, the learning is executed according to its evaluation functions and learning parameters. We should give SLA suitable evaluation functions and the learning parameters. For this, we should evaluate the total activity of MAS and change and determine these factors. If the total activity of MAS is calculated by Bottom-Up approach, it is very difficult because the coordinative relations are complex in

changeable environment. Then we evaluate the MAS's total performance by the winning rates in 2-players game environment. The winning rate represents the adaptation to problems which opponent MAS generate. This evaluation approach is a relative fitness, but we suppose that it is suit for the evaluation of MAS in changeable environment.

In next section, we describe our game environment, Competition for food between ant colonies.

2. Competition for Food between Ant Colonies

Our game is in the class of multi players game. First, we would like to formalize this game. Broadly speaking, this game has 1 continuous game field, 2 colonies, and some foods. Each colony is consisted of ants and their formicaries. In this game, this 2 colonies contest the number of foods which ants carry to their nest.

$$\widetilde{C_i} = \left\{ A^i_1, A^i_2, \cdots, A^i_{m_i}, \overbrace{Nest^i} \right\} \qquad (1)$$

$$\left| \widetilde{C_i} \right| = m_i \qquad (2)$$

$$nest^i_j \in \overbrace{Nest^i} \qquad (3)$$

$$nest^i_j = \left(nex^i_j, ney^i_j \right) \qquad (4)$$

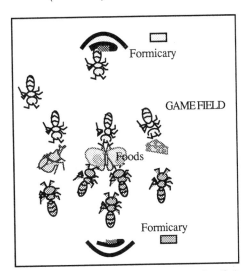

Fig. 1 Competition for Food between Ant Colonies

where $\widetilde{C_i}$ means i-th colony, $\overbrace{Nest^i}$ shows the formicary set of colony i, nex^i_j, ney^i_j are the nest absolute x & y positions. Each ant is represented as follows.

$$A_j^i(t) = \left\{ Px_j^i(t), Py_j^i(t), Rn_j^i(t), Tr_j^i(t), Vc_j^i(t) \right\} \qquad (5)$$

where $A_j^i(t)$ is the agent j of team i at time t, $Px_j^i(t), Py_j^i(t)$ means its locations on this game field, $Rn_j^i(t), Tr_j^i(t)$ indicate abilities of $A_j^i(t)$, $Vc_j^i(t)$ represents movement of $A_j^i(t)$. $Rn_j^i(t)$ is running ability and $Tr_j^i(t)$ shows traction ability of agent. The following definitions represent the remain parts of our game, food. Food $F_k(t)$ is consisted of location term and movement vector $Sp_k(t)$. $Sp_k(t)$ is determined by agents which carry k-th food as equation (9).

$$\widetilde{F} = \{F_1, F_2, \cdots, F_n\} \qquad (6)$$

$$|\vec{F}| = n \qquad (7)$$

$$F_k(t) = \left\{ Px_j^F(t), Py_j^F(t), Sp_k(t) \right\} \qquad (8)$$

$$Sp_k(t) = \kappa \sum_{Pull(A_j^i(t), F_k(t))\, =\, true} Tr_j^i(t) \cdot Vc_j^i(t) \qquad (9)$$

This equation (9) suggests that agents can carry food faster when agents carry a food coordinately than when an agent carry it by itself. Where κ is a constant, the function $Pull(A_j^i(t), F_k(t))$ judges a possibility that agent $A_j^i(t)$ can carry food $F_k(t)$. When food $F_k(t)$ is satisfied with the following condition (10), colony i gets food k.

$$sqrt\left(\left(nex_j^i - Px_k^F(t)\right)^2 + \left(ney_j^i - Py_k^F(t)\right)^2 \right) \neq 0.0 \qquad (10)$$

3. The Learning Agent
3.1 construction policy

In this, we would like to construct our agent which is not omniscient. And our each agent has learning mechanism based on Stochastic Learning Automata(SLA), which is one of reinforcement learning.

Usually, we can divide planning forms into 2 categories. One is the way which a planner builds plans for all agents, the another is the way which each agent make a plan for itself. Generally, the later can generate plans faster than the former, but the later's plans sometimes are not appropriate totally because there is no supervisor. Then we should pay attentions for this coordination of plans which agents generate selfish.

For this coordination, we suppose that sufficient replanning time when their plans are not appropriate totally is earned by the high planning speed at each agent.

And our agent does not use all information on game field. In real world, in sometimes, we cannot know all information which we need. Then our agent is not omniscient and it observes self state and all information about foods. The agents does not observe other ants states irrespective of enemy or team mates.

There are many reinforcement schema. Usually, Q-learning need more sufficient stability of environment than SLA. And agents should acquire several strategies to win. For this 2 reasons, we use Stochastic Learning Automata(SLA). This learning scheme is very simple and needs evaluation function, but it's robustness of parameters is great.

3.2 The Learning Agent

In Fig.6, we show the information flow of each agent "ant". This flow is consisted of 5 steps.

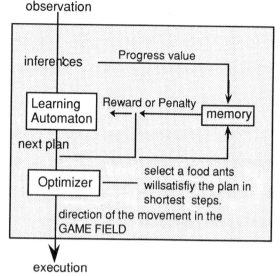

Fig. 2 Flow in an Ant of an agent.

p1; Observation step. The information of observation of agent $A_j^i(t)$ is

$$Ob_j^i(t) = Px_j^i(t) \cup Py_j^i(t) \cup Vc_j^i(t) \cup \widetilde{F} \qquad (11).$$

p2; Recognition step. From the observation and the last output of SLA, determine the now environment state. For this determination, we introduce 5 inferences.

$$\widetilde{inf}_j^i = \left\{ inf_{j1}^i, inf_{j2}^i, inf_{j3}^i, inf_{j4}^i, inf_{j5}^i \right\} \qquad (12)$$

$$inf_{jk}^i \mid Ob_j^i(t) \Rightarrow R_{jk}^i \subseteq \mathcal{R} \qquad (13)$$

The inf_{j1}^i is an inferences function which infers the number of foods that its colony will take. The second inference function inf_{j2}^i calculates the consuming time in the condition of inf_{j1}^i. The inf_{j3}^i, inf_{j4}^i are corresponds to inferences about enemy colony's food and consuming time respectively. Finally, the fifth inference function inf_{j5}^i deduces the number of foods which interest no ants. From these inferences, each ant obtains real number inference results R_{jk}^i.

But we suppose that these results cannot represent its ant' environment state. These results represent the an environment state of ants's colony. But an environment state of an ant in its colony is not represent sufficiently. We think that under appropriate coordinated movement, actions which ants select are satisfied with demands from team mates relatively. Ants execute necessary and sufficient actions. Then, we should add information which represent an agent's role among a colony. In this, we use the last SLA output $\alpha_j^i(t-1)$ as this role information.

This SLA's input states are made by division of the Cartesian product of the inference results R_{jk}^i and the role information $\alpha_j^i(t-1)$.

$$\widetilde{\phi}_j^i = \left\{ \phi_{j1}^i, \phi_{j2}^i, \cdots, \phi_{j432}^i \right\} \qquad (14)$$

After the inference, each ant selects an corresponding state ϕ_{jl}^i from $\widetilde{\phi}_j^i$. In this step, there is only one state ϕ_{jl}^i which satisfy the following condition.

$$\phi_{jl}^i \supseteq \bigcup_{k=1}^{5} R_{jk}^i \cup \alpha_j^i(t-1) \qquad (15)$$

p3; Action selection step. Each ant selects action $\alpha_j^i(t)$ from action set $\widetilde{\alpha}_j^i$ statistically according to probability vector $\widetilde{P}_{jl}^i$ of the input state ϕ_{jl}^i (selected at **p 2**).

$$\boldsymbol{\widetilde{P}}_j^i = \left\{ \widetilde{P}_{j1}^i, \widetilde{P}_{j2}^i, \cdots, \widetilde{P}_{j432}^i \right\} \qquad (16)$$

$$\widetilde{P}_{jl}^i = \left\{ P_{jl1}^i, P_{jl2}^i, \cdots, P_{jl5}^i \right\} \qquad (17)$$

$$\widetilde{\alpha}_j^i = \left\{ \begin{array}{c} NO\_MARK, SPEED\_UP, CARRY \\ COLLECT\_FOOD, DEADLOCK \end{array} \right\} \qquad (18)$$

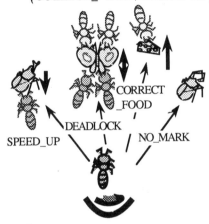

Fig. 3 The plans.

The elements of $\widetilde{\alpha}_j^i$ are called as PLAN as ant's destination. Concretely speaking, *NO_MARK* indicate foods without any ants. *SPEED_UP* means foods which are carried by team mates, and *COLLECT_FOOD* means foods which are carried by opponents. This categorization of foods is determined by threshold processing and foods which are not satisfied with this 3 plans are called as *DEADLOCK*.

p4; Direction determination step. The selected plan $\alpha_j^i(t)$ represents a kind of food as destination and $\alpha_j^i(t)$ does not point at a point on the game field. We must transfer $\alpha_j^i(t)$ to one point on the game field. Then we suppose that the point is equal to the location of the food that the ant can achieve the selected plan fastest. (Optimizor in Fig.7) Every ant goes to this point using its abilities, $Rn_j^i(t), Tr_j^i(t)$.

p5; Learning step. Reinforcement the probability vector of SLA according to the improvement of progress value. The progress value corresponds to the progress of the colony. The value is calculated from the mentioned inference results R_{jk}^i. Usually in SLA model, reinforcement is executed in every observation time. But in our model, the reinforcement is not executed in every times. The reinforcement of our model is executed when the action is changed because ants may keep same actions under appropriate coordination (Fig.8). As you see, in Fig.8, at time i, agent selected plan "A" and kept plan

"A" until time k. In this case, the ant calculates progress values at time i and time k. The calculation method is shown in (30).

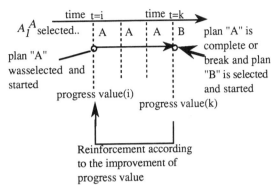

Fig. 4 The reinforcement timing.

$$\begin{array}{llll} if & nowAwayFood > startAwayFood & then & progress = -2 \\ if & nowAwayFood < startAwayFood & then & progress = +2 \\ if & nowAwayTime > startAwayTime & then & progress = +1 \\ if & nowAwayTime < startAwayTime & then & progress = -1 \\ if & nowGetFood > startGetFood & then & progress = +2 \\ if & nowGetFood < startGetFood & then & progress = -2 \\ if & nowGetTime < startGetTime & then & progress = +1 \\ if & nowGetTime > startGetTime & then & progress = -1 \end{array} \qquad (19)$$

where "start" means the starting time, "now" means the last time, "GetFood" and "AwayFood" indicate the its side colony's expected number of food, opponent's expectation respectively. For example,

" *if nowGetFood > startGetFood then progress = +2*" represents if the number of expected foods of its side colony at the last time is larger than the number at the starting time, add 2 to its progress value.

If the progress value is larger than 0, the reinforcement signal 1 is send to the SLA part and reinforce as follows:

$$if \left(\left(P_{jkl}^i + reward/100.0 \right) \geq 1.0 \right)$$

$$P_{jk*}^i \Leftarrow P_{jk*}^i$$

$$if \left(\left(P_{jkl}^i + reward/100.0 \right) < 1.0 \right)$$

$$P_{jkl}^i \Leftarrow P_{jkl}^i + reward \cdot (1.0 - P_{jkl}^i)/100.0$$

$$P_{jkx \neq l}^i \Leftarrow P_{jkx \neq l}^i (1.0 - reward/100.0) \qquad (20)$$

where the reward is learning rate.

4. EXPERIMENTS

First, we would like to test the basic learning ability of the our agent. If our agent is constructed accurately, it will be getting rare to happen the occasion which a penalty signal is generated in each agent. There are 2 colonies with 5 agents respectively in a game field. Their formicaries are simplified as a line(snap 8 of Fig.10). Each ant's starts a random-point on their formicary-line. This start position is changed randomly in every games. An ant needs about 6 time steps to reach its nearest food. The traction ability

$Tr_j^i(t)$ is almost 80% of $Rn_j^i(t)$. This setting of experiment is same in the following all experiments.

In Fig.5, the progress of the occurrence of penalty signal is shown. As you see, the occurrence of penalty signal is getting rare. From this, we suppose that this framework is proper.

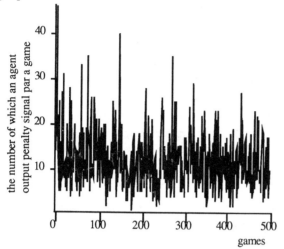

Fig. 5 Learning convergence.

Second, the learning ability of our colony is to be confirmed. For this verification, 4 colonies are introduced. Colony 1,2,3 have 4,3,2 agents with learning ability respectively. Colony 4 has 4 agents without learning ability. But all agents have a same matrix of SLA which an agent acquires in a battle against 4 agents colony. Then, they tend to carry free foods and they do not know team play. In Fig.6, the total winning rates against Colony4 is shown. As you see, our learning colonies can acquire coordinated motions.

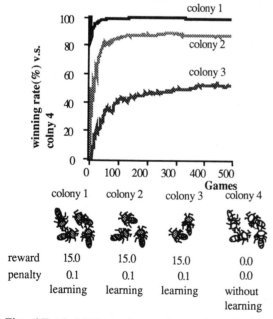

Fig. 6 Total abilities against random action selection colony.

Next, we check the adaptability against change of environment. Until 200th game, colony1 fights with colony5. Colony 5 has 4 agents without learning ability. An agent of

the colony5 carries a food in the ration of 40% when it can carry the food. By this property, Colony5 can carry all foods in a finite time. On 200th game, an agent of colony1 is dead. By this death of an ant, some of acquired coordinated motions may not be able to be generated after 200th game because all actors for coordinated motions does not appear on the stage. Then, the remaining agents must generate affectable coordinated motions which can be played by themselves only. In Fig.7, we suppose that our agents can reform coordinated motions quickly.

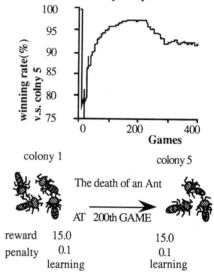

Fig. 7 Reform coordinated motions against new environment.

Colony4 and 5 may not have so affectable strategies. Then we would check the learning ability against hard environment. A new colony6 with 11 agents without learning is introduced. But they had learned sufficiently as a colony in battle against their copy and each agent includes the acquiring matrix of SLA. In Fig.9, a winning rate of colony7, which is consisted of 11 agents with learning without a priori SLA matrix, against colony6 is indicated. As increase of the number of agent in a colony, the contribution of an agent is getting modest and it is getting impossible for each agent to recognize its action's contribution. And as colony6 is strong, the almost all actions generated by colony7 will be given penalty signals. In Fig.8, as you see, the progress of winning rate is very low but finally colony7 conquer colony6.

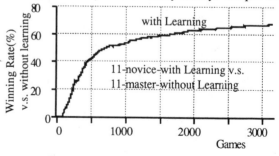

Fig. 8 Learning in the hard environment.

Finally, we show the generated team play in a computer simulation. A word of caution is necessary in explaining this. The following descriptions (1~8) are subjective observations by us. We just want to understand the behavior of our colonies. There are 2 teams, W&Y, consisting of 5 ants. Each ant in the Y-team has the matrix data of an SLA which was made from the competition of 1 ant v.s. 5 ants during 1000 games. Thus, the ants of the Y-team have acquired a pattern for carrying "free food". The Y-team does not learn in this game setting. The W-team has not been in any competitions until this 0-th game. It has been learning in this game, and their reward and penalty factors are settled at 0.15 and 0.1 respectively. Now it is the 151th game of the competition between W and Y. In the following, we explain their movements. We pick up several moments during the 151th game from the computer screen (Fig.10).

1, Game start (time = 6, 151-th game); We allocate 7foods in the center of the Field. Each team consists of 5 ants; one team is set under(Y-team), the other is upper(W-team). The Y-team has acquired the pattern of carrying "free" foods, but it does not learn in this game. The W-team is learning from the 0-th game under a reward of 15.0, and a penalty rate of 0.1. Until the 150-th game, the W-team had learned sufficiently and is capable of winning about 90% as like in graphs in Fig.6. The ants of the teams are of almost uniform ability in, running and pulling, but overall the Y-team has some advantages.

2, Arrive at foods (time = 21); They arrive at the foods at the 21st step. Now we suppose that The W-team is shadowing the Y-team. In short, if the W-team carries the "w× 3"food, the W-team will lose contact with the other 3 foods until coming back from the queen room. Then theW-team starts to move.

3, The straggle for position (time = 23); One of The W-team walks away from the "far-right "food and approaches others. And another ant of the W-team moves towards the center to block ants from the Y-team. While the W-team is moving, the Y-team does not carry and just look on. Then the w-team gets an advantage.

4, Start carrying foods (time=27); After getting an advantage, the W-team starts to carry foods but some ants stay at the center to block the movements of the Y-team. Furthermore, the ants that stay towards move to the "Y-team carrying" food at the center and give pressure.

5, Fake motions (time=33); 2 ants of the W-team carrying food decide that there is no chance of getting away food by the Y-team, one ant keeps on carrying and the other comes back to center to carry foods in coordinated with the other ants. At that moment, the ant of the W-team who is following an ant of the Y-team peels away and returns to the two Y-team ants that are carrying on the "far right" food. But his previous quarry makes a mistake. He does not follow the W-team ant and disappears off the field below.

6,Time= 41; The Y-team makes mistakes again. The two carrying food on the "far-right" mistakenly abandon it in fond of the movement of their team member who has just dropped out of the field. Furthermore, the W-team ant abandons its struggle for one food against the two Y-team ants in the center, enabling it to carry away 4 foods in coordination with its team members. This gives the W-team a big advantage.

7, Time=54 ;The W-team almost wins.

8,Time=87; The W-team continues to carry off foods.

5. Conclusions

In this study, we approach the learning coordinated motions of team plays in a dynamically changeable environment containing uncertain factors, such as opponents's reactions and abilities, using a distributed system. Therefore we propose a reactive planning system using reinforcement learning and show the effect of this system for the fast acquisition of team plays in a small-size-CFAC.

But there are the remainder. From these experiments, we can confirm the basic learning ability of this agent and colony. But we should discuss more about their environment because we must prepare more stronger colony as learning environment than the present one. One approach is the battle against its copy. Concretely speaking, by the fight with a colony with same learning ability, we would like to supply such more harder environment than the present colony. We expect to occurrence of the strongest colony by co-evolution. The following graph shows the progress of the winning rate of this battle against the copy. Our future interest is the acquisition of coordinated motions under a period of stable winning growth. We cannot show results about the occurrence of high-level colony. But the total ability against colony5 of a learning colony with L_{RP} is getting down in proportion to the number of games(almost 30000 games).

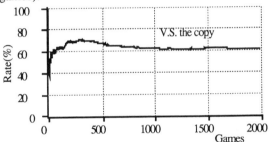

Fig. 9 Learning against a learning colony with same learning ability.

References

[1] Colorni,A., Dorigo,M., and Maniezzo,V.: An investigation of some properties of an "Ant algorithm".In *Parallel Problem Solving from Nature,2*,Elsevier Science Publishers, 1992.

[2] Colorni,A., Dorigo,M., and Maniezzo,V.: Distributed Optimization by Ant Colonies.In *Proceedings First European Conference on Artificial Life*,The MIT press 1991.

[3] Collins,R.,J. and Jefferson,D.,R.: AntFarm;Towards Simulated Evolution.In *Artificial Life 2,SFI Studies in the Sciences of Complexity,vol.X.*,Addison-Wesley,1991.

[4] G. Theraulaz, S.Goss, J.Gervet&J.L. Deneubourg.:Task differentiation in Polistes wasp colonies:a model for self-organising groups of robots. .In Simulation of Animal Behavior:From Animal to Animats,J.-A Meyer& S. Wilson, Mit Press, Cambridge, 1990.

[5] Naredra,K. and Thathachar,M.A.L. Learning Automata An Introduction,Prentice Hall, 1989.

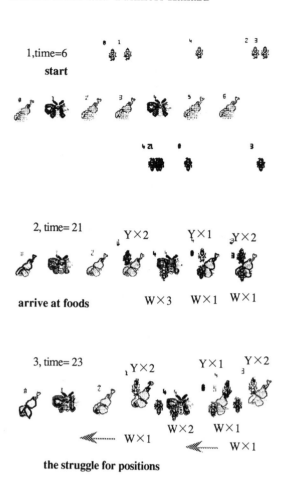

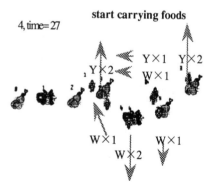

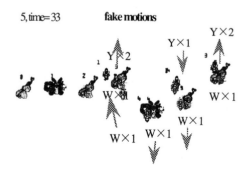

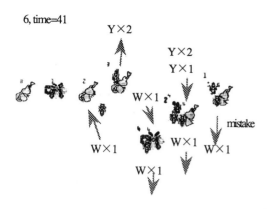

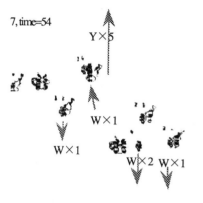

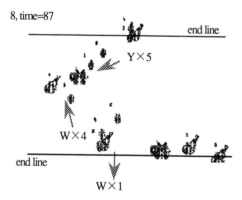

Fig. 10 The snap shots.

APPLIED ADAPTIVE BEHAVIOR

Emergent Colonization and Graph Partitioning

Pascale Kuntz, Dominique Snyers

Télécom Bretagne

Laboratoire d'Intelligence Artificielle et Systèmes Cognitifs

B.P. 832, F-29285 Brest Cedex, FRANCE,

e-mail : Dominique.Snyers@enst-bretagne.fr

Abstract

The classical optimization problem of graph partitioning is transformed into a problem of dynamical co-adaptation of species. An artificial society of autonomous animats from different species is created and the species co-adaptation leads to a territorial colonization coinciding with this solution of the optimization problem. We experimentally verify that our model is minimal for the set of rules controlling the society for this graph partitioning problem. Simulation results also show the relevance and robustness of this new distributed algorithm.

1 Introduction

The study of natural systems from physics, biology, economy or chemistry shows that their complexity does not necessarily depend on the complexity of their parts nor on the complexity of their intrinsic dynamics [16]. Self-organization is the fundamental concept underlying those results; it is considered here as the emergence of a collective global order from a population of elements interacting with each other (see [15] for a precise formulation). Many natural systems, and those artificial systems trying to simulate them, display some kind of emerging structures or behaviors through a self-organizing process with no explicit *a priori* definition (e.g. [8]).

The territorial colonization is one of those emergent properties shared by many biological systems from the most complex organisms of the animal world to the simplest ones like bacteria. Different colonies emerge from the competition among individuals from the same or from different species, and this competition often arises because of the spatial distribution of some limited resources. A colony means here " a group of organisms which is partially clustered, relatively stable in size and over time, and exhibiting high levels of interactions amongst its members" [1].

Territorial colonization in natural or artificial systems composed of some agents moving in an environment does not necessarily rely on a high level organization amongst agents; colonization emerges from simple decentralized agents with no or very few communication between them, also called "reactive agents" [7]. Several cases of such space structuring agents without any *a priori* explicit knowledge of their goals can be found in insect societies; these are particular cases of the self-organization phenomenon called "the swarm intelligence" by entomologists.

In this article, we use this "swarm intelligence" paradigm to develop a new algorithm for solving a classical problem from combinatorial optimization: the graph partitioning problem. We create a purely artificial ecological system with no biological correspondence whose adaptation matches the resolution of the graph partitioning problem by self-organization. This problem consists of finding an optimal partition, with unknown cardinality, of the set of vertices from a weighted graph. The optimal partition minimizes the sum of the weights associated with edges with both extremities in the same class or equivalently maximizes the sum of the weights associated with edges between vertices in different classes. A typical application of this problem is represented by the distribution of tasks on processors of a parallel computer in order to minimize the communication cost between processors. Each task corresponds to a graph vertex and the weights between vertices is inversely proportional to the communication flow between two tasks. The task distribution thus regroups on the same processor the tasks with a high degree of communication by partitioning the associated graph. Another instance of this graph partitioning problem applied to classification is used here. It is known to be $\mathcal{NP}$-complete [12], [10] and was tackled with many heuristics (polyhedral methods, tabu search, simulated annealing, genetic algorithms ... see [11], [4], [18] for more details).

The new distributed algorithm for solving this problem is based on a swarm intelligence model governing the co-adaptation of several different species. A population of animats from different species evolves on the graph vertices taken as the environment, reproduces and competes for territory. This territorial colonization is governed by a majority rule, assigning a vertex to the species in majority. The set of vertices colonized by a species corresponds to a class of the graph partitioning problem. Therefore, the global partition emerges from the local movements of animats which are themselves totally unaware of the global goal.

Section 2 briefly describes the notion of "swarm intelligence" and its recent applications in combinatorial optimization. Section 3 gives the precise microscopic rules of our model of colonization by co-adaptation. Parameter values are found in Section 4 and simulation results are presented in Section 5 with some comments on the asymptotic behavior of the system.

2 Swarm Intelligence and Combinatorial Optimization

In the last few years, researchers have shown how insect colonies can be seen as a natural model of collective problem solving. Entomologists dwell on the spontaneous emergence of global structures through local interactions between insects and their immediate environment only. The analogy between some classical problems of combinatorial optimization and the behavior of insect societies has recently given rise to some new algorithms (shortest path finding between objects on a surface [20], [14], traveling salesman problem [3], clustering [5], [6] , [13]).

The specification of those problems depends on the biological or artificial nature of the underlying domain (see [6]). In the case of natural systems, it corresponds to the *a posteriori* identification of some particular biological functions. When this concept of swarm intelligence is extended to artificial systems, the problem is *a priori* defined and its internal rules must be chosen at the microscopic level to lead the system to some macroscopic behaviors corresponding to the solution of the problem at hand. We recognize here the more general distinction between the algorithmic complexity of a problem and the complexity of natural systems emphasized by H.Atlan [2] , I.Stengers and I. Prigogine [19]. The complexity of a problem is evaluated by its difficulty to be solved by an automatic procedure; the goal is clearly *a priori* defined and only the most efficient procedure to achieve this goal needs to be found. On the contrary, the complexity of natural systems cannot be established from any *a priori* known finality; this finality is even, in many cases, the object of the investigation itself. Concerning problem solving through swarm intelligence, the solution to a problem is considered as a particular state of the swarm-environment system in which the functional consequence is achieved, being either *a priori* or *a posteriori*.

One of the major peculiarities of the swarm functional logic lies in the mutual co-determination of both the animat society and its environment. Self-organization of a system indeed, can be based on the notion of *stigmergy*, introduced by Grasse [9] for the study of the termite nest building. He showed how communication between workers is not necessarily required to perform global tasks. Only some kind of interactions between workers and their environment are needed. Coordination emerges from an autocatalytic chain retroaction between stimuli and responses: workers modify the environment by producing new stimuli which lead them to new responses modifying in turn the environment until some kind of structure emerges. In this case, as pointed out by G. Théraulaz and J. Gervet [22], [21], "the environment plays the rôle of a spatio-temporal memory keeping track of the swarm past actions while selecting its own dynamic regime." From this duality, the problem can be solved either by organizing the environment or by structuring the society of animats.

3 The Co-adaptation Model

3.1 The Clique Partitioning Problem

Let $G = (V, E, w)$ be a complete graph with a set V of n vertices and a set E of edges weighted by the function $w : E \to \Re$ (weights may be negative thus). The problem consists in finding a partition $P = (V_1, \ldots, V_p)$ of the set V in p classes ("cliques"), p not being given, minimizing

$$f(P) = \sum_{k=1}^{p} \sum_{\substack{(u,v) \in E \\ u \in V_k, v \in V_k}} w(u,v)$$

This combinatorial optimization problem is seen here through the study of a dynamic model based on the adequation between the partitioning of G and the colonization of each vertex of V, on which, evolve moving reactive animats from different species. This colonization mechanism arises from a competition between species based on the majority rule: a colony is seen here as a set of vertices with the same species in majority. The model of swarm intelligence developed here leads, in a finite discrete time interval T, to the emergence of a particular colonization that coincides with a "good" partitioning of G in terms of f (the intrinsic $\mathcal{NP}$-completeness of the clique partitioning problem does not allow us to always insure optimality): we talk of *optimal behavior* on T. The explicit computation of f is not required; the optimal behavior emerges from a stimergitic self-organizing mechanism.

This mechanism is activated by a motion strategy, a reinforcement procedure and an aging mechanism identical for all animats. The motion strategy favors animat moves keeping animats within their own colony or escaping distinct colonies. Locally favorable moves (i.e. when an animat , moves to a vertex colonized by its own species) are reinforced by a reproduction function such that new generations globally improve the territorial colonization. Older generations progressively disappear because of an aging mechanism.

3.2   Animats and Environment Characteristics

Let S be the finite set of species, $\mathcal{T}$ the discrete time space and $\mathbf{e} : \mathcal{T} \to S^n$ the function giving e^v, the species in majority on each vertex v of V. The society environment is then entirely determined by the quadruple $(V, E, w, \mathbf{e})$. At each time t, an animat x from the society is defined by its time invariant species $\mathbf{e}(x)$, its position $\mathbf{v_t}(x)$ defined by the vertex of G on which it is located, its age $\mathbf{a_t}(x)$ specifying its life expectancy and a binary function of satisfaction $\mathbf{s_t}(x)$ triggering the reproduction mechanism. This mechanism depends on a function $\mathbf{r_t}$, common to all animats, and an heuristic $\mathbf{h}$ to resolve the cases of equality in the species in majority on a vertex.

3.2.1   Initialization

The number of different species q is taken to be superior or equal to the number of cliques in the optimal partitioning of G ($q \geq p$); new species cannot be created but species can disappear. Initially, the animats are uniformly distributed between species and assigned to random graph vertices.

In order to increase the discrimination between incident edge weights on a vertex v, weights associated with edges $(u, v) \epsilon G(v)$, where $G(v)$ is the set of vertex v incident edges, are transformed through a sigmoid function whose center and slope respectively depend on mean and standard deviation between weights associated with edges in $G(v)$; this transformation is noted $\tilde{w}_v(u, v)$.

3.2.2   The age function $\mathbf{a_t}$

The age x of each animat increases by one unit every iteration, and any of its move from vertex $\mathbf{v_t}(x)$ to vertex $\mathbf{v_{t+1}}(x)$ causes additional aging. An animat disappears when its age exceeds a given threshold $Amax$. At a given time t therefore, the age of x is defined by

$$\mathbf{a_t}(x) = t + m(\mathbf{v_t}(x))$$

where $\begin{aligned} m(\mathbf{v_t}(x)) &= 0 \text{ if } x \text{ stays on } \mathbf{v_t}(x) \\ m(\mathbf{v_t}(x)) &= K.\tilde{w}_{\mathbf{v_t}(x)}(\mathbf{v_t}(x), \mathbf{v_{t+1}}(x)) \\ &\quad \text{if } x \text{ moves from } \mathbf{v_t}(x) \text{ to} \\ &\quad \mathbf{v_{t+1}}(x)(\text{with } K \text{ constant} > 0). \end{aligned}$

This strategy lowers the risks of being trapped in local extrema. The disappearance of the first generation

animats pushes the system out of the initial configuration ($t = 0$) and further generation deaths successively propel the system toward a solution closer to the optimum.

3.2.3   Satisfaction Function $\mathbf{s_t}$

An animat x is considered to be satisfied at time t when it is located on a vertex colonized by its own species (i.e. a vertex on which the species is in majority). At time t its satisfaction function is given by:

$$\begin{aligned} \mathbf{s_t}(x) &= 1 \text{ if } \mathbf{e}(x) = e^v(t), \\ \mathbf{s_t}(x) &= 0 \text{ otherwise.} \end{aligned}$$

3.2.4   The Reproduction Function $\mathbf{r_t}$

When an animat x is satisfied ($\mathbf{s_t}(x) = 1$) on a given vertex $\mathbf{v_t}(x)$ the reproduction function reinforces the positive situation by creating on this vertex a number R of animats of the same species as x. These new animats are initialized with an age 0. The reproduction function is thus defined by:

$$\begin{aligned} \mathbf{r_t}(x, \mathbf{v_t}(x)) &= R \text{ if } \mathbf{e}(x) = e^{\mathbf{v_t}(x)}(t), \\ &= 0 \text{ otherwise.} \end{aligned}$$

Hence, when an animat moves from vertex $\mathbf{v_t}(x)$, on which the species in majority is identical (resp. different) to its own, to vertex $\mathbf{v_{t+1}}(x)$ associated with different (resp. identical) majority species, R animats are created on vertex $\mathbf{v_t}(x)$ (resp. $\mathbf{v_{t+1}}(x)$).

3.2.5   Equality Case Heuristic $\mathbf{h}$

If $m, m > 1$, species are in majority with the same cardinality on vertex v, the equality heuristic h decides between those species. Given $e_t^1, \ldots, e_t^m$ the species in majority at time t on v and $W_{v,i}$ the local contribution to the global optimization criterion of vertex v for the species i is:

$$W_{v,i} = - \sum_{(u,v) \epsilon G(v)} lw(u, v)$$

with $\begin{aligned} lw(u, v) &= \tilde{w}_v(u, v) \text{ if } e^u(t) = e_t^i \\ &= 0 \text{ otherwise.} \end{aligned}$

Relative to this global criterion, the best species has a minimal contribution $W_{v,i}$. This species is artificially made the majority by adding on v, a given number of animats of that species (this number is independent of t).

When a vertex v looses its population and becomes empty, new animats are once again created on v following the same procedure with $m = q$. This is the only way to reactivate extinct species which proves to be very important in the case of clique with one vertex only, i.e. with few reinforcements.

Graph	Vertex nbr.	Opt. sol.	Opt. clique nbr.
G1	30	-2608	4
G2	36	-1684	7
G3	34	-1928	3
G4	40	-2608	4
G5	158	-145640	6
G6	145	-143636	3

Table 1: Data set

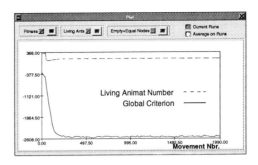

Figure 1: Mean evolution in time of the global criteria and of the number of animats

3.2.6   The Motion Strategy of an Animat

The Animat Selection
The distributed characteristic of this algorithm is simulated on a sequential machine by a Monte Carlo procedure for activating animats. An animat x is randomly selected and is allowed to move with a given probability:

$$Prob(x, move) = \frac{\mathbf{a_t}(x)}{Amax}.$$

Destination Vertex Selection
Selecting the destination vertex for animat x relies on whether the animat is located on a vertex colonized by its own species $\mathbf{s_t}(x) = 1$ or not.

Case 1 : $\mathbf{s_t}(x) = 1$
Movements maintaining x in the same colony are favored by selecting destination vertex $\mathbf{v_{t+1}}(x)$ with a probability inversely proportional to the $(\mathbf{v_t}(x), \mathbf{v_{t+1}}(x))$ edge weight. This corresponds to minimizing the sum of the weights associated with edges with both extremities in the same clique.

Case 2 : $\mathbf{s_t}(x) = 0$
Departure from the colony is favored by selecting destination vertex $\mathbf{v_{t+1}}(x)$ with a probability proportional to the $(\mathbf{v_t}(x), \mathbf{v_{t+1}}(x))$ edge weight. This corresponds to the maximization of the sum of the weights associated with edges between vertices in different cliques.

4   Model Parameters and Validation

4.1   The Model Sensibility to Parameters

This species co-adaptation model has been tested on real life data from [10] (see data set characteristics on Table 1). Any result presented in the sequel represents the mean value computed from 50 runs of 2000 animat movements.

This co-adaptation model depends on 5 parameters: the initial number of animats (N), the maximum age before death ($Amax$), the reproduction rate (R), the number of species in initial population (q) and the influence of movement on aging (K). Those parameters essentially depend on the graph dimension. The optimal values found for graph G1 have been kept for G2, G3 and G4 (because of similar graph dimensions). For graph G5 and G6, those values have been transformed proportionally to the graph dimension. Optimal values $Amax^\star$, $R^\star$, $q^\star$ and $K^\star$ have been chosen by a hill climbing method: starting from quadruple (N, R, q, K), parameter $Amax^\star$ was chosen first followed by $R^\star$, $q^\star$ and $K^\star$ successively.

Maximal Age.   This parameter determines the death frequency between generations. At a certain time, depending on this maximal age parameter, the whole population disappears leading to a strong reorganization of the society comparable to some avalanche phenomena (figure 1). During this avalanche phenomena many cases of multiple species in majority on the same vertex occur, and therefore, the society adaptability is improved thanks to heuristic **h**. If the phenomenon comes too early ($Amax < 30$) the reproduction is almost inexistent, and therefore, most of the animats disappear at the same time leaving many empty vertices; determining the species in majority on those empty vertices is then strongly correlated with heuristic **h**. If this phenomenon comes too late ($Amax > 200$) reproduction becomes too abundant before the first avalanche and the second generation freezes the system in a local optimum close to the initial random configuration. We have chosen $Amax = 50$ for G1, G2, G3, G4 and $Amax = 150$ for G5 and G6.

Initial population size.   The influence of the initial population size ($t = 0$) on its adaptability is proportional to the parameter $Amax$ (figure 2). Optimal values ($Amax^\star = 50, N^\star = 300$) lead to multiple avalanches in the number of heuristic **h** activations (figure 3) and every such avalanche successively pushes the system closer to the optimal state. We have chosen $N^\star = 300$ for small graphs and $N^\star = 2000$ for the larger ones.

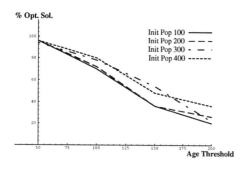

Figure 2: Influence of the initial population size and of the maximal age

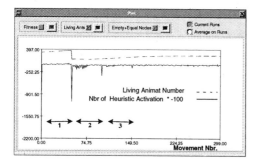

Figure 3: Mean number of calls to heuristic **h** as a function of time

Birth rate. This parameter controls the size of the new generation following an avalanche. Its value does not seem to be critical as long as it is large enough (figure 4); we choose $R^\star = 3$.

Initial number of species. The best results are obtained when the initial number of species slightly outnumbers the clique number p associated with the optimal partitioning (figure 5). Such a value gives a greater degree of freedom to the system for escaping local optimum. We have chosen $q^\star = 6$ for G1 (where $p = 4$).

Influence of the animat motion. The strategy for vertex selection (cfr. §3.2.6) increases the probability of animat x, that has already moved, being, at time t, on a

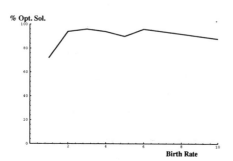

Figure 4: Influence of the birth rate

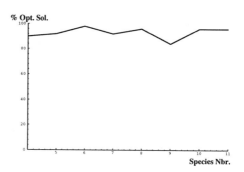

Figure 5: Influence of the initial number of species

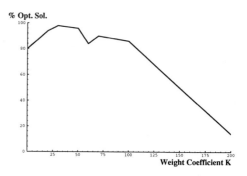

Figure 6: Influence of the animat motion

vertex v with a species in majority corresponding to its ($\mathbf{e}(x) = e^v(t)$). Every motion of an animat augments its chance to release new animats of the same species in $t' > t$. For $K = 0$ this effect disappears since, in that case, all first generation animats have the same probability of moving. For $K > 100$, the moving animats die too fast for being able to modify the initial configuration (figure 6) . $K^\star = 30$ was chosen.

4.2   Model Experimental Validation

The relative importance of every function governing the co-adaptation of species is analyzed here (local motion strategy, $\mathbf{h}$, $\mathbf{r_t}$ and $\mathbf{a_t}$). Seven simplified models have been designed for that purpose by deactivating one or more of these functions. Table 2 gives the mean number of optimal solutions found on 50 runs of graph G1 with the same parameter set as before.

Without the local motion strategy – replaced by a random selection of destination vertices – the only heuristic $\mathbf{h}$ leads to the optimal solution once on 50 runs. When combined with the local motion strategy this rate reaches 10/50. Adding reproduction also requires the introduction of an aging mechanism. Indeed on the one hand, any uncontrolled growth in the animat number continuously modifies the environment without necessarily approaching the optimal solution. On the other hand, lack of aging forbids species to disappear, which is often necessary to find the optimal solution when the initial number

Opt. sol. nbr.	Selection	h	r_t	a_t
1		*		
0	*			
10	*	*		
0		*	*	
0	*		*	*
38		*	*	*
48	*	*	*	*

Table 2: Number of optimal solutions found on 50 runs for G1 with the simplified models.

Graph	Opt. sol.	Success	Mean crit.	Iter. nbr.
G1 (n=30)	-2608	98%	-2607.7 *(2.3)*	456 *(376)*
G2 (n=36)	-1684	92%	-1683 *(4.3)*	350 *(210)*
G3 (n=34)	-1928	100%	-1928 *(0)*	385 *(218)*
G4 (n=40)	-2068	92%	-2044 *(81.4)*	579 *(413)*
G5 (n=158)	-145640	86%	-145607	635 *(188)*
G6 (n=145)	-143636	80%	-143589	574 *(167)*

Table 3: Results of the algorithm on each test graph. The last two columns indicate mean values on 50 runs, and between parentheses, the corresponding standard deviation.

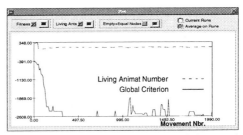

Figure 7: Asymptotic behavior of the model

of species q is not equal to the optimal number of clique. Dually, heuristic **h** is the only mechanism able to reactivate extinct species; without it, the system is often attracted by suboptimal states with a suboptimal number of species. Let us note that species extinction arises frequently when the optimal graph G partition contains some cliques of small cardinal, therefore generating only a few birth.

Results shown on table 2 corroborate the relative importance of all these functions in our co-adaptation model for the clique partitioning problem. The importance of heuristic **h** is stressed which allows us to find the delicate optimal partitioning for graph G1. (G1 has a unique vertex clique.)

5 Simulation Results

We see in Table 3 that more than 92 % of trials lead to the optimal solution for small graphs (less than 40 vertices) and more than 80 % for larger graphs (150 vertices). Moreover, the standard deviation of the fitness function on 50 runs shows how close from the optimal solution we stay. Concerning computer implementation, cpu time optimization has not been our main motivation. Table 3 however, shows that, in a sequential implementation, the mean number of iterations (in terms of animat moves) required for convergence toward the optimal solution is absolutely acceptable.

Convergence of this algorithm, is by no means a static property but the macroscopic consequence of a dynamic population distribution. The experimental study of the models asymptotic behavior (figure 7) shows an aperiodic oscillation of the environment states around their optimal state. The optimal state is by far the most frequently visited one. Therefore, we could redefine the optimal behavior as the most frequent state during a given time interval taken after some transients. The optimal behavior characterization does not require any global criterion computation.

An analysis of the dynamics of our system (animats, environment) in terms of species adaptation shows survival as the main implicit goal of species. Following the animat governing rules, survival is ensured by its reproduction function whose mean birth rate increases with the number of vertices its species has colonized. In our case, the environment is finite (the graph has a finite number of vertices) and territorial colonization therefore, results in an implicit competition between species.

6 Conclusion

In this article, we have proposed a model of co-adaptation leading to a territorial colonization. This colonization behavior emerges by self-organization without any *a priori* fitness function computation; this model represents an example of *intrinsic adaptation* as introduced by Packard [17]. This evolutionary process of intrinsic adaptation has been used here for solving the classical problem of a graph partitioning in clique of minimal weights. We have created an artificial society of autonomous animats of different species whose optimal behavior coincides with the solution of the optimization problem. On the data sets used in this article, our approach seems to compete rather positively with other well known techniques; we would like now to systematically compare our results with those from tabu search, simulated annealing [4] and genetic algorithms [18]

Concerning algorithmic complexity, this new method shows two interesting advantages: on one hand, the problem solution emerges by self-organization without ever computing explicitly the global criterion, and on the other hand, it is an intrinsically distributed procedure. Our current research also investigates its implementation on a parallel machine.

References

[1] A.M. Assad and N.H. Packard. Emergent colonization in an artifical ecology. In F. Varela and P. Bourgine, editors, *Proc. of the 1st Ecal Conference*, 1991.

[2] H. Atlan. L'intuition du complexe et ses théorisations. In F. Fogelman Soulié, editor, *Colloque de Cerisy: Les théories de la complexité*. Seuil, 1991.

[3] A. Colorni, M. Dorigo, and V.Maniezzo. An investigation of some properties of an ant algorithm. In R. Männer and B. Manderick, editors, *Proc. of Parallel Problem Solving from Nature*. Elsevier Science Pub., 1992.

[4] S.G. de Amorin, J.P. Barthélemy, and C.C Ribeiro. Clustering and clique partitioning: Simulated annealing and tabu search approaches. *Journal of Classification*, 9:7–41, 1992.

[5] J.L. Deneubourg, S. Goss, N. Franks, A. Sendova-Franks, C. Detrain, and L. Chretien. The dynamics of collective sorting: Robot-like ants and ant-like robots. In *Proc. of 1st int. conf. on Simulation of Adaptive Behavior*, Paris, 1990.

[6] J.L. Deneubourg, G. Theraulaz, and R. Beckers. Swarm-made architectures. In F. Varela and P. Bourgine, editors, *Proc. of the 1st ECAL*, Paris, 1991.

[7] J. Erceau and J.Ferber. L'intelligence artificielle distribuée. *La Recherche*, 233:750–758, 1991.

[8] S. Forrest. Emergent computation: Self-organizing, collective and cooperative phenomena in natural and artificial computing network. In *Emergent Computation*. North-Holland, 1990.

[9] P Grasse. La reconstruction du nid et les coordinations interindividuelles; la théorie de la stigmergie. *Insectes sociaux*, 35:41–84, 1959.

[10] M. Grötschel and Y. Wakabayashi. Facets of the clique partitioning polytope. *Mathematical Programming*, 46:367–387, 1990.

[11] P. Hansen, B. Jaumard, and E. Salanville. Partitioning problems in cluster analysis: A review of mathematical programming approaches. In *Conf. of the Internatinal Federation of Classification Societies*, Paris, September 1993.

[12] M. Krivanek and J. Moravek. $\mathcal{NP}$-hard problems in hierarchical-tree clustering. *Acta Informatica*, 23:311–323, 1986.

[13] E. Lumer and B. Faieta. Diversity and adaptation in populations of clustering ants. In *Proc. of 3rd int. conf. on Simulation of Adaptive Behavior*, Brighton, 1994.

[14] B. Manderick and F. Moyson. The collective behavior of ants: An example of self-organization in massive parallelism. In *Proc. of the AAAI Spring Symposium on Parallel Models of Intelligence*, Stanford University, CA, 1988.

[15] G. Nicolis and I. Prigogine. *Self-Organization in Non-Equilibrium Systems*. Wiley, New-York, 1977.

[16] G. Nicolis and I. Prigogine. *Exploring Complexity: an Introduction*. W.H. Freeman and Co., 1989.

[17] N. Packard. Intrinsic adaptation in a simple model for evolution. In *Proc. of the 1st Artificial Life Conf.Int.*, Los Alamos, NM, September 1987.

[18] D. Snyers. Clique partitioning and genetic algorithms. In *Proc. of Int. Conf. on Neural Networks and Genetic Algorithms*, Innsbrück, April 1992.

[19] I. Stengers and I. Prigogine. *Entre le temps et l'éternité*. Fayard, 1989.

[20] T.R. Stickland, C.M. Tofts, and N.R.Franks. A path choice algorithm for ants. *Naturwissenchaften*, 79:567–572, 1992.

[21] G. Théraulaz and J. Gervet. Principes fonctionnels de l'intelligence en essaim et modèles de computation collective chez les insectes sociaux. In *Proc. of 2sd Congrès de systémique*, Prague, 1993.

[22] G. Théraulaz, S. Goss, J. Gervet, and J.L. Deneubourg. Task differentiation in polistes wasp colonies: A model for self-organizing groups of robots. In *Proc. of 1st int. conf. on Simulation of Adaptive Behavior*, Paris, 1990.

Diversity and Adaptation in Populations of Clustering Ants

Erik D. Lumer[1,2,*]**and Baldo Faieta**[2]

[1] *Center for Nonlinear Phenomena and Complex Systems*
Université Libre de Bruxelles, C.P. 231
Blvd. du Triomphe, B-1050 Brussels, Belgium
and
[2]*Zetes Electronics*
Da Vinci Science Park, 3 rue de Strasbourg, B-4, 1130 Brussels, Belgium

Abstract

In this paper, we introduce a new method for structuring complex data sets into clusters. The method relies on local actions in a population of simple, ant-like processes, so that global data structures emerge in a self-organized fashion. The model provides a setting to explore the role of diversity and local adaptive behavior in shaping the collective *phenotype* of the population.

1 Background

Population thinking in biology dates back at least to Darwin's seminal work on the principles of natural selection [1]. More recently, the study of insect societies or the immune system, to name only two examples in the biological realms, have focused on the qualitatively distinct properties which can arise at the collective level as a result of local processes. The possible functional relevance of these global states and their constraining coupling to the local processes from which they emerge has prompted the development of new theories and techniques to elucidate the micro-macro links.

In particular, the advent of powerful computers over the past two decades has offered an experimental setup in which to explore some of the basic population effects exhibited in biological systems. At the same time, natural systems have begun to provide powerful insights toward the design of distributed forms of computation [2, 3]. The basic idea is to search for simple behavioral rules at the individual level which translate into an overall population "phenotype" that embodies the result of some computation. Whenever such rules are found, they open up the possibility to exploit the intrinsic parallelism in collections of locally interacting processes that perform in the absence of centralized controls. Several classical problem-solving and optimization tasks have recently been dealt with in such a fashion, from chrypt-arithmetic problems [4], to the sorting of objects in segregated piles [2], to the optimal partitioning of graphs [5], among others.

The work described in this paper explores several issues of general relevance to collective behavior and self-organization in populations, in particular the functional role and ecological expression of population diversity and individual behavioral adaptation. The study is carried on in the specific context of a novel approach to exploratory data analysis, akin to cluster analysis and multidimensional scaling, which provides a clear set of performance metrics against which different populations of clustering ant-like processes can be compared. In the next subsection, we review an earlier study of ant-like colonies by Deneubourg and colleagues [2] which inspired the present model. We then briefly introduce standard approaches to structuring multidimensional data sets, as well as some more recent development in this area, prompted by the need to support explorations in complex information spaces such as large textual databases.

This should set the stage for the present work. A more complete description of the task domain, along with the outgrowth of a practical clustering system, is beyond the scope of this paper, and is being reported elsewhere [6]. Instead, in the following sections, we focus on the self-organized properties in populations of simple autonomous processes. Section 2 describes the individual processes in our system, the basic rules governing their behavior, and the environment in which they evolve. In section 3, we introduce an element of diversity in the population, and endow the individual ant-like agents[1] with memory and context-dependent behavior. We then present the results from stochastic simulations of the model. Measures designed to track the dynamics of the self-organized clustering are applied to populations with varying de grees of diversity and individual complexity. Finally, we close with a discussion of our results and in-

---

*Present address: The Neurosciences Institute, 3377 North Torrey Pines Court, La Jolla, CA 92037

[1]We use the terms agent, process, and ant interchangeably. The latter is used for convenience only; it is not meant to imply any biological realism in our model agents.

dicate future developments.

1.1   Collective Sorting in Ant-Like Colonies

In section 2, we will introduce a distributed clustering method for multidimensional data sets inspired by a recent study of the manner in which ant colonies sort their brood [2]. In the model of Deneubourg and coworkers, lightweight ant-like agents move at random on a 2-d grid on which objects have been scattered. The agents do not communicate with each other and can only perceive their surrounding local environment. When they bump into an object, the probability that they pick it up decreases with the density of and similarity with other objects in the vicinity. Likewise, the probability of dropping an object carried by an agent is an increasing function of a simple similarity measure within a local region. This simple behavior, combined with a positive feedback from the environment which is reshaped by the the ongoing collective action, translates into the organization of initially dispersed objects into stacks of identical elements.

Deneubourg and coworkers restricted their studies to environments made of either identical objects or two distinct types of objects. Thus, the collective "phenotype" of their ant colonies was one of sorting, a fairly trivial computational task to carry on a conventional computer, although quite remarkably performed by social insects in the absence of central controls. Nevertheless, as we will show in section 3, their algorithm can be generalized to objects which differ along a continuous similarity measure, leading to a novel clustering method for multidimensional data sets with quite interesting properties. Before we turn to this algorithm, we briefly recall what cluster analysis and multidimensional scaling techniques are about.

1.2   Structuring Data and Explorations in Complex Information Space

Clustering and scaling techniques have been widely used in a variety of domains, as a way to probe underlying structures in complex data sets [7]. In particular, these techniques have seen a renewed interest in the context of information access. Indeed, in complex information spaces, such as text databases, it is important to provide means of representing the overall structure of the data sets, so as to support effective explorations of their content [8, 9]. Furthermore, some effort has been put in developing methods which reorganize data sets in real time, so as to allow ongoing interactions between an information system and its user.

The problem that cluster analysis addresses is the following one [7]: given a set of elements, and a similarity measure between pairs of elements, find an algorithm for grouping elements in clusters, so that similar elements end up in the same cluster. In general, each datum

may be represented as a point in some high-dimensional space, and the number of clusters is not known a priori. Clearly, this problem does not have a best solution, and many statistical techniques have been proposed.

There are two major families of clustering methods: the hierarchical ones, in which clusters are formed by a process of agglomeration or division, and the partitioning methods, such as the k-means algorithm in which elements are allowed to move between clusters at different stages of the analysis, so as to join the cluster with the nearest centroid. In the partitioning methods, this process continues iteratively until convergence is reached with a predefined number of clusters. Hierarchical methods are computationally expensive, but analyze the data at different levels of granularity, while the faster partitioning methods establish clusters devoid of internal structure.

Multidimensional scaling represents a different class of numerical techniques which extract some global structure out of data sets. These methods are designed to construct a map displaying a faithful representation of the relationships between a collection of elements, given only a matrix of pairwise distances. Typically, the map will be in two or three dimensions, so as to allow its visualization. In addition to well established multidimensional scaling methods [10], recent stochastic techniques, such as simulated annealing [11], can be used in building global maps which minimize some "stress" function, although their computational cost is still very expensive.

As this brief survey indicates, effective exploratory data analysis imposes a trade-off between, one the one hand, responsiveness, and on the other, the complexity of representations constructed by structuring methods. In this context, the intrinsic parallelism in the self-organizing process of collective sorting motivates the search for similar paradigms to structure more complex data sets. In the next section, we develop such a process.

2   Self-Organized Clustering

We model the basic ants and their environment as follows. Ants perform a random walk on a 2d-grid, on which elements have been laid out at random, so that a site in the grid is occupied by at most one element. In fact, the dimensions of the grid are such that its number of sites exceeds the number of elements by roughly an order of magnitude. Furthermore, the number of elements exceeds the number of ants by at least another order of magnitude, so as to translate ants actions over a short period of time into small fluctuations of the environment.

The simulation evolves in discrete time steps. At each step, an ant is selected at random and can either pick or drop an element at its current location, given that there is either an element at that location or that the ant is carrying one, respectively. Assuming that an unloaded ant comes across an element, the probability of picking that element increases with low density and decreases with the similarity of the element vis-a-vis the other elements in a small surrounding area. (In what follows, we define this area as a square of $d \times d$ nodes) . Accordingly, the probability of picking an element, say i, is defined as

$$P_{pick}(i) = (\frac{k_p}{k_p + f(i)})^2 \qquad (1)$$

where k_p is a constant and $f(i)$ a local estimation of the density of elements and their similarity to i.

By the same token, the probability that an ant-like process will drop a carried element should increase with the density of similar elements in its surrounding area. A simple functional relation which satisfies this tendency, and the one being used here, is given by

$$P_{drop}(i) = \begin{cases} 2f(i) & \text{if } f(i) < k_d \\ 1 & \text{otherwise} \end{cases} \qquad (2)$$

where k_d is a constant. In the probabilities for manipulating elements expressed by P_{pick} and P_{drop}, the density dependent function $f(i)$ for an element i, at a particular grid location, is defined as

$$f(i) = \begin{cases} \frac{1}{d^2} \sum_j (1 - d(i,j)/\alpha) & \text{if } f > 0 \\ 0 & \text{otherwise} \end{cases} \qquad (3)$$

In this expression, the sum extends over all the elements in the local area surrounding element i, and $d(i,j)$ measures the dissimilarity between the pair of elements (i, j). The constant α scales the dissimilarities. For the sake of concreteness, let us assume here that the elements can be represented as points in an n-dimensional space, so that $d(i,j)$ is simply the euclidian distance between i and j. The normalizing term d^2 equals the total number of sites in the local area of interest, and introduces a density dependency in $f(i)$. As a result, the maximum of f is reached if and only if all the sites in the neighborhood are occupied by identical elements (i.e. $d(i,j) = 0$), in which case $f = 1$. Whenever a loaded ant decides to drop its element, it looks for the first empty site in its vicinity in which to do so. A time step finishes with the selected ant moving to one of its four adjacent nodes, each direction of motion being equally likely.

In summary, the simulation consists in cycling through a loop involving: 1) the selection of an ant, 2) if appropriate, the manipulation of a local object by that ant, and 3) a random unitary displacement on the grid. We contend that the collection of ants so-defined performs a heuristic mapping of the data set onto the 2-d grid. This mapping amounts to a dynamic organization of data in a fashion halfway between a cluster analysis - in so far as elements belonging to different concentration areas in their n-dimensional space end up in different clusters - and a multidimensional scaling, in which an intracluster structure is constructed. Notice, however, that the relative positioning of clusters on the grid is arbitrary[2].

_____
[2]By relaxing the global positioning constraints, we are able to

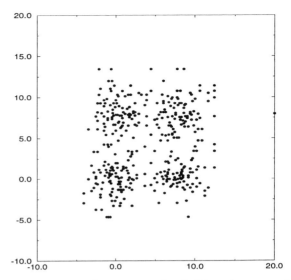

Figure 1: Data Set composed of 400 points sampled with equal probabilities from 4 gaussian distributions. The distributions are defined according to: $(N(0,2), N(0,2))$, $(N(0,2), N(8,2))$, $(N(8,2), N(0,2))$, and $(N(8,2), N(8,2))$.

This process is illustrated in the following example. We generated a 2d data set composed of 400 points sampled with equal probability from one out of four bivariate gaussian distributions. The distributions have identical variances but shifted means. The actual scatter plot of the sampled points in their 2d space is shown in figure 1 and the properties of the distributions are indicated in the accompanying caption. The data points were laid out at random locations on a 52x52 grid, populated by 40 ants. The other parameters of the simulation are indicated in the caption of figure 2a, which shows the initial distribution of data points on the grid. Notice that each element in this figure is labeled according to its originating distribution for illustrative purpose only. This information is not available to the ants. Figure 2b shows the layout of elements on the grid after 50 cycles of the simulation, each cycle being composed of 10,000 ant selections. As can be seen, the data points are clustered into patches , each one made of points issued mostly from a single statistical distribution. However, the number of patches exceeds and thus poorly reflects the number of distributions underlying the data set.

In the next section, we discuss ways in which the colony can be modified to fix this discrepancy. We also investigate how the speed at which stable structures are constructed depends on the properties of individual members of the colony. To close this section, let us emphasize that all the results presented below have

_____
devise a faster algorithm. Also, in the context of textual databases, the relative positioning of coarse clusters is likely to be meaningless.

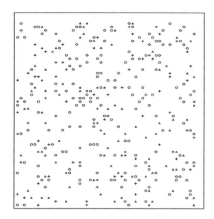

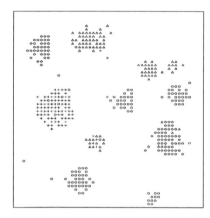

Figure 2: Layouts of elements on a 52x52 grid. Elements sampled from different distributions are represented by different symbols. a (top): Initial layout. b (bottom): Layout after 50 cycles using a population of basic clustering agents.

been verified to hold qualitatively for a variety of data sets, including those embedded in higher dimensions. For instance, we have applied successfully our algorithm to synthetic data sets embedded in an 8-dimensional space. Performance seems rather independent of the size of the data set provided that the following criterion is met: sampling size must be sufficiently large to produce locally dense sets of similar points, that is to say the average number of points differing from a given one by less than the constant α must be of the order of the sensing surface d^2 of an agent moving on its grid.

3   Population Diversity and Local Adaptive behavior

In this section, we shall introduce and compare three variants of the basic population of clustering ants considered above. First, we substitute to the homogeneous population one made of individuals possessing different displacement speeds and sensitivities to object similarities. Also, we endow the ants with an evanescent memory for locations where they recently succeeded in dropping an element. Finally, we consider the impact of individual behavioral changes at the collective phenotipic level.

Before we turn to this study, let us introduce a number of dynamic measures to track the unfolding of the clustering process. We compare various runs by means of three measures. First, we compute at each cycle the spatial entropy on the grid, and this, at different granularities. This measure informs us of the relative order on the grid, so that larger clusters will translate into lower entropies [13]. Such a measure, while correlating well with the visual feedback that an animation of the run provides, does not indicate whether similar points end up at neighboring locations on the grid in agreement with the underlying statistics of the data set. This possibility is measured by a criterion of global fit, which is simply an average over all the measures $f(i)$ for a given layout on the grid. Finally, the temporal profile of the total number of drops is recorded as a measure of the effectiveness of object manipulations performed in a colony.

3.1   Diverse vs. Homogeneous Populations

It is often argued that diversity plays a crucial role in shaping up the properties of populations. One obvious biological role of diversity is as a source of variability in selectionist systems. However, from a computational view, the issue has received attention only sporadically (e.g. [4, 12]).

Our system offers a nice domain in which to quantify the impact of diversity at a macroscopic level. Indeed, we introduce variability by virtue of a range of paces, comprised between 1 and V_{max}, the latter being defined as the quantal displacement of an ant in a single time step along a given grid axis. At the same time, the pace is coupled in an inverse manner to the pickiness of an ant: fast moving ants have a more liberal measure of similarity, while slow moving ants are very selective in their similarity criterion. This trend is expressed quantitatively in the following manner. Let v be the pace of an ant. The local density function f computed by that ant now reads as

$$f(i) = \begin{cases} \frac{1}{d^2} \sum_j (1 - \frac{d(i,j)}{\alpha + \alpha(v-1)/V_{max}}) & \text{if } f > 0 \\ 0 & \text{otherwise} \end{cases} \quad (4)$$

As an example, a population of ants is built by selecting for each individual a pace chosen uniformly in the range (1,6). Figure 3a shows the result of their clustering after 50 cycles. The data and initial conditions are identical to those associated with figures 2. Notice now that most of the elements are distributed across only four clusters, in a way which reflects their underlying statistical distributions. Figure 3b shows the equivalent layout using a homogeneous population of ants moving at a median pace of 3 sites/step. We observe in this case a larger number of clusters. The differences between the two populations is further characterized in figures 4a-c. In figure 4a, we compare the time course of the mean fit for the two populations. While the plot indicates a more rapid stabilization of the overall fit in the homogeneous population, the saturation takes place at a value which is inferior to the one in the diverse population. The faster convergence of elements in the homogeneous population is co nfirmed in figure 4b, where the spatial entropies are shown. Notice that the slightly lower entropy of the grid organized by homogeneous ants is an artifact of the proximity between two pairs of large, although distinct clusters. Finally, figure 4c indicates that the better clustering achieved by the diverse population involves a smaller number of manipulations.

These results are observed in a number of runs with different initial conditions and for a variety of data sets. The diverse population seems to outperform a homogeneous one for the following reason: the fast, sloppy ants rapidly seggregate elements on a coarse scale, as they tend to bring elements somewhat in the right "ballpark". On the other hand, the slow and picky ants act more locally, by sorting and placing elements with greater care.

Finaly, let us point out that the clustering process is density dependent in the n-dimensional space of the data sets. Indeed, the largest concentrations of element to appear on the grid, in fact the nucleuses for the surviving clusters, correspond to data points near the peaks of their original distribution, as such points are sampled more often.

3.2 Agents with Short-Term Memory

In runs presented in the previous subsections, the ants were endowed with a memory for the m most recent elements dropped, along with their new location. (In these runs, the memory was set to $m = 8$). When a new element is picked by an ant-like process, a comparison is made with the elements in memory, and the ant automatically goes toward the location of the memorized element most similar to the one just collected. This behavior leads to the formation of a smaller number of statistically equivalent clusters, a desirable property indeed. Figures 5a-c illustrate the impact of varying the memory size in individuals forming a diverse population. As we can see, the quality of the clustering depends strongly on the size of the memory buffers, with performance peeking for a memory size of around six items.

3.3 Behavioral Switches

Although the clustering process is stochastic, and allows for ongoing fluctuations at a micro-scale, it is basically irreversible in that the spatial entropy gradually decreases

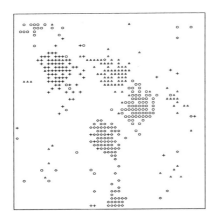

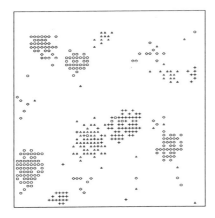

Figure 3: Layouts after 50 cycles. a (top): Diverse population of agents with paces in the range (0,6) and individual memory buffers for up to 8 items. b (bottom): Homogeneous population of ants with same memory setting as in fig. 3a.

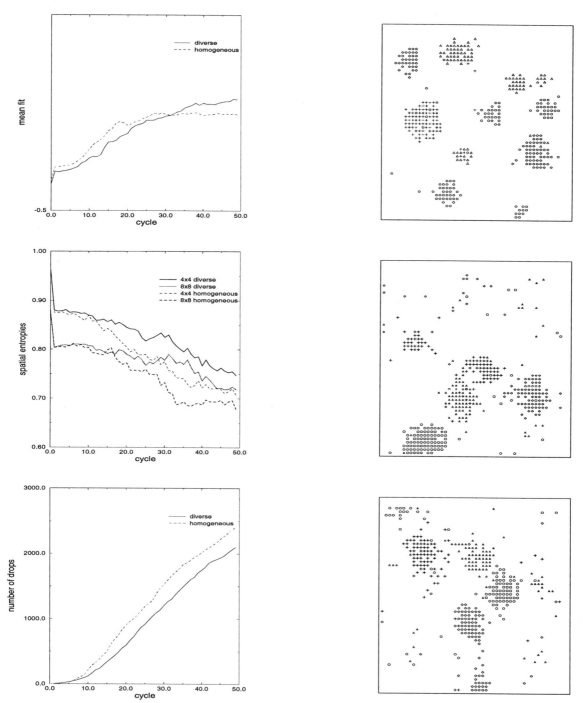

Figure 4: Analysis of performance for runs shown in figures 3. a (top): Average fit as a function of time. b (middle): Time course of spatial entropies computed over ensembles of squared areas of dimensions 4x4 and 8x8, respectively. c (bottom): Aggregate number of drops in the population as a function of time.

Figure 5: Global effect of individual memory sizes. a (top): m=0. b (middle): m=4. c (bottom): m=8.

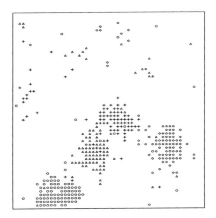

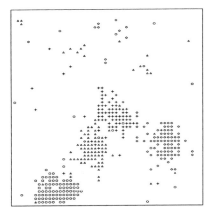

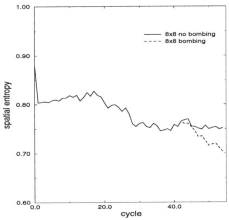

Figure 6: Self-regulated behavioral switching from gathering elements to destroying clusters. a (top): Grid shortly after an ant has begun destroying the upper left cluster. b (middle): 5 cyles later. Ants have reverted to gathering the disseminated elements. c (bottom): As a result, elements issued from the same statistical distributionend up in the same cluster.

with time. As elements get positioned in an acceptable neighborhood, they become less likely to be moved again towards another location. Accordingly, the ants will pick and drop fewer elements as time goes on. This latter property can be exploited in an adaptive behavior which introduces a sort of annealing in the system. Thus, we modify the individual agents so that each one can switch from gathering elements to destroying clusters if it hasn't manipulated an element for more than a preset number of cycles.

The ensuing collective dynamics is illustrated in figures 6a-c. The leftmost figure should be compared with figure 5b, which showed the clusters built after 50 cycles by diverse agents with a memory buffer sized to 4 items. In the present case, the grid is displayed after 55 cycles. One can see that the upper left clusters has been destroyed, and that this results in a regrouping of its elements in a single cluster, as illustrated in figure 6b after 60 cycles of the simulation. Indeed, following this action by a single agent, most of the other processes will engage in gathering the disseminated elements, thus preventing for a while any further destruction of clusters.

4   Conclusions

In this paper, we presented a simple model of clustering, which is performed in a fully decentralized fashion by a population of simple processes. This model offers a controlled setting in which to evaluate how changes in local properties translate into different performance at the system level. In particular, we observed that diverse populations of clustering agents consistently outperform homogeneous groups. Furthermore, we found that local behavioral changes, based on prior experience, can be manipulated to produce desired macroscopic effects. We have considered two kinds of adaptations, on the one hand via a memory for relevant locations, and on the other hand, in the form of behavioral switches regulated by the global feedback from the environment.

Interestingly enough, clusters which uncover global structures in a data set are constructed by local agents with no mutual interactions other than indirectly via the environment which they modify. This collective process amounts to a heuristic mapping of a possibly high-dimensional and sparse data set onto a plane, in a way which preserves neighborhood relationships as much as possible. In this plane, the emergent structure of a data set can be readily seen. Clustering is nonparametric, insofar as the number of constructed clusters is not specified a priori. This property stands in contrast with the parametric nature of most clustering algorithms. Notice also that the same collective process can be generalized to more complex environments, such as landscapes and 3d lattices [6].

These observations suggest that our mechanism could be integrated in a continuously evolving system used to visualize, organize and analyze interactively unstructured data sets. As a matter of fact, the experiments presented here have allowed us to derive a novel clustering algorithm and system, which capture this functionality. Preliminary studies applied to textual databases have been encouraging, and further results will be reported in the near future [6].

Acknowledgement

The authors would like to thank J.L. Deneubourg for many fruitful discussions about the work presented in this paper. They are also grateful to G. Nicolis at the University of Brussels and A. Wirtz at Zetes Electronics for providing a forum in which this work could be developed. This research was supported by a grant from Zetes Electronics.

References

[1] Darwin, C. (1859) "On the origin of species by means of natural selection of favoured races in the struggle for life". London: Murray

[2] J.L. Deneubourg, S. Goss, N. Franks, A. Sendova-Franks, C. Detrain, and L. Chretien (1991) "The dynamics of collective sorting robot-like ants and ant-like robots", in Proc. of the 1st Conf. on Sim. of Adaptive Behavior

[3] B.A. Huberman ed. (1988) "The Ecology of Computation", North-Holland, Amsterdam

[4] S. Clearwater, T. Hogg, and B.A. Huberman (1992) "Cooperative Problem Solving", in Computation: The Micro-Macro View, B.A. Huberman ed., World Scientific Press

[5] P. Kuntz and D. Snyers (1993), "Ant Colonies and Self-Organizing Graph", submitted paper

[6] B. Faieta and E.D. Lumer, "Exploratory data analysis via self-organization", in preparation

[7] A.K. Jain and R.C. Dubes (1988) "Algorithms for clustering data", Prentice Hall

[8] D.R. Cutting, D.R. Karger, J.O. Pederson, and J.W. Tukey (1992) "Scatter/Gather: a cluster-based approach to browsing large document collections", in Proc. SIGIR92

[9] M. Chalmers and P. Chitson (1992) "Explorations in information visualizations", in Proc. SIGIR92

[10] J.B. Kruskal (1964) "Multidimensional scaling by optimizing goodness of fit to a nonmetric hypothesis", Psychonometrika 29

[11] S. Kirpatrick, C.D. Gelatt, and M.P. Vecchi (1983) "Optimization by simulated annealing" vol. 220 (4698)

[12] N.A. Nowak and K. Sigmund (1993) "Tit for tat in heterogeneous populations", Nature, vol. 355, pp. 250-252

[13] H. Gutowitz (1993) "Complexity-seeking ants", in Proc. ECAL 1993

AUTHOR INDEX